What's New In This Edition

Microsoft continues to refine and extend the functionality of its immensely popular FrontPage Web site authoring and management suite with the release of FrontPage 98.

Microsoft FrontPage 98 Unleashed, Third Edition has been completely revised and updated to keep you informed of the additional components and technologies and how to best take advantage of them.

Completely new material for this edition includes:

- Designing Web Sites with Themes, Chapter 14
- Getting the Most from the Clip Art Gallery, Chapter 15
- Working with the Microsoft Image Composer, Chapter 16
- Creating Great Images with Image Composer, Chapter 17
- Enhancing Your Images with Effects, Chapter 18
- Optimizing Your Images and Color Palettes, Chapter 19
- Working with GIF Animator, Chapter 20
- Creating and Designing Image Maps, Chapter 21
- Designing Pages with Dynamic HTML, Chapter 40
- Using Push Channels, Chapter 41
- Web to Database Connectivity with FrontPage 98, Chapter 42
- Advanced Database Set Up and Custom Scripts, Chapter 43
- Working with SQL and Database Management Systems, Chapter 44
- Moving Up to Visual InterDev, Chapter 45
- Using IIS with FrontPage 98, Chapter 53
- Using Other Web Servers with FrontPage 98, Chapter 54

Microsoft® FrontPage™ 98

Third Edition

William R. Stanek, et al.

201 West 103rd Street
Indianapolis, IN 46290

UNLEASHED

International Standard Book Number: 1-57521-349-4

Library of Congress Catalog Card Number: 97-68010

2001 2000 99 98 4 3 2

Interpretation of the printing code: the rightmost multi-digit number is the year of the book's printing; the rightmost single-digit, the number of the book's printing. For example, a printing code of 98-1 shows that the first printing of the book occurred in 1998.

Composed in AGaramond and MCPdigital by Macmillan Computer Publishing

Printed in the United States of America

Trademarks

President *Richard K. Swadley*

Publisher and Director of Acquisitions *Jordan Gold*

Executive Editor *Beverly M. Eppink*

Managing Editor *Patrick Kanouse*

Indexing Manager *Johnna L. VanHoose*

Director of Marketing *Kelli S. Spencer*

Product Marketing Manager *Kim Margolius*

Marketing Coordinator *Linda B. Beckwith*

Acquisitions Editor
Beverly M. Eppink

Development Editor
Bob Correll

Production Editor
Andrew Cupp

Copy Editors
Margaret Berson
Chuck Hutchinson
Bart Reed

Indexers
Greg Pearson
Kelly Talbot
Craig Small
Christine Nelson

Technical Writer
Steve Banick

Technical Reviewers
Brad Meyers
Bill Vernon
Michael Watson

Editorial Coordinators
Mandie Rowell
Katie Wise

Technical Edit Coordinator
Lorraine E. Schaffer

Resource Coordinators
Deborah Frisby
Charlotte Clapp

Editorial Assistants
Carol Ackerman
Andi Richter
Rhonda Tinch-Mize
Karen Williams

Cover Designer
Jason Grisham

Book Designer
Gary Adair

Copy Writer
David Reichwein

Production Team Supervisor
Brad Chinn

Production
Mike Henry
Linda Knose
Tim Osborn
Staci Somers
Mark Walchle

Overview

Introduction **xxxv**

Part I FrontPage Basics

1 Introducing FrontPage 98 **3**

2 Using the FrontPage Explorer **13**

3 Working with the FrontPage Editor **37**

Part II Creating Web Pages with FrontPage 98

4 Creating Web Pages with FrontPage 98 **51**

5 Working with Links and Lists **71**

6 Creating Richer Web Pages with HTML Features **89**

7 Enhancing Your Web Pages with Images—The Easy Way **107**

Part III Web Page Layout and Design with FrontPage 98

8 Designing Tables with FrontPage 98 **139**

9 Creating Frames **155**

10 Editing and Enhancing Your Frames **169**

11 Designing Pages with Style Sheets **185**

12 Advanced Page Layout with Style Sheets **203**

13 Working with Active Elements: Banners, Hit Counters, and More **215**

Part IV Web Page Graphic Design and Image Composer

14 Designing Web Sites with Themes **233**

15 Getting the Most from the Clip Art Gallery **249**

16 Working with the Microsoft Image Composer **273**

17 Creating Great Images with Image Composer **287**

18 Enhancing Your Images with Effects **317**

19 Optimizing Your Images and Color Palettes **335**

20 Working with GIF Animator **357**

21 Creating and Designing Image Maps **385**

Part V Forms and Advanced Form Handling

22 Working with Forms **403**

23 Getting More from the Form Page Wizard **419**

24 Handling Form Output and Saving the Results **427**

25 Validating Forms **449**

26 Search Engines and Indexing Your Web Site **459**

Part VI Templates, Wizards, and FrontPage Components

27 Creating Web Pages with FrontPage Templates **469**

28 Guest Books and Feedback **477**

29 Instant Web Sites with FrontPage 98 **487**

30 Building a Discussion Web **495**

31 Creating a Customer Support Web **511**

32 Creating a Project Web **523**

33 Establishing a Corporate Presence **533**

34 Automation with FrontPage Components **545**

35 User Registration and Restricted Webs **559**

Part VII Adding Dynamic Content to Your Web Page

36 Scripting with VBScript **575**

37 Creating Interactive Page Controls with ActiveX **599**

38 Scripting with JavaScript **623**

39 Adding Java Applets to Your Web Page **643**

40 Designing Pages with Dynamic HTML **663**

41 Using Push Channels **677**

Part VIII Working with Databases

42 Web to Database Connectivity with FrontPage 98 **697**

43 Advanced Database Setup and Custom Scripts **713**

44 Working with SQL and Database Management Systems **739**

45 Moving Up to Visual InterDev **763**

Part IX Web Site Management with FrontPage Explorer

46 Organizing Your Pages **783**

47 Managing Your Web **803**

48 Configuring Firewalls and Proxies **815**

Part X Web Servers and FrontPage 98

49 Using the Personal Web Server **827**

50 Personal Web Server Administration **845**

51 Working with Server Extensions and Multihoming **863**

52 Administering FrontPage Server Extensions **875**

53 Using IIS with FrontPage 98 **889**

54 Using Other Web Servers with FrontPage 98 **895**

Part XI Advanced Development for FrontPage 98

55 Introducing the FrontPage Developer's Kit **915**

56 Customizing FrontPage Menus **927**

57 Creating Your Own Templates **939**

58 Creating Your Own Wizards **949**

59 Programming the Wizard **961**

Part XII Appendixes

A Installing FrontPage 98 **977**

B Troubleshooting FrontPage 98 **983**

Index **995**

Contents

Introduction xxxv

Part I FrontPage Basics

1 Introducing FrontPage 98 3

What Is FrontPage 98 and Why Do You Need It? 4
Creation and Management of Web Pages 4
The Personal Web Server and the FrontPage Server Extensions ... 7
Microsoft Image Composer, Themes, and the Clip Art Gallery ... 7
Templates, Wizards, and FrontPage Components 9
Using Page Templates 9
Using Wizards 9
Using FrontPage Components 9
Web Technologies Supported by FrontPage 98 10
Summary 12

2 Using the FrontPage Explorer 13

Working with the FrontPage Explorer 14
Starting the FrontPage Explorer 14
Examining the Root Web 15
Views Explained 16
Using the Navigation View 16
Using the Folders View and All Files View 17
Using the Hyperlinks View 18
Using Other Views 20
A Quick Look at the Explorer Menus and Toolbar 20
Using the File Menu 20
Using the Edit Menu 21
Using the View Menu 21
Using the Tools Menu 22
Using the Help Menu 24
Using the Explorer Toolbar 24
Working with Webs in the Explorer 25
Creating Webs 25
Opening Existing Webs 27
Editing Webs 28
Deleting a Web 28
Using and Displaying Hidden Documents in a Web 28
Publishing and Copying a Web 29
Importing and Exporting Files and Webs 29
Importing an Existing Web 30
Exporting Files 32

File Manipulation in the Explorer 33
Deleting Files from the Current Web 33
Renaming and Moving Files 33
Associating Files with Editors 34
Summary 36

3 Working with the FrontPage Editor 37

Working with the FrontPage Editor 38
Starting and Using the FrontPage Editor 38
Editor Views 38
Editing Pages 39
Opening Existing Pages 40
Saving Pages 42
Using the Menu 43
Using the File Menu 43
Using the Edit Menu 44
Using the View Menu 44
Using the Go Menu 45
Using the Insert Menu 45
Using the Format Menu 45
Using the Tools Menu 45
Using the Table Menu 46
Using the Frame Menu 46
Using the Window Menu 46
Using the Help Menu 46
Using the Toolbar 47
Summary 48

Part II Creating Web Pages with FrontPage 98

4 Creating Web Pages with FrontPage 98 51

What Is HTML? 52
Creating a Page 53
Setting Page Properties 54
Working with the General Tab 55
Customizing the Appearance of Your Page 57
Customizing Your Colors 61
Defining Font Colors 62
Setting Margins 63
Customizing Pages with Meta Properties 64
Designing the Page 66
Creating Headings 67
Creating Paragraphs 68

Aligning the Text 69
Summary 70

5 Working with Links and Lists 71

Using Links 72
Using Relative Paths in Links 73
Using Direct Paths in Links 74
Using Links Within Documents 75
Creating Links with FrontPage 98 76
Creating a Link 76
Creating a Link from the FrontPage Explorer 77
Editing Links with FrontPage 98 78
Changing a Link's URL 78
Deleting a Link Partially or Completely 78
Following a Text Link 78
Creating and Editing Bookmarks with FrontPage 98 79
Labeling a Bookmark 79
Creating a Link to a Bookmark 79
Changing or Deleting a Bookmark 79
Visiting a Bookmark 80
Using Lists 80
Creating Lists 82
Bulleted Lists 82
Definition Lists 84
Numbered Lists 85
Nesting Lists and Collapsible Outlines 87
Changing a List Type 87
Summary 88

6 Creating Richer Web Pages with HTML Features 89

Using Line Breaks and Horizontal Lines 90
All About Line Breaks 90
All About Horizontal Lines 92
Adding Visual Variety to Your Documents 94
Using Superscripts and Subscripts 98
Working with Font Types 98
Working with Font Sizes 99
Adding Comments to Your Documents 101
Using Special Characters 102
Using Addresses 103
Using Formatted Text 104
Summary 105

7 Enhancing Your Pages with Images—The Easy Way 107

Using Images in Your Web Pages ... 108
Working with Images in FrontPage 98 ... 109
Importing Images ... 112
Cutting, Copying, and Pasting Images ... 114
Saving an Image to the Current Web ... 115
Using Background Images ... 115
When and How to Use Images ... 117
Using Alternate Text ... 119
Sizing Your Images ... 120
Placing Images in Your Documents ... 121
Sizing Images to Fit Your Needs ... 125
Designing Highlights with Images ... 126
Additional Enhancements for Images ... 128
Image Formats ... 129
Using GIF ... 130
Using JPEG ... 131
Creating Your Own Images ... 132
Using Color Maps ... 133
Interlacing GIFs ... 134
GIFs with Transparent Backgrounds ... 135
Summary ... 136

Part III Web Page Layout and Design with FrontPage 98

8 Designing Tables with FrontPage 98 139

Table Design ... 140
Creating a Table Using the FrontPage Editor ... 141
Drawing Your Own Table ... 141
Letting FrontPage 98 Help You Create the Table ... 142
Inserting Rows or Columns ... 144
Inserting a Table Caption ... 144
Editing, Deleting, and Merging Table Elements ... 145
Deleting Table Elements ... 145
Splitting Table Elements ... 145
Merging Cells, Rows, and Columns ... 147
Resetting Table Properties ... 147
Advanced Property Settings for Cells ... 148
Advanced Property Settings for Groups of Cells ... 149
Adding Color to Your Table ... 150
Adding Color to an Entire Table ... 150
Adding Color to Part of a Table ... 151
Adding Background Images to Your Table ... 151
Summary ... 153

9 Creating Frames 155

Frame-Enhancing Your Documents 156
Working with Frames: The Basics 156
Building the Frames in the FrontPage Editor 157
Adjusting and Dividing the Frames 158
Defining an Alternate Document 159
Saving and Using Your Frames Page 160
Using Frame Templates 161
Banner and Contents Page 161
Contents Page 162
Header, Footer, and Footnotes Pages 162
Header, Footer, and Contents Page 164
Horizontal and Vertical Split Pages 164
Top-Down, Three-Level Hierarchy Page 165
Nested Three-Level Hierarchy Page 165
Summary 167

10 Editing and Enhancing Your Frames 169

Customizing Your Frames 170
Naming Frames 171
User Adjustment of Frames 171
Optimizing the Frame Size 171
Frame Margins 173
Targeting Frames and New Windows from Links 173
Targeting Basics 173
Fine Tuning the Targeting 174
Creating Borderless Frames 175
Implementing Borderless Frames 176
Design Considerations For Borderless Frames 177
Putting the Borderless Design to the Test 179
Tips for the Banner and Contents Template 179
Tips for the Contents Template 180
Tips for the Header, Footer, and Footnotes Templates 180
Tips for the Header, Footer, and Contents Template 181
Tips for the Horizontal and Vertical Split Templates 182
Tips for the Top-Down Three-Level Hierarchy Template 182
Tips for the Nested Three-Level Hierarchy Template 183
Summary 183

11 Designing Pages with Style Sheets 185

What Are Style Sheets and How Are They Used? 186
How Does FrontPage 98 Support Style Sheets? 187
Which Browsers Support Style Sheets? 188

How to Use In-line Style Sheets ... 189
Defining the Style for an Individual Element ... 189
Defining the Style for a Group of Elements ... 189
Defining the Style for an Entire Page ... 190
How to Use Header-Defined Style Sheets ... 190
Defining Style in the Header ... 190
Streamlining Header Styles with Grouping ... 193
Editing Header-Defined Styles ... 193
Style Sheet Basics ... 194
Decorating Your Text with Fancy Styles ... 194
Using Font Styles ... 195
Adjusting Space Between Text Elements ... 196
Using Font Faces ... 197
Using Font Sizes ... 200
Summary ... 201

12 Advanced Page Layout with Style Sheets 203

Showing Your True Colors with Styles ... 204
Using Colorful Backgrounds and Text ... 204
Using Images in Backgrounds ... 205
Cool Spacing Techniques with Style Sheets ... 208
Getting the Most out of Margins ... 208
Using Borders and Padding ... 211
Playing with the Text ... 212
Summary ... 213

13 Working with Active Elements: Banners, Hit Counters, and More 215

Tracking Hits ... 216
Tips for Placing the Hit Counter on the Page ... 216
Setting Up the Counter ... 216
Using Scrolling Marquees ... 218
Positioning a Marquee ... 218
Sizing and Coloring a Marquee ... 219
Animating a Marquee ... 219
Using Netscape Plug-Ins and Embedded Multimedia Objects ... 221
Seamless Incorporation ... 222
Full Functionality ... 222
Maximum Flexibility ... 224
Working with Hover Buttons ... 225
Adding Stylish Text and Linking the Hover Button ... 225
Coloring and Sizing the Button ... 225
Adding Effects ... 226
Adding Sounds and Images ... 227

Managing Your Banner Ads 227
Sizing and Placing Banners 228
Adding Transitions to the Banner Ads 228
Adding Images and Linking 229
Summary 230

Part IV Web Page Graphic Design and Image Composer

14 Designing Web Sites with Themes 233

Viewing and Selecting Graphical Themes 235
Deciding on an Appropriate Theme for Your FrontPage Web 239
Adding Your Own Graphical Themes 241
Finding the Graphical Theme Files 243
Modifying Colors 243
Modifying Graphical Images 244
Modifying Font Families and Colors 246
Summary 247

15 Getting the Most from the Clip Art Gallery 249

Image Formats Supported by Clip Gallery 250
Inserting a Clip Art Image from the Clip Gallery 252
Using Clip Gallery's Advanced Features 253
Using the Find Feature to Locate Images 254
Adding, Deleting, and Modifying Keywords 255
Organizing, Adding, Deleting, and Renaming Categories 257
Adding and Deleting Clip Art Images and Clip Packages 262
Using the Update Feature 269
Summary 271

16 Working with the Microsoft Image Composer 273

Some Terms You Should Know 274
Invoking Image Composer from within FrontPage 98 275
The Image Composer Desktop 276
The Image Composer Toolbar 277
The Image Composer Toolbox and Color Swatch 280
The Image Composer Menu 282
Summary 285

17 Creating Great Images with Image Composer 287

Creating Sprites 288
Setting the Sprite Color 288
Using the Text Tool 289
Using the Shapes Tool 291
Using the Cutout Tool 296
Using the Paint Tool 300

Opening and Saving Compositions 304
Opening Existing Compositions 305
Starting a New Composition 306
Saving Compositions and Selections 306
Inserting Sprites 311
Scanning Sprites into Image Composer 312
Manipulating and Combining Sprites 312
Positioning Sprites 312
Resizing and Cropping Sprites 313
Rotating, Flipping, and Aligning Sprites 314
Grouping Sprites 315
Working with the Stack 315
Summary 315

18 Enhancing Your Images with Effects 317

Texture Transfer 318
Using the Effects Tool 321
Applying the Effects 321
Arts and Crafts 322
Color Enhancement 323
Distort 323
Gradient 324
Outlines 327
Paint 327
Patterns 328
Photographic 329
Sketch 331
Surface 332
Adding Plug-Ins 332
Using the Paint Tool 334
Summary 334

19 Optimizing Your Images and Color Palettes 335

Using FrontPage Editor's Image Tools 336
Using Restore and Undo with Images 336
Adding Text to Your Images 338
Adding Transparency to Your Images 341
Cropping Your Images 343
Washing Out Your Images 344
Making Your Images Black and White 346
Rotating, Reversing, and Flipping Your Images 346
Adjusting Contrast 347
Adjusting Brightness 347
Adding Beveled Frames 348

Selecting File Format 350
Reducing File Size 350
Resampling Your Images 354
Summary 356

20 Working with GIF Animator 357

Concepts of GIF Animation 359
Using GIF Animator 360
Creating the Background 361
Preparing the Foreground 365
Creating the Frames 366
Loading the Frames into GIF Animator 370
Working with the Animation 373
Point of View 381
Animation in Place 381
Showing the Passage of Time 382
Smooth Versus Sudden Change 383
Where to Find Animated GIFs 383
Summary 383

21 Creating and Designing Image Maps 385

Client-Side Versus Server-Side Image Maps 388
Setting the Image Map Style 389
Adding Hotspots 390
Adjusting Existing Hotspots 394
Changing the Position of a Hotspot 394
Changing the Size of a Rectangle or Circle Hotspot 394
Changing the Shape of a Polygon Hotspot 395
Changing the Link to Which a Hotspot Points 396
Deleting a Hotspot 397
When to Use Image Maps 398
Designing the Best Image Map 399
Summary 399

Part V Forms and Advanced Form Handling

22 Working with Forms 403

What Forms Are and Why You Want to Use Them 404
Form Design 405
Creating the Form 406
Hidden Fields in Forms 408
Adding Input Fields to the Form 408
Using One-Line Text Boxes 409
Using Password Fields 410
Using Scrolling Text Boxes 411

Using Check Boxes and Radio Buttons 412
Using Drop-Down Menus 415
Using Push Buttons 416
Summary 417

23 Getting More from the Form Page Wizard 419

Using the Form Wizard 420
Defining Page Title and URL in the Form Page Wizard 420
Adding, Modifying, and Removing Form Elements 421
Selecting the Type of Input 422
Presentation Options 422
Output Options 423
Finishing the Page and Closing the Form Page Wizard 424
An Overview of Input Types 424
Summary 426

24 Handling Form Output and Saving the Results 427

Handling Form Output 428
Handling Form Output Yourself 428
Using a Form Handler to Process the Output 430
Customizing the Form Results 431
Setting Up the File Results Tab 431
Setting Up the E-mail Results Tab 433
Setting Up the Confirmation Page Tab 434
Saved Fields Tab 436
Working with Custom Scripts 439
Choosing a Programming Language for Your CGI Scripts 440
Using UNIX Shell 441
Using C/C++ 443
Using Perl 444
Why Use CGI Scripts? 445
How CGI Scripts Work 446
Using CGI Scripts with FrontPage 98 446
The Action Field 447
The Method Field 447
The Encoding Type Field 448
Summary 448

25 Validating Forms 449

How Does the Validation Process Work? 450
Selecting a Scripting Language for Validation 451
What Types of Form Information Can Be Validated? 451
Validating Input from Radio Buttons 451
Validating Input from Drop-Down Menus 453

Validating Input from One-Line and Scrolling Text Boxes 454
Validating Text Data Types 455
Validating Numeric Data Types 456
Restricting the Length of Data Entries 457
Checking Input Values 457
Summary 458

26 Search Engines and Indexing Your Web Site 459

Introducing Search Engines and Indexed Databases 460
What Are Search Engines and How Are They Used? 460
What Are Indexers and How Are They Used? 460
Working with the Search Bot 461
Adding the Search Bot to Your Web 463
Creating the Search Page 463
Configuring the Search Bot and the Search Form 463
When Not to Use the Search Bot 465
Summary 466

Part VI Templates, Wizards, and FrontPage Components

27 Creating Web Pages with FrontPage Templates 469

Saving Time with Templates 470
Basic Templates 471
Normal Page 471
Frequently Asked Questions 472
Table of Contents 473
Bibliography 474
Pages with Newspaper and Magazine Style Layout 475
Search Page 475
Confirmation Forms 476
Summary 476

28 Guest Books and Feedback 477

Creating and Using a Guest Book 478
Getting Started with the Guest Book 478
Enhancing the Guest Book 480
Customizing the Guest Book Entries 481
Building a Better Guest Book 482
Updating the Guest Book 482
Creating the Guest Book Confirmation Page 483
Using the Guest Book 483
Getting Feedback 484
Creating a Feedback Page 484
Customizing the Feedback Results 485
Summary 486

29 Instant Web Sites with FrontPage 98 487

Saving Time with Instant Web Sites 488
Creating an Instant Site 489
A Quick Look at FrontPage Webs 492
Summary 493

30 Building a Discussion Web 495

What Are Discussion Groups? 496
  Open-Ended Discussion Groups: The Usenet Model 496
  Pros and Cons of Open-Ended Discussion Groups 496
  Restricted Discussion Groups: The BBS Model 497
  Pros and Cons of Restricted Discussion Groups 497
  Which One Is Right for You? 498
Creating a Discussion Group 498
  The Discussion Board as a New Web 498
  Features of the Discussion Board 499
  Configuring the Submission Form 500
  Different Types of Discussion Boards 501
  Organizing the Table of Contents 501
  Look and Feel 502
  Finishing the Web Creation 504
How Discussion Groups Are Logged and Updated 504
  Posting and Replying to Messages 504
  How Threading Works 506
  Where the Files Are 506
Managing Discussion Groups 508
  Traditional Group Handling 508
  Deleting Individual Messages 508
  Modifying Individual Messages with FrontPage 98 509
Summary 509

31 Creating a Customer Support Web 511

Using the Customer Support Web 512
The Welcome Page 512
The What's New Page 513
The FAQ Page 514
The Bug Reporting and Information Page 515
The Suggestions Page 516
The Download Page 517
The Discussion Area 519
The Search Page 520
The Technical Notes Page 521
Summary 521

32 Creating a Project Web 523

Using the Project Web ... 524
The Project Home Page ... 524
The Members Page ... 525
The Schedule Page ... 526
The Status Page ... 527
The Archive Page ... 528
The Search Page ... 529
The Discussions Area ... 530
Summary ... 531

33 Establishing a Corporate Presence 533

Examining the Corporate Presence Web ... 534
Determining the Pages for Your Web ... 535
Choosing Topics for Your Home Page ... 535
Defining the What's New Page ... 536
Creating Product and Service Pages ... 537
Creating the Feedback Form ... 538
Creating the Table of Contents Page ... 539
Creating a Company Standard ... 540
Adding an Under Construction Icon ... 541
Adding the Company Name and Contact Information to Your Pages ... 542
Choosing a Presentation Style ... 543
Creating a Task List ... 544
Summary ... 544

34 Automation with FrontPage Components 545

How to Use FrontPage Components ... 546
How Do FrontPage Components Work? ... 547
Using the Confirmation Field Component ... 548
  Associating Fields with Values ... 548
  The Confirmation Field Component in Action ... 549
Using the Include Page Component ... 551
Using the Scheduled Image Component ... 552
Using the Scheduled Include Page Component ... 554
Using the Substitution Component ... 555
  Using Default Configuration Variables ... 555
  Defining New Configuration Variables ... 556
Summary ... 557

35 User Registration and Restricted Webs 559

Working with Restricted Webs ... 560
Accessing Restricted Webs ... 560

Creating a Members-Only Web 561
Setting Up the Web for Registration 561
Configuring the Registration Component 563
Creating a Closed Web for Specific Users 565
Creating User Accounts in the FrontPage Explorer 565
Creating Computer Accounts in the FrontPage Explorer 566
Restricting Groups in the FrontPage Explorer 569
Summary 571

Part VII Adding Dynamic Content to Your Web Page

36 Scripting with VBScript 575

Learning VBScript 576
Putting VBScript to Work for You 577
Adding Scripts to Your Page 580
VBScript Basics 580
Variables 581
Arrays 582
Arithmetic Operators 583
Comparison Operators 585
Strings 586
Comments 587
Controlling Flow with Conditionals 587
Controlling Flow with Looping 589
Going Beyond the Basics with VBScript 591
Basic Procedure Classes 591
System Procedure Classes 594
Summary Example 596
Summary 598

37 Creating Interactive Page Controls with ActiveX 599

What Is ActiveX? 600
ActiveX Background 600
ActiveX Core Technologies 601
Using ActiveX and ActiveX Controls 602
Placing ActiveX Controls on a Web Page 605
ActiveX Controls You Can Use 605
Adding the Control 607
Setting Common Properties of Controls 608
Setting Unique Properties of Controls 609
Using ActiveX with VBScript 613
Changing Object Properties with Method Calls 613
Accessing a Control's Methods 615
Using Events of a Control 618
Summary 622

38 Scripting with JavaScript 623

Getting to Know JavaScript 624
Why Is JavaScript So Hot? 624
How to Use JavaScript Now 625
JavaScript Fundamentals 626
Working with Variables 626
Working with Data Types 627
Working with Strings 627
Working with Arrays 628
Working with Functions 628
Working with JavaScript Objects 630
Performing Calculations in JavaScript 630
Using Arithmetic Operators 630
Using Comparison Operators 632
Using Assignment Operators 633
Using Logical Operators 634
Controlling Flow with Conditionals 635
Using the `if` Structure 635
Using the `if...else` Structure 635
Nested `if` Structures 636
Using Conditional Expressions 636
Controlling Flow with Looping 637
Using `for` Loops 637
Using `while` Loops 637
Using `continue` and `break` Statements 638
Using JavaScript in Your Web Page 638
Writing and Printing to the Page 639
Displaying the Current Date and Time 640
Controlling Browser Behavior 641
Summary 642

39 Adding Java Applets to Your Web Page 643

Getting to Know Java 644
Java Safety 644
Platform Independence 645
The Truth About Java-Powered Pages 646
Why Is Everyone So Hyped About Java? 646
How to Use Java Now 647
How Applets and Applications Are Different 647
Using an Applet on a Web Page 647
Getting the Tools You Need to Create Applets 650
Packages in the Development Kit 650
Tools in the Development Kit 652

Configuring an Applet Editor for FrontPage 653
Compiling Java Programs 653
Using a Graphical Compiler 654
Using a Command-Line Compiler 654
Creating Java Applets 654
An Object and Class Primer 654
Applet ABCs 655
Displaying with `paint` 655
Using the Complete Applet 658
Working with Images in Java 659
Using the Java AppletViewer 661
Summary 662

40 Designing Pages with Dynamic HTML 663

Text Animation 664
Page Transitions 667
Collapsible Outlines 668
Dynamic Labels and Access Keys for Form Fields 670
A Lack of Standards 670
The Document Object Model 671
Dynamic Styles 671
Dynamic Content 672
Absolute Positioning and "2D Layout" 673
Data Binding 674
Summary 676

41 Using Push Channels 677

Creating Push Channels 678
The Channel Definition Format 679
Using the Channel Definition Wizard 680
Managing Multiple Channels 688
Designing Push Channel Content 691
Learning by Looking 692
Learning from Tutorials and References 693
Facing Dual Standards 694
Summary 694

Part VIII Working with Databases

42 Web to Database Connectivity with FrontPage 98 697

Web Database Access: Past and Present 698
Creating ODBC Data Sources 699
Database Access with Internet Database Connector Pages 702
Creating the Template File 702

Creating IDC Files with the Internet Database Connector Wizard 705
Viewing the Results 708
Database Access Using Active Server Pages 709
Creating a New Active Server Page 710
Running the Database Region Wizard 710
Summary 712

43 Advanced Database Setup and Custom Scripts 713

The Internet Database Connector Wizard's Advanced Options 714
The Query Tab 714
The Connection Tab 716
The Limits Tab 717
The Driver Specific Tab 717
Using a Database Search Form 718
Creating A Database Search Form 718
Searching with the Internet Database Connector 721
Searching with Active Server Pages 723
Introducing the ActiveX Data Objects 725
The ADO Object Model 726
ADO `Collections` 727
The `Connection` Object 727
The `Recordset` Object 729
The Command Object 733
Using the ActiveX Data Objects 734
Opening an ADO Connection 735
Creating an ADO Recordset 736
Summary 738

44 Working with SQL and Database Management Systems 739

The Reader's Club Case Study 740
Creating the Reader's Club Web Site 741
Using Microsoft Access 97 to Create the Database 742
Designing the Database 743
Creating the Data Tables 743
Defining the `RdrClubDSN` ODBC Datasource 748
Generating Web Files with Microsoft Access 97 749
Generating Internet Database Connector (IDC) Files 749
Testing the IDC Files 751
Adding Database Functionality to the Reader's Club Site 752
Using Microsoft Query to Generate SQL Statements 753
Creating Internet Database Connectivity Files with FrontPage 98 756
The Database Region Wizard 759

Migrating to SQL Server 760
Summary 761

45 Moving Up to Visual InterDev 763

What Is Visual InterDev? 764
Should I Use Visual InterDev or FrontPage 98 to Develop and Maintain My Web Site? 766
How Does Database Connectivity Differ Between FrontPage 98 and Visual InterDev? 767
Data Source Name Files 768
FrontPage Internet Database Connector and HTML Template Pages 768
Visual InterDev `global.asa` Files 770
The Newest Data Object Layer: Active Data Objects 771
The Database Development Environment of Visual InterDev: Visual Data Tools 771
Using ActiveX Controls to Access Databases in Visual InterDev .. 773
Building a Database-Driven Active Server Page with Design Time ActiveX Controls 774
Setting Up the Active Server Project 774
Building the Active Server Page 775
Populating the Table with the Data Range Controls 776
Building Database-Driven Active Server Pages with the Visual InterDev Data Form Wizard 779
Summary 780

Part IX Web Site Management with FrontPage Explorer

46 Organizing Your Pages 783

Shared Borders 785
Planning Your Page Organization 786
Understanding Page Relationships 786
Applying Page Relationship Theory 788
Creating the Web 790
Navigation Bars in FrontPage Editor 794
Modifying the Navigation Structure 799
Odds and Ends 801
Summary 802

47 Managing Your Web 803

Automatic Web Updates 804
Manual Web Updates 805
Using Variables and Includes 810
Summary 814

48 Configuring Firewalls and Proxies 815

Firewalls 816
Protection 817
Access Control 817
Security 817
Privacy 818
Logging and Statistics 818
Proxies 819
Proxy Service 819
How Proxies Work with Web Servers 820
Using Proxies and Firewalls with FrontPage 820
Defining Proxies 821
When FrontPage 98 Uses Proxies 821
Encryption 822
Accessing Your Server 822
Accessing Your External Server from Inside the Firewall 822
Accessing Your Server from Outside the Firewall 822
Summary 823

Part X Web Servers and FrontPage 98

49 Using the Personal Web Server 827

Why You Might Need a Web Server 828
Why an Individual Might Need a Web Server 828
Why an Individual Might Not Need a Web Server 828
Why Organizations Might Need a Web Server 829
Why Organizations Might Not Need a Web Server 829
Why Use the Personal Web Server? 829
Installing the Personal Web Server 830
Specifying a Directory 830
Checking Your Connection 830
Defining the Administrator 832
Starting the Personal Web Server 832
Running HTTP and FTP Services 834
Configuring and Running the FTP Service 834
Configuring and Running the HTTP Service 836
Internet Security Issues 837
Remote Access 837
Content Control 838
CGI Scripts 838
Intranet Security Issues 838
Content Control 838
CGI Scripts 839

Working with Access Controls 839
Controlling Access with User and Computer Accounts 839
Setting Global and Unique Access Controls 840
The Authentication Process 842
Internal Authentication 842
External Authentication 843
Summary 843

50 Personal Web Server Administration 845

Being a Webmaster 846
Webmaster as Web Author 846
Webmaster as Network Administrator 846
Combining Both Jobs 847
FrontPage Support for Webmasters 847
Configuring the Server 847
Settings in the `httpd.cnf` File 848
Settings in the `srm.cnf` File 849
The `mime.typ` File 852
The `access.cnf` file 854
The Basics of Web Server Administration 856
Administering the Personal Web Server from the Command Line 857
Managing and Verifying Links 859
Verifying Links 859
Recalculating Links 861
Summary 862

51 Working with Server Extensions and Multihoming 863

Using the Server Extensions 864
What Are the Server Extensions? 864
What Servers Can Use the Extensions? 865
Getting Help with the Server Extensions 866
Installing and Upgrading the Server Extensions 867
Installing the Server Extensions on Windows 95 and Windows NT 867
Installing the Server Extensions on UNIX 868
Multihoming 869
What Is Multihoming? 869
Multihoming Methods 869
Listening for Other Hosts 870
Connecting FrontPage 98 to a Multihomed System 870
Configuring FrontPage 98 871
Summary 873

52 Administering FrontPage Server Extensions 875

Exploring the Server Extension Administration Tools 876
Local Server Extension Administration 876
Local Administration with `fpsvradm` 877
Local Administration with `fpwinsvr` 882
Remote Server Extension Administration 884
Enabling Remote Administration 885
Remote Extension Administration with `fpremadm` 885
Remote Extension Administration with the Web-Based Forms 886
Summary 888

53 Using IIS with FrontPage 98 889

Introducing Internet Information Server 890
Version Considerations 890
Features 891
System Requirements 891
Installing the FrontPage Server Extensions for IIS 892
Summary 894

54 Using Other Web Servers with FrontPage 98 895

Reasons for Using Other Web Servers 896
Key Considerations for Using FrontPage 98 with Other Web Servers 897
Assessing the Server's Scalability, Reliability, and Responsiveness 898
Establishing Priorities for Server Functions 898
Developing a Budget 899
Determining the Feasibility of Using the Same Server 899
Evaluating the Level of Support of FrontPage Web Hosting Companies 900
Defining Processes for Transferring Content 900
Summarizing the Key Considerations 901
Using FrontPage 98 When the Server Extensions Are Unavailable 901
WebBot Functions That Rely on FrontPage Server Extensions 901
Server Compatibility Issues 902
Issues with Transferring Files and Content 903
Creating New FrontPage Webs on Other Servers 904
Using WebSite 1.1 for Windows 95 to Host Your FrontPage Webs 904
Some Quick Troubleshooting Steps 907

Updating Non-FrontPage Webs to Work with FrontPage 98 908
Updating Content on FastTrack Server 2.01 for Windows NT 908
Testing Your FrontPage Webs with a Browser 911
Summary 912

Part XI Advanced Development for FrontPage 98

55 Introducing the FrontPage Developer's Kit 915
Using the FrontPage Developer's Kit 916
Obtaining and Installing the FrontPage Developer's Kit 917
What's in the FrontPage Developer's Kit 917
The Template Examples 918
The Wizard Examples 918
The FrontPage Developer's Kit Utilities 919
Examining the CGI Scripts 922
Designer HTML and WebBot Extensions 923
Summary 925

56 Customizing FrontPage Menus 927
Menus: Do You Love Them? 928
What You Need to Know Before You Start 928
Getting Started with the Registry Editor 929
Creating New Menus 930
Building a Custom Menu for the FrontPage Editor 930
Building a Custom Menu for the FrontPage Explorer 934
Summary 938

57 Creating Your Own Templates 939
Templates: A Basic Overview 940
Template Directories 940
Creating the Parameter File 941
Creating Page and Frameset Templates 945
Creating Web Templates 946
Using the Web Template Maker 946
Creating a Web Template by Hand 946
Summary 948

58 Creating Your Own Wizards 949
The Basics of Creating Wizards 950
Wizard Directories 950
Creating the Parameter File for Wizards 951
Creating Your Wizard's Interface 952
Tracking Wizard Parameters Using Temporary Files 952
Input Parameters 953
Environment Parameters 954

Output Parameters 955
Putting Temporary Parameter Files into Perspective 955
Determining Where Your Wizard Should Look for Key Files 957
Using OLE Automation in Your Wizards 958
Summary 959

59 Programming the Wizard 961

Establishing a Connection to the OLE Server 962
Checking the Status of the Explorer When Necessary 963
Writing HTML Pages to Files 964
More OLE Automation with FrontPage 98 966
Using OLE Automation with the FrontPage Explorer 966
Using OLE Automation with the FrontPage Editor 969
Using OLE Automation with the FrontPage To Do List 971
Summary 973

Part XII Appendixes

A Installing FrontPage 98 977

Running the Installation 978
Choosing Installation Options 979
Testing the Personal Web Server 982

B Troubleshooting FrontPage 98 983

Solving Problems with the Editor 984
Problems Saving a Web Page 984
Image Map Display Problem 985
Forms and Text 985
Solving Problems with the Explorer 986
Problems Accessing a Local Web 986
Problems Accessing Remote Web Pages 986
Web Pages Don't Exist 987
Solving Problems with the Personal Web Server 987
Changing Port Numbers 987
Problems with Internet Information Server 988
Problems Accessing Web Pages 988
Solving Problems Accessing Your Web: No Network Access 989
Can't Access a Local Web 990
Can't Open a Web 990
Solving Problems Accessing Your Web on the Network 990
Solving Problems Publishing Your Web 991
Problems Moving Your Web 992
Missing Files 992
Unable to Connect to Web Server 993

Index 995

Acknowledgments

Special thanks to my wife and family, who continue to put up with the tappety-tap of my keyboard at all hours of the day and night. Without your support, *Microsoft FrontPage 98 Unleashed, Third Edition* wouldn't have been possible. Yes Junior, daddy's finished, so let's go to the beach! :-)

—*William Robert Stanek*

First, I give thanks to God for the many blessings that we so often do not see. Second, to my mother Phyllis, who raised me against all odds. Third, to my wife and family, who support my weekends spent away from them as I write this stuff. And finally, to three teachers I've had in what seems like a lifetime of academia. I had many good teachers, but three who never accepted anything short of excellence and stretched my mind to places I had never imagined. Thank you Donald Ellison, Charles Maxwell, and A.R. Marudarajan for always raising the bar.

—*Keith Leavitt*

Dedication

To all our friends for their love and support.

—*David and Rhonda Crowder*

I dedicate this work to my wife, Rosemarie, and my sons, Eric and Justin. You are each wonderful blessings from God to me.

—*Keith Leavitt*

About the Authors

Lead Author

William Robert Stanek (`director.net@worldnet.att.net`) is a leading Internet technology expert, an award-winning author, and a top Web site designer. Over the years, his practical and thorough advice has helped Web publishers, programmers, and developers all over the world. A few of the books William has written include: *Netscape One Developer's Guide, Peter Norton's Guide to Java Programming,* and *Web Publishing Unleashed, Professional Reference Edition.*

While many Internet books provide partial examples and perhaps a few working programs, William prefers to work with a balanced load of teaching examples and real-world examples that help you develop practical and usable skills. In his books, you will find complete solutions for your Web development and publishing needs. This book you hold in your hands is no exception. In this book, you will find everything you need to build your Web site or home page.

Beyond books, William is also a regular columnist and feature writer for magazines. Throughout 1997, he was a contributing editor and columnist for the Web Database Developer column in *Dr. Dobb's Sourcebook*; topics he covered included Web-database connectivity with LiveWire, scripting ODBC Web-database solutions, and writing Web-database scripts with CGI. William is also a contributor to *PC Magazine*, and you'll sometimes find his work in the PC Tech section. A sample of work in *PC Magazine* includes "Spotlight on JavaScript," "VBScript 2.0 and JavaScript 1.2," "VRML: 3D for the Web," and "Energizing Your Web Pages," in the June, August, and September issues from this year.

As a publisher and writer with over a decade of hands-on experience with advanced programming and development, William brings a solid voice of experience on the Internet and Web development to his many projects. His years of practical experience are backed by a solid education, which includes a Master of Science in Information Systems and a Bachelor of Science in Computer Science. When he is not writing or designing Web sites for the Fortune 1000, William enjoys spending time with his family. His favorite time of the day is when he steals a few minutes to read to the youngest.

William served in the Persian Gulf War as a combat crew member on an electronic warfare aircraft. During the war, he flew on numerous combat missions into Iraq and was awarded 9 medals for his wartime service, including one of our nation's highest flying honors, the Air Force Distinguished Flying Cross. William wrote Chapters 1–13, 22–39, 48–52, 55–59, and Appendixes A and B.

Contributing Authors

David and Rhonda Crowder were hypertext pioneers and have been involved in the online community for over a decade. Their company, Far Horizons Software, a Web site design firm, created the award-winning LinkFinder and NetWelcome sites. They and their cats live in Miami, Florida. David and Rhonda wrote Chapters 14–21, 40, 41, 46, and 47.

Craig Eddy currently resides in Richmond, VA. He is a Senior Developer for Pipestream Technologies, Inc., which is a leading producer of sales force automation and customer information management software. Craig specializes in Visual Basic, SQL Server, Microsoft Access, and Web site development. He has been an author for *Access 95 Unleashed, Office 95 Unleashed, VBScript Unleashed, Access 97 Unleashed, Sams' Teach Yourself Access 97 in 24 Hours,* and *Microsoft Visual InterDev Unleashed,* as well as co-author of *Web Programming with Visual Basic.* Craig is also involved in developing worldwide product distribution networks, and can be reached at `craig.eddy@cyberdude.com`. Craig wrote Chapters 42, 43, and 53.

Armando Flores is an Information Technology Architect for Coral Gables Consulting Group in South Florida, where he specializes in cross-platform systems integration (mainframe, midrange, client/server and Web). Armando enjoys the unique perspective of having worked for IBM and KPMG Peat Marwick as a Systems Engineer, Instructor, and Consultant. His current interests are design and implementation of Distributed Objects System. Armando is a Microsoft Certified Professional and can be reached via e-mail at `aflores@cgcg.com`. Armando wrote Chapter 44.

Keith Leavitt is the manager of Advanced IT Evaluation and Development at the Southern California division of a large aerospace firm. He holds BS and MS degrees in Electrical Engineering from Southern Illinois and California Polytechnic Universities, respectively. Keith wrote Chapter 45.

Edward J. Lee (`ejlee@cgcg.com`) is a principal with Coral Gables Consulting Group, a Microsoft Solution Provider company he co-founded in 1994. Edward has 17 years of experience in large-scale systems implementations and IT management consulting, and his areas of expertise include information technology planning and application development. During the past two years, he has focused on designing new Web-based applications and on extending legacy applications to the Web. Edward has had several speaking engagements, including a presentation on "Corporate Security on the Internet" at the Greater Miami Chamber of Commerce kick-off meeting in 1995, and "A Framework for Developing a Client/Server Strategy" at the Spring 1993 NetCom/Micro Solutions Exposition in Miami. Prior to launching his own firm, he was employed by IBM and EDS, where he played a number of technical roles in application development projects. Edward received his MBA from the Babson College Graduate School of Business in Wellesley, MA, and he holds an undergraduate business degree from Boston University. Edward wrote Chapter 54.

Tell Us What You Think!

As a reader, you are the most important critic and commentator of our books. We value your opinion and want to know what we're doing right, what we could do better, what areas you'd like to see us publish in, and any other words of wisdom you're willing to pass our way. You can help us make strong books that meet your needs and give you the computer guidance you require.

Do you have access to the World Wide Web? Then check out our site at `http://www.mcp.com`.

As the team leader of the group that created this book, I welcome your comments. You can fax, e-mail, or write me directly to let me know what you did or didn't like about this book—as well as what we can do to make our books stronger. Here's the information:

Fax: 317-581-4669
E-mail: `mtaber@mcp.com`
Mail: Mark Taber
Comments Department
201 W. 103rd Street
Indianapolis, IN 46290

Introduction

Web technologies are changing so rapidly that it is hard for mere mortals to keep up. So much has taken place in the past year that we had to go back to the drawing board and start over. We changed so much that we challenge anyone with a previous edition of the book to find a chapter in this new edition that hasn't changed. We hope that you'll reward our efforts to bring you the best of the best by buying this book and telling your friends about it.

True to form, Microsoft has put together a class act with the Web development tools you'll find in FrontPage 98. FrontPage 98 is designed so that novices and experts alike can create advanced Web pages using the latest technologies, including dynamic HTML, push, style sheets and much more. FrontPage 98 moves Web publishing a giant step ahead with a keen emphasis on design. You'll find lots of new features to help you create powerful Web pages with designs that will make the competition green with envy.

As you read this book, you will learn how to take advantage of the many features of FrontPage 98. We have taken great care to provide invaluable tips and pour our expertise into every page of *Microsoft FrontPage 98 Unleashed, Third Edition.* Today's Web publishers have powerful resources at their fingertips, and this book shows how to use every one of them.

Who Should Read This Book

Microsoft FrontPage 98 Unleashed, Third Edition is for anyone who wants to publish on the Web or who has considered publishing on the Web. Although this book is intended for those with a casual to accomplished knowledge of the Internet and the World Wide Web, the plain English approach makes this book perfect for just about anyone. We truly hope you find this book to be invaluable as you plot your course to success in Web publishing.

How This Book Is Organized

Microsoft FrontPage 98 Unleashed, Third Edition is designed to be the most comprehensive resource guide to FrontPage 98 available anywhere. Chapter by chapter, you will learn everything you need to know to design and publish dazzling Web pages with FrontPage 98.

In this new edition, we decided to get rid of the background information that introduced the Net, the Web, and publishing basics. Readers told us through their comments that they don't want this information, so we focus on the stuff you need right up front. In Chapter 1 you'll learn about the tools FrontPage 98 provides. Chapter 2 shows you step by step how to master FrontPage's WYSIWYG tool for managing your Web pages. Chapter 3 shows you the tasks you need to learn to become proficient with the all-important FrontPage Editor.

Part II, "Creating Web Pages with FrontPage 98," explores everything you need to know to create a cool Web page that is complete with multimedia features. Chapter 4 is a power primer for creating Web pages with FrontPage 98. You will find useful tips, expert advice, and a strong emphasis on design. Chapter 5 shows you how to add links and lists to your Web pages. Chapter 6 helps you jazz up the page with extras, like multicolored text and horizontal rules. Chapter 7 tells you when, how, and why to use images.

After you've worked with FrontPage 98 for a while, you will be ready to move on to advanced issues, like page layout and design. Part III, "Web Page Layout and Design with FrontPage 98," takes a comprehensive look at the issues you need to know to create powerful pages just like a real pro. Chapter 8 explores one of the hottest elements in Web publishing—tables. Tables are powerful aspects of any page and can help you control layout of text and images.

Because readers told us that they want to know more about frames, there are now two extensive chapters that cover every aspect of Web page design with frames. Similarly, readers told us that they wanted to know more about style sheets. Style sheets give you sophisticated control over the placement of elements on the page. Because style sheets are so powerful, yet not entirely easy to use, we've expanded our coverage of style sheets into two hands-on chapters that will teach you everything you need to know.

Part IV, "Web Page Graphic Design and Image Composer," takes page layout and design a step further by focusing on graphic design. Too often, graphic design is overlooked, yet your images tell the world about your Web publishing skills. There's no reason a beginner can't design graphics like a pro, and there's no reason a pro has to try to learn graphic design for the Web on his own. Chapter 14 helps you learn a powerful new feature of FrontPage 98 called themes. A theme is a design blueprint for all the pages of a Web site, and FrontPage 98 includes dozens of ready-to-use themes that have been designed by a group of experts. FrontPage 98 also includes an extensive Clip Art Gallery. In Chapter 15 you learn how to do more and go farther using the Clip Art Gallery.

Because readers told us that they want to learn more about Microsoft Image Composer—the handy image design tool included with FrontPage 98—we bolstered our coverage of Image Composer to three expansive chapters that will teach you the ins and outs of Image Composer's every feature. These chapters cover creating images with sprites, using image effects, improving your images, and optimizing your image's color palettes for the Web.

Form creation and design is another area of Web publishing that is difficult to master. In this new edition, we've rounded out our coverage of forms to five comprehensive chapters. Chapter 22 helps you learn how to work with forms in FrontPage 98. Chapter 23 tells you how to go the distance with the Form Page Wizard. Chapter 24 takes an inside look at form handlers. Chapter 25 explores form validation. Chapter 26 covers indexing and how to add a full-text search capability to your Web site.

Part VI, "Templates, Wizards, and FrontPage Components," explores three of the hottest features of FrontPage 98 and how they make Web publishing a snap. Here, we've again expanded our coverage from a mere three chapters in the previous edition to nine chapters that now focus on specific tasks and how you can accomplish them. You'll learn how to build a discussion forum, how to build a restricted web, how to create a guest book, and lots more.

Beyond HTML, a whole world of hot technologies is waiting to be put to use. In Part VII, "Adding Dynamic Content to Your Web Page," you will learn how to use all the latest and hottest Web publishing technologies—all of which are now supported directly by FrontPage 98. Chapter 36 covers VBScript. Using ActiveX and integrating ActiveX with VBScript is the subject of Chapter 37. Chapter 38 shows you how to use JavaScript in your Web pages. Chapter 40 explores animation, page transitions, and everything else dynamic HTML has to offer. Chapter 41 teaches you the ins and outs of push technology, and after reading it, you will be able to create and manage a push channel like a pro.

Next we explore Web-database connectivity, a fairly new topic for FrontPage publishing. Through four hands-on chapters, we take you step by step through everything you need to know to use your database with FrontPage 98. Chapter 42 tells you how to search and update your database from the Web. Chapter 43 explores advanced set up and custom scripts. Chapter 44 is a hands-on project that takes you through the entire implementation process with a sample database. Chapter 45 explores Visual InterDev, and how you can use it with FrontPage 98.

Although managing your Web site is the key topic of Part IX, "Web Site Management with FrontPage Explorer," the section covers much more. You'll learn how to organize your Web pages, how to manage your Web site, how to configure firewalls, and how to set up proxies.

Part X, "Web Servers and FrontPage 98," takes a close look at how you can use servers with FrontPage. The server included with FrontPage 98 is called the Personal Web Server. In Chapter 49, you learn all about using the Personal Web Server with FrontPage 98. Chapter 50 explores everything you need to know to administer the Personal Web Server. Because you might not be able to use the Personal Web Server, the next two chapters explorer remote administration with the FrontPage server extensions. In these chapters, you'll learn all about the new FrontPage Server Extension Resource Kit, multihoming, and more. Chapter 53 takes a detailed look at how you can use Microsoft Internet Information Server with FrontPage 98. Chapter 54 rounds out the section with a look at using other servers with FrontPage 98.

Customizing FrontPage 98 with the FrontPage Developer's Kit is the subject of Part XI, "Advanced Development for FrontPage." Chapter 55 introduces you to the features of the FrontPage Developer's Kit. Chapter 56 tells you how you can customize FrontPage menus. Chapter 57 tells you how to create your own templates. Chapters 58 and 59 provide a detailed look at creating your own wizards. Not only will you be able to use these templates and wizards with FrontPage 98, but you can also share the templates and wizards with other FrontPage publishers.

IN THIS PART

- Introducing FrontPage 98 *3*
- Using FrontPage Explorer *13*
- Working with the FrontPage Editor *37*

PART I

FrontPage Basics

CHAPTER 1

Introducing FrontPage 98

by William Robert Stanek

IN THIS CHAPTER

- What Is FrontPage 98 and Why Do You Need It? *4*
- Templates, Wizards, and FrontPage Components *9*
- Web Technologies Supported by FrontPage 98 *10*

Microsoft FrontPage 98 is an easy-to-use tool for creating and managing Web sites. It is the authoring and management tool of choice for thousands of people around the world. FrontPage 98 is used by people who thought they would never be able to establish a presence on the Web due to the complexity of creating and managing a world-class Web site and by old pros who like the convenience and ease of use FrontPage 98 offers.

As Microsoft Office users will see, FrontPage 98 utilizes the very familiar Microsoft Office interface. In fact, FrontPage 98 is the only Web site creation and management tool that is a member of the Microsoft Office family of applications. All the tools included in FrontPage 98 are also part of one complete package and you will find that it is surprisingly easy to become a Web publisher using FrontPage 98.

As yet the first authoring tool created for nonprogrammers that is robust enough for professional web developers, FrontPage 98 provides everything you need to design, publish, and manage your Internet or intranet Web site. Responding to the need for powerful, easy-to-use web creation tools, FrontPage 98 provides web authoring and editing features that help you create rich, dynamic Web sites.

What Is FrontPage 98 and Why Do You Need It?

Web technologies are growing at a phenomenal rate. When once there was only Hypertext Markup Language (HTML), now there is Dynamic HTML, cascading style sheets, ActiveX controls, plug-ins, applets, scripts, and much more. Keeping pace with this ever growing array of technology is confusing. Enter FrontPage 98, an integrated what-you-see-is-what-you-get (WYSIWYG) tool suited for creating and managing Web sites that is well ahead of the competition.

The following is a list of the key tools within FrontPage 98:

- FrontPage Editor and FrontPage Explorer, which you will use to create and manage Web pages
- Personal Web Server and FrontPage Server Extensions, which you will use to test your Web pages and to serve them to the world
- Image Composer, which you will use to create and edit images

Creation and Management of Web Pages

FrontPage 98 includes two powerful tools for creating and managing Web pages using a WYSIWYG authoring environment, the FrontPage Explorer and the FrontPage Editor. Not only does the FrontPage authoring environment display documents in a style that mirrors the style of the actual published documents, but the FrontPage Explorer and FrontPage Editor are also very easy to use.

The FrontPage Explorer, as shown in Figure 1.1, presents your Web site in a manner similar to the Windows Explorer and simplifies Web site creation and maintenance, particularly for complex sites. The FrontPage Explorer gives you multiple ways to view your site. Each of the various views provides a different type of overview of the Web site. To access any of the various views, you simply click on one of the view icons shown in the left side of the screen displayed in Figure 1.1. In all, there are seven views.

When you first start the Explorer, the Navigation View and the File View are displayed as shown in Figure 1.1. As you can see, Navigation View provides a hierarchical representation of your Web site with icons that indicate the various pages in your web. You can expand the view to various levels in the page hierarchy or collapse the view for a higher-level picture. File View lists all the files and folders associated with the current web. You can sort this list by name, title, size, type, modification date, editor, and any comments you've added. You will learn more about views in Chapter 2, "Using the FrontPage Explorer."

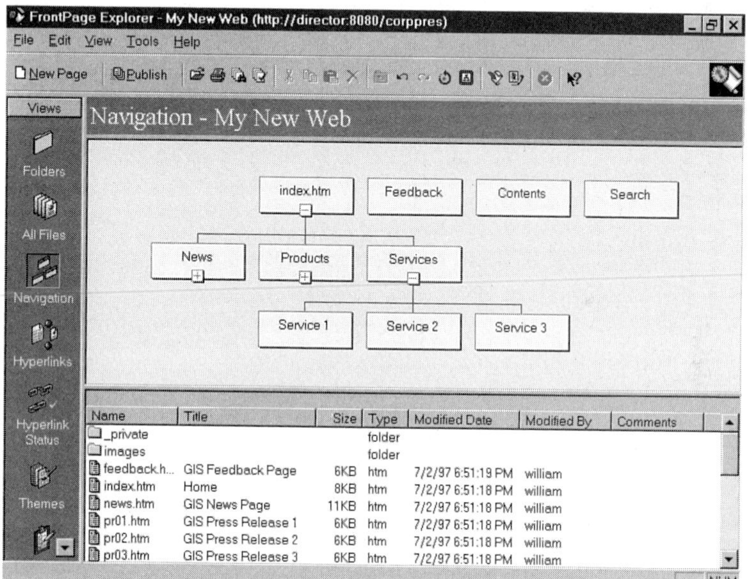

FIGURE 1.1.
The FrontPage Explorer is a hot graphical display tool.

Another FrontPage Explorer feature is the drag-and-drop interface, which lets you create a link by simply dragging a page or image icon to a specific place on a page in the FrontPage Editor. With the FrontPage Editor (shown in Figure 1.2), you can create your Web pages in a fully WYSIWYG environment. Because FrontPage 98 supports all standard file formats and protocols, you can link to any file, such as MPEG or PDF, as well as link to any FTP site, Gopher site, or newsgroup.

Also, as you can see from Figure 1.2, the FrontPage Editor fully supports image formats and displays images as you will see them in your published Web page. In fact, you can import any of more than a dozen common image formats into your Web page, and based on your selection, FrontPage 98 will automatically convert these images to a format that can be used in your browser.

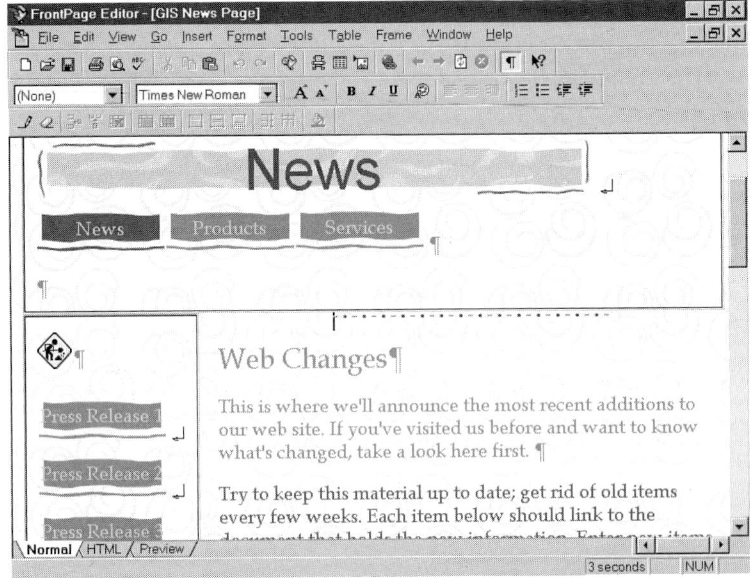

FIGURE 1.2.
The FrontPage Editor enables WYSIWYG authoring at its best!

One of the best features of the FrontPage Editor is the inline frames editor shown in Figure 1.3. Using the inline editor, you can view and edit all the frames in a frame-enhanced web at the same time. No more switching back and forth between pages or worrying about frame sources at all. Because you can manipulate the size of any frame using the mouse, there is no more guess work in determining the frame size.

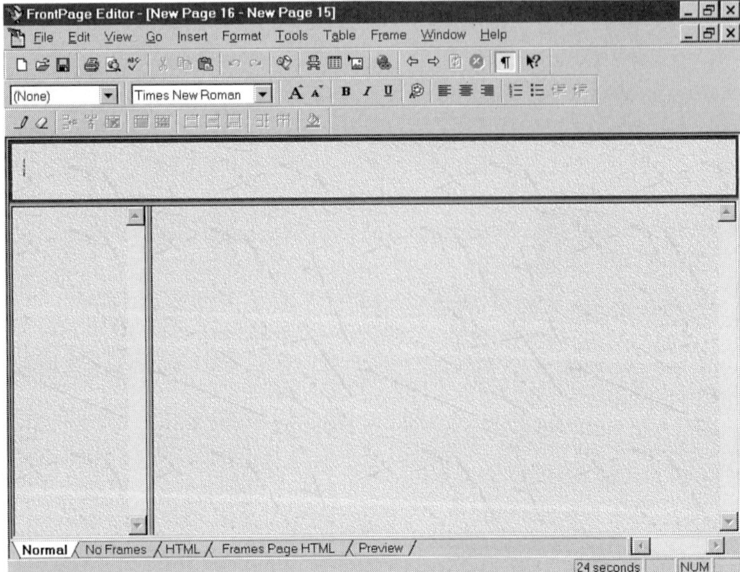

FIGURE 1.3.
The inline frames editor makes frame-enhancing your documents easy.

If you're not a crazed fan of frames, don't worry, because there are lots of other great features in FrontPage 98 that make Web publishing a snap. Using the table drawing tool, you can create a table complete with rows and columns simply by drawing the table on the screen with the mouse. Using active elements, you can add rotating banners, hit counters, animation, video, and more to your Web page at the touch of a button. FrontPage 98 also supports dynamic HTML, cascading style sheets, scripting, and advanced database connectivity.

The Personal Web Server and the FrontPage Server Extensions

Thousands of Web publishers face the complex task of keeping their sites up-to-date. With addresses to Web sites and pages changing every day, it is a frustrating task simply to keep sites current. FrontPage 98 introduces integrated tools that virtually do the job for you. For example, using a feature called Verify Hyperlinks, you can tell FrontPage 98 to verify every link in your entire Web site. FrontPage 98 examines local and remote links in the background while you go on to other tasks. When it finishes, you will see a complete report of all invalid and questionable links. Using a single interface, you can then update these links automatically for specific pages or for all pages in your Web site. This ends the task of individually chasing down broken links.

While not having to chase down broken links is great, you couldn't perform this magic trick without the Personal Web Server and the FrontPage Server Extensions. Behind the scenes these key FrontPage tools are hard at work to make your life as a Web publisher easier. In addition to making it possible to verify links in your pages, the server and the extensions enable most of the advanced features of FrontPage 98.

The Personal Web Server fully supports the Hypertext Transfer Protocol (HTTP) and the Common Gateway Interface (CGI) standards. If you don't have a Web server, you can use the Personal Web Server to serve one Web site or a dozen Web sites to the Internet community. If you already have a Web site, you can use the FrontPage Server Extensions to integrate your existing Web site with FrontPage 98. The extensions do much more than simple integration. They let you effortlessly copy or post your Web site between platforms and to other servers while still allowing you to use all the wonderful features of FrontPage 98.

CAUTION

You must install the FrontPage Server Extensions in order for FrontPage 98 to work properly with your Web server. For more information on the FrontPage Server Extensions see Chapter 51, "Working with Server Extensions and Multihoming."

Microsoft Image Composer, Themes, and the Clip Art Gallery

One of the biggest complaints from users who had previous versions of FrontPage was the poor support for advanced graphic and Web site design. Starting with FrontPage 97, Microsoft added the Image Composer to the line-up of tools found in FrontPage. The Image Composer allows you to create Web-ready images using advanced sprite technology. With sprites, each text and graphical element of an image is a separate component that you can easily manipulate.

Image Composer sports features that rival those of the best image creation tools on the market. Image Composer also includes a large library of ready-to-use images. For FrontPage 98, Image Composer has been completely updated and many of the difficult design tasks are now much more intuitive. You will learn all about Image Composer in Part IV, "Web Page Graphic Design and Image Composer."

Beyond the many images that are available in image composer, FrontPage 98 now sports a complete clip art gallery with hundreds of images that you can easily add to your Web pages. However, images are only one part of the clip art gallery; there are also pictures, sounds, and videos.

The increased emphasis on Web site design is very evident when you examine the Web site themes that are now a part of FrontPage 98. Using themes, you can add a specific look and feel to all your Web pages. A sample theme set is shown in Figure 1.4.

Amazingly, FrontPage 98 includes dozens of different themes. Each theme has its own set of images for banners, buttons, bullets, navigation, and more. Each theme also uses style sheets to coordinate colors for backgrounds, text, headers, and links in all your Web pages. Because every aspect on the page is designed to work with the theme you have chosen, there is no more guessing if a certain text color works with the background color you have chosen. See Chapter 14, "Designing Web Sites with Themes," for more information.

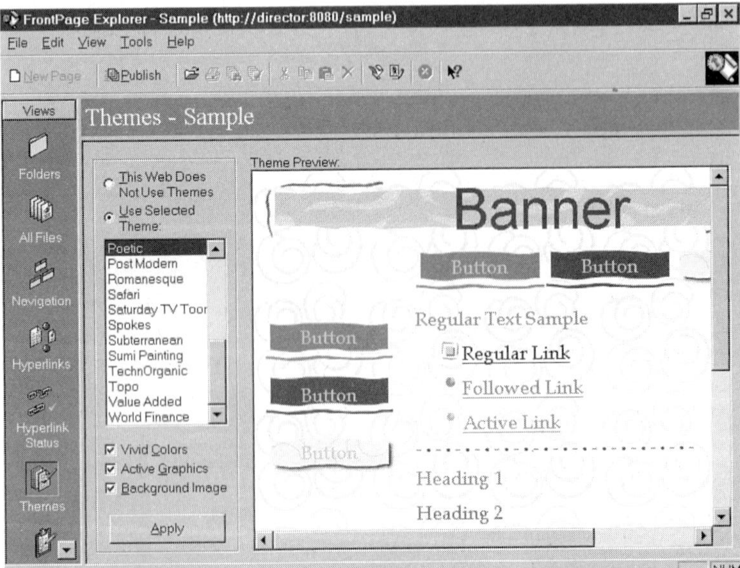

FIGURE 1.4.
Themes make it easy to create Web sites with a terrific design.

Templates, Wizards, and FrontPage Components

Beyond page editing and web creation, you should learn additional FrontPage publishing concepts. As you will quickly learn when you delve into FrontPage 98, templates, wizards, and FrontPage Components are at the heart of FrontPage 98. Without these elements, you simply cannot use FrontPage 98 as it was meant to be used.

Using Page Templates

When you create a page or a web in FrontPage 98, you usually base the page or web on a template. FrontPage 98 includes dozens of templates designed to make content creation a snap. You will find two types of templates in FrontPage 98: page templates and web templates.

A page template is an outline for a specific type of page, such as a home page or a customer survey page. A web template contains outlines for a specific set of pages, such as all the pages that relate to a business-oriented Web site. Usually, templates for webs and pages contain guidelines that make development easier. Just as there are very basic templates, such as the normal page template, there are also very advanced templates, such as the template for a customer support web. See Part VI, "Templates, Wizards, and FrontPage Components" for more information on templates.

Using Wizards

Some pages and webs you create in FrontPage 98 are very complex. To ensure that anyone can create these complex pages and webs without problems, FrontPage 98 includes powerful tools called wizards. Wizards help you automatically generate content. All you have to do is start the wizard and follow the prompts. As with templates, FrontPage 98 includes two types of wizards: page wizards and web wizards.

You can use page wizards to create documents with forms and scripts. Forms allow you to collect information from the reader. Scripts allow you to customize your pages for individual users and browsers as well as to add interactivity to your Web pages. A page wizard also helps you create a home page.

You can use web wizards to create entire webs with dozens of pages. FrontPage 98 includes two powerful web wizards: the Corporate Presence Wizard and the Discussion Web Wizard. Using the Corporate Presence Wizard, you can create a site that is designed to help you establish a presence on the Web. Using the Discussion Web Wizard, you can create a web with multiple discussion groups that company employees and customers alike can use to discuss topics of interest.

Using FrontPage Components

At the touch of a button, FrontPage Components (also known as WebBots) allow you to add advanced capabilities to your Web site, including interactive forms, navigation bars, text searches, and discussion forums. FrontPage Components offer drop-in interactive functionality, which greatly streamlines the development process and eliminates the need to write your own scripts or add complicated HTML commands. No programming is involved at all.

In FrontPage 98, you will find more than a dozen Components. Another name for a FrontPage Component is simply a bot. You can think of each bot as a program that runs when needed. Bots automate complex administration processes and eliminate the need to write your own scripts or add complicated HTML commands.

Before FrontPage introduced FrontPage Components, administration of world-class Web sites was the realm of those who earned the name Webmaster by being the best at what they did. Great Webmasters know how to create scripts that process the input of forms. With a bot, you can collect the results from forms, automatically add navigation bars, create pages with full text searches, allow registered users to access key areas of your web, and do just about anything else that once only a skilled Webmaster could do.

FrontPage Components are great for most publishing tasks. However, they cannot do advanced follow-on processing of input from forms, and they cannot help you generate content based on the type of the user's browser. In some instances you might have to use a custom script. Fortunately, FrontPage 98 allows you to create scripts written with either VBScript or JavaScript.

Web Technologies Supported by FrontPage 98

Although FrontPage 97 was a great improvement over FrontPage 1.1, FrontPage 97 still wasn't up to date with current Web publishing trends. One of the most notable technologies that FrontPage 97 did not support was cascading style sheets. As unbelievable as it seems, FrontPage 97 also lacked support for some of the HTML extensions in Internet Explorer—Microsoft's own browser.

Fortunately, this time around Microsoft did things right and FrontPage 98 features full support for current Web technologies and the major extensions to those technologies. A list of all the technologies supported by FrontPage 98 follows:

- **HTML 4.0:** Frames, tables, forms, and all the other goodies are fully supported.
- **HTML Extensions:** Background images, marquees, sound tracks, and many other extensions to HTML are fully supported.
- **Java Applets and Netscape Plug-ins:** Easy to add and manipulate applets and plug-ins.
- **ActiveX Controls and Active Elements:** Full support for ActiveX and Active elements such as rotating banners and hit counters.
- **Web Scripting with JavaScript and VBScript:** Features a scripting wizard for automatically generating scripts, validation routines, and more.

- **Database Connectivity:** The Database Wizard makes it easy to access and manage databases from the Web.
- **SSL Support:** Security controls are built into FrontPage 98 and the Secure Socket Layer protocol is directly supported.
- **Cascading Style Sheets:** Take advantage of all the features of style sheets without having to worry about complex markup tags.
- **Image Scanning:** Allows you to scan images into the FrontPage Editor using a scanner, digital camera, or video camera.
- **Dynamic HTML:** Supports transitions, special effects, and animation using Microsoft's Dynamic HTML specification.
- **Proxies and Firewalls:** Built-in support for configuring proxies and firewalls.
- **Push Technology and CDF:** Makes creating and managing push content channels with Microsoft's Channel Definition Format very intuitive.

Because publishing your Web site with previous editions of FrontPage wasn't as easy as it should have been, the FrontPage Explorer and the Web Publishing Wizard have now been completely integrated (see Figure 1.5). A new button on the FrontPage Explorer toolbar allows you to easily publish your FrontPage web to local and remote Web sites. Because the publishing process has been streamlined and made more intuitive, many of the problems with publishing your FrontPage web have been eliminated.

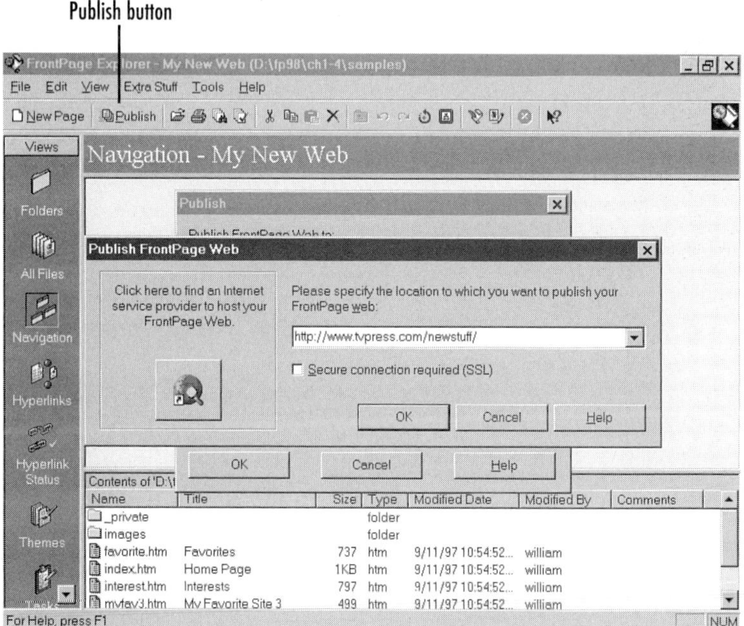

FIGURE 1.5.
The Web Publishing Wizard is now integrated with the FrontPage Explorer.

Summary

FrontPage 98 is a terrific tool for creating Web pages and managing Web sites. FrontPage 98 includes: the FrontPage Editor, the FrontPage Explorer, the Personal Web Server, and the Microsoft Image Composer. Anytime you want to create Web pages, you will use the FrontPage Editor. To manage your FrontPage webs, you will use the FrontPage Explorer. When you want to test out your pages or serve them to the world, you will need the Personal Web Server. Finally, you can use the Image Composer whenever you want to jazz up your Web pages with images.

Using the FrontPage Explorer

by William Robert Stanek

CHAPTER

IN THIS CHAPTER

- Working with the FrontPage Explorer *14*
- Views Explained *16*
- A Quick Look at the Explorer Menus and Toolbar *20*
- Working with Webs in the Explorer *25*
- Importing and Exporting Files and Webs *29*
- File Manipulation in the Explorer *33*

You simply cannot get the most out of FrontPage 98 without mastering the Explorer. The Explorer is command central when it comes to FrontPage 98; you will use the Explorer to perform most of your Web site management and maintenance tasks. The Explorer is also the main interface to everything that FrontPage 98 has to offer. You'll use the Explorer to start the FrontPage Editor, the Microsoft Image Composer, and the Personal Web Server.

The chapter begins with a quick look at the Explorer views, menus, and toolbar, and then takes a close look at various Explorer tasks for working with collections of Web pages called webs. Beginners should use this chapter as a starting point, because it takes a close look at using the Explorer. However, if you don't like or don't need step-by-step instructions, by all means, skip this chapter. Part I is the only section of the book that dwells on the basics. If you need help installing FrontPage 98, take a look at Appendix A, "Installing FrontPage 98."

Working with the FrontPage Explorer

The Explorer is your primary means of creating and managing FrontPage *webs.* Webs are collections of pages organized within a common directory structure. You'll also use the Explorer as your interface to other tools within FrontPage 98. Starting these tools from the Explorer is easy. To start the Editor, just click the Show FrontPage Editor button on the Explorer's toolbar. To start the Image Composer, click the Show Image Editor button on the Explorer's toolbar.

Starting the FrontPage Explorer

Before you run the FrontPage Explorer, you should make sure that the Personal Web Server or another Web server is installed on your PC. If you installed the Personal Web Server with FrontPage 98, the Personal Web Server should start automatically the first time you try to access a web in the FrontPage Explorer. If you are using a different Web server, you need to install the FrontPage Server Extensions for the server in order to use the extended features of FrontPage 98. You can find more information on servers and the server extensions in Part X, "Web Servers and FrontPage 98."

Starting the FrontPage Explorer is as easy as double-clicking the Explorer icon in the FrontPage folder. However, if you don't have the FrontPage folder in view, you can access the FrontPage Explorer through the taskbar's Start menu. Typically, an icon for Microsoft FrontPage is added to the Programs menu. In Windows, click the Start button, go to Programs, then select FrontPage Explorer.

When you first start the FrontPage Explorer, you see the Getting Started dialog box. Using this dialog box, you can create a new web or open an existing web. Although the Getting Started dialog is useful, you can tell FrontPage 98 to load the last web used in the previous session instead of displaying this dialog box. To do this, select the Always open last web check box in the lower-left corner of the dialog box. When opening a web in the FrontPage Explorer, you are typically prompted for a user name and password that was created when you installed FrontPage 98 or your server extensions.

Examining the Root Web

When you install FrontPage 98, the main directory for your web contains your *root web*. The root web is a starting point for content on your new Web server. All the webs you create based on templates and wizards are placed in subdirectories in the main directory for the root web.

The root web has a single Web page called `default.htm` and several related folders. You can access any of the folders related to this web simply by double-clicking the folder icon or folder name. To load the index page into the FrontPage Editor, double-click its file icon or name.

To access the root web in your browser, you must use the Personal Web Server or install the FrontPage Server Extensions for your current Web server. If the Personal Web server is running on your PC, you can access the root web by typing in the URL address of your server. For example, if your server is called `www.mydom.com`, `you can access your local server using the following URL:`

```
http://www.mydom.com/
```

However, if your server is called `www.mydom.com`, and you installed the server on port 8080, you can access this local server using the following URL:

```
http://www.mydom.com:8080/
```

Similarly, when you publish your web on your Internet service provider's Web server or if you are on a networked system, you can view the default document in your browser using one of these URLs:

```
http://www.yourcompany.com/
http://www.your_service_provider.com/~you
```

CAUTION

Before you make your web accessible to others, you want to replace the default page for the root web with the home page to your site.

Although it is a good idea to test documents in your browser, you get a much better picture of what is in the root web by using the FrontPage Explorer. To open the root web in the FrontPage Explorer, select File | Open FrontPage Web. The Getting Started dialog box appears, letting you select the `Root Web` from the list box. If your Root Web does not appear in the list, click the More Webs button to open the Open FrontPage Web dialog box. Select your Web server from the drop-down box or enter its address in the text box, then click the List Webs button. Generally, the root web will be the first web shown in the list of available webs (see Figure 2.1).

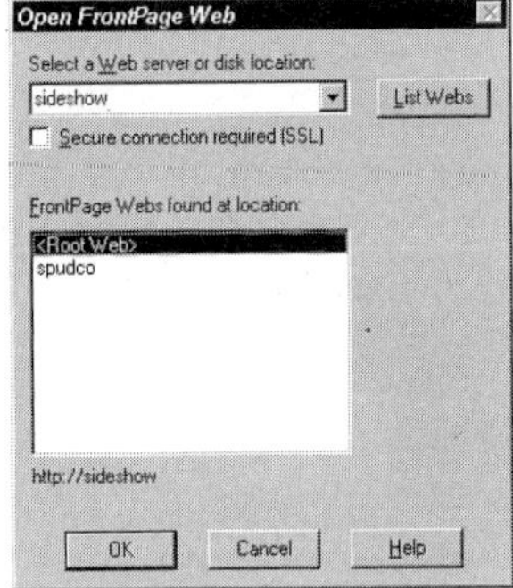

FIGURE 2.1.
The Open FrontPage Web dialog box.

Views Explained

The FrontPage Explorer provides you with many different ways to work with your webs through views. Each view simply provides a different way of looking at a web. Some views are good for getting an overall picture of a web. Other views are good for looking at specific aspects of a web. You can switch views by clicking one of the view buttons in the Views panel of the FrontPage Explorer, or by choosing the appropriate view from the View menu.

Using the Navigation View

The default view for creating new sites in the FrontPage Explorer is Navigation View (see Figure 2.2). If you are not currently in Navigation view, you can change to it by clicking the Navigation button in the Views panel. The Navigation View is split into two distinct areas, which are the Navigation pane and the Contents pane. The Navigation pane appears in the top right of the Explorer window and provides a textual picture of all the web pages. In Navigation View, links among web pages are shown in hierarchical fashion, which is sort of like a graphical map of your web. By viewing the graphical map, you get a clear idea of how pages within the web are linked together. The Contents pane appears in the lower right of the Explorer window. The Contents pane provides a list of all files and folders in the current web. You can rely on the Contents pane to tell you about all the files in a web. Together, these panes provide an at-a-glance picture of everything in your web.

In the Navigation View, you can expand and shrink the levels of the page hierarchy. Whenever you see a plus sign, it means you can expand the hierarchy to see another level of detail within the web. Whenever you see a minus, it means you can shrink the hierarchy to see less detail. To expand or shrink the view, simply double-click the plus or minus sign.

TIP

Each Explorer view has a different shortcut menu associated with it that allows you to quickly perform common functions associated with the view. To access the shortcut menu, right-click over a view pane. You will find that the shortcut menus make the Explorer much easier to work with.

FIGURE 2.2.
Initial view of the root web in the FrontPage Explorer.

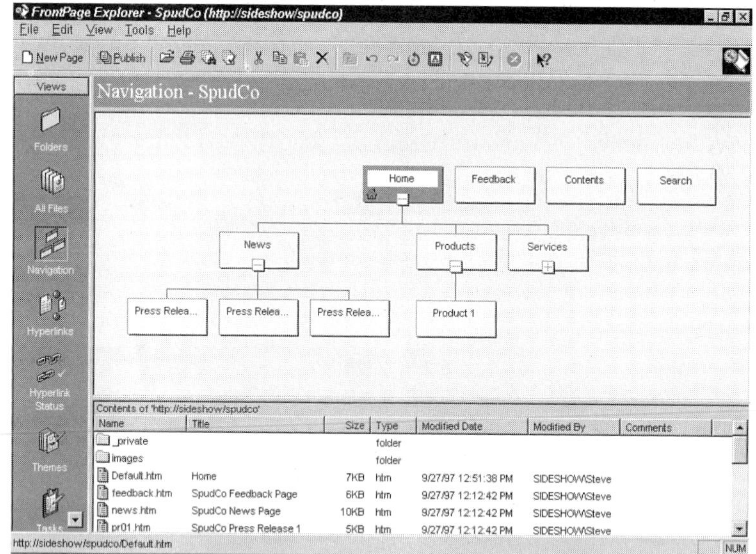

Using the Folders View and All Files View

In addition to the primary views, you can use the Folders View and the All Files View. If you want to look at specific files within a web, you can rely on these views to help you out.

When you select the Folders View (see Figure 2.3), you see a list of all the folders and files in the web. Folders are listed on the left and files within the current folder are listed on the right. You'll use this view when you want to work with files in individual folders.

When you select the All Files View, you see a list of all the files in the web. Instead of separate windows for folders and files, the specific folder for a file is just another column in the contents description. You'll use this view when you want to browse or search through all the files in a web.

Both the Folders View and the All Files View display summary information of the files used in the current web. As you can see from Figure 2.3, the information summarized in the Folders View is quite extensive and is organized into a directory tree structure. To see the contents of a folder, double-click the folder.

The column title bars are more than decoration. You can click any of the column title bars to order your files based on the information in the column. By default, your folders and files are organized alphabetically by title. You can, for example, click the file's Name title bar to alphabetize by filename.

All the columns can be resized as well. To resize a column, move the mouse pointer over the title bar area so that it is between the column you want to resize and the column that follows it. When you do this, the mouse pointer changes to a pointer with arrows on both ends. Now click and hold the left mouse button and drag the dividing bar to resize the column. When the column is sized appropriately, release the left mouse button.

You can easily edit the files in the Folders View. Just move the mouse pointer over an item summarizing information for the file, and double-click the left mouse button. The FrontPage Explorer opens the file for editing using the editor you configured for the file type.

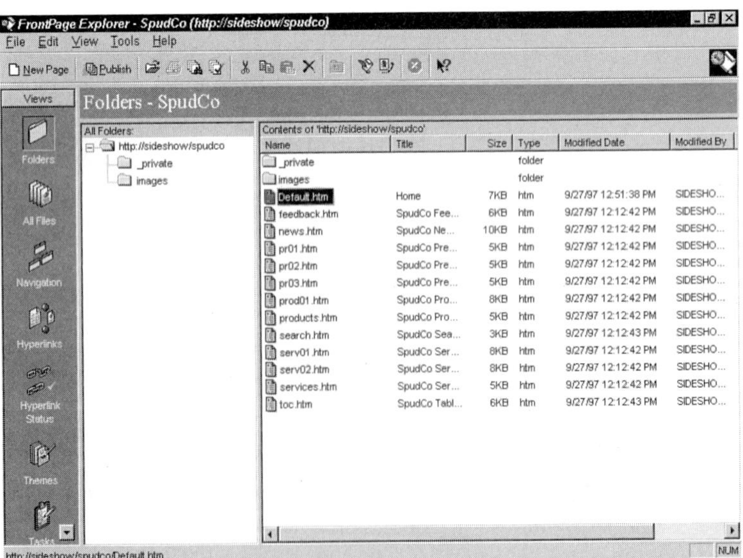

FIGURE 2.3.
The Folders View displays information about the files in your web.

Using the Hyperlinks View

The Hyperlinks View is a combination of the Outline and Hyperlink Views that were a part of FrontPage 97. Here, the views are simply combined to create a single two-pane view (see Figure 2.4). You'll use the Hyperlinks View when you want to examine the way pages within a web are linked together at various levels of detail.

The left pane of the Hyperlinks View displays your web as an outline, starting with the home page. You can tell that a document is the home page for the web because the icon shaped like a house replaces the document icon. By expanding the outline for a particular page, you can see the hypertext links and images within the page.

NOTE

Images used in the web are displayed only if the Hyperlinks to Images option is selected on the View menu.

The right pane depicts the organization of your web graphically. When you select a page in the left pane, a graphical picture associated with the document is displayed in the right pane. Links to and from the selected document are shown with a line. The line ends with an arrow that symbolizes the relationship between the linked documents. Just as you can expand and shrink the file list in the left pane, you can also expand and shrink the levels of linking in the right pane. Simply click a plus sign to see more detail and the minus sign to see less detail.

You can easily edit any file shown in the Hyperlinks View. All you have to do is double-click the file's icon, and it opens for editing, using the editor you configured for the file type. You can double-click a web page to open it for editing in the FrontPage Editor. You can also click an image to open it for editing using the Image Composer or any other image editor that you configured for use with FrontPage 98.

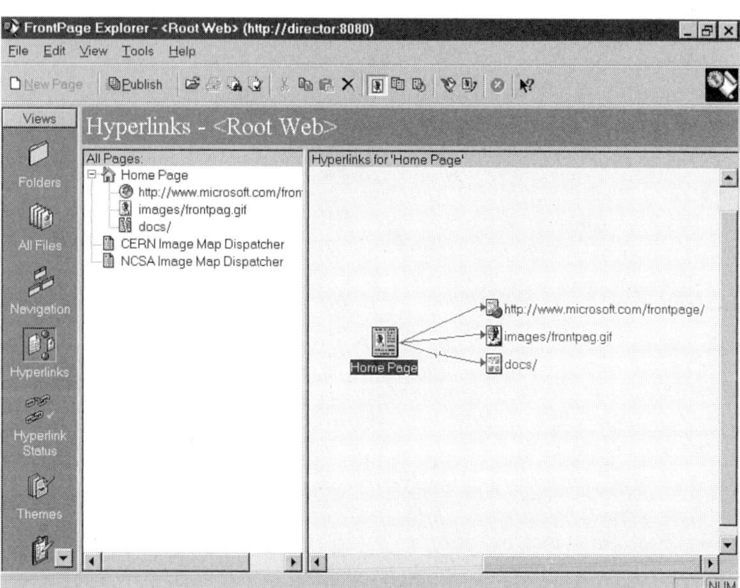

FIGURE 2.4.
The Hyperlinks View displays an outline and a graphical depiction for your web.

Using Other Views

The FrontPage Explorer has three additional views that you'll use from time to time. The following are these views:

- Hyperlink Status—Provides a quick summary of the status of all links in a web
- Themes—Allows you to assign a theme to the current web
- Tasks—Allows you to view tasks that you need to complete for the current web

You'll use the Hyperlink Status and Tasks views to help you maintain and manage your webs. You'll use the Themes View to assign or change the theme for a web.

CAUTION

If you assign a theme to a web, every single page in the web will be updated to reflect the current theme. Further, any page you create in the FrontPage editor while that web is open will also have elements reflecting the current theme. To learn more about themes, see Chapter 14, "Designing Web Sites with Themes."

A Quick Look at the Explorer Menus and Toolbar

FrontPage Explorer has five pull-down menus and a fairly extensive toolbar.

NOTE

Menu and toolbar items that are grayed out cannot be selected. These grayed-out options become available when you perform an action that makes them usable. For example, most of the options in the Explorer's menus are grayed out until you open a web or create a new web.

Using the File Menu

You use the File menu whenever you want to manipulate webs. This menu also lets you import files to the current web or export files from the current web.

You can create a web in a snap by selecting the New option. Then, when you want to work on your killer web site again, you can select the Open FrontPage Web option. Other options on the menu allow you to close, publish, or delete the current web.

You can use the Import option to bring existing documents, images, and other resources into the current web. This is how you let FrontPage 98 know you have existing resources that you want to work with. You can also export any selected document from the current web in

FrontPage 98. Generally, you export documents from FrontPage 98 when you want to save them in an alternate location.

The printing options are new to FrontPage 98. Using these options, you can print the Navigation View. The numbered options at the bottom of the menu allow you to quickly access webs you previously opened in FrontPage 98. The Explorer tracks the last four webs you opened. You can reopen these webs by clicking the web name in this menu.

Using the Edit Menu

You use the FrontPage Explorer's Edit menu when you want to manipulate files. Generally, the actions you can choose are limited based on the view you use. Some of the basic tasks on this menu allow you to select all the files in a web as well as to undo or redo previous actions.

The Cut, Copy, and Paste options allow you to move files around your web. Because FrontPage 98 automatically updates file paths for you, you don't have to worry that moving a file to a different location will cause problems in your web.

The Delete option lets you delete a file that is selected in any of the Explorer's views. Whenever you try to delete a file, the Explorer warns you that the document will be deleted permanently and asks you to confirm that you want to delete the file.

The Rename option allows you to rename a file. Although renaming a file usually invalidates hypertext links within your web, FrontPage 98 is smart enough to automatically update all pointers to the file within other documents of the current web when you rename a file.

The Open option allows you to open a selected document for editing in the FrontPage Editor. Another way to open files in the Explorer is with the Open With option, which lets you select an editor you've configured for use with FrontPage 98. The Open With option is very useful when you want to open files that are not in HTML format. For example, you can use it to edit a VRML document used in your web. Instead of starting your editor, searching for the document, and opening the document for editing, you simply select the document and use the Open With option to open the document with one of your chosen editors.

When you are in Tasks View, the Do Task option lets you perform the action associated with a task on your web's To Do list. A To Do list helps you manage the tasks related to creating and running a web. You can also mark the task as completed.

The final option on the Edit menu is Properties. When you use this option, the Explorer opens the Properties dialog box. This dialog box has two properties pages, which you can access by clicking the tabs labeled General and Summary.

Using the View Menu

The View menu is basically another way to change views in the Explorer. You can also use the menu to see a task history and to refresh the current web. Sometimes, when you access webs on another server, you'll find that the web did not completely display in the Explorer views. If this happens, use the Refresh option. Often when you change views, extra options are added to the View menu.

In Hyperlinks View, you'll find extra options on this menu. To see images used in the web, select the Hyperlinks to Images option. To see links every time they appear in the web, select the Repeated Hyperlinks option. To see links within pages, called *bookmarks*, select the Hyperlinks Inside Page option.

The menu is also changed when you are in Navigation View. You can expand the view of the web completely, size the view to fit the current window, or rotate the view.

Using the Tools Menu

The Tools menu lets you perform web management functions. The Spelling option allows you to check the spelling of documents in your web. You can check the spelling in a single document or in all the documents in your web. When spell checking multiple pages from the FrontPage Explorer, you can have a series of tasks added for each page containing misspelled words. You can use these tasks to track which documents you need to fix.

FrontPage 98 doesn't perform cross-web spell checking of your documents in the same way it does normal spell checking. When it finds documents with misspelled words, it lists them in the Spelling dialog box as it scans them. You can edit any of the documents by double-clicking the related entry in the Spelling dialog box or by selecting the document's entry and clicking the Edit Page button.

With the Verify Hyperlinks option, you can check the validity of all the links in your web, including links to resources on the Internet. A similar command is the Recalculate Hyperlinks option. This option searches the current web for links and dependencies and then updates the links and text index related to the web. You use this option to update the Explorer views when you add or change the content of a web in the Editor.

The Shared Border and Define Channels options are a bit confusing without a firm understanding of some advanced publishing concepts. When you work with navigation bars, you can use the Shared Border option to display borders shared between pages. You use the Define Channels options to create push channels. You'll learn more about push channels in Chapter 41, "Using Push Channels."

The next set of options in this menu displays FrontPage tools. The Show FrontPage Editor option starts the Editor, if it is not already started, and displays it. Similarly, the Show Image Editor option starts and displays your image editor of choice, which is usually Image Composer.

The Web Settings option opens the Web Settings dialog box, which contains server configuration pages that you can access with tabs labeled Parameters, Configuration, Advanced, Language, and Navigation. The Parameters tab lets you add keywords and values that you can insert into documents in any web using the Substitution WebBot. Using the Configuration tab, you can check server information and change the name and title for a web. The Advanced tab lets you configure the type of validation scripts and image maps you want to use with your webs. The Language tab lets you select the default language and encoding for documents, such as U.S. English. The Navigation tab lets you set text labels for any navigation bars used in your web.

To set permissions for your webs, you use the Permissions option. This option is available only if you run the Personal Web Server and the server is properly configured. When you set permissions for webs, you set permissions for the root web and all webs in folders under the root web.

The Permissions dialog box has three tabs. The Settings tab lets you set access permissions for the current web. The Users tab lets you add and remove accounts for those who manage webs, those who create documents for the web, and those who can use the web. The Computers tab lets you restrict access to documents based on IP address and provides controls for Web administrators, content authors, and end users.

NOTE

The Settings tab of the Permissions dialog box is not available if the root web is the current web. The Settings tab allows you to base permissions on the root web settings, which are only valid in webs other than the root web. Because all access and control permissions are based on settings in the root web, the Users and Computers tabs are editable only when the current web is the root web.

The Change Password option allows you to change the password for the current user login. As a security precaution, to change the password, you must first enter the password you originally used to log in.

NOTE

You can only change passwords if you run the Personal Web Server and the server is properly configured.

By selecting Options from the Tools menu, you access a general purpose dialog box with three tabs: General, Proxies, and Configure Editors. The General tab lets you toggle the display of warnings and the Getting Started dialog. The Configure Editors tab lets you configure additional editors for use with FrontPage 98. Using the Proxies tab, you can set up a firewall between your network and the Internet. The purpose of the firewall server is to shield your network.

Using the Help Menu

The Help menu is pretty self-explanatory. To access FrontPage's comprehensive help documentation, you use the Microsoft FrontPage Help option. The Microsoft on the Web option accesses the FrontPage area of the Microsoft Web site. If you aren't connected to the Web when you select this option, FrontPage 98 will launch your browser and initiate a connection. The About Microsoft FrontPage Explorer option displays information on your version of FrontPage. From the About Microsoft FrontPage Explorer dialog box, you can run a network test using the Network Test tool.

Using the Explorer Toolbar

Compared to the FrontPage Editor, the icons on the Explorer's toolbar are very basic. If you are familiar with Microsoft Office, you probably recognize many of the icons. The following is a summary of the icons and their uses:

Icon	*FrontPage Menu Option*	*Description*
New Page	New Page	Starts the FrontPage Editor with a page based on the normal page template open and ready to edit
Publish	FrontPage Web	Starts the publishing process for the current web
	Open FrontPage Web	Opens an existing web
	Print Navigation View	Prints the navigation view of the current web
	Cross File Find	Finds text in the current web
	Cross File Spelling	Spell checks documents in current web
	Cut	Cuts the selected file(s)
	Copy	Copies the selected file(s)
	Paste	Inserts the file(s) from the clipboard

Icon	*FrontPage Menu Option*	*Description*
	Delete	Deletes the selected file(s)
	Up One Level	In Folder View, allows you to go up one level
	Show FrontPage Editor	Displays the FrontPage Editor
	Show Image Editor	Displays the Microsoft Image Composer
	Stop	Tells the Explorer to stop trying to load a web or page
	Help	Displays online help documentation when you click a button, menu, or window after selecting this icon

Working with Webs in the Explorer

This section discusses webs and the directory structure associated with webs. Whenever you want to manipulate webs, you do so in the FrontPage Explorer. Webs contain sets of pages and resource files, such as images, sound files, and video files. All the pages and resource files in webs are organized into easy-to-manage directory structures.

Creating Webs

You create, edit, and manage webs in the FrontPage Explorer. To create a web, select File | New | FrontPage Web. This opens the New FrontPage Web dialog box, shown in Figure 2.5. Now you can tell FrontPage 98 what type of web you want to create. Usually, you will want to base your new web on one of the following Explorer web templates or wizards:

- Corporate Presence Wizard—Helps you create a web site designed for a company that plans to offer products or services on the WWW
- Customer Support Web—Creates a customer support web, which is also called a help web or a technical support web
- Discussion Web Wizard—Helps you create a web-based discussion group for posting and displaying user messages
- Empty Web—Creates a web without any pages

- Personal Web—Creates a personal web, with pages including your interest, photos, and favorite Web sites
- Project Web—Creates a web that helps you manage projects, such as software development

NOTE

To get the most out of these and other wizards and templates, take a look at Part VI, "Templates, Wizards, and FrontPage Components."

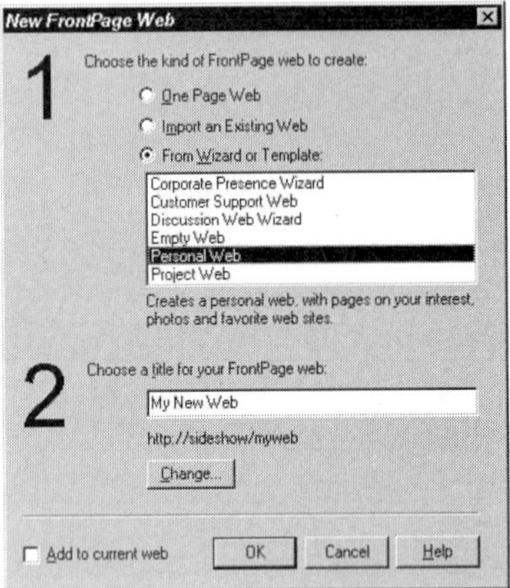

FIGURE 2.5.
Creating a new web.

After you choose the type of web you want to create, give your web a name and select a location for the web. Because you probably don't want to use the default location, click the Change button. You can now enter a new location for the web in the Change Location dialog box (see Figure 2.6).

To use a specific Web server for the new web, enter the full URL path to the server and a folder on the server for the web, such as the following:

```
http://www.your_isp.com/projects
```

In this example, the new web will be created in the `projects` directory of the `www.your_isp.com` server. If you want to create a web without using a server, simply enter a file path for the web, such as the following:

```
d:\mywebs\project
```

Here, the web will be created in the `mywebs\project` folder of the D hard drive. Note that whenever you create a web using an existing folder, FrontPage 98 will convert the folder to a FrontPage web.

FIGURE 2.6.
Selecting a location for your new web.

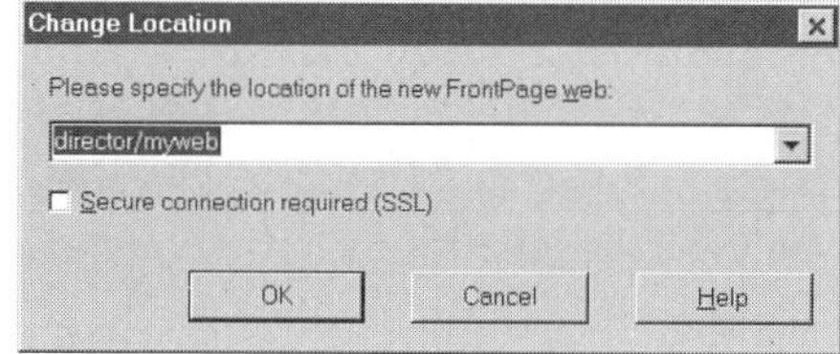

Opening Existing Webs

FrontPage 98 can access any web you created on local or remote systems. To open a web, select Open FrontPage Web from the File menu in the FrontPage Explorer. The Getting Started dialog box appears, letting you select the Root Web from the list box. If your Root Web does not appear in the list, click the More Webs button to open the Open FrontPage Web dialog box. Select your Web server from the drop-down box or enter its address in the text box, then click the List Webs button. Using the Open FrontPage Web dialog box shown in Figure 2.7, you can specify the location of the web you want to use by entering the URL address of a server or the path to a folder on your file system.

Simply enter the URL or file path directly into the Select a Web server or disk location field. After you select a server or folder, click the List Webs button to see a listing of available webs for the server or folder you chose. Keep in mind that all FrontPage servers and folders have root webs. Whenever you create webs within a root web, you actually create a subdirectory to use with FrontPage 98. When you click the List Webs button, these subdirectories are listed.

Sometimes when you try to open a web, you cannot establish a connection to the web's server. If this happens, you see a connection error. To clear up the error, you should check the following points:

1. Make sure that the Personal Web Server is started or that you've installed the proper FrontPage Server Extensions.
2. If you want to access a remote server, be sure you are connected to the network or to the Internet.

FIGURE 2.7.
Opening a web in the FrontPage Explorer.

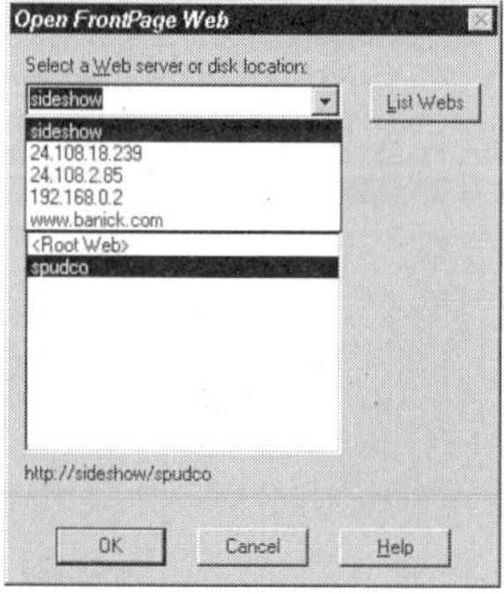

Editing Webs

Because webs represent complex structures of pages and files, editing webs is very different from editing individual pages. Generally, when you edit a web, you manipulate the web's attributes. Attributes for a web include its title, name, and location.

The two primary attributes for a web are its title and name. The only use for the web title is as an identifier in the FrontPage Explorer. Otherwise, the web title is not used anywhere else. For this reason, when you create a web, the web title is usually set to a default value, such as My New Web.

The web name, on the other hand, identifies part of the URL path to the files in the web. When you change a web's name, you actually move the web to a new subdirectory.

You can change a web's title and name using the Configuration tab of the Web Settings dialog. To open this dialog box, select Web Settings from the Tools menu in the FrontPage Explorer.

Sometimes, you want to create subdirectories for files and pages within a web. If so, change to a view that shows folders and filenames. Choose New from the File menu and then select Folder on the submenu.

FrontPage 98 creates a new folder with the folder name highlighted for editing. Now, enter a name for your folder. You can move pages, images, and other files into the new folder. When you do this, FrontPage 98 automatically updates all references to the files.

Deleting a Web

Occasionally, you need to delete a web and all the files associated with the web. To delete a web, select Delete FrontPage Web from the File menu in the FrontPage Explorer. After you delete a web, there is no way to get the web back.

Using and Displaying Hidden Documents in a Web

You can create directories that are hidden from users. These directories use the underscore as the first character of a directory name, which means that they are private and available only to the web's administrator. Often when you create a web, you have files that users should not access or view directly. In this case, you move the files to a directory users cannot access, such as `_private`.

As a Web administrator, you might need to view and edit files in private directories. To show these directories in the FrontPage Explorer views, you use the Advanced tab of the Web settings dialog box. Select the Show Documents in Hidden Directories field, and then click the OK button.

When you make changes in the Advanced tab, the Explorer asks you if you want to refresh the web. When you refresh a web, the FrontPage Explorer instructs the server to retrieve the web with the new settings, make updates as necessary, and build a new text index for the web.

Publishing and Copying a Web

Publishing and copying a web to a new location is essentially the same task. To get started, click the Publish button or select File | Publish FrontPage Web. The Publish FrontPage Web dialog box allows you to publish a web to a server or copy a web to a file system (see Figure 2.8). All you need to do is enter the URL or file path for the published web and click OK. Afterward, FrontPage will copy all your files to the new destination.

The next time you publish the web, FrontPage 98 will give you the option of publishing only files that have changed. Publishing only the files that have changed is a time-saving feature.

NOTE

Although FrontPage 98 distinguishes between copying a web to your file system and copying a web to a server, there really is no difference in how the web is copied. However, when you copy a web to a local or remote server, you are publishing the web and making it available for others. When you copy a web to your file system, you are copying the web to a new location that will probably not be accessed directly by users.

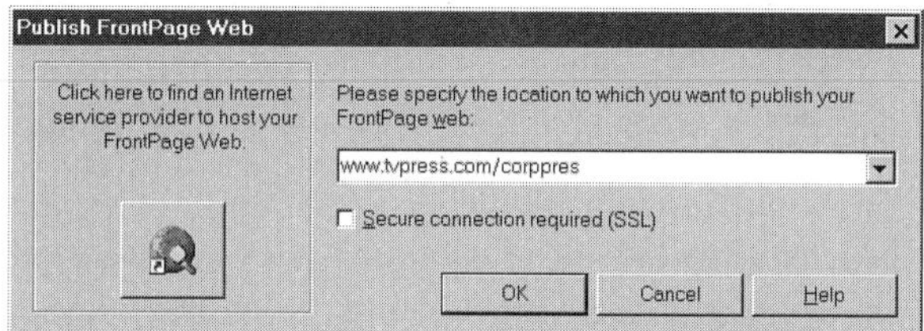

FIGURE 2.8.
Publishing a web.

Importing and Exporting Files and Webs

The FrontPage Explorer is your import/export specialist. Whenever you want to bring files into a web or move them out of a web, you'll rely on the Explorer's import and export features.

Importing Files to the Current Web

If you have already published on the WWW, you probably have web pages and images on your hard drive. When you want to use these files in FrontPage 98, you should import them for use in a specific web. This makes the files easier to manage and makes it possible for you to get all the benefits of FrontPage 98.

You can import files of any type in the Explorer. When you import text-based documents that are in a format other than HTML, the Explorer does not convert the page to HTML format. If you want to convert a text-based document to HTML format, you should open the page in the FrontPage Editor, then save it to the current web.

NOTE

Be sure to configure an editor for all files you import that are not in an HTML or standard image format. To learn how to configure editors for use in FrontPage 98, see Chapter 3, "Working with the FrontPage Editor."

Before you import files, start the FrontPage Explorer and make the web to which you want to add the files the current web. From the Explorer's File menu, select Import to open the Import File to FrontPage Web dialog box. Initially, almost all the dialog box's buttons are grayed out; you need to add files to the import list before you can use the other options. Your first step is to select the files you want to import.

You can select files in two ways. Using the Add File button, you can select individual files to import. Using the Add Folder button, you can select entire folders to import. You can even import from another Web site with the From Web button (which is explored below, in the section, "Importing an Existing Web"). Another useful button on the Import dialog box is the Edit URL button, which allows you to change the URL associated with a file you are importing.

After you select files for importing, they are displayed in the import list until they are removed from the list with the Remove button or imported into the current web with the OK button. Because of this, you can click the Close button to close the dialog box. Exit the Explorer and then restart the Explorer, and the files are still on the import list.

TIP

A common error you might see when importing files is that the file already exists on the current web. If you replace a file, you overwrite the file in the current web.

Importing an Existing Web

The Import Web Wizard is a handy tool to get to know. Using this wizard, you can create a new FrontPage web from an existing web. Your first step is to open the New FrontPage Web dialog box, and then select Import an Existing Web. The Import Web Wizard dialog box allows you to import a web from your file system or from an actual web on another server (see Figure 2.9). If you do not know the file path to the source web, click the Browse button. To include subfolders within the web, select the Include Subfolders check box.

The Import Web Wizard dialog box is similar to other dialog boxes. Using the buttons labeled Back and Next, you can move backward or forward through the Wizard pages, respectively. Using the Cancel button, you can exit the Wizard without importing the web.

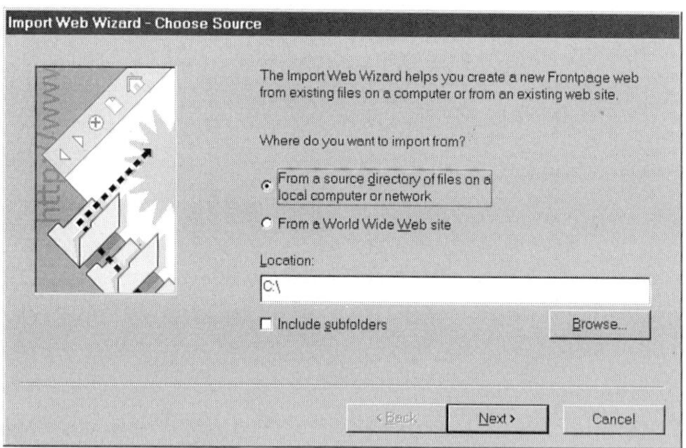

FIGURE 2.9.
Selecting a web to import.

After you select a source web, click the Next button. How the Import Web Wizard works next depends on where your source web is located. If you are importing a Web site from a live Web server by a URL, you are provided a screen like the one shown in Figure 2.10. Using this page of the Import Web Wizard, you can limit the amount of the source Web site that you want to download. You can choose to limit how many levels of the Web site will be transferred, how many total kilobytes, or limit to text and images for the download. If you are importing your site from your file system, the Import Web Wizard shows you a complete list of files that you are about to import (see Figure 2.11). You can exclude individual files from the list by selecting the filename in the list and then clicking the Exclude button. By holding down the Ctrl or Shift key, you can select groups of files to exclude. To bring back all files from the original unedited list, click the Refresh button. You can then edit the list of files again.

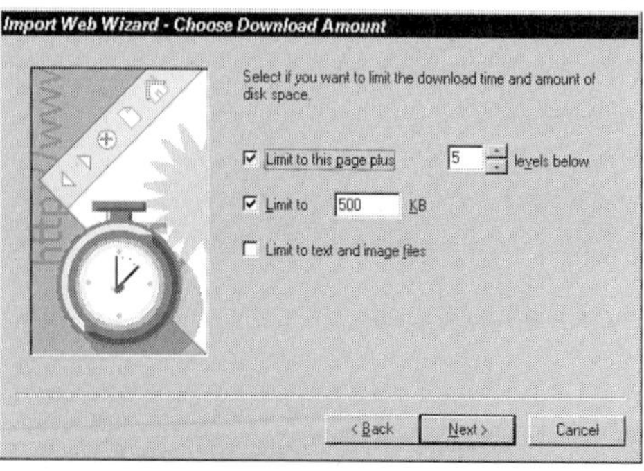

FIGURE 2.10.
Setting limits on the download.

When you are satisfied with your choices, click the Next button. This brings you to the final wizard page (see Figure 2.12). All you need to do is click the Finish button, and the Import Web Wizard imports the files and creates the new web for you.

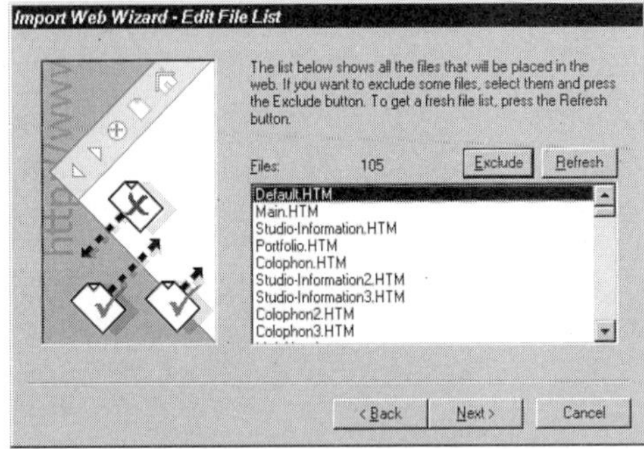

FIGURE 2.11.
Editing the file list.

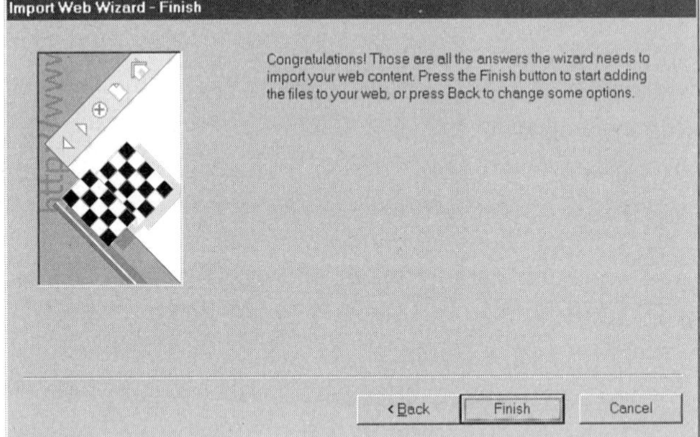

FIGURE 2.12.
To import files and create the new web, click the Finish button.

Exporting Files

Just as you might need to import files for use with FrontPage 98, sometimes you want to export files from FrontPage 98. When you export files from FrontPage 98, you really only save the files to a location other than the web they are stored in. Although you could use the Save As function of the FrontPage Editor to perform the same task, the reason to use the Explorer to export files is that you can export files without opening them.

To export files, select the file in any view and choose the Export option of the File menu. If you are using a view that shows filenames, you can select multiple files for exporting.

NOTE

If a page you are exporting contains images or other objects, the Explorer displays a dialog box asking if you want to save the images and objects with the page. Saving these objects with your page ensures that you have everything you need to publish the page in one place.

File Manipulation in the Explorer

Because the Explorer is designed to handle administration tasks, file manipulation is a big part of the Explorer's bag of tricks. You'll use the Explorer to delete, rename, and move files. You'll also use the Explorer to configure editors for use with specific file types.

Deleting Files from the Current Web

Deleting files from the current web is easy but not necessarily intuitive. When you want to delete a file, you should not do so using the Windows Explorer or at the system prompt. You should only delete files in the FrontPage Explorer.

To delete a file, select the file in any of the views and then use the Delete option on the Edit menu. The FrontPage Explorer asks you to confirm that you want to delete the files; if you do, click the Yes button.

TIP

Whenever files are listed by filename, you can select multiple files for deletion. After selecting the first file by clicking it, hold down the Ctrl key to select additional files. You can select a group of consecutively listed files by clicking the first file you want to select and then moving the mouse pointer to the last item and holding the Shift key as you click the left mouse button.

Renaming and Moving Files

You should use the FrontPage Explorer to rename files. To rename a file, you can use any view that shows the file by name. Simply select Rename from the Edit menu or right-click and select Rename from the pop-up menu. After you select the Rename option, you can edit the file name (see Figure 2.13). When you are finished, click a different file for the change to take effect.

Switching to the FrontPage Explorer to rename a file might not seem logical. After all, you could use the Save As option on the FrontPage Editor's File menu to create a new file. However, the old file the page is based on still exists at its original location. To make sure that there is only one copy of the file in a web, you need to switch to the FrontPage Explorer.

Moving files around the current web is also accomplished in the FrontPage Explorer. To move a file, left-click its entry, hold the mouse button, and drag the file to its new location.

The FrontPage Explorer only allows you to move files to existing folders within the current web. If you want to move a file to a new folder within the current web, you should create the folder before trying to move the file. To create a new folder, select New from the File menu, and then select New Folder. Be sure to give your folder a name that helps you identify its contents.

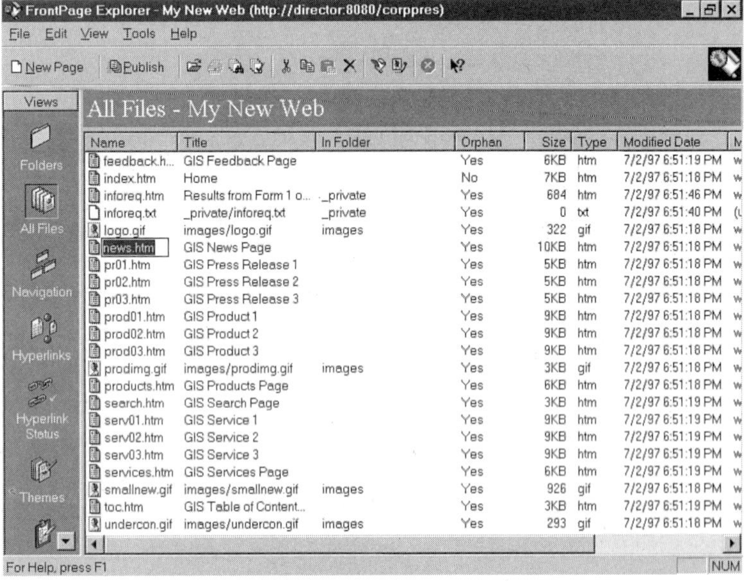

FIGURE 2.13.
Renaming files in the FrontPage Explorer.

When you move files around in a web, other pages in the web are often affected, especially if there are links pointing to the file you are moving. Fortunately, the Explorer automatically tracks all links to files in your webs, and if moving the file invalidates links in other files, the Explorer gives you the option of automatically updating links to the file.

Associating Files with Editors

Most files end with a three- or four-letter extension that identifies the file type or the formatting of the file, such as HTML documents that end with the `.htm` or `.html` extension. The FrontPage Explorer uses the file extension to determine which editor to use with the file you want to open for editing.

Using the FrontPage Explorer, you can configure additional editors for use with FrontPage 98 by selecting Options from the Tools menu. This opens the dialog box shown in Figure 2.14. As shown, select the Configure Editors dialog box to see a list of all currently configured editors and the associated file extensions.

Currently, the Windows Notepad is configured as the editor of choice for all miscellaneous file types. To add an editor to the list, click the Add button in the Configure Editors tab. As you can see from Figure 2.15, the Explorer displays a dialog box in which you can configure the editor. In the File Type field of the Add Editor Association dialog box, enter the three- or four-letter extension that identifies the type of file you will use the editor with. In Figure 2.15, you can see that the user is configuring an editor for use with PCX images, so the file type is `PCX`.

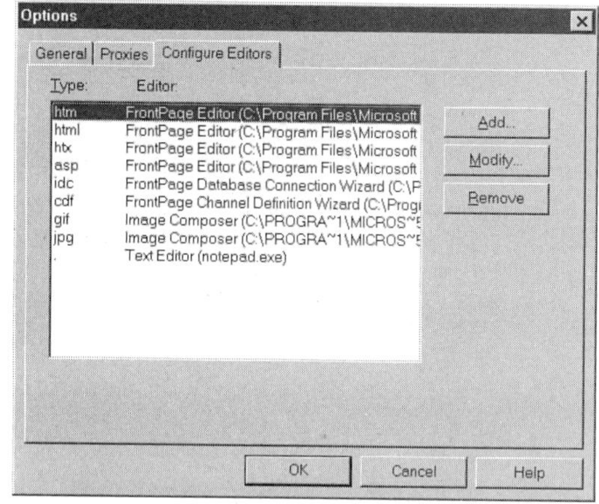

FIGURE 2.14.
The Configure Editors tab shows the editors configured for use with FrontPage 98.

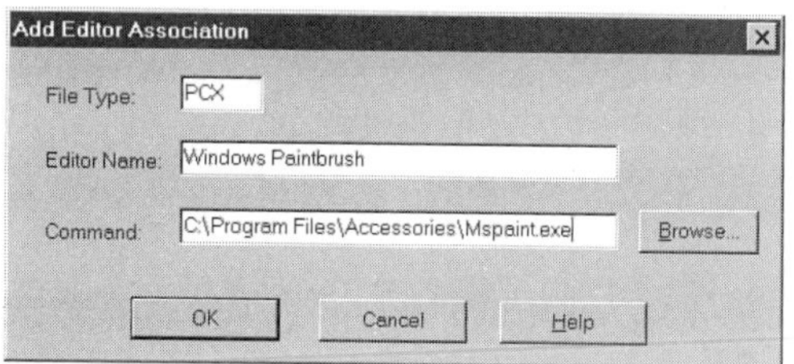

FIGURE 2.15.
To add editors, you must specify the file type.

In the Editor Name field, enter a name for the editor. The name does not have to be the actual name of the program; rather, it is the name with which you want to identify the editor. In the Command field, enter the full path to the editor's binary executable file. If you do not know the path, click the Browse button, and the Explorer displays a dialog box that enables you to browse your file system.

NOTE

Although most editors can be used with multiple file types, the Explorer allows you to configure only one file type at a time. You should go through the configuration process one time for each file type you plan to use with the editor.

At any time, you can make changes to editor definitions or remove them from the editor list. After selecting an editor you want to change, click the Modify button in the Configure Editors dialog box. This opens a dialog box labeled Modify Editor Association. To remove an editor from the list, select it and then click the Remove button.

Summary

The FrontPage Explorer is a powerful tool that you use to create and manage webs. Although webs are more complex than pages, FrontPage 98 has great features that make creating, editing, and deleting webs easy. The Explorer is also your command central for FrontPage 98; you can use the Explorer to start the FrontPage Editor, the Personal Web Server, and the Image Composer.

CHAPTER

Working with the FrontPage Editor

by William Robert Stanek

IN THIS CHAPTER

- Working with the FrontPage Editor 38
- Using the Menu 43
- Using the Toolbar 47

The most basic contents of your FrontPage webs are the individual pages that make up the web. Your tool of choice whenever your want to work with Web pages is the FrontPage Editor. Because this chapter covers basic concepts, advanced users might want to skim the chapter for key points.

Working with the FrontPage Editor

You can use the FrontPage Editor to create and edit pages. Pages are HTML documents that can contain references to images, sound, and even video files.

Starting and Using the FrontPage Editor

The easiest way to start the FrontPage Editor is to launch the FrontPage Editor from the FrontPage Explorer. To do this, click the Show FrontPage Editor button on the Explorer's toolbar. The Editor button depicts a red feather quill and a scroll.

Most menus in the FrontPage Editor are not available when you first open the editor. To activate these menus, you need to open an existing page or create a new page. Even when pages are loaded into the editor, you will find that some of the options are grayed out. These grayed-out options are not available until you perform a specific action. For example, the Paste option is not available until you place an object on the Clipboard using the Cut or Copy options.

Before you create or edit a page in the FrontPage Editor, you should load a web into the FrontPage Explorer. By loading a web into the Explorer, you tell the FrontPage Editor that this web is the current web. From then on, all pages you create in the Editor will be saved to the current web and all pages in the current web will be available for editing.

Editor Views

Just as the FrontPage Explorer has several different views, so does the FrontPage Editor. When you first load a page into the editor, you are in Normal view, which is indicated by a tab at the bottom of the editor window (see Figure 3.1).

Next to the Normal view tab, you will find two other tabs, called HTML and Preview, which allow you to access the HTML and Preview views respectively. If you want to view or edit the HTML markup for a page, simply click the HTML tab. If you want to preview the page with all its elements displayed, select the Preview tab.

In the Preview view, you view the page in the FrontPage Editor just as it should look in your favorite Web browser. Thus, all the comments and other formatting marks that you see in Normal view are not displayed.

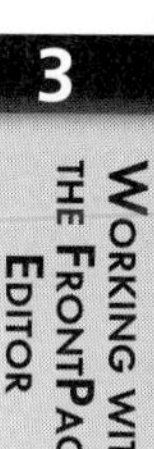

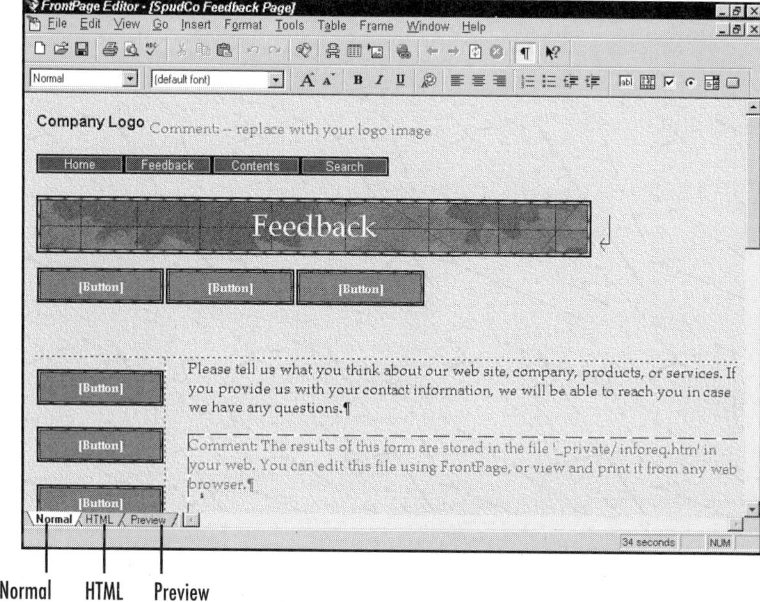

FIGURE 3.1.
The FrontPage Editor has three views.

Editing Pages

Before you can edit a page, you must first create it. You can start by opening the FrontPage Editor. To do so, click on the Show FrontPage Editor button in the FrontPage Explorer toolbar. This launches the FrontPage Editor and by default creates a new Web page based on the Normal page template. At a later time you can customize this template, but for now you can work with what you've got. If your FrontPage web uses a theme, it is applied to your new page.

If you want to create a page that isn't based on the normal page, open the New dialog box in the FrontPage Editor by selecting New from the File menu. Now you can choose a template or wizard on which to base your page by double-clicking when the pointer is over the template or wizard title (see Figure 3.2). Alternatively, you can use the arrow keys on your keyboard to highlight a template or wizard and then press Enter to make a selection.

As you might have imagined, when you want to edit pages, you will be using the FrontPage Editor. You enter text just as you do in any word processor. Because the editor is a WYSIWYG tool for creating Web pages, behind the scenes it is generating HTML markup for your page as you enter text, formatting, and images. You can add dozens of HTML elements to your pages with the FrontPage Editor. You will learn how to add these elements to pages in Part II, "Creating Web Pages with FrontPage 98."

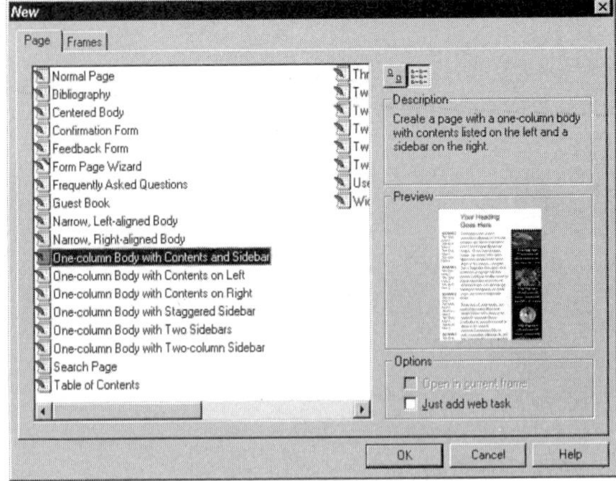

FIGURE 3.2.
Selecting a template or wizard for your new page.

Opening Existing Pages

When you select Open from the File menu to open an existing page, you see a dialog box that lets you access files based on their location. You can open files from the current web, files on your hard drive, or files on the World Wide Web (WWW). The Open page dialog box is set up to access files from the current web, which is the web you currently have open in the FrontPage Explorer. If there is no current web, the FrontPage Editor displays your operating system's standard Open File dialog box.

As shown in Figure 3.3, you can type a URL directly into the URL field to retrieve a local or remote file. Alternately, you can click the Find File button to access your file system's Select File dialog box. You can search the WWW for a remote page by clicking on the browser button in the lower right corner of the dialog box. Use of this button requires your system to have a default Web browser (such as Microsoft Internet Explorer), as defined for the operating system. When you install a new Web browser, it should automatically ask you if you want it to become your default Web browser.

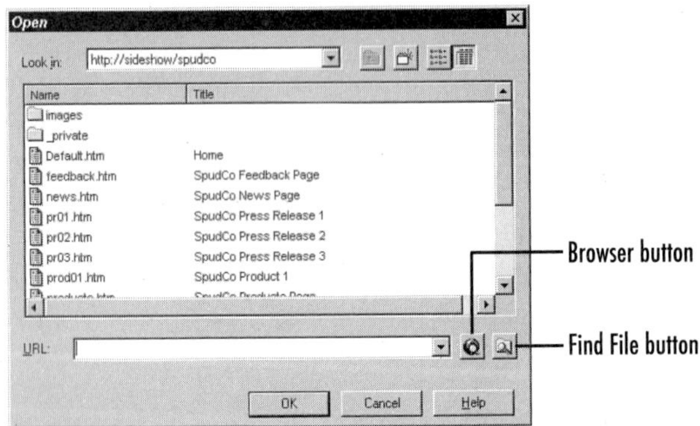

FIGURE 3.3.
Accessing current FrontPage webs with files listed by name and title.

The Look in field of the Current FrontPage Web tab is somewhat deceptive. You cannot use it to search your file system. Instead, this list contains folders within the current web that you've visited, and using this field, you can quickly re-visit a folder within the current web.

To the right of the Look in field is a button that allows you to go up one level in the folder hierarchy. You can only use this button when you previously moved down the folder hierarchy by double-clicking folders within the current web.

The FrontPage Editor supports multiple file and document formats. When you open files in a format other than HTML, the FrontPage Editor converts the page to HTML format. Formats supported by the FrontPage Editor include the following:

HTML (`.htm`, `.html`, `.htx`, `.asp`, `.htt`)

Rich Text Format (`.rtf`)

ASCII text (`.txt`)

Microsoft Excel (`.xls`, `.xlw`)

Windows Word 2.0/6.0/95/97 (`.doc`)

Microsoft Works (`.wps`)

WordPerfect 6.x (`.wpd`, `.doc`)

Most document formats are automatically converted to HTML. The converted page is formatted as closely as possible to the original layout. Pages in ASCII text format are not automatically converted. Before the editor converts the page, you must specify how you want the page to be formatted using the dialog box shown in Figure 3.4. Using the radio buttons within the dialog box, you are given the option to import the text in one of four fashions.

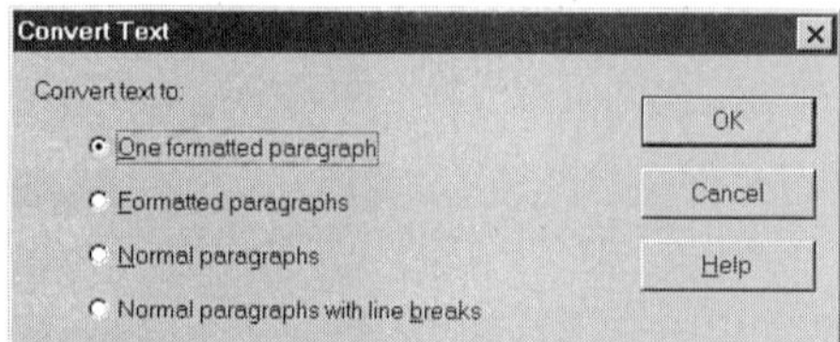

FIGURE 3.4.
Selecting a style for ASCII text pages.

Usually, you want to use the default option, which attempts to import the page with paragraph returns intact. The following is a summary of each of the options:

One formatted paragraph	Your page is imported as formatted text, and paragraph returns are not always preserved. This is the default option.
Formatted paragraphs	Your page is imported as formatted text with paragraph returns preserved.

Normal paragraphs	Your page is imported as text using the normal text style, and paragraph returns are not always preserved.
Normal paragraphs with line breaks	Your page is imported as text using the normal text style, and paragraph returns are preserved.

NOTE

The difference between normal text and formatted text is the font the browser uses. Normal text is displayed with the standard proportional font, such as Times Roman, used by the browser. Formatted text is displayed with a non-proportional font like the one most typewriters use, such as Courier.

Saving Pages

To save a page in the FrontPage Editor, select either Save or Save As from the File menu. All pages are saved to the location you opened them from, which is usually the current web. Because a new page has yet to be named, the Save As dialog box is opened when you select Save from the File menu. If you do not have a web active in the FrontPage Explorer, you will only be able to save the page to your file system.

All pages you create in the FrontPage Editor are given a default title and file name. Usually, you will want to enter a new title and filename. Enter the title in the Title text box. The title should describe the contents of the page. Enter the filename in the URL text box. This filename will be part of the document's URL (in addition to the path and server name). The filename should end with an `.htm` or `.html` extension, which identify the page as an HTML document. When you are finished, click OK to save the page to the current web.

The Save As dialog box enables you to save pages as files or as templates. To save the page as a template, click the As Template button, which creates a new page template based on the contents of your page. When saving your page as a template, you are prompted with the Save As Template dialog box, which allows you to define a Title, Name, and Description for your new template. If you want to save over an existing template, click the Browse button to select the template by name. When your template has been saved, you can create pages based on this template using the New Page dialog box.

NOTE

If your newly saved page on your hard drive contains images or other objects, the FrontPage Editor allows you to save the attached images and objects with the page. Saving these objects with the page ensures that you have everything you need to publish the page in one place (typically a subdirectory in your web or on your hard drive).

Using the Menu

If you've used the FrontPage Editor, you probably know the menu is quite extensive. This section does not examine the many options in detail. Instead, it examines the basic menus that are not discussed in other chapters and provides an overview of other menus.

NOTE

Most menus in the FrontPage Editor are not available until you have a file open for editing, typically from the FrontPage Explorer. Even when pages are loaded into the editor, you will find that some of the options are grayed out. These grayed-out options are not available until you perform a specific action. For example, the Paste option is not available until you place an object on the Clipboard using the Cut or Copy options.

Using the File Menu

You can use the File menu whenever you want to manipulate files. The menu also lets you view file properties and printer settings.

The first section of the File menu is for creating, opening, and closing files. To create a new page, select the New option. To close the current page, select the Close option.

The File menu allows you to save pages in one of three ways. You can save the page to its current filename and location using the Save option. This means if you opened the document from the current web, the document is saved to the current web. If you opened the document from a file on your hard drive, the file is saved to its location on the hard drive and not to the current web. If you want to save a file to the current web that you opened from a file on your hard drive or an external location on the Internet, you should use the Save As option. You can also use the Save As option to save to a new location for a file opened from the current web. To save all the files currently open in the FrontPage Editor, select the Save All option.

Using the Preview in Browser option, you can preview the current page in your browser. Other options let you check page setup for printing, preview the document before printing, and print the document. You have similar options for working with a fax.

To examine properties associated with a page, you can use the Page Properties option. Page properties relate to the page title and base location, background images and sounds, margins and language settings, and custom META tags. Page properties are different from the page settings used for printing the document that you see if you select the Page Setup option.

The Send option lets you send the current file as an e-mail attachment. This is great if you want to get a document to someone quickly.

The numbered options at the bottom of the menu allow you to quickly access files you previously opened. The FrontPage Editor tracks the last four files you opened. You can reopen these files by clicking the filename in this menu.

The final menu option lets you exit the FrontPage Editor and closes all open files. If you've made changes to files, the FrontPage Editor displays a prompt asking whether you want to save the files.

Using the Edit Menu

You use the Edit menu when you want to perform editing functions such as cut, copy, or paste. Two terrific features of the FrontPage Editor are multilevel undo and redo. With multilevel undo and redo, the FrontPage Editor tracks when you use any options that affect the content of the current page and allows you to undo them one by one. If you undo something by mistake, you can select the redo option to put the FrontPage Editor back in its previous state. Sometimes, the undo or redo options are not available. This usually happens when there is nothing to undo or redo. However, some actions can't be recovered, and if you try to undo or redo them, the FrontPage Editor does not let you.

You use many of the other options in the Edit menu just as you use them in your favorite word processor. You use the Cut option to remove selected text, images, and resource references from the page and copy them to the Clipboard. The Copy option copies selected items to the Clipboard. When they are on the Clipboard, you can use the Paste option to insert the items into the page at the current insertion point.

The Clear option is a simple delete function that erases selected text, images, and resource references. Because these items are not placed on the Clipboard, you need to be careful when using this option.

To find text referenced in the current page, you can use the Find option. To search for and replace text referenced in the current page, you can use the Replace option.

The Add Task option adds a task related to the current page to the Task list. When you select this option, the Editor opens the New Task dialog box. The Task list helps you manage the tasks related to creating and running a web.

The Bookmark, Hyperlink, and Unlink options create and manipulate hypertext references on your pages. Links and bookmarks are explained in Chapter 5, "Working with Links and Lists." Finally, the Properties option lets you specify properties for a selected HTML element, such as a table.

Using the View Menu

You use the View menu to add or remove toolbars from the command area. The toolbars are examined later in this chapter.

Using the Status Bar option, you can add or remove the status area at the bottom of the FrontPage Editor's display window. The status area displays command summaries and other key information.

The Format Marks option is similar to the show and hide formatting option in Microsoft Word. Using this option, you can see line breaks and other formatting that are not usually displayed. By default, this option is always on when you open a new page.

Sometimes when you access a page, you find that the file did not completely display in the FrontPage Editor. If this happens, use the Refresh option.

Using the Go Menu

Much like your Web browser, the FrontPage Editor lets you move forward and backward when editing multiple documents and following links. Within the FrontPage Editor you can follow a link within your page by holding the Control key while clicking a link. Using the Go menu, you can move forward and backward in the Editor to previously viewed documents. You can also use the Go menu as a shortcut to open your Mail or News client, as well as your Contacts list.

Using the Insert Menu

The Insert menu adds HTML elements to the current page. You will learn all about these elements in Part II, "Creating Web Pages with FrontPage 98."

Using the Format Menu

You use the Format menu to add character and paragraph formatting to your pages. In Part II you learn how to use character and paragraph formatting.

Using the Tools Menu

The Tools menu includes many miscellaneous functions, such as the spell checker and thesaurus. Even though Microsoft Office isn't required, FrontPage 98 uses the Office spell checker and thesaurus (not surprising, because FrontPage is part of the Office family of products).

The AutoThumbnail command lets you create a smaller version of an image (a thumbnail) and link it to the original image. You can create a thumbnail by selecting an image and choosing the AutoThumbnail command from the Tools menu, or by selecting an image and pressing CTRL+T. Below the AutoThumbnail command is the Shared Borders menu item. This command lets you control the Shared Borders for your entire Web site or just the page you are editing. You can choose to add or remove the shared borders for the top and bottom and left and right of the page.

The next set of options on this menu displays FrontPage tools. The Show FrontPage Explorer option starts the FrontPage Explorer, if it is not already started, and displays it. The Show Image

Editor launches the default image editor (typically Microsoft Image Composer). You can define the default image editor in the FrontPage Explorer via the Configure Editors tab of the Tools|Options dialog box.

The final option sets default font options for character set, font face, and MIME encoding. You can also define the AutoThumbnail settings.

Using the Table Menu

The Table menu adds tables to the current page. Chapter 8, "Designing Tables with FrontPage 98," explores the table creation and design process. Most of the options in the table menu are grayed out if you haven't started a table in the current document.

Using the Frame Menu

When you are looking to work with frames, FrontPage 98 gives you an entire menu to play with. Chapter 9, "Creating Frames," provides you with comprehensive information on designing pages with frames and how to use these features of the FrontPage Editor. If you are not working with a frames-based page, every option but New Frames Page is grayed out.

Using the Window Menu

You use the Window menu to change the way pages are organized in the FrontPage Editor and access any open pages. Using the Cascade option, you can arrange all open pages in overlapping windows for easy access. This option is especially useful when you have three or more pages open and you want to switch among them.

With the Tile option, you can resize all open pages in windows that are completely visible in the FrontPage Editor's main viewing area. When you have a lot of open pages, the Tile option is not as useful as the Cascade option. For this reason, you should use the Tile option when you have four or fewer pages open, and you want to easily move among them.

If you have a number of windows minimized within the FrontPage Editor, you can use the Arrange Icons option to tidy up the stack of minimized windows at the bottom of the FrontPage Editor window. This is especially convenient when you are trying to work with a large number of files, while still remembering where each one is.

The numbered options at the bottom of the menu allow you to quickly access any files currently open. Although the Editor only lists the first nine open pages, you can use the More Windows option to access any other open pages.

Using the Help Menu

You use the Help menu to display information about the FrontPage Editor and to access the online help system. To access FrontPage's comprehensive help documentation, use the Microsoft FrontPage Help option. The Microsoft on the Web option accesses the FrontPage area of the

Microsoft Web site. The About Microsoft FrontPage Editor option displays information about your version of FrontPage.

Using the Toolbar

The FrontPage Editor has one of the most extensive toolbars you will find in any application. In all, there are six toolbars: Standard, Format, Image, Forms, Table, and Advanced. You can add and remove any of the toolbars by selecting the appropriate options in the View menu. Because the toolbars are independent elements, you can move them to any area of your screen.

To change the location of a toolbar, move the mouse pointer over the toolbar, but not on top of any of the toolbar's icons, and click and hold the left mouse button. Now you can drag the toolbar to a new location on the screen. When the toolbar is where you want it, release the mouse button. From then on, the toolbar displays in the new location.

TIP

If you're like me and you want to see all the toolbars at once, try moving the tool bars you use the least to the bottom of Editor window. When you move a tool bar just above the status bar, the tool bar is cleanly integrated into the FrontPage Editor window.

The most versatile toolbar is the Standard toolbar (see Figure 3.5). This toolbar has icons for many of the most commonly used FrontPage Editor menu options. From this toolbar, you can open, save, and print pages. You can also performed editing functions such as cut, copy, paste, undo, and redo.

FIGURE 3.5.
The FrontPage Editor's Standard toolbar.

The Format toolbar, shown in Figure 3.6, includes most of the options you use to manipulate the layout of your pages. You can use the icons on this toolbar for adding text highlights, aligning, and indenting.

FIGURE 3.6.
The FrontPage Editor's Format toolbar.

When you add images to your pages, you use the Image toolbar shown in Figure 3.7. You want to use this toolbar when you create image maps or transparent GIFs.

FIGURE 3.7.
The FrontPage Editor's Image toolbar.

When you add forms to your pages, you use the Forms toolbar, shown in Figure 3.8. The icons in this toolbar let you add input fields to your forms with the click of a button.

FIGURE 3.8.
The FrontPage Editor's Forms toolbar.

With the Advanced toolbar shown in Figure 3.9, you can quickly add advanced features to your pages. Advanced features supported include ActiveX controls, Java applets, client- and server-side scripts, and plug-ins.

FIGURE 3.9.
The FrontPage Editor's Advanced toolbar.

You will use the Table toolbar shown in Figure 3.10 whenever you create or edit tables. I recommend using this toolbar instead of the table menu—it will save you time.

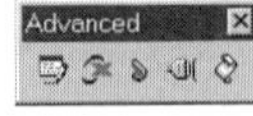

FIGURE 3.10.
The FrontPage Editor's Table toolbar.

Summary

As you have seen, getting started with the FrontPage Editor is fairly easy. You will rely on the FrontPage Editor to help you create terrific Web pages. Now that you've learned Editor basics you are ready to move on to more advanced topics, like creating your own Web pages.

IN THIS PART

- Creating Web Pages with FrontPage 98 *51*
- Working with Links and Lists *71*
- Creating Richer Web Pages with HTML Features *89*
- Enhancing Your Web Pages with Images—The Easy Way *107*

PART

Creating Web Pages with FrontPage 98

CHAPTER 4

Creating Web Pages with FrontPage 98

by William Robert Stanek

IN THIS CHAPTER

- What Is HTML? 52
- Creating a Page 53
- Setting Page Properties 54
- Designing the Page 66
- Creating Headings 67
- Creating Paragraphs 68
- Aligning the Text 69

Traditionally, to create a great Web site you needed to be a heady mix of programmer, artist, and gearhead. Web site creation simply wasn't meant for the everyman (or woman). Thankfully, with FrontPage 98 you can now step into the exciting realm of web design without having your eyes glaze over. With a firm understand of how to use FrontPage 98, and some HTML design concepts under your belt (all handily provided to you in this book), you're ready to dazzle the world!

What Is HTML?

When Tim Berners-Lee envisioned the World Wide Web, he envisioned it having a common and easy-to-use interface that would allow anyone to publish to it. To accomplish this, he and others at the European Laboratory for Particle Physics (CERN) developed the Hypertext Markup Language (HTML), which is based on a subset of the Standard Generalized Markup Language (SGML). SGML was created as a means of formatting documents (typically academic papers) for printing and distribution. SGML is based on the concept of *document type definitions* (DTDs) to provide instructions on how the content should be formatted. Using SGML as the basis of HTML ensured that the new markup language for the Web was rooted in a solid standard that was already proven to be a cross-platform solution.

Only the essential elements of SGML were adopted to form the original specification for HTML. This drastically reduced the complexity of the original HTML specification and reduced the overhead for transferring hypertext documents over the network. Another advantage of using SGML as the basis for HTML was that SGML DTDs provided an easy way to extend the HTML standard. It was the intent of the developers of HTML to create a language for Web documents that was initially simple, yet could grow more complex over time.

BROWSERS: WINDOWS TO THE WEB

You'll see references to HTML and the format of markup code throughout this book, and you might wonder why. Although FrontPage 98 automatically puts your documents in HTML format, you should know the basic structure of HTML and the level of HTML used in your document at any particular time. This helps you understand what is going on behind the scenes and why your document might not look the way you want it to in a particular browser. (To see the actual HTML markup, click the HTML tab in the FrontPage Editor.)

A browser is a software application that enables you to access the Web. You can think of a browser as your window to the Web. Change your browser and you get a whole new view of the Web.

Whenever you a create page in FrontPage 98, you should view the page in several different browsers. Because of the dramatic changes in HTML over the years, you cannot expect your pages to look the same in different browsers. Often, you'll find that your pages look slightly different in a different browser, especially if you use an older version of a browser. Using your comparisons, you can then make a conscious decision on what is more important–the readability and usability of your page, or the design itself. Each Web site has different objectives. If your site relies heavily on your design, you might need to find the time to tweak your page design so that it works with a wide cross section of browsers, without introducing anomalies. For example, font sizing and placement differ greatly among not only Web browsers (such as Microsoft Internet Explorer and Netscape Navigator/Communicator), but also platforms (Windows versus Apple Macintosh).

As with anything, successful research can translate into a successful result. With more experimentation and practice, you will be able to create sites that minimize the conflicts among browsers and platforms, making a site that everyone can enjoy and appreciate.

NOTE

Successful authoring of a Web site relies on a basic comprehension of how Web pages work. Although FrontPage 98 shields you from the mundane aspects of the Hypertext Markup Language, to make authoring easier you should have at least a rudimentary understanding of how HTML works. To help you in your web development, consider the following HTML resources from Sams.net Publishing:

- *Teach Yourself Web Publishing with HTML in 14 Days, Professional Reference Edition* by Laura Lemay.
- *HTML and CGI Unleashed, Professional Reference Edition* by John December and Mark Ginsburg.

Creating a Page

Creating a page in the FrontPage Editor is easy—simply select File|New or press Ctrl+N. You can now select a template for your new page using the dialog box shown in Figure 4.1.

To help you decide which of the many templates you want to use, the New Page dialog box has the Description area and the Preview area. The brief descriptions and the preview of the page's outline are usually all you need to get on your way. Still, getting the most out of each of the templates is covered in Part VI, "Templates, Wizards, and FrontPage Components."

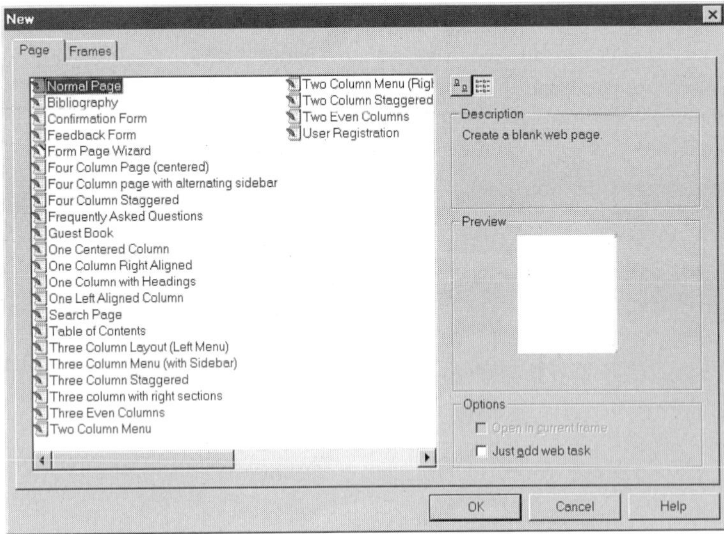

FIGURE 4.1.
Creating a page using a template. FrontPage 98 gives you several templates to choose from.

Setting Page Properties

Now that you have a new page, look at its default properties. All pages, even new pages, have default attributes. Figure 4.2 shows the Page Properties dialog box. Each input area lets you define attributes for markup tags used in the HEAD element of your documents.

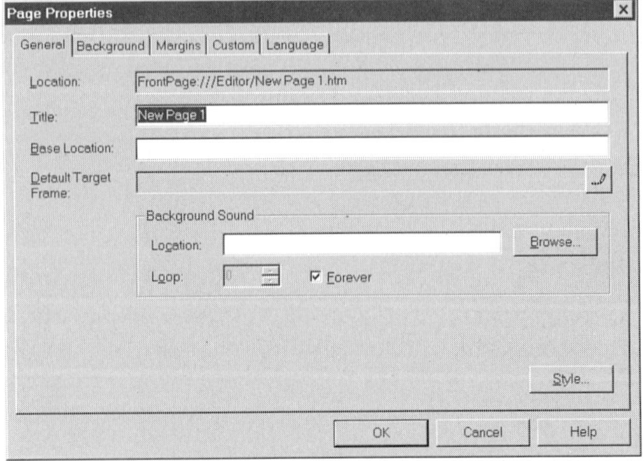

FIGURE 4.2.
Setting page properties.

To set page properties, select Page Properties from the File menu. Alternatively, you can click the right mouse button and then select Page Properties from the submenu that appears.

FrontPage 98 allows you to define attributes for the HEAD element tags without learning the specifics of each tag. Not only does the point-and-click interface save you frustration, but it also saves you time. Most of the input fields pertain to setting base attributes for the document, such as the background color. If you've played the color guessing game with your HTML pages before, you know how cool it is to see a color palette and select a color from this palette at the touch of a button.

The following sections teach you how to use these properties. Admittedly, setting page properties by pointing and clicking is easy. What is not so easy is knowing why and when to use these page properties.

Working with the General Tab

The General tab of the Page Properties dialog box is the catch all for page properties. Using this page, you can check a page's filename. You can set a document title, base location, and default target frame. You can even select a background sound for the page.

Page Location

By default, FrontPage 98 bases the document uniform resource locator (URL) on the name of the template used to create the document, on the path to the current web, and sometimes on the content of the page (such as the first line of text). If you refer back to Figure 4.2, you see that the title for the page is set to `New Page 1`. After you save the page, the URL to the page appears in the Location field. A typical URL for this page could be the following:

```
http://127.0.0.1/test/index.htm
```

In the preceding, `http` specifies that the document is transferred using the Hypertext Transfer Protocol. The Internet Protocol (IP) address `127.0.0.1` is the numeric equivalent of the host name for the local machine. This is just as easy for the computer to interpret as an actual host name, such as `mcp.com`. In fact, all host names are equated to numeric addresses by networked computers anyway. `test` is the name of the primary directory on the local host that contains your files for this web. The final part of the page URL is the name of the file. If you look in the `test` directory in the FrontPage web's folder, you see the file `index.htm`.

Because the URL property is grayed out in the properties window, you cannot update this field directly. If you want to change the filename, you must select Save As from the File menu and make the changes in the pop-up window, as shown in Figure 4.3.

If the document you are working with is not a new page, you should only change the filename using the FrontPage Explorer. Otherwise, you may end up with duplicate files.

Document Titles

You define document titles in the General tab of the Page Properties dialog box. By default, FrontPage 98 bases the document title on the name of the template used to create the document. If you refer back to Figure 4.2, you'll see that the default title for Normal Page is New Page 1.

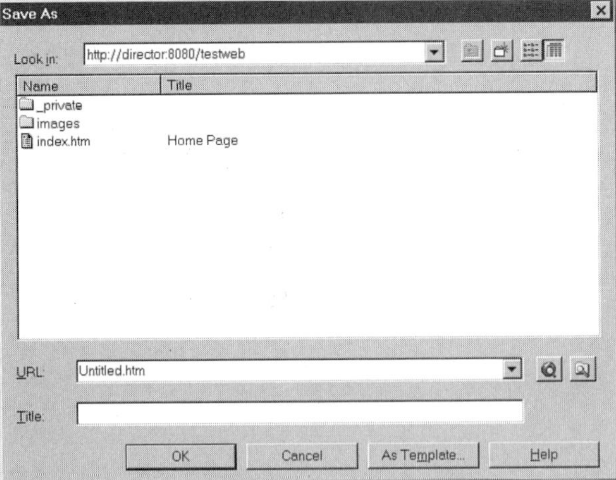

FIGURE 4.3.
Changing the filename.

The rules for titles are simple. Each document can have only one title. Your title should be short, but descriptive. A general rule to follow for the length of the title is 65 characters or less. If your title is over 65 characters in length, it might get truncated when the document is displayed. Additionally, the title can contain no extra formatting or markup. This means it should only contain plain ASCII characters.

TIP

Think carefully about the title for your document and the information it provides to readers. The title is the most referenced component of any document. It appears on a user's bookmark or hot list, which contains a list of a user's favorite online places saved for future reference. The title also appears on the user's history list, which is a list of places visited during the current session. Most search engines list the page title in the query results. Furthermore, most Web browsers prominently display the document title as well.

Because the title might be referenced separately from your document by the user, it should provide insight into the contents or topic of the document. A good title for an extreme sports service in Australia is Extreme Sports Australia. Depending on the focus of the document, a better title might be Extreme Sports in Australia and New Zealand or Extreme Sport Experiences in Australia and New Zealand.

Using Base Locations

The Base Location property on the properties page allows you to set a base URL for your page. Usually, you access files on a local Web server using a relative file path. When you use a relative path to locate a file, you are locating the file in relation to the current file. Although this is the normal way to use relative paths, you can define a base path for all relative links in your document.

Using the Base Location property, you can tell the browser to locate files in relation to a specific path that could actually point to a remote server. You could define a base path as follows:

```
http://mcp.com/
```

The base path example tells the browser to add `http://mcp.com/` to all relative links in the document. You'll find that defining a base path is most useful when your document is available at two different locations and you want to relate them to documents at a specific location. For example, you could publish your home page at a free Web mall without changing relative addresses to absolute addresses.

Whenever a user accesses the sample document, no matter where the document is actually located on the Web, any links the user follows lead him to pages at the `mcp.com` Web site. The base path also ensures that other relative paths on the page are valid at the new site, including the path to the images on your page.

Using the previously defined base path, the relative references `vpbg.htm`, `vpttl11.gif`, `bboard.gif`, and `vphp.htm` are interpreted as the following:

```
http://mcp.com/vpbg.htm
http://mcp.com/vpttl11.gif
http://mcp.com/bboard.gif
http://mcp.com/vphp.htm
```

Setting a Default Target Frame and Background Sound

The Default Target Frame property on the properties page is used with frame-enhanced pages. You'll find a more thorough discussion of frames in Chapter 10, "Editing and Enhancing Your Frames."

Customizing the Appearance of Your Page

Most browsers display Web pages with a default background color—but why settle for ordinary when you can add images and living color to the background or spiff up your text and links with color as well. FrontPage 98 introduces a powerful what-you-see-is-what-you-get (WYSIWYG) interface for selecting the background images and colors to be used in your documents.

In the Page Properties dialog box, click the Background tab to set the background and colors for your new page. Figure 4.4 shows two basic ways to do this. You can get the background and colors from another page, or you can specify your own background and colors.

NOTE

If you use themes in your page, the colors and background are already determined for you. Therefore, to change the colors and background, you must either change your theme or decide not to use themes at all for either the current page or the entire web site.

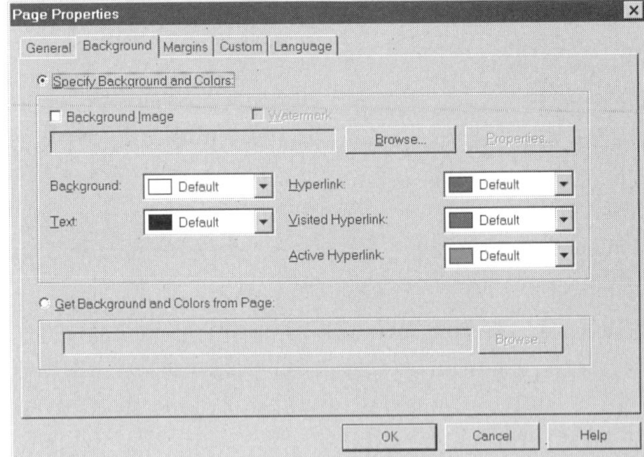

FIGURE 4.4.
Using the Background tab to set colors and the background.

Getting a Background and Colors from Another Page

One page property on the Background tab you might be tempted to use often is Get Background and Colors from Page. This property lets you set background images, background colors, and color definitions for text and links based on another page. To use this property, enable the Get Background and Colors property on the Property page by clicking the checkbox beside the property label. Next, specify the name of the file you want to use as the source for these settings. If you don't know the name of a file, you can use the Browse button to view a list of all HTML documents in the current web.

NOTE

Notice that when you enable the Get Background and Colors property, the properties for background images, background colors, text colors, and link colors are grayed out. This tells you these properties cannot be set at the present time and any current settings for these properties are not used.

Although the process of basing color and background definitions on another document seems fairly straightforward, this is a good example of FrontPage 98 shielding the publisher from the complexities of what's actually taking place. If you use this feature, the file you name is used as the style sheet for the current document.

Using Background Images and Watermarks

Background images are set using the Background tab of the Page Properties dialog box. With the Background Image property, you can specify an image to be used as the background for the document. The image is tiled or repeated to fill the background area. You can use tiling to create design effects using small images. The best image formats to use for background images are Graphical Interchange Format (GIF) and Joint Picture Experts Group (JPEG), which are fully supported by all graphics-capable browsers.

You enable this property for editing by clicking the Background Image checkbox beside the property label, as shown in Figure 4.5. Then, to specify a background image in FrontPage 98, enter the filename of the image you want to use. If you don't know the name of a file, you can use the Browse button to view a list of available images. Using background images in your pages is discussed in detail in Chapter 7, "Enhancing Your Web Pages with Images—The Easy Way."

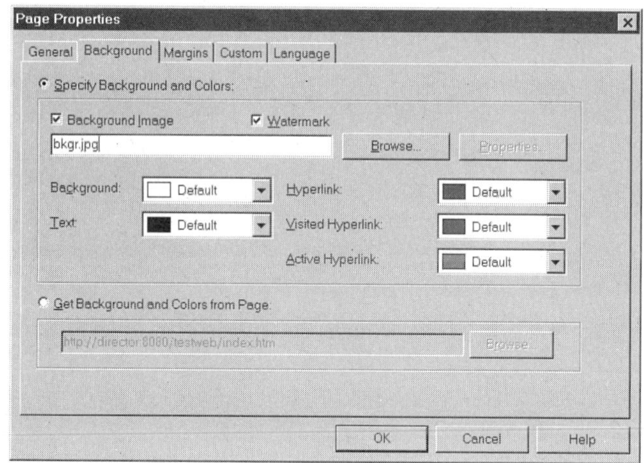

FIGURE 4.5.
Using background images.

Usually, your background pattern scrolls with the page. Using FrontPage 98, you can create background patterns that do not scroll. Nonscrolling background patterns are called *watermarks*. Watermarks are much more effective than the traditional scrolling backgrounds. To create a watermark, activate the Watermark property. Watermarks are supported by all browsers that are compliant with Internet Explorer 2.0 extensions (namely Microsoft Internet Explorer 2.0, 3.0, and now 4.0+).

Using Background Colors

The Specify Background and Colors property allows you to specify a color for the background using the Background tab of the Page Properties dialog box. To select a background color, activate the Background property's drop-down list by clicking and holding the left mouse button. As you see in Figure 4.6, you can then select one of the available colors. Initially, you have 18 choices. The Default value returns the background color to the browser default. If the color you want is listed in the initial list, select it.

To access additional colors, select the Custom value. You'll see a pop-up window similar to the one shown in Figure 4.7. You can now select a custom color.

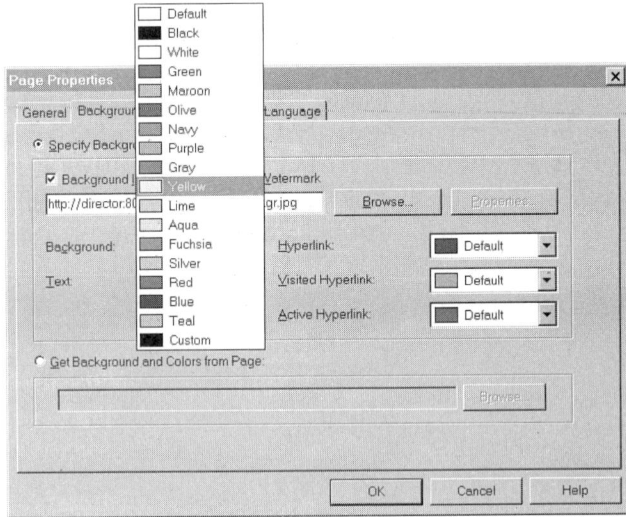

FIGURE 4.6.
Using background colors.

With the additional color palette open, FrontPage 98 gives you 48 colors from which to choose. The currently selected color is highlighted by a thin black border. To select a different background color, move the mouse pointer to the color you want to use, click the left mouse button, and then click the OK button.

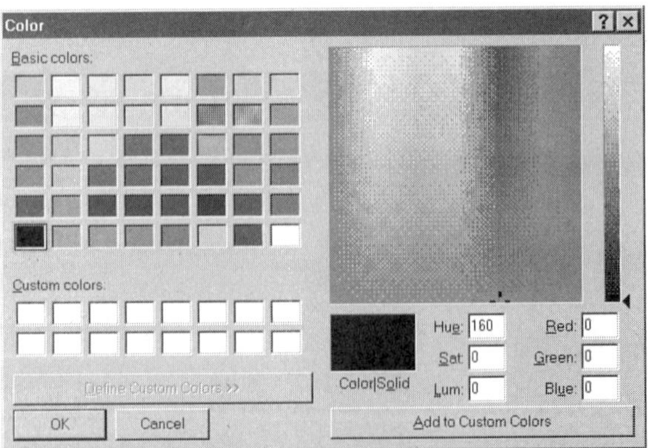

FIGURE 4.7.
Accessing additional background colors.

TIP

FrontPage 98 allows you to set a background color and a background image for the same document. I highly recommend you use this feature when you want to ensure that your pages are displayed in a unique way. If the background image cannot be displayed for any reason (for example, because the user turned off the auto load image feature of her browser), the background color you specified is displayed. Additionally, if you do not specify a background color and the background you specified cannot be displayed, the browser does not use your color assignments for text and links. This fail-safe method ensures that the browser doesn't use text and link colors that conflict with the standard gray background.

Using Text and Link Colors

By default, the color of the font used in your documents is either black or it is set by the user to a specific color using his browser color preference settings. However, black text on a black background is unreadable. When you use background images or colors, you usually need to specify the color for text and links to ensure that the text and links are readable.

To ensure that text and links on the page are readable no matter what background color or type of image you use, FrontPage 98 allows you to set text and link colors using the following properties:

`Text`	Specifies the color for normal text
`Hyperlink`	Specifies the color for links that are unvisited
`Active Hyperlink`	Specifies the color for active links
`Visited Hyperlink`	Specifies the color for visited links

To select a color for text or links, use the Background tab of the Page Properties dialog box and then activate the property's drop-down list by clicking and holding the left mouse button. Initially, you have 18 choices. The Default value returns the background color to the browser default. If the color you want is listed in the initial list, select it.

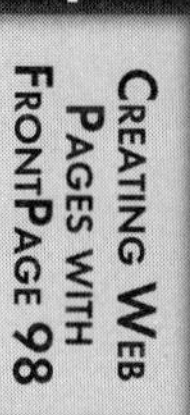

To access additional colors, select the Custom value. FrontPage 98 lets you select from a palette of 48 basic colors. The currently selected color is highlighted by a thin black border. To select a different background color, move the mouse pointer to the color you want to use, click the left mouse button, and then click the OK button.

Customizing Your Colors

If the 48 colors in the basic palette aren't enough, you can create custom colors for text, links, and backgrounds. FrontPage 98 also lets you store values for up to 16 custom colors for use in your other pages.

To create a custom color, click the property you want to associate the color with and then choose the Custom color value. This opens the Color dialog box shown previously in Figure 4.7.

You define custom colors using one of the following methods:

- Specify the red, green, and blue values associated with the custom color using the Red, Green, and Blue edit fields. Valid values are 0 through 255.
- Specify the hue, saturation, and luminosity values using the Hue, Saturation, and Luminosity edit fields. Valid values are 0 through 255.
- Set hue and saturation values using the color cube by clicking and dragging the mouse across the color spectrum field. Then, set the luminosity value by moving the triangle pointer up or down in the vertical color bar to the right of the color spectrum field.

The Color/Solid field displays the dithered and solid colors that correspond to your current color selection. When the custom color is set to your liking, click the Add to Custom Colors button to use the value for the current property.

TIP

If you want to save the custom color, select a rectangle in the Custom Colors grid, create your custom color, and then click the Add to Custom Colors button.

Defining Font Colors

When you set a font color, you change the color of text within your page and override the default text color you set in the Page Properties dialog box. Start by moving the pointer to where you want to insert text in the new color or by selecting text to change to the new color.

Although you set the font color using the same dialog box you use to set custom colors for the page, the way you access this color window is different. To access the color window, you choose one of the following methods:

- Select the Text Color button on the Format toolbar. This button has an artist's palette with a capital A beneath it.
- Open the Edit menu and select Font Properties. In the Font dialog box, activate the Color property's drop-down list by clicking and holding the left mouse button. Select the Custom color value. If the text you wish to change colors is part of a FrontPage Component function (such as a timestamp), Font Properties isn't an option from this menu.
- Select the Font option from the Format menu to open the same Font Properties dialog box as the previous method.

NOTE

Although the capability to assign font colors is extremely useful, the use of color in publications has always caused problems. Some color combinations just don't go together—for example, purple, green, and hot pink text all on the same Web page would be unattractive. Don't use color in your publication because you can; instead, use color as a design technique to enhance your page.

When using colorful text in Web publications, you should follow three general rules:

1. Use basic colors for text whenever possible, such as black, gray, red, yellow, green, blue, and white.
2. Ensure that your font colors are readable on the background you chose.
3. Limit the number of colors you use on any single page, and if practical, follow the same color scheme throughout your publication. Four colors are usually sufficient.

Setting Margins

Margins can enhance the appeal of your pages by making them more distinct. Settings margins for your page is easy with the Margins tab of the Page Properties dialog box. (See Figure 4.8.)

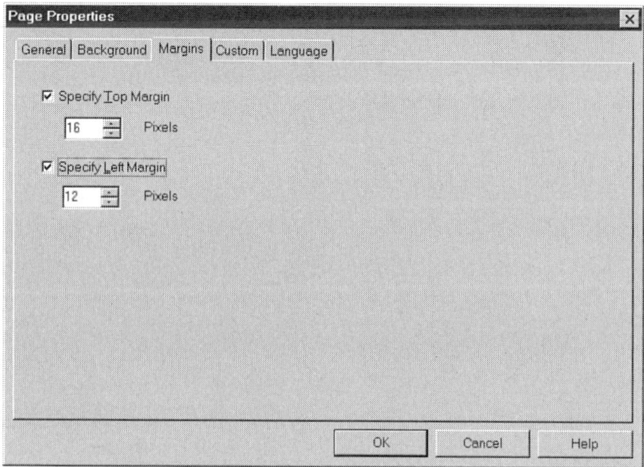

FIGURE 4.8.
Setting margins.

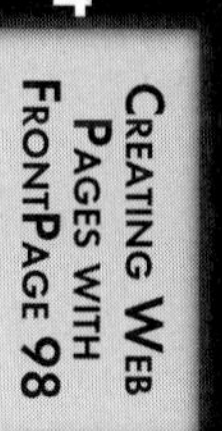

The first step is to select the checkbox related to the margin you want to set. To set the top margin, select the Specify Top Margin field. To set the left margin, select the Specify Left Margin field.

Next, set the width of the margin by entering a numeric value directly in the input field or by using the up- and down-arrow buttons. The width of the margin is set in pixels. If the top margin is set to 50, there are 50 pixels of space between the top of the page and the topmost element on the page.

NOTE

Currently, Internet Explorer 3.0/4.0 is the only browser that support margins used in this manner. For a more widely supported way of setting page margins, see Chapter 12, "Advanced Page Layout with Style Sheets."

Customizing Pages with Meta Properties

Using the Custom tab of the Page Properties dialog box, you can enter meta information for your pages. As shown in Figure 4.9, all pages created in FrontPage 98 have default meta values. Typically, the first meta value pertains to the type of document and character set in use. An additional meta value states that the page was generated with FrontPage 98. You can add new meta information using the button labeled Add.

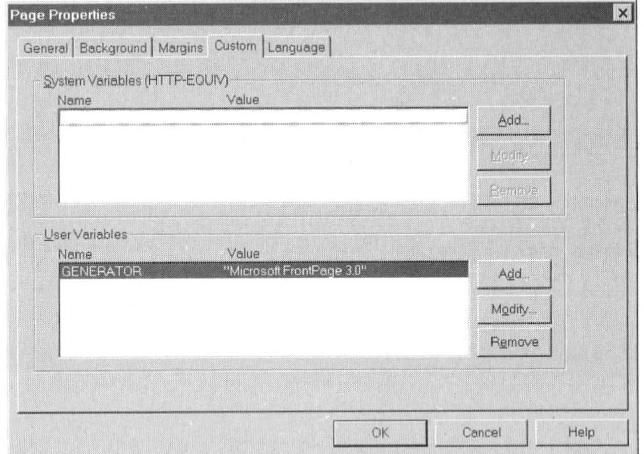

FIGURE 4.9.
The Custom tab lets you define meta values. By default, FrontPage 98 always inserts a meta value stating that FrontPage was indeed used to author this page.

When you click the Add button, you see the dialog box shown in Figure 4.10, where you can enter the meta information and an associated value.

When a client application requests an HTML document, a Web server usually passes the document with a response header prepended. This header is separate from the HTML HEAD element and contains information the client needs to interpret the document. Sometimes, you want to modify the standard header or create your own header for special situations. Other times, you want to provide information to the client that you could not pass using standard HTML elements.

Using the META property, you could pass this extra or specialized information in the HEAD element of a document. The server retrieving the document includes this information in the response header for the client's use.

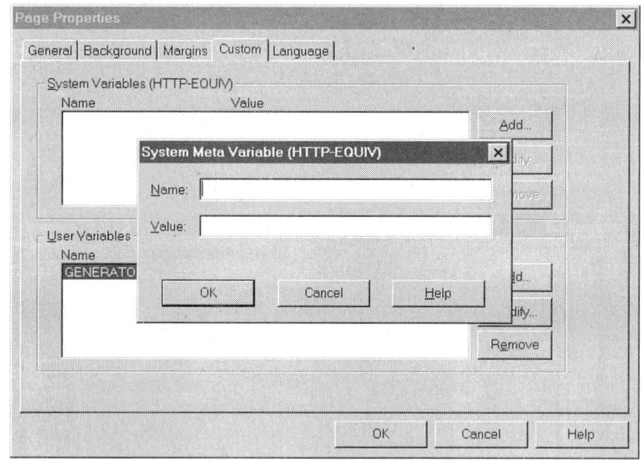

FIGURE 4.10.
Adding meta information.

Two types of variables are associated with the `META` property:

- System variables
- User variables

System variables allow you to specify information to be included in the response header using the `HTTP-EQUIV` attribute. When you use system variables, you should use a valid HTTP header name and supply a value for it.

If you do not know the valid HTTP header name or do not want to supply a header name using `HTTP-EQUIV`, you should use a user variable instead. User variables allow you to reference meta information. FrontPage 98 uses the standard user variable `generator` and sets an associated value that tells anyone viewing the HTML markup for the page that it was generated using Microsoft FrontPage 98.

In general, you use the `META` property only when there isn't a more standard HTML tag you can use to provide the information. Using the `expires` system variable, you can specify an expiration date for your document. A Web server adds this meta information to the document's response header as

```
Expires: Mon, 31 Dec 1998 10:00:00 HST
```

Using the `keywords` system variable, you can set keywords for the document, such as `publishing`, `books`, and `magazines`. A Web server adds this meta information to the document's response header as

```
Keywords: Publishing, Books, Magazines
```

Using the `refresh` system variable, you can specify a time interval that the client should re-request the file, such as every 30 seconds. A Web server adds this meta information to the document's response header as

```
Refresh: 30
```

If you use user variables, the server does not generate a response header. Some information you might want to pass in this way includes an e-mail address for the document's author, the date the document was published, and other information not specifically addressed by other HTML tags. You can specify the e-mail address of the document's author with a user variable called `author` and the document's publication date with a user variable called `published`.

Designing the Page

Well-designed documents achieve their impact from simplicity of design. They are organized in a way that is coherent and flowing. Yet, designs that seem simple and natural to the reader are often the result of intense efforts to make them seem this way. You can use many techniques to structure the document in powerful, yet uncomplicated ways.

Sometimes, it is not what you have on the page that helps convey your message, but what you do not have. Empty space on the page makes material easier to read and helps focus the reader's attention on your ideas. Interestingly enough, it is the separation of the material that creates the emphasis and draws the reader's attention. Two key components of the page that can help you create white space are paragraphs and headings.

Browsers typically display an empty space between paragraphs, so a page with many paragraphs has more white space. You should use short paragraphs the most and long paragraphs the least. A short paragraph has fewer than six lines. A long paragraph has ten or more lines. Varying the length of paragraphs is a key technique for keeping the reader's attention. If you use the same paragraph length repeatedly, even the most lively material seems monotonous.

Browsers also display an empty space between headings. Using headings, you can divide the document into sections or topics. A document broken into topics looks more manageable and interesting. Headings help the reader identify the main points of the document at a glance. They also help the reader quickly find topics of interest.

Color is another key feature you can add to the document. Most browsers display your document on a gray background. Netscape has introduced an extension that enables you to add images and color to the background. Other Netscape extensions enable you to specify the color of text and links. If you plan to enhance your documents specifically for users with browsers that use Netscape extensions, the background color element can be a good extension to manipulate.

Often the best way to add color to the page is through graphic images. A few pictures placed strategically on the page can dramatically increase the impact of the page. Your pictures do not have to be sophisticated or high resolution. Simplicity is usually best. You should place the images so that they focus the reader's attention on the key aspects of the page. For example, place a small eye-catching graphic at the beginning of a key paragraph. Adding pictures to your documents is featured in Chapter 7.

Creating Headings

By using headings, you can better organize your ideas. The chapters of most nonfiction books use many levels of headings. You usually find chapter headings, sections headings that pertain to each major topic, and subheadings pertaining to subtopics. Headings appear in a bold type that is larger than the normal font size. The size of the font is often related to the level of the heading. Chapter headings use the largest font size, section headings use a slightly smaller font size, and so on. The boldfaced text at the top of this section is an example of a subtopic heading level.

HTML enables you to create up to six levels of headings. HTML headings display in bold type. In general, a level one heading uses the largest font of heading sizes, and a level six heading uses the smallest font of heading sizes. Browsers typically insert a space before and after the heading. This white space is proportional to the size of the heading. Figure 4.11 shows how the FrontPage Editor displays the six heading levels.

FIGURE 4.11.
Using headings in your pages.

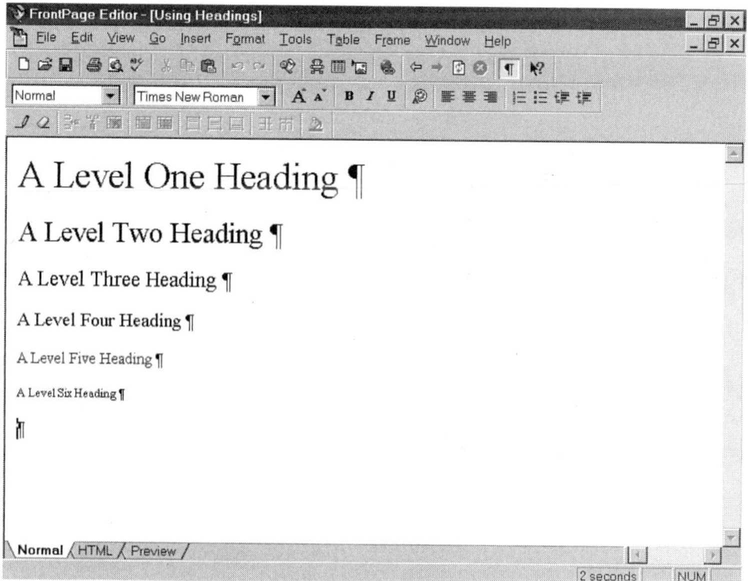

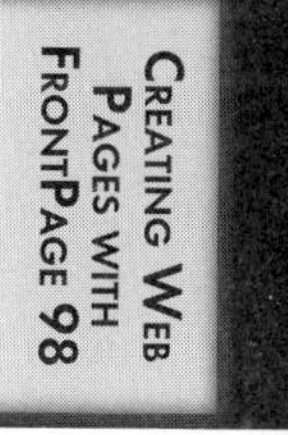

You set the heading level in FrontPage 98 using a pull-down menu on the Format toolbar. To make selections from the pull-down menu, click and hold your mouse button and then move the mouse pointer up or down. The pull-down menu that allows you to set text properties is in the left corner of the Format toolbar, shown in Figure 4.12.

To add a heading to your document, move the cursor to the point where you want to insert the heading or select the text you want to format in a particular heading and then select a heading level from the Format toolbar's pull-down menu. Another way to set heading levels is to open the Format menu and select Paragraph. This invokes the Paragraph Properties window, which you can use to set the heading level at the current insertion point.

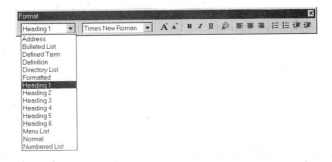

FIGURE 4.12.
Selecting a heading level using the Format toolbar.

NOTE

As the Web publisher, you only have direct control over font size by using style sheets. Because style sheets are only supported in the more recent browsers (such as Microsoft Internet Explorer 3.0+ and Netscape Communicator 4.0), the majority of Web publishers can only control the relative size of a font. With relatively sized fonts, the size of the font is determined by configurations set up in the browser displaying the document, and font sizes are consistent relative to each other and the main text. Most browsers display visible differences only in heading levels one to four. Consequently, a level four heading is often displayed in the same font size as level five and six headings.

Creating Paragraphs

After years of casual or professional writing, you might find that some processes of writing are automatic. You probably don't think about the need to place a period at the end of a sentence or why we use apostrophes in contractions. Similarly, when you start a new paragraph, you probably add a blank line, indentation, or both to separate the new paragraph from the previous one without giving much thought about why. You add the blank line or indentation because it makes sense, and because it is what your grammar teacher told you to do. Blank lines and indentations serve to visually separate the paragraphs and break up the document.

In HTML, the way to visually break up the document into paragraphs is to use the paragraph tag <P>. When a browser sees the paragraph tag, it ends the current line and inserts a blank space before inserting the text or object following the paragraph tag.

FrontPage 98 eliminates the need to insert tags and allows you to add paragraphs just as you would with any word processor—by using the normal format. If you change text formats, you can use the Format toolbar's pull-down menu to set the format back to normal.

NOTE

Keep in mind that when you add empty paragraphs to your document, FrontPage 98 adds special markup that ensures your document is displayed with the spacing you select.

Aligning the Text

FrontPage 98 offers push button ease for changing the alignment of all text elements. To align a paragraph, heading, or other text element on the page, just move the insertion point to the text element you want to align and then select the alignment you want to use from the Format toolbar, as shown in Figure 4.13. Alternatively, you can select any portion of the text element and then select the alignment you want to use from the Format toolbar. Three alignment options are currently available: Center, Align Right, and Align Left.

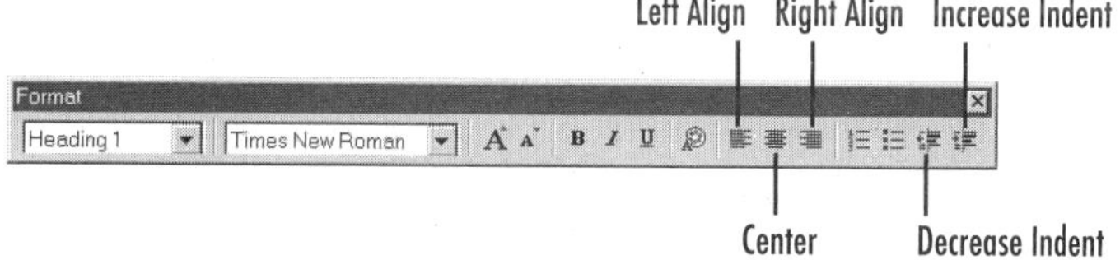

FIGURE 4.13.
Using the Format toolbar to select text alignment.

You can also indent text using the Format toolbar's Increase Indent button. Each time you click this button, the FrontPage Editor indents the text element about an inch. To decrease the indentation, use the Decrease Indent button.

AN INSIDE LOOK AT TEXT ALIGNMENT

Behind the scenes, FrontPage 98 is hard at work ensuring that the text alignment works with the widest range of browsers. Text alignment is a feature of HTML that was originally introduced by Netscape Navigator. Originally, the Navigator only allowed you to center text using a unique tag. Unique tags present problems to Web publishers because they aren't supported by some browsers. When the designers of HTML implemented text alignment, they did not adopt the Netscape tag for centering text. For this reason, when FrontPage 98 centers text, it inserts both the HTML and Netscape tags for centering. This ensures your text is centered in nearly every current browser.

To achieve text indentation, FrontPage 98 adopts a favorite trick of the Web publishing gurus, which is bending the rules to meet your needs. Here, the developers of FrontPage 98 needed a way to indent text. They knew that if they inserted an HTML BLOCKQUOTE element, browsers would indent the text without altering the style of the text. To indent multiple levels,

continues

continued

FrontPage 98 actually inserts multiple `BLOCKQUOTE` elements. An unfortunate side effect of using the `BLOCKQUOTE` element to create indentation is that it can cause strange results with some HTML elements. For example, alignment of your images and other web objects might be drastically affected. Although this problem is more a function of how FrontPage 98 terminates HTML elements when starting a new element, it is a problem you should be aware of.

Summary

FrontPage 98 makes Web publishing easy. Using the techniques discussed in this chapter, you can create simple, yet effective Web documents. Although dozens of HTML tags are used to create the features discussed in this chapter, FrontPage 98 allows you to create pages without worrying about tags and their attributes. Not only does this save you time, it also allows you to concentrate on building the visual impact of your documents.

Working with Links and Lists

by William Robert Stanek

IN THIS CHAPTER

- Using Links 72
- Creating Links with FrontPage 98 76
- Editing Links with FrontPage 98 78
- Creating and Editing Bookmarks with FrontPage 98 79
- Using Lists 80
- Creating Lists 82

To increase the interactive nature of your document, you can create links to other documents within your site or on the Web. You can also create internal links in your document that help guide readers to key parts of your publication. You can add to your document any of several types of lists that add to the visual impact of the document by clearly organizing material.

Using Links

The Web without links wouldn't really be the Web. A page without links would not be interactive, so now it is time to put the "hyper" into hypertext. Most Web documents contain hypertext links. Links act as pointers to other resources or files in your site or on the Web. Using links, you can connect text, graphic images, and multimedia objects to your documents. The great thing about hypertext linking is that linked text, images, or objects can be located anywhere on the Web, which means you can add images to your document that don't even reside on your Web server. For example, if you create a resource guide to the latest in cutting-edge Web technologies, you might want to reference another Web site. You could use the logo at the top of the page to link to the Sams Web site.

To link to the page and image, you need to know the URL of the image and the URL of the Web site. These URLs are as follows:

```
http://www.mcp.com/sams
http://www.mcp.com/images/logo_id.gif
```

Although links might look like a tangled mess, the mess can be easily untangled. Links tell the browser where to send a request for a particular file. Initially, the browser does not care what type of file it is supposed to retrieve; it simply attempts to retrieve the file. To get to a file, browsers need to know the location of the resource. The resource's location is specified as a Uniform Resource Locator, commonly called a URL.

The first URL in the preceding example tells the browser to use the hypertext transfer protocol to access a file on the `www.mcp.com` Web server. Here, the file is the base document in the `writing` directory. The second URL tells the browser to use the hypertext transfer protocol to access a file called `logo_id.gif` on the `www.mcp.com` Web server. Here, the file is a graphic image in the `sams` directory. URLs such as these that have complete address information enable you to link your documents to files on other Web servers.

The address in a link is not visible unless the mouse pointer is over the anchor text or graphic. The anchor is the portion of the link that is visible when a browser displays the document. To activate a link, you move your mouse pointer over the anchor and click the left mouse button. If a line of text is the anchor, the reader can click the text to activate the link. If an image is the anchor, the reader can click the image to activate the link. You can also create an anchor that uses both text and an image. More information on using images and linking to images can be found in Chapter 7, "Enhancing Your Web Pages with Images—The Easy Way."

Text links generally appear in blue letters and images with links have a blue border around them. In Figure 5.1, the first link uses text to anchor the link in the document. The reader clicks `The Writer's Gallery` to activate the link. The second link uses an image to anchor the link in the document. The reader clicks the image to activate the link. The third link combines a text and image anchor. The reader clicks either the text or the image to activate the link.

FIGURE 5.1.
Using text and images to create links.

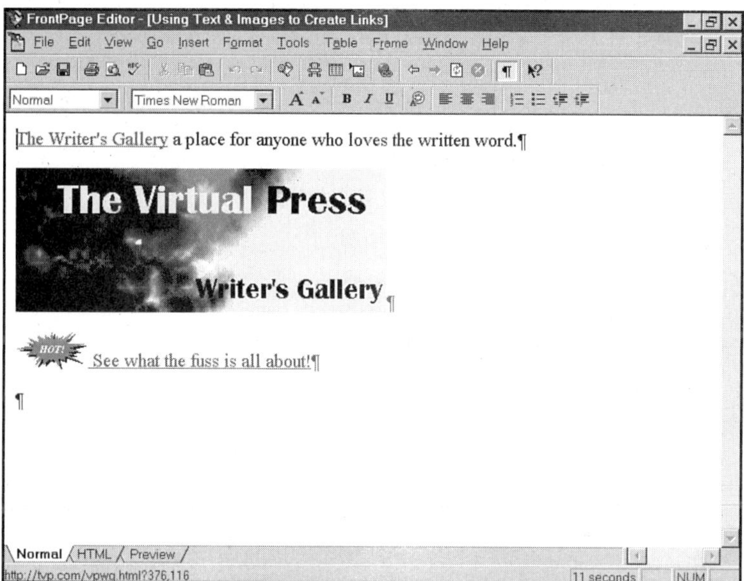

As you can see, hypertext links to text and objects can be the most powerful features on your document. You can add links to your document in three key ways:

- Using relative paths to files in links
- Using direct paths to files in links
- Using links called bookmarks within your documents

Using Relative Paths in Links

You can access *local files*—files on your local Web server—using a relative file path. URLs with relative file paths generally do not name a protocol or a Web server in the link. When you use a relative path to locate a file, you locate the file in relation to the current file. Being able to access a file in relation to the current file implies that you have already accessed a file on a particular Web server.

You can use relative file paths in three key ways:

- A file in the current directory.

  When you click a link with the following URL path, your browser expects to find the file `orders.html` in the current directory:

  ```
  orders.html
  ```

- A file in a parent directory of the current directory.

  The following file is located in the directory above the current directory:

  ```
  ../orders.html
  ```

  This file is located two directories above the current directory:

  ```
  ../../orders.html
  ```

- A file in a subdirectory of the current directory.

  This file is in the subdirectory called `info`:

  ```
  info/orders.html
  ```

TIP

Good links do not say "click here." A "click here" link disrupts the flow of the text and the natural thought processes. The interactive nature of the Web is such that you should never have to say "click here." Build hypertext links into the text and by doing so, you will create documents that flow.

When using links, keep in mind that links are highlighted in the document. Typically, links are shown in underlined blue letters that make them stand out from surrounding text.

Using Direct Paths in Links

Another way to access files is directly. You do this by specifying the complete path to the file you want to access. Although you must specify the protocol to be used for files directly accessed on a non-local Web server, you do not have to specify the protocol for files directly accessed on a local Web server.

Because only the complete path to the file must be specified there are two key ways to access files directly:

- Specify the full path to the file, including the transfer protocol.

  The following file could reside on a non-local server:

  ```
  http://www.unitedmedia.com/comics/dilbert/index.html
  ```

- Specify the full path to the file excluding the transfer protocol.

  The following file must reside on a local server:

  ```
  /comics/dilbert/index.html
  ```

TIP

Designing good links is easy when you know the basics of using relative and direct paths. The key is to keep the anchor text for the link short but descriptive. Usually this text should be three to five words describing the link in a way that is clear to the user. Anchor text can be the key words of a sentence, but sometimes you might want the anchor text to include an entire short-but-descriptive sentence. Later sections of this chapter show how you can better organize links using lists and menus.

Using Links Within Documents

Internal document links are called *bookmarks*. Bookmarks can provide powerful navigation mechanisms for your readers and are especially useful in long documents. Using bookmarks can provide you ways to quickly jump to key sections of any document.

Creating links within documents is a two-part process. First, you specify a link with a key word in a form similar to other links you have seen. The next step is to label the location within the document to which you want the reader to jump.

The key word used in the link and anchor name must match exactly. When a user activates a bookmark, the section you labeled is displayed. If the bookmark is within the current document, the browser quickly searches the document for the label containing a key word that matches the key word in the link. When the browser finds the matching key word label, the browser displays the corresponding section of the document. If the internal link is within a different document, the browser loads the document and then searches for the label that matches the key word in the link. The location of the label relative to the link in the document does not matter. As long as the label is within the body of the document, the browser finds it.

Using bookmarks, you can create an index for your document, such as the one shown in Figure 5.2. If you click the `Overview` link, your browser searches for the key word `Overview`. When your browser finds the key word, the section associated with the key word is displayed. In the example, the browser scrolls forward and displays the overview section of the document. The ellipses show where actual document content belongs.

You can specify bookmarks to other documents in many ways. Using relative paths and key words, you can access specific locations in documents on the local Web server. Using direct paths and key words, you can access specific locations in documents located anywhere on the global Web.

You can use relative paths with bookmarks in three key ways:

- A bookmark to a file in the current directory
- A bookmark to a file in a parent directory of the current directory
- A bookmark to a file in a subdirectory of the current directory

FIGURE 5.2.
After you activate a link, your browser jumps to a section associated with the key word.

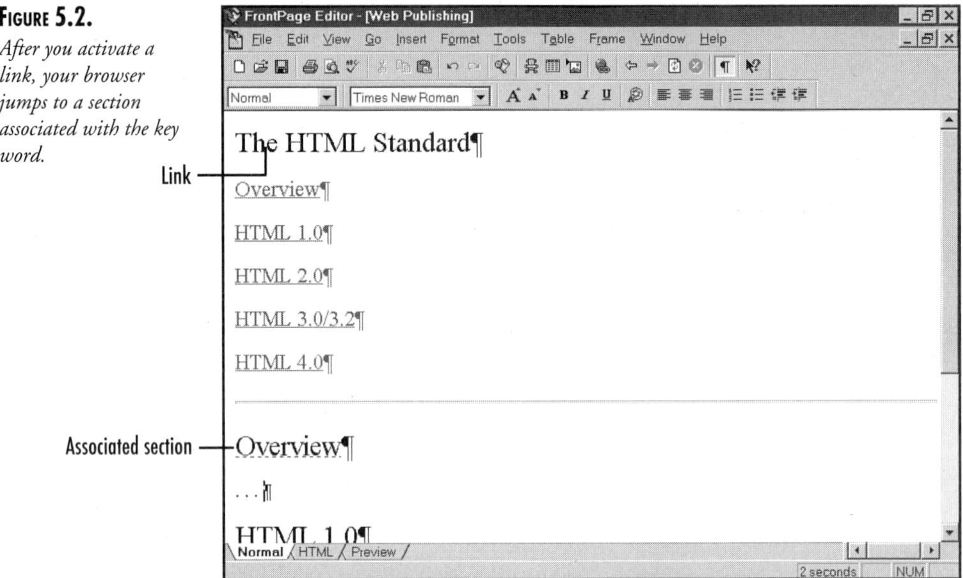

You can use direct paths with internal links as well. The two key ways you use internal links with direct paths are the following:

- Append the bookmark to the full file path that includes the transfer protocol.
- Append the bookmark to the full file path that excludes the transfer protocol.

CAUTION

Be careful when specifying internal links to someone else's document. Web documents tend to change frequently, and a key word label that is specified today might not be there tomorrow.

Creating Links with FrontPage 98

FrontPage 98 offers a very friendly interface for creating links and bookmarks. This section takes you step-by-step through these processes.

Creating a Link

You can easily create links in the FrontPage Editor. In the Editor, select the text that identifies the link and then either choose Hyperlink from the Edit menu or click the Standard Toolbar's Create or Edit Hyperlink button. Either opens the Create Hyperlink dialog box shown in Figure 5.3. Now, all you need to do is enter a URL in the URL field.

If you don't know the URL you want to use, FrontPage 98 displays a list of files in the current web and provides buttons that you can use to search for the URL (see Figure 5.3). Here are some of the ways you can select resources to which you want to link:

File in Current Web: Click the name and FrontPage 98 will enter the URL for you.

File on the Web: Using the Use your Web Browser to select a page or file button, you can search the web for a URL. When you find the page you are looking for, simply return to the FrontPage Editor and the URL will be filled in for you.

File on your disk: Using the Make a hyperlink to a file on your computer button, you can search your disk for a file you want to use.

Add mail reference: Use the Make a hyperlink that sends E-mail button to create a mailto: reference, which tells the reader's browser to open a create-mail session.

Create a new page and link to it: Use the Create a page and link to the new page button to add a new, blank page to your Web site and link to it.

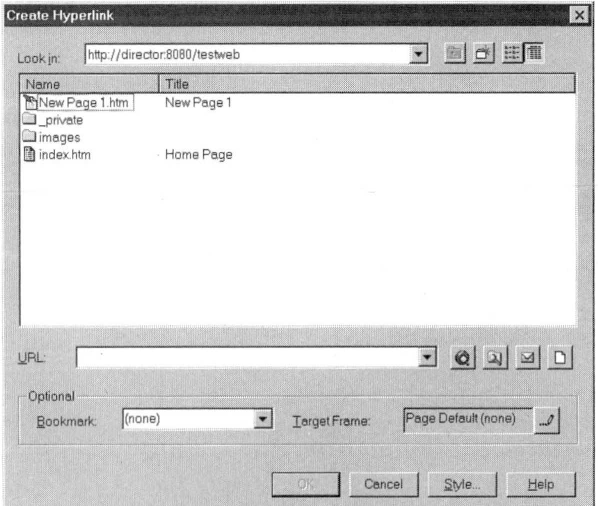

FIGURE 5.3.
Creating a link.

Creating a Link from the FrontPage Explorer

FrontPage 98 also lets you create a link from any open page to another page in the current web using the FrontPage Explorer. In the FrontPage Explorer, select the page to which you want to link. Hold the left mouse button and then drag the mouse pointer from the FrontPage Explorer to the line in the FrontPage Editor at which you want to create the link. Release the mouse button.

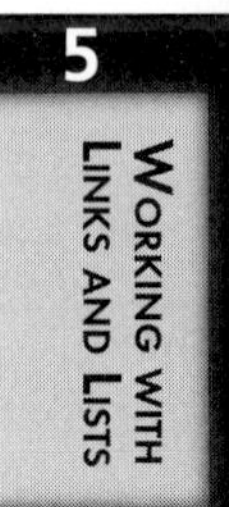

FrontPage 98 creates the link to the page on the line you chose. The anchor text for the link is the name of the page you linked from. The best way to create a link from the FrontPage Explorer to the FrontPage Editor is to resize them so they can be displayed side by side.

Editing Links with FrontPage 98

Any link you create can be updated, changed, or deleted as necessary. This section guides you through the link editing process.

Changing a Link's URL

FrontPage 98 enables you to easily change a link. In the FrontPage Editor, place the pointer anywhere in the text containing the link, or select any part of the link and then either chose Hyperlink from the Edit menu or click the Create or Edit Link button. Either opens the Edit Hyperlink dialog box. You can now change the link.

Deleting a Link Partially or Completely

To delete an entire link in the FrontPage Editor, select the text for the link or the linked object then choose, Remove formatting from the Format menu. The FrontPage Editor deletes the link but not the text or object associated with the link.

To delete part of a link in the FrontPage Editor, select the text from which you want to delete the link and then choose Remove formatting from the Format menu. The text will no longer be a part of the link.

Following a Text Link

Sometimes before you edit a link, you want to see where the link leads. FrontPage 98 enables you to follow a link from an open page to the targeted page or bookmark. If the page is not already open in another window, the FrontPage Editor opens the target page for editing and makes it the active page. If the link is to a bookmark, the FrontPage Editor displays the section of the page containing the bookmark. If the target page is not in the current web, FrontPage 98 opens a copy of the page that you can save to the current web.

To follow a link in the FrontPage Editor, place the pointer anywhere in the text containing the link or select any part of the link and then hold Ctrl and click the mouse. After following a link, you can follow the link back to its source by clicking the Back button. When you do this, the FrontPage Editor opens the source page and displays the section of the page containing the source of the link.

NOTE

Following a link from the FrontPage Editor to a page or resource on the World Wide Web might take a long time. The FrontPage Editor does not time out because it assumes that the page link is valid and that the server the resource resides on is valid. If FrontPage 98 doesn't display your page, click the Stop button.

Creating and Editing Bookmarks with FrontPage 98

Because bookmarks are links within documents, you create and edit them using a slightly different technique than what you use with other links. Creating a bookmark is a two-part process that involves labeling the bookmark and creating a link to the bookmark.

Labeling a Bookmark

When you label a bookmark, you give the bookmark a name. Simply select one or more characters of text and then select Bookmark from the Edit menu. This opens the Bookmark dialog box.

In the Bookmark Name field, enter the name of the bookmark. The bookmark name can include spaces but must be unique within the document. Because the name must be unique in the current document, the Bookmark dialog box shows you a list of bookmark names you've already defined. When you are done, click the OK button.

Creating a Link to a Bookmark

After a bookmark is labeled, you can create a link to it. To create a link to the bookmark, select the text or image that you want to use as the link. Next, open the Create Hyperlink dialog box by clicking on the Create or Edit Hyperlink button.

To link to a bookmark on the current page, place a pound-sign character (#) between the bookmark name and the page URL as shown in Figure 5.4. FrontPage 98 will fill in the optional Bookmark field as you type. Here the URL is `#hello` and the bookmark label is `overview`.

To link to a bookmark in a different page, simply enter the URL to the page containing the bookmark, then place a pound-sign character (#) between the bookmark name and the URL. If you wanted to create a bookmark link to a page in the current web called `home.htm`, the value you enter in the URL field would look something like the following:

```
home.htm#tester
```

Changing or Deleting a Bookmark

Changing or deleting a bookmark in the FrontPage Editor is easy. To do so, select the bookmark and then choose Bookmark from the Edit menu. This opens the Bookmark dialog box.

To change the name of the bookmark's label, simply enter the new name. To delete the bookmark, click the Clear button. When you are done editing the bookmark, click the OK button.

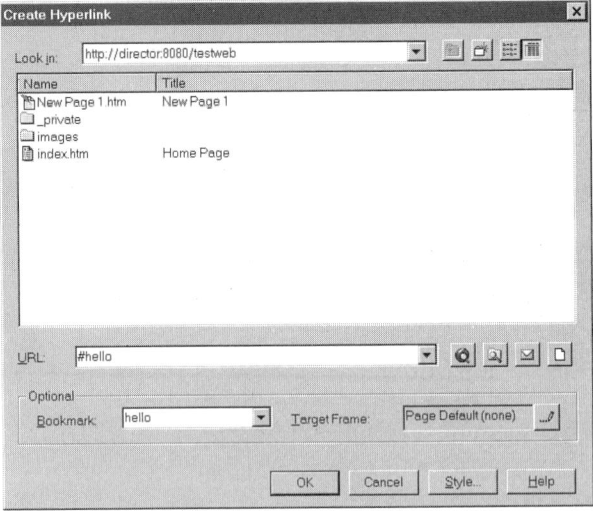

FIGURE 5.4.
Creating a bookmark.

Visiting a Bookmark

You can visit a bookmark on the current page or on another page using the FrontPage Editor. When you visit a bookmark on the current page, the corresponding link does not have to exist. However, when you visit a bookmark on another page, there must be a link to that page and the page must have a label that corresponds to the key word in the link.

To visit a bookmark on the current page, select any text and then choose Bookmark from the Edit menu. In the Other Bookmarks on this Page field, select the bookmark that you want to visit and then click the Goto button. The FrontPage Editor displays the section of the page containing the bookmark you selected. You can close the Bookmark dialog box by clicking the OK or Cancel button.

To visit a bookmark on another page, place the pointer anywhere in the link and then hold Ctrl and click the mouse. The FrontPage Editor opens the new page and displays the section of the page containing the bookmark you selected.

Using Lists

Lists are one of the most useful tools in your writing and publishing toolkit. Lists can give a clear order to your ideas and add to the visual impact of your document. You can use lists to grab the attention of readers, especially those readers who might be simply browsing or Web-surfing your site in a quest to find new and interesting places to visit.

The best lists are designed for a specific purpose. For example, the steps discussed in this chapter for creating a Web document would make a great list:

- Develop a strategy.
- Define the document structure.
- Create the document.
- Add features to the document.
- Proof the document.
- Test the document.
- Publish the finished document.

This type of list is called a *bulleted list.* Bulleted lists are often used to outline goals, objectives, or tasks that have no specific order. Bulleted lists are also called unordered lists. This list, however, is in a specific order, so a bulleted list is not the best way to present it.

A better way to present the list of steps for creating a Web document is to number the list:

1. Develop a strategy.
2. Define the document structure.
3. Create the document.
4. Add features to the document.
5. Proof the document.
6. Test the document.
7. Publish the finished document.

This type of list is called a *numbered list.* Numbered lists are used when tasks must be performed in a specific order. Numbered lists are also called ordered lists.

Lists are also used in the glossary section found in many nonfiction books. A glossary contains a list of key words and their definitions. You can use definition lists whenever you want to associate a key word with a concept or definition. Many definition lists look something like the following:

1. HTML

   Hypertext Markup Language

   The Hypertext Markup Language is a formatting language (based on the Standard Generalized Markup Language) that enables you to format information in visually appealing ways without sacrificing ease of use and the potential for wide distribution.
2. SGML

   Standard Generalized Markup Language

   The Standard Generalized Markup Language forms the basis for most markup languages and is an advanced language with few limitations.

3. VRML

   Virtual Reality Modeling Language

   Virtual Reality Modeling Language is an advanced markup language (based on the Open Inventors ASCII File Format) that enables you to create multidimensional documents.

Although the three fundamental types of lists are strongly supported by the HTML standard, the standard defines two additional types of lists designed primarily for programmers. You can use menu lists to list the contents of program menus. You can use directory lists to list the contents of directories. Menu lists and directory lists have fallen into disuse and are poorly supported by browsers. If you use a menu or directory list, the chances are very high that your browser will display the list following the rules for another list type. It is generally not a good idea to use menu or directory lists.

Creating Lists

The FrontPage Editor enables you to create the five list types defined in the HTML standard. However, like Web browsers, the Editor only uniquely supports the three primary types—bulleted lists, numbered lists, and definition lists. For this reason, the sections that follow focus only on the primary list types.

Bulleted Lists

Bulleted lists outline goals, objectives, or tasks with no specific order. When your browser sees the beginning of a bulleted list, it takes the following two actions:

- Starts a new line
- Inserts a character called a bullet before the listed item

As Figure 5.5 shows, bulleted lists are generally single spaced. Although most browsers display the bullet as a large solid dot, the actual size and shape of the bullet might be different in your browser. Text browsers, such as Lynx, display the bullet as an asterisk. Other browsers use a different symbol for the bullets at each level of nested lists.

Creating bulleted lists with the FrontPage Editor is a three-step process. The first step is to begin the list. To begin a bulleted list at the insertion point, click the Bulleted List button or select Bullets and Numbering from the Format menu.

When you select Bullets and Numbering from the Format menu, the List Properties dialog box is displayed. To display this dialog box at any time, right click, then select List Properties from the pop-up menu.

FIGURE 5.5.
A sample bulleted list.

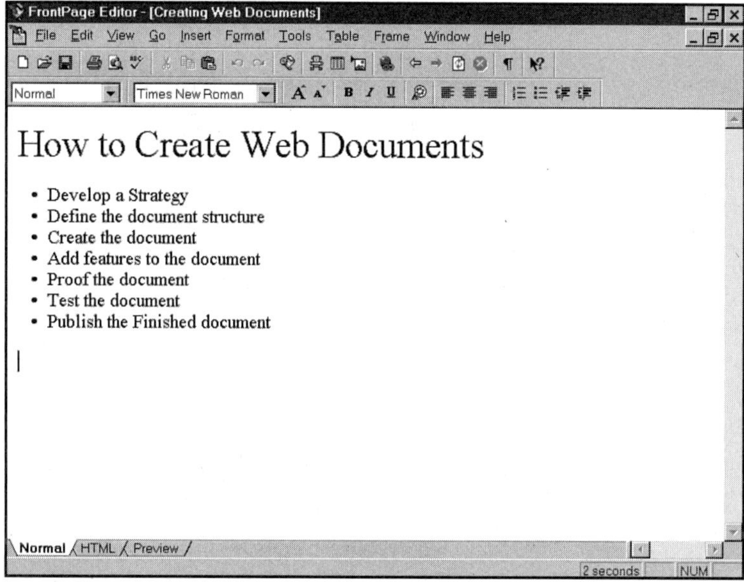

> **NOTE**
>
> You can work strictly with the current list type by selecting List Item Properties from the pop-up menu. Right click then select List Item Properties.

Using the Image Bullets tab shown in Figure 5.6, you can define a graphic image to use as your bullet. If your current web has a theme, you will probably want to use images from the current theme. Otherwise, specify your own image to use.

FIGURE 5.6.
Selecting the bullet image.

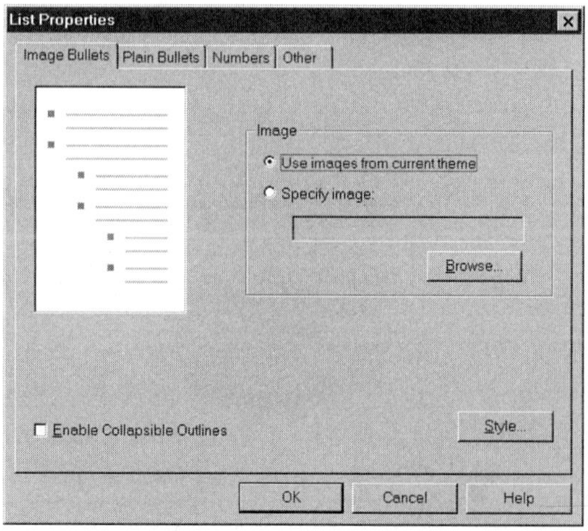

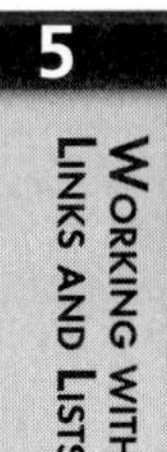

Using the Plain Bullets tabs shown in Figure 5.7, you can select the shape of bullets for the list. Simply click the graphical icon that depicts the type of bullet you want to use.

FIGURE 5.7.
Selecting the shape of your bullets.

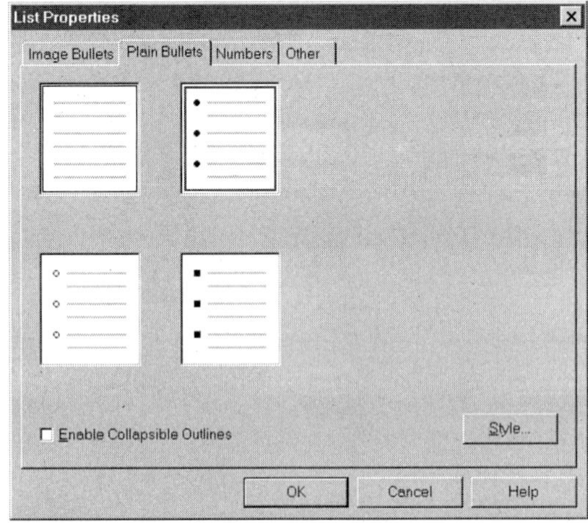

The second step is to enter your list items. FrontPage 98 automatically continues the list for you. To add a list item, simply press Enter.

The final step is to end the list. When you want to end the list, press Enter twice or press Ctrl+Enter.

FrontPage 98 also enables you to reformat existing text as a bulleted list. To do this, select one or more paragraphs and then click the Bulleted List button or select Bullets and Numbering from the Format menu.

Definition Lists

A definition list is generally for glossary terms and their definitions, but that does not mean you must use glossary lists for this strict purpose. You can use glossary lists whenever you want to associate a key word, phrase, or sentence with a concept. Each item in a definition list contains two elements:

- A key word called the *definition title*
- The definition called the *definition data*

As the example in Figure 5.8 shows, glossary lists are usually formatted with the terms and definitions on separate lines. The terms are aligned with the left margin, and the definitions are indented. Additionally, all aspects of glossary lists are generally single spaced.

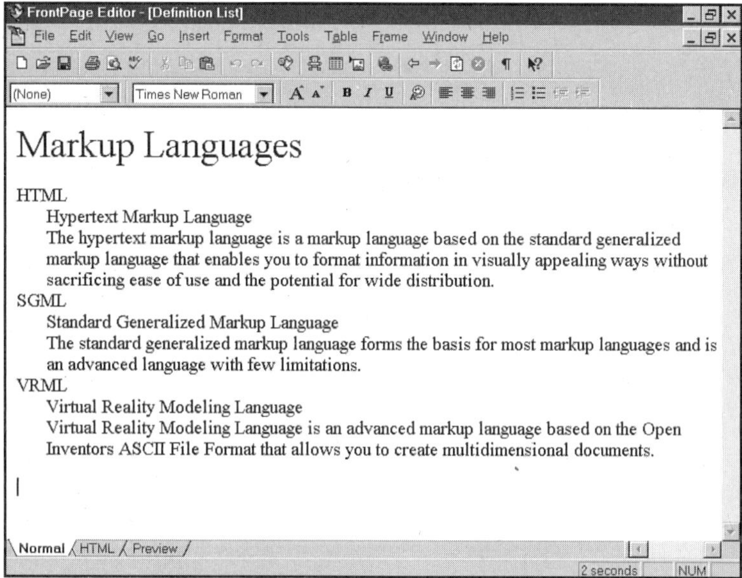

FIGURE 5.8.
A sample glossary list.

To create a definition list with the FrontPage Editor at the insertion point, choose Definition from the Format toolbar's Change Style pull-down list. The Change Style pull-down list is the first pull-down list on the Format toolbar. This inserts the appropriate markup to begin the definition list.

Now you can enter a key word or phrase you want to define. After you press Enter, you can enter a definition for the term. You can continue to add terms and definitions to the list in this fashion. To end the list at any time, press Enter twice or press Ctrl+Enter.

TIP

The easiest way to enter more than one definition for a term is to insert a line break. As you might recall, you insert line breaks by pressing Shift+Enter.

Numbered Lists

Numbered lists are also called ordered lists. Each item in an ordered list is consecutively numbered or lettered. Letters are used only when you nest lists. When a browser sees the beginning of an ordered list, it does three things:

1. Starts a new line
2. Indents the text of the list item
3. Puts the appropriate number or letter in front of the list item

As you can see from the example in Figure 5.9, numbered lists are single spaced like other types of lists discussed earlier. You should use numbered lists when tasks must be performed in a particular order or when you want to add specificity to the list. When you number a list of resources such as those shown in Figure 5.9, you add specificity to the list. Instead of the list being just another list of resources, the list represents the 12 reference works you wish were on your bookshelf.

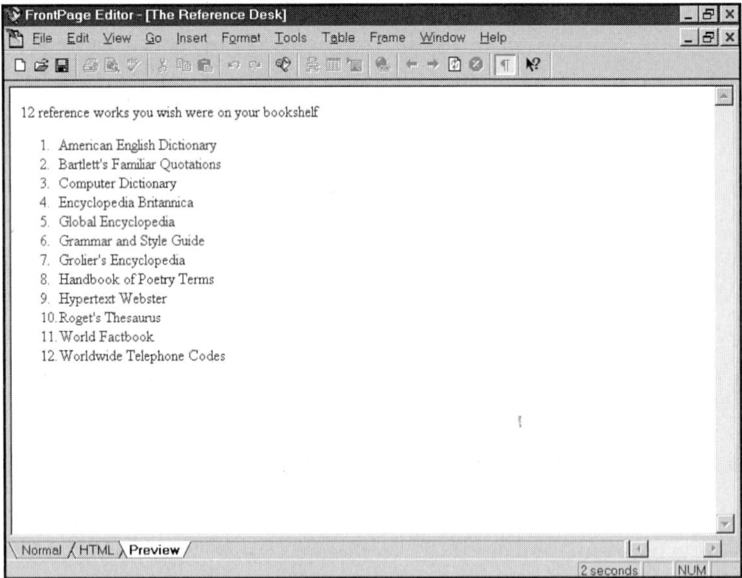

FIGURE 5.9.
A sample numbered list.

Creating numbered lists with the FrontPage Editor is similar to creating bulleted lists. The first step is to begin the list. You do this by clicking the Numbered List button or selecting Bullets and Numbering from the Format menu.

When you select Bullets and Numbering from the Format menu, you see the dialog box shown in Figure 5.10. To display this dialog box at any time, right click, then select List Properties from the pop-up menu. If the Numbers tab is not active, display it by clicking the tab label. To select the type of sequencing for the list, click the graphical icon that depicts the alphabetic or numeric sequencing you want to use.

Sometimes you want to start your numbered list at a specific value, especially if you are continuing a list from a previous section of the page. You can use the Start At field of the Numbers tab to select a specific start count for the sequence.

FrontPage 98 enables you to reformat existing text as a numbered list. To do this, select one or more paragraphs and then click the Numbered List button or select Bullets and Numbering from the Format menu.

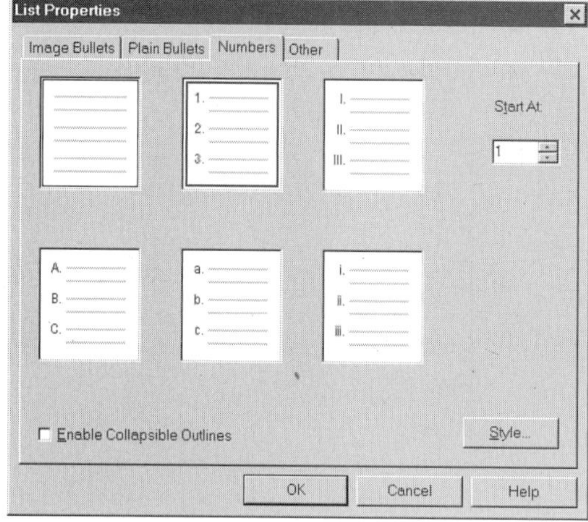

FIGURE 5.10.
Selecting the alphabetic or numeric sequencing of your list.

Nesting Lists and Collapsible Outlines

A nested list is a list inside another list. In HTML, you nest a list by including the entire structure for a list within your current list. For example, you could put bulleted lists within your numbered list structure.

To create a nested list, move the insertion point to where you want the nested list to begin. Next, follow the procedures for creating the type of list you want to insert. When you are finished, press Enter twice to end the nested list. You might have to press Enter a third time to get back to the previous list type. If you press Enter a fourth time, you end the previous list type as well.

A new option in FrontPage 98 is the capability of enabling collapsible outlines. A collapsible outline is an outline that the user can expand or shrink. To expand an outline that is collapsed, all the user has to do is double click the outline. Afterward, the user can shrink the outline by double clicking again.

Collapsible outlines are a feature of dynamic HTML as implemented in Internet Explorer versions 4.0 or later. You can create a collapsible outline simply by nesting lists within a list and then selecting the Enable Collapsible Outlines checkbox on the Other tab of the List Properties dialog box (see Figure 5.11). The Other tab is only available after you create a list.

Changing a List Type

FrontPage 98 enables you to quickly change one list type to another list type. For example, you can change a bulleted list to a numbered list or a numbered list to a bulleted list.

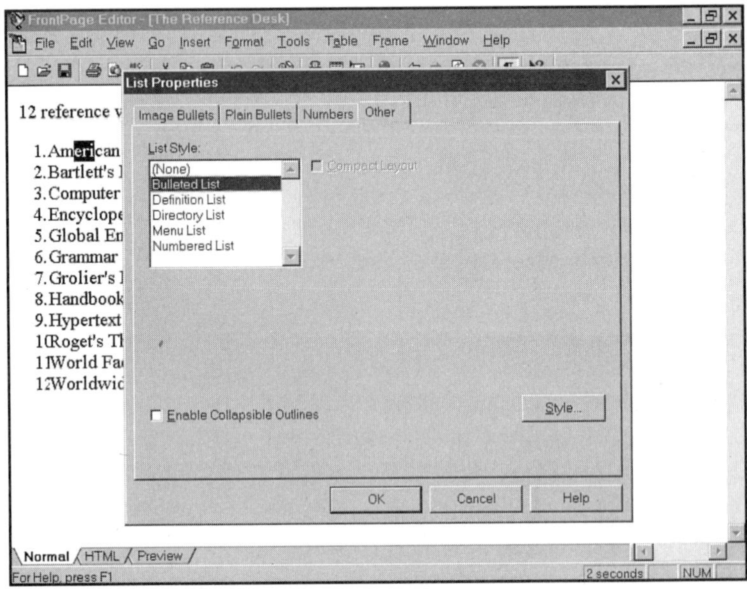

FIGURE 5.11.
Creating a collapsible outline.

To change a list type, select the entire list you want to change by moving the mouse cursor over the list, then right click and select List Properties from the pop-up menu. In the Other tab of the List Properties dialog box, select the new list type and then click the OK button.

NOTE

Because FrontPage 98 changes only the formatting of the outermost select list, the formatting of any nested lists is retained. Also, when you change a list to a definition list, all list items are changed to the format for definitions, not terms.

Summary

Basic techniques that add to the visual impact and interactivity of the document include using lists, hypertext links, and bookmarks. Lists add to the visual impact of the document by clearly organizing material. Hypertext links increase the interactive nature of your document. Bookmarks guide readers to key parts of your publication.

Creating Richer Web Pages with HTML Features

by William Robert Stanek

IN THIS CHAPTER

- Using Line Breaks and Horizontal Lines *90*
- Adding Visual Variety to Your Documents *94*
- Using Superscripts and Subscripts *98*
- Working with Font Types *98*
- Working with Font Sizes *99*
- Adding Comments to Your Documents *101*
- Using Special Characters *102*
- Using Addresses *103*
- Using Formatted Text *104*

A key ingredient for success in Web publishing is the ability to create documents with high visual impact and a high level of interactivity. Basic techniques that add to the visual impact of the document include using line breaks to create a column of text and using horizontal lines to visually divide the document into sections. You can add visual variety to the page by changing the font type and size of text. Most basic documents also use character styles, comments, special characters, and text elements such as preformatted text or addresses.

Using Line Breaks and Horizontal Lines

Sometimes the features that seem very basic are not. Line breaks enable you to break a line without adding a space between the lines. Horizontal lines are graphical lines drawn across the width of the document. Although line breaks and horizontal lines might seem straightforward, they both have many advanced features.

All About Line Breaks

You can use the simple facility of a line break to format text on your document in many creative ways. Sometimes you don't want a space between lines of text, or you want to highlight an example by breaking the line and starting a new line showing the example.

Consider this example. The following text has no line break, so text runs together all on the same line:

```
This section will contain: An introduction to the document
```

Now consider an example with a line break, as in the following:

```
This section will contain:
An introduction to the document
```

You can also use line breaks to format your text into a column or simple list. Not only does text formatted in a column add to the visual impact of the document, but it also gets the reader's attention.

To add a line break with FrontPage 98, press Shift+Enter, or optionally choose Line Break from the Insert menu. Behind the scenes, FrontPage 98 adds the appropriate markup for the line break.

The following example shows you a simple list. Each line is typed in, followed by a `Shift+Enter` to create the line break:

```
Our on-line publications include:
Books
Magazines
Newspapers
Newsletters
```

You can use line breaks inside other text formatting without affecting the font or style of the previously declared formatting. If you insert a line break into a heading, the text before and

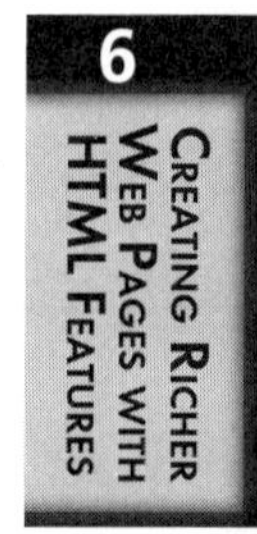

after the break is formatted in the style and font of a heading. All the line break does is start a new line, like the carriage return on a typewriter.

Netscape introduced an extension to line breaks that enables you to clear the margins after a line break. This enhancement is extremely useful when you want to clear the left, right, or both margins after placing an image on the page. If you do not clear the margins, the text might be aligned in a column to the left or right of the image. In FrontPage 98, you specify the clear margin attribute after you insert the line break. This attribute is ignored by Microsoft Internet Explorer.

If you have format marks turned on (View | Format Marks), you can select the line break symbol by double-clicking it and then press Alt+Enter. This invokes the Break Properties window. As you can see from Figure 6.1, this properties window has a series of radio buttons that enable you to set line break properties.

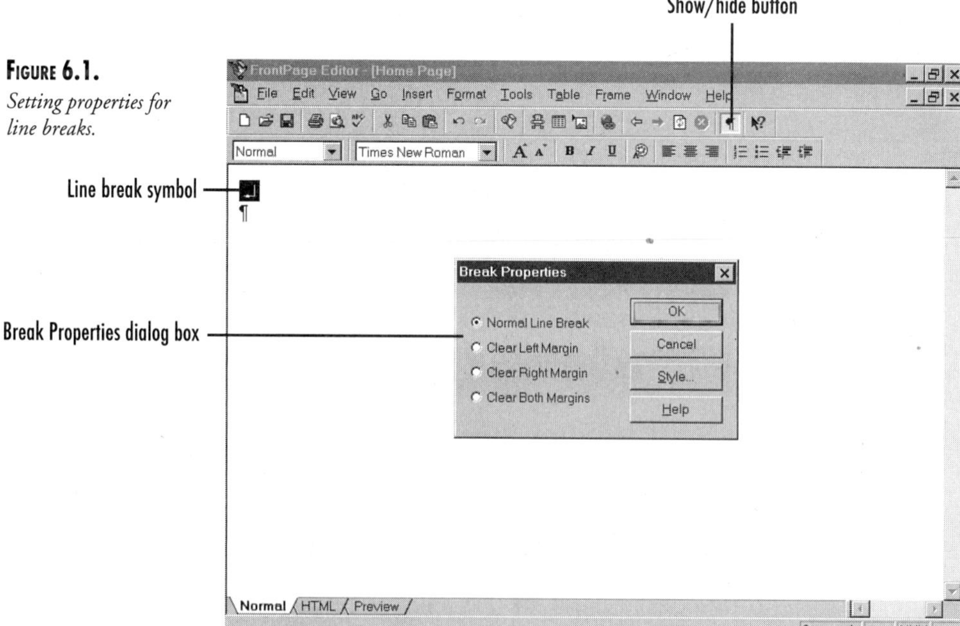

FIGURE 6.1.
Setting properties for line breaks.

NOTE

You can only see format marks such as line breaks if the Format Marks option of the View menu is selected.

In addition to creating more useful ways to break up text and images, you can use a newer tag to ensure that text stays together. A *non-breaking space tag* ensures that two words appear on the same line with no line breaks. A non-breaking space is useful to ensure that text is formatted as you want it to be, but keep in mind that users might have to scroll their browser windows to finish reading the line of text.

To insert a non-breaking space, press Shift+Space.

All About Horizontal Lines

Another way to easily add to the visual impact of the document is to use a horizontal line. The two basic styles of horizontal lines are *shaded* and *unshaded*. Because shaded lines appear to be engraved into the document and add a more special touch, unshaded lines aren't used very often.

Wherever the horizontal line should appear in the text of your document, open the Insert menu and select Horizontal Line. The great thing about horizontal lines is that you can use them to divide your document visually into sections. However, you should use horizontal lines sparingly. Too many horizontal lines in the document can spoil the effect. Therefore, use them to highlight or to help the reader better identify the major sections of the document.

Figure 6.2 depicts a combined example using line breaks and horizontal lines. Although the figure shows only the outline of the document, you can see how horizontal lines can divide the document into four major sections (with the fourth beyond the visible window display).

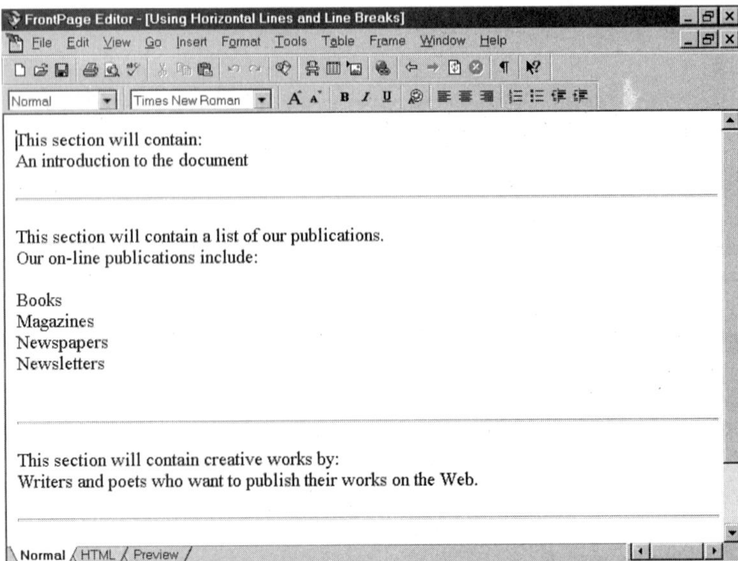

FIGURE 6.2.
You can break up the document using horizontal lines and line breaks.

Horizontal lines become helpful design tools as HTML evolved. With these extensions, you can size the horizontal rule to make the separation of topics and subtopics on your pages more distinct. The size of a horizontal line is defined in terms of pixels.

To separate topics and subtopics visually, you could use one size value for main topics and another size value for each level of subtopics. You should experiment with line sizes in your publications. A size of five pixels is usually sufficient to separate main topics, and a size of two pixels is usually sufficient for subtopics. To set horizontal line properties, select a horizontal line you've added to the document and press Alt+Enter. This opens the dialog box shown in Figure 6.3.

FIGURE 6.3.
Setting horizontal line properties.

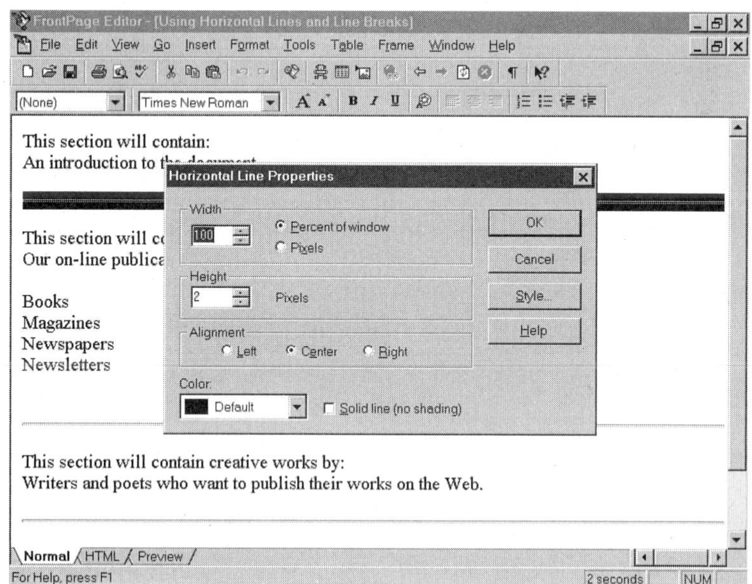

You can align a horizontal line with the left margin, right margin, or center of the page. You can define the length of the horizontal line in pixels or as the percentage of the browser's window width. By combining the two attributes, you can create powerful effects, such as the one shown in Figure 6.4.

NOTE

Keep in mind that some older or non-traditional browsers might ignore the sizing and alignment values for horizontal lines. These browsers also display the multiple horizontal lines in the example as ordinary horizontal lines. It is best to use multiple horizontal lines only on pages that are displayed by newer browsers.

FIGURE 6.4.
Fancy uses of horizontal lines.

By default, the color of horizontal lines is set to the color of the background. You can override this default by selecting a specific color value for the horizontal line. As with other elements that use color, the Color field of the Horizontal Line Properties dialog box has a pull-down list for selecting any of 16 basic colors. The Default value lets you return to the browser default color. The Custom value opens the Color dialog box, which allows you to choose from an expanded selection of colors, or create your own custom colors.

Some Web publishers want to make their documents stand out from other documents on the Web and use graphical lines based on GIF images instead of the standard horizontal line. These graphical lines, although visually appealing, have a major drawback in that readers with text-only browsers see no line break at all. To a reader with a text-only browser, documents with graphical lines based on images have no subdivisions, which is a problem.

Adding Visual Variety to Your Documents

A Web document that contains only paragraphs and headings is boring. Often, you want to highlight and emphasize key sections of the text. To do this, you can use a special set of HTML tags called *character style tags*. Character style tags highlight your text using techniques such as boldface and italics. Unlike heading and paragraph tags that insert white space into the document, character style tags do not insert whitespace, which makes it possible to use character style tags within other tags to highlight a single word or a group of words.

FrontPage 98 enables you to select commonly used character styles directly from the Format toolbar. These styles include bold, italics, and underline. You can also add these and other character styles with the Font dialog box. To open the Font dialog box, select Font from the Format menu. Also, you can click the right mouse button and then select Font Properties on the pop-up menu that appears.

HTML has two subsets of character style tags: *physical styles* and *logical styles.* Physical styles tell the browser the precise format to display. HTML defines physical styles for bold, italics, underlined, strikethrough, and monospace typewriter type. A browser accessing documents containing physical styles attempts to display the text using the strict format you have specified. If it is unable to do so, it might substitute another style for the one you are using, or worse, it might ignore the tag and display the text in the standard style. Consequently, when you want to make sure text is highlighted, use logical styles. Logical styles are the preferred method of adding highlights to Web documents.

Unlike physical style tags, logical style tags do not specify a strict format. They tell your browser how the text should be used and let the browser display the text according to a set of configurations specific to the browser. The logical assignment of the style to the browser ensures that your text is highlighted in the document in some way. HTML defines logical styles for citations, samples, definitions, code, variables, keyboard input, emphasized text, and strongly emphasized text.

FrontPage 98 does not organize styles as specified by the standard. Styles are grouped into regular styles and special styles. These generic style groupings include both physical and logical styles, which might lead to confusion if a browser doesn't support what FrontPage 98 calls a regular style.

Just as with your favorite word processor, some regular style formats are directly accessible from the Format toolbar. Regular styles include emphasized, strongly emphasized, underlined, strikethrough, and monospace type. Browsers usually display emphasized text in italics and strongly emphasized text in bold type. Because these are defined as purely physical styles in HTML, the exact style is determined ultimately by the browser.

Because the logical styles are preferred to the physical styles, the actual markup for bold and italics text is placed in the special style section. Despite what the Format toolbar indicates, when you select the I or B button, you are using emphasized text and strongly emphasized text.

Netscape introduced blinking text, and it has been a subject of controversy ever since. Imagine, for a moment, an entire paragraph or an entire page blinking on and off while you are trying to read it. Text blinking on and off is like a tiny neon sign on your page that attracts the reader's eyes. Sometimes blinking text is good. You draw the reader's attention temporarily to a key area of the page. At other times, blinking text is bad. It distracts the readers while they are trying to read the text on the page. The controversy surrounding the blinking text might be the reason the Internet Explorer does not support this feature.

TIP

The key to using blinking text is to confine it to a small area of your page and to be sure that it only affects a few key words.

Other styles in the special style section are not universally supported by all browsers. Consequently, these styles are rarely used. The following is a list of styles in the special style section:

Citation	Indicates the text is a citation. Most browsers display this style in italics.
Code	Indicates that text is computer code or a program sample. Most browsers display this style in a monospace font such as Courier.
Definition	Indicates that you are defining the highlighted word. Most browsers display this style in italics.
Keyboard	Indicates text that a user would type on the keyboard. Most browsers display this style in a monospace font such as Courier.
Sample	Indicates a sample of literal characters. Most browsers display this style in a monospace font such as Courier.
Variable	Indicates that text is a variable name such as those used in computer programs. Most browsers display this style in italics.

The Font tab of the Font dialog box supports the most commonly used styles (see Figure 6.5). In the Font Style field, you see options for the Regular, Italic, Bold, and Bold Italic styles. In the Effects field, you see options for the Underline, Strikethrough, and Typewriter styles. You can combine any of the styles used in the Font tab. The Sample area of this tab gives you a preview of how your chosen style affects text.

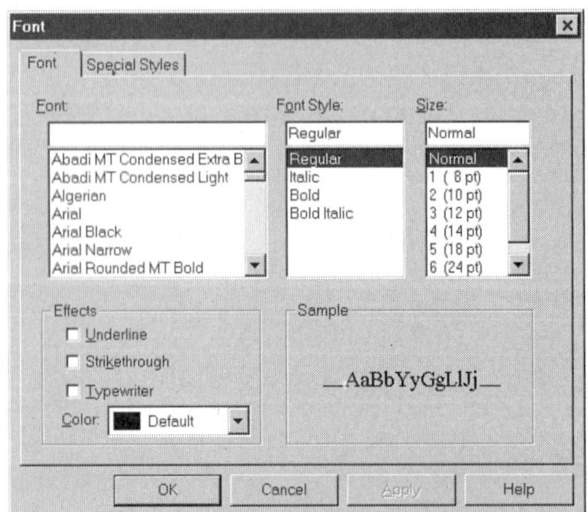

FIGURE 6.5.
Setting commonly used text styles.

The Special Styles tab of the Font dialog box supports the styles you'll use less frequently (see Figure 6.6). To insert a style, activate the checkbox associated with the style by clicking it. Although the Special Styles tab lets you combine styles, you generally should not. As with the Font tab, the Sample area of the Special Styles tab gives you a preview of how your chosen style affects text.

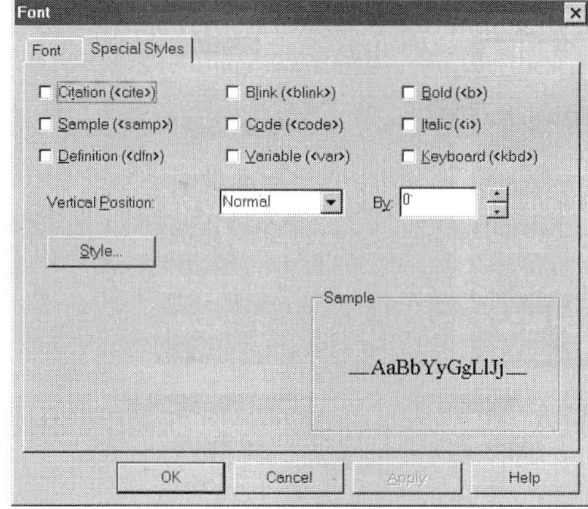

FIGURE 6.6.
Setting special text styles.

Figure 6.7 shows an example of how styles are displayed in FrontPage 98 and in most browsers.

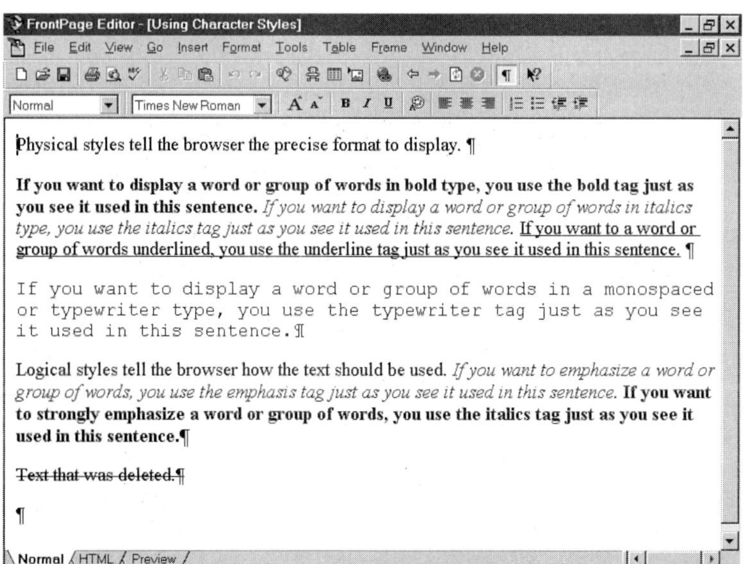

FIGURE 6.7.
A demonstration of various styles.

Using Superscripts and Subscripts

By using superscript and subscript text, you can add more variety to the textual portions of your page and create more advanced documents. You display superscript text by raising the vertical alignment of the associated text. Similarly, you display subscript text by lowering the vertical alignment of the associated text.

FrontPage 98 allows you to add superscripts and subscripts using the Font dialog box, which is shown in Figure 6.8. To access this dialog box, select Font Properties from the Format menu or click the right mouse button and then select Font Properties on the pop-up menu that appears. Next, select the Special Styles tab.

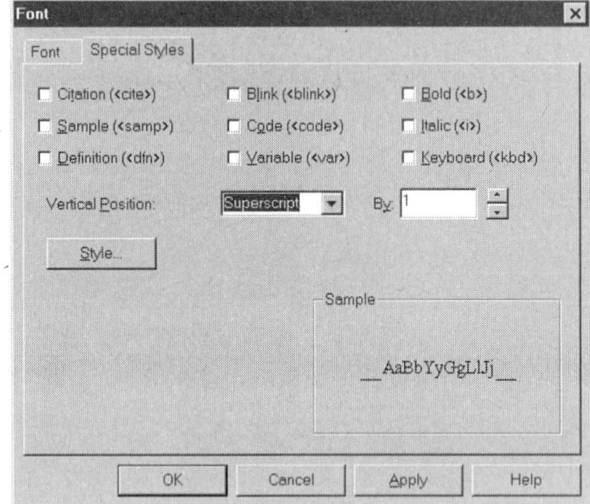

FIGURE 6.8.
Setting superscript and subscript values.

On the Special Styles tab is a field labeled Vertical Position. Initially, the vertical position of any text element is normal. You can change this position to superscript or subscript using the pull-down list provided.

FrontPage 98 allows you to specify the number of points the alignment is offset. In this way, you can create multiple levels of superscript or subscript text. To set the level of the superscript or subscript, adjust the value in the By field.

Working with Font Types

The type of font used to display the text on your page is usually set in the user's browser. This gives the user control over the font face. Often, you as the publisher want to use a certain font face for headings, such as the highly readable Arial, and another font face for paragraph text, such as Century Schoolbook. You might want to use a decorative font, such as Augsburger Initials, to create a fancy first letter for the first word of a paragraph.

Advanced browsers give the publisher relative control over font type. FrontPage 98 also supports font typing. If the font type is available on the user's system, the specified font is used to display your text. If the font type is not available on the user's system, the default font as specified in the user's browser is used to display your text.

FrontPage 98 uses the default font type unless you specify otherwise. You add unique fonts as you create pages by selecting a font type from the Format toolbar. When you want to change fonts, you simply select a new font from the Format toolbar. Behind the scenes, FrontPage 98 adds all the necessary markup.

Another way to add font types is after you create a page. Select a section of text and then select a font type for the text.

TIP

A key concept in using fonts in your Web publications is to limit the number of font styles you use on any single page. To be consistent, you should also limit the number of fonts you use throughout the publication. A good rule of thumb is to use no more than three different font styles on any page. You should also try to use the same fonts throughout the publication.

WARNING

Keep in mind that if you are choosing to specify a particular font for your Web page, the visitor must have that font installed on his system to see the page as you intended. Try to choose standard or easily obtainable fonts for your site.

Working with Font Sizes

The original HTML specification had no way to define a specific font size to use. This is primarily because the font size is traditionally controlled by configurations in the user's browser, and the user is the one who selects the font size she would like to use for viewing Web documents. Using various heading levels, Web publishers had some control over font size. Generally, you could use a level one heading to create text with an approximate font size of 36, you could use a level two heading to create text with an approximate font size of 24, and so on. However, this still didn't give Web publishers accurate control over font sizes, especially if the publisher wanted to change font size in the middle of a line of text.

Web browsers corrected this shortcoming by allowing Web publishers to define the font size relative to a base font size. You can define the size for the font using values between 1 and 7. A value of 1 indicates the smallest text. A value of 7 indicates the largest text. The default value of 3 usually corresponds to the size of standard text on the page.

FrontPage 98 allows you to quickly decrease or increase the size of selected text using the Decrease Text Size and Increase Text Size buttons of the Format toolbar. You can also use the Font dialog box to set the size of select text. To access this dialog box, select Font Properties from the Format menu. You can also click the right mouse button and then select Font Properties on the pop-up menu that appears. As shown in Figure 6.9, the Font tab of the Font dialog box has a field labeled Size. You can use this field to adjust the relative size of selected text.

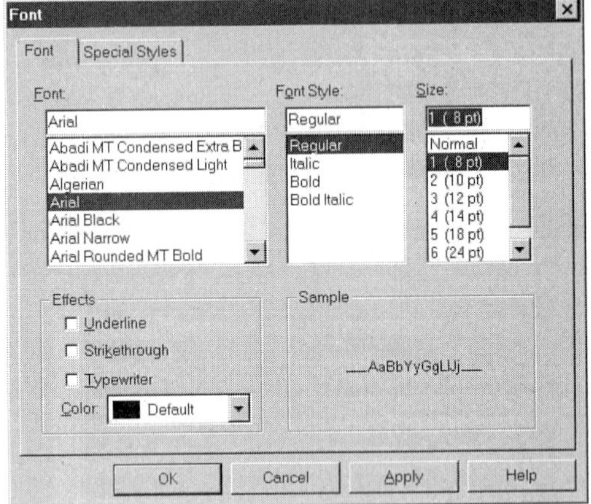

FIGURE 6.9.
Using the Font dialog box to adjust the size of text.

Being able to adjust the font size is very handy. A small font size is useful for disclaimers or copyright notices that should appear on the page but not eat up page space. A large font size is useful when you want to draw attention to specific keywords or paragraphs of text. You can adjust the font size to create a large first letter for keywords or the first word in a paragraph. You can also create word art by adjusting the font size within words or sentences, as shown in Figure 6.10.

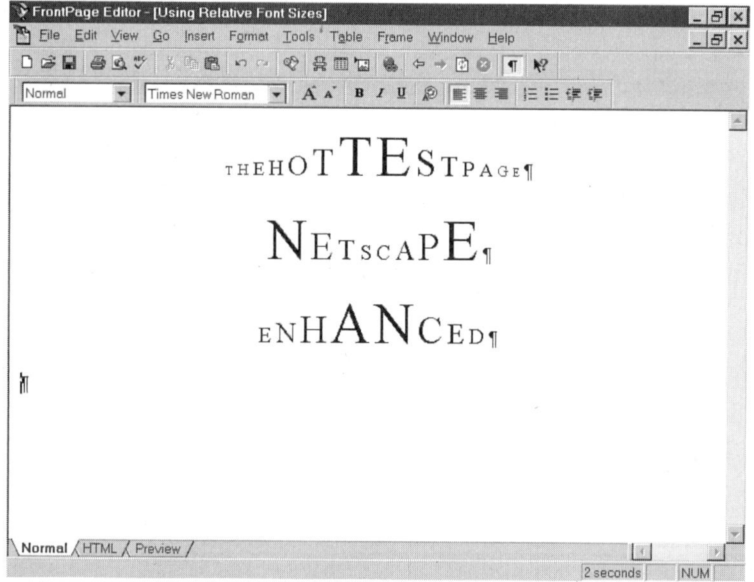

FIGURE 6.10.
Creating word art with relative font sizes.

Adding Comments to Your Documents

If you are a programmer or have looked at the printout of a computer program, odds are you have seen comments inserted in code. Comments are used in computer code to make notes or explanations to anyone who might see the code. Even the original programmer finds the comments useful when changes or additions to the code are necessary, especially if they come up months or years after originally writing the program. Programmers use comments because working through the logic of code every time it must be changed is a waste of time and resources.

Web publishers can similarly use comments to save time and resources when making changes and additions to HTML documents. You can use comments to track the update history of the document; make notes about text, links, or objects in the document; or pass information to anyone who might be reading the source code. Comments are not displayed by the browser with the text and objects on the page and are only viewable if you look at the source code for the document.

In FrontPage 98, you add comments by selecting FrontPage Component from the Insert menu, then choosing Comment from the FrontPage Component dialog box. You can now enter your comments as shown in Figure 6.11. When you are finished, click the OK button.

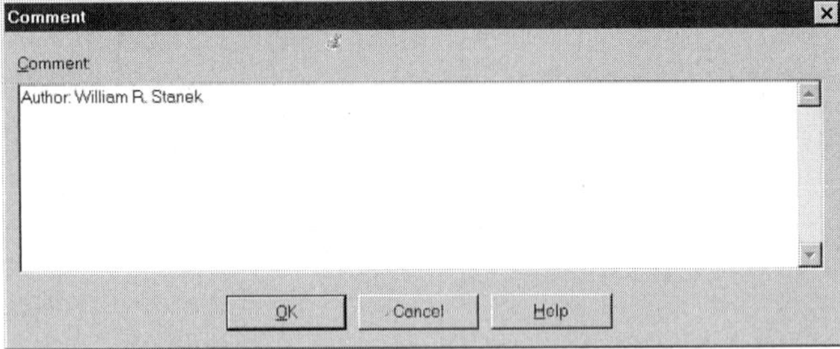

FIGURE 6.11.
Adding comments to your page.

FrontPage 98 inserts your comments on the page. Although this text can be viewed from the FrontPage Editor, it is not displayed by a Web browser unless the reader views the HTML markup for the page. Annotation text is displayed in purple and retains the character size and other attributes of the current paragraph style.

TIP

Comments are inserted in the page using a simple WebBot called the annotation bot. When you move your pointer over the annotation text, you see a robot icon. This icon indicates that a WebBot is embedded in the page. You access an edit window associated with the bot by double-clicking when the robot icon is visible. Double-clicking when the robot icon is visible opens the Comment dialog box.

Using Special Characters

In HTML, special characters are also called entities. The two types of entities are character entities and numeric entities. Character entities use actual text characters to define the special character, such as `"` for the double quotation mark symbol. Numeric entities use numbers to define the special character and add a hash mark before the number, such as `|` for the vertical bar (|) symbol. The numbers used with numeric entities correspond to character positions in the ISO Latin I character set.

With FrontPage 98, using special characters in your Web document is easy, and you don't have to memorize character values. Wherever the special character should appear in the text of your document, you simply open the Insert menu, select Symbol, and choose a character to insert (see Figure 6.12).

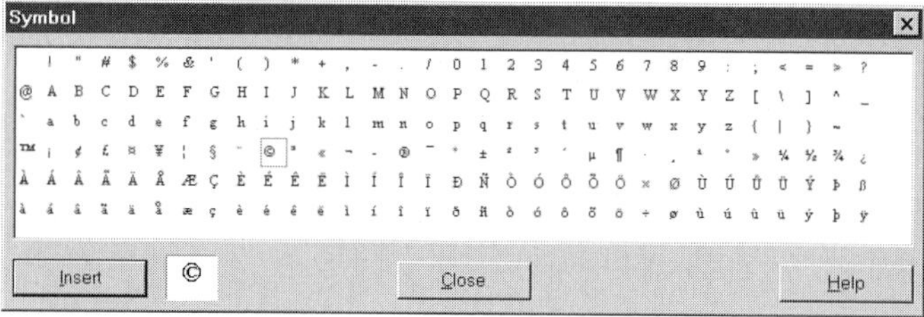

FIGURE 6.12.
Selecting a symbol to insert.

When a browser sees that special character, the browser interprets the character and displays the corresponding symbol, if possible. For example, when a browser reads the entity value `|`, it displays the vertical bar symbol.

> **NOTE**
>
> In HTML, you must use entity values for any characters used in markup tags, which include the following symbols: #, <, >, and &. Fortunately, FrontPage 98 automatically inserts these special characters for you.

Using Addresses

In HTML, addresses get special attention. Browsers typically display address text in italics with a paragraph break before and after the address. No other special formatting is associated with addresses.

To add an address to your document, move the cursor to the point where you want to insert the address or select the text you want to format as an address and then select Address from the Format toolbar's pull-down menu.

Another way to add an address is to open the Format menu and select Paragraph. This brings up the Paragraph Properties dialog box, which you can use to add address formatting at the current insertion point. While this dialog box is open, you can also select an alignment for the address with the Paragraph Alignment field, as shown in Figure 6.13.

> **TIP**
>
> An address entered in multiple lines using the Enter key has a lot of empty space. This is a function of HTML formatting and not a fault of FrontPage 98. To avoid extra spacing type Shift+Enter, which inserts a line break.

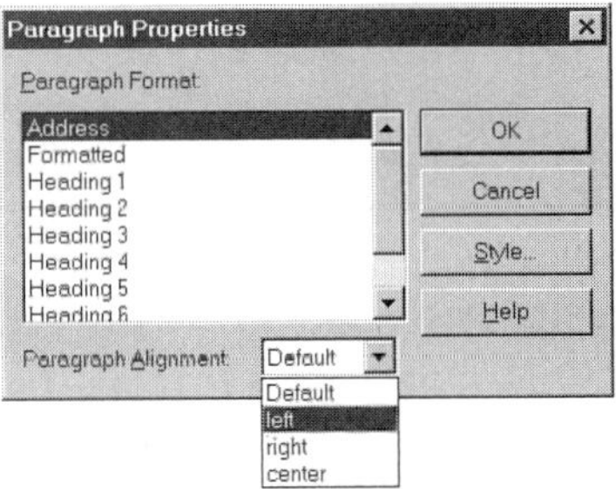

FIGURE 6.13.
Selecting an alignment for address text.

Using Formatted Text

Defining a section of text as formatted is extremely useful and enables you to use standard ASCII text formatting techniques to format text in your documents. In a section of text declared as formatted, you can use any of your favorite ASCII spacing tricks, including tabs, multiple tabs, multiple spaces, and multiple blank lines, without fear that a browser will discard them. Usually, formatted text is displayed in a monospaced font such as Courier.

When you use formatted text, the FrontPage Editor really works overtime. Not only is the editor adding HTML tags, but it is also inserting ASCII formatting that is saved with your document. Figure 6.14 shows a sample document with formatted text.

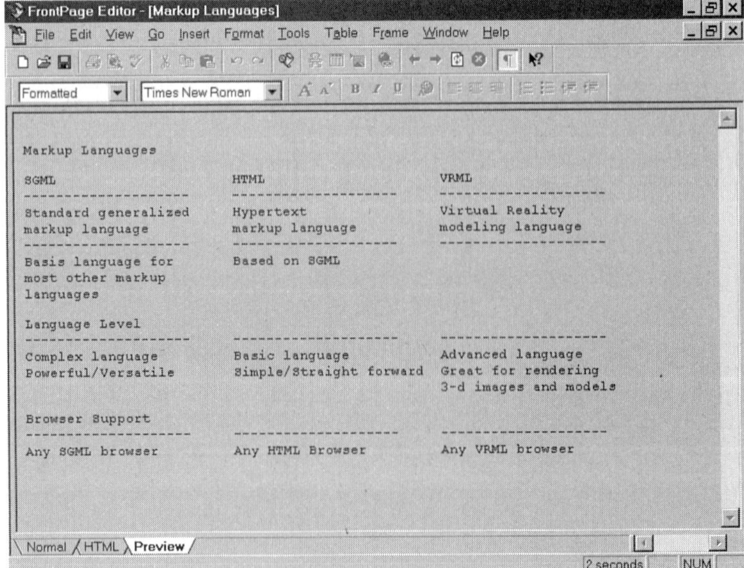

FIGURE 6.14.
A document with formatted text.

To add formatted text to your document, move the cursor to the point where you want to insert the formatted text or select the text you want to be in this format and then select Formatted from the Format toolbar's pull-down menu.

Another way to add formatted text is to open the Format menu and select Paragraph. This brings up the Paragraph Properties dialog box, where you can add formatted text at the current insertion point.

CAUTION

When using preformatted text, keep in mind that monospaced fonts appear much wider than proportional fonts. Proportional fonts use the amount of screen space proportional to their size, which means that an *i* uses less screen space than a *w*. In a monospaced or nonproportional font, each letter uses the same amount of screen space.

Summary

The ability to create documents with high visual impact is essential to your success as a Web publisher. You can add variety to you page using line breaks, horizontal lines, and character styles. You can also add variety by changing font type and size.

Enhancing Your Pages with Images—The Easy Way

by William Robert Stanek

IN THIS CHAPTER

- Using Images in Your Web Pages 108
- Working with Images in FrontPage 98 109
- Importing Images 112
- Cutting, Copying, and Pasting Images 114
- Saving an Image to the Current Web 115
- Using Background Images 115
- When and How to Use Images 117
- Using Alternate Text 119
- Sizing Your Images 120
- Placing Images in Your Documents 121
- Sizing Images to Fit Your Needs 125
- Designing Highlights with Images 126
- Additional Enhancements for Images 128
- Image Formats 129
- Creating Your Own Images 132

Images are the key to unleashing the power of your Web publications. Everywhere you look on the Web, you find images. Web publishers use images to enhance their pages and get the reader's attention. You can use thumbnail icons to create highlights and navigation mechanisms. You can use computer-designed images as logos, page titles, illustrations, and maps to the hot features at your site. You can use digitized photos to convey your message in a way that is more powerful than text alone. These photos can help sell your products and services and can even show the rest of the world what your part of the world looks like.

Using Images in Your Web Pages

Adding images to your Web pages is easy and can be accomplished using either external images or inline images. Readers access external images by activating a hypertext link to the image, such as a link that says `67 Chevy fire-engine red`.

When a reader clicks the link, the image downloads to his computer. If an image viewer is available and configured for use in the reader's browser, the image displays. If an image viewer is not available, the image is stored on the reader's hard disk for later viewing.

Although adding external images to your Web publications is as easy as providing a link to the image, it does require forethought and a fundamental understanding of image formats and related concepts. Browsers know which image viewer to launch based on the file type extension (`.jpeg`, `.gif`, and so forth) of the external image referenced in your document. When a reader accesses a link to a GIF image, the browser checks a configuration table to see which application should display the image, which is why your web files should always be named with the appropriate extension. If the file is in GIF format, name it with a `.gif` extension. If the file is in JPEG format, name it with a `.jpeg` or `.jpg` extension.

Unlike external images that are not displayed directly, inline images can be viewed directly. When a reader with a graphics-capable browser accesses your page, the images can automatically load with the text on the page. When you add an image to a page, you specify the location of the image by using a URL. The URL can be a relative path such as `67chevy.gif`, or it can be a full path such as `http://www.mydom.dom/usr/images/gifs/67chevy.gif`.

All image files are in a specific format. The two most popular image formats on the Web are GIF and JPEG. All graphics-capable browsers support both the GIF and JPEG formats. Beyond support for GIF and JPEG, FrontPage 98 supports images in the following formats: BMP (Windows and OS/2), EPS, MAC, MSP, PCD, PCX, RAS, TIFF, WMF, and WPG. These additional formats are popular formats for graphic design tools, image packages, and shareware image libraries.

Whenever you use any of these additional image formats, FrontPage 98 converts the image to either the GIF or JPEG format depending on the number of colors in the image. FrontPage 98 converts images with 256 or fewer colors to GIF and images with more than 256 colors to JPEG. The section "Image Formats" later in this chapter discusses image formats in more detail.

When you specify an image, you can also specify alternate text to display in place of the image. Readers with a text-only browser see the alternate text instead of the image. If you do not specify alternate text, readers with a text-only browser see a note that marks the location of the image on the page, such as `[IMAGE]` .

Browsers handle inline images in many different ways. Some browsers load all text and associated images before displaying any part of your document. Some browsers display text and graphics as they read in your document. Other browsers load and display the textual portions of the page, leaving placeholders where the images go, and then retrieve the images one by one. A few advanced browsers let the reader select options for displaying the components of the page.

Individual browsers handle inline images in many different ways, but all graphics-capable browsers provide readers with a mechanism for turning off the automatic image-loading feature of the browser. This nice feature for readers means more work for Web publishers.

Before you add inline images, there are many concepts you should consider. The most important matters you should think about are when and how to use images in your publications.

Working with Images in FrontPage 98

FrontPage 98 provides terrific control over images and enables you to see all the images your page contains as you edit it. You can use images in two key ways: insert them directly into a page or import them into your web for future use. All images come from one of three sources: the current web, an external source such as the World Wide Web, or a local file.

NOTE

In this book, you will find many other chapters to help you work with images. For tips on optimizing images and color palettes as well as using elements on the image toolbar, see Chapter 19, "Optimizing Your Images and Color Palettes." For tips on working with image maps, see Chapter 21, "Creating and Designing Image Maps."

Using the FrontPage Editor, you can easily insert images from the current web. The first step is to move the insertion point where you want the image inserted and then choose Image from the Insert menu or click the Insert Image button located on the Standard toolbar. This opens the dialog box shown in Figure 7.1.

You can easily create links in the FrontPage Editor. In the Editor, select the text that identifies the link and then either choose Hyperlink from the Edit menu or click the Standard toolbar's Create or Edit Hyperlink button. This opens the Create Hyperlink dialog box shown in Figure 6.3. Now, all you need to do is enter the URL to the image in the URL field.

If you don't know the URL of the image you want to use, FrontPage 98 displays a list of files in the current web. FrontPage 98 also provides buttons that you can use to search for the image. Here are some of the ways you can add images:

File in Current Web—Click the name and FrontPage 98 will enter the image URL for you.

File on the Web—Click the Use your Web Browser to select a page or file button, and you can search the web for the image URL.

File on your disk—Click the Select a file on your computer button, and you can search your disk for an image you want to use.

Clip Art—Click the Clip Art button to access the Microsoft Clip Art Gallery; the Clip Art Gallery has hundreds of web-ready images you can use.

Scan—Use the Scan button if you want to scan in a digital image using a scanner, digital camera, or a video camera; FrontPage 98 assumes you have all the necessary hardware to scan in the image.

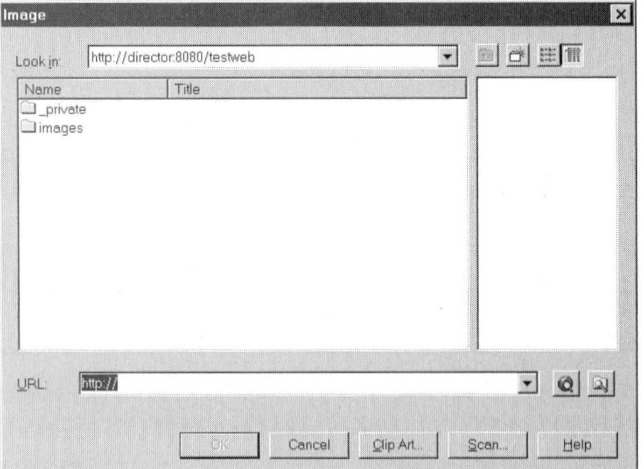

FIGURE 7.1.
The Image dialog box.

After you add an image, you can define attributes for the image by clicking the image, then right-clicking and selecting Image properties from the pop-up menu. This opens the Image Properties dialog box (see Figure 7.2). Image properties define exactly how the image will be used in the Web page. As you can see from the figure, the Image Properties dialog box has three tabs: General, Video, and Appearance.

Properties in the General tab define the image source, alternative representations, and default hyperlinks. Properties in the Video tab define a dynamic source to display instead of the image in compliant browsers, such as Internet Explorer. Properties in the Appearance tab define how the image will appear on the page.

Although you will find specific tips for using each of these attributes later in the chapter, Table 7.1 gives you a quick overview of image attributes and their uses.

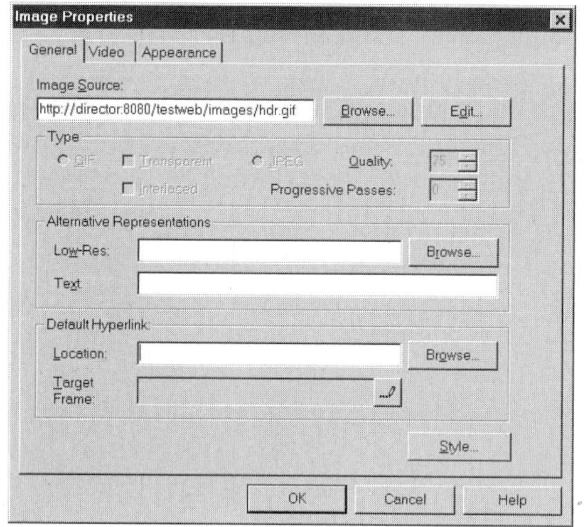

Figure 7.2.
Assigning image properties.

Table 7.1. Image attributes and their uses.

Tab	*Property*	*Use*
General	Image Source	Sets the image source file URL.
	GIF	Sets the image type to GIF.
	Transparent	Used only with GIF images; indicates image has transparent background.
	Interlaced	Used only with GIF images; indicates the image is interlaced for faster display while loading.
	JPEG	Sets the image type to JPEG.
	Quality	Used only with JPEG images; indicates the quality of the image.
	Progressive Passes	Used only with JPEG images; indicates the number of passes in rendering the image.
	Low-Res	Sets a low-resolution image to display before loading and displaying a high-resolution image; speeds up display of page. (Netscape only.)
	Text	Sets text to display if the image is not loaded for any reason. Also used as the tooltip mouseover in newer web browsers.
	Location	Links the image to a resource at the given location.
	Target Frame	Targets a specific frame for the hyperlink.

continues

Table 7.1. continued

Tab	*Property*	*Use*
Video	Video Source	Sets a dynamic source video for the image.
Appearance	Alignment	Sets the position of the image in relation to text and other elements on the page.
	Border Thickness	Sets the width of the image border; used with images that are linked to other resources.
	Horizontal Spacing	Sets the width of the whitespace to the left and right of the image.
	Vertical Spacing	Sets the width of the whitespace above and below the image.
	Specify Size	Allows you to set specific width and height for the image.
	Width	Sets the width of the image.
	Height	Sets the height of the image.
	Keep Aspect Ratio	Keeps the current aspect ratio in case the image is resized.

Importing Images

Using the FrontPage Explorer, you can import images for future use in the current web. Keep in mind that when you insert an image that is not in the GIF or JPEG format, FrontPage 98 converts the image to either GIF or JPEG format. Because FrontPage 98 stores all files by web on your file system, you generally should not edit the original image file. However, if you do edit the file in its original location, you must import the image again so FrontPage 98 can store the updated image.

In the FrontPage Explorer, choose Import from the File menu. This opens the Import File to FrontPage Web dialog box, which is shown in Figure 7.3. Before you specify files to import, only four options are available in this dialog box: Add File, Add Folder, Close, and Help.

When importing images, you generally do not want to use the Add Folder button. Instead, you use the Add File button. Clicking this button opens the Add File to Import List dialog box, which is shown in Figure 7.4. Using the Look In drop-down list, you can select the folder you want to browse. FrontPage 98 displays a list of files that match the current file type selected in the Files of type field.

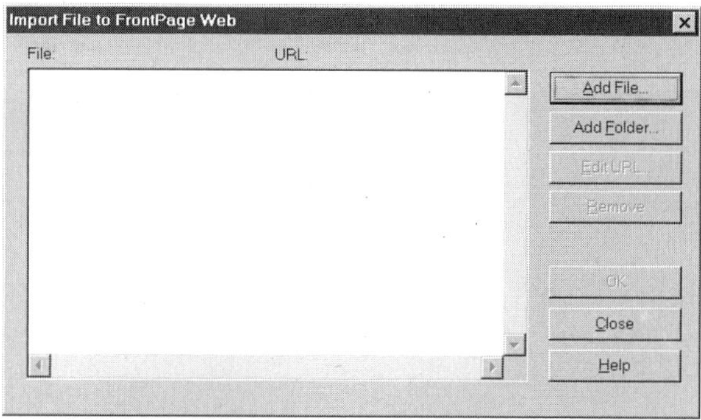

FIGURE 7.3.
Importing files.

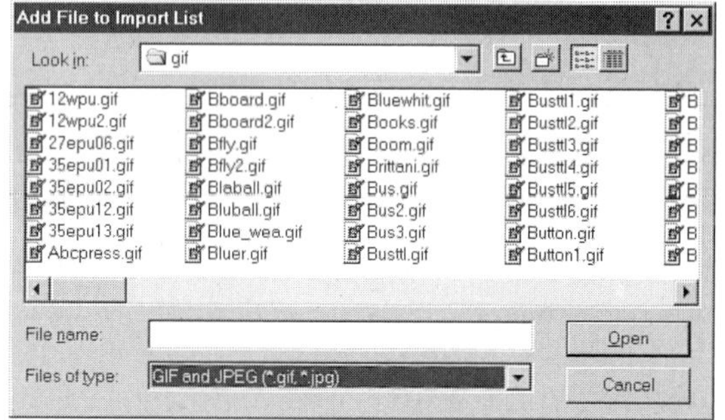

FIGURE 7.4.
Adding files to the import list.

If you know the name of the image you want to import, you can enter the name in the File name field. If you do not know the name of the image, you can browse folders until you find the image you are looking for. When you find the image, you can add it to the list of files to import by double-clicking the filename, selecting the filename, and then clicking the Open button, or typing the filename and then clicking the Open button.

TIP

FrontPage 98 enables you to select multiple files for importing. By holding down the Ctrl key and clicking the left mouse button on a filename, you can add files to your import list. Using the Shift key and the mouse, you can select a group of files listed consecutively. To do this, click the left mouse button on the first file you want to select, move the mouse pointer to the last file you want to select, and hold down the Shift key as you press the left mouse button.

When there are files in the import list, the FrontPage Explorer displays them in the Import File to FrontPage Web dialog box as shown in Figure 7.5. FrontPage 98 adds the filenames and their locations to a file for safekeeping. This enables you to import some or all of the files at a later date. To remove a file that you added to the import list by mistake or otherwise do not want to import, select the image's filename from the import list and click the Remove button.

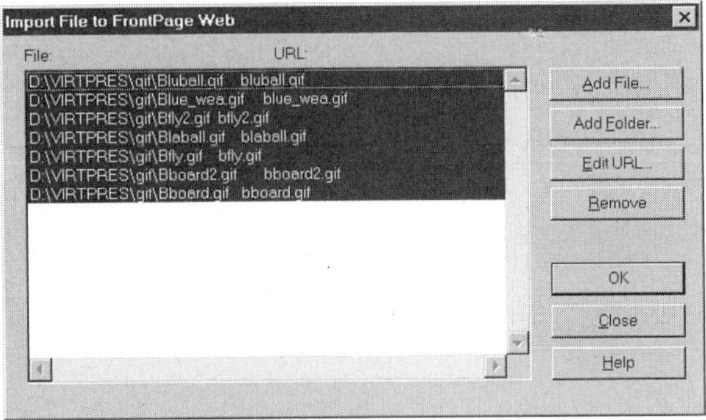

Figure 7.5.
A list of files to import.

You should note that all the buttons in the dialog box are active when there are files to import. By default, the Explorer selects all the files for importing. By clicking the OK button with all the files selected, you can import all the files at once. Using the techniques for selecting multiple files, you can select a group of files to import. When you start importing files, the OK button changes to a Stop button. The Stop button enables you to stop importing files to the current web at any time.

If a conflict occurs when you are importing files, FrontPage 98 displays a warning. To continue importing files, you must make a selection. In this case, you select Yes to replace the existing file with the one you are importing and No to keep the existing file.

By default, the FrontPage Explorer imports all images to a subdirectory called `images` within the current web's main directory. To change this default, you need to edit the image's URL path using the Edit URL dialog box (click the Edit URL button). Unfortunately, you have to set a new path individually for each image you are importing. Any links or WebBots in documents within the current web are updated to use the new path to the image.

Cutting, Copying, and Pasting Images

When you edit your documents in the FrontPage Editor, you often want to manipulate images just as you would text. FrontPage 98 enables you to do so using the familiar cut, copy, and paste mechanisms you find in most word processors. Before you can cut, copy, or paste an image, you need to select it.

You can select an image by doing any of the following:

- Click the image.
- Move the pointer to the left or right side of the image and then click and hold the left mouse button and drag the pointer over the image.
- Move the insertion point to the left or right side of the image and then press Shift+left-arrow key or Shift+right-arrow key.

> **TIP**
>
> If you press the Delete key when the image is selected, the Editor removes it from the page, and the only way to get the image back is to use the Undo function. When you delete an image in this way, the image is removed from the page but is not copied to the Clipboard.
>
> You can delete an image without selecting it first. One way to delete an image without selecting it first is to move the insertion point after the image and press the Backspace key.

When the image is selected, you can use the cut, copy, or paste button on the Standard toolbar or access these functions from the Edit menu. When you cut an image, it is removed from the page and copied to the Clipboard. When you copy an image, it is copied to the Clipboard but is not removed from the page.

When an image is on the Clipboard, you can insert it using the Paste button or by selecting Paste from the Edit menu. Because Windows shares the Clipboard between programs, you can cut an image from your favorite paint program and paste it directly into your document. If the image is not in the GIF or JPEG format, the FrontPage Editor automatically converts the image to either GIF or JPEG format. Images with 256 or fewer colors are converted to GIF. Images with more than 256 colors are converted to JPEG. These formats are discussed in detail later in the chapter in the "Image Formats" section, which explains why FrontPage 98 handles images in this way.

Saving an Image to the Current Web

FrontPage 98 tracks all changes to images for you. Any images you've inserted into your document from a file, pasted from the Clipboard, or altered in the current document can be imported to the current web when you save the document. However, the FrontPage Editor does not automatically import the images. Generally, the Save Image to Web dialog box is displayed for each image that was inserted or updated since the page was last saved to the web.

By default, the Editor saves all images to a subdirectory called `images` within the current web's main directory. To change this default, you need to edit the image's URL path.

Using Background Images

Page backgrounds are a graphic designer's dream come true. To add a background image, all you have to do is specify an image to be used as the background for the page. The image is tiled or repeated to fill the background area. You can use tiling to create design effects using small images. The best image formats to use for background images are GIF and JPEG, which are fully supported by leading browsers such as Netscape Navigator and Internet Explorer.

To add a background image, open the Page Properties dialog box and click the Background tab. Select the Background Image check box, and you can enter a relative or absolute URL to the image in the text input field provided (see Figure 7.6).

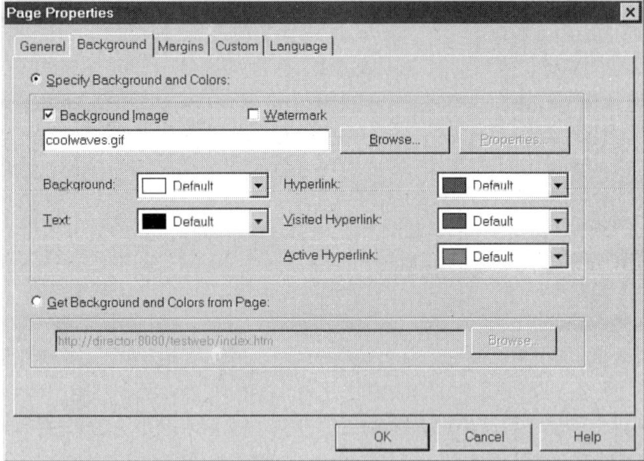

FIGURE 7.6.
Inserting a background image.

The key to using backgrounds in your pages is to make sure the background does not interfere with the readability of the page. Figure 7.7 shows how background images can add pizzazz to your Web pages without interfering with the readability of the page. The background image is a grouping of five animals: an eagle, a seal, an ape, a wolf, and a polar bear. Because the original image did not fill the browser's window, it is tiled.

FIGURE 7.7.
Add pizzazz to your pages with backgrounds.

A popular technique to use when adding backgrounds is to create the illusion that the image runs along the margin (see Figure 7.8). With your cool graphic in the margin, you can be sure that it won't interfere with the readability of the page. The trick to the illusion is a spacing technique that makes it seem as if the background image is only in the left margin when in fact it extends across the full width of the browser's window.

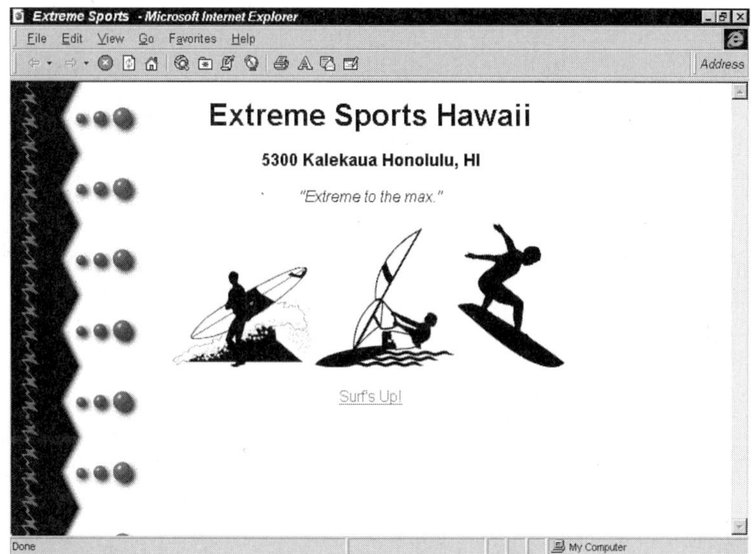

FIGURE 7.8.
A popular technique for backgrounds is creating a margin along the left side of the window.

To ensure the background image is only tiled vertically, the image should be at least 1200 pixels wide. 1280×1024 is the most popular high-end screen resolution. Following this advice, you put dark graphics in the left margin that are 100 to 200 pixels wide and combine them with a light (usually white) graphic 1000 to 1100 pixels wide that completes the effect. You could also reverse this and put light graphics in the left margin that are 100 to 200 pixels wide and combine them with a dark graphic 1000 to 1100 pixels wide.

FrontPage 98 includes clip art that you can use for backgrounds. To access these background images, open the Page Properties dialog box, select the Background tab, and then click the Browse button. This opens the Select Background Image dialog box, which is identical to the Image dialog box covered extensively in previous sections. Because you want to use clip art backgrounds, click the Clip Art button.

When you find a background image you want to use, double-click it. This closes the Select Background Image dialog box and inserts the full path to your chosen background image in the Background Image text input field. Later when you save the page, FrontPage 98 displays a prompt that asks you to confirm that you want to save the image to a file. Generally, you want to click the Yes button, which ensures the background image file is copied to the current web.

When and How to Use Images

As you've seen, adding images to your publications is easy, yet this ease of use makes for easy abuse as well. Your inline images should supplement text and enhance the document but rarely replace text on the page. One of the most important choices you as the Web publisher have to make is determining when and how to use images. You can use images in your publications in dozens of ways. Before you add an image to the publication, however, you should ask yourself three questions:

- Why you are using the image?
- Does the image add to the impact of the page?
- Does the image help the reader?

Creating images, even simple images, for use in Web documents is an art form that is largely misunderstood even by professionals. You will find many Web documents with images that are horribly designed and actually lessen the impact of the documents they are in. Many more Web documents have images designed by the skilled hands of graphic designers that fail to create the desired impact because they are over-designed. A common and mistaken philosophy for many of these poorly designed documents is that bigger and more is better. Bigger and more is not better.

When you create images, use a design and style that fit the purpose of the document. Often simple low-resolution images work just as well as advanced high-resolution images. Nothing gets the reader's attention faster than well-designed and well-placed images. You should use images in your Web documents when they

- Accent the page
- Highlight key ideas
- Serve a specific purpose

Images can highlight the textual portions of the page. Graphic titles and logos can be eye-opening introductions for your publications. Small images can accent key ideas or concepts. Illustrations, figures, and pictures can support key points discussed in the publication.

Images that serve a specific purpose are the most useful. By putting an image tag inside a hypertext link, you can create images that act as links to other documents. If you use a series of images, you can create a simple menu to key pages at your site. Sometimes images can even be the only element on the page. If the image contains hot areas that are mapped to specific pages at your site, a single image can act as your site's menu. In this way, the image can act as the doorway to key areas at the site.

Other questions you should ask yourself when adding images to your page include these:

- How large is the image file and how long does it take the average user to download?
- How many images are there already on the page, and does the image fit in with the images on the page?

These issues have more consequence than you might think. The more features you add to the page, the longer it takes for the page to load into the reader's browser. If you add too many features, the reader might get impatient and choose another site to visit. Consequently, for large images, you might want to consider using a small image called a *thumbnail* that links to the large image or even a simple text link to the image. You can create a thumbnail using an image or painting program (such as Image Composer) to shrink the original, larger image to a smaller size. With a thumbnail ready, you can insert it into your Web page just like any other image. Also, as you will see later in the discussion of color maps, some images just aren't compatible with each other and cause conflicts that can dramatically affect the way readers see your page.

The best Web publications are user-friendly and highly interactive. You can add images to your pages to make them more friendly and more interactive.

Using Alternate Text

Providing ways for readers who cannot or choose not to view images to enjoy your site is a key concept in the design of your documents. Users with text-only browsers and users who turn off the automatic image-loading feature of their browsers cannot see your images. Consequently, for these users, you want to provide alternate features in addition to your images.

EDITING TECHNIQUE

Sometimes you want to include alternate text that the reader can see in place of your images. You do this in the Image Properties dialog box. To display this dialog box, select the image and then press Alt+Enter or right-click, and then select Image Properties from the pop-up menu. In the Alternative Representations area of the dialog box, enter the text you want the reader to see when the image is not displayed. For the fire-engine red '67 Chevy, you could specify the alternate text "Fire-engine red '67 Chevy with mag wheels."

TIP

Double-clicking an image automatically opens the default image editor, which is usually Image Composer. If you want to change the default image editor, you can use the Windows Explorer File Types tab to do so. File types can be set by doing the following steps:

1. Open a folder using the Windows Explorer.
2. Choose View|Options to open the Options dialog box. Click the File Types tab.
3. Select an existing file type for your images (such as JPEG Image) and click the Edit button.
4. In the actions list, select `open` and click the Edit button.
5. Select a new application to associate to this file type by clicking the Browse button.
6. Confirm your changes by clicking OK to close the Editing action dialog box, clicking OK to close the Edit File Type dialog box, and clicking OK to close the Options dialog box.

When you specify alternate text, readers see the text instead of the `[IMAGE]` note telling them an image is on the page. Browsers typically display alternate text for images in brackets. However, telling the reader that a picture of a car is on the page might not enhance the reader's perception of the page. Again, you should add features to increase the impact of the page. A better way to provide information about images is to use several descriptive words that help readers see the image in their mind's eye.

NOTE

Internet Explorer and some other browsers display the alternate text whenever you move the pointer over the image. Because of this, you can use the alternate text to describe the resource an image is linked to as well.

If telling the reader what the image contains doesn't enhance the page, you can remove the reference to the image. Usually, you use an empty alternate text assignment to do this. However, FrontPage 98 does not allow this. As a result, you can insert a space as the text, which effectively replaces `[IMAGE]` with `[ ]`.

Often, images are essential to the understanding of concepts explored in your documents. Although readers with text-only browsers cannot view your inline images, you might want to make key images available both as inline and external images. For example, if you are comparing the hot new design of your latest product to a competitor's product, a digitized photo can support your claims and help you sell the product. Although users with text-only browsers cannot display inline images, they probably can display external images using an image viewer to display the picture.

Sizing Your Images

The physical size of your images in terms of bytes is extremely important. Every inline image you include must be loaded when the page is accessed, and a 15K image takes a lot longer to download than a 3K image. However, slow-loading graphics aren't necessarily large graphics; they are high-resolution graphics or graphics with many colors. A very large four-color image at low resolution downloads faster than a small 256-color image at high resolution.

A good rule to follow when adding images to your Web pages is the 14-second rule. The 14-second rule has the average user in mind. Currently, the average user accessing the Web has a 28,800bps modem. If you analyze this statistically, use the median so extremes won't have a large effect on the outcome. The current trend is toward 28,800bps, with many Web users accessing at 9600bps/14,400bps and an increasing number accessing at 33,600bps and 56,000bps. The philosophy at the heart of the rule is that if it takes longer than 14 seconds under the best of conditions to download all the objects in your document, you might want to restructure your document so it downloads in 14 seconds or less.

Fourteen seconds is really the average (median) value in a frustration window that weighs poor performance and slow access speeds at one end and the top performance and access speeds at the other end. Don't use the rule as an absolute. Use it as a reality check to help you develop user-friendly pages. This is the basic precept of the rule—make sure your pages are user friendly by valuing the user's time. After most users have browsed the Web for a while, they discover that there is nothing more frustrating than waiting for thousands of bytes of graphics to load. You might want to follow this rule to satisfy your visitors.

NOTE

To test the 14-second rule, make sure that the automatic image-loading feature of your Web browser is turned on and then try loading one of your Web documents. Use a modem speed of 28,800bps. If it takes more than 14 seconds under optimal conditions to fully load all text and graphics–assuming no other time-delaying features are adversely affecting the download–look at the document and see what is slowing the load time. Consider modifying the offending element. Note that your Web documents load faster for you because of your proximity to the site. If it takes you 14 seconds to download the document, it will probably take users at disparate sites a lot longer.

One way to avoid putting byte-hogging graphics on a page is to use thumbnail images. Using thumbnail images is a great way to link to large images and other resources. The notion of a thumbnail describes how these resources are included in your documents. You use a small image to lead to something bigger, such as a large image or another resource. To avoid using an external viewer, you could link the thumbnail image to an HTML document that features the large version of the image.

To make an image clickable, you have to insert the image into a link. You can do this in the FrontPage Editor by selecting the image, then opening the Image Properties dialog box. Afterward, enter the link in the Default Hyperlink Location field of the General tab. At any time, you can specify a new link in the Location field. To browse documents you might want to link to, you can use the Browse button that is beside the Location field. This button opens the Edit Hyperlink dialog box.

EDITING TECHNIQUE

Placing Images in Your Documents

The way you place objects on the page is as important as the colors and sizes you choose for your images, especially when you are aligning text and images. All images in HTML are placed on the page using a specific alignment. By default, FrontPage 98 aligns the bottom of the image with the bottom of any text element that might be associated with the image.

In the Appearance tab of the Image Properties dialog box, you can specify a more precise alignment for your images. Figure 7.9 shows the Image Properties dialog box with the Alignment drop-down list active. As you can see, you can choose from nine alignments.

Figure 7.10 illustrates a few examples of how you can take advantage of alignment in your Web

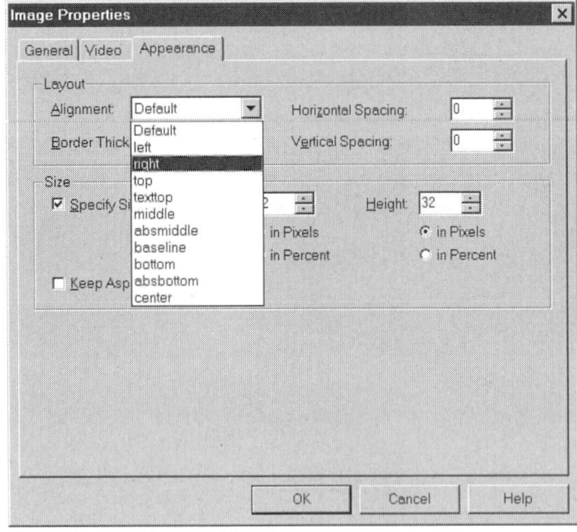

FIGURE 7.9.
Specifying the alignment of images.

page.

These values align text and images in ways contrary to what you might think when you see the

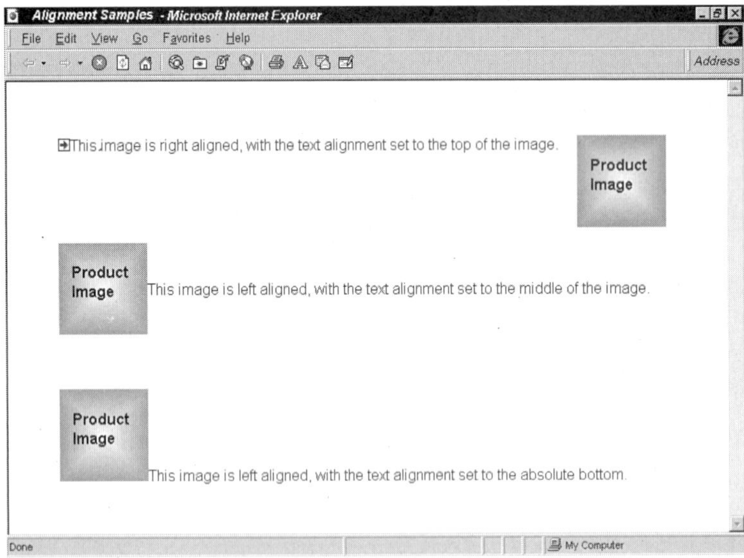

FIGURE 7.10.
Various alignments of text and images.

values. For example, the `MIDDLE` value does not align the middle of the image with the middle of the text. The `MIDDLE` value aligns the middle of the image with the bottom of the text, which produces a slightly off-center effect. The `TOP` value does not precisely align the top of the image with the tallest elements in the associated text. The `TOP` value generally aligns the text and the image along an imaginary line slightly above the text. Similarly, the `BOTTOM` value does not align the bottom of the image with the lowest element in the text. The BOTTOM value generally aligns the image and text along the baseline of the text. Text elements such as an *h* are aligned along the baseline, and text elements such as a *g* extend below the baseline.

One reason the BOTTOM value is the default alignment is that text does not wrap around images. This means that if you align a long line of text with the top of the image, part of your text is aligned with the top of the image and the remainder of the text is displayed below the image. Consequently, you should only use the TOP and MIDDLE alignment values to align a single short line of text with an image.

Many of the remaining alignment values originally were introduced by Netscape to correct the shortcomings of the standard HTML alignments. These alignment values behave exactly as their names imply they should. The value of TEXTTOP aligns the top of the image with the top of the tallest element in the line of text associated with the image. The value of ABSMIDDLE aligns the center of the image with the center of the line of text associated with the image. The value of ABSBOTTOM aligns the bottom of the image with the bottom of the line of text associated with the image. The value of BASELINE aligns the base of the image with the baseline of the text associated with the image, which is exactly how the value of BOTTOM handles text and image alignment.

HTML 3.2 and HTML 4.0 enable you to use two additional alignment values, which can be used to align an image and a paragraph of associated text into columns. The LEFT value puts the image in the left margin and wraps the text around the right side of the image. The RIGHT value puts the image in the right margin and wraps the text around the left side of the image.

By aligning text and images into columns using these alignments, you can create documents with rich layout and styles that merge the image into the text of the document in ways more powerful than previously possible. To get the text to wrap around only the left or right side of the image, you make the image the first element in a short paragraph of text.

As you can see in Figure 7.11, the image is in the left column and the paragraph text is in the right column. This was achieved by using LEFT horizontal alignment and TEXTTOP vertical alignment. Keep in mind that any subsequent text is aligned with the image until the left margin is clear.

Images and text are aligned with minimal spacing. This spacing sometimes makes the text difficult to read. One way to increase the spacing and make the image more useful is to include the image in a hypertext reference, as shown in Figure 7.12. The image shown has a border around it that clearly separates it from the associated text, and it is also clickable.

As Figure 7.12 shows, you can get the text to wrap around two or three sides of the image using alignment values of LEFT or RIGHT. To do this, you insert a line of text before the image tag. Your browser should display complete lines of text before inserting the image. However, if you follow this approach, you want to preview the document using a standard (13-inch) screen size on a Macintosh system or a standard (640×480) video mode on a DOS/Windows system.

Another useful HTML feature you can use when aligning images and text is the line break.

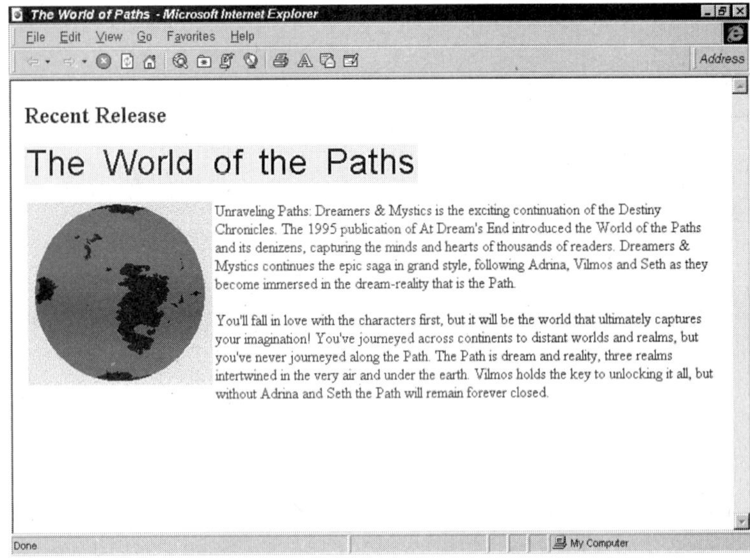

FIGURE 7.11.
Aligning text and images into columns.

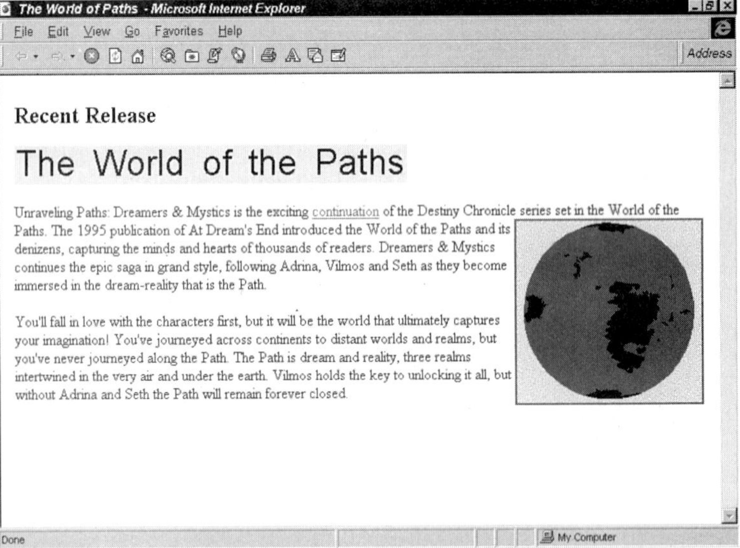

FIGURE 7.12.
Merging the image into the text.

Using the CLEAR attribute of line breaks, you can insert a clean break into the column of text associated with the image. The text before the line break is aligned with the image in a column. The text after the line break is inserted when the margin is clear. If the image is aligned with the left margin, you should select a value of Clear Left in the Line Break Properties dialog box. If the image is aligned with the right margin, you should select a value of Clear Right in the Line Break Properties dialog box.

By default, FrontPage 98 inserts HTML markup that tells your browser the width and height of the image. This is useful for advanced browsers that load the text of a document first and leave an appropriately sized space where the image is located when the document finishes loading. These attributes are also useful for precisely sizing your images to fit the needs of the document.

Sizing Images to Fit Your Needs

The ability to shrink or enlarge images on the fly is extremely useful. You can create a menu of images that are consistently sized without creating new files to contain the resized images. You can then reuse the same images later in the document at their original sizes or sized to suit your needs without loading new image files. This is convenient for you and reduces the download time of your document.

Using the Appearance tab of the Image Properties dialog box, you can adjust the width and height of an image. The first step is to select the Specify Size check box. Next, enter a width and height for the image in pixels or as a percentage of the browser's window. When you are finished, click the OK button and FrontPage 98 updates and resizes the image.

For example, if the original size of the image is 200×190, you can shrink the image by defining a new width and height as shown in Figure 7.13.

FIGURE 7.13.
Resizing images.

Designing Highlights with Images

Other reasons for adding images are to highlight your page and showcase your ideas. Most pages on the Web use images to introduce the page. These images range from simple text on a colorful background to eye-popping 3D images. Both types of images are fine when used for the right reasons. The image you use to introduce your documents should fit in with your publishing style, the subject matter you discuss in the document, and the content of related documents. When starting out, simple is usually best.

Although your style of publishing will be different from that of other Web publishers, you should generally follow a unified design within pages of the same publication. One of the key areas you want to focus on is the color scheme for images used in your documents, which is an area of Web publishing that is all too often overlooked. As you look at the colors you plan to use in your images, key in on the colors used in backgrounds and in text. These are the colors you want to limit.

You could follow a similar color scheme for all the images at your site. In this way, your pages have a familiar look to readers. You could also follow a color scheme for pages associated with a certain publication or key areas at your site. In this way, each publication at your site has a familiar look to readers, and they have a visual cue when they enter a new area. The key concept here is to look at the colors you plan to use in a particular document's images and ask yourself if they work well together and if the colors help the reader. Here is an example of colors that don't work well together: a title page that features a logo with a green background and blue text, header titles with a white background and red text, and other images on the page with gray backgrounds and yellow text.

You might also want to use consistent sizing of key images from page to page. This concept also helps to give your pages a familiar feel and look. For example, you could make the graphical titles for your pages 150×350 pixels and the graphical subtitles for your pages 75×350 pixels. In this way, your titles and subtitles are positioned in the same location on the screen. Figure 7.14 shows how the concepts of introducing your document with an image, using a color scheme, and using consistent sizing could be used in your Web documents.

Another way to design highlights for the same document is to use the images as a graphical menu. Figure 7.15 shows the graphical menu for the redesigned document. This technique provides quick access to the key areas at your Web site.

If you use graphical menus in your publications, provide a text-based way for readers to access the menu. You might be surprised to find that text-based alternatives to graphical menus help all the readers who visit your site, especially those who are impatient and don't want to wait for your images to load. An interesting outcome of placing an image inside a hypertext reference is that whenever the associated alternate text is displayed, it is clickable anchor text. This provides readers using text-only browsers with a way to access other pages at your site. It also helps readers with graphics-capable browsers who might have switched off automatic image loading, as well as those readers with browsers that display alternative text while the image is downloading.

FIGURE 7.14.
Introducing your documents with images.

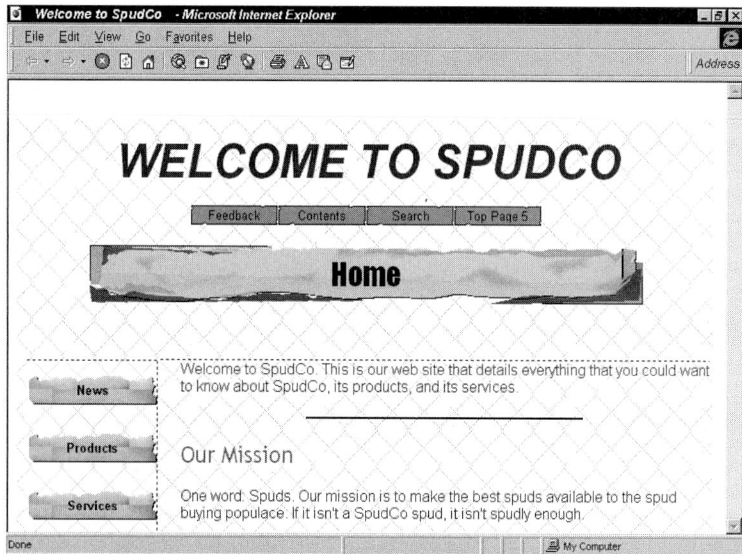

FIGURE 7.15.
Designing a graphical menu.

Figure 7.16 shows how the alternate text used in the previous example is displayed in a browser. As you can see, the alternate text forms a simple menu that readers can use to access key areas at the site. Without the alternate text, the reader using this browser is lost.

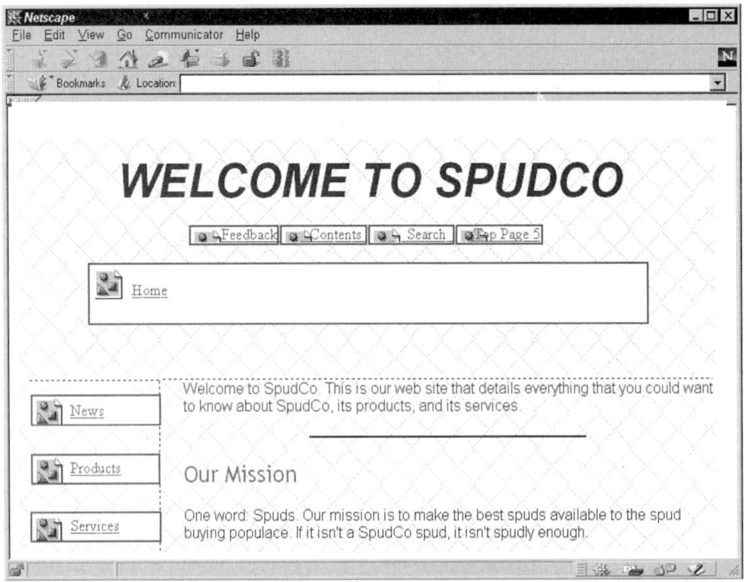

FIGURE 7.16.
Providing alternate text for your graphical menus.

Graphical menus aren't the only way you can provide readers with navigation mechanisms. Many Web publishers use a standard set of small icons to provide readers with access to pages at their sites. The most common navigation icons are variations of the left, right, up, and down arrows. The left arrow is generally used to provide quick access to the previous page. The right arrow provides quick access to the next page. The up arrow provides quick access to the home or top-level page. The down arrow provides quick access to the next level page.

Additional Enhancements for Images

FrontPage 98 supports additional enhancements for images, which enable you to specify the following factors:

- The width of the border surrounding an image that is linked to a resource
- The vertical space around the image
- The horizontal space around the image
- An alternate low-resolution image to load first

These attributes are fully supported by Netscape and Internet Explorer. You can set values for these attributes using the Image Properties dialog box.

Usually, browsers display a border around all images that are linked to another Web resource. Both Web users and publishers alike consider this border to be distracting in most instances. Because of this, FrontPage 98 sets the width of borders around images to zero, which tells the browser not to display a border at all if possible. In recent months, this has become the favorite setting for most Web publishers.

However, sometimes you want the image to have a distinct border. In the Layout area of the Image Properties dialog box is the Border field. You can use this field to set the pixel size of the border to be drawn around an image.

Also in the Appearance tab of the Image Properties dialog box are the Horizontal spacing textbox and the Vertical spacing textbox. You can use the Horizontal spacing textbox to increase the pixel size of the horizontal margins surrounding the image. Similarly, you can use the Vertical spacing textbox to increase the pixel size of the vertical margins surrounding the image. Spacing is used to put whitespace between multiple images or text. If you use these spacing techniques, you generally do not want to use a border around the image.

Finally, specifying a low-resolution image is a time-saver that reduces the wait time and makes it possible for other elements on the page to be displayed before a high-resolution image is displayed. On the first pass through the document, Netscape-capable browsers load the images specified as low-res sources. When all other images in the document are loaded, the image specified in the Image Source field is loaded. Browsers that do not support low-res sources load the image specified by the Image Source field.

In the Image Properties dialog box, click the General tab. You find low-res field in the Alternate Representations area. You can use this field to specify the name of a low-resolution image. The Browse button opens the Insert Image dialog box, which enables you to specify the name of any image imported to the current web or the absolute path to an external image.

TIP

Try to keep your low-resolution image small in terms of byte size. A 2K low-resolution image loads many times quicker than your 25K high-resolution image. Netscape- and Internet Explorer-enhanced browsers fade in the high-resolution image over the low-resolution image. The best low-resolution images act as placeholders and are the same size as the high-resolution image. In this way, the text on the page doesn't shift when the high-resolution image is displayed.

Image Formats

Dozens of image formats are in use. Each computer platform includes its own popular format and usually several other popular formats. Drawing and design applications have their own proprietary formats. Some formats have become de facto standards because of their tremendous popularity. Other formats are so specialized that only a small group of users benefit from them. Maneuvering through this maze of formats can be a nightmare if you create images for specific groups of users. Just when you think you have the right formats available for the right group of users, another group of users comes along. Fortunately, only two image formats are in wide use on the Web: GIF and JPEG.

Using GIF

The graphics interchange format developed by CompuServe Information Service is the most widely supported and used image format in the world. All graphics-capable browsers support GIF, as do most drawing, design, and image processing programs. As you might expect, GIF is the favorite format for Web publishers.

Three variations of the GIF format are in use. The original specification, GIF87a, has been around since 1987. Because of its many advantages over other formats, GIF87a quickly became a de facto standard. Creators of drawing programs quickly discovered how easy it is to write a program that decodes and displays GIF images. GIF images are compressed to 20 to 25 percent of their original size with no loss in image quality, using a compression algorithm called LZW. Smaller images require less disk space to store, use less network bandwidth, and download faster. Additionally, because the LZW algorithm can be quickly decoded, images display almost immediately after downloading.

The next update to the format was the GIF89a specification. GIF89a added some useful features, including transparent GIFs. Using transparent GIFs, you can create images that seem to float on the page because they have a transparent background. (See the section on transparent GIFs, "GIFs with Transparent Backgrounds," later in this chapter for more information.)

All browsers support both the GIF87a and GIF89a formats, which is great news for Web publishers. The only drawback is that you can only use 256 colors in a single image. Although this limitation is restricting, it is actually good in most instances. Most images use only a few colors. This is especially true for icons, bullets, or other small features used to accent the page. Most computer systems can display only 256 colors. If you use only 256 colors, the computer does not have to dither the image to create the illusion of additional colors. An image with fewer colors that does not have to be dithered is displayed faster, uses less disk space, and also downloads more quickly. GIF is ideal for images with flat color, such as text. GIF is less ideally suited to photographs and similar color-rich images.

Recently, there has been a lot of controversy over the LZW compression used by GIF images. This compression technology is patented to the Unisys Corporation. In January 1995, Unisys announced that developers using the GIF format in their applications might have to pay a licensing fee. A licensing fee for GIF images could apply to millions of software applications, including your favorite browser. As you might imagine, software developers around the world were in an uproar for months following the announcement. Some developers were so outraged that they removed support for GIF images from their applications. Other developers went in search of alternatives.

One alternative software developers looked to is GIF24. GIF24 has wide support from the Internet user community as well as from CompuServe Information Service. Unlike the original GIF specifications that support only 256 colors, GIF24 supports true 24-bit color, which enables you to use more than 16 million colors. One drawback to using 24-bit color is that most computers currently support only 256 colors. Before a 24-bit image can be displayed on an 8-bit screen, it must be dithered, which requires processing time and might also distort the image.

GIF24 uses a compression technique called PNG, and because there should never be a licensing fee associated with PNG, software developers are gladly turning to GIF24. In the coming months, you should start to see drawing, design, and image processing programs that support GIF24.

EDITING TECHNIQUE

After you insert a JPEG image into a document, you can convert it to GIF format. To do this, select the image you want to convert and then open the Image Properties dialog box. In the Type area of the General tab is a field labeled GIF. When you check this field and click the OK button, FrontPage 98 automatically converts the image from JPEG to GIF. Keep in mind that the number of colors in the image might be reduced and that the byte size of the image file might become larger.

Using JPEG

JPEG is a standard for still image compression that was developed by the Joint Photographic Expert Group. The goal of the JPEG members was to create a standard for storage and transmission of photograph-quality images. JPEG supports true 24-bit color.

True 24-bit color means that each pixel displayed on the screen has 24 bits of information associated with it. There are over 300,000 pixels on an average-size screen, so you can imagine how quickly truecolor images can eat up your hard disk space. Fortunately, JPEG is a compression standard that uses powerful compression algorithms to dramatically reduce the disk space requirements for the image. Some images can be reduced to a twentieth of their original size.

Compressing an image into such a small size has its drawbacks. The first drawback is that JPEG compression is *lossy*, meaning that some information in the image is lost in the compression. The JPEG format was created primarily for photographs, so it is ideally suited for natural scenery where compression strips out information that the eye does not need. Depending on how the image is compressed, this loss of information might or might not be perceivable. Another drawback to compressing the image into a small space is that it generally takes longer to decode the image for viewing. However, the actual time period for the decoding depends on the user's system and the amount of compression.

As you consider using JPEG compression for your images, you should consider carefully the types of images that you will compress. Although JPEG enables you to use brilliant colors and provides quality support for complex images and digitized photographs, JPEG was not designed to be used for simple images with few colors. JPEG compression might distort simple images, especially if the image has few colors or large areas of the same color. Also, JPEG compression is not as effective as GIF in reducing the size of simple images. A simple image compressed with JPEG compression is much larger than the same image compressed using GIF.

Because of the drawbacks to JPEG compression, JPEG was not widely supported until recently. One of the issues driving the growth of JPEG use is the controversy surrounding the GIF compression algorithm LZW. The controversy caused many software developers to take another look at JPEG. Most popular browsers, including NCSA Mosaic, Internet Explorer, and Netscape Navigator, let you use inline JPEG images.

TIP

A great place to learn more about JPEG is the JPEG FAQ. You can find the JPEG FAQ on the Web at the following location:

```
http://www.cis.ohio-state.edu/hypertext/faq/usenet/jpeg-faq/top.html
```

After you insert a GIF image into a document, you can convert it to JPEG format. To do this, select the image you want to convert and then open the Image Properties dialog box. In the Type area of the General tab is a field labeled JPEG. When you check this field, an additional field labeled Quality displays. After you select a setting for quality, click the OK button.

Quality settings are often used with compression as a reality check describing the trade-off you want to make between the resulting file size and the image quality. The range for quality settings in FrontPage 98 is from 1 to 99. The higher the quality setting, the larger the resulting file is and the better the image quality. The default quality setting is 75.

Quality settings can be confusing because a quality setting of 75 does not mean that the resulting file will have 75 percent of the information. Compression ratios—which FrontPage 98 sets automatically—describe how much information to squeeze out of the file. The quality setting is used to keep the ratio of compression realistic when compared to your need for a usable image. Generally, your goal should be to select the lowest quality setting that meets your needs.

Creating Your Own Images

You can create images using drawing, design, and image processing programs. Although commercial image creation tools, such as Photoshop, are powerful and fully featured, shareware drawing tools, such as Paint Shop Pro, provide general-purpose image creation solutions. FrontPage 98 includes a terrific image editor called Image Composer.

Using image tools, you can create a simple graphical title or logo in a few minutes. You can use image tools to alter existing images to meet your publishing needs and to convert these images from other formats to the GIF or JPEG formats for use as inline images. You can easily create and modify images, but you can dramatically improve the quality and friendliness of your images through

- Proper use of color maps
- Interlacing GIFs when necessary
- Using GIFs with transparent backgrounds when necessary

Using Color Maps

Color maps are one of the biggest problem areas in image design. All images have color palettes associated with them that define a set of colors for the image. Each color displayed on the screen is loaded into a color map that tracks colors displayed on the screen at any one time. A computer with an 8-bit display uses a color map that can hold 256 color values. A computer with a 24-bit display uses a color map that can hold 16.7 million color values.

Some computer systems reserve a subset of values in the color map for the standard display. Windows systems reserve 20 values in the color map to display standard colors. In addition to reserved colors, any colors currently displayed on the screen are allocated in the color map. This means if your browser display takes up only part of the screen and other applications are running, the combined set of colors displayed on the screen by all the applications running is allocated in the color map.

Although you can create 24-bit images with 16.7 million colors, most computers display only 8-bit images with 256 colors. This means when you create an image that uses 16 million colors, most computers displaying the image have to dither the image to create the illusion that there are extra colors in the image when in fact only 256 colors are displayed.

The distortion of the image caused by the dithering is often the least of your problems. Only 256 colors can be displayed at once on an 8-bit color display. This means there is a conflict in the color map if the first image uses all 256 colors and the next image displayed on the screen at the same time uses additional colors. These additional colors are mapped to the closest color value in the current color map, which can produce strange results. Your brilliant red is mapped to orange, or even green, if that is the closest color value available in the current color map.

Some browsers try to solve the color mapping problem by limiting the number of colors any single image can use. This enables you to display more inline images on the screen at once. However, the cost of this trade-off is high. If your images use 256 colors and the browser restricts each image to a maximum of 50 colors, the images have to be dithered to 50 colors each. The result is often a large reduction in the quality of your image.

The best way to ensure that your documents have no color map problem is to use a common color map for all images in a particular document. If you are creating original images, most drawing programs let you select a palette of 256 colors to work with. You can add colors or change color definitions in the palette by removing or altering existing color definitions in the palette. After you are done working with the palette, you should save it, if possible, for future reference and use with your images.

Using a single color palette is easy if you are creating original images, but it is not easy if you are incorporating existing images into your documents. One way to overcome this problem is to use an image processing toolkit that can merge the color palettes used in multiple images to a common color palette.

Unfortunately, mapping multiple images to a single color palette is useful only when the images either contain few colors or already use a similar set of colors. This is because the image processing tool merging the color palettes generally merges the colors using a best-guess algorithm that tries to analyze how multiple colors that are close in value can best be merged into a single color value. Sometimes the tool guesses right and there is no distortion of your images. Other times, the tool guesses wrong and your image is distorted. Ultimately, if your images contain few colors in the first place or use similar maps, there is little reason to merge the color maps. For simple images like these, you might want to preview your document using multiple browsers and worry about a conflict in the color map only when you find one.

Another way to fix the color mapping problem is to reorganize your document so that images with conflicting color maps cannot be displayed on the screen simultaneously. This solution to a color mapping problem is simple and fast.

Finally, a great way to avoid potential color map problems is to limit your use of colors in the images you create. For example, if you use a particular shade of red in one image, use the same shade of red in other images. In a palette of 16.7 million colors, there are probably 50 shades of red that are so close in hue that it is difficult to tell them apart. You can also track the values associated with colors in a table. When you are designing additional images for a particular document and want to use consistent colors, having color values at hand can be invaluable. You will learn more about color palettes in Chapter 19, "Optimizing Your Images and Color Palettes."

Interlacing GIFs

An advanced feature you can incorporate into your GIF images is *interlacing.* Interlaced GIFs are displayed in four stages. As if you were zooming in on something from far away, during each stage, the image gets progressively more detailed until the image is finished loading. This is accomplished by separating the lines of pixels in the image into four groups of lines that are interlaced and displayed in stages. Your television and possibly your monitor display images in this manner.

Many experienced Web publishers do not understand the value of interlacing images. Interlaced images are time-savers to readers and are especially useful when you use large images in your documents. As the image loads in stages, readers can decide when they have seen enough of the image. Based on what they've seen, they might continue reading the document, they might make another selection, or they might wait to see the image finish loading. Readers value their time, and if you value their time as well, your documents will be friendly and well-perceived.

Older versions of browsers might not display GIFs in stages. Whether the image is a noninterlaced GIF or an interlaced GIF, these browsers wait until the entire image is downloaded and then display the GIF. Although not all browsers display interlaced GIFs in stages, all browsers can display interlaced GIFs.

Creating an interlaced GIF in FrontPage 98 is as easy as selecting Interlaced from the Type area of the Image Properties dialog box. Be sure to save the updated image when you save your page.

GIFs with Transparent Backgrounds

Using a GIF with a transparent background, you can create an image that appears to float on the page. This is extremely useful when you want to create a fancy title, logo, icon, or image that does not use a solid colored or rectangular background. Creating a GIF with a transparent background is easy. The first step is to assign a color to the image's transparency index.

The color value assigned to the transparency index indicates which color from the image's color map should be transparent. When a browser displays an image with a transparent background, it changes all occurrences of the color value in the transparency index to the color value for the background of the document. The best images to convert to GIF89a format are those with a single background color. This is important because you can only assign one color value to the transparency index, and if your image has several background colors, only one color will be transparent. Figure 7.17 shows the difference between an image with a normal background and one with a transparent background.

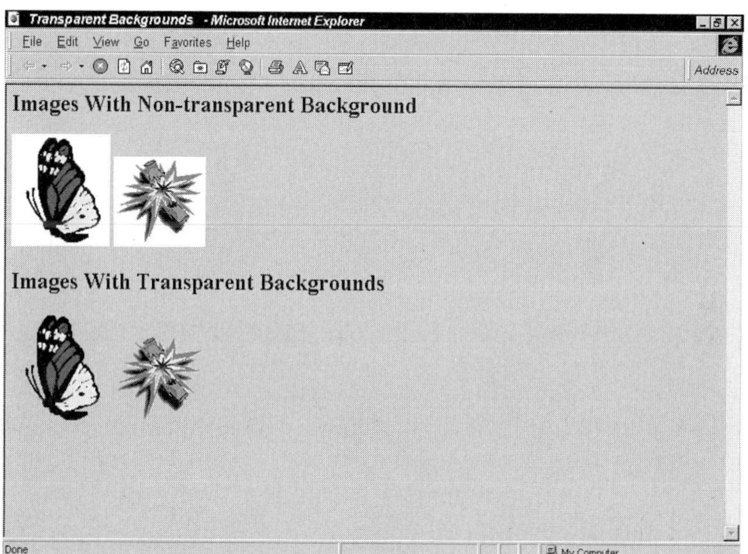

FIGURE 7.17.
Images with transparent backgrounds appear to float on the page.

You should also make sure that your background color appears nowhere else in the image. Any part of your image that uses the color value specified in the transparency index is displayed in the background color for the page. To avoid this problem, you should be sure that your images have a unique background color. When you are creating new images, this is easy. You simply select a color you do not plan to use in the image.

CAUTION

Although some Web publishers tell you to select an outrageous color for your background, such as hot pink, you should never use a color that you do not want the world to see if for some reason your image is not displayed with a transparent background. Not all browsers can display your image with a transparent background, and if you use an outrageous color, someone somewhere will see your image with that hot pink background. Instead of using an outrageous color, you should use a neutral color such as the gray background used by most browsers. The RGB color value for the background color used by most browsers is 190, 190, 190. Using this color value ensures that your images do not look ridiculous if the transparent background is not displayed and also makes your GIFs appear to have transparent backgrounds on browsers that do not support transparent GIFs.

You can easily create an image with a transparent background in the FrontPage Editor. However, the image must be inserted into the current document. To make a color in the image transparent, use the following steps:

1. Select the image that you want to have a transparent background.
2. Click the Make Transparent button on the Image toolbar.
3. Move the tip of the pointer to the color in the image that you want to make transparent, and then click the left mouse button.
4. When you view the properties of the image, the Transparent field is checked.

An image can have only one transparent color. You can change the transparent color at any time by repeating the steps in the preceding list and simply selecting a new color. If you select a new transparent color, the previous transparent color is returned to its original color. If you try to set a transparent background on an image that is not in GIF format, the FrontPage Editor prompts you to convert the image to GIF format. Keep in mind that the number of colors in the image might be reduced and that the byte size of the image file might become larger.

NOTE

If you make a mistake when selecting a transparent color and decide you don't want any color to be transparent, you can return the transparent color to its original state simply by selecting it again or by opening the Image Properties dialog box and deselecting the Transparent field.

Summary

Everywhere you look on the Web, you find Web publications that use images. You can use images to add highlights, navigation mechanisms, logos, page titles, illustrations, and maps to the hot features at your site. Although there are many image formats, the primary image formats in use on the Web are JPEG and GIF.

PART

IN THIS PART

- Designing Tables with FrontPage 98 *139*
- Creating Frames *154*
- Editing and Enhancing Your Frames *169*
- Designing Pages with Style Sheets *185*
- Advanced Page Layout with Style Sheets *203*
- Working with Active Elements: Banners, Hit Counters, and More *215*

Web Page Layout and Design with FrontPage 98

CHAPTER

Designing Tables with FrontPage 98

by William Robert Stanek

IN THIS CHAPTER

- Table Design *140*
- Creating a Table Using the FrontPage Editor *141*
- Inserting Rows or Columns *144*
- Inserting a Table Caption *144*
- Editing, Deleting, and Merging Table Elements *145*
- Resetting Table Properties *147*
- Advanced Property Settings for Cells *148*
- Advanced Property Settings for Groups of Cells *149*
- Adding Color to Your Table *150*
- Adding Background Images to Your Table *151*

Tables are omnipresent in Web sites for one specific reason—they are one of the best ways for you to organize information effectively. No doubt you have seen tables at work on your favorite Web pages, even if you weren't aware that they were there. Tables let you take information—text or even images—and control its appearance to the visitor. Tables are an incredibly powerful tool for controlling layout, giving you more control over your presentation. This chapter shows you how to create tables and use tables effectively in your pages.

Table Design

Tables are one of the most valued features in the HTML specification. In general, a table has a caption and one or more rows of data organized into columns. The columns of data contain individual cells. Each individual cell is either a header or a data set. Although a table can have several levels of headings, all headings serve to identify the data sets contained in the body of the table. Some tables also have footers. Footers are used to make annotations within the table. Thus, tables have three basic parts: header, body, and footer.

Web publishers have no direct control over the size of the window used to display a table, which means that table data defined in absolute terms, such as pixels or characters, could easily get obscured or clipped. To avoid this problem, authors can define column widths in relative terms as well as absolute terms.

By defining a table in relative terms, you can specify a size that is a percentage of the current window size. The browser displaying the table sizes the table accordingly, using the currently defined font. The default size for a table is the current window size.

Tables can be used to contain more than just raw text. You can use tables in other ways as well. You can do any of the following:

- Add background images to a table
- Add lists to a table
- Build forms within a table
- Create tables within a table

Traditionally, tables are used to organize data sets like those shown in Figure 8.1. Although the table shown in the figure is very useful, tables can be powerful additions to your pages if you can think beyond the bounds of tradition.

As you work with tables, keep in mind that FrontPage 98 supports the table model set forth in the HTML 4.0 specification. Although this table model is rich in features, most older browsers cannot use the advanced extensions. Specifically, if you use table colors, background images, and custom border colors, older browsers usually display your table without these features. To point out possible compatibility problems, I will usually refer to these features as *advanced.*

To test advanced tables that you develop in FrontPage 98, I recommend that you access your Web page using the most current version of Internet Explorer or Netscape Navigator. This way, you can see how your page will look in the best of conditions. Afterward, you should test the table in an older browser, such as Internet Explorer 2.0 or Navigator 2.0. That way, you can see how your page will look in less than optimal conditions.

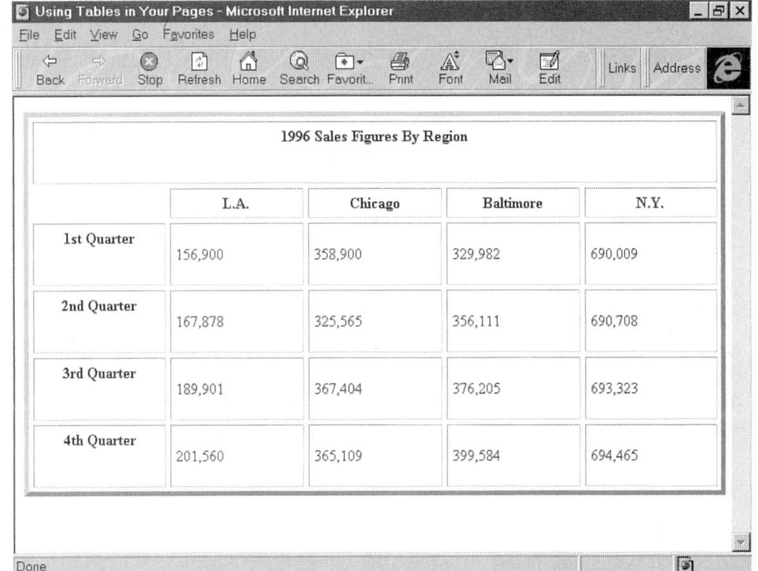

1996 Sales Figures By Region				
	L.A.	Chicago	Baltimore	N.Y.
1st Quarter	156,900	358,900	329,982	690,009
2nd Quarter	167,878	325,565	356,111	690,708
3rd Quarter	189,901	367,404	376,205	693,323
4th Quarter	201,560	365,109	399,584	694,465

FIGURE 8.1.
Tables can be used to organize textual information into a readable format.

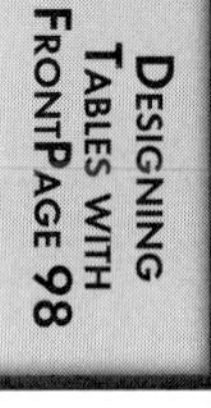

Creating a Table Using the FrontPage Editor

Whenever you work with tables, you should have the Table toolbar active, so be sure to choose View|Table Toolbar. After the toolbar is active, you can easily create and edit your tables using the buttons provided. One of the most useful features of FrontPage 98 is the Draw Table tool (the pencil icon on the Table toolbar). Using this tool, you can draw a table complete with multiple rows and columns by sketching its outline.

Although the table drawing tool is useful, FrontPage 98 provides another way for you to create tables: by choosing Table|Insert Table. When you use this option, you define the table and all its elements using a dialog box and let FrontPage 98 draw the table for you.

Drawing Your Own Table

When you want to create a table freehand, the table drawing tool comes in handy. To start your table, first make sure that the Table toolbar is enabled from the View menu (View|Table Toolbar) and click the Draw Table button. After you move the pointer to the place where you want the upper-left corner of the table to start, click and hold the mouse button and then size the table by dragging the pointer. When you release the button, FrontPage 98 creates the table using the default settings.

The following are some quick tips for working with the drawing tool:

Adding Rows	Move the pointer to the place where you want to add the row. Click and hold the mouse button; then drag the pointer down until the dashed drawing line extends to the full height of the table.
Adding Columns	Move the pointer to the place where you want to add the column. Click and hold the mouse button; then drag the pointer left or right until the dashed drawing line extends to the full width of the table.
Changing Table Height	Move the pointer over the lower border. Click and hold the mouse button; then drag the pointer up or down.
Changing Table Width	Move the pointer over the right border. Click and hold the mouse button; then drag the pointer left or right.
Changing Cell Height	Move the pointer over the cell's upper or lower border. Click and hold the mouse button; then drag the pointer up or down.
Changing Cell Width	Move the pointer over the left or right border. Click and hold the mouse button; then drag the pointer left or right.

Letting FrontPage 98 Help You Create the Table

When you are fairly certain of the size of your table and the numbers of rows and columns for the table, you might want to let FrontPage 98 draw the table for you. To do so, access the Insert Table dialog box by choosing Table|Insert Table. Then you can use the Insert Table dialog box to define the basic layout of your table (see Figure 8.2). In the Size panel, you specify the number of rows and columns for the table, and FrontPage 98 determines the number of cells needed to fill the table.

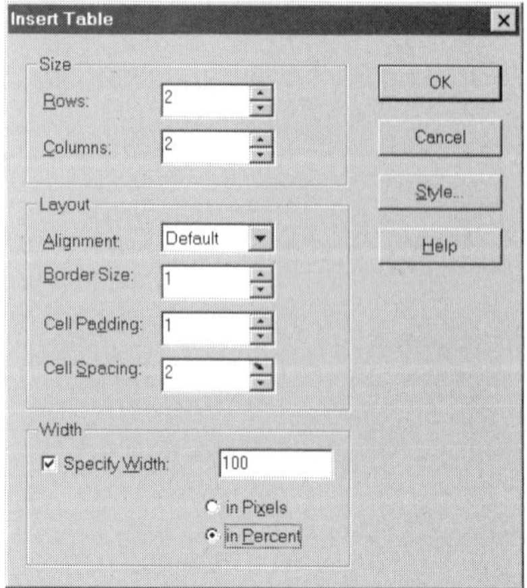

FIGURE 8.2.
The Insert Table dialog box lets you determine your table's attributes.

Next, take a look at the Layout panel of the dialog box. Text in your documents can flow around tables. By default, tables are aligned with the left margin, and text is displayed on the right side of the table. You can also align tables with the right margin, which causes text to be displayed on the left side of the table. Although you sometimes want text to appear on one side of the table, you can place the table in the center of the page, in which case no text flows around the table. To set the alignment of the table, use the Alignment drop box.

Most tables have borders. To set the pixel width of the border, use the Border Size text box (you can also use the spin wheels beside the text box to determine a value). Generally, you should use a value between 1 and 5. When you use a value of 1, the border is very thin and serves as a slight accent to the table. When you use a value of 5, the border is a strong feature that dominates the table.

If you don't want the table to have a border, use a value of 0 to remove the border completely. When you use tables to align elements on your page, you might want to remove the table border.

In terms of the readability of your table, *cell padding* and *cell spacing* are the most important attributes you define for the table. Cell padding specifies the spacing within data cells. Cell spacing specifies the spacing between data cells. You specify padding and spacing in pixels as well.

In the Width panel of the Insert Table dialog box, you specify the relative or absolute width of a table. The default width is the current window size. You can specify the width in pixels (absolute width) or as a percentage of the current window size (relative width). To ensure that the table will be resized to fit the dimensions of the screen, you should use a relative width.

Despite all the advances in computer technology, the most commonly used screen size is 640×480 (800×600 if you are lucky) on Windows systems and a close approximation on Mac systems (aproximately 512×512 on some systems). Many machines are capable of higher, yet most users are not knowledgeable about how to change their resolution. On high-end workstations, a common screen size is 1280×1024. A table with a relative width of 50 percent has a width of about 240 pixels at a screen size of 640×480 and a width of about 512 pixels at a screen size of 1280×1024. Here, the table has consistent but relative proportions, and whitespace appears around the table, which usually works best with tables that use only text.

When you combine text and graphics, or if you need cells of a specific size, you might want to define the table width in pixels. To ensure that your table is easy to read at all screen sizes, you should use a width of no more than 480 pixels and size all elements of the table accordingly. If you use a pixel size larger than 480, anyone using a screen size that isn't as wide will have to use a scrollbar to view parts of your table, which can make a large table unwieldy. Thus, as you create your tables, you should consider the frustration of the user who has to scroll both horizontally and vertically to access bits and pieces of the table data.

Inserting Rows or Columns

You can always add rows or columns to a table after you've created it, and the easiest way to do so is to model the new row or column after an existing row or column. Start by clicking a cell and dragging the pointer until the row or column is highlighted. Next, click the Insert Row or Insert Column button on the Table toolbar. FrontPage 98 then extends the table and inserts an identically sized row or column.

When you want to add more than one row or column, first move the insertion point to the cell in the table where you want to add the new row or column; then choose Table|Insert Rows or Columns. The Insert Rows or Columns dialog box then appears.

By default, the dialog box appears as shown in Figure 8.3. With the Rows radio button selected, you can insert one or more rows either above or below the current insertion point. With the Columns radio button selected, you can insert one or more columns either to the left or right of the current insertion point.

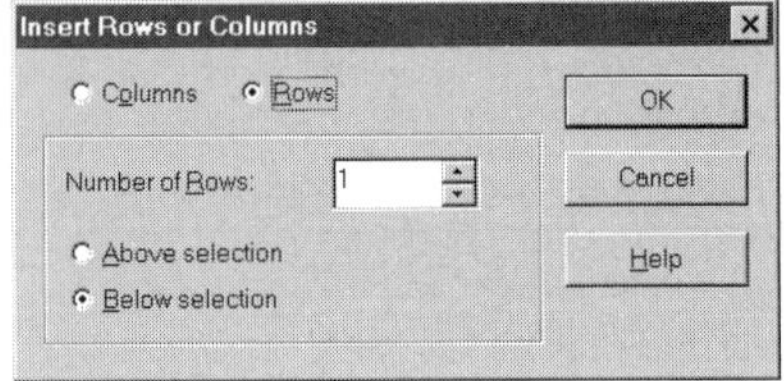

FIGURE 8.3.
Inserting rows.

Inserting a Table Caption

After you specify how you want the basic components of the table to look, you might want to add a *caption* to the table. A caption provides an explanation or description of the data sets contained in a table. To insert a caption, click to select the table and then choose Table|Insert Caption. The FrontPage Editor moves the insertion point above the table so that you can add the caption.

You also can adjust the appearance and location of the caption. To change the default settings for the caption, select the caption by clicking in the area of the caption. You know that the caption is selected because the Editor highlights a portion of the caption. While the caption is selected, you can open the Caption Properties dialog box by choosing Table|Caption Properties. In this dialog box, you can set two basic properties to change the alignment of captions either above or below the table (see Figure 8.4).

Although captions are centered above the table automatically, you can change the alignment of the caption using the Align Left and Align Right buttons on the Format toolbar. To add highlighting to the caption, you can use bold text.

FIGURE 8.4.
Setting caption properties.

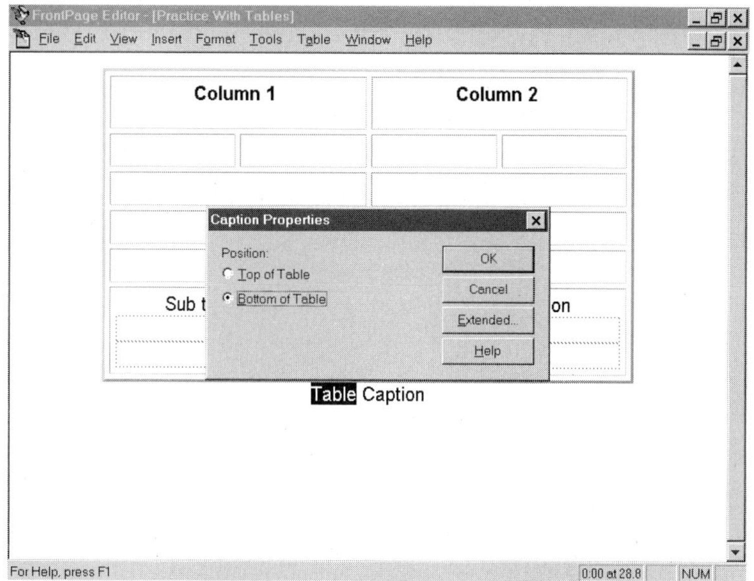

Editing, Deleting, and Merging Table Elements

FrontPage 98 enables you to manipulate all the table elements in whole or in part, but you must first select the element you want to manipulate. To do so, move the insertion point to the cell, row, column, or table you want to manipulate, and then choose the appropriate item from the Table menu. To select an individual data cell, choose Select Cell. To select a row of cells, choose Select Row. To select a column of cells, choose Select Column. To select the entire table, choose Select Table.

If you like using the mouse or keyboard, you can select cells by

- Clicking and dragging the mouse within the table
- Holding Shift and using the arrow keys within the table

Deleting Table Elements

With the table element selected, you can delete it or edit its properties. To delete the selected table element, click the Delete Cell button. You can copy the selected element to the buffer or cut the element out of the table. After the element is on the buffer, you can paste it anywhere in the page, and the FrontPage Editor creates a new table based on that element.

Splitting Table Elements

After you select a cell, row, or column, you can split it into additional cells, rows, or columns. To do so, click the Split Cells button. The Split Cells dialog box then appears, as shown in

Figure 8.5. After you finish splitting the table element by making a selection here, click the OK button. Any data in the table element when it is split generally stays in the original cell in which it was located.

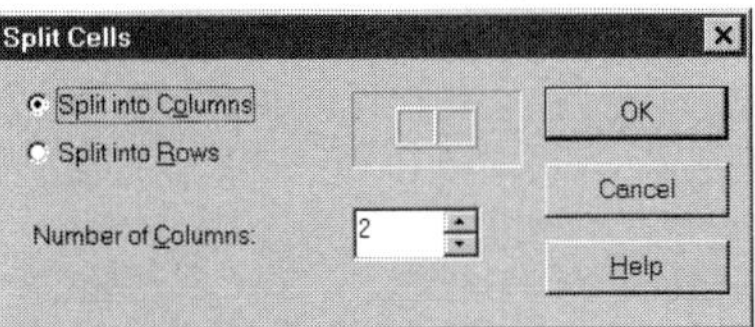

FIGURE 8.5.
Splitting cells into additional columns and rows.

To add rows to the selected area, select the Split into Rows radio button, and select the total number of rows you want in each selected element. For example, if you select one cell and want to add another cell row, enter `2` in the Number of Rows field.

To add columns to the selected area, select the Split into Columns radio button, and select the total number of columns you want in each selected element. For example, if you select one cell and want to add another cell column, enter `2` in the Number of Columns field.

Figure 8.6 shows an example of splitting rows and columns. The first table has two columns and two rows. In the second table, the original first row is split into four columns. You can make this change by selecting the first row and entering `2` in the Number of Columns field in the Split Cells dialog box. In the third table, the original first column is split into two columns. You can make this change by selecting the first column and entering `2` in the Number of Columns field in the Split Cells dialog box.

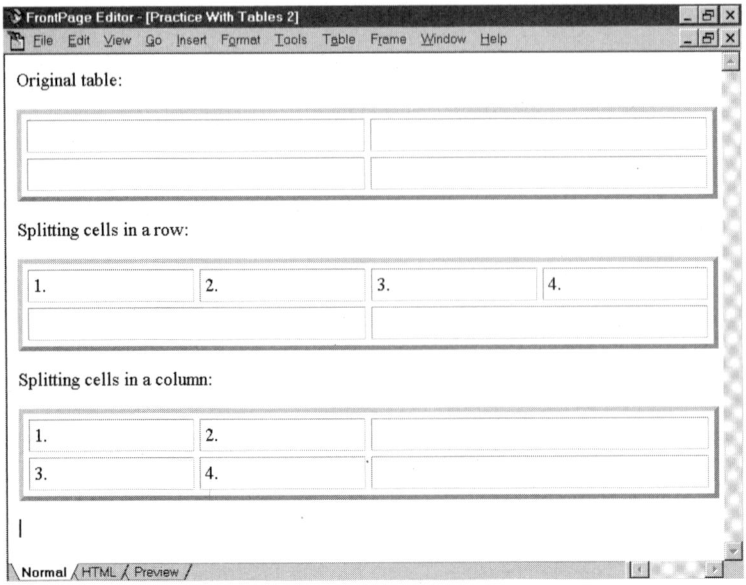

FIGURE 8.6.
An example of splitting cells.

Merging Cells, Rows, and Columns

After you select two or more table elements, you can merge them into a single cell, row, or column. To do so, choose Merge Cells from the Table toolbar. Then the data that was once split between two or more cells, rows, or columns is merged into a single element.

You can also merge cells using the Erase tool on the Table toolbar. Using the Erase tool, you can click and drag the pointer to erase internal cell borders and thus merge cells.

Resetting Table Properties

After you create a table, you can reset most of its default characteristics at any time. To do so, move the insertion point anywhere in the table and choose Table|Table Properties. The Table Properties dialog box then appears, as shown in Figure 8.7.

FIGURE 8.7.
Resetting table properties.

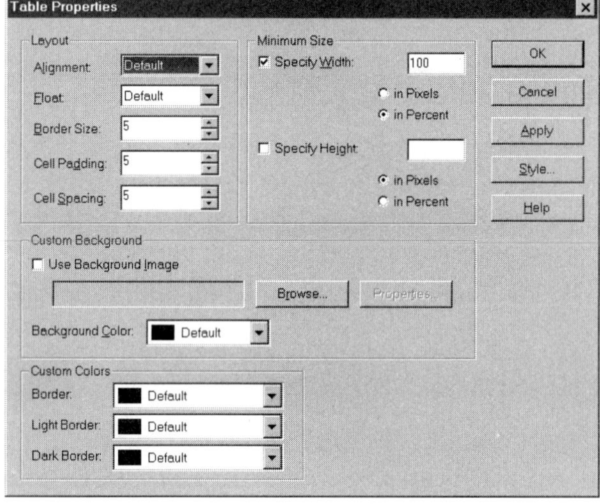

The Table Properties dialog box has many of the same elements as the Insert Table dialog box. However, as you can see from Figure 8.7, you cannot change the number of columns or rows in this dialog box. One reason for this restriction is to protect the data cells in the table from accidental deletion.

To set the alignment of the table, use the Alignment field. To set the pixel width of the border, use the Border Size field. To specify the spacing within data cells, use the Cell Padding field. To specify the spacing between data cells, use the Cell Spacing field. You can also specify a relative or absolute width of a table. The default width is the current window size. You can specify the width in pixels or as a percentage of the current window size.

You can check to see what effect individual layout changes have by using the Apply button. Then, when you're sure that you like the new layout for the table, click the OK button.

Advanced Property Settings for Cells

In general, two types of cells are used in tables: *data cells* and *heading cells*. Data cells contain the numbers, facts, and statements to display in the table. Heading cells contain headings for sections, columns, and rows. When you create a table in the FrontPage Editor, all cells are defined as data cells by default.

Other defaults are assigned to the cells when they are created as well. These settings pertain to the layout, width, and span of each cell. To set new properties for a cell, move the cursor to the cell and then open the Cell Properties dialog box by choosing Table|Cell Properties. This dialog box is shown in Figure 8.8. The great thing about this dialog box is that, as you make changes, you can see how they affect the table by using the Apply button. Because clicking this button does not close the dialog box, you can then make further changes and test them as well.

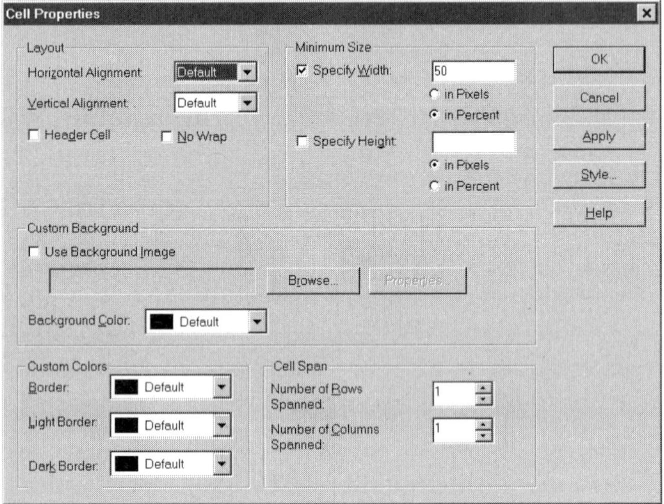

FIGURE 8.8.
Setting cell properties.

In the Layout panel of the Cell Properties dialog box, you can specify the alignment of data within a cell and whether a cell is a heading or data cell. Header cells have different properties than data cells. For example, heading cells are displayed in bold type, and data cells are displayed in normal type. Other differences have to do with the alignment within cells. The default horizontal alignment for heading cells in a table is centered. The default horizontal alignment for data sets in a table is the left margin. The default vertical alignment for both heading cells and data cells is middle.

To change the alignment settings, you use the Horizontal Alignment and Vertical Alignment fields in the Cell Properties dialog box. Three vertical and three horizontal alignment settings are available. The vertical alignments are top, middle, and bottom. The horizontal alignments are left, center, and right.

Usually, column width is determined by the number of characters in the first heading or data set in the column. FrontPage 98 overrides this function by specifying a relative width for each column that depends on the number of columns in the table. For example, in a table with two columns, FrontPage 98 generally assigns the relative width of 50 percent of the table size to each column; in a table with three columns, FrontPage 98 generally assigns the relative width of 33 percent of the table size to each column; and so on.

You can override this default with either a relative or absolute value. Relative values are expressed as a percentage of the table size. Absolute values are expressed in pixels. Using relative widths is usually better than using a width based on pixels. It saves you the trouble of trying to ensure that your table is readable and usable regardless of the screen size. It enables you to manipulate an individual column size to fit the user's needs. It also enables you to remove or add columns without recomputing the pixel width. You can set the width of a cell in the Minimum Size panel of the Cell Properties dialog box.

FrontPage 98 gives you advanced control over the placement of cells within your tables. Usually, cells span only one row and one column, yet by specifying the span of a cell, you can create cells that span several columns or rows. You can set the row span and column span of a selected cell in the Cell Span panel of the Cell Properties dialog box.

Both heading cells and data cells can span multiple columns and rows. You can use heading cells that span multiple columns to create major headings for sections of a table. If a heading spans several columns, and you define subheadings for those columns, you need cells that span multiple rows for any columns with only one level of heading. That way, you can ensure that the headings and cells line up appropriately.

Advanced Property Settings for Groups of Cells

After you define the individual cells that make up a table, you might want to specify general rules for groups of cells within the table. However, the attributes assigned to a particular cell usually apply only to that cell. If your table has 30 cells, you have to define the properties for each cell, and setting properties for 30 cells one at a time is tedious.

To set properties for multiple cells, move the insertion point to the column or row with cells that you want to set with similar properties. Next, choose either Table|Select Column or Table|Select Row, and then choose Table|Cell Properties. When you set cell properties, the properties are applied to all selected cells. After you finish setting cell properties, click the Apply button to confirm your changes and then the OK button to close the dialog box.

Using this technique, you can easily add row and column heading cells to your table. To add a column of heading cells, select the column of cells where you want to place headings, and then in the Cell Properties dialog box, activate the Header Cell checkbox. To add a row of header cells, select the row of cells where you want to place headings, and then in the Cell Properties dialog box, activate the Header Cell checkbox. After you finish setting cell properties, click the Apply button to confirm your changes and then the OK button to close the dialog box.

You can also select cells by row and column using the mouse. To select a row of cells, move the cursor to the left-hand border of the table. When you see the cursor change to a black arrow pointing right, click the left mouse button. To select a column of cells, move the cursor to the top border of the table. When you see the cursor change to a black arrow pointing down, click the left mouse button.

After you select cells, you can manipulate the selection. To select additional cells, move the pointer into a cell, press Shift, and then click the left mouse button. Similarly, you can deselect a cell by moving the pointer into a cell, pressing Ctrl, and then clicking the left mouse button.

Adding Color to Your Table

You can add splashes of color to an entire table or to individual elements in the table. The key to using color in your tables is to use it sparingly, and you should always test the readability of your text when used with a new color. If the text is unreadable, select the text and then change the color of the text using the `color` property.

Adding Color to an Entire Table

To define colors for an entire table, first choose Table|Table Properties. The two panels of the Table Properties dialog box that help you add color to tables are Custom Background and Custom Colors.

In the Custom Background panel, you can select a background color for all data and header cells in the table. From the Background Color pull-down list, you can choose color values. If you use the default value, the `color` property is set to use the browser default. If you use the custom value, FrontPage 98 displays the Color dialog box.

In the Custom Colors panel, you can add unique border colors to your table. Most browsers display tables using a shading effect around the border. Generally, the top and left side of the border have lighter shading than the bottom and right side of the border. This shading creates a 3D effect. To define shading for the light border (generally the top and left side of the table border), select a color from the pull-down list for the Light Border field. To define shading for the dark border (generally the bottom and right sides of the table border), select a color from the pull-down list for the Dark Border field.

You can remove the shading and use a single border color by selecting a specific color from the pull-down list for the Border field. Keep in mind that specific shading overrides the value of the Border field. If you want to use a single border color, set the Light Border and Dark Border fields to the default value. For example, the table defined using the settings shown in Figure 8.9 has a color conflict. Because of this conflict, the Light Border and Dark Border field values override the `color` value set for the Border field.

FIGURE 8.9.
Color properties can sometimes conflict.

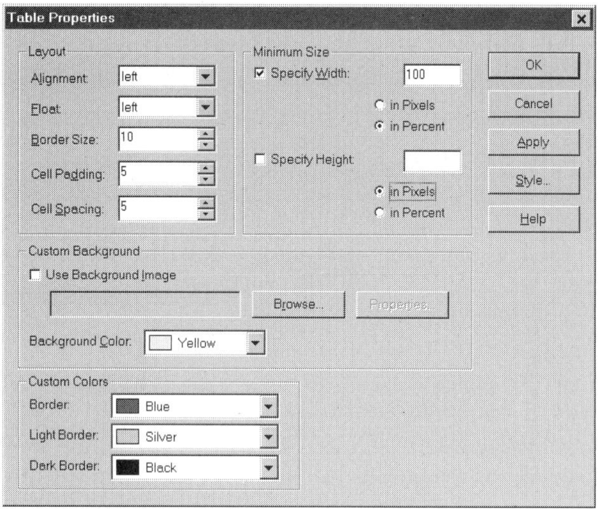

Adding Color to Part of a Table

Using the Cell Properties dialog box, you can add color to individual data and heading cells. To do so, first choose Table|Cell Properties. Like the Table Properties dialog box, the Cell Properties dialog box has two panels to help you add color. The key difference is that, for individual cells, the light and dark borders pertain to the inner borders of the cell.

To create a contrast between the shading of the table and the shading of cells, the light and dark borders for cells are reversed. Therefore, the Dark Border field affects the top and left cell borders, and the Light Border field affects the bottom and right cell borders.

TIP

You can assign the same color settings to more than one cell. To do so, you must select the cells before you open the Cell Properties dialog box.

Adding Background Images to Your Table

In addition to supporting colors in tables, you can also add images to table backgrounds. If you want to use the image as a background for an entire table, assign the background image using the Table Properties dialog box. If you want to use the image as a background for an individual cell, assign the image using the Cell Properties dialog box.

When you select the Use Background Image checkbox in either the Table Properties or Cell Properties dialog box, the input text field becomes editable. You can then enter the absolute or relative URL path to the background image file. If you don't know the path to the background image, click the Browse button.

NOTE

As with page backgrounds, the background image for your table should be in GIF or JPEG format to get the widest compatibility with compliant browsers.

Figure 8.10 shows how you can use background images in tables. When you combine unique page colors or backgrounds with a table that has backgrounds, be sure to check the table for readability. The table shown in the figure worked great against a white background. Yet when the page color was changed to black and the text color was changed to white, a conflict occurred in the readability of the table. To correct the readability problem, text within the table was changed to black.

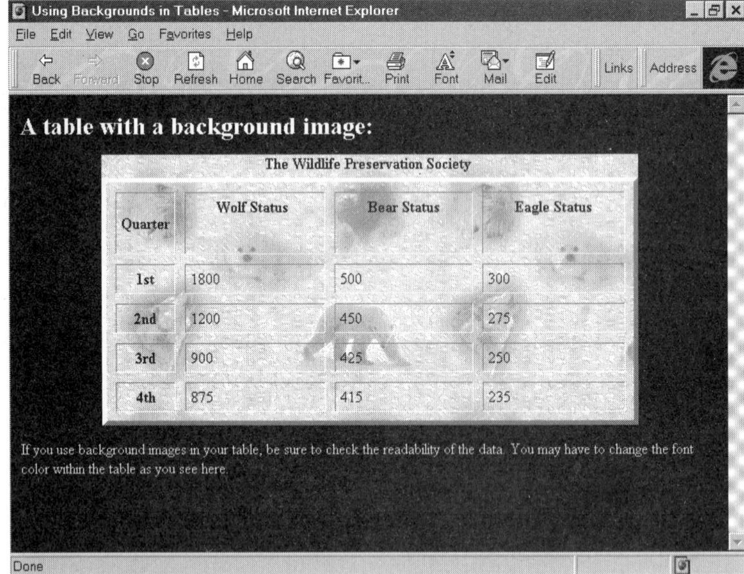

FIGURE 8.10.
Using background images in your tables.

Summary

Tables are one of the most dynamic elements ever added to the HTML standard. With FrontPage 98, you can quickly and easily create powerful tables with precisely controlled layout. Most tables have a caption and one or more rows of data organized into columns. The columns of data contain individual cells. Each individual cell is either a heading or a data set. Although a table can have several levels of headings, all headings serve to identify the data sets contained in the body of the table. Use tables to add pizzazz to your Web pages!

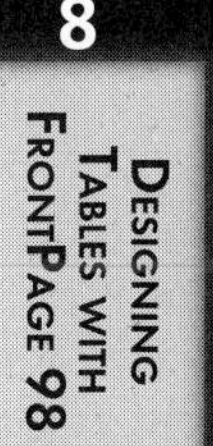

CHAPTER

Creating Frames

by William Robert Stanek

IN THIS CHAPTER

- Frame-Enhancing Your Documents *156*
- Adjusting and Dividing the Frames *158*
- Defining an Alternate Document *159*
- Saving and Using Your Frames Page *160*
- Using Frame Templates *161*

Since the addition of frames to the HTML menagerie, they have become one of the biggest boons—and banes—for Web developers and surfers alike. Frames allow you to create documents with multiple independent "regions," somewhat akin to independent windows. Each frame is in its own right a mini-Web browser, viewing a separate page of content. Your frames can have scroll bars, size manipulators and borders, and even headers or footers. The FrontPage Editor makes creation of frames-based pages a simple task. However, as easy as it is to create frames with the FrontPage Editor, you still should carefully study this chapter to make sure that you are creating frames for the right reasons.

Frame-Enhancing Your Documents

Frames enable you to create documents with multiple windows. Now that frames are part of the HTML specification, all HTML 4.0-compliant browsers support frames. Browsers that support frames include most versions of Netscape Navigator and Internet Explorer.

Working with Frames: The Basics

The best thing about frames is that they let you, as a Web developer, create a unique page that is not limited to one top-down, left to right scrolling screen. And for those older browsers that do not support frames, you can create a different document that is used by browsers that cannot use frames, separate from your document that is used by frames-capable browsers.

Each frame is identified by a unique source. The source can be any type of document, but it typically consists of HTML pages. The frame-enhanced page in Figure 9.1 uses three window frames. The contents of each mini-window come from a separately defined HTML document merged into a common window using frames.

The common window for frames is referred to as the frame source page, and it is a separate document that defines the size and attributes of each frame. Thus, creating the page shown in Figure 9.1 requires the following four documents:

- A frame source page
- Three HTML pages, one for each frame

In the example, the left-side frame was created from a document containing a title image. The right-side frame is the primary frame; as shown here, it contains the contents of a home page created specifically for Netscape Navigator 3+ and Internet Explorer 3.0+ browsers. The bottom frame contains a text-based menu. When a menu item is clicked, the contents of the associated document are normally loaded into the main frame. The ability to click links in one frame and load the associated resource in another page is handled using targets. A target is simply the window or frame into which you want to load a resource.

As you can see from the example, some of the frames have horizontal and vertical scrollbars that readers can use to access the additional material in the document. Although scrollbars usually are displayed when needed, you have control, as the publisher, over when and how scrollbars are displayed.

FIGURE 9.1.
A frame-enhanced page.

You do not have to frame-enhance all the pages at your Web site. A key concept in designing publications for frames is to define frames only on the main page that readers use to access the publication. This can be your home page or any top-level page at your site. Using a top-level page reduces the amount of work you must do to frame-enhance your site and enables you to use frames as they were meant to be used.

Building the Frames in the FrontPage Editor

EDITING TECHNIQUE

To create a frame-enhanced page, select New from the File menu or press Ctrl+N; then, in the New Page dialog box, click the Frames tab. You can now select a template for your frame-enhanced page. Although you can use the Preview window of the New Page dialog box to help you decide which template to use, I've put together a brief overview of the frame templates to help you visualize what the finished page will look like. You will find this overview of the frame templates in the section of this chapter titled "Using Frame Templates."

After you select a frame template, FrontPage 98 will initialize the FrontPage Editor, and there will be one editing area for each of the frames in your page (see Figure 9.2). Now, you have the option of using an existing page as the source for your frames or telling FrontPage 98 to create a new page for the frame. Because you don't want to haphazardly blend pages together, you will probably want to step back and plan out how you want the frame-enhanced page to come together before you start piecing documents together.

If you want to work on each frame separately, you could create separate pages in the FrontPage Editor, then set the initial page for each frame so that it points to the correct source. The advantage of creating each frame as a separate page is that you do not have to work within the restricted area of the divided window, which can free your creativity. The disadvantage is that you do not see how everything comes together until the pages are actually merged, and you will not know if text, images, and other elements will fit in the areas you've designated for the frames.

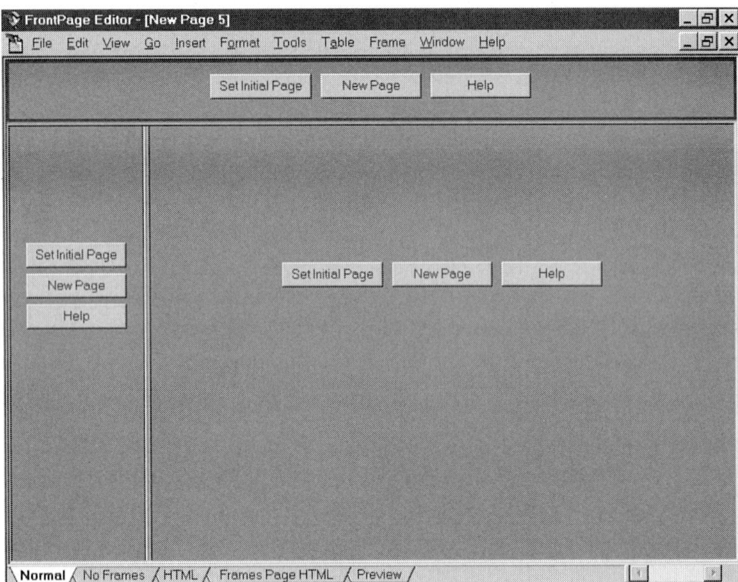

FIGURE 9.2.
Getting started with frames in the FrontPage Editor.

If you want to work on the frames together, you can roll up your sleeves and dive in by creating a new page for each frame. The advantage of creating the frames together is that you can see how various aspects of each frame work with the other frames. The disadvantage is that you might develop tunnel vision, where you size elements to fit within the confines of the frame and forget that everything about the frame size is adjustable. Further, although the FrontPage Editor does a good job of creating a representative area for each frame, the frames will probably be sized differently when viewed in a browser.

After you consider how you will create your frame-enhanced page, take another look at Figure 9.2 and note the new tabs at the bottom of the Editor window. The No Frames tab allows you to create a page that will be displayed by browsers that do not support frames. The Frames Page HTML tab displays the frame source page, which contains the markup that defines the size and attributes of each frame. Sizing and setting frame attributes are explored in the next section.

Adjusting and Dividing the Frames

At first glance, the way you divide a browser window into frames can seem confusing. This is because window frames are organized much like a table, with each window divided into one or more rows and columns. The way rows and columns of frames are organized depends on the template you start out with. However, you are not stuck with the frames as defined by the template.

You can break any individual frame into several smaller frames. To do this, select the frame by clicking while the pointer is over the frame. Now that the frame is selected, you can break it into smaller sections using the Split Frame option of the Frame menu. Using the Split Frame dialog box, you can split the frame into two rows or two columns. As shown in Figure 9.3, you will need to set the initial page or create a new page for the frame you just created.

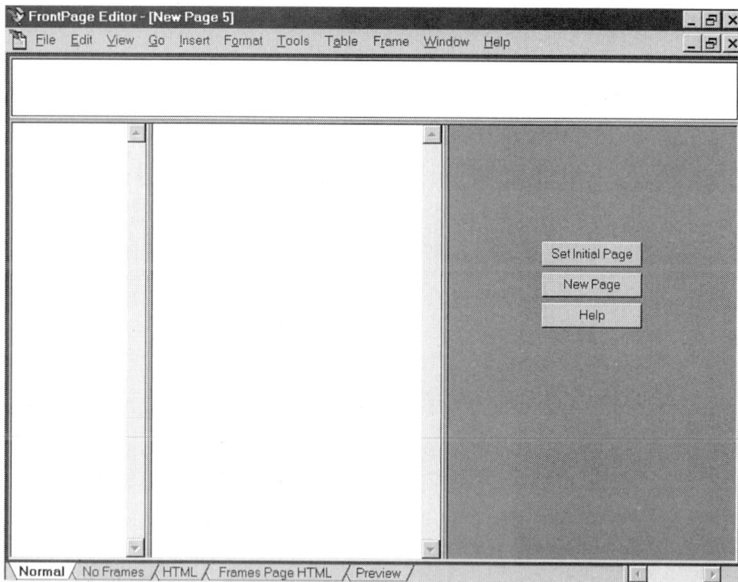

FIGURE 9.3.
After you split a frame, you will need to define the page for the frame.

If you decide that you don't want a frame in the window, you can use the Delete Frame option of the Frame menu. Because FrontPage 98 might not be able to undo your action, be sure that you select the right frame before you use this option.

With your document broken into frames and subframes, you can work on sizing the frames. As you can see from Figure 9.3, each frame is separated by a grid line. You can move these horizontal and vertical grid lines to resize any frames in your document. To do this, move the pointer to the grid line you want to resize. The arrow pointer changes to the resize pointer—a pointer with arrows on either end. If you press and hold down the left mouse button, you can drag the grid line to resize the frame.

Defining an Alternate Document

When you are done defining individual frames, you should create a page for browsers that are not capable of using frames. This page is called the No Frames page. Browsers that can't use frames include older versions of popular browsers like Netscape Navigator and Internet Explorer, as well as current versions of many other browsers.

It is always a good idea to define an alternate source document. There is no point in creating a page that arbitrarily excludes a group of Web users. However, if you do not specify an alternate page, FrontPage 98 inserts a warning to users who cannot view the frame-enhanced document that tells them the page uses frames, which is a feature not supported by their browsers.

Creating a No Frames page that is better than the default is a snap. With your frame-enhanced page loaded into the Editor, click the No Frames tab. You can now create the No Frames page. To get a quick start, try loading the original page before you frame-enhanced it into the FrontPage Editor, then copy the entire page and paste it into the No Frames page of your new frame-enhanced page. If this is a completely new page, you can still base the frames page on any page you've already created. Just load it into the FrontPage Editor, copy it to the Clipboard, and paste it onto the No Frames page.

Saving and Using Your Frames Page

Now that you are well on your way to creating a wonderful frames page, you probably want to save your page and access it in your browser. Unfortunately, saving your frames page can be a bit confusing, especially if you have lots of frames. The first time you save the frames page using the Save or Save As option of the File menu, you will need to name the frame source page and each page that you created using the New Page option.

FrontPage 98 asks you to name each new page in turn, then asks you to name the frame source page. You will know which frames page you are naming because the dialog box has a Summary icon that highlights the frame being saved (see Figure 9.4). You will know you are saving the frame source page because there will be no Summary icon. If you close the page and want to modify the frames page later, you can use the URL to the frame source page to access the entire set of frames.

Because the frame source page is the page visitors to your Web site will access, you want to carefully select the URL you will use for this page. You also want to think about the URLs for the individual frames as well, especially if you plan to feature more than one frames page at your Web site. Here's why: Let's say you create a frames page with three frames. You name the frame source page `coolstuff.htm`; the side frame, `side.htm`; the banner frame, `banner.htm`; and the main frame, `main.htm`. Visitors to your Web site will access your frames page using its complete URL, such as `http://www.you.com/coolstuff.htm`. When they access the page, each page loads into the visitor's browser.

After your success with the first frames page, you decide to create another frames page. You call this page `freestuff.htm` and divide it into two frames. The small left frame is called `side.htm` and the main frame is called `main.htm`. Oops, you've just tried to point to the same page URLs as the other frames page. To steer clear of potential naming problems, you should use page names that will help you identify the frameset for each page. For example, the pages for coolstuff.htm you could name coolside.htm, coolbanner.htm, and coolmain.htm. Similarly, for freestuff.htm, you could use the names freemain.htm and freeside.htm. These more distinct page names will make it easier to identify and maintain your frame-enhanced pages.

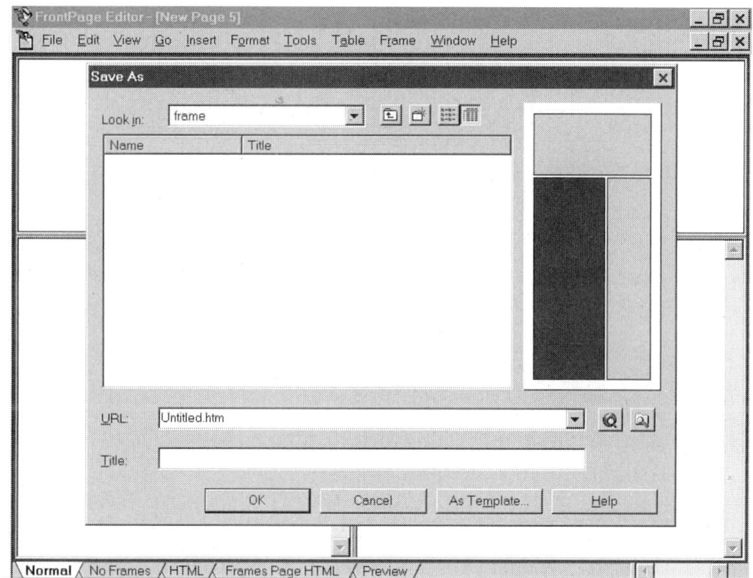

FIGURE 9.4.
FrontPage highlights the frame you are saving.

Using Frame Templates

FrontPage provides quite a few templates designed to make using frames easier. Because these templates are named, sized, and already have targets, most of the setup work is done for you. So, if you can find a template that meets your needs, you can be well on your way to creating a great frames page with a limited amount of fuss.

Banner and Contents Page

The Banner and Contents template creates a document with a banner at the top, a Table of Contents Frame, and a Main Frame (see Figure 9.5). The Banner Frame targets the Table of Contents Frame and should contain the Main navigation links. When a user clicks a link in the Banner Frame, the user's browser loads the referenced document into the Table of Contents Frame.

The Table of Contents Frame targets the Main Frame and should contain links to the main pages in the current section of the web or to all the bookmarks in Main Frame's current page. When users click a link in this frame, their browsers load the referenced document into the Main Frame.

The Main Frame does not target any other frame and should contain the main information. When users click a link in this frame, their browsers load the referenced document into the Main Frame, which overwrites the existing source document.

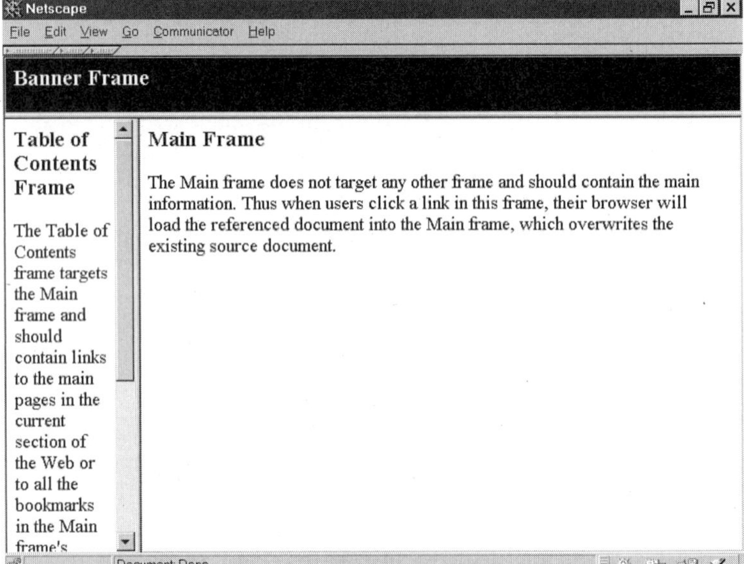

FIGURE 9.5.
A page with Banner and Table of Contents Frames.

Contents Page

The Contents template creates a document with a Table of Contents Frame and a Main Frame (see Figure 9.6). The Table of Contents Frame targets the Main Frame and should contain links to the main pages in the current section of the web or to all the bookmarks in the Main Frame's current page. When users click a link in this frame, their browsers load the referenced document into the Main Frame.

The Main Frame does not target any other frame and should contain the main information. When users click a link in this frame, their browsers load the referenced document into the Main Frame, which overwrites the existing source document.

Header, Footer, and Footnotes Pages

The Header, Footer, and Footnotes templates are very basic templates that create similarly styled pages. All three templates are divided into a large Main Frame and a small sub-frame like the one shown in Figure 9.7. The main differences between these templates is how the page is divided and how the frames are linked together:

Header   Creates a page with a small frame at the top of the window that targets the Main Frame.

Footer	Creates a page with a small frame at the bottom of the window that targets the Main Frame.
Footnotes	Creates a page with a small frame at the bottom of the window frame; the Main Frame targets the Footnotes Frame. To access footnotes related to the text, users click links in the Main Frame and the corresponding footnotes are displayed in the Footnotes Frame.

FIGURE 9.6.
This page uses a Table of Contents Frame along the left, and a Main Contents Frame on the right.

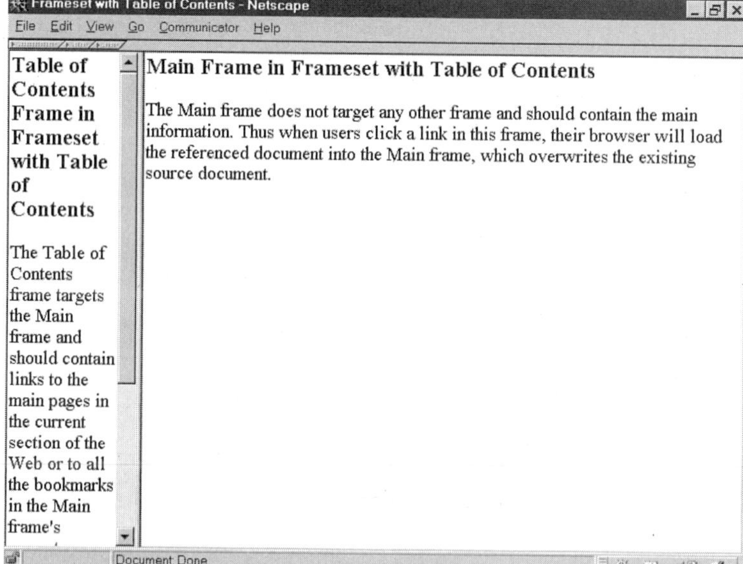

FIGURE 9.7.
A page with a Footnotes Frame.

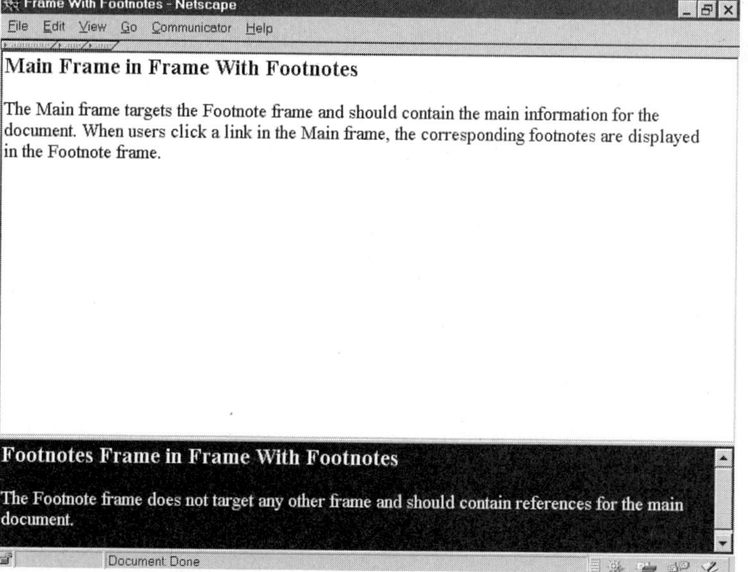

Header, Footer, and Contents Page

The Head, Footer, and Contents template creates a document with navigation bars at the top and bottom, a Table of Contents Frame, and a Main Frame (see Figure 9.8). Navigation bars are usually image map banners. Both navigation bars target the Table of Contents Frame and should contain the main navigation links. When users click a link in either navigation bar, their browsers load the referenced document into the Table of Contents Frame.

The Table of Contents Frame targets the Main Frame and should contain links to the main pages in the current section of the web or to all the bookmarks in the Main Frame's current page. When users click a link in this frame, their browsers load the referenced document into the Main Frame.

The Main Frame does not target any other frame and should contain the main information. When users click a link in this frame, their browsers load the referenced document into the Main Frame, which overwrites the existing source document.

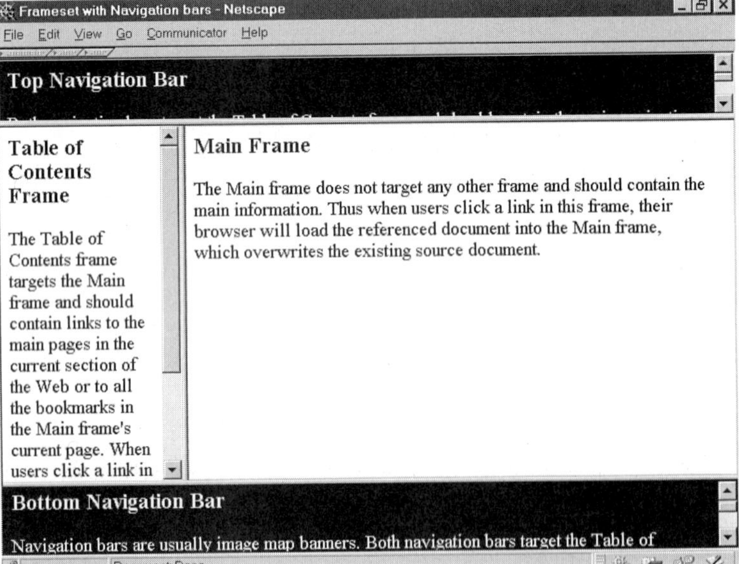

FIGURE 9.8.
A page with header, footer, and contents frames.

Horizontal and Vertical Split Pages

The Horizontal and Vertical Split templates are used to divide a page into two independent frames of equal size (see Figure 9.9). Using the Horizontal Split template, you create a page with two rows. Using the Vertical Split template, you create a page with two columns.

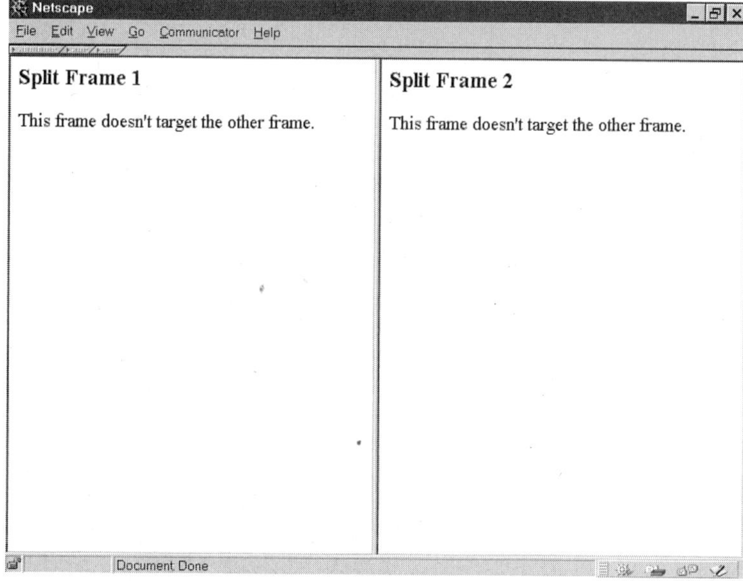

FIGURE 9.9.
A page divided into two frames.

Top-Down, Three-Level Hierarchy Page

The Top-Down, Three-Level Hierarchy template creates a page split into three frames (see Figure 9.10). The top frame targets the middle frame and should contain the main sections of your web. When users click a link in the top frame, their browsers load the referenced document into the middle frame.

The middle frame targets the bottom frame and should contain links to the main subsections of the web or to all the bookmarks in the bottom frame's current document. When users click a link in this frame, their browsers load the referenced document into the bottom frame.

The bottom frame does not target any other frame and should contain the detailed information at your site. When users click a link in this frame, their browsers load the referenced document into the bottom frame, which overwrites the existing source document.

Nested Three-Level Hierarchy Page

The Nested Three-Level Hierarchy template creates a document with a nested hierarchy split into three frames (see Figure 9.11). The left frame targets the right top frame and should contain the main sections of your web. When users click a link in the left frame, their browsers load the referenced document into the right top frame.

The right top frame targets the right bottom frame and should contain links to the main subsections of the web or to all the bookmarks in the right bottom frame's current document. When users click a link in this frame, their browsers load the referenced document into the right bottom frame.

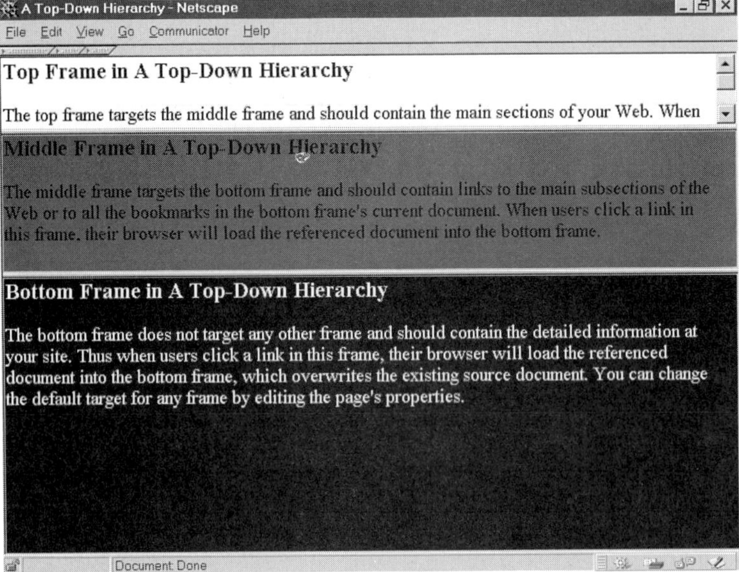

FIGURE 9.10.
A page with the Top-Down, Three-Level Hierarchy frames.

The right bottom frame does not target any other frame and should contain the detailed information at your site. When users click a link in this frame, their browsers load the referenced document into the right bottom frame, which overwrites the existing source document.

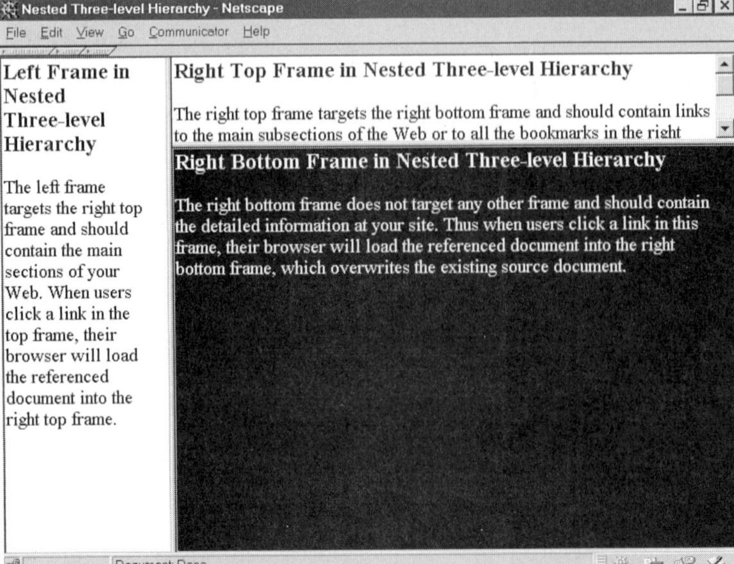

FIGURE 9.11.
A page using the Nested Three-Level Hierarchy frames.

Summary

Frames are more than mini-windows within the larger browser window. In fact, they are the gateway to an entirely new way to publish on the Web. As you have seen, creating frames-enhanced pages with FrontPage 98 is easy. You start by selecting a frames template as the basis for the page. Then you adjust the frames until they are sized and styled as you like them. Afterward, you should create a No Frames page so users with browsers that don't support frames can enjoy your page as well.

Editing and Enhancing Your Frames

By William Robert Stanek

IN THIS CHAPTER

- Customizing Your Frames 170
- Targeting Frames and New Windows from Links 173
- Creating Borderless Frames 175
- Putting the Borderless Design to the Test 179

If you are just getting started in Web publishing, the frame templates are great starting points. When you use the frame templates, you don't have to worry about advanced setup of the frames because it has all been done for you. The design of the frame interface is already developed. The handling of links within frames is already defined. The frame properties are already set to preset values.

Although the frame templates are great starting points, they may not provide the look and feel that you want for your frame-enhanced page. To change the look and feel of the frames, you need to examine how you can optimize frame properties, how frames are named and targeted, and other design issues.

Customizing Your Frames

You can control every aspect of your frame-enhanced page from the way they are named to the way they are targeted. You can add scrollbars to frames, control the thickness of the frame grids, and define the margin spacing around frames as well. All these features of frames are controlled by setting frame properties within FrontPage 98. Because each frame is defined separately, you need to customize each frame's properties individually.

With the frames page open in the editor, right-click over the frame you want to customize, and then choose Frame Properties from the pop-up menu. After you set the properties of the current frame, you will probably want to set properties of each of the other frames in turn. As you can see from Figure 10.1, the Frames Properties dialog is fairly extensive. These properties break down into the following groups:

- Properties for naming the frame
- Properties for sizing the frame
- Properties for setting the margin size
- Properties for setting options

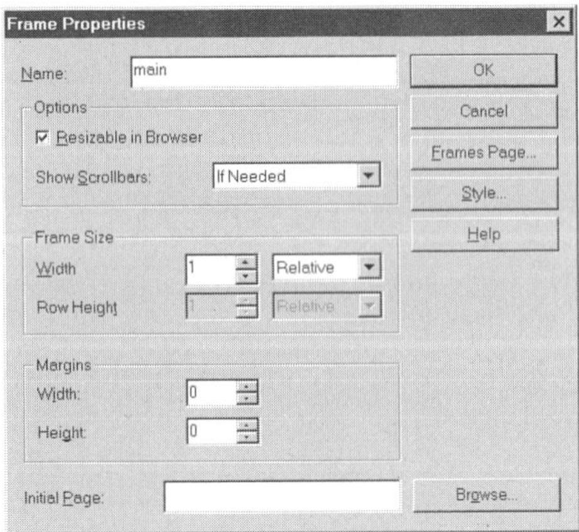

FIGURE 10.1.
Use the Frame Properties dialog to customize your frames.

Naming Frames

The Name field in the Frame Properties dialog is important because the frame name plays a key role in how your frames interact with other frames and windows. When you use the frame templates, each of the default frames is already named. Whenever you add new frames, you should assign the frame a name. To name a frame, enter a keyword in the Name field of the Frames Properties dialog. The best names for frames are short but descriptive, such as Main, Side, or Menu.

After you assign a name to a frame, that frame can be targeted by other frames. Usually, these frames are on the same page. For example, your page could have a main section named Main and a menu section targeted at the Main frame. In this way, when a user clicks a hypertext reference in the menu, the corresponding document is loaded into the Main frame.

You can target a frame by setting the Default Target Frame field in the Page Properties dialog box associated with the source page. The value for the Default Target Frame field should be the name of the frame you want to target. This means that the Name field for each frame you are defining is very important and should be uniquely specified for all frames in a page.

User Adjustment of Frames

Users can adjust frames in two key ways: by using scrollbars and by resizing the frame. In general, users want to be able to manipulate your frames, especially if they are using a screen size other than the one you created the publication for. However, you can turn these features on or off using the Resizable in Browser check box and the Show Scrollbars field of the Frame Properties dialog.

By default, the size of all frames can be adjusted by the user. Users can adjust frames by moving the pointer over a frame edge, holding down the left mouse button when the resizing icon appears, and dragging the frame edge to a new position. You can turn the resizing feature off by deselecting the Resizable in Browser check box. Keep in mind, though, that even a single frame that cannot be resized affects the adjustability of other frames in the window.

The browser usually decides whether a window should have scrollbars. If the entire source document is visible in the frame, the browser automatically displays the frame without scrollbars. If the entire source document is not visible in the frame, the browser automatically displays the frame with scrollbars. Older browsers display both horizontal and vertical scrollbars regardless of whether both are needed.

To control when scrollbars are displayed, use the Always and Never options of the Show Scrollbars field. If you don't want a particular frame to ever be displayed with scrollbars, use the Never option. If you want a particular frame to always have scrollbars, use the Always option.

Optimizing the Frame Size

Using the inline frame editor, you can adjust the size of individual frames without having to deal with the Frame Properties dialog. The editor is easy to work with and can help you quickly adjust frame sizes, but the editor doesn't show you exactly how the frames will look in other browsers or at other screen sizes.

To test the frames page, you can use the Preview in Browser option of the File menu. Select the browser you want to use and the window size, and then click the Preview button. As you will probably discover when you preview the page, the frames will be distorted at some screen sizes. This is because frames can be sized using either *absolute* or *relative* values. Absolute values are defined in pixels, such as the frame is 100 pixels wide. Relative values generally are defined in relation to other frames or the current window.

You can adjust the height and width of a frame using the Frame Size area of the Frame Properties dialog. Because of the way frames are divided into rows and columns, you won't always be able to set both the width and height of a frame. For example, if a frame is the only one on the current row (fills the window width), you can only set the height of the frame.

Generally, you want to use absolute sizing for frames to ensure that elements within a frame are displayed fully. If you create a frames page that uses the nested three-level hierarchy template, you may want to size the left frame to accommodate the width of a graphical menu. Suppose that images in the menu are 100 pixels wide. Here, you probably don't want the frame width to be less than 100 pixels, so you would set the width of the left frame to at least 100 pixels.

Although defining frame size in pixels may seem the easiest way to size a frame, it is never a good idea to define all the frames in terms of pixels. The size of the browser window can vary substantially, depending on the display mode and sizing being used. Further, your browser may override the values you have assigned in order to fill the whole window, which can cause a distortion of your frame-enhanced page. Consequently, you should use fixed pixel values with relative values. For example, set the menu frame to 150-pixel width and the main frame to a relative width.

Relative values are usually expressed as a percentage of the total window size. When you use percentages, you assign a value between 1 and 100. The following are some examples of relative sizing with percentages for a window divided into two frames:

- Create a small side frame and a large main frame by setting the width of the side frame to 10% and the width of the main frame to 90%.
- Create two frames of equal width by setting the width of the left frame to 50% and the width of the right frame to 50%.

NOTE

If the total of all percentages assigned is greater than 100, the values are scaled down to 100. If the total of all percentages assigned is less than 100, the relative sizes are scaled up to 100, and in this way, the relative-sized frames are given the extra space.

To use relative scaling, you use an asterisk with or without a value. An asterisk with no associated value is interpreted as a request to give all remaining space in the row or column to the frame you are creating. An asterisk with a value in front of it is used to scale how much relative space to assign to a frame. A frame with the value "3*" would get three times as much relative space as other frames assigned with a relative value. Because you are scaling a frame relative to other frames, relative scaling usually should be used with one of the other sizing methods. The following are some examples of using relative scaling for a window divided into three frames:

- Assign the first frame a screen width of 10%, the second a screen width of 25%, and the third a relative width of *.
- Assign the leftmost frame a pixel width of 100, the next frame a relative width of *, and the third frame a pixel width of 100.

Frame Margins

To set the frame margin (or spacing), use the Margins area of the Frame Properties dialog. The Height field controls the top and bottom margin sizes for the frame. The Width field controls the frame's left and right margin sizes. If you use a value of zero in either of these fields, your browser displays the frame with a default margin so that frame edges do not touch. Because the browser default margin size can vary, you may want to assign a specific margin size.

Targeting Frames and New Windows from Links

You can define how frames interact, that is, the way links in one frame target another frame. Using targets, you can open resources in any frame of the current window or open an entirely new window if necessary.

Targeting Basics

Most of the frame templates already have targets defined. When you add frames to these templates or want to change the default behavior of your frames page, you need to work with targets. A target is a window or frame into which you want to load a linked resource. If links in your side frame are targeted at the main frame, clicking a link in the side frame tells a browser to load the related resource for the link in the main frame.

You identify a target frame using the name assigned to the frame when you created it. So, be sure to write down the names of the frames used in your page. Armed with the frame names, you are ready to set up targets for the frames. You can assign targets in one of two ways:

- Assign a default target
- Assign a target to a specific link

Assigning a Default Target

The easiest way to assign a target for links in a frame is to use a default target. In this way, you do not have to insert target information for each individual link in the frame. You simply assign the default target and press on.

To set the default target for the current frame, right-click in the frame, and then select Page Properties. In the General tab, click the Edit button of the Target Frame field to open the Target Frame dialog. Now enter the name of the frame you want to target in the Target Setting field (see Figure 10.2).

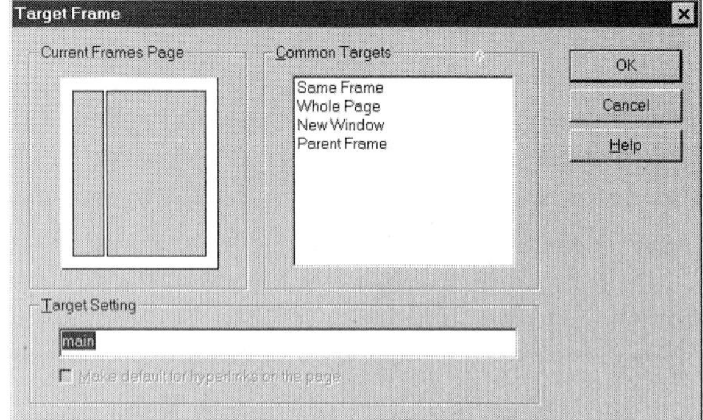

Figure 10.2.
Assigning a default target to a frame is easy.

Assigning a Target to a Specific Link

Using a default target makes it easier to get your frames page up and running. But sometimes you don't want a link to use the default. To override the default target for a frame, all you need to do is assign a new target to any link you want to change. Thus if you want to target most of the links to a single frame called Main and some links to a frame called Footer, you can easily do this. You would set the default target to Main, then edit the target assignment for each link that should target the Footer frame.

To assign a target to a specific link, select the text or image that identifies the link and then press Ctrl+K for the HyperLink option of the Edit menu. Next, click the Edit button of the Target Frame field to open the Target Frame dialog. Now enter the name of the frame you want the link to target in the Target Setting field.

Fine Tuning the Targeting

You're probably thinking that there's got to be more to targeting. After all, what's this Common Targets area in the Target Frame dialog all about? Well, you use the common targets to fine-tune the way you target frames, and you'll find that common targets are especially handy when you don't want to target a named frame. The following are the common targets currently defined:

Same Frame — Target the current frame. When you click a link, the associated resource is loaded into the current frame. FrontPage 98 assigns the value of `_self` in the Target Setting field. `_self` is a code used by browsers to target the same frame.

Whole Page — Get rid of the current frames page and load this page into a full window. When you click a link, the associated resource is

	loaded at the top of the window hierarchy, which ensures it is always a full window. FrontPage 98 assigns the value of _top in the Target Setting field. _top is a code used by browsers to target the top (or whole) window.
New Window	Load the associated resource into a new browser window. When you click a link, the associated resource is loaded in a separate browser window, just as if you had started a new browser and typed in the URL. FrontPage 98 assigns the value of _new in the Target Setting field. _new is a code used by browsers to spawn a new browser window.
Parent Frame	Load this link over yourself and reset the window. When you click a link, the associated resource is loaded over the current frames page. FrontPage 98 assigns the value of _parent in the Target Setting field. _parent is a code used by browsers to target the frame source page associated with the current frame.

Instead of using the New Window target, I recommend targeting a specifically named window, such as Window2, which tells the browser to open a named window and target all links to this window. Using the window name, you can target the new window from other frames as well and avoid opening multiple secondary windows that confuse the user.

The most used relationships are _top and _parent, which serve similar purposes. Using the _parent or _top relationship, you can force the browser to reset the window entirely and avoid loading a frame document within the current frame. You want to use one of these relationships whenever you have a link that leads to a page containing frame assignments. For example, if lower-level documents reference your home page, you can assign the target of the link as _parent or _top to avoid getting a frame within a frame.

Most people don't give a hoot about the exact difference between the _parent relationship and the _top relationship. So, to these people I say, use _top and go on with life. However, if you use frames extensively and rely on sets of frames within frames, the difference between these two relationships can be extremely important.

When you use _parent, only the frame source page associated with the current frame is overwritten. Thus if you had a left frame with its own frame set and a right frame with its own frame set, you could load a new page or a new frame set into the left frame only, and the right frame would remain unchanged. On the other hand, if you use the _top relationship, the new page or new frame set would be written to the top of the window hierarchy, and both sets of frames would be overwritten.

Creating Borderless Frames

If you've been working with frames for a while, you know that one of the most common user complaints related to frames is that the frames clutter the screen and make the page seem difficult to navigate. Screen space is very important to users and when you cram two, three, or four frames into a limited space, you make the entire page seem like a house built entirely of closets. No one likes to be jammed into a closet. You can take your frames page out of the closet and into the mainstream using borderless frames. Borderless frames get rid of unnecessary frame borders and scrollbars, freeing up screen real estate and giving your page a cleaner, more professional look.

Contrary to popular opinion, creating borderless frames isn't a task you should tackle without careful forethought. Sure, to remove the border around frames, all you need to do is set a few options and go about your merry way. But unless you redesign your frames page or better yet, design the page for borderless frames in the first place, your frames page probably won't be displayed as you would like. In fact, unless you understand the design techniques that go into achieving a true borderless frames page, your page will probably be displayed with frame borders.

Beyond design problems, another stumbling block for borderless frames is browser support. The only browsers that support borderless frames are Internet Explorer (version 3.0 or later) and Netscape Navigator (version 3.0 or later). Browsers that do not support borderless frames will ignore the borderless attributes and continue to display the frame border. Before the discussion turns to specific design techniques you should consider, the next section covers how to tell Internet Explorer and Navigator that your frames page should be displayed without borders.

Implementing Borderless Frames

Creating borderless frames would be much easier if both Microsoft and Netscape were on the same sheet of music, but as you might expect as the browser war heats up, both developers decided to follow different paths when they implemented borderless frames. Unfortunately, for Web publishers, the different implementations mean extra work. Fortunately, FrontPage 98 supports borderless frames as implemented in Internet Explorer. You can create borderless frames for Internet Explorer by setting properties of the frame source page in the FrontPage Editor.

With the frames page open in the Editor, right-click any frame, and then select Frame Properties. Click the Frames Page button. This opens the Page Properties dialog for the frame source page. Now, click the Frames tab and deselect the Show Borders check box as shown in Figure 10.3. When you deselect the Show Borders check box, FrontPage 98 sets the Frame Spacing to zero. Generally, you should leave this value set to zero. Close all open dialog boxes and save the page.

Now, you have a page that will display frames without borders if possible in Internet Explorer. To tell Netscape Navigator to display the page with borderless frames, you have to go a completely different route. Start by clicking the Frames Page HTML tab to display the markup that defines the frames in your page. Find the line that begins with the following text:

```
<frameset
```

FIGURE 10.3.
Setting up borderless frames for Internet Explorer.

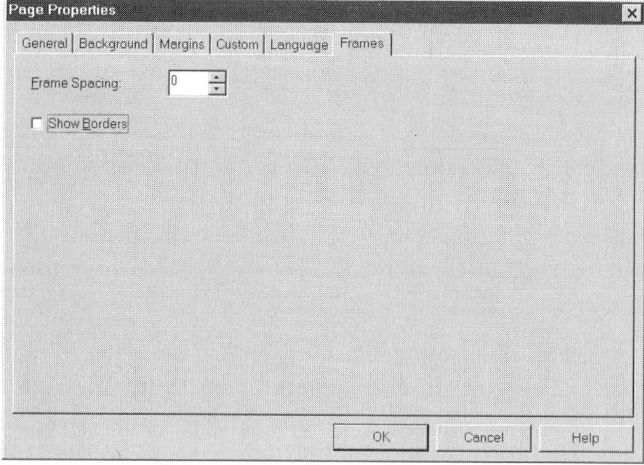

On this same line, there should be an assignment for frame spacing, such as the following:

```
framespacing="0"
```

Insert a space after this assignment, and then add the following:

```
border="0"
```

Follow this assignment with a space to create a line of markup that should look similar to the following:

```
<frameset framespacing="0" border="0" rows="50,2*">
```

As with most HTML, if the browser does not understand an attribute, it ignores it. You can use this combination of the Netscape and Internet Explorer methods for borderless frames without any fear of causing problems with either browser.

TIP

Don't worry about the row or column assignment that completes the line of markup; it will vary depending on your frames page. Just be sure you don't overwrite it.

Click the Normal tab and save the page. You are finished. Keep in mind browsers that don't support borderless frames will display your document in a traditional frame style.

Design Considerations For Borderless Frames

Telling your browser to use borderless frames isn't the only step you need to take to ensure your frames page is indeed displayed without borders. You also need to ensure the page follows a sound design that makes it possible for a browser to display frames without borders. This design should be developed with multiple browsers, multiple platforms, and multiple users in mind.

Browsers use screen space for menus, toolbars, scrollbars, and the like. Although these accessories generally are configurable based on user preferences, you need to consider how much screen real estate these extras use up in the best and worst of conditions. Menus and toolbars are usually displayed in the top margin and eat up between 50 and 150 pixels of screen space. Horizontal and vertical scrollbars within frames take up about 10 to 15 pixels. Although status bars on the bottom margin usually take up 15 to 25 pixels, some browsers let you remove the status bar completely.

Because screen space requirements for browser interfaces usually aren't standardized across platforms, you also need to consider that different platforms may have different interfaces. For example, Windows 95 has a taskbar at the bottom of the screen. The taskbar takes up about 25 pixels in the best of conditions.

Different users probably have different browser options and viewing preferences, which can also be driven by the platform they use. They also probably have different monitors. So it doesn't matter if you have a 21" screen and can use a screen size of 1280×1024 pixels. Most other users are stuck with a screen size of about 640×480 pixels or 800×600 pixels, and when you develop your borderless frames, you should keep the least common denominator in mind.

For a site on the Internet where you have no control over who visits, you should develop the borderless frames for a screen size of 640×480 pixels. Don't forget to account for space eaters like menus and toolbars. In the best of conditions, on a 640×480 screen size, the actual viewing space is about 630×430 and in the worst of conditions, the viewing space is about 625×305.

For a site on an intranet where you know who is visiting, you can adjust the conditions to meet your environment. Suppose you have a mixture of PCs and high-end workstations with the lowest resolution being 800×600. In the best of conditions, on a 800×600 screen size, the actual viewing space is about 790×550 and in the worst of conditions, the viewing space is about 785×525.

Now that you know the viewing space you have to work with, you should design the content of the borderless frames with this viewing space in mind. For example, if you determine that the width of a frame you will use is 100 pixels, you would ensure that images, tables, and other elements in the frame are no wider than 100 pixels.

Although I've examined the viewing space as a whole, the width of the viewing space is usually the most limiting constraint. If the width of all your frames exceeds the width of the viewing space, your frames will be displayed with scrollbars. Further, if the width of an element in a frame is wider than the frame itself, the frame will be displayed with a scrollbar. The height of your frames and the elements within the frames play a similar role in determining whether your page is displayed without borders.

NOTE

Keep in mind that unless you specifically set the Show Scrollbars option of the Frame Properties dialog to Never, borders and scrollbars will be added if the content of a frame is larger than the area dedicated to the frame. Because you generally want users to be able to use your page and all its resources, you shouldn't turn off the scrollbars feature without careful forethought about the consequences.

Putting the Borderless Design to the Test

Although the goal is to create a more professional-looking page, reducing the clutter and cleaning up a page with borderless frames doesn't mean the page won't have scrollbars. After all, the main portion of your page will probably have a lot of information that users will want to get at and they won't want to get at it in tiny bites that preserve the sanctity of your borderless frames. For this reason, you may want to design your page with the prospect that your main frame will be displayed with a vertical scrollbar.

With borderless frames, you will usually want to use some absolute values to size frames, especially for header, footer, and menu frames. However, because it is never a good idea to define all the frames in terms of pixels, at least one frame in the page should have a relative size. Usually this relative-sized frame is your main frame.

To get a better understanding of how to work with borderless frames, try applying the techniques I've discussed throughout the chapter to the frame sets that come with FrontPage 98. Because many of the templates have similar designs, you probably want to jump to a specific section that covers the template you plan to use.

Tips for the Banner and Contents Template

In the banner and contents template, you have three frames: a banner at the top of the window, a contents frame, and a main frame. To get the borderless frames effect, size the banner frame and the contents frame using absolute sizing and the main frame using relative sizing.

Try to keep the images in the banner frame small. Restrict the height and the width so the banner is no larger than 625×125 pixels. You may want to center the banner to make sure that the frame design looks good at various screen sizes. Remove borders around the banner even if it is clickable. Keep in mind that a thin banner (625×80) will look much better at a screen size of 640×480 than a thick banner (625×125). Size the frame appropriately based on your banner size. If your banners are 625×100 pixels and are displayed without borders, give the frame a width of 100 pixels.

The table of contents frame is your menu and may have text and graphic elements. If you want this frame to be displayed without borders, both height and width are constraints. Make sure the frame is wide enough so you can present the necessary navigation links without them seeming cramped but not so wide as to make the main frame seem small. Remember, you are creating your frames page for those working with the smallest screen sizes, and 640 pixels isn't a lot of space. A good width for this frame is 150 pixels or less.

Height is another problem for the contents frame. To figure out the maximum height for this frame, you need to subtract the height of the banner frame from the available space. If you try to design for the worst case scenario, you aren't left with a lot of room here, so I say go with the average of about 430 pixels of usable space at 640×480. If your banner frame has a height of 100 pixels, the height of all the elements in the contents frame should be 330 pixels or less. To meet this goal, you may need to reduce the font size of any text in this frame.

The main frame is where your primary data is displayed. Generally, you want this frame to fill the remaining space and have a scrollbar if necessary. To follow this advice, use relative sizing and a width of *.

Tips for the Contents Template

When using the contents template, you have two frames: a contents frame and a main frame. If you want to incorporate borderless frames, size the contents frame using absolute sizing and the main frame using relative sizing.

The contents frame act as your menu and can have text and graphic elements. Both height and width are constraints if you want this frame to be displayed without borders. Make sure the frame is wide enough so that you can present the necessary navigation links without them seeming cramped but not so wide as to make the main frame seem small. Keep in mind that you are creating your frames page for those working with the smallest screen sizes, and 640 pixels isn't a lot of space. A good width for this frame is 150 pixels or less.

As with the banner and contents template, height is another problem for the contents frame. If you try to design for the worst case scenario, you aren't left with a lot of room here, so I say go with the average of about 430 pixels of usable space at 640×480, and the height of all the elements in the contents frame should be 430 pixels or less. To meet this goal, you may need to reduce the font size of any text in this frame.

As before, the main frame is where your primary data is displayed. You want this frame to fill the remaining space and have a scrollbar if necessary. To follow this advice, use relative sizing and a width of *.

Tips for the Header, Footer, and Footnotes Templates

The header, footer, and footnotes templates are divided into a large main frame and a small subframe. If this page is your home page or a top-level area page, you may want to size the main frame and the subframe so that they have no borders or scrollbars. For other pages, you probably only want the subframe to appear without borders.

If you use the header, footer, and footnotes frames as they were intended to be used, you will probably want to keep these frames small. For a header, restrict the height to 150 pixels or less, and size any text and images within this frame to fit this limitation (see notes in previous section for banner tips). The best footer and footnotes frames are very small, so restrict the height to 100 pixels or less for optimal impact and size any text and images within this frame to fit this limitation.

If you want the main frame to be borderless, height is the main problem area. To figure out the maximum height for this frame, you need to subtract the height of the subframe from the available space. When you design for the worst case scenario, you aren't left with a lot of room here, so I say go with the average of about 430 pixels of usable space at 640×480. If your sub-frame has a height of 100 pixels, the height of all the elements in the main frame should be 330 pixels or less. To meet this goal, you may need to reduce the font size of any text in this frame.

Tips for the Header, Footer, and Contents Template

In the header, footer, and contents template, you have four frames: a header frame at the top of the window, a contents frame, a main frame, and a footer frame at the bottom of the window. To get the borderless frames effect, size the header, contents and footer frames using absolute sizing and the main frame using relative sizing.

The header frame is where you usually display banners, a graphical image map, or a site logo. I'll refer to the combined images and text that make up this frame as the header element. Try to keep the header element small. The combined height and width of the header element should be no larger than 625×125. You may want to center the header element to make sure that the frame design looks good at various screen sizes. Remove borders around the images even if they are clickable. Keep in mind that a thin header element (625×80) will look much better at a screen size of 640×480 than a thick header element (625×125). Size the frame appropriately based on the size of the header element. If your header element is 625×100 and is displayed without borders, give the frame a height of 100.

The footer frame is where you usually will display copyright or contact information. The best footer frames are very small, so restrict the height to 100 pixels or less for optimal impact and size any text and images within this frame to fit this limitation.

The table of contents frame provides additional links and information. If you want this frame to be displayed without borders, both height and width are constraints. Make sure the frame is wide enough so that you can present the necessary navigation links without them seeming cramped but not so wide as to make the main frame seem small. Remember, you are creating your frames page for those working with the smallest screen sizes and 640 pixels isn't a lot of space. A good width for this frame is 150 pixels or less.

Height is another problem for the contents frame. To figure out the maximum height for this frame, you need to subtract the height of the header and footer frames from available space. If you try to design for the worst case scenario, you aren't left with a lot of room here, so I say go with the average of about 430 pixels of usable space at 640×480. If your header and footer frames have a combined height of 175 pixels, the height of all the elements in the contents frame should be 255 pixels or less. To meet this goal, you may need to reduce the font size of any text in this frame.

The main frame is where your primary data is displayed. Generally, you want this frame to fill the remaining space and have a scrollbar if necessary. To follow this advice, use relative sizing and a width of *.

Tips for the Horizontal and Vertical Split Templates

In the split templates, you have two frames split either horizontally or vertically. If you are using a horizontal split, follow the tips in the section titled, "Tips for the Header, Footer, and Footnotes Templates." If you are using a vertical split, follow the tips in the section titled, "Tips for the Contents Template."

Tips for the Top-Down Three-Level Hierarchy Template

The top-down three-level hierarchy template gives you three frames: a top frame, a middle frame, and a bottom frame. To incorporate borderless frames you need to size the top and middle frames using absolute sizing and the main frame using relative sizing.

The top frame is where you usually display banners, a graphical image map, or a site logo. I'll refer to the combined images and text that make up this frame as the *header element.* Try to keep the header element small. The combined height and width of the header element should be no larger than 625×125. You may want to center the header element to ensure that the frame design looks good at various screen sizes. Remove borders around the images even if they are clickable. Keep in mind that a thin header element (625×80) will look much better at a screen size of 640×480 than a thick header element (625×125). Size the frame appropriately based on the size of the header element. If your header element is 625×100 and is displayed without borders, give the frame a height of 100.

The middle frame is where you usually will display the primary navigation links. Make sure the frame is wide enough so that you can present the necessary navigation links without them seeming cramped but not so wide as to make the middle frame seem small. Remember, you are creating your frames page for those working with the smallest screen sizes, and 640 pixels isn't a lot of space. A good height for this frame is 150 pixels or less.

The bottom frame is where your primary data is displayed. Generally, you want this frame to fill the remaining space and have a scrollbar if necessary. To follow this advice, use relative sizing. However, if you want the bottom frame to be borderless, height is the main problem area. To figure out the maximum height for this frame, you need to subtract the height of the top and middle frames from the available space. If you try to design for the worst case scenario, you aren't left with a lot of room here, so I say go with the average of about 430 pixels of usable space at 640×480. If your top and middle frames have a combined height of 180 pixels, the height of all the elements in the main frame should be 250 pixels or less. To meet this goal, you may need to reduce the font size of any text in this frame.

Tips for the Nested Three-Level Hierarchy Template

If you use the three-level hierarchy template, you have three frames: a left frame, a right top frame, and a main frame. To add borderless frames, size the left and right top frames using absolute sizing and the main frame using relative sizing.

The left frame is your menu and logo area. Make the frame wide enough so that you can present the necessary navigation links and images without them seeming cramped but not so wide as to make the others frame seem small. Remember, you are creating your frames page for those working with the smallest screen sizes, and 640 pixels isn't a lot of space. A good width for this frame is 150 pixels or less.

The right top frame is where you usually display banners, a graphical image map or a site logo. I'll refer to the combined images and text that make up this frame as the header element. Try to keep the header element small. The height of the header element should be no larger than 125 pixels. To figure out the maximum width for this frame, you need to subtract the width of the left frame from the available space. If the left frame has a width of 150 pixels, the width of all the elements in the main frame should be 480 pixels or less. To meet this goal, you may need to reduce the font size of any text in this frame.

The main frame is where your primary data is displayed. Generally, you want this frame to fill the remaining space and have a scrollbar if necessary. To follow this advice, use relative sizing and a width of *.

Summary

As the publisher and page designer, you can control the look and feel of the frames page by adjusting the properties of each frame. You decide how frames are organized and whether they have borders. You decide if links in a frame target other frames or open a brand new window. Although FrontPage 98 makes it easier to set and change frame properties, you still need to carefully plan out how the frames page comes together, especially if you want to use borderless frames.

CHAPTER 11

Designing Pages with Style Sheets

by William Robert Stanek

IN THIS CHAPTER

- What Are Style Sheets and How Are They Used? *186*
- How to Use In-line Style Sheets *189*
- How to Use Header-Defined Style Sheets *190*
- Style Sheet Basics *194*
- Decorating Your Text with Fancy Styles *194*

Better control over the design aspects of your page is what style sheets offer, and the Cascading Style Sheets level 1 specification lives up to the promise—well, mostly. With style sheets, you can set specific font size, face, and color anywhere in your Web page. You can add and change background colors to highlight sections of text. You can control margins and spacing around text and graphical elements. You can even control the placement of design elements and the style of borders to display around everything from paragraphs of text to images to tables. FrontPage 98 integrates new CSS features into the FrontPage Editor, making it easier to take advantage of this standard that has become part of the next generation of Web browsers.

What Are Style Sheets and How Are They Used?

Style sheets are a dream come true for Web publishers who wish their Web pages could use some of the advanced design and layout techniques offered by popular desktop publishing software. With style sheets, you can specify design and layout parameters for every element in your Web page.

Adding a style sheet to your page is easier than you might think. Compare the page shown in Figure 11.1 to the page shown in Figure 11.2. Both pages have the same content. The first page uses a style sheet that gives the page a unique look. The second example is a plain old run-of-the-mill HTML page without a style sheet. The difference between these pages is striking, especially if you view them in living color with your browser.

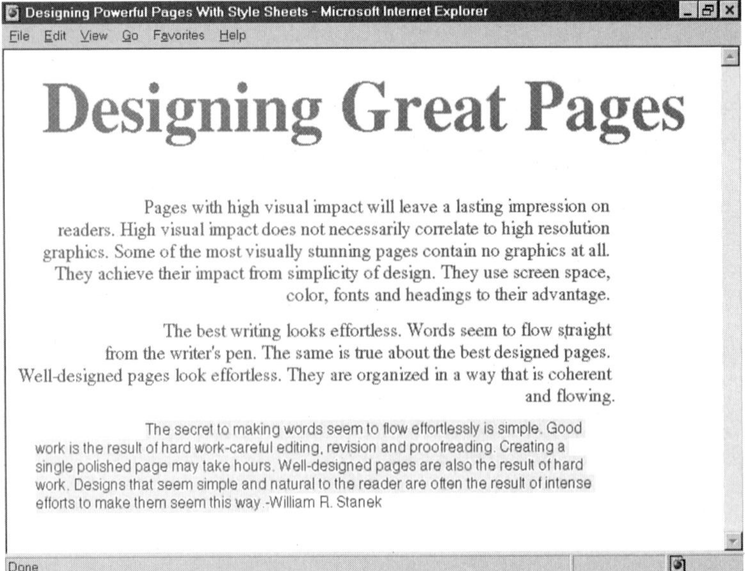

FIGURE 11.1.
Adding style to your pages.

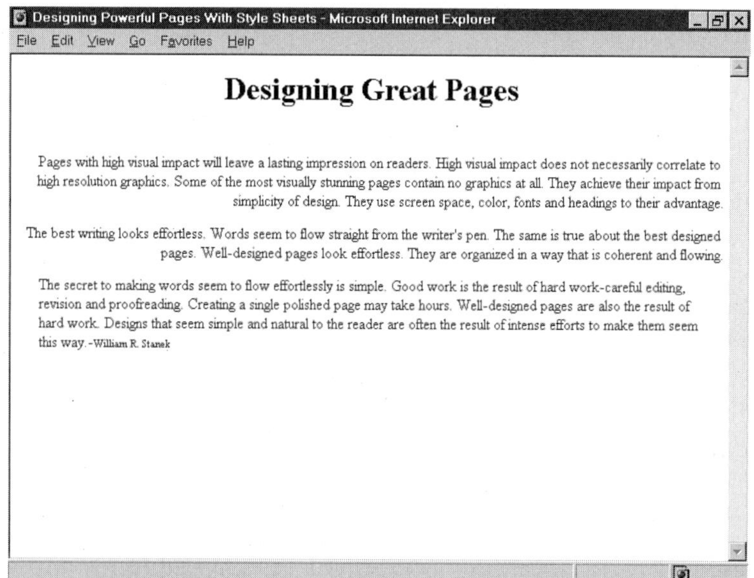

FIGURE 11.2.
A page without style.

The style sheet used in Figure 11.1 sets the following design parameters:

- All level 1 headings are in 45-point Times Roman and displayed in brown.
- All standard paragraphs are in 12-point Times Roman and displayed in blue.
- All paragraphs are to be right aligned.
- The right margin for paragraphs is set to one inch.
- All block quotations are in 10-point Helvetica and displayed in black.
- Highlighting with a yellow background is added to all block quotations.

In earlier chapters, you saw that FrontPage 98 allows you to specify font type, color, and size. So you may be wondering what the difference is between the extensions and style sheets. What style sheets offer you as a Web publisher are additional options and, for some attributes such as font face, better control over which fonts are used. As you read through this chapter, you will find many additional areas in which style sheets provide better control over aspects of layout and text.

Now that I've whetted your appetite, take a closer look at:

- How FrontPage 98 supports style sheets
- Which browsers support style sheets

How Does FrontPage 98 Support Style Sheets?

FrontPage 98 is the first edition of FrontPage to feature built-in support for style sheets as defined in the Cascading Style Sheets Level 1 specification. Although you don't need to learn the ins and outs of CSS1, you should know that FrontPage 98 doesn't give you the full gamut of options offered by the style sheet specification. Using traditional style sheets, you can define all of your style parameters in the page header, which allows you to easily define how each element within a page should look. FrontPage 98 supports header-defined style sheets in a limited way, which I will discuss later in the chapter in the section titled "How to Use Header-Defined Style Sheets."

Defining a style sheet within the page header is only one way you can add style to a Web page. The style sheet specification also allows you to define style parameters in a separate document that can be imported into any page at your Web site. Importing style sheets allows you to apply a single style sheet to multiple pages, which adds a consistent look and feel to your Web site. Although you can use the same style information in every Web page in your site, external style sheet files let you coordinate this consistency with minimal effort. With themes (covered in Chapter 14, "Designing Web Sites with Themes"), FrontPage 98 implements a similar concept, but uses a different means to achieve the consistent look and feel.

The third and final way to use style sheets is to add style parameters to individual elements within a page. FrontPage 98 features full support for this in-line style notation. Using the in-line notation, you can add style to a paragraph of text, a table, or any other element, but you cannot define a style for all paragraphs, all tables, and so on. Further, when you place in-line style notations throughout your page, you lose the greatest benefit of style sheets: the ability to separate the presentation from the content. That said, I would like to believe that the developers of FrontPage chose this route for style sheets on purpose. Typically, designers use in-line and header-defined style sheets to add highlights to a page but not to add style to an entire Web site or area at a Web site. When you want to use style on a grander scale, you should use FrontPage themes.

Which Browsers Support Style Sheets?

Although style sheets are one of the most innovative features to come along in the short history of HTML and the Web, support for style sheets is sporadic at best. Only the latest and greatest browsers support style sheets, and as you might have already guessed, these browsers are Internet Explorer (version 3.0 or later) and Netscape Communicator and Navigator (version 4.0 or later). In one of these browsers, your style sheets should be displayed just as you defined them. However, due to minor inconsistencies, some style sheet features may not be displayed correctly in either Internet Explorer or Netscape Navigator. For example, Internet Explorer 3.0 won't display vertically tiled background images, which is a feature you can add with style sheets. In a non-compliant browser, your style assignments are simply ignored. Here, the browser displays its default style or follows enhancements you've made elsewhere. For example, if you assign a background image and color using standard features, and then define a blue background for paragraph text using style sheets, the blue background for paragraph text would not be displayed, but the standard background color and image would be displayed.

Despite all this, style sheets remain one of the best features you can add to your Web page. My advice is to go in with your eyes wide open. Use style sheets when you want to achieve an advanced layout and design that will knock the viewers' socks off, but make sure your pages have a sound design that works in many different types of browsers.

How to Use In-line Style Sheets

FrontPage 98 allows you to customize the look of every element in your Web page. You can add in-line style assignments to headers, paragraphs, tables, images, quotes, addresses, lists, and more. You define style assignments in one of three ways:

- Define the style for an individual element.
- Define the style for a group of elements.
- Define the style for the entire page.

Defining the Style for an Individual Element

To add style to an individual element, such as a paragraph of text, right-click anywhere within the element, then select the Properties dialog for the element from the pop-up menu. Within the Properties dialog for the element, you will see a Style button. Click this button to display the Style dialog box shown in Figure 11.3. After you make your style assignments, close all the open dialog boxes. FrontPage 98 inserts the style assignments.

FIGURE 11.3.
Defining inline styles with the Style dialog box.

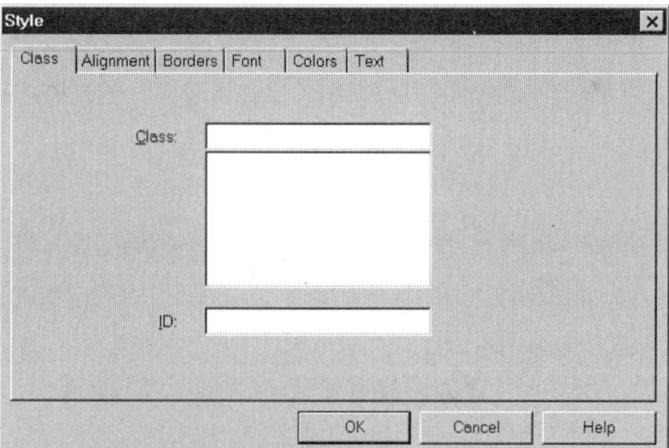

Defining the Style for a Group of Elements

FrontPage 98 also allows you to add style to a group of similar elements. Start by selecting the elements you want to update by clicking the first element in the group, then dragging the mouse until the last element in the group is highlighted. Now, you can make style assignments for all the selected elements.

Immediately after you release the left mouse button, right-click to display the pop-up menu. Select the appropriate properties dialog, then click its Style button. After you make your style assignments, close all the open dialog boxes. FrontPage 98 applies the style assignments to the group of elements.

TIP

Once you set the style assignment for a text element, such as a paragraph, FrontPage 98 will automatically assign the style to consecutive elements you create. For example, if you want to continue the style in the next paragraph, all you need to do is press the Enter key when you finish typing the paragraph, and FrontPage 98 will start a new paragraph using the current style.

Defining the Style for an Entire Page

The final way you can use in-line style sheets is to apply them to the entire page. When you use style sheets in this way, you are assigning a default look for all elements in the page. Generally, you can override these assignments by making new assignments for individual elements within the page.

To define a default style for the page, right-click anywhere in the page, then select Page Properties from the pop-up menu. Open the Style dialog by clicking the Style button. After you make your style assignments, close all the open dialog boxes. FrontPage 98 applies the style assignments to all the elements on the page.

How to Use Header-Defined Style Sheets

Defining the style of elements using the in-line notation is great, but labor-intensive. You have to define the way each element looks, and whenever you change elements, you have to make new style assignments for the new element. Do you really want to wade through the Style dialog many times to define the look of every single element on your Web page? Surely, there must be a better way of assigning style to a Web page, and there is. You can separate the presentation from the content with header-defined style sheets.

Defining Style in the Header

Using header-defined style sheets, you define the way each element will look in the page header. Thus instead of defining the style of each element within the text of the page, you define the way a particular element will look in the header, and you need do so only once. With a header-defined style sheet, you can define the style for all paragraphs in the page with a single style assignment.

Afterward, you need do nothing more and all paragraphs in your page will automatically use the style assignment. You can take this wonderful simplicity further by making a header-defined style assignment for every type of element used in your Web page. Now all the elements in your page have a custom look and feel. Can you see how this could be useful?

Now for the bad news, which you must've known was coming. Although FrontPage 98 allows you to create header-defined style sheets, the creation process isn't entirely intuitive and definitely not for the novice. To get started, open the Format Stylesheet dialog by selecting Stylesheet from the Format menu. As you can see in Figure 11.4, this dialog box is a free-flow text dialog with actual markup. The tags you see are used as follows:

`<style>`	Marks the start of the header-defined style sheet.
`<!--`	Marks the start of a comments section. Comment markup is used to hide your style definitions from browsers that don't understand style sheets.
`-->`	Marks the end of the comments section.
`</style>`	Marks the end of the header-defined style sheet.

NOTE

Although you should never need to change the default markup, you may need to edit your style assignments within these tags.

FIGURE 11.4.
For header-defined style sheets, use the Format Stylesheet dialog box.

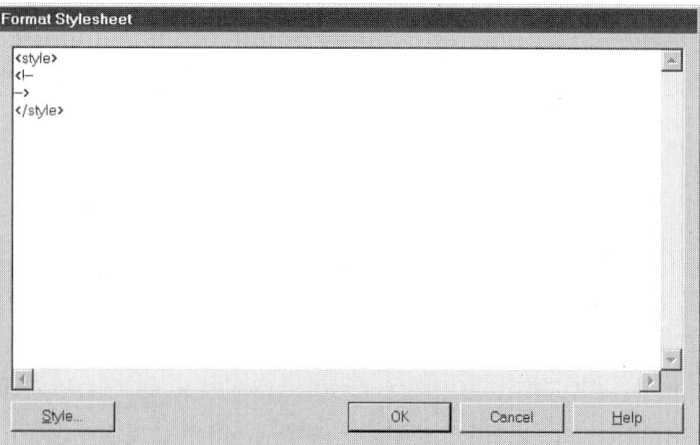

The next step is to move the insertion pointer so it is after the start comment tag. To make the style assignments easy to read, I recommend starting a new line. You can do this by pressing Enter when you move the insertion point. Now, you need to think about the element or elements you want to make stylish. You'll need to refer to each element by its unique identifier, called a *selector*. The selector for paragraphs of text is P, which is simply the markup tag for the element without the first and last characters (<>). A complete list of elements and their selectors is shown in Table 11.1.

Table 11.1. Selectors for page elements.

Element Name	*Selectors*
Addresses	ADDRESS
Applet	APPLET
Block Quote	BLOCKQUOTE
Data cell within table	TD
Definition in glossary	DD
Embedded objects	EMBED
Glossary list	DL
Header cell within table	TH
Hypertext link	A
Image	IMG
Item in list	LI
Level 1 heading	H1
Level 2 heading	H2
Level 3 heading	H3
Level 4 heading	H4
Level 5 heading	H5
Level 6 heading	H6
Numbered list	NL
Ordered list	OL
Paragraph text	P
Preformatted text	PRE
Row within table	TR
Table caption	CAPTION
Table	TABLE
Term within glossary	DT
Unordered list	UL

Enter the identifier for the element you are defining, and then click the Style button. You will now see a Style dialog similar to the one used for in-line style assignments. Use the fields in this dialog box to define the style for the current element. Click the OK button when you are finished. FrontPage 98 inserts the necessary style assignments into the Format Stylesheet dialog. The style assignment for the current element includes all the markup within the curly brackets ({}). To define a style for a different element, move the insertion point to a new line, then repeat the preceding steps.

When you are finished with all style assignments, close the Format Stylesheet dialog box. FrontPage 98 inserts the style assignments into the page header. You can update these style assignments at any time by reopening the Format Stylesheet dialog box.

Streamlining Header Styles with Grouping

Every textual or graphical element in your Web page can have a unique look. Following what I've outlined so far for style sheets, you would apply one style parameter to each element. For example, to set the color of all headings to brown, your style assignments in the Format Stylesheet dialog would look like the following:

```
<STYLE>
<!--
H1  {color: brown}
H2  {color: brown}
H3  {color: brown}
H4  {color: brown}
H5  {color: brown}
H6  {color: brown}
-->
</STYLE>
```

Defining each style element separately would mean some very large style sheets and would also increase the downloading time of your page. Fortunately, you can combine like definitions by grouping them in a comma-separated list, such as the following:

```
<STYLE>
<!--
H1, H2, H3, H4, H5, H6 {color: brown}
-->
</STYLE>
```

If you wanted to group styles for paragraph text and addresses, you would do the following:

1. Open the Format Stylesheet dialog.
2. Move the insertion pointer so it is after the start comment tag.
3. Enter the following characters:

   ```
   P, ADDRESS
   ```

4. Click the Style button.
5. Make your style assignments using the Style dialog.
6. Close the Style dialog.

Editing Header-Defined Styles

Editing header-defined styles isn't rocket science, but it isn't necessarily intuitive either. After you make style assignments, the assignments are inserted into the page header. You can view these assignments using the HTML tab of the FrontPage Editor. Although you could edit the assignments in the HTML view, I don't recommend doing that. Instead, open the Format Stylesheet dialog by selecting Stylesheet from the Format menu. Move the insertion point to the line containing the reference to the element whose style assignments you want to change. If you want to change the style assignments for paragraph tags, move the insertion point to the line containing the P identifier. Then click the Style button.

Now, all you need to do is change the style assignments. When you are finished making the necessary changes, close the Style dialog, and FrontPage 98 will update the style assignments for you.

Style Sheet Basics

When you open the Style dialog from any element's properties dialog box, you see a properties box with a confusing array of options. There are five common tabs, each with lots of cryptic choices, with one additional tab in the element properties Style dialog box. The following is a brief rundown of what you will use each of the tabs for:

Class	Allows you to create sets of style rules that you can apply to elements in your pages by referencing the class type. This tab does not appear in the Style dialog box opened from the Format Stylesheet dialog.
Alignment	Helps you define the spacing, positioning, and margins for an element.
Borders	Used to define stylish borders for an element.
Font	Sets the font and/or font family to be used with the element.
Colors	Sets the background and foreground colors for the element; also lets you define background images and positioning of those images.
Text	Allows you to manipulate the style of text within an element.

Because using style sheets is more about design than anything else, it doesn't make sense to simply run through all the options in these tabs. Instead, I have divided the discussion into several broad areas based on the design techniques you will use rather than the divisions within the Style dialog. The discussion begins in this chapter with a look at designing with text, then continues in the next chapter with a look at color and spacing techniques. This approach will allow you to focus on good design rather than tabs and confusing options.

Decorating Your Text with Fancy Styles

The font you use defines the way text looks. Before the advent of desktop publishing, the number of fonts publishers used was limited. Each new font included in the publication cost the publisher money. Some companies specializing in creating fonts charged thousands of dollars for a single font and, consequently, even in the early days of computing, fonts were still expensive.

Fortunately, this is not true today. The power of type was unleashed in the early days of the desktop publishing revolution. Now you can buy fonts for pennies, and there are thousands to choose from.

Using Font Styles

Beyond the uppercase and lowercase characters that make up fonts, fonts have many different characteristics. You can use normal, bold, italic, and bold italic. These different font types add emphasis and carry meanings. Italic type, with its forward-slanting appearance, is often used for emphasis for important information, quotations, or captions. Bold type, easily distinguished by being considerably darker than normal text, stands out and is often used for headings. Bold and italic type are generally considered harder to read in large blocks of text.

Style sheets give you control over font characteristics with five fields of the Text tab: Weight, Style, Variant, Transform, and Decoration (see Figure 11.5). Using the Weight field, you control the boldness of text on the page, which can make text lighter or darker. Using the Style field, you control the style of the font as normal, italic, or oblique. Using the Transform field, you specify whether text is displayed in all uppercase letters, all lowercase letters, or title case. Using the Decoration field, you can use the popular and not-so-popular overlining and blinking techniques for marking text.

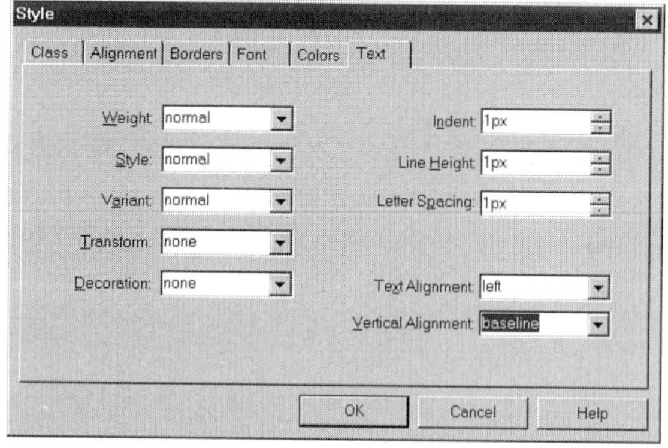

FIGURE 11.5.
Adding font styles to your text is handled with fields in the Text tab.

Because most of the font styles can be achieved using standard techniques that don't require style sheets, I recommend sticking to the basic options on the FrontPage Editor's toolbar. However, the discussion of style sheets would not be complete without taking a brief look at these font options.

The weight for regular text is normal. You can adjust the boldness of the text with these relative values:

lighter	Displays text in one step lighter than regular text for this element
bolder	Displays text in one step darker than regular text for this element

You can also use the value bold, which is the same as selecting Bold on the FrontPage Editor's toolbar, or you can set the weight to a specific numeric value. A weight of 100 is the lightest value and a value of 900 is the darkest value.

The default style of text on the page is normal. You can change the style of the font to normal, italic, or oblique. While you are setting font style, you may want to consider using the small-caps style variant. In small-caps, all lowercase letters are displayed as small capital letters. Small-caps are best used with headings or newspaper-style text.

To change the case of text, you can use the Transform field with these values:

capitalize	Displays the first character of each word in uppercase (which is title case).
uppercase	Displays all characters in uppercase.
lowercase	Displays all characters in lowercase.
none	Displays all characters in default style and eliminates an inherited style for the case that you may have defined for the whole page.

Decorating text is one of the most controversial style elements for fonts. Although you may want to add underlining or strikethrough to text, you probably want to stay away from overlining text and blinking text. Overline text can be confusing because it is not a normal part of text. Use a horizontal rule instead. Blinking text can be annoying because it makes text seem like a neon sign. Definitely avoid blinking text if you can help it. Ideally, if you choose to use blinking text, try to minimize your use of it to short phrases or single words that require attention. Usually blinking text is used for clickable items; avoid using it when an item is not clickable.

The most (and some would argue the only) useful option out of all the options available for these five fields is, interestingly enough, the none option for the Decoration field. Using this option, you can remove the underlining of hypertext links. Your hypertext links will still be highlighted using the colors you've specified; they just won't be underlined. From a design standpoint, removing the underlining of text links is often a good idea. Underlining is distracting. Any time you can remove the distraction of underlining, yet retain the functionality and ease of navigation, definitely consider this tactic.

Adjusting Space Between Text Elements

With style sheets, you can give clear separation to text elements, such as paragraphs and headings, by adjusting the spacing and alignment of the elements. Going back to the Style dialog box (see Figure 11.5), you will find five fields on the right side of the Text tab: Indent, Line Height, Letter Spacing, Text Alignment, and Vertical Alignment.

You can indent the first line of each block level element using the Indent field, which adds a style to your text never before seen in Web publications. If you wanted to indent the first line of a paragraph 50 pixels, you would set the Indent field to 50.

The Line Height field allows you to set the space before and after a text element as well as between lines of text within the element. Normally, line height is a factor of font size and element type. A level 1 heading has more space between it and other elements than a paragraph.

Paragraphs with 14-point text have more space between consecutive lines of text than paragraphs with 10-point text.

By setting the line height to a specific value, you can adjust the space between lines of text as well as the space between various elements. Sometimes you will find that you can make a page more readable by increasing the spacing between lines of text. Just as you may want to open up a page with spacing, you may find that you need to crunch more text into a smaller area. In this case, decrease the line height.

Playing with the line height can get you into trouble. Always remember that line height is tied to font size and element type. If you make the line height too small, lines of text will overwrite each other. As a general rule, the line height in pixels should be at least twice as large as the current font size. Once you've adjusted the line height to this pixel size, you can adjust it slightly up or down to meet your needs.

Another way to enhance the appearance of text elements is by adjusting the spacing between individual characters with the Letter Spacing field. Spacing is set as the number of pixels between characters of text. Use this spacing technique to help you fill a certain area with text or make text more compact.

The final two fields (Text Alignment and Vertical Alignment) are generally the same as the alignment options available from the FrontPage Editor's toolbar and menu. Whenever possible, you should rely on the standard techniques for implementing these design styles. The exception is the wonderful text alignment value of justify, which allows you to justify text, just as you can in your favorite word processor. Justified text is a great design feature when you want paragraphs and text elements to have a consistent flow and look.

Although justified text usually makes the finished product look better, it can mean more work for you as the publisher. Justified text does not work well with non-proportional fonts. Justified text can leave gaping holes in your text, and you will often see large areas with no text where a short line is stretched to fill the window. You will probably want to fix each of these lines by hand or try to rework the wording of the text.

Using Font Faces

Fonts come in thousands of styles given names by their designers. Many font styles in use today are hundreds of years old. Fonts like Baskerville have been around since 1766. Some types that are considered modern first appeared over 100 years ago. Others, like Castellar, Contemporary Brush, and BriemScript have only been around for a few decades.

The name of a font sometimes conveys a message about the style of the font, but not always. Fonts like Ransom, Futura, Century Gothic, and NuptialScript carry distinct messages about the style. Fonts such as New Century School Book, Contemporary Brush, Courier New, and Times New Roman all seem to be saying they are a modern reworking of a classic font. Thousands of other font faces simply have a name that may or may not convey a meaning to you.

TIP

The font you choose for the main text does not have to be the font you use in headings. Some fonts were meant to be used in headings. Some fonts were designed to be decorative. Other fonts were designed to be used in normal text. The key to selecting a good font style is to use a font that is easy to read under a variety of conditions and works well for the purpose for which you plan to use it.

A key concept in using fonts in your publications is to limit the number of font faces you use on any one page. For the sake of consistency, you should also limit the number of font faces you use throughout the publication. A good rule of thumb is to use no more than three different font faces on any page and, if possible and practical, to use the same fonts throughout the publication.

To specify the font face, you use the Font tab of the Style dialog (see Figure 11.6). Font families are specified either by a precise name, such as New Century Schoolbook, or in terms of a general font style, such as serif. If the font type is not available on the user's system, the default font as set in the user's browser is used to display your text. When you specify a font face, you select the font name from the selection list, and FrontPage 98 inserts it into the Font field.

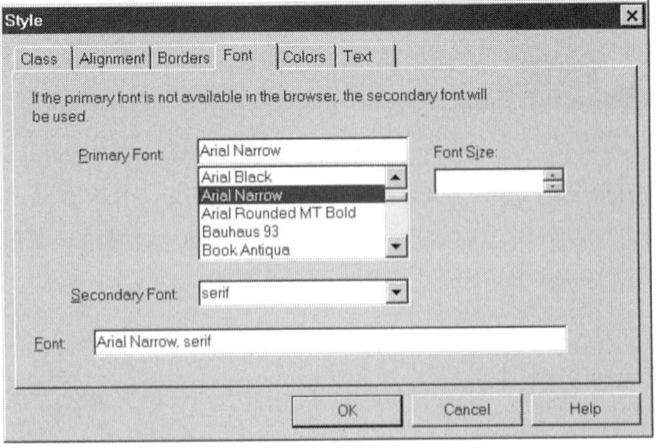

FIGURE 11.6.
Font faces are defined in the Font tab of the Style dialog.

Two fonts really aren't a lot when you are trying to achieve perfection. You can specify additional fonts to use simply by entering them after the primary and secondary font. Be sure to separate each font name with a comma. To learn the value you must use for a particular font, select it in the Primary Font or Secondary font field and write down the value FrontPage 98 uses.

When you use multiple fonts, the browser will attempt to use each font face in turn until it finds one that can be used to display your text. If none of the specified font faces is available, the default font is used. You can specify multiple font types using the Font field as follows:

Arial Narrow, Lucida Handwriting, Times New Roman, serif

CREATING TEXT APPEAL

The fonts you use define the way text looks in your documents. Fonts have many different characteristics and are classified in three key ways: by family, proportionally as monospace or proportional, and stylistically as serif or sans-serif.

Normal, bold, and italic type form a basic font family. A font family is simply a group of related fonts. Some font families include combinations, such as bold italic type. These different font types add emphasis and carry meanings.

Most typewriters use *monospace* type. In monospace type, each alphabetic or numeric character takes up the same space. A monospaced "l" takes as much space as a monospaced "w." Monospace type is easy to read and great for tired eyes. Another kind of type is *proportional* type. With proportional type, each alphabetic or numeric character takes up only the space it needs. Today, most fonts are proportional. Using proportional type, you can add visual variety to your text.

Serifs are the stylistic flourishes, like cross strokes or curves, added to the end of the strokes in a character. *Sans* is a French word that means without. Thus, *sans-serif* fonts do not have stylistic flourishes. Serif fonts are the primary fonts used in books, magazines, and newspapers because they are easier to read. For a classical or traditional look, you should use serif fonts. Sans-serif fonts have a more contemporary look and are often used for book or magazine titles, captions, and headings. You may want to use a sans-serif font for headings and a serif font for normal text. Traditional belief is that readers have an easier time reading large passages of text using serif fonts, while headings are more effective using sans-serif fonts.

Unfortunately, font faces are not universal across platforms. If you want to ensure your text has a certain style, you should use a general font style. Here are some examples of general font styles with examples of a font that may be used by the user's system:

serif	A generic font family with stylish flourishes, such as Times Roman
sans-serif	A generic font family without stylish flourishes, such as Helvetica
cursive	A font that looks handwritten, such as Lucida Handwriting
ransom	A contemporary font family, such as Western or Fantasy
monospace	A non-proportional font family, such as Courier

An example using the various font families is shown in Figure 11.7.

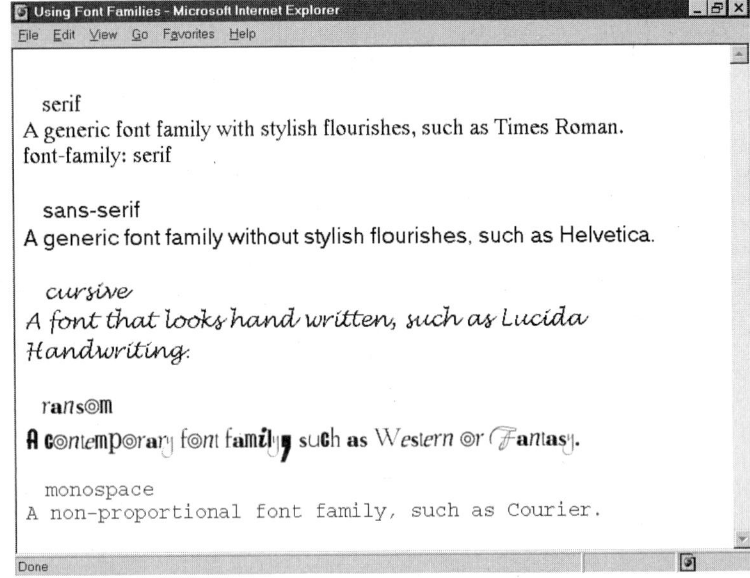

FIGURE 11.7.
Using font families in your page.

Using Font Sizes

Fonts come in many sizes. The larger the type size, the larger the type. Font size is specified in units called *points.* A point is a printing unit that equals approximately 1/72 inch. However, the true size of the font really depends on how the font was designed. Words in 10-point type using one font may not be the same as words in 10-point type in another font. This ambiguity in font sizes is something that goes back to the earliest days of printing, when printers designed their own type and different systems of point sizes were in use in different countries.

The most common point size for material designed to be read on a computer is 12 points. This is a good size for the main textual portions of the publication. Other common sizes range from 9 to 12 for the main text. Two rules of thumb for font size are

Do not make the type size so small that the reader has to squint to read.

Do not make the type size so large that the reader feels he has to sit across the room from the screen.

Instead of relying on the user's browser to change the size of text relative to other text, you can specify a specific point size for the text. To do this, you will use the Font Size field in the Font tab. An example using font size is shown in Figure 11.8.

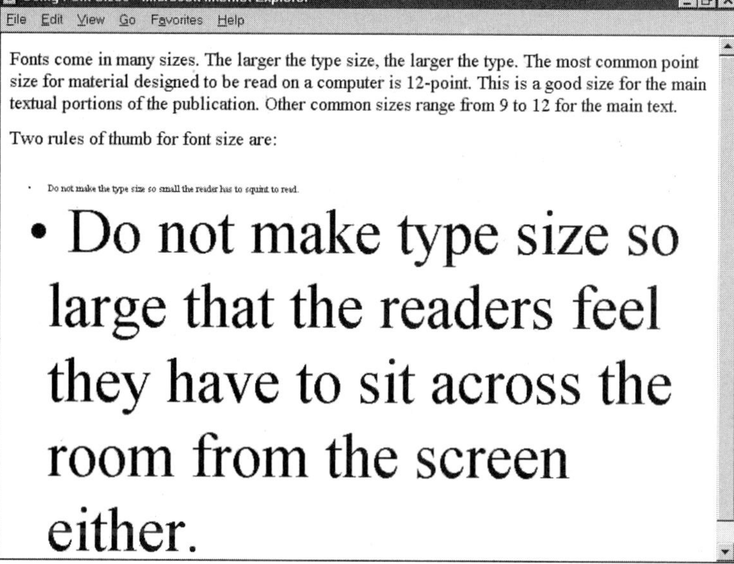

FIGURE 11.8.
Sizing your text just the way you want it.

Summary

Style sheets enable you to customize your Web pages and control just about every aspect of the layout and design of your page. When you use style sheets, you need to remember that only the most advanced browsers support these extended features. With this in mind, you should design a great page first and then design style sheet extras for advanced browsers.

12

Advanced Page Layout with Style Sheets

by William Robert Stanek

IN THIS CHAPTER

- Showing Your True Colors with Styles *204*
- Cool Spacing Techniques with Style Sheets *208*

The previous chapter just scratched the surface on how to use style sheets. Working with font styles and faces is only one area where style sheets offer terrific alternatives. Now look at how you can use style sheets to do advanced page layout and design. I'll start the discussion with a look at designing with color. Afterward, I'll cover spacing techniques you can use to layout your page.

Showing Your True Colors with Styles

You can easily add splashes of vivid color to your pages using style sheets. Color can be added to text, backgrounds, and images used in your pages.

Using Colorful Backgrounds and Text

When you want to work with color you will rely on the Colors tab of the Style dialog box to help you get the job done (See Figure 12.1). The two primary drop-down boxes you will use to add color to your pages are the Foreground Color drop-down box and the Background Color drop-down box. The Foreground Color field is used to set the color of text, and the Background Color field sets the background color the text is displayed against.

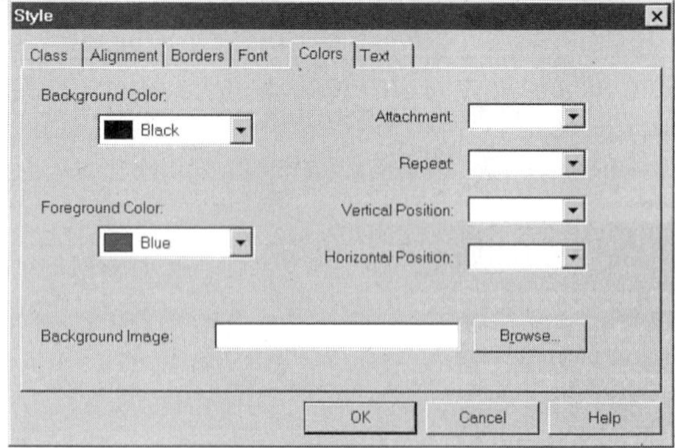

FIGURE 12.1.
Working with the Colors tab.

With the wide range of colors available, there are bound to be conflicts. This is especially true when you use color combinations with text and backgrounds. For example, lightly colored text against a white background is almost always a poor combination.

TIP

Increasingly, Web pages are printed, for future reference or to allow the user to read the page in her free time. For this reason, you might want to consider the readability of your page when printed. Many color combinations work on screen, but don't print well.

In the example shown in Figure 12.2, the screen displays black text against a yellow background. In print it is difficult to read the colorful text used in this example; however, the page works better on screen. This is a good example of contrast problems that might occur only on printed Web pages. If you were concerned about readability in print, you would need to select different colors.

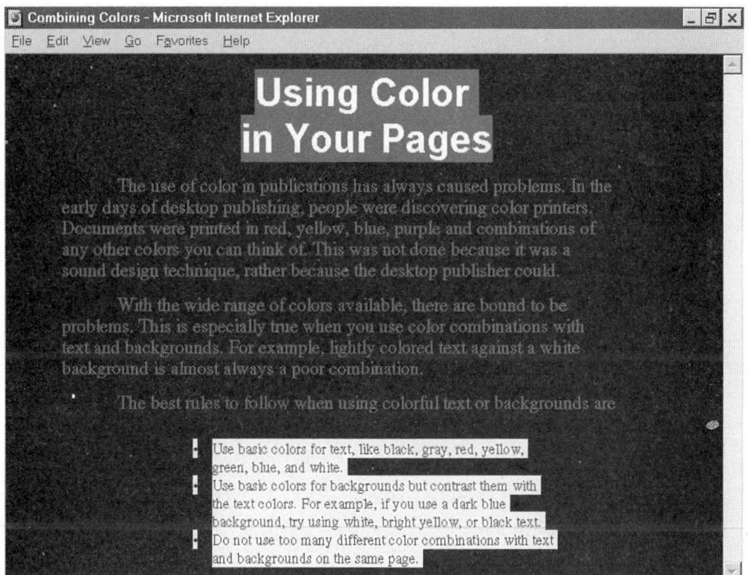

FIGURE 12.2.
Color combinations that work on screen might be difficult to read in print.

Using Images in Backgrounds

In addition to using colors with backgrounds, you can also specify an image to display in the background. Although, in theory, you can add a background image to any text element, most browsers only allow you to add the image to the body of the page. To specify the background image using style sheets, right click. Then select Page Properties from the pop-up menu. Afterward, click the Style button in the Page Properties dialog box. If you are designing for an advanced browser that allows you to add background images to text elements, you can define the image using the Background Image drop-down box of the Colors tab.

By default, background images are tiled to fill the current element and are overlaid on top of any specified background color. This allows you to combine a background color and a floating image in the background. To avoid a conflict, assign the background image in the Style dialog box for the page and the background color in the Page Properties dialog box.

As you might expect, the style sheet specification allows you to precisely define how and where a background image will be displayed. To control the tiling of the image, you can use the Repeat drop-down box with the following settings:

repeat	Repeats the image both horizontally and vertically in the background
repeat-x	Repeats the image along the x axis (horizontally) in the background
repeat-y	Repeats the image along the y axis (vertically) in the background
no-repeat	Does not repeat the image in the background; instead, displays it on the window only one time

With the Attachment drop-down box, you can specify that the image scrolls in the background, which is the current default for background images. To make the image fixed on the page, use the fixed value from the same drop-down box. Fixed images are similar to the watermarks supported by Internet Explorer. As you might recall, watermarks remain in the background even when you scroll the page. If you've never used watermarks, this is definitely a design technique to perfect, especially when you consider that a relative few Web publishers have discovered and implemented this feature.

The most powerful feature offered for background images is precise positioning using keywords. When you use keywords, you tell the browser a preset location to use for placing background images. You position background images using the Vertical and Horizontal Position drop-down boxes. The Vertical Position drop-down boxes settings are as follows:

top	The vertical position of the image starts on the top of the element's window.
center	The vertical position of the image starts in the middle of the element's window.
bottom	The vertical position of the image starts at the bottom of the element's window.

The Horizontal position field's settings are as follows:

left	The horizontal position of the image starts on the left side of the element's window.
center	The horizontal position of the image starts in the middle of the element's window.
right	The horizontal position of the image starts on the right side of the element's window.

By combining Repeat and Attachment values with various Horizontal and Vertical Positions, you can create some neat design effects that deviate from the traditional stale background images. Table 12.1 shows some interesting combinations that you might want to try.

Table 12.1. Creative combinations for tiling background images.

Repeat Value	*Vertical Position*	*Horizontal Position*	*Attachment*	*Description*
repeat-x	center	left	fixed	Leaves the first half of the window empty and then repeat the image only on the X axis.
no-repeat	center	center	fixed	Centers a single non-scrolling background image on the page.
repeat-y	top	right	scrolling	Creates vertical tiling in the right margin. This is a popular design technique for backgrounds when combined with left-aligned text, tables, and images for a powerful effect.
repeat-y	top	left	scrolling	Creates vertical tiling in the left margin. This is also a popular design technique when combined with offset text, images, or tables for a powerful effect.
repeat-x	bottom	left	fixed	Adds a fixed background image to the bottom of the browser window.

Aside from choosing relative positions (left, right, and center) Figure 12.3 shows the second choice for creating combinations. The image is tiled along the y axis using the value repeat-y and placed precisely on the page with vertical positioning. To ensure the paragraph text is not displayed on top of the image, the left margin is indented.

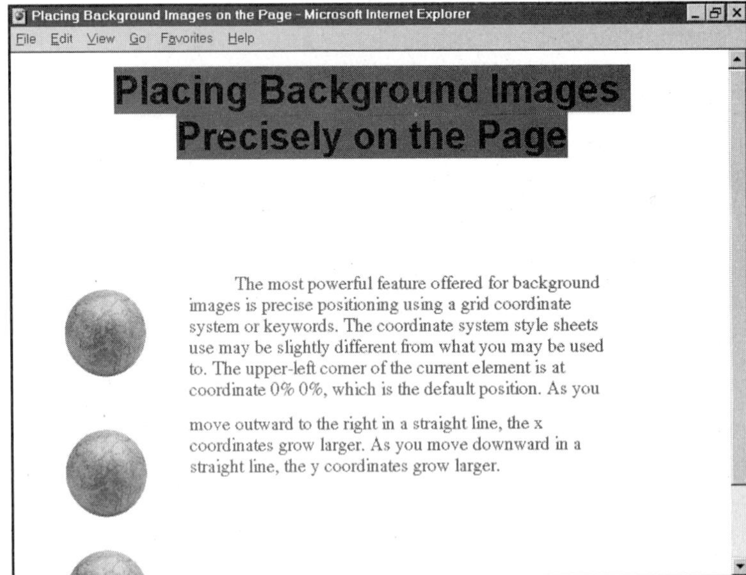

FIGURE 12.3.
Precisely placing background images on the page.

Cool Spacing Techniques with Style Sheets

I like to use spacing techniques to add flair to the page. This section shows how you can use the same spacing techniques in your pages to control the margins size, line spacing, word and letter spacing, and more.

Getting the Most out of Margins

Sometimes it isn't what you have on-screen that conveys your message, but what you don't have on-screen. Empty space on the screen makes the material easier to read by drawing the reader's attention to the area of the screen that does contain material. The separation of material creates emphasis and compels the reader to pay attention to the central text or images.

Using space effectively is not a new idea. In traditional publications, graphic designers carefully balance the amount of empty space on the page in order to emphasize material. They do this by using wide margins whenever possible. Open your favorite text book and you will probably find that the top margin is smaller than the bottom margin. Next compare the margins on two opposing pages. You might find that on the left-hand page the left margin is wide and the right margin near the binding is narrow. On the right-hand page the left margin near the binding is narrow and the right margin is wide. Print publications are usually designed this way to make them more visually appealing.

Some of the ways you can use screen space to enhance your Web pages include the following:

Creating offset text columns with tables.

Using a wide left margin and a narrow right margin.

Indenting the first line of every paragraph.

You can vary these techniques to fit your publication needs. If you want off-center text to the left, do so—or use a wide right margin and a narrow left margin.

A page that is entirely graphical can also benefit from spacing techniques. If text is secondary to an image on the page, the center piece of the page should be the image. Then, you can design the page to enhance the value of the image. The key is to use space in a way that enhances the design and draws attention to what you want to emphasize.

These and many more spacing techniques can be achieved with style sheets, and you can add spacing techniques to elements on your page using the Alignment tab of the Style dialog box (see Figure 12.4). To adjust the width of the margins, you will use the text boxes in the Margins area of the Alignment tab. These text boxes include the following:

Left	Sets the size of the element's left margin in pixels
Right	Sets the size of the element's right margin in pixels
Top	Sets the size of the element's top margin in pixels
Bottom	Sets the size of the element's bottom margin in pixels

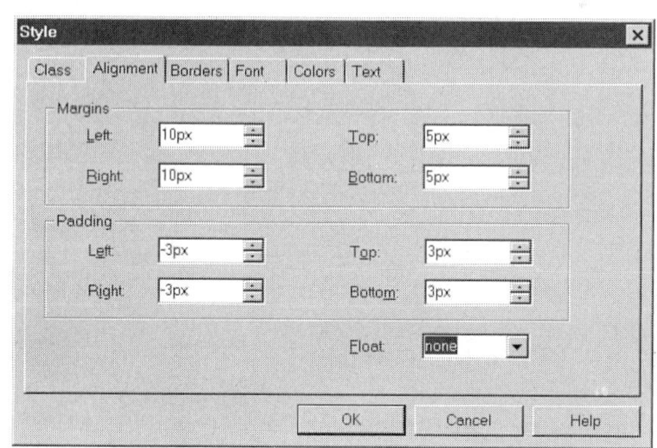

FIGURE 12.4.
Use the text boxes of the Alignment tab to set margins. You can opt to use the spin wheel controls beside each text box to set a value.

You can create powerful spacing effects by changing the margins within the body of your page. One way to do this is to alternate the margin widths of various paragraphs of text (see Figure 12.5). On the page in Figure 12.5, the first and third paragraph have a wide right margin and the second paragraph has a wide left margin.

To achieve this affect, the following margin values were used for the first paragraph:

Left	25 pixels
Right	200 pixels

The following margin values were used for the second paragraph:

Left	200 pixels
Right	25 pixels

Also note some of the other style enhancements to the page. The font for paragraph text is set to Arial. The font for headings is set to Helvetica and is placed on a yellow background.

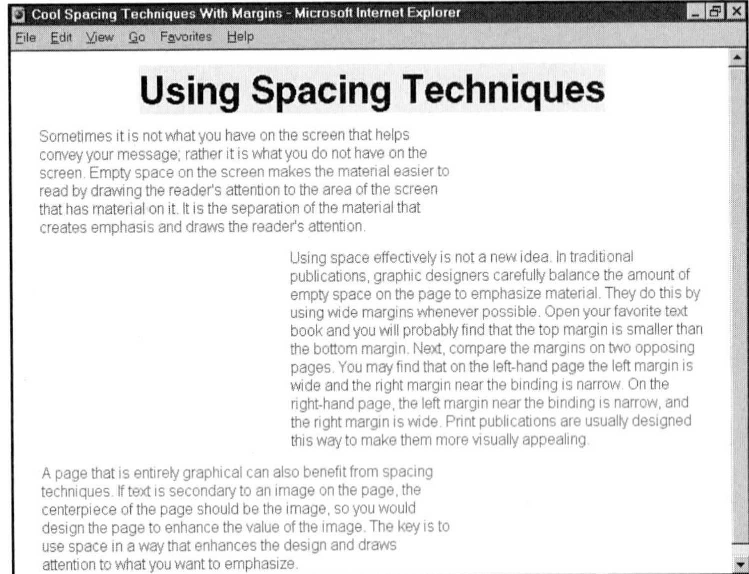

Figure 12.5.
Cool spacing techniques using margins.

HOW GRAPHIC DESIGNERS USE GRIDS

By adjusting margins for text and graphical elements, you can create grids. The grid system is a way of designing pages that can help you create a uniform and symmetrical look to the published page. Graphic designers have used the grid system to design pages for many years. Using the grid system, you break the page into columns. Text, graphics, and other objects on the page are lined up within the columns.

A simple page could be broken into three grid columns. Complex pages could be divided into 10 or more grid columns. The number of imaginary grid columns depends on the type and number of objects you are placing on the page.

For example, a newsletter could be divided into three grid columns. Header and title information could go across the whole top of the page, meaning this text would be in all three grids. Pictures could be aligned in the first or leftmost grid. Text could be placed in columns two and three.

Although the grid system is used primarily in print publications, it also makes sense to use the grid system in electronic publications. Your publication should not look like an angry mess on the reader's computer screen. The pages of your publication should be pleasing to look at. Using the grid system helps you add symmetry to your pages.

Using Borders and Padding

Borders provide another way to enhance your page with a popular spacing technique. To set border style, size, and color, you will use the Borders tab of the Style dialog box (see Figure 12.6). As you can see from the figure, there is a set of related drop-down boxes and text boxes that allows you to set individual aspects of the border around an element.

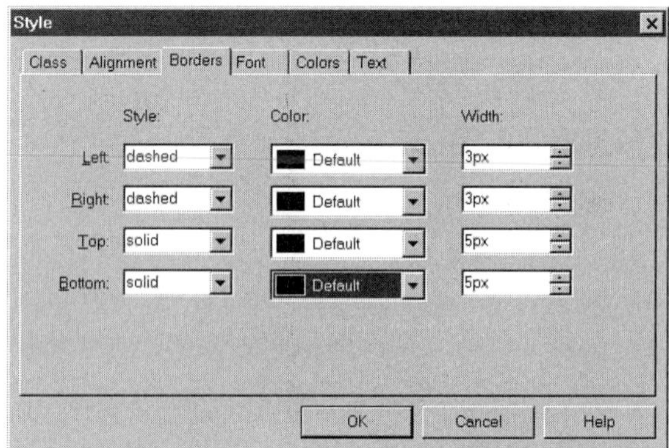

FIGURE 12.6.
You can add borders to any element in your page using the Borders tab.

To add a unique style to the border, you can use any of the following values for the Style pull-down menus:

none	Draws no border
dashed	Draws the border as a dashed line
dotted	Draws the border as a dotted line
solid	Draws the border as a solid line
double	Draws the border as a double line
groove	Draws the border as a 3D line
ridge	Draws the border as a raised 3D line
inset	Draws the border as an inset 3D line
outset	Draws the border as an outset 3D line

You can add color to the border simply by selecting a color value in the Color pull-down menu. Think carefully before you change this to a value other than the default. Most browsers use a border color that is based on the color of the background. If you change this default color for the current element, will the border color clash with the colors you have chosen for backgrounds, images, and text?

You set the width of the border in pixels, and you might find that a thick top and bottom border works well with a thin left and right border. Try various combinations of border style and width until you achieve the effect you are looking for.

To increase the spacing between borders and content, you can use the text boxes in the Padding area of the Alignment tab. Like other spacing text boxes, there is a set of related fields for padding the left, right, top, and bottom areas of the content. Generally, the best way to set the padding is to use the same value for all the text boxes.

Another way to give your pages a unique look is to adjust the spacing between letters. You can adjust the spacing between letters to give a monospace look to a proportional font face or to create long banner-like headings. To adjust the spacing between letters, you use the Letter Spacing text box of the Text tab.

Playing with the Text

Style sheets create entirely new ways to enhance your pages. Some of the best style sheet controls are those that let you play with the text on the page. As you set off to use style sheets, don't be afraid to experiment.

One of my favorite ways to jazz up the text on the page is to create tip and note boxes. By adding background colors to offset text, you can create a shaded box like those used with notes, tips, cautions, and warnings. The following is one way you could set up a neat note box for a page with a white background:

Create your note text.

Open the Style dialog box and click the Colors tab.

Set the Background Color drop-down box to Silver, and set the Foreground Color drop-down box to Blue.

Click the Margins tab.

Set the left margin to 200 pixels, and set the right margin to 20 pixels.

Click the Font tab.

Set the primary font to Lucida Handwriting, and set the secondary font to cursive.

A sample page using these techniques is shown in Figure 12.7. After you take a look at this example, head off and have some fun with style sheets.

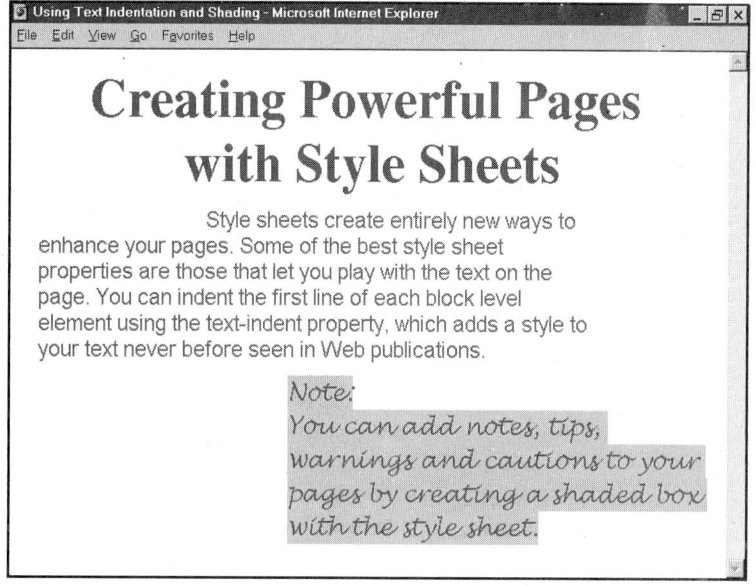

FIGURE 12.7.
Using indentation and shading to jazz up your page.

Summary

With style sheets, decorating your page with fancy styles has never been easier. Finally, you can use any font face, type, size, or color you want. You can easily add color to text, backgrounds, and images used in your pages. You can even boost the impact of your pages with cool spacing techniques.

Working with Active Elements: Banners, Hit Counters, and More

by William Robert Stanek

IN THIS CHAPTER

- Tracking Hits *216*
- Using Scrolling Marquees *218*
- Using Netscape Plug-Ins and Embedded Multimedia Objects *221*
- Working with Hover Buttons *225*
- Managing Your Banner Ads *227*

If something about Web publishing could make you stand up and cheer, it would be the active elements that are now a part of FrontPage 98. With the introduction of these drop-and-go elements, CGI scripts for small and medium-sized publishers may be relics of the past. After all, why would you want to pull your hair out trying to install and configure scripts when you can just drop the functionality you need into your page and go on with life?

The active elements you will learn how to use in this chapter include: hit counters, scrolling marquees, hover buttons, and rotating banners. If you've never worked with these elements before, don't worry; everything you need to get started is explored right here. Because plug-ins are another form of active element, I've also added a section on using Netscape plug-ins.

Tracking Hits

One of the most popular ways to track activity on the Web is with a hit counter. Hit counters are used to silently track how many times a particular page has been accessed. When you think about it, the term hit counter is a bit of a misnomer. You aren't really tracking hits; you are tracking page views—how many times a page has been viewed or accessed. To extend this point, imagine a visitor that arrives at your Web site and decides to refresh the page (for whatever reason) 10 times. Your hit counter will increment once each refresh, not truly reflecting the number of visitors.

Tips for Placing the Hit Counter on the Page

Before you add a hit counter, you should consider where and how to place the counter on your page. Most counters are placed at the bottom of the page, just before any copyright or contact information. Placing the counter at the bottom of the page ensures that the counter will be seen, but won't be a prominent part of the page. On the other hand, if you want to tout your site's statistics, you might want to place the hit counter at the top of the page, just after your header and banner information.

Usually, you will want to center the counter on the page, which makes the counter stand out. Because the counter displays only a numeric value, such as 1500 or 001500, you probably want to add descriptive text before or after the counter as well. Here are some examples of text you may want to use with a hit counter:

Total Hits

Hits Since `[insert a date here]`

Total Page Views

This page has been accessed `[insert hit counter]` times.

Setting Up the Counter

Adding a hit counter to your page is easy. To get started, open the Hit Counter Properties dialog by selecting Insert|Active Elements|Hit Counter. As shown in Figure 13.1, you can now set the parameters for the counter.

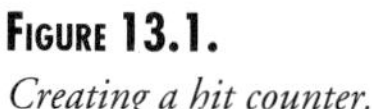

FIGURE 13.1.
Creating a hit counter.

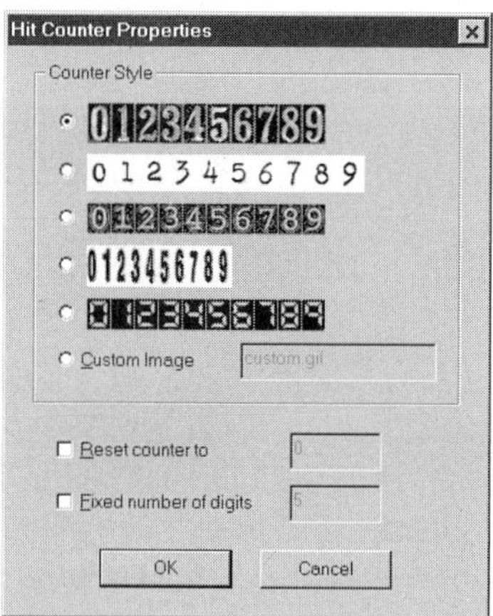

The first step is to select a style for your counter. FrontPage 98 provides several different styles for the counter. Choose a style that fits your personal tastes and your Web page. Some of the styles have a black background and other styles have a white background. If you want to make the counter blend in well, use colored styles and backgrounds that match your page. For example, a counter style with a black background blends well on a page with a black background but stands out clearly on a page with a white background.

If you want to go with the default values, you need do nothing more. Simply click the OK button, and FrontPage 98 will insert a reference to your hit counter in the page. The reference looks like this:

```
[Hit Counter]
```

By default, the value of the counter is set to zero and is displayed as a single digit. So the first time you visit the page, the counter will read 1. Whenever you want to change the settings for the counter, all you need to do is load the page in the FrontPage Editor and double-click the counter reference.

Overriding the default values is easy. If you don't want to go with the default counter settings, you can set the counter to a specific value. Select the Reset counter to check box, then enter a value in the associated input field. You can set or reset the value of the counter at any time. To set the counter to display 25000 hits the first time the page is accessed, you would set the reset field to 24999.

Often, you will want the counter to display with a fixed number of digits, which can make the counter stand out more. Instead of reading 100 hits, your counter could read 00100 hits—sort of like an odometer in a car. To set the counter to a fixed number of digits, select the Fixed number of digits check box and enter the number of digits in the associated input field. Usually, you will want to display at least five digits.

Using Scrolling Marquees

Scrolling marquees are moving banners that scroll across the screen. Using this feature of Internet Explorer (marquees do not appear in Netscape Navigator or Communicator), you can provide readers with real-time information such as stock reports, sports scores, and late-breaking news. You can also animate advertisements and any other type of information you want to provide at the site.

Marquees are animated billboards in cyberspace. Although marquees can be located anywhere within the body of your HTML document, the key to using marquees is to position them smartly in an area where they are not a distraction. The best locations for scrolling marquees are in the top or bottom portion of a document. In this way, the marquee is seen either immediately or when the user is nearly finished reading the page.

The development team at Microsoft did a great job of ensuring scrolling marquees aren't as distracting as blinking text. To do this, they provided a number of controls over how a marquee is animated, sized, and positioned. More importantly, you can control when a marquee ceases to scroll.

To add a basic marquee to your page, select Insert|Active Elements|Marquee. This opens the Marquee Properties dialog box shown in Figure 13.2. In the Text field, enter the message to scroll and click the OK button. FrontPage 98 inserts the marquee following the defaults for positioning and behavior.

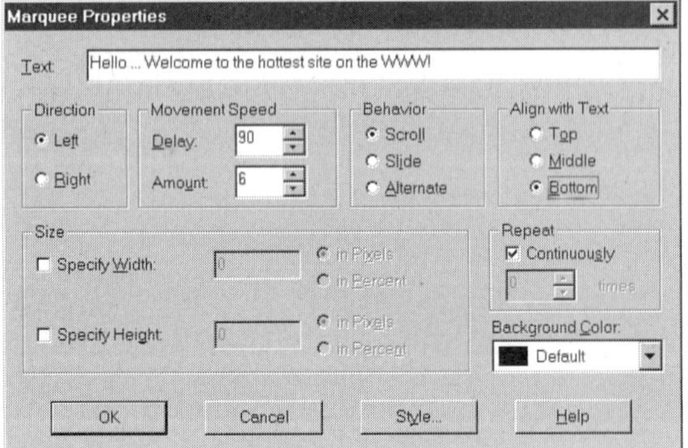

FIGURE 13.2.
Creating a scrolling marquee.

Positioning a Marquee

Think of a marquee as an object on the page whose position can be fine-tuned. The outline of the marquee in the FrontPage Editor is highlighted with a dashed line. Click the marquee once to manipulate the marquee in your page. On both ends and in the middle of a selected marquee are resizing points. If you move the pointer to a resizing point and click and hold the left mouse button, you can resize the marquee by dragging the pointer. If you move the pointer to a different area of the marquee and click and hold the left mouse button, you can drag the marquee to a new location on the page.

Using the Align with Text field of the Marquee Properties dialog box, you can specify how text around the marquee is aligned. Three values for this field enable you to align text around the marquee with the top, middle, or bottom of the marquee. When the marquee does not fill the width of the browser's window, you'll find these values very useful.

Sizing and Coloring a Marquee

Unless otherwise specified, marquees occupy only a minimum amount of screen space. You can reserve a larger area for the marquee using the Specify Width and Specify Height fields of the Marquee Properties dialog box. You can specify the width of a marquee as an absolute value in pixels or as a relative percentage of screen width. Similarly, the height of a marquee can be specified as an absolute value in pixels or as a relative percentage of screen height.

Usually, you want your marquee to run along the full length of the window. This makes the marquee easier to read and follow. The marquee defined in Figure 13.3 occupies 25% of the screen height and 100% of the width.

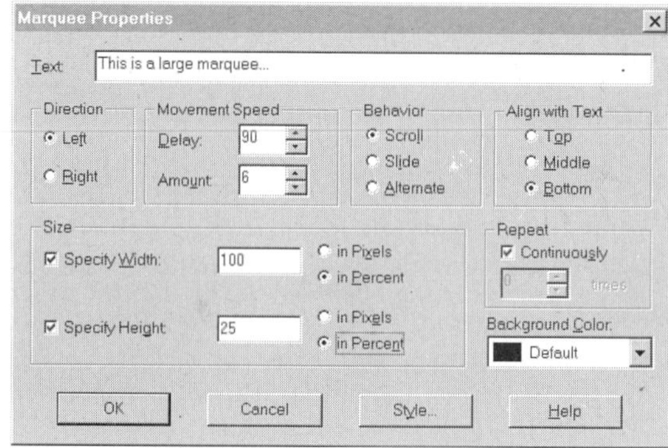

FIGURE 13.3.
Adjusting the width and height of a marquee.

Setting the marquee text off from other text on the page is often important. To clearly differentiate between the area reserved for the marquee and other text, you can use the Background Color property. As with other color properties, a pull-down list lets you access predefined colors.

Make sure that your scrolling message is readable against the background color you choose. If it is not, you might want to change the color for text on the page or change the background color of the marquee.

Animating a Marquee

You can control the way marquees move across the screen. Usually, marquees scroll in from the right, move all the way across the screen, and go completely off. You can use four key areas to alter the movement of the marquee: Behavior, Direction, Repeat, and Movement Speed.

The Behavior area helps you animate the marquee in unique ways. Scroll is the default behavior. A sliding marquee starts completely off one side of the screen, scrolls all the way into position, and then stops. An alternate marquee starts completely off one side of the screen, scrolls in until it touches the far margin, and then moves back and forth within the area reserved for the marquee.

Using the Direction radio button set, you can change the direction the marquee scrolls. By default, marquees scroll from left to right. If you select Right, the marquee scrolls from right to left.

By default, marquees continuously scroll across the screen. If you deselect the Continuously value of the Repeat field, you can define how many times a marquee repeats. Setting the repeat field to a finite value helps to ensure that your scrolling message isn't distracting.

Two properties control how fast a marquee moves across the screen. Use the Amount text box to specify the number of pixels the marquee moves each time it is drawn on the screen. Use the Delay text box to specify the wait in milliseconds between each successive redraw. Figure 13.4 shows the properties for a slow-moving marquee, and Figure 13.5 shows the properties for a fast-moving marquee.

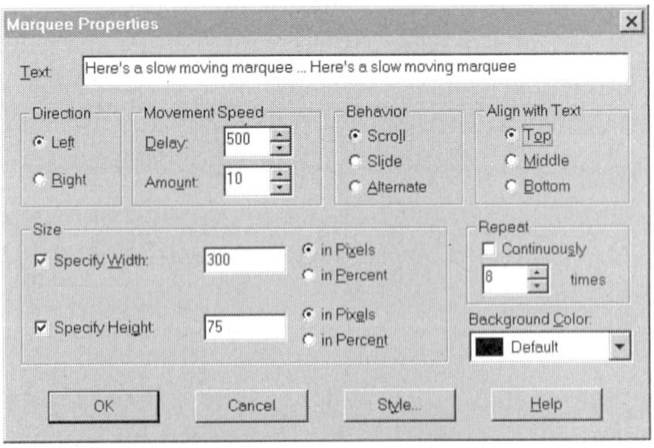

FIGURE 13.4.
A slow-moving marquee.

Marquee Properties

Text: Here's a slow moving marquee ... Here's a slow moving marquee

Direction: (•) Left ( ) Right

Movement Speed: Delay: 500 Amount: 10

Behavior: (•) Scroll ( ) Slide ( ) Alternate

Align with Text: (•) Top ( ) Middle ( ) Bottom

Size: [x] Specify Width: 300 (•) in Pixels ( ) in Percent; [x] Specify Height: 75 (•) in Pixels ( ) in Percent

Repeat: [ ] Continuously 8 times

Background Color: Default

OK Cancel Style... Help

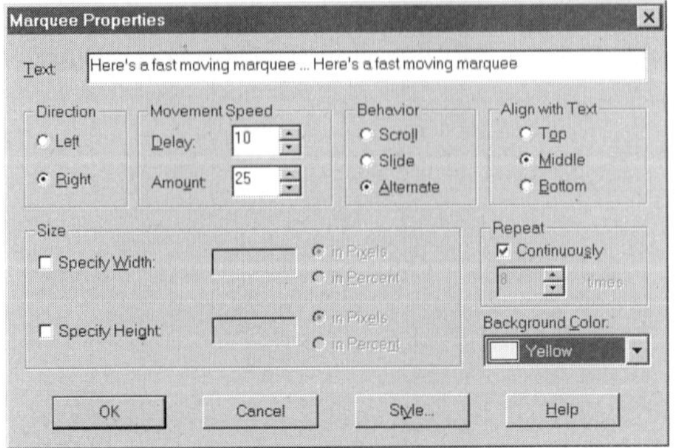

FIGURE 13.5.
A fast-moving marquee.

Using Netscape Plug-Ins and Embedded Multimedia Objects

Netscape *plug-ins* extend the capabilities of the browser and provide native support for new data types. Plug-ins are player or reader modules for software applications that are created specifically for use with the Netscape Navigator. Because Internet Explorer features a plug-in compatibility mode, most plug-ins will work in Internet Explorer as well. Check with the vendor and make sure you are using the right version of the plug-in.

Most plug-ins are designed to be used on a specific platform, such as Windows 95 or Macintosh. However, some plug-ins, such as those programmed in Java, can be platform-independent. You can find Netscape plug-ins for Macromedia Director, Apple QuickTime movies, Adobe Acrobat PDF documents, Microsoft Video for Windows, and Java. Although plug-ins are created primarily by third-party vendors, they provide features which, when merged with the baseline features, are indistinguishable to the user. This means the end user can use a plug-in without worrying about why or how the plug-in is activated and what happens when the plug-in is activated.

The way you incorporate files for use with plug-ins is by selecting the Advanced submenu and then selecting the Plug-In menu item. You find Advanced as an option on the Insert menu of the FrontPage Editor.

The Plug-In Properties dialog box is shown in Figure 13.6. Most of the plug-in properties are set to acceptable default values automatically. The key fields you want to fill in are Data Source and Message for Browsers without Plug-in support. You use the Data Source field to enter the URL path to the data file you want to use. The message for browsers without plug-in support is displayed whenever a browser cannot run Netscape plug-ins.

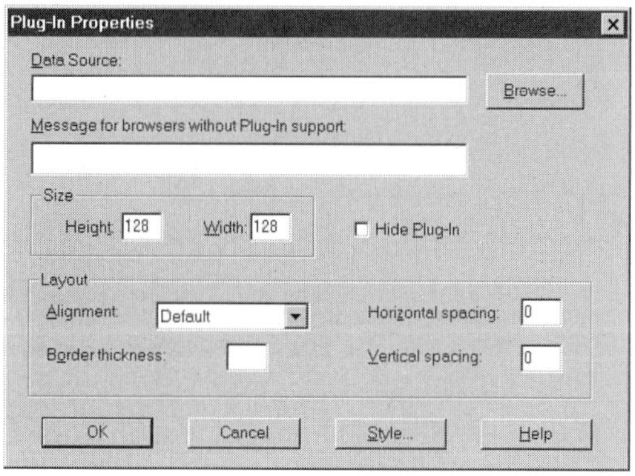

FIGURE 13.6.
Setting properties for plug-ins.

Netscape designed plug-ins with three things in mind:

- Plug-ins should be seamless for users.
- Plug-ins should be fully functional across platforms.
- Plug-ins should offer plug-in writers maximum flexibility.

Seamless Incorporation

Plug-ins are seamless because they are configured like built-in helper applications. If the plug-in is available, it is used without opening a separate window to display the output. The output of the plug-in is displayed in the current window. If a plug-in is not available, the browser looks in the helper application configuration table to find an application that can display the object in-line. The output of the helper application is also displayed in the current window.

This design concept enables you to embed any type of object into your Netscape-enhanced documents. For example, if your browser is configured to use Windows Paintbrush to display PCX-formatted images, the embedded element shown in Figure 13.7 starts Windows Paintbrush, builds the image called `TIGER`, and displays the image wherever and however you placed it in the current document.

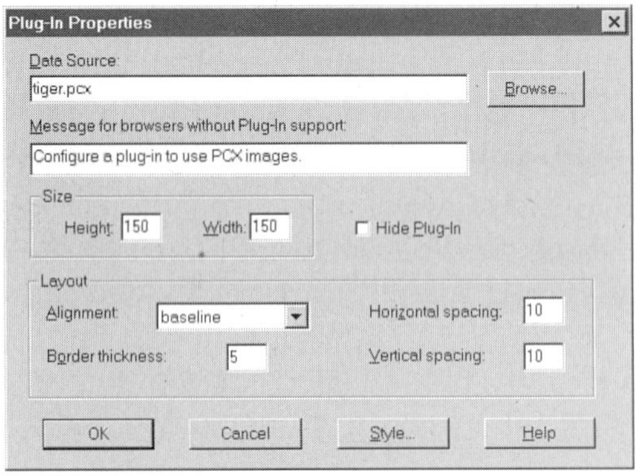

FIGURE 13.7.
Using a plug-in to display PCX images.

Full Functionality

The functionality of plug-ins is also important. The values you pass to plug-ins are platform-independent, meaning a property that is valid for a Windows 95 version of a plug-in should be valid for a Macintosh version of the plug-in. Regardless of platform, plug-ins can be used in one of three modes:

- Embedded
- Full-screen
- Hidden

In embedded mode, the output of the plug-in is placed in the current window. This means embedded objects are a part of a larger HTML document and can be used just like GIF and JPEG images. You can use embedded plug-ins with in-line video, animation, graphic objects, and anything else you want to display within the current window. A key concept with embedded plug-ins is that they can be highly interactive. For example, if the plug-in allows for it, you could use all the controls for dynamic sources and apply them to your embedded object.

You can use embedded objects like any other type of object on the page. To adjust the size of the embedded object, you use the Height and Width properties of the Size field. Figure 13.8 shows how you can embed a 100×100 image in BMP format. Keep in mind that as long as the user has a plug-in capable of handling images in BMP format, the plug-in executes and the image displays.

FIGURE 13.8.
Using a plug-in to display BMP images.

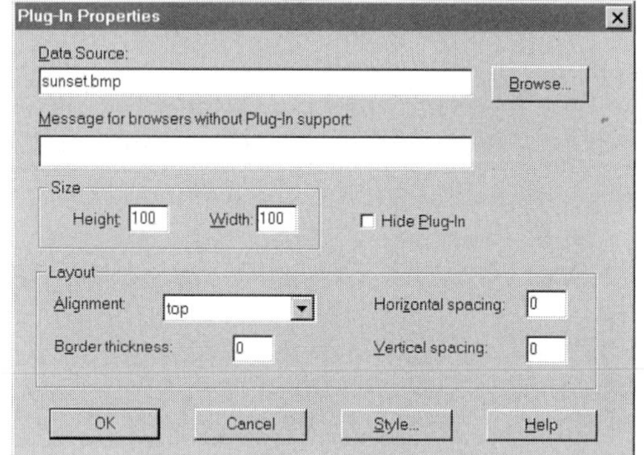

In full-screen mode, the output of the plug-in fills the browser's inner window but leaves the user controls in place. Therefore, users have full access to Netscape's pull-down menus, toolbar, directory buttons, and the URL window.

You do not need to enter special size properties for full-screen plug-ins. Full-screen plug-ins are sized automatically and can be used with any type of object, including video, animation, and graphic objects. The Adobe Acrobat plug-in uses the full-screen mode. Using the Acrobat plug-in, you can access PDF documents.

Figure 13.9 shows how you can use a PDF document as a data source. As long as the user has the Adobe Acrobat plug-in, the PDF document displays automatically.

In hidden mode, the output of the plug-in is not seen on the screen. You can use hidden plug-ins with any files that users do not have to see to experience, such as an audio file. You can also use hidden plug-ins to perform background functions, such as decrypting or decompressing files for display. If you want to use a hidden plug-in, select the Hide Plug-In field.

FIGURE 13.9.
Using a plug-in to display PDF documents.

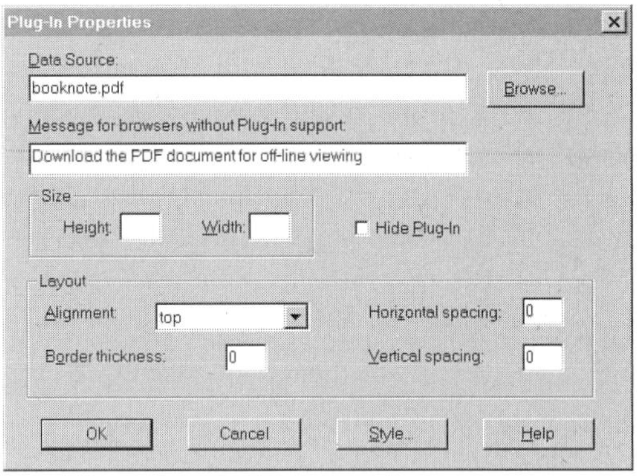

Maximum Flexibility

Using the properties in the Layout area, you can precisely place your plug-in. The Alignment property lets you specify how the plug-in is aligned with text on the same line or area of the page as the plug-in. In the pull-down list for the Alignment property, you see eleven alignment values including the default. Because these are the same alignment values used with images, you'll find a complete discussion of these values in Chapter 7, "Enhancing Your Pages with Images—The Easy Way."

The Border Thickness property determines the thickness of the border drawn around embedded objects that are linked to other resources. You specify border thickness in pixels. A value of 5 for this property indicates that the plug-in should have a 5-pixel wide border drawn around it if it is linked to another resource.

The spacing around your plug-in is also important. As with borders, you specify the amount of horizontal and vertical space in pixels. Horizontal spacing is the area above and below your plug-in. Vertical spacing is the area to the left and right of the plug-in.

When you add a plug-in to a page, the FrontPage Editor inserts an image that depicts a piece of a jigsaw puzzle. You can double-click this image to open the Plug-In Properties dialog box.

Click the plug-in icon once to manipulate the size and position of the plug-in. On both ends and in the middle of a selected plug-in are resizing points. If you move the pointer to a resizing point and click and hold the left mouse button, you can add vertical and horizontal spacing by dragging the pointer. If you move the pointer to a different area of the plug-in icon and click and hold the left mouse button, you can drag the plug-in to a new location on the page.

TIP

Many plug-ins have unique properties beyond these basic layout settings. You can specify values for unique properties directly in the HTML markup. After you add the plug-in to the page, click the HTML tab. Now you can edit the markup for the plug-in and add any attributes and values.

Working with Hover Buttons

Multimedia madness has reached a new height with hover buttons. Using a hover button, you can create a button that comes to life when the pointer hovers over it. These so-called hover buttons are complete with text labels, special effects, alternating images, and sounds that all depend on the state of the hover button. Because hover buttons can be linked to a specific page at your Web site, you will usually want to use a hover button as a menu option or navigation tool. To get started with hover buttons, open the Hover Button dialog by selecting Insert|Active Elements|Hover Button. You can now set the properties for the hover button.

Adding Stylish Text and Linking the Hover Button

Although the special effects and sounds for hover buttons are terrific extras, the most important aspect of a hover button is its text label. The text for the button should be a single descriptive word or a short phrase that tells where the button leads. You set the label text for the button using the Button text field.

After you set the button's label, you may want to select a specific font type, size, and color for the text label, so click the Font button to display the Font dialog shown in Figure 13.10. Because of the limitations in font types for button text, the Font pull-down list does not provide an extensive list of font faces for the button. Change the font style and size to suit your needs. Keep in mind that you may need to change the size of the button to accommodate the changes to the text label, or conversely, you may need to resize the label text to fit your button.

FIGURE 13.10.
Defining the font type, size, and color for the button's text label.

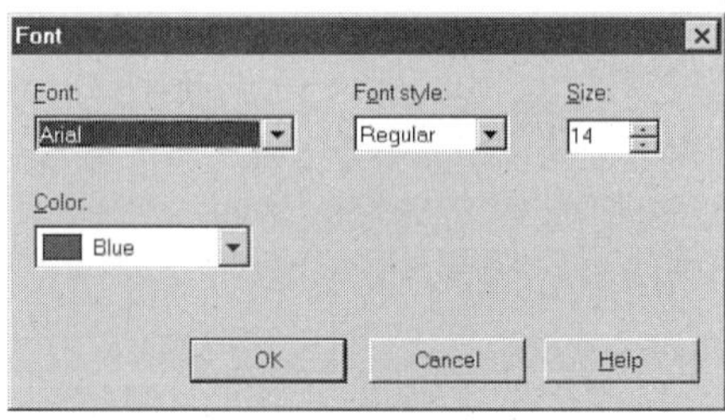

Next, you should specify the page or resource that is accessed when the button is clicked. Use the Browse button to help you find the URL you want to use. If the page or resource is not at your Web site, be sure to use a complete URL.

Coloring and Sizing the Button

After you add the text label to the button and the link, close the Hover Button dialog box and take the hover button for a test drive. For now, forget about the way the button looks and concentrate on how it fits on your page. Click the button once to select it. You should now see the resize points on the button. If you move the pointer to a resizing point and click and hold the left mouse button, you can resize the button by dragging the pointer. If you move the pointer to a different area of the button and click and hold the left mouse button, you can drag the button to a new location on the page.

As you are sizing the button, check the label text to see if the font size is correct. You may need to increase or decrease the font size of the button text. Or you may want to change the text so that it is shorter or longer as appropriate for your needs. Keep in mind that less text is usually better and that if you plan to add images to the button, you will need space for these images as well.

Once you have the button sized and positioned where you want it, double-click the button to open the Hover Button dialog. You can now fine-tune the size of the button using the Width and Height fields. If you plan to use a group of hover buttons to form a menu or navigation bar, use a specific size for each button. For buttons that are stacked vertically, you will usually want all buttons to have the same width. For buttons that are lined up horizontally, all buttons should have the same height.

Next, define the color of the button using the Button color field. If you want the button to have the same background color as the page, set the Background color field to Default. Otherwise, you can set the background to a specific color. Because there are so many colors involved here, be sure to put the colors to the Love/Hate test. View the page in your browser; if you love the colors, leave them alone. If you hate the colors or if they cause a color conflict, change them.

Adding Effects

Hover buttons are designed to come to life when you move the pointer over them. The animation of hover buttons is made possible with visual and lighting effects, such as color fill and glow. To add an effect, click the Effect pull-down list as shown in Figure 13.11 and select one of the available effects.

Each effect is tied to a specific color called the *effect color*. Generally, the button will move between the button color you have chosen and the effect color using the designated effect. To make the effect subtle, use an effect color that is close in hue to the button color, such as a blue button color and a navy blue effect color. To increase the emphasis of the effect yet ensure the hover isn't distracting, use an effect color and button color that are different but not at opposite ends of the color spectrum, such as yellow/red, yellow/green, or blue/green.

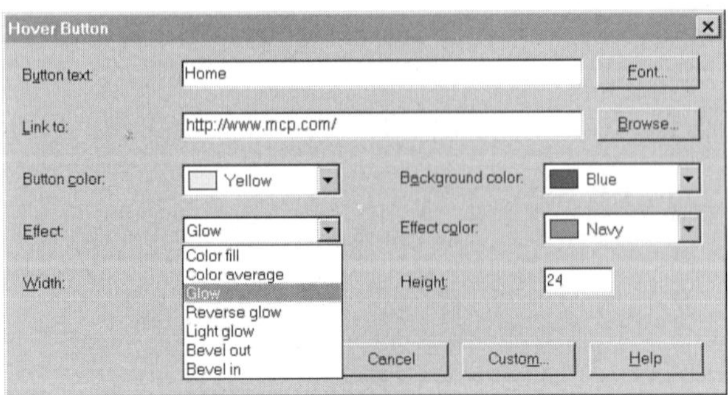

FIGURE 13.11.
Adding effects to the hover button.

Adding Sounds and Images

Your hover button can have sounds and images associated with it as well. To add these extras, open the dialog shown in Figure 13.12 by clicking the Custom button of the Hover Button dialog.

FIGURE 13.12.
Adding sounds and images to the hover button.

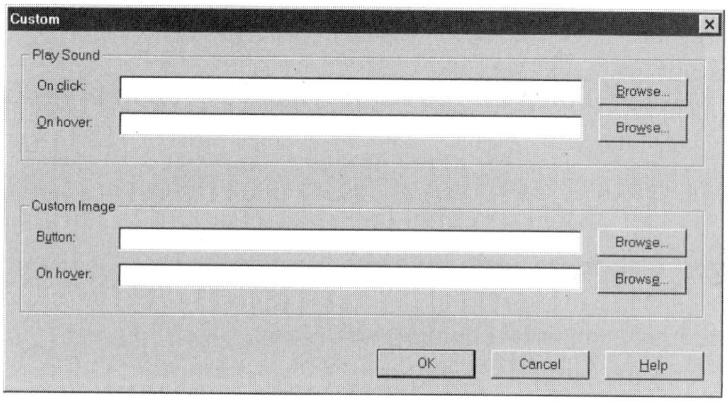

Sounds are used with hover buttons in one of two ways. The sound is played either when the button is clicked or when the pointer is over the button. Use the On click field to define a sound to play when the button is clicked and the On hover field to define a sound to play when the pointer is over the button. Enter the URL to a sound file or use the Browse button to help you find a sound file.

Sometimes you may want to use alternating images for a button instead of a visual effect. With images, the image is either displayed by default or when the pointer is over the button. Use the Button field to define a default image for the button and the On hover field to define a image to display when the pointer is over the button.

If you decide to combine alternating images with visual effects, test the page in several different browsers. I have found that sometimes the changing colors in the visual effects when combined with the multiple colors of a button's images can cause color conflicts. Be sure to test the button in the default state as well as with the pointer over the hover button.

Managing Your Banner Ads

A banner is an image that you use to advertise on the Web. With FrontPage 98's built-in support for banner ad management, working with banners has never been easier. Not only does FrontPage 98 allow you to easily add banners to any page, but it also helps you manage your banners effectively. To activate the Banner Ad Manager, select Insert|Active Elements|Banner Ad Manager in the FrontPage Editor.

Sizing and Placing Banners

Before you start working with banners, you should consider where you want to place banners on your page and how you will size the banner. Most banners are placed at the top of the page immediately after the header or title images for the page. Banners are sometimes placed at the bottom of the page as well.

Whenever you use top- or bottom-placed banners, you will probably want to size the banner so that it is a prominent element on the page. Popular sizes for top or bottom-placed banners are 440×50 and 400×50. These are the banner sizes used by most banner exchanges. Another popular size for this type of banner is 468×60, which is a size often used for paid banner advertising.

If you want to break with tradition and move away from the mainstream page design techniques, try placing banner ads in a column on the left or right side of the browser window. Here, you would use small banner ads, such as banners that are 220×50 or 200×50. If you place these banners in a fixed borderless frame, you can ensure the ads are always visible yet retain the flexibility for rotating and changing banners easily.

After you determine the size of your banner ads, you can set this size in the Width and Height fields of the Banner Ad Manager (see Figure 13.13). By sizing the banners within the Ad Manager, you ensure that all your banners are displayed at the same size regardless of their actual size. Because resizing images can sometimes distort them, you will probably want to size the images exactly anyway, but at least you don't have to worry about accidentally giving a banner the wrong size.

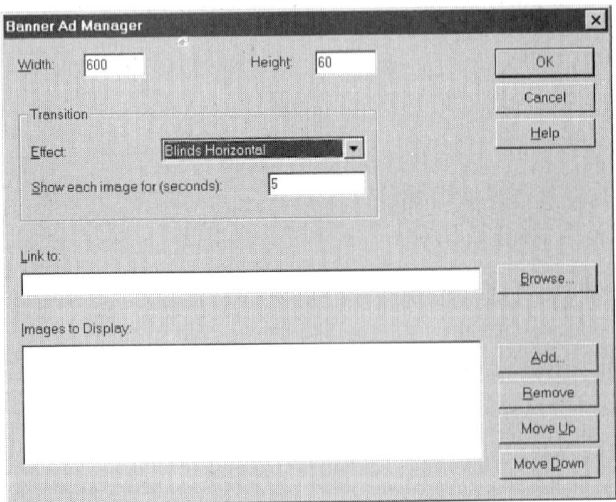

FIGURE 13.13.
Sizing your banners.

Adding Transitions to the Banner Ads

The next thing you should consider before you add banners to your page is whether and how you will want to rotate your banner ads. The Banner Ad Manager is best used to rotate banners frequently while the user is visiting your Web site. If you don't want FrontPage 98 to rotate banner ads automatically, you don't need the Banner Ad Manager. When you want to rotate banners on a scheduled basis, such as daily or weekly, you don't need the Banner Ad Manager either and will want to use the Scheduled Image FrontPage component instead.

Using the Ad Manager, you can define how often banners are rotated as well as a transition effect to use. You define the length of time to display each banner in seconds, and you can run into problems here. If you change banners too often, you run the risk of annoying users. So, you generally want to show each banner for a fairly long duration, say, 30 seconds or more. Remember, the user's browser has to download each image, which can slow the loading of other elements on the page.

The effects the Banner Ad Manager offers are great for making smooth and professional transitions between successive banners. Each transition effect has its own appeal, and the best way to see which transition you like is to try them out. That said, my personal favorites are Box In and Box Out.

Adding Images and Linking

Although the task of rotating the banners is completely automated, you need to tell the Banner Ad Manager which banners to use. You do this using the Images to Display area of the Banner Ad Manager dialog. Use the Add button to add an image to the rotation list. Use the Move Up and Move Down buttons to manipulate the order of the images. If you need to remove a banner from the rotation, highlight it and click the Remove button.

Before you dive in, keep in mind that banners are displayed in the order listed. In the example shown in Figure 13.14, three banners are set to display. These images will be displayed in the following order: `banner1.gif`, `banner2.gif`, then `banner3.gif`. Because the Ad Manager will continuously loop through the banners, you do not need to enter a specific banner more than once.

TIP

If you give banners a number suffix as shown in the example, you will have an easier time keeping track of the order of the banners.

Now that you've got your banners all dressed up and nowhere to go, you should define a link for the banners. This link will be used whenever one of the banners is clicked. Unfortunately, the Banner Ad Manager does not let you give each banner its own link, so for now, you are stuck with a single link.

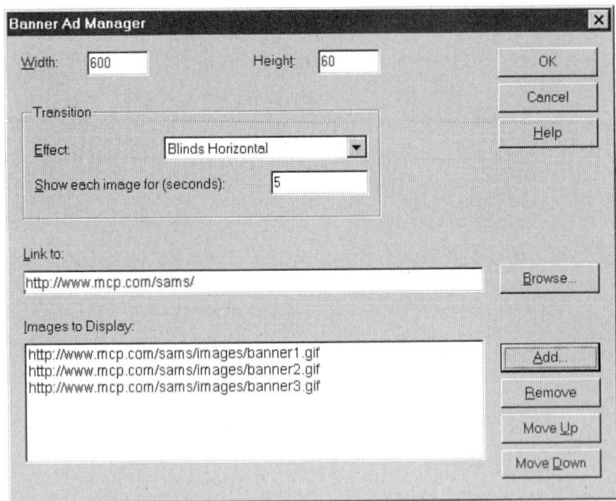

FIGURE 13.14.
Setting the banners to rotate.

Still, you can make the best of this situation by linking the banner to an advertising information page or a menu page. With an advertising information page, you provide information about your site's advertisers along with links to each advertiser's Web site. With a menu page, you provide lists of resources and links to where they can be found at your Web site or at other Web sites.

Summary

Active elements are great for adding innovative extras to your Web pages without having to resort to scripting. Using a hit counter, you can track page accesses for all the world to see. With marquees, you can add moving banners to your pages. With plug-ins, you can extend the functionality of your browser. Using a hover button, you can add an animated button to the page that is complete with multimedia enhancements. In addition to these nifty extras, you can use the Banner Ad Manager to automatically rotate banner ads for you, which makes it possible for publishers of all sizes to effectively manage advertising.

IV PART

IN THIS PART

- Designing Web Sites with Themes *233*
- Getting the Most from the Clip Art Gallery *249*
- Working with the Microsoft Image Composer *273*
- Creating Great Images with Image Composer *287*
- Enhancing Your Images with Effects *317*
- Optimizing Your Images and Color Palettes *335*
- Working with GIF Animator *357*
- Creating and Designing Image Maps *385*

Web Page Graphic Design and Image Composer

Designing Web Sites with Themes

by David and Rhonda Crowder

IN THIS CHAPTER

- Viewing and Selecting Graphical Themes *235*
- Deciding on an Appropriate Theme for Your FrontPage Web *239*
- Adding Your Own Graphical Themes *241*
- Modifying Colors *243*
- Modifying Graphical Images *244*
- Modifying Font Families and Colors *246*

Graphical themes are a new feature added to FrontPage 98. They are, in a sense, the other side of the coin to templates (see Part VI, "Templates, Wizards, and FrontPage Components"). While templates allow you to quickly and easily establish a basic structure and page content for a FrontPage Web site, themes lay down a basic, consistent, graphical pattern for all the pages in the Web site. Themes ensure that each page in the Web site looks as though it belongs as part of the whole, and a user moving from page to page feels constantly at ease, recognizing all the different elements from previous experience.

You can save development time by using the predesigned themes because they already have the characteristics of the major elements of Web pages worked out in a pleasing, coherent blend. Otherwise, you would either have to go over each page making the adjustments by hand, or develop your own style sheets (see Chapter 12, "Advanced Page Layout with Style Sheets"). Graphical themes, in fact, are put together with cascading style sheets that have been created by Microsoft's own highly experienced Web designers.

Cascading style sheets allow Web developers to easily control the appearance of Web pages. The characteristics of every single element of HTML can be set in advance in a style sheet. Then, when that style sheet is attached to a Web page, the page's elements change to reflect the definitions established in the style sheet.

For example, you could define the `<H1>` heading style to be Arial font, 24 points in size, and blue in color. Then, if you attached that style sheet to a Web page, any text between `<H1>` and `</H1>` tags would appear in 24-point, blue Arial. Nothing more is needed by way of definition in your HTML code, just the plain `<H1>` tags, because all the other details are already spelled out in the style sheet.

What is particularly nice about this approach is that you can change the appearance of every `<H1>` tag in all the Web pages attached to that style sheet simply by changing the one definition in the style sheet. With the earlier approach, you would have to search for and alter each occurrence of the tag individually throughout your entire site.

Style sheets are a development of the World Wide Web Consortium (W3C), which defines the standard. Although Internet Explorer 3.0 offered some limited support for style sheets, the full implementation was not available until the 4.0 and higher versions of both Microsoft Internet Explorer and Netscape Navigator.

CAUTION

When you apply a graphical theme to your Web site, it will change all your previous settings for covered elements. If you have an element you do not wish to change, but still want to use the theme for the rest of your Web site, you will have to use FrontPage Editor to open each page where that element is found and use the appropriate FrontPage tools to manually override the settings. For example, if you used a theme in which Heading 2 is a larger font than you want, you can select the characters in that heading and adjust their size downward using the Decrease Text Size button in the toolbar.

You cannot, however, alter the background image or color on a per page basis; FrontPage automatically removes the Background notebook tab from the Page Properties dialog box when you apply a theme.

Another, more advanced, approach—discussed later in this chapter—is to modify the theme itself so that the element or elements you want to change are applied differently.

Viewing and Selecting Graphical Themes

Themes are accessed through the Views bar. When you click on the Themes button, the main window to the right of the Views bar is filled with the themes selection bar and the Theme Preview window (see Figure 14.1). If your currently selected FrontPage Web site does not have a theme applied to it, the Theme Preview window will be blank and the This Web Does Not Use Themes radio button will be selected by default. In this case, you must click on the Use Selected Theme radio button (if your currently open Web already uses themes, this button will already be selected). These radio buttons are located at the top of the themes selection bar. You must have an open FrontPage web for the theme to be applied; you cannot select a theme and then create a web for it.

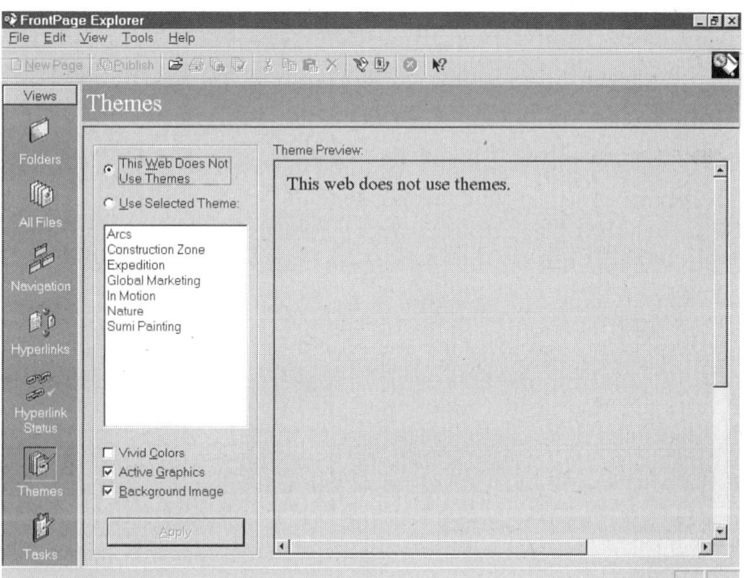

FIGURE 14.1.
The Themes View.

You can also reach a nearly identical window (see Figure 14.2) by selecting Format|Themes from the menu in FrontPage Editor. Note that you must have a Web page open or the Format menu is not available. This Choose Theme dialog box is only applicable to the open page rather than to the FrontPage web as a whole, and any theme chosen here overrides the web's theme, but only for that page. The basic options are that the page does not use themes, that it uses the theme applied to the web in FrontPage Explorer, or that it uses a different theme selected in the Choose Theme dialog box. Otherwise, it is functionally identical to the FrontPage Explorer's themes view.

TIP

If you click on any theme name while the This Web Does Not Use Themes radio button is selected, the Use Selected Theme radio button will be automatically selected.

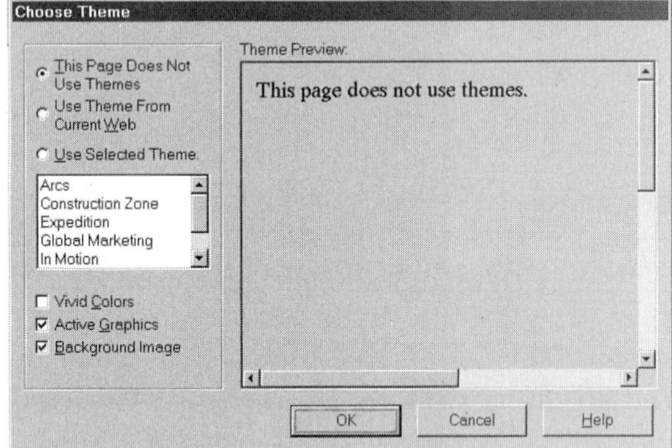

FIGURE 14.2.
The Choose Theme dialog box in the FrontPage Editor.

The names of the available themes are found in the large list box that comprises most of the themes selection bar. To view one of the themes, simply click the name and, after a few moments, the representation of that theme's elements will appear in the Theme Preview window.

After selecting a theme, the Theme Preview window shows the appearance of various items (see Figures 14.3 and 14.4 for examples of the appearance of different themes) so you can know in advance what your Web site will look like if you apply a particular theme to it.

TIP

After a theme has been selected, you can use the up and down arrow keys to scroll from one theme example to another. However, there is a drawback to this approach, because it takes a little bit of time for each example to be displayed. Therefore, the arrow key scrolling is a bit jerky, because FrontPage attempts to load an example for every theme name you pass along the way to the one you want. Unless you want to view each theme sequentially, use the mouse pointer to select the theme you want.

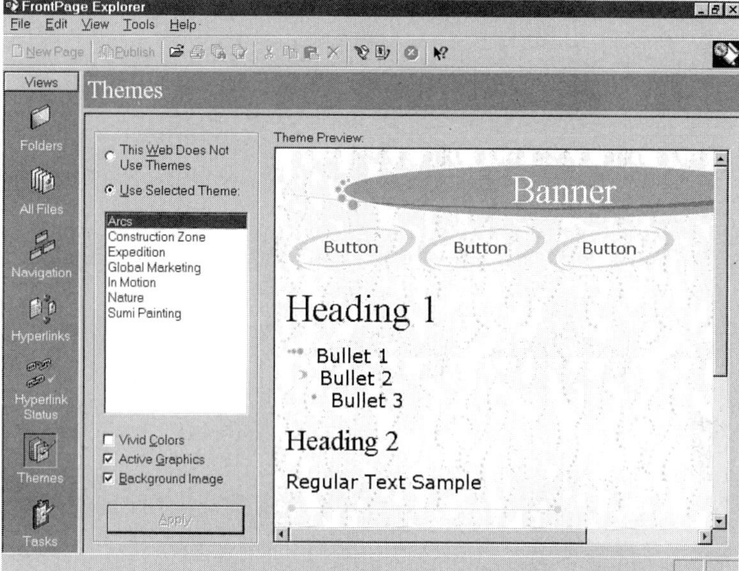

FIGURE 14.3.
Arcs theme example.

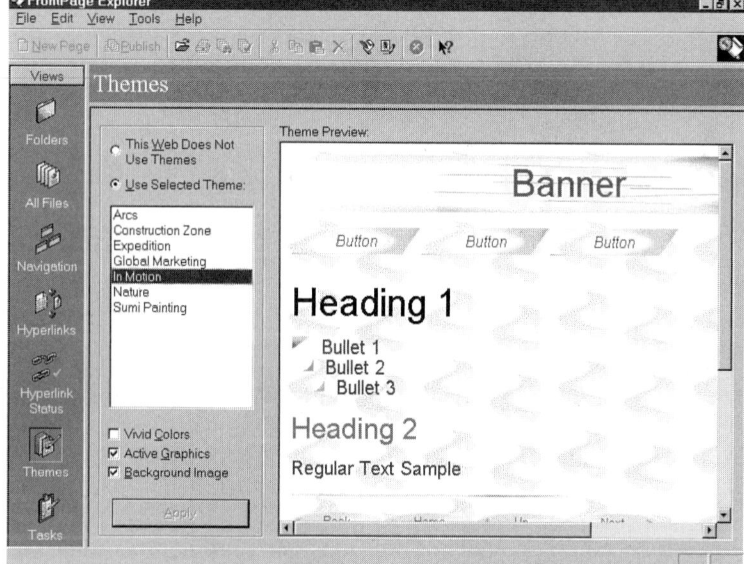

FIGURE 14.4.
In Motion theme example.

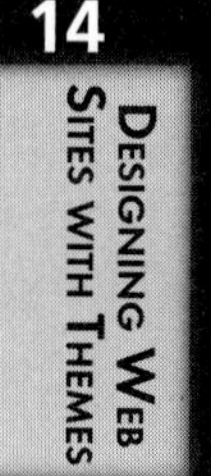

The themes available to the Theme Preview window are

- Banners
- Buttons
- Heading 1

- Heading 2
- Bullet 1
- Bullet 2
- Bullet 3
- Regular Text
- Horizontal Line (separator image)
- Navigation Bar (Back & Next, Home, Parent)
- Regular Link
- Followed Link
- Active Link
- Background Color/Image

In addition, though representations of them are not shown in the Theme Preview window, the following items are also controlled by the themes style sheets:

- Heading 3
- Heading 4
- Heading 5
- Heading 6
- Table Border Color (Light)
- Table Border Color (Dark)

At the bottom of the themes selection bar, there are three check boxes and one button:

- Vivid Colors check box: Click this to select (or deselect) an alternate, but similar, color scheme for the selected theme.
- Active Graphics check box: Click this to select (or deselect) a display with alternate GIF images. These might be animated bullets; buttons that show different images for normal, hovered, or pushed; and so on.
- Background Image check box: Click this to toggle the background image on and off.
- Apply button: Click this button to apply the selected theme to your FrontPage Web. This will take a few moments (how long depends on the speed of your system), during which the status bar at the bottom of your screen will read "Applying theme." When the theme application process is completed, the status bar will read "Theme applied."

TIP

If you click the Apply button, but afterward decide you do not want to use any graphical theme, or if you want to totally remove a previously existing theme, click the radio button labeled This Web Does Not Use Themes and then click the Apply button. This will completely remove all themes from the selected Web.

If, on the other hand, you simply wish to change themes rather than to remove all themes from your Web entirely, just select the one you desire from the list box and click on the Apply button. The new theme will overwrite the old one.

NOTE

For those interested in pursuing the details of the cascading style sheets Microsoft uses for the graphical themes, FrontPage uses the file named `graph0.css` in the appropriate directory (see the section on modifying themes below) by default. Clicking the Active Graphics check box causes FrontPage to use the file named `graph1.css` instead.

In a similar fashion, clicking the Vivid Colors checkbox causes FrontPage to use the file named `color1.css` instead of the default file `color0.css`.

Deciding on an Appropriate Theme for Your FrontPage Web

The graphical appearance of your Web carries a powerful, though nonverbal, message to everyone who views it. For example, the Arcs theme, with its bright pastel colors, relatively thin font, and narrow horizontal lines and balled endings, contrasts strongly with the Global Marketing theme. The latter, while not exactly somber, is designed to give a more solid feeling, using darker tones, heavier lettering, square lined background, and thicker, blockier horizontal lines. Each of these designs carries with it a certain feeling, just as different types of music or different styles of clothing do.

It is a good idea when designing a Web site to bear in to whom you want the Web site to be attractive, and select themes accordingly. Think about who they are, how they act, and what they wear. Are you aiming for an audience of corporate financial executives? If so, then bear in mind that these are people who do not, as a rule, wear bright or flashy clothing. They generally live their lives according to a fixed and unvarying pattern, and they are often suspicious of innovation. A Web site designed to be bright and flashy, or which gives a feeling of instability, will probably not appeal to them. The Global Marketing theme was made for them.

On the other hand, the In Motion theme, with its forward slanting buttons, windblown navigation bar, and swirling background, is absolutely perfect for a more progressive audience such as artists or writers. The movement metaphor could also be successfully applied to some business situations, such as an entrepreneurial organization that sees itself as "going places" or to companies that specialize in transportation or travel.

The artists who designed these themes have already put a great deal of work into developing meaningful symbols for you to use on your sites. With just a few clicks of a mouse button, you can turn even a simple textual site into a beautifully done design.

An example of an industrial Web page (using the Construction Zone theme) is presented in Figure 14.5 and, to balance the coin and show the versatility of FrontPage themes, an example of an environmental site (using the Nature theme) is presented in Figure 14.6.

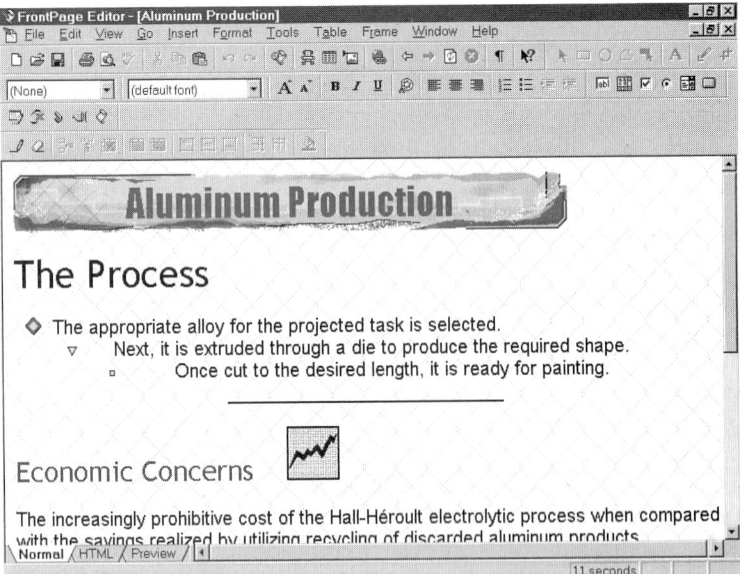

FIGURE 14.5.
Construction Zone theme example.

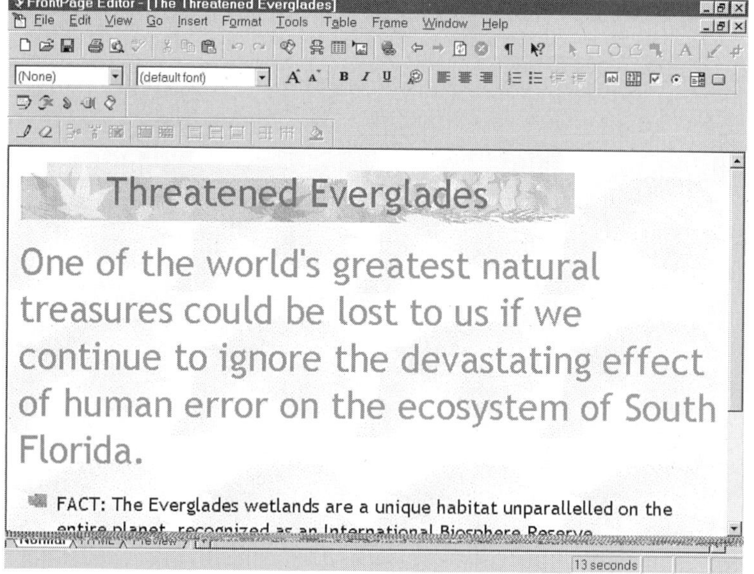

FIGURE 14.6.
Nature theme example.

Adding Your Own Graphical Themes

As mentioned earlier in this chapter, graphical themes are put together with cascading style sheets. This means, of course, that if you want to go beyond the themes that come with FrontPage, you can modify the supplied themes or even create your own (for details on how style sheets work, see Chapter 12).

For instance, you might want to use the Global Marketing theme for an international banking client, but the client naturally might want the bank's logo to be the banner at the top of every page. Using the process outlined below, you could solve this problem by simply substituting a scanned image of the logo for the appropriate file.

TIP

There are two ways you can modify the themes. You can changing the cascading style sheets, or if you are uncomfortable with modifying style sheets, you simply can replace the original GIF files in the appropriate folder with images of your own to which you give the same filenames as in the Microsoft created style sheets. The latter approach can only be used to change the graphical elements, such as buttons and bullets; so if you want to change font types, background colors, and so forth, you will have to work with the settings in the cascading style sheets.

CAUTION

Make sure to make a backup copy of any theme folder, style sheet file, or GIF image file you are going to modify or replace in case you later need to restore it.

To add your own customized graphical theme to the listing in the themes selection bar, you need to first choose a unique name for your theme. Next, using Windows Explorer, add a new folder under the following path:

```
C:\Program Files\Microsoft FrontPage\themes
```

TIP

If your theme name is short, use it for the folder name; otherwise, use a shortened form of it. See the section later in this chapter titled "Finding the Graphical Theme Files" for examples of how Microsoft has handled its theme names.

Once you have done that, copy the files from the folder of the theme you want to change into your new folder. From now on, you will be working only with the copied files in your new folder; the originals will be left alone.

Next, you need to change the name of the `.inf` file to be the same as your folder name. For example, if your custom theme is in `C:\Program Files\Microsoft FrontPage\themes\mytheme`, your `.inf` file must be named `Mytheme.inf` in order for FrontPage 98 to recognize it.

NOTE

Microsoft has followed the pattern of naming the folder with all lowercase lettering and the `.inf` file with initial uppercase lettering in most instances. While varying this scheme does not seem to affect the functionality of customized themes (as evidenced by the cases where Microsoft doesn't follow it and proven by experimentation), it is probably best to stick with it. There are no cases where Microsoft uses more than eight letters for a folder name or `.inf` file name.

Now, load the newly named `.inf` file into Notepad (or your favorite text editor) and change the line with the title to reflect your new theme name. This does not have to be exactly the same as the name you used for your folder and `.inf` file, but it should, of course, be similar. For instance, you could use `title=My New Theme` for the `.inf` file named `Mytheme.inf`. The words after `title=` will be the ones shown in the list box in the themes selection bar, so keep the title short enough to fit in it (about 16 to 17 characters maximum).

Finally, save the modified .inf file. Start FrontPage Explorer and verify that your new theme is now listed along with the originals. You are now ready to modify the theme to suit yourself.

CAUTION

You should use Notepad or some similar text editor to make the changes to the files you are modifying, because the results must be saved in plain ASCII format. If you must use a word processor, make certain to save the files as text. Otherwise, the word processing program will insert formatting codes into the file, which will interfere with your purposes.

CAUTION

When modifying the .inf file, you might not be able to double-click its name in the file listing to bring up Notepad, because due to the file extension Windows might attempt to launch utilities supplied from other programs related to .inf files instead. If this occurs, you might have to run Notepad or your preferred text editor and load the file from within the editor.

Finding the Graphical Theme Files

The files for the supplied graphical themes are located in folders of `C:\Program Files\Microsoft FrontPage\themes` (assuming you have FrontPage on your C: drive and have followed the standard installation procedure; if you have not installed FrontPage in the default folders, you will need to adjust the folder addresses accordingly). The folder names for each theme are obvious (the Arcs theme is in `arcs`, for instance), though there are sometimes abbreviations to keep the folder names to the 8-character standard Microsoft has used here (for example, Construction Zone is in `construc` and Sumi Painting is in `sumipntg`).

Modifying Colors

Colors are listed in the RGB (red, green, blue) notation system. Both the Standard Colors (`color0.css`) and the Vivid Colors (`color1.css`) files have the same elements in them, although the color values differ, of course.

Table 14.1 gives the common name of the element and the variable name whose value you will need to modify to change the color of the element in the graphical theme.

Table 14.1. Elements in files `color0.css` and `color1.css`.

Element	*Variable*
Normal Link	`a:link`
Visited Link	`a:visited`
Active Link	`a:active`
Background color	`body {background-color}`
Body text	`body {color}`
Table border (light)	`table {table-border-color-light}`
Table border (dark)	`table {table-border-color-dark}`
Heading 1	`h1`
Heading 2	`h2`
Heading 3	`h3`
Heading 4	`h4`
Heading 5	`h5`
Heading 6	`h6`

For example, say you wanted to change the color of the `<H1>` heading in the theme you have created by copying the files from the Arcs theme. You would load the file `color0.css` (this file affects only the normal colors; if you want to change the Vivid Colors setting, you need to load `color1.css`) into Notepad (or any other ASCII text editor) and look for the following code:

```
h1
{
        color: rgb(0,0,0)
}
```

All you need to do is to change the RGB triplet from the preset black (0,0,0) to the desired color (red, for example, would be 255,0,0). Then, save the file in ASCII format. The color change is complete at that point and will show up in your custom theme.

Modifying Graphical Images

Unlike the color files, the graphical elements vary between the Standard Graphics (`graph0.css`) and the Active Graphics (`graph1.css`) files. Although several elements are the same, the Active Graphics setting requires more images.

Tables 14.2 and 14.3 give the common name of the element and the variable name whose value you will need to modify to change the GIF image associated with the element in the graphical theme.

NOTE

The background image is not in either of the graphics files, but is found in the file named `theme.css`; the variable is `body{background-image}`.

Table 14.2. GIF elements in file `graph0.css` (Standard Graphics).

Element	*Variable*
Horizontal Line	`separator-image`
Bullet 1	`list-image-1`
Bullet 2	`list-image-2`
Bullet 3	`list-image-3`
Banner Image	`nav-banner-image`
Navigation button (horizontal) normal	`navbutton-horiz-normal`
Navigation button (horizontal) pushed	`navbutton-horiz-pushed`
Navigation button (vertical) normal	`navbutton-vert-normal`
Navigation button (vertical) pushed	`navbutton-vert-pushed`
Navigation bar Home button normal	`navbutton-home-normal`
Navigation bar Next button normal	`navbutton-next-normal`
Navigation bar Back button normal	`navbutton-prev-normal`
Navigation bar Parent button normal	`navbutton-up-normal`

Table 14.3. GIF elements in file `graph1.css` (Active Graphics).

Element	*Variable*
Horizontal Line	`separator-image`
Bullet 1	`list-image-1`
Bullet 2	`list-image-2`
Bullet 3	`list-image-3`
Banner Image	`nav-banner-image`
Navigation button (horizontal) normal	`navbutton-horiz-normal`
Navigation button (horizontal) hovered	`navbutton-horiz-hovered`
Navigation button (horizontal) pushed	`navbutton-horiz-pushed`
Navigation button (vertical) normal	`navbutton-vert-normal`

continues

Table 14.3. continued

Element	*Variable*
Navigation button (vertical) hovered	`navbutton-vert-hovered`
Navigation button (vertical) pushed	`navbutton-vert-pushed`
Navigation bar Home button normal	`navbutton-home-normal`
Navigation bar Home button hovered	`navbutton-home-hovered`
Navigation bar Home button pushed	`navbutton-home-pushed`
Navigation bar Next button normal	`navbutton-next-normal`
Navigation bar Next button hovered	`navbutton-next-hovered`
Navigation bar Next button pushed	`navbutton-next-pushed`
Navigation bar Back button normal	`navbutton-prev-normal`
Navigation bar Back button hovered	`navbutton-prev-hovered`
Navigation bar Back button pushed	`navbutton-prev-pushed`
Navigation bar Parent button normal	`navbutton-up-normal`
Navigation bar Parent button hovered	`navbutton-up-hovered`
Navigation bar Parent button pushed	`navbutton-up-pushed`

If you want to change the image used for the horizontal line in the theme you have created by copying the files from the Arcs theme, you load the file `graph0.css` (this file affects only the standard graphics; if you want to change the Active Graphics setting, you need to load `graph1.css`) into Notepad (or any other ASCII text editor) and look for the following code:

```
separator-image: url(arcsepd.gif);
```

Next, you need to change the name of the image URL from the current image to the desired one. For example, change `arcsepd.gif` to `newhline.gif` (you must also copy the image file into the same theme directory as the `.css` file). Now, save the file in ASCII format. The graphics change is complete at that point and will show up in your custom theme.

Modifying Font Families and Colors

Table 14.4 gives the common names of the font elements and the names of the associated variables whose value you will need to modify in order to change those fonts. These are found in the files `graph0.css` and `graph1.css`.

In each case, you are able to set the font family, color, text alignment, and vertical alignment of the fonts.

Table 14.4. Font elements in files `graph0.css` and `graph1.css`.

Element	*Variable*
Banner text font	`.mstheme-bannertxt`
Horizontal Navigation bar text fonts	`.mstheme-horiz-navtext`
Vertical Navigation bar text fonts	`.mstheme-vert-navtext`
Home Navigation button text fonts	`.mstheme-navtxthome`
Next Navigation button text fonts	`.mstheme-navtxtnext`
Back Navigation button text fonts	`.mstheme-navtxtprev`
Parent Navigation button text fonts	`.mstheme-navtxtup`

For example, say you wanted to change the banner text font in the theme you have created by copying the files from the Arcs theme. You load the file `graph0.css` (this file affects only the normal fonts; if you want to change the Vivid Colors fonts, you need to load `graph1.css`) into Notepad (or any other ASCII text editor) and look for the following code:

```
.mstheme-bannertxt
{
        font-family: times new roman;
        color: rgb(0,0,0);
        text-align: center;
        vertical-align: middle;
}
```

To change any of the settings, just replace the value after the colon. For example, you could change the font family by changing `times new roman` to `verdana` or the color by changing the RGB triplet after `color:`. You could change the horizontal alignment of the text by altering the value after `text-align:` (for example, from `center` to `left`) and the vertical alignment by changing the one after `vertical-align:` (perhaps from `middle` to `top`). Then save the file in ASCII format. The change in font values is complete at that point and will show up in your custom theme.

NOTE

Although the colors for the Heading elements (`h1`, `h2`, and so on) are set in the files `color0.css` and `color1.css` (refer to Table 14.1), the font families for these elements are set separately in the file `theme.css`.

Summary

Graphical themes are a quick and easy way to create a FrontPage Web that is a coherent artistic whole. This chapter covered how to view, select, and apply themes to your Web, as well as design considerations relating to your Web's content. You also learned how to adapt and modify the supplied themes, changing colors, fonts, and images.

Getting the Most from the Clip Art Gallery

by David and Rhonda Crowder

IN THIS CHAPTER

- Image Formats Supported by Clip Gallery 250
- Inserting a Clip Art Image from the Clip Gallery 252
- Using Clip Gallery's Advanced Features 253

FrontPage 98 comes with a collection of clip art you can use to spruce up your Web pages. Much more important than just another bunch of images, however, is the Clip Gallery itself. It is a FrontPage Editor feature that enables you to not only view and insert the included clip art, but to maintain a searchable database of the clips. You can also add and delete clips to and from the database, modify the search keywords, and control which categories images are placed in—you can even add whole new categories of your own.

Image Formats Supported by Clip Gallery

The Clip Gallery is not limited to just bitmapped image formats—it supports vector graphics as well (see Tables 15.1 and 15.2). Bitmapped image files represent an image as a fixed series of dots, each with an assigned color value. These colored dots, when displayed on a computer screen as pixels, create a picture of fixed height and width; changing the size of the image can result in tremendous distortion and a blocky appearance. Vector images, on the other hand, are created from mathematical formulas that define the characteristics of lines, curves, and so on. The height and width of vector images are not fixed like bitmapped images, but can be changed at will. Unlike the blocky appearance of enlarged bitmapped images, vector images retain their smooth appearance when their size is altered.

CAUTION

Microsoft uses its own peculiar definitions in Clip Gallery; they refer to vector graphics as "clip art" and bitmapped graphics as "pictures"—a distinction you are very unlikely to find elsewhere. Generally speaking, outside of FrontPage 98, "clip art" is used to refer to any image of any graphics type if its purpose is to be added to a publication in place of in-house artwork, and "picture" is any image at all.

Table 15.1. Vector image file types supported by Clip Gallery.

File Type	*File Extension*
CorelDraw	`.cdr`
Computer Graphics Metafile	`.cgm`
Micrografx Designer/Draw Plus	`.drw`
Enhanced Metafiles	`.emf`
Encapsulated PostScript	`.eps`
Windows Metafile	`.wmf`
Word Perfect Graphics Metafile	`.wpg`

Table 15.2. Bitmapped image file types supported by Clip Gallery.

File Type	*File Extension*
Windows Bitmap	`.bmp`
FlashPix	`.fpx`
Graphics Interchange Format	`.gif`
JPEG	`.jpg`
PictureIt!	`.mix`
Kodak PhotoCD	`.pcd`
PC Paintbrush	`.pcx`
Macintosh PICT	`.pct`
Portable Network Graphics	`.png`
Tagged Image Format File	`.tif`

TIP

Clip Gallery does not recognize alternate file extensions. For example, if you get a file named `image.jpeg`, you will have to change it to `image.jpg` before you can import it.

Regardless of the original format of the image file, however, it will be automatically converted when you save the Web page you inserted it into in FrontPage Editor. Images 8 bits or under will be converted to the GIF image format, and to JPEG if they are over 8 bits. The reason for this is that the major Web browsers do not recognize—and therefore will not display—most image file types. The two exceptions to this automatic conversion are GIF files and JPEG files. Obviously, GIF files do not need to be converted to their own format, and, because both of these image types are recognized and displayed by both Netscape Navigator and Microsoft Internet Explorer, there is no need to convert a JPEG file to anything else, either. Generally speaking, JPEG files tend to be much smaller than equivalent GIF files, anyway.

NOTE

To clarify the point, it is not the actual image you are importing that is converted to a GIF file, but a copy of it, which is saved to your working folder along with the Web page you are working on. The original image file remains untouched in its original file format, still in its original folder location.

Inserting a Clip Art Image from the Clip Gallery

The basic procedure for inserting a piece of clip art into a Web page from within FrontPage Editor consists of just a few simple steps. After you have placed the cursor at the point in your Web page where you would like to insert the clip art image, choose Insert|Clipart from the menu. This will bring up the Clip Gallery. (See Figure 15.1.)

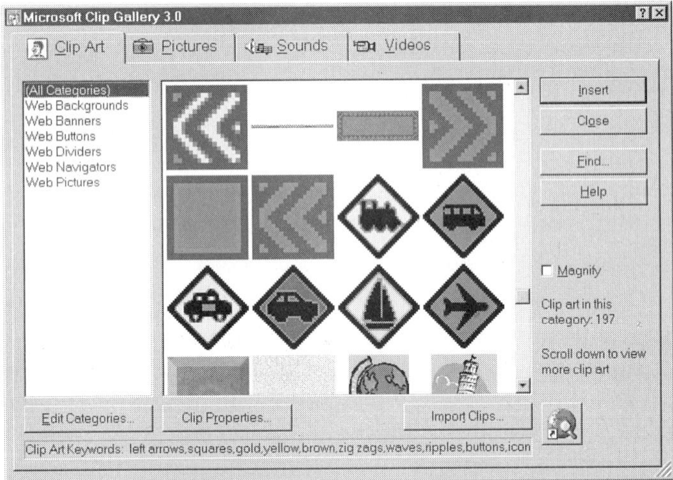

FIGURE 15.1.
The FrontPage Clip Gallery.

TIP

Although you can also access the clip art via the Insert Image command (menu or toolbar button), this is a much more cumbersome approach, requiring you to either add the image files one at a time via the standard folder and file selection method, or to cancel the folder view and click the clip art button to access the Clip Gallery. It is easiest to stick with the Insert|Clipart menu selection.

Next, click the notebook tab labeled Clip Art if you want to select your images from the vector graphics files. If you want to use the images from the bitmapped graphics files, then click the notebook tab labeled Pictures (see the Caution box earlier for an explanation of these labels). For our current purposes, ignore the Sound and Video notebook tabs.

The list box on the left side allows you to choose which categories of pictures are shown in the selection area. The default selection is All Categories, but you can click one of the categories to limit the number of images displayed. As you try new categories, thumbnail versions of the images in the category you have selected will appear in the image display window. These thumbnail images are called "previews" in FrontPage 98. You will find that some images will appear in more than one category.

TIP

The number of pictures in the selected category is shown to the right of the image display window, just below the Magnify check box.

Select the image you want to insert by clicking it. If you do not see an image you want to use, you can use the scroll bar on the right side of the image display window to view more images in the current category, or you can select another category entirely.

If you want to view a larger version of the thumbnail image, click the Magnify check box. As long as it is checked, any thumbnail you select will be magnified; the unselected images are not affected (to turn off the magnification effect, simply click the check box again so that the check mark is gone). The selected image, though magnified, is still small enough so that you can click any of the other images, and even though it overlaps the surrounding images a bit, there is always enough of the others showing for you to select them instead.

To insert the selected image on your Web page, either double-click the one you want or just click the Insert button. If the image was originally a file other than a GIF or JPEG file, there will be a brief moment when a conversion routine will run as the importation is completed. The image you have selected will be placed on the Web page you are working on and Clip Gallery will close automatically, returning you to FrontPage Editor.

TIP

To replace one clip art image on your Web page in FrontPage Editor with another, select the one you want to get rid of, open Clip Gallery, then simply insert the new one just as if you were inserting it into an unused portion of your Web page. The new clip art image will overwrite the old one. An image that is inserted over another image will not retain any of the settings of the old image (such as washout, sizing, and so on); you are starting all over with the new one.

Using Clip Gallery's Advanced Features

Clip Gallery does more than just provide a list of images to insert. It has many more advanced functions. Most of these relate to its database side, including the built-in Find feature that enables you to search for keywords associated with the preview images, the ability to place images into differing—or even multiple—categories, and even the capacity to create entirely new categories for filing images. You can also augment the existing images by importing new ones to Clip Gallery from a variety of sources, such as existing clip art collections.

Using the Find Feature to Locate Images

Each clip art image has several keywords associated with it. For example, the picture of a black pair of scissors pointing to the left has the keywords `left arrows`, `scissors`, `black`, `buttons`, `icons`, and `Web graphics` associated with it. When you are viewing images, the keywords belonging to a particular image you have selected will be shown at the bottom of the Clip Gallery.

To search for an image by keyword, click the Find button to the right of the preview display window. This will bring up the Find Clip dialog box. (See Figure 15.2.)

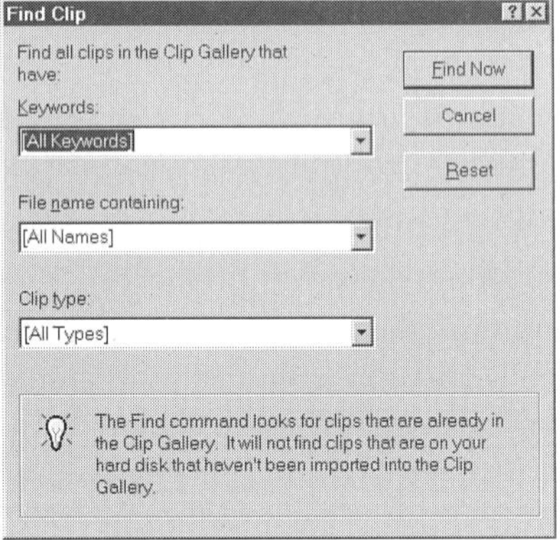

FIGURE 15.2.
The Find Clip dialog box.

You can search by keywords, filename, or clip type (file format type), or any combination of the three. In the first two of these cases, a portion of the correct keyword or filename will still result in a match. For instance, if you type the keyword search term "gol," then you'll find all files with "gold" or "golf" keywords attached to them, as well as any other terms that contain this string. The filename search is not as useful, because the images supplied with FrontPage 98 have names like `WB00320_.GIF` rather than descriptive filenames; however, if you add clip art from other sources that do use filenames that give a hint of the image contents, this feature could be of great value. The file format type is selected from a drop-down list box, so you cannot search for something like all file formats with a "g" in them.

CAUTION

In the beta versions of FrontPage 98, the database can become jumbled, especially when deleting image previews, and the keywords can get attached to images other than the ones they originally belonged to. One hopes this problem will be fixed in release versions.

There is no provision in Clip Gallery's database search function for multiple search terms, nor for Boolean searches. Therefore, you cannot use the Find feature to look for "gold AND button." You would have to look for either one keyword or the other. Although you *can* use more than one word, this is possible only in the case of a phrase that would need to be matched exactly (such as "Web graphics").

NOTE

By way of example, you could, if you wanted to, use all three approaches at once and search for a file that contained the keyword `button`, a filename containing the string `WB023`, and of the `.gif` file type.

Despite FrontPage 98's distinction between vector graphics ("clip art") and bitmapped graphics ("pictures"), the categories for the Find feature are the same regardless of which notebook tab you have selected.

If the search term you have chosen cannot be matched in the image database, you'll see a message stating, "The Clip Gallery could not find any clips that match your criteria." If the keyword or other criteria you have chosen is a match, then the thumbnail images of the associated files will appear in the image box.

After you run Find for the first time, a new category will be added called "(Results of Last Find)." The contents of this category, of course, change with each new Find operation you run. You can insert a piece of clip art from this new category just as you would from any of the regular ones. This is a temporary category, however, and will exist only until you close Clip Gallery; if you reopen Clip Gallery, the results of your last search operation will be gone, and the category will not appear again until you run another search operation.

Adding, Deleting, and Modifying Keywords

You might want to make changes to the keywords as they originally stand. For instance, say you have a banner image that you decide to use for a client from Taiwan who publishes cookbooks dedicated to Chinese cuisine. In that case, the existing keywords such as "banner," "Web graphics," and so forth are not going to be adequate to describe what that image means to you. Clicking the Clip Properties button at the bottom of Clip Gallery will bring up the Clip Properties dialog box. (See Figure 15.3.)

NOTE

You can also access the Clip Properties dialog box by right-clicking the image you want to add keywords to and then selecting Clip Properties from the pop-up menu that appears.

FIGURE 15.3.
The Clip Properties dialog box.

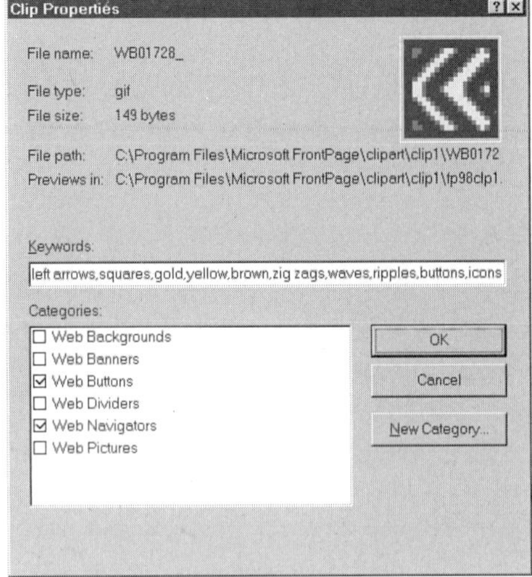

Adding Keywords

Click in the edit box labeled Keywords and place the cursor where you want to add the new keywords. There is no requirement for any particular order to the keywords, so you do not need to alphabetize, nor does capitalization matter, because the `Find` function is not case sensitive. Separate each keyword or keyword phrase with a comma, but do not put any space after the comma before beginning the next keyword. The space is not needed and will merely become an unnecessary and useless part of the keyword. You should not put a comma after the last keyword.

TIP

There is a limit of 90 characters total (including the commas between the keywords and any spaces in keyword phrases) for all the keywords associated with any one image file. If you are going to add your own, you might find that you do not have enough room; therefore, you'll probably want to delete any of the existing ones you do not need. Keep your own new keywords as short as possible, as long as the shortened form is still useful to you.

So, for the example of the cookbook client, you would probably want to add such keywords as `cookbook,Taiwan,Chinese food` to the banner image. Even that simple addition puts 28 more characters into the keyword listing, so you can see how important it is to choose your keywords carefully.

Deleting and Modifying Keywords

Although the keywords that show at the bottom of the Clip Gallery cannot be edited, the ones in the Clip Properties dialog box can. As with any other editable text, you can delete the ones you want to get rid of by highlighting the text and pressing the Delete key or by placing the cursor after them and using the destructive Backspace key, or any other normal text deletion method.

In the same manner, to modify a keyword term, simply select the portion you want to replace and then type over that portion just as you would with any other editable text.

Organizing, Adding, Deleting, and Renaming Categories

If the provided categories of Web Backgrounds, Web Banners, Web Buttons, Web Dividers, Web Navigators, and Web Pictures are not suitable for your purposes, you can always add your own, change the names of the existing ones, or delete entire categories.

Even if you are perfectly satisfied with the default category setup, you might still find that it is convenient for you to group some images together at some point; for instance, for a project that uses certain graphics over and over, or if you need to import images into Clip Gallery. Or, you may just want to move an image from one category into another.

Whatever your reasons, FrontPage 98 can fulfill your needs with powerful, but simple, methods for organizing your clip art.

Organizing Categories

Although it is possible to just pile every bit of clip art into a single category, or to just select All Categories and use the Find button, if you work with a large number of custom images, it is far better to exercise professional care and put in the time and effort to organize things properly to begin with, giving thought to organizing categories for maximum efficiency in image retrieval. Even if you only want to use the supplied images, you might want to establish your own categories for certain ones of them, or relocate them from their default category to another one.

Select an image and then click the Clip Properties button at the bottom of the Clip Gallery. When the Clip Properties dialog box appears, you'll notice that at the bottom beneath the keywords there is a listing of all available categories (with the dual exceptions of the "(All Categories)" and "(Results of Last Find)" categories, which are hard-coded and cannot be manipulated like the other ones. Some of the check boxes before the category names are checked and some are not. The categories that are checked are the ones that contain a reference to the selected image. If there are more categories than will fit in the listing, then a scroll bar will appear, enabling you to scroll up and down the list to view them all.

To remove an image from a category, click the check box containing a check mark; to add an image to a category, click the blank check box in front of the category name to which you want to add the image, and a check mark will appear.

You can put an image in more than one category by simply clicking multiple check boxes, and you can transfer an image from one category to another by checking the category you want to add it to and then unchecking the category you want to remove it from. There is no transfer of the physical image file; merely a change in the notations in the Clip Gallery database.

TIP

If you uncheck every listed category, the image is still not removed from the database itself. It will still reside in both the "(All Categories)" category and—if you previously ran a `Find` that matched the image—the "(Results of Last Find)" category (this last one is temporary, because the contents of the Results category are automatically cleared when you close Clip Gallery). These two categories are different from the others in that they are hard-coded and cannot be deleted by the user. If you select the image in either of those categories and click the Clip Properties button, it will show that it is not assigned to any category. If you do wish to delete the image from the database, you must follow the procedure in the section "Adding and Deleting Clip Art Images and Clip Packages," later in this chapter.

Adding Categories

To add your own categories to Clip Gallery, you need to access the New Category command. This can be done in three different ways:

- Place the pointer in the category listing in Clip Gallery and then right-click and select New Category from the pop-up menu that appears.
- Click the Edit Categories button at the bottom of Clip Gallery beneath the category listing to bring up the Edit Category List dialog box (see Figure 15.4); then click the New Category button.
- While in the Clip Properties dialog box, click the New Category button. This approach also has the advantage of automatically placing the currently selected image into the new category, whereas the first two methods listed above will create empty categories.

With any of these methods, you'll invoke the New Category dialog box (see Figure 15.5). Simply type the name of the category you wish to create into the edit box and then click the OK button. If you change your mind before finishing this procedure, just click the Cancel button or press the Escape key and you'll be returned to the Clip Gallery or the Clip Properties dialog box, whichever you invoked the New Category dialog box from.

CAUTION

If you use the Clip Properties' New Category button approach, then you should make sure to bear in mind that the creation of a new category is a totally separate action from any changes you make to the image's properties. Once you have clicked the New Category button, typed a name into its edit box, and hit the OK button, then the category has been created already, even though you can still abort any other changes you might have made in the Clip Properties dialog box by just hitting the Cancel button. The only effect this cancellation has on the new category is that the addition of the image reference to it is not completed; what you have done in this case is to create a category with nothing in it, just as though you had used one of the other two methods outlined earlier. The only way the image reference is added to the new category is if you click the OK button in Clip Properties.

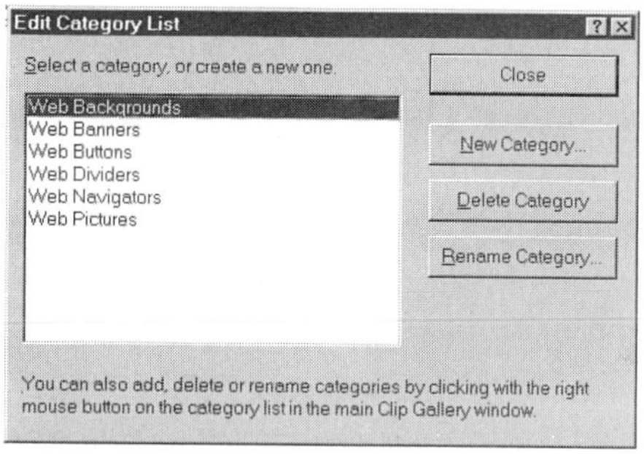

FIGURE 15.4.
The Edit Category List dialog box.

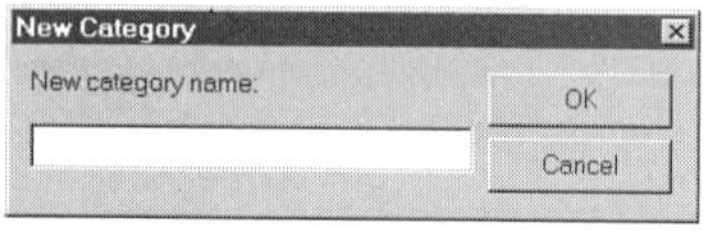

FIGURE 15.5.
The New Category dialog box.

TIP

The categories listing follows the common standard of ASCII alphabetization, where numerals and most of the usual nonalphabetic characters (including the parentheses characters) come before the letter A. Microsoft uses this fact to keep the "(All Categories)" choice at the top of the list box and "(Results of Last Find)" right under it, whereas all other categories are stacked below these two.

continues

continued

Because the top choice in the Categories list box is automatically the default choice, you can create a new default category by simply taking advantage of this convention and naming your category using any of the ASCII characters that come before "(". These include the blank space, as well as the following characters:

```
! " # $ % & '
```

Because all the supplied categories begin with the word "Web," you can, of course, also use the characters

```
) * + , - . / @ \ ] ^ _ '
```

and all the letters from A to V, as well as the numbers 0 through 9, to place categories under the "(All Categories)" and "(Results of Last Find)" categories but before the main supplied categories. You could even go ahead and use "(" to create a new default category just as long as the description of your category came before "(All"–such as the name "(ABC)".

Deleting Categories

To remove categories from Clip Gallery, you need to first select the category you want to delete by clicking it in the category listings; then you need to access the Delete Category command. This can be done in two different ways:

- Place the pointer in the category listing in Clip Gallery and then right-click and select Delete Category from the pop-up menu that appears.
- Click the Edit Categories button at the bottom of Clip Gallery beneath the category listing to bring up the Edit Category List dialog box (refer to Figure 15.4); then click the Delete Category button.

With either of these methods, you'll receive a message box asking you if you are sure you want to delete the selected category. Click the Yes button to complete the deletion or the No button to cancel the deletion.

CAUTION

If you delete a whole category, then every image in that category will instantly be entirely removed from the database. The only exception to this is any image that is also listed in another category or categories. You'll receive a warning message to this effect when you delete a category that will give you the option to abort the deletion. The warning message does not necessarily mean that there are any images that will be removed; it will appear even if every image in the category is also contained in other categories.

Although removal from the Clip Gallery database does not mean that the actual image files are deleted (they will still remain on your drive), you would still be faced with the hassle of having to import again any images lost under these circumstances. Because the keywords for those images would be lost through the process of category deletion, you would also have to reenter all of them for each and every image.

You should exercise great care when deleting categories. If you do have some images you want to keep, but still need to get rid of the category and most of the images, then you should either go through each image and add it to another category (see procedure in "Organizing Categories" earlier in the chapter) or just transfer them to another category, thus removing it from the category to be deleted but preserving it within the overall database.

If you do not wish to spend the time to carefully recategorize each image you want to keep, one good approach to quickly avoid the lost image problem would be to simply create a holding category for the time being. Just create a new category, call it "holding," and transfer the images you want to keep into it before deleting the category they were previously located in. You can then transfer the images into more appropriate categories at your leisure at some later time. Of course, you can delete the "holding" category when you're done with it, too.

Renaming Categories

To rename categories in Clip Gallery, you need to first select the category you want to rename by clicking it in the category listings; then you need to access the Rename Category command. This can be done in two different ways:

- Place the pointer in the category listing in Clip Gallery and then right-click and select Rename Category from the pop-up menu that appears.
- Click the Edit Categories button at the bottom of Clip Gallery beneath the category listing to bring up the Edit Category List dialog box (refer to Figure 15.4); then click the Rename Category button.

With either of these methods, you'll invoke the Rename Category dialog box (see Figure 15.6). Simply type the new name for the selected category into the edit box and then click the OK button. If you change your mind before finishing this procedure, just click the Cancel button or press the Escape key, and you'll be returned to the Clip Gallery.

FIGURE 15.6.
The Rename Category dialog box.

Adding and Deleting Clip Art Images and Clip Packages

You are not limited to using only the clip art provided with Clip Gallery. You can always, of course, still insert any image you want from any source you have into a Web page (see Chapter 7, "Enhancing Your Web Page with Images—The Easy Way"). However, you can also store images in Clip Gallery for easier retrieval and management.

You can import images from your hard drive, CD-ROMs, from specially prepared "clip packages" designed to work with Clip Gallery, and even from a special Web site that Microsoft has set up called "Clip Gallery Live."

NOTE

To be precise, the images themselves are not imported to Clip Gallery; actually, it is information about their characteristics and location that is added to the Clip Gallery database of clip art, along with a thumbnail copy of the image, called a "preview."

Therefore, if you have an image on a CD-ROM or floppy disk, you can leave it there, without copying it to your hard drive, but the disk with the image on it must be available (and placed in the same drive it was originally in) if you want to be able to actually import the image into FrontPage Editor.

You can, of course, copy the actual image file onto your hard drive if you prefer before importing the information about it into the Clip Gallery database. You might even want to establish a special folder to hold images for this purpose.

Importing Clip Art to Clip Gallery

To import image information into the Clip Gallery database, click the Import Clips button at the bottom of Clip Gallery. This will bring up the Add Pictures to Clip Gallery dialog box. (See Figure 15.7.)

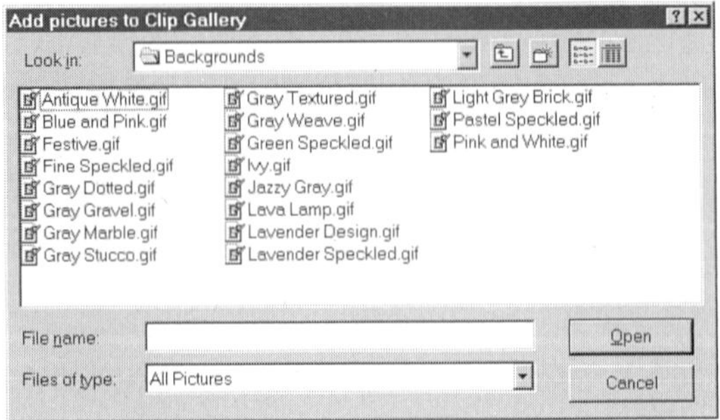

FIGURE 15.7.
The Add Pictures to Clip Gallery dialog box.

TIP

If you have the option to, it can save disk space if you import JPEG files (commonly having the extension `.jpg`), because they are often smaller than GIF files of the same image, depending on the color depth of the original.

TIP

If you select a category in the list box before you import an image, that category will be automatically selected in the Clip Properties dialog box.

From the Add Pictures to Clip Gallery dialog box, select the image file format type (if known) from the drop-down list box labeled "Files of type:" at the bottom. If you do not know the file format of the image or images you want to add, or if you want to add files of more than one format, then just leave the default All Pictures selection in place.

If the folder displayed does not contain the file(s) you want to add to Clip Gallery, change to the one that does.

Now select the file you want to import (its name will then appear in the File name edit box) and then click the Open button. If the files are not GIF or JPEG formats, a conversion routine will run briefly and then the Clip Properties dialog box will be displayed. If you have decided to import multiple files, there will be slight differences in the dialog box in order to accommodate the different importation needs (see Figures 15.8 and 15.9 as well as the Note following them).

TIP

If you want to import more than a single file at a time, then hold down the Ctrl key and click the files you want. You can also hold down the Shift key to do this, but in that case, the files must be sequential; with the Ctrl key, you can select files without also selecting the ones in between them.

In either case, all the filenames you have selected will be shown in the File name edit box.

Enter any keywords you want to add for the image. If there is a blank check box before a category you want to add the image to, then click it to check it; if there is a checked check box before a category you do not want to add the image to, click it to uncheck it. If you want to create a new category for the image, click the New Category button and follow the procedure outlined in the section titled "Adding Categories," earlier in the chapter. In this case, the image will be automatically added to the new category. Click OK to complete the importation.

If you have imported more than one image, the next one will be displayed (the images display in the filenames' reverse alphanumeric order, last to first). You'll need to add keywords and make category selections for each image.

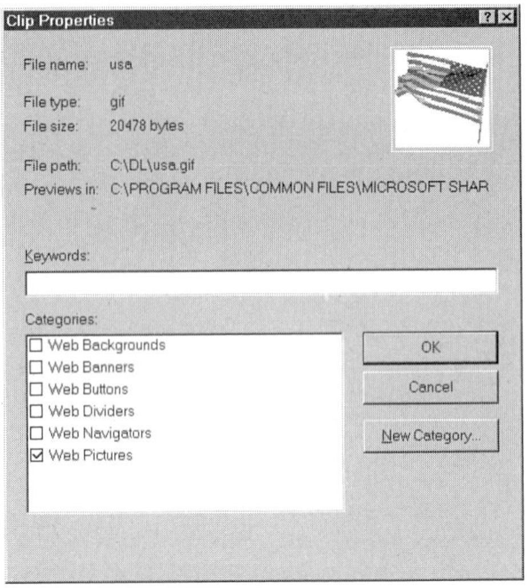

FIGURE 15.8.
The Clip Properties dialog box with a single imported clip.

Clip Properties
File name: usa
File type: gif
File size: 20478 bytes
File path: C:\DL\usa.gif
Previews in: C:\PROGRAM FILES\COMMON FILES\MICROSOFT SHAR
Keywords:
Categories:
☐ Web Backgrounds
☐ Web Banners
☐ Web Buttons
☐ Web Dividers
☐ Web Navigators
☑ Web Pictures
OK
Cancel
New Category...

FIGURE 15.9.
The Clip Properties dialog box with multiple imported clips.

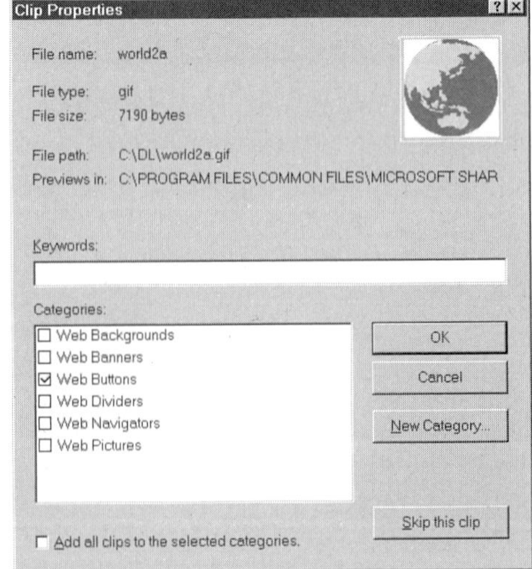

NOTE

For multiple images, there are two further options to consider. If you do not want to import a particular image, you can click the button labeled Skip this clip. The importation for that particular image will be canceled, and the Clip Properties for the next one will be displayed. *Do not* click the Cancel button to skip a single image that is part of a multiple image importation; that will cancel the entire operation, and you'll have to start over.

The other option is a check box in the lower-left corner labeled Add all clips to the selected categories. This is a time-saving device, but it has a catch. If you are importing a series of images that you want to go into the same categories, this will keep you from having to manually click all the appropriate check boxes for each image. The major drawback with this method is that you cannot enter keywords for any of the images if you click this check box. If you click the OK button while this check box is selected, all the images will automatically be imported one after the other. You'll have to go into the appropriate category and select each image individually, click the Clip Properties button, and enter the keywords afterward if you choose this approach.

Importing Clip Art from Clip Packages

A clip package is a clip art collection specially designed to work with Clip Gallery. They are already preset with keywords, categories, and preview images. To import the previews from clip packages, there is a different procedure from importing images.

First, instead of selecting the image file format type, choose Clip Gallery Packages from the drop-down list box labeled "Files of type:" at the bottom. If the folder displayed does not contain the clip package you want to add to Clip Gallery, change to the one that does.

Next, select the clip package you want to import (its name will then appear in the File name edit box); then click the Open button. When you are finished, click the Close button.

Importing Clip Art from the Clip Gallery Live Web Site

You can access a Web site called "Clip Gallery Live" that Microsoft has created to support Clip Gallery. From there, you can download new images. (See Figure 15.10.)

To connect to Clip Gallery Live from within Clip Gallery, just click the icon button on the bottom-right side that shows a globe with a magnifying glass in front of it (which is exactly the same symbol as the shortcut icon for the Microsoft Internet Explorer Web browser). This will launch your default Web browser and connect it with the site. The first time you do this, you'll be presented with a dialog box that asks you if you have Web access. To avoid this happening during subsequent Clip Gallery Live accesses, click the check box labeled "Don't show this message again." Then click the OK button to proceed, or click the Cancel button to abort the operation.

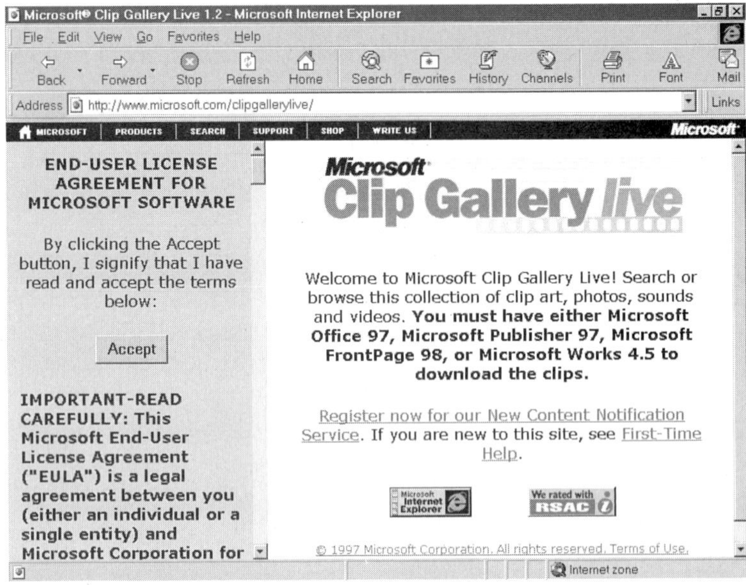

FIGURE 15.10.
The Clip Gallery Live Web site.

To use the Clip Gallery Live site, you must first agree to abide by the terms and conditions on the left side. Click the Accept button.

You can either browse the images by category or search them by keyword (see Figures 15.11 and 15.12). By default, you are in browse mode to start with, so clicking the Browse button has no effect in this situation. If you want to enter search mode, click the Search button. To return to browse mode, click the Browse button.

Under the Browse and Search buttons are icon-style buttons corresponding to the notebook tabs in Clip Gallery: Clip Art, Pictures, Sounds, and Videos (as mentioned at the beginning of this chapter, Microsoft uses its own peculiar definitions in Clip Gallery; they refer to vector graphics as "clip art" and bitmapped graphics as "pictures"). Once again, the sound and video are not germane to our current purposes.

In browse mode, you are presented with a drop-down list box under the heading, "Select a category." Categories here range from "Academic" to "Weather." Select the one you are interested in and then click the button labeled Go (or press the Enter key). The first 12 images in that category will be displayed on the right. To access further images (a dozen at a time), scroll down and click the right arrow. From subsequent screens, click the left arrow to go back and the right arrow to go forward. When you find an image you want to download, click the filename beneath it. When Internet Explorer asks you what you want to do with the file, click the Open this file from the Internet radio button, then click OK. The image, with keywords and categories already assigned, will be downloaded straight into Clip Gallery in `.wmf` format. There will be a new category called "(Downloaded Clips)" and, if the new images are registered in categories you do not currently have in Clip Gallery, the new categories will be created automatically as well.

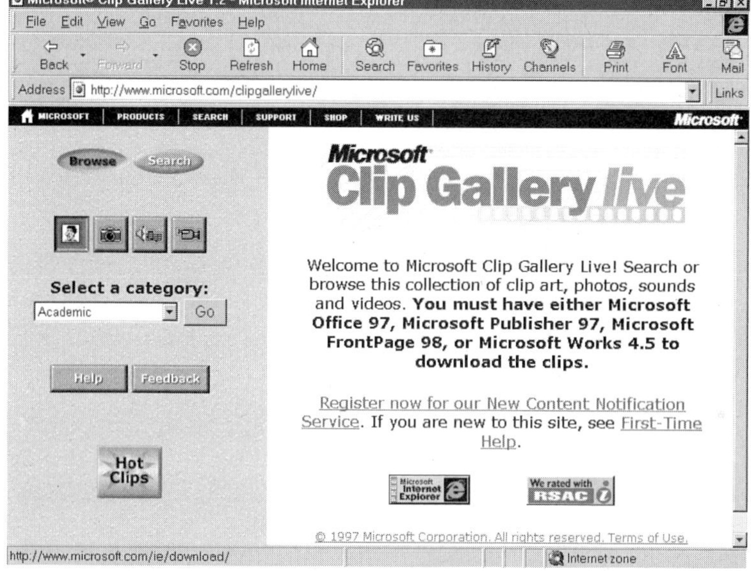

FIGURE 15.11.
The Clip Gallery Live Web site's Browse screen.

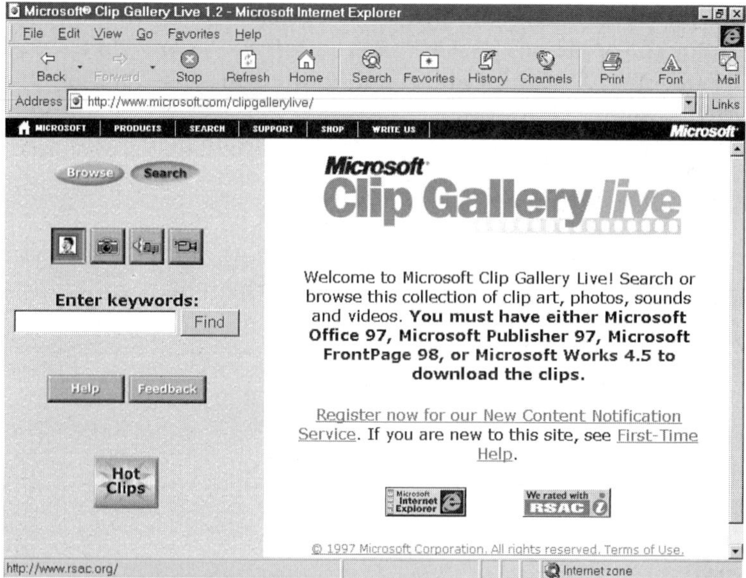

FIGURE 15.12.
The Clip Gallery Live Web site's Search screen.

This is the only procedure you can use; if you just download the image the normal way, it will be in a useless `.cil` format.

NOTE

The Clip Gallery Live Web site is designed to work with Microsoft Internet Explorer. In order to use it with Netscape Navigator, you must tell Navigator about Microsoft's new `.cil` file type for downloading these images. The easiest way to do this is to attempt to download an image. When Netscape tells you that it is an unknown file type, click the Pick App button. From the resultant Configure External Viewer dialog box, click the Browse button. Go to the `c:\program files\common files\microsoft shared\artgalry\` folder and double click on the file `artgalry.exe`. This will return you to the Configure External Viewer dialog box, where you should now click OK. As with Internet Explorer, you should now choose to open the file rather than to save it to disk.

Buttons labeled Help and Feedback provide, respectively, information on how to use the site, and an opportunity to tell Microsoft how you feel about it and what you would like to see included in the future.

A button labeled Hot Clips at the bottom left shows a variety of images from varying categories.

In search mode, everything looks the same as in browse mode, with the exception that the Select a Category list box and the Go button are replaced with the Enter Keywords edit box and the Find button. Of course, you enter the keywords for your search in the edit box and then click the Find button (or press the Enter key). Unlike with Clip Gallery itself, Clip Gallery Live's search function allows you to use multiple keywords (try "clouds" and then try "clouds rain" to see the effect this has).

The download procedure is the same as for the browse mode.

Using FrontPage 97 Clip Art in FrontPage 98's Clip Gallery

If you installed FrontPage 98 over FrontPage 97, then, even though your old clip art isn't displayed in Clip Gallery, it is still there on your hard drive right where it used to be. You just need to import it into Clip Gallery and assign it to a category.

The clip art categories have changed from what they were in FrontPage 97. Instead of the old lineup of Animations, Backgrounds, Bullets, Buttons, Icons, Lines, and Logos, FrontPage 98 has the following lineup:

- Web Banners
- Web Buttons
- Web Dividers
- Web Navigators
- Web Pictures

There are a couple of obvious category similarities between the two versions: Button images should go into the Web Buttons category, and Lines should go into the Web Dividers category. Beyond that, it is probably best to just create new categories that match the old ones.

The old clip art from FrontPage 97 is located in the following directories:

Animations: `C:\Program Files\Microsoft FrontPage\Clipart\Animations`

Backgrounds: `C:\Program Files\Microsoft FrontPage\Clipart\Backgrounds`

Bullets: `C:\Program Files\Microsoft FrontPage\Clipart\Bullets`

Buttons: `C:\Program Files\Microsoft FrontPage\Clipart\Buttons`

Icons: `C:\Program Files\Microsoft FrontPage\Clipart\Icons`

Lines: `C:\Program Files\Microsoft FrontPage\Clipart\Lines`

Logos: `C:\Program Files\Microsoft FrontPage\Clipart\Logos`

Deleting Clip Art Previews from Clip Gallery

To delete a preview (image reference and thumbnail image) from the database, select the image you want to remove and press the Delete key. You'll be asked to confirm the deletion. Click the Yes button to confirm; click the No button to cancel the deletion.

You can also delete an image reference from the database by right-clicking the image you want to get rid of and then selecting Delete Clip from the pop-up menu that appears.

When you delete a preview, it is not the same as deleting the file. Deleting a preview simply removes the thumbnail image from Clip Gallery and removes the reference in the database. In order to delete the actual file on your hard drive, you need to use Windows Explorer or a graphics program with file deletion capability.

CAUTION

If you delete a preview, then the keywords and category assignments are lost and must be reentered if you import the image again.

Using the Update Feature

A number of circumstances can affect the reliability of the image database information in Clip Gallery. Files can be moved, they can be deleted, or they can be altered or even replaced by a new image with the same filename.

Clip Gallery deals with this problem by providing the Update feature. When you invoke Update, it will scan the disk and check the current listing of all the files in the Clip Gallery database against the real situation it finds on your drive.

To invoke the Update feature, right-click any preview image, then select Update Clip Previews from the resultant pop-up menu. The Update dialog box will appear. (See Figure 15.13.)

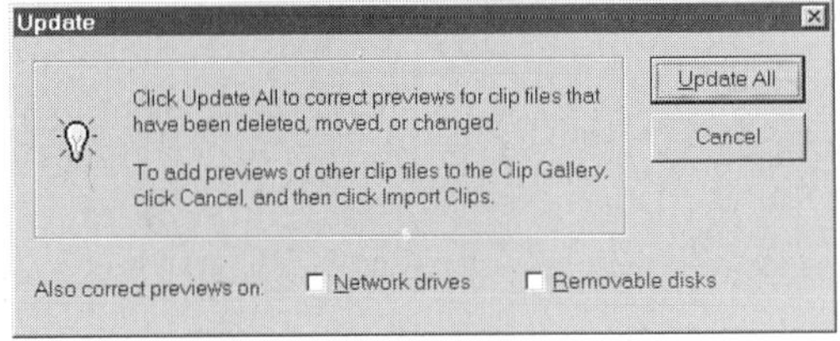

FIGURE 15.13.
The Update dialog box.

If you need to check only the images on your hard drive, then simply click the Update All button (there is no provision for updating only the selected image). If you also need to check images on another type of drive, such as on a network drive or on external disks in floppy drives or zip drives, then click the appropriate check boxes at the bottom of the dialog box before you click the Update All button.

If a file has been moved, then a dialog box (see Figure 15.14) will appear notifying you that "The Clip Gallery cannot find the following file:". At this point, you have four choices. If you choose to update the location, you'll be presented with a standard File Open dialog box. Because this lacks the convenient browse feature that makes it so easy to find files in some dialog boxes, you'll have to know the new location of the file and manually switch to it. When you find the correct folder, click the Open button and Clip Gallery will update the preview database to amend the location of the file. There is no provision for locating a file that has been renamed. If the file has a new file name, you will have to reimport it under the new one after removing the old preview.

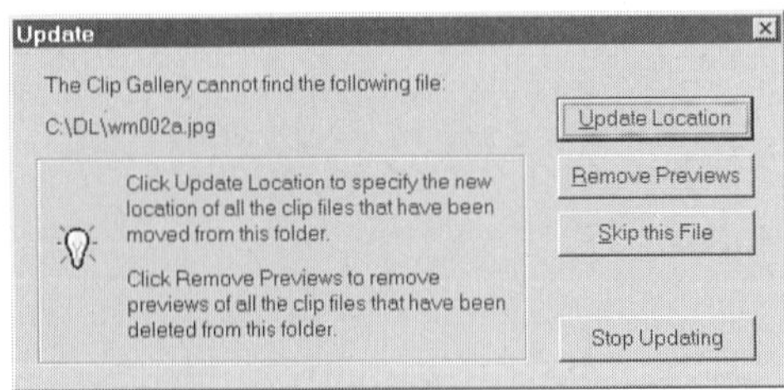

FIGURE 15.14.
The Update dialog box when Clip Gallery cannot find your file.

If you opt to remove all the previews that Clip Gallery cannot find on the disk, you forego any opportunity to update a location. All references to any files that are not in their original location will be deleted (there is no provision for removing only the one image reference).

If you click the Skip this file button, then Update will continue looking for other altered or missing files, but it will not deal with the currently displayed one at all. The result of this is that when you select that image in Clip Gallery and click Clip Properties, the old location information will still be there, but the file length will be set to zero.

If you choose to stop the update process, the entire operation is canceled.

When the process is complete, a message box will inform you that "The Clip Gallery has finished updating your previews."

NOTE

If you have selected the check box for an external drive, then the Update process will remind you that you need to insert the appropriate disk in the drive Clip Gallery has in its database.

Summary

The Clip Gallery is a very useful tool for managing clip art images. It can manage a database of images consisting of many different file formats, but all of these will be converted to GIF format when they are inserted into FrontPage Editor and saved—except for GIFs and JPEGs. The Clip Gallery database provides an easy way to organize disparate images into handy categories, and images can be imported from a variety of sources—including a specially dedicated Microsoft Web site—into the database. A variety of utility routines exist for database management, including the ability to place images into multiple categories, create new categories, modify or delete categories, add keywords, and perform searches. Thumbnail images, called "previews," are displayed, and image information can be added, deleted, or modified. The Update feature can be used to deal with changes in the image files.

Working with the Microsoft Image Composer

by David and Rhonda Crowder

IN THIS CHAPTER

- Some Terms You Should Know 274
- Invoking Image Composer from within FrontPage 98 275
- The Image Composer Desktop 276

The Microsoft Image Composer is a full-featured graphics program that can successfully compete with a number of commercial programs currently on the market. One major difference between Image Composer and similar programs that cost hundreds of dollars is that you already own it—it comes free with FrontPage 98.

Image Composer is an updated version of the old Altamira Composer program, which has been optimized for the creation of Web graphics. You can draw your own images from scratch using a variety of tools; you can create everything from ovals and complex curves to airbrush paintings and pencil sketches. You can also import existing images in a variety of formats. Images can be combined if you choose, or you can manipulate their colors, shapes, and transparency. Also, you can take advantage of Image Composer's built-in special effects to do some truly amazing things to spice up humdrum images.

FrontPage users have found Image Composer to be one of the most useful Web tools in their arsenal, and it is such an impressive program that there are even those developers who are not FrontPage users who have bought FrontPage solely because they can get Image Composer that way.

This chapter will cover the basic operation of Image Composer, its major concepts, the layout, menus, and toolbars. Subsequent chapters will go into greater depth on the details of sprite usage, image effects, and color palettes, as well as show you how to get the most out of FrontPage Editor's image-handling tools.

Some Terms You Should Know

Image Composer works a bit differently than a common paint program because it is "object oriented." Its basic building blocks are called "sprites." Each element (or, more properly, "image object") in a composition is a sprite. If you insert a GIF image into the composition, it becomes a sprite. If you draw a shape across the GIF, that is another sprite. Each sprite has its own independent properties, and the composition as a whole is the combination of all its sprites. Sprites will be covered in detail in Chapter 17, "Creating Great Images with Image Composer," but this is a term you'll need to know from the beginning.

Although Image Composer does not create three-dimensional images, you need to consider three dimensions in working with the composition. As with the "layers" concept in programs such as Photoshop (actually, Altamira Composer, the forerunner of Image Composer, was first with this concept, and Photoshop and the others followed), Image Composer has what is called the "stack" (also known as the z-order, from the x-y-z coordinate system, where x runs left to right, y runs up and down, and z can be viewed as running from the front of the monitor to the back of it), which determines which sprites are on top of or underneath the others.

Another concept you might not be familiar with from other graphics programs is "channels." Microsoft officially defines a channel as "a medium for transferring color information to the pixels of a display monitor." However, you might as well just think of channels as the basic color segments of an image. Image Composer has four channels. Three of these are obvious and easy to understand—red, green, and blue, which are the basic building blocks of RGB color images. This is the system used by all the common computer monitors currently in use. The fourth channel, however, is called "alpha," and its value determines the opacity or transparency of a sprite.

The alpha channel becomes a very important consideration when you have several sprites stacked on top of one another. The greater the degree of transparency of the top sprite, the more you can see through it to the sprites beneath. Therefore, the alpha channel can be used to totally alter the appearance of a composition.

NOTE

If you are technically minded, you might be interested to know that the red, green, and blue channels are 24-bit, whereas the alpha channel is 8-bit.

Invoking Image Composer from within FrontPage 98

You can use Image Composer as a standalone program, or you can launch it while you're working on a Web page in FrontPage Editor, or modifying a FrontPage web in FrontPage Explorer.

In either FrontPage Editor or FrontPage Explorer, you can select Tools|Show Image Editor from the menu. In FrontPage Explorer, you can also click the Show Image Editor button in the toolbar (see Figure 16.1); for reasons known only to Microsoft, this button is not in the toolbar for FrontPage Editor, so you will have to use the menu selection method from it.

TIP

An alternative method of launching Image Composer is to double-click an image in a Web page you are working on in FrontPage Editor. Additionally, you can double-click an image's filename in FrontPage Explorer's Folder view, All Files view, or Navigation view. It is possible to launch via a similar method from the Hyperlinks view, as well, but you must double-click the image icon in that case, rather than the filename. The advantage to this approach is that the image you have selected will be automatically loaded into Image Composer. If you use the toolbar or menu method, Image Composer will launch with an empty workspace.

FIGURE 16.1.
The Show Image Editor button in FrontPage Explorer.

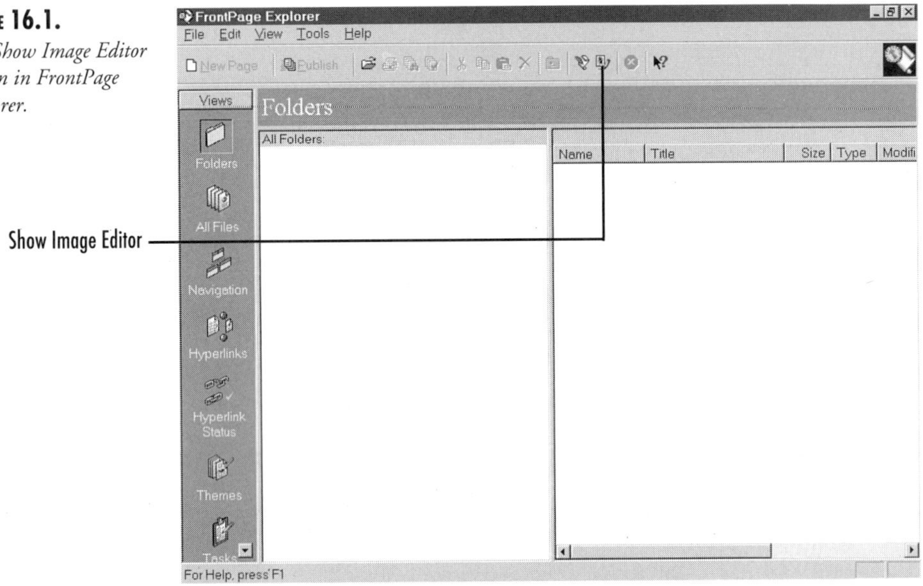

Show Image Editor

CAUTION

Be aware that each time you double-click an image or filename, or use the toolbar or menu approaches, a new instance of Image Composer is launched. Depending on your computer system, this could seriously overload your resources, and perhaps even cause your computer to crash. To prevent this problem from occurring, make sure to close Image Composer each time you finish working on an image (after you have saved it, of course).

The Image Composer Desktop

The Image Composer "desktop" is the total program interface (see Figure 16.2). It consists of the control elements (menu, toolbar, toolbox, and color swatch) through which you issue commands to the program; the status bar, which passes messages from the program to you about its functions; and the composition space and workspace, which have already been discussed.

One more critical concept is necessary before we begin—the difference between the workspace and the composition space. Unlike a typical graphics program, Image Composer has two working areas. The workspace is the total screen area that is not devoted to menus, toolbars, and so on. The composition space, however, is the portion of the workspace in the center of things. It is white and 420×275 pixels in size by default (although both of these settings can be changed). The area of the workspace outside the composition space is a holding tank for anything you want to keep handy, but isn't currently being used in the composition itself.

FIGURE 16.2.
Microsoft Image Composer desktop.

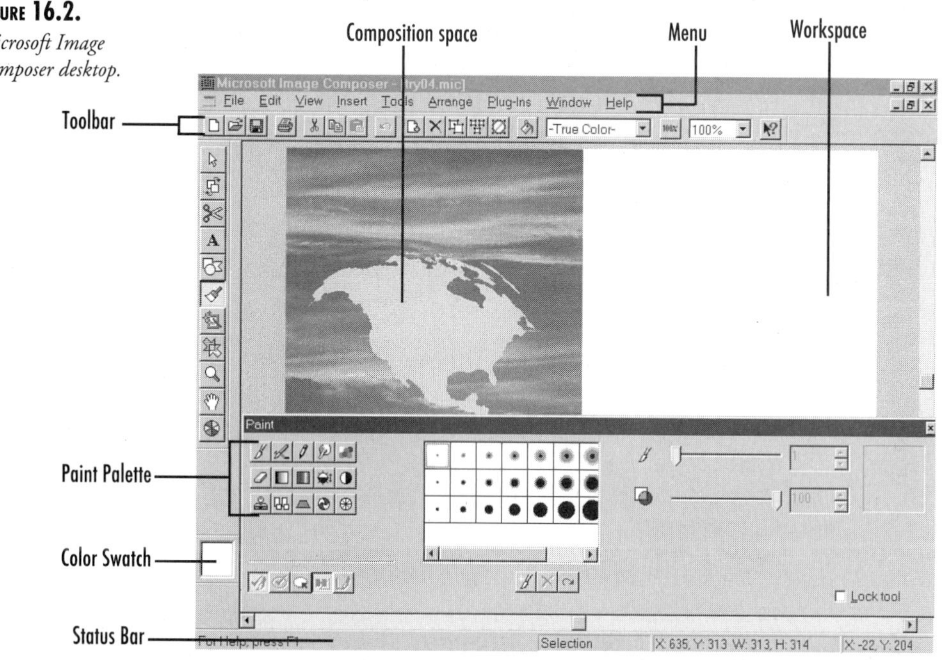

TIP

It is helpful in understanding this concept if you think of a composition as a collage. The composition space is the piece of paper to which you are gluing the different elements, and the workspace is the table on which the paper rests. The elements you haven't glued into place yet are arranged on the table, all around the paper.

This becomes very important when you save your work. If you save it as a bitmapped image (such as a GIF file), the only parts that are kept are the ones that are in the composition space; everything else is thrown away. In order to maintain the entire workspace intact between sessions, you must save the file in the Microsoft Image Composer format (`.mic`).

Finally, when you access any of the tools Image Composer has available, a box will open from which you can make various choices relating to the tool; these are known as palettes (not to be confused with the color palette).

The Image Composer Toolbar

The toolbar contains the basic file-handling and image-editing commands, such as Open, Save, Cut, Copy, Undo, and so on. (See Figure 16.3 and Table 16.1.)

CAUTION

The Undo command, it cannot be emphasized enough, has only a single level; that is, it will only undo the most recent change you have made.

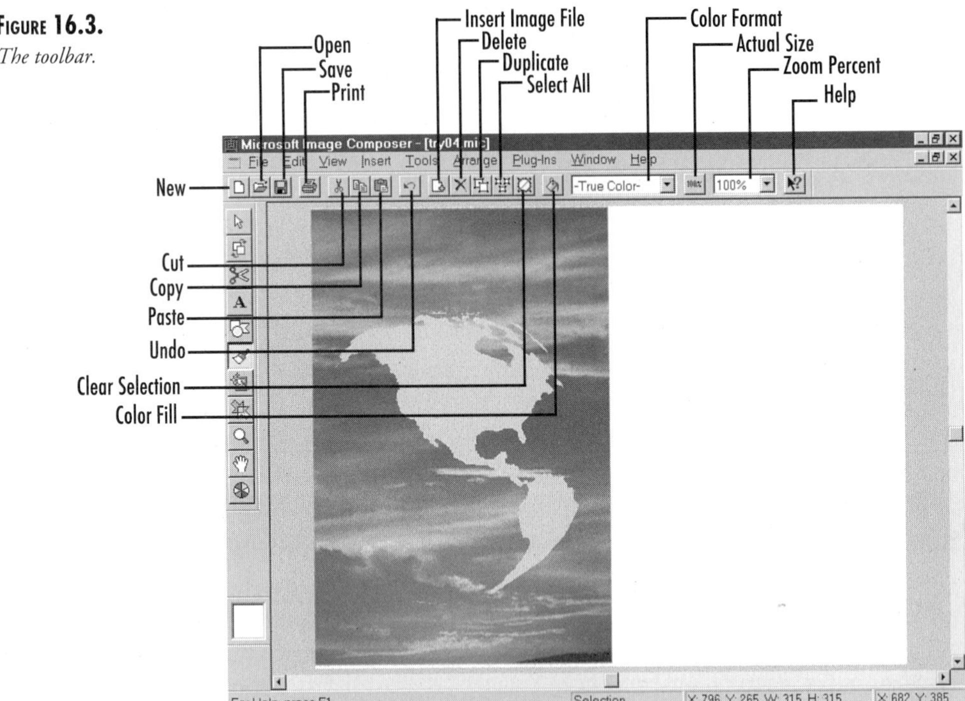

FIGURE 16.3.
The toolbar.

Table 16.1. Toolbar buttons.

Button	*Function*
New	Clears the current composition and begins with an empty one.
Open	Clears the current composition and loads an existing one.
Save	Saves the current composition to disk.
Print	Prints the current composition.

Button	*Function*
Cut	Deletes the currently selected sprite and places a copy of it in the Clipboard.
Copy	Places a copy of the currently selected sprite in the Clipboard.
Paste	Places a copy of the Clipboard contents into the current composition.
Undo	Reverses the most recent action taken.
Insert Image File	Adds an existing image to the current composition.
Delete	Deletes the currently selected sprite without copying it to the Clipboard.
Duplicate	Performs a simultaneous Copy and Paste, placing a copy of the currently selected sprite into the composition, offset slightly from the original.
Select All	Simultaneously selects all sprites in the composition.
Clear Selection	Cancels any and all current selections.
Color Fill	Changes all non-transparent pixels in selected sprite to color-in-color swatch.
Color Format	Switches among black and white, grayscale, true color, and so on.
Actual Size	Resets zoom percentage to 100%.
Zoom Percent	Sets zoom factor ranging from 10% to 1,000%.
Help	Activates the Help pointer. Placing the Help pointer over any item and then clicking the left mouse button results in a context-sensitive Help screen for that item.

TIP

To make the icons in the toolbar larger (this has no effect on the toolbox), select View|Toolbars from the menu. In the resultant Toolbars dialog box (see Figure 16.4), click the check box labeled Large Icons in order to have easier-to-see buttons on the toolbar. This will make your workspace smaller by a fraction of an inch, but the increased ease of use in the toolbar is worth it.

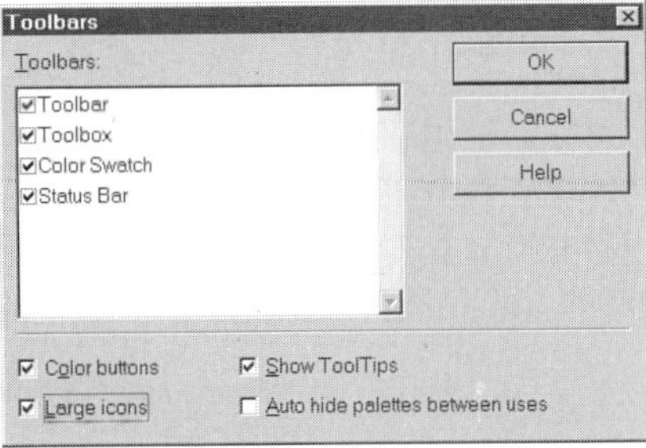

FIGURE 16.4.
The Toolbars dialog box.

This dialog box considers all the command elements of the Image Composer desktop to be "toolbars," whether they are called such anywhere else or not. Therefore, here is where you will choose whether or not to display the various elements. The check boxes next to each desktop element's name should be checked if you want it to be displayed, or unchecked if you want to remove it from the desktop. If elements are removed from the desktop, their commands must be accessed from the menu choices. You can always change the settings later if you change your mind, thus restoring the removed elements to the desktop.

Two further check box options available here are Color Buttons and Show ToolTips. The first is in case you would like grayscale buttons in the toolbar (once again, this does not affect the toolbox); the second turns on and off the floating tips that display if you rest the pointer on a button for a few moments (the slightly more detailed tips in the status bar remain active).

One final checkbox is the Auto hide palettes between uses option. If you check this, any visible tool palette will disappear when you begin working on your composition. This is useful, because the palette would otherwise obscure part of the composition space. To bring back the palette, simply place the mouse pointer in the status bar.

CAUTION

The auto hide feature only works when the palette is in the default position at the bottom of the workspace. If you move it to another location, it will only go gray instead of blanking out. To solve this problem, select View | Dock Tool Palette from the menu, which will return the palette to its default position.

The Image Composer Toolbox and Color Swatch

The toolbox contains the tools for image creation and manipulation, such as adding text, creating shapes, imposing graphic effects, and so on (see Figure 16.5 and Table 16.2). Each of these buttons, when clicked, brings up a window called a "palette" (no relation to color palettes, by the way—refer back to Figure 16.2) that provides you with the detailed options available for the particular tool. The color swatch, although technically not part of the toolbox, is located directly beneath it in the same panel, so it is included here.

FIGURE 16.5.
The toolbox and color swatch.

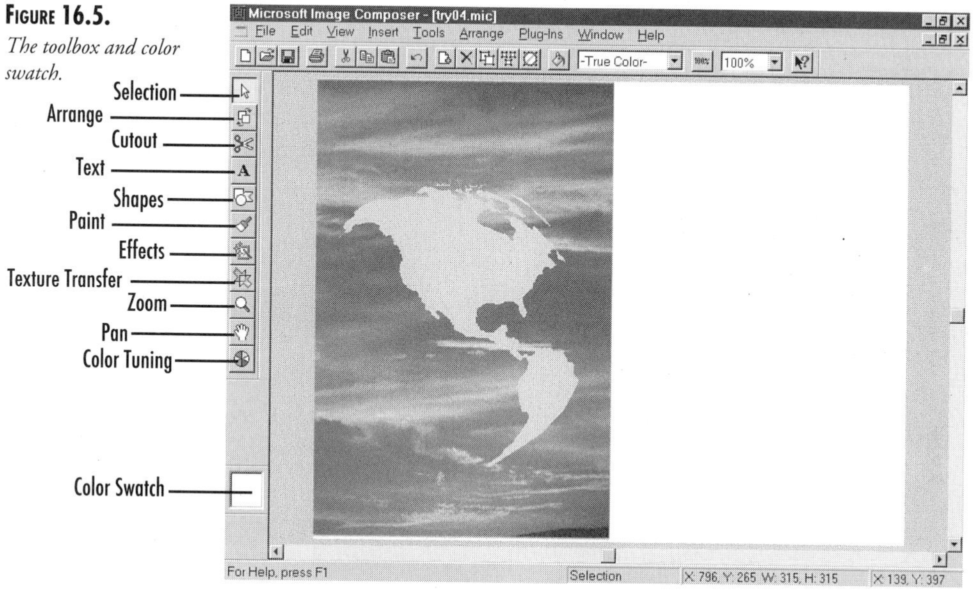

Table 16.2. Toolbox buttons and the color swatch.

Button	*Function*
Selection	Allows pointer to be used for sprite selection.
Arrange	Allows you to adjust the width and height of a sprite, or to crop it. Additional options include rotating, flipping, and aligning, moving sprites backward and forward in the stack, and grouping/ungrouping sprites.
Cutout	Provides tools for cutting out areas from sprites. Like the Shape tool, it allows you to create rectangles, ovals, spline curves, and polygons, but removes these shapes from the selected sprite instead of adding them to the composition. Also has Select Color Region tool for extracting all areas of the same color from a sprite.
Text	Enables you to enter a single line of text (up to 80 characters in length) in any font you have into the composition (see the following Tip).
Shapes	Provides tools for drawing rectangles, ovals, spline curves, and polygons.
Paint	Provides a variety of freehand painting tools (brush, pencil, airbrush, and some special effects, such as dodge and burn), as well as a custom brush designer.

continues

Table 16.2. continued

Button	*Function*
Effects	Gives a wide variety of effects (such as watercolor and sponge) to make sprites look as though they were painted on a canvas. Also has a variety of other effects, such as edge enhancement and color gradients.
Texture Transfer	Transfers pixels from one sprite to another.
Zoom	Enables you to click your composition to zoom in or Ctrl+click to zoom out.
Pan	Lets you drag the composition to another position.
Color Tuning	Adjusts brightness, hue, contrast, and saturation of colors. Also allows you to work on highlights and shadows, as well as a histogram of the selected sprite.
Color Swatch	Brings up the color palette from which you choose the current color.

The Image Composer Menu

As with most other Windows programs, the menu in Image Composer is largely duplicated by the program's buttons and other non-menu controls. Also, many of the menu choices are common to all Windows programs. For these reasons, and because most people prefer the use of buttons to menus, we dealt with the toolbar and toolbox first. There are, however, some things that are available solely through the menu. These exclusive menu choices are the only ones that are covered in Table 16.3.

The menu bar includes the following choices: File, Edit, View, Insert, Tools, Arrange, Plug-Ins, Window, and Help. The Arrange menu is the only one with no exclusive menu choices.

Table 16.3. Functions exclusive to the menu.

Menu	*Menu Choice*	*Function*
File	Save As	Saves the entire composition under a new name.
	Save Selection As	Saves the selected sprite under a new name.
	Save Copy As	Saves copy of the current composition without affecting current file name.

Menu	*Menu Choice*	*Function*
	Save for the Web	Invokes wizard to help optimize image for Web site use.
	Composition Properties	Displays information about the width, height, color space, and so on for the current composition.
	Composition Setup	Enables you to set width, height, and color for composition space (either for the current composition or for all future compositions).
	Scan Image	Enables you to select or operate a TWAIN-compliant scanning source.
	Send	Puts a copy of the current composition into an e-mail message.
Edit	Paste Special	Pastes objects from the Clipboard into the composition, with options as to image type.
	Copy Channel	Copies the settings from the red, green, blue, or alpha channel.
	Paste Channel	Pastes the settings from a previously copied red, green, blue, or alpha channel.
	Broadcast Channel	Creates a grayscale image of the selected sprite.
	Properties	Displays information about the width, height, color space, and so on for the currently selected sprite. Can also be accessed via Alt+Enter keys.
View	Center on Composition Space	This command puts the center of the composition space into the center of the workspace. Can also be accessed via the Home key.
	Center On Selection	This moves the composition so that the selected sprite is in the center of the workspace. Can also be accessed via the F8 key.

continues

Table 16.3. continued

Menu	*Menu Choice*	*Function*
	Fit Composition Space to Selection	Resizes composition space to size of selected sprite.
	Composition Guides	Shows grid lines in workspace.
	Lock Composition Guides	Prevents composition guides from being repositioned.
	Toolbars	This brings up the Toolbars dialog box (see the section titled, "The Image Composer Toolbar").
	Toggle Palette View	This will remove any open palette from the workspace. Can also be accessed via the F2 key.
	Dock Tool Palette	If the palette has been moved from its default position, this command will return it.
Insert	From PhotoCD	Just like the Insert Image File button, this command allows you to import images into the composition, except that this specifically requires a Kodak PhotoCD format disk to import from.
Tools	Options	Allows you to change various settings such as the default size and color of the composition guide, the path to an alternate plug-in directory, whether or not scroll bars are active, and so on.
	Microsoft GIF Animator	If you have this program installed, it will show up on the Tools menu listing.
Plug-Ins	Repeat Last Plug-In	Repeats the entire sequence from your most recent use of plug-ins.
	Impressionist	Accesses options for a plug-in that comes with Image Composer.
Window	New Window	Opens a new window on the current composition (see the following Caution).

Menu	*Menu Choice*	*Function*
Help	Microsoft Image Composer Help Topics	Opens the Help file.
	Learning Microsoft Image Composer	Opens tutorial on using Image Composer.
	Common Tasks	Quick reference to Image Composer tools.
	Keyboard Short Cuts	Shows a listing of keyboard short cuts.
	Microsoft on the Web	Takes you to the official Microsoft Image Composer support Web site.

CAUTION

The Window|New Window command does not create a copy of the active composition, but simply allows you to see more than one view of it. Therefore, although you can pan, zoom, and so on without affecting any other windows, any change you make to the sprites in one window takes place in the other ones as well.

Summary

Microsoft Image Composer is an object-oriented graphics program. Its basic building blocks are image objects called "sprites." Image Composer can import images from, and save to, a wide variety of file types. Special effects can be used to enhance images. Sprites can be combined or stacked on top of one another, and their color and transparency can be varied. These features are controlled through use of the menu, toolbar, toolbox, and color swatch.

Creating Great Images with Image Composer

by David and Rhonda Crowder

IN THIS CHAPTER

- Creating Sprites 288
- Opening and Saving Compositions 304
- Inserting Sprites 311
- Scanning Sprites into Image Composer 312
- Manipulating and Combining Sprites 312

Sprites are the individual elements that comprise a composition in Image Composer. The theory and capabilities of sprites were covered in Chapter 16, "Working with the Microsoft Image Composer" (refer to the figures in Chapter 16 for the location of buttons and tools mentioned in this chapter). In this chapter, you will get practical, hands-on experience in working with sprites, from opening existing compositions to scanning new ones.

Creating Sprites

Image Composer provides only two official ways to create sprites. With a little cheating, however, there is a third way. The two official methods are to use the text tool and the shapes tool. The first, of course, simply puts text into the composition. The shapes tool provides basic rectangles and ovals, in addition to the more complex possibilities inherent in polygons and spline curves. The third way is more like the traditional paint program, using the paint tool.

Setting the Sprite Color

Before jumping into sprite creation, you should note that there is one thing all sprites have in common. Whether text or shapes, whatever you create will show up in the currently selected color. To change this color, click the color swatch (the large, colored square at the bottom of the toolbox buttons). This will bring up the Color Picker dialog box (see Figure 17.1).

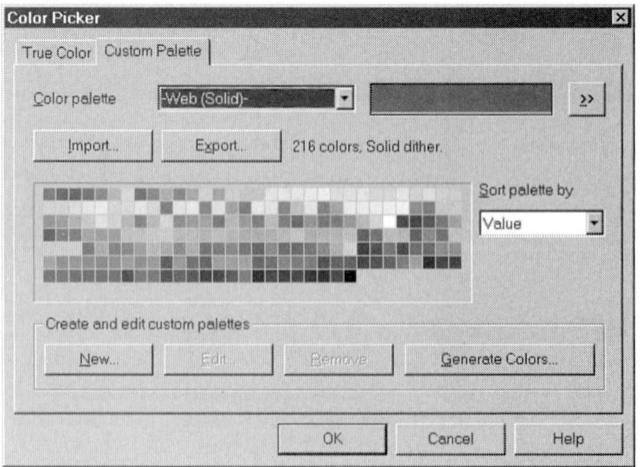

FIGURE 17.1.
The Color Picker dialog box.

The uses and limitations of color palettes will be covered in greater detail in Chapter 19, "Optimizing Your Images and Color Palettes." For our current purposes, simply click the color you want to use for your sprite and then click the OK button. The color in the box will change, indicating your new choice, and anything created from now until you change the color again will be in that color.

Using the Text Tool

Clicking the Text button brings up the text palette (see Figure 17.2). This palette shows information on the currently selected font: font, style, size, and script (script will usually default to Western).

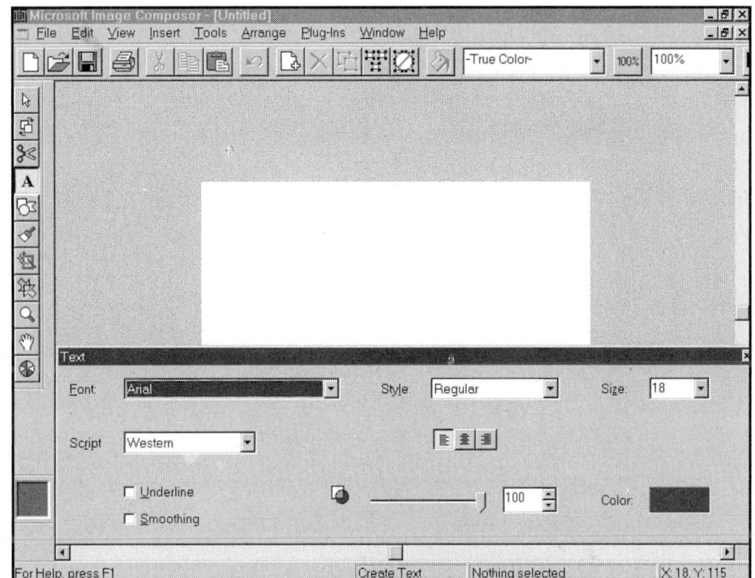

FIGURE 17.2.
The Text palette.

There are a number of ways to change the settings for a font. you can choose a new one by clicking the arrow on the drop-down Font list. You'll be presented with a list of the available fonts on your system.

You can choose the font style from the drop-down list in the center of the dialog box by clicking the one you want. Typically, this will include Regular, Italic, Bold, and Bold Italic, although some fonts will not have all these styles available.

You can select the size from the drop-down list on the right side. These measurements are in points. A point is 1/72 of an inch.

There are some other controls in the text palette. In the center of the text palette are three buttons for aligning the text. The one on the left is for left alignment, the one in the center is for center alignment, and the one on the right is for right alignment. You can also click on the check boxes in the lower left corner if you want the text to be underlined or if you want to smooth the edges (the latter effect is minimally noticeable).

As is common with Image Composer tools, the text palette has an opacity setting (at the bottom center of the palette). By default, this is set to 100%, or normal, full solidity. If you want to set a greater degree of transparency for your text, set this to a lower amount. This setting is most effective if you are planning to place your text over some other graphical element; otherwise, it simply has the effect of lightening the text.

Finally, you can click the color display in the lower right corner to bring up the color picker and choose a different color for your text.

To create text, simply place the mouse pointer where you want to put the text and click the left mouse button. This will create a resizable text box (see Figure 17.3). Now all you have to do is type. If the text doesn't fit quite right, just click on one of the drag handles around the text box and, holding the left mouse button down, move it until the box is the size you need. The lettering in the text is in the currently selected color and has a transparent background.

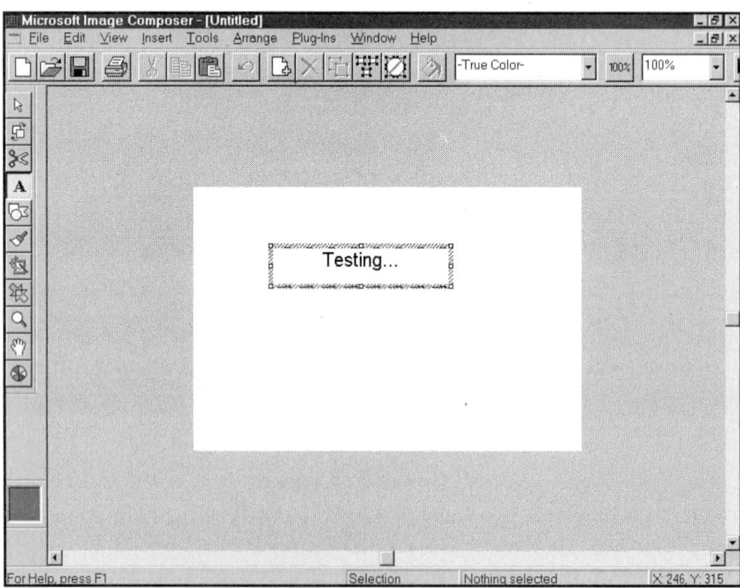

FIGURE 17.3.
The text sprite.

If you want to change anything about the text, just select the text box and alter the appropriate setting in the text palette. This can be done even after you have finished creating the text.

Choosing the Right Font

As with any graphical element, you must give careful thought to choosing the right font for the impression you want to create with your Web site. A delicate, flowery font in a pastel color will not be appropriate for a financial services site, nor will a straight, bold font in basic black do for an artist's Web page. Try several fonts and styles and see how they fit your intended purpose.

Using the Shapes Tool

The Shapes tool allows you to render both fixed shapes and hand-drawn ones. Figure 17.4 shows the shapes palette. The buttons on the left of the palette are where you select the type of shape with which you want to work. From top to bottom, they are Rectangle, Oval, Curve, and Polygon. The Curve and Polygon buttons are the ones you use to create hand-drawn shapes; polygons consist entirely of a series of straight lines. Either one can be used to create open or closed shapes.

FIGURE 17.4.
The Shapes palette.

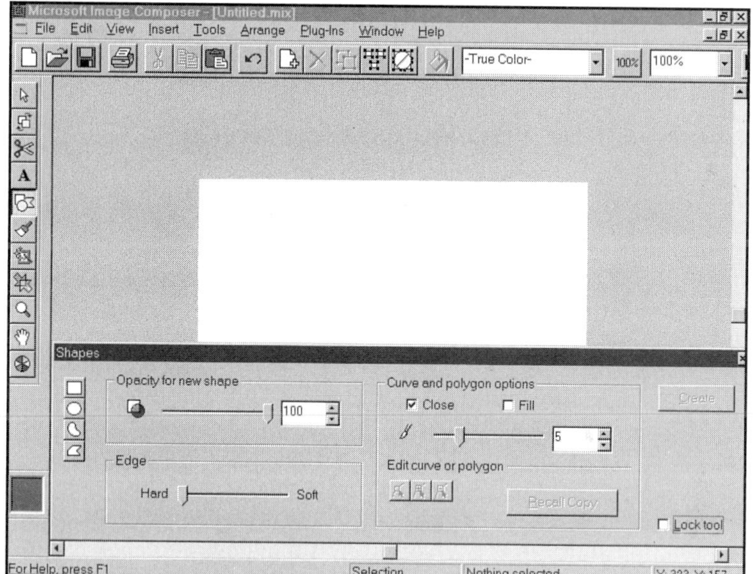

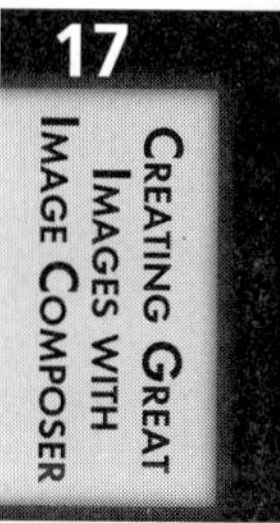

The Opacity setting determines the degree of transparency in the shape. The higher the number, the greater the solidity. The Curve and Polygon options apply only to those particular shapes and are, therefore, dealt with in the sections on those topics.

On the upper right side is the Create button. It finalizes your shape and places it into the composition; until this button is pressed, you can still edit the shape (see Figure 17.5).

The check box in the lower right corner of the shapes palette, labeled Lock tool, locks the selected shape button down; otherwise, it will be automatically deselected when the shape is rendered. This is useful when you intend to draw several different instances of the same type of shape. When you are finished, however, remember to uncheck Lock tool so that you can again use the mouse pointer to select objects; otherwise, you'll only be able to keep drawing shapes.

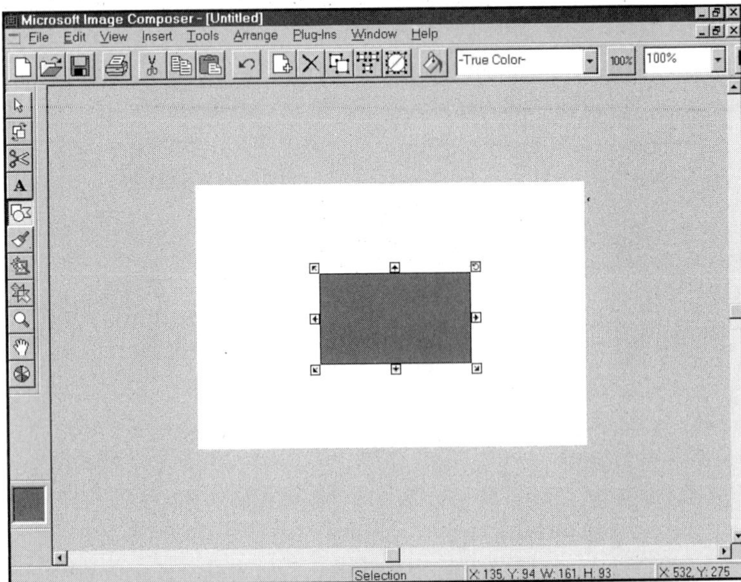

FIGURE 17.5.
A rendered shape.

Creating Rectangles

To create a rectangular shape (see Figure 17.6), you first need to select the color you want the rectangle to be (see the section titled, "Setting the Sprite Color"). Next, click the Rectangle button on the Shapes palette and set Opacity to the desired setting.

Place the pointer (which now shows a rectangle under the arrow to indicate which shape you are working with) on the composition at the point you want to start the first corner of the rectangle.

While holding the left mouse key down, drag the pointer in any direction until the rectangle is the size and shape you desire. An outline rectangle will follow the pointer as you drag, showing how the finished shape will appear. When you are satisfied, release the mouse button and click the Create button to complete the operation. The completed rectangle will be created.

Creating Ovals

To create an oval shape (see Figure 17.7), follow the same procedure as for creating a rectangular shape, except click the Oval. The pointer will show an oval under the arrow to indicate which shape you are working with.

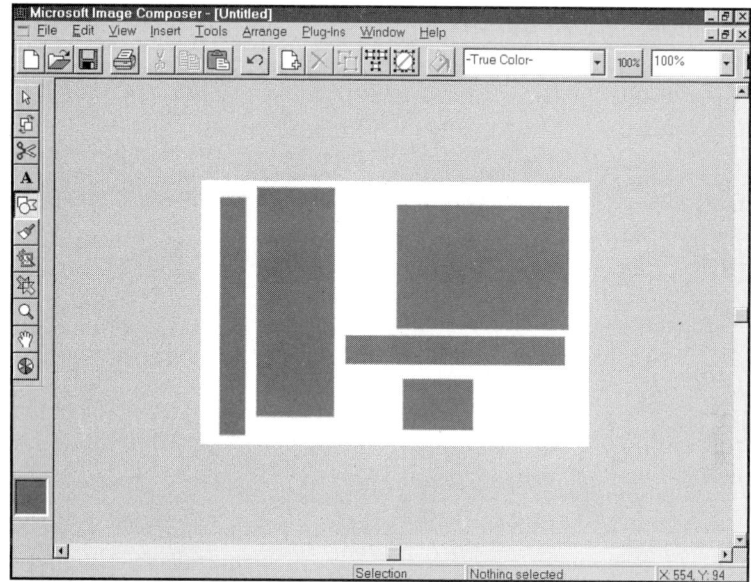

FIGURE 17.6.
Some rectangular shapes.

FIGURE 17.7.
Some oval shapes.

Creating Spline Curves

To create a curve shape (see Figure 17.8), you should first select the color you want the curve to be (see the section titled, "Setting the Sprite Color"). Next, click the Curve button on the Shapes palette and set Opacity to the desired setting.

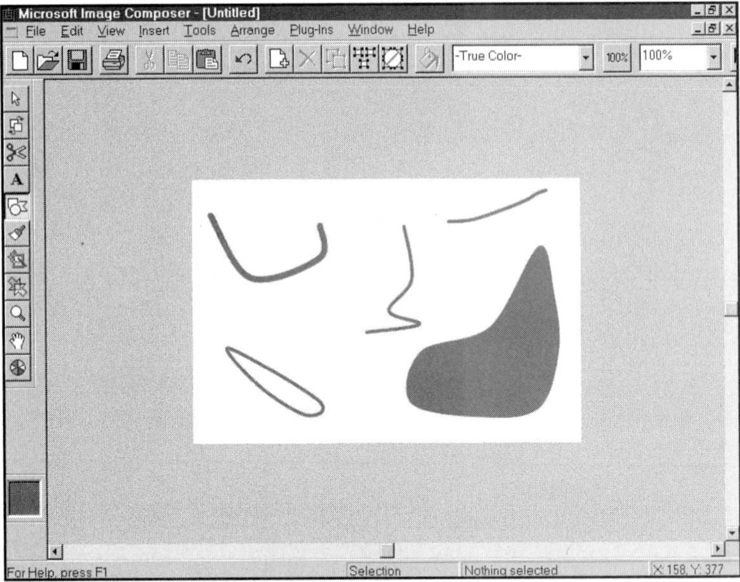

FIGURE 17.8.
Some curve shapes.

Set the line width to a number from 1 to 20 (the smaller the number, the thinner the line). If you want to create a closed shape, check the Close check box. Otherwise, make sure it is unchecked. If you are just beginning to work with curves, it is probably best for you to work with an open shape to get the feel of how it works before tackling the more complex closed curve approach.

If the Close option is selected, you need to decide whether you want the curve figure to be filled (with the currently selected color and opacity, just like the outline), or whether you want only the outline to be drawn. Check the Fill check box to make a solid figure; uncheck it to make it hollow.

Now you're ready to actually draw the curve. Place the pointer (which now shows a wavy line under the arrow to indicate which shape you are working with) on the composition at the point you want to start the curve. Click the left mouse key once to set the first point, then move the pointer to another point and click again. A straight line will appear between the two points (even though this tool generates curves, it needs at least three points to do so; therefore, the line between the first two points has no curve to it).

Move the pointer to yet another point and click again. If you are working with an open curve, the line between all the points now acquires a curve to it. If you have selected a closed curve, you'll see an airfoil shape appear when you check the third point as Image Composer closes the figure. With every point you add to the line from now on, a new curve will be created based on the relationship among the new point and the two preceding it. You can see this clearly with an open curve as the curve follows along with each new point; with a closed curve, every time you click a new point within your composition, you'll watch the shape of the near portion of the figure change.

If you're not satisfied with the shape, you can click the buttons under the label, Edit curve or polygon *prior to* clicking the Create button. The first edit button, Move points, allows you to click a point (represented by the small boxes that appear as you move your pointer around the shape) and drag it to a new position, thus altering the shape. The middle button, Add points, lets you place the pointer where you want to insert a new point and do so by pressing the left mouse button. The new points can then be moved just like the previously existing ones to alter the shape. The third button, Delete points, lets you remove points from the shapes. To remove a point, place the pointer on the one you want to delete and press the left mouse button. You can only delete points until you are down to two (when you are all the way back to a straight line).

Before a shape is created, you can right-click to bring up a menu with the Move, Add, and Delete points commands. When you are satisfied with the shape, click the Create button to complete the operation. The completed curve will be created.

Creating Polygons

To create a polygon shape (see Figure 17.9), follow the same procedure as for creating a curve shape, except that you click the Polygon button instead of the Curve button. The pointer will show a polygon under the arrow to indicate which shape you are working with. The only difference between them is that, with polygons, you are working with straight lines rather than with curves.

Recalling Curves and Polygons

What do you do if you have created a complex curve or polygon, then rendered it, but aren't satisfied with the end result? One approach is to do the whole thing over again—however, there is an easier solution. Although you cannot edit a curve or polygon after it is rendered, you can edit a recall of it.

A *recall* is a copy of the most recently created curve or polygon sprite. To get a recall, just open the Shapes palette and click the Recall Copy button. It does not matter if you have created a rectangle or oval sprite in the meantime. You can even use another tool entirely (for instance, you can add text to the composition) and still come back to the Shapes palette and recall the last curve or polygon. A copy of it will appear in exactly the spot it was created (even if you have since moved it), ready for editing.

Just follow the procedure outlined above to edit the recall version.

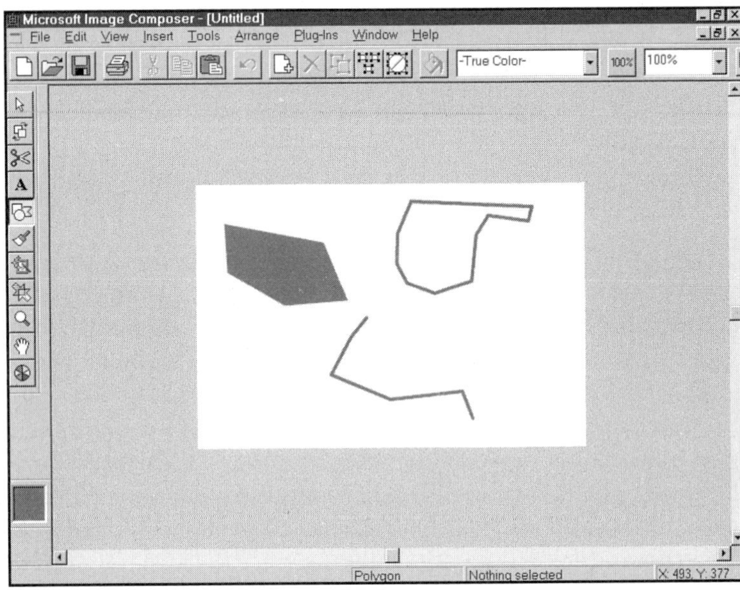

FIGURE 17.9.
Some polygonal shapes.

Using the Cutout Tool

The Cutout tool (see Figure 17.10) is essentially identical to the Shapes tool, but with a bit of a twist. Instead of creating shapes, it either erases or copies the portion of the sprite it is drawn on top of. The shapes you create with the Cutout tool are the same as with the Shapes tool: rectangle, oval, curve, or polygon.

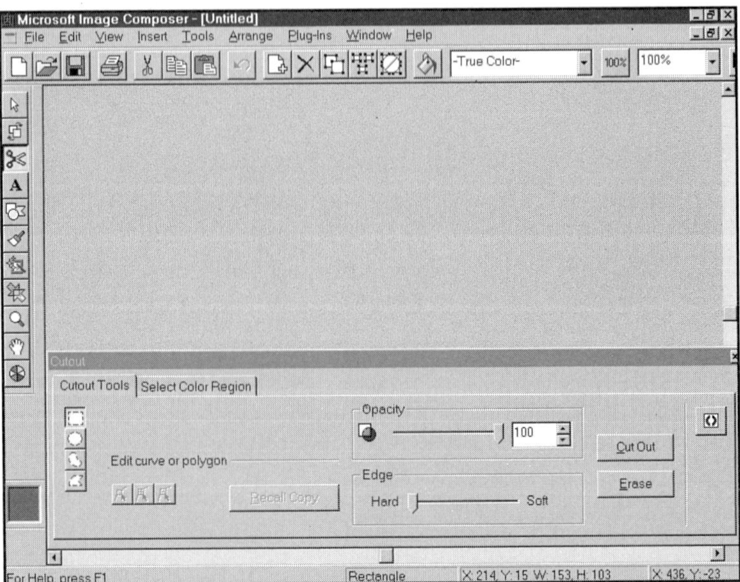

FIGURE 17.10.
The Cutout tool.

Whether it erases a section of that shape or copies the portion of the sprite underneath it depends on your choices under Selection. The Cut Out button creates a copy of the area of the underlying sprite that is within the borders of the shape (for example, you can copy a rectangular section from a map this way, or copy an oval from a family portrait to create an old-fashioned look). The cutout becomes a new sprite, which can then be moved away from its original location. The original sprite from which the cutout was made remains unchanged (see Figure 17.11).

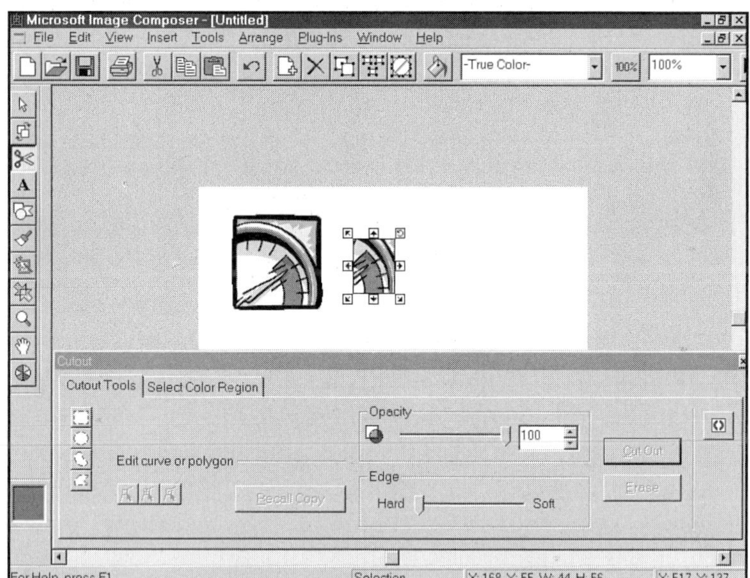

FIGURE 17.11.
A Cutout shape.

> **TIP**
>
> You can use curve and polygon cutouts to copy some unusual shapes such as continental outlines from maps.

The bottom button, Erase, on the other hand, does affect the underlying sprite. It cuts a hole in it, using the shape you have overlaid on it as a cutout template (see Figure 17.12). You do not have to cut out only from the center of the sprite, but can lop off edges as well.

The opacity setting is critical with Cut Out and Erase. If it is set to 100, then everything works simply as described above. If it is set to a lower number, then things get a little bit more complicated. With Add, your copy will be a pale shadow of the object you are extracting from. With Delete, you will effectively just lighten the area covered by the shape instead of boring a hole through it.

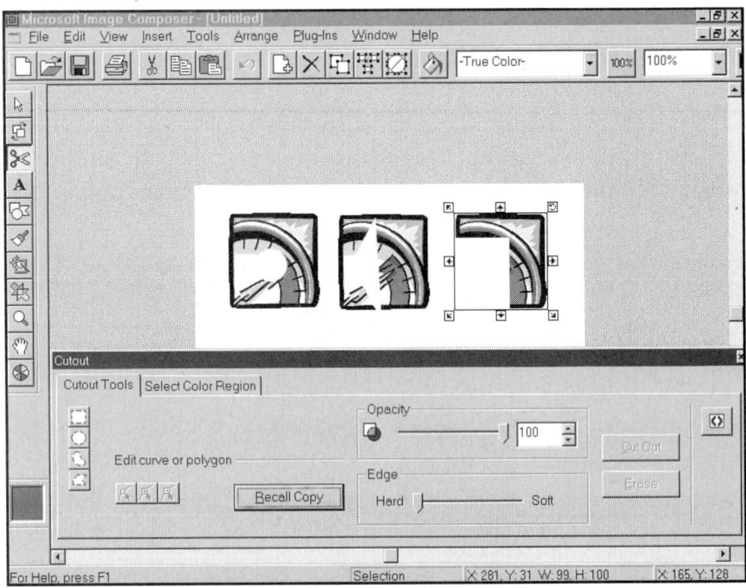

FIGURE 17.12.
Some erased shapes.

TIP

The currently selected color does not matter, as it will affect neither an extraction nor an erasure.

There are two other interesting additions to the basic Shapes tools. The first is the Stencil tool. It creates an inverted copy of the selected sprite (see Figure 17.13). The transparent areas of the sprite are filled with the currently selected color, and the opaque areas are set to full transparency.

The second interesting tool is found on the second tab. Click the Select Color Region tab to access it (see Figure 17.14). This tool creates a new sprite by duplicating only selected colors from the source sprite. The select color region tool looks like a magic wand.

To use it, first select the sprite you wish to lift color areas from. Next, click the select color region button. Make sure the Add radio button is selected in the Selection panel.

If you want to select all areas of the same color throughout the entire sprite, make sure the Global radio button is selected in the Search Mode panel. If you want to select only those areas of the same color that abut the pixels you are clicking, select the Local radio button.

In the selected sprite, Click the color you wish to lift. It will be highlighted in the currently selected color from the color picker. This is a merely a guide so you can see what areas have been selected; when you extract the selected colors, they will be the original colors from the source sprite.

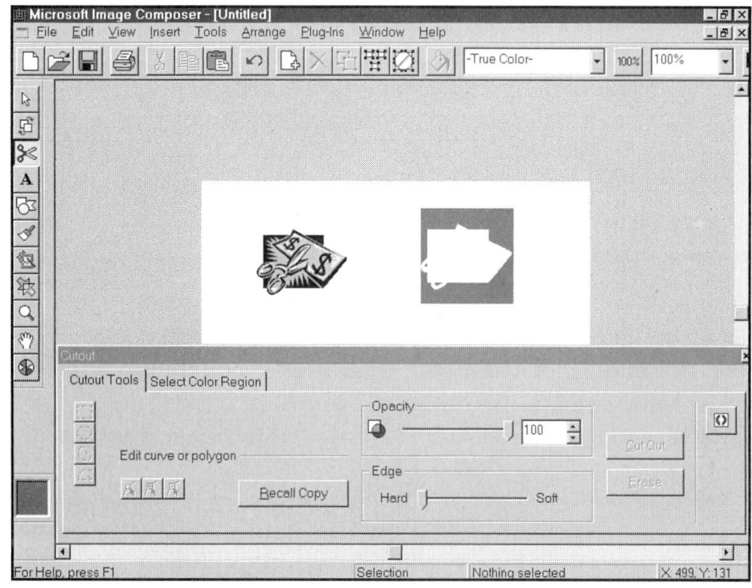

FIGURE 17.13.
A stencil.

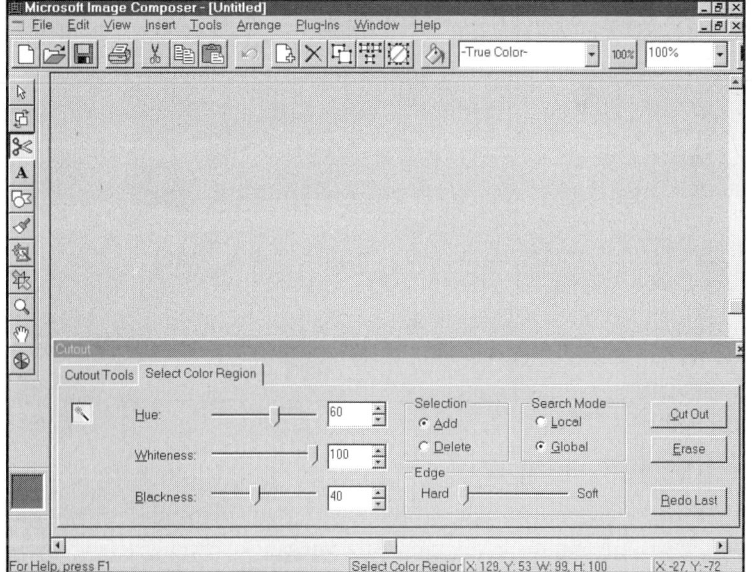

FIGURE 17.14.
The Select Color Region palette.

If you click a color and decide you do not want it after all, click the Delete radio button in the Selection panel, then click the Redo Last button. Your last selection will be undone. Make sure you click the Add radio button again before proceeding.

If the tool selects more or less color area than you want, follow the procedure in the preceding paragraph to undo the damage, then adjust the Hue, Whiteness, and Blackness sliders (located on the left side of the palette), and try again until you get the selection you want.

When you are satisfied with the selection, click the Cut Out button. You will need to move the newly extracted sprite off the original one to see it.

If you want to remove the selected color regions from the original sprite, click the Erase button instead of the Cut Out button.

Figure 17.15 illustrates a sprite before and after color region processing. In this example, we have lifted the ocean sections of the Western hemisphere from a globe. The resultant image is the same map, but with the land areas transparent; that sprite has been overlaid on a sunset, which shows through the former land areas.

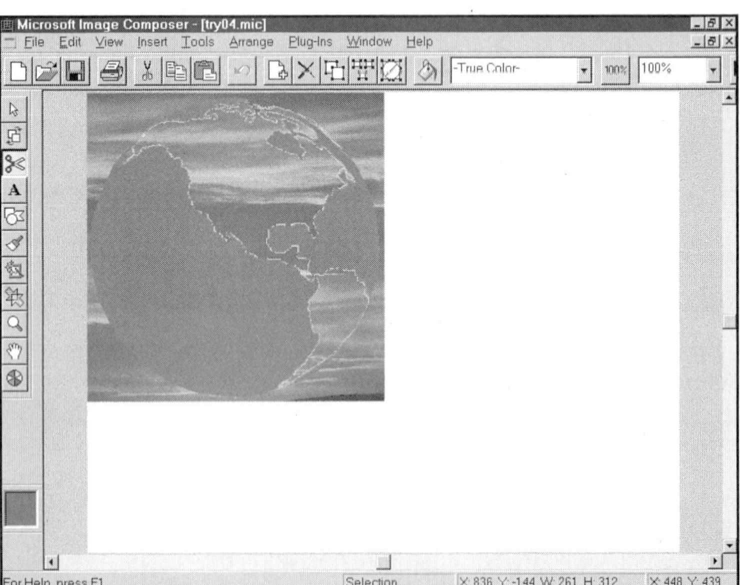

FIGURE 17.15.
A color region cutout sprite.

Using the Paint Tool

If you start with a blank composition, you have a blank canvas on which to work. If you try to use the Paint tool on it, though, you will quickly find that you are unable to paint on that canvas. The Shapes tool works fine, as does the Text tool, but nothing else has any effect at this point, unless you want to zoom and pan with a plain white composition space.

The reason for this lack of options is that Image Composer is designed to work by importing or creating sprites. One catch is that only the Shapes and Text tools create sprites. The Paint tool only works when you use it on an existing sprite; it is not intended to be used for the creation of sprites, but for their modification. Therefore, it is impossible to paint on the composition space.

What do you do if there is no suitable image file for you to import and work on? If the composition you want to create can't be done with rectangles, ovals, and so forth? You can create a sprite from scratch, using only the options available in the Paint palette, with one small twist. If you want to draw your own sprite by hand, you need to create your own sprite canvas. Just draw a rectangle shape in order to have a "canvas" to work on (see the section titled, "Using the Shapes Tool").

NOTE

We have included two sample sprite canvases in the Companion Web Site for this book. One is 420×275 pixels, the same size as the default composition space (filename: `Canvas_420_by_275.gif`). The other is 600×60 pixels, the same size as a banner image in a FrontPage graphical theme (filename: `Canvas_600_by_60.gif`). Both are white, but you can change the color or size to suit yourself.

Whether you are starting from scratch or modifying existing artwork, the Paint palette (see Figure 17.16) has a lot to offer. It has four basic drawing tools—paintbrush, airbrush, pencil, and eraser—but a variety of other capabilities as well. These are all found in the Paint Effect grid on the left side of the Paint palette, and an overview of them is given in Table 17.1. Moving the pointer slowly over the grid will give you the names of the tools.

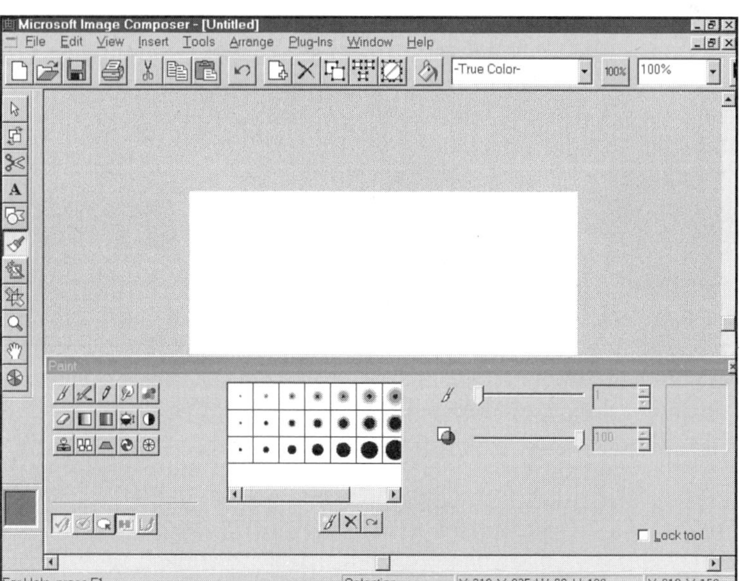

FIGURE 17.16.
The Paint palette.

To the right of this is the paintbrush selection grid, from which you can choose a brush of the size and shape you want simply by clicking it.

The three buttons immediately beneath the paintbrush selection grid control the Brush Designer, which is dealt with in a separate section entitled, "Using the Brush Designer."

Farther right are the sliders for choosing brush size and opacity. On the extreme right side is a graphical representation of the currently selected brush showing its shape and size.

Table 17.1. Paint effect grid tools.

Tool	*Purpose*
Paintbrush	Simulates a paintbrush, giving a broad stroke of paint
Airbrush	Simulates an airbrush, causing a spray-painted effect
Pencil	Simulates a pencil, giving a single-pixel hard line
Smear	Simulates the action of a finger rubbed on a painted picture, mixing nearby colors together
Impression	Similar to Smear, Impression runs colors together
Erase	Turns pixels transparent, thus removing them from the image
Tint	Applies a light coating, or wash, of color to the area
Colorize	Covers the area in a new color without changing the contrast
Dodge-Burn	Simulates photographic developing technique, resulting in lightening or darkening of particular areas
Contrast	Increases or decreases the contrast of a given area
Rubber Stamp	Copies the portion of a sprite under the current paintbrush; the copy can then be used as a paintbrush or stamp
Transfer	Copies an entire sprite that you can then paint onto another sprite either in part or in whole (see the following note)
Mesa	Supposed to alter pixels to appear wrapped around a truncated cone; actually just smears them
Vortex	Alters pixels to appear as though they were twisted
Spoke Inversion	Inverts every other stroke in affected area

There are also six tools, detailed in Table 17.2, that determine the painting effect of the selected brush.

Table 17.2. Brush effect grid tools.

Tool	*Purpose*
Use Brush	Use a shape from the standard or custom brush selections to paint with.
Use Template	Use a shape copied from a sprite to paint with.
Set Template	Choose which sprite to copy brush shape from.
Over	If Over is selected, painting is done over all areas of the sprite; if Over is deselected, painting is only done on nontransparent pixels.
Continuous Strokes	Applies a steady flow of paint when moving brush.

Most of these tools are pretty straightforward in usage. Just select the tool, drag the brush around the selected sprite (or just click the sprite for a very localized effect), and the effect takes place. A couple of them, though, need a little bit of explanation.

To lighten with the Dodge-Burn tool, use the slider to choose a positive number; to darken, use a negative number. This is not as backward as it seems; in the original photographic technique for which this effect is named, you darken an area by lessening the amount of light reaching the developing paper, and lighten it by allowing more light to reach it.

The reverse is true with contrast. Contrast is lessened with a negative number and increased with a positive one.

To use the Transfer tool, first select a sprite, click another sprite, and then paint the second image onto the first.

NOTE

The special effects here (such as Mesa, Vortex, and so on) are generally not as impressive as the ones of the same name in other tools, because they are applied to a very small area via the paintbrush rather than to the sprite as a whole.

Using the Brush Designer

If none of the default brush types suits your purposes, Image Composer provides a tool to assist you in creating your own custom brush design. The three buttons below the paintbrush selection grid are the way you control brush design and maintenance. The first one is the New Brush button, and it is used to open the Brush Designer (see Figure 17.17). The middle one is the Delete Brush button, and it is used to delete a selected brush from the paintbrush selection grid. The last one is the Reset to Defaults button, and it is used to completely remove all custom brushes from the grid.

CAUTION

Be very careful about using the Reset to Defaults button. It is better to take the time to individually judge and remove any undesired custom brushes with the Delete Brush button than to just wipe them all out, perhaps losing some you'll later have to re-create.

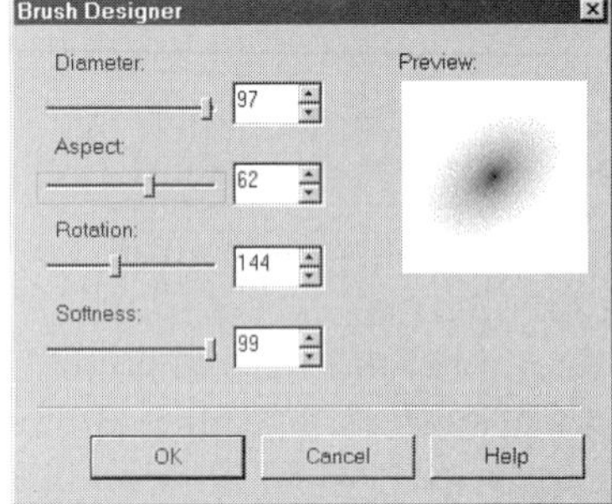

Figure 17.17.
The Brush Designer.

There are four attributes you can set for your custom brushes in Brush Designer, and are as follows:

- **Diameter.** Diameter can range from 1 to 100. The higher the number is, the larger the brush is.
- **Aspect.** Defines the brush's shape. Values can range from 1 to 100. Within this range, shapes can change from a nearly flat line at 1 to an oval at 50 and a circle at 100.
- **Rotation.** Sets the angle at which the brush sits. Can range from 0 to 360 degrees. Rotation occurs in a clockwise manner when increasing and counterclockwise when decreasing. If you have a round brush (diameter=100), there is no effect when changing the rotation.
- **Softness.** Sets the amount of falloff at the brush's edges. Values can range from 0 to 100. A setting of 0 gives a very soft edge around a hard core about half the diameter of the total. A setting of 100 gives a totally hard edge with no falloff whatsoever.

When you have set these values to your satisfaction, click OK. The custom brush you have just designed will now appear in the paintbrush selection grid and will continue to be available for future operations until you delete it.

Opening and Saving Compositions

There are two distinctly different approaches to starting a project with Image Composer: either opening an existing composition or starting a completely new one. Because Image

Composer's tools are strongest in the area of image manipulation and modification, it is easiest to begin with an existing image or images and work from there. The Image Composer sprite library provides a good starting point, or you can use the supply of clip art available. You can also scan in photographs, artwork, and so on, using a TWAIN-compliant scanner or other input device.

However, Image Composer also offers the computer artist the ability to create his or her own images from scratch.

Opening Existing Compositions

If you want to open an existing composition, you have a choice of file types, which are listed in Table 17.3. To open an existing composition, click the Open button, then select the folder that contains the composition you want to open. Next, double-click the filename of the desired composition.

> **TIP**
>
> In addition to Image Composer compositions, you can open other kinds of image files as well. Once these files are opened, Image Composer will treat them as a composition. The composition space will be set to the size of the first file opened.

Table 17.3. Supported formats for the Open command.

File Type	*File Extension*
Altamira Composer	`.acc`
Windows Bitmap	`.bmp`
Windows Device Independent Bitmap	`.dib`
FlashPix	`.fpx`
Graphics Interchange Format	`.gif`
JPEG	`.jpg`, `.jpeg`
Microsoft Image Composer	`.mic`
Microsoft Picture It!	`.mix`
Portable Network Graphics	`.png`
Photoshop	`.psd`
Targa	`.tga`
Tagged Image Format File	`.tif`, `.tiff`

Starting a New Composition

Image Composer starts up with a blank composition space. However, if you are already using the program and you want to start a new composition, click the New button. Your active composition will be instantly replaced by a blank composition space, unless you have made changes since you last saved it.

If you have made changes, you'll be asked if you want to save the changed version. Click the Yes button to save the composition, or the No button to discard the recent changes.

Saving Compositions and Selections

There are five separate methods for saving your work: Save, Save As, Save Selection As, Save Copy As, and Save for the Web. Whereas the basic Save command (the only one for which there is a button on the toolbar) will simply save the current composition with its current name and settings in the default `.mic` file format, the other methods present you with various options.

NOTE

If you elect to save a composition that is as yet unsaved, it's the same as if you had chosen the Save As command.

The Save As Command

When you save a composition using File | Save As, the file type you select has an important impact. Although you can save in a variety of formats (see Table 17.4), only the Microsoft Image Composer (`.mic` file) or Photoshop (`.psd` file) options will preserve all the elements in your composition. The Photoshop option also allows you to choose not to save the composition space itself (or to save it as a background layer). Although it will, by default, save all the sprites outside the composition space, you can override this by unchecking the checkbox (see Figure 17.18).

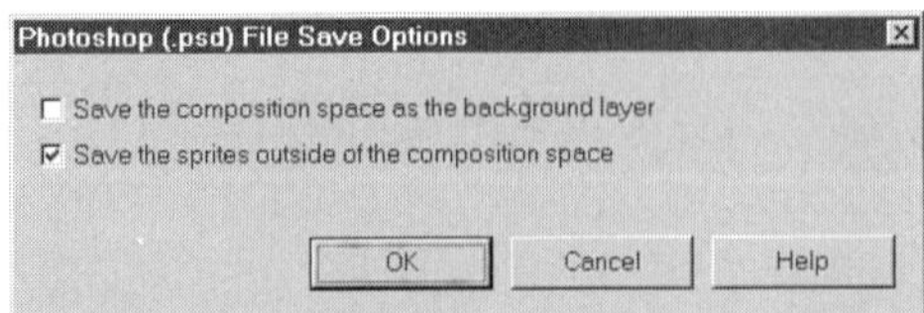

FIGURE 17.18.
The Photoshop (.psd) File Save Options dialog box.

If you save it as a regular bitmapped file (`.gif`, `.jpg`, and so on), only the information in the composition space itself is kept; all the other sprites in the workspace outside the composition space are discarded. In addition, the composition is permanently flattened into a single sprite, thus you lose the ability to work with individual sprites or any sprite groups you might have created (see the section titled, "Manipulating and Combining Sprites," for information on sprite groups).

One further consideration is that different file formats have varying color formats possible (for example, true color, grayscale, and so on). Depending on the file format you choose, you can also select which color format to save the composition in.

TIP

Because you are presumably developing graphics for use on the World Wide Web, you'll want to save the finished image as either a `.gif` or `.jpg` file—those are the only ones the major browsers will recognize. However, you might want to modify the image at a later date, or use a portion of it in another composition. To maintain your future options to utilize all of Image Composer's image manipulation features, make sure to save a copy as a `.mic` file and then save another copy as either `.gif` or `.jpg`. That way, if you want to do further work on the image, you can reopen the Image Composer version with all the sprite information intact.

Table 17.4. Supported formats for the Save As command.

File Type	*File Extension*
Windows Bitmap	`.bmp`
FlashPix	`.fpx`
Graphics Interchange Format	`.gif`
JPEG	`.jpg`
Microsoft Image Composer	`.mic`
Microsoft Picture It!	`.mix`
Portable Network Graphics	`.png`
Photoshop	`.psd`
Targa	`.tga`
Tagged Image Format File	`.tif`, `.tiff`

The Save Selection As Command

The Save Selection As command is used to save a sprite or group of sprites as a bitmapped file. As the name implies, you must first click a sprite to select it (or hold down the Ctrl key and click several sprites to select multiple objects simultaneously). When you choose File | Save Selection As, only the selected object or objects will be saved.

NOTE

The supported formats for the Save Selection As command are the same as for the Save As command in Table 17.4, except that you cannot use the `.mic` or `.psd` options.

The Save Copy As Command

The Save Copy As command allows you to make a backup copy of your composition without saving the current one. This command saves the composition under any filename you select, but does not change the filename of the current composition. The same file formats are supported as for the Save As command (see Table 17.4).

The Save for the Web Command

The Save for the Web command launches a wizard that is designed to help you optimize your graphics for presentation on the World Wide Web (see Figure 17.19).

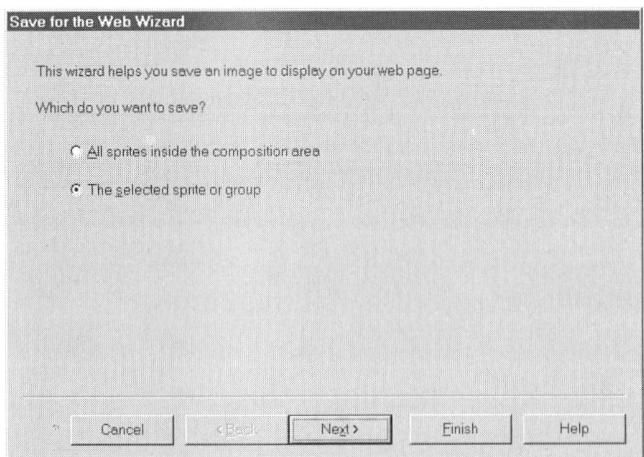

FIGURE 17.19.
The Save for the Web Wizard.

Your first choice is whether to save all the sprites inside the composition space or only those that are currently selected. Sprites outside the composition space cannot be saved with the wizard. Click the Next button to proceed.

If your sprites have transparent areas, the dialog in Figure 17.20 will appear. By default, the transparency is left intact, but you can choose to fill the transparent areas with a background color instead. Click the Next button to proceed.

If you have opted for the default and kept the transparency intact, the dialog in Figure 17.21 will appear, asking whether your Web page has a solid or tiled background. Click the appropriate radio button. If you have chosen a solid color, you can click the Color button to bring up the color picker and specify which solid color your Web page uses. Click the Next button to proceed.

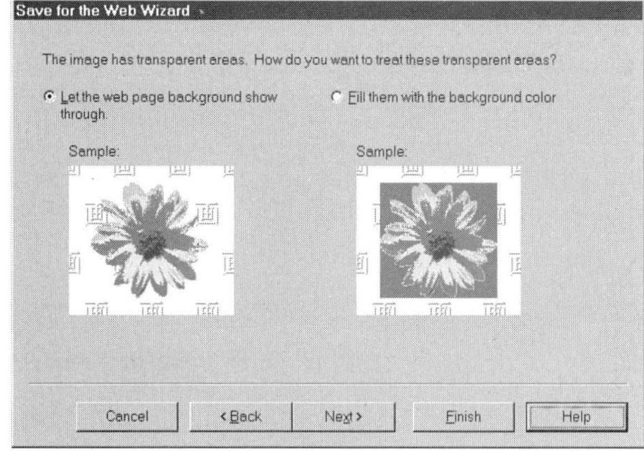

FIGURE 17.20.
Transparency dialog box of Save for the Web Wizard.

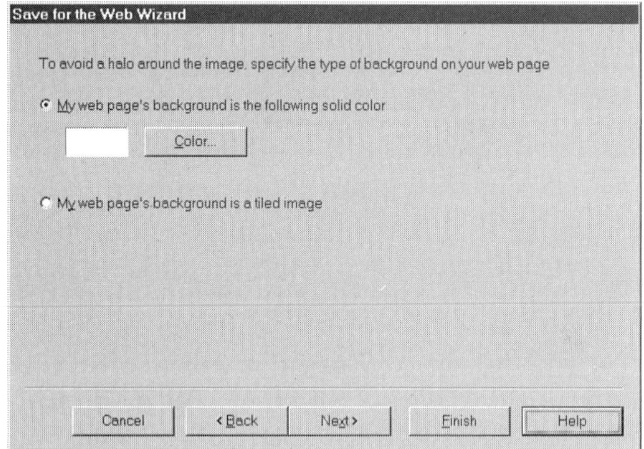

FIGURE 17.21.
Web page background dialog box.

If, on the other hand, you chose to give up the transparency and have it filled in, the dialog in Figure 17.22 will appear. Click the Color button to choose the color that will fill in the transparent areas, then click the Next button to proceed.

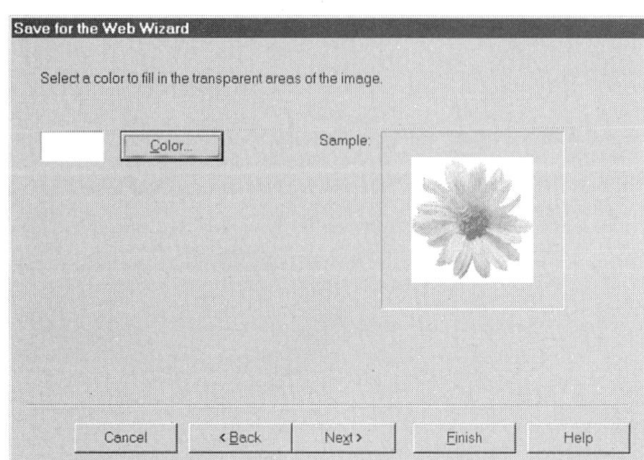

FIGURE 17.22.
Transparency fill in color dialog box.

If the image you have decided to save has no transparency, or if you decided to fill in the transparency, then the dialog in Figure 17.23 will appear. The purpose is to determine the best compromise between image quality and download speed. The Connection speed drop-down menu allows you to choose various types of connections, such as 28.8k modem, 128k Full ISDN, and so on. The different types of images you can save the file as are shown, along with the download times at the currently selected connection speed. As you choose different speeds, the download time changes accordingly. Click on the image you believe represents the best compromise, then click the Next button to proceed.

FIGURE 17.23.
Size and image quality dialog box.

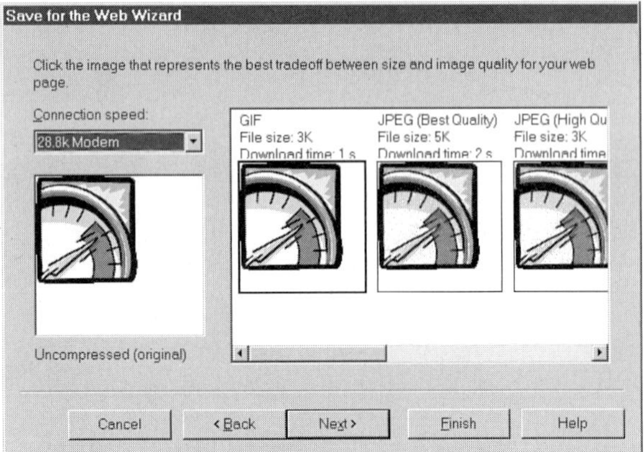

The final part of the wizard (see Figure 17.24) shows a summary of the choices you have made. If you have changed your mind about any of them, use the Back button to return to the earlier dialogs and change them. Otherwise, click the Save button to finish. This will open a standard save dialog box (see Figure 17.25). The settings in the save dialog box will reflect the choices you made while using the wizard.

FIGURE 17.24.
Summary dialog box.

Save for the Web Wizard

When you click Finish, a Save dialog is displayed in which you specify the name and location for the image file. Based on your selections in the preceding screens, the Wizard will fill in the following Save options for you

Format

File type:	GIF
Color palette:	-Web (Dithered)-
Compression:	Not available for GIF
Transparency:	Yes
Transparent color:	(R: 255, G: 0, B: 255)
Composition space color:	(R: 255, G: 255, B: 255)

When you want to save an image for the Web without using this Wizard, click Save Copy As... or Save Selection As... on the File menu.

Cancel | < Back | Next > | Save | Help

FIGURE 17.25.
Save dialog box.

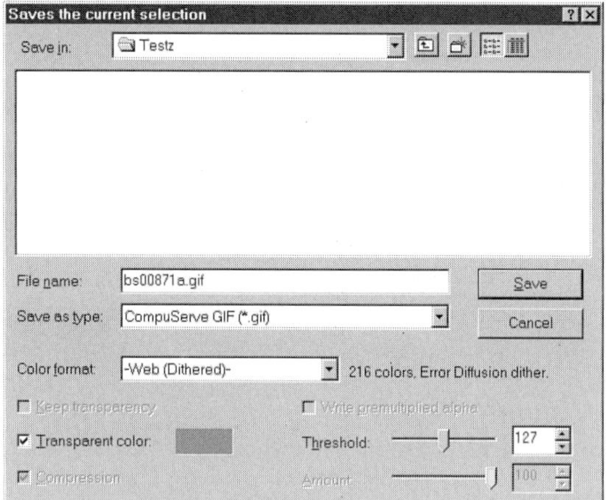

Inserting Sprites

Inserting a sprite is very similar to opening a file, with the difference that the image is added to the current composition rather than replacing it. To insert an image as a sprite, click the Insert Image File button. As with the Open command, you select the folder that holds the image you want to add and then double-click the appropriate filename. Supported file formats are listed in Table 17.5.

Table 17.5. Supported formats for the Insert Image File command.

File Type	*File Extension*
Altamira Composer	`.acc`
Windows Bitmap	`.bmp`
Windows Device Independent Bitmap	`.dib`
Graphics Interchange Format	`.gif`
JPEG	`.jpg`, `.jpeg`
Microsoft Image Composer	`.mic`
Kodak PhotoCD	`.pcd`
Photoshop	`.psd`
Targa	`.tga`
Tagged Image Format File	`.tif`, `.tiff`

Inserted images are automatically selected, thus removing any active selections in your current composition.

NOTE

An *inserted* `.mic` file, unlike an *opened* one, does not retain its identity as a separate composition, but is simply broken into several individual sprites that become part of the current composition.

You can also paste the contents of the Clipboard as a sprite. This gives you the ability to include the graphic output of other programs in an Image Composer composition. It can also be used for adding screen captures to your work.

Scanning Sprites into Image Composer

Image Composer has the capability to use TWAIN-compliant scanners to scan images into your composition as sprites. If you have a single scanning device, then the menu choice File|Scan Image|Acquire Scan will bring up your TWAIN scanner controls. If you have multiple TWAIN devices, you'll first need to use the File|Scan Image|Select Scan Source menu option to choose which one to use.

Manipulating and Combining Sprites

A composition is most often made up of several different sprites. In fact, "composite image" might be a more accurately descriptive term. When sprites are combined, attention must be paid to not only their content and position, but to their size, transparency, and placement in the stack. Although content is a personal design decision, some basic rules for handling the other factors can be very useful.

Positioning Sprites

Every sprite that is opened or inserted (as well as every newly created text object) appears initially in the upper-left corner of your composition. Because it is difficult to imagine much use for a composition where everything but items created with the Shape tool remained there, you'll doubtless want to move these sprites into other positions. To do so, place the pointer on the sprite, hold down the left mouse button, and drag the sprite to its new place.

There are some tools on the Arrange palette (see Figure 17.26) that are useful in positioning sprites. They are located on the upper-left side (with icons of houses on them), the fifth, sixth, and seventh buttons from the left. From left to right, these are Set Home Position, Return to Home Position, and Lock/Unlock Position.

The "home position" is the position at which the sprite enters the composition. In the case of ones that are opened or inserted, the home position is the upper-left corner of the composition space. The same is true in the case of shapes created with the Shapes tool (although you would think that the home position would be wherever they are drawn). If you click the Return to

Home Position button, then no matter where you have repositioned a sprite, it will leap back to the upper-left corner of the composition space.

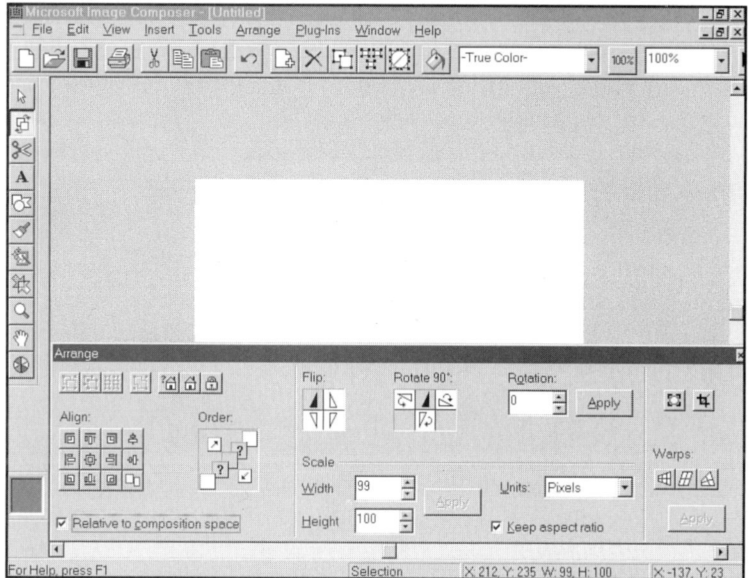

FIGURE 17.26.
The Arrange palette.

The solution to this is to use the Set Home Position button. Select a sprite and click this button. Wherever the sprite is, is its new home position. Henceforth, if you move it and then click the Return to Home Position button, this is the point it will return to. This feature can be very useful if you are experimenting with various placements, but are as yet uncertain about them.

The last button, Lock/Unlock Position, will keep a sprite from moving no matter what you do. The only way to move it again is to select it and click the Lock/Unlock Position button again. In the meanwhile, the sprite cannot be dragged and will not respond to the Return to Home Position button.

Resizing and Cropping Sprites

All sprites are surrounded by a "bounding box." This box has handles you can click and drag to interactively resize the image. In addition, the Arrange palette allows you to adjust the width and height of a sprite, or to crop it. There are two buttons on the far upper right side of the Arrange palette that are very important.

The bounding box will automatically change size along with any adjustments you make to the sprite, so the first of these buttons, Fit Bounding Box, might not seem at first to make sense. However, if you erase a portion of the sprite, the bounding box does not change size. It is necessary in this case to use the Fit button to return the bounding box to outlining the true borders of the sprite.

The second button, Crop/Extend, is more intuitive. Just as you can extend a sprite by dragging one of the handles along the bounding box, you can do so by clicking this button and then changing the settings in the edit boxes labeled Width and Height, after which you click the Apply button. There are two options associated with this task. The first is whether you are extending by absolute pixel width (the default setting) or are extending by a percentage. Select which you prefer from the drop-down list box labeled Units. The second option is whether to keep the existing proportions relatively the same when you change the size. To do so, make sure the check box labeled Keep Aspect Ratio is checked (this check box also controls whether this ratio is retained if you drag the bounding box handles to resize the sprite).

The one catch to the Crop/Extend button is that you cannot crop a sprite using the width and height settings in the Arrange palette (if you attempt this, you'll only shrink the sprite, not crop it). You must, after clicking it, use the handles on the bounding box. Instead of dragging them outward as you would to enlarge the sprite, you drag them inward until only the portion of the sprite you want to keep is showing.

Rotating, Flipping, and Aligning Sprites

There are three separate methods for rotating sprites. The first, the straight interactive approach, is to use the upper-right handle on the bounding box (the one with a circular arrow). If you click this handle and move the pointer, the sprite will turn in the direction you drag (clockwise if you move the pointer down or right, counterclockwise if you move up or left).

The two other methods are on the Arrange palette. The easiest way is to click the Rotate icons. The one on the upper-left will rotate the sprite 90 degrees counterclockwise; the one on the upper-right will rotate it 90 degrees clockwise; and, finally, the one on the bottom will rotate it 180 degrees.

The way to have more precise control over of degrees rotated is to change the settings in the Rotation box. You can scroll the numbers five at a time, or you can change them by typing in any number you want. When you have the settings as you want them, click the Apply button.

You can also flip the sprite horizontally, vertically, or both at once by clicking on the Flip icons to the right of the Rotate icons.

Aligning Sprites

The sprite alignment tools are in a cluster on the far left side of the Arrange palette. The Align tools are composed of 12 buttons, each of which causes a different alignment between objects. As you move your mouse pointer over these buttons, a help balloon will pop up telling you what each does. If you place your pointer over the first button in the top row, for example, the help balloon will say Upper Left Corners. Each button also has a descriptive image on it that shows the type of alignment it performs.

If the check box labeled Relative to composition space is checked, then the selected sprite will be aligned to the composition space. If this check box is not checked, you will need to select two sprites for alignment; the second one selected will be aligned with the first sprite selected.

Grouping Sprites

Sprites can be combined into a single group by selecting as many as you want to add and then clicking the Group button in the Arrange palette. A group can be moved as if it were a single sprite.

Ungrouping is accomplished very easily—just select the group and then click the Ungroup button. The Explode button works much the same way, with one major exception. If a group is composed of other groups (subgroups), the Ungroup button will leave the subgroups intact; the Explode button will take both the group and all subgroups apart.

One final button in this set is the Flatten button. Flattening a group makes it into a single sprite. Once a group has been flattened, it cannot be ungrouped or exploded ever again.

Working with the Stack

When sprites are not overlapping one another, it is easy to think of them as all on the same plane, but this is not the case. Each one actually occupies its own plane, and every sprite is either in front of or behind other sprites. The order of sprites is known, appropriately enough, as the "stack."

This becomes readily apparent when two or more sprites overlap. The order of overlapping sprites can be critical when composing an image, applying transparency values, and so on.

To change the order of sprites, select the one you want to move. You can use the Order icon on the Arrange palette or just click the right mouse button to access a menu with the same choices on it. Either way, you can move the selected sprite forward or backward one plane at a time, or you can send it straight to the farthest or closest plane.

Summary

This chapter covers the nuts and bolts of sprite handling, from opening and inserting existing sprites to creating new ones and how to save either kind. The Text tool, Shapes tool, and Paint tool are covered in depth, including how to utilize extraction, transparency, and various paint effects. This chapter also covers the topics of rotating and flipping sprites as well as aligning and grouping them.

CHAPTER 18

Enhancing Your Images with Effects

by David and Rhonda Crowder

IN THIS CHAPTER

- Texture Transfer *318*
- Using the Effects Tool *321*
- Adding Plug-Ins *332*
- Using the Paint Tool *334*

Image Composer provides a full range of special effects to enhance your images. It offers tools to modify images with drop shadows, color gradients, vortex warps, watercolor appearance, and just about anything else you can imagine. If the wealth of built-in effects isn't enough to satisfy you, you can add more, because Image Composer supports Photoshop-compatible plug-ins, such as Kai's Power Tools.

NOTE

Photoshop is a graphics program with similar features to Image Composer, but which costs several hundred dollars. Kai's Power Tools are a popular add-on to Photoshop (and other graphics programs) that provides sophisticated special effects, many of which duplicate the ones built in to Image Composer.

Texture Transfer

You use the Texture Transfer tools to copy images or portions of images, or to copy channel information from one sprite to another. The Texture Transfer controls are shown in Figure 18.1. As you can see, each tool button is a graphic that shows a demonstration of the effect it represents. A few of the tools have additional options, but the opacity slider is the main option common to all (for a description of opacity, see Chapter 17, "Creating Great Images with Image Composer").

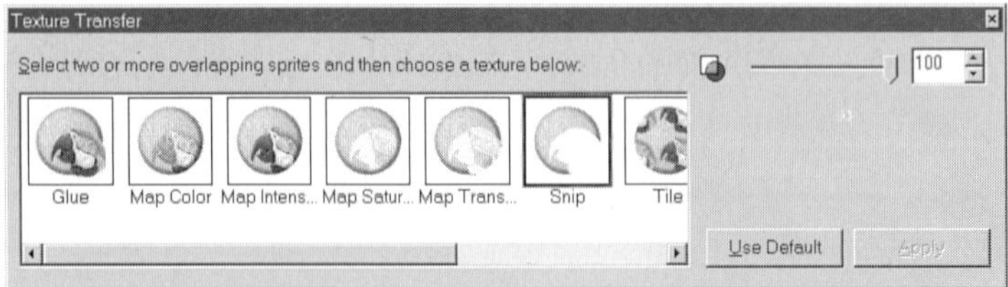

FIGURE 18.1.
The Texture Transfer palette.

To use these tools, follow these steps:

1. Select the sprite you want to copy from (called the *source sprite*). While holding down the Shift key, select the one you want to copy to (called the *destination sprite*). Both sprites should now be selected (see Figure 18.2). The first sprite selected will always be the source sprite.
2. Click the Texture Transfer button in the toolbar.
3. Select the type of transfer you want by clicking the appropriate button (see Table 18.1).
4. Set the opacity to the amount you want.

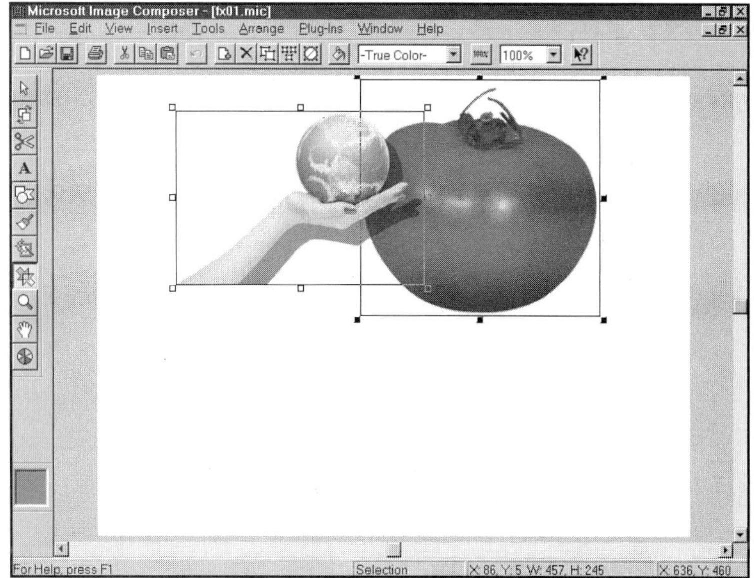

FIGURE 18.2.
Two selected sprites.

5. Set other options, if any, required by the particular type of transfer you're using.
6. Click the Apply button. The operation is now complete.

NOTE

For the Texture Transfer tools to function, the source sprite and the destination sprite must be in contact. It does not matter which one is on top. You need to move one of them to view the results of the operation.

Table 18.1. Texture Transfer effects.

Effect	*Function*
Glue	Copies the source sprite's opaque pixels only to the destination sprite, replacing the destination sprite's transparent pixels.
Map Color	Copies the Red, Green, and Blue channel information from the source sprite to the destination sprite.
Map Intensity	Sets the destination sprite to the same intensity value as the source sprite.
Map Saturation	Sets the destination sprite to the same saturation value as the source sprite.

continues

Table 18.1. continued

Effect	*Function*
Map Transparency	Copies the Alpha channel information from the source sprite to the destination sprite.
Snip	Erases the opaque pixels of the destination sprite where they overlap the opaque pixels of the source sprite.
Tile	Covers the opaque pixels of the destination sprite with as many rows of the source sprite that will fit (see the following tip).
Transfer Full	Copies all the source sprite's pixels, both opaque and transparent, to the destination sprite.
Transfer Shape	Copies the source sprite's opaque pixels only to the destination sprite without replacing the destination sprite's transparent pixels.

TIP

When tiling (see Figure 18.3), you should usually keep the source sprite much smaller than the destination sprite. Also, tiling is the one exception to the rule that the source and destination sprites must be touching; you can use any sprite anywhere in the composition as a tile source.

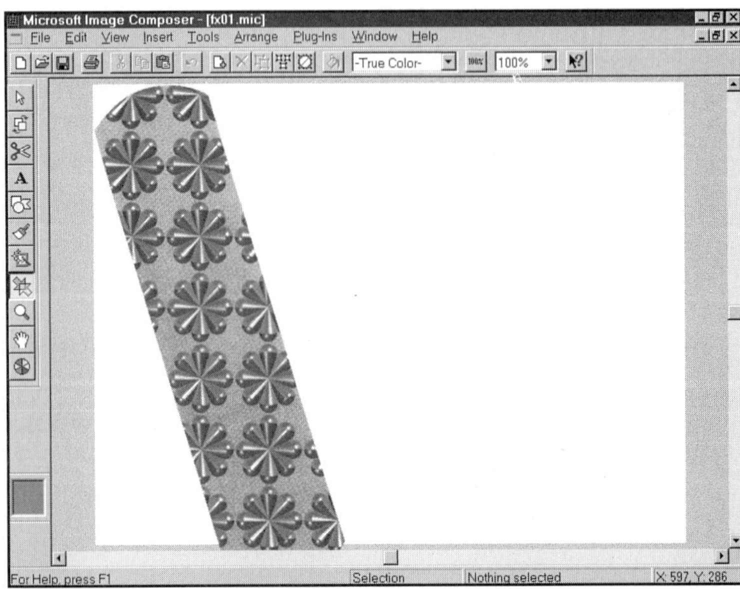

FIGURE 18.3.
An example of tiling.

Using the Effects Tool

The Effects palette consists of two notebook tabs. The first one (see Figure 18.4) is labeled Effects, and contains clickable image buttons that show examples of the effects they represent.

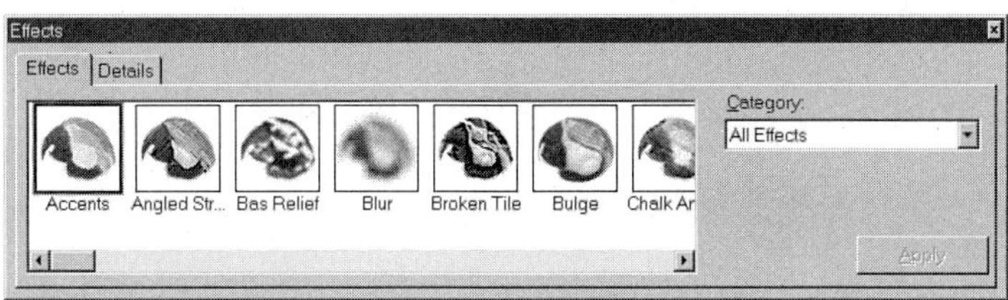

FIGURE 18.4.
The Effects tab.

On the right side of the Effects tab is a drop-down menu labeled Category. These category choices consist of Arts & Crafts, Color Enhancement, Distort, Gradient, Outlines, Paint, Patterns, Photographic, Sketch, and Surface. In addition to these basic categories, there are also the All Effects and Popular categories. The former shows every single effect available, while the latter shows only those few effects that Microsoft believes to be the most popular ones. All of the effects in Popular effects are also found in other categories from which they are taken.

As you select each different category, the image buttons change to show representations of the different tools available within that category.

The other tab on the Effects palette is labeled Details (see Figure 18.5). This tab has the controls for changing any optional settings the chosen effect might have. The controls in the Details tab change depending on your choice of effects. For many, the only choice is the degree of opacity.

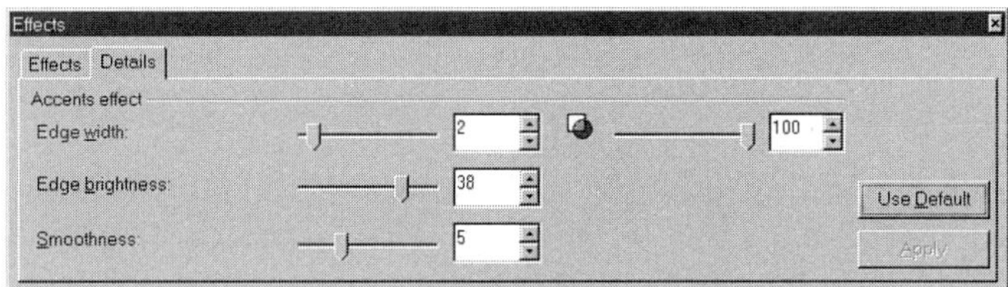

FIGURE 18.5.
The Details tab.

Applying the Effects

Every effect, regardless of category, is applied with the following procedure:

1. Select the sprite to which you want to apply the effect.
2. Select the category of effect you want to use from the Categories drop-down menu.
3. Click on the image representing the effect you want.
4. Click the Details notebook tab.
5. Set the opacity to the amount you want.

6. Set other options, if any, required by the particular type of art effect you're using.
7. Click the Apply button. The effect is then applied to your selection.

TIP

Both the Effects and Details tabs have Apply buttons, but they work a bit differently. The Apply button on the Effects tab simply applies the effect each time you push it, and multiple applications will layer on one another. The Apply button on the Details tab, however, undoes the previous application before applying the new one.

Arts and Crafts

The Arts and Crafts category (see Figure 18.6) presents a number of different tools that emulate crafts techniques, such as paper cutouts, stained glass, stamping, and so on. Table 18.2 lists the various effects in this category.

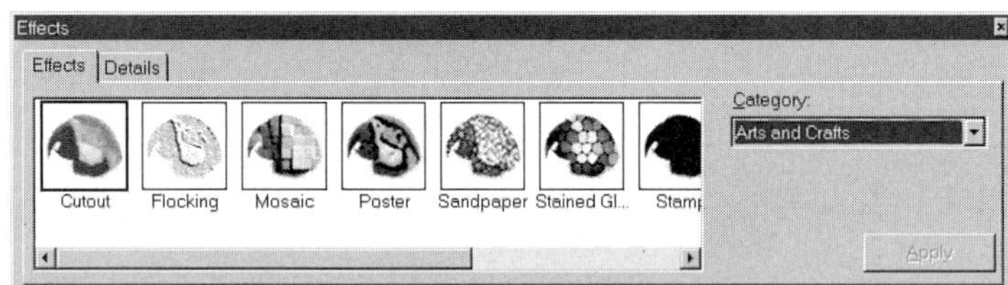

FIGURE 18.6.
Arts and Crafts effects.

Table 18.2. Arts and Crafts effects.

Effect	*Function*
Cutout	Looks as though it is made of cut out colored paper
Flocking	Looks like it was printed on blotting paper
Mosaic	Looks like it was made of mosaic tiles
Poster	Standard posterization effect
Sandpaper	Looks like it was printed on sandpaper
Stained Glass	Looks like it is made of stained glass
Stamp	Plain silhouette-like effect as though made from a rubber stamp
Stone Print	Looks like a two-color photocopy
Torn Edges	Looks like it was stamped from a cut out sponge

Color Enhancement

The Color Enhancement category (see Figure 18.7) presents several tools for making color alterations. Table 18.3 describes the various effects in this category.

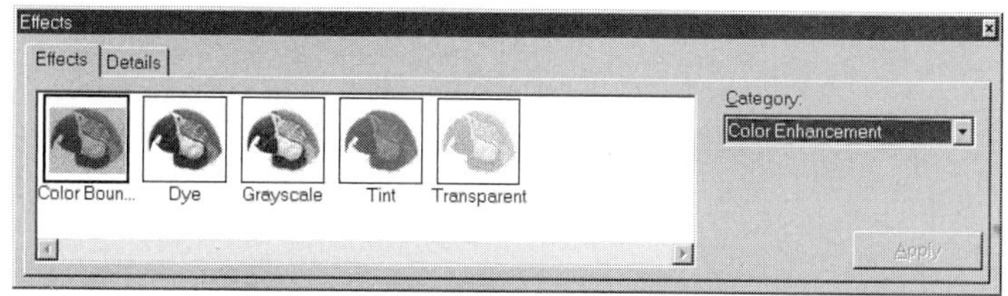

FIGURE 18.7.
Color Enhancement effects.

Table 18.3. Color Enhancement effects.

Effect	*Function*
Color Bounding Box	Changes both opaque and transparent pixels to the currently selected color.
Dye	Changes all opaque pixels but black and white ones to the currently selected color.
Grayscale	Changes color ramp to grayscale ramp. Has no user-definable values.
Tint	Changes opaque pixels only to the currently selected color.
Transparent	Changes the sprite's transparency. Values range from 0 to 100. A setting of 0 renders the sprite totally transparent; a setting of 100 causes no change.

Distort

The Distort category (see Figure 18.8) presents different tools for warping the shapes of sprites. Table 18.4 describes the various effects in this category.

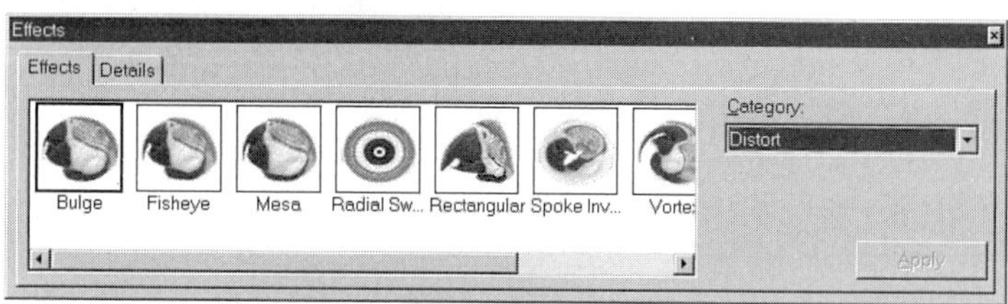

FIGURE 18.8.
Distort effects.

Table 18.4. Distort effects.

Effect	*Function*
Bulge	This effect either spreads out a sprite's center, or squishes it in, depending on the setting.
Fisheye	Much like Bulge, this effect spreads or contracts the center of a sprite; values less than 100 contract, and values over 100 expand.
Mesa	Positive values simply swell the sprite in a circular pattern; negative values show the mesa shape.
Radial Sweep	This effect slices the center line of pixels from the sprite and then repeats it to make a disk shape. You can set the angle of the slice taken to negative values for counterclockwise, positive values for clockwise.
Rectangular	Stretches a sprite into a combination boxy/curved shape, using sine, cosine, or linear knee functions. With this effect, as with Wave, you can work with X or Y axes, or both.
Spoke Inversion	This effect is like Radial Sweep, but it takes several slices and then swaps the inner and outer edges of them.
Vortex	This effect swirls a sprite by chosen degree; negative degrees swirl counterclockwise and positive degrees swirl clockwise.
Wave	Makes a sprite into a snakelike shape. You can set X and/or Y axes, wave frequency and amplitude, and create symmetrical waves.

Gradient

The Gradient category (see Figure 18.9) presents only a single tool, the Gradient (Square). Utilizing four colors, it creates a gradual blend. You can create your own custom blends, as well as use the supplied ones.

FIGURE 18.9.
Gradient effect.

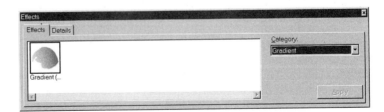

This is a much more complex tool than most of the others, and requires some care to achieve a really good effect. To use the Gradient tool, do the following:

1. Select the sprite you want to fill.
2. Make sure that Gradient (Square) is selected in the Effects palette.
3. Click the Details tab (see Figure 18.10).

FIGURE 18.10.
Gradient details tab.

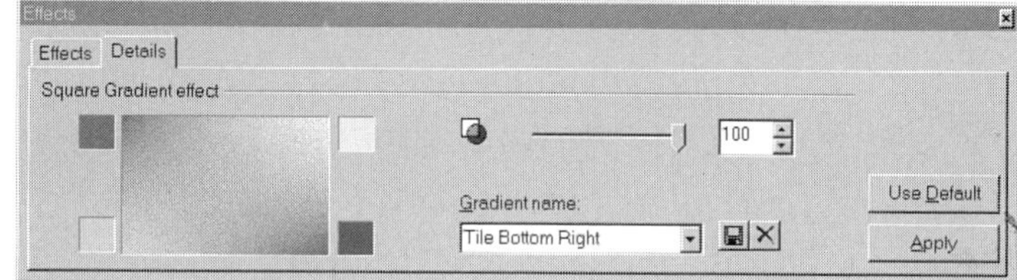

4. Set the opacity to the amount you want.

TIP

If you set the opacity to 100, the selected sprite is simply filled with solid color, overwriting all texture and shading. Unless you want to wipe out the underlying image, experiment with opacity settings under 100.

5. Choose a blend from the drop-down list labeled Gradient Name. A representation of the selected blend is shown on the left side. If none of the blends suits your purposes, see below to learn how to create custom blends.
6. Click the Apply button. The selected sprite is then filled with the chosen blend, as shown in Figure 18.11.

To create your own custom gradient, follow these steps:

1. Click one of the small color boxes at the corners of the gradient display box on the Detail tab. The Color Picker dialog box then appears, as shown in Figure 18.12.
2. Click the color you want to use for that corner of the blend.
3. Click OK.
4. Repeat Steps 1 through 3 for each of the other corners.

The colors you choose then blend into a new gradient.

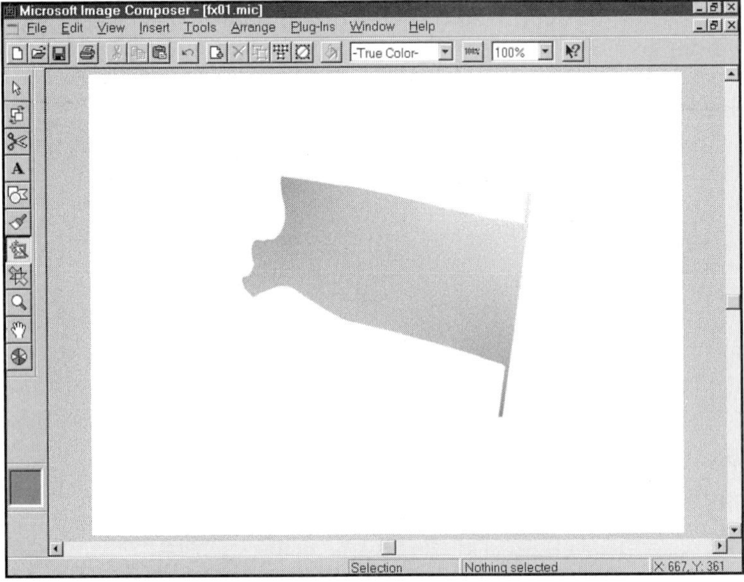

FIGURE 18.11.
A sprite with a gradient applied.

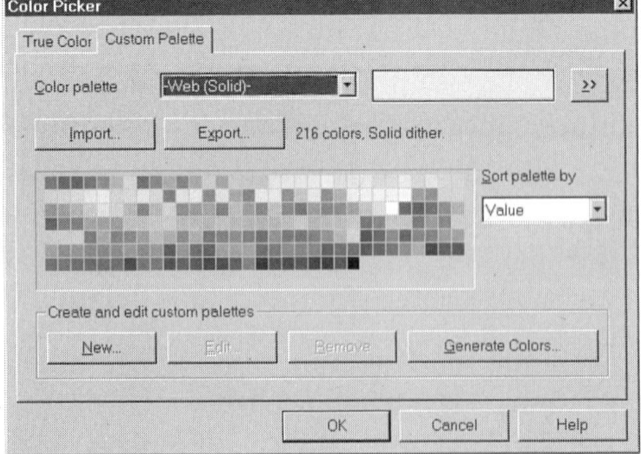

FIGURE 18.12.
Color Picker dialog box.

TIP

You don't have to use four different colors when creating a custom blend. If you want a two-color gradient that shades evenly from top to bottom, rather than a four-color one, make each of the top colors identical. Do the same for the bottom colors. For example, you can set both top corners to red and both bottom corners to blue. You can vary this approach to create left-to-right gradients as well, or use only three colors instead of four for an unusual effect.

Outlines

The Outlines category (see Figure 18.13) offers tools for manipulating various edge effects. Table 18.5 describes the various effects in this category.

FIGURE 18.13.
Outlines effects.

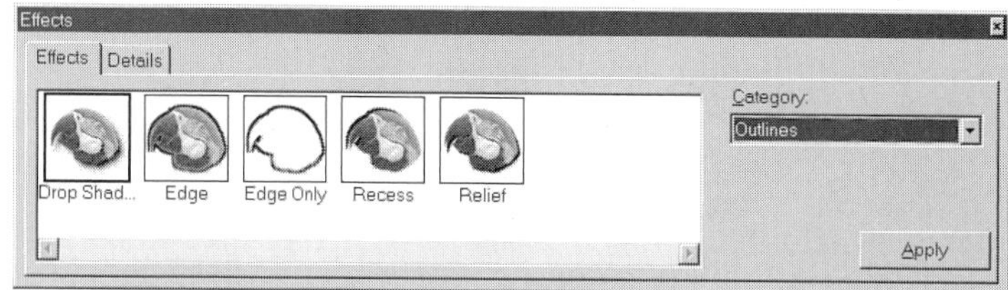

Table 18.5. Outlines effects.

Effect	*Function*
Drop Shadow	Creates variable shadow effect. You can set X and Y offsets (positive only), opacity, and choose shadow color.
Edge	Outlines the sprite with a halo effect. You can set edge thickness, opacity, and color.
Edge Only	Just like Edge, except that the sprite is removed, leaving only the halo outline.
Recess	Makes sprite appear to sink back. No adjustable settings.
Relief	The opposite of Recess. Makes sprite appear to push forward.

Paint

The Paint category (see Figure 18.14) presents a variety of simulations of painterly effects. The Paint effects names are thoroughly descriptive of the actual effect applied—Watercolor, Paint Daubs, Sprayed Strokes, and so on. Table 18.6 lists the various effects available in the Paint category.

FIGURE 18.14.
Paint effects.

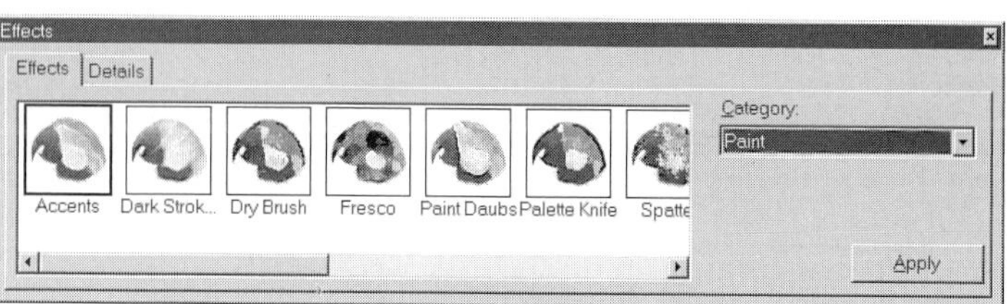

Table 18.6. Paint effects.

Effect	*Function*
Accents	Highlights the edges of the sprite
Dark Strokes	Uses diagonal black and white brush strokes
Dry Brush	Reduces color detail at edges
Fresco	Short, rounded dabs are applied
Paint Daubs	Looks like a series of paint strokes
Palette Knife	Looks as though painted with a palette knife
Spatter	Gives an airbrush effect
Sponge	Looks like paint was applied with a sponge
Sprayed Strokes	Looks like spray paint
Sumi-e	Simulates Japanese ink painting
Underpainting	Layers two copies of the sprite over one another; the bottom one looks like it was painted on brick
Watercolor	Looks like watercolor painting
Wet Paper	Looks as though sprite were painted onto wet paper

Patterns

The Patterns category (see Figure 18.15) essentially consists of variations on three themes: bars, checkerboards, and noise (random dot patterns). Table 18.7 lists the various effects in this category.

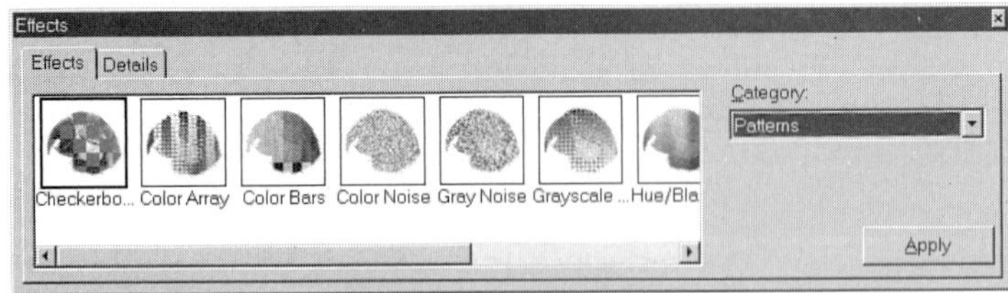

FIGURE 18.15.
Patterns effects.

Table 18.7. Patterns effects.

Effect	*Function*
Checkerboard	Adds a checkerboard appearance
Color Array	Adds a color checkerboard appearance
Color Bars	Looks like a TV test pattern
Color Noise	Random color dots

Effect	Function
Gray Noise	Random grayscale dots
Grayscale Array	Adds a grayscale checkerboard pattern
Hue/Blackness	Like Color Bars, but gets darker toward the bottom
Hue/Whiteness	Same as Hue/Blackness, but gets lighter toward the bottom
Stripes	Adds a striped appearance

As always, it is important to remember to set the opacity so that the patterns do not totally obliterate the underlying sprite. Aside from the opacity considerations, you should bear in mind the shape and texture of the sprite when choosing a pattern. For example, because most of the patterns are strong vertical or horizontal designs, they look terrible when applied to a sprite with strong diagonals, as you can see in Figure 18.16.

FIGURE 18.16.
A sprite with a conflicting pattern applied.

Perhaps the highest and best use of these patterns is for text and other flat, monocolored images.

Photographic

The Photographic category (see Figure 18.17) presents effects that are designed to simulate standard photographic manipulation and filtering techniques. Table 18.8 describes the various effects in this category.

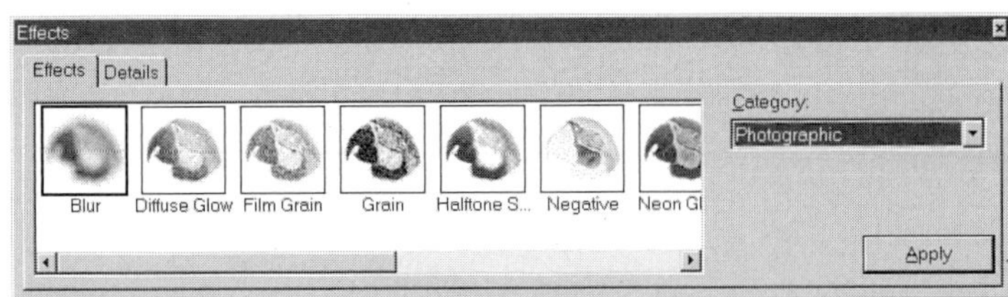

FIGURE 18.17.
Photographic effects.

Table 18.8. Photographic effects.

Effect	*Function*
Blur	Blurs selected sprite from the edges inward. The amount of blur depends on the settings; the higher the number, the greater the blur. You can blur in X or Y dimensions, or both at once.
Diffuse Glow	Applies a diffusion filter, resulting in an image as though seen through dirty glass.
Film Grain	Gives an appearance of old-style film grain, heavier on the darker areas.
Grain	Similar to film grain, but with more user control, such as vertical and horizontal grain.
Halftone Screen	Produces an effect like newspaper photographs composed of tiny dots; can also use circles and lines instead of dots.
Negative	Reverses all colors, creating a color negative effect. Has no user-definable values.
Neon Glow	Creates a hot, glowing effect.
Sharpen	The opposite of blur. Increases contrast between neighboring pixels.
Sharpen Lite	The same as Sharpen, but less of it.
Soften	Essentially the same as Blur, but considerably less of it. Works by decreasing contrast between neighboring pixels.
Transparent	Changes the sprite's transparency. Values range from 0 to 100. A setting of 0 renders the sprite totally transparent; a setting of 100 causes no change.

TIP

The Blur effect can be very useful for creating a three-dimensional effect in a composition. You can apply the blur effect to the background images while leaving the foreground images sharp.

Also, you can use the Sharpen effect repeatedly on the same sprite to produce a grain effect.

Sketch

The Sketch category (see Figure 18.18) presents some more simulations of traditional artist's techniques. Table 18.9 lists the various effects available in the Sketch category.

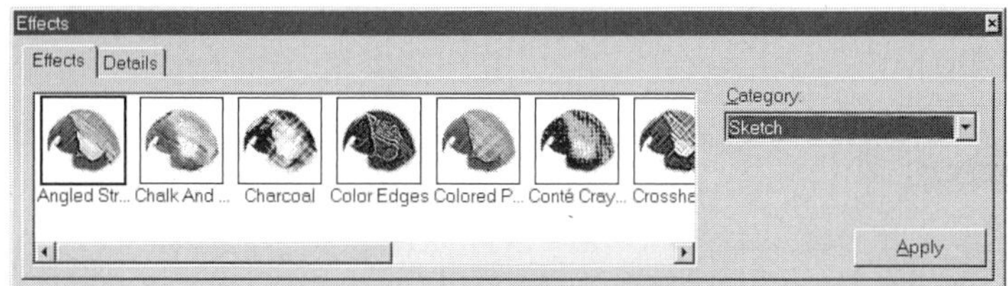

FIGURE 18.18.
Sketch effects.

Table 18.9. Sketch effects.

Effect	*Function*
Angled Strokes	Paints sprite in diagonal strokes
Chalk and Charcoal	Looks as though both chalk and charcoal were used
Charcoal	Looks like sprite was drawn with charcoal
Color Edges	Makes sprite black and white, then adds colored highlights
Colored Pencil	Looks like sprite was drawn with colored pencils
Conte Crayon	Looks like sprite was drawn with a crayon
Crosshatch	Gives sprite a crosshatched appearance
Fine Marker	Looks like sprite was drawn with a Flair
Rough Pastels	Looks like sprite was drawn with pastel chalk
Smudge Stick	Looks like smudge stick was used
Technical Pen	Looks like sprite was drawn with a Rapidograph

Surface

The Surface category (see Figure 18.19) simulates the appearance of several different materials. Table 18.10 lists the various effects available in the Surface category.

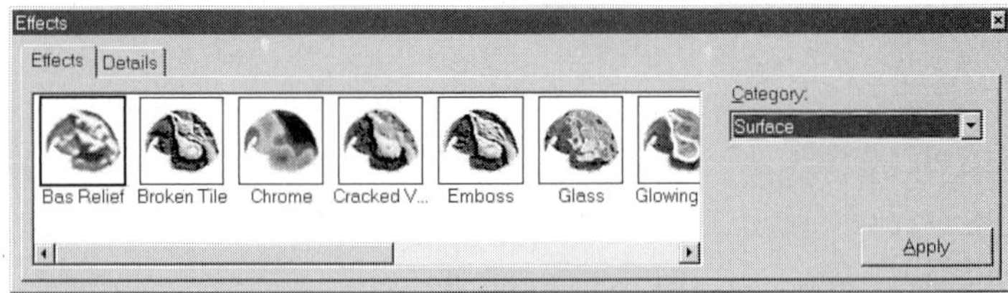

FIGURE 18.19.
Surface effects.

Table 18.10. Surface effects.

Effect	*Function*
Bas Relief	Creates a bas-relief effect
Broken Tile	Looks like sprite was made of broken tiles
Chrome	Looks like sprite is made of chrome
Cracked Varnish	Looks like cracked plaster
Emboss	Gives sprite a raised, 3D appearance
Glass	Looks as though you are looking at it through a dirty window
Glowing Accents	Adds glowing edges to the sprite
Plaster	Like emboss, but with bumps and dips
Plastic Wrap	Looks as though it is wrapped in cellophane
Ripple	Looks like sprite is underwater
Rough Textures	Makes sprite look like it was painted on burlap

Adding Plug-Ins

Image Composer can use many Photoshop-compatible plug-ins (see the following caution, however). To add them, you should install them in the `PlugIns` folder. If you installed Image Composer on your C drive with the default choices, the path would be `C:\Program Files\Microsoft Image Composer\PlugIns`. If you do not want to install them in this folder, or if you already have some plug-ins installed in other folders for use with other programs, Image Composer allows you to name one alternative folder in which it will look for plug-ins. To do so, follow this procedure:

1. Choose Tools|Options.
2. In the resulting Options dialog box, click the Plug-Ins tab, as shown in Figure 18.20.

FIGURE 18.20.
Setting the optional plug-ins folder choice.

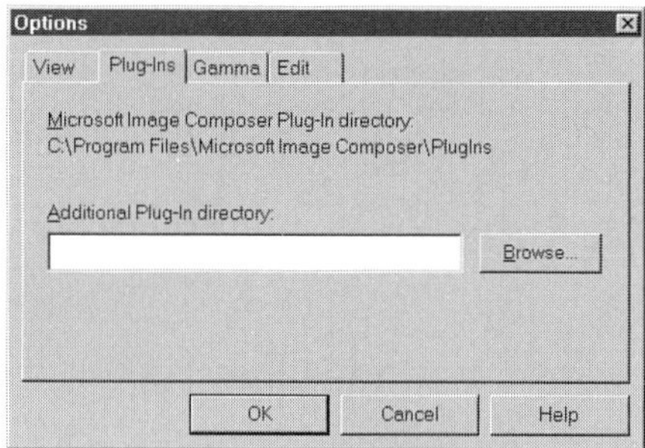

3. If you know the folder location, type it into the text box labeled Additional Plug-In directory. If you do not know its location, click the Browse button. After you find the folder, double-click its name or click OK, and it is added.

CAUTION

Image Composer works with filter plug-ins only; it does not work with import/export plug-ins. You should probably check with the publisher of any Photoshop plug-in to be certain that it follows version 2.5 of the Photoshop plug-in filter interface. Better yet, get a demo copy from the publisher, and try it before spending your money. Most plug-in publishers maintain Web sites, so you can probably download a demo for free.

The Impressionist plug-in, which is included with Image Composer, duplicates many of the built-in features of Image Composer's own special effects tools (for example, chalk, charcoal, Sumi-e, watercolor, and so on). Yet, it adds some others (such as geometric and marker) that make it worthwhile on its own. Even with the areas of duplication, the Impressionist plug-in provides a number of different effects that Image Composer does not, and it has an easy-to-use interface that includes a preview feature, as you can see in Figure 18.21.

To use the Impressionist plug-in, you must first have a sprite selected. Next, select Plug-Ins|Impressionist|Impressionist from the menu. After you have made your effects selection, click the Apply button. The effect you chose will be applied to the selected sprite.

If you wish to repeat the same effect without going through the entire procedure, simply select a sprite, then choose Plug-Ins|Repeat Last Plug-In from the menu. This can be done with the original sprite for compound effects, or with a different, newly selected sprite.

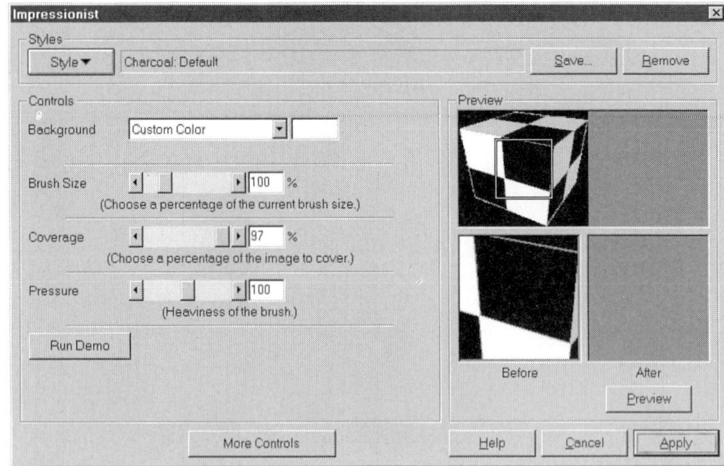

FIGURE 18.21.
The Impressionist interface.

Using the Paint Tool

The Paint tool (see Chapter 17 for a detailed description of the Paint tool) offers some of the same effects available from the Effects tool, but with an important difference. Whereas the Warps and Filters tool applies the effects to an entire sprite, the Paint tool applies them to only a limited area depending on brush size. These tools are as follows:

- Tint
- Colorize
- Mesa
- Vortex
- Spoke Inversion

Summary

Image Composer's special effects tools are Texture Transfer and Effects. In addition, the Paint tool provides some localized effects.

This chapter provides step-by-step instructions and example illustrations that show how, using these tools, you can alter the color and appearance of sprites in a number of ways, from applying painterly effects such as watercolor to distortions such as wave effects.

Optimizing Your Images and Color Palettes

by David and Rhonda Crowder

IN THIS CHAPTER

- Using FrontPage Editor's Image Tools *336*
- Selecting File Format *350*
- Reducing File Size *350*

Earlier chapters covered the basic techniques for creating and adding images to your FrontPage web. Once the images are on the page, though, FrontPage 98 adds a wealth of new image editing and enhancement tools for you to use. In addition to these tools, this chapter also discusses the factors you need to consider to get the highest performance and best appearance from your Web images.

Using FrontPage Editor's Image Tools

If the FrontPage Editor image toolbar (see Figure 19.1) is not showing, select View | Image Toolbar from the menu. It will now appear on the upper right. The first five buttons deal with creating and managing image map hotspots, and are covered separately in Chapter 21, "Creating and Designing Image Maps."

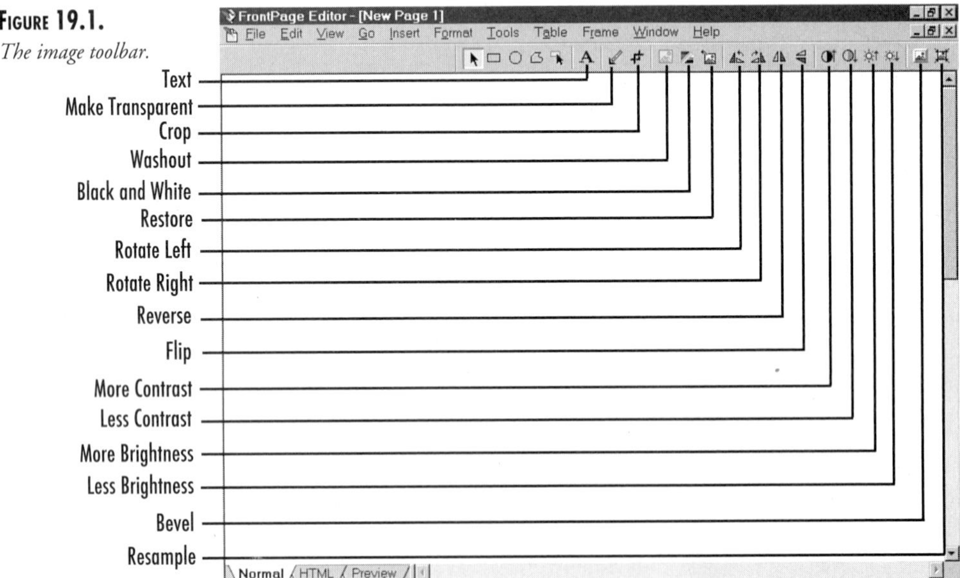

FIGURE 19.1.
The image toolbar.

Using Restore and Undo with Images

Before you start making changes to images, it's important to understand how to recover from alterations you are unhappy with. In addition to the standard Undo button, you also have the use of the Restore button on the image toolbar. Each approach has slightly different characteristics, and each has its advantages and disadvantages.

The Restore Button will undo all changes made to an image as long as you have not yet saved the page since you made them. After you have saved the page, the Restore button will base all later restorations on the newly saved image. Every time you save, Restore starts from scratch.

CAUTION

Always, always, always keep a separate copy of the original image, either in a different folder on your hard drive or on a floppy disk.

The Restore command works on an image whether you have made a single change or even if you have made multiple changes. For instance, you could flip an image, then change the contrast, make it into a black-and-white picture, crop it, and rotate it a couple of times. The Restore button will still undo all these changes with just a single click.

The one exception to this is the Text command. Text added to an image must be manually deleted. Neither the Restore button nor the Undo button will remove a text label from an image. The reason for this is that the text label does not actually become a part of the image, but is laid over it. Thus, the image itself is not changed and there is nothing to restore from. Why the Undo button does not affect this, though, is a mystery.

You do not have to use the Restore button immediately after a change is made. Even if you have worked on another image in the meantime, you can still restore any image on the page. Just click the image you want to restore to its original state. Once it is selected, click the Restore button.

Of course, you can also use the Undo button to manually step back through image changes one by one, just as with any other kind of work you do in FrontPage Editor. Unlike the Restore button, this technique will work even after saving the page.

However, the Undo button is a general purpose approach, not one specifically designed for working with images. Thus, in contrast to the Restore button, you cannot tell it which image to work on. It will simply back up step by step through all the things you have done, so if the image you need to change was not the most recent work you have done, the Undo button will have to undo all the work you have done since then before it reaches the image changes. As mentioned earlier, like the Restore button, Undo has no effect on the Text command.

So, when do you use which button? Restore is useful only when you need to start all over again with an image, or are at least willing to do so. Other than using the button during early experiments, when you are still familiarizing yourself with the other image buttons, it is probably best to use it when you decide that you have taken a wrong tack and an image has become totally unworkable.

Undo, on the other hand, is only useful when backing up step by step will not destroy other work. It is the clear choice if, for example, you have just used the Washout button and immediately realize that you do not like the results, but do not want to undo the changes you made just before the washout was applied. If, however, you have finished with an image, then done lots more work on the page before deciding you want to go back to an earlier version of the image, the Undo button would probably be a poor choice because you would have to give up all the intervening work in order to get back to the image changes. You would have to decide in such a case which approach would be less trouble for you; to use Undo and have to redo the other work or to use Restore and have to redo the image.

In addition to the two buttons dedicated to correcting changes, you can also use a few simple tricks to reverse most changes without resorting to the more drastic measures. For example, if you have flipped an image and want to put it back upright, just flip it again. The same principle works with rotations as well; if you have rotated an image right and want it back, just rotate it left (or three more times to the right). Don't want the contrast you added earlier? Use the Less Contrast button on the image to reverse the effect. Finally, the Black and White button is a toggle switch, so you can revert to color by simply hitting it again.

Adding Text to Your Images

Whether used as callouts, internal captions, or part of the artwork itself, text labels can enhance images in many ways. Careful use of fonts, color, and phrasing can turn a humdrum image into an eye-catching piece of communication.

NOTE

FrontPage Editor cannot add text to JPEG images. If you want to add it to one, you will have to convert it to GIF format first. To do this, right-click the JPEG image, then select Image Properties from the pop-up menu. This will bring up the Image Properties dialog box (see Figure 19.2). To convert from JPEG to GIF, just click the GIF radio button and hit the OK button.

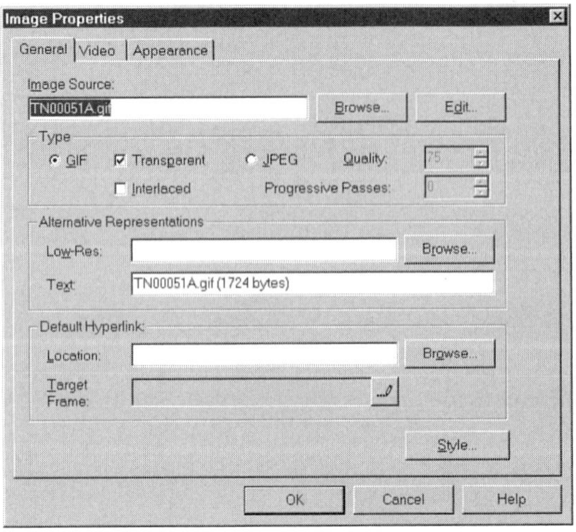

FIGURE 19.2.
Image Properties dialog box.

Not every image needs text, though, and there are some points you should consider before adding it. For one thing, most images used on the World Wide Web are smaller than their counterparts in printed media due to the increased demands that larger images place on Net connections. In order to speed up download time, image size is often the first thing sacrificed. If you add text to an image, that text must be sized to fit within the boundaries of the image. Is it still easily readable? If it is too small, there is no point to adding it, and your best solution would probably be to use an external caption for the image, or to use the text in the main body of your Web page, referring to the image for clarity.

If the image is too small and you still want the text in the image itself, then you will have to resize the image to make it larger. However, resizing a bitmapped image can result in serious degradation of image quality. If the original of the image is larger than the version you are using on your Web page, you are in luck; just replace the smaller image. Or, if it is in a vector format that can be scaled without degradation in the originating program, you can then save the new larger version as a GIF and import it into FrontPage 98. You can also try the Resample command in FrontPage Editor; depending on the image and the degree of resizing, it can often produce an acceptable enlargement (see the section titled "Resampling Your Images"). Otherwise, you have an insurmountable problem and should probably look for another image entirely.

Does the image have a place where text would stand out? It does not have to be a white background with bold black lettering on it, but a busy, cluttered image is not conducive to good textual enhancement. It is best to choose an area of solid color, or at least one with relatively few color changes, to place your text so it will stand out. If the background is dark, use light color for the text; if it is light, use dark colors for the text. If it is intermediate, then experiment with different colors; complementary colors (for example, red on blue) usually work best in such a situation. Also, see the section titled "Washing Out Your Images" for another possible solution.

You can add text labels to an image by using the following procedure:

1. Select the image you want to add the text to.
2. Click the Text button in the image toolbar. A text box with sizing handles will appear in the center of the selected image (see Figure 19.3).
3. Type the desired text. The text box will dynamically expand as you type; it is only limited by the width of the image. When you are finished, click anywhere outside the text box.

If you want to move the location of the text, simply place the pointer within the text box, hold down the left mouse button, and drag it into a new position.

If you do not like the default text, you can change the font type, size, and color by clicking the text. This will bring up the text box. Next, either use the buttons in the Format toolbar (see Chapter 4, "Creating Web Pages with FrontPage 98") or select Format|Font from the menu and make your changes by using the Font dialog box (see Figure 19.4).

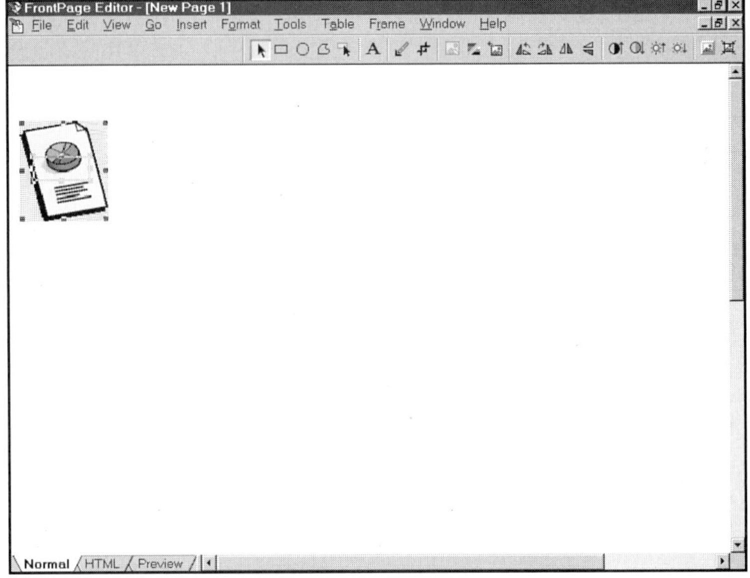

FIGURE 19.3.
Image with text box.

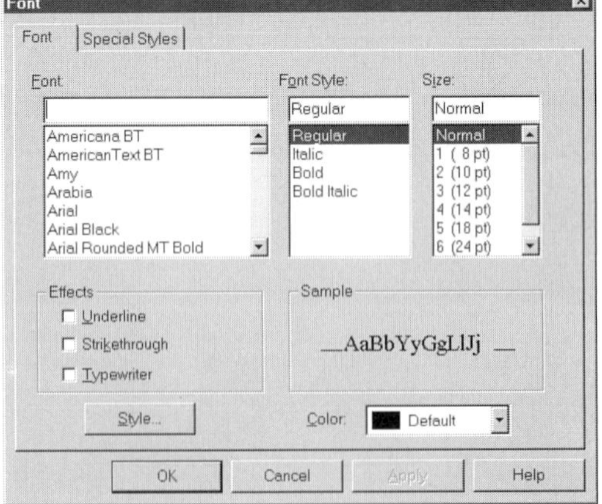

FIGURE 19.4.
The Font dialog box.

CAUTION

If you want to delete text you have added to an image, be aware that the Restore and Undo commands will have no effect. Instead, you must click the image, then click the text box, then press the Delete key. You can probably skip the second step because the text box should be active when you select the image, but occasionally it is not, and pressing the Delete key at that point will remove the image instead.

NOTE

You cannot right-click the text box in an image and bring up the Font Properties dialog box from the pop-up menu the way you can with regular text elsewhere on the page.

Adding Transparency to Your Images

Images as a whole are invariably rectangular in shape. In most cases, though, the main portion of the artwork in the image is not rectangular. This means that there is some area around the artwork between it and the edges of the rectangular image that is just plain background, and this background usually doesn't fit in too well with the design of a Web page. The only real exception is when you have a plain white page and the image has a plain white background.

The result of this is that any image inserted on a Web page that has a colored background or a background image is set off within a box (see Figure 19.5). There might be times when you want to do this deliberately for design effect, but it is common practice to eliminate this extraneous background and, with it, the boxy appearance.

FIGURE 19.5.
Image without transparency.

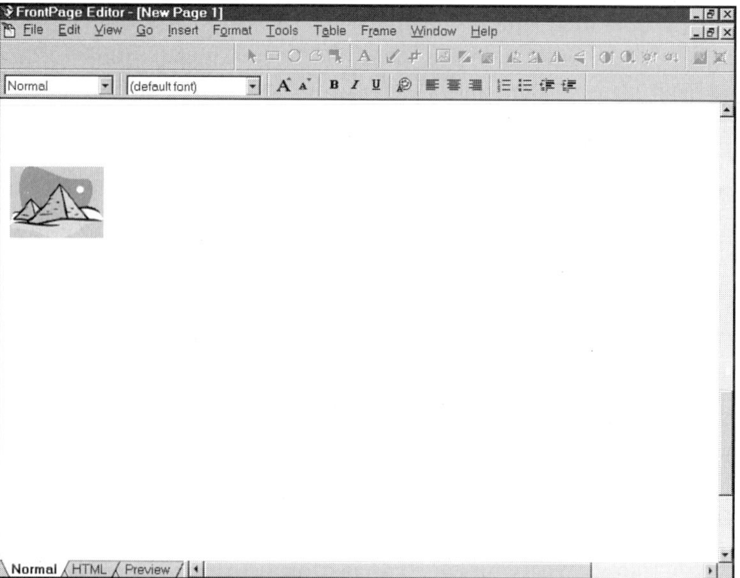

This is done by making the image background transparent so that the Web page behind can show through (see Figure 19.6). Currently, this is only possible with GIF images; JPEGs do not support transparency.

FIGURE 19.6.
Image with transparent background.

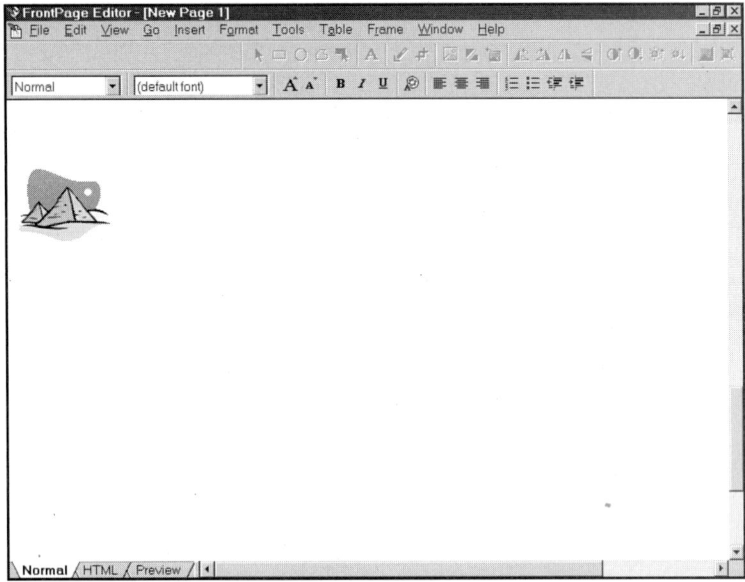

Clip art imported from the Clip Gallery in GIF format already has transparency in effect. Depending on your choices in Image Composer, images from that program might or might not have transparency (this is also true of other similar graphics programs). However, sometimes, you can lose that feature in FrontPage Editor. Applying washout to an image, for example, or converting a GIF image to a JPEG (even if you later convert it back to a GIF) will cause this. And, of course, there are tons of sources of images that do not have transparent backgrounds. Or, for your own artistic design reasons, you might even want to have the rectangular outline showing while you make an internal color transparent (see Figure 19.7).

FrontPage Editor provides the Make Transparent button to solve this problem. This is likely the easiest approach to this problem that you will ever find in any program. Simply click the button in the image toolbar, then click the color you want to make transparent. That's really all there is to it.

When you select a color other than the (transparent) background in images that already have transparency applied (like the ones from Clip Gallery), the formerly transparent background will be rendered in medium gray because, unfortunately, you cannot make more than one color transparent. If you change your mind after selecting one, you can either restore or undo the change, or, if you just want to restore the old transparent background, you can simply select the Make Transparent button once more and click the medium gray to make it transparent again.

If you are dealing with a JPEG image and want transparency, you will have to convert it to a GIF first, then apply the transparency tool.

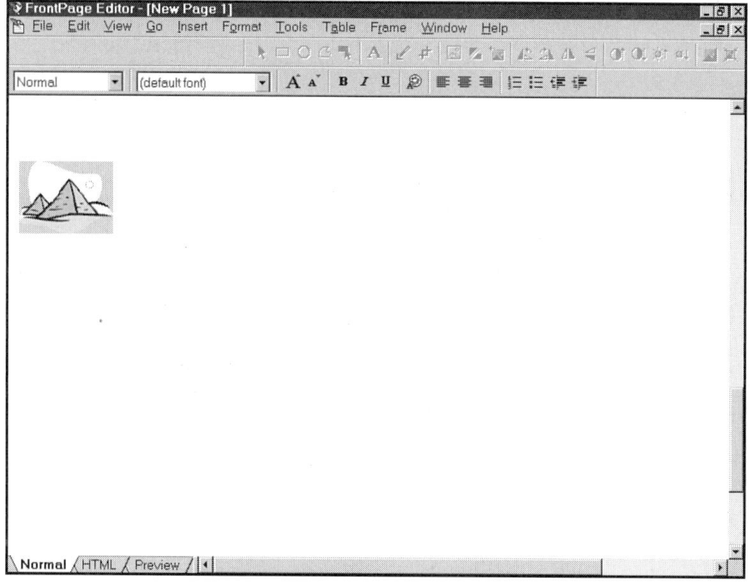

FIGURE 19.7.
Image with internal transparency.

If you want to completely remove all transparency from an image, the simplest way to do it is to convert the GIF to a JPEG, but not all images look best as JPEGs (see the section titled "Selecting File Format"). The best way to do it is to just remove the transparency setting from the GIF image entirely.

With either approach, start by right-clicking the image, then select Image Properties from the pop-up menu. This will bring up the Image Properties dialog box (see Figure 19.2). To convert from GIF to JPEG, just click the JPEG radio button and hit the OK button (for full information on setting JPEG image options, see Chapter 7, "Enhancing Your Web Page with Images—The Easy Way"). To just remove the transparency while leaving the GIF a GIF, click the check box labeled Transparent to uncheck it, then hit the OK button.

Cropping Your Images

Cropping is the art of cutting out all extraneous parts of an image to concentrate on the real meaning you want to convey. It may be necessary for a variety of reasons. You might want to focus on a single individual in a group photograph, for instance, or to pull out a piece from a montage. Perhaps there is just a portion of a larger piece of artwork that perfectly fits your needs, or a scanned image may have a border you hadn't noticed before. Whatever the reason, if you want to remove everything but part of an image, here's how to do it:

1. Select the image you want to crop.
2. Click the Crop button in the image toolbar. A box will appear, drawn through the sizing handles, surrounding the image (see Figure 19.8).

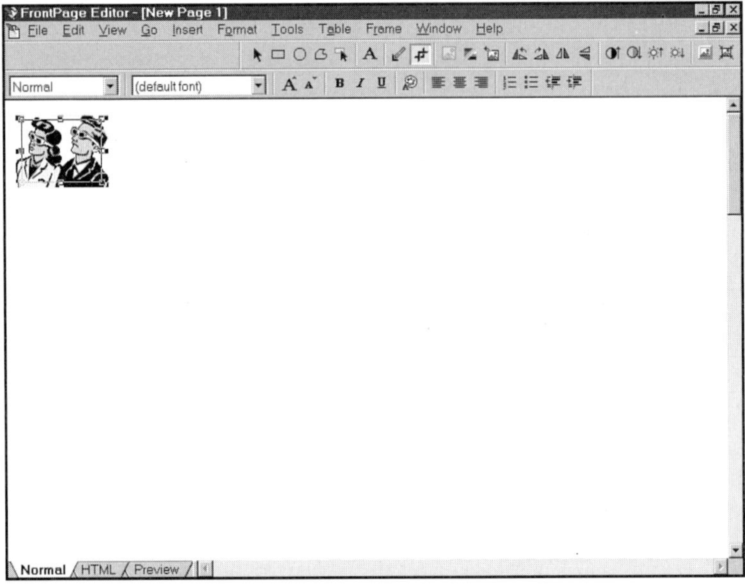

FIGURE 19.8.
The crop box.

3. Place the pointer on one of the sizing handles. When the pointer changes from the regular arrow to a double arrow, press the left mouse button and, while holding it down, drag the box until it frames only the portion of the image you want to keep, and then release the mouse button. If you cannot get the box just right with only one sizing handle, you can move the pointer to a different sizing handle after releasing the mouse button, and repeat as many times as necessary.
4. You can move the cropping box around the image by placing the pointer inside the box, depressing the left mouse button, and dragging it to a new location. When you have it positioned as you want, release the mouse button.
5. Steps 3 and 4 can be repeated as often as necessary.
6. To actually make the crop, place the mouse pointer inside the cropping box and double-click the left mouse button (or hit the Enter key). All areas of the image outside the crop box will be deleted. You can use the Restore button if you do not like the results.

Washing Out Your Images

The Washout command is perhaps the best thing that could ever have happened to background images, even though you may want to use washed-out images in many other situations. It simultaneously lowers both brightness and contrast drastically, resulting in a pale version of the original that is still pastel-faithful to the original colors. You will recall the discussion of contrast problems in the section titled "Adding Text to Your Images": With washout applied, text that once was lost in the overall image now leaps to the fore (see Figures 19.9 and 19.10). This tool is wonderfully useful for background images in tables, or for image-based buttons.

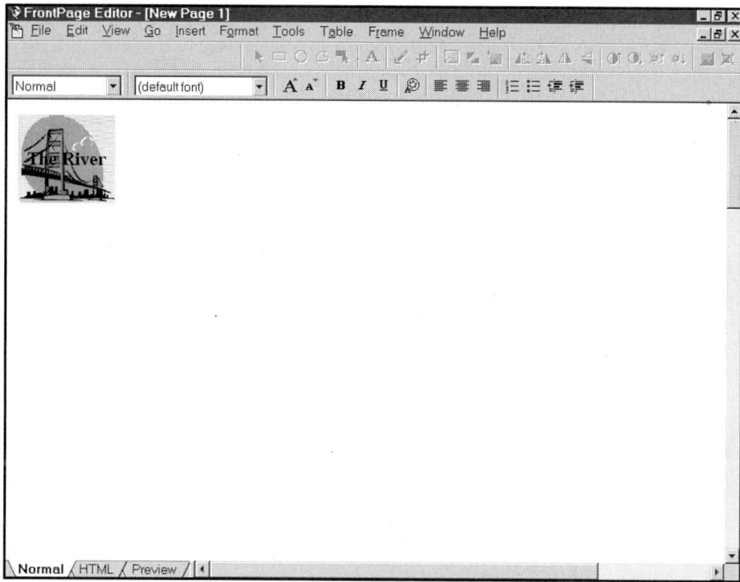

FIGURE 19.9.
Text on original image.

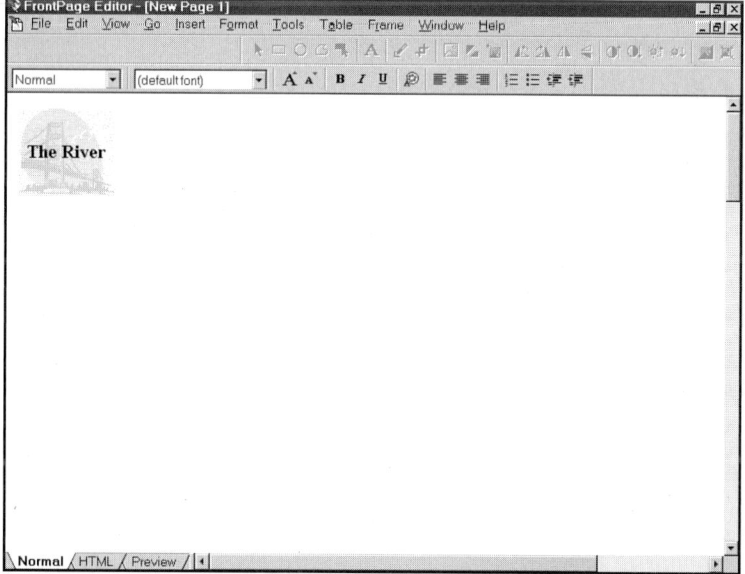

FIGURE 19.10.
Text on washed-out image.

Applying the Washout command is extremely simple. Just select an image, then click the Washout button in the image toolbar.

TIP

The Washout command will undo transparency in GIFs. To restore it, apply the Make Transparent command to the light gray background in the washed-out image.

NOTE

You can wash out a background image for the entire page by simply clicking the Washout button when no other images are selected (it does not affect the situation if you have selected text or some other page element, just as long as it is not an image). The command, however, will not work on the background image if you have a theme applied, but only on one specified in the Page Properties dialog box.

Making Your Images Black and White

The Black and White button does not actually do what it says; instead of making a two-color image, it creates a grayscale version of a color image. Although it is hard to imagine a great deal of use for this command in the color-intensive World Wide Web, it can be useful in creating background images, especially in concert with the Washout command.

To apply the Black and White command, select an image, then click the Black and White button in the image toolbar.

Like washout, Black and White can be applied to background images, with the same restrictions.

Rotating, Reversing, and Flipping Your Images

You can change the orientation of an image easily by using the Rotate Left, Rotate Right, Reverse, and Flip buttons on the image toolbar (see Figure 19.11).

The Rotate commands turn an image 90 degrees at a time; thus, four Rotate commands in a row will return an image to its original state. Reverse and Flip will show mirror images (left-right and top-bottom, respectively). All are applied in the usual simple manner: select the image, then click the appropriate button. As long as the image remains selected, you can keep on rotating, flipping, or reversing it—or any combination of these—endlessly.

Like the Washout and Black and White commands, rotation, flipping, and reversal can be applied to background images, with the same restrictions.

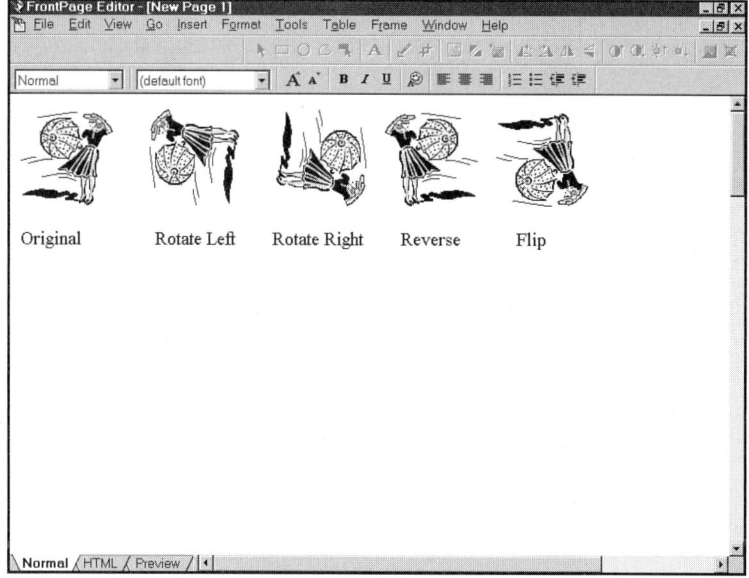

FIGURE 19.11.
Image subjected to rotation, reversal, and flipping.

Adjusting Contrast

The More Contrast and Less Contrast command buttons allow you to adjust the relative importance between pixels of different values in your images. As you increase contrast, differences between pixel values are emphasized until subtleties fade away entirely and you are left with a simplistic line rendering of your image in basic colors; as you decrease it, differences between pixel values are minimized until you finally reach a solid black image.

As with the other commands in the image toolbar, you simply select the image and then repeatedly click the More Contrast or Less Contrast buttons until you reach your desired goal.

Like the Washout, Black and White, and orientation commands, contrast changes can be applied to background images, with the same restrictions.

Adjusting Brightness

The More Brightness and Less Brightness buttons allow you to adjust the light values in your images. With each click on the More Brightness button, colors in your image are lightened until, if you hit the button enough times, white is the only remaining color; as you click the Less Brightness button, the colors are darkened with each click until you are left with nothing but black.

TIP

Neither command has any effect on the transparent color. The brightness buttons can therefore be used, in addition to making minor value adjustments, to create silhouette images (see Figure 19.12). Obviously, the background color in these cases must contrast for the silhouette to show; a white silhouette on a white background is invisible, for instance. It should also be noted that not all images are suitable for silhouettes (see Figure 19.13).

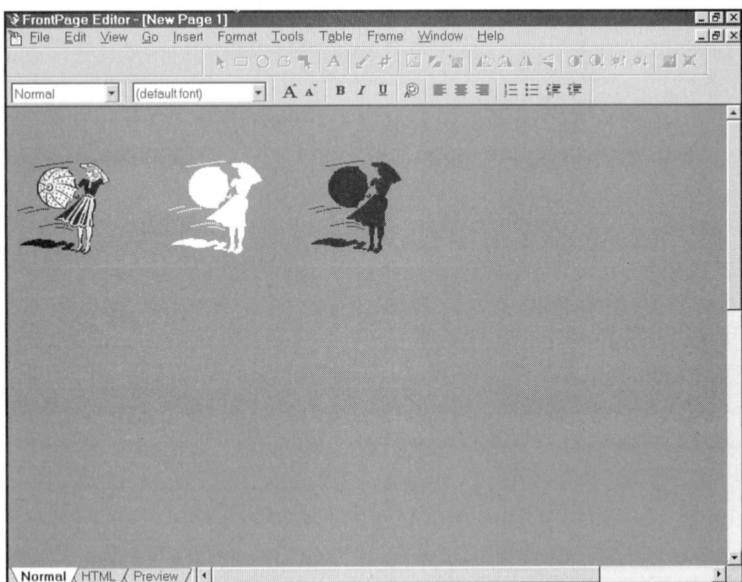

FIGURE 19.12.
Silhouetting an image.

As with the other commands in the image toolbar, you simply select the image and then repeatedly click the More Brightness or Less Brightness buttons until you reach your desired goal.

Like the Washout, Black and White, orientation, and contrast commands, brightness changes can be applied to background images, with the same restrictions.

Adding Beveled Frames

The Bevel command, although useful for making quick buttons out of images, is not very impressive. If you select an image, then click the Bevel button, a shaded border with a 3D look to it will be wrapped around the image (see Figure 19.14). It is in plain gray and white, with the apparent light source from the upper left. You have no control over the color, border width, position of apparent light source, or anything else. Due to the white portion of the bevel, you cannot use it effectively on a white page. Also, part of the image itself shows up wrapped over the beveled edge, so choose or draw your pictures carefully if you want to use the bevel effectively.

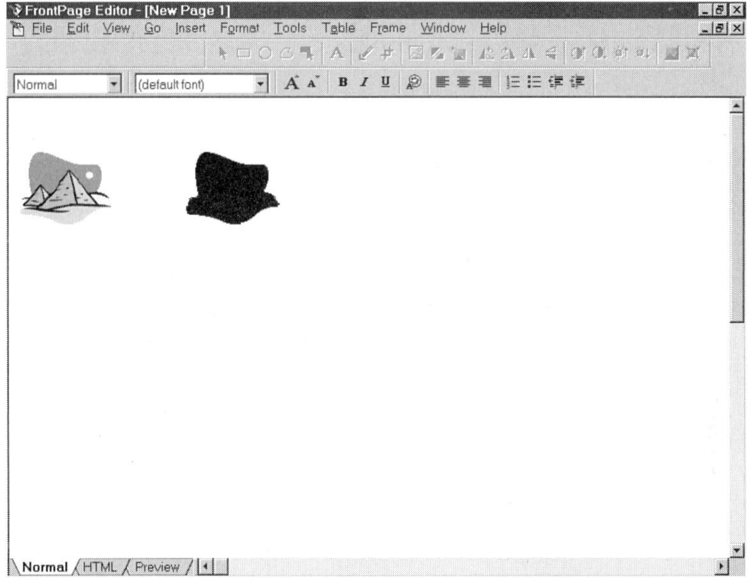

FIGURE 19.13.
A poor choice for silhouetting.

> **TIP**
>
> If you go into the Image Properties dialog box and give the image a border before you bevel it, you can improve its appearance.

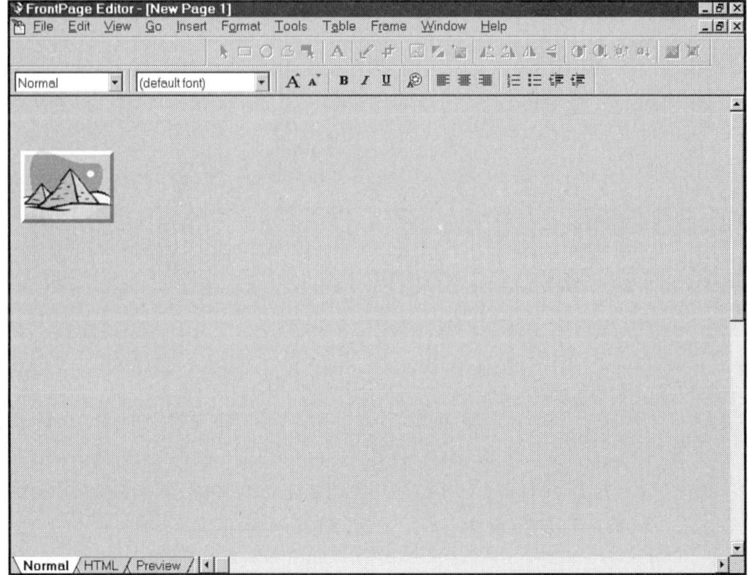

FIGURE 19.14.
A beveled image.

Selecting File Format

Although newer formats, like the Portable Network Graphics (PNG) format, which is designed to replace the GIF file format, will probably eventually take hold, FrontPage designers are left to deal with the two current standards, GIF and JPEG.

Due to the nature of their respective capabilities and configurations, GIF files are better for sharp images with fewer colors (screen captures, presentation charts, icons, and so on), and JPEG files are better for images with many colors and subtle gradations of shades (fine art, scanned photographs, and so on). This is because JPEG files, by their nature, are designed to work best on truecolor images with subtle changes between sectors. GIFs, on the other hand, are limited to a maximum of 256 colors. JPEGs, which represent everything in an image by a series of mathematical curves, are inherently poor at handling sharp edges. Also, there is invariably some degree of image degradation with the approximations involved in the JPEG format, whereas GIFs faithfully represent every pixel in the original image.

Therefore, you must look carefully at an image before deciding which file type would work best with it. Is it mostly a few colors? Is it filled with sharp changes of color, or does it contain mostly gentle changes? Is file size a major consideration, or is it palpably nonexistent?

If the image absolutely requires transparency or embedded text, then it must be a GIF, no question about it because only GIF files support these approaches to images.

On the other hand, if the image cries out to be represented in JPEG format, then text and transparency must take a back seat to the necessities of subtleties in transition and/or the need for truecolor representation.

When it comes to displaying a partial image on connection, either the interlaced GIF or the progressive JPEG offer equivalent solutions. Although neither one will actually speed up connection or download times, either one will provide a lower quality representation of the image in question right off the bat, gradually sharpening until the image is full quality. Although, as noted, this has no effect on practical questions of connectivity, it may well keep an otherwise bored viewer connected.

Reducing File Size

When it comes to file size, there is no question about it; JPEG is king. Except in very rare cases, a given GIF file is larger than the equivalent JPEG file. Faced with those situations where the GIF file is the preferred method, such as when text or transparency is a required element, the FrontPage designer must look for ways to reduce the size of the GIF file. Of course, you can always simply reduce the size of the file, but if this is not a viable option for your particular situation, you should try the color reduction approach.

Unfortunately, FrontPage 98 does not directly support color reduction for images. However, Image Composer, though not as straightforward about it as other programs like Photoshop, does indirectly offer color reduction through the use of custom color palettes.

Actually, any time you load an Image Composer sprite (which is a truecolor image) and save it as a GIF, you are already performing a color reduction, from 16.7 million possible colors to a maximum of 216. No, that is not a typo. There are not 256 colors, but 216 available with an Image Composer GIF. The reason for this is that Image Composer uses a group of colors that has been called by various names such as Browser Safe Palette, Common Browser Palette, or Safety Palette; it is known in Image Composer as the Web Palette using the Balanced Ramp or limited amount of colors. These 216 colors are ones which—at least in theory—the major browsers will represent with absolute accuracy on any system, whether it be hi-color, truecolor, or simple SVGA. The Web Palette has two versions: solid and dithered.

The solid version is best used, of course, for images with relatively small numbers of solid colors. The dithered version can accommodate, with little loss of clarity, subtle images based on truecolor technology.

Dithering is the process of simulating colors that are present in the image, but not available in the browser's palette. If the user has enabled dithering in his browser, then it will blend several pixels of different colors in a small area in an attempt to create an approximation of the unavailable color (for the sake of argument, say that orange is not available in the browser's palette; in that case, dithering would solve the problem by mixing pixels of red and yellow in close proximity). The result is usually good enough to fool the eyes of the viewer into believing that the missing color exists, although quality varies greatly from one image to another. If the user has not enabled dithering, the image will be displayed with an unfortunately large amount of posterization (see Figures 19.15 and 19.16).

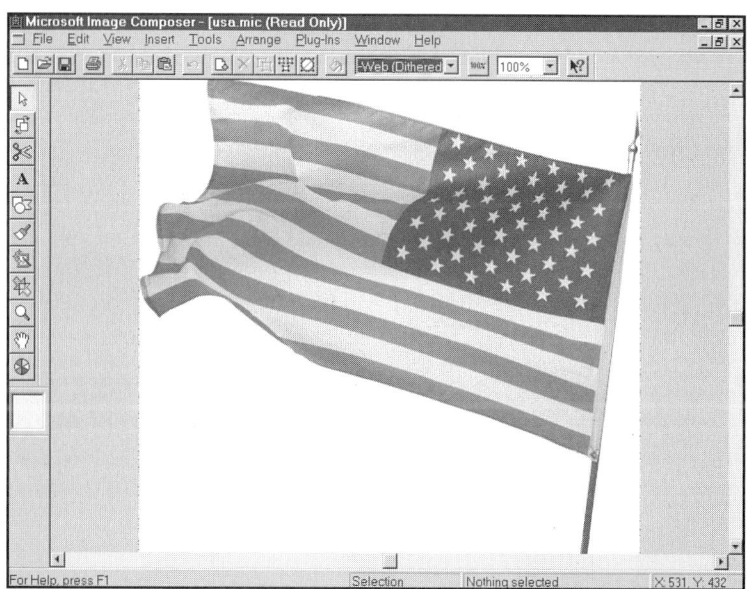

FIGURE 19.15.
Image with dithering.

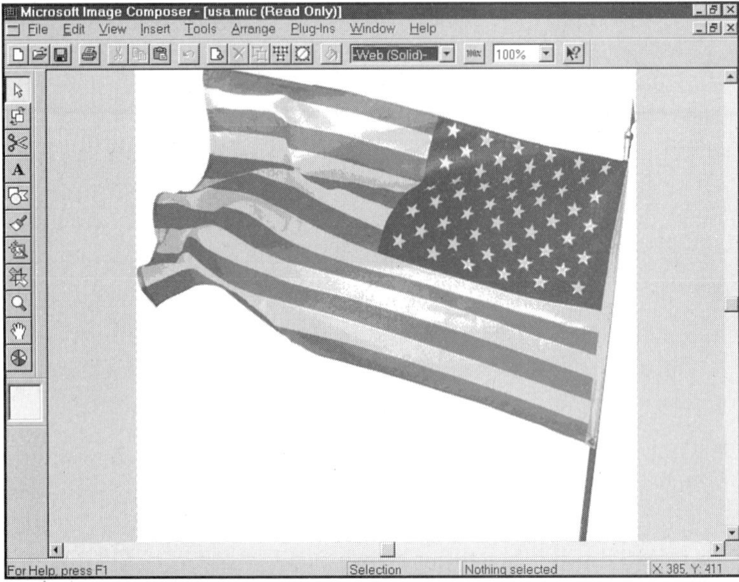

FIGURE 19.16.
Image without dithering.

> **NOTE**
>
> The reason that there are 216 colors is that a palette of colors is best represented by a cube of a whole number. 6×6×6 = 216; the next highest whole number, 7, if cubed, takes you over the 256 color mark, and thus out of range of the 8-bit graphics systems, which many Web surfers still use. With a PC running Windows, you could actually function quite nicely with 236 colors because Windows reserves 20 colors for the operating system, but there is no whole number cube root of 236, so the remaining 20 colors are just plain thrown away in the interests of symmetry.

To apply these concepts to color reduction of GIF images, the same principles can be applied to reduction of one GIF to another, just as easily as when applied from a truecolor image to a GIF. It is unfortunate that Microsoft did not include these alternate palettes with Image Composer, but it is easy enough to create them for yourself as custom color palettes.

Because the supplied palettes accommodate the 256-color palette (or as close as you can get to it in practical terms), you will probably want to create custom palettes for 128 colors, 64 colors, 32 colors, and so forth. Because these numbers leave more than enough room to deal with the 20 colors Windows must reserve for itself, you need not worry about the cube root situation.

To create a custom color palette, follow these steps:

1. Click the Color Swatch. This will bring up the Color Picker dialog box (see Figure 19.17).

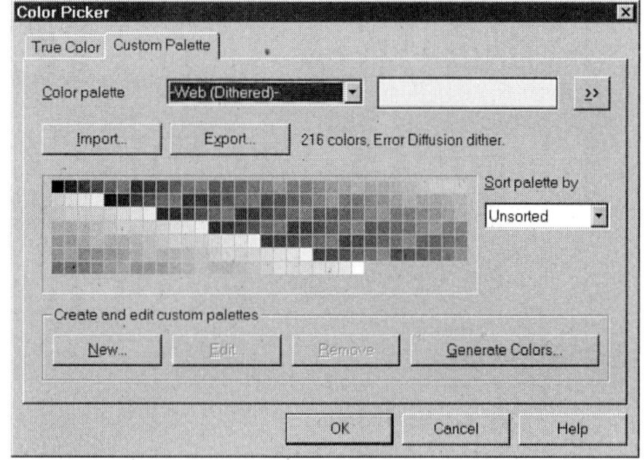

FIGURE 19.17.
The Color Picker dialog box.

2. In the Create and Edit Custom Palettes section, click the New button. This will bring up the New Color Palette dialog box (see Figure 19.18).

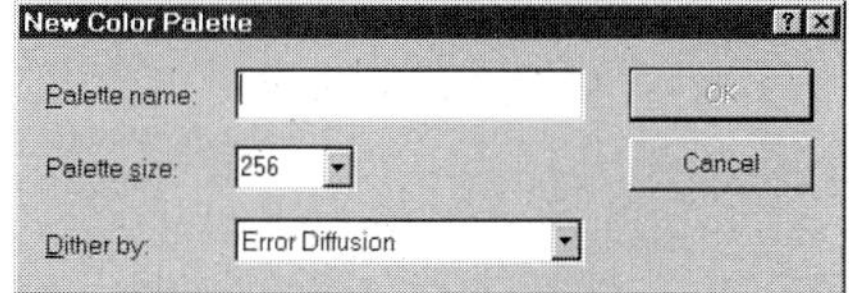

FIGURE 19.18.
The New Color Palette dialog box.

3. Under Palette Name, type the new name (for example, `128_solid_palette`).
4. From the drop-down list box, select the number of colors represented in the new palette (for example, 128).
5. From the drop-down list box, select the type of dithering this particular palette will use (for example, solid).
6. Click the OK button to complete creation of the palette. You will now be returned to the Color Picker dialog box.
7. Click the Generate Colors button. This will bring up the Generate Colors dialog box (see Figure 19.19).

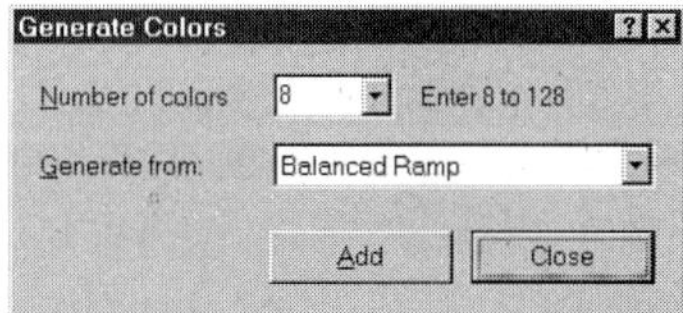

FIGURE 19.19.
The Generate Colors dialog box.

8. Under Number of Colors, select the appropriate number for the custom palette you are creating (for example, 128).
9. Under Generate from, select Balanced Ramp.

10. Click the Add button to complete the task.
11. If, at this point, you get the Generate Colors warning box, click the OK button to proceed.
12. Click the Close button in the Generate Colors dialog box.
13. By default, the new palette is unsorted. If you want it to be sorted by Hue, Saturation, Value, Red, Green, or Blue, then select the appropriate value from the Sort palette by drop down list box.
14. Click the OK button to establish your new palette.

Your new palette will now be available for Save As, Save Selection As, and Color Format commands.

Resampling Your Images

Resizing an image in FrontPage Editor has no effect at all on the file size of that image. This is because FrontPage 98 does not actually alter the image at all, but simply changes the `width` and `height` settings in the `<img src>` tag within the HTML code it generates for that image (see Chapter 7 for a discussion of these items). To permanently alter the actual size of the image—and, therefore, of the file—you must resample the image after resizing it.

Resampling has two basic benefits. First, it will reduce the file size of an image you have resized to be smaller than it originally was, thus saving disk space and speeding downloading time. Second, it will improve the appearance of an image you have resized to be larger (technically, it does this with reduced images also, but the act of reducing an image already hides many of its flaws, so the effect is not so noticeable as with enlarged images). It also has one real drawback: it will *increase* the file size if you have made the image larger. Thus, if the quality of an enlarged image is acceptable for your purposes, it is best not to resample it.

TIP

If you have a large, grainy image, reducing the image size and resampling can result in both a clearer image and a smaller file size.

The images in Figure 19.20 demonstrate the reduction aspect. The first image is 315 pixels square and has a file size of 7,190 bytes. After resizing and resampling, as shown in the second, smaller image, it is 105 pixels square and the file size has been reduced to 3,229 bytes. Note that, although the area of the image has been reduced nine times, the file size is only a little less than half that of the original.

Figure 19.21 illustrates the effect of resampling on an enlarged image. Because the quality effect is much greater on an enlarged image, we have also included the intermediate stage of the image. The first image is 100×57 pixels and has a file size of 2,335 bytes. The second image has been enlarged to 300×171 pixels, but with no increase in file size. It has, of course, a blocky appearance due to the enlargement. The third image is the same pixel size as the second, but after resampling, it now has a file size of 22,492 bytes. It also has a much better appearance than the plain enlargement does. As with the reduction example, the area of the image was changed by a factor of nine (enlarged nine times, though, rather than reduced), but the file size change was much more drastic than with a reduction. Instead of a little better than 50% reduction in file size, you now have almost 1,000% increase. Clearly, although resampling can vastly improve the quality of enlarged images, the tradeoff in file size may not be worth it.

The actual method of resampling is, like the rest of the FrontPage image tools, very easy. Just resize an image, then click the Resample button.

FIGURE 19.20.
Reduced and resampled image.

TIP

Because you may want to have exact control over the pixel size of an enlarged image, there is something you should be aware of. There is an odd exception to the rule that enlarging an image without resampling does not increase file size. The rule holds true if you resize using the sizing handles, but if you use the Image Properties dialog box, and resize the image using the Specify size option (on the Appearance notebook tab), then FrontPage 98 will create a separate, slightly larger file for the enlarged image. You can avoid this situation by first enlarging an image with the sizing handles, and then using the Image Properties dialog box to change the size; no new file will be created if you do this.

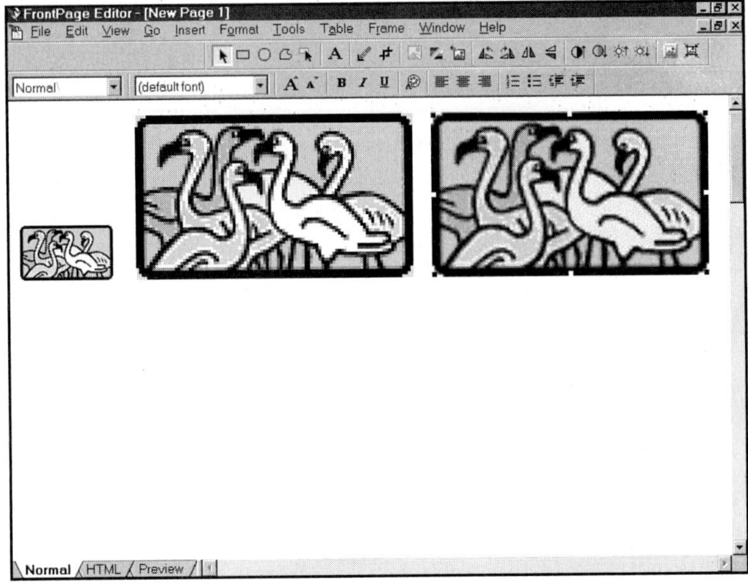

FIGURE 19.21.
Enlarged and resampled image.

Summary

This chapter first deals with recovering from changes to images, then covers the use of FrontPage Editor's image tools, ranging from the somewhat tricky Text command to the use of transparency and washout, rotation, contrast, and so on. It then discusses the selection of file formats for various purposes, the reduction of file size and color depth, as well as resampling images.

CHAPTER 20

Working with GIF Animator

by David and Rhonda Crowder

IN THIS CHAPTER

- Concepts of GIF Animation 359
- Using GIF Animator 360
- Point of View 381
- Animation in Place 381
- Smooth Versus Sudden Change 383
- Where to Find Animated GIFs 383

GIF Animator, once a stand-alone offering of Microsoft, has been officially added to the FrontPage suite of programs as of FrontPage 98. Intended to work hand in hand with Image Composer, it enables you to add the power of animated GIFs to Web sites. It is universal in its application, so the resulting animation files can also be used with non-FrontPage Web sites, or even be viewed in many offline graphics programs.

Animated GIFs offer the most effective way to include simple animation on your site, taking much less room than dedicated animation formats and requiring no special plug-in software for your visitors to enjoy them. The GIF is simply downloaded to your visitors' systems along with the other images on the page they are viewing, and runs in their browser (giving you the extra benefit of no load on your server, unlike some other animation approaches). Although you are not going to be able to develop the kind of animation you see in sophisticated videos like *The Mind's Eye* or *The Lawnmower Man,* you can still do some surprisingly good effects that will add greatly to the appeal of your site.

The original GIF 87a standard barely mentioned in passing that multiple images were possible. When it was updated from the 87a version to the 89a version, the official document noted that "The Graphics Interchange Format is not intended as a platform for animation, even though it can be done in a limited way." Ironically, GIFs have since become the standard for animation on the World Wide Web, and a large number of graphics programs now support this approach.

As you might have guessed, the GIF 87a standard was published in 1987 and the GIF 89a standard in 1989. A number of years have passed since then, and despite the development of the new PNG (Portable Network Graphics) or "Ping" file format, the GIF 89a file format has remained the venue of choice for animation on the Web. PNG files, though they are viable replacements for GIFs in other ways, such as file size and interlacing, do not support animation. The Multiple Network Graphics (MNG) or Ming file format, however, is an extension of the PNG file, and will support animation, but it is still in a state of flux at this time. For those interested in following the development of this format, which will at some point replace the GIF 89a file format, you can access the specification at `ftp://swrinde.nde.swri.edu/pub/mng/documents/`.

NOTE

GIF files use the Lempel-Ziv-Welch (LZW) compression algorithm, which is owned by the Unisys Corporation. In 1995, despite years and years of royalty-free development on this graphics standard, Unisys announced that they would henceforth collect royalties from developers utilizing the GIF format. The good news about all this legal brouhaha is that neither end users nor online services are affected by the problem. Basically, unless you are developing a graphics program utilizing the GIF format, you do not need to worry about it. As a FrontPage developer, you can rest assured that this is Microsoft's problem, and they have already dealt with it. All you need to worry about is creating good animation.

Concepts of GIF Animation

The actual technique by which GIF animations create an illusion of movement to the human eye is an old-fashioned method. As in traditional cel animation, the illusion of motion is created by rapidly displaying a series of slightly different images. In fact, all the apparent motion on any kind of screen, whether television, movie, or computer, is ultimately done in this way. In the case of a film, the sequential images are a series of photographic slides strung together in a film reel, each projected onto a screen for a fraction of a second. Whether this series of images is a recording of an actual event or a recording of carefully prepared artwork is of no consequence; the human brain translates them into active, fluid motion.

To get a good handle on the best uses of this method, use your VCR to record some cartoons, preferably from the golden age of cartooning, like the old Bugs Bunny and Road Runner cartoons. Most modern cartoon animation is very poor quality compared to these; with vastly increased production costs, studios today cut corners, tending toward simplistic backgrounds and unrealistic character movement. Play the tape back at slow speed, paying careful attention to how various effects were achieved using both major and minor differences in imaging. You can do the same with real life events or television shows, but you will miss out on the little touches that a truly gifted animator can bring to a cartoon, and that is essentially what GIF animation is—a very short cartoon.

To prepare an animation, you must first, of course, conceive of an event. Next, you need to break that event down. What are the essential parts of it? How do they interact? What can be left out and still leave enough material to coherently express the event? Remember that you must balance the needs of the artwork against the size of the finished file. You are not presenting reality here, with all its detail and texture, but a distillation of reality.

For example, say you want to show a sailboat moving across the sea. In real life, there would be swells or perhaps even waves causing the boat to move up and down and yaw from side to side. The sails might flutter in a contrary breeze, and the wake would be disturbed by both wind and waves. The sea itself would show a variety of shadings of color, and the sun could throw highlights from reflecting off the waves. The mast and sails would cast shadows across both deck and sea. The crew would not be sitting totally still like mannequins, either. If you attempted to put all this into a GIF animation, however, the resulting file would be so large that, to put it mildly, it would be untenable for a Web site.

COMPANION Web site

So, to make the concept fit the needs, strip it down to its basics. You need a sea, of course, and the sky, but these can be represented effectively by a couple of plain blue patches of different shades. There has to be a boat, but leave out the sail movement and forget the crew entirely. Now, all you have to do is start the boat at one side of the image and move it step by step to the other side (see Figure 20.1). To see this simple animation, load the file `boatmove.gif` from the Companion Web Site that accompanies this book.

FIGURE 20.1.
A simple animation.

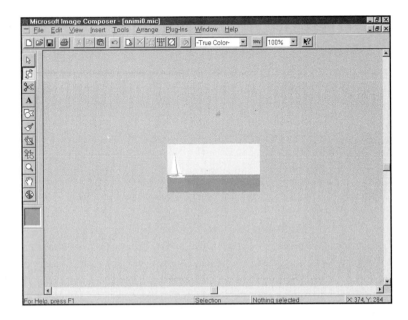

It might take some trial and error, but once you have the minimum number of elements that will still fulfill the original vision, you have everything you need to make your GIF animation work. Now, all that remains is the nitty-gritty of putting it together.

Using GIF Animator

GIF Animator, with its easy-to-use interface and straightforward integration with FrontPage 98, is a viable approach to adding animation to your site—as long as you use it in concert with Image Composer or Windows Explorer. As a stand-alone program, it has serious design flaws, which are discussed in later sections of this chapter.

You can invoke GIF Animator from within Image Composer by selecting Tools|GIF Animator from the menu. The window this opens is unresizable, and contains the full GIF Animator interface in the form of a toolbox, three notebook tabs (only one of which shows at first), and a frame display (see Figure 20.2).

CAUTION

Each time you click the GIF Animator menu choice, a new instance of the program is instantiated. If you need to switch back and forth between Image Composer and GIF Animator, use the toolbar.

FIGURE 20.2.
GIF Animator.

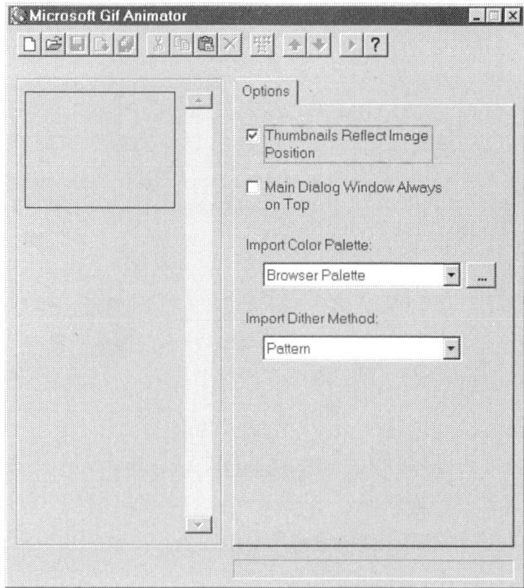

The following tutorial walks you through the construction of the `boatmove.gif` animation. You will be using Image Composer to create the frames from which the animation will be built, so that you can take advantage of its special features, and then you will add the frames to GIF Animator to finalize the animated GIF image.

First, you will need to put in a cyan rectangle for the sky. For the sea, you will actually be using two different, but essentially identical, blue rectangles. This way, you can hide the keel of the sailboat, and the lower portion of its hull, through layering of sprites. It is true that you could simply erase the lower part of the sailboat, thus creating the same effect, but this way, they will be kept hidden when you want them to be, but still be available later if you decide you need them to create a particular effect. Plus, it is also a good technique you may want to use in other animations.

Creating the Background

To begin, set the composition area in Image Composer to the following dimensions: 200×100 pixels. This is to keep the animation within reasonable bounds for any visitor's screen size, and ultimately to keep the file size down to manageable levels. To accomplish this, select File|Composition Setup from the menu, then click the notebook tab labeled Current Composition (see Figure 20.3). Set the width to 200 pixels and the height to 100 pixels in the appropriate edit boxes, and then click the OK button.

> **TIP**
>
> Because you can't alter the size of the images in GIF Animator, that means if you are not creating the images yourself to a specific size, but bringing in clip art, you have to alter each individual image before it goes in.

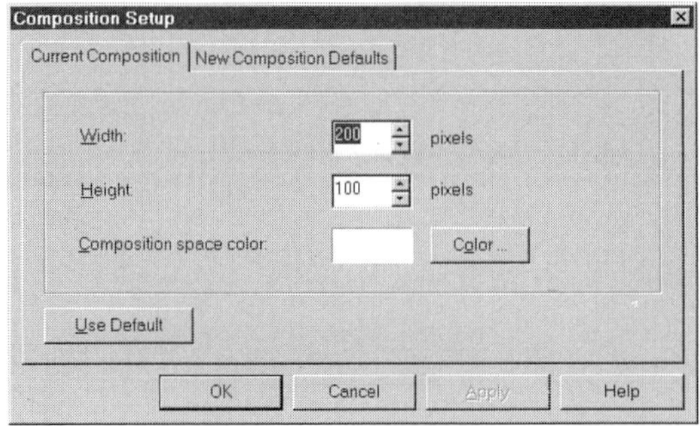

FIGURE 20.3.
The Composition Setup dialog box.

The rectangles are created using Image Composer's Shapes tool (for details on the tools in Image Composer, see Chapter 16, "Working with the Microsoft Image Composer"). The cyan rectangle for the sky should take up the upper two-thirds of the composition area, so you need to make it 200×66 pixels in size and position it at the top of the composition area. The technique for accomplishing this is as follows:

1. Click the Color Swatch to open the Color Picker dialog box.
2. From the color palette, select a light blue color for the sky (see Figure 20.4), then click OK.

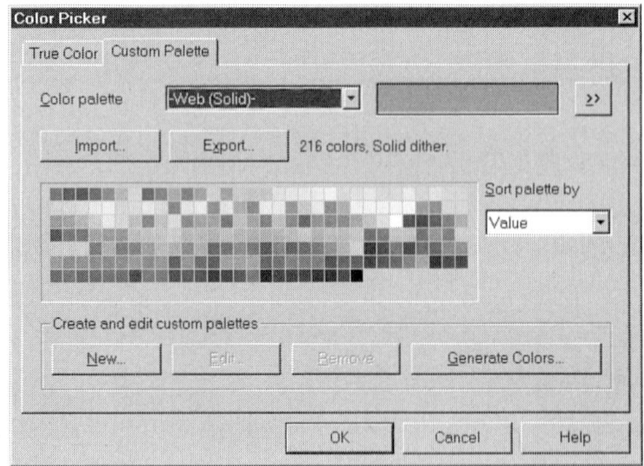

FIGURE 20.4.
The Color Picker dialog box.

3. Click the Shapes tool to bring up the Shapes palette (see Figure 20.5).

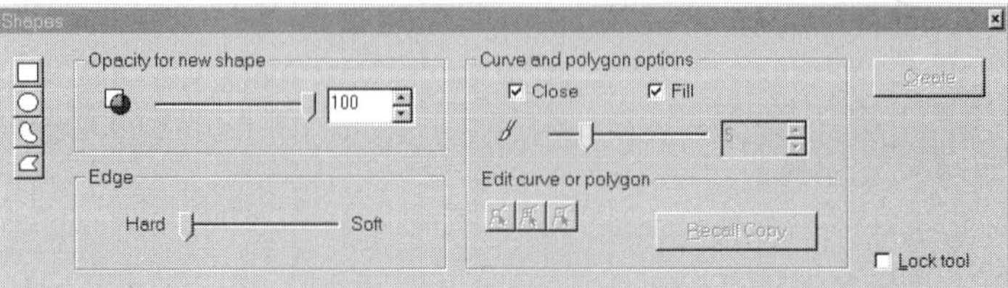

FIGURE 20.5.
The Shapes palette.

4. Click the Rectangle button.
5. Place the mouse pointer in the upper-left corner of the composition area and, while holding down the left mouse button, drag until you have covered approximately the area you want the sky to cover. Although you can read the width and height in the status bar as you draw the rectangle (the numbers after W and H), you do not need to be overly concerned about exactitude, because the size can be fine-tuned later. Release the mouse button and click the Create button in the Shapes palette.
6. Click the Arrange tool to bring up the Arrange palette (see Figure 20.6).

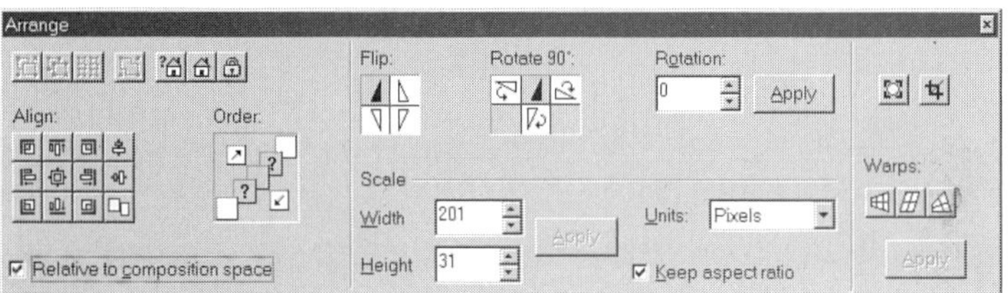

FIGURE 20.6.
The Arrange palette.

7. Select the sky rectangle in your image.
8. Under Scale, set the units to pixels, click the check box labeled Keep aspect ratio to uncheck it, then type in 200 for the width and 66 for the height. Next, click the Apply button immediately to the right of the height and width boxes.
9. To position the sky exactly, use the Align tools on the left side. The Align tools are composed of 12 buttons, each of which causes a different alignment between objects. As you move your mouse pointer over these buttons, a help balloon will pop up telling you what each does. If you place your pointer over the first button in the top row, for example, the help balloon will say Upper Left Corners. Each button also has a descriptive image on it that shows the type of alignment it performs. Make sure that the check box labeled Relative to composition space is checked; this will make sure that the sky is aligned with the composition space, rather than another sprite. Next, click the Upper Left Corners button. The sky should now fit perfectly (see Figure 20.7).
10. Repeat Steps 1 through 9 for the sea, but select a deeper blue color for it. Also, set it to a size of 200×30 pixels. When aligning it, click the Lower Left Corners button instead (it is the first button in the bottom row). The image should now look like Figure 20.8. The small space between sky and sea is intentional; as mentioned earlier, you are deliberately creating layered sprites, and the next step will be to fill it in.
11. Next, follow the same procedure in Step 10 for creating a smaller slice of sea, this one 200×4 pixels. Align it horizontally by clicking the Left Sides button (the first button in the center row). To place it vertically, so that it exactly covers the open space between sky and sea, you can either select it and move it manually by pressing the up and down arrow keys, or follow Step 12.

FIGURE 20.7.
Image with sky in place.

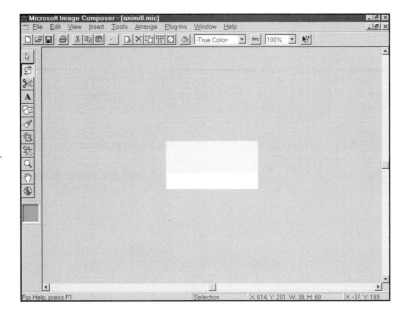

FIGURE 20.8.
Image with sky and partial sea in place.

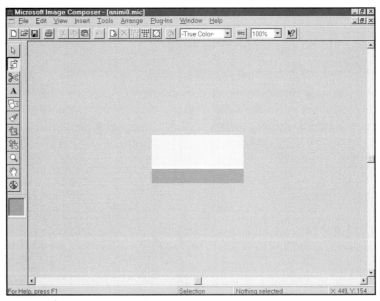

12. First, select the large sea rectangle. Then, while holding down the Shift key, select the small sea rectangle (it must be done in this order). Both will now be selected. Uncheck the Relative to composition space check box so it is blank, then click the Touch Edges button (the fourth button in the bottom row). The small sea rectangle will now fill the formerly empty space between sea and sky, and the background for the animation is complete (see Figure 20.9).

FIGURE 20.9.
Completed background image.

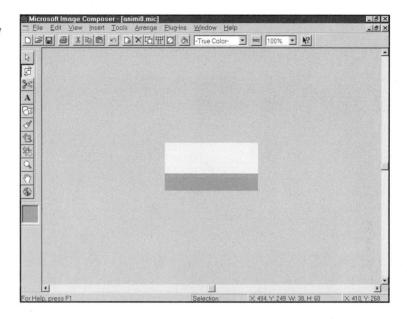

CAUTION

The Scale tool in the Arrange palette is slightly inaccurate, so when you use it, you might not get exactly the dimensions you want. You might need to adjust the figures for width and height by anywhere from one to three pixels in order to make sprites of the same nominal width or height actually be the same size. For example, if two sprites are each listed in the Scale tool as being 100 pixels in width, but you can tell at a glance that they are slightly different widths, you should increase the numbers in the width setting for the smaller one until they actually match on the screen (perhaps at 101, 102, or 103). It is helpful to set the Zoom Percent to 300% or better to magnify the differences when making adjustments.

Preparing the Foreground

To add the sailboat to the image, follow this procedure:

1. Insert the image `sailboat.gif` from the Companion Web Site, then drag it into the composition area, placing it so that the hull is just below the sky rectangle (see Figure 20.10). You do not have to be absolutely precise because you will be adjusting the position next. This placement allows the sailboat to be mainly depicted against the sky, while still appearing to be in the sea. COMPANION Web site
2. Select the large sea rectangle at the bottom of the image, then click the Arrange tool to bring up the Arrange palette. Use the Order tool to move the sea to the front of the z-order by clicking the To Front box. Depending on how you have placed the boat, at

least part of the bottom of it should be obscured. In terms of layers, the boat is now in front of the sky and the small sea rectangle, and it is behind the large sea rectangle. The effect is to embed the boat in the sea.

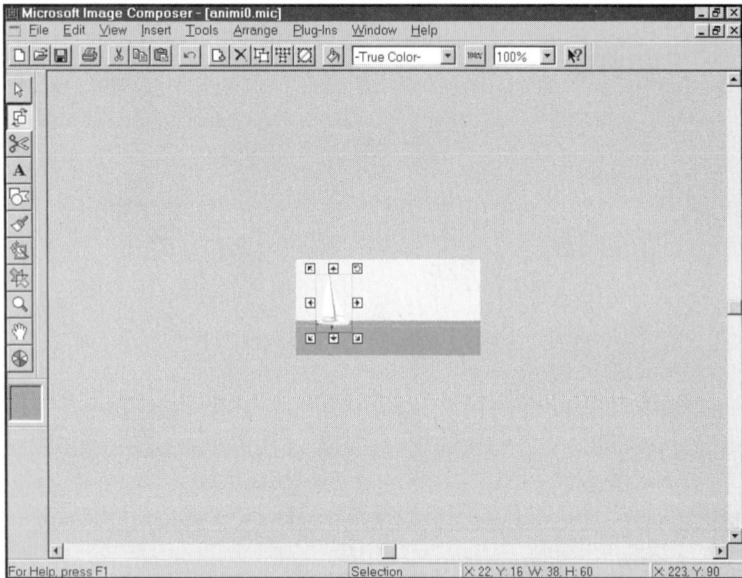

FIGURE 20.10.
Boat placement.

3. If the boat is too high, then part of the keel will be showing; if it is too low, then it will appear to be sinking. To adjust the position until it is just right, select the boat, then use the up and down arrow keys to move it until you have it the way you want it (see Figure 20.11).
4. Once the boat is positioned vertically, use the left arrow key to move it just barely out of the composition area (see Figure 20.12). You are now ready to begin the animation.

Creating the Frames

Because the animation needs to start with an empty sea, save this image as `boat01.gif` (because the boat itself is out of the composition area, it will not be part of the saved GIF file). To do this, select File|Save As from the menu, then select CompuServe GIF (`*.gif`) from the Save As Type drop-down list box. Next, click the Save button. At this point, you will be warned that this format will not have all the advantages of the Image Composer `.mic` file format and will not save any sprites outside the composition area (see Figure 20.13); because this is your intention, just click OK to proceed. You will have to do this for each of the frames you save.

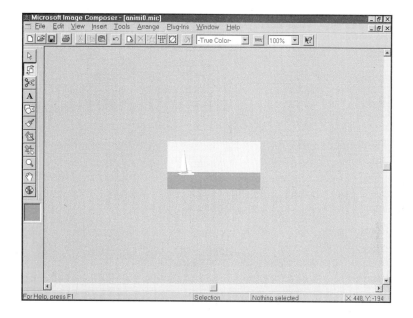

FIGURE 20.11.
Layered composition.

FIGURE 20.12.
Ready to begin the animation.

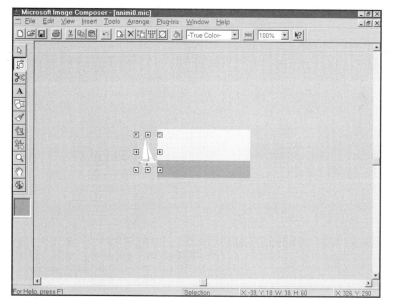

FIGURE 20.13.
File Format Limitation dialog box.

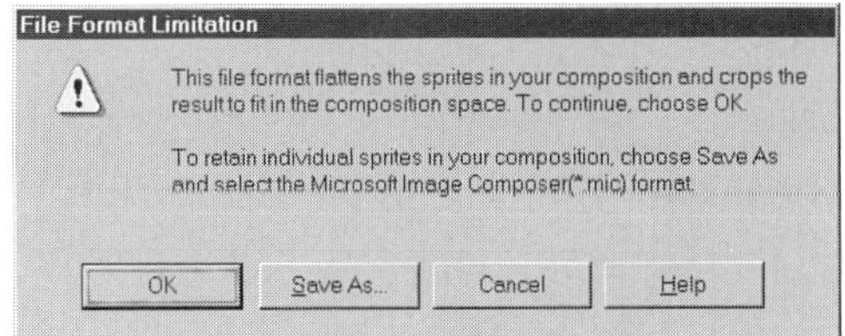

The animation will also need to end with an identical image. However, because you usually do not know at this time exactly how many frames you are going to need to complete an animation, it would be premature to assign a number to the ending frame. There are two approaches you can use to solve this problem. The first is to save the file again as `boatxx.gif`, then use Windows Explorer to rename the file when you are finished, replacing the `xx` with an appropriate number. The second, simpler, approach is to wait until all the other frames are finished. Because in this animation you are not going to change the background image during the course of it, but simply move a sailboat across it, the final step will be to move the last bit of the sailboat off the background, thus leaving it empty, just as the first frame was. At that point, you can save it, knowing the proper number to use.

NOTE

The purpose of having identical beginning and ending frames in this animation is so that it can be looped more smoothly. This approach gives a slightly longer fraction of a second during which there is no boat in the scene than if the final frame simply showed the last bit of the stern of the boat. Thus, there is an impression of a series of boats sailing past rather than one boat jumping from side to side.

From here, it is a fairly simple, though tedious, matter to move the boat forward, pausing every now and then to shoot a new frame. You will be moving the boat ten pixels at a time, so press the right arrow key 10 times, then save the image as `boat02.gif`. Again, the portion of the boat that is not yet on the composition area will not be saved. Repeat this process, saving a new GIF (making sure you increment the filename—`boat03.gif`, `boat04.gif`, and so on) for every 10 pixels of forward movement, until the boat is entirely off the composition area on the right side. Figures 20.14 through 20.16 illustrate the beginning, middle, and end of this process. As described earlier, when the boat is totally off the composition area, you will shoot the final frame. You will get approximately 25 frames, depending on exactly where you positioned the sailboat for the beginning frame.

FIGURE 20.14.
The first frame.

FIGURE 20.15.
The middle frame.

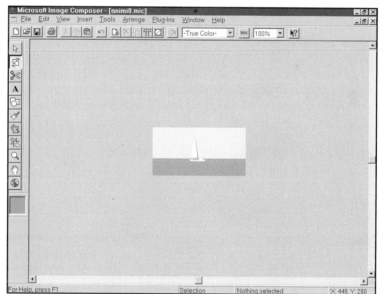

FIGURE 20.16.
The last frame.

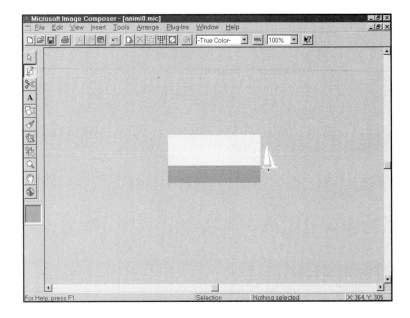

Loading the Frames into GIF Animator

Although it is possible to import all the images into Image Composer, then drag and drop them into GIF Animator (this is the official Microsoft approach), it is actually easier to drag them in from Windows Explorer. With this method, the filenames give you a good reference point for which ones go in which order, whereas simply viewing the images in Image Composer, it is a little more difficult to tell one frame from another (especially if you have very little difference among the images). Also, in Image Composer, imported images all land in the same spot, and using the Windows Explorer method saves you the time and trouble of manually sorting them into order before beginning.

Open Windows Explorer and resize it so that it takes up the left side of the desktop, and then open GIF Animator and position it so it is on the right side (see Figure 20.17).

Now, simply click the filename `boat01.gif` and, while holding down the left mouse button, drag it into the open frame in GIF Animator, and then release the button to drop it there. The results should look like Figure 20.18. Note that GIF Animator has automatically created the next frame for you to drop the next image into. Also, note that the first frame is now labeled Frame #1, whereas the new frame has no label. Each sequential frame will be automatically numbered as you drop images into it (see Figure 20.19).

FIGURE 20.17.
Windows Explorer and GIF Animator.

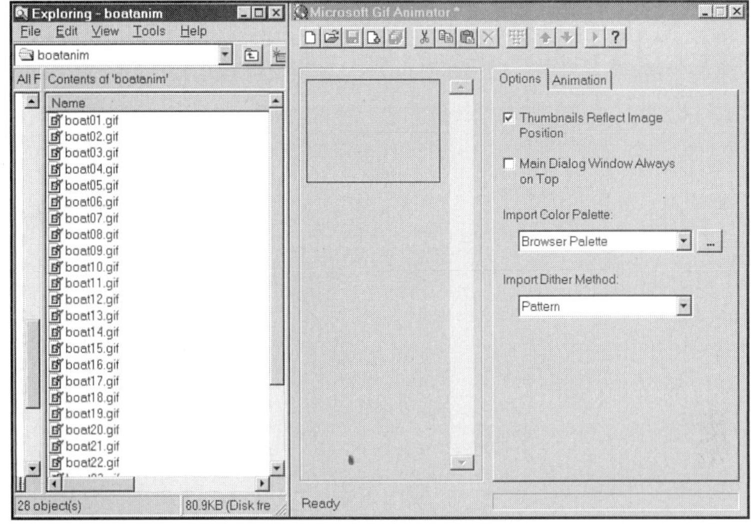

TIP

Because GIF Animator does not label frames with the filenames of the images dropped into them, it is a good idea to give your files names that have sequential numbers as you did with `boat01.gif`, `boat02.gif`, and so on. This way, it is easy to keep track of which image needs to go into which frame. Also, make sure the numbers start with 1, because GIF Animator's frame numbering sequence does so.

FIGURE 20.18.
GIF Animator with first frame filled.

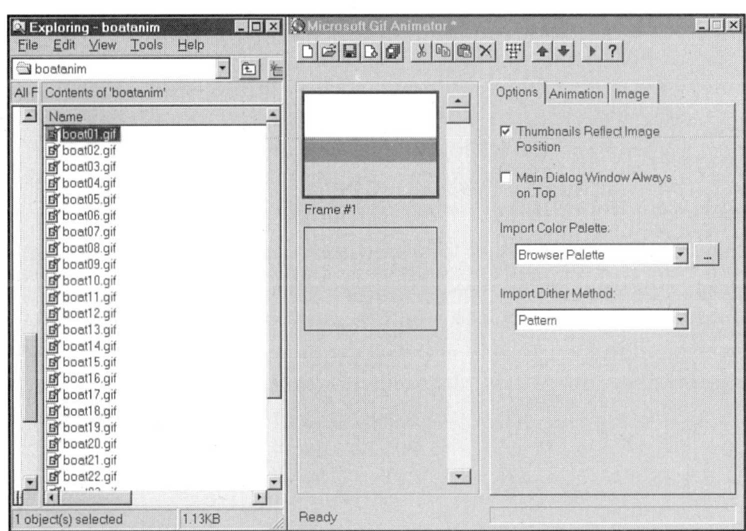

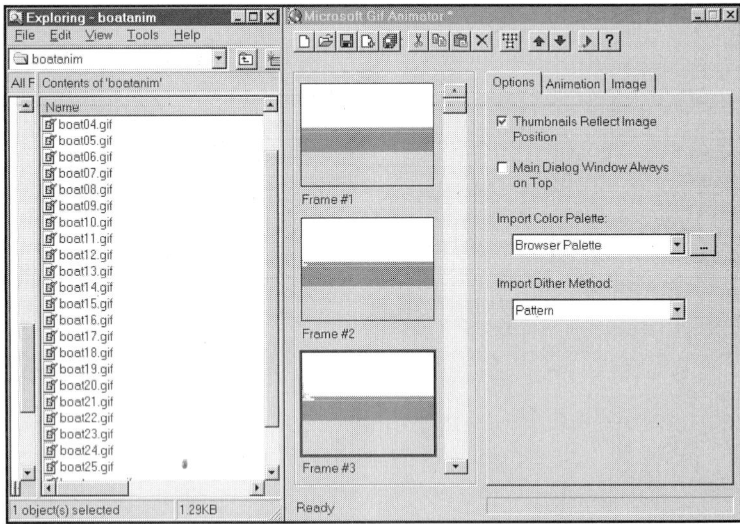

FIGURE 20.19.
GIF Animator with several frames filled.

Continue to drag and drop images into the empty frame. After the third frame is filled, you will discover one of the most annoying features of GIF Animator: when you have filled up the last frame, it does not automatically roll up to show you the empty frame; you have to click the scroll bar every time you want to add an image.

When you have completed dragging and dropping all the images in the animation, click the Save button and save the file as `boatmove.gif`. It is a good idea to set up a separate folder for each animation and include both the individual images and the completed animation there.

Improving the Animation

You could do a number of things to add improvements to this animation. Shooting a frame for every 5 pixels of movement instead of every 10 would smooth out the motion, for instance. Adding a wake behind the boat would give more of a feel of actual movement, a sense that the boat, rather than just being shoved from one side to the other, is interacting with another element in the image, is actually in the sea, and thus would lend a touch of reality to the formerly static water in which it travels. A sun could be added to the sky in order to more fully realize the background, or perhaps the boat could sail in front of an island on the horizon. A shark fin might cut the water, either following the boat or moving against the flow in counterpoint. Perhaps the boat doesn't make it to the far side, but capsizes, showing the formerly hidden keel as it rolls over and sinks. Use your imagination and see what you can do, but remember that every complication you add increases the file size of the completed animation. This basic animation creates only a 16K file, though, so you have plenty of room to maneuver.

Working with the Animation

Now that the animation exists, you can begin to use the features of GIF Animator. In addition to the frame sequence you are already familiar with, the controls consist of a toolbar and three notebook tabs. This section describes the toolbar first (see Figure 20.20).

FIGURE 20.20.
The GIF Animator toolbar.

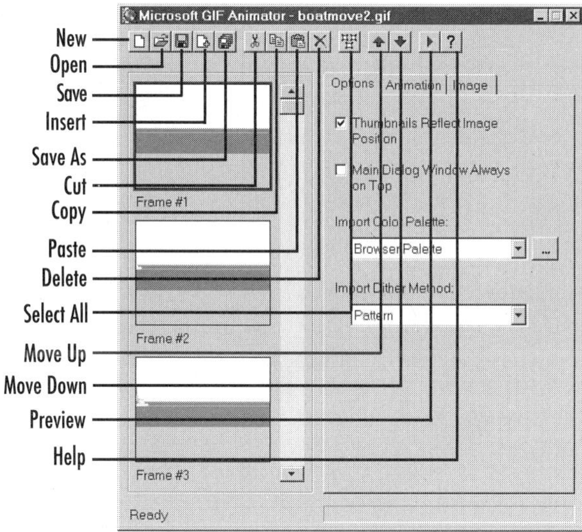

The Toolbar

The New button is basically useless; all it does is clear the current animation (if it has not been saved, you will be prompted to save it). Because you cannot create animation frames within GIF Animator, the New button's only use is in the unusual event that you have already created frames for several different animations, and want to load the first set of frames into GIF Animator, save the animation file, then move right on to loading the next set of frames. Because it is very rare for this situation to occur, you will not have much need for this button.

The Open button, on the other hand, is one you'll get a lot of use from. It loads an animated GIF file into GIF Animator, automatically replacing any saved material already in it. If the animation currently in GIF Animator has not yet been saved, you will be prompted to save it first. The constituent images that comprise the total GIF will be broken down into the frames in GIF Animator, ready for you to work with.

> **TIP**
>
> Because an excellent method for studying animated GIFs is to use GIF Animator to dissect other artists' work, you can simply open one of theirs just as you would one of your own, and you can see exactly how it was done.

The Save button, of course, saves your animated GIF file. The first time you do this with a new animation, you will be presented with the usual choices of name and folder. Unless a file is new, however, it will simply save the file without allowing you to choose details. If you later decide to save it under a different name or location, you will have to use the Save As button, which is located on the far side of the Insert button.

CAUTION

Image Composer cannot save a multi-image GIF file. You must use GIF Animator to save one. In fact, you cannot even open an animated GIF in Image Composer; all you will get is the first frame, and if you attempt to save it from that program, that is all that will be saved; if you have not changed the filename, that means that the animation will be destroyed.

The Insert button allows you to import a single GIF image and place it in your animation sequence. The image will be placed into the frame immediately before the currently selected one, moving everything from the selected frame down one. It is not active until an animation exists.

CAUTION

GIF Animator has two very serious problems. The first of these is that you can only import a single frame at a time; there is no facility for mass importation, no way to select more than one file. Although it is true that you can drag and drop multiple files at a time either from Image Composer or from Windows Explorer, there is no rhyme or reason to the results when the files are dropped into GIF Animator. The second flaw—and this is so bad that one is at a loss to imagine what the designers of this program had in mind at the time—is that you cannot add images sequentially with its Insert button. Any image that is inserted into GIF Animator using its Insert button will be placed *before* the currently selected image. The empty frame cannot be selected. Thus, you are forced to construct an animated GIF backwards and, because you are also forced to do it one frame at a time, the task can be unbelievably tedious unless you have very few frames to fill. The backwards construction problem, at least, can be solved by using the drag-and-drop approach or by placing a dummy image in the first frame, then always selecting the dummy image (which will continue to move down with each insertion) to insert a new image.

The Cut, Copy, Paste, and Delete buttons work with the clipboard just as in every other Windows program. The only difference with GIF Animator is that the Paste button works just like the Insert button in its actions, placing the pasted image into the frame preceding the selected one and moving everything down one frame. You can also paste images copied from other programs.

TIP

If you want to insert an image into GIF Animator when it has no animation in it (when it is first started or when you have just pressed the New button), the Insert button will not work, but you can still use the Paste button to add one from the clipboard.

The Select All button is used when you want to apply changes to every image, rather than just one or a few.

CAUTION

When using the Select All button, occasionally—not often, but occasionally—any changes you make to the settings contained in one notebook tab will not take unless you first click a different notebook tab.

The Move Up and Move Down buttons change the position of an image in the animation sequence. To use them, select the image you want to move. For each click on a Move button, the selected image will move up or down one frame; the other frames will automatically shift to accommodate its new position.

The Preview button lets you see the animation as it will work with the current settings. Clicking it brings up the Preview box (see Figure 20.21). This is very useful for trying different settings and checking out their effects prior to actually saving the file.

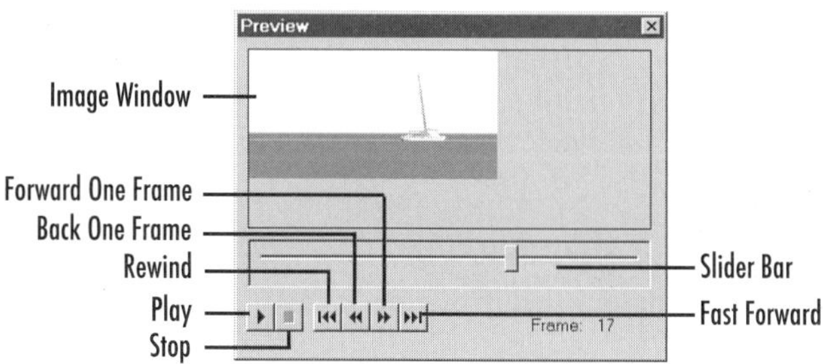

FIGURE 20.21.
Preview image.

When the Preview box first appears, the animation is automatically running. To stop it, click the Stop button. To start it running again, click the Play button. The remaining buttons are used only when the animation is stopped, and each changes the frame being viewed in a different way. The Rewind button sets the animation to the first frame; the Fast Forward button, despite its name, does not fast forward the animation, but advances it instantly to the final frame. The other two buttons step the animation backward and forward frame by frame, but, unfortunately, they must be clicked again and again to step through the movement; holding them down has no effect beyond the first click.

More useful is the slider bar, which is found above the buttons. As you have probably noticed, it moves along with the animation, indicating its progress as it plays or is stepped forward and backward. However, it has more functionality than this; you can also use it to move the animation smoothly in both directions by clicking it and dragging it backward and forward.

The Options Tab

The Options notebook tab (see Figure 20.22) is the only one available when you first start up GIF Animator. The other two become available only when you load an existing animation or start a new one by using paste or drag and drop.

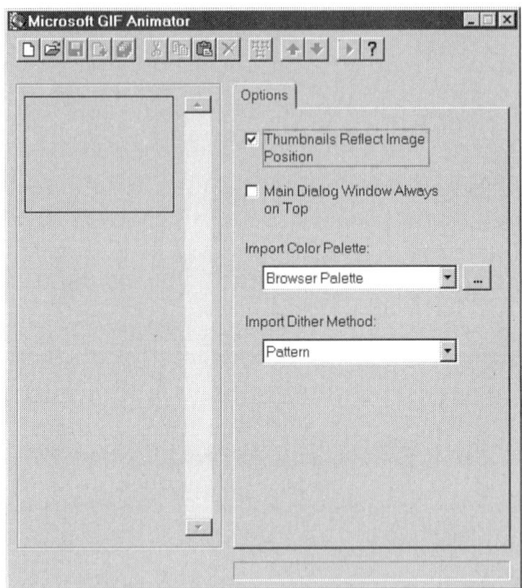

FIGURE 20.22.
The Options notebook tab.

The check box labeled Thumbnails Reflect Image Position works in concert with elements on the two other notebook tabs and will be dealt with in the section titled "Positioning Your Images."

The check box labeled Main Dialog Window Always On Top actually means that GIF Animator is always on top of other programs if this is checked. This is a useful setting for drag-and-drop activities.

The drop-down list box labeled Import Color Palette has built into it two settings: Browser Palette (the default) and Optimal Palette. The first option causes a single palette to be generated for the entire animation and is the same as the Safety Palette discussed in Chapter 19, "Optimizing Your Images and Color Palettes." The second uses a single palette for each frame in the animation; because some animations use widely varying colors between frames, this can give the best color results, but can result in a much larger file. You can also click the ellipsis to the right of the list box to import any other palette you want to (see Figure 20.23), which will be added to the drop-down list box choices. To use it instead of one of the built-in choices, just select it like the others.

FIGURE 20.23.
Importing a new palette.

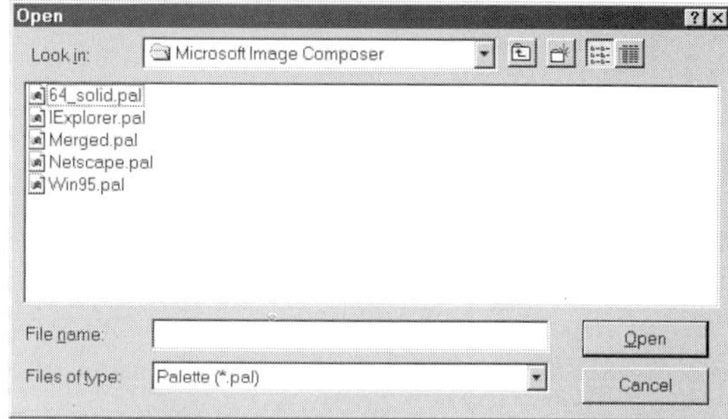

The Import Dither Method drop-down list box offers the various dithering options available (see Chapter 19 for a discussion of dithering).

The Animation Tab

The Animation notebook tab (see Figure 20.24) controls the overall settings for the animation.

FIGURE 20.24.
The Animation notebook tab.

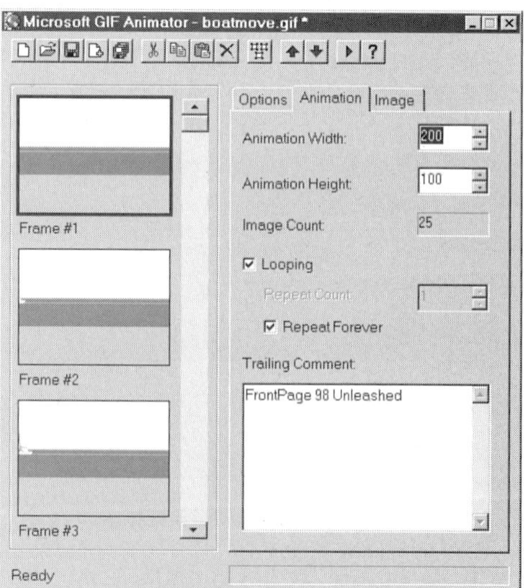

The boxes labeled Animation Width and Animation Height display the size of the current animation's largest frame. Beyond this, they work in concert with elements on the two other notebook tabs, and are dealt with in the section titled "Positioning Your Images."

CAUTION

If you insert (or paste, or drag and drop) an image that has greater dimensions than the animation, the Animation Width and Animation Height will be permanently changed to reflect the larger size, even if you later delete the larger image from the frame.

The Image Count tells how many frames are in the animation. It is informational only, of course, and cannot be changed except by adding or deleting images.

If you want your GIF animation to run only a single time when loaded, then make sure the check box labeled Looping is unchecked. To set the animation to run more times, check this box, then either select a number of times under Repeat Count or click the check box labeled Repeat Forever to create an endlessly running animation.

TIP

The repeat count is not the same as the number of times the image will be shown; it is the number of times it will be repeated, that is, how many times it will be shown after the first time. For example, if you want your animation to run 10 times, set the repeat count to 9, not 10.

The Trailing Comment allows you to add text information, which will not be part of the viewable animation, but which will be included internally in the GIF file. You might want to place copyright statements here, or your company contact information.

The Image Tab

The Image notebook tab (see Figure 20.25) is theoretically designed for control of individual frames. However, you will probably not want to use most of its settings except for the total animation. To apply the particular effect to all the frames, first click the Select All button in the toolbar. To apply it to one or several frames, select them individually.

The first thing you will find is the information on the width and height of the currently selected frame. This is for information only, and cannot be altered; GIF Animator has no provision for resizing images.

The Left and Top settings work in concert with elements on the two other notebook tabs, and are dealt with in the section titled "Positioning Your Images."

The Duration setting controls how many hundredths of a second the frame is displayed before the next one comes on. This is one of those settings that is usually kept the same for all frames in an animation.

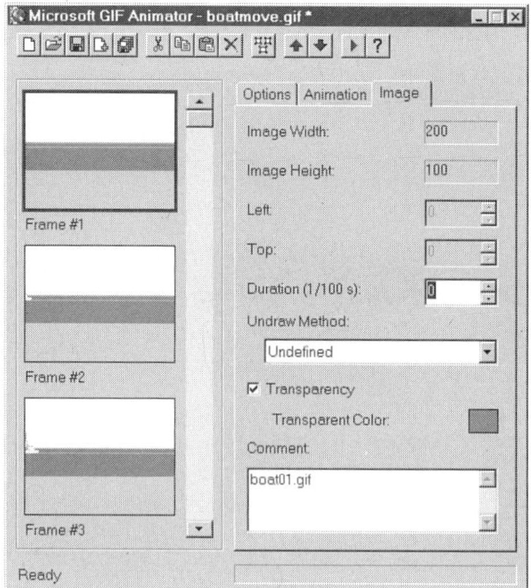

FIGURE 20.25.
The Image notebook tab.

However, there may be times when you will want a particular image to remain on screen longer than others. Obviously, you could achieve this effect by having several identical frames shown in a row, but changing the duration so that a single frame remains longer is a much more economical approach to file size.

Alternatively, you may want to create a speeded-up section within your animation. In this case, the way to do it would be to change the duration so that those frames ran faster than the animation as a whole.

The Undraw Method can be very important. This defines how the program displaying your GIF animation will handle the problem of the displaying your subsequent images on top of the previously shown image. Generally, animation frames are all the same size, the images are the same size as the frames, the images do not move within the frames, and there is no transparency in the background of the images. If this is the case, then it does not matter what undraw method you use, and the default Undefined is as good as any.

However, if you are going to change any of those factors, you will need to take into account what method is used to remove the previous image. In most cases, you'll want to choose Restore Background for the cleanest animation. This totally removes the previous image and gives a clean slate on which the next one is drawn. However, if you want to create a trail effect, you will need to choose Leave in order to have the images laid over one another (see Figure 20.26), because this method will not erase the previous image (see the section entitled, "Positioning Your Images" for information on achieving this effect). Restore Previous is basically the same as Leave, but it has been known to cause display troubles on occasion, so just stick with the Leave option.

FIGURE 20.26.
Trail effect made with Leave option.

The Transparency check box is best left alone. Transparency should be set long before the images are ever loaded into GIF Animator. However, if you want to, you can change whether a frame or the entire animation has transparency, and what color is transparent. Simply click the Transparency check box to uncheck it, and transparency is gone. You should be aware that this will, in most cases, mess up your images, causing a rectangular block of previously invisible background color to surround some element.

You can also change which color is transparent. Clicking the color square brings up the Global Palette (see Figure 20.27). Just click the color you want to make transparent for the image or animation, then click the OK button.

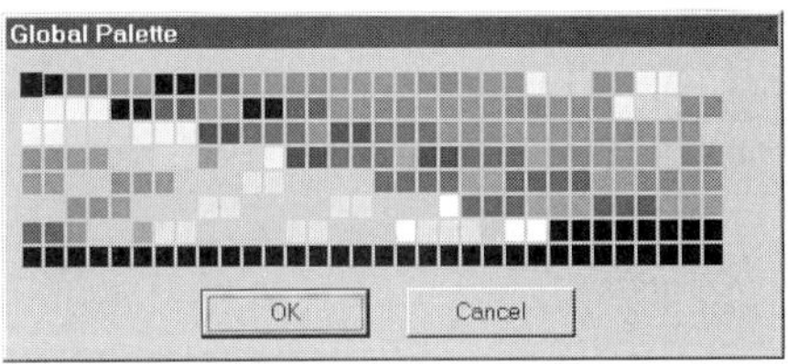

FIGURE 20.27.
Global Palette.

The Comment edit box is similar to the Trailing Comment on the Animation notebook tab, except that it is limited to the specific image or images that are currently selected.

Positioning Your Images

Total control of the position of your images in GIF Animator requires the use of all three notebook tabs. In order to take charge of this, you must first check the check box labeled Thumbnails Reflect Image Position in the Options notebook tab.

Next, in the Animation notebook tab, you must set the Animation Width and Height settings. These are initially locked into the largest dimensions of your imported frames, and cannot be decreased, but only increased. Increasing these dimensions does not actually scale the images themselves to a larger size, but simply sets a larger frame around the animation. Because GIF Animator has no facilities for scaling the GIF images, the utility of this function is not immediately apparent until you look at the Left and Top settings on the Image notebook tab.

These settings enable you to place the image, which is by default set at the upper-left corner (or 0,0) position, anywhere you want within the wider frame you have created. You can use the Select All button to set all the images within a larger framework than originally designed, or you can move one image at a time within that framework, creating special effects like the trailing effect in Figure 20.26, or any other animation within the animation effect you may imagine. Remember, however, that all three of these notebook tabs must work in concert for any of this to take place.

Point of View

Most animations have a moving object against a static background. There is no reason, however, why the focal object cannot remain stationary and the background be put into motion, as in the view of a car's driver out the windshield.

For that matter, there is no reason why both the focal object of the animation and the background cannot be animated independently. Is the viewpoint from the outside or the inside of the moving object? Does the background move, or is it static, or do both the object and the background move?

Animation in Place

In addition to the typical usage of GIF animation, wherein an object is moved from one place to another, changes can be made to take place in a stationary object, such as a flashing icon, an odometer, or even more elaborate objects like an erupting volcano.

Another type of nontraditional animated artwork you can create with animated GIFs is a flashing montage. With the montage approach, the different images in the animation, instead of being slightly progressed versions of the same picture, are totally different from one another. In this case, the usual approach of making sure that all the images have the same height and width need not apply. The resultant animated GIF will have the height set to the same measure as the tallest constituent image and the width set to the same measure as the broadest one. Thus, if you have three images measuring 16×32, 74×64, and 58×102, the final animated GIF composed of them will have a width of 74 and a height of 102.

COMPANION Web site

Of course, in order to have a coherent piece of artwork, the images, though different, should express a theme. You could, for example, use a series of images about baseball, football, basketball, and so on to make a montage for a sports news site. Or you might collect a group of drawings of females for a site celebrating womanhood. A collection of state flags would be appropriate for an American history site. The possibilities are endless. These three examples are illustrated in the files `sports.gif`, `celwoman.gif`, and `statflag.gif` on the Companion Web Site that accompanies this book.

`Statflag.gif`, by the way, is a good example of how you must sometimes trade off image quality for file size. This is an unusual situation, requiring 50 frames with no way to leave any out. At the original size of these images, the completed animation file would be over a quarter of a megabyte in size. Of course, this is way too large, so the images had to be reduced. Even at this smaller image size, the total file is around 60K, about as large as you want to get for current download times. `Celwoman.gif` has only 11 frames and is 48K, and `sports.gif`, with 9 frames, is 20K, much more in line with what you want to try for.

TIP

If you do use different sizes of constituent images, make sure that you choose Restore Background for the undraw method, in order to avoid having bits and pieces of previous images cluttering up the display of subsequent ones.

CAUTION

Neither Netscape Navigator nor Internet Explorer will correctly display an animation composed of differently sized frames if the GIF is embedded in an HTML page by the `<img src>` method (which is what happens when you use the Insert Image button in FrontPage 98). FrontPage Editor fails to properly read the information on height and width, instead setting it to the size of the first frame, and then it sets and distorts all subsequent frames to that size as well. Nor can you solve this problem by setting the height and width tags manually to the greatest size, because that will lock all the frames to the largest possible size. Eliminating the tags will not work, either; this is always a poor idea, and fails to solve the problem in any event. The way to get around this limitation is to set up a hyperlink to the image. When your visitors click the link, either browser will properly display the different frames.

Showing the Passage of Time

One particularly powerful use of "animation in place" is to show the passage of time, whether by sand pouring through an hourglass, changes in the settings of digital or analog clocks, sun and moon rising and setting while light and dark come and go, or any other method you can imagine to express the differences.

Smooth Versus Sudden Change

Depending upon the particular event, a series of gradual changes in the images may be presented to create a smooth motion, as in the case of a bird flapping its wings, or the change may be sharp and sudden, as in the case of a firecracker exploding. The former approach, of course, requires more images in the animation, thus drastically increasing file size.

Where to Find Animated GIFs

As mentioned previously, the best way to learn about animated GIFs is to view the work of others. Table 20.1 presents a premier selection of Web sites specializing in animated GIFs. Each was taken from our LinkFinder Red Hot Links award-winning list of animated GIF sites.

Table 20.1. Animated GIF sources.

Name	*Location*
Animated Art for Netscape	`http://www.geocities.com/SiliconValley/Park/7276/index.html`
Animated GIF Artists Guild	`http://www.agag.com/`
Badger's Animated GIF Gallery	`http://www.vr-mall.com/anigifpd/anigifpd.html`
Bill's Animated GIF Collection	`http://www.gifanimations.com/`
Dr. Fun's Page of Animations	`http://www.drfun.com/ani.htm`
Tru Realities	`http://trureality.com/`
Wagon Train Animated GIFs	`http://dreamartists.com/animated.htm`
Web Wizard's World Animation Station	`http://www.geocities.com/SiliconValley/Park/8100/animfram.htm`

Summary

GIF Animator was once a stand-alone product, but has now been added to the FrontPage suite of programs. Designed to work in concert with Image Composer to create animated GIF files, it allows you to add animation to your site without the high overhead of other methods. GIF animations follow the same tried-and-true methods used by the cel animations of cartooning, creating an illusion of motion by the rapid display of slightly differing frames. The process of breaking down an event into its constituent parts is the key to good animation.

This chapter offers examples of how to construct animations from background to realistic movement, using Image Composer's special features. It then shows how to load the individual images into GIF Animator's frames, and goes into detail on how to use GIF Animator's various features to manage and modify the animation, as well as how to use these features to create special effects. It describes various techniques for creating different kinds of animations, offering examples along the way, and concludes with a listing of Web sites offering animations you can study.

CHAPTER 21

Creating and Designing Image Maps

by David and Rhonda Crowder

IN THIS CHAPTER

- Client-Side Versus Server-Side Image Maps *388*
- Adding Hotspots *390*
- Adjusting Existing Hotspots *394*
- When to Use Image Maps *398*
- Designing the Best Image Map *399*

"A picture is worth a thousand words." Nowhere is this more true than with image maps. Image maps are a useful sort of visual shorthand that allows one picture to replace an entire menu of hyperlink choices. Instead of facing rows or columns of text endlessly listing all the possible connections among (or within) Web pages, you just look at a picture and click the part you want.

What should an image map look like? As you roam the Web, it sometimes seems that there are as many answers to that question as there are image maps in existence. Some are actual maps, showing the layout of continents, housing developments, or college campuses. Some are abstract works of art with embedded text. An image map of a library bookshelf might have you clicking different volumes to access various subjects. The possibilities are infinite (see Figures 21.1, 21.2, and 21.3).

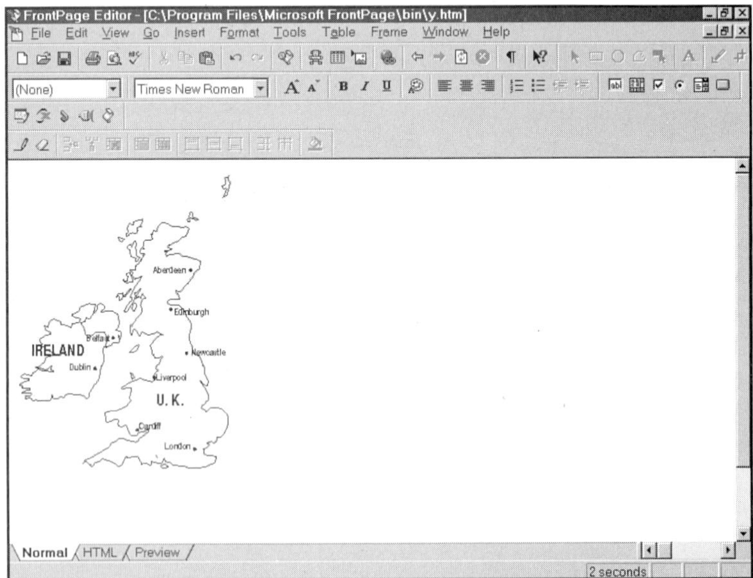

FIGURE 21.1.
Standard map style image map.

The one thing all image maps have in common is that several areas of the image are keyed to a hidden menu of links to different URLs. Really, they are nothing more than a logical extension of the idea of hyperlinked images; they just have more than one link per image. However, there is an extra level of complexity involved with image maps when compared to normal image links. When there is only one URL possible per image, no special computation is involved beyond simple link processing. When image maps make it possible to add several links to a single image, there has to be a method to distinguish them.

FIGURE 21.2.
Artistic style image map.

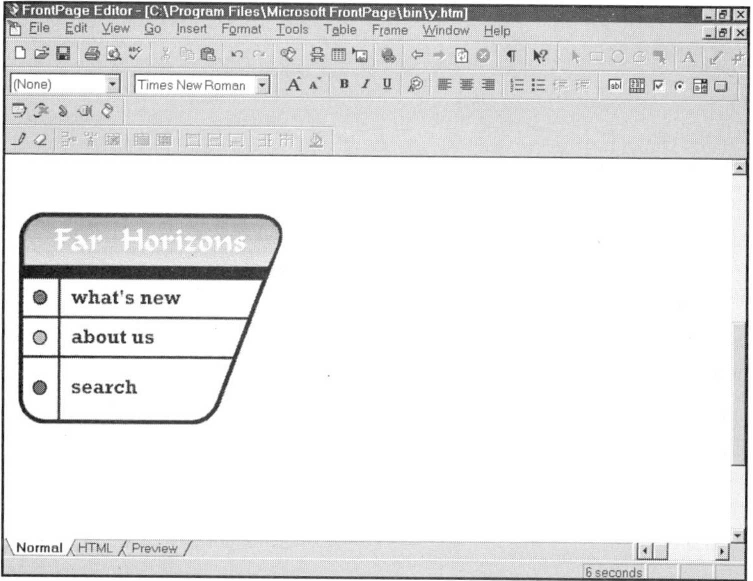

FIGURE 21.3.
Book style image map.

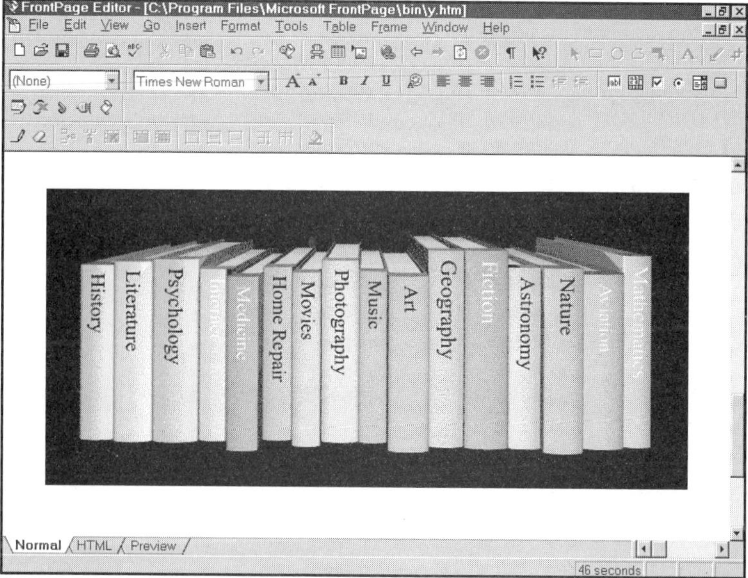

The solution to this is to keep track of the position of the pointer within the image, and to tie the xy coordinates (see Figure 21.4) of that position to a list of possible links. For instance, a different URL would be triggered if the pointer were between 0,0 and 20,10 than if it were between 0,11 and 20,20. At first, only rectangular areas could be supported, but other shapes were soon added.

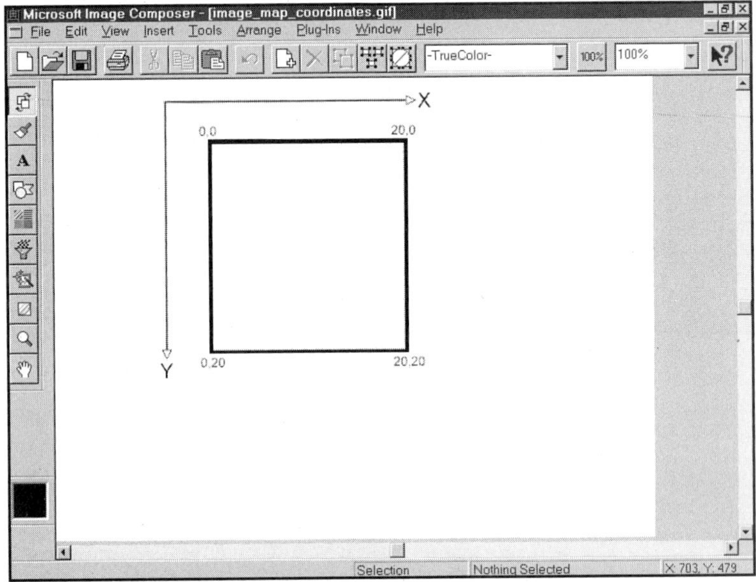

FIGURE 21.4.
Image map coordinates.

> **NOTE**
>
> You might notice that the xy coordinate system used by image maps is different from the one you learned in geometry class, but is standard in computer graphics. FrontPage 98 places the zero point for both x and y in the upper-left corner instead of the lower-left corner, and there are no negative values possible. Also, while the value of x increases the farther right you go, just like the old, familiar method, the value of y increases as you go downward, not upward, which is forced by the fact that you are starting at the top instead of the bottom.

Client-Side Versus Server-Side Image Maps

There are two approaches to generating responses from image maps. The earlier method was for the server to compute the URL from the pointer's xy coordinates. The main drawback to this server-side approach was that it placed an extra load on the server and that, consequently, it was slower than the newer method of client-side image maps. The performance degradation was not significant with only a small number of users, but a busy Web site could impact server performance dramatically if several visitors simultaneously were using image maps.

Following the current trend to shift the computing burden away from the server to the client system, client-side image maps were developed to solve this problem. Web browsers were made that took care of the necessary computations on the visitors' systems rather than on the server they were connected to. The result is greater convenience for both sides, as the server load is reduced and the image map computation speed is increased.

While the newer versions of both Netscape Navigator and Microsoft Internet Explorer support client-side image maps, this is not true of all Web browsers (both Netscape and IE have supported server-side image maps from the first; IE has supported client-side from its first version, and Netscape has from version 2.0 onward). When deciding whether to employ client-side or server-side image maps, Web designers must take into account the type of browser used by most of their visitors.

If server performance is a critical issue for the site on which you are working, and most of the visitors are using one of the major browsers, it is probably best to go with the client-side approach, bearing in mind that some of the people coming to your site will be unable to use your image maps. Whether to provide an alternate menu for these people, or to simply put in links to the Microsoft and Netscape sites so they can download compatible browsers, is a design decision you must make.

If, on the other hand, you have all the server power you could ever possibly use, and a small group of users committed to a less well-known Web browser (for instance, in a small company's net setup), the server-side approach is the obvious choice.

Most web designers will find themselves somewhere between these two extremes, but the Web is rapidly tending toward client-side image maps as the norm. FrontPage 98 allows you to choose either server-side, client-side, or both approaches.

Setting the Image Map Style

You need to let FrontPage 98 know what types of image maps you want it to use on your web. If you do decide to use server-side image maps, you must also tell FrontPage 98 what type of server you are using. If you are uncertain, contact your network administrator or Internet Service Provider (ISP). In addition to the servers from Microsoft and Netscape, FrontPage 98 offers support for both NCSA (National Center for Supercomputing Applications) and the World Wide Web Consortium's CERN. The popular Apache server is considered to be NCSA.

Tell FrontPage 98 which type or types of image maps you want by doing the following:

1. Open your web in FrontPage Explorer.
2. From the menu, select Tools|Web Settings.
3. In the FrontPage Web Settings dialog box (see Figure 21.5), click the Advanced tab.

FIGURE 21.5.
The FrontPage Web Settings dialog Box.

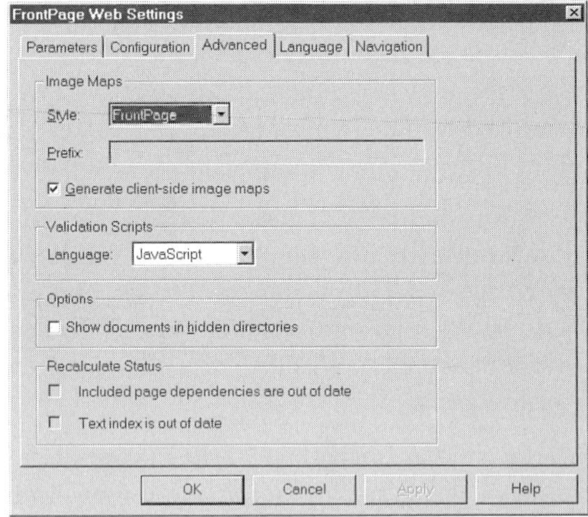

4. If you want only client-side image maps, select None in the drop-down list labeled Style, then make sure the check box labeled Generate Client Side Image Maps is checked. If it isn't, click it.
5. If you want only server-side image maps, select the appropriate server in the drop-down list labeled Style, then make sure the check box labeled Generate Client Side Image Maps is not checked. If it is, click it.

   There is an edit box labeled Prefix underneath the Style box. Depending on which server you select, you might need to enter the directory containing your server-side CGI handler. Default directories are provided for the NCSA and CERN servers. If you are not certain about this, check with your network administrator or ISP.
6. If you want both types of image maps, follow the procedure in Step 5, but make sure the Client Side check box is checked.
7. When you are finished, click the OK button.

Adding Hotspots

Each link area within an image map is called a hotspot. Hotspots are added using the image map buttons in FrontPage Editor's toolbar (see Figure 21.6). The three buttons cover most of the possibilities for highlighting shapes within your images. They are rectangles, circles, and polygons. Although there is no spline option for irregular curves, you can, with a little patience, use the polygon tool to follow a curve closely enough.

FIGURE 21.6.
The image map buttons.

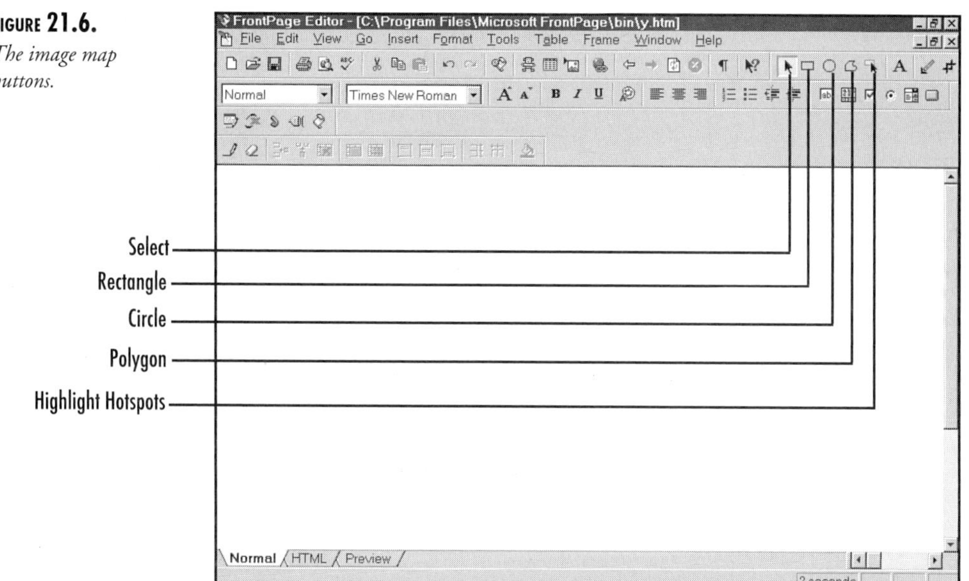

NOTE

The areas outside hotspots can either be left nonfunctional as far as clicks are concerned, or you can set a default hyperlink just like you would with any hyperlink image. If you set a default hyperlink, any clicks outside hotspots, but within the image, will link to the default hyperlink.

To make a hotspot within an image, use the following technique:

1. On the active page, select the image that you want to turn into an image map.
2. Click the hotspot shape button (rectangle, circle, or polygon) that will allow you to best outline the chosen portion of the image where you will be placing the hotspot.
3. For the rectangle, place the pointer at any of the four corners of the area you want to make into a hotspot. While holding the left mouse button down, move the pointer in any direction until the box surrounds the hotspot area (see Figure 21.7). Release the mouse button when you are satisfied.

   For the circle, place the pointer at the center of the area you wish to draw a circle around. Then, while holding the left mouse key down, drag the circle until it is the size you want (see Figure 21.8). Release the mouse button when you are satisfied.

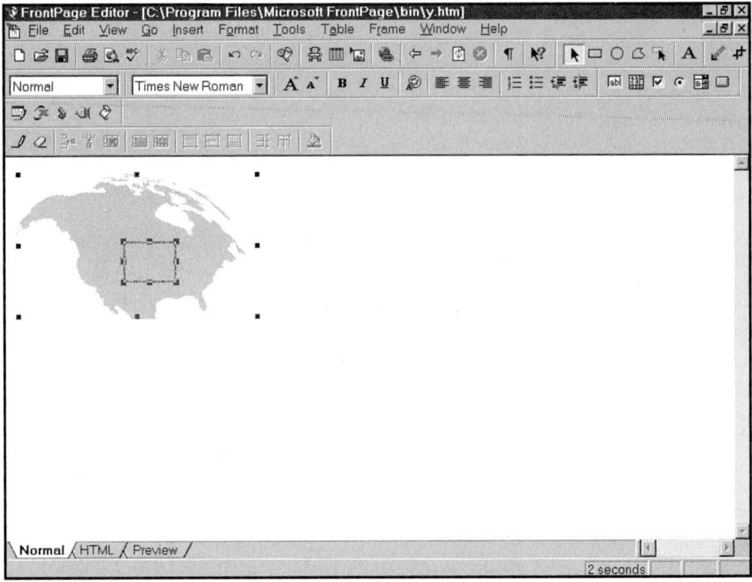

FIGURE 21.7.
The rectangle hotspot.

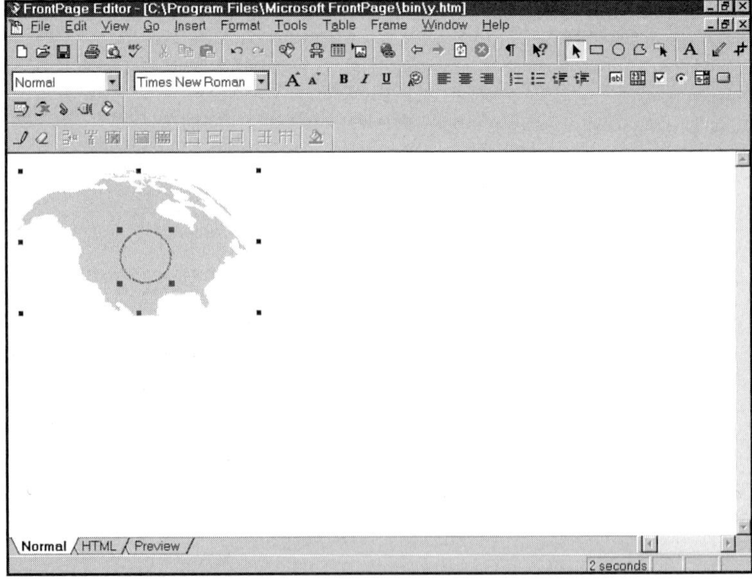

FIGURE 21.8.
The circle hotspot.

For the polygon, click at any point on the perimeter of the shape, and then move the pointer to another point (preferably one at which the shape's outline changes direction) and click again. A line will appear connecting the two points, and more will appear as you add more points (see Figure 21.9). Continue to play this high-tech connect the dots game until you have returned to your starting point.

FIGURE 21.9.
The polygon hotspot.

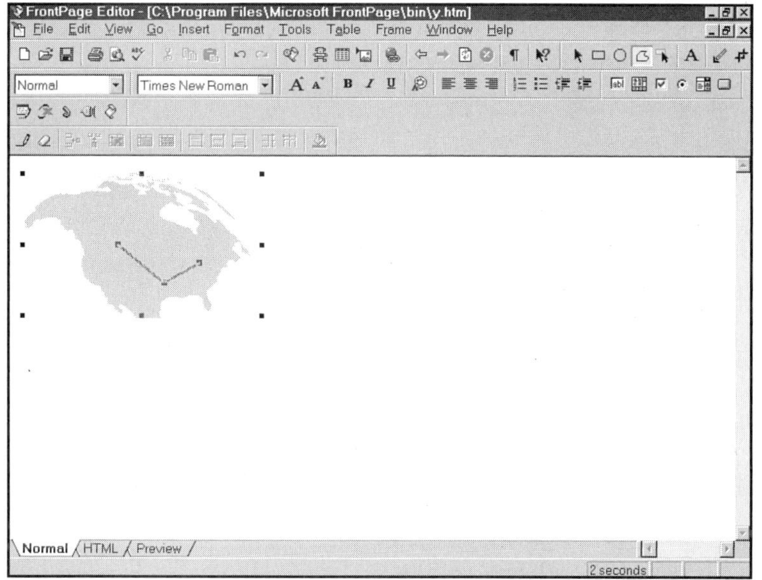

4. When the hotspot outline has been drawn, the Create Hyperlink dialog box will appear (see Figure 21.10). This is the same dialog box you use to create ordinary hyperlinks (see Chapter 5, "Working with Links and Lists"), and the technique is the same; you are, after all, creating just another ordinary hyperlink, regardless of the fact that there are several of them embedded in a single image.

FIGURE 21.10.
The Create Hyperlink dialog box.

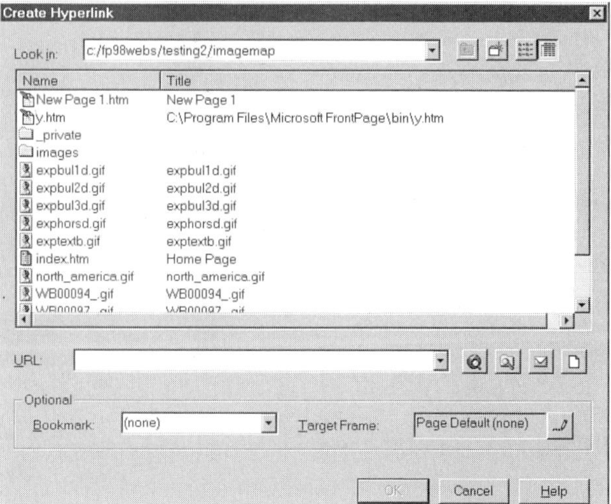

5. After you have completed your hyperlink choices, click the OK button. The operation is now complete.
6. To add more hotspots to the image, repeat Steps 1 through 5.

NOTE

After you have added a hotspot, it becomes visible when you select the image map in FrontPage Editor's Normal view. The fifth button in the image map tools is the Highlight Hotspots button (refer to Figure 21.6). It can be toggled on and off with a mouse click. When it is active (depressed), the image part of the image map is blanked out and only the hotspots are visible.

Adjusting Existing Hotspots

Because nothing on a Web page is ever cast in stone, you will probably, at some time, want to make changes to hotspots you have created. Fortunately, this situation was foreseen, and the solutions are easy to implement.

Changing the Position of a Hotspot

You might need to change the position of a hotspot, if the image it is a part of has textual elements that change. Whatever your reasons, the following shows how to do it:

1. Select the image that contains the hotspot you want to move. The outlines of all the hotspots in that image will appear.
2. Place the mouse pointer *inside* the hotspot, not on the outline of it.
3. Press and hold the left mouse button. While holding it down, move the pointer to the desired location within the image. The hotspot image will drag along with it.
4. When you are satisfied with the new position, release the mouse button.

CAUTION

When you depress the left mouse button, sizing handles will appear on the outline of the hotspot. Do not drag on these handles unless you wish to resize the hotspot.

Changing the Size of a Rectangle or Circle Hotspot

You can fine-tune the coverage of rectangle or circle hotspots by enlarging or reducing them. The following is the procedure:

1. Select the image that contains the hotspot you want to resize. The outlines of all the hotspots in that image will appear.

2. Place the mouse pointer either inside the hotspot or on the outline of it and press the left mouse button. Sizing handles will appear on the outline of the hotspot.
3. For a rectangle, place the pointer on a handle on the side of the rectangle you want to resize. When you are over a handle, the pointer will change into a double arrow. Now press and hold the left mouse button. While holding it down, move the pointer in the direction you want to expand or contract the rectangle. The side of the outline you have selected will follow along. Changing the length of the sides of a rectangle also changes its shape, of course, unless you change all sides equally.
4. For a circle, follow the procedure in Step 3, except that it does not matter which sizing handle you drag on, since a circle has no sides. The entire circle will expand or contract as you move the pointer. There is no way to change the shape of the circle; if you want an oval, you will have to approximate it with a polygon.
5. When you are satisfied with the size, release the mouse button.

FIGURE 21.11.
Resizing a circle hotspot.

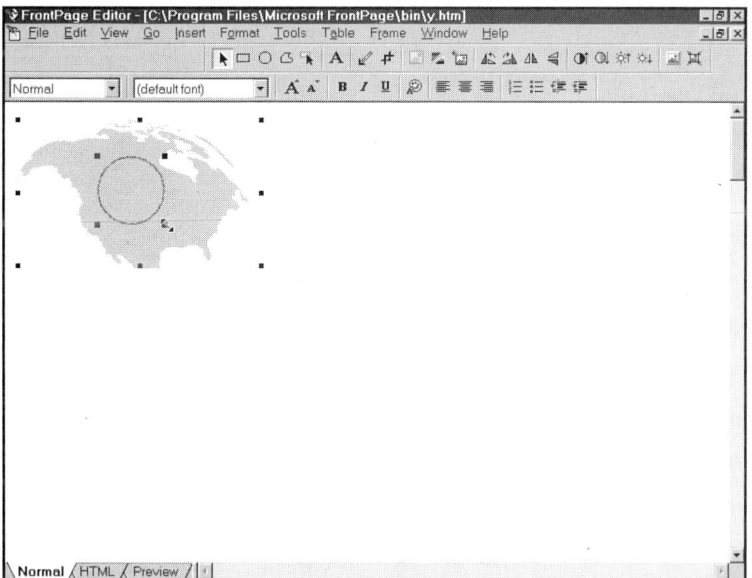

Changing the Shape of a Polygon Hotspot

Just as with rectangles and circles, polygons sometimes need a bit of adjustment. The following is how to do it:

1. Select the image that contains the polygon hotspot you want to reshape. The outlines of all the hotspots in that image will appear.
2. Place the mouse pointer either inside the hotspot or on the outline of it and press the left mouse button. Sizing handles will appear on the outline of the hotspot.

3. Place the pointer on a handle anywhere on the outline of the polygon you wish to reshape. When you are over a handle, the pointer will change into a quadruple arrow. Now, press and hold the left mouse button. While holding it down, move the pointer the direction in which you wish to move the point. The two lines leading from the point you have selected will follow. This is called rubberbanding. When you are satisfied with the new position of the point, release the mouse button.
4. Repeat Step 3 until you have achieved the shape you desire.

NOTE

Due to the nature of polygons, there is no simple procedure to change the size of one, just the shape. If you want to maintain the same shape, but achieve a new size, you will have to drag each point to a new position. It's a bit tricky, but with careful attention you can manage a shape that, while larger or smaller, is pretty much the same shape as the original.

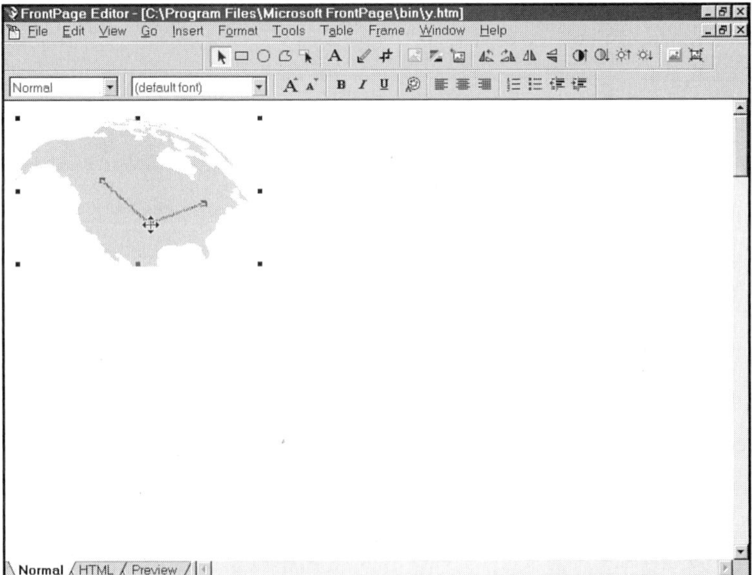

FIGURE 21.12.
Redoing a polygon hotspot.

Changing the Link to Which a Hotspot Points

Even if everything is fine with the image and the hotspot layout, you might need to change the URL to which a hotspot points. The following is the method for doing this:

1. Select the image that contains the polygon hotspot you want to change. The outlines of all the hotspots in that image will appear.

2. Place the mouse pointer either inside the hotspot or on the outline of it and press the left mouse button. Sizing handles will appear on the outline of the hotspot.
3. Place the pointer inside the hotspot you want to work with and click the right mouse button.
4. From the resulting pop-up menu, select Image Hotspot Properties, which will bring up the Edit Hyperlink dialog box (see Figure 21.13).
5. Change the URL in the same manner you would for any hyperlink (see Chapter 5).

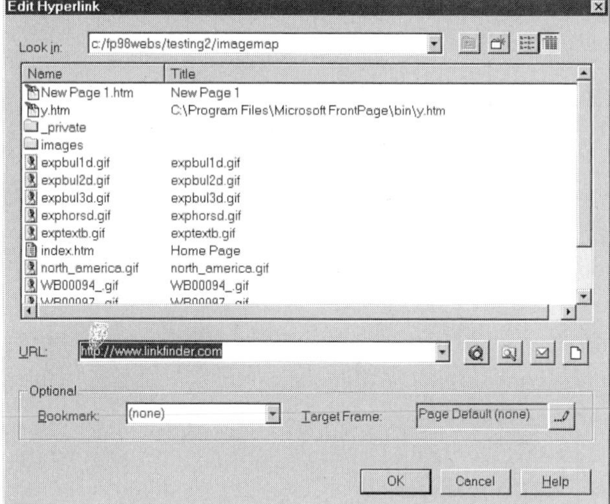

FIGURE 21.13.
The Edit Hyperlink dialog box.

Deleting a Hotspot

If resizing or changing the URL isn't enough, you might find that you want to get rid of a hotspot entirely. Here is how to do it:

1. Select the image that contains the polygon hotspot you want to delete. The outlines of all the hotspots in that image will appear.
2. Place the mouse pointer either inside the hotspot or on the outline of it and press the left mouse button. Sizing handles will appear on the outline of the hotspot.
3. Press the Delete key.

When to Use Image Maps

Image maps can be used to link to anything a normal hyperlink can, such as to Web pages within your site or in other sites, other images, and even other image maps. In fact, there is no reason you couldn't build an entire hierarchy of image maps.

Of course, there is still a place for textual hyperlinks. If you have only two or three links, the plain listing will probably be quite sufficient. However, if you have multitudinous links to provide, an image map is probably your best answer.

Bear in mind, however, that image maps are images. Granted, this should be obvious, but it means that the idea behind the image map must be one that can be grasped visually.

If, for example, you have a set of links that is best expressed in geographic coordinates, or through vivid graphical representations, an image map is definitely your best approach. The following are some examples of these situations:

- A chain of stores with several locations could use an image map. The image map could include links that lead to the address, telephone number, hours of operation, and so on, for each location.
- A multi-web site, such as a varied group of artists, all of whom have banded together to support one another's efforts, could use an image map. The image map could link to the photographer's Web site through a snapshot embedded in the image, the musician through an instrument, and so on.
- A clothing store could utilize an image of a model wearing its latest creations. Clicking the shoes would bring up a Web page detailing color, price, availability, and so on, of shoes. Clicking the skirt would bring up similar information about that item, and so forth.
- A mega-corporate Web site could use images suggestive of the products with which they deal (see Figure 21.14, for an example). A picture of a factory could lead to the manufacturing segment, an image of a band could lead to the entertainment industry, a pasture with cattle could lead to the dairy segment, and so on.

Avoid using an image map when your links cannot be coherently expressed using a visual representation. Most sites, for instance, have a page of reciprocal links to other sites that cover the same or related subjects; it is difficult to imagine how a picture could be developed that would properly express this.

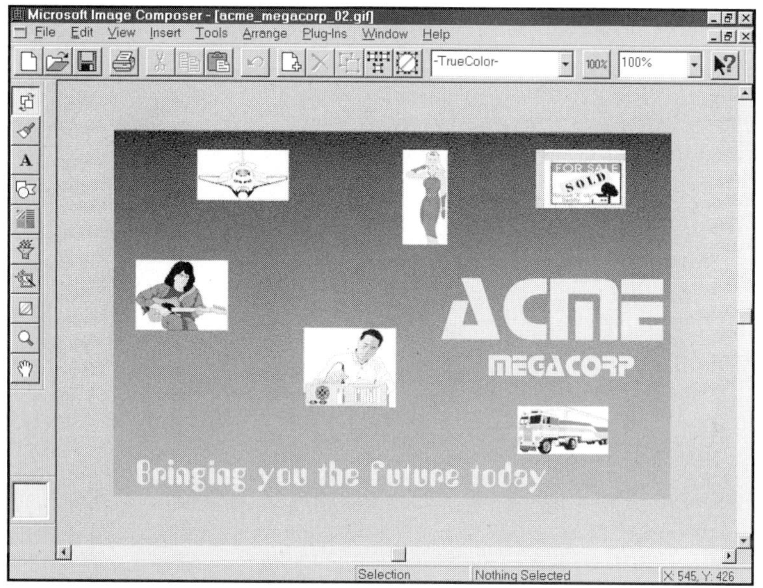

FIGURE 21.14.
A corporate image map example.

Designing the Best Image Map

Before any hotspots can be added, of course, you need an image to make into an image map. You need to consider elements such as the reputation and public posture of the organization running the Web site, the organization of the material, and the possibilities inherent in the subject matter.

You also need to look at practical matters such as how many hotspots can be coded into one image. The number of hotspots is limited mainly by design considerations; too few and your users will become frustrated trying to hunt all the hotspots down; cram too many in and the image map becomes uselessly confusing.

In the end, the best image map is the one a visitor to your site finds easy to use.

Summary

Image maps are a tool that replaces endless menus of hyperlinks with a single, coherent, and visual approach. They can have varied applications and representations. This chapter discusses the different types of image maps and the client-side versus the server-side approaches to deploying them. It offers a detailed series of steps for creating and modifying the hotspots, which are the core of image maps. The chapter then goes on to a discussion of practical application and approaches to designing hotspots.

Part V

Forms and Advanced Form Handling

IN THIS PART

- Working with Forms 403
- Getting More from the Form Page Wizard 419
- Handling Form Output and Saving the Results 427
- Validating Forms 449
- Search Engines and Indexing Your Web Site 459

CHAPTER 22

Working with Forms

by William Robert Stanek

IN THIS CHAPTER

- What Forms Are and Why You Want to Use Them *404*
- Form Design *405*
- Creating the Form *406*
- Hidden Fields in Forms *408*
- Adding Input Fields to the Form *408*

In previous chapters, you learned how to create wonderful Web publications that include pictures, image maps, videos, and sound tracks. So now that you've created the beginnings of a wonderful publication, how do you get feedback, comments, and praise from visitors that will make all your hard work worthwhile? The answer is easy—add a fill-out form to an appropriate place in your Web publication and invite your readers to participate.

HTML 2.0 introduced forms, and Web publishing has never been the same. Forms are the primary way to add interactivity and two-way communication to your Web publications. They provide friendly interfaces for inputting data, searching databases, and accessing indexes. To submit a fill-out form, the user only has to click on the Submit button. Your forms can contain pull-down menus, push buttons, text, and graphics.

In this chapter, you'll learn all about forms—what they are, how to use them, and much more.

What Forms Are and Why You Want to Use Them

In our daily lives, we see forms all the time:

- The forms you fill out at the doctor's office
- The credit card bills that require you to fill in the dollar amount in tiny boxes, subtly reminding you to make sure to include all the zeros that go along with the digit
- The surveys and questionnaires you receive in the mail
- The personality compatibility polls you can find in magazines at the checkout counter

Although you might not think of these items as forms, all of them require you to fill in information or make selections from groups of numbered or lettered items. When you submit a printed form, someone on the receiving end has to file these forms away. In an increasingly computerized world, this usually means entering the information into a database or spreadsheet. Major companies hire dozens of people for the specific task of entering the thousands of forms that flood the company every day into the company database. This is a huge expense and a tremendous burden on the company.

Now imagine a virtual office where thousands of forms are entered into the company database every day without a single worker. The forms are processed efficiently, almost instantly, and the customer can get feedback within seconds of submitting a form. The cost for what otherwise would be a mammoth undertaking is just a few hours—the time it takes you to design a fill-out form and add a FrontPage Component or CGI script (see Chapter 24, "Handling Form Output and Saving the Results," for more information) to process the information.

Using forms, you open a two-way communication channel between you and the visitors to your Web publications. Visitors can send comments directly to you. You can add a WebBot or create CGI scripts to process the input automatically. In this way, readers can get immediate results. You can e-mail the input to your e-mail address. This way, you can respond to readers' questions and comments easily and personally. You can also set up a script to process the input, give results to the reader, and send yourself e-mail.

The scripting part of the process runs in the background, and the fill-out form is what the reader sees up close and personal. Readers can interact with forms by entering information in the spaces provided, by making selections from pull-down menus, by activating push buttons, and by submitting the data for instant processing. Figure 22.1 shows a simple form with areas for text entry. This form is used to enter product orders online and was created with the Form Page Wizard in less than five minutes.

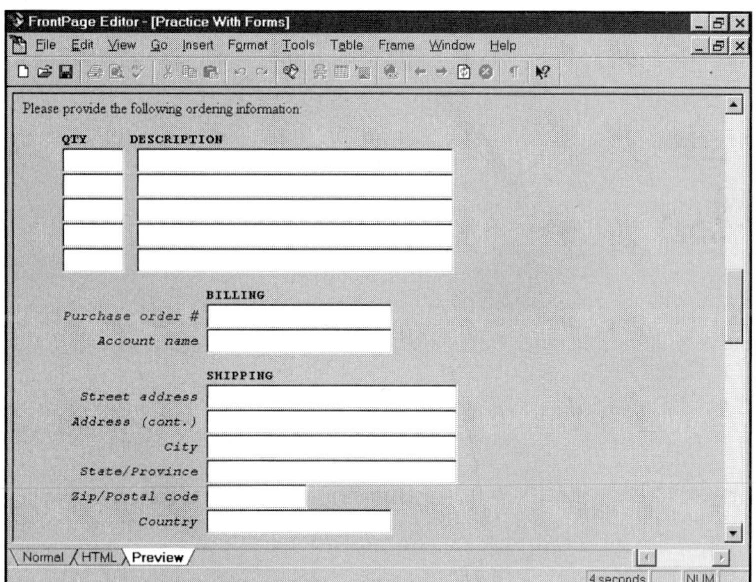

FIGURE 22.1.
An online order form.

Form Design

Although creating a form is easy, designing a good form is not always easy. Some publishers use generic, all-purpose forms that fail because the form wasn't designed with a specific purpose in mind. For example, if you are looking to get information from your visitors for online purchasing, you need a form that concentrates on getting the pertinent data, such as their name, shipping and billing addresses, their payment information, and what exactly they are ordering. It is less crucial to find out what they think of your Web site or their educational experience. The key to designing forms is to use them for a specific purpose. When you want to get feedback from readers, you create a form for reader feedback. When you want to take orders online, you create a form for submitting online orders.

Designing forms that are useful to readers and to you as the publisher should be your primary goal. A form that is useful to readers will be used. A form that is useful to you as the publisher makes your job easier. The key to creating forms that are useful to readers and you as the publisher is also in form design. As you go through the steps for designing forms, keep the following guidelines in mind:

- A form that is useful and appealing to the reader (assuming that they want to fill it out to get something out of the process) typically has the following characteristics:
  - Friendly
  - Well organized
  - Sized correctly
- A form that is useful to you (assuming it requests the required information) as the publisher typically does the following:
  - Uses uniquely named and easily identifiable keywords for fields
  - Allows for brevity of processing and quick indexing whenever possible
  - Provides subtle guidance to the reader on the amount of input you are seeking

With these rules in mind, you should always provide descriptions along with form fields. As with print forms, the descriptions for fields should be brief. This makes the form easier to read.

Here's an example of a wordy field description:

You should enter your full name in the adjacent text window using your first name, middle initial, and last name as appropriate.

Here's a better field description:

Please enter your name (First, Middle Initial, Last).

Input fields should be correctly sized to ensure that they are usable. A good field size ensures that all key information entered by the user is visible in the input area. For a telephone number, you can define the input field to be 12 characters in length. This allows customers to enter their phone number and area code. If a reader puts parentheses around the area code, the length of the input field should be stretched to 14 characters. If the reader lives in another country, the length of the input field should be stretched to at least 16 characters.

The form itself should be correctly sized and well organized to ensure that readers will take the time to fill it out. A good form balances the number of fields against the length of the fields. This means that a form that requires lengthy input from readers should have few fields, and a form that requires the reader to make many selections but requires limited actual input should have many fields.

Creating the Form

FrontPage 98 provides both a manual method and an automatic method for creating forms and setting up form elements. Using the manual method, you build the form using FrontPage's WYSIWYG interface. Using the Form Wizard, FrontPage 98 guides you through every step of the form creation process, making the process mostly automated. To give you a solid understanding of how forms work, this chapter focuses first on the manual form-building process and then on the automated process.

Within a form, you can use any valid HTML element. Although multiple forms can be on a single Web page, you cannot create subforms within a form. Primarily, this is because the form must be submitted to be processed in a specific manner.

EDITING TECHNIQUE

FrontPage 98 lets you set these properties for forms using the Form Properties box, which is shown in Figure 22.2. You can access this properties box whenever you add a push button element by clicking the Form button in the element's properties box or by opening the element's properties box and clicking the Form button. Using the Form Properties dialog box, you define how the results of the form will be saved and used as well as what the user sees after submitting the form. Saving and using the results of a form is covered in Chapter 24.

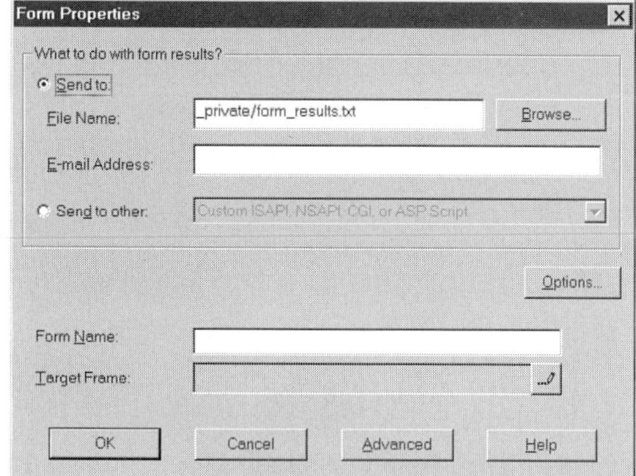

FIGURE 22.2.
Setting form properties.

To ensure that users submit valid information, you can validate form fields. When you validate a form, you check the contents of the form for accuracy and completion. The validation process ensures that you get the information you need from your customers, which in turn ensures the integrity of any databases based on the form input. To learn how to validate forms, see Chapter 25, "Validating Forms."

Putting this all together, your road map for creating and working with forms should go like this:

1. Create the form fields—either manually or with the Form Page Wizard.
2. Determine how results will be used and how the submission will be confirmed for the user.
3. Add validation to the form (if any).

Hidden Fields in Forms

You can set hidden fields using the Form Properties box. Hidden fields are not displayed and are only useful to provide essential input to a processing script, database, or file. Hidden elements have two attributes:

`Name`	The keyword associated with the input field
`Value`	The value of the field

Use hidden fields as a way to identify the form used to submit an entry or to insert vital information before each entry in a flat file or database. For example, if you want to pass the version number of the form or the page that the information was passed from, you could place the information in a hidden field to be passed on to you, transparent to the visitor. To add a hidden field, click the Advanced button in the Form Properties dialog box. This displays the Advanced Form Properties dialog box (see Figure 22.3). Click the Add button to define hidden fields. After you've added your hidden values, you can modify or remove them at any time.

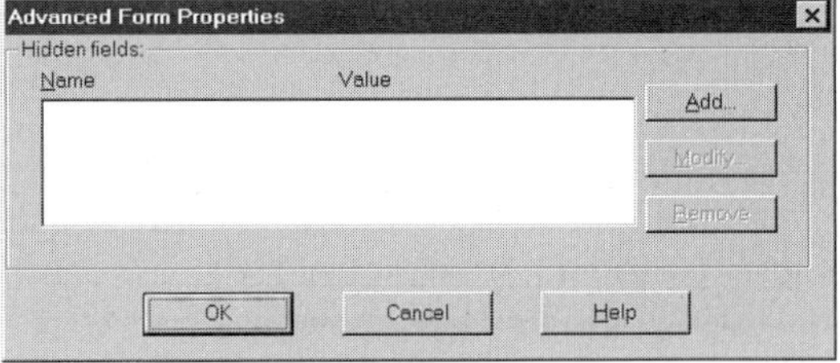

FIGURE 22.3. *Adding a hidden form field.*

Adding Input Fields to the Form

Before you create your first form in the FrontPage Editor, you should activate the Forms toolbar. You can do this by selecting Forms Toolbar from the View menu. The Forms toolbar has six buttons that are used to add the six key form elements:

- One-line text boxes and password fields
- Scrolling text boxes
- Check boxes
- Radio buttons
- Drop-down menus
- Push buttons

These elements are designed specifically for use within forms and are what make fill-out forms useful and interactive. Associated with each form element is a keyword that describes the type of data the element expects and a value input by the user.

Although the keyword cannot include spaces, the input from the user can. For example, a form element can ask for the user's full name. A keyword describing this element could be called `full_name`, and a user could submit the value "William R. Stanek." You can then store this input into a database, a flat file (typically a text file containing your data), or an HTML document.

> **NOTE**
>
> The Form button used to open the Form Properties dialog box is only accessible from a push button element's properties box. The primary reason for this is that push buttons are usually used to submit forms. On other form element dialog boxes, you'll see a button named Validate instead of the Form button. This button is used with field validation.

Using One-Line Text Boxes

EDITING TECHNIQUE

One-line text boxes are basic input fields for text. To insert this form element, click the One-line Text Box button on the Forms toolbar. After the element appears, right-click the text box button and choose Form Field Properties. This opens the Text Box Properties dialog box shown in Figure 22.4. After you define the properties for this element and click the OK button, the element is inserted into your document.

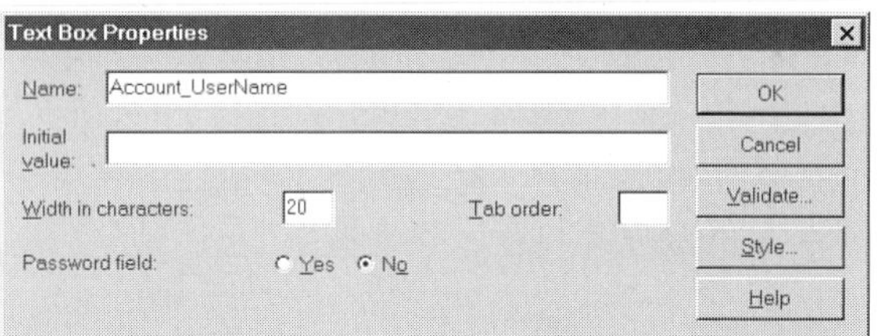

FIGURE 22.4.
Defining properties for a one-line text box.

As you can see, the Text Box Properties dialog box is used to define settings for the one-line text box you are creating. Here are the fields:

Name	The keyword associated with the input field (for example, `Account_UserName`).
Initial value	An initial value for the field that will be displayed in the text area. The user can add to this information and, if necessary, delete the information to enter new information.
Width in characters	The width of the input field, expressed as the number of characters for the text area (for example, `20`).

Tab order	The order in which the field is accessed using the Tab key. For example, if this field is set to 1, the field will be the first field accessed when the tab key is used.
Password field	Sets the field to a password field; see the next section for more information.

TIP

At any time, you can reopen the properties dialog box associated with an input field by double-clicking the input field.

TIP

A sample form that uses one-line text boxes is shown in Figure 22.5.

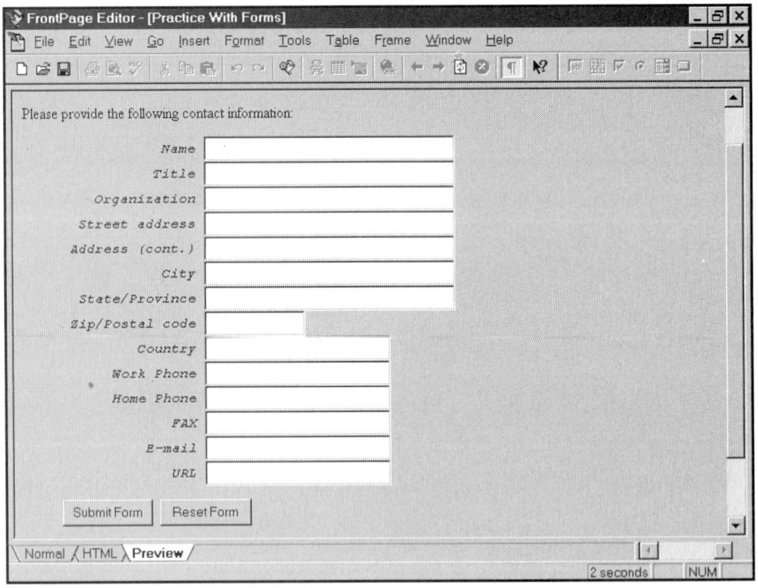

FIGURE 22.5.
Using one-line text boxes.

Using Password Fields

To allow users to enter password information without revealing the password to onlookers, you can create a Password field. A password field is a one-line text box with the Password field radio button selected. (See Figure 22.6.)

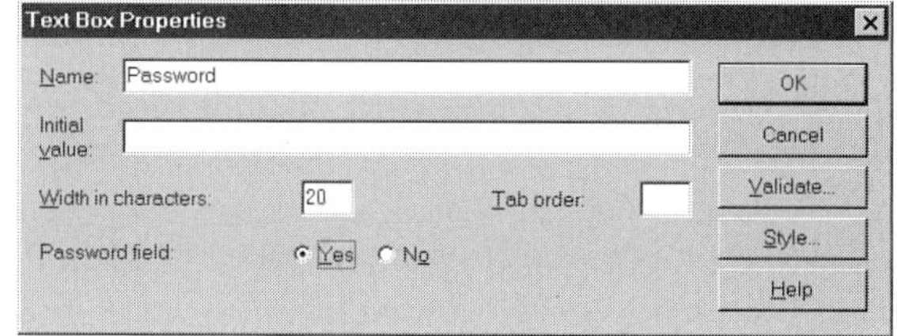

FIGURE 22.6.
Defining properties for a password field.

All text entered in a password field is seen as asterisks. The asterisks are used only to mask the characters and do not affect how the text is passed to your gateway script. By combining a password input field and an input field for the user's login ID, you can pass this information to a script or WebBot that validates the user's access to protected areas of your Web site (see Figure 22.7). For a complete look at the user registration process, refer to Chapter 35, "User Registration and Restricted Webs."

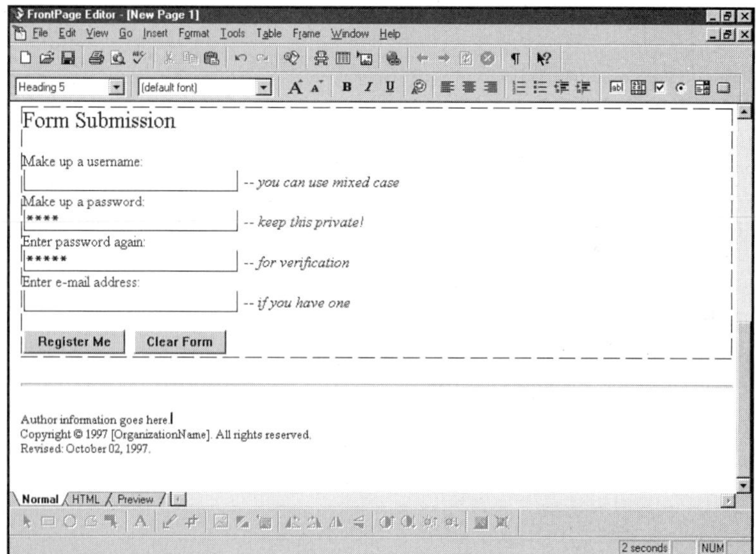

FIGURE 22.7.
Using a password field in a form.

Using Scrolling Text Boxes

Scrolling text boxes have more functionality than the one-line text boxes because they enable you to define text windows of any size to display on the screen. Text windows can be used to input large amounts of data. Although the size of the window is defined in rows and columns, you have no real control over how much data the user can enter into the window. This is because text windows have vertical and horizontal scroll bars that enable the user to scroll left to right as well as up and down.

Scrolling text boxes can have default text. Default text provided for a text window is displayed exactly as entered. Although the user can erase any default input if necessary, initial input should be used primarily to save the user time.

To insert this form element, click the Scrolling Text Box button on the Forms toolbar. This opens the Scrolling Text Box Properties dialog box shown in Figure 22.8. After you define the properties for this element and click the OK button, the element is inserted into your document.

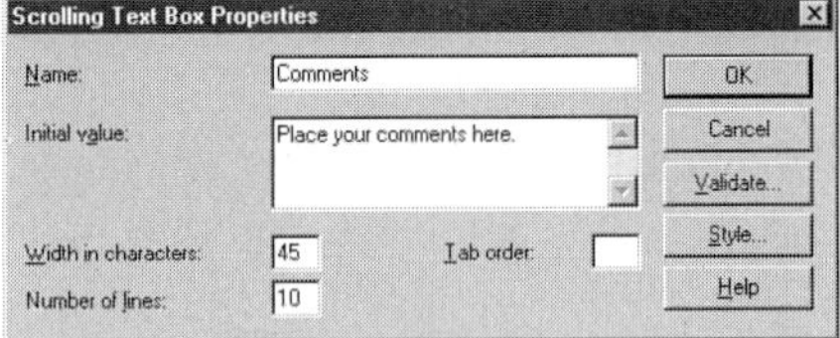

FIGURE 22.8.
Defining properties for scrolling text boxes.

As you can see, the dialog box is used to define settings for the scrolling text box you are creating. Here are the fields:

Field	Description
Name	The keyword associated with the input field.
Initial value	An initial value for the field that will be displayed in the text area. The user can add to this information and, if necessary, delete the information to enter new information. The initial value cannot be a list of text.
Width in characters	The width of the input field expressed as the number of characters for the text area.
Tab order	The order in which the field is accessed using the Tab key.
Number of lines	The height of the text window in number of lines.

A sample form that uses scrolling text boxes is shown in Figure 22.9.

Using Check Boxes and Radio Buttons

The check box input field creates a box that can be checked by a user. The radio button input field creates a circular button that can be checked by a user. Some browsers display selected check boxes and radio buttons using text—an x for a check box and a round bullet for a radio button. Other browsers display check boxes and radio buttons as graphical push buttons with a 3D flair.

Although the primary difference between a check box and a radio button might seem to be their shape, there is a fundamental difference in the way they behave. Check boxes allow users to make multiple selections. Radio buttons, on the other hand, allow users to make only one selection.

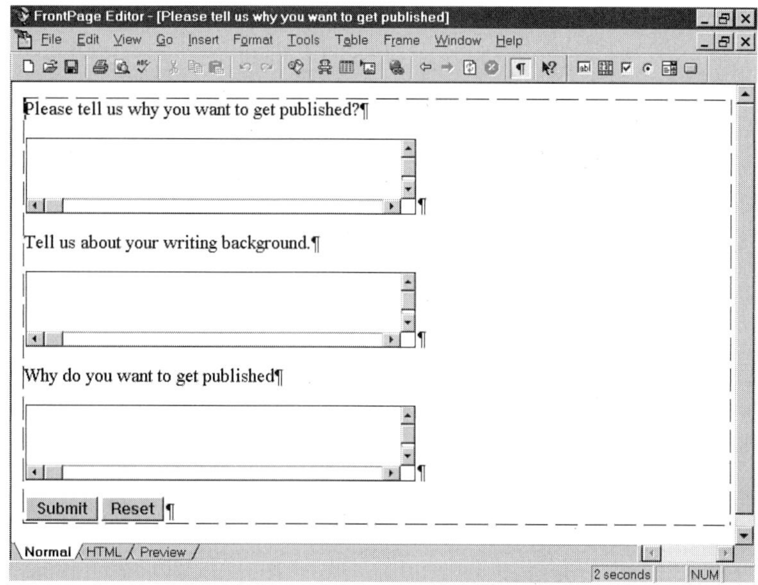

FIGURE 22.9.
Using scrolling text boxes.

With this in mind, you want to use radio buttons with a single associated keyword value when the user should make only one selection, such as a choice of A, B, or C. You want to use check boxes with multiple associated keyword values when the user can make multiple selections, such as a choice of all or any of A through E.

For each check box or radio button element, you must specify the default properties. The Radio Button Properties box is shown in Figure 22.10. After you define the properties for this element and click the OK button, the element is inserted into your document.

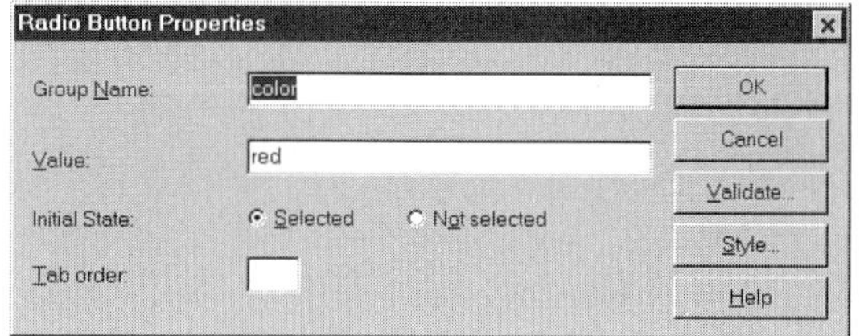

FIGURE 22.10.
Defining properties for radio buttons.

Here are the fields you can set in this dialog box:

Group Name	The keyword associated with a group of radio button input fields.
Value	The value to assign if the user activates the check box or radio button.

Selected	The check box or radio button is automatically selected when viewed. The best use of this attribute is for default options that can be unchecked if necessary.
Not selected	The check box or radio button is not selected when viewed and can be checked by the user.
Tab order	The order in which the field is accessed using the Tab key.

The dialog boxes associated with check boxes and radio buttons are nearly identical. The only difference is that the Check Box Properties box lets you specify a name and the Radio Button Property box lets you specify a group name.

Figure 22.11 depicts how check boxes and radio buttons can be used in a form. The check box groups will accept multiple responses, but the radio button groups will only accept a single response.

NOTE

Keep in mind that although the value and label for radio buttons and check boxes are sometimes set with the same keyword or phrase, labels and values are not used in the same way. A label is the text that the reader sees. A value is the actual value passed to the form handler.

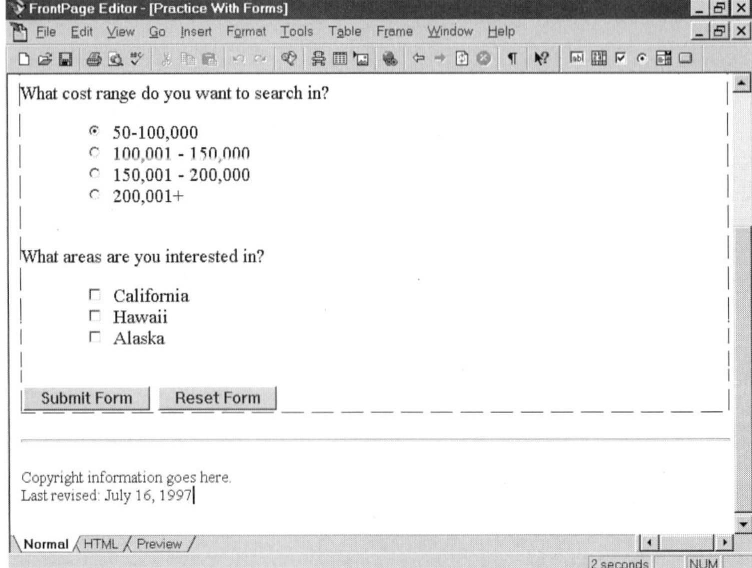

FIGURE 22.11.
Using radio buttons and check boxes.

Using Drop-Down Menus

Creating drop-down menus for your forms is more difficult than creating other elements. Each element in a drop-down menu is a selection. In some menus, all the selections are completely visible on the screen. In other menus, some or most elements are hidden until the reader activates the menu.

To insert this form element, click the Drop-Down menu button on the Forms toolbar. This opens the Drop-Down Menu Properties box shown in Figure 22.12. After you define the properties for this element and click the OK button, the element is inserted into your document.

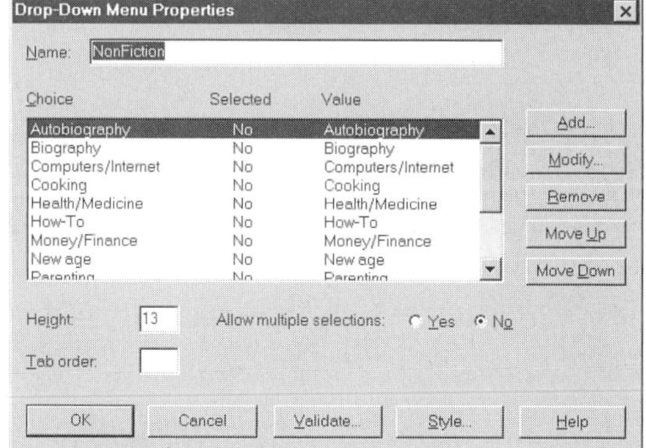

FIGURE 22.12.
Defining properties for drop-down menus.

As you can see, this dialog box has a lot of options. You use the Name field to specify a keyword for the selection menu. The Add button is used to add selections to the menu. Each selection is identified by a word or phrase the user can select, a value associated with this choice, and the initial state. By default, the value associated with the choice is set to the keyword you have used to identify the choice. The initial state of the choice is either selected or not selected.

The Height field is used to set the number of menu selections displayed on the screen without the user having to activate the drop-down menu. By default, the user can select only one option from the menu. To allow the user to make multiple selections, select the Yes button in the Allow multiple selections field. Most browsers allow you to make multiple selections by holding down the control button on the keyboard and clicking with the left mouse button when the pointer is over the additional item you want to select.

Figure 22.13 shows several types of selection menus. The first example shows a drop-down menu with the selections hidden. The second example shows a menu with all selections displayed on the screen by default. Onscreen menus occupy more space. You should consider using onscreen menus when the user can make multiple selections and pull-down menus when the user can only make one selection. The final example shows a menu with part of the selections displayed and part of the selections hidden. The scroll bar can be used to access additional items.

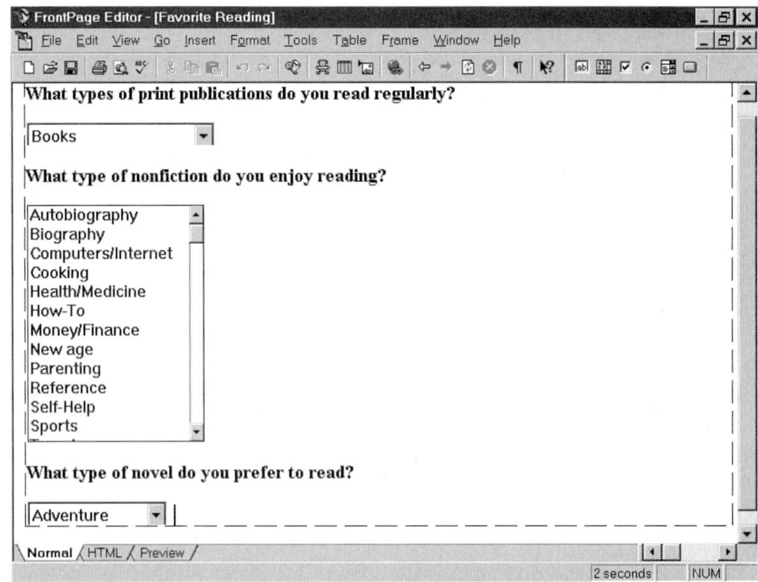

FIGURE 22.13.
Using drop-down menus.

To add selections to your menu, click the Add button on the Drop-Down Menu Properties box. This opens the Add Choice dialog box shown in Figure 22.14.

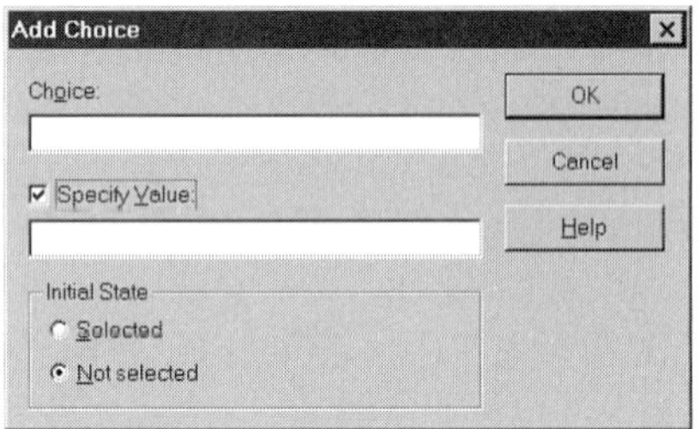

FIGURE 22.14.
Adding selections to the menu.

After you've added selections, you can modify those selections, manipulate their order, or remove them using the buttons in the Drop-down Menu Properties box. To do this, select the item you want to edit and then click on the appropriate button.

Using Push Buttons

Push buttons allow you to submit or clear a form. The Push Button Properties dialog box is shown in Figure 22.15.

To open this dialog box, select Push Button on the Forms toolbar. After you define the properties for this element and click the OK button, the element is inserted into your document.

By default, Reset buttons are labeled with the value of `Reset` and Submit buttons are labeled with the value `Submit`. You change the default value in the Push Button Properties box by specifying a new label in the Value/label field (for example, Clear Form or Submit Form).

FIGURE 22.15.
Defining properties for push buttons.

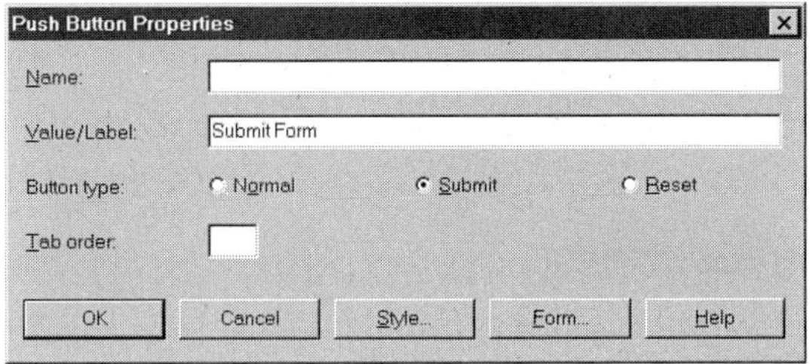

Using the Name field, you can track which Submit button a user clicked. This provides another way of tracking the precise form used to submit input. Figure 22.16 shows a sample form with Submit and Reset buttons. As you see, each form only needs one Submit button and one Reset button.

FIGURE 22.16.
Using push buttons.

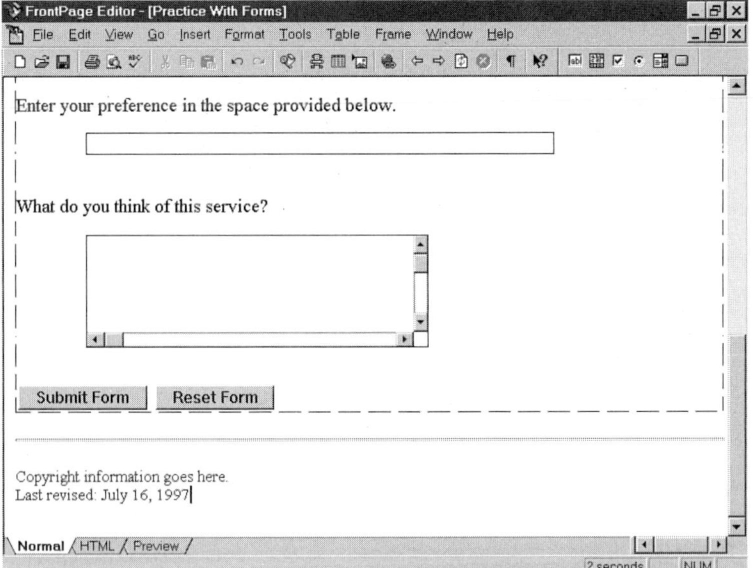

Summary

Forms add interactivity and provide friendly interfaces for entering data, searching databases, and accessing indexes. Designing forms that are useful to readers and to you as the publisher should be your primary goal. Using the FrontPage Editor, you can quickly add form elements using the Forms toolbar.

CHAPTER 23

Getting More from the Form Page Wizard

by William Robert Stanek

IN THIS CHAPTER

- Using the Form Wizard 420
- An Overview of Input Types 424

Now that you know how to create forms, the next topic is how the form creation process can be automated to perfection. The Form Page Wizard is optimized for creating forms with common types of inputs. This chapter is a walk-through of everything the Form Wizard has to offer.

Using the Form Wizard

You will use the Form Page Wizard when you want to create a new page that uses a form. To launch the Form Wizard, select New from the File menu or press Ctrl+N while inside of the FrontPage Editor. Then click the Form Page Wizard option in the New File dialog box. This displays the Form Page Wizard dialog box shown in Figure 23.1. Finally, click OK to launch the Wizard.

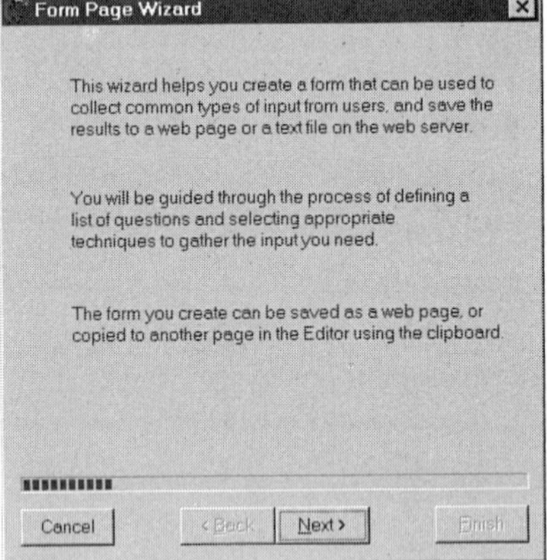

FIGURE 23.1.
The FrontPage Form Wizard allows you to create several different types of forms.

The buttons at the bottom of the dialog box are standard throughout the form creation process. At any time, you can move to the previous or next phase of the creation process using the Back or Next buttons. When you've fully defined the form, you can click the Finish button and the FrontPage Editor will create the form you've designed. You can determine how far along you are in the process by the status indicator located just above the button row.

Defining Page Title and URL in the Form Page Wizard

To begin, click the Next button. As you can see from Figure 23.2, the first step is to name the page and define a URL for the page. Because the form page will be saved to the current web, you should ensure that you use a unique URL and title. By having unique titles and URLs you can keep track of your pages more easily, which pays dividends when organizing your site as a whole.

FIGURE 23.2.
With the Form Page Wizard you can control many aspects of your eventual file, including the page's title and URL.

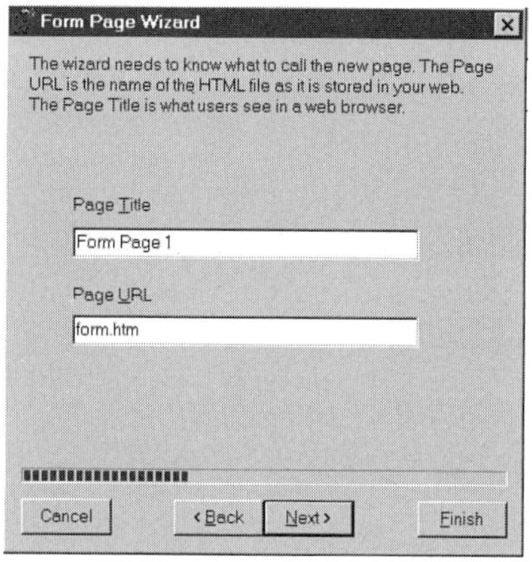

Adding, Modifying, and Removing Form Elements

After you've told FrontPage where to store the page in the current Web, click the Next button to continue. Figure 23.3 shows the dialog that lets you control form elements. From this page, you can add, modify, and remove form elements using the Add, Modify, and Remove buttons, respectively. When you first create a new form, the field listing area should be empty. However, if you click the Add button you're offered a choice of several form queries, along with the textual prompt in which you would like to couch them.

After you've added two or more form elements, you can modify the order of a selected element using the Move Up and Move Down buttons. To completely erase all form elements and start over, you can use the Clear List button.

FIGURE 23.3.
Form element definition and editing dialog box.

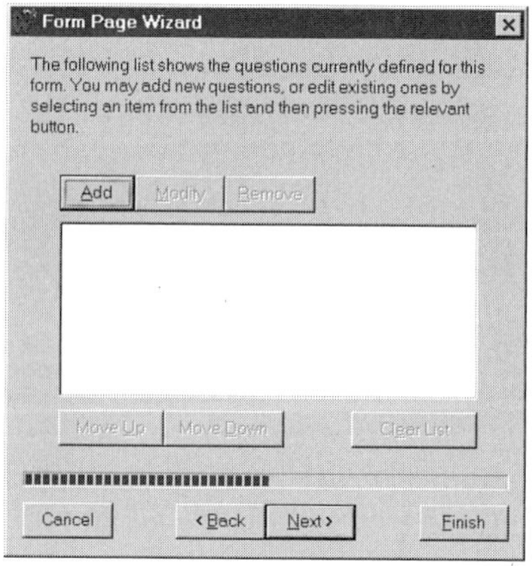

Selecting the Type of Input

Most forms ask the user a series of questions. The Form Page Wizard enables you to select from a list of common questions used in forms. To access this list, click on the Add button. You can now select the type of information you want to collect from the user.

As you can see from Figure 23.4, the associated page has three sections. The first section provides a selectable list of common information collected from users. The second area provides a brief description of the input fields the Form Page Wizard will generate based on the information type. The third section enables you to edit the question associated with the information type.

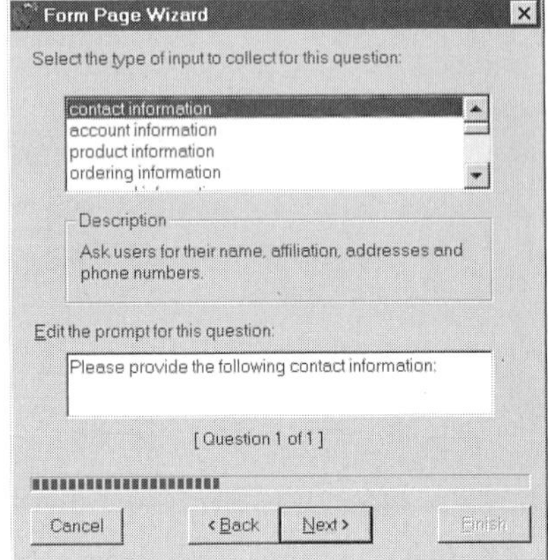

FIGURE 23.4.
The input selection dialog box.

After selecting the type of input you'd like to collect, click the Next button. This displays a page that you can use to select specific input fields related to the form question, such as name, address, and phone number. Figure 23.5 shows the input fields you can select for contact-related information. For a complete overview of the input type page, see the section of this chapter titled, "An Overview of Input Types."

To define another question or set of input fields for the form, click the Next button to return to the original Form Element Definition dialog. From there, you can click Add to start the form creation process over again.

Presentation Options

When you have finished defining element sets for the form, proceed to the Presentation Options page using the Next button. As you can see from Figure 23.6, this page enables you to specify the overall format for form questions, and will also generate a table of contents for the page. Usually, form questions are formatted as a numbered list and you might want to use this format as well.

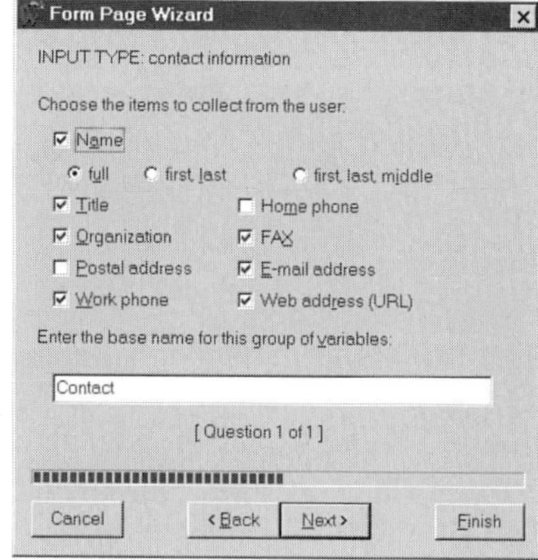

FIGURE 23.5.
Input field definition dialog box.

To help you create visually appealing forms, FrontPage uses two general presentation techniques. By default, your form elements are aligned using an HTML table. Because some older browsers cannot handle tables, you can also create the form using formatted text.

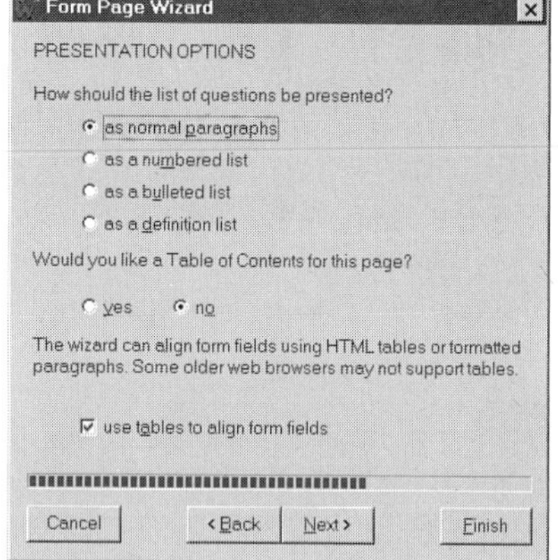

FIGURE 23.6.
Presentation Options dialog box.

Output Options

After specifying the presentation options, click the Next button to select the output options. The Output Options page is shown in Figure 23.7. By default, the Form Page Wizard saves the results from a form in a Web page called `formrslt.htm`. You can change the default setting to save the results to a file or specify a CGI script that will process the form results. You can also change the default filename for the results by entering the name of the file without the HTML extension in the appropriate field.

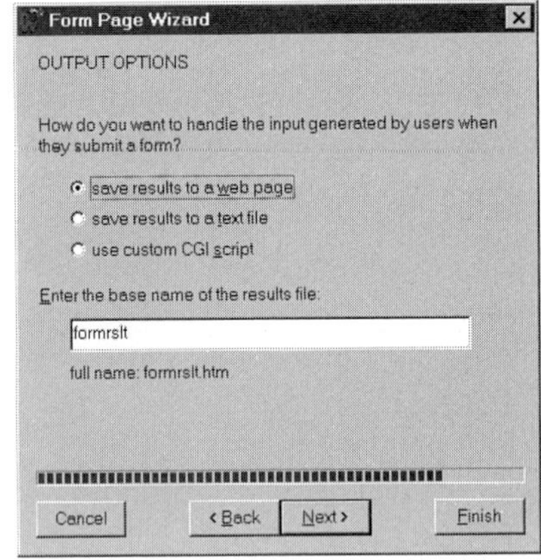

FIGURE 23.7.
Output Options dialog box.

Finishing the Page and Closing the Form Page Wizard

To finish the Page and close the Form Wizard, click the Finish button. You can do this from any page within the Form Wizard. FrontPage will now create your form.

An Overview of Input Types

The input types are the heart of the Form Page Wizard. Without the input types, the wizard wouldn't be useful. Table 23.1 provides you with a quick reference cheat sheet for determining which input types you will want to use in a form.

Table 23.1. Quick reference cheat sheet for input types.

Input Type	*Data Requested*	*Description*
Account information	User name Password	Used to set up an account login or registration form.
Contact information	E-mail address Fax Home Phone Name Organization Postal address Title Web address Work phone	Used to gather contact and address information from users.
Ordering information	Billing information List of products Shipping address	Used to set up an online ordering form.

Input Type	*Data Requested*	*Description*
Personal information	Age Eye color Hair color Height ID number Name Sex Weight	Used to collect personal information for identifying and describing the user.
Product information	Model Platform and version Product code Product name Serial number	Used to enter product information or register a product online.
One of several options	Drop-down menu Radio buttons List	Helps you create a selection menu, radio button group, or list.
Any of several options	Check boxes	Helps you create a group of check boxes.
Boolean	Check box Yes/no radio buttons True/false radio buttons	Helps you create input fields with either/or options.
Date	mm/dd/yy dd/mm/yy Free format	Helps you create input fields for entering dates in a validated format.
Number	Set maximum length Set currency prefix	Helps you create input fields for entering numeric values.
Paragraph	None	Helps you create scrolling text boxes.
Range	Scale of 1–5 Bad, poor, average, fair, good Range from disagree strongly to agree strongly	Helps you create input fields for data entered in a range of preset values.

continues

Table 23.1. continued

Input Type	*Data Requested*	*Description*
String	Set maximum length	Helps you create standard one-line text boxes.
Time	hh:mm:ss am/pm hh:mm:ss 24-hour Free format	Helps you create input fields for time in a validated format.

Summary

With the Form Page Wizard, you can create advanced forms in fewer than five minutes. FrontPage includes other powerful form-based tools beyond the Form Page Wizard. Using the Validation WebBot and the Scripting Wizard, you can automatically generate validation routines for your forms. Using the Internet Database Connector Wizard, you can connect your databases to the Web. You can use these tools to meet many of your most advanced Web publishing needs.

CHAPTER 24

Handling Form Output and Saving the Results

by William Robert Stanek

IN THIS CHAPTER

- Handling Form Output 428
- Customizing the Form Results 431
- Working with Custom Scripts 439
- Choosing a Programming Language for Your CGI Scripts 440
- Why Use CGI Scripts? 445
- How CGI Scripts Work 446

Before the advent of FrontPage, processing input from a form required a CGI script. As anyone who has created a CGI script knows, CGI scripts can range in complexity from a simple 15-line script that processes basic input to a 1,000-line script that performs advanced processing. FrontPage 97 introduced more powerful *WebBots* that automatically process the input of forms for you. These WebBots perform the basic-to-intermediate-level scripting tasks used most frequently by Web publishers. In FrontPage 98, WebBots are commonly referred to as *FrontPage Components*. The two terms are essentially interchangeable for all. With FrontPage Components, most Web publishers will never have to create a CGI script again—unless they want to.

For those of you who don't know, CGI stands for Common Gateway Interface, a popular and common method of adding programming functionality to Web pages. Essentially they are small subprograms that can communicate with the Web server while it assembles your Web page. For example, if you had a CGI process that would insert the user's name into every page, it would call that CGI script every time a page was served to the user. WebBots are a more specialized example of a CGI-like application.

Handling Form Output

You can define how you want to handle form output using the Form Properties box, which is accessible by right clicking anywhere in a form and selecting Form Properties from the pop-up menu. Just as the form creation process in FrontPage 98 is either mostly automated or mostly manual, so is the form handling process.

Whenever you handle output from a form, you are generally relying on the Personal Web Server or the FrontPage Server Extensions. If you aren't using the Personal Web Server or the FrontPage Server Extensions, the only form handler you should use is a custom script. For more information on custom scripts see the section titled, "Working with Custom Scripts."

Handling Form Output Yourself

Handling the output of a form yourself is easy. All you need to do is decide if you want to send the output to a named file, to an e-mail address, or to both a named file and an e-mail address. You define this using the Send to field of the Form Properties dialog box (see Figure 24.1).

When you send the output to a file, you can specify an HTML page or an ASCII text file. Ideally, you will use an HTML page when you want to be able to check current form submissions simply by loading in your browser a Web page containing the form results. Use an ASCII text file when you want to save the results in a format that is easily manipulated. You can place the form output file in a private directory to keep it hidden from prying eyes. To do this, save the file to the private folder that is a part of most Webs by adding the folder name to the File Name field value, such as `_private/results.txt`.

FIGURE 24.1.
Configuring the form results for files and e-mail.

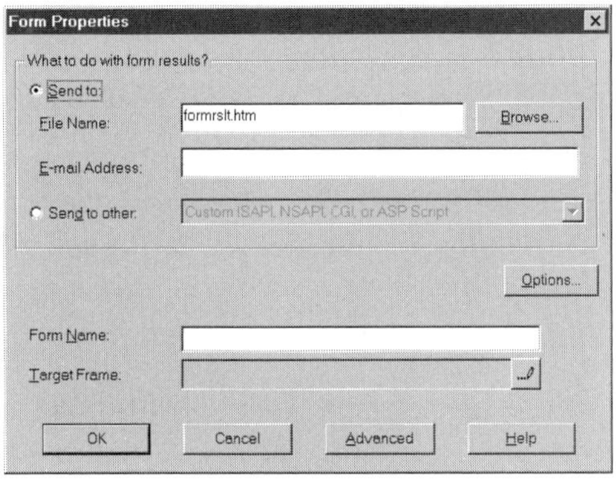

Because FrontPage 98 automatically generates the necessary file for you, you don't need to worry about creating the Web page or text file. However, you should write down the filename so you can access the form data submitted by users.

You can also send the output as an e-mail message to any e-mail address you specify. All you need to do is fill out the E-mail Address field with a valid address, such as `user@domainname.com`. If you specify a file name and an e-mail address, FrontPage 98 will send the output to both places.

Here is a walk through of the form creation and configuration process, to help you put together a more complete picture of the form creation and handling process. The creation process always starts with creating a form, such as the one shown in Figure 24.2. Here, the form has a single scrolling text box that allows users to enter comments anonymously.

FIGURE 24.2.
A basic comments form.

After creating the form, go on to define the form properties. If you wanted the result to go to a Web page called `formrslt.htm`, you would enter this filename in the File Name field of the Form Properties dialog box. Now whenever users submit comments, the results are sent to this page.

Because you haven't defined any other configuration settings, any results submitted using this form are formatted like those in Figure 24.3. Later, I will show you how to get lots more information from even the simplest form, such as the date of submission, the browser type, and lots more.

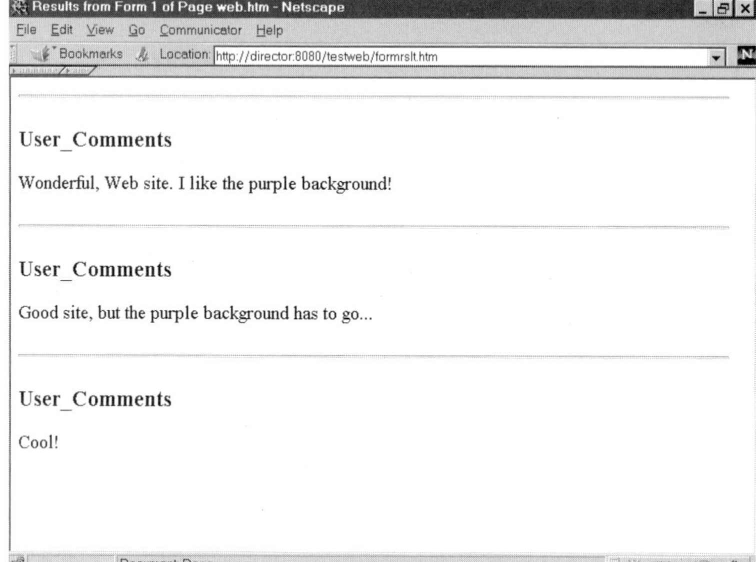

FIGURE 24.3.
The form results are logged in the file specified.

Using a Form Handler to Process the Output

Being able to send the output of a form to a file or e-mail address is great, but sometimes you want to process the output directly. FrontPage 98 provides several different methods to process output from form handlers. Form handlers available to you include custom scripts, the discussion form handler, and the registration form handler.

To select a form handler, activate the Send to other radio button in the Form Properties dialog box. After you choose a form handler from the pull-down menu, click on the Options button to define settings for the handler (see Figure 24.4). Each handler has unique properties and must be set up separately.

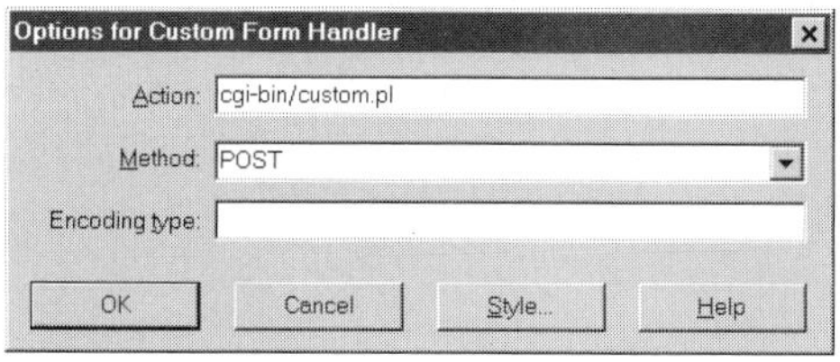

FIGURE 24.4.
The Options for Custom Form Handler dialog box lets you specify your own handler for your form.

Custom scripts are external programs that run on the Web server. Although you can use custom scripts to process the input from forms, you must program your own form handling solution. For more information, see the section of this chapter titled, "Working with Custom Scripts."

A discussion form handler is used with discussion Webs, which allow users to post messages to a discussion area and read messages from other users. Creating discussion groups and using the discussion form handler is the subject of Chapter 30, "Building a Discussion Web."

Often you will want to restrict access to an area of your site or require users to register before they can use key areas of your site. You can use the registration handler to do this. For detailed information on using the registration handler, see Chapter 35, "User Registration and Restricted Webs."

Customizing the Form Results

Customizing the form results allows you to define what users see after they submit a form and how the output of the form is recorded. You can customize the form results any time you save the results to a file, send the results in an e-mail message, or use a form handler. Make certain that you are back to sending the form data to a file instead of a specific handler. Otherwise, the Options display will be quite different, depending on what method of form handling you had chosen. Because the discussion form handler and the registration form handler are discussed in other chapters of this book, this section focuses on customizing form results when you decide to handle the results on your own.

After you open the Form Properties box, click the Options button to customize the form results. You will see a dialog box with four configuration pages that you can access by clicking on the corresponding tab. Although it is usually best to specify how you want the results of a form to be saved when you first create the form, you can update this information at any time by loading the page in the FrontPage Editor, changing the form properties settings, and then saving the page again.

Setting Up the File Results Tab

Typically the first tab you will set defaults for is the File Results tab. As you can see from Figure 24.5, the File Results tab has many options.

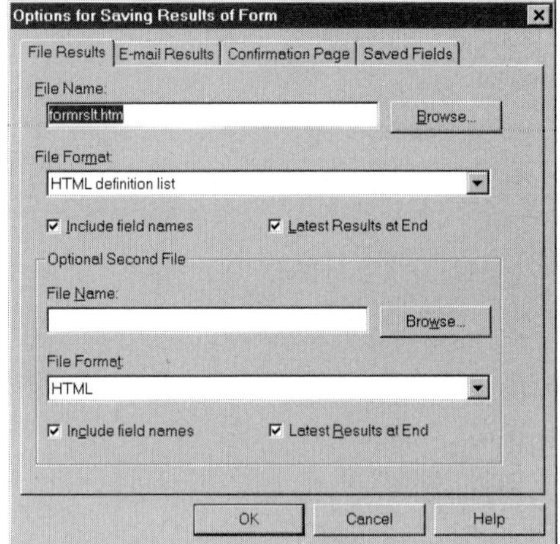

FIGURE 24.5.
Defining the format of results.

If the Send to radio button is selected, you can use the File Name text box to specify the name of the file to store the results. This text box is essentially the same as the File Name field of the Form Properties dialog box. For this reason, if you change this value, the value of the File Name field is also changed. If this file does not exist, FrontPage 98 will create the file.

The File Format field enables you to select the format of the results file from a drop-down list. You should choose the format carefully. If you are unsure of the format you will want your data in, it might be best to experiment with file formats on your local Web. The default format is normal text formatted as HTML paragraphs. The complete list of formats for results includes the following:

- **HTML.** Results are stored in an HTML document and formatted as HTML paragraphs. This is the default format.
- **HTML definition list.** Results are stored in an HTML document and formatted using a definition list. The field names are stored as terms, and values input by the user are indented like definitions.
- **HTML bulleted list.** Results are stored in an HTML document and formatted using a bulleted list.
- **Formatted text within HTML.** Results are stored as formatted text in an HTML document.
- **Formatted text.** Results are stored in ASCII text format without HTML markup.
- **Text database using comma as a separator.** Results are stored in plain ASCII text file with a comma separating field names and values. This is a good format to use with a database or other application.

- **Text database using tab as a separator.** Results are stored in plain ASCII text file with a tab separating field names and values. This is a good format to use with a database, spreadsheet, or other application.
- **Text database using space as a separator.** Results are stored in plain ASCII text file with a space separating field names and values. This is another good format to use with a database or other application.

When the Include field names box is checked, both the name and the value of each form field is saved to the results file. When this box is not checked, only values are written to the file.

If the Latest Results at End box is checked, FrontPage 98 adds the newest results to the end of the results file. Otherwise, the newest results are displayed first. Because you usually want to see the latest results without having to scroll through all the old messages, you probably want this box to be unchecked.

A terrific feature of the File Results tab is the Optional Second File area, which allows you to specify a second file for the results. In this way, you can store the results in an easy to read format such as HTML and an easily manipulated format such as text with commas for field separators.

Setting Up the E-mail Results Tab

When you want to receive a copy of the form results via e-mail, you will use the E-mail Results tab (see Figure 24.6). The first three areas are fairly self-explanatory, especially if you've read the description of the fields in the File Results tab. The E-mail Message Header area is where the E-mail Results tab really gets interesting. Unlike traditional mailto: references used in forms, FrontPage 98 allows you to add a subject line and a reply-to e-mail address to the e-mail results message.

You can use the Subject Line to alert you to the contents of the message and to automatically file results data. To file results data into folders for you, use the configure filter option of your favorite e-mail program. If your e-mail program doesn't support filters, you might want to try Eudora or even Netscape Navigator mail.

You can use the Reply-to Line to fill in address information should you ever want to reply to an e-mail results message. Here, you will probably want to base the value on a form field name, so be sure to check the Form Field Name check box. The form field name is the actual name you assigned to a form field. For example, if you created a form with an e-mail address field that you named UserAddress, you would enter UserAddress in the Reply-to Line field. Then, if you replied to an e-mail message, the user's e-mail address will be entered in the reply-to field of your message automatically.

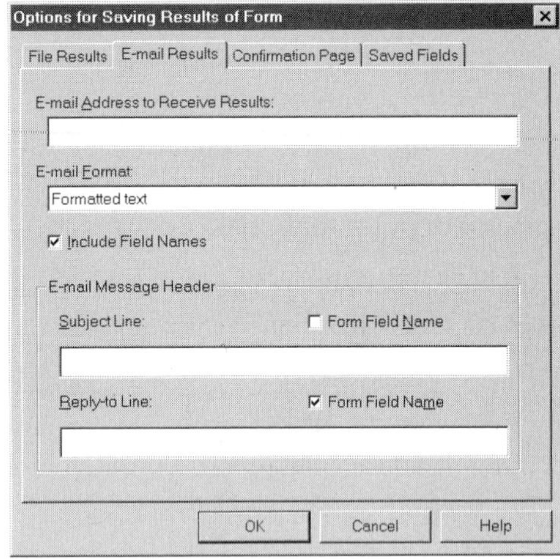

FIGURE 24.6.
Defining the format of results sent in e-mail messages.

Setting Up the Confirmation Page Tab

The purpose of the Confirmation Page tab is to let you specify the URL of a confirmation page (see Figure 24.7). Whenever a user submits a form, the confirmation page is displayed to show that the form was submitted successfully.

The overwhelming majority of Web publishers use confirmation pages, and you probably will want to as well. The reason confirmation pages are so popular is they allow you to ensure that the process completes smoothly. They let the user know the procedure actually worked and whatever information they submitted has been recorded, so that they do not try to submit the information more than once. For this reason, if you do not specify a confirmation page, FrontPage 98 creates one automatically. To select your own confirmation page, click the Browse button.

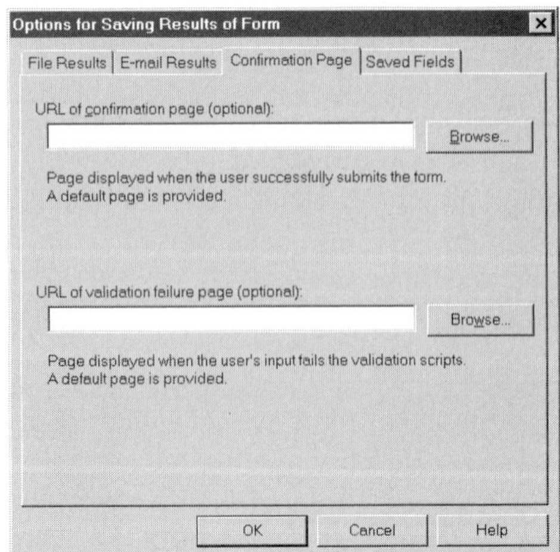

FIGURE 24.7.
Setting the URL to a confirmation page.

Often, you will find that the default confirmation page is all you need. Now take a look at an actual form and a corresponding confirmation page generated by FrontPage 98. Figure 24.8 shows the form submission page. As you can see, this page lets users enter a full name, e-mail address, and other information.

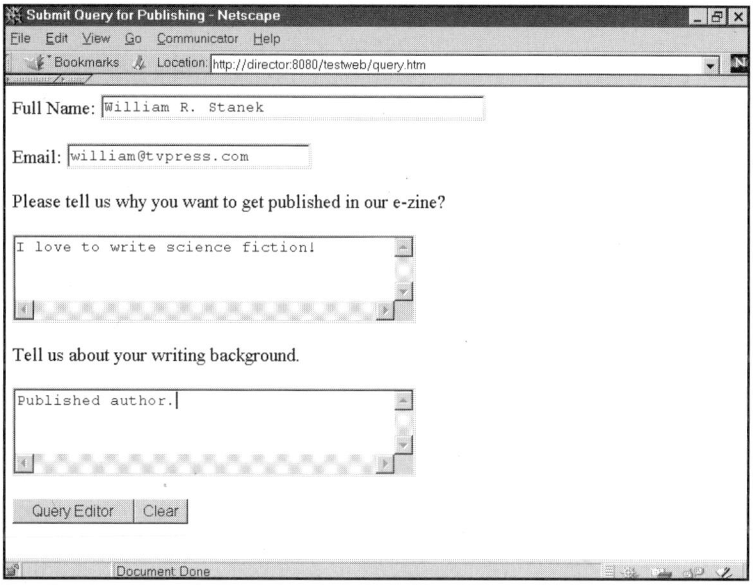

FIGURE 24.8.
An interrogative page using forms created in the FrontPage Editor.

When the form is submitted, the user sees a confirmation page like the one shown in Figure 24.9. Here, the user's entries are confirmed and the user is thanked for the submission.

If you don't like cookie-cutter format, you can create your own confirmation page. To do this, start a new page in the FrontPage Editor and enter the message you want the user to see.

EDITING TECHNIQUE

Anytime you want to base part of the text on the results, you will need to use the Confirmation Field WebBot. To access this WebBot, select Insert|FrontPage Component, then choose Confirmation field. You can now enter the name of an input field whose value you want to insert into the page. If you had a field named EmailAddress, you would enter this name. Click OK.

Now the Confirmation Field WebBot will insert a reference to this field. You can double-click on the reference to edit the associated field name. Now when the confirmation page is displayed as a result of a form submission, the value of the EmailAddress field will be entered into the body of the page exactly where you told the Confirmation Field WebBot to put it.

FIGURE 24.9.
The confirmation page that complements the form submission page.

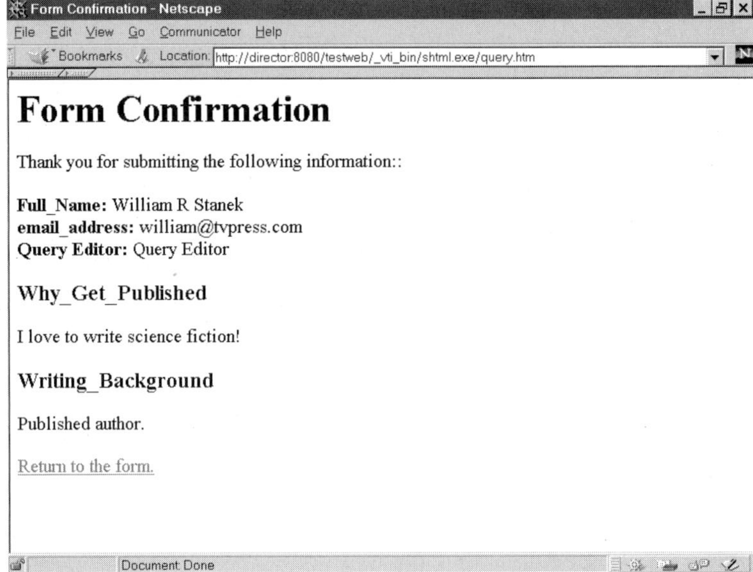

Saved Fields Tab

Normally only the value of the form fields are saved with the form results. However, FrontPage 98 lets you save additional information with the results, which you might find helpful when you process or analyze the results (see Figure 24.10). This information is appended after the form data and includes the following:

- **Browser type.** The type of browser accessing the page as specified by the browser.
- **Date.** The date the form was submitted.
- **Remote computer name.** The name of the remote computer used to submit the form.
- **Time.** The time the form was submitted.
- **User name.** The name of the user accessing the page; this is filled in only for forms submitted on a restricted web.

The Browser type field is one of the most useful fields you can save. You can use this field to examine the browser version, platform, operating system, and language related information. When you select the Browser type check box, values you see in your results files will look like the following:

```
Mozilla/4.0 (Win95; U)
```

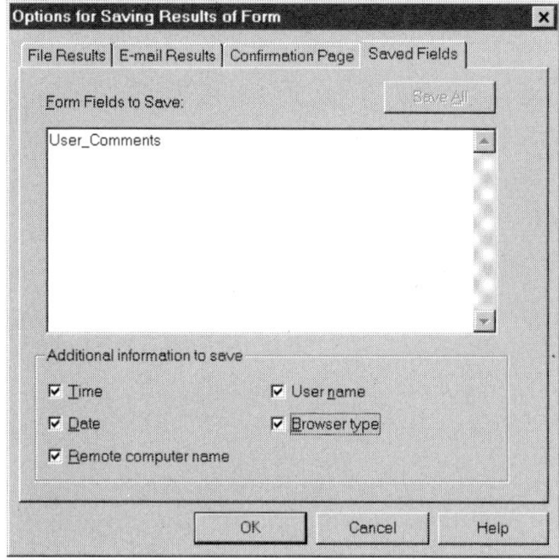

FIGURE 24.10.
Add additional fields to the results.

If you've never worked with custom scripts before, this value probably looks strange. The following is a breakdown of the value:

Mozilla	Refers to the browser's internal application name. Mozilla is the code name for the Netscape Navigator browser.
4.0	Refers to the specific version of the browser. Here, Netscape Navigator version 4.0.
Win95	Refers to the operation system running the browser. Here, the operating system is Windows 95.
U	Country code for the browser version. Here, the browser was created for use in the U.S. You might also see an I, which is a country code for the international version of a browser.

A summary of values you might see for the Browser Type field is shown in Table 24.1. As you can see from the table, Internet Explorer does use the code name Mozilla in some instances. This happens because Internet Explorer has a Netscape Navigator emulation mode.

Table 24.1. Understanding Browser Type values.

Return Value	*Description*
`Mozilla/3.0 (compatible; MSIE 4.0; Macintosh)`	Internet Explorer 4.0 emulating Navigator 3.0 on a Macintosh system
`Mozilla/3.0 (compatible; MSIE 4.0; Windows 95)`	Internet Explorer 4.0 emulating Navigator 3.0 on a Windows 95 system

continues

Table 24.1. continued

Return Value	*Description*
`Mozilla/3.0 (compatible; MSIE 4.0; Windows NT)`	Internet Explorer 4.0 emulating Navigator 3.0 on a Windows NT system
`Mozilla/4.0 (Macintosh; I; 68K)`	Navigator 4.0 on a 68K Macintosh
`Mozilla/4.0[de] (WinNT; U)`	German language version of Navigator 4.0 on Windows NT
`Mozilla/4.0b2 (X11; I; IRIX 5.3 IP22)`	Navigator 4.0 Beta 2 on a UNIX X Window system running IRIX 5.3
`Mozilla/4.0Gold (Macintosh; I; PPC)`	Navigator 4.0 Gold on a PowerMac

An example that shows these additional fields added to the results page is shown in Figure 24.11. I highly recommend tracking most or all of the additional information if you plan to do any analysis of traffic to your Web site.

FIGURE 24.11.
Add additional fields to the results.

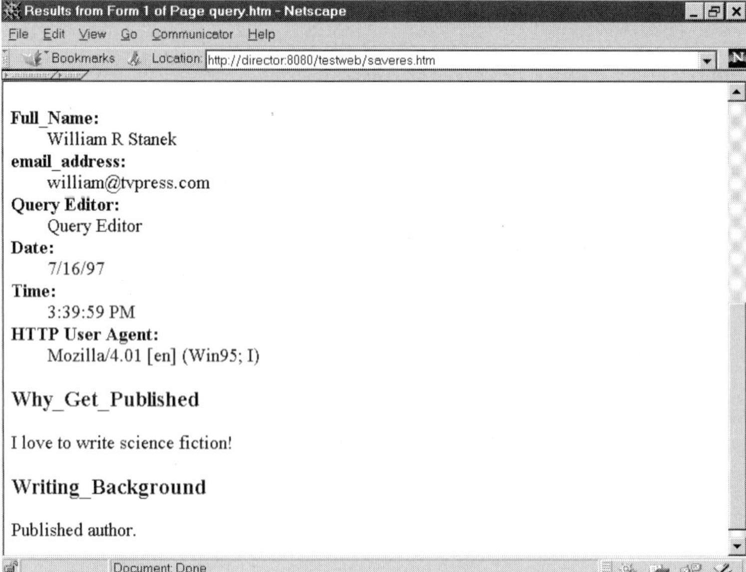

Working with Custom Scripts

Using custom scripts, you can create powerful, personalized, and professional Web publications that readers can really interact with. The most common type of script you will create when working with form processing is a CGI script. CGI scripts are external programs that act as gateways between the Web server and other applications. You can use CGI scripts to process input from readers, and thus open a two-way communication channel with your readers. Reader input can be data from fill-out forms, keywords for a database query, or values that describe the reader's browser and connection.

NOTE

For some pregenerated CGI scripts that you can freely integrate into your web site, visit `http://www.worldwidemart.com/scripts/`.

Although FrontPage 98 enables you to easily add WebBots to pages that use forms, WebBots generally do not perform any post-submission processing. With CGI scripts, you can process input from forms automatically and generate output directly to the reader, based on the results of the processing.

CGI scripts are external programs that run on the Web server. You can use CGI scripts to create highly interactive Web publications. The standard that defines how external programs are used on Web servers and how they interact with other applications is the common gateway interface. The three keywords that comprise the name of the standard—common, gateway, and interface—describe how the standard works:

Common. By specifying a common way for scripts to be accessed, CGI enables anyone, no matter their platform, to pass information to a CGI script.

Gateway. By defining the link or gateway between the script, the server, and other applications, CGI makes it possible for external programs to accept generalized input and pass information to other applications.

Interface. By describing the interface, or the way external programs can be accessed by users, CGI reduces the complex process of interfacing with external programs to a few basic procedures.

The developers of CGI worked these key concepts into the CGI standard to create a powerful and extendible advanced feature for Web publishers that shields readers of your publications from its complexities. The reader only has to click an area of an image map or submit a fill-out form after completing it. Everything after the click of the mouse button seems to happen automatically, and the reader doesn't have to worry about the how or why. As a Web publisher, understanding how CGI scripts work is essential, especially if you want to take advantage of the ways CGI can be used to create powerful Web publications.

Although the reader sees only the result of the submission or query, behind the scenes many things are happening. The following is a summary of what is taking place:

1. The reader's browser passes the input to the Web server.
2. The server, in turn, passes the input to a CGI script.
3. The CGI script processes the input, passes it off to another application if necessary, and sends the output to the Web server.
4. The Web server passes the output back to the reader's browser. The output from a CGI script can be anything from the results of a database search to a generated, completely new document based on the reader's input.

On UNIX systems, CGI scripts are located in a directory called `cgi-bin` in the `.usr` file system and CGI utilities are located in a directory called `cgi-src` in the `.usr` file system. On other systems, your Web server documentation will explain in what directories CGI scripts and utilities should be placed.

Choosing a Programming Language for Your CGI Scripts

CGI scripts are also called *gateway scripts.* The term *script* comes from the UNIX environment, in which shell scripts abound, but gateway scripts don't have to be in the format of a UNIX script. You can write gateway scripts in almost any computer language that produces an executable file. The most common languages for scripts are the following:

AppleScript
Bourne Shell
C Shell
C/C++
Java
Perl
PHP/FI
Python
Tcl
Visual Basic

The best programming language to write your script in is one that works with your Web server and meets your needs. Preferably, the language should already be available on the Web server and you should be proficient in it (or at least have some knowledge of the language). Keep in mind, most user input is in the form of text that must be manipulated in some way, which makes support for text strings and their manipulation critically important.

The easiest way to determine if a language is available is to ask the Webmaster or system administrator responsible for the server. As most Web servers operate on UNIX systems, you might be able to use one of the following UNIX commands to check on the availability of a particular language:

```
which
```

```
whereis
```

You can use either `which` or `whereis` on UNIX systems. You would type `which` or `whereis` at the shell prompt and follow the command with a keyword on which you want to search, such as the name of the programming language you want to use. To see if your UNIX server supports Perl, you could type one of the following:

```
which perl
```

```
whereis perl
```

As Perl, C/C++, and UNIX shell are the most popular languages for scripts, the sections that follow look briefly at these languages, with emphasis on why and when to use them. Each section contains a checklist for features and systems supported, which can be interpreted as follows:

- **Operating System Support.** The operating systems on which the language can be used.
- **Programming Level.** The difficulty of the language to use and learn.
- **Complexity of Processing.** The complexity of the tasks you can process with the language.
- **Text-Handling Capabilities.** The ability of the language to manipulate text and strings.

Using UNIX Shell

Operating system support: UNIX

Programming level: Basic

Complexity of processing: Basic

Text-handling capabilities: Moderately Advanced

The UNIX operating system is in wide use in business, education, and research sectors. There are almost as many variations of the UNIX operating system as there are platforms that use it. You will even find that platforms produced by the same manufacturer use different variants of the UNIX operating system. For example, DEC has variants for the DEC-Alpha, DECstation, and DEC OSF.

What these operating systems have in common is the core environment on which they are based. Most UNIX operating systems are based on Berkeley UNIX (BSD), AT&T System V, or a combination of BSD and System V. Both BSD and System V support the following three shell scripting languages:

Bourne shell

C shell

Korn shell

TIP

You can quickly identify the shell scripting language used by examining the first line of a script. Bourne shell scripts generally have this first line:

```
#!/bin/sh
```

C shell scripts generally have a blank first line or the following:

```
#!/bin/csh
```

Korn shell scripts generally have this first line:

```
#!/bin/ksh
```

All UNIX shells are interpreted languages, which means the scripts you create do not have to be compiled. Bourne shell is the most basic shell. C shell is an advanced shell with many features of the C programming language. Because Bourne shell uses a completely different syntax than C shell, scripts written in Bourne are not compatible with scripts written in C. If you create a script in Bourne shell and later want to use C shell to interpret the script, you must rewrite the script for C shell.

Many programmers often want to merge the simplicity of Bourne shell with the advanced features of C shell, and this is where Korn shell comes in handy. Korn shell has the same functionality as the Bourne shell and also incorporates many features of the C shell. Any shells you've written in Bourne shell can be interpreted directly by the Korn interpreter. This saves time rewriting a script when you later find you want to use a feature supported by Korn. Although the Korn shell is gaining popularity, Bourne and C shell are the two most widely used UNIX shells.

Some differences in Bourne, C, and Korn shell are visible only if you are at the shell prompt and using a particular shell. You can change your current shell any time from the shell prompt by typing the following:

`/bin/sh` to change to Bourne shell

`/bin/csh` to change to C shell

`/bin/ksh` to change to Korn shell

Usually, you will see differences among the various shells immediately. For example, the default command prompt for Bourne shell is the dollar sign, while the default command prompt for C shell is usually your host name and user ID followed by a colon. Beyond this, C shell supports a history function, aliasing of commands, and many other controls that the Bourne shell does not. However, to the CGI programmer, these differences are generally not important. Your primary concern should be the features that the shell directly supports and how scripts behave when executed in the shell.

Bourne shell is the smallest of the shells and the most efficient. Consequently, a Bourne shell script will generally execute faster and use fewer system resources. When you want more advanced features, such as arrays, you will want to use Korn shell. Korn shell has more overhead than Bourne shell and requires a few more system resources. When you want to make advanced function calls or assignments, you will want to use C shell. Because C shell is larger than Bourne and Korn shell, scripts written in C shell generally have higher overhead and use more system resources.

Take note that shell scripting is generally considered to be less secure and robust than traditional programming. This is because the commands are essentially operating system functions that have been extended to suit a particular purpose. If you are creating a script that handles either high security or high traffic operations, you might want to reconsider and choose a more rugged solution.

Although UNIX shells have good built-in facilities for handing text, such as sed, awk, and grep, they are not as powerful or extensible as traditional programming languages. You should consider using shell scripts when you want to perform simple tasks and moderately advanced text or file manipulation.

Using C/C++

Operating system support: UNIX, DOS, Windows, Macintosh, and others

Programming level: Advanced

Complexity of processing: Advanced

Text-handling capabilities: Advanced but awkward

When you want your scripts to perform complex tasks, you call in the big guns. Two of the most advanced languages used in CGI scripts are C and C++. C is the most popular programming language in use today. C++ is the object-oriented successor to C. Both C and C++ are advanced programming languages that require you to compile your scripts before you can use them. A major advantage of C and C++ is that they enjoy widespread use, and versions are available for virtually every operating system you can think of.

The primary time to use C (rather than C++) is when your scripts must execute swiftly and use minimal system resources. C was developed more than 20 years ago, and has been gaining popularity ever since. CGI programmers use C because compiled C programs are very small—tiny compared to programs with similar functionality developed in other languages. Small programs use minimal system resources and execute quickly. However, C is a very complex language with difficult-to-use facilities for manipulating text. Therefore, if you are not proficient in C, you should be wary of using C to perform advanced text string processing.

The primary time to use C++ is when certain functions of your scripts will be reused and when long-term development costs are a major concern. C++ is an object-oriented language that enables you to use libraries of functions. These functions form the core of your CGI scripts and can be reused in other CGI scripts. For example, you can use one function to sort the user's input, another function to search a database using the input, and another function to display the output as an HTML document. However, C++ is an object-oriented language that is very different from other languages. If you have not used an object-oriented language before, are not familiar with C, and plan to use C++ for your CGI scripts, you should be prepared for a steep learning curve.

Using Perl

Operating system support: UNIX, DOS, Windows, Macintosh, and others

Programming level: Advanced

Complexity of processing: Advanced

Text handling capabilities: Very Advanced

If you want to be on the inside track of CGI programming, you should learn and use the Practical Extraction and Report Language (Perl). Perl combines elements of C with UNIX shell features such as awk, sed, and grep to create a powerful language for processing text strings and generating reports. Because most of the processing done by CGI scripts involves text manipulation, Perl is rapidly becoming the most widely used language for CGI scripts. As with C and C++, a major advantage of Perl is its widespread use. Versions of Perl are available for virtually every operating system you can think of. You can use Perl to perform the following tasks:

- Easily manipulate files, text, and processes.
- Extract text strings and manipulate them in complex ways.
- Quickly and easily search files, databases, and indexes.
- Print advanced reports based on the data extracted.

Perl, like Bourne and C shell, is an interpreted language. However, Perl does not have the limitations of most interpreted languages. You can use Perl to manipulate extremely large amounts of data, and you can quickly scan files using sophisticated pattern-matching techniques. Perl strings are not limited in size. The entire contents of a file can be used as a single string. Perl's syntax is similar to C's. Many basic Perl constructs, like `if`, `for`, and `while` statements, are used just as you use them in C.

TIP

Like a UNIX shell script, a Perl script will usually specify the path to the source routines in the first line. Therefore, the first line of a Perl script should specify the path to where Perl is installed on the system. This path is usually one of the following:

```
#!/usr/local/perl

#!/usr/local/bin/perl
```

Perl is surprisingly easy to learn and use, especially if you know the basics of C or UNIX shell. Perl scripts are usually faster than UNIX shell scripts and slightly slower than compiled C/C++ scripts. You should use Perl whenever you have large amounts of text to manipulate.

Why Use CGI Scripts?

At this point, you might be worried about having to program. You might also be wondering why you would want to use gateway scripts at all. These are valid concerns. Learning a programming language isn't easy, but depending on what you want to do, you might never have to program at all. Dozens of ready-to-use CGI scripts are freely available on the Web. Often you can use these existing programs to meet your needs.

The primary reason to use CGI scripts is to automate what would otherwise be a manual and probably time-consuming process. Using CGI scripts benefits both you and your reader. The reader gets simplicity, automated responses to input, easy ways to make submissions, and fast ways to conduct searches. Gateway scripts enable you to automatically process orders, queries, and much more. CGI programs are commonly used for the following purposes:

- Process input, typically search strings, and output a document containing the results of the search.
- Validate user identification and password information and grant readers access to restricted areas of the Web site.
- Process input from image maps and direct the reader to associated documents.
- Add the reader's feedback or survey responses to a database or index.
- Track visitors to Web pages and post continually updated numbers to the Web page as it is accessed.
- Generate documents based on the type of browser the reader is using.
- Perform post-submission processing and possibly output results for the reader.

FrontPage WebBots perform many of the things that CGI scripts are used for. In fact, the only common CGI tasks FrontPage has not automated are the last three items in the previous list.

How CGI Scripts Work

Gateway scripts are used to process input submitted by readers of your Web publications. The input usually consists of environment variables that the Web server passes to the gateway script. Environment variables describe the information being passed, such as the version of CGI used on the server, the type of data, the size of the data, and other important information. Gateway scripts can also receive command-line arguments and standard input. To execute a CGI script, the script must exist on the server you are referencing. You must also have a server that is both capable of executing gateway scripts and configured to handle the type of script you plan to use.

Readers pass information to a CGI script by activating a link containing a reference to the script. The gateway script processes the input and formats the results as output that the Web server can use. The Web server takes the results and passes them back to the reader's browser. The browser displays the output for the reader.

The output from a gateway script begins with a header containing a directive to the server. Currently there are three valid server directives: `Content-type`, `Location`, and `Status`. The header can consist of a directive in the format of an HTTP header followed by a blank line. The blank line separates the header from the data you are passing back to the browser. Output containing `Location` and `Status` directives usually are a single line. This is because the directive contained on the `Location` or `Status` line is all that the server needs, and when there is no subsequent data, you do not need to insert a blank line. The server interprets the output, sets environment variables, and passes the output to the client.

Any transaction between a client and server has many parts. These parts can be broken down into the following eight steps:

1. Client passes input to a server.
2. Server sets environment variables pertaining to input.
3. Server passes input as variables to the named CGI script.
4. Server passes command line input or standard input stream to CGI script if present.
5. Script processes input.
6. Script returns output to the server. This output always contains a qualified header, and contains a body if additional data is present.
7. Server sets environment variables pertaining to output.
8. Server passes output to client.

Using CGI Scripts with FrontPage 98

FrontPage enables you to set properties for forms using the Form Properties dialog box. To use a CGI script, select the Send to other radio button, then choose the Custom ISAPI, NSAPI, CGI, or ASP Script form handler. Next, click the Options button. This opens the Options for

Custom Form Handler dialog box shown in Figure 24.12. As you can see, this dialog box has three fields: Action, Method, and Encoding Type. The next three sections discuss the values you can use for these fields.

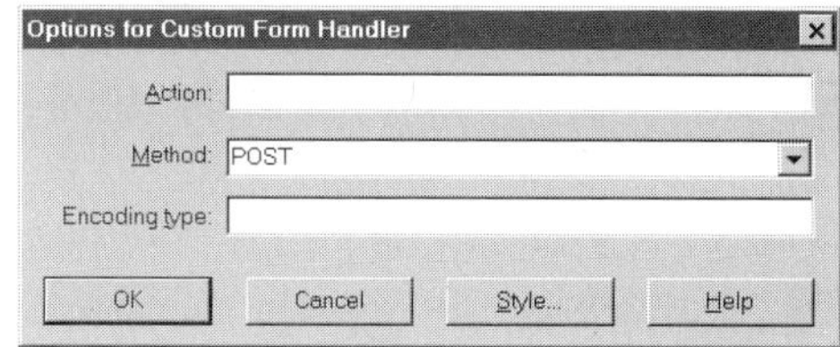

FIGURE 24.12.
The Options for Custom Form Handler dialog box is where you will specify parameters for your CGI script.

The Action Field

The Action field specifies the action to be performed when a form is submitted. As a form without a defined action will not be processed in any way, you should always specify a value for the Action field. You can define an action for your forms to be a URL to an executable CGI script and a form action.

By specifying the URL to a gateway script, you can direct input to the script for processing. The URL provides a relative or an absolute path to the script. Scripts defined with relative URLs are located on your local server. Scripts defined with absolute URLs can be located on a remote or local server. Most CGI scripts are located in the `cgi-bin` directory. You could access a script called `query.pl` in the `cgi-bin` directory by setting the Action field to the following:

```
http://www.mcp.com/cgi-bin/query.pl
```

The Method Field

The Method field specifies the way the form is submitted. There are currently two acceptable values:

```
GET
POST
```

The preferred submission method is `POST`, the default value used by FrontPage 98. `POST` sends the data as a separate input stream via the server to your gateway script. This enables the server to pass the information directly to the gateway script without assigning variables or arguments. Using this method, there is no limit to the amount of data that can be passed to the server.

`GET` appends the retrieved data to the script URL. The script URL and the data are passed to the server as a single URL-encoded input. Assigning the data to variables on a UNIX system means passing the data through the UNIX shell. The number of characters you can send to UNIX shell in a single input is severely limited. Some servers restrict the length of this type of input to 255 characters, which means you can append only a limited amount of data to a URL before truncation occurs. You lose data when truncation occurs, and losing data is a bad thing. Consequently, if you use `GET`, you should always ensure that the length of data input is small.

The Encoding Type Field

The Encoding type field specifies the MIME content type for encoding the form data. The client encodes the data before passing it to the server. The reason for encoding the data from fill-out form is not to prevent the data from being read, but rather to ensure that input fields can be easily matched to key values. By default, the data is `x-www-form-encoded`. This encoding is also called URL encoding. If you do not specify an encoding type, the default value is used automatically.

Although in theory you can use any valid MIME type, such as `text/plain`, most forms on the Web use the default encoding, `x-www-form-encoded`. MIME stands for Multipurpose Internet Mail Extensions. HTTP uses MIME to identify the type of object being transferred across the Internet. The purpose of encoding is to prevent problems you would experience when trying to manipulate data that has not been encoded in some way.

You do not have to set a value for this field. However, if you wanted to strictly specify the default encoding, you would set the Encoding type field to the following value:

```
x-www-form-encoded
```

Summary

FrontPage 98 makes it easy to handle form output and save the results without programming any code. So when you need to use forms, your best bet is to rely on FrontPage 98. However, if you need to go all out, you can use CGI to create a custom script. Whenever you create a form, you define the options for saving the results. You might also want to create your own confirmation page.

CHAPTER 25

Validating Forms

by William Robert Stanek

IN THIS CHAPTER

- How Does the Validation Process Work? *450*
- Selecting a Scripting Language for Validation *451*
- What Types of Form Information Can Be Validated? *451*
- Validating Input from Radio Buttons *451*
- Validating Input from Drop-Down Menus *453*
- Validating Input from One-Line and Scrolling Text Boxes *454*

When you validate a form, you check the contents of the form for accuracy and completion. The validation process ensures that you get the information you need from your customers, which in turn ensures the integrity of any databases based on the form input.

How Does the Validation Process Work?

The traditional way to validate a form is with a custom script. The custom script resides on the server and processes input submitted by a user. If the form is not filled out properly, the custom script creates a correction page that allows the user to correct or update the original data. After the data is updated or corrected, the user can resubmit the data, which is once again validated. This sometimes circular process between the server and the client browser is resource and time intensive—not to mention frustrating for users.

Enter FrontPage 98 and its built-in support for client-side validation of forms. With client-side form validation, there is no back-and-forth processing between the server and the client browser. All validation takes place on the user's system, which is efficient as well as time-saving.

Just as you need a script to validate your form on a server, you also need a script to validate your form on the end-user's system. For cross-platform compatibility, your script must be written in a client-side scripting language such as VBScript or JavaScript. Server-side languages are more platform specific and don't have as much of a general base as most scripting languages.

NOTE

You can learn more about VBScript and JavaScript in Part VII, "Adding Dynamic Content to Your Web Page."

Although you normally would need to write a validation routine on your own, FrontPage 98 can help you automate the validation process. Using components of the Script Wizard, FrontPage automatically generates routines to validate any form you create. Absolutely no programming is involved. You simply tell FrontPage the acceptable parameters for form elements and the Script Wizard generates your script.

TIP

The Script Wizard works in conjunction with the Validation WebBot. Together they fully automate the script generation process based on the parameters you select. This means the Validation WebBot and the Script Wizard run silently in the background. Although the Validation WebBot is used strictly for form validation, you can use the Script Wizard to generate other types of scripts. To learn more, see Chapter 38, "Scripting with JavaScript."

When you add validation to a form, you specify which fields are validated. The primary reason for this is that validation is handled in different ways for each type of form element. Individual validation of form fields also provides greater freedom. If a form has 10 fields and only one field is vital, you can add validation to the single vital field without adding validation to the other fields. If a form has five fields and all are vital, you can add validation to each field, but you must do so one field at a time.

A form is validated when a user clicks the form's Submit button. If a user does not properly complete a validated form field, he sees a prompt telling him to complete the form field and resubmit the form. If a user does not properly complete multiple validated form fields, he sees a single prompt telling him to complete the fields.

Selecting a Scripting Language for Validation

FrontPage can automatically generate validation scripts in either JavaScript or VBScript. By default, FrontPage is set to create validation scripts using JavaScript. Primarily this is because JavaScript is more widely supported than VBScript.

You can change the scripting language default in the FrontPage Explorer. To do so, select Web Settings from the Tools menu. Then in the Web Settings dialog box, click the Advanced tab. You can now set the default scripting language using the Language field's pull-down menu. Valid options are VBScript, JavaScript, and None. Only use the None option if you want to rely exclusively on the Validation WebBot, in which case your server must have FrontPage Server Extensions installed for use.

What Types of Form Information Can Be Validated?

FrontPage enables you to validate input from radio buttons, drop-down menus, one-line text boxes, and scrolling text windows. You cannot validate input from check boxes, push buttons, or images used as push buttons. If you think about it, these exclusions make sense.

Unlike radio buttons, check boxes are not grouped together, which allows the user to make multiple selections or no selections. Because all possibilities are acceptable, there is nothing to validate. Push buttons, whether they are regular or graphical, have only one associated action. The push button either submits or clears the contents of a form, and there is no need to validate pushing the button.

Validating Input from Radio Buttons

Although radio buttons are similar to check boxes, radio buttons are grouped together and only one radio button in a group can be selected. These properties of radio buttons are handled automatically by your browser. The problem with radio buttons is that in a traditional form, the publisher usually selects a default state. The default state ensures that a choice is selected when the form is submitted for processing.

With validation, you no longer need to rely on a default state. You simply validate the radio buttons in the group. If none of the radio buttons are selected when the form is submitted, a prompt appears telling the user to make a selection for the radio button group. Thus you will use validation of radio buttons to ensure that the user has made a choice. For example, if you want to gather statistical data about the average age of users who visit your site, you could use radio buttons with specific age ranges such as:

Under 18

19-25

26-35

Over 35

If you let users submit forms with a default option for age, you might be getting misleading information. Instead of most users falling into your default age group of 19–25 as you hoped, your data is misleading because some percentage of users are simply accepting the default and submitting the form. To get accurate data, you can use validation.

Before you add validation to a group of radio buttons, remove the default state. The default is selected when displayed in the FrontPage Editor. Thus for any radio button that is selected when displayed in the FrontPage Editor, you need to edit the associated properties dialog box and change the Initial State field to Not Selected. This ensures that the validation process can work.

Start by opening a page that contains your form; then open the properties dialog box for any radio button in the group to which you want to add validation. You can access the properties by selecting the radio button and then right clicking. The properties can be chosen from the pop-up menu that will appear. When you add validation to any radio button in a group, validation is added to the entire group. Click the Validate button. This opens the dialog box shown in Figure 25.1.

To turn on validation, select the check box labeled Data Required. In the Display Name field, enter a name for the radio button group. This name is used as part of the prompt users will see if they don't make a selection for this group. Close all open dialog boxes and validation is added to all radio buttons in the related group. Remember that this will only work if the radio buttons' default status is turned off.

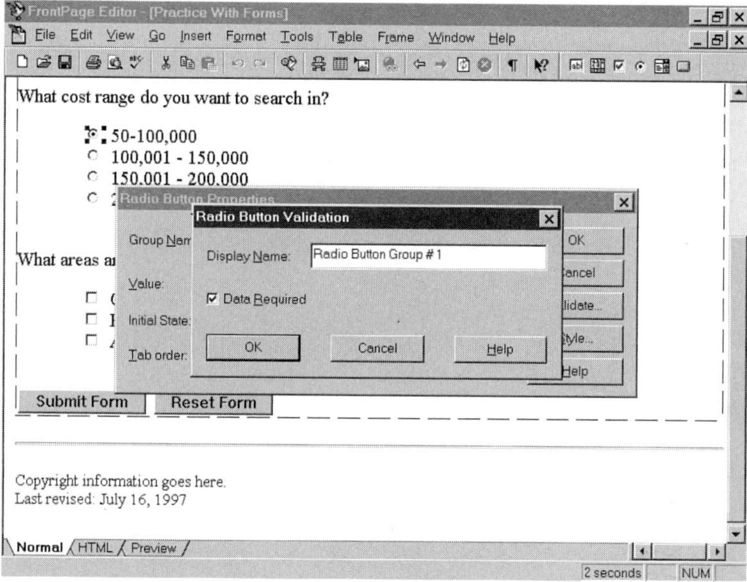

FIGURE 25.1.
Adding validation to a group of radio buttons.

Validating Input from Drop-Down Menus

In forms, drop-down menus typically allow users to make one or more selections. To give users a pointer that they should make a selection, the first menu item is often a dummy item that reads something like: Make a Selection. This means that sometimes you do not want the first menu item to be selected.

With validation, you can ensure that users make a selection on the drop-down menu, and disallow the first item as a valid selection. To add validation to a drop-down menu, open the page that contains your form and open the properties dialog box for the drop-down menu you want to validate. Click the Validate button. This opens the dialog box shown in Figure 25.2.

To turn on validation, select the checkbox labeled Data Required. In the Display Name field, enter a name for the drop-down menu. This name is used as part of the prompt users will see if they do not make a selection for this group. If you want to disallow the first menu item, select the check box labeled Disallow First Item. When you close all open dialog boxes, validation is added to your drop-down menu.

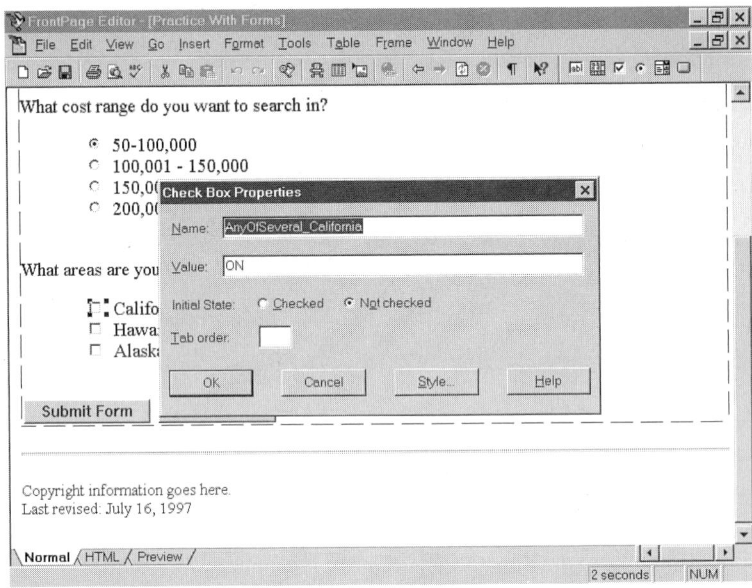

FIGURE 25.2.
Adding validation to a drop-down menu.

Validating Input from One-Line and Scrolling Text Boxes

When you think about it, one-line text boxes and scrolling text boxes serve almost identical functions. You use both types of text boxes to gather input from users. This input can be a mixture of alphabetic and numeric characters, such as an address, phone number, or comments.

Text boxes are the most versatile fields for your forms and, similarly, validation routines for text boxes are extremely versatile. Without validation, there is no way to restrict what the user enters into your text fields. For example, instead of the user's phone number, you get a bunch of Xs or you get a phone number without the area code. With validation, you can set the specific type of data you want to obtain. You can set minimum and maximum lengths of fields. You set the format for numeric data. You determine the acceptable range of values.

Because text box validation is extremely versatile, setting the validation parameters for text boxes is more involved than with other input fields. Start by opening the properties dialog box for the text box you want to validate. Click on the Validate button. This opens the dialog box shown in Figure 25.3. You can now define validation parameters for the text box.

FIGURE 25.3.
Adding validation to one-line and scrolling text boxes.

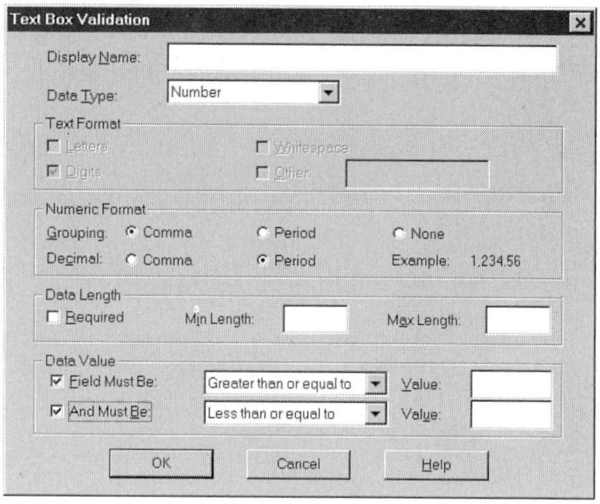

At the top of the dialog box are two key fields: Display Name and Data Type. As with other validated fields, the Display Name field is used as part of the prompt users see if they do not enter valid data for the text box. The Data Type field allows you to determine the acceptable types of data for the text box.

Initially, the Data Type field is set to No Constraints. This means there are no constraints on the type of data the user can enter into the text box. You can add constraints by making a selection from the associated pull-down menu. The other options on this menu are Text, Number, and Integer.

Selecting the Text option allows you to set further options in the Text Format area of the dialog box. Similarly, selecting the Number option allows you to set additional options in the Numeric Format area of the dialog box. Integer is a restrictive option that ensures only whole integers can be entered and disallows the entry of decimal values.

At first, it might not seem obvious at what time you would choose one data type over another and you might be tempted to simply use the No Constraints option. The key here is to use the data type that makes the most sense for the type of information you want to gather from the user. If there truly are no constraints for the text box—as in the case of comments—use the No Constraints option. Otherwise, use a more limiting constraint.

Validating Text Data Types

The text data type is great for addresses, phone numbers, and dates. When you select the text data type, properties in the Text Format field become available. You can select any combination of the following properties:

Letters. Allows the user to enter alphabetic characters into the text.

Digits. Allows the user to enter numeric characters into the text box.

Whitespace. Allows the user to enter spaces. Without selecting this option, you are effectively restricting the user's entry to a single word or number.

Other. Allows you to specify the additional characters that can be entered into the text box without causing an error in validation. Typical characters you might add include commas, periods, hyphens, and back slashes.

When you create address elements in forms, you will usually have separate elements for street address, city, state, country, and ZIP code. Here are some guidelines you can use for acceptable text formatting and validation:

Street address. Select the Letters, Digits, Whitespace, and Other fields. In the Other field enter `.-/`.

City. Select the Letters, Whitespace, and Other fields. In the Other field enter `-`.

Country. Select the Letters, Whitespace, and Other fields. In the Other field enter `-`.

ZIP code. Select the Digits and Other fields. In the Other field enter `-`.

You can use the Text data type to validate phone numbers as well. The guidelines you use for formatting depend on the style of phone number you expect. Here are typical styles for phone entries paired with formatting constraints you might want to use:

(XXX)XXX-XXXX. Select Digits and Other. In the Other field enter `()-`.

XXX-XXX-XXXX. Select Digits and Other. In the Other field enter `-`.

TIP

Be sure to give the user an example of the format you expect, such as: Please enter your phone number in the format 123-456-7890.

Another use for the text data type is for validating date entries. As with phone numbers, you should state explicitly the style you expect, such as dd/mm/yy. If you wanted data entries to be in this format, select the Digits and Other fields. In the Other field enter: `/`.

Validating Numeric Data Types

Numeric data is great for strict number entries and can be in integer or decimal format. As you know, integers are whole numbers such as 3, 5, and 7. Decimals are numbers such as 3.5 or 4.25. Because it doesn't make sense to allow entry of decimals with integers, the Decimal field is grayed and not applicable if you select the Integer data type. If you select the Number data type, both the Grouping and Decimal fields are usable in the Numeric Format field.

The Grouping field allows for entries of multiple numbers separated by commas or periods. If you select None for the Group field, multiple number entries are not acceptable.

The Decimal field defines whether the decimal place is expressed as a comma or a period. Although the period is the traditional designator in the U.S., the standard is different in other countries.

If you try to change either field, you will notice that the Grouping and Decimal fields are interrelated—you cannot group with commas and express the decimal place as a comma, or group with periods and express the decimal place as a period. Based on your selections the Example field will display a sample number that adheres to the conventions you've defined.

Restricting the Length of Data Entries

Using the Data Length area of the Text Box Validation dialog, you can set restrictions on the minimum and maximum length of the text entry. Checking the minimum length of data helps ensure that users enter correct information. For example, if you are looking for a phone number with area code, a valid entry would be at least 12 characters long. Checking the maximum length restricts the user from entering too much information.

By setting the minimum and maximum lengths to the same value, you ensure the user enters the exact number of characters you expect. Going back to the date entry example in the format dd/mm/yy, you would want the acceptable minimum and maximum length to be 8 characters. Be sure to select the check box labeled Required to ensure that your length rules are enforced.

TIP

As you try to determine the acceptable values for input, keep your international visitors in mind. For example, international phone numbers with country codes are longer than 12 characters.

Checking Input Values

Validation really pays off when you need to ensure entries are within specific value ranges. Using the Data Value field, you can ensure both numeric and alphabetic entries are within acceptable ranges. If you are looking for an answer between 1 and 100, you do not want values less than 1 or more than 100. If you want the user to choose answer A, B, or C, you do not want him to enter D.

You can check for parameters within specific ranges using two validation constraints:

Field Must Be. Use this constraint to specify the start of the acceptable range.

And Must Be. Use this constraint to specify the end of the acceptable range or an additional constraint.

To specify the start of the range, select the Field Must Be check box. Then enter a starting value for the range in the Value field. Finally, select the applicable rule, such as the entry must be greater than the specified value.

To specify the end of the range or an additional constraint, select the And Must Be check box. Then enter a constraining value for the range in the Value field. Finally, select the applicable rule, such as the entry must be less than the specified value.

Summary

By validating form fields, you can ensure the data submitted in a form is what you expect it to be. Whenever you validate form fields, you are relying on the FrontPage WebBot or a script to perform the necessary validation. Because all of this process takes place on the user's computer, the user doesn't have to go through the monotony of back-and-forth processing between the server and the client browser.

Search Engines and Indexing Your Web Site

by William Robert Stanek

IN THIS CHAPTER

- Introducing Search Engines and Indexed Databases *460*
- Working with the Search Bot *461*
- Adding the Search Bot to Your Web *463*
- When Not to Use the Search Bot *465*

The hypertext facilities of the World Wide Web put the world's most powerful search engines at your fingertips. Search engines are the gateways to the vast storehouses and databases available on the Web. Thousands of Web search engines are used every day, and if you've browsed the Web, you know that online searches are easy to perform. You simply enter keywords and press Enter, and the search engine takes over.

FrontPage 98 includes a powerful search engine in the form of a WebBot. This WebBot, called the Search bot, provides a full text-searching capability for your Web site. When the user submits a form containing search words, the Search bot returns a list of all pages in the current web that contain matches for the search words. When you want to add a search engine to your web with minimum fuss, the Search bot is the way to go.

Introducing Search Engines and Indexed Databases

A *search engine* is an application specifically designed and optimized for searching databases. Search engines can race through megabytes of information in nanoseconds. They achieve this terrific speed and efficiency thanks to an application called an indexer.

An *indexer* is an application specifically designed and optimized for indexing files. Using the index built by the indexer, the search engine can jump almost immediately to sections of the database containing the information you are looking for. Thus, creating an indexed database of documents at your Web site requires two applications: a search engine and an indexer.

What Are Search Engines and How Are They Used?

Hundreds of search engines are used in commercial and proprietary applications. Search engines are usually part of a larger application, such as a database management system.

When Web publishers looked for indexing and searching solutions, they looked at the search engines available and found that most of them were not well suited for use on the World Wide Web, primarily because these search engines weren't designed to be used on distributed networks.

One solution Web publishers did find is the *Wide Area Information Server*, or *WAIS*. WAIS is a database retrieval system that searches indexed databases. The databases can contain just about any type of file, including text and HTML. The WAIS interface is easy to use and you can perform a search on any topic simply by entering a keyword and pressing Enter. When you press Enter, the WAIS search engine takes over. The FrontPage Search bot is based on WAIS and allows you to search your web with keywords.

What Are Indexers and How Are They Used?

The index for *Microsoft FrontPage 98 Unleashed* is an invaluable resource for quickly finding information in this book. Using the index, you can quickly find the topic or subtopic you want to learn more about. You do this by following an alphabetical listing of keywords selected by an indexer who combed the manuscript in search of the gems you would be interested in.

The indexer used the text of the entire book to create an alphabetical list of keywords and related concepts. The alphabetical listing is broken down into categories and subcategories. The first categories are broad and divided based on the letters A to Z. Next, the broad categories are subdivided based on keywords. The keyword categories are sometimes further divided based on related concepts. For quick reference, a page number is associated with keywords and their related concepts. You've probably noticed that articles (such as a, an, and the) and prepositions (such as in, with, and to) are never listed in the index. This is because the indexer has a list of hundreds of common words that should be excluded from the index because they occur too often to be helpful.

A computer-coded indexer builds an index in much the same way. The indexer application uses a list of common words to figure out which words to exclude from the index, searches through the list of documents you specified, and finally builds an index containing the relevant associations among the remaining words within all the specified documents. As most indexers build a full-text index based on your documents, the index is often larger than the original files. For example, if your Web site has 15MB of data in 125 documents, the indexer would create an index slightly larger than 15MB.

Whenever you create a web in FrontPage 98, a text index is automatically created. Any time you save a new page to the web or recalculate links in your web, FrontPage 98 updates this text index.

Working with the Search Bot

The Search bot enables you to easily perform searches within your web. To do this, the Search bot relies on an indexer to create a text index for your web. The indexer creates the text index using the document files found in the public folders of your web. Because the indexer ignores private folders, you do not have to worry about private data showing up in search results. Using the Search bot, you can enter a query using the simple one-box form (see Figure 26.1).

By default the Search bot finds all documents matching any keyword you enter in the query box. You can enter as many keywords as you want on the query line. Because the search is not case-sensitive, the keywords do not have to be capitalized as shown. If you type in two keywords, the Search bot assumes that you want to search on either word. Therefore, to search the index for documents containing either `WAIS` or `Web`, you could use the following:

```
WAIS Web
```

Although you could specify the `OR` explicitly in a search, such as `WAIS OR Web`, you generally do not have to. Again, this is because the `OR` is assumed whenever you do not specify otherwise. To search the index only for documents containing both `WAIS` and `Web`, you could use the following:

```
WAIS AND Web
```

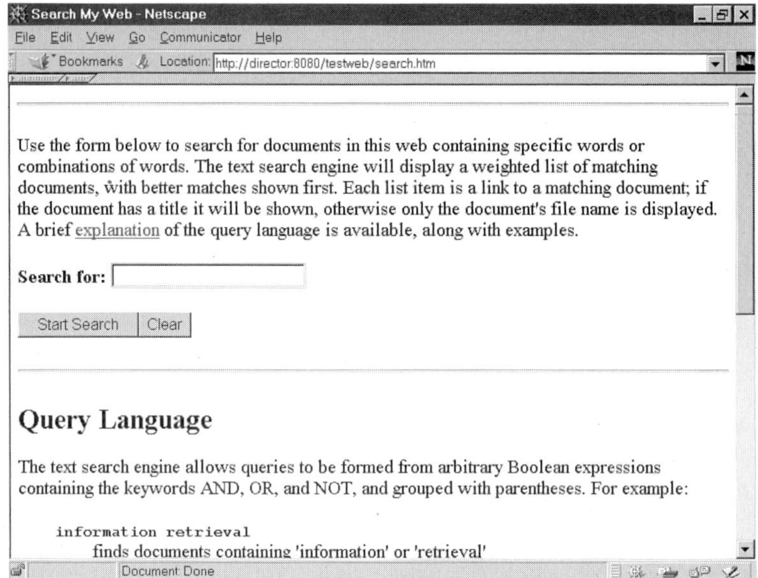

FIGURE 26.1.
The FrontPage 98 Search bot.

Here, the `AND` tells the Search bot you are only interested in documents containing the words `WAIS` and `Web`. You can combine the basic functions of logical `OR` and logical `AND` in many ways. Because you will often be searching for material on a specific subject, you can use multiple keywords related to the subject to help you get better results on your searches. For example, if you are looking for publishers on the Web, you might try the following keywords:

```
book
fiction
magazine
nonfiction
publisher
publishing
```

The Search bot also allows you to search for a file that contains one word but not another. The search word you use to perform a selective search is `NOT`. Using the following search, you could find pages containing the keyword `WAIS` but not the keyword Web:

```
WAIS NOT Web
```

The final type of search you can perform with the Search bot is to search for word prefixes using the asterisk character. To search for words starting with `info`, you would use the following search:

```
info*
```

If you use the default configuration for the Search bot, the search results are returned as you see them in Figure 26.2. Here, you see a one-line summary of each page containing the search parameters; included in the summary are the page title, page modification date, and file size.

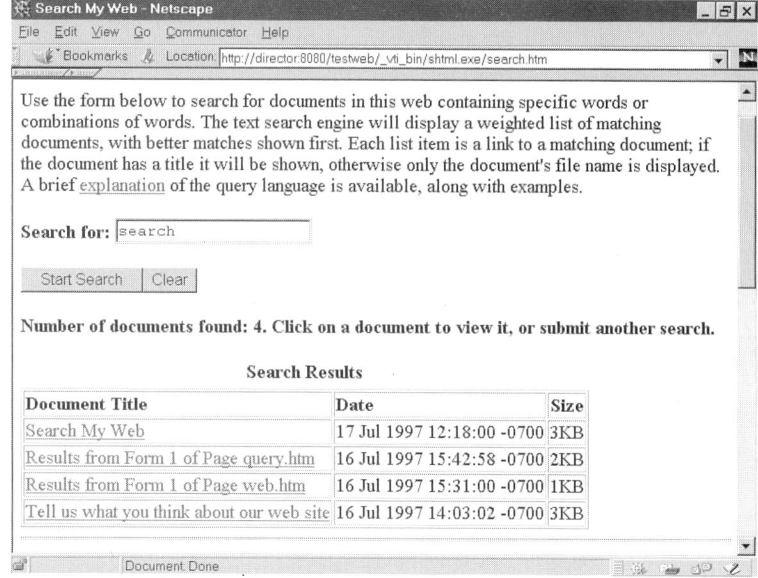

FIGURE 26.2.
The results of a search using the default setup.

Adding the Search Bot to Your Web

The Search bot provides a full text-searching capability for your web. Any document files that you do not want users to search, such as header and footer pages, should be placed in a subdirectory called `_private`. The Search bot does not search in this directory. You can add the Search bot to your web in a separate search page or as part of any page you want.

Creating the Search Page

To create a separate search page, open the New dialog box, then select the Search Page template. When you use the Search Page template, you do not need to make any further modifications. Your search page will look just like the one shown in Figure 26.1 and the search results will be formatted just as you see them in Figure 26.2.

The Search bot can also create its own search form in any page that you choose. To insert the Search bot and its associated search form into a page, open the page for editing in the FrontPage Editor, then select Insert|Active Elements|Search Form. This opens the Search Form Properties dialog box. If you simply click OK right now, you will end up with a search interface like the one shown in Figure 26.1 and your search results will be formatted just as you see them in Figure 26.2.

Configuring the Search Bot and the Search Form

To customize the search form and the search results, change the Search bot's default property values. To do this, double-click the search form. Now, you can use the Search Form Properties dialog box to configure the Search bot and the search form. This dialog box has two tabs: Search Form Properties and Search Results.

The Search Form Properties tab, displayed in Figure 26.3, lets you specify the way the search form looks in your Web page. The form is very simple, with a label for the input box, a one-line text box that accepts input, and two labeled buttons. To change the way the form looks, simply change the default labels. Here's a list of the fields and how they are used:

Label for Input	The label for the one-line text box. The default is Search for:.
Width in Characters	The width of the one-line text box. By default the character width of the text box is 20.
Label for "Start Search" Button	The label for the button that starts the search. The default is Start Search.
Label for "Clear" Button	The label for the button that clears the form. The default is Reset.

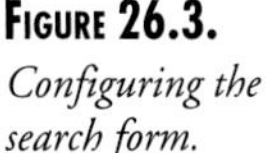
FIGURE 26.3.
Configuring the search form.

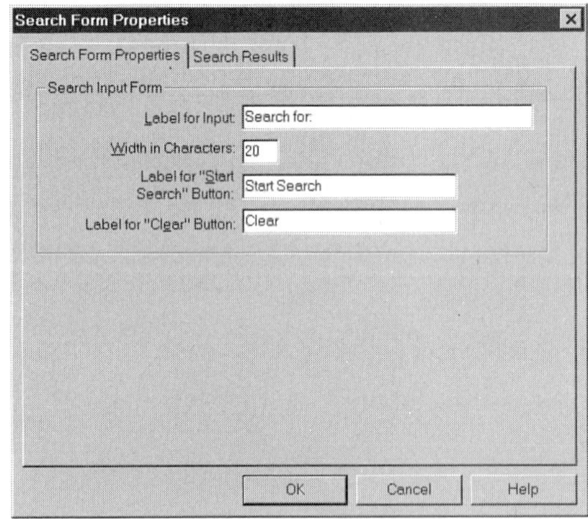

The Search Results tab, displayed in Figure 26.4, defines the ways you can manipulate the results of a search. You can modify these criteria within the Search Results tab. Results appear based on matches for the search words and can be ranked by the following criteria:

Word List to Search	Use the keyword `All` to allow users to search all the document files in this web, except those placed in hidden folders. If the web has a discussion group, enter the name of the discussion group folder to allow users to search only entries in the discussion group.

Score (Closeness of Match)	The scoring mechanism tries to rank the relevancy of the page based on the number of times the search words appear on the page.
File Date	The date the file was created or the last time the file was updated.
File Size (in K bytes)	The size of the file.

TIP

Although scoring is the most common way to rank the relevancy of files, many Web publishers prefer to use all three ranking statistics. The file's modification date tells the user how current the document is. The file's size indicates how much data the file contains.

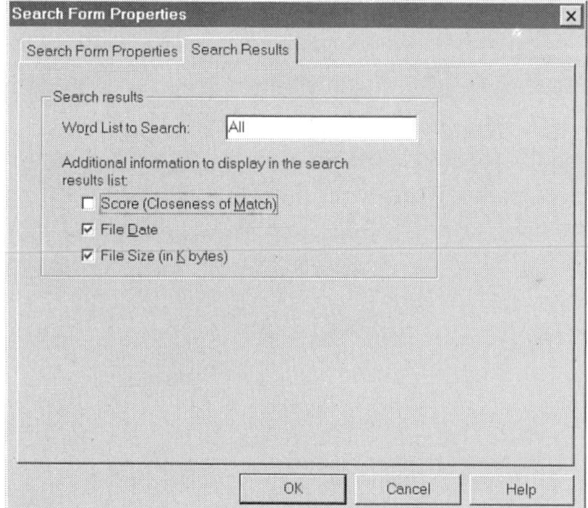

FIGURE 26.4.
Configuring the search results.

When Not to Use the Search Bot

Although the Search bot is a great search engine, the following are two specific instances in which you might have to (or want to) use a different type of search engine:

- When you cannot use FrontPage Server Extensions with your current Web server software, or do not plan to install the server extensions for your server
- When you have advanced or unique needs for which the Search bot is not well suited

In the first case, you will probably know immediately that you cannot use the Search bot. However, before you decide against the Search bot, obtain the most current list of servers supported by FrontPage 98 extensions. You might be pleasantly surprised when you discover that extensions are available for your server and you have only to download and install them. You can find this list of available server extensions in the FrontPage area of Microsoft's Web site, at the following address:

```
http://www.microsoft.com/frontpage/
```

In the second case, you might have a more difficult time determining when the Search bot will not meet your needs. Full-text searches are powerful, and the results are displayed quickly using the Search bot. In most cases, the Search bot is exactly what you need at your Web site. However, if your needs are advanced or unique, the Search bot will not meet your needs. For example, if you want to display the search results in a customized format that includes a list of keywords used in the matching pages, you would not want to use the Search bot.

When you have advanced needs, you will want to look at installing your own search engine. Generally, the search engine will be in the form of a custom script that you must install on your server.

Summary

When you want to add a search engine to your Web site, the FrontPage Search bot makes the job a snap. Text searches of your web depend on the FrontPage indexer to work overtime behind the scenes to keep your web's text index up to date. The Search bot itself handles the job of using the search keyword to find what users are looking for.

VI
Part

In This Part

- Creating Web Pages with FrontPage Templates 469
- Guest Books and Feedback 477
- Instant Web Sites with FrontPage 98 487
- Building a Discussion Web 495
- Creating a Customer Support Web 511
- Creating a Project Web 523
- Establishing a Corporate Presence 533
- Automation with FrontPage Components 545
- User Registration and Restricted Webs 559

Templates, Wizards, and FrontPage Components

CHAPTER 27

Creating Web Pages with FrontPage Templates

by William Robert Stanek

IN THIS CHAPTER

- Saving Time with Templates 470
- Basic Templates 471
- Search Page 475
- Confirmation Forms 476

FrontPage 98 includes dozens of templates to help you create powerful Web pages. Not only will creating Web pages with templates save you time, but the templates themselves are guides that can help you design better pages. This chapter discusses the basics of using templates, with emphasis on how to use them as the basis for Web pages both within your corporate intranet and on the World Wide Web. Even if you do not plan to use templates, you should read this chapter to gain an understanding of the types of pages used on corporate intranets and Web sites.

Saving Time with Templates

A template is an outline for a specific type of page that often contains guidelines to make development of the page easier. Although these guidelines do not ask specific questions concerning design and layout of the page, they do cover the major issues you should consider when developing a specific type of page. Because these templates were designed by a team of experts, you gain from them valuable insight into the specific areas your page should cover.

As you know, you create pages in the FrontPage Editor. To base a new page on a template, select New from the File menu and then choose the template on which you want to base your page. Alternatively, you can press Ctrl+N.

Using a template, you can cut an hour or more off the development time of a single page. Webmasters who maintain their own site or a corporate intranet site will find the time savings invaluable, especially when they complete complex projects ahead of schedule and under budget. In the fast-paced profession of Web site design, where cost is usually the deal maker or breaker, the savings you can pass on to your customers by starting with a template could make all the difference in landing the contract.

Generally, all templates include default headings and text that you usually have to replace with headings and text specific to your document. To better understand how templates can save you time and money, let's look at the templates used in FrontPage. By examining each of the templates, you will gain a thorough understanding of what types of pages are used at Web sites and how those pages are designed.

NOTE

When you create documents with templates, FrontPage 98 automatically adds comments that guide you through the process of designing the page. To allow you to see the page as it will appear in the reader's browser, these preset comments do not appear in the figures in this chapter.

Basic Templates

FrontPage 98 includes a set of basic templates that help you create advanced pages at the click of a button. You will find that these templates are the ones you will use most often. The following is a list of a few of the FrontPage 98 templates:

- Normal Page
- Bibliography
- Confirmation Form
- Feedback Form
- Frequently Asked Questions
- Guest Book
- Search Page
- Table of Contents
- User Registration

A few of these templates are explored in this chapter.

Normal Page

If you have been following the examples in this book, you have probably already used the Normal Page template. All this template does is create a blank page for you. By default, the Normal Page template is selected when you open the New dialog box. To use this page, you simply press Enter or click the OK button without making a selection.

To redefine the Normal Page template, select Save As from the File menu. In the Save As dialog box, click As Template. This opens the dialog box shown in Figure 27.1. By default, the template name is that of the template you are using currently. If you want to redefine the template, click OK. When FrontPage 98 displays a warning dialog box that asks whether you really want to overwrite the template, select Yes.

TIP

Not only can you redefine templates in FrontPage 98, but you can also create entirely new templates. Webmasters who maintain multiple sites might want to define variations of the Normal Page template for use with each of their sites. In this way, you can start with a base page for each of your webs.

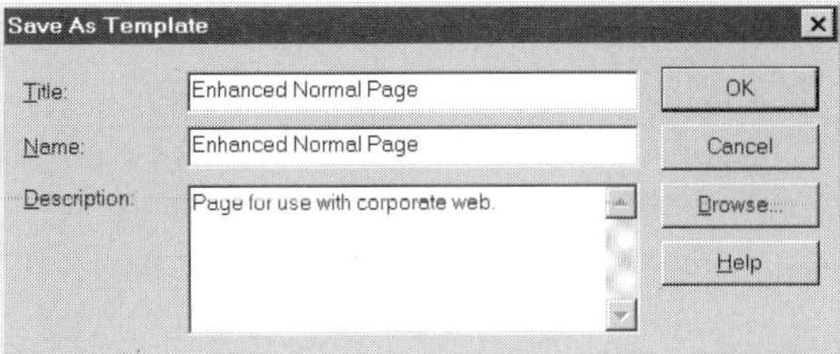

FIGURE 27.1.
Redefining a template.

Frequently Asked Questions

Frequently Asked Questions (FAQ) pages are very common on the Web. Generally, a FAQ is a list of frequently asked questions and their answers. Although an FAQ can cover a broad range of loosely related topics, usually an FAQ exhaustively explores a single topic, such as how to make an MPEG movie, or the options in digital sound. Many companies that sell commercial software products develop FAQs that explore the uses and benefits of the products.

Figure 27.2 shows the Frequently Asked Questions template. Again, you should carefully replace the title text so you do not accidentally delete links and bookmarks. You should add new questions to the end of the Table of Contents section, and then add a new section in the body of the document that answers each question. The goal behind creating a FAQ is to answer every question that a user commonly has. If your business or Web site leaves users scratching their heads in puzzlement, take advantage of the FAQ template to clear the mist.

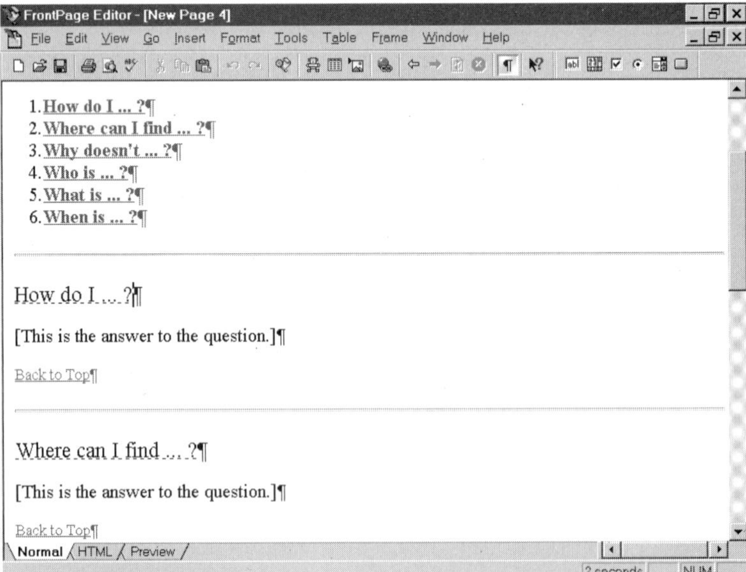

FIGURE 27.2.
The Frequently Asked Questions template.

To save time when entering a new question, you can copy the entire text of a previous question and then update the associated link properties. To save time when creating a new section, you can copy one of the existing sections and then update the associated bookmark information. Be sure that both the link name in the Table of Contents section and the bookmark name in the new section match.

Throughout the document, you will find links labeled Back to Top. Readers can use these links to jump to the top of the Page Title bookmark.

Table of Contents

Like an index, a table of contents is useful but usually difficult to build and maintain. FrontPage 98 allows you to instantly add a table of contents to your web using the Table of Contents template.

FrontPage 98 builds the table of contents by examining all the links contained in the top-level page you specify and then recursively examining the lower level pages for links to other pages. If the web contains pages that are not linked to any other page, these pages are either excluded (by default) or included (by selecting a property setting when you build the table of contents).

To build a table of contents for the current web, either create a new page based on the Table of Contents template or select Insert|Table of Contents. To set properties for the table of contents, open the Table of Contents Properties box shown in Figure 27.3, by double-clicking the table of contents section.

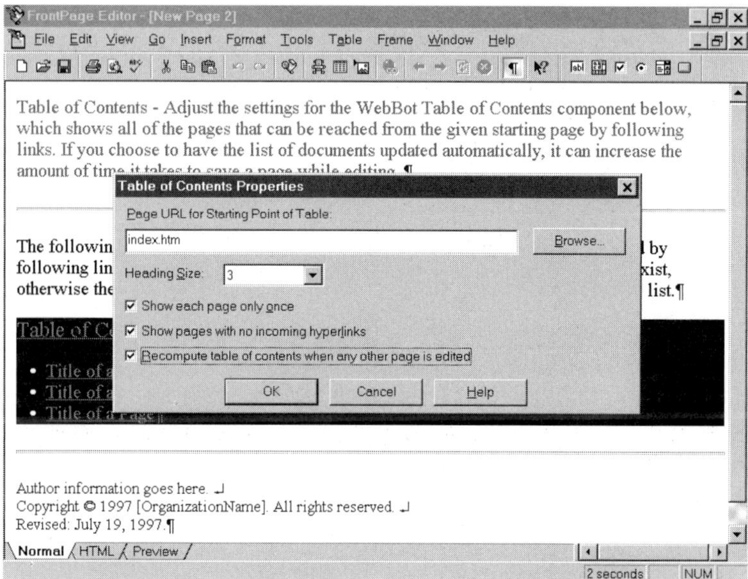

FIGURE 27.3.
Setting properties for the table of contents page.

Each of the fields in the properties box enables you to customize the table of contents. You can use these fields as follows:

`Page URL for Starting Point of Table`	Enables you to specify the URL of the Point of Table top-level page you want to build the table of contents from. If you do not know the page URL, click the Browse button to get a list of pages in the current web.
`Heading Size`	Enables you to specify the size of the heading to use for the first entry in the table of contents. If you want no headings, select none.
`Show each page only once`	Ensures that each page appears only once in the table of contents. Otherwise, pages linked from more than one page will be listed once for each link.
`Show pages with no incoming hyperlinks`	Ensures pages that have no internal links are not displayed.
`Recompute table of contents when any other page edited`	Ensures that the table of contents is automatically updated when any page in the Web is edited.

NOTE

Rebuilding the table of contents can be a time-consuming process, especially for large webs. You can manually regenerate the table of contents by opening and saving the page containing the table of contents.

Bibliography

The Bibliography template is shown in Figure 27.4. You will use this template to create a bibliography for your online publication. Unlike print publications, your online publication can contain hypertext links to the bibliography page. You can also include links to additional reference sites or to works on the Web. Whenever you are reproducing material from another source (be it Web, print, or another medium), be sure to include a bibliography entry. Using the FrontPage 98 template, you can make short work of giving credit where credit is due.

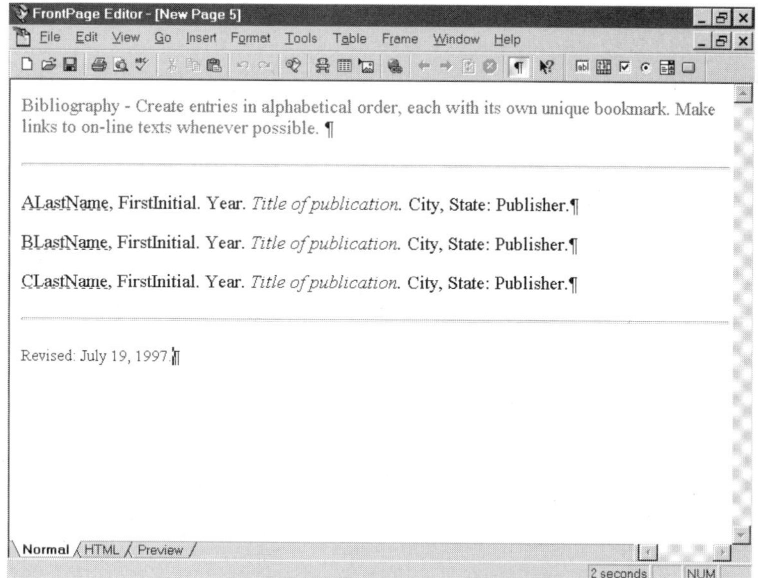

FIGURE 27.4.
The Bibliography template.

Pages with Newspaper and Magazine Style Layout

If you are looking to create a Web page that is more than a simple up-down, left-right layout, FrontPage 98 has many templates for creating pages with advanced layouts. These templates emulate conventional print publications, like a newspaper. In the New dialog box, these are the templates that mention columns and menus in their titles, such as the Two Column Body with Contents on Left template. When you have advanced page design needs or when you want to create a page that has a well-designed layout, the column and menu templates are usually good starting points. Be careful when using these templates in tight screen real-estate, especially if you are using shared borders throughout your Web site.

Search Page

The Search Page template creates a page that lets you search through the full text of your Web site. Whenever you save a Web page or recalculate links, FrontPage 98 creates a text index for your site. Using the Search bot and the search page, you can allow users to access and retrieve information from this index.

If you plan to use a search page, the Search Page template is the perfect starting point. The template page includes the search form and detailed information on the search process and query syntax. (See Chapter 26, "Search Engines and Indexing Your Web Site," for complete details.)

Confirmation Forms

Whenever a user submits a form, a confirmation page can be displayed to show that the form was submitted successfully. This page uses a FrontPage Component, called the Confirmation Field bot, to automatically insert values for input fields.

Most Web publishers use confirmation pages, and you probably will want to as well. You can use the Confirmation Form template as the basis for your default confirmation page. Be sure to update the page to reflect the fields in your form. (Configuring the Confirmation Field bot is covered in Chapter 34, "Automation with FrontPage Components.")

NOTE

Keep in mind that if you do not specify a confirmation page, FrontPage 98 creates one automatically. You define the URL to the confirmation page in the Confirmation tab of the Options for Saving Results of Form box. On the page with the form for which you would like to create a confirmation page, open the Form Properties box, and then access the Options for Saving Results of Form box by clicking the Options button. From there, go to the Confirmation tab. In the URL of Confirmation Page field, enter the name of the confirmation page.

Summary

Old and new Web publishers alike might want to base their pages on an appropriate template. Not only will creating Web pages with templates save you time, but the templates themselves are guides that can help you design better pages. You can use them to publish on the corporate intranet or on the World Wide Web.

For information on creating your own templates and customizing existing templates, see Chapter 57, "Creating Your Own Templates."

CHAPTER 28

Guest Books and Feedback

by William Robert Stanek

IN THIS CHAPTER

- Creating and Using a Guest Book 478
- Building a Better Guest Book 482
- Getting Feedback 484

Getting input to your site from visitors is important. Using guest books and feedback forms, you can learn what users really think of your Web site. A guest book is a simple method of collecting opinions and comments about your site; its operation mirrors a traditional hotel guest book almost exactly. While comments in a guest book are generally displayed for all the world to see, feedback is usually private and not shared. So when you set about creating a guest book or feedback form, you really need to consider whether you want a public or private forum. As you surf the Web, you will find that many sites use guest books. Guest books have been around for centuries, and it should be no surprise that Web entrepreneurs adopted the idea to obtain both a listing of visitors and comments from those visitors.

Creating and Using a Guest Book

Creating and using a guest book is not a simple act. Traditionally, you need some advanced functionality to store and retrieve the guest book entries and information. It's also important to realize how and why you would want to use a guest book. If you don't want comments from your users, and are just incorporating a guest book because it's a fad, then you probably don't need one.

Getting Started with the Guest Book

Using the Guest Book template, you can create a guest book instantly. All you need to do is open a new page based on the Guest Book template and save it to your web. Now you have a Guest Book like the one shown in Figure 28.1.

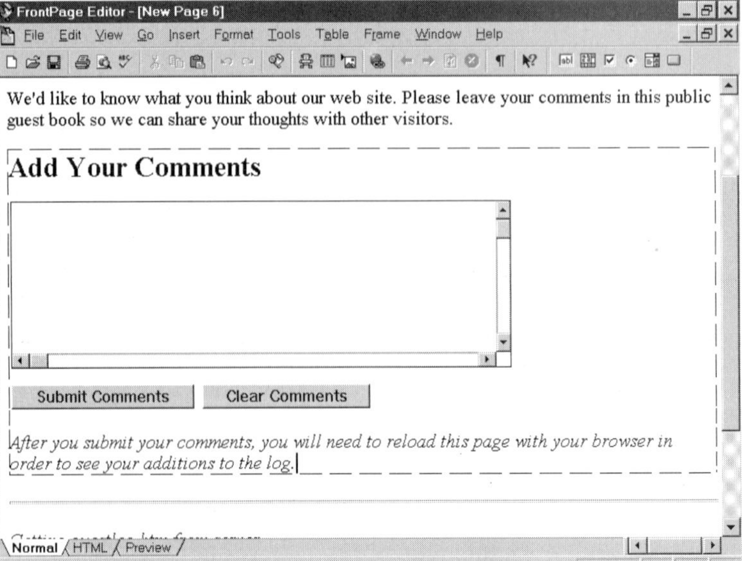

FIGURE 28.1.
The Guest Book template.

If you do nothing else, your guest book entries will be logged in a page called `guestlog.htm` and the text of this log page will be automatically included in the body of the guest book entry page. Thus, when users access the guest book entry page, they will see the submission form and current guest book entries. After users submit a new entry, they will need to reload the page to see their entry. As you will see, this simple yet functional solution is easily modified to give your guest book and your web a more sophisticated look and design.

The mechanism that automatically includes the text from the log page is called an Include Page Component, or simply the Include bot. You will find this component hidden at the bottom of the guest book page, between the two horizontal lines immediately after your guest book form. To see the current settings for the bot, double-click the component found between the two horizontal lines to bring up the properties box shown in Figure 28.2.

NOTE

While you can use the Include Page Components Properties box to define the name of the page to include in the guest book, the page URL should always match the file name you assign in the Send to text box of the Form properties box. Also, unless you have more than one guest book in the current web, there is really no reason to change the default setting and filename.

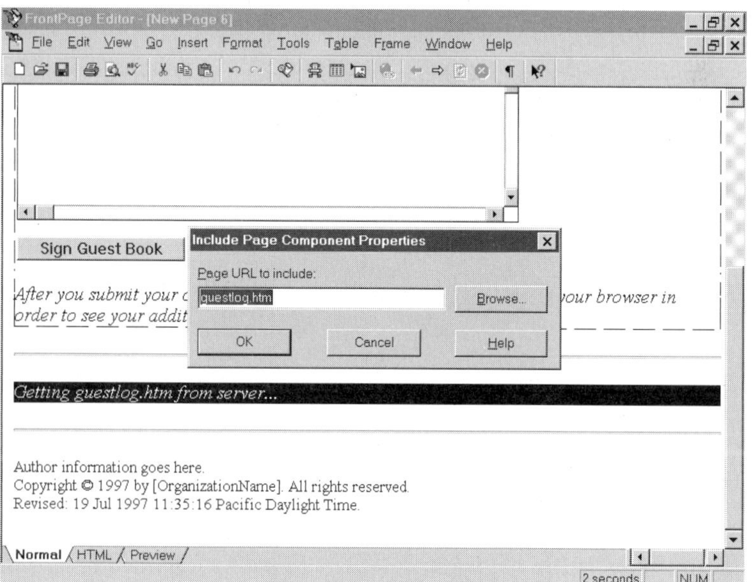

FIGURE 28.2.
Working with the Include bot.

Enhancing the Guest Book

Because the default template for the guest book is very plain, you definitely want to jazz it up a bit. To start, I recommend you add a level one header to the page that says something like `Please Sign Our Guest Book` or `We Welcome Your Comments for Our Guest Book`.

Next, you probably want to change the default text on the push buttons. The submission button currently reads `Submit Comments` and the reset button reads `Clear Comments`. Definitely change that to something better; after all, this is a guest book not really a feedback form. For the submission button, you might want to use something like `Sign Guest Book` or `Add Entry to Guest Book`. For the reset button, you might want to use `Clear` or `Start Over`. You can change all of these by selecting the button in question and then right-clicking on it. You should then choose Form Field Properties from the pop-up menu that appears. From there, you can change all sorts of aspects of the button's appearance, including its label.

Because most guest books ask a user to fill in his name and e-mail address, you should add a way for a users to enter this information. Two input fields should do the trick. Be sure to insert descriptive text before the input fields and give the input fields appropriate field names.

An example of an enhanced guest book is shown in Figure 28.3.

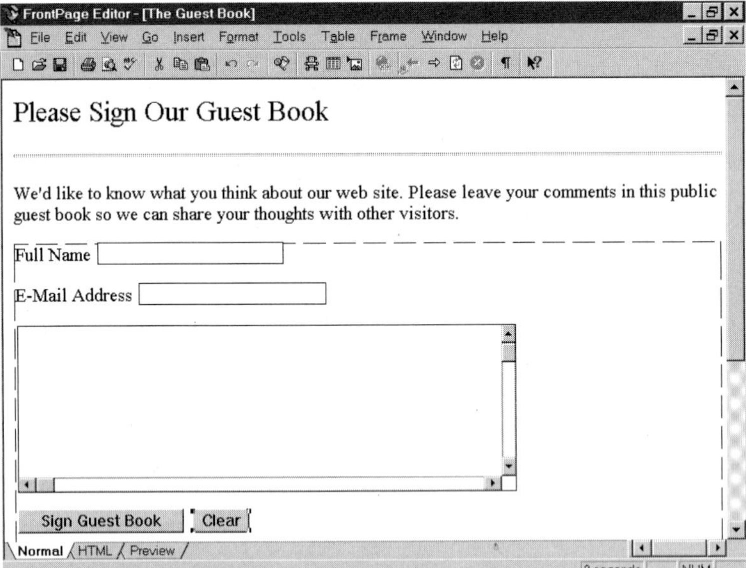

FIGURE 28.3.
An updated guest book.

Customizing the Guest Book Entries

As I stated earlier, guest book entries are sent to a file called `guestlog.htm` by default. You can change this file name using the Form Properties box (see Figure 28.4). To access this properties box, right click anywhere on the form and select Form Properties from the pop-up menu. Any time you change the filename for logging guest book entries, you should also update the Include bot properties so that it points to this file. Generally, you will want to make no other changes to the main Form Properties box.

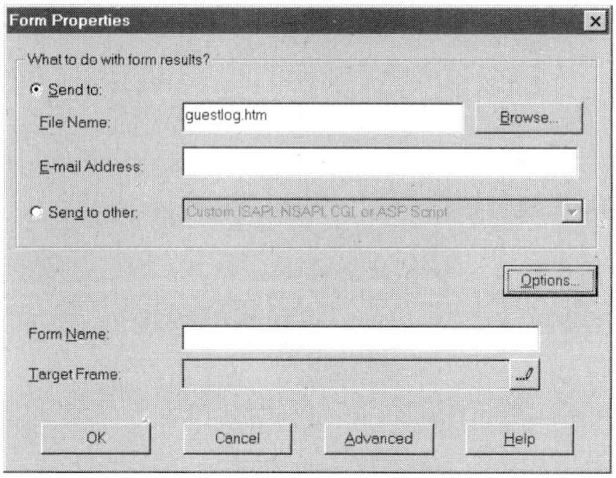

FIGURE 28.4.
Selecting the file for logging guest book entries.

Next, you can customize the format of guest book entries. Click the Options button in the Form Properties box. Using the File Results tab, you can select a new format for guest book entries. Generally, you will want to use one of these formats:

- **HTML.** Log guest book entries formatted as HTML paragraphs.
- **HTML definition list.** Log guest book entries using a definition list format.
- **HTML bulleted list.** Log guest book entries using a bulleted list format.
- **Formatted text within HTML.** Log guest book entries as preformatted text.
- **Text Database using Space as separator.** Log guest book entries with a space as the delimiter.

By default, the guest book logs entries are in chronological order with the latest entries at the end of the file. Because you will usually want to see the most recent entries first, deselect the Latest Results at End check box.

The Saved Fields tab lets you change the style of guest book entries. Generally, the only additional information you want to save with a guest book entry is the Time and Date information. The Remote Host information is nice, but it will often be an IP address that makes no sense. Furthermore, because the User Name field is only valid in restricted webs, this field will be blank unless the guest book is a part of a restricted web.

After you make configuration changes, save the guest book page and give it a test run.

Building a Better Guest Book

To give your guest book and your web a more sophisticated look and design, you will probably want to change how the guest book works. Unlike the simple guest book solution implemented with the Guest Book template, a well-designed guest book would let users know that their submissions have been accepted and wouldn't make users reload the guest book to see their entries. Following the steps in this section will show you how to build a better guest book.

NOTE

Although giving the guest book a makeover is fairly easy, you don't need to change how the guest book works at all if you are satisfied with the original guest book.

Updating the Guest Book

Start by loading your guest book entry page into the FrontPage Editor. Now delete the Include bot from the bottom of the page. To do this, click the text inserted by the Include bot, then press Delete or the backspace key.

Next, right click the form and select Form Properties on the pop-up menu. Click the Options button and go to the Conformation Page tab as shown in Figure 28.5. Enter the URL of a confirmation page, such as `logged.htm`. Click OK. At this point, don't worry about the error that says you haven't created the confirmation page yet.

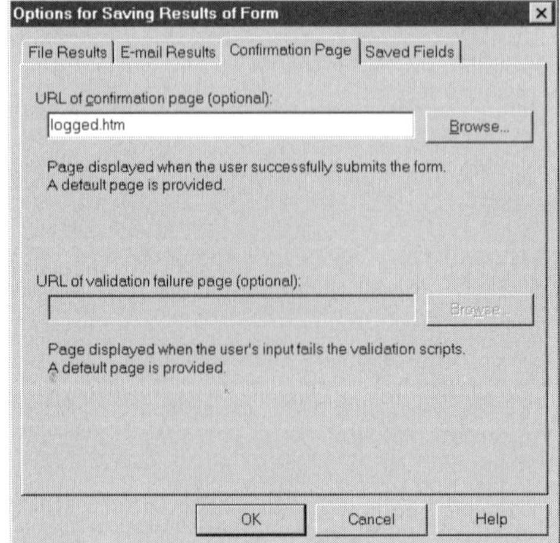

FIGURE 28.5.
Enter the URL of a confirmation page.

Creating the Guest Book Confirmation Page

After you update and save the guest book entry page, you need to create the confirmation page. To do so, start a new page based on the Normal page template. Now add a confirmation message to the page, such as the one shown in Figure 28.6.

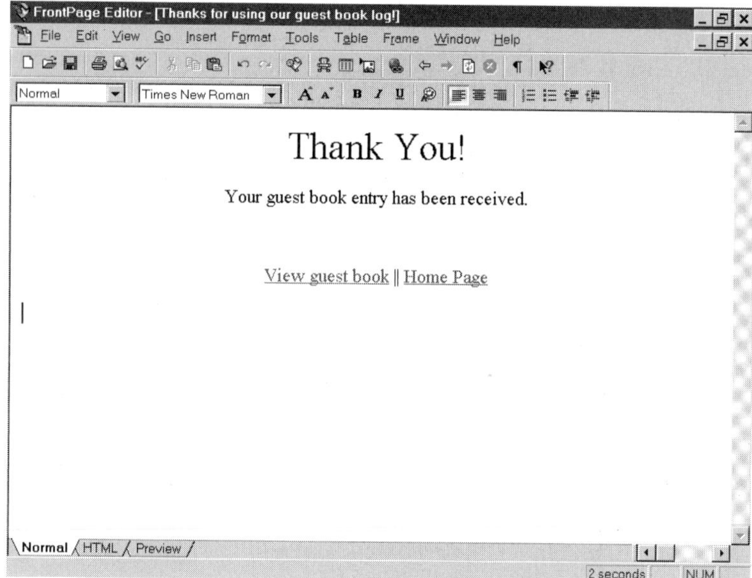

FIGURE 28.6.
A sample guest book confirmation page.

Finish the page by adding a link that leads to the guest book entries, which is now a separate page. The page URL you link to should be the same page URL you entered in the Send to field of the Form Properties box. If you didn't change the default guest log page, the URL is `guestlog.htm`. You can also add a link that lets users access your home page.

When you are finished creating the confirmation page, save it using the page URL you specified in the Confirmation Page tab, such as `logged.htm`. Be sure to give the page an appropriate title when you save it.

Using the Guest Book

To ensure the guest book is accessible, add links to the guest book from your home page or other pages at your Web site. Now, when a user makes an entry in the guest book, he will see the confirmation page and can then access the newly updated guest book.

Getting Feedback

Getting feedback from visitors is essential. If you don't want to use a public forum like the guest book, you should definitely add a feedback page to your web. In this way, you can learn what visitors like and don't like. You can get the all important suggestions for improving your Web site and much more.

Creating a Feedback Page

Creating a feedback page with FrontPage 98 is easy. All you have to do is select the Feedback Form template from the New page dialog box. As you can see from Figure 28.7, the Feedback Form template provides a good starting point for some of the questions you might want to ask visitors to your Web site.

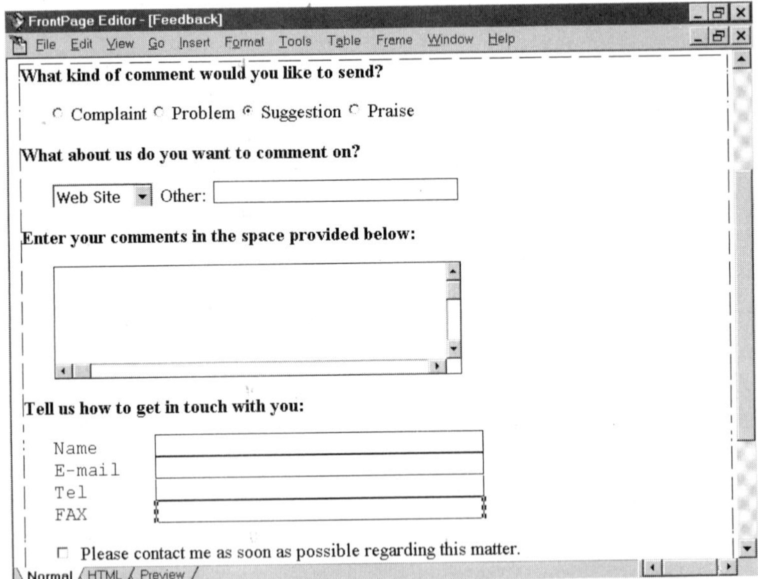

FIGURE 28.7.
The Feedback Form template.

Without making any changes to the feedback page, you can get complaints, suggestions, problems, and praise that pertain to your Web site, your company, your products, and your services. Although this is great for a corporate Web site, most Web publishers will want to remove the entire section concerning what the user wants comment on. An alternative would be to change the values of the selection menu, so the values fit in with your Web site and the pages you publish.

Other changes you might want to make to the feedback page of a personal web include the following:

- Delete the input fields for telephone and FAX.
- Move the personal contact fields to the beginning of the form.

Further, unless you really want to get back to people who submit feedback, you should delete the final check box or, at the very least, reword the associated text so that users aren't expecting an immediate response.

Customizing the Feedback Results

By default, feedback results are stored in a text database with fields separated by tabs. The destination file is `feedback.txt` in a private directory. You can change these settings using the Form Properties box. Other settings you might want to check include the saved fields and the confirmation page.

If you use the default settings, submissions will be saved with all the additional information, which includes time, date, remote computer name, user name, and browser type. Because no one but you will see the feedback results, you might as well use all the additional information. However, keep in mind that you can't rely on the user name field to tell you the user's name or e-mail address.

If you do not create a confirmation page, users will see a default confirmation page created by FrontPage 98. Rather than use a default page, you should create a confirmation page like the one shown in Figure 28.8. If you want to add to the page confirmation fields that show what the user entered, see the section on the Confirmation Field bot in Chapter 34, "Automation with FrontPage Components."

FIGURE 28.8.
A sample feedback confirmation page.

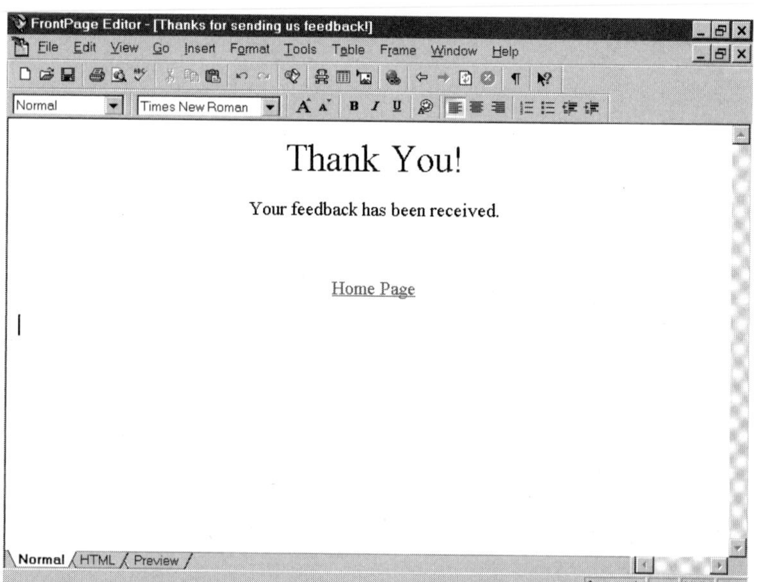

Summary

Guest books and feedback forms are great for getting input from visitors to your Web site. Use a guest book when you want the input to be available to anyone visiting your site. Use a feedback form when you want a private means for getting input from visitors.

CHAPTER 29

Instant Web Sites with FrontPage 98

by William Robert Stanek

IN THIS CHAPTER

- Saving Time with Instant Web Sites 488
- Creating an Instant Site 489
- A Quick Look at FrontPage Webs 492

With the ready-to-use Web sites included in FrontPage 98, you can create an instant Web site that will dazzle the masses. These ready-to-use Web sites appear in the form of familiar Microsoft Wizards. They bring new definition to the meaning of quick site generation and range from basic one-page sites to advanced sites with dozens of pages. This chapter discusses how to create an instant Web site that will meet your needs whether you plan to set up a complete corporate intranet or a site on the World Wide Web. Even if you do not plan to use an instant Web site, you should read this chapter to gain an understanding of the various sites you can create to establish your Web presence. To compliment this chapter, you can also refer to Chapter 27, "Creating Web Pages with FrontPage's Templates."

Saving Time with Instant Web Sites

You can create a wide range of Instant Web sites with Web site templates and web wizards. As you might expect, you can build basic webs with Web site templates and advanced webs with wizards. A Web site template contains outlines for a specific set of pages, such as all the pages that relate to a customer support web. Using this Web site template, you then can go through and customize the individual pages as needed. Web site templates are a pre-canned solution for Web site creation, allowing you to adopt the format and organization for your own site. A web wizard, on the other hand, helps you automatically generate content for a complex web. The web wizard takes you through several steps by asking questions relevant to the type of Web site you want to create. When you are done answering questions and choosing options in the wizard, the wizard then proceeds to take that information and create a customized site based on your choices. A web wizard site still follows a canned mentality (there are, after all, only so many options), but it does have a more distinct identity than a web site template.

Both web site templates and wizards contain helpful guidelines to make easier the development of a particular type of site. As with page templates, the guidelines provided do not ask specific questions concerning design and layout of the page. However, they do cover just about every major issue you should consider when developing a specific type of site. This gives you valuable insight into the specific areas your site should cover. Figure 29.1 and 29.2 illustrate two sample instant sites. These sites showcase how easy it is to create attractive and full-featured Web sites with FrontPage 98.

The basic appeal to using Web site templates or web wizards is to help you create a satisfying site quickly. When you are new to web design, or if you do not have a great deal of time, creating a completely new Web site from the ground up can be intimidating, time consuming, and frustrating. These templates and wizards have already been created by Microsoft to account for a logical organization and structure, as well as the most commonly relevant information. You can use the sites created by the Web site templates and wizards to flesh out your own ideas and steer you in the right direction for your own site. You might not choose to use every aspect of the site that is created, but it can help you get your site established with a little less effort.

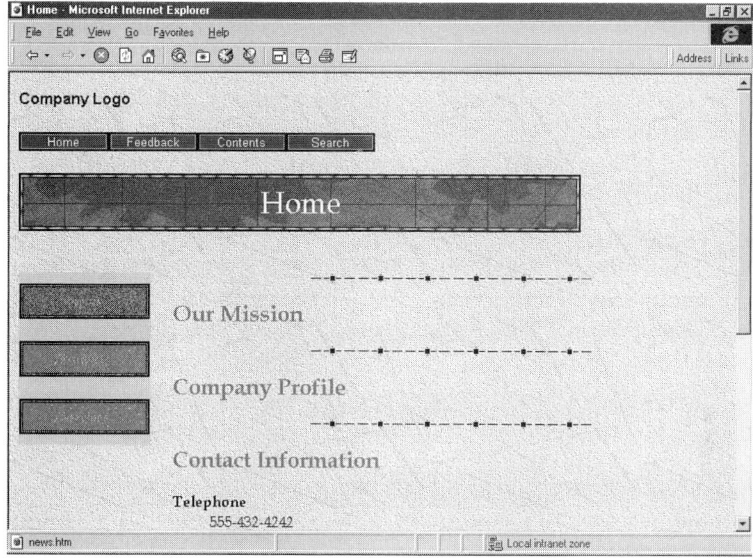

FIGURE 29.1.
The FrontPage Web site templates make creating great sites quick and easy.

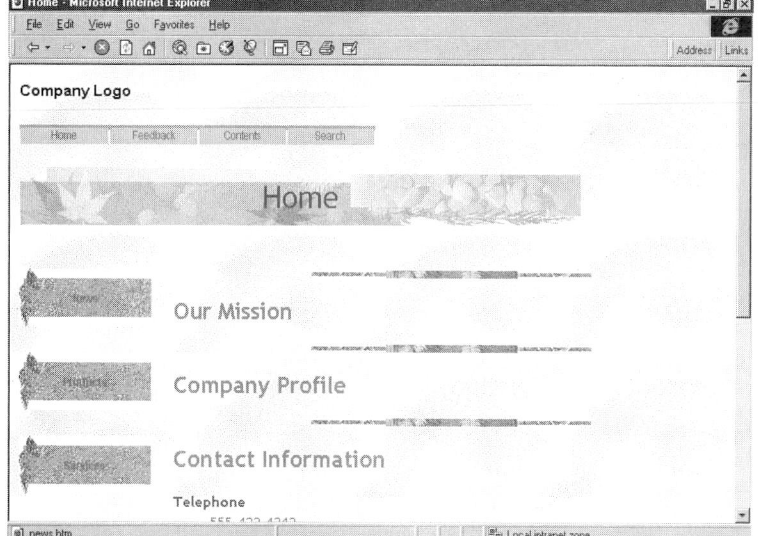

FIGURE 29.2.
Each instant Web site can be customized to suit your needs.

Creating an Instant Site

As mentioned before, when you want to create an instant site you can use either the FrontPage Web Wizards or Web site templates. The key difference between a web wizard and a Web site template is how FrontPage 98 creates the site. The subsequent chapters in this section (Chapter 30, "Building a Discussion Web," Chapter 31, "Creating a Customer Support Web," Chapter

32, "Creating a Project Web," and Chapter 33, "Establishing a Corporate Presence") all discuss in detail using the individual Web site templates and wizards to create a Web site. Before you leap into those chapters, let's cover some of the basics of creating your instant site.

All web wizards and Web site templates are accessed from the FrontPage Explorer, via the New FrontPage Web dialog box (shown in Figure 29.3). To access the New FrontPage Web dialog box, choose File|New|FrontPage Web in the FrontPage Explorer. If you are already at the Getting Started dialog box, click on the Create a New FrontPage Web radio button and then click the OK button. The New FrontPage Web dialog box provides you with two steps to get started in creating your Web site. The first step in creating your instant site is to choose what kind of site you want to create. When you click the From a Wizard or Template radio button, you can select a Web site template or web wizard from the list box. Each different entry represents a unique Web site template or web wizard. Typically, the name of the wizard or template is clear enough to indicate what type of site you would be creating if you selected it. When you select an entry in the list, a brief description of your choice appears below the list box. Use this to spot the right template or wizard for you.

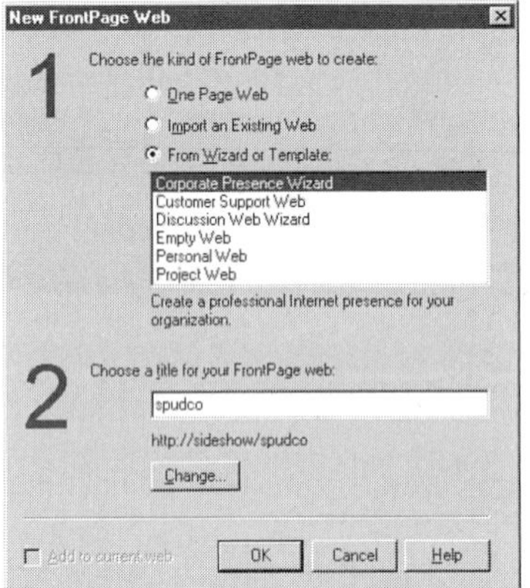

FIGURE 29.3.
The New FrontPage Web dialog box is where it all starts for instant Web sites.

After you have your template or wizard selected, you can proceed to the second step. The second step involves telling FrontPage 98 where to create your new Web site. Using the text box at the bottom of the New FrontPage Web dialog box, you can enter a name for your new Web site. This name is used in conjunction with your server's name to create the URL (address) for your new Web site. As you type in the text box, the URL below the text box updates to reflect your new name. If, for some reason, the URL shown below the dialog box is incorrect, you can click the Change button to open the Change Location dialog box (shown in Figure 29.4). This dialog box is used to enter a new URL for your new Web site. This should be entered in the form of `http://`*`yourservername`*`/`*`yourwebname`*. By clicking OK, you return to the New FrontPage Web dialog box with your URL updated.

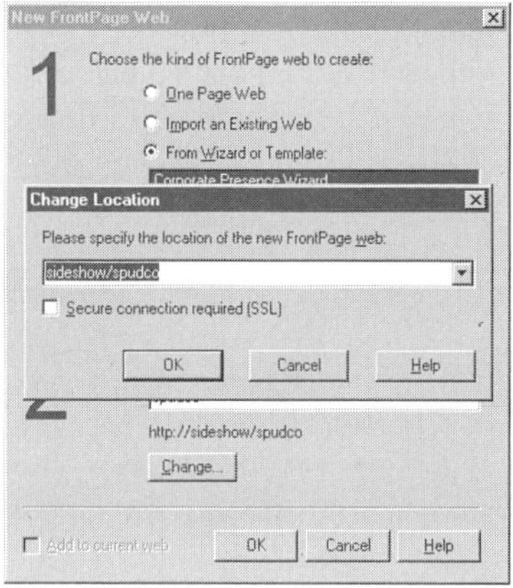

FIGURE 29.4.
The Change Location dialog box is used to enter a new URL for your site.

After you have determine what type of Web site you want to create and where it will be created, you are ready to tell FrontPage 98 to start creating your site. Click the OK button to begin the creation of your Web site. What happens next depends on what Web site template or wizard you selected. When you select to create an instant Web site with a Web site template, FrontPage 98 dutifully creates a new Web site using the example provided by the template. You are not prompted for any additional information and will have to customize the Web site manually in the FrontPage Editor. If you selected a web wizard, the process is somewhat more involved.

Web wizards act much like wizards in other Microsoft programs. You are taken step by step through the process of carrying out an action. You indicate that you are ready to proceed to the next step by clicking the Next button, or that you want to return to the previous step by clicking the Back button. The length of the wizard depends on the type of site you are creating, and what questions it will ask. One of the most convenient aspects of FrontPage 98's web wizards is that they will remember what you entered the next time you run the wizard. This is especially convenient if you are creating sites for the same company or with the same information. Figure 29.5 depicts a FrontPage web wizard in action.

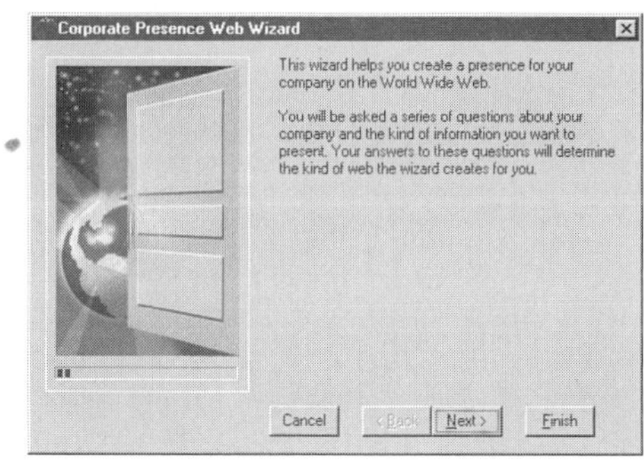

FIGURE 29.5.
The Corporate Presence Web Wizard.

When you have completed the prerequisite steps in the web wizard, the wizard will indicate you have finished entering information. Your only option to continue will be to click the Finish button, where FrontPage 98 will take the information you gave the wizard and create your Web site. Upon completion of the creation of your site, you then are able to customize your site much like you would a web template site or a site you built yourself.

EDITING TECHNIQUES FOR WIZARD PAGES

FrontPage wizards understand a whole range of editing commands, including cut, copy, paste, and undo. This allows you to select text on any wizard page and copy it to the clipboard, paste text from the clipboard into a field, and unerase text that you accidentally deleted.

The following demonstrates how you can use these editing commands:

- **Cut.** Select the text and then press Ctrl+X. This action places text on the clipboard.
- **Copy.** Select the text and then press Ctrl+C. This action places text on the clipboard.
- **Paste.** With text on the clipboard, move to the field into which you want to paste text, and press Ctrl+V.
- **Undo.** You can undo a paste, cut, or other deletion of text by pressing Ctrl+Z.

Because the clipboard is a standard object, you can copy text to the clipboard in other applications and then paste it into a wizard field. For example, you can copy the company phone number from a MS Word document and paste it into a relevant wizard field.

Each instant web contains default pages and images that you can use as a road map to help you design a terrific site. Most webs have at least one top-level page. A top-level page, like a home page, is the page that most visitors start on and use to access other areas of your web.

To better understand how instant webs can save you time and money, this chapter includes a look at each of the Web site templates and wizards available in FrontPage. By examining each of the available Web sites, you can gain a thorough understanding of what types of sites you can build and how the sites are designed.

NOTE

When you create sites with web templates and wizards, FrontPage 98 automatically adds comments that guide you through the process of designing the page.

A Quick Look at FrontPage Webs

The One-Page and Empty webs are the most basic webs available. If you have been following the examples in this book, you have probably already used the one-page web. When you use the one-page web, the FrontPage Explorer creates a web with a single page based on the normal page template. By default, the One-Page web is selected when you open the New Web dialog box. To use this web, you simply press the Enter key or click OK without making a selection.

The Empty web, as the name implies, creates a new web that has no contents. You can use the empty web when you want to create a new site from scratch. However, with all the ready-to-use webs available, I do not know why you would ever want to use this web.

Granted, the One-Page and Empty webs are remarkably uncomplicated entities, however, the remaining webs are anything but simple. You can use these webs to establish a corporate presence, create a discussion web, and much more. When you have advanced Web site needs, you should look to these webs to provide you with quick solutions. The following is a quick look at the remaining webs:

Discussion Web Wizard. This wizard helps you quickly create a web-based discussion area where participants can post and read messages. This process is done step by step, thanks to the wizard interface. See Chapter 30.

Customer Support Web. The Customer Support Web template creates a customer support web based on a pre-defined template. You can then use the FrontPage Editor to customize each individual page. See Chapter 31.

Personal Web. If you are looking to create your own personal Web site, this Web site template can help you out in organizing information about your interests, web site links, and photographs.

Project Web. Another Web site template, the Project Web creates a web designed to help you develop and discuss a project. This includes a web-based discussion area where participants can post and read messages. See Chapter 32.

Corporate Presence Wizard. This lengthy wizard helps you quickly create an extensive business-oriented Web site to promote products and services. See Chapter 33.

Summary

Creating an instant Web site is easy with the Web site templates and wizards included in FrontPage 98. A Web site template contains outlines for a specific set of pages, such as all the pages that relate to a customer support web. A wizard helps you automatically generate content for a complex web, such as one that would help you build a presence on the World Wide Web. Both Web site templates and web wizards contain helpful guidelines to make development of intranet and Web sites easier.

CHAPTER 30

Building a Discussion Web

by William Robert Stanek

IN THIS CHAPTER

- What Are Discussion Groups? *496*
- Creating a Discussion Group *498*
- How Discussion Groups Are Logged and Updated *504*
- Managing Discussion Groups *508*

No matter how big an organization becomes, it always needs to hear from its customers, whether it's through customer response forms or the total sales every month. If you're already on the Web, one useful method for getting customer feedback is a discussion board. Discussion boards often allow users and your own employees to communicate with each other. Whether it contains a gripe session or troubleshooting help, a discussion board is useful for any organization. Personal web sites can take advantage of discussion boards too, be they for hobbyists or just plain chat.

What Are Discussion Groups?

Despite its rather straightforward definition, a discussion group can take many different forms. Some groups are open-ended, where anybody and everybody can post to them. With another kind of group, the authorship is much more regulated, and user accounts are explicitly given. I'll briefly cover the good and bad points for using each kind of group. Perhaps the best way to compare open-ended and restricted discussion groups is with talk radio. Some talk-radio shows air nationally, and consequently, you hear a broad spectrum of opinions, on topic or not. With a local talk show, the topic can be more focused to a particular audience. This isn't to imply that one is necessarily better than the other—just that they are different.

Open-Ended Discussion Groups: The Usenet Model

One aspect of the Internet that many people find enjoyable is Usenet. On Usenet, anybody and everybody can read and write to each other in public on almost any topic they want. This makes Usenet a great public forum where you can get, or give, help to anybody on the Net. The only real problem with Usenet is the sheer bulk of its entirety; Usenet has well over 12,000 newsgroups. Each of these newsgroups generally has a different topic from the other groups on Usenet.

Pros and Cons of Open-Ended Discussion Groups

Probably one of the best aspects of Usenet is its complete openness. Because anybody can post anything, all opinions are heard equally. Consequently, if a point is argued or defended well, the author will probably command respect, which makes it possible for minority opinions to be exposed to everybody at large. In this respect, Usenet is great for allowing everyone a complete perspective on any given topic. Another benefit of an open-ended discussion group is the many different viewpoints from the rest of the Internet. If you have a problem with something and you live far from civilization, Usenet can bring you a great deal of help. You don't necessarily need to drive many miles just to get an opinion; you can simply post your query to Usenet. Its many inhabitants typically respond with some useful answers.

The obvious downside of an open-ended discussion forum such as Usenet is the easy abuse of it. It's far too easy for people to post topics that are unrelated to a particular newsgroup. Anybody who's read Usenet long enough knows how annoying chain letters and advertisements can be. These messages are often posted to entirely too many newsgroups, most of which have nothing to do with the article in question. Another downside of a discussion group such as Usenet is that everybody can post. Without someone to regulate what's posted, there is little accountability. What this means is that literally anybody can write to almost any Usenet newsgroup and disrupt the ongoing discussions.

Usenet does have some moderated newsgroups where the content is filtered. With moderated newsgroups, a small number of people are in charge of all posts that appear in a particular newsgroup. That's not to say that only a handful of people actually write the content; rather, they are the editors. A post bound for a moderated newsgroup is routed to the moderator, who then decides whether it should be posted to the entire newsgroup. This allows a moderator to filter out all the venom and pointless arguments. Some people dislike the concept of a moderator, claiming that the moderator is imposing his own viewpoints on a newsgroup. Although this is certainly true, a moderated newsgroup has few realistic alternatives. It is almost impossible to present completely objective information in a newsgroup with only one moderator.

Restricted Discussion Groups: The BBS Model

Another popular model for a discussion group is a restricted discussion forum. This model is frequently seen in BBSs (bulletin board systems) around the country. The big difference between the two models of discussion groups is how many people can access them. Although almost anybody on the Internet can access Usenet, very few people can access BBS discussion groups. This isn't to say that BBSs are actively restrictive; it's just that each one is located in its own particular area. Consequently, the users closest to a BBS will be able to participate in that system's discussion. The rest of the country, and indeed the world, is left out because of prohibitive long distance phone bills.

Pros and Cons of Restricted Discussion Groups

On the whole, restricted discussion groups tend to be more focused. They're usually more focused not only on content, but also on information. Because the discussion group participants have been filtered already, there are fewer voices to be heard. This means that most mainstream opinions are heard and no extremes. If you post a query to a restricted discussion group, you might or might not get an answer. If you send that same message to a Usenet newsgroup, you'll almost always get a reply. In Usenet, you'll get an answer, whether it's right or wrong. Also, depending on the criteria for restricting access to a discussion group, the content could be very helpful. The moderator of a moderated discussion group within Usenet has a certain style, and he'll impose it over his group. If a BBS catered to only writers, any queries about writing hints or the like garner more useful replies. On Usenet, whether people know something or not, they'll volunteer their opinions.

The downside of a restricted discussion group is its lack of information. Suppose you wanted to ask for car help on a BBS devoted to writing; chances are, you wouldn't get too much help. You might have to go to a car BBS or post the question to an open-ended forum, such as Usenet. Another downside to a restricted discussion board is the problem of stagnation. After a while, all the old hats at a BBS tend to dominate the discussion boards. Because the discussion has fewer participants, there tend to be fewer new topics. Most of the old timers have already expressed their opinions to each other, and few want to explain themselves again. Open discussion boards tend to have a constantly changing mix of new participants.

Which One Is Right for You?

With all this talk about discussion boards, you're probably trying to figure out which one is right for you. As with anything else, it all depends on what you want to do with it. If you're the Webmaster in charge of setting up a corporate Web site, you might want an open-ended discussion board. This allows users of your product to freely and openly talk to your employees, as well as other users. They can exchange useful information for technical support, upcoming releases, and the like. Although anybody can post anything they want, you can easily moderate the newsgroup.

You can opt for a private discussion board if you're the Webmaster for only a particular group within your company. This allows only the customers that your group serves to participate. Although there is more work involved with creating user accounts for everybody, the discussion remains more focused. Your customer can ask questions of your group, and replies are focused to that particular person. Any technical support is very personalized and appropriate to the customer. Another benefit of a closed-off discussion board is the capability to disseminate proprietary information.

Creating a Discussion Group

One of the more difficult tasks for a traditional Webmaster is creating a discussion board, because of the amount of time required for setting it up and writing the CGI scripts. After you finish these tasks, you can easily export and modify the board for anybody else who needs it. It is the initial creation that is difficult. Fortunately, FrontPage 98 takes a great deal of the difficulty out of creating discussion boards.

The Discussion Board as a New Web

Probably the easiest way to create a discussion board is to create a new web for it. From the FrontPage Explorer, simply choose File|New FrontPage Web and select the Discussion Web Wizard option. Next, specify how you want to create the web and enter a name for the web. You can add a discussion area to the current open web by selecting the Add to Current Web checkbox. After you log in as the Webmaster for this web, you're presented with an introductory screen (see Figure 30.1). The Discussion Web Wizard asks you a series of questions. Based on your answers, the wizard creates a new discussion board that is tailored to your choices.

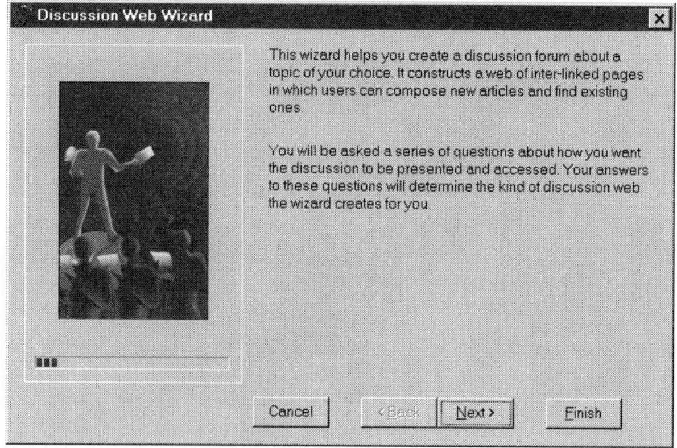

FIGURE 30.1.
FrontPage 98 makes creating a discussion board a simple matter of going through a wizard.

Features of the Discussion Board

The FrontPage Discussion Web Wizard offers a great deal of power for what it does. It features a number of options that you can easily disable or enable at creation time. For example, the first choices you have when you start the wizard are what primary options to enable (see Figure 30.2). You can let every user see a list of the current discussion by enabling the Table of Contents option. Similarly, you can allow people to search the text of messages by turning on the Search Form option.

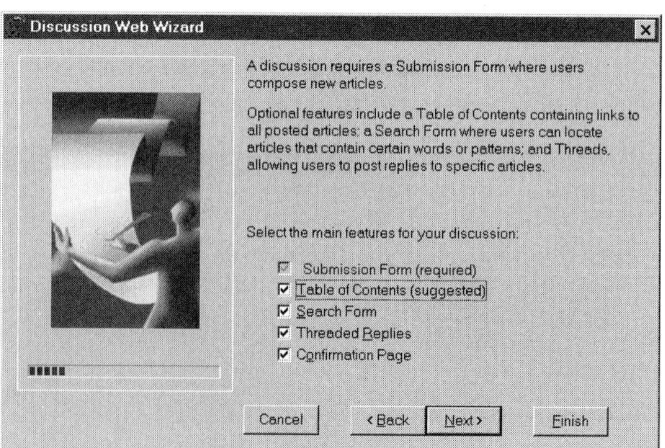

FIGURE 30.2.
You can enable or disable a wealth of features from this dialog box.

One of the most useful features of any newsreader is the capability to display threads. A thread is a series of messages that are each related to each other. When you follow a thread from the beginning, you can see where the topic started and where it began to diverge. Particularly large discussions have many subthreads running through them. When people first load your discussion board, you can allow them to see the existing threads by checking the Threaded Replies option. The Confirmation Page is a simple Web page that tells the author that his message has been posted.

After you've specified what main features you want enabled, you can type in the name of the board itself. FrontPage 98 automatically converts your input into the name of a folder. The folder that is created holds all the data files related to this discussion board. The name of the folder is displayed under the title you specify for the discussion forum (see Figure 30.3). Be sure to make a note of the name of the folder that FrontPage 98 creates.

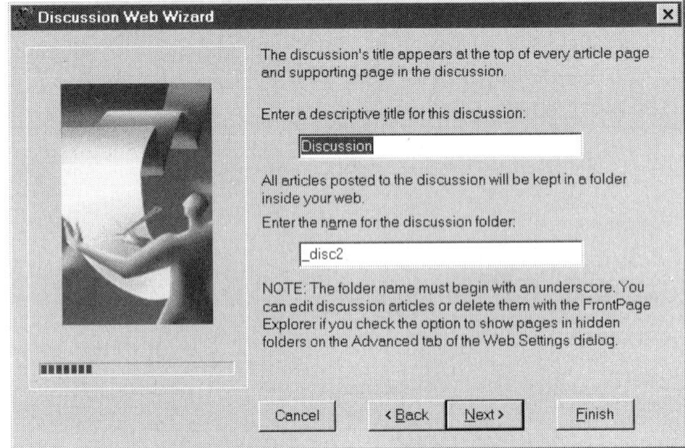

FIGURE 30.3.
Organizing discussion groups and their files along a folder mentality saves you both work and heartache.

Configuring the Submission Form

Submitting messages to the discussion web is handled with forms. After you give the web a title, you need to select the default input fields for this form. As you can see from Figure 30.4, there are three different configurations for the input form. To understand what fields you might need, you need to understand what these fields are generally used for.

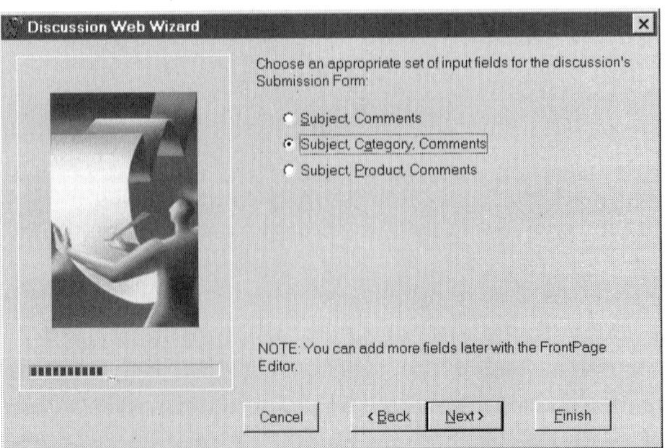

FIGURE 30.4.
Select the appropriate field for your discussion forum.

The four default fields are Subject, Comments, Category, and Product. The Subject field is the most important field. All threads are organized and responded to by subject. The Comments field is a text box that you use to enter comments on the topic of discussion. The

Category and Product fields provide pull-down lists that can be used to sort discussion topics by category name or product type.

TIP

If you want to use the Category and Product fields, you should edit the discussion submission form in the FrontPage Editor immediately and enter meaningful items in the pull-down list.

Different Types of Discussion Boards

After you have chosen the categories that are included in each message, as detailed in the previous section, you need to determine the security level of your discussion group. This decision is displayed in Figure 30.5, which asks the very simple question of whether you want a private discussion board. The default is to create an open discussion forum so that anybody can post to it. You can change this by clicking the Yes option. If you restrict access to your discussion board, FrontPage 98 prompts you. It reminds you that the web in which the discussion board resides must be restricted. If you've made the discussion board a separate web, this won't be a problem.

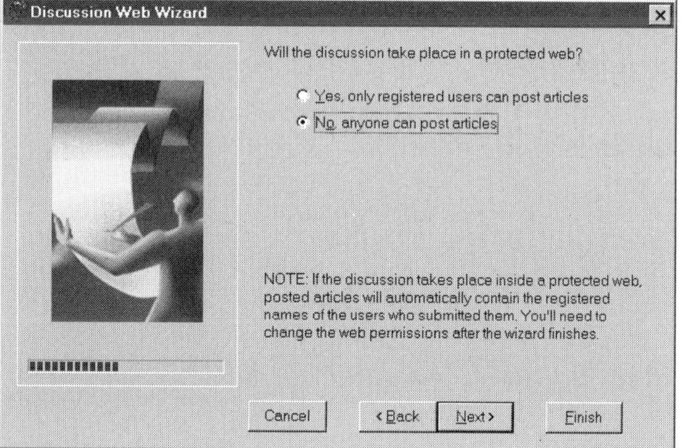

FIGURE 30.5.
You can specify whether the discussion board should be private.

Organizing the Table of Contents

The next two questions the wizard presents to you relate to the Table of Contents (see Figure 30.6 and Figure 30.7). You can specify how the messages are listed, as well as whether the discussion board is the home page for the web. The second option allows you to easily create a discussion board in an existing web. If you do not want to overwrite the existing home page, select No.

CAUTION

If you accidentally choose Yes to overwrite the existing home page, the Discussion Web Wizard will overwrite your existing home page. Be careful!

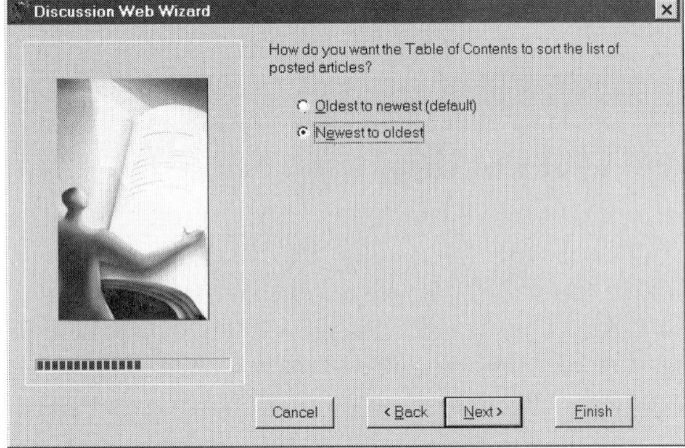

FIGURE 30.6. *Select the method of sorting for the discussion list.*

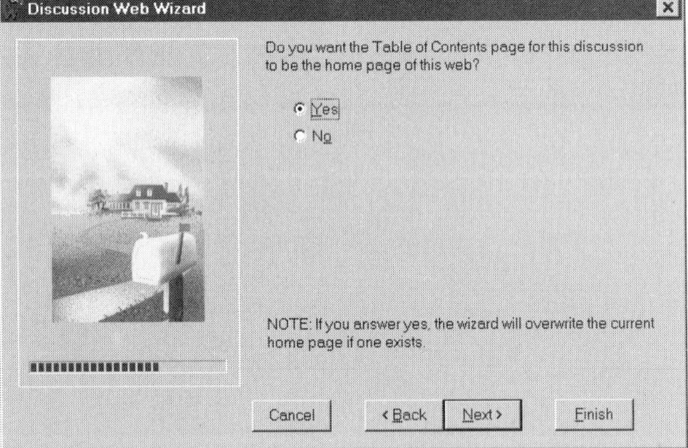

FIGURE 30.7. *From here you can assign the table of contents as this discussion's home page.*

Look and Feel

FrontPage 98 also enables you to easily control the look and feel of the discussion board with the next three questions the wizard asks you. If you've enabled message searching on this discussion board, the wizard asks you how search results should be displayed (see Figure 30.8).

The next question is probably the most important look-and-feel issue you have to deal with (see Figure 30.9). You're given the ability to specify a theme for all the Web pages in the discussion board. Using a theme, you can control the background color or image for the pages and you can control various link colors. Although this might not sound impressive, it makes all your messages appear in a consistent fashion. For sites that are run by an organization, it's imperative that the Web pages have a consistent look; this option from FrontPage 98 achieves this consistency.

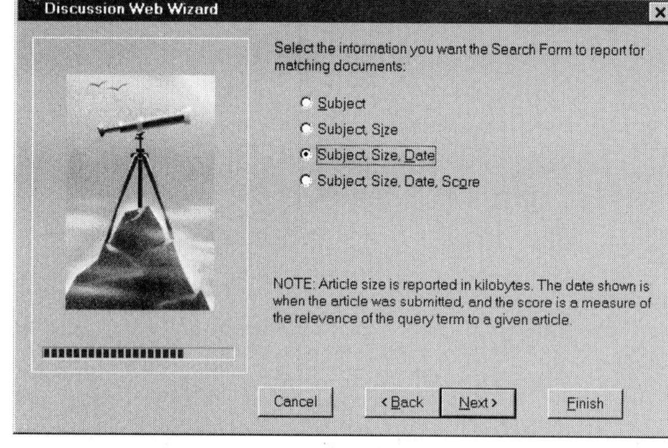

FIGURE 30.8.
Using the Discussion Web Wizard you can set how detailed a search users can enact. As coarse as Subject only, or as detailed as Subject, Size, Date, and Score.

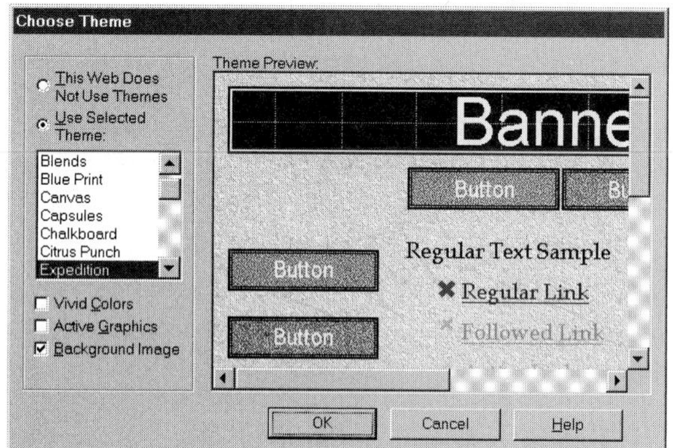

FIGURE 30.9.
By choosing a theme, you can control how all the Web pages in the discussion board will look.

After you indicate your theme preference for the discussion board, you see the dialog box displayed in Figure 30.10. This dialog box enables you to control how each message in the discussion board is displayed—not the general color and look and feel, but the general layout. You can have FrontPage 98 use general Web pages so that all browsers can view your board. If you want to target users who have frames-capable browsers, you can specify frames-specific layouts. If you choose to use frames, you can indicate the size and shape of each frame (see Chapter 10, "Editing and Enhancing Your Frames").

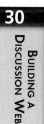

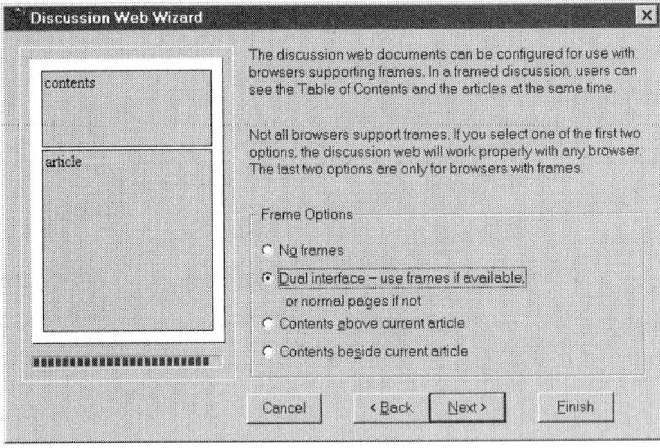

FIGURE 30.10.
You can choose to use frames or generic Web pages for the layout of each message.

Finishing the Web Creation

On the last wizard page displayed (see Figure 30.11), the Discussion Web Wizard shows the titles of the main pages of your web. These main pages should match the configuration settings you've chosen in the web creation process. To create the web, click the Finish button.

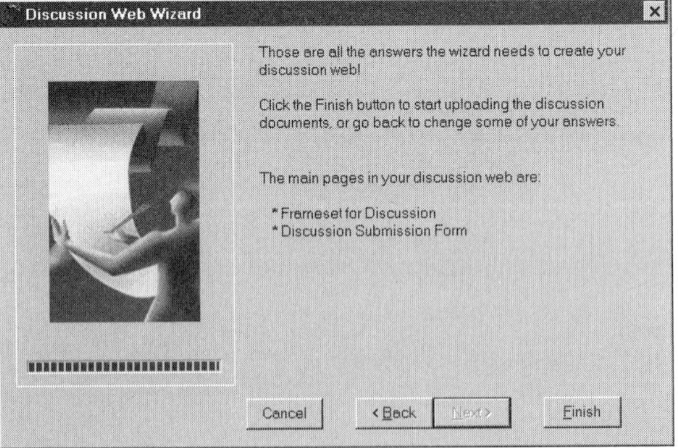

FIGURE 30.11.
Note the main pages for your Web and then click the Finish button.

How Discussion Groups Are Logged and Updated

After you've answered all the Discussion Web Wizard's questions, your discussion board is created. People can access your discussion forum and post whatever they want. Typically, you'll want to post some sort of welcome message before everybody else posts. This acts as a springboard to spur other people to write in your discussion board.

Posting and Replying to Messages

Your new discussion board is updated every time anybody posts to it. When someone accesses your Web page, she sees a display similar to Figure 30.12. Any messages are displayed under the first horizontal rule. You can post a new message to the discussion board by clicking the

Post button. You see a new window where you simply enter the information in the form fields (see Figure 30.13). After you're done, you click the Post Message button at the bottom of the Web page. If you're currently viewing a message, you can also reply to it. This opens a window similar to Figure 30.13. The main difference is that the Subject field has already been filled in for you. You can simply type your message as if you were posting a new message.

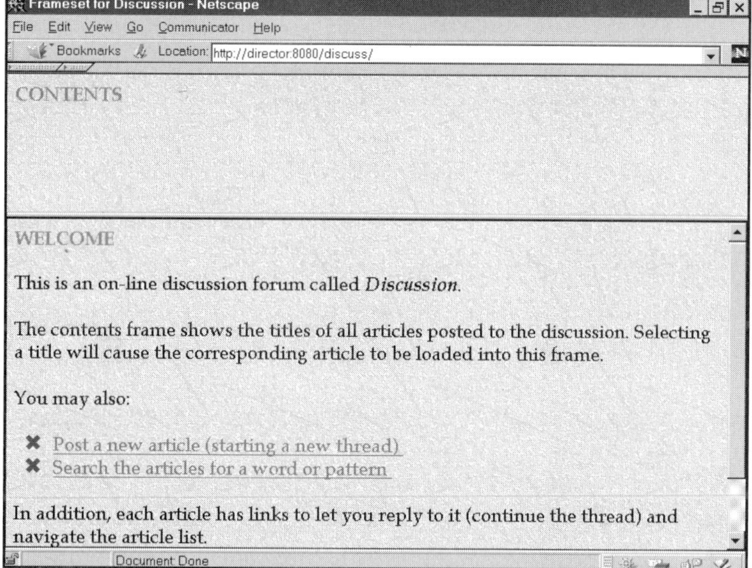

FIGURE 30.12.
This newly created discussion board is waiting for someone to contribute something.

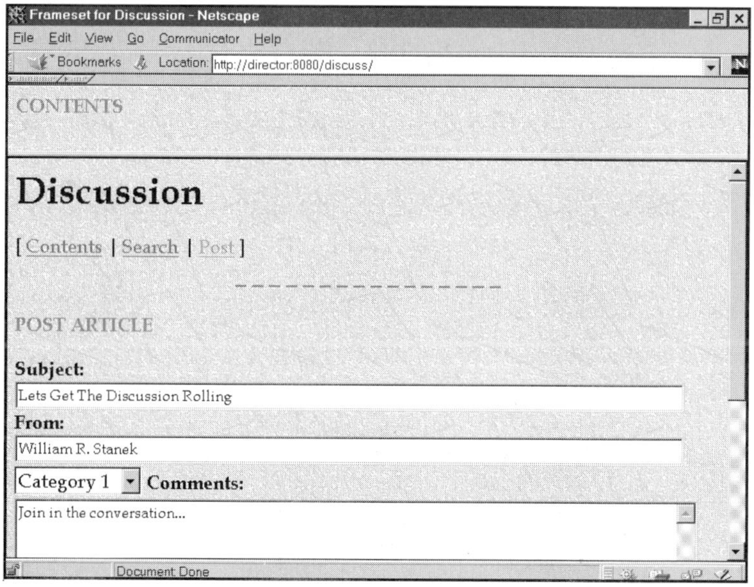

FIGURE 30.13.
When you post a new message, you have to enter the subject, your name, and the message.

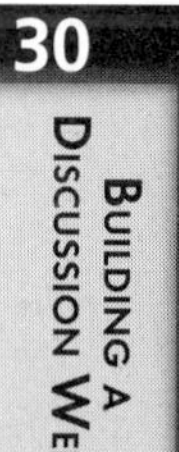

NOTE

If the discussion board you're creating is password-protected, users won't have to fill in their usernames. These fields are filled in automatically by FrontPage 98 for each poster.

How Threading Works

When you first create the discussion board, you can enable FrontPage 98's threading ability. If used, threads allow users to more easily follow flows of discussions as they evolve. Each reply message is placed at the end of the thread in relation to the original message. As more and more people reply to the different articles in the thread, subthreads develop. FrontPage 98 displays all threads by indenting each article in a particular subthread (see Figure 30.14). Those articles in the same thread are points in which the thread separated into another tangent. It's very likely that subthreads will develop subthreads of their own. When you reply to any message, it adds to the thread or subthread.

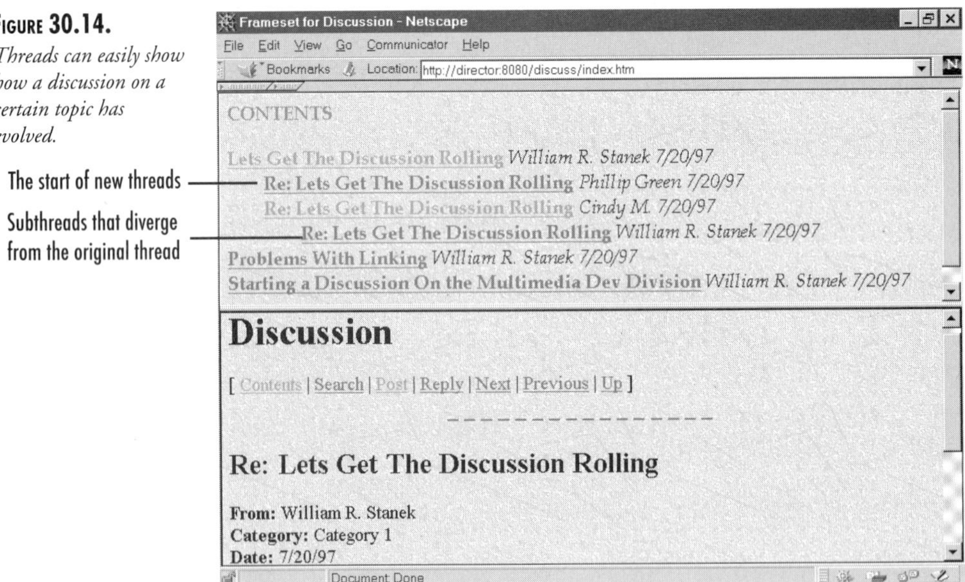

FIGURE 30.14.
Threads can easily show how a discussion on a certain topic has evolved.

Where the Files Are

FrontPage 98 keeps track of all the files for a discussion group in one location. During the creation process for a discussion board, you're asked to name the board. When you enter a name, the name is modified and used as the folder name (refer to Figure 30.3). All the data files associated with a discussion board are stored in that folder. Generally speaking, the files are stored in `\FrontPage Webs\Content\`*`webname`*`\`*`discussion board name`*. Table 30.1 has a list of all the critical files that each discussion board depends on and where they're located.

Table 30.1. Disk location for discussion board data files.

File Location (Relative to `\FrontPage Webs\Content\` *`Web Name`)*	*Purpose*
`\Group Name`	The name you gave the discussion board under the `Web name` web.
`\xxxx_cfrm.htm`	After a user posts an article, this Web page indicates that the post was received. This file is not created if you disable the option during the creation of the discussion board.
`\xxxx_post.htm`	This is the Web page that users use when they want to post an article to your discussion group.
`\xxxx_srch.htm`	This is the Web page that users use when they want to search the discussion board. This file is only created if you want to let people search your discussion board.
`\index.htm`	The main index page for the discussion board.
`\_private\xxxx_ahdr.htm`	This file holds the header that appears at the top of posted articles. This file has links to Next, Previous, Reply, and Up.
`\_private\xxxx_aftr.htm`	This file holds the footer that appears at the bottom of posted articles. By default, this page is blank.
`\_private\xxxx_head.htm`	The generic header for all messages. By default, it contains everything up to, and including, the first horizontal rule.
`\_private\xxxx_foot.htm`	The generic footer for all messages. By default, it contains everything after, and including, the last horizontal rule.
`\_private\xxxx_styl.htm`	The sample Web page that has the color configuration for all messages.
`\Group Name\########.htm`	The actual body for the message of the corresponding article number.
`\Group Name\_vti_cnf\########.htm`	This file holds various information about the corresponding article, including relational links, creation date, and related information.
`\Group Name\_vti_shm\########.htm`	The file contains the page that's presented when somebody wants to reply to an article.

Managing Discussion Groups

Another daunting task in managing a discussion group is maintaining it. You have to be able to check the content of the messages and change them if necessary. You might also want to purge old articles because of disk space considerations or simply because they're old. Whatever the case might be, you'll sometimes need to perform some form of maintenance on the board. Although FrontPage 98 doesn't give you direct capabilities to manage your discussion board, it does simplify the task.

Traditional Group Handling

Traditionally, most Web-based message board systems had a small set of functions accessible to the moderator. He could easily delete messages or entire threads from a discussion board. Occasionally, he had the power to directly modify the content of each message. This typically wasn't necessary because the moderator often had direct access to the Web pages that made up the articles. In fact, in many cases, the role of a moderator was played by the Web administrator.

Deleting Individual Messages

One of your jobs as moderator of the discussion board is removing messages. Sometimes, somebody will post something offensive or inappropriate that must be removed. Other times, you might want to remove a message because it's too old to be relevant. Regardless of the need, FrontPage 98 provides an easy mechanism for removing any unwanted message.

Simply get a Folder View of the entire discussion board and then change to the private directory containing the discussion messages. This directory is named after the title of the web. For example, if the title of the web is Customer Support, the directory name is `_cussup`. All messages posted by users are named `########.htm` with the `#` characters representing digits (see Figure 30.15). To find the article you don't want, you can expand the Title section so you can read the full subject of each message. Highlight the message you want to delete, click the right mouse button, and select the Delete option. The message is removed and all links are updated accordingly. That means that if the article was in the middle of a thread, the Next and Previous links are fixed.

NOTE

To see files in a hidden or private directory, you must select the Show documents in hidden directories checkbox in the Advanced tab of the Web Settings dialog box. You can access this dialog box by selecting Tools|Web Settings.

After a message is deleted, there is no method for retrieving it. If you need to keep a backup of the message, such as for archiving purposes, save the message first.

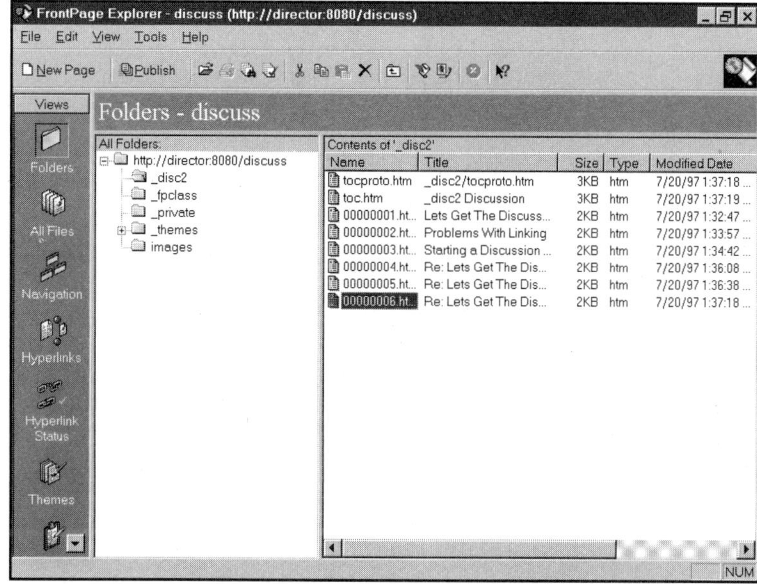

FIGURE 30.15.
Deleting unwanted threads is easy.

Modifying Individual Messages with FrontPage 98

Another job of a moderator is modifying an existing message. For whatever reason—the author used too many profanities, wrote a rambling message, or whatever—you might have to change some messages. This task is also intuitive using FrontPage Explorer. Because each article in the discussion board is a Web page, simply get a Folder View of the discussion forum. Next, select the article number that you want to change and highlight it. Click the right mouse button and select the Open option, which loads the article into the FrontPage Editor. Alternately, you can simply double-click the article. Now edit and save the article as you would any other Web page.

> **TIP**
>
> If you modify an article, be sure to let people know that you've changed it. It's generally considered good form to do this so that the author doesn't get blindsided. He might have written one thing, but someone could argue with him over an edit that you made. Be sure to include some text in the edited text that indicates that you modified the original and why.

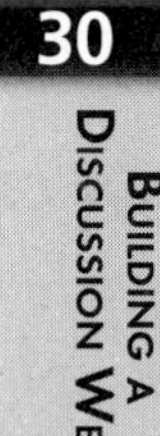

Summary

Discussion boards can be very useful tools for any organization, large or small. It allows both employees and users to talk about whatever interests them. Because you'll be creating the discussion board, you can control the direction of the discussion. FrontPage 98 provides a very easy-to-use wizard mechanism for creating many types of discussion forums. You can control everything from the general look and feel to what features are enabled.

In addition to providing various aesthetic controls, FrontPage 98 also gives you tools with which you can work on your discussion group. You can decide whether the discussion board is open to everybody or restricted in its access. FrontPage 98 also gives you full editorial control over the content of the discussion board. You can delete existing articles or simply edit them. You accomplish all of this without any special interface from FrontPage 98. FrontPage 98 is flexible enough to handle all your modifications and adjust all affected files.

CHAPTER 31

Creating a Customer Support Web

by William Robert Stanek

IN THIS CHAPTER

- Using the Customer Support Web 512
- The Welcome Page 512
- The What's New Page 513
- The FAQ Page 514
- The Bug Reporting and Information Page 515
- The Suggestions Page 516
- The Download Page 517
- The Discussion Area 519
- The Search Page 520
- The Technical Notes Page 521

Hundreds of companies have online customer support areas. An online customer support area can serve your customers 24 hours a day, 365 days a year. Customers can access the area when they have problems, regardless of whether it is 3 a.m. or noon. FrontPage 98 can support a large number of people for a long period of time, all without anyone having to pick up a phone.

Using the Customer Support Web

The Customer Support Web is a fairly advanced web, with over 20 related documents designed to help you provide world-class customer support. Ideally, this web would be a separate area of a larger site and not your only presence on the Web.

You can create the Customer Support Web simply by selecting the Customer Support Web from the New dialog box in the FrontPage Explorer. Because this web is a template, all the pages are created for you automatically. After you create the web, be sure to select a theme for it. The rest of the chapter takes a look at each of the pages in the Customer Support Web.

The Welcome Page

The top-level page of the Customer Support Web is called the Welcome page and appears in Figure 31.1. The Welcome page, like most pages in this web, has three main "sections" on the screen: header, body with sidebar, and footer.

A Navigation Bar bot adds the standard sidebar menu to the document. You cannot update

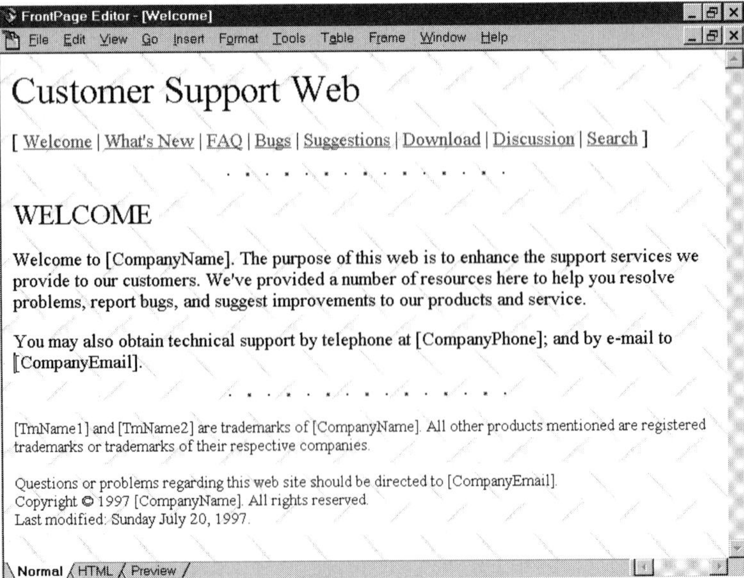

FIGURE 31.1.
The Welcome page.

this sidebar without updating all documents within this web that use the shared border. To see which page you should update, select the menu in the sidebar by clicking it, then open the Navigation Bar Properties box by double-clicking the left mouse button or pressing Alt+Enter. As you can see, the sidebar includes links to all the key areas of the Customer Support Web. Generally, you will not want to update the header itself.

Unlike the other sections of the page, you can (and should) edit the body of the document. Because the purpose of this page is to welcome visitors and tell them about your services, you should include two to three paragraphs describing the features of your online Customer Support Web.

When the document is generated, a timestamp is added to it. You should make the document yours right away by filling in all the blanks. Start by replacing the text in brackets with text appropriate for your company. If you do not like the style of the timestamp, you can change this by opening the TimeStamp bot's properties box. You can also update or change the timestamp's generation criterion from here.

The What's New Page

The What's New page of a Customer Support Web has slightly a different goal and scope from the What's New page on your main web. The page should track product updates, the availability of patches, release schedules, and other product-related information.

Figure 31.2 shows the What's New page. You will want to update the body text of this page immediately if you want people to take your customer support area seriously. The main body section contains links to the Download page and the Technical Notes page. The easiest way to update the link text is to place the insertion point within the link text, type in your new link text, and delete what's left over. If you do not update the link text in this way, you might accidentally delete the link. Another way to change the URL is to click anywhere within the URL field (within the FrontPage Editor's Normal view) and then right-click. From there, you should be able to choose to view the hyperlink's properties.

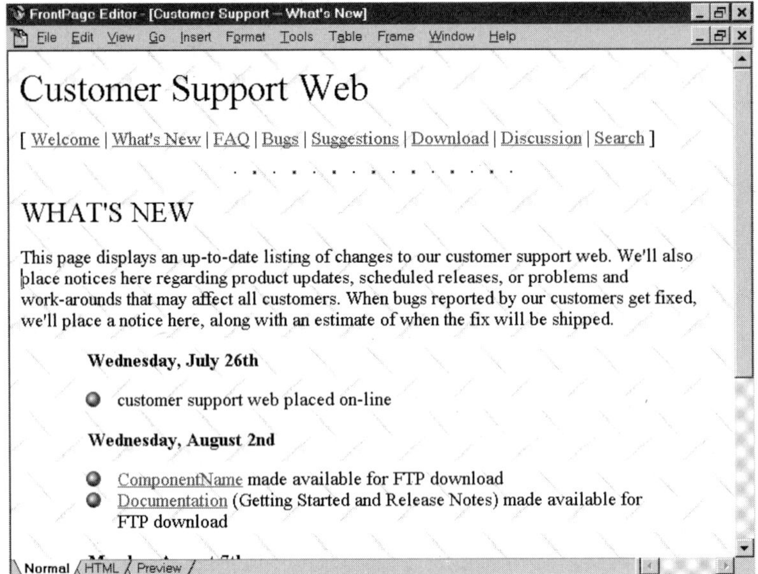

FIGURE 31.2.
The What's New page.

The FAQ Page

A FAQ is a list of frequently asked questions and their answers. Your Customer Support Web should contain a comprehensive FAQ page that answers common questions that your support staff handle. You might also want to include tips and tricks that make using your software, products, or services easier. The FAQ page included in the Customer Support Web and shown in Figure 31.3 is a starting point.

If you do not already have a list of commonly asked questions, ask your support team to help you make the list. They will probably be very glad to help you, especially when they consider how the page will make their jobs easier.

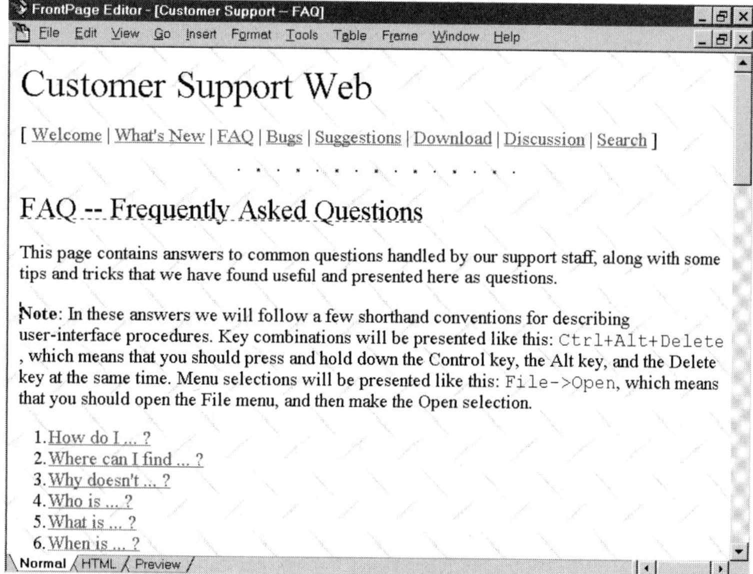

FIGURE 31.3.
The FAQ page.

The Bug Reporting and Information Page

Very few software products do not have bugs. Bugs are software glitches, the worst of which cause systems to crash. The purpose of the Bugs page shown in Figures 31.4 and 31.5 is two-fold. Customers should be able to report bugs they have found in the software so you can fix them. Customers should also be able to see a list of known bugs.

Most customer support areas include a bug reporting and information page for each major product that the company produces. Ideally, you would not only list the known bugs, but would also tell the customer how to get around each bug and perhaps where to download a patch that fixes the bug.

Lastly, the existence of a bug page reassures the customer that you're constantly testing and revising your product, and that if a problem comes up, it doesn't go unconquered for very long. Note that you can manipulate the bug report form in much the same way you can any form, as you learn in Chapter 23, "Getting More from the Form Page Wizard."

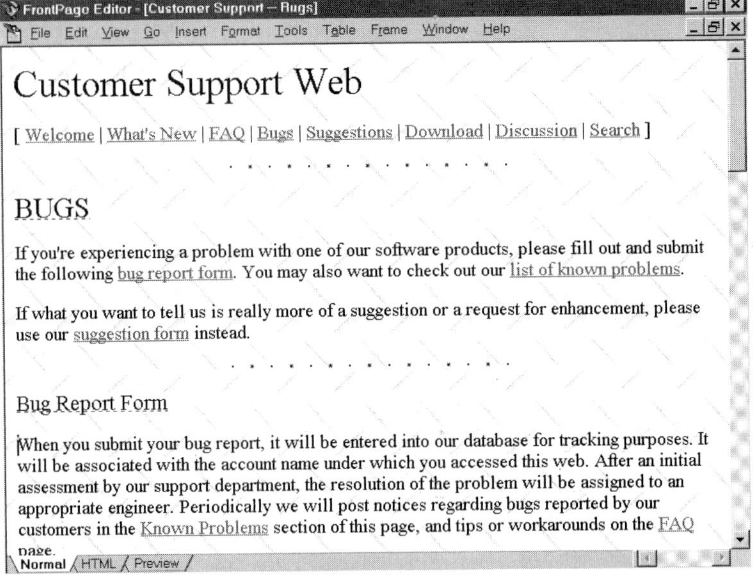

FIGURE 31.4. *Customers should be able to report bugs quickly and easily on the Bugs page.*

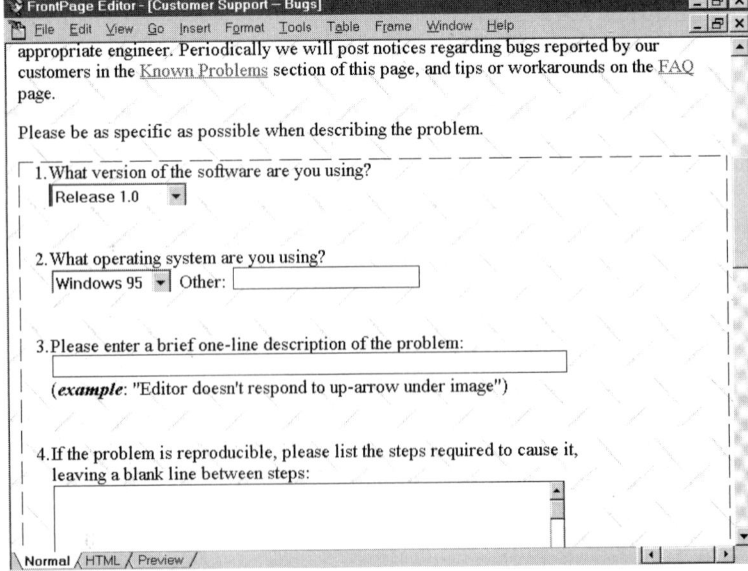

FIGURE 31.5. *On the Bugs page, customers should be able to find a list of known bugs.*

The Suggestions Page

A Suggestions page opens an extremely important communications channel with your customers. While you will certainly get suggestions that won't be useful, you might be surprised at how many truly wonderful ideas your customers have for enhancing your products and improving your customer service. The Suggestions page shown in Figure 31.6 allows customers to make suggestions concerning your Web site, company, products, service, support, and even your marketing style.

FIGURE 31.6.
Suggestion pages are a great way to learn from your customers.

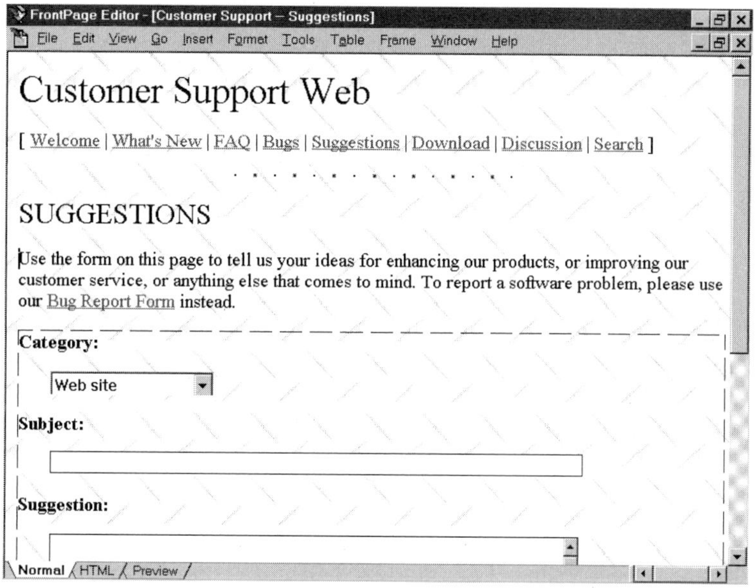

The Download Page

The Download page provides a common area for downloading patches, updates, and other customer support-related files. As Figure 31.7 shows, the first segment introduces the page and provides a link to the file formats bookmark. The next section is an index for the updates, patches, and other files that the reader can download from this page. You should replace the link titles with more appropriate text.

When a reader clicks on a link in the Contents section, his browser displays the appropriate bookmark within the document, such as those shown in Figure 31.8. The Navigation bot will always arrange a series of navigation tools across the top of the page, depending on the user's location within the web. When providing files on the Web, it's helpful to use some form of compression to reduce download time. This shows that you are considerate of the customer's time.

TIP

You should provide files in at least two compressed formats if possible, such as ZIP and compressed TAR. ZIP is an extremely popular compression technique. Zipped files can be decompressed on just about any system as long as the reader has an unzip utility. The compressed tape archive (TAR) format is another popular format. While TAR utilities are available for most systems, the TAR format is primarily for readers who access the Web via a UNIX-based server.

Both ZIP and TAR are compression formats that essentially allow files to travel at sizes smaller than their original dimensions. You can't execute a compressed file, but you can copy and move it, thus having archives take up less space than they normally would. There are many shareware applications that can extract and distill both ZIP and TAR documents.

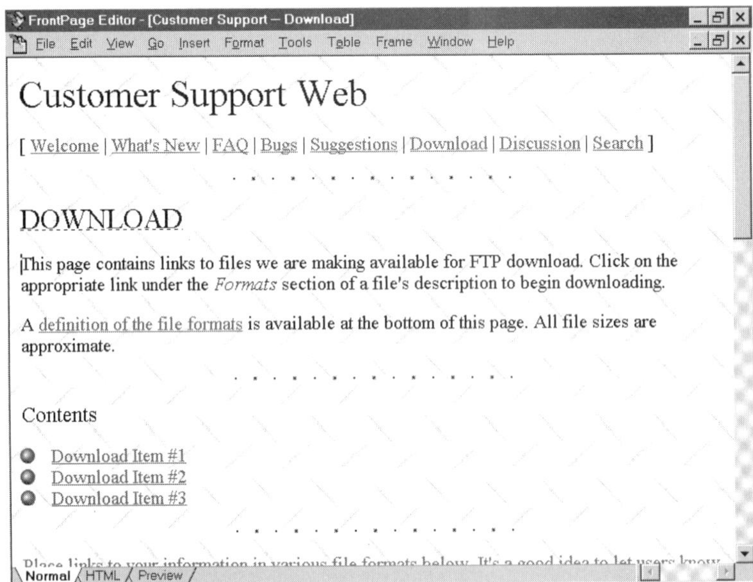

FIGURE 31.7.
A template for allowing the downloading of updates and enhancements.

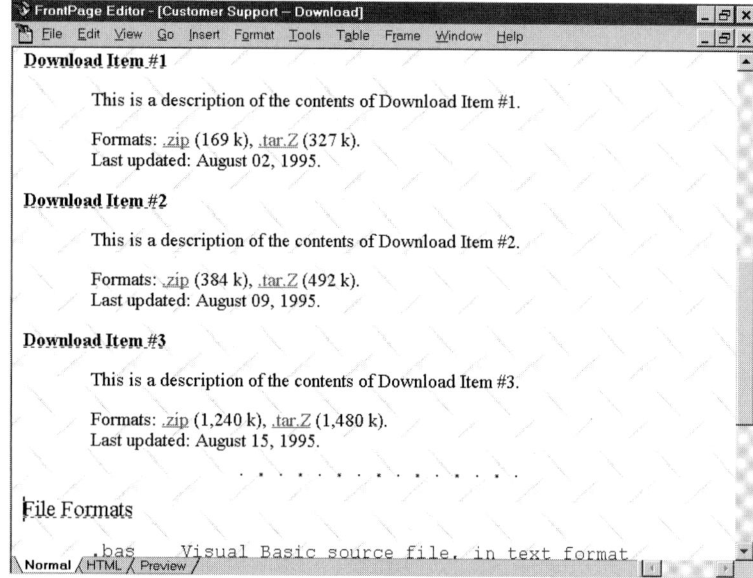

FIGURE 31.8.
The Navigation component allows the user to move easily from page to page.

The Discussion Area

No Customer Support Web would be complete without a Discussion area in which company employees and customers can discuss your products. This area contains four pages: a Home page, Table of Contents, Search page, and Posting page. The Home page for this area is the same page the reader accesses when he clicks on the Discussion link from another area of the web.

The centerpiece of the discussion area is the page shown in Figure 31.9. On this page, readers can post material to the Discussion area. All current postings to the discussion group are available from the Table of Contents page. The table of contents updates whenever new material is posted. Readers can also search through the postings using a Search page. To return to the normal customer support areas, click on the Home hyperlink.

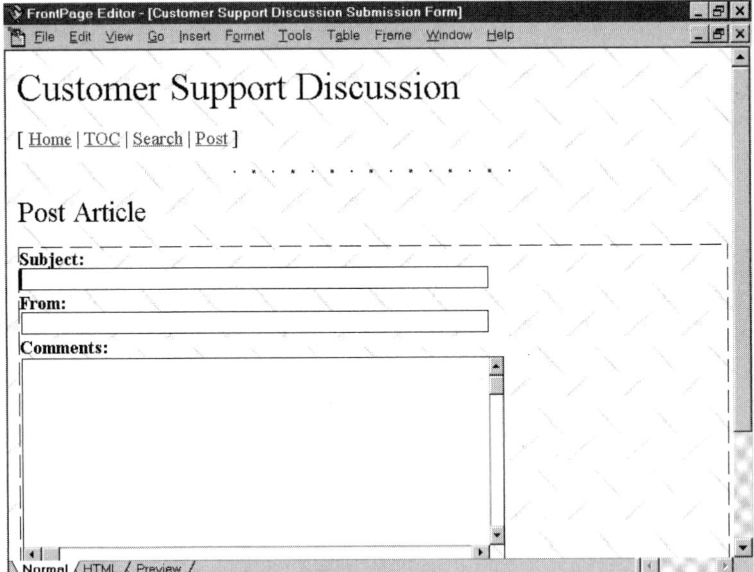

FIGURE 31.9.
Posting to the Customer Support Discussion area.

The Search Page

The Search page lets readers search through the full text of your Customer Support Web. Whenever you save a page or recalculate links, FrontPage 98 creates a text index of your site. Using the Search bot and the Search page, you can allow users to access and retrieve information from this index.

The Search page is partially shown in Figure 31.10. A great thing about this page is that it includes detailed information on the query language used in the search process.

FIGURE 31.10.
Search the Customer Support Web.

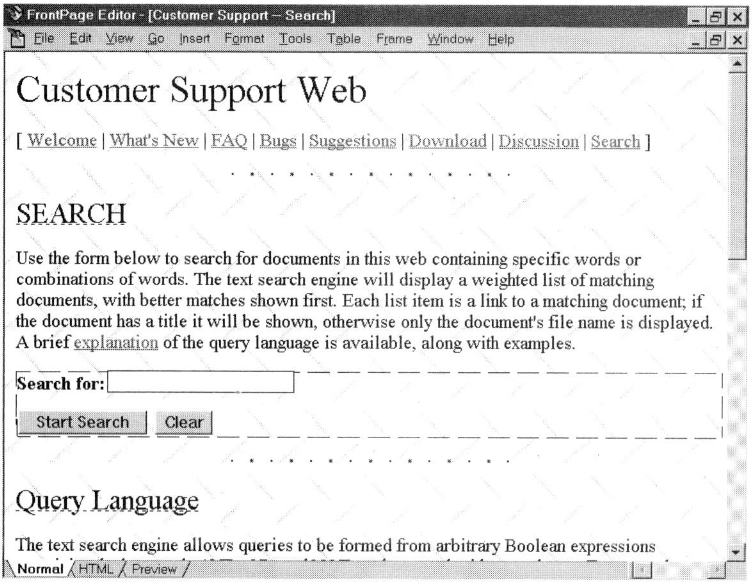

The Technical Notes Page

Hidden amongst the many pages provided with the Customer Support Web is the Technical Notes page. It is used to describe problems and solutions. Initially, this page is accessible only from the What's New page. However, if you plan to provide technical notes to your readers, you should add links to the page throughout the support web. For example, you might want to create links to this page from the Bugs page and the Download page.

Summary

The Customer Support Web uses a template to instantly create an advanced web. When you want to create an area to support customers' needs and receive feedback from customers, the Customer Support Web is a great choice.

Creating a Project Web

by William Robert Stanek

IN THIS CHAPTER

- Using the Project Web 524
- The Project Home Page 524
- The Members Page 525
- The Schedule Page 526
- The Status Page 527
- The Archive Page 528
- The Search Page 529
- The Discussions Area 530

No matter what company or department you work in, you arc probably a part of one or more projects. Your project team's goal is to get the job done, whether the job entails designing a new car, developing an application, or putting together an advertising campaign. FrontPage 98's Project Web can help you ensure that your project stays on track and accomplishes its goals.

Using the Project Web

Just as you might not want to release information on your boss and those you supervise, you probably would not want the general public to know the status of the company projects. Thus, the Project Web is another Web best suited for the corporate intranet. The Project Web includes the following:

- A home page where you can list what's new with the project and provide access to key pages within the web.
- A page where you can list the members of the project team and their contact information.
- A page for your schedule, complete with sections for events, milestones, and deliverables.
- Two discussion areas for tracking discussions related to the project.
- An archive page so you can reference and link to all the documents generated by the project team and its members.

You can create the project web simply by selecting the Project Web from the New Web dialog box in the FrontPage Explorer. Because this web is a template, all the pages are created for you automatically. After you create your Project Web, be sure to choose a theme for the web.

The Project Home Page

The top-level page of this web is called the Home page and appears in Figure 32.1. This page provides a starting point for the Project Web and lists what's new with the project. Like most pages in this web, the project Home page has three main sections: a header, a body, and a footer.

A FrontPage component creates the standard document and formatting. Keep in mind that if you alter the shared borders for this page, you are modifying them for the entire site. However, unlike the navigation and timestamp information, you can (and should) directly edit the body text of the document. Start by replacing the default text with text that is specific to your project. Remember, a lot of people use FrontPage, so it's probably quite embarrassing to be caught with all the default "insert company name here" stuff on your live Web site.

FIGURE 32.1.
The project Home page.

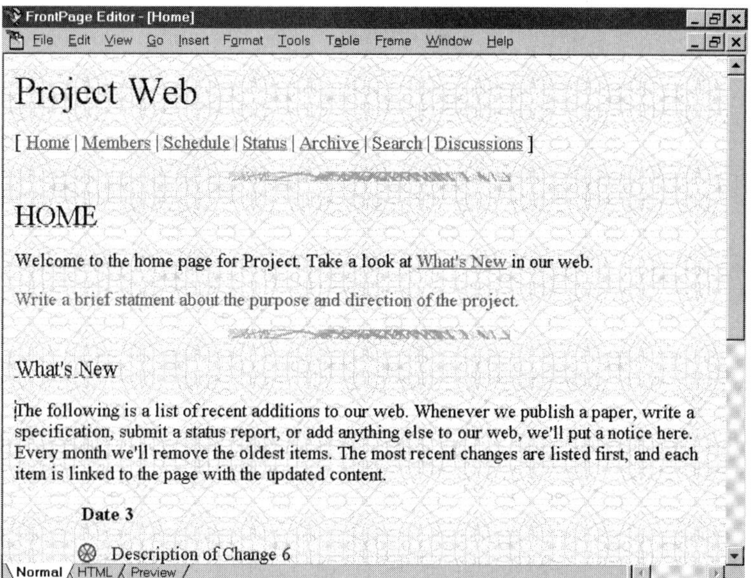

The Members Page

You can use the Members page to create a complete listing of the members of the project team. The page consists of two main sections. The first section, shown in Figure 32.2, contains an index of member names linked to the detailed listing shown in Figure 32.3. As shown, the second section can contain photos and contact information for each member of the project team.

The members section can be expanded to be much more than just a collection of the people who work on a particular project. You can use it to highlight your company's softball team, or to show what everyone dressed up as at the office Halloween party. All of the pages contained within the project web are extensible.

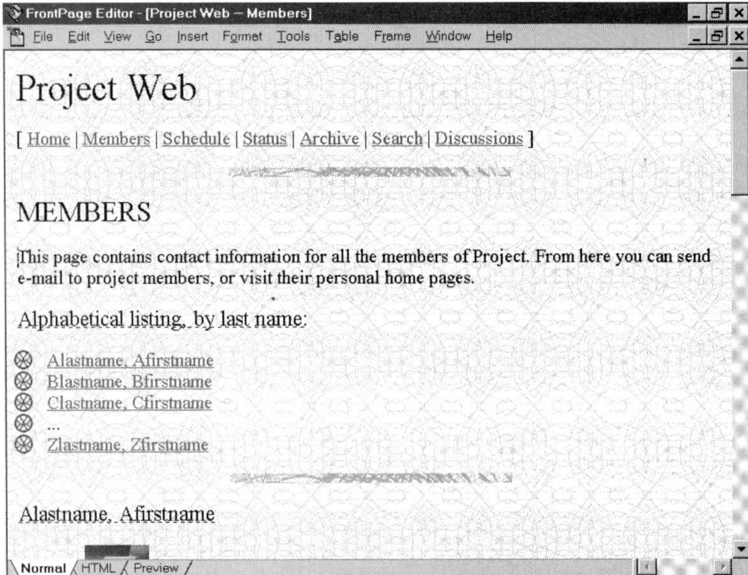

FIGURE 32.2.
The index on the Members page.

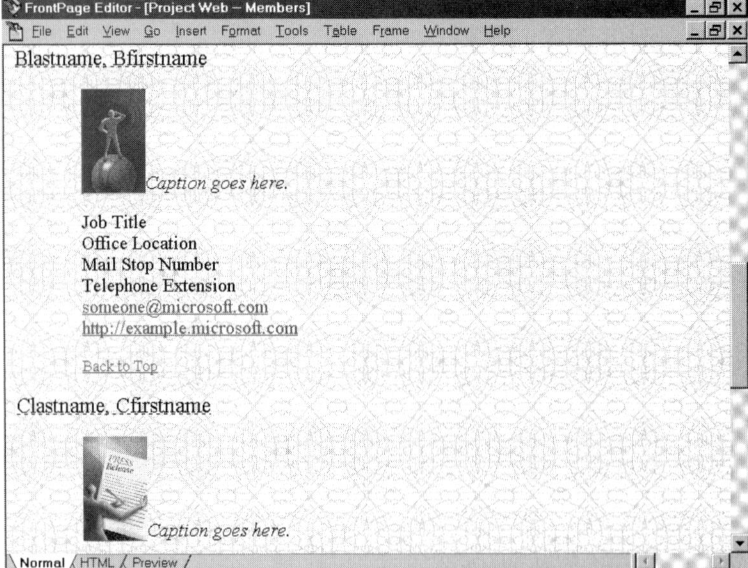

FIGURE 32.3.
Member information.

The Schedule Page

The Schedule page helps the project stay on track. Figure 32.4 shows part of the Schedule page. The page displays a week-by-week prioritized list of items on which the team is working.

Use the concepts that the page introduces to help you develop a schedule page suitable for your project. Project team members can use the schedule page as a quick reference for all the events, milestones, and deliverables related to the project.

What makes the Schedule page powerful is the fact that it's central. No one person possesses or can view the schedule. If maintained properly, you can set and meet goals within a team setting and still be able to maintain a semblance of discipline.

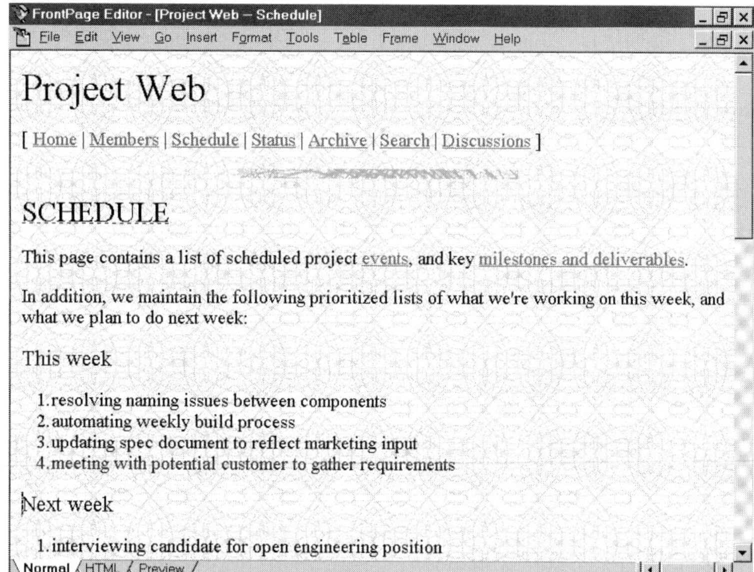

FIGURE 32.4.
The Schedule page.

The Status Page

Another key page in the Project Web is the Status page, shown in Figure 32.5. The Status page helps all the members of the project team track the monthly, quarterly, and yearly reports for your project. Management might also find it useful to track the Status page as a reference.

If the Schedule page tells you what you'll be doing, the Status page tells you what you have done. This is a valuable tool for tracking successes and failures among projects, as well as a handy history to help you learn from experience.

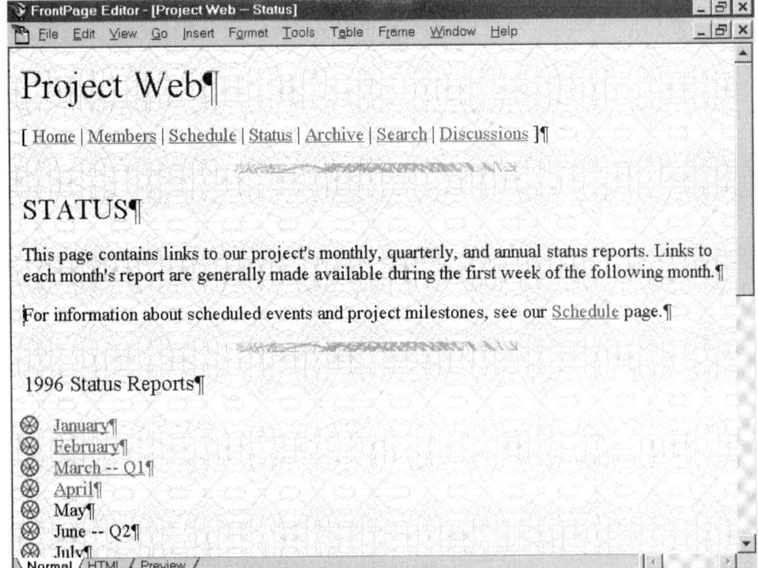

Figure 32.5.
The Status page.

The Archive Page

The Archive page provides a common area for referencing and linking to all the documents that the project team and its members generate. You can also use it to create links to software and utilities that the members of the project team might need. Figure 32.6 shows the introduction to the Archive page. The remaining sections of the page are organized much like the Download page in Chapter 31, "Creating a Customer Support Web."

FIGURE 32.6.
The Archive page.

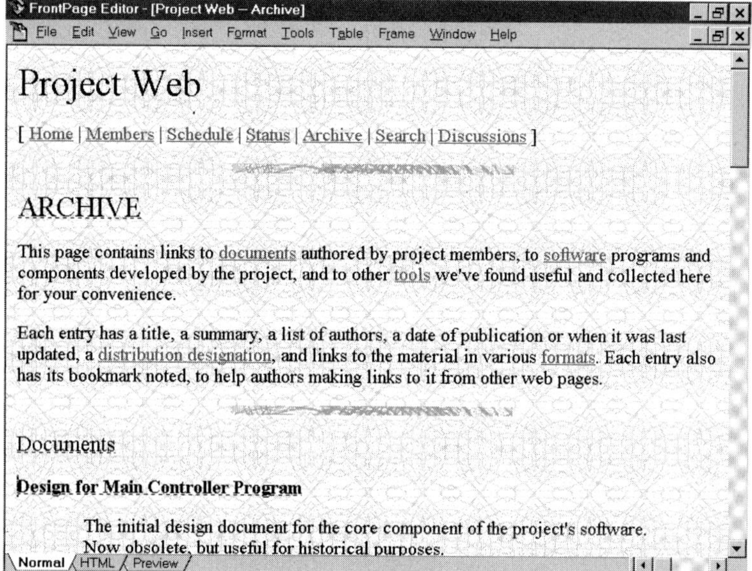

The Search Page

The Search page lets project members search through the full text of your Project Web. Whenever you save a page or recalculate links, FrontPage 98 creates a text index to your site. Using the Search component and the Search page, you can enable users to access and retrieve information from this index. The Search page is partially shown in Figure 32.7.

Searching can save you a lot of time, especially when embarking on new projects. If you know vaguely what another team has done, but don't have the specifics, you can most likely search them out. For example, you might learn that the previous team's attempt at a similar project failed because the hardware demands were too high for the computers at the time. Armed with this knowledge, you can try and trim down the requirements for your own project.

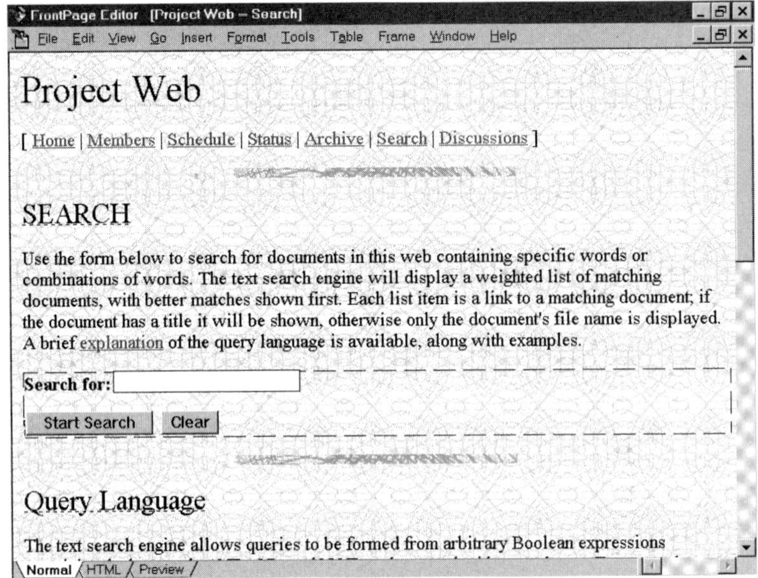

FIGURE 32.7.
Search the Project Web.

The Discussions Area

As shown in Figure 32.8, the Project Web includes two complete Discussions areas. The first discussion relates to project requirements. The second discussion builds a knowledge base for the project by tracking common questions and answers. While you could redefine the purposes of these discussions simply by changing the text where appropriate, the requirements and knowledge base discussions are great for most projects.

Each Discussions area contains four pages: a home page, a table of contents, a search page, and a posting page. The home page for the area is the same page the reader accesses when he clicks on the Discussions link from another area of the Web.

Your navigation decisions from the Discussions front entry are somewhat limited. What if you wanted to add a few more options? Normally, you would need to edit the file and add your own hyperlinks and URLs. In this case, all you have to do is edit the properties of the Navigation component. To do so, double-click on either of the Navigation components on the page, either the top button row or the left column of buttons. From there, choose the Same Level radio button. What you should see is a much more expanded selection of possible destinations from this page, and all without you writing a single line of code. If you're confused by the Same Level, Parent Level language, go look at your Project web in the Navigation view from the FrontPage Explorer. You should quickly figure out that the pages are linked in hierarchies, and all the menu items on the same horizontal hierarchy as the discussion group (Members, Status, Archive, Search, Schedule) will appear when you choose that option from the Navigation component properties. Parent options are those that are above the current level in hierarchy.

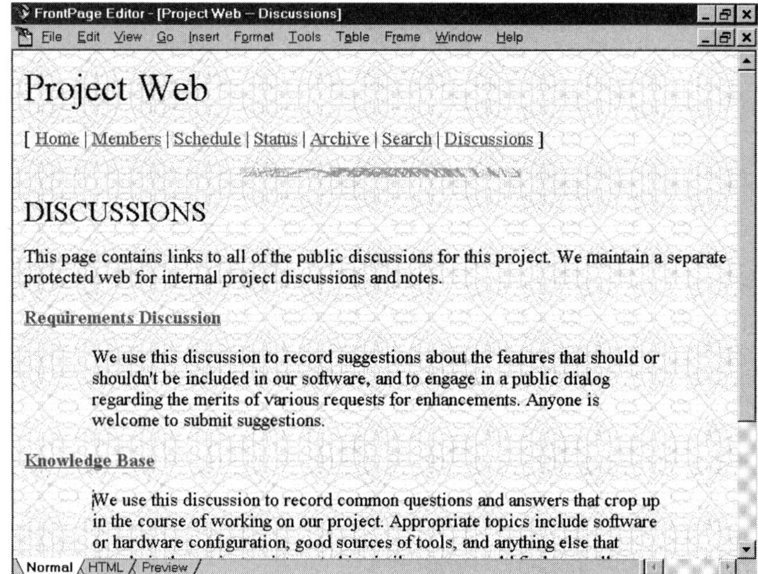

FIGURE 32.8.
The Project Web includes two discussion areas.

Summary

Using the Project Web to help you develop and promote a company project is a great idea. Because the Project Web is designed as a place for project team members to discuss the project and to brainstorm, you will probably want to use the Project Web on a corporate intranet or on a restricted web.

CHAPTER 33

Establishing a Corporate Presence

by William Robert Stanek

IN THIS CHAPTER

- Examining the Corporate Presence Web *534*
- Determining the Pages for Your Web *535*
- Choosing Topics for Your Home Page *535*
- Defining the What's New Page *536*
- Creating Product and Service Pages *537*
- Creating the Feedback Form *538*
- Creating the Table of Contents Page *539*
- Creating a Company Standard *540*
- Adding an Under Construction Icon *541*
- Adding the Company Name and Contact Information to Your Pages *542*
- Choosing a Presentation Style *543*
- Creating a Task List *544*

The Corporate Presence Web is by far the most advanced web included with FrontPage 98. In fact, it is so advanced that you need a Web Wizard to help you build it. As the name implies, this web is designed to help your company (or the company you work for) establish a presence on the Web. The Corporate Presence Web is designed to be your company's main site on the World Wide Web. FrontPage 98's Corporate Presence Web can help you built the site, step-by-step.

Examining the Corporate Presence Web

The key pages of the Corporate Presence Web include the following:

A corporate home page

A table of contents page

A What's New page

Press release pages

A directory of your company's products and services

Pages for individual products and services

Pages for obtaining feedback from your customers

A search page

The pages included in this web are similar to the pages in other webs. What makes this web unique and powerful is that just about every aspect of the web can be tuned to your needs via the wizard.

To start a Corporate Presence Web, select New from the File menu (or press Ctrl+N), and then choose the Corporate Presence Web Wizard from the New dialog box. Next select the name of your Corporate Presence Web. After you enter this information, FrontPage 98 launches the Corporate Presence Web Wizard.

Figure 33.1 shows the first page of the Corporate Presence Web Wizard. The buttons at the bottom of the dialog box are standard throughout the web creation process. At any time, you can move to the previous or next phase of the creation process using the Back or Next buttons. When you have fully defined the web, click the Finish button and the FrontPage Editor creates the web you have designed.

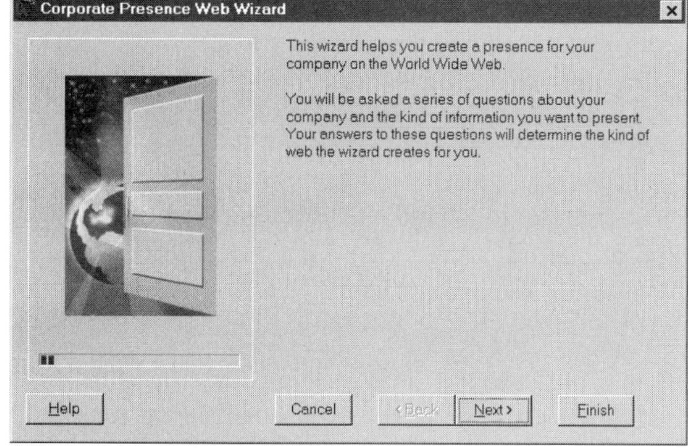

FIGURE 33.1.
Getting started with the Corporate Presence Web Wizard.

Determining the Pages for Your Web

Now that you have started the Corporate Presence Web Wizard, click the Next button. This displays the wizard page shown in Figure 33.2, from which you can select the type of pages you want to include in your web.

Keep in mind that the pages you create with the wizard are based on templates designed specifically for the Corporate Presence Web. In most cases, you will want your Corporate Presence Web to include all of the possible pages.

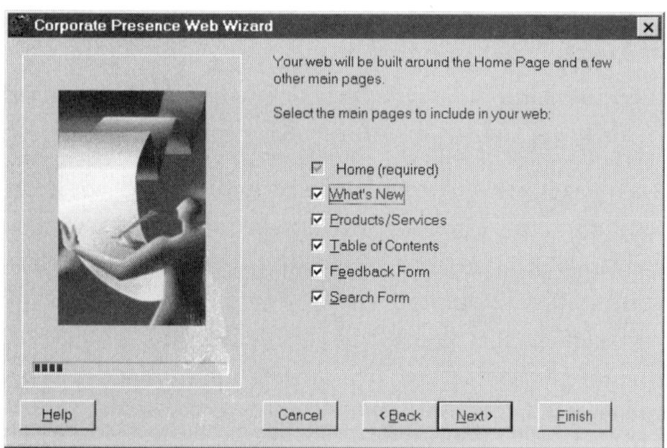

FIGURE 33.2.
Select the type of pages you want to use in your web.

Choosing Topics for Your Home Page

After you have selected the types of pages for your web, you can continue by clicking Next. The next page in the Corporate Presence Web Wizard lets you select the topics you want to appear on the corporate Home Page.

As the wizard dialog shown in Figure 33.3 implies, the Home Page is the first page most visitors to your web will see. For this reason, you should let visitors know immediately what your company does and what the company represents.

Small to mid-sized businesses should include the company mission and profile on the Home Page, because some users who visit might not be familiar with the company. However, most large businesses will want to include the company mission and profile on a separate company background page. Still, I recommend selecting all the available topics. You can always delete sections you do not want to use later.

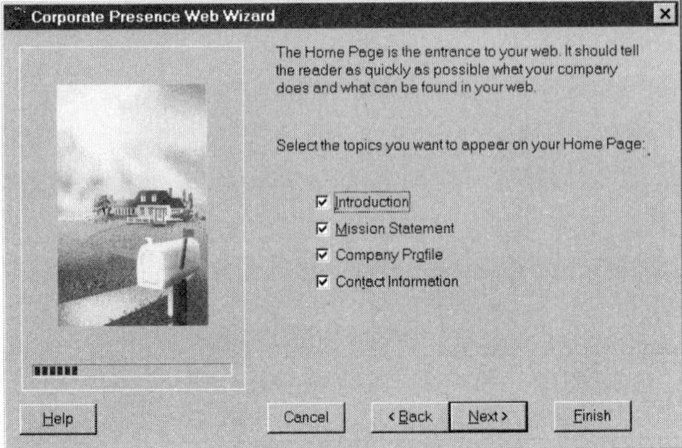

FIGURE 33.3.
Select topics for your Home Page.

Defining the What's New Page

If you chose to include a What's New Page, the wizard next displays the screen shown in Figure 33.4. This page helps you choose topics for your What's New Page.

What's New Pages usually provide readers with an updated history of a Web site, and are often one of the most visited pages. You can also use the What's New Page to tell your potential customers about new developments within the company, which is a powerful tool for establishing your corporate presence in cyberspace. For this reason, the Corporate Presence Web Wizard includes changes to the Web site, a directory of press releases, and recent reviews of the company all on the same page. This is a winning combination, and you will probably want to use all three topics on your What's New page.

FIGURE 33.4.
Selecting topics for your What's New Page.

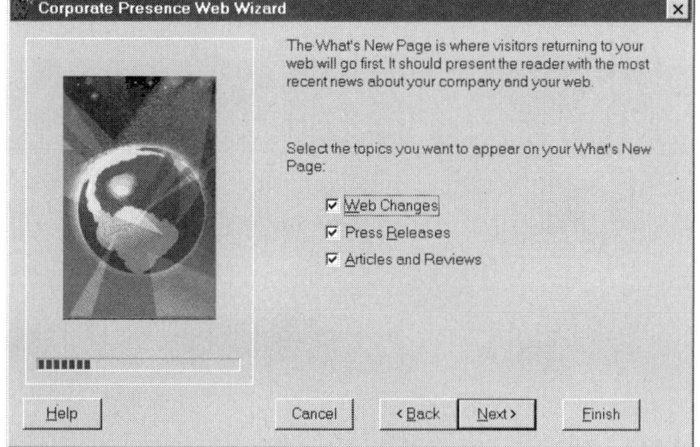

Creating Product and Service Pages

If you selected the products and services option earlier, clicking Next takes you to the dialog box shown in Figure 33.5. Most companies sell products or services; some companies offer both. In this section of the setup wizard, you can choose how many Products pages and Services pages you want to create.

NOTE

Zero is an acceptable value for the Products and Services fields. If you enter a zero in one of the fields, you will not be able to select the related options in later setup stages. If you enter a zero in both fields, you will skip the wizard sections that relate to products and services.

FIGURE 33.5.
Creating Product Pages and Service Pages.

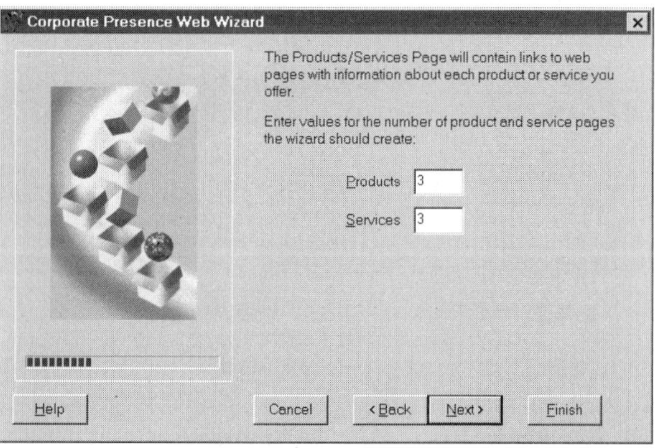

After entering the number of Product Pages and Service Pages you would like the wizard to create, click the Next button. As you can see from Figure 33.6, the wizard then lets you select the topics for your pages.

Keep in mind that you are specifying default topics for all Product Pages and Service Pages. If you are unsure about the type of product or service information you would like to provide on the Web, select all the available options and make a determination when you see the completed templates.

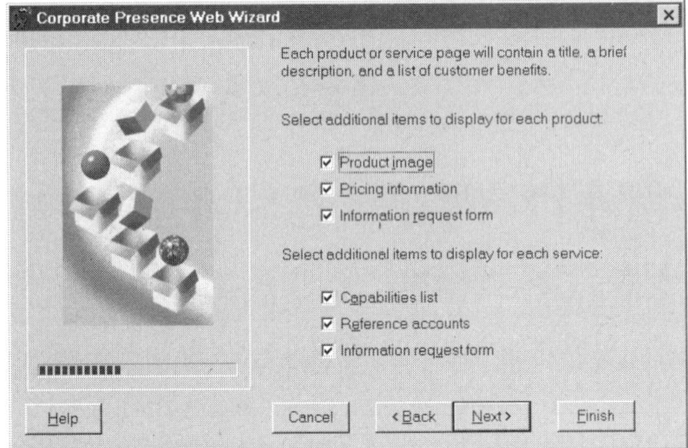

FIGURE 33.6.
Selecting topics for the Product Pages and Service Pages.

Creating the Feedback Form

Getting feedback from customers is extremely important, which is why the Corporate Presence Web Wizard creates a Feedback Form for you. As you can see from Figure 33.7, the Feedback Form will enable you to collect a lot of information from the reader—perhaps too much. If you really want to know what visitors think, do not ask them for too much personal information. Their e-mail addresses and perhaps their full names should suffice in most instances.

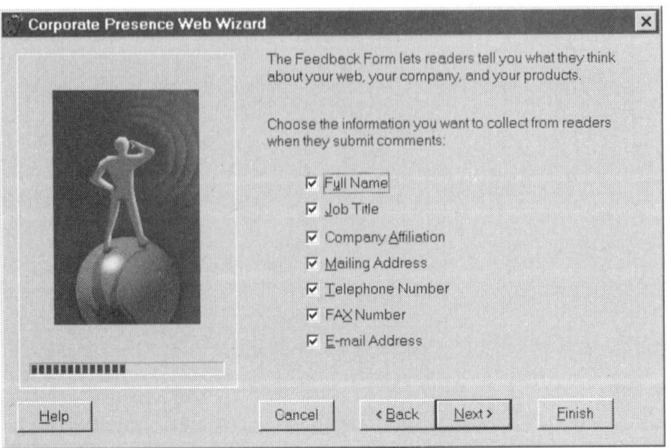

FIGURE 33.7.
Determining input for the Feedback Form.

As shown in Figure 33.8, you can store the data gathered from the Feedback Form in two key formats: ASCII text (tab-delimited) or HTML (web page). Data in a text format is easily manipulated, which is good if you want to do any follow-up processing. Data in HTML format is easy to read, but not easily manipulated. You can change this selection later by opening the page in the FrontPage Editor and changing the properties associated with the Feedback Form.

FIGURE 33.8.
Storing feedback data.

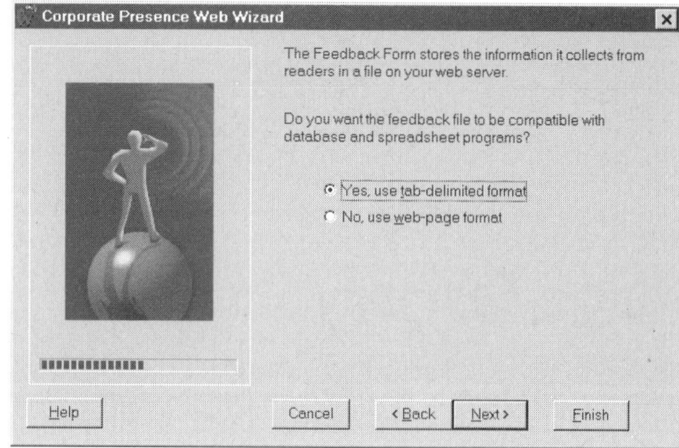

Creating the Table of Contents Page

Like an index, a table of contents for a Web site is useful but usually difficult to build and maintain. FrontPage 98 automates this process and enables you to build a Table of Contents Page that is automatically updated when you make changes to the web structure. As shown in Figure 33.9, you can also create links to pages in the web that are not linked to other pages and identify top-level pages with a bullet.

NOTE

Although I recommend using this page, it could grow unwieldy if your site has a lot of pages. If that happens, you might want to remove the FrontPage component that is making automatic updates to the page. (Load the page in the FrontPage Editor, click the table of contents text, and then press Delete). You might also want to delete links to low-level pages.

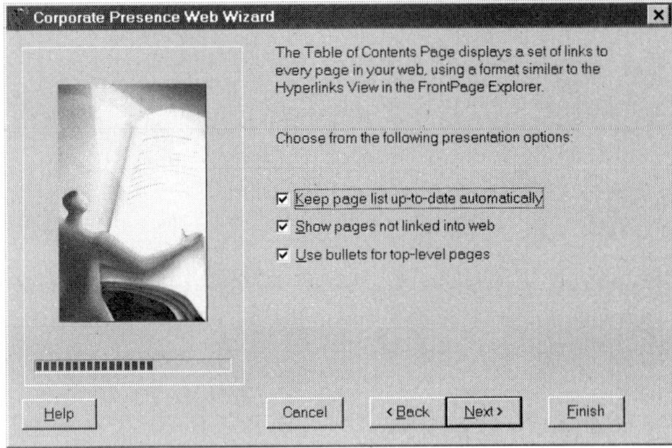

FIGURE 33.9.
Determining the style of the Table of Contents Page.

Creating a Company Standard

You can determine how intrusive or subtle your company's presence will be on the future Web site. The Corporate Presence Web Wizard gives you seven different variables to control how strongly your company is represented. The following seven choices are divided into two different categories (as displayed in Figure 33.10):

- **Your company's logo** (at the top of the page). This controls whether your company's logo will be automatically inserted at the top of every page within the site.
- **Page title** (at the top of the page). This controls whether the title of the page is automatically inserted at the top of the page as an aid to navigation.
- **Links to your main web pages** (at the top of the page). This controls whether links to your other corporate sites will be automatically inserted at the top of every page. If you don't have any other sites, your choice is obvious.
- **Links to your main web pages** (at the bottom of the page). This is identical to the previous item, except that the links in question would appear at the bottom of each page instead of the top. If you have both selected, each link will appear twice.
- **E-Mail address of your Webmaster** (at the bottom of the page). This controls whether you have an e-mail address at the bottom of every page that links to your Webmaster's address.
- **Copyright notice** (at the bottom of the page). This controls whether a legal copyright notice protecting your company's ownership of the site's contents will appear at the bottom of every page.
- **Date page was last modified** (at the bottom of the page). This controls whether a timestamp displaying the last time of modification is inserted into the bottom of every page.

Common sense is the prerequisite for using these elements. If you are already incorporating a graphic that has your company's logo in it (as a banner perhaps) in every page, then having the logo on top of every page is somewhat redundant. The same is true of having links to your other corporate sites on both the bottom and top of your pages. Double the links does not necessarily means double the goodness. A bare minimum for most companies is copyright, Webmaster address, and date last modified. Each is important to the end user in one way or another. Copyright warns them against stealing your work, the Webmaster address reassures them that they can reach someone, and the last modified date tells them if changes have been made to the site since the last time they were there.

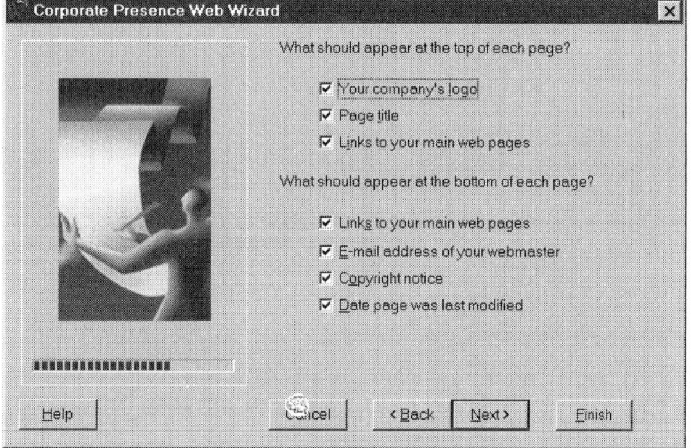

FIGURE 33.10.
Defining standard headers and footers.

Adding an Under Construction Icon

As you can see from Figure 33.11, the next page enables you to add an Under Construction icon to unfinished pages. This serves as a visual cue to visitors that the page is not finished yet. When you first create your web, most of your pages will be unfinished, so if you decide to use this icon, it will likely appear in a lot of places.

CAUTION

The Under Construction icon is extremely frustrating for users, especially if it is used in many places on your web site. After all, who wants to browse a site where every link leads to a dead end? So, instead of publishing an unfinished site, polish your web presence until it shines and *then* publish it.

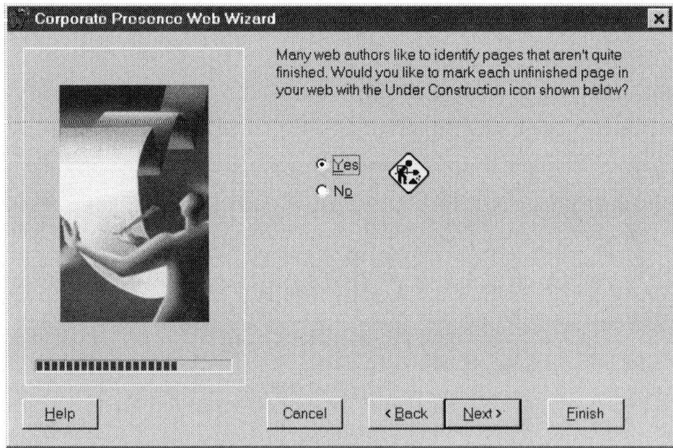

FIGURE 33.11.
Adding an Under Construction icon.

Adding the Company Name and Contact Information to Your Pages

Your company name plays an important part in building your Web presence. All of your pages should include either the full name of your company or an abbreviated name. Some of your pages should include the company's address as well. To avoid the tedium of having to add this information to dozens of pages, the Corporate Presence Web Wizard lets you define this information using the wizard dialog shown in Figure 33.12.

You must not leave any of these fields blank. Therefore, if you click Next and any of these fields are empty, the FrontPage Explorer displays a prompt that tells you to fill in the missing field. After you specify this information, the wizard takes care of adding it to pages where needed.

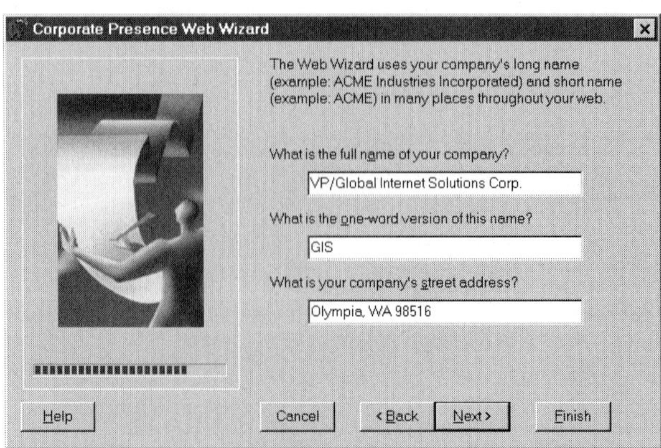

FIGURE 33.12.
Adding key information to your pages.

Contact information beyond the company's address is also important. On the next page, shown in Figure 33.13, you specify phone, FAX, and e-mail addresses. Again, because this information must appear on key pages within your web, you cannot leave any of these fields blank, which means that you would need to fill in the two blank fields on the page shown in Figure 33.13 before you advance to the next stage of the Corporate Web wizard setup.

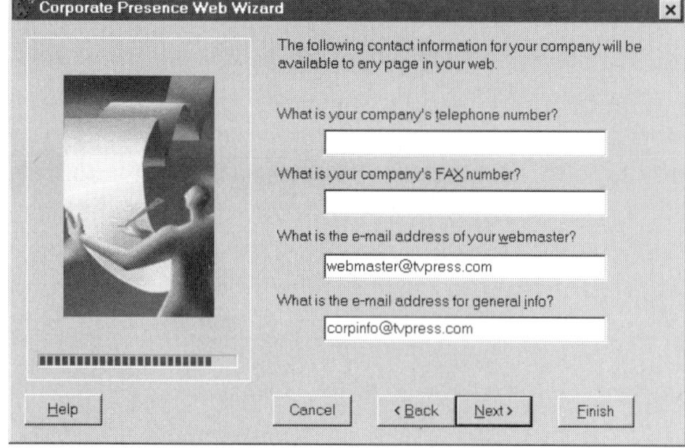

FIGURE 33.13.
Completing the necessary contact information.

Choosing a Presentation Style

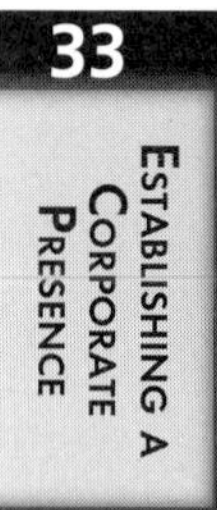

The next page in the wizard lets you select a theme for all the pages in your web. Keep in mind that the theme applies to just about every aspect of your web. Generally, the wizard creates graphics for the following:

Backgrounds

Header and footer page links

Default page title graphics

Fancy horizontal rules

Buttons

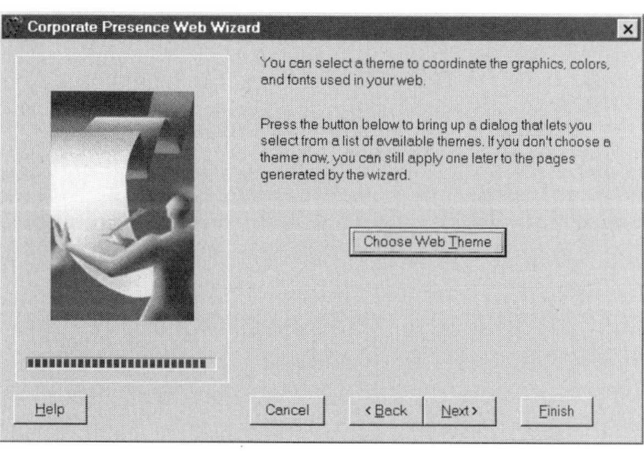

FIGURE 33.14.
Selecting a theme.

Creating a Task List

The final page in the Corporate Presence Web Wizard enables you to automatically generate a task list for your new web. The task list contains a list of tasks that you should perform to complete the web. You should generate the task list, because it gives you a clear idea of what you need to do next.

Now that you are done defining your web, click the Finish button. When you do this, the wizard starts creating your web. After the wizard creates your web, it generates the task list. If you created all the available pages, you have a task list with items similar to the one shown in Figure 33.15. Use this list as a guideline to help you complete the design of your web. After you complete the tasks on your task list, look at and edit each and every page in your web.

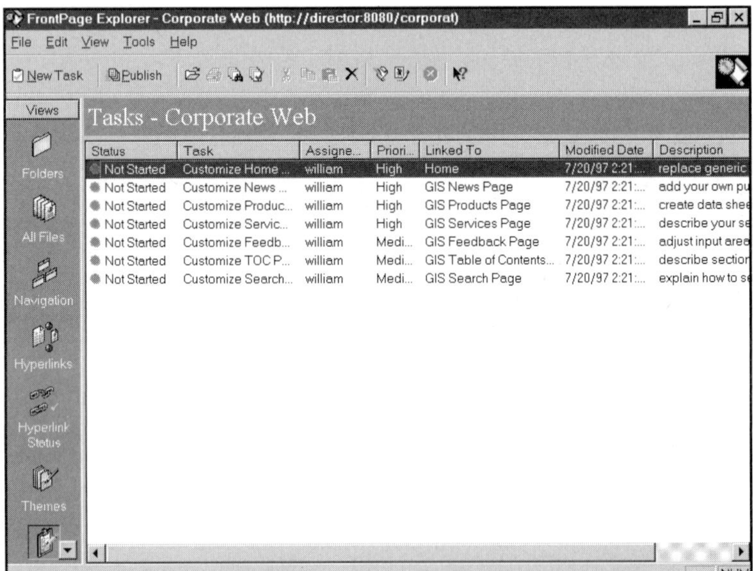

FIGURE 33.15.
Use the task list to help you complete the design.

Summary

Establishing a corporate presence on the Web is a fairly easy task. All you need to do is start the Corporate Presence Web Wizard and follow its step-by-step walk through of the web creation. When you are finished creating the web, be sure to examine and update each and every page in the web.

Automation with FrontPage Components

by William Robert Stanek

IN THIS CHAPTER

- How to Use FrontPage Components *546*
- How Do FrontPage Components Work? *547*
- Using the Confirmation Field Component *548*
- Using the Include Page Component *551*
- Using the Scheduled Image Component *552*
- Using the Scheduled Include Page Component *554*
- Using the Substitution Component *555*

FrontPage Components greatly streamline the development process and eliminate the need to write your own scripts or add complicated HTML commands. With a FrontPage Component, sometimes called a *WebBot* or simply a *bot*, you can collect the results from forms, automatically add navigation bars, create pages with full text searches, allow registered users to access key areas of your Web site, and much more. No programming is involved at all.

How to Use FrontPage Components

Throughout this book, you have learned about FrontPage Components (previously known as WebBots). As you have seen, you can use components to automate many Web publishing tasks.

The FrontPage Editor makes the process of adding FrontPage Components to pages easy. The first step is to move the insertion point where you want to place the component. Next, click the Insert FrontPage Component icon (the robot) on the Standard toolbar, or choose Insert|FrontPage Component. In the Insert FrontPage Components dialog box, shown in Figure 34.1, select the component you want to use by double-clicking the appropriate keywords.

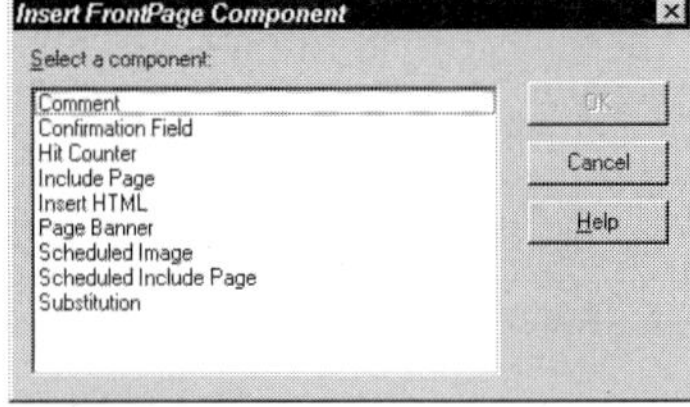

FIGURE 34.1.
The Insert FrontPage Component dialog box is used to add components to your page.

You can access the following components from the Insert FrontPage Component dialog box:

Comment	Inserts a comment into the page; comments are not displayed with the page and are viewable only if you examine the HTML source code. For more information, see Chapter 6, "Creating Richer Web Pages with HTML Features."
Confirmation Field	Confirms a user's entry into a form field; used with a confirmation page. You learn how to use the Confirmation field component in this chapter.
Hit Counter	Counts the number of times a page has been accessed. For more information, see Chapter 36, "Scripting with VBScript."
Include Page	Inserts the contents of a Web page into the current page; generally used to add headers, footers, and banners. You learn how to use the Include Page component in this chapter.

Insert HTML	Inserts a section of HTML that will not be validated in the FrontPage Editor; used to add markup that FrontPage 98 doesn't support directly.
Page Banner	Adds a graphical or text banner to the page.
Scheduled Image	Allows you to schedule when an image will be displayed in a Web page and when it will be replaced by a different image. You learn how to use the Scheduled Image component in this chapter.
Scheduled Include Page	Allows you to schedule when a page will be included in a Web page and when it will be replaced by a different included page. You learn how to use the Scheduled Include component in this chapter.
Substitution	Allows you to replace a section of text with a value you specify; used to update all the pages in a web quickly with preset flags and values. You learn how to use the Substitution component in this chapter.

Although you can access most of the components from the FrontPage Components window, you can access some components only when you use a specific template or active element. Components that aren't directly accessible generally handle background processing. For example, the Table of Contents component runs in the background any time your table of contents page is loaded into a browser, and the Registration component is invoked whenever you try to access a restricted web.

In FrontPage 98, the FrontPage Component maintenance process is also easy. When you move your mouse pointer over an area of a page containing a component, the pointer changes from an arrow to a robot. The robot icon indicates that a component is embedded in this area of the page. You access a Properties dialog box associated with the component by double-clicking when the robot icon is visible. With this dialog box open, you can change the characteristics of the component.

How Do FrontPage Components Work?

You can think of a FrontPage Component as a program or script that runs when needed. Some components affect your Web site only when you add or update the component in the FrontPage Editor. They therefore have no effect when a user browses the web. Most FrontPage Components automatically update themselves at runtime. As a result, the components either run immediately when viewed or start when the user performs an action in the page, such as submitting a fill-out form. Components that run immediately make updates to the page in browsers and in the FrontPage Editor.

All FrontPage Components that automatically update themselves at runtime depend on FrontPage server extensions. Therefore, you must either use the Personal Web Server to provide Web services or install the FrontPage server extensions for your server.

CAUTION

If you cannot use the FrontPage server extensions with your server, you will have problems with many of the FrontPage Components. The following are the primary components to watch out for:

Confirmation Field component

Discussion component

Registration component

Save Results component

Search component

Hit Counter component

These components execute when a user submits a fill-out form, and the do not work without the FrontPage server extensions. Other components might present problems as well because they add material to the page when loaded into a browser.

Using the Confirmation Field Component

The Confirmation Field component echoes a user's input to a form on a special page called a *confirmation page.* You can create confirmation fields for all your forms except those that execute a custom CGI script.

You can specify the confirmation page at any time by accessing the Form Properties box. Click the Options button and then the Confirmation Page tab. Then enter the URL of your confirmation page.

Associating Fields with Values

In Chapter 22, "Working with Forms," you explored how to create forms. As you might recall, each input field has two attributes:

`Name`	The keyword associated with the input field
`Value`	The value of the field

When you create a form, you should note the names of each field that you want to echo on a confirmation page. With this list of field names, you can open your confirmation page and insert the Confirmation Field component as appropriate. You must insert one component for each field that you want to confirm.

TIP

To view the properties for any field, open the Properties dialog box associated with the field by moving the mouse pointer over the field and double-clicking.

To use this component, select Confirmation Field from the Insert FrontPage Component dialog box. You then see the dialog box shown in Figure 34.2. In the Name of Form Field to Confirm field, enter the name of the form field (radio button, text box, and so on) you want to echo on this page. For all form fields except radio buttons, use the name in the Name text box. For radio button fields, use the name in the Group Name field. When you are finished, click the OK button.

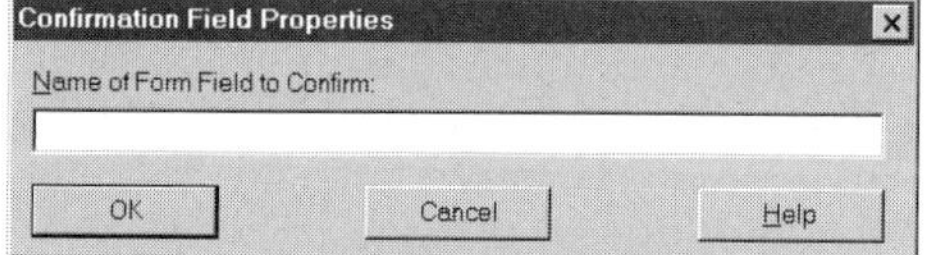

FIGURE 34.2.
Using the Confirmation Field component.

NOTE

You should use the Confirmation Field component only on form confirmation pages. When the user displays the page, the Confirmation Field component updates the field, and your page appears with appropriate values.

The Confirmation Field Component in Action

Before you use the Confirmation Field component, you should create a fill-out form such as the one shown in Figure 34.3. This form lets registered users submit questions to the company's customer support staff. The form asks for key information that confirms the identity of the user.

You should appropriately name each input field in the form. For this example, the fields you want to track are the user's account number and e-mail address. To verify the field names, you can open the Properties dialog box associated with the input field. Figure 34.4 shows the Text Box Properties dialog box for the input field for the user's account number. Note that the name of the field is `Account_number`. You should write down all the field names on a piece of paper.

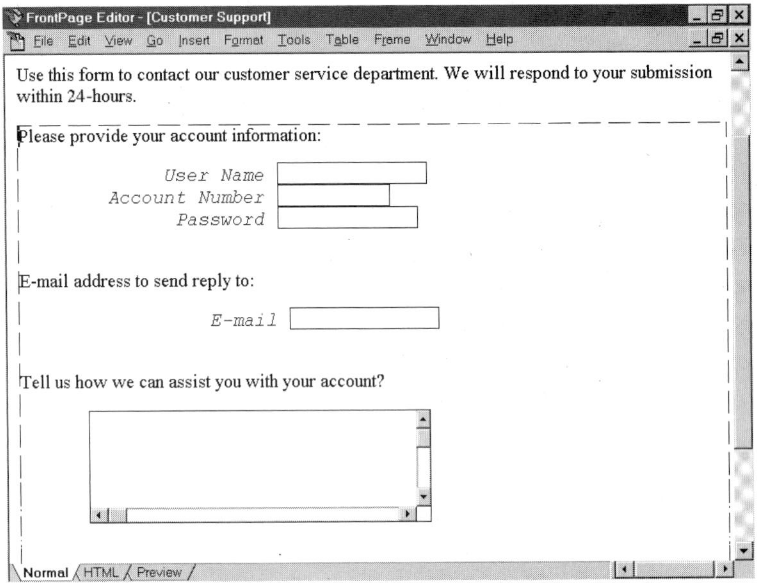

FIGURE 34.3.
A customer support form for registered users.

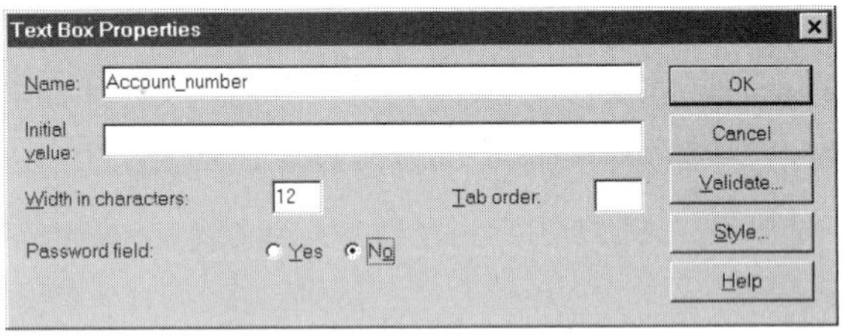

FIGURE 34.4.
Verifying field names.

Next, you should ensure that you have set a URL for the confirmation page. Afterward, you can create a confirmation page such as the one shown in Figure 34.5. When you insert the Confirmation Field component, the component asks you to enter the name of the field, which is then inserted into the page within square brackets. This page has two confirmation fields, one for `Account_number` and one for `Account_email`. You can update the properties of these components at any time by moving the mouse pointer over the confirmation field and double-clicking.

NOTE

At the bottom of Figure 34.5 is a two-link navigation menu within square brackets. Do not confuse the confirmation fields in square brackets with a similar technique used to highlight navigation links.

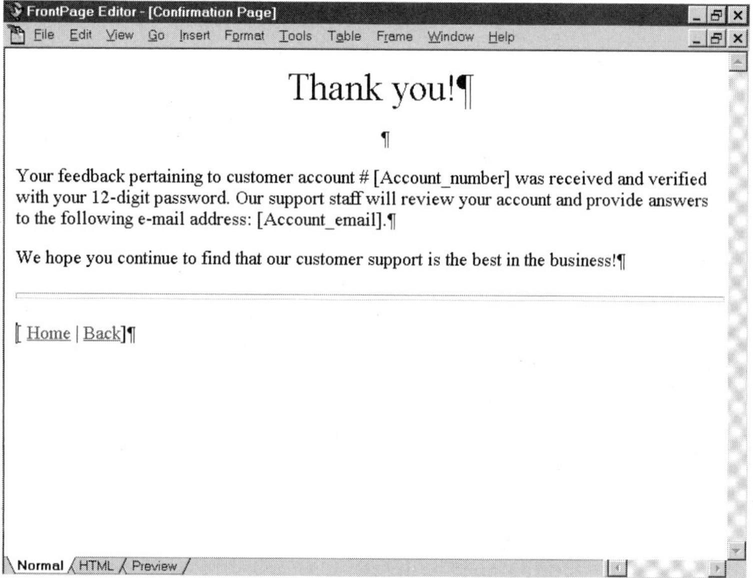

FIGURE 34.5.
A typical confirmation page.

Using the Include Page Component

The Include Page component helps you create standardized page sections throughout your web by enabling you to merge a page into an existing page. You use this function in many of the pages created with the web templates and wizards to add standard elements to pages.

When you view a page in a browser or in the FrontPage Editor, all Include Page components are replaced with the contents of the pages they reference. These pages can come from the same web, or from an entirely separate Web site. If you change the contents of a page referenced by an Include Page component, the change is made to every page in the web that has the Include Page component inserted in it.

> **TIP**
>
> Sometimes you might not want a page that you are including to be accessible to those who visit your Web site. If this is the case, create a subdirectory called `_private` within your Web site and store the page in this directory. Visitors to your web cannot access files in the `_private` directory.

To insert the Include Page component into a page, click the Insert FrontPage Component icon on the Standard toolbar, or choose Insert|FrontPage Component. On the Insert FrontPage Component dialog box, select the Include component by double-clicking Include Page. The dialog box shown in Figure 34.6 then appears.

FIGURE 34.6.
Using the Include Page component.

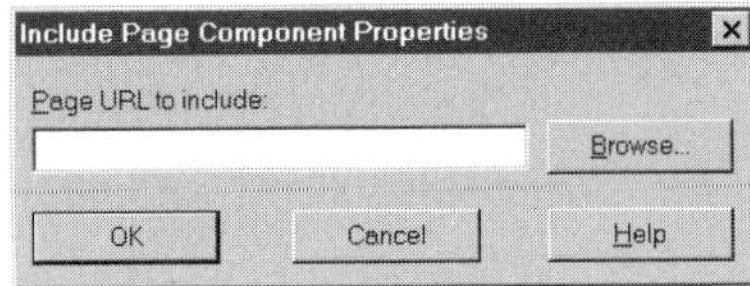

In the Include Page Component Properties dialog box, enter the URL of the page to include. If you don't know the URL of the page, click the Browse button to select a URL from a list of page URLs in the current web. When you are finished, click OK.

TIP

Keep in mind that you can use the Include Page component to insert the contents of a page outside of your current FrontPage web. You could use this to insert pages from another Web site, such as a search engine.

When you close the Properties dialog box, you see a message telling you that FrontPage 98 is retrieving the included page and inserting it into the current page. You cannot edit any elements included in the current page. You must open and edit the page that you are including to make any changes.

TIP

You can insert material before an Include Page component that is the first element on the page. Simply move the insertion point before the included elements and press Enter.

Using the Scheduled Image Component

Sometimes you might want to display images at your site for a specific period of time. For example, an advertiser wants to run an ad in your magazine for two weeks. You sign the advertiser to a contract stating this fact and ask him to specify the start date of the advertisement. Armed with this information, you place a Scheduled Image component on the pages where the ad will appear and schedule it so that the ad begins on the advertiser's start date, displays for 14 days, and then is replaced with your standard logo.

The preceding example illustrates one instance in which you might want to use the Scheduled Image component. Obviously, you might want to use this component at many other times. The primary reason to use this component is to include an image in a page with the intent of replacing the image at a later date and time.

CAUTION

The Scheduled Image and Include Page components execute only when changes occur to a web. Thus, to ensure that the Scheduled Image or Include Page component runs when you want it to, you should make some type of change to your web daily, such as incrementing the value of a configuration variable.

To insert the Scheduled Image component into a page, click the Insert FrontPage Component icon on the Standard toolbar, or choose Insert|FrontPage Component. In the Insert FrontPage Component dialog box, select the Scheduled Image component by double-clicking Scheduled Image. The dialog box shown in Figure 34.7 then appears.

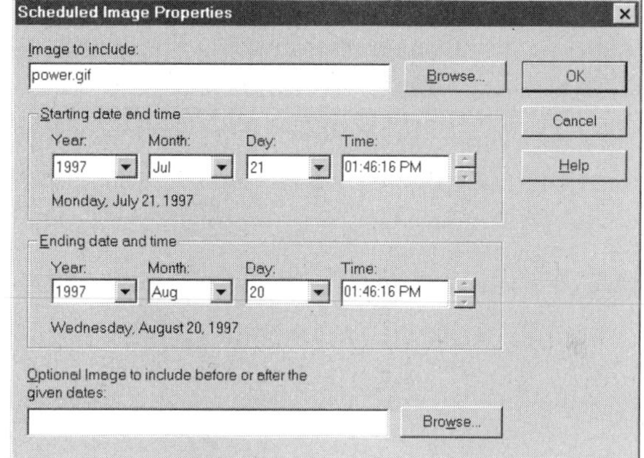

FIGURE 34.7.
Using the Scheduled Image component.

In the Scheduled Image Properties dialog box, enter the URL of the image to include. If you don't know the URL of the image, click the Browse button to select a URL from a list of images in the current web.

TIP

You can schedule an image from a Web site separate from your own using a complete URL, such as `http://www.mcp.com/sams/images/logo.gif`.

Next, you can specify the dates when the image should appear on the page. In the Starting date and time panel, enter the starting date using the drop-down lists to select the year, month, day, and time as appropriate. Initially, the starting date and time are set to the current date and time.

NOTE

If the starting date and time are equal to or earlier than the current date and time, the image appears on the page immediately.

In the Ending date and time panel, enter the date to stop including the image. Initially, this field is set to a calendar date approximately 30 days from the current date. The final option you can define is for an optional image to display when the included image is not being displayed. Click the Browse button to select a URL from a list of images in the current web. Click OK to close the Properties dialog box.

Using the Scheduled Include Page Component

Sometimes you might want to display a standard header, footer, or section of a page for only a specific period of time. With the Scheduled Include Page component, you can insert a page into the current page for a fixed time period.

To insert the Scheduled Include Page component into a page, click the Insert FrontPage Component icon on the Standard toolbar, or choose Insert|FrontPage Component. On the Insert FrontPage Component dialog box, select the Scheduled Include Page component by double-clicking Scheduled Include Page. Alternatively, you can select Scheduled Include Page and then click the OK button or press Enter on the keyboard. As you can see from Figure 34.8, you configure this component almost identically to the way you configure the Schedule Image component.

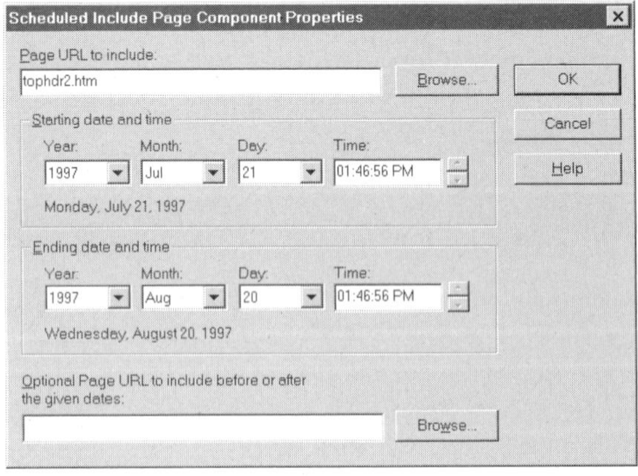

FIGURE 34.8.
Using the Scheduled Include Page component.

In the Scheduled Include Page Component Properties dialog box, enter the URL of the page to include. If you don't know the URL of the page, click the Browse button to select a URL from a list of pages in the current web. Next, specify the dates when the Include should appear in the page. In the Starting date and time panel, enter the starting date. If the starting date and time is earlier than the current date and time, the page appears immediately.

In the Ending date and time panel, enter the date to stop including the page. You can also define a page to display before and after the scheduled page appears. Click the Browse button to select a URL from a list of pages in the current web. When you are finished, click OK to close the Properties dialog box.

Using the Substitution Component

Just as you might sometimes want to insert standard headers and footers into your pages, you might also want to include standard segments of text. For example, most pages include contact information. Wouldn't it be great to be able to change the contact information instantly if one of the addresses is no longer valid? Well, with the Substitution component, you can make instant updates to your pages.

To insert the Substitution component into a page, click the Insert FrontPage Component icon on the Standard toolbar, or choose Insert|FrontPage Component. In the Insert FrontPage Component dialog box, select the Substitution component. You then see the dialog box shown in Figure 34.9. From the Substitute with pull-down list, you can select any of the default configuration variables as well as any configuration variables that you have added to the web.

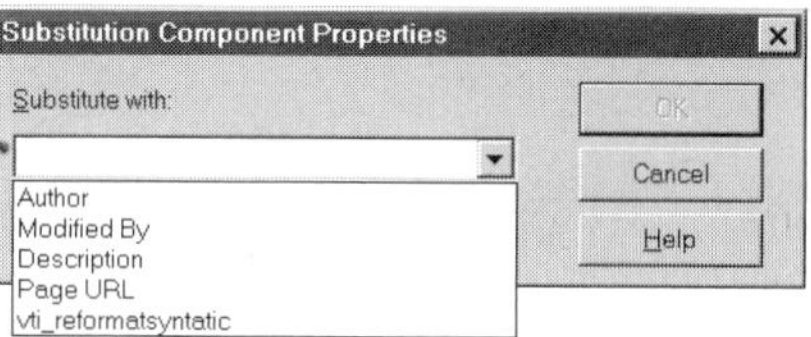

FIGURE 34.9.
Using the Substitution component.

Using Default Configuration Variables

When a user views a page containing a Substitution component, the component replaces a temporary variable with its value. This variable is called a *configuration variable* because the Web administrator can configure it and it is valid throughout the web.

FrontPage 98 tracks key information for all pages created, such as who created the page and who last modified the page. To view the settings for the default variables associated with any page, select the page in the FrontPage Explorer, and then open the Properties dialog box by choosing Edit|Properties or by pressing Alt+Enter. You can use these variables within your own web, thanks to the Substitution component. Figure 34.10 illustrates these variables.

To use these any of these variables (as well as some other built-in variables) within the Substitution component, you can select them from the Substitution Component Properties dialog box. You are given the following choices to substitute:

FIGURE 34.10.
The FrontPage Explorer's Properties dialog box.

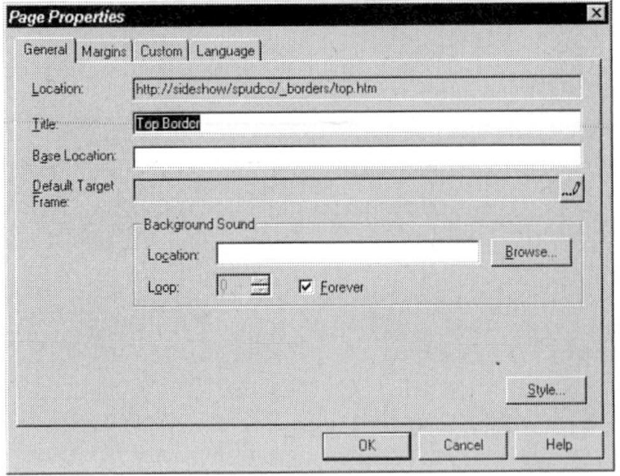

`Author` — The user name of the person who created the page, as defined in the Created by field of the FrontPage Explorer's Properties dialog box.

`ModifiedBy` — The user name of the person who most recently modified the page, as defined in the Modified by field of the FrontPage Explorer's Properties dialog box.

`Description` — A description of the current page, as defined in the Comments field of the FrontPage Explorer's Properties dialog box.

`Page-URL` — The page URL of the page, as defined in the Page URL field of the FrontPage Explorer's Properties dialog box.

Defining New Configuration Variables

To define new configuration variables, you start by choosing Tools|Web Settings in the FrontPage Explorer to open the Web Settings dialog box shown in Figure 34.11. The Web Settings dialog box has five tabs. The Parameters tab shows any user-defined configuration variables, and you can use it to add, modify, and remove user-defined configuration variables.

FIGURE 34.11.
The Parameters tab.

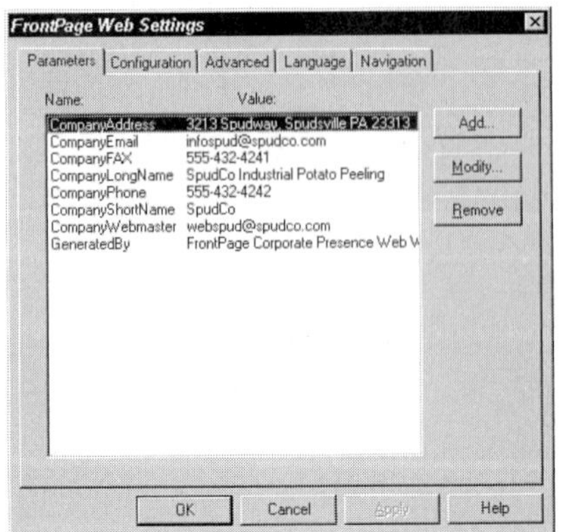

To add a configuration variable, click the Add button, which opens the Add Name and Value dialog box, which is shown in Figure 34.12. In the Name field, enter the name of the configuration variable you want to define. Although the name can be any length, it cannot contain the colon character (:). In the Value field, enter the value you want associated with the new configuration variable. The value can be a text string of any length. When you are finished, click the OK button. Repeat the procedure to define additional configuration variables.

NOTE

Select templates and web types create additional variables automatically. These include the company name (as defined by the Corporate Presence Wizard), address, what the web page was generated by, and more.

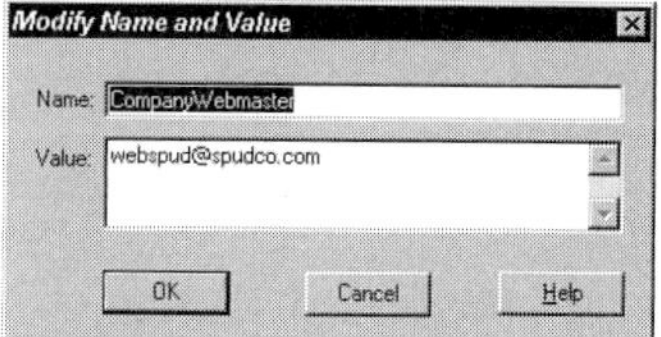

FIGURE 34.12.
Defining new configuration variables.

Summary

FrontPage 98 includes more than a dozen FrontPage Components. Components are useful for automating even the most advanced tasks and can be easily added to any page. Some components affect your web only when you add or update the components in the FrontPage Editor. Most FrontPage Components automatically update themselves at runtime. Components that run immediately make updates to the page in browsers and in the FrontPage Editor.

All components that automatically update themselves at runtime depend on FrontPage server extensions. Therefore, if you plan to use FrontPage Components that execute at runtime, you must either use the Personal Web Server to provide Web services or install the FrontPage server extensions for your server.

CHAPTER 35

User Registration and Restricted Webs

by William Robert Stanek

IN THIS CHAPTER

- Working with Restricted Webs 560
- Accessing Restricted Webs 560
- Creating a Members-Only Web 561
- Creating a Closed Web for Specific Users 565
- Restricting Groups in the FrontPage Explorer 569

Often you might want to control access to an area of your web or to an entire Web site, especially if you want to get paid subscriptions to your Web site. Setting up a restricted web without a lot of help isn't easy. Fortunately, FrontPage 98 fully supports the creation of webs with controlled access and user registration.

Working with Restricted Webs

By default, all users have access to your web. Using a restricted web, however, you can create a members-only area of your web. You restrict access to a web in two key ways:

- You can require users to register before entering a restricted web.
- You can allow only users registered by the Web administrator to access a restricted web.

The first method allows any user to access a web as long as he or she registers beforehand. A user typically can register by using a simple registration form that asks him or her to select a user name and password, which means access to the web is virtually unlimited. Generally, this type of web is known as a *members-only web*. The primary reason to use this type of web is that it allows you to track the number of registered users for your web. Sites such as C|Net (`www.cnet.com`) use this number to tout the popularity of their Web sites.

The second method allows only a specific set of users to access a web. The Web administrator grants these users access, and each user must specify the user name and password that the administrator assigned in order to enter the web. At any time, the Web administrator can revoke the access privileges. Generally, this type of web is known as a *closed web*. The primary reason to use this type of web is that it allows you to set up a controlled-access web for remote users. Businesses often use this type of web to allow a specific group of workers to access business data they need to perform their daily tasks. Whether the closed web is part of the corporate intranet or the Internet is up to you.

Accessing Restricted Webs

When a user tries to enter a restricted web, the Registration component asks him or her to enter a user name and password using the dialog box shown in Figure 35.1. If the user is not registered with the web and tries to enter information in this dialog box, the Registration component takes the user to a page set up for registration failures. For a members-only web that simply tracks the number of members, the failure page usually includes a link to a registration form.

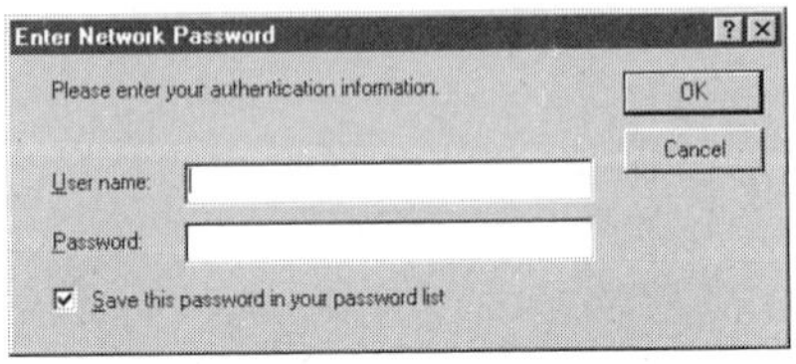

FIGURE 35.1.
A user must specify a user name and password to access a restricted web.

If the user is registered with the web, the Registration component grants access to the web and remembers the user name and password throughout the current session. However, the next time the user visits the web, he or she will be prompted again for a user name and password, which again will be good for an entire session.

Creating a Members-Only Web

Usually, when you create a members-only web, you simply want to track the number of members for your web. You can use the membership totals to tell the world about the popularity of your web. When you also require users to enter personal contact information, you get insight into who is visiting your Web site and where these users come from. These vital statistics can help you target the content of your web and sell advertising.

Creating a members-only web is fairly easy. You start by setting up the web for registration. Next, you configure the registration form and the Registration component. Finally, if you don't like the default confirmation and registration failure pages, you should create your own.

Setting Up the Web for Registration

To allow users to register for a web, you must create a registration form. Because of the way permissions are set, you should always register users using a form page located in the Root web. This form should grant them access to another web at your site.

If your Web site is at `www.mcp.com`, then your Root web is at `http://www.mcp.com/`. To register users for the `corppres` web at `http://www.mcp.com/corppres/`, for example, you create a registration form that is located in the base web, such as `http://www.mcp.com/registr.htm`.

In the FrontPage Explorer, open the web for which you want to register users and then choose Tools|Permissions. The Permissions—(webname) dialog box then appears, as shown in Figure 35.2. On the Settings tab, select the Use unique permissions for this web radio button, and then click the Apply button.

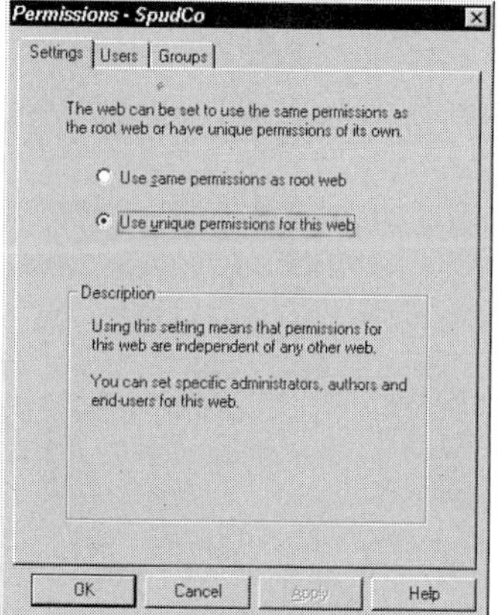

FIGURE 35.2.
Setting web permissions.

Next, on the Users tab, which is shown in Figure 35.3, select the Only registered users have browse access radio button, and then click the OK button to close the dialog box.

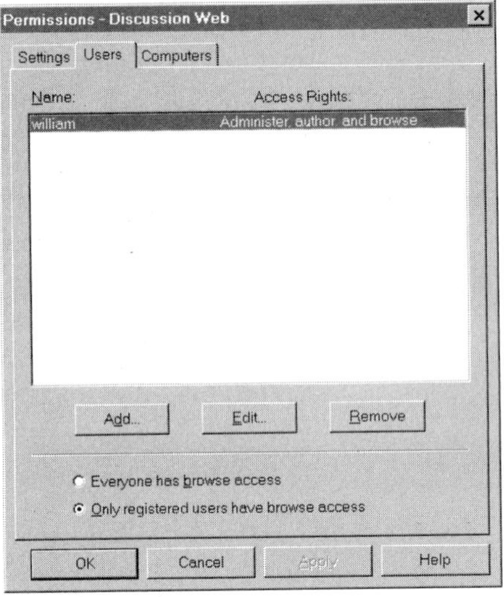

FIGURE 35.3.
Setting user permissions.

Next, you need to open the Root web. You can do this by choosing File|Open FrontPage Web to open the Getting Started dialog box. Select the Open an Existing FrontPage Web radio button and select the web server's root web, identified by the name `<Root Web>` in the web listing. If you have more than one root web listed, select it to identify the server below the list box. If you want to open an entirely new server's root web, click on the More Webs button to provide a new web server's address. Click OK to open the selected web. With the Root web as your current web, you can now open a new page in the FrontPage Editor and save it to the Root web. Start by choosing File|New. In the New dialog box, select the User Registration template, and click the OK button.

You can use the page created by the editor as the basis for your registration page. Delete any text that you don't want to include, and change the text associated with the registration form as appropriate for your web. Next, check the names associated with each input field.

The field names must exactly match the names used by the Registration handler (which you will create shortly). If they do not match, users cannot register for your web. Unfortunately, the Registration component is not smart enough to ensure that these fields match, and whenever users try to register, the component will display a failure page with a misleading error message such as `You must specify a user name.`

Configuring the Registration Component

Now that you have created a registration page, you need to configure the Registration component for use on your web. With the registration page open, right-click the form and then choose Form Properties from the pop-up menu. The Registration Form Handler should be selected in the Send to other radio button. Next, click the Options button to define options for the handler. The dialog box shown in Figure 35.4 then appears.

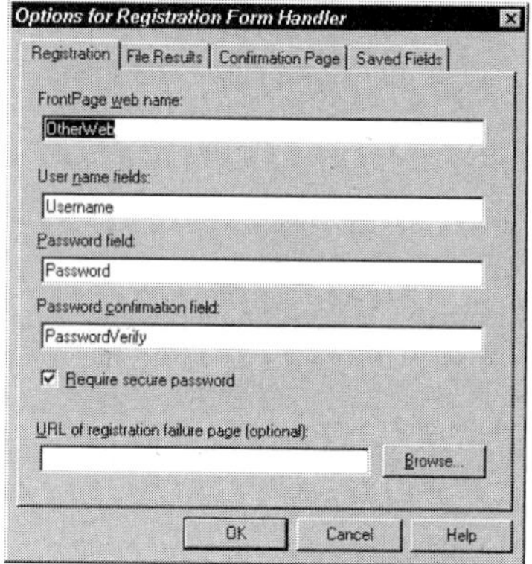

FIGURE 35.4.
Configuring the registration handler.

As you can see from Figure 35.4, the Registration handler has four configuration pages. You can access them by clicking the Registration, File Results, Confirmation Page, or Saved Fields tab. Although the Registration tab contains unique settings, the other tabs are exactly the same as those used for forms.

The first tab you should look at is the Registration tab. In the FrontPage web name text box, verify the name refers to the web for which you are registering users. The name must match the web name as shown in the Open Web dialog box.

TIP

As with other forms, all data submitted using the registration form is saved to a file. By default, the registration form data is saved as a text database with tabs separating fields. You can check and change these settings in the File Results tab of the Form Properties Options dialog box. Using the data file, you can determine how many users are registered at your web. By adding additional fields to the registration form, such as an address field, you can learn more about the people visiting your web.

All registration forms should have user name, password, and password confirmation fields. You should verify that the field names you used in your registration form match those shown in the Registration tab. If they do not match, enter the correct field names.

If you want to ensure that users have passwords that follow sound security practices, check the Require secure password field. In FrontPage 98, a secure password has six or more characters and does not partially match the user name.

The final field for which you might want to specify information is the URL of registration failure page field. All registration forms use default failure pages unless you specify another page. Figure 35.5 shows a failed registration using the default failure page. Although the default page is fairly basic, it gets the job done.

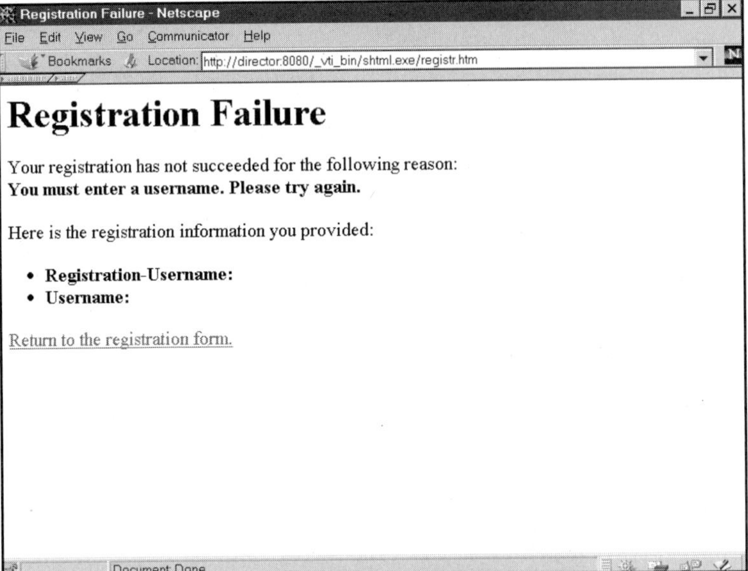

FIGURE 35.5.
The default page for failed registrations.

Next, you should review the settings in the other tabs. The key field you should check is the URL for the confirmation page in the Confirmation Page tab. All registration forms use default confirmation pages unless you specify another page.

Figure 35.6 shows a confirmed registration using the default confirmation page. This page confirms the user's registration and lets them access the restricted web. To ensure that users can register for your web, your home page in the Root web should have a link to the registration page.

FIGURE 35.6.
The default page for confirmed registrations.

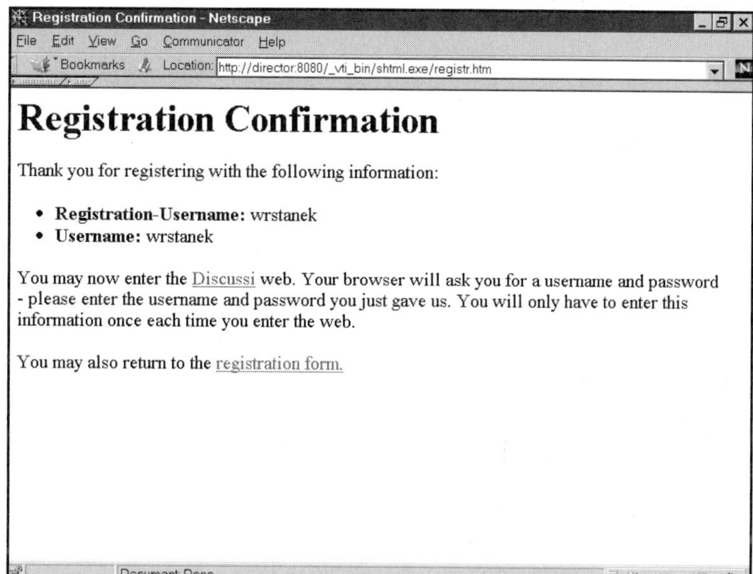

Creating a Closed Web for Specific Users

A closed web is designed to be used by a specific group of users, such as your company's research group. To ensure the integrity of the closed web, you probably should preregister all the users. In this way, you, as the Webmaster, create all the accounts and assign the users' passwords.

To create a closed web, you start by restricting access to the web. In the FrontPage Explorer, open the web for which you want to register users, and then choose Tools|Permissions. The Permissions—(webname) dialog box then appears. On the Settings tab, select the Use unique permissions for this web radio button, if it isn't selected already. Click the Apply button if you have made any changes. Next, on the Users tab, give browse access to registered users only by selecting the Only registered users have browse access radio button.

After you restrict access to the web, you need to set up accounts. You can use two types of accounts: user accounts and computer accounts.

Creating User Accounts in the FrontPage Explorer

You create user accounts on the Users tab of the Permissions—(webname) dialog box. This dialog box shows an alphabetical list of all users who have access to the current web. To the right of each user's name is a list of his or her access privileges. The access privileges match the three categories of access controls. For users who can only browse the web, `Browse` is listed by their names. For users who can create pages, `Author` and `Browse` are listed by their names. For users who can administer webs, `Administer`, `Author`, and `Browse` are listed by their names.

To add a new user, click the Add button at the bottom of the Users tab. The dialog box shown in Figure 35.7 then appears.

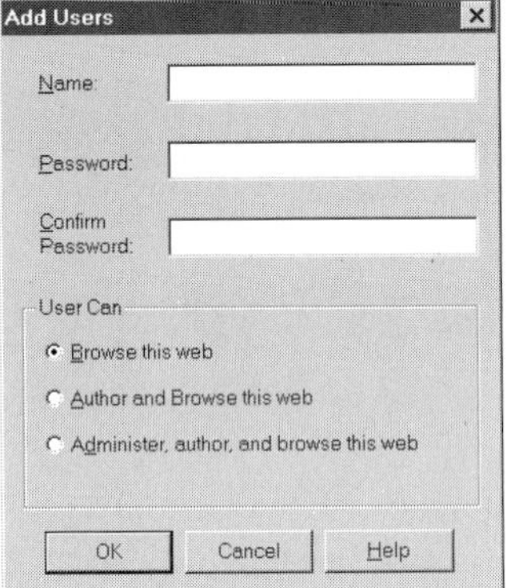

FIGURE 35.7.
Creating user accounts.

In the Name field of the Add Users dialog box, enter a user name for the account. Typical user names combine the first letter of a user's first and middle name with the last name. If the user has a long last name, you use only a portion of the last name. In this way, all user names are a specific length, such as eight characters. To create an account for William Robert Stanek, for example, you can use the user name `wrstanek`.

In the Password field, assign the user a password. For security purposes, all passwords should be unique and at least eight characters in length. Because FrontPage passwords are case sensitive, you can combine uppercase and lowercase characters in your passwords. For strict security, passwords should contain a mixture of alphanumeric and non-alphanumeric characters. After you enter the password, re-enter it in the Confirm Password field.

The final step in the account creation process is to set user privileges. Select the appropriate access privileges for the type of account you're creating. When you're done, click OK to close the Add Users dialog box and add the account.

After you create an account, you can change permissions at any time by selecting the account in the Users tab and then clicking the Edit button. This opens the Edit Users dialog box and lets you select new permissions with a radio button. The only way to change a user's password is to log in as that user and choose Tools|Change Password in the FrontPage Explorer. Alternatively, you can select the account, click the Remove button to erase the account, and then re-create the account.

Creating Computer Accounts in the FrontPage Explorer

Computer accounts are not used like user accounts. Instead of granting privileges, you are setting the maximum allowable privilege based on the location of the computer. Restricting access to your Web site based on the location of a computer makes your Web site more secure.

Using computer accounts, you can ensure that only users of the internal network—your intranet—have permission to use the web.

> **NOTE**
>
> Computer accounts are not available if your web server is Microsoft Internet Information Server, Microsoft Peer Web Services, or Microsoft Personal Web Services. For the IIS family of web servers you can restrict access on a *groups* basis, explained later in this chapter in the section, "Restricting Groups in the FrontPage Explorer."

To create computer accounts, you use the Computers tab of the Permissions—(webname) dialog box. As you can see in Figure 35.8, the Computers tab is almost identical to the Users tab. However, accounts are organized numerically by IP address instead of alphabetically.

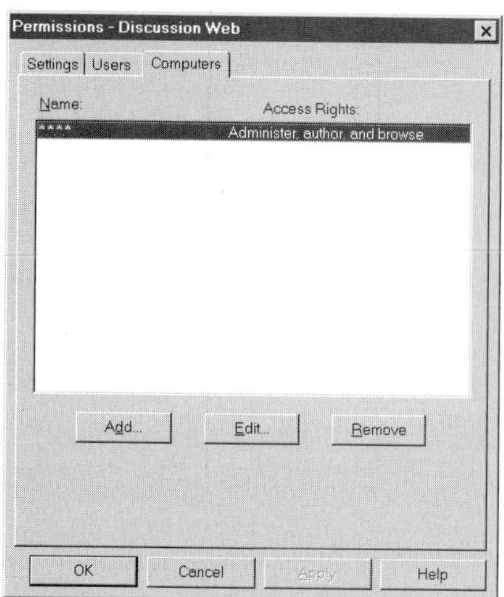

FIGURE 35.8.
Checking computer accounts.

IP addresses are broken down into period-separated fields. The value of these fields can tell you a great deal about the classification and structure of the computer to which it refers. Part of the address identifies the network to which the computer is attached, and part of the address identifies the host computers attached to the network. Any field of the IP address that contains an asterisk is a wildcard that allows any value to make a match for that field.

When you install FrontPage 98, a default computer account is set with all fields as asterisks. Therefore, any computer can be used to access your Web site.

If you are at all concerned with security, your number-one priority is to close off this gaping security problem. The first step is to grant the computer you're currently using full access rights to the Web server. To do so, click the Add button at the bottom of the Computers tab. The

Add Computer dialog box then appears, as shown in Figure 35.9. In the IP Mask field, enter the full IP address of your computer without using any asterisks. Because this account should have full privileges, select the Administer, author, and browse this web radio button. Close the dialog box by clicking the OK button. Then click the Apply button at the bottom of the Permissions dialog box.

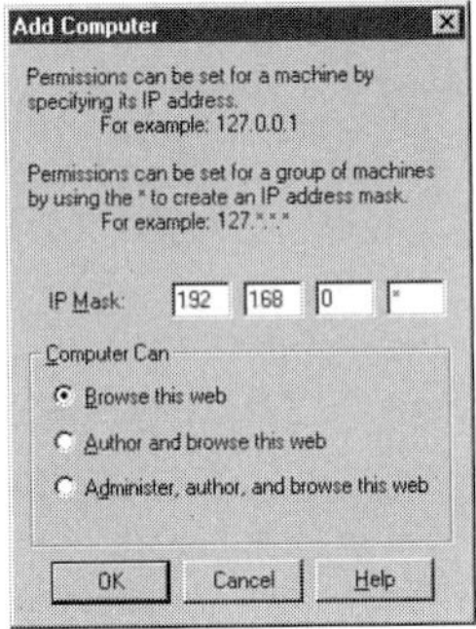

FIGURE 35.9.
Adding new computer accounts.

Afterward, you should create an account with administrator privileges for the local loopback, which is usually `127.0.0.1`. This way, you can ensure access to the server when you are logged directly into the Web server console.

Next, you should grant the appropriate level of privileges for computers within your network. Enter the IP address information that identifies your network to a level you feel comfortable with. You can use asterisks for some fields. If your network is

```
192.2.8
```

with host computers on your network identified as

```
192.2.8.1
192.2.8.2
192.2.8.3
192.2.8.4
192.2.8.5
192.2.8.6
192.2.8.7
192.2.8.8
192.2.8.9
```

you could create a computer account using the value

```
192.2.8.*
```

If you have multiple subnets, you can create individual computer accounts for each subnet as shown previously. You can also use another asterisk field. For example, if you have three subnets

```
192.2.7
192.2.8
192.2.9
```

you can create a computer account using the value

```
192.2.*.*
```

If you allow remote access from computers not connected to your internal network, you should create a separate computer account for each computer. This account should have a fully qualified IP address, meaning you use no asterisks.

The final step is to change the access privileges for the default computer account. If you permit access to users outside the internal network, edit this account and change the level of access to Browse This Web radio button in the Add Users dialog box. If you do not permit access by outside users, remove the default account.

After you create an account, you can change permissions at any time by selecting the account on the Computers tab of the Permissions dialog box and then clicking the Edit button. This opens the Edit Computer dialog box so that you can modify the permissions for the computer account. To erase an account, select it and then click the Remove button.

Restricting Groups in the FrontPage Explorer

When your Web server is a member of the Microsoft Internet Information Server family of web servers, you can choose to restrict access on a groups basis. Groups are a Windows NT grouping of similar accounts, sharing similar permissions. A Windows NT user account can be a member of several different security groups, sharing the permissions for each group. Using the FrontPage Explorer, you can restrict access to your Web site by restricting what permissions particular groups have. The Groups tab of the Permissions—(webname) dialog box, as shown in Figure 35.10, is used to control group permissions. This dialog box shows an alphabetical list of all of the Windows NT groups that have access to the current web. To the right of each group's name is a list of its access privileges. The access privileges match the three categories of access controls. For users who belong to a group that can only browse the web, `Browse` is listed by the group name. For group members who can create pages, `Author` and `Browse` are listed by the group name. For users who can administer webs, `Administer`, `Author`, and `Browse` are listed by their group's name.

NOTE

Restriction of groups is only available if your web server is Microsoft Internet Information Server, Microsoft Peer Web Services, or Microsoft Personal Web Server. For non-IIS based Web servers, you can restrict access on a computer basis (as explained in the section, "Creating Computer Accounts in the FrontPage Explorer").

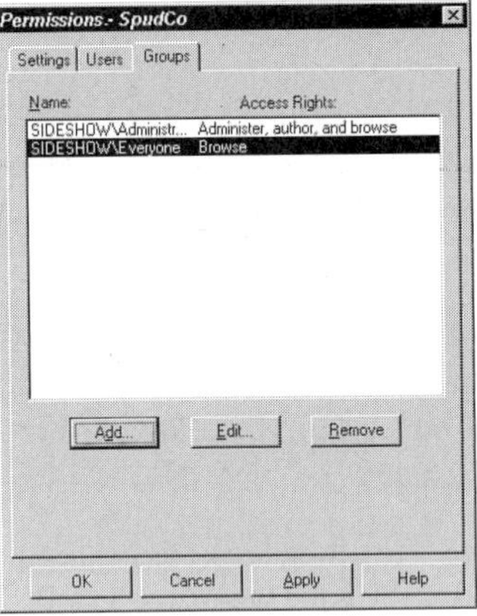

FIGURE 35.10.
Restricting access with groups.

By default, the groups list contains the group `Everyone` and the `Administrators` group. The `Everyone` account contains every user account in the Windows NT domain, while the `Administrators` account refers to all users within the domain that hold administrator permissions. Keep in mind that this is Windows NT account groupings and permissions. To add a new group to the list, click the Add button to open the Add Groups dialog box, shown in Figure 35.11. The Obtain list from drop box is used to select the Windows NT domain from which to obtain account information. Select the group (or groups) name from the Name list box, and click the Add button to add them to your web permissions list. Use the Users Can radio button set to select the permissions for the newly added group or groups.

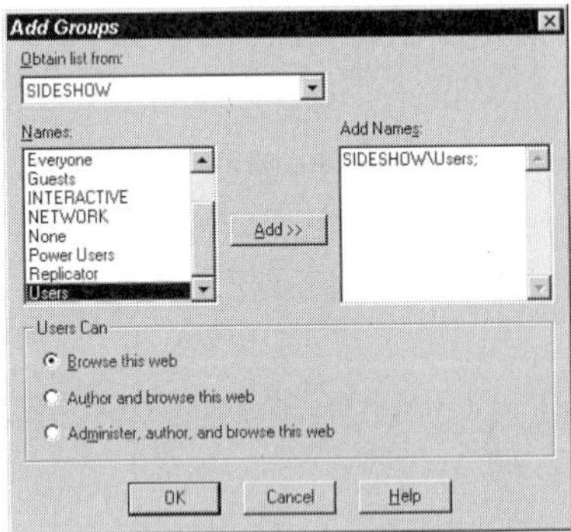

FIGURE 35.11.
The Add Groups dialog box lets you specify permissions for NT user groups in your web.

At a later time, if you want to modify the permissions for a group, select it and click the Edit button to open the Edit Groups dialog box. This dialog box lets you modify the permissions for an existing group. Finally, to remove a group from the permissions list, select it from the list and click the Remove button.

TIP

The Everyone group contains all users, including the anonymous user account used by the web server. This group should be the first account you modify permissions for if you are concerned about security.

Summary

When you want to control access to a web, you should use a restricted web. By allowing users to register for the web, you create a members-only web, which allows you to track the number of members and member information. Although members-only webs are great, you do not have complete control over who uses the web. If you want to have complete control over a web, you should use a closed web. With a closed web, you, as the Webmaster, create accounts for the web and thus control who has access to the web.

Part VII

Adding Dynamic Content to Your Web Page

IN THIS PART

- Scripting with VBScript *575*
- Creating Interactive Page Controls with ActiveX *599*
- Scripting with JavaScript *623*
- Adding Java Applets to Your Web Page *643*
- Designing Pages with Dynamic HTML *663*
- Using Push Channels *677*

CHAPTER 36

Scripting with VBScript

by William Robert Stanek

IN THIS CHAPTER

- Learning VBScript 576
- Putting VBScript to Work for You 577
- Adding Scripts to Your Page 580
- VBScript Basics 580
- Going Beyond the Basics with VBScript 591
- Summary Example 596

Microsoft's Visual Basic Script, also called VBScript, offers the functions of a programming language and the simplicity of a technology streamlined for the Web. With VBScript, you can bring your Web pages to life with real-time interaction; you no longer have to wait for a server to respond to button clicks and mouse movements. A click of a button gets an instant reaction, and the movement of the mouse pointer over an object brings the object to life.

FrontPage 98 integrates Visual Basic into its most basic functions, allowing you to add scripting power to your Web pages. The FrontPage Editor comes with a basic entry device that allows you to insert scripts into your pages, executable on either the server or the client's browser.

When you enhance your Web pages using VBScript, you insert scripts directly into your pages. Because VBScript is a subset of Microsoft's Visual Basic, your scripts resemble programs written in Visual Basic. If you aren't a programmer, don't worry. The wonderful thing about VBScript is that you can easily learn and use this simple programming language. Many Web publishers who aren't programmers use VBScript to enhance their Web pages.

Learning VBScript

If ever a programming language should have been adopted for use on the Web, it's Visual Basic. Microsoft's Visual Basic is founded on the simplest programming language ever designed, called BASIC. Extending the simplicity of BASIC to a more structured and modern object-oriented programming approach made Visual Basic a smashing success story. A language that understands objects—such as buttons, toolbars, and menus—and is easy to use is a dream come true for programmers.

When the developers at Microsoft redesigned Visual Basic for the Web, they knew they had to get rid of the massive overhead associated with Visual Basic programs. They therefore had to streamline every aspect of Visual Basic and keep only the essentials of the language.

Like most basic programming languages, VBScript is an interpreted language, which is both good news and bad news. The good news is that you don't need to compile your scripts as you would with a program written in C or C++. Your scripts are directly interpreted, line by line, when they're executed in the user's browser. The bad news is that before a user can run your scripts, he or she needs a VBScript interpreter, which is part of the standard Internet Explorer browser package. It's installed automatically when the user installs Internet Explorer.

Although Microsoft's Internet Explorer 3.0 and later versions include VBScript interpreters, most other browsers don't. However, an add-on module for Netscape Navigator 3.0 or later supports VBScript. Netscape Navigator users need to install this add-on module before they can fully use your VBScript-enhanced pages. To learn more about this plug-in, visit `http://www.ncompasslabs.com/`.

After you learn about VBScript, you're ready to learn how to use one of FrontPage 98's most advanced features: the Script Wizard. With the Script Wizard, you can generate scripts automatically. You don't need to know VBScript to use Script Wizard. However, you will better understand how to generate scripts automatically if you know how VBScript works.

Putting VBScript to Work for You

The possible uses for VBScript in your Web pages are endless. You can use scripts to create forms that change in response to users' questions; these customized forms could tailor orders, surveys, and customer support to the customers' needs. The results from VBScript-enhanced forms can be processed locally by the users' browsers or can be passed on to a server script for further processing.

You also can use VBScript to add interactive menus and buttons to the page. When a user makes a menu selection, portions of the page can change in response to the selection. At the click of a button, a dialog box can open to answer the user's question, offer helpful hints, or prompt the user when errors occur. Figure 36.1 shows a sample dialog box.

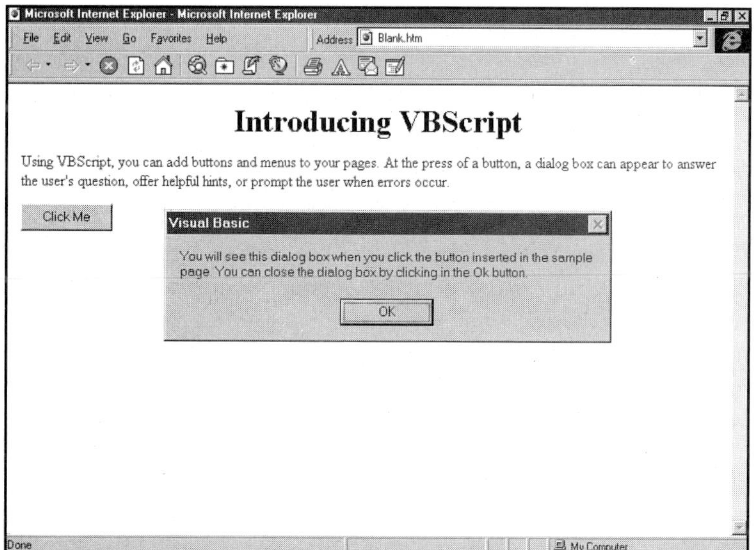

FIGURE 36.1.
Using VBScript to display dialog boxes.

To add these graphical objects to your pages, you use the basic controls offered by HTML forms. In the example, the form element is a button—named `cmdButton`—displayed with the label `Click Me`.

By combining the form elements you learned about in Chapter 22, "Working with Forms," you can easily create interactive Web pages complete with buttons, text fields, text areas, radio buttons, and check boxes. Later in this chapter, you learn more about adding controlled objects to your VBScript-enhanced pages.

You can display the dialog box associated with the button in Figure 36.1 by using the following code:

```
Sub cmdButton_OnClick
```

```
    Msgbox "You will see this dialog box when you click the button inserted
in the sample page. You can close the dialog box by clicking in the Ok button."

End Sub
```

By examining this code, you can see how VBScript works. The name of the button is `cmdButton`; an event related to it is called `OnClick`. When the button is clicked, the subroutine `cmdButton_OnClick` is executed automatically. VBScript features many ways of automatically handling user events, such as button clicks, mouse movement, and detecting when the pointer is over an object. The `Msgbox` statement tells the user's browser to display a dialog box with the contents you define between the quotation marks.

NOTE

VBScript is not case sensitive. Therefore, `cmdButton`, `cmdbutton`, and `CMDBUTTON` all refer to the same subroutine.

VBScript is great for crunching numbers, too. You can create a script to perform calculations, such as computing your annual salary based on wages and investment income or determining the time it will take to travel from one city to another.

With CGI, the user would have to fill out a form, submit the form to a server, and then wait for the server to respond. When the server finishes the calculations, the results would then be sent back to the client, which would display the results. As you know from earlier discussions on CGI, the results are usually displayed on a separate results page. With VBScript, all this back-and-forth processing is eliminated. The user can fill out a form and see the results instantly—and on the same page!

The sample page shown in Figure 36.2 uses VBScript to compute the sales tax on an order. The user simply enters the appropriate values and clicks a button, which causes a script to compute and display the results.

Although the script used to perform the calculation shown in Listing 36.1 is longer than the preceding script example, the script has a fairly basic structure. Simply put, the script accepts three values and displays the results after computations are made. If all this description seems like Greek to you, don't worry because this is just an example.

Listing 36.1. Calculating costs and sales tax.

```
Sub cmdCost_OnClick()

Dim State
Dim tripLength
Dim tripParty
Dim Cost
Dim Tax
```

```
Dim Total

tripLength = tripDays.Value
tripParty = tripSize.Value
State = resState.Value

If tripLength = 0 Then
    MsgBox "Please enter the length of your getaway."
    Exit Sub
End If
If tripParty = 0 Then
    MsgBox "Please enter the number of people in your party."
    Exit Sub
End If

Cost = 75.00 * tripLength * tripParty

If State = "HI" Then
     Tax = Cost * 0.07
Else
     Tax = 0
End If

Total = Cost + Tax

tripCost.Value = Cost
tripTax.Value = Tax
tripTotal.Value = Total

End Sub
```

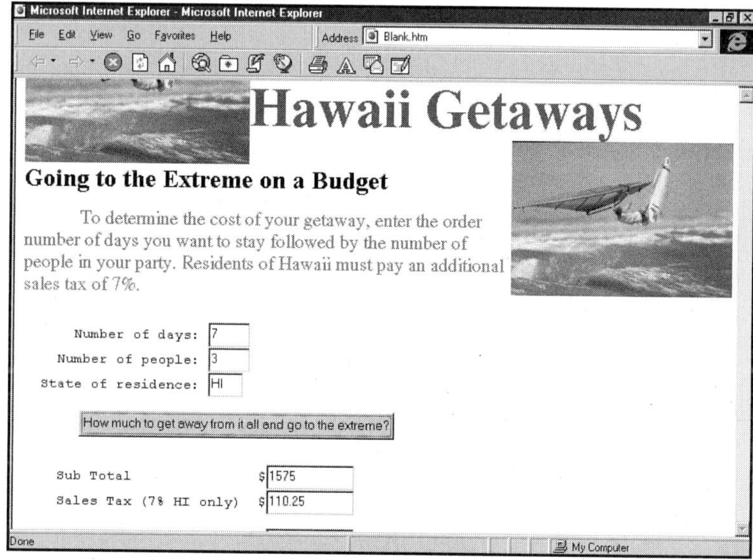

FIGURE 36.2.
Using VBScript to compute sales tax.

As a VBScript developer, you have an expanded role in Web publishing and might need to modify options in your browser for this new role. Most browsers consider VBScript to be a form of active content. Because running active content can present security concerns, the capability to run scripts is sometimes disabled. Check your browser's preferences or settings to ensure that the browser can use scripts.

Adding Scripts to Your Page

Just as you use the FrontPage Editor to create pages, you use the FrontPage Editor to create pages with scripts. Start by opening an existing Web page or creating a new page to which you want to add a script; then move the insertion point to the place where you want the script to run. Generally, you should place scripts wherever you will use them to add content or updates to the page.

After you determine where you want to add a script, choose Insert | Advanced | Script. You then see the dialog box shown in Figure 36.3. In the Language area of the dialog box, select the radio button labeled VBScript. Selecting this option sets a property that tells the reader's browser you're using the VBScript language. For now, enter your scripts directly in the input area provided. When you're finished, click the OK button.

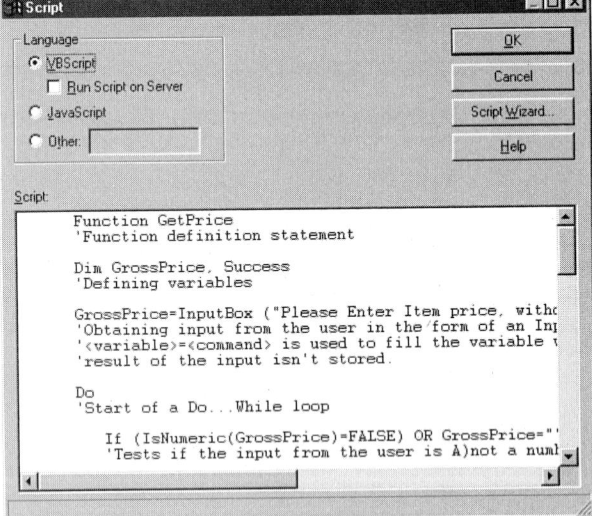

FIGURE 36.3.
Using the FrontPage Editor's Script dialog box to create scripts.

VBScript Basics

The syntax and structure of programs written in VBScript are like a familiar shoe for anyone who has programmed before. This is true regardless of which programming language you might have used. BASIC was originally invented as a teaching language, because the essential roots of programming could be easily explored in the language's simple syntax. Anyone who has had any programming experience will find that the concepts they are familiar with are easily exported to VBScript.

Variables

You can easily create a variable in VBScript by giving the variable a name. If you assign a name to a variable, you can later refer to the variable by name in your code. You can declare variables in two ways: explicitly or implicitly.

When you declare an explicit variable, you tell VBScript with the keyword `Dim` that you're creating a variable, and after the `Dim` keyword, you add the variable name. `Dim` is an abbreviation of Dimension, which should help you remember the keyword. When using `Dim`, you are giving dimension to your variables. If you want to explicitly declare a variable called `eValue`, for example, you use the following:

```
Dim eValue

eValue = 10
```

When you implicitly declare a variable, you use the variable without first declaring it, so you don't need to use the `Dim` keyword. VBScript creates the variable for you as necessary. If you want to use a variable called `iValue` implicitly, for example, you use the following:

```
iValue = 150
```

By default, VBScript allows you to mix implicit and explicit variables in your code. The problem with this capability, however, is that any variable name is assumed to be valid. For example, if you use a variable called `iValue` and later assign a value to a variable called `iVale`, VBScript creates instances of both variables, even if `iVale` is a typographical error for `iValue`. To avoid this problem, you can set the `Explicit` option.

Using the `Explicit` option forces you to declare all variables explicitly with the `Dim` keyword and ensures that your variables are valid. This option should be the first element in your script:

```
Option Explicit

Your script here.
```

As most programmers know, when you use variables in a program, you typically must state the type of variable. If the variable is used with integers, you declare the variable as an `Integer`; if the variable is used with strings, you declare the variable as a `String`. However, typing variables appropriately can lead to problems in code and also can create a complex structure that increases the overhead required for programs.

So that you can avoid problems and streamline VBScript, VBScript automatically allocates a variable type to any variables you use in your programs. Variable types used by VBScript include `Boolean`, `Byte`, `Integer`, `Long`, `Single`, `Double`, `Date`, `String`, `Object`, `Error`, `Empty`, and `Null`.

Generally, if you use a whole number, such as `5` or `8`, with a variable, VBScript creates the variable as an `Integer`. Variables with values that use decimal points, such as `3.5` or `5.82`, are usually assigned as double-precision floating-point values—`Doubles`. Variables entered with a mixture of alphabetical and numeric characters, such as `H2O` or `4-H`, are created as `Strings`.

Because VBScript can automatically convert between some variable types, most variable conflicts are eliminated. However, if you try to add a string variable to a numeric variable type, you get an error. Consequently, if a variable has alphanumeric characters, don't try to perform numeric calculations with it.

NOTE

Before performing calculations, you can make sure that variables are numeric by using the `IsNumeric` function. This function returns a value of `true` if the variable is numeric and `false` if it isn't. The following sample code checks for a numeric variable:

```
If IsNumeric(Value1) = True Then
    Value2 = Value1 + 5
```

A set of related functions checks other variable types: `IsDate`, `IsEmpty`, `IsNull`, `IsNumeric`, `IsArray`, and `IsObject`.

Arrays

Arrays allow you to group related sets of data together. When you create an array, you must specify its number of dimensions.

VBScript allows you to create arrays with up to 60 dimensions. A one-dimensional array is like a column of tabular data; a two-dimensional array is like a spreadsheet with rows and columns; and a three-dimensional array is like a 3D grid that takes time and space into account.

You can create a one-dimensional array from a single column of tabular data. If the column has 20 data points, you can declare the array as follows:

```
Dim myArray(19)
```

NOTE

Arrays always begin at `0` and end at the number of data points in the array minus 1. Therefore, an array with `20` data points is initialized as `Array_Name(19)`.

You can create a multi-dimensional array from the cells of a spreadsheet. If the spreadsheet has three columns, each with five rows of data points, you can declare the array as follows:

```
Dim myArray(2,4)
```

If you want to get the value of a specific cell in the spreadsheet, you can use the following:

```
myValue = Array_Name(columns -1, rows -1)
```

In this statement, `columns` is the column position of the cell, and `rows` is the row position of the cell. If you want to know the value of the cell in column 1, row 4, for example, you can use the following:

```
myValue = myArray(0,3)
```

Although these sample arrays have fixed sizes, you can also size arrays dynamically. This way, you can use input from users to drive the size of the array. You can declare a dynamic array as follows:

```
Dim dynamicArray()
```

Later, you can tell VBScript the size of the array by using the `ReDim` function in one of these two ways:

```
ReDim dynamicArray(iCount - 1)

ReDim dynamicArray(columnCount - 1, rowCount - 1)
```

NOTE

After you create an array at a specific dimension, you can't change the dimensions. If you create a two-dimensional array, for example, you can't change it later to a three-dimensional array.

To determine the size of an array at any time, you can use the `UBound` function, which returns the array's upper boundary. The following example returns the upper boundary of the array in a message box:

```
Dim myArray(99)
Dim x
For x = 0 to UBound(myArray)
     myArray(x) = "Initial"
Next
Msgbox "The upper boundary of the array is" & UBound(myArray)
```

Arithmetic Operators

You perform calculations in VBScript in much the same way you write out calculations in longhand. The only difference is that you usually assign the result to a variable.

To add numbers, use the + operator, as shown in these two examples:

```
Result = 1 + 5

Result = ValueA + ValueB
```

To subtract numbers, use the `-` operator, as these two examples show:

```
Result = 5 - 1

Result = ValueB - ValueA
```

To multiply numbers, use the `*` operator; here are two examples:

```
Result = 2 * 4

Result = ValueA * ValueB
```

To divide numbers, use the `/` or `\` operator, as shown in the following examples:

```
Result = 2 / 4

Result = ValueA / ValueB

IntegerResult = ValueA \ ValueB
```

The difference between `/` and `\` is the type of division. The traditional `/` divides normally, returning a decimal number with remainder (if applicable). The `\` operator will discard the remainder and return only the integer segment. For example, `5 / 2 = 2.5` but `5 \ 2 = 2`.

In division, you often have a remainder. Because you might want to perform calculations based on the remainder, you need a way to determine it. In VBScript, you do so by using the `Mod` function. For the following expression, the value of the result is set to `1`:

```
Result = 7 Mod 2
```

To multiply by an exponent, use the `^` operator. This example is the same as 3×3×3×3:

```
Result = 3 ^ 4
```

You can also use this example, which is the same as `ValueC * ValueC`:

```
Result = ValueC ^ 2
```

You can negate a value by using the `-` operator, as shown in these two examples:

```
Result = -2 * 3

Result = -ValueA * ValueB
```

When you mix operators, VBScript performs calculations using the same precedence order your high school math teacher taught you. For example, multiplication and division in equations are carried out before subtraction and addition, as shown in these examples:

$3 + 2 \times 6 = 15$

$2 \div 2 + 3 = 4$

$(2 + 3) \times 6 = 30$

The complete precedence order of operators is shown in Table 36.1. According to the table, exponents have the highest precedence order and are always calculated first, although items in parentheses will be processed first and their results then applied in arithmetic order.

Table 36.1. The precedence order of arithmetic operations.

Order	*Operation*
1	Exponents (^)
2	Negation (-)
3	Multiplication (*) and Division (/ and \)
4	Remainders (Mod)
5	Addition (+) and Subtraction (-)

Comparison Operators

When you perform comparisons, you check for certain conditions, such as "Is A equal to B?" To perform comparisons in VBScript, you use a set of comparison operators that aren't much different from the comparison operators used in math every day. The only difference is that, in your scripts, you typically use a control flow, such as conditional looping, with your comparison. For example, if A is equal to B, you will perform a specific task; if A is not equal to B, you will perform a different task.

To see whether a variable is equal to another variable or to a specific value, use the equal sign. The following example checks for equality:

```
if myValue = 0 Then
   Msgbox "The variable is set to zero."
if myValue = Input Then
   Msgbox "The values are equal."
```

To see whether variables aren't equal, use the inequality operator, as shown in this example:

```
if myValue <>0 Then
   Msgbox "The variable is NOT set to zero."
if myValue <>Input Then
   Msgbox "The values are NOT equal."
```

To check whether one variable is less than or greater than another variable, use the less than and greater than operators. You can check for values greater than or less than a variable as follows:

```
if myValue < 0 Then
   Msgbox "The value is less than zero."
if myValue > 0 Then
   Msgbox "The value is greater than zero."
```

Another type of comparison you can perform is to see whether a variable is less than or equal to a value. Likewise, you can see whether a variable is greater than or equal to a value. The following example shows this type of comparison:

```
if myValue <= Input Then
   Msgbox "myValue is less than or equal to Input."
if myValue >= 0 Then
   Msgbox "The value is greater than or equal to zero."
```

NOTE

There is no set precedence order for comparison operators. Comparisons are always performed from left to right.

When you compare objects, such as buttons, you use a special comparison operator called `Is`. By using the `Is` operator, you can see whether two objects are equivalent. The operator returns a result that is `true` if the objects are equivalent or `false` if they aren't. This example shows how you can check whether the object reference `cmd_Button` refers to the object `Button`:

```
Result = cmd_Button Is Button
If Result = True Then
    Msgbox "The objects are equivalent."
Else
        Msgbox "The objects are NOT equivalent."
```

You can also perform the comparison directly in the control flow statement:

```
If cmd_Button Is Button Then
    Msgbox "The objects are equivalent."
Else
        Msgbox "The objects are NOT equivalent."
```

Strings

Strings are sets of alphabetical and numeric characters. In VBScript, you can use strings in many ways. Because VBScript automatically types variables for you, you don't need to declare a variable as a string. You can declare a variable this way:

```
Dim aString
```

Later, you can define a string value for the variable as follows:

```
aString = "This is a String."
```

Often, you might want to add strings together. For example, if a user enters his or her full name as three separate variables representing the first, middle, and last name, you might want to add these strings together. Although you may see scripts that use the + operator to concatenate strings, the normal operator for string concatenation is the `&` operator. With the `&` operator, you can add strings together as follows:

```
fullName = firstName & " " & Middle & " " & lastName
```

Sometimes you also might want to display the value of a string in a message box. To do so, you also use the `&` operator, as shown in the following sample code:

```
bString = "Cool"
Msgbox "The value of the string is: " & bString
```

This code displays a dialog box with the following message:

```
The value of the string is: Cool
```

Comments

Just as you can add comments to HTML markup, you can add comments to your VBScript code. To add comments, use the single quotation mark. All text after the single quotation mark and on the same line is interpreted as a comment. Here are some examples of using comments in your code:

```
'This variable holds the first name of the customer
Dim firstName
'This variable holds the middle name of the customer
Dim Middle
'This variable holds the last name of the customer
Dim lastName
```

Controlling Flow with Conditionals

In much the same way as traffic lights control the flow of traffic on the street, conditional instructions control the flow of instructions in your code. In the following sections, I describe several of these instructions.

if...Then

If you want to execute a set of instructions only when a certain condition is met, you can use an `if...Then` condition. You can control the execution of instructions based on a `true` condition as follows:

```
if condition = True Then
  A = B
End If
```

You also can use an `if...Then` condition in the following way:

```
if condition Then
  A = B
End If
```

You can control the execution of instructions based on a `false` condition as follows:

```
if condition = False Then
  A <> B
End If
```

You can also use this form:

```
if Not condition  Then
  A <> B
End If
```

You can extend the `if...Then` condition with the `Else` and `ElseIf` statements. The `Else` statement offers an alternative when a condition you specify isn't met. Here's the structure of an `if...Then...Else` condition:

```
if homeRun = True Then
    Msgbox "The condition has been met."
Else
    Msgbox "The condition has not been met."
End If
```

To add more conditions, you can use the `ElseIf` statement. In this way, each additional condition you add to the code is checked for validity. The following example uses the `ElseIf` statement:

```
if firstValue < 0 Then
  Msgbox "The value is less than zero."
ElseIf firstValue = 0 Then
  Msgbox "The value is equal to zero."
ElseIf firstValue = 1 Then
  Msgbox "The value is equal to one."
ElseIf firstValue = 2 Then
  Msgbox "The value is equal to two."
ElseIf firstValue = 3 Then
  Msgbox "The value is equal to three."
ElseIf firstValue = 4 Then
  Msgbox "The value is equal to four."
Else
  Msgbox "The value is greater than 4."
End If
```

Select Case

Checking for multiple conditions with the `ElseIf` structure can be tedious. When you want to check more than three conditions, you should probably use the `Select Case` statement. Using the `Select Case` structure, you can transform the last example in the preceding section into code that's clearer and easier to understand:

```
Select Case firstValue
   Case < 0
     Msgbox "The value is less than zero."
   Case 0
     Msgbox "The value is equal to zero."
   Case 1
     Msgbox "The value is equal to one."
   Case 2
     Msgbox "The value is equal to two."
   Case 3
     Msgbox "The value is equal to three."
   Case 4
     Msgbox "The value is equal to four."
```

```
   Case Else
     Msgbox "The value is greater than 4."
End Select
```

If you compare the `ElseIf` example and the `Select Case` example, you can see that the `Select Case` example requires less code and has a simpler structure. You can apply this same structure any time you want to check for multiple conditions. Here's another example of `Select Case`:

```
Select Case Abbrev
   Case "HTML"
     Message "The HyperText Markup Language."
   Case "SGML"
     Message "The Standard Generalized Markup Language."
   Case "VRML"
     Message "The Virtual Reality Modeling Language."
   Case Else
     Message "You have entered an abbreviation not known to the system."
End Select
```

Controlling Flow with Looping

Sometimes you might want to execute a section of code repeatedly. In VBScript, you can do so in three ways:

- Execute a code segment for a specific count by using `For...Next` looping
- Execute a code segment while a condition is met by using `Do While` looping
- Execute a code segment until a condition is met by using `Do Until` looping

In the following sections, you examine how to use these control flow elements.

For...Next

To execute a code segment for a specific count, use `For...Next` looping. The structure of `For...Next` is as follows:

```
For Counter = Start to Finish
   insert code to repeat
Next
```

You can easily use `For...Next` looping in your code. The following example uses this structure to initialize an array of 20 elements:

```
For x = 0 to 19
   aStruct(x) = "Unknown"
Next
```

After the `For...Next` loop is executed, all 20 elements in the array are initialized to the value `Unknown`. To make the `For...Next` loop more versatile, you can step through the counter at specific intervals. To do so, add a positive or negative value after the `Step` keyword. The following example sets the array positions `0`, `2`, `4`, `6`, and `8` to `Even`:

```
For x = 0 to 8 Step 2
   aStruct(x) = "Even"
Next
```

This loop sets the array positions 3, 6, and 9 to Multiple:

```
For x = 3 to 9 Step 3
   aStruct(x) = "Multiple"
Next
```

When you use a negative step value, you should reverse the normal order of the counter. Therefore, instead of going from the lowest value to the highest value, you go from highest to lowest:

```
For x = 8 to 0 Step -2
   aStruct(x) = "Even"
Next

For x = 9 to 3 Step -3
   aStruct(x) = "Multiple"
Next
```

Do While

To execute a code segment while a condition is met, use Do While looping. The structure of this loop is as follows:

```
Do While condition
   insert code to repeat
Loop
```

As long as the condition is met, the loop is executed. To break out of the loop, you must change the condition at some point within the loop. Here's an example of a Do While loop that changes the status of the condition:

```
Do While homeRun = True

   If basesLoaded Then
      Message "Great time to hit a home run."
   ElseIf Balls = 3 And Strikes = 2 Then
      Message "Go for it!"
   Else
      homeRun = False
   EndIf

Loop
```

By placing your condition at the top of the loop, you make sure that the loop is executed only if the condition is met. Sometimes, you might want to execute the loop at least once before you check the condition; to do so, you can place the check for the condition at the bottom of the loop, as shown in this example:

```
Do

   If basesLoaded Then
      Message "Great time to hit a home run."
   ElseIf Balls = 3 And Strikes = 2 Then
      Message "Go for it!"
   Else
      homeRun = False
   EndIf

Loop While homeRun = True
```

Do Until

If you want to execute a loop *until* a condition is met instead of *while* a condition is met, use `Do Until` looping, as shown in this example:

```
Do Until condition
    Insert code to repeat
Loop
```

To make sure that the loop is executed at least once, you can use the following structure:

```
Do
    Insert code to repeat
Loop Until condition
```

Here's another example of a `Do Until` loop:

```
Do

   If basesLoaded Then
      Message "Great time to hit a home run."
   ElseIf Balls = 3 And Strikes = 2 Then
      Message "Go for it!"
   Else
      homeRun = False
   EndIf

Loop Until homeRun = True
```

NOTE

If you compare the `Do While` loops in the preceding section to the `Do Until` loops in this section, you can see that the logic for both types of loops is similar. The key difference is in how the logic is applied. In a `Do While` loop, code is executed *while* a condition is met; in a `Do Until` loop, code is executed *until* a condition is met.

Going Beyond the Basics with VBScript

As you've learned throughout this chapter, programming with VBScript is fairly straightforward. To go beyond the basics, take a look at how to group sections of code into procedures.

Basic Procedure Classes

Procedures you create in VBScript are groups of statements that perform a particular task. After creating a procedure, you can call it from different locations in your code. After the procedure finishes executing, control returns to the code that called the procedure, and your script continues executing from there.

The two basic classes of procedures are

- **Functions.** Procedures that return a value to the caller.
- **Subroutines.** Procedures that don't return a value to the caller.

Functions

Functions—procedures that return a value to the statement that called them—are useful in your scripts. When you create a function, you can define parameters required to execute the function. *Parameters* are optional variables that you can use to pass values to the function.

The following is the basic structure of a function:

```
Function functionName(argument1, argument2, ..., argumentN)
   Insert function code here.
End Function
```

You can use functions in your code as follows:

```
Function getName
   Dim goodName
   Do While goodName = ""
      goodName = InputBox "Enter your full name:"
   Loop
   getName = goodName
End Function
```

In this example, `getName` is the name of the function. Because the function accepts no parameters, none are defined after the function name. A temporary variable called `goodName` is created to make the code easier to follow and debug. The temporary variable is used to store the user's input. After the user enters a valid name, the `Do While` loop is exited. The value the user entered is assigned to the function, allowing the value to be returned to the calling statement.

CAUTION

Variables used within functions or subroutines are temporary variables. These variables exist only within the scope of your function or subroutine, so the term *local variables* is another name for variables used within procedures.

You can call a function in one of these two ways:

```
Call getName()

fullName = getName()
```

Another way to call a function is within a statement:

```
Msgbox "The name you entered is: " getName()
```

When you don't have any parameters to pass to the function, the parentheses are optional:

```
fullName = getName
```

To better understand how parameters are used, try creating a function that converts a time entry to seconds. This function, called `countDays`, accepts four parameters: `nYears`, `nDays`, `nHours`, and `nMinutes`. Because these parameters are passed directly to the function, you don't need to create temporary variables in the function. The code for the function `countSeconds` is as follows:

```
Function countSeconds(nYears, nDays, nHours, nMinutes)
   Dim tempSeconds
   tempSeconds = ((365 * nYears + nDays) * 24 + nHours) * 3600 + 60 * nMinutes
   countSeconds = tempSecounds
End Function
```

When you call this function, the parameters are mandatory and must be entered in the order defined. Here's a statement that calls the `countSeconds` function:

```
numSeconds = countSeconds(1,69,24,5)
```

NOTE

You can break out of a function and return to the caller at any time by using the `Exit Function` statement. This statement is useful when a predetermined condition has been met and you want to return to the calling statement without finishing the function's execution.

Subroutines

You can also use subroutines in your scripts. A *subroutine* is a procedure that can be called anywhere in the code but doesn't return a value to the caller. You can pass parameters to a subroutine just as you do to a function.

The structure of a subroutine is almost identical to the structure of a function:

```
Sub subroutineName(argument1, argument2, ..., argumentN)
   Insert subroutine code here.
End Sub
```

You can use subroutines in your code as follows:

```
Sub displayError(errorMessage)
   MsgBox "Error: " & errorMessage
End Sub
```

In this example, displayError is the name of the subroutine. The subroutine expects one parameter to be passed to it; this parameter holds the error message to display to the user.

You can call the displayError subroutine in one of these two ways:

```
Call displayError("You have entered an invalid message.")

displayError("You have entered an invalid message.")
```

When you don't have any parameters to pass to the subroutine, the parentheses are optional:

```
Call displayWarning
```

NOTE

You can break out of a subroutine and return to the caller at any time by using the Exit Sub statement. When you use this statement, control is returned to the calling statement without finishing the subroutine's execution.

System Procedure Classes

Beyond the basic procedure classes are system classes. The two system classes for procedures are events and methods.

Events

An *event* is a subroutine executed automatically by the system when a certain condition exists. There are events for mouse clicks, mouse movements, clicks of buttons, and so on. You refer to events with a control name and an event name, separated by the underscore character, as follows:

```
myButton_OnClick
```

Here, the control name is myButton, and OnClick is the event name.

The following event is executed automatically when a button labeled cmdButton is clicked:

```
Sub cmdButton_OnClick

    Msgbox "You will see this dialog box when you click the button inserted
in the sample page. You can close the dialog box by clicking in the Ok button."

End Sub
```

OnClick is certainly one of the most used events, but it's not the only event you can use. Other events you can use and their meanings are shown in Table 36.2.

Table 36.2. Event procedures and their uses.

Event Name	*Use*
`onAbort`	Executed when the loading of an object is aborted
`onBlur`	Executed when an object is deselected
`onChange`	Executed when a user changes the value of an object by making a selection
`onClick`	Executed when an object, such as a button, is clicked
`onError`	Executed when an error occurs during the loading of an object
`onFocus`	Executed when an object is active
`onLoad`	Executed when an object is loaded
`onMouseOut`	Executed when the mouse pointer was over an object and then moves away
`onMouseOver`	Executed when the mouse pointer moves over an object
`onReset`	Executed when a form is reset
`onSelect`	Executed when an object is selected
`onSubmit`	Executed when a form is submitted
`onUnload`	Executed when an object is unloaded

Methods

Just as subroutines and functions are similar, so are events and methods. *Methods* are normally used to cause events to occur in the code rather than as a result of interaction with the user. Therefore, a method is a controlled event. Unlike user-driven events, controlled events aren't executed automatically.

Although you can call a method, you must refer to it by the object to which it relates. To call a method, use the following syntax:

```
objectName.methodName
```

`objectName` is the name of the object you're referring to, and *`methodName`* is the name of the method you want to execute.

One way to use a method is to simulate button presses during a product tutorial. Instead of the user driving the event, you simulate the event to trigger an identical response.

```
Sub myButton_OnClick

     Msgbox "You will see this dialog box when you click the button inserted
in the sample page. You can close the dialog box by clicking in the Ok button."

End Sub
```

Then you can execute the event with the code:

```
myButton.Click
```

Summary Example

In order to better illustrate the principles you've learned thus far, go over this summary example. It covers some of the basic concepts you've learned, and provides a concrete example of some of the syntax. Essentially, it's an overly commented long block of code that you can refer back to when trying to create your own applications. This example is not meant as a real-world application. For example, there should be far more validation checking of the user's input to make certain that it isn't beyond a certain range. The following code makes a simple application that gets a price from a user, then applies a user-defined sales tax to it, and returns a net price.

Listing 36.1. VBSEG_39.HTM—The listing example in its entirety.

```
<html>

<head>
<title>New Page 1</title>
<meta name="GENERATOR" content="Microsoft FrontPage 3.0">
</head>

<body>

<p><script language="VBScript"><!--

  Function GetPrice
  'Function definition statement

  Dim GrossPrice, Success
  'Defining variables

  GrossPrice=InputBox ("Please Enter Item price, without a dollar sign $","Price
➥Entry Box",0)
  'Obtaining input from the user in the form of an Input box. Note that
  '<variable>=<command> is used to fill the variable with information. Otherwise,
  'the result of the input isn't stored.

  Do
  'Start of a Do...While loop

   If (IsNumeric(GrossPrice)=FALSE) OR GrossPrice="" Then
   'Tests if the input from the user is A)not a number and B)not empty
   'Then goes on to to get data from user once more.
   'Note presence of a monitor variable, in the form of SUCCESS.

    MsgBox "Please enter a valid value."
    GrossPrice=InputBox ("Please Enter Item price, without a dollar sign $","Price
➥Entry Box",0)
    Success=FALSE
```

```
    Else
    'If data passes tests above then it's valid and the process can continue
     Success=TRUE
    End If
    'Terminating the If statement

   Loop While Success=FALSE
   'Closing the loop. Note the condition comes at the end, ensuring that the loop
   'will execute at least once.

   GetPrice=GrossPrice
   'This returns the variable after the function ceases running
   End Function

   GrossPrice=GetPrice()
   'Calling the GetPrice function. Results are stored in GrossPrice

   document.write "You entered the price as : $" & GrossPrice & ". Now you may:"
   'Writing text to the HTML document instead of using Message Boxes
  --></script> </p>

<p align="center"><input type="BUTTON" name="CmdGetTax" value="Calculate will
➥Tax">  <input type="BUTTON" name="CmdFinish" value="Finish"> <script
➥language="VBScript"><!--

 Sub CmdGetTax_OnClick
 'Note that CmdGetTax only runs when you click the button, hence "OnClick"

   Dim Tax, NetPrice, Success

   Tax=InputBox ("Enter the tax percentage as a decimal number between 0 and
➥1.","Tax Entry Box",0.07)

   Do
    If (IsNumeric(Tax)=FALSE) Then
     MsgBox "Please enter a number and not text"
     Tax=InputBox ("Enter the tax percentage as a decimal number between 0 and
➥1.","Tax Entry Box",0.07)
     Success=FALSE
    Else
     NetPrice = GrossPrice * (Tax + 1)
     'Calculating tax

     Success=TRUE
    End If
   Loop While Success=FALSE

   document.write "At " & (Tax*100) & "% tax your final price is $" & NetPrice & "."
   'Note how you can influence a variable without actually changing it. The
   '(Tax*100) Statement produces a percentage number, but leaves the actual Tax
unchanged.
 End Sub
</script> <script
language="VBScript"><!--

 Sub CmdFinish_OnClick
```

continues

Listing 36.1. continued

```
  document.write "Your untaxed price is $" & GrossPrice & "."
 End Sub
</script></p>
</body>
</html>
```

Summary

VBScript is a powerful tool for enhancing your Web pages. Because it's so easy to use, learning VBScript basics, such as how to perform calculations or how to concatenate strings, is a snap. These basic concepts are the building blocks to more advanced subjects such as controlling the flow through your scripts and creating procedures.

CHAPTER 37

Creating Interactive Page Controls with ActiveX

by William Robert Stanek

IN THIS CHAPTER

- What Is ActiveX? *600*
- Using ActiveX and ActiveX Controls *602*
- Placing ActiveX Controls on a Web Page *605*
- Using ActiveX with VBScript *613*

Creating documents that come to life before your eyes is what Microsoft's ActiveX is all about. ActiveX-enabled pages can feature powerful yet easy-to-use interfaces that merge virtual reality, 360-degree control over video, real-time audio, and even games into Web pages. ActiveX is based on the powerful innards of the Windows operating system, bringing a new level of complexity to Web pages that otherwise might be difficult to attain. Although there are inroads for ActiveX on other platforms (namely MacOS and UNIX), ActiveX does not offer true cross-platform compatibility. However, if you are authoring for a Windows 95 or NT based audience, particularly on intranets, ActiveX could be just the trick to power-up and activate your Web site.

In this chapter, you explore ActiveX, the control components that make it work, and how to activate your Web pages with ActiveX.

What Is ActiveX?

At the heart of ActiveX is a concept for merging technologies by using an enhanced object linking and embedding (OLE) interface. OLE is certainly not a new technology; it is a fundamental component in the Windows 95/NT architecture. ActiveX is OLE for the Internet.

ActiveX Background

ActiveX has garnered a lot of attention. Although it has failed to steal the spotlight from Java, ActiveX has proven to be an appealing option for many developers catering to Windows-based visitors and intranets. To help spread the word about ActiveX to the farthest reaches of cyberspace, Microsoft maintains a comprehensive home page for ActiveX, as shown in Figure 37.1. You can find the ActiveX home page at this site:

```
http://www.microsoft.com/activeplatform/
```

Microsoft based ActiveX on the Component Object Model (COM), which allows objects to communicate with each other by using links. Object linking is central to OLE, used widely in Windows applications. COM also forms the basis of both OLE and ActiveX, but OLE and ActiveX serve different functions. OLE is designed for use on desktop computers and carries way too much overhead to use on the Internet. ActiveX, on the other hand, trims down COM to make object linking practical for Internet use.

When the developers at Microsoft redesigned object linking for the Internet, they streamlined COM delivery considerably—so much so, that ActiveX components with compression are smaller than their OLE counterparts. ActiveX also introduces incremental rendering of components and asynchronous connections. Incremental rendering helps users see almost instantaneous results during downloading, and asynchronous connections speed up downloading considerably.

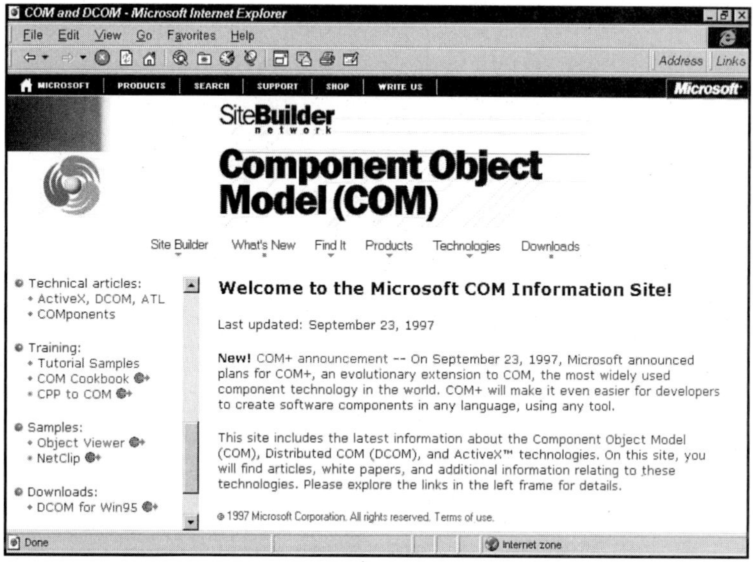

FIGURE 37.1.
The ActiveX home page at Microsoft.

ActiveX Core Technologies

ActiveX is the key to integrated technologies for both clients and servers; its core technologies include the following:

- ActiveX controls
- ActiveX scripting
- ActiveX documents
- The ActiveX server framework

The ActiveX server framework is designed specifically for servers, but ActiveX scripting, ActiveX documents, and ActiveX controls are designed for clients, such as browsers. As Figure 37.2 shows, these core technologies work together to give you live content on the Web.

ActiveX controls are the key to adding live and interactive multimedia to your Web documents. With ActiveX controls, you can embed and execute software applications in a Web page that lets users view and interact with movies, animation, and audio. You can create ActiveX controls with any developer tool that supports OLE, such as Visual C++, Visual J++, and Visual Basic.

ActiveX controls are used to extend the capabilities of your Web page through the embedding of applications in your documents. Typically, when an ActiveX-capable browser (such as Internet Explorer 3.0+) encounters an embedded control that is not currently installed, it is automatically retrieved and installed for you. Just as Netscape lets third-party developers create plug-ins for their Netscape Navigator browser, Microsoft allows third-party developers to create new

ActiveX controls. Hundreds of ActiveX controls are available from Microsoft and from third-party developers. Fortunately, Microsoft maintains a page on which you can find listings of available controls. Follow the links to the Component Gallery from the main ActiveX Platform page.

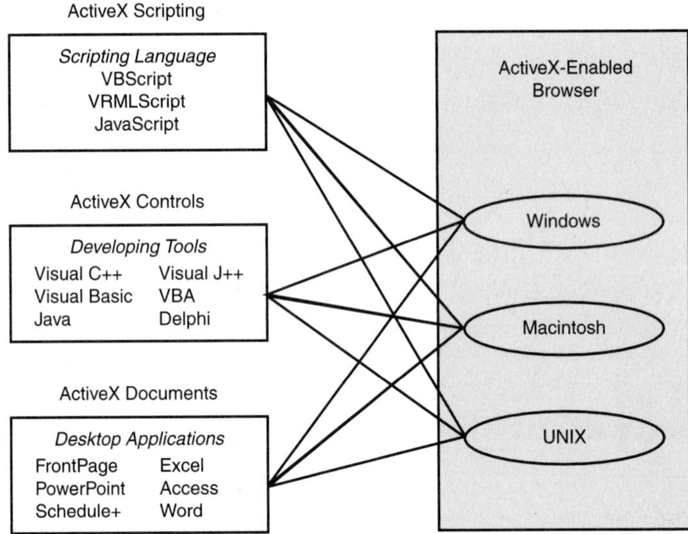

FIGURE 37.2.
ActiveX technologies work together.

Client-side scripting languages have gained considerable popularity due to their powerful and far reaching effects. These client-side languages let you as a developer create interactive client-side logic and programs to extend your Web page. Two of the most popular scripting languages are JavaScript and VBScript. With ActiveX scripting, you can use any client-side scripting language that is supported by the Web browser in your documents. You can also link your client-side scripts to Java applets, embedded applications, and ActiveX controls.

With ActiveX documents, you can import documents formatted for Word, Excel, PowerPoint, Schedule+, Access, and many other applications into your Web pages. These documents are imported by using a special viewer inserted into the browser's viewing window. This viewer has its own toolbars, menus, and interface.

The key to ActiveX documents is that the application the document is formatted for must be OLE-compliant. As long as an application is OLE-compliant, you can use ActiveX document technology.

Using ActiveX and ActiveX Controls

At heart, ActiveX is a Windows 32-bit technology for Windows 95 and NT. Microsoft has been working with development partners to bring the power of the Active Platform to other operating systems, at least in part. Microsoft Internet Explorer 3.0 and 4.0 are available for

MacOS, and in part support ActiveX controls. UNIX ports of the ActiveX architecture and the IE browser are forthcoming, and promise the same near-cross platform compatibility that the MacOS version offers. The true hindrance to cross-platform ActiveX controls is the controls' tight reliance on the features and functions of the Windows operating system.

The showcase browser to support ActiveX is Internet Explorer. When you use Internet Explorer, you don't have to get any special software to enable ActiveX. However, Internet Explorer 4.0 provides you with several levels of security dependent on the zone you are using (for example, a private intranet on a LAN or the Internet). You need to insure that your browser is set to allow you to use ActiveX controls. You can change the security level in your browser by opening Security Tab in the Internet Options dialog box from the View menu. The Security tab gives you a drop box to select your zone (presumably Internet zone), and four radio buttons for controlling security. These radio buttons reflect the following levels:

- **High (most secure).** Exclude content that could damage your computer. The browser prevents you from encountering possibly harmful content, such as ActiveX controls, scripts, and plug-ins.
- **Medium (more secure).** Warn before running potentially damaging content. You will be issued a warning when you encounter ActiveX controls, scripts, and plug-ins, and have the option to avoid downloading it.
- **Low.** Do not warn before running potentially damaging content. Internet Explorer does not offer any warnings or restrictions on possibly harmful content.
- **Custom (for expert users).** Base security on settings you choose. With this option enabled, you can click the Settings button to personalize your browser's behavior when you encounter ActiveX controls, scripts, plug-ins, and more.

Internet Explorer isn't the only browser to support ActiveX. Netscape Navigator users can download a plug-in called NCompass Script Active. With NCompass Script Active installed, you can use VBScript, most ActiveX controls, and ActiveX documents similar to Internet Explorer. To get the current version of NCompass Script Active, visit NCompass Labs at this site:

```
www.ncompasslabs.com
```

If you visit the Microsoft SiteBuilder Network (`http://www.microsoft.com/sitebuilder`), you can get your first taste of how easily you can get and install a new control. Unlike plug-ins, ActiveX controls are readily and immediately available when you visit a page that uses a control because the ActiveX specification requires that all controls support self-registration. To demonstrate this capability, see how the SiteBuilder Network controls are installed in a browser. The first step is to visit the SiteBuilder Network. As you can see in Figure 37.3, when you reach a page containing a control, your browser immediately retrieves and starts to install the control, provided you have allowed such an action in your security settings. You might be prompted to allow the installation, or if you have selected to disallow ActiveX controls by accident, the controls are not downloaded.

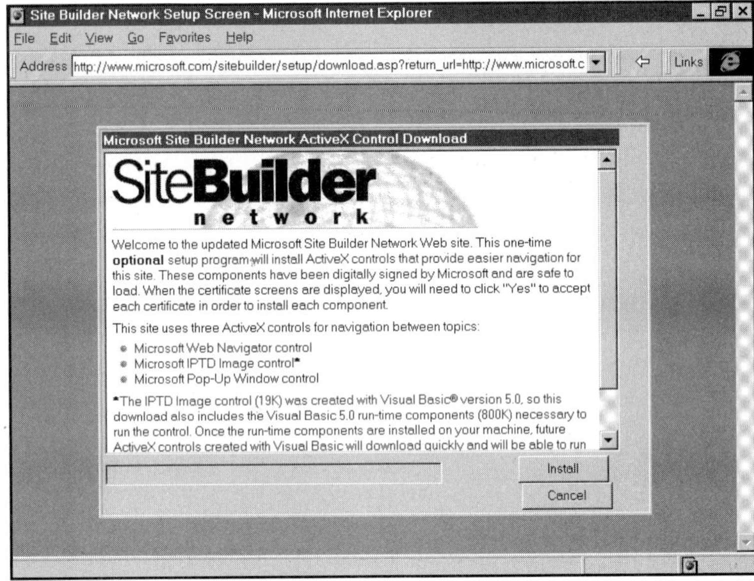

FIGURE 37.3.
Internet Explorer installs components automatically if you don't already have them.

After the browser completely downloads the control, you see an authentication window like the one shown in Figure 37.4. If you choose to continue with the installation, the control is instantly added and available for use; if you choose not to, the control is discarded and your system is left untouched.

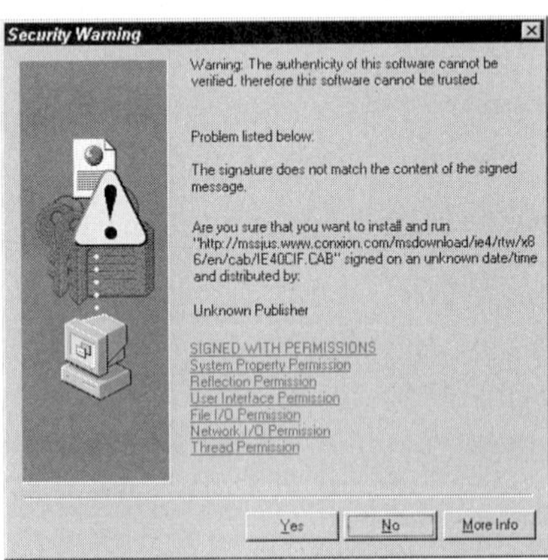

FIGURE 37.4.
Each control requires that you confirm its installation. Authentication information is signed to the control.

Most controls download and install very quickly, especially at 28.8 Kbps or faster. If you log on the Internet with a slower modem, you'll be glad to know that you need to download a control only once. After that, the control is always available for use on your system. When your browser downloads a control, and you choose to install it, the control is registered in the Windows Registry (a registry for applications on your system).

Placing ActiveX Controls on a Web Page

Adding controls to your page isn't always easy, especially if you don't know the acceptable properties, events, and methods for the control you want to use. At this point, FrontPage integration with ActiveX comes in handy, as you discover in the following sections.

ActiveX Controls You Can Use

Microsoft includes dozens of ActiveX controls with FrontPage 98. Yet if you have ever used other ActiveX-compliant products, you probably have several dozen controls available on your system. For example, when you install Internet Explorer 3.0 or 4.0, approximately a dozen new controls are made available on your system. Furthermore, some controls you install depend on other controls. As a result, when you install one control, several controls are actually installed on your system.

Table 37.1 shows a list of some common controls that are typically installed when both FrontPage 98 and Internet Explorer are available on your system. When dealing with known controls, FrontPage 98 lists the appropriate parameters for the control. When dealing with a control that FrontPage 98 does not consider known, you must manually provide your own parameters, with no prompting from FrontPage 98 itself.

Table 37.1. Common controls.

Control Name	*Description*
ActiveMovie control	Plays video files.
ActiveX Image control	Displays images in multiple formats, including JPG, GIF, BMP, metafile, and wavelet.
Animated Button	Creates an animated button from sequences of an AVI video file.
Calendar control	Adds an interactive calendar.
Chart control	Creates charts and graphs from data.
Gradient control	Creates horizontal lines with gradient coloring.
Label object	Creates text labels that can be rotated.
Marquee control	Creates a window for scrolling marquees.
Macromedia Active Shockwave	Allows you to use Shockwave files.
ActiveX Hot Spot control	Creates clickable regions on a page.
Menu control	Creates a menu that can be easily accessed.
Popup Window control	Creates a pop-up window for tips, notes, and warnings.

continues

Table 37.1. continued

Control Name	*Description*
Popup Menu control	Creates a pop-up menu for easy site navigation.
Preloader control	Loads documents, images, and other media files in the background so they are instantly available when needed.
Stockticker control	Displays data that changes continuously.
Timer	Allows you to create timed events that are used to add or remove elements from the page.
ViewTracker	Generates events that can be used to tell when controls are in the viewable part of the browser's window.
Web Browser control	Control for displaying any ActiveX document within a page. These documents can include Word documents, Excel spreadsheets, and Access tables.

Many of the controls available from Microsoft deal with Form elements. These controls provide alternatives to using intrinsic HTML controls that depend solely on VBScript and are in a group of controls called Microsoft Forms 2.0. Table 37.2 shows a listing of these controls.

Table 37.2. Microsoft Forms 2.0 controls.

Control Name	*Description*
Checkbox control	Adds a checkbox to the page
Combobox control	Adds a drop-down list to the page
Command Button control	Adds a push button to the page
Frame control	Creates a scrollable picture frame for manipulating images
Image control	Adds an image within a form
Label control	Adds a text label to the page
Listbox control	Adds a scrollable list of options to the page
Multipage control	Allows you to use multiple pages that can be accessed with buttons or tabs; similar to the TabStrip control
Option Button control	Adds a radio button to the page
Scrollbar control	Adds scrollbars to the page
Spin Button control	Adds to the page a button that can be rotated
TabStrip control	Lets users reach several pages with tabs that can be clicked

Control Name	*Description*
Textbox control	Adds a text entry field or text window to the page
Toggle Button control	Adds a button with a toggle state, such as on and off, to the page

You use form controls as you would use intrinsic HTML controls. For example, you can use the Checkbox control to add a checkbox that uses ActiveX to respond to the user's selections. However, you might find that using intrinsic HTML controls with VBScript is much easier than using ActiveX form controls. For this reason, I recommend using only the form controls with unique features, including the MultiPage control, the Spin Button control, and the TabStrip control.

Adding the Control

EDITING TECHNIQUE

You are not limited to the controls that FrontPage 98 intrinsically knows. Any ActiveX Control registered on your system can be used in your Web pages. You add ActiveX controls to your pages in the FrontPage Editor. After you move the insertion point to the place where you want to add the control, click the ActiveX control button from the Advanced toolbar. The dialog box shown in Figure 37.5 then appears.

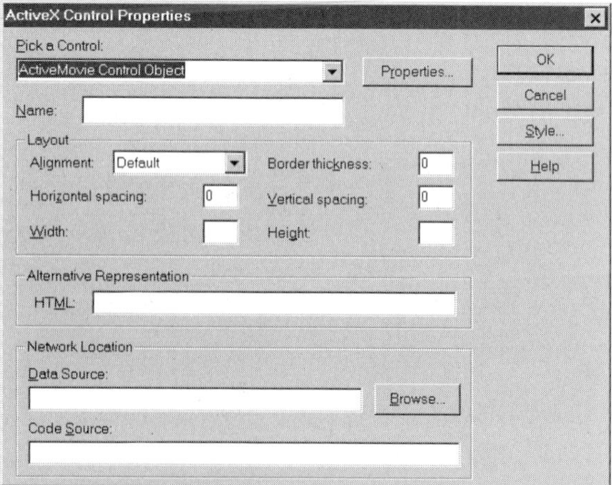

FIGURE 37.5.
Setting properties for ActiveX controls.

From the Pick a Control pull-down list, you can quickly select any control registered on your system. Keep in mind this list shows all controls currently registered on your system.

After you select a control from the list, you need to set properties for the control. Although properties listed in the ActiveX Control Properties dialog box are common to all controls, properties you access by clicking the Properties button are unique properties for the control you're using. How your control is displayed in the FrontPage editor depends on the control itself.

If possible, FrontPage 98 displays the control exactly as it will be shown in the user's browser. Otherwise, you see an icon for the control you've added to the page. Typically this is a white box icon with the name of the control.

Setting Common Properties of Controls

Not only do controls added to your page need to be uniquely known by your system, they also need to be uniquely identified on the page so that they can be interactive. To do so in the ActiveX Control Properties dialog box, enter a unique name for the control in the Name text box. You use this name to refer to the control in your scripts. Remember that this name should be unique for this control on each page it appears in your site.

Uniquely identifying each control you add becomes more important when you add several controls to the same page because scripts interact with individual controls referred to by object. Therefore, if you add two Label controls to a page, each control must be uniquely identified.

The properties in the Layout panel of the ActiveX Control Properties dialog box aren't new. You have seen them used many times before, especially with images. These properties are used exactly as discussed in previous chapters. For your convenience, they are summarized in Table 37.3.

Table 37.3. Common layout properties for ActiveX controls.

Property Name	*Description*
Alignment	Determines the alignment of the object
Border Thickness	Determines the border width to use if the object is a hyperlink
Height	Sets the object's height
Horizontal Spacing	Sets the horizontal spacing around the object
Vertical Spacing	Sets the vertical spacing around the object
Width	Sets the object's width

If you refer back to Figure 37.5, you'll see the three fields I haven't defined yet:

HTML

Data Source

Code Source

The HTML text box allows you to insert HTML markup and text to be displayed by browsers that do not support ActiveX controls. Ideally, you will add content to make up for what the readers can't see. Unfortunately, FrontPage 98 does not create the markup for you, and you must enter your own markup tags and text directly in the HTML field, up to a maximum of 254 characters.

Controls you add to the page may need to refer to data files. You use the Data Source field to tell the control the name of the data file. For example, the ActiveMovie control plays movies and needs to know the name of the movie you want it to play. You can enter the data source using an absolute or relative URL.

Earlier, you learned that all ActiveX controls must be self-registering, which ensures that users can get controls without any problems. To enable self-registering, you must tell the client where to get the source code for a control that isn't registered on a user's system; the Code Source property comes in here. You use it to specify the absolute URL path to the control's source code.

Consider the example of the Macromedia Flash control, which is used to add multimedia excitement to Web pages. The URL for the Flash control is:

```
http://active.macromedia.com/flash/cabs/swflash.cab
```

After the URL path, add the version and build of the control you're using, as follows:

```
http://active.macromedia.com/flash/cabs/swflash.cab#version=2,1,0,7
```

Then assign the URL path and the version information to the Code Source property.

TIP

Finding the URL path for the control's source code and version information isn't always easy. The best way to make sure that your pages refer to the control's most current version is to visit the control developer's Web site and examine the markup source code for samples that use the control.

Setting Unique Properties of Controls

You can set unique properties for a control by clicking the Properties button near the top of the ActiveX Control Properties dialog box. Some controls have dozens of unique properties. Although FrontPage 98 lets you add any type of control to your page, that doesn't mean that the FrontPage Editor understands all the properties the control uses. For this reason, when you click the Properties button, one of two things happens, depending on whether the control is known or new.

Known Controls

If the FrontPage Editor knows what properties the control uses—as read from a configuration file—a dialog box that lists all the control's properties appears. When this dialog box is available, setting individual properties is often as easy as clicking the property listing until the value you want to use is displayed.

Figure 37.6 shows the Properties dialog box for the Calendar control. You learn more about properties for commonly used controls in the next section.

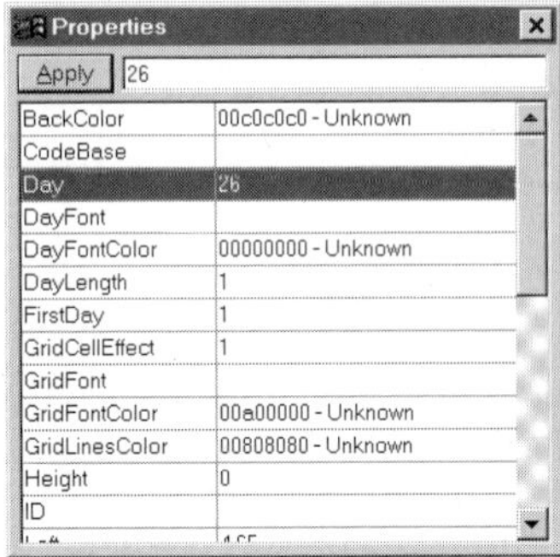

FIGURE 37.6.
If FrontPage 98 knows the properties for the control, you see a Properties dialog box like this one.

As you can see in Figure 37.6, the Properties dialog box contains two columns of entries for each property that you can set for the control. The first column shows the name of the property, and the second column shows the property's default value. Not all properties have default values, though.

Clicking an entry in the Properties dialog box allows you to edit a text value associated with the property. You enter this text in the text entry field at the top of the dialog box. If another window is associated with the property you've selected, a button is displayed to the right of the text entry field. Clicking this button opens a dialog box for the property, but you can also double-click the property entry to display this dialog box.

When you click a property that accepts only specific values, such as On or Off, values are entered for you automatically. Each click of the mouse moves you through the value selections.

Just about any control you use has properties that set default colors for text, backgrounds, and highlights. Now take a look at how you can define color-related properties. Most properties that set colors have a related Color dialog box in which you can select colors by using a graphical interface. When the Color dialog box shown in Figure 37.7 is open, you can choose a color simply by clicking it. After you make a color selection, close the Color dialog box by clicking the OK button. Then the active property is set to the color you selected.

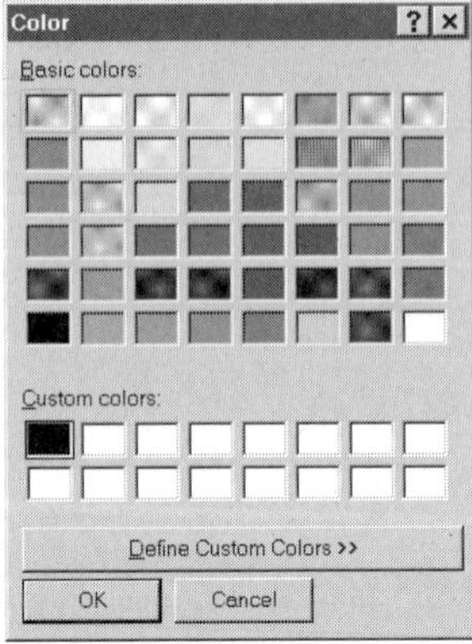

FIGURE 37.7.
Setting a property to a specific color.

If the 48 colors in the basic palette aren't enough, you can create and store values for up to 16 custom colors to use for other controls or control properties. To create a custom color, click the Define Custom Colors button near the bottom of the Color dialog box. As you can see in Figure 37.8, this action adds a new area to the Color dialog box.

FIGURE 37.8.
Customizing your colors.

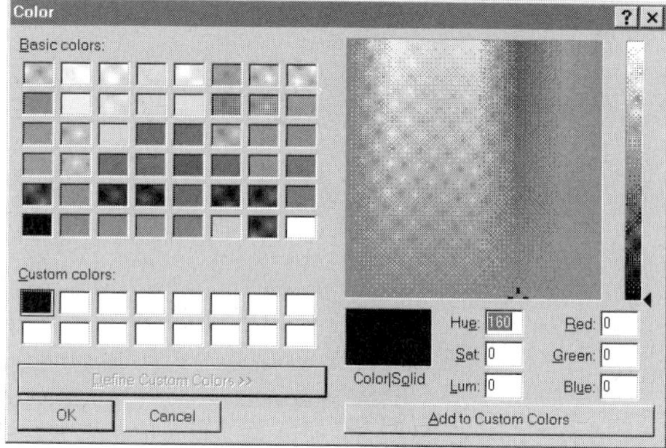

You define custom colors by using one of the following methods:

- Specify the red, green, and blue values for the custom color by filling in the Red, Green, and Bluetext boxes. Valid values are between 0 and 255.
- Specify the hue, saturation, and luminosity values in the Hue, Saturation, and Luminosity text boxes. Valid values are between 0 and 255.
- To set hue and saturation values by using the color cube, click and drag the mouse across the color spectrum field. To set the luminosity value, move the triangle pointer up or down in the vertical color bar to the right of the color spectrum field.

The Color/Solid field displays the dithered and solid colors that correspond to your current color selection. After you set the custom color to your liking, click the OK button to use the value for the current property.

TIP

If you want to save the custom color, select a rectangle in the Custom Colors grid, create your custom color, and then click the Add to Custom Colors button.

New Controls

After you click the Properties button in the ActiveX Control Properties dialog box, if the FrontPage Editor does not know what properties the control uses, you see a generic dialog box that lets you set parameters for the control (see Figure 37.9).

FIGURE 37.9.
If FrontPage 98 doesn't know the properties for the control, you see a dialog box like this one.

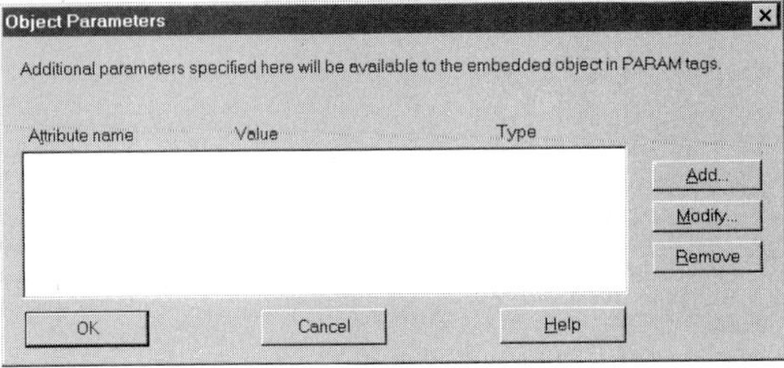

When the Object Parameters dialog box appears, FrontPage 98 depends on you to enter valid parameters for the control. A parameter is like any other property, meaning parameters have names and accept values. With parameters, you can also sometimes define a media type.

To add parameters, you click the Add button. The Edit Object Parameter dialog box then appears, as shown in Figure 37.10. In the Name text box, you enter the name of the parameter you're setting. In the Value area, you select a radio button that corresponds to the type of parameter you're setting and then enter information related to the parameter type.

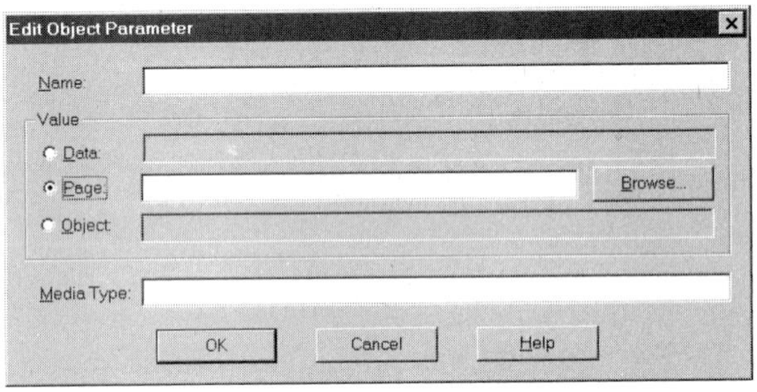

FIGURE 37.10.
Editing parameters for the control.

Data type parameters use strings or numeric values. For example, the Label control uses a parameter called `FontSize` that expects a numeric value. This numeric value is a `Data` type. To use a 12-point font with the Label Object, you enter `FontSize` in the Name field, select the Data radio button, and enter **`12`** in the related input field.

Page type parameters generally, but not always, refer to HTML documents, which is the reason that you must also specify a media type. Media types follow the MIME standard. For example, the ActiveMovie control uses a page type parameter called `FileName`. To use this property, you enter **`FileName`** in the Name field and then select the Page radio button. In the input area for the Page type, you enter the actual filename, such as `myMovie.avi`. Here, you enter **`video/x-msvideo`** in the Media Type field.

Object type parameters generally refer programmatically to other objects, which could be another control on the page. For example, suppose that you have two Label controls on the page.

The control named `labelA` can refer to the control named `labelB`. In this case, in the Name field, you enter the name of the parameter, such as `Reference`, select the Object radio button, and then enter the name of the object in the input area.

Using ActiveX with VBScript

Just as you can't create applications or controls—such as menus and buttons—without a development language, you can't create fully interactive Web pages without a scripting language and controls; ActiveX and VBScript enter the picture at this point. ActiveX and VBScript are the perfect partners.

ActiveX supplies the foreground functions, such as the menus, buttons, and other controls users see, hear, and experience; VBScript provides the background functions, gluing the controls together and allowing them to call script methods and respond to events.

Changing Object Properties with Method Calls

With VBScript, you can easily change the properties of an ActiveX control. All you need to do is access the control by using the name identifier you assigned to it. This unique identifier, which is the value assigned to the Name field in the ActiveX Control Properties dialog box, is used to create a reference to the control you're adding to the page.

Using the unique name of the control, you can change any of its properties by referring to the property specifically in a method call to the control. For example, if a control called `LabelA` has a property called `FontName`, you can set the `FontName` property in your script this way:

```
Sub setFontName
     LabelA.FontName = "Arial"
End Sub
```

NOTE

Determining the acceptable properties for a control you have downloaded over the Internet isn't an easy task unless you have documentation. If you have a control you want to use in your Web pages, you should visit the control developer's Web site to get detailed documentation for the control.

To explore this concept further, take a look at the Calendar control. You place a control on the page by choosing Insert|Advanced|ActiveX Control in the FrontPage Editor. Alternatively, if the Advanced toolbar is open, you can simply click the ActiveX control button.

Create a page for the control in the FrontPage Editor. Open the ActiveX Control Properties dialog box, and then select the Calendar control from the Pick a Control pull-down list. If the Calendar control isn't available on your system, don't worry. This example uses Calendar Control 8.0. Follow the discussion and refer to the figures provided.

Start by naming the control `Calendar1`. Then set the Width of the control to 450 pixels and the height of the control to 350 pixels. Also set the Border thickness to 0. Leave the rest of the settings with their default values as you see in Figure 37.11.

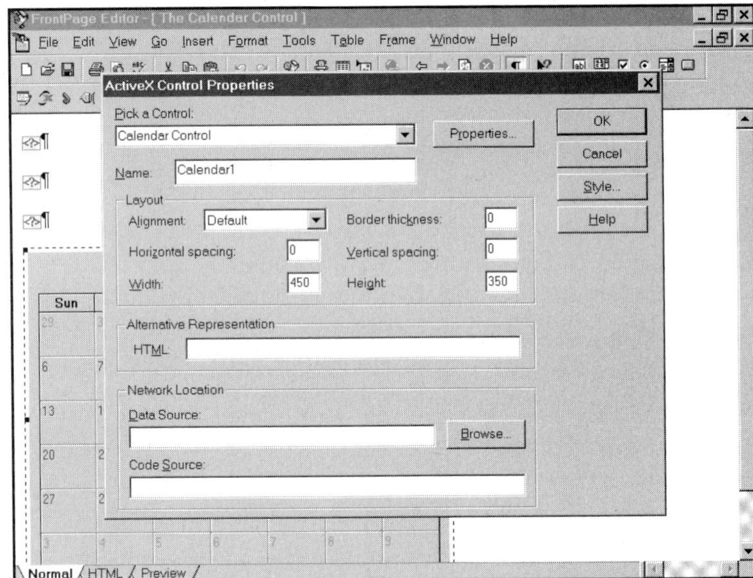

FIGURE 37.11.
Creating a Calendar control.

You can set many properties for the Calendar control, such a default day, month, and year. To set these properties, first click the Properties button to open the Properties dialog box. Then you can set properties for the day, month, and year by doing the following:

1. Double-click the Day field, and enter `31` in the text input area. Press Enter.
2. Double-click the Month field, and enter `12` in the text input area. Press Enter.
3. Double-click the Year field, and enter `1997` in the text input area. Press Enter.

Next, you can close all open dialog boxes and save the page. If you add some text to describe the control, you get a page similar to the one shown in Figure 37.12.

You can access the same `Day`, `Month`, and `Year` properties in a script by using method calls. As you can see in Listing 37.1, you need one method call for each property you want to set.

Listing 37.1. Setting control properties.

```
' Add main body of script here

Sub setCalendar
     Calendar1.Year = 1997
     Calendar1.Month = 1
```

```
    Calendar1.Day = 1
End Sub

'Add more subroutines here
```

When the `setCalendar` routine of the script is executed, the properties for the calendar control are set, and the control updates instantly.

To have the properties set automatically when your page is loaded, you do not use a subroutine. Instead, you place the properties before the main body of the script as follows:

```
Calendar1.Year = 1997
Calendar1.Month = 1
Calendar1.Day = 1
' Add main body of script here
```


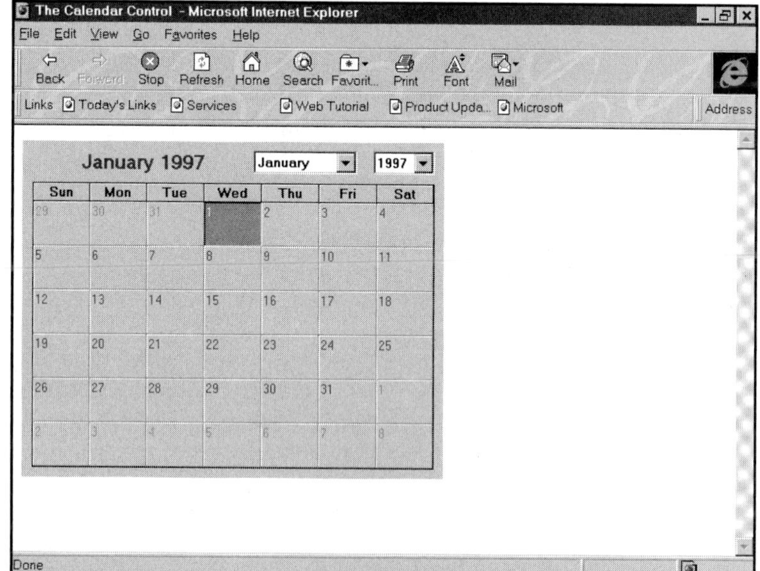

FIGURE 37.12.
The finished page with your control.

Accessing a Control's Methods

Many controls have methods you can access. Methods differ from properties because they're generally used to perform or simulate an action. For example, the Calendar control contains methods for moving around the calendar. Using these methods, you can advance or go back to another day, month, or year.

Documentation for a control should describe any methods it uses. To access a control's method, you use the same technique you use to change a control's property. The only difference is that, instead of using a property name, you use a method name as follows:

```
Sub prevDay
     Calendar1.PreviousDay
End Sub
```

Some methods accept parameters, so you can pass parameters to a method by placing them in parentheses. Each parameter in parentheses is separated by a comma:

```
Sub paramPassing
     paramControlA.setupBox("What are you trying to do?",
➥"Insure you use proper values")
End Sub
```

Other methods can return values to your script. Procedures that return values are called *functions*, and generally, functions return results you want to evaluate or store, such as this one:

```
Sub storeResult
     result = paramControlA.setup
End Sub
```

Using intrinsic HTML controls, you can add more functions to the Calendar control. As you see in Figure 37.13, button controls that allow users to easily manipulate the calendar have been added to the page. Here, methods of the Calendar control are used to update the calendar when any of the buttons on the page are clicked.

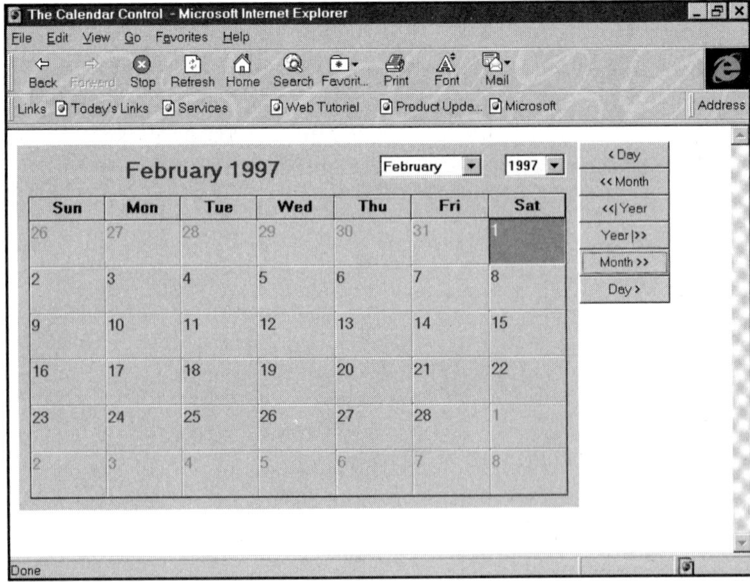

FIGURE 37.13.
This page uses a script to access the control's methods.

You can create a similar page following these steps:

1. Create a page for the Calendar control.
2. Open the ActiveX Control Properties dialog box, and then select the Calendar control from the Pick a Control pull-down list.

3. Name the control `Calendar1`.
4. In the Layout area, set the Alignment to Left.
5. Set the width of the control to 500 pixels and the height of the control to 380 pixels.
6. Set the horizontal spacing to 1 to pad the spacing between the ActiveX control and the nearest text or other object.
7. Add the control to the page by clicking OK to close the ActiveX Control Properties box.
8. The insertion point should be on the right side of the control. Without pressing any other keys, add a push button to the page. From the Forms toolbar (View|Forms Toolbar), click the Push Button icon to insert a new push button. Repeat this step until you have six push buttons on the right side of the control.
9. Double-click the first push button. In the dialog box that appears, set the Name field to `PreviousDay`. Set the Value field to `< Day`. Then confirm that the Normal button type is selected. Click OK to close the dialog box.
10. For the second push button, set the Name field to `PreviousMonth`. Set the Value field to `<< Month`. Again, confirm that the Normal button type is selected and click OK to close the dialog box.
11. For the third push button, set the Name field to `PreviousYear`. Set the Value field to `<<| Year`. Confirm the Normal button type and click OK to close the dialog box.
12. For the fourth push button, set the Name field to `NextYear`. Set the Value field to `Year |>>`. As with the previous push buttons, confirm that the Normal button type is selected and click OK to close the dialog box.
13. For the fifth push button, set the Name field to `NextMonth`. Set the Value field to `Month >>`. Confirm the Normal button type and close the dialog box by clicking OK.
14. For the sixth push button, set the Name field to `NextDay`. Set the Value field to `Day >`. Finally, confirm that the Normal button type is selected and click OK to close the dialog box.
15. Choose Insert | Advanced | Script to open the Script dialog box in which you can create a script. Be sure that VBScript is selected as the language type. Then enter the following code:

```
    Calendar1.Year = 1997
    Calendar1.Month = 1
    Calendar1.Day = 1

Sub PreviousDay_OnClick
    Calendar1.PreviousDay
End Sub

Sub NextDay_OnClick
    Calendar1.NextDay
End Sub
```

```
Sub PreviousMonth_OnClick
     Calendar1.PreviousMonth
End Sub

Sub NextMonth_OnClick
     Calendar1.NextMonth
End Sub

Sub PreviousYear_OnClick
     Calendar1.PreviousYear
End Sub

Sub NextYear_OnClick
     Calendar1.NextYear
End Sub
```

After you save the page, load it into your browser. You can do this by choosing the File|Preview in Browser command. As long as the browser supports ActiveX and VBScript, you can interact with the Calendar control. Study the script that enables this interaction. You also can use similar techniques with other controls.

Using Events of a Control

Just as your scripts can react to user events such as button clicks, your scripts can also react to a control's events. Most controls have events driven by interaction with users. If you use events of the Label Object control, your scripts can react to mouse movements or clicks of mouse buttons.

The way you handle an event, such as a mouse click, is up to you. When a user clicks a mouse button over a Label control, your script could rotate the label, display a message box, change the caption for the label, or even dynamically update the document.

To handle an event, you must create a subroutine in your script to execute when the event is triggered. The name of the subroutine must include the identifier of the control to which the event relates, followed by an underscore character, and then the name of the event, such as the following:

```
Sub labelA_Click

labelA.caption = "Mouse click detected"

End Sub
```

In this example, the name of the control whose event you want to handle is `labelA`. The event related to the control is `Click`. Therefore, when the control is clicked, the subroutine `labelA_Click` is automatically executed; it sets the value of the control's caption to `Mouse click detected`.

With event-related actions, you can create highly interactive pages. A mouse click on a control can drive other events or updates in other controls. For example, you can add two Label controls to a page. When you click one label, the label updates itself and the other label as well.

In the following example, clicking `labelA` changes the angle and caption for itself and another label on the page called `labelB`:

```
Sub labelA_Click

labelA.angle = labelA.angle + 5
labelB.angle = labelB.angle - 5
labelA.caption = "Mouse click detected"
labelB.caption = "Why not click on me?"

End Sub
```


As Figure 37.14 shows, you can take interaction between Label Object controls a step further. In this example, two Label Object controls are added to a Web page. When you click either control, the caption of the active control is set to `Click`, and the angle of the captions for both controls is changed, which makes the labels rotate in different directions. When you double-click either control, the caption of the active control is set to `Double click`, and the angles for the controls are interchanged and updated.

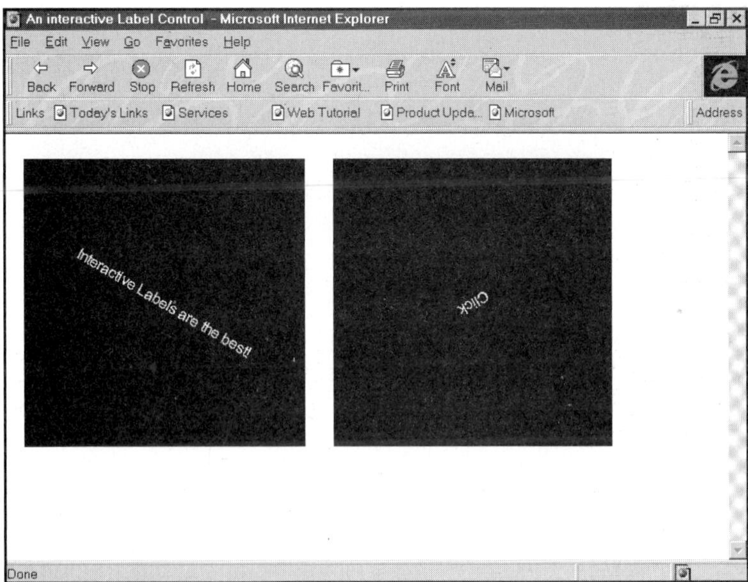

FIGURE 37.14.
This figure demonstrates how a control's events can be controlled by a script when an event is triggered.

The following steps show how you can create a similar page:

1. Create a new page.
2. Open the ActiveX Control Properties dialog box, and then select the Label Object control from the Pick a Control pull-down list. Then follow steps 2A through 2D.
   A. Name the control `labelA`.
   B. In the Layout area, set the alignment to Left.

   C. Set the width of the control to 300 pixels and the height to 300 pixels.
   D. Set the horizontal and vertical spacing to 10.

3. Open the Object Parameters dialog box for the control by clicking the Properties button. Then follow steps 3A through 3G.
   A. Click the Add button to open the Edit Object Parameter dialog box. Enter the value **`Angle`** in the Name text box. Enter **`0`** in the Data text box. Click the OK button to close the dialog box.
   B. Click the Add button to open the Edit Object Parameter dialog box. Enter the value **`Alignment`** in the Name text box. Enter **`4`** as the Data text box's value. Click the OK button to close the dialog box.
   C. Click the Add button to open the Edit Object Parameter dialog box. Enter the value **`BackStyle`** in the Name text box. Enter **`1`** in the Data text box. Click the OK button to close the dialog box.
   D. Click the Add button to open the Edit Object Parameter dialog box. Enter the value **`Caption`** in the Name text box. Enter **`Interactive Labels are the Best!`** in the Data text box. Click the OK button to close the dialog box.
   E. Click the Add button to open the Edit Object Parameter dialog box. Enter the value **`FontName`** in the Name text box. Enter **`Arial`** as the Data text box's value. Click OK to close the dialog box.
   F. Click Add to open the Edit Object Parameter dialog box. Enter the value **`FontSize`** in the Name text box. Enter **`10`** as the Data text box's value. Click OK to close the dialog box.
   G. Click Add to open the Edit Object Parameter dialog box. Enter the value **`ForeColor`** in the Name text box. Enter **`#FFFFFF`** in the Data text box. Click the OK button to close the dialog box
   H. Click the OK button to close the Object Parameters dialog box.

5. Add the control to the page by clicking OK to close the ActiveX Control Properties dialog box.
6. Move the insertion point to a new line.
7. Open the ActiveX Control Properties dialog box again, and then select the Label Object control from the Pick a Control pull-down list. Then follow steps 7A through 7D.
   A. Name the control `labelB`.
   B. In the Layout area, set the alignment to Left.
   C. Set the width of the control to 300 pixels and the height to 300 pixels.
   D. Set the horizontal and vertical spacing to 10.

8. Open the Object Parameters dialog box for the control by clicking the Properties button. Follow steps 8A through 8G.
   A. Click the Add button to open the Edit Object Parameter dialog box. Enter the value **`Angle`** in the Name text box. Enter **`180`** in the Data text box. Click the OK button to close the dialog box.
   B. Click the Add button to open the Edit Object Parameter dialog box. Enter the value **`Alignment`** in the Name text box. Enter **`4`** as the Data text box's value. Click the OK button to close the dialog box.
   C. Click the Add button to open the Edit Object Parameter dialog box. Enter the value **`BackStyle`** in the Name text box. Enter **`1`** in the Data text box. Click the OK button to close the dialog box.
   D. Click the Add button to open the Edit Object Parameter dialog box. Enter the value **`Caption`** in the Name text box. Enter **`Labels can react to user-driven events`** in the Data text box. Click the OK button to close the dialog box.
   E. Click the Add button to open the Edit Object Parameter dialog box. Enter the value **`FontName`** in the Name text box. Enter **`Arial`** as the Data text box's value. Click the OK button to close the dialog box.
   F. Click the Add button to open the Edit Object Parameter dialog box. Enter the value **`FontSize`** in the Name text box. Enter **`10`** as the Data text box's value. Click the OK button to close the dialog box.
   G. Click the Add button to open the Edit Object Parameter dialog box. Enter the value **`ForeColor`** in the Name text box. Enter **`#FFFFFF`** in the Data text box. Click the OK button to close the dialog box.
   H. Click the OK button to close the Object Parameters dialog box.
9. Choose Insert|Advanced|Script to open the Script dialog box in which you can create a script. Be sure that VBScript is selected as the language type. Enter the following code:

```
Sub labelA_Click

labelA.angle = labelA.angle + 5
labelB.angle = labelB.angle - 5
labelA.caption = "Click"

End Sub

Sub labelB_Click

labelA.angle = labelA.angle - 5
labelB.angle = labelB.angle + 5
labelB.caption = "Click"

End Sub

Sub labelA_DblClick
```

```
labelA.angle = labelB.angle + 20
labelB.angle = labelA.angle - 20
labelA.caption = "Double Click"

End Sub

Sub labelB_DblClick

labelA.angle = labelB.angle - 20
labelB.angle = labelA.angle + 20
labelB.caption = "Double Click"

End Sub
```

Save the page and load it into your browser. Test the controls by clicking them. A single click should have different results than a double-click. Study the script to see how it performs, and use similar techniques in your own scripts.

Summary

You can use FrontPage's easy access to ActiveX integration to create exciting and lively Web pages. By using ActiveX components that are closely tied to scripts, you can add a new level of interactivity to your Web site that otherwise might not have been possible. ActiveX is an appealing option for many developers, especially those who are freed from the constraints of cross-platform compatibility. As ActiveX grows in popularity and power, undoubtedly you will find the use for more and more components in your Web pages.

CHAPTER

Scripting with JavaScript

by William Robert Stanek

IN THIS CHAPTER

- Getting to Know JavaScript *624*
- JavaScript Fundamentals *626*
- Working with Functions *628*
- Working with JavaScript Objects *630*
- Performing Calculations in JavaScript *630*
- Controlling Flow with Conditionals *635*
- Controlling Flow with Looping *637*
- Using JavaScript in Your Web Page *638*

JavaScript is a scripting language that is included in HTML pages to increase their interactivity. This interactivity runs the gamut from alert boxes and status bar messages to complex menu systems and form validation.

Getting to Know JavaScript

JavaScript is more closely related to a programming language than to HTML tags. JavaScript cannot exist, however, outside HTML. To function, it must be included as part of a page.

For example, JavaScript enables the HTML author to respond to user-initiated events, such as mouse clicks and form activity, without the need for client/server interaction. The result provides quicker operation for the end user and less load on the server.

Although you can find similarities between Java and JavaScript, the languages are different and are intended for different uses. A simple form-handling routine that requires a significant amount of coding in Java represents a basic task for JavaScript. Here, JavaScript bridges the gap by enabling HTML authors to implement basic HTML functionality and interactivity without hours and hours of writing code.

The other side of the coin for JavaScript means that you have a much smaller set of objects, methods, and properties to work with, and they all focus on dealing with HTML content. For example, JavaScript cannot control network connections or download files.

Why Is JavaScript So Hot?

Although JavaScript is based on a programming language, it is simple enough to be within easy reach of anyone who feels comfortable with HTML coding. It greatly expands the capabilities of typical HTML pages without a great deal of hassle.

To see just how easily you can create a script in JavaScript, open an existing Web page in the FrontPage Editor. Click the Advanced toolbar's Insert Script button. Select JavaScript as your language in the Script dialog box, and then enter the following in the script input area:

```
document.writeln("This page last changed on "+document.lastModified)
```

Close the Script dialog box and save the page. The FrontPage Editor inserts the script into the page when you close the Script dialog box.

Next, load the page in your browser. Without any further communication with the server, JavaScript accesses the page's modification date and displays it for the user. You don't need to remember to update a line of HTML or include a link to a CGI script; after the JavaScript line appears, the process is automatic.

The information is obtained from the file itself. Each file has a set of basic information about itself, including size, date and time of last modification, and file type. The JavaScript simply looked at the file's properties to determine the last time it had been changed, and passed that information on to the Web page.

JavaScript also enables you to manage multiple frames effectively. Although a page cannot be redrawn, you can control the content in other frames by loading them with new URLs or managing form input.

One major JavaScript feature is revealed in its capability to handle forms and their elements. JavaScript can validate and check the information on a form before it is sent to the server, saving valuable processing and communication time. Client-side form processing also localizes the process, making it much harder for end users to send incompatible data that could cause damage to the server.

Additional characteristics now represent a part of form elements in the shape of events and event handlers. For push buttons and text boxes, the page author can check for mouse clicks, changed text, and focus and even change the content of form elements. In addition, submission of forms and other information is controlled by substituting custom actions for the standard submit button formats.

How to Use JavaScript Now

FrontPage 98 fully supports JavaScript. You can use JavaScript to validate your forms before submitting them to a server. You can also use the Scripting Wizard to generate scripts written in JavaScript automatically.

For users to take advantage of your JavaScript-empowered pages, they need to use browsers with JavaScript interpreters. The current browser choices include Netscape Navigator (2.0 and later) and Microsoft Internet Explorer (3.0 and later).

TIP

As with many sites that provide a host of technologies, some of which are mutually exclusive, offering your page in a generic version shows good manners if crucial content is not usable with a non-JavaScript browser. You can also offer a link to sites on which a compatible browser is available for downloading.

A problem can develop when a user views a page embedded with JavaScript statements with a non-compatible browser. A non-compatible browser ignores the scripting tags and displays the JavaScript commands as any other text. For a document including any length of JavaScript, the result produces a screen full of commands and characters otherwise unintelligible to the user. To prevent an older or non-compatible browser from incorrectly processing your JavaScript code, you can use HTML comment tags so that FrontPage 98 hides the script from the user's browser, thus clearing up the potential problem.

As JavaScript compatibility changes, you can use the following text to see whether a browser you want to use is JavaScript compatible:

1. Create a new page in the FrontPage Editor. Use the title `JavaScript Test Page`.
2. With the insertion point at the beginning of the page, open the Script dialog box and select JavaScript as your scripting language. Then enter the following script:

```
function checkJS () {
    alert("This browser is JavaScript-compatible.");
}
```

3. Close the Script dialog box. Insert a level one heading with the following text:

```
Checking for JavaScript compatibility.
```

4. With the insertion point at the end of the page, open the Script dialog box again, and select JavaScript as your scripting language. Then enter the following script:

```
checkJS();
```

5. Close the Script dialog box, and save the page. You can open the page in any browser you want to test. If the browser is JavaScript compatible, you see the alert box shown in Figure 38.1. Otherwise, the browser itself will tell you that it's JavaScript incompatible.

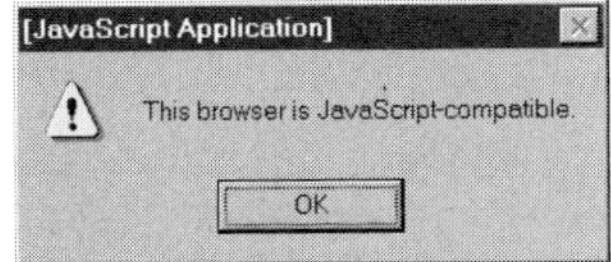

FIGURE 38.1.
Testing for JavaScript compatibility.

With proper placement and use, JavaScript can add vital functionality to your HTML pages without interfering with the capability of non-compatible browsers to interpret a document. Remember, if your page depends on JavaScript for including crucial information or operability, warning users and supplying a generic version of the document will show them a common courtesy.

JavaScript Fundamentals

JavaScript is a powerful and versatile scripting language that can work wonders in your Web pages. As you have seen, JavaScript is easy to use and work with. Like most programming languages, JavaScript has a specific syntax for statements, expressions, and control flow. You use these basic structures as building blocks to more advanced subjects.

Working with Variables

In JavaScript, variable names are case sensitive, which means that `Var1`, `var1`, and `VAR1` all refer to different named containers for values. Although variable names can include alphabetic and numeric characters as well as the underscore (_) character, they cannot include spaces or punctuation characters. Further, variable names must begin with an alphabetic character or the underscore character.

In JavaScript, you can declare variables as global or local. By default, variables you declare outside a function are global, meaning that they can be accessed by statements located anywhere in the current script and by other scripts in the same HTML page. Variables declared within a function cannot be accessed outside the function, meaning that the variables are local to the function and are not accessible outside the function.

Variables are generally initialized with the `var` keyword. However, the `var` keyword is optional for global variables and mandatory for local variables.

Working with Data Types

Unlike programming languages with rigid syntax, JavaScript supports *loose typing.* Normally, when you use variables in a program, you must state the type of variable. If the variable is used with integers, for example, you declare the variable as an integer. If the variable is used with strings, you declare the variable as a string. Typing variables appropriately can lead to problems in code and also creates a complex structure that increases the overhead required for programs.

To avoid problems and make programming easier, JavaScript automatically allocates a variable type to any variables you use in your programs. JavaScript automatically converts between variable types whenever possible, which eliminates most variable conflicts. However, if you try to add a string variable to a numeric variable type, you will usually have problems. You will also have problems if JavaScript expects a string and you reference a numeric variable. You can find solutions for these problems in the next section.

Working with Strings

Because JavaScript automatically types variables, you don't need to declare a variable as a string. Yet for JavaScript to recognize a variable as a string, you must use single or double quotation marks to enclose the value associated with the variable, as in this example:

```
myString = "Creating a String."
```

In your scripts, you might often need to add strings together. For example, if a user enters his full name as three separate variables representing his first, middle, and last name, you might want to join these strings together. To do so, you use the + operator to concatenate the strings, as in this example:

```
userfullname = firstname + " " + middlename + " " + lastname
```

Keep in mind that if you enclose numeric values within quotation marks, JavaScript still interprets the values as strings. Therefore, you can get strange results when you try to add values together.

Working with Arrays

An array is like a table that you can use to group related sets of data together. In JavaScript, your table can have one column of data and as many rows as you need. If you want to create an array to hold the names of the seven continents, for example, you can declare the array as follows:

```
continents = new Array(6)
```

Arrays always begin at `0` and end at the number of data points in the array minus 1. Thus, an array with seven data points is initialized as `Array_Name(6)`.

After you define an array, you can insert values for elements in the array. The most basic way to do so is to use individual statements that reference the array element by its index. Listing 38.1 shows an example of setting values for the zones array.

Listing 38.1. Setting values for an array.

```
continents = new Array(6)
continents[0] = "North America"
continents[1] = "South America"
continents[2] = "Australia"
continents[3] = "Asia"
continents[4] = "Africa"
continents[5] = "Antarctica"
continents[6] = "Pangea"
```

After you set values for array elements, you can easily access those values in your scripts. You do so by referencing the array element by its index, as in this example:

```
aValue = continents[3]
```

As a result of the previous statement, the `aValue` variable is set to `Asia`.

Working with Functions

Functions are extremely useful elements in your scripts. A function is a procedure that returns a value to the statement that called it. When you create a function, you can define parameters that are required to execute the function. Parameters are optional variables that you can use to pass values to the function.

The basic structure of a function is as follows:

```
function functionName(parameter1, parameter2, ..., parameterN) {
   //Insert function code here.
}
```

NOTE

A comment is a block of text that won't be interpreted by the script handler. You can set a comment by prefacing it with //. Comments are also invaluable for debugging and documentation purposes, especially if someone else will eventually have to work with your code.

You can use functions in your code as follows:

```
function ObtainAddress() {
   var userAddress
   while (userAddress == "") {
      userAddress = prompt("Please enter your address.","")
   }
   return userAddress
}
```

In this example, `getAddress` is the name of the function. Because the function accepts no parameters, none are defined after the function name. A temporary local variable called `userAddress` is created to make the code easier to follow and debug. The temporary variable is used to store the user's input. After the user enters a valid name, the `while` loop is exited. The value the user entered is returned to the calling statement. Generally, all functions return one or more values using the `return` statement.

It's important to note that local variables will not survive the conclusion of a function. As soon as that function completes its task and returns whatever values, all the variables it used to get that far are lost, unless they are returned to the main program. The advantage to this is that all the variables used by your functions don't linger, clogging up memory space. The disadvantage is that those variables will only exist for a short period of time until they are erased or otherwise stored.

You can call a function by using the following:

```
ObtainAddress()
```

You could also use the following:

```
userAddress = ObtainAddress()
```

The difference between the two methods of calling the function is a simple one. The first method simply executes the function, without regard to storing the return variable (if any). The second method has a variable equal the result of the function, therefore trapping and storing the return value.

The reason you'd want to use the first method is also simple. Use the first method in functions that don't need to return variables. If you have a function that only updates the screen, or perhaps scrolls a marquee along the bottom of a browser window, you don't need specific return values. On the other hand, if your function gets a user's name, address, or credit card number, you'd definitely want to store that information.

Working with JavaScript Objects

The power and simplicity of JavaScript comes from its use of objects. Objects are simply containers that can be described by the events, methods, and properties associated with them. With JavaScript, as with other object-based programming languages, you can work with objects in a variety of ways. You can use built-in objects, like the window object. You can create new objects based on the built-in objects, like a new window. You can also define your own objects with unique events, methods, and properties. However, because JavaScript is not a true object-oriented programming language, objects do not inherit properties, events, or methods of higher objects in the hierarchy. Therefore, all object references must be explicit.

When you insert scripts into pages, keep in mind that all JavaScript objects are created when they are loaded into your Web page. If you try to use an object that has not yet been created, JavaScript generates an error.

Whenever you use JavaScript to work with HTML elements, such as windows, frames, forms, images, hypertext links, and plug-ins, you work within the scope of the JavaScript's main object hierarchy. JavaScript includes several objects that do not follow a precise object hierarchy. These objects include arrays, dates, functions, math functions, and strings.

Performing Calculations in JavaScript

Math in JavaScript is similar to math in Java and C++, which means that JavaScript has several operators. If you routinely perform calculations in scripts, you will find that most of these operators are invaluable. JavaScript operators can be broken down into five broad categories: arithmetic operators, comparison operators, assignment operators, logical operators, and bitwise operators.

Using Arithmetic Operators

You use arithmetic operators to perform simple functions such as addition and subtraction. You use the + operator to add numbers together. The following two examples show addition:

```
theAnswer = 5 + 4

theAnswer = aValue + bValue
```

You use the - operator to subtract numbers. The following two examples show subtraction:

```
theAnswer = 40 - 5

theAnswer = bValue - aValue
```

You use the * operator to perform multiplication, as shown in the following two examples:

```
theAnswer = 2 * 5

theAnswer = aValue * bValue
```

You use the / operator to divide numbers, as shown in these two examples:

```
theAnswer = 32 / 4

theAnswer = cValue / dValue
```

Often, in division you have a remainder. Because you might want to perform calculations based on the remainder, you need a way to determine it. In JavaScript, you do so by using the modulus operator (%). Consider the following expression:

```
theAnswer = 7 % 2
```

Here, the value of the result is set to 1.

You can negate a value by using the unary negation operator (-). The following two examples show how to negate values:

```
theAnswer = -3 * 5

theAnswer = -bValue
```


When you mix operators, JavaScript performs calculations using the same precedence order your high school math teacher taught you. For example, multiplication and division in equations are carried out before subtraction and addition. Consider these examples:

```
6 + 3 * 5 = 21

2 / 2 + 3 = 4
```

The complete precedence order of arithmetic operators is shown in Table 38.1. Negation operators have the highest precedence order and are always calculated first.

Table 38.1. The precedence order of arithmetic operations.

Order	*Operation*
1	Negation (-)
2	Multiplication (*) and division (/)
3	Remainders (%)
4	Addition (+) and subtraction (-)

Another way to perform simple arithmetic operations is to increment or decrement values by using unary operators. Typically, if you want to increment a value by 1, you write a statement as follows:

```
aValue = aValue + 1
```

Another way to write this value is to use the increment operator (++), as in this example:

```
++aValue
```

The result of the preceding statement is that `aValue` is incremented by 1. Similarly, you can decrease the value of `aValue` by using the decrement operator (--), as in this example:

```
--aValue
```

When you use the increment or decrement operator in a statement, the placement of the operator is extremely important. The result of this statement is that `aValue` and `bValue` are set to 6:

```
bValue = 5
aValue = ++bValue
```

The JavaScript interpreter reads the statement as "Add 1 to `bValue` and store the result in `aValue`." Because the ++ occurs before the variable label, the interpreter increments the variable and then stores it in `aValue`.

If you change the position of the increment operator to

```
aValue = bValue++
```

the JavaScript interpreter reads the statement as "Set `aValue` equal to `bValue` and then add 1 to `bValue`." The result is that `aValue` is set to 5, and `bValue` is incremented to 6. In this case, the interpreter hits the instruction to store `bValue` in `aValue` first, and then increments `bValue`.

As you can see, the difference between a prefix operator, such as `++aValue`, and a postfix operator, such as `aValue++`, is subtle, yet they yield completely different results.

Using Comparison Operators

You use comparison operators to check for certain conditions, such as A is equal to B. Generally, you use a control flow, such as conditional looping, in conjunction with your comparison. For example, if A is equal to B, you perform a specific task; if A is not equal to B, you perform a different task.

When you're performing comparisons, you often compare objects as well as numeric and textual data. To see whether a variable is equal to another variable, you use the comparison operator (==). The operator returns a result that is `true` if the objects are equivalent or `false` if they are not equivalent. Here is an example that checks for equality:

```
if myValue == varA
   //The variables are equal
```

To see whether variables are not equal, you use the inequality operator (!=), as in the following example:

```
if myValue != varA
   //The variables are not equal
```

To see if one variable is less than or greater than another variable, you use the less than (<) and greater than (>) operators. You can check for values greater than or less than a variable as follows:

```
if myValue < varA
   //myValue is less than varA
if myValue > varA
   //myValue is greater than varA
```

Another type of comparison you can perform is to see whether a variable is less than or equal to (<=) a value. Likewise, you can see whether a variable is greater than or equal to (>=) a value. The following example shows this type of comparison:

```
if myValue <= varA
   //myValue is less than or equal to varA
if myValue >=.varA
   //myValue is greater than or equal to varA
```


Using Assignment Operators

Assignment operators are useful for assigning values to named variables. Some assignment operators such as the equal sign (=) are used in just about every statement you will write. Other assignment operators, such as divide by value (/=), are used rarely—if at all. Table 38.2 lists all the assignment operators.

Table 38.2. Assignment operators.

Operator	*Description*
=	Equals
+=	Add by value
-=	Subtract by value
*=	Multiply by value
/=	Divide by value
%=	Modulo by value
&=	Bitwise And by value
|=	Bitwise Or by value
^=	Bitwise XOr by value
<<=	Shift Left by value
>>=	Shift Right by value
>>>=	Zero Fill by value

As with the increment and decrement operators, you can use assignment operators to save some typing. Instead of typing

```
g = g + 7
```

You can type

```
g += 7
```

Although both statements perform the same operation, the second statement does so with less typing on your part. Saving a few keystrokes becomes increasingly important in long scripts and in series of repetitive statements. Listing 38.2 shows examples of how you can use the most common assignment operators in your scripts.

Listing 38.2. Assignment operator examples.

```
myVar = 2;      // assigns to myVar the value 2

myVar %=5;      // assigns to myVar the result of myVar % 5

myVar *=3;      // assigns to myVar the result of myVar * 3

myVar /=6;      // assigns to myVar the result of myVar / 6

myVar -=1;      // assigns to myVar the result of myVar - 1
```

Using Logical Operators

Logical operators are great for performing several comparisons within a control flow. For example, if you want to see if A is greater than B and if C is less than B before you perform a calculation, you use a logical operator.

Like comparison operators, logical operators return either `true` or `false`. Generally, if the operation returns `true`, the script interpreter performs a set of statements. Otherwise, you skip the statements or perform other statements.

The most commonly used logical operators are logical `And` (`&&`) and logical `Or` (`||`). These operators merge the results of two comparisons to produce a `true` or `false` value. The logical `And` returns a `true` value only when both comparisons return a `true` value. The logical `Or` returns a `true` value when either or both comparisons return a `true` value.

The final logical operator available in JavaScript is called `Not` (`!`). You use the `Not` operator to change a Boolean value from `true` to `false` or from `false` to `true`. Generally, when you use the `Not` operator, you should use parentheses as follows:

```
If !(A < B) then
//execute this code
```

Listing 38.3 shows how to use logical operators in your scripts.

Listing 38.3. Using logical operators.

```
varA = 5
varB = 10
varC = 2
varD = 15
if varA > varC && varB < varD then
   //the result is true
if varA > varB && varC < varB then
   //the result is false because both sides
   //of the comparison don't evaluate to true
if varA > varB || varC < varB then
   //the result is true because at least one side
   //evaluates to true.

var green = 5
var red = 10
If !(red < green) then
   //Because 10 is less than 5, the initial comparison evaluates to false.
   //Using the Not operator, the result is changed to true.
```

Controlling Flow with Conditionals

When you want to execute a set of instructions only if a certain condition is met, you can use `if` or `if...else` structures.

Using the `if` Structure

Using the `if` structure, you can control execution based on a `true` or `false` condition. You can control the execution of instructions based on a `true` condition as follows:

```
if (condition) {
   //then condition is true
   //and statements between the curly brackets {} are executed.
}
```

Using the `Not` operator (`!`), you can also control the execution of instructions based on a `false` condition, as in this example:

```
if (!condition) {
   //then condition is false
   //and statements between the curly brackets {} are executed.
}
```

Using the `if...else` Structure

You can extend the `if` condition with the `else` statement. The `else` statement provides an alternative when a condition you specified is not met. The structure of an `if...else` condition is as follows:

```
if (condition) {
   //condition is true
   //and statements between these curly brackets {} are executed.
```

```
}
else {
   //condition is false
   //and statements between these curly brackets {} are executed.
}
```

Nested if Structures

To add more conditions, you can nest `if` statements or use logical operators. In this way, additional conditions you add to the code are checked for validity. The following example shows nested `if` statements and how you can replace the nested statements with logical operators. The logical `And` (`&&`) operator often eliminates the need to nest `if` statements, which creates cleaner, more sophisticated-looking code. Here's an example:

```
//Nested if statements
if (conditionA) {
   if (conditionB) {
   //condition A and B are true
   //and statements between these curly brackets {} are executed.
   }
}

//Replacing a nested if statement with a logical operator
if (conditionA) && (conditionB) {
   //condition A and B are true
   //and statements between these curly brackets {} are executed.
}
```

Using Conditional Expressions

Often you use conditionals to assign values to variables based on certain conditions. Suppose that you run an online order center from which users can purchase CDs or cassettes at a fixed price. When a user orders a CD, the price is $10.99. When a user orders a cassette, the price is $8.99. You can use an `if` statement to assign the price as follows:

```
if (type="CD") {
   price = 10.99
}
else {
   price = 8.99
}
```

A cleaner and more elegant way to perform `if...else` conditional assignments to variables is to use a conditional expression. Conditional expressions allow you to replace the entire `if...else` conditional with a single statement. Using a conditional expression, you can replace the `if...else` structure for the online order example with the following:

```
var price = (type = "CD") ? 10.99 : 8.99
```

You read the preceding statement as follows: "If the condition is true, then set the price to 10.99; otherwise, set the price to 8.99."

Controlling Flow with Looping

Sometimes you might want to execute a section of code repeatedly. In JavaScript, you can do so in two ways:

- Execute a code segment for a specific count using `for` looping.
- Execute a code segment while a condition is met using `while` looping.

Using `for` Loops

To execute a code segment for a specific count, you use `for` looping. The structure of `for` is as follows:

```
for (initialize counter;  condition; update counter) {
   insert code to repeat
}
```

You can easily use `for` looping in your code. The following example uses this structure to initialize an array of 20 elements:

```
for (x = 0; x < 20; x++) {
   aStruct(x) = "Unknown"
}
```

This `for` loop does the following:

- Initializes the counter to zero
- Sets the condition that the loop should continue as long as `x` is less than 20
- Increments the counter by 1 during each iteration of the loop
- Initializes the value of all 20 elements in the array to `Unknown`

Using `while` Loops

To execute a code segment while a condition is met, you use `while` looping. The structure of a loop that checks for a `true` condition is as follows:

```
while (condition) {
   insert code to repeat
}
```

The structure of a loop that checks for a `false` condition is as follows:

```
while (!condition) {
   insert code to repeat
}
```

As long as the condition is met, the loop is executed. To break out of the loop, therefore, you must change the condition at some point within the loop. Listing 38.4 shows an example of a `while` loop that changes the status of the condition.

Listing 38.4. Using `while` loops.

```
//This loop will continue as long as homeRun = true
while (homeRun) {

   if basesLoaded {
      alert ("Great time to hit a home run.")
   }

   else {

      if Balls = 3 && Strikes = 2 {
      alert ("Go for it!")
      }

   }

   else {
      homeRun = False
   }

}
```

Using `continue` and `break` Statements

When you're working with conditional looping, you often might want to break out of a loop or continue with the next iteration of the loop. Appropriately, the `break` statement allows you to end the execution of a loop, and the `continue` statement allows you to begin the next iteration of a loop. Whenever your script begins the next iteration of the loop, the condition is checked, and in `for` loops, the counter is updated as necessary.

```
For (x = 0; x < 20; x++) {

       If (x%2==0) {
  document.writeln("Even numbers will continue.")
  continue
  }

       If (x%2==1){
  document.writeln("Odd numbers stop the loop!")
  break
  }
```

The `continue` command jumps the loop to its next iteration, usually because of a successful condition. The `break` command exits the loop entirely, usually because of an error or unique response.

Using JavaScript in Your Web Page

You will find many uses for JavaScript, and more continue to appear all the time as developers experiment with the possibilities opened with interactive HTML. In the following sections, I show you a few examples to get you started.

Writing and Printing to the Page

Many of the examples earlier in this chapter showed that you could use JavaScript to write to the page. If you follow and test this example, you should get a fair idea of the different ways you can use JavaScript to write to the page:

1. Open a new page in the FrontPage Editor. Use the title `Practicing with JavaScript`.
2. With the insertion point at the beginning of the page, open the Script dialog box and select JavaScript as your scripting language. Then enter the following script:

```
function printMessage(msgStr) {
    document.writeln("<HR>");
    document.writeln(msgStr);
    document.writeln("<HR>");
}
alert("Function is loaded and ready.");
```

3. Close the Script dialog box. Insert a level one heading with the following text: `Welcome to my JavaScript page`. Press Enter.
4. Open the Script dialog box again, and select JavaScript as your scripting language. Then enter the following script:

```
printMessage("I just called a function from the body.");
```

5. Close all open dialog boxes by clicking their OK buttons. Save the page.

   Figure 38.2 shows how this page looks in a browser.

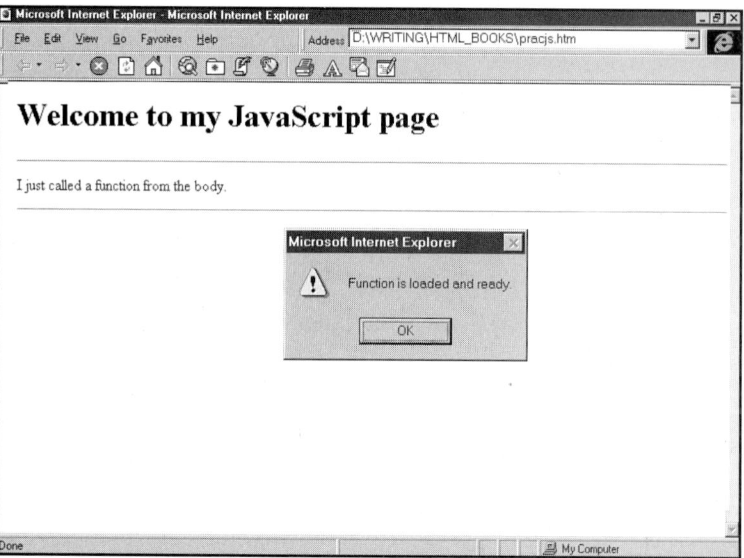

FIGURE 38.2.
Writing to a Web page.

What happens here is that you're addressing the Web page directly as a document. The `document.writeln` command inserts text into the document just as if you had typed it within a text editor. In this case, it inserts the instructions to create two horizontal lines in a Web page (the <HR> tags) and a brief selection of text (`msgStr`). What's important to note is that you can insert this text as the Web page renders. That means you can stick variables in there as well as text.

Displaying the Current Date and Time

The number of ways to display the time on your Web page is growing. Most of these methods involve server-side includes or objects dependent on helper applications. JavaScript offers live access to the system date and allows you to display the current time through a form field when it's used in conjunction with a timer feature.

Displaying a live clock is a common use of JavaScript's capability, and creating it is not much harder. You just insert the script shown in Listing 38.5, using the Script Wizard.

Listing 38.5. A live clock function using JavaScript.

```
var timerID = null;
var timerRunning = false;

function startclock ()    {
 stopclock();
 time();
   }

function stopclock ()   {
 if(timerRunning)
 clearTimeout(timerID);
 timerRunning = false;
   }

function time ()    {
   var now = new Date();
   var mName = now.getMonth() + 1;
   var dName = now.getDay() + 1;
   var dayNr = ((now.getDate()<10) ? "0" : "")+ now.getDate();
   var ampm = (now.getHours() >= 12) ? " P.M." : " A.M."
   var hours = now.getHours();
   hours = ((hours > 12) ? hours - 12 : hours);
   var minutes = ((now.getMinutes() < 10) ? ":0" : ":") + now.getMinutes();
   var seconds = ((now.getSeconds() < 10) ? ":0" : ":") + now.getSeconds();

       var DayDateTime=(" "
       + hours
       + minutes
       + seconds
       + " "          + ampm         );

 window.status=DayDateTime;
     timerID = setTimeout("time()",1000);
```

```
     timerRunning = true;    }

function clearStatus()   {
 if(timerRunning)
 clearTimeout(timerID);
 timerRunning = false;
 window.status=" ";
}
```

To initialize the clock, you need to use the Script Wizard. Here are the necessary steps:

1. Open the Script dialog box, and enter the script in Listing 38.5. Be sure that JavaScript is selected as the language type.
2. Click the Script Wizard button in the Script dialog box. Select the Code View radio button at the bottom of the dialog box.
3. In the Select an Event area of the Script Wizard dialog box, double-click the window element, and then select the `onLoad` event by clicking it. In the text area for editing scripts, enter the following:

   ```
   startClock()
   ```

The clock then starts running when the page is loaded by the browser. It does so by calling a function called `startClock()`. The `startClock()` function in turn calls the `Time()` function. The `Time()` function then inserts the current time into the browser's status bar.

NOTE

You won't be able to see this effect in the FrontPage Editor Preview mode, as the effect requires a full browser that includes a status bar. Load up your latest version (3.0+) of either Netscape Navigator or Internet Explorer to test the clock.

Controlling Browser Behavior

One of the important and powerful capabilities of JavaScript is controlling various aspects of browser behavior and appearance. This feature comes in handy for implementing demonstrations and tours by adding the capability to spawn new browser windows with controllable levels of functionality.

The command syntax to create a new browser window is

```
windowVar = window.open("URL", "windowName" [, "windowFeatures"])
```

where the terms are defined as follows:

- `windowVar` represents the name of a variable that holds the information about the new window.

- `URL` refers to an address for the contents of the new window and can be blank.
- `windowName` represents how the window is referred to in frame and window references.
- `windowFeatures` provides a list of the individual features of the browser that should be included or excluded. If this parameter is blank, all features are enabled. If only some features appear, any unmentioned features are disabled.

To include a feature, use the syntax *`windowFeature`*`=yes` or *`windowFeature`*`=1`. Conversely, to disable a feature, use *`windowFeature`*`=no` or *`windowFeature`*`=0`.

The features include the following:

- `toolbar` for the row of buttons at the top of the screen
- `status` for the message bar at the bottom of the browser
- `scrollbars` for the buttons and slides to control the part of the document viewed when it exceeds the window boundaries
- `resizable` for user control over the size of the browser window
- `width` and `height` in pixels for the initial size of the window
- `menubar` creates the menu at the top of the window if true
- `location` creates a URL entry field if true
- `directories` creates the standard Navigator directory buttons, such as What's New and What's Cool, if true

For example, you can insert this code to open a plain window with hotlink-only navigation:

```
//Setting one feature automatically sets all non-mentioned features to false.
window.open("URL", "windowName", "toolbar=no")
```

Summary

JavaScript adds new functionality and interactivity to HTML pages that in the past you could attain only through learning CGI scripting languages such as Perl. By switching the bulk of interactive behavior to the client side, the use of JavaScript has also improved the perceived speed of World Wide Web sites as seen by the user. Although JavaScript does have its nuances and idiosyncrasies, taking the time to learn JavaScript pays off because you can support Web pages with dramatically improved features and functions that users will want to visit again and again.

CHAPTER 39

Adding Java Applets to Your Web Page

by William Robert Stanek

IN THIS CHAPTER

- Getting to Know Java 644
- The Truth About Java-Powered Pages 646
- How to Use Java Now 647
- Getting the Tools You Need to Create Applets 650
- Configuring an Applet Editor for FrontPage 653
- Compiling Java Programs 653
- Creating Java Applets 654
- Working with Images in Java 659
- Using the Java AppletViewer 661

Java has brought the promise of interactivity and cross-platform programming to the Web. Introduced over two years ago, Java offers portability and powerful programming potential for all Web developers. Nearly anything you could imagine can be programmed in Java and added to a Web page, including sound, animations, and application interaction. Java has helped promote a change in the way developers think about the World Wide Web, similar to the way the World Wide Web changed the way people think about the Internet.

Getting to Know Java

Java is an object-oriented programming language developed by Sun Microsystems, Inc. Although Java was not initially conceived as a way to expand the interactivity and capability of Web pages, people quickly saw how the platform-independent nature of Java made an ideal fit with the nature of the Internet.

In the past, when an author developed a page with special content beyond the constraints of HTML, she had to make an important decision: either use helper applications or shift the necessary processing to the server. The first solution meant that some content was inaccessible to some users if they didn't have the helper application or if a helper was unavailable for their system. The second solution meant excluding some content because inherently slow modem lines made animation and sounds unworkable over normal network connections.

Enter Sun's Java. By utilizing a key feature of Java—platform independence—Java applets can implement sound, animation, spreadsheets, e-mail applications, guest books, and virtually anything else you can program, regardless of platform.

Java Safety

Running in a distributed environment, such as an intranet or the World Wide Web, requires safeguards for client computers; a potentially hostile piece of code can do a great deal of damage by erasing files, formatting disks, and creating other types of damage. Given the way applets are implemented—automatic load and run—you need to ensure the integrity of any piece of code distributed to a broad and uncontrolled audience.

As a Web page author using Java, you have the responsibility to ensure that your applets are clean. The best way is to get them only from trusted sites. Be careful about picking up applets anywhere you find them—the hard drive you save may be your own.

PROGRAMMERS LOVE A CHALLENGE

Java is not bulletproof. As quickly as it was proclaimed secure, a dedicated group of programmers went to work to find security holes, and they found them. Through cooperative efforts between Sun, Netscape, Microsoft, and others, most of these security problems were taken care of, but it's still a dangerous world.

You can do a few things to protect yourself and your system:

- Use only the most up-to-date versions of software. This includes using the most recent version of Java for your coding efforts.
- If your system allows screening applets at the firewall, take advantage of it. If there are applets you'd like to use, make them available internally.

As discussed earlier, the compiled bytecode is checked extensively for illegal operations and verified again on the host system before the applet is run. Although these security features limit the scope and capabilities of an applet, they also help ensure security against Trojan horse viruses and other shenanigans by less-than-scrupulous programmers.

With all the security features built in, you don't want to implement word processors, spreadsheets, or other interactive applications within the context of a browser. If you require these programs, consider building a full Java application, which does not contain the security restrictions of an applet.

Although no system can guarantee 100% security, Java goes a long way to ensure the protection of client systems from its applets. It uses three security procedures to make the end user safe from malicious attacks:

- Bytecode verification
- Memory layout
- File access restrictions

Bytecode Verification

After a piece of Java code is loaded into memory, it enters the interpreter, where it is checked for language compliance before the first statement is executed. This process protects against corruption or changes to the compiled code between compile time and runtime.

Memory Layout

Next, the memory layout is determined for each of the classes, preventing would-be hackers from forging access by deducing anything about the structure of a class or the machine it's running on. Memory allocation is different for each class, depending on its structure and the host machine.

File Access Restrictions

After that, the interpreter security continues to monitor the activity of the applet to make sure it doesn't access the host file system, except as specifically allowed by the client or user. You can extend some implementations of this specific feature to include no file access at all.

Platform Independence

The platform-independence feature is probably the most important one. One compiled piece of Java code can run almost identically on any platform with a Java compiler. This includes users of Microsoft Windows, MacOS, most UNIX variants, and OS/2. By its very nature, Java does not contain any implementation-specific syntax. This format means a byte is an 8-bit integer and a float is a 32-bit IEEE 754 floating-point number, no matter where the applet runs.

With object-oriented code, Java takes advantage of a special programming feature that allows programmers to upgrade capabilities by simply adding a new class. When an applet is upgraded, it is not always necessary to reload the entire applet. A small additional class may be all that's needed.

The Truth About Java-Powered Pages

When Java was first released in 1995, if you wanted to do something nifty on your Web page with an applet, you needed two things:

- Enough programming language experience to learn Java
- Users with the HotJava browser to view your applet because it wasn't yet supported by Netscape or Microsoft

Fortunately, this situation didn't last long. Thousands of programmers and Web developers became interested in Java and before long, applets were available everywhere. Netscape adopted Java compatibility for its 2.0 release of Navigator. This decision was followed closely by Microsoft, which included Java support as part of its 3.0 release of Internet Explorer.

HotJava is available but remains a distant choice in the browser market. Although easily customized using Java classes, it's still pretty slow. Sun is not attempting to compete with the Big Two and instead focuses on intranet and custom markets.

With plenty of applets and Java-compatible browsers, making a Java-powered page is as simple as including an applet definition within your HTML document. To wave the Java banner, many page authors also include the Java-powered icon as part of the page with the applet or links to other Java pages.

Why Is Everyone So Hyped About Java?

Java holds a great deal of promise for the World Wide Web and computers in general because it provides a solution to the problem of incompatible platforms. The Internet and intranets are no longer expected to include similar or directly compatible machines (all UNIX, all Macintosh, or all PC). Because it has a neutral architecture, the same application written in Java can be used by anyone on the network, without concern for what kind of machine the developer used.

For stand-alone applications, Java's object-oriented structure provides an easy method to upgrade. The class for the upgrade or extension of the application is downloaded into the appropriate class library; then you can run the updated features.

With its modeling capabilities, Java represents a good choice for implementing advanced Web capabilities and content, such as virtual reality sites or Web crawlers powered by intelligent agents.

How to Use Java Now

The simplest way to implement Java is through embedding applets in your HTML pages. A wide variety of applets are already available for inclusion, including the animation applet included with the Java Development Kit and a plethora of "ticker" display applets.

How Applets and Applications Are Different

Java applications work similarly to stand-alone programs, such as your browser or word processor. They don't require a third-party intermediary, such as HotJava or the AppletViewer. Applets require a Java-compatible browser or the AppletViewer for viewing. They operate similarly to other objects embedded in HTML documents, such as Shockwave or RealAudio files, which require assistance to run.

Because applets run on a host system, they are especially suspect and lead to several key security restrictions. Applets have limited capability to interact with their host platform. An applet cannot write files or send files to a printer on the local system. In addition, it cannot read local files or run local applications. Although no system is 100% secure, Java goes to great lengths to ensure the integrity of applets generated under its banner.

JAVA APPLETS AND JAVASCRIPT

It has been said a million times, but if you have just started using Java, it bears repeating. Java isn't JavaScript. JavaScript isn't Java.

Java, in applet or application form, is a compiled language with classes and inheritance. HTML pages can include a reference to Java applets, which then get downloaded and run when a compatible browser finds the tag.

JavaScript is an object-based, client-side scripting language developed by Netscape, but it does not include classes or inheritance. JavaScript exists on the HTML page and is interpreted by a compatible browser along with the rest of the page.

Although they share some common syntax and terminology, the two items work differently and have different uses. Confusing Java and JavaScript leads to a steeper learning curve.

Using an Applet on a Web Page

Using applets on a Web page requires a two-part process. First, you must make sure your classes and related files, such as images and audio clips, appear in a directory accessible to the HTML page. One common location is in a `classes` subdirectory of the HTML documents.

Second, the applet tag that refers to the class is inserted in the Web page, along with any parameters the applet needs to function.

NOTE

If your browser is not Java-compatible, the applet section of the HTML page is ignored.

Setting Applet Properties

To add an applet to your page, start by clicking the Advanced toolbar's Insert Java Applet button. This opens the Java Applet Properties dialog box shown in Figure 39.1.

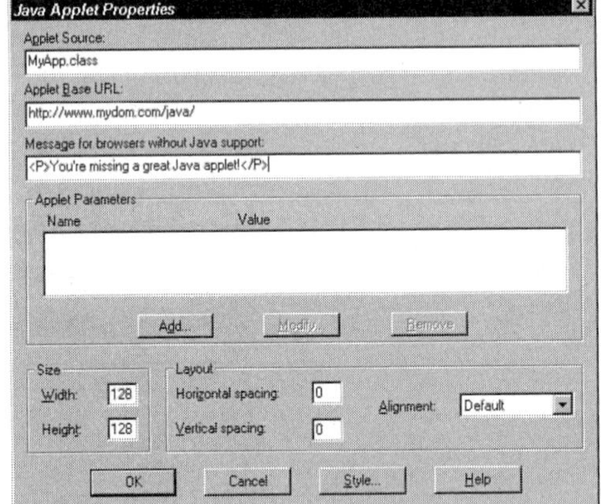

FIGURE 39.1.
Setting applet properties.

Although it looks as if you have a lot of options, they're actually simple. The Applet Source field provides your browser with the filename for the compiled applet, such as `myApp.class`. The Applet Source field can contain only the filename for the applet, not a path to a filename. If the applet code resides in a directory other than the one the HTML document is in, you must fill in the Applet Base URL field to indicate the path to the applet, such as `www.`*`yourserver`*`.com/apps/`.

A key field you should fill in is the Message for browsers without Java support field. Browsers that don't support Java display whatever you place in this field. As you see in Figure 39.1, this field can contain text and markup.

Telling your browser where to find the applet usually isn't enough. Most applets also require a set of parameters to control their actions. Without parameters, applets could not communicate with each other, and you could not pass general-purpose values to applets. You'll learn more about parameters in the next section.

You can work with applets like any other type of object on the page. To adjust the size of the applet, you use the Height and Width properties of the Size field. Using the properties of the Layout field, you can precisely place your applet on the page. The Alignment property lets you specify how the applet is aligned with text on the same line or area of the page. In the drop-down list for the Alignment property, you see nine alignment values, which are the same alignment values used with images.

The spacing around your applet is also important. You specify the amount of horizontal and vertical space in pixels. Horizontal spacing is the area above and below your applet. Vertical spacing is the area to the left and right of the applet.

When you add an applet to a page, the FrontPage Editor inserts a large icon that has the letter J in bold letters. You can double-click this icon to open the Java Applet Properties dialog box. Click the icon once to manipulate the size and position of the applet. On both ends and in the middle of a selected applet are resizing points. If you move the pointer to a resizing point and click and hold the left mouse button, you can add vertical and horizontal spacing by dragging the pointer. If you move the pointer to a different area of the applet icon and click and hold the left mouse button, you can drag the applet to a new location on the page.

Passing Parameters to Applets

Parameters pass information to the applet about its environment and how it should behave in the current HTML document. Some applets have one method of running and don't accept any parameters. Most, however, contain some user-definable parameters that can be changed.

Check any documentation supplied with the applet to see what's available. There is no limit to the number of parameters you can include within an applet tag.

Use the Applet Parameters area of the Java Applet Properties window to work with parameters. Parameters are set in name/value pairs like most extensions. Click the Add button to add new parameters. Click the Modify button to modify the currently selected parameter. Use the Remove button to delete the currently selected parameter.

To add a parameter to an applet, click the Add button, which opens the dialog box shown in Figure 39.2. In the Name field, enter the name of the parameter you are setting. In the Value field, set the parameter to a specific value.

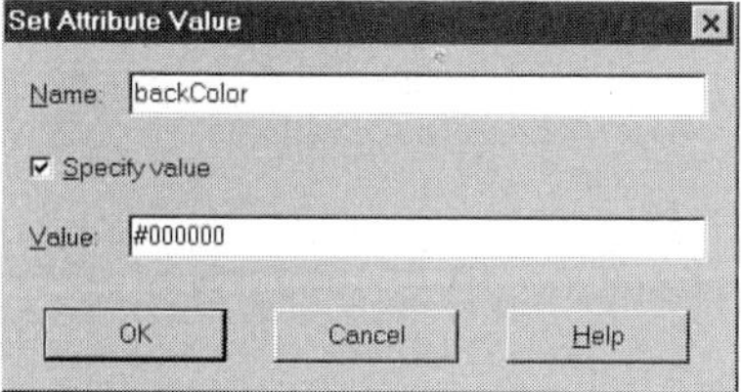

FIGURE 39.2.
You can set several different parameters for your applet, including specific attributes (in this case the background color).

Parameter names are case-sensitive and must exactly match the parameter names in the applet. If the applet does not provide exceptions for mismatched data types, an incompatible value could cause the applet not to function. For example, if a parameter looks for an integer and you enter a text string, the applet could fail to operate.

This process has one small complication. You'll notice that FrontPage 98 defines all parameters within quotation marks, meaning all parameters are passed as strings. What gives?

The nuance is that parameters are always sent to applets as strings, regardless of how you represent them in the parameter tag. The conversion to the appropriate data type happens inside the applet. The moral to this story is to make sure the value you send will convert to the right type.

More on Messages for Browsers Without Java Support

When an incompatible browser is interpreting an HTML document, it ignores any tags it doesn't understand. In this case, that includes the applet and its parameters. However, the browser ignores them one at a time instead of finding the closing applet tag and ignoring everything in between. When the browser reaches elements you've defined in the Message for browsers without Java support field, the browser knows what to do and handles any additional elements perfectly.

TIP

Make sure the actual size of your image matches the dimensions of the applet. If the size defined in the image tag is different from the actual size, it could be distorted on the viewer's screen.

This is an easy way to substitute content for users who don't have Java-compatible browsers. Although all the benefits of Java are lost, at least the users have something to view, even if it's a message saying that they should get a Java-capable browser.

Getting the Tools You Need to Create Applets

The first item needed for writing applets is the Java Development Kit, commonly referred to as the JDK. The JDK is currently available for most operating systems, including Sun Solaris, OS/2, AIX, Windows 3.1, Windows 95/NT, and Macintosh. You can obtain the JDK by visiting JavaSoft on the Web at

```
http://www.javasoft.com/
```

Packages in the Development Kit

The JDK is a wonderful resource. It includes many different code libraries that save you time and help you develop code more easily. Table 39.1 summarizes the core code libraries and their uses.

Table 39.1. Core code libraries included in the JDK.

Package	*Description*
`java.lang`	The core set of the classes for the Java language that provide basic functions, such as string and array handling
`java.applet`	A set of the classes that relate to the applet environment and are generally used when viewing applets
`java.awt`	A set of the classes that provide graphical interface tools such as buttons, controls, scrollbars, and windows
`java.awt.image`	A set of classes related to using images
`java.awt.datatransfer`	A set of classes for data transfer classes and methods
`java.beans`	A set of classes for the JavaBeans specification (`http://java.sun.com/beans/spec.html`)
`java.io`	A set of the classes that provide standard input/output and file I/O utilities
`java.lang`	A set of classes for internationalization
`java.math`	A set of classes for mathematical functions and procedures
`java.net`	A set of the classes that provide tools for accessing networks by protocols, such as FTP, Telnet, and HTTP
`java.rmi`	A set of classes for remote method invocation, for creating Java-to-Java programs
`java.security`	A set of classes for Java security functions and applet signing
`java.sql`	A set of classes for Java interaction with SQL databases
`java.text`	A set of the classes that provide functions for text management
`java.util`	A set of the classes that provide core utility functions such as encoding/decoding, hash tables, and stacks
`sun.tools.debug`	A set of the classes that provide debugging functions and tools

Tools in the Development Kit

You will also find most of the tools you need to work with Java right in the JDK. You use these tools to create Java bytecode, view your programs, and debug your code. Table 39.2 shows a brief summary of the key tools and their uses.

Table 39.2. Key developer's tools in the JDK.

Tool Name	*Executable*	*Description*
Java AppletViewer	`appletviewer`	Used to view applets without a Web browser
Java interpreter	`java`	Runs Java bytecode
Java compiler	`javac`	Compiles Java programs into bytecode
API documentation	`javadoc`	Creates API documentation generator in HTML format from Java source code
Java header and stub	`javah`	Creates C language header file generator and stub files from a Java class, which allows your Java and C code to interact
Java class file	`javap`	Disassembles Java files disassembler and prints out a representation of Java bytecode
Java language debugger	`jdb`	Helps you find and fix problems in your Java code
Java runtime interpreter	`jre`	An end-user's tool for running Java programs
RMI class generator	`rmic`	Generates stub and skeleton classes for objects implementing the `java.rmi.remote` interface
RMI remote registry	`rmiregistry`	Starts a remote object registry on a specified port
Version naming system	`serialver`	Returns the version of one or more classes
Internationalization tool	`native2ascii`	Converts non-Unicode Latin-1 source code files to Unicode Latin-1
JAR tool	`jar`	Combines multiple files into a single Java archive (jar) file

Tool Name	*Executable*	*Description*
Digital signing tool	`javakey`	Generates digital signatures for archive files and manages the database of entities and their signatures

Configuring an Applet Editor for FrontPage

Although you cannot use the FrontPage Editor to write applets, you can use your favorite text editor or word processor. To configure a text editor for use with FrontPage, follow these steps:

1. Start the FrontPage Explorer.
2. Open the Options dialog box by selecting Tools|Options. Click the Configure Editors tab.
3. With the Configure Editors tab active, click the Add button.
4. In the File Type field, enter `java`.
5. In the Editor Name field, enter the name of the text editor.
6. In the Command field, you need to enter the actual path to the executable for the text editor, such as

   ```
   c:\windows\notepad.exe
   ```

Now you can access Java source files directly from the FrontPage Explorer. All you need to do is double-click a Java source file ending with the `.java` extension, and FrontPage 98 automatically loads the file into your text editor. When you have finished editing the file, be sure to save it in ASCII text format.

Compiling Java Programs

All Java source files that you save as ASCII text with the `.java` extension must be compiled to bytecode before you can use them in a Web page. To compile your Java programs, you use the Java compiler. When you compile the source with the `.java` extension, the Java compiler creates a separate file for each class in your program. These compiled class files are named with the `.class` extension. If an application has more than one class file, you should always invoke the Java interpreter with the name of the class containing the main method.

Although compiling applications on the Macintosh is as easy as dragging the `.java` file onto the compiler, other system owners should not be too envious. On other systems, `javac` is a command-line program. Because the command line offers a simplified interface and streamlined design, the version of `javac` for UNIX, Windows 95/NT, and OS/2 is actually much more versatile.

Using a Graphical Compiler

Following are the steps you use to compile a Java program using a graphical compiler:

1. Drop the `.java` file onto the compiler, or select Open from the compiler's File menu.
2. The compiled output file(s) with the `.class` extension is generally placed in the same directory as the source.

Using a Command-Line Compiler

Here are the steps you use to compile a Java program using a command-line compiler:

1. Change to the directory containing the source code and type the following at the command prompt:

   ```
   javac yourProgram.java
   ```

   yourProgram`.java` is the actual file name of your Java program, such as `javac Jompanion.java`.
2. The compiled output file(s) with the `.class` is generally placed in the same directory as the source.

Creating Java Applets

Creating Java applets is easier if you already have a background in programming. With Java's tight structure, the basic format of an applet is fairly straightforward. This section walks you through an example.

TIP

You can access online tutorials and documentation for Java and object-oriented programming at the following:

`http://www.javasoft.com/`

An Object and Class Primer

Java is *object-oriented*, meaning that Java programs are built out of sections of code that package data with the instructions that affect it. A *class* is the template from which objects are created.

Think of it as a suburban neighborhood of cookie-cutter tract houses. All the houses begin as a blueprint, and every house uses the same one. You can't live in a blueprint, so you have to put the concrete, lumber, pipes, wire, and drywall together to build a house. In Java, this is called *instantiation*, and an instance of the blueprint is called an *object*. Many houses (objects) are built from the same blueprint (class).

Simple enough, right? Now it's time to move a little dirt and get your fingernails dirty.

Applet ABCs

At its simplest, an applet consists of two parts—a class declaration and a `paint` method. The following snippet contains a breakdown of the common elements for any applet:

```
import java.awt.Graphics;

public class MyApplet extends java.applet.Applet {
    public void paint (Graphics g) {
       your statements here;
    }
}
```

The first line includes a copy of the `Graphics` class from Java's Abstract Windowing Toolkit (AWT), which contains the methods needed for putting graphics, including text, lines, and dots, on the browser screen. This line may also be represented as `import java.awt` if more than the `Graphics` class is used.

Second, the actual applet is declared. It is public, meaning it is available to any other class, and it is a subclass of Java's `Applet` class, which provides the behavior necessary for interaction with the host browser.

The third section defines a method called `paint`, which the Java interpreter uses to put the information on the screen. It is public to the class, and `void` indicates that it does not return a value when it is completed. Its one parameter is an instance of the `Graphics` class imported on the first line of the program, which is referred to as `g`. This reference could just as easily be called bob or hammer, but `g` is the commonly used convention.

Displaying with `paint`

Now that the applet is defined, you need to make it do something. For the `paint` method, include the following line

```
g.drawString("Have a nice day.",50,25);
```

such as

```
import java.awt.Graphics;

public class MyApplet extends java.applet.Applet {
    public void paint (Graphics g) {
      g.drawString("Have a nice day.",50,25);
    }
}
```

After compiling the code and inserting it into an HTML document, you get something that looks like Figure 39.3.

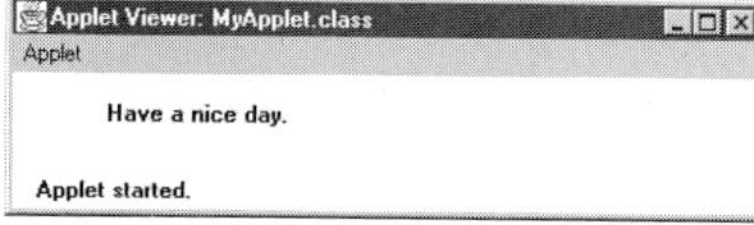

FIGURE 39.3.
`MyApplet` *displays a simple message on the screen.*

TIP

To test your applet, you can use a browser such as Netscape Navigator (2.0 or later) or Microsoft Internet Explorer (3.0 or later). Another alternative is the Java AppletViewer, which is provided with Java Development Kit. For more information, see "Using the Java AppletViewer" later in this chapter.

Of course, applets can do much more. By including some other AWT classes, you can make the text look better. First, you need the classes that control the font and display color:

```
import java.awt.Font;
import java.awt.Color;
```

Now, after the class declaration, create a variable to hold a new setting for the text:

```
Font f = new Font("TimesRoman",Font.ITALIC,24);
```

After the `paint` method declaration, use the `Graphics.set` methods to set the display before writing to the screen:

```
g.setFont(f);
g.setColor(Color.red);
```

The complete source for the applet is now

```
import java.awt.Graphics;
import java.awt.Font;
import java.awt.Color;

public class MyApplet extends java.applet.Applet {
    Font f = new Font("TimesRoman",Font.ITALIC,24);
    public void paint (Graphics g) {
       g.setFont(f);
       g.setColor(Color.red);
       g.drawString("Have a nice day.",50,25);
    }
}
```

With this extra bit of effort, the applet now looks like Figure 39.4.

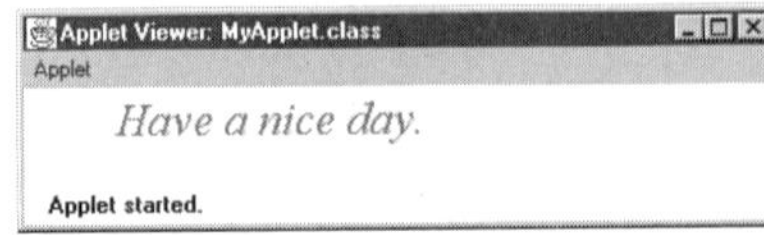

FIGURE 39.4.
`MyApplet` *now displays in a larger font in red and italics after some minor revisions to the code.*

Again, this example is limited. The addition of a parameter to control the string makes it more useful to the HTML author. After the class declaration, declare the message as a variable:

```
String message;
```

A new method is also required to initialize the value of `message`.

APPLET ACTIVITIES

In addition to `paint`, four major activities exist in the life of an applet. If any are omitted, default versions are provided in the `Applet` class. This setup is called *inheritance*. Providing new methods in the applet is called *overriding*.

The first activity is *initialization*, accomplished with the `init` method: `public void init() {...}`. This activity occurs once, immediately after the applet is loaded. Initialization includes creating objects, setting graphics, or defining parameters. It can happen only once in the applet's life.

The second activity is starting, accomplished with the `start` method: `public void start() {...}`. After initialization, activity begins. This activity can also happen if a user activity stopped the applet. Starting can happen many times in the life of an applet. The `paint` method is invoked somewhere in this method. The next activity is stopping, accomplished with the `stop` method: `public void stop() {...}`. This activity can be an important method to include because by default the applet continues running and using system resources, even after the user has left the page with the applet. Like start, stopping can occur many times in the course of execution.

The last activity is destroying, accomplished with the `destroy` method: `public void destroy() {...}`. Destroying means that an applet throws out its own garbage after completing execution—when the applet is no longer needed or the user exits the browser. Java provides adequate coverage in this department, so you don't need to override this method unless you want to return specific resources to the system.

Initializing the `message` parameter requires overriding the `init` method for the applet:

```
public void init() {
    this.message = getParameter("message");
    if (this.message == null) {
        this.message = "Your message here."; }
    this.message = "A note from Java: " + this.message;
}
```

This method retrieves the value of the parameter in the HTML document. If a parameter named `message` is not found, then the value is null and `message` is set to the default string, Your message here.

TIP

Java is case-sensitive for all of its variables, even when passed back and forth as parameters. Remember, Bob isn't bob.

Now you need to update the paint method so that it uses the string defined in init, rather than the literal string in the drawString method:

```
g.drawString(this.message);
```

Using the Complete Applet

The complete listing for MyApplet appears in Listing 39.1. Note the use of the parameter in the init method. Enter this listing in your text editor. Save the file as ASCII text in the same directory as the HTML page you use to display the applet. The file name must be MyApplet.java. Compile the applet.

Listing 39.1. A simple applet for displaying text on-screen.

```
import java.awt.Graphics;
import java.awt.Font;
import java.awt.Color;

public class MyApplet extends java.applet.Applet {
    Font f = new Font("TimesRoman",Font.ITALIC,24);
    String message;

    public void init() {
        this.message = getParameter("message");
        if (this.message == null) {
            this.message = "Your message here."; }
        this.message = "A note from Java: " + this.message;
    }

    public void paint(Graphics g) {
        g.setFont(f);
        g.setColor(Color.red);
        g.drawString(this.message,50,25);
    }
}
```

To use this applet, follow these steps:

1. Create a new page in the FrontPage Editor.
2. Open the Java Applet Properties window by clicking the Advanced toolbar's Insert Java Applet button.
3. Set the Applet Source field to MyApplet.class.
4. Set the width to 400 and the height to 50.
5. If the class file is not in the same directory as the HTML document that uses the applet, you must set the Applet Base URL property.
6. To set your own display message, you must set a parameter for the applet. Click the Add button. Enter message in the Name field. Then enter the message you want to display in the Value field.
7. Close all open dialog boxes and save the page.

Working with Images in Java

Loading and displaying images in Java is an easy task, thanks to the `Image` class in `java.awt`. The first method to work with in `Image` is `getImage`, which loads the image from the Internet to your applet.

TIP

Images are not integrated with the applet. Currently, Java supports only GIF and JPEG image files.

To load the image file, `getImage` needs to know where to find it. You have two ways of indicating this:

- A URL object with the complete server and path information, such as `http://www.wossomatta.edu/java/images/rocky.gif`.
- A URL object with the base information (`/java`) and a string with the path or filename of the image file (`images/rocky.gif`).

Although the first method appears to be much simpler, it is not very flexible. If the location of the image changes, you have to change the source code and recompile the applet.

The second form is the preferred method and includes two options for establishing the base URL:

- `getDocumentBase()`—Returns a URL based on the directory of the HTML document that contains the applet.
- `getCodeBase()`—Returns a string representing the directory of the applet. Its value is dependent on the `CODEBASE` attribute in the `<APPLET>` tag. If the applet is stored in the same directory as the HTML document, this value is empty.

Here are a few examples of how `getImage` works:

- `Image pict = getImage(new URL("http://www.wossomatta.edu/java/images/rocky.gif"));`

  This uses a hard-coded URL to retrieve the image. If the location of the image changes, you need to change the source code and recompile the class in order for the applet to find the file.

- `Image pict = getImage(getDocumentBase(), "images/boris.gif");`

  This applies the path information to the end of the base URL of the HTML document containing the image. If the file is in the document root, then `getDocumentBase` might be `http://www.pottsylvania.gov/`, and the entire URL to the image file is `http://www.pottsylvania.gov/images/boris.gif`.

- `Image pict = getImage(getCodeBase(), "images/boris.gif");`

  Assume the HTML document information is the same as the prior example, and now the applet is stored in the directory `javaApplets`. Here's the breakdown on what is where:

  Document—`http://www.pottsylvania.gov/`

  Applet—`http://www.pottsylvania.gov/javaApplets/`

  Image file—`http://www.pottsylvania.gov/javaApplets/images/boris.gif`

It's important to note one thing at this point—the applet has only loaded the image; it hasn't done anything with it. It only exists as an `Image` object called `pict`. You display it using a method from the `Graphics` class:

```
public void paint(Graphics g) {
    g.drawImage(pict,10,10,this);
}
```

NOTE

You may have noticed the `this` parameter in the `drawImage` method. The `this` parameter refers to the current instance of an object.

That's all there is to it. This form of `drawImage` displays `pict` with the top-left corner at the coordinates 10,10. You can also add a second set of numbers to define the width and height of the image when it's painted, enabling you to make it fit anywhere you want.

TIP

Expect image degradation when you expand or contract an image far beyond its original size. Changing the height-to-width ratio also distorts the image.

The entire applet to display the image (see Figure 39.5) is shown in Listing 39.2. The Animator applet uses these basic operations to display a series of images, which give the appearance of motion.

Listing 39.2. A simple applet to load and display an image.

```
import java.awt.Graphics;
import java.awt.Image;

public class showPict extends java.applet.Applet {

image pict;

public void init() {
    pict = getImage(getCodeBase(),"images/garden.gif");
```

```
    }

    public void paint(Graphics g) {
        g.drawImage(pict,10,10,this);
    }

}
```

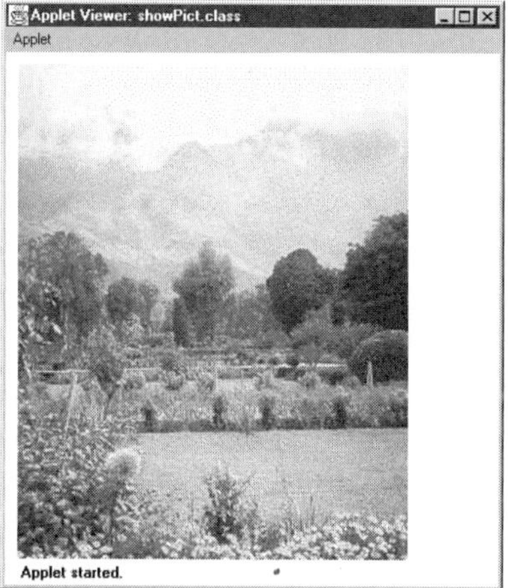

FIGURE 39.5.
The `showPict` *applet loads an image from the* `images` *subdirectory of the* `javaApplets` *directory.*

Using the Java AppletViewer

During applet development and testing, sometimes it's easier to bypass the unnecessary overhead of a browser. If your browser doesn't support applets, you still need a way to view the applets. At this point, the Java AppletViewer comes in handy. With the AppletViewer, only the applet is displayed; the rest of the HTML is ignored.

The AppletViewer searches the HTML document for the `<APPLET>` tag, such as what's shown in Listing 39.3. Keep in mind that FrontPage 98 automatically adds the markup you see whenever you add an applet to a Web page in the FrontPage Editor.

Listing 39.3. A simple HTML document containing an applet tag.

```
<HTML>
<HEAD>
<TITLE>The animation applet</TITLE>
</HEAD>
<BODY>
<APPLET CODE="Animator.class" WIDTH=460 HEIGHT=160>
<PARAM NAME=imagesource VALUE="images/beans">
<PARAM NAME=endimage VALUE=10>
<PARAM NAME=pause VALUE=200>
</APPLET>
</BODY>
</HTML>
```

Using the information contained within the tag, the AppletViewer opens a window and runs the applet. Other HTML information on the page is ignored—only the applets appear.

The Java AppletViewer is distributed with the Java Development Kit and is found in the same directory as the Java compiler and interpreter. To run the command-line version of the AppletViewer, use the following steps:

1. Create a document with an applet in the FrontPage Editor.
2. From a command line prompt, type

   `appletviewer[path/]filename.html.`

   If the AppletViewer launches from the same directory as the HTML document, you don't need the path name. Otherwise, the path is relative to your current location in the directory structure. The extension `.htm` is also valid for the viewer.
3. Any applets found in the HTML document are loaded and run, with each applet in its own instance of the AppletViewer.
4. Although you cannot change the initial parameters contained within the HTML page from the AppletViewer, you can start the applet from the beginning by choosing Applet|Restart. To load it again from memory, select Applet|Reload.
5. Leave the applet by choosing Applet|Quit on the AppletViewer's toolbar.

To view an applet with the graphical version of the AppletViewer, you can do one of the following:

- Drag and drop an HTML document with the `.html` extension onto the AppletViewer icon.
- Click the AppletViewer icon. Once the AppletViewer is started, select File|Open Local.

Summary

Java use keeps spreading quickly as more and more hardware and software manufacturers pledge support to the language and concepts. Even if you never have the chance to delve deep into the intricacies of building an applet or application from scratch, an understanding of the basics will help you take full advantage of the powerful capabilities available.

CHAPTER 40

Designing Pages with Dynamic HTML

by David and Rhonda Crowder

IN THIS CHAPTER

- Text Animation *664*
- Page Transitions *667*
- Collapsible Outlines *668*
- Dynamic Labels and Access Keys for Form Fields *670*
- A Lack of Standards *670*
- The Document Object Model *671*
- Dynamic Styles *671*
- Dynamic Content *672*
- Absolute Positioning and "2D Layout" *673*
- Data Binding *674*

Dynamic HTML brings a new standard of pizzazz and interoperability to the formerly static existence of the World Wide Web. FrontPage 98 currently provides direct support for animation of text and other page elements, page transitions, collapsible outlines, and the addition of dynamic labels to form fields. In addition to these built-in capabilities, Web developers can, through the use of scripting, add even more dynamic functionality to their pages.

As an example, designers used to have to set form input to a fixed length, which created numerous difficulties. For example, to set up a text input box for street addresses, designers had to guess at the maximum workable length that would both fit without distorting the layout of the form and still leave enough space for even the most exotic addresses. Dynamic HTML, however, allows overflow input to scroll beyond the limits of the text box. Because this capability is built in to FrontPage 98 and Internet Explorer, you don't need to invoke it deliberately.

Text Animation

FrontPage 98's animation feature allows you to create Web pages with elements that fly or drop into place, spiral about the page, and zoom in and out. Despite the fact that it is called "text animation" in most references to it, the technique is not limited to text but can be successfully applied to most objects. For example, you can also animate the following objects:

- Banner ads
- Confirmation fields
- Forms
- Hit counters
- Hover buttons
- Images
- Marquees
- Symbols
- Timestamps
- Videos

NOTE

Although you can apply the "text animation" technique to images as well, the images do not become true animations in the sense that the images themselves remain static. Text animation simply changes the position of a page element following a predetermined pattern. Thus, your image zooms or spirals, or it comes in from the left or the right of the page, but the artwork itself does not change. If you want to animate the actual artwork, you need to use another approach, such as with GIF Animator. (See Chapter 20, "Working with GIF Animator.")

A few caveats apply. As far as forms are concerned, all elements can be animated except for drop-down menus. The Search form, being a WebBot instead of a normal form, is an exception; it cannot be animated. Also, a video runs while it moves into place; if it is a short, non-looping run, it might finish running before it reaches its intended position, thus possibly spoiling the video's effect.

TIP

If animation of these objects is apparently not working, check to see whether some property of the object might prevent either movement or visibility of movement. For example, a marquee whose width is the same as the full page does not do anything if it is animated with a "fly from right" command because it has no room to move. To allow the movement from the right, you have to reduce the size of the marquee to less than the screen width. The same marquee, if animated with a "fly from bottom" command, works fine because it already takes up less than the full screen.

In addition to search forms and drop-down menus, a few other objects cannot be animated, such as horizontal lines and the table of contents. Regular tables are not capable of animation either.

For most of its effects, text animation takes advantage of the capability of JavaScript and dynamic HTML to set the exact screen position of page elements. (See the section "Absolute Positioning and '2D Layout.'") Using a set of preprogrammed changes in position, the animation setting allows you to use three different basic types of positional changes: flying from different page locations, spiraling, and flying word by word.

The first animation effect, flying, causes a page element to first appear from a chosen spot on the page and then travel a straight line to its established page position. You can choose from eight possible options.

In the case of the first four options (bottom, left, right, and top), the starting point from which the element moves is determined by its ultimate destination. For example, if an image is in the middle of the page, and you choose for it to fly in from the top, it begins its descent from the middle of the top of the page; if it is near the right side, then it begins its drop from near the right side, and so on.

With the last four options (bottom-left, bottom-right, top-left, and top-right), the starting point is fixed for all elements. Thus, all objects, no matter the destination point, come from the bottom-left corner if you choose bottom-left fly-in. Unlike the first four options, whose travel patterns always make a right angle to one side or another of the page, the last four options can move at any angle dictated by the need to draw a straight line from a corner to the destination point.

The second effect, spiraling, causes the element to appear in the top-left corner of the page and then loop clockwise into its final position, sometimes moving off-screen depending on the location of the destination point.

Flying by word works much the same as normal flying but is workable only with text. In this effect, a sentence (or selected group of words) is moved into its ultimate destination position a word at a time. The only options for this animation technique are to fly in from the top right or bottom right, or to drop in. In the fly-in cases, any angle of flight can be achieved, depending on the destination position of the element; the drop-in option works the same as a fly-in from the page top, in that each word begins its journey directly above its ultimate destination point and then falls down until it is locked into place.

The zoom-in and zoom-out animation techniques do not depend, like the other approaches, on absolute positioning, but on resizing the page elements in question. Zooming in is achieved by beginning with a reduced image of the page element, which is then enlarged to achieve its normal size. Zooming out works in the reverse manner, beginning with an enlargement of the element, which is then shrunk to its real size.

To use any of these animation methods, you follow the same procedure; only the exact menu choice differs. First, select the page element or elements you want to animate. Next, choose Format|Animation and then click the option you want to use (see Figure 40.1). To remove animation from a page element without deleting it, choose Off from the Animation menu.

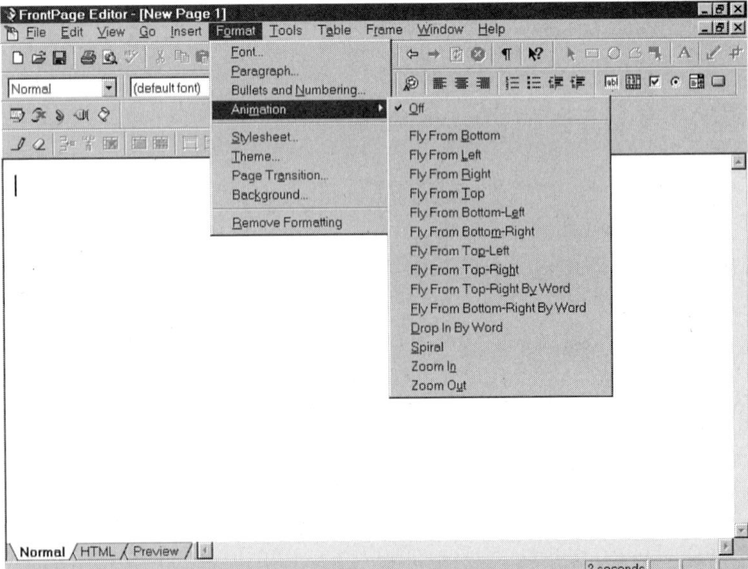

FIGURE 40.1.
Animation menu options.

CAUTION

If you delete an object to which you have applied "text animation," you must be careful to make sure you also remove the paragraph mark (carriage return) from that line along with it. Otherwise, there is still a non-breaking space ( ) in the HTML code that still holds the animation data for the element you have deleted. If this happens, the results are not actually visible but still result in animation activity, thus slowing down the presentation of your page.

Animation methods can be mixed for different elements, even within an overall larger framework. For example, you can animate a form as a whole or individually animate each element in the form. Say you have a form with a text input box, a radio button, a check box, and a couple of buttons. The text box can fly in from the top, the radio button from the bottom-left corner, the check box from the right side, and the buttons could be made to spiral in.

Page Transitions

Page transitions allow you to choose from a variety of flashy, sophisticated special effects. These effects take place when a visitor to your site either enters or leaves a particular page for which you have coded transitions.

Choose Format|Page Transition to open the Page Transitions dialog box, which is shown in Figure 40.2. You can choose from one of the many transitions available, such as horizontal blinds or random dissolve, and then type in the number of seconds you want the effect to last in the Duration text box. Next, you need to choose under what circumstances you want the effect to take place. The options are to show the effect on Page Enter or Page Exit. These choices present two minor, technical variations: you can also choose to show the effect when a visitor to your site enters or leaves the site via the chosen page.

FIGURE 40.2.
Page Transitions dialog box.

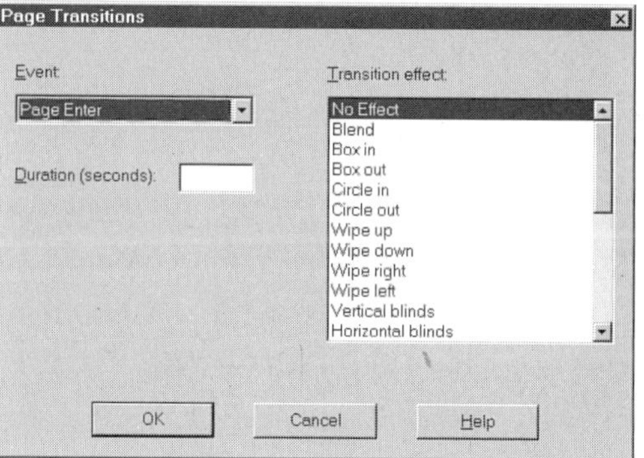

NOTE

FrontPage has difficulties with Page Transitions. At the time of this writing, the settings do not hold.

Collapsible Outlines

You are already used to working with collapsible outlines (sometimes called *dynamic outlining*). Windows Explorer uses them for expanding and contracting views of folders and subfolders. WinHelp uses them in the same manner for viewing the table of contents of help files.

FrontPage 98 can turn any list object—whether numbered, bulleted, or imaged—into a collapsible outline, as you can see in the example shown in Figure 40.3.

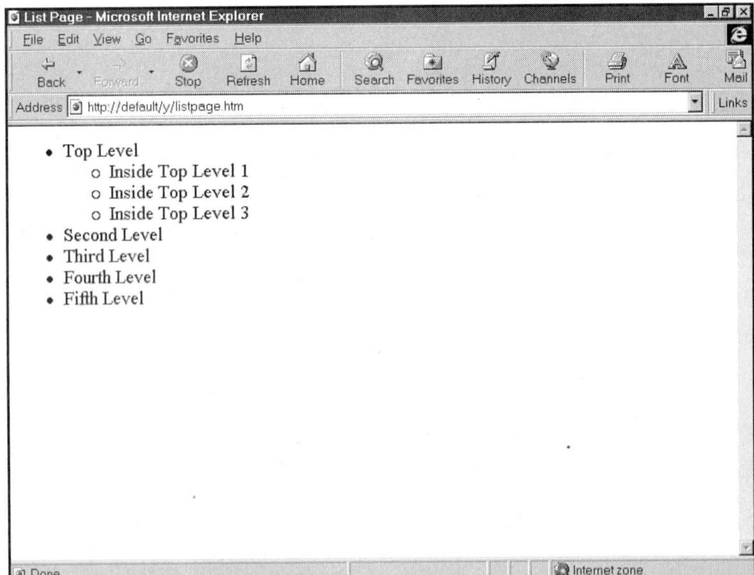

FIGURE 40.3.
A collapsible outline.

To implement a collapsible outline on an HTML list, just right-click any portion of a list and select List Properties from the pop-up menu (see Figure 40.4).

When the List Properties dialog box appears, as shown in Figure 40.5, click the Enable Collapsible Outlines check box on the appropriate notebook tab. Then click the OK button to create the outline.

FIGURE 40.4.
Pop-up menu.

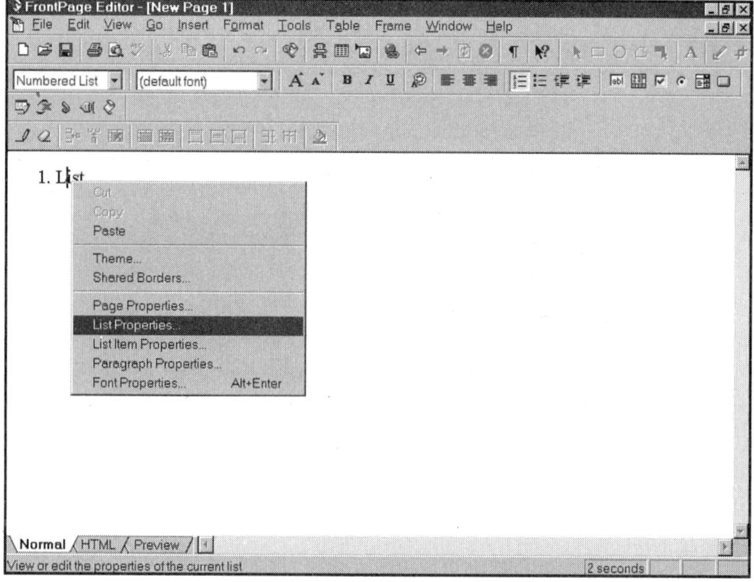

FIGURE 40.5.
List Properties dialog box.

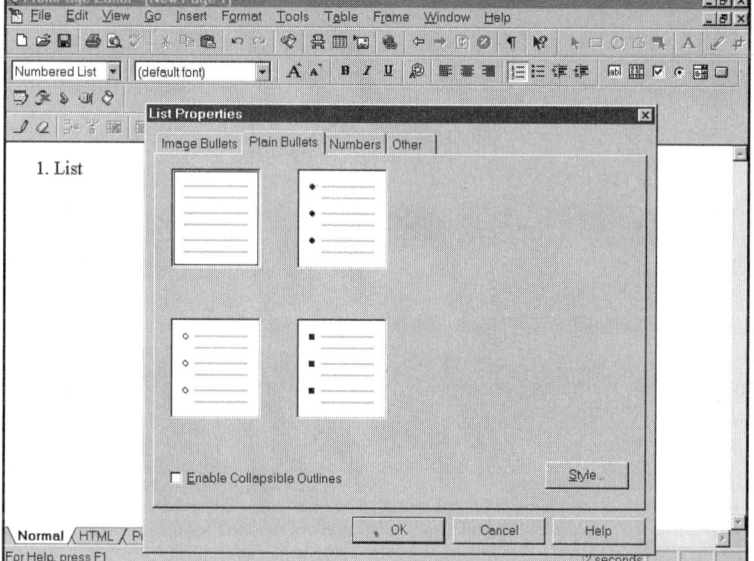

Dynamic Labels and Access Keys for Form Fields

You are probably used to being able to click the label next to a check box or radio button in Windows programs and having the selection made just as though you had clicked on the form element itself. FrontPage 98 now brings these dynamic approaches to the Web. To make your forms use clickable labels, just select both the label and the form element it is next to, and then choose Insert|Form Field|Label.

Another new capability dynamic HTML brings to FrontPage 98 form field labels is the *access key*. Again, it is an old friend. You have no doubt employed this capability many times, as when you press Alt+F to access the File menu. As with the usual Windows method, the key used along with the Alt key is the same as the underlined letter in the menu or dialog box option.

To implement this capability, simply highlight the letter you want to use for the access key, and then click the Underline button on the toolbar. This way, you can create in an Alt+key combination.

CAUTION

Be careful in choosing the letter for the access key. If you choose the same letter for two different form labels, the behavior of Internet Explorer could be erratic. There is also a problem if you assign an access key that is already in use in either FrontPage or any Web browser with which your page might be viewed. In that case, the access key will interfere with the normal operation of the program (Alt+F for accessing the file menu, for example). FrontPage does not and cannot warn you about these types of conflicts.

Clickable labels and access keys can be used independently or in tandem on the same form element labels.

To remove either or both of these dynamic functionalities from a label, select both the affected label and its form element, and then choose Insert|Form Field|Remove Label. (This option is only visible if you have previously created a clickable label.) If you're removing an access key, you must also highlight the access letter and click the Underline button on the toolbar to remove the underlining from it.

A Lack of Standards

The "leading edge" of computer technology is often referred to sardonically as the "bleeding edge" for a good reason. Dynamic HTML is a classic case. First, very few people can actually agree on what it is. Even most Web developers are surprised to learn that, officially speaking, no such thing as "Dynamic HTML" exists. The World Wide Web Consortium (W3C), the official standards body for the WWW, has no such thing as a "Dynamic HTML Working Group."

Dynamic HTML means different things to different people. Netscape uses it to mean one thing, Microsoft another, and they do not, currently at least, agree on many points. The most critical point of disagreement has been over what object model to use, though both sides seem to be headed toward settling on the Document Object Model currently being developed by the W3C.

To further confuse the issue of just what Dynamic HTML is, both sides agree that it is not even HTML. To quote the W3C, the various proposals for the Document Object Model, "do not propose any new HTML tags."

So what exactly is dynamic HTML? It is, in the absolute broadest sense, any method by which HTML-based Web pages can be lifted from their current static paradigm. In a more practical definition, it is the use of scripting languages to access and control the various elements in a Web page. Because this book is devoted to Microsoft-based Web development, this chapter focuses solely on Microsoft's version of Dynamic HTML, covering the basics of how it works and then showing some specific examples of how it can be put into action along the way.

The Document Object Model

The Document Object Model was developed by the W3C. Like nearly everything else about the World Wide Web, its form is tentative, subject to the tugs and pulls of different schools of thought and the vicissitudes of committee development.

If you have ever used JavaScript, you already have a basic understanding of the Document Object Model because it is an extension of the JavaScript approach to controlling page elements. Basically, JavaScript gave control of the characteristics of many page elements and allowed developers to initiate events based on user interaction with them. In dynamic HTML, these capabilities are greatly enhanced. The developer can have control over every single element on a page and can program events for them all.

Although there might seem little to get excited about when considering the possibilities of an `onmouseover` event for an `<h3>` tag, the capability to totally control everything in an HTML document—and to react to anything at all the user does within it—is actually quite a stunning development in Web technology. Essentially, it allows an HTML document to become not just a display piece, but an actual application in itself.

Dynamic Styles

Cascading style sheets were the first step in gaining greater control over the appearance of various elements on a Web page. The dynamic styles approach takes this capability one giant step further: Web designers can now not only alter the style and position of any element at will, but they also can cause this change to happen as a result of user activity.

For example, the color, size, font type, and so forth of body text can be set via CSS. However, this approach still leaves the text absolutely static. The following code illustrates the difference between it and dynamic HTML.

NOTE

Dynamic HTML is not opposed to cascading style sheets but can—and often does—work in concert with them.

To observe this code at work, open a new Web page in FrontPage Editor, click the HTML tab at the bottom of the screen, and type the code into the area between the `<body>` and `</body>` tags, save it, and then click the View in Browser button in the toolbar to see it in Internet Explorer. You can also use the menu options to choose Insert|Advanced|Script and then type the script. You should follow the same procedure for all the sample code snippets. For details on the use of script languages with FrontPage 98, see Chapter 36, "Scripting with VBScript," and Chapter 38, "Scripting with JavaScript."

```
<p onmouseover="this.style.fontStyle='normal';"
onmouseout="this.style.fontStyle='italic';">
This font will change style.
</p>
```

When viewed in Internet Explorer, this font changes from normal to italic as you place the pointer over it. It then changes back again when you move the pointer away from it.

Although you could also use this technique to change other styles than the font style, such as font size, you should be very careful when altering a font during a `mouseover` event. The following variation changes the size of the font instead:

```
<p onmouseover="this.style.fontSize='12pt';"
onmouseout="this.style.fontSize='24pt';">
This font will change size.
</p>
```

Viewed in Internet Explorer, this line of text behaves erratically, not due to any bug, but due to the fact that, as the font size increases and decreases with mouse movement, the point at which the mouse pointer is over it changes; a spot on the Web page that is outside the boundaries of the 12-point font is still within the boundaries of the 24-point font. The only way this font expansion example behaves as intended is if the pointer is brought in from the upper-left side because that point never changes. (Actually, you could bring it in anywhere along the top, as long as you don't go beyond the point where the end of the sentence is in the original, smaller font.)

Dynamic Content

With Dynamic HTML, the content of Web pages is no longer locked in at load time but can be altered at any time at the will of the designer, just like the position of elements can be. Modifications, additions, and deletions can be programmed, and the other content of the document will automatically adjust to the new situation without further server access.

The following code causes an image to be displayed when a sentence is moused over and then to vanish when the mouse pointer moves off the sentence. The second sentence changes position to reflect the state of visibility of the image.

```
<p onmouseover="manreading.style.display='';"
➥onmouseout=manreading.style.display='none';">This text will cause an image to
➥be displayed when you mouse over it.</p>
<div id="manreading" style="display: 'none';">
<p><img src="pe02086a.gif" width=100 height=87;"></p>
<p>This text will move to accommodate the appearance or disappearance of
➥the image.</p>
</p>
```

Absolute Positioning and "2D Layout"

The ability to control precisely where an element actually appears on an HTML page was first achieved with the Netscape <LAYERS> tag. That tag's approach, in the experience of many designers, required a bit too much complexity, yet the results were worth the trouble. Web designers had long wanted for the chance to have the kind of layout control their colleagues in the print media were used to, and they finally had it.

With the advent of the W3C's Document Object Model, the layers concept of absolute positioning has been taken up and the technique simplified. The <LAYERS> tag is now held in less favor than previously and will probably ultimately go the way of the <BLINK> tag, but unlike that unlamented annoyance, it holds its place in the history of the Web.

You can very clearly see the tremendous value of absolute positioning in form design. Where form elements previously landed pretty much as they pleased, leaving a haphazard and ragged appearance (unless they were embedded in a table that could be used in a limited way to force them to line up), dynamic HTML allows the form designer to control the exact placement of every element perfectly.

In addition to being able to place any element an exact number of pixels from the top or left, Web developers could also use layers (as you would guess from the name) to place elements in front of or behind one another. This capability was also brought along into the Document Object Model. For reasons that defy understanding, Microsoft documentation continually refers to this function as "2D Layout" and even speaks of "the ability to provide content in two dimensions." It is, of course, actually 3D layout, providing the capability to place page elements along the x, y, and z axes.

If you have ever worked with graphics applications such as Photoshop or Microsoft Image Composer (the latter is part of the FrontPage 98 suite of programs and is dealt with in other chapters of this book), then you are already familiar with the necessary concepts. Briefly, the x axis runs from the left to the right of the page, and the y axis runs from the top to the bottom. To visualize the z axis, you need to forget the old concept of the page as a single sheet. Now you can view a Web page as a series of sheets, each on top of the other, and the z axis runs from the front to the back.

When various elements are placed in different positions on the z axis, the result is really very much like a series of transparencies that, when combined on an overhead projector, produce a composite image on a screen.

However, the difference between the original concept of layers and the current use is that, instead of a series of pages atop one another, with each page containing certain elements, the x, y, and z-order of any and every element on a page can be set, modified, and changed again and again, each moving forward, backward, side to side, and up and down in a dance that is different for every user.

To illustrate the use of z-order, you can make two images move in front of and behind one another. Enter the following text into the head of your document:

```
<style type="text/css">
#imageone {position: absolute; left: 0; top: 50; z-index: 1}
</style>
<style type="text/css">
#imagetwo {position: absolute; left: 0; top: 50; z-index: 2}
</style>
```

Next, enter the following in the body (substitute your own images in place of the sample image files):

```
<div id="imageone">
<p><img src="TN00051A.gif" width="101" height="88"></p>
</div>
<div id="imagetwo">
<p><img src="HH01478A.gif" width="100" height="99"></p>
</div>
<p onmouseover="imageone.style.z-index = 3;"
➥onmouseout="imageone.style.z-index = 1;">This will flip the two images to
➥different levels.</p>
```

NOTE

Depending on your particular application in dynamic HTML, you might want to consider one other thing: there are actually four dimensions. In addition to the *x*, *y*, and *z* of height, width, and depth is *t*, or time. Just as the *z-order* determines which items are in front of or behind the others, the sequence or progression in which events occur through time might be considered to be the *t-order*.

Data Binding

With data binding, dynamic HTML offers a new level of easy database functionality to Web developers. Binding data sources such as comma-delimited files tables yields a rich new capacity for user interaction, with all the activity taking place on the client machine.

Data can be bound to, in theory at least, almost any object (a few exceptions exist, such as password fields and submit and reset buttons), but forms and tables offer the most useful common functionality, being used respectively for data input and output.

In addition to comma-delimited databases, dynamic HTML can bind to other common data sources such as ODBC, JDBC, and so on, through Data Source Objects (DSOs), which function as database connection controls. DSOs provide a local database engine with data sorting, filtering, and viewing capabilities.

Microsoft has a selection of these DSOs available in the Data Source Object Gallery on its Web site. The DSO that dealt with here is the Tabular Data Control (TDC), which comes with Internet Explorer 4.0 and is installed automatically along with it. The TDC is specifically designed to work with comma-delimited files.

The first step, of course, is to have a data source. You can create a file like the following simple example in any database management program, spreadsheet, or word processor. (The option to save it as a comma-delimited file may be phrased as "ASCII," "comma-separated-value," or "CSV," and so on.)

```
NAME,ADDRESS,PHONE
Ralph Richardson,123 Anywhere Street,555-2222
Susan Pinkerton,321 Elm Avenue,555-1111
Debbie Robards,456 Main Street,555-3333
```

Next, you must add the data source object to the page. The following example is typical of the basic approach. It first establishes an ID for the object and then, through the classid, tells Internet Explorer to use the Tabular Data Control. The next line tells where to find the data source file. This value is a URL and can be a fully detailed one or, as here, a relative one; this one says to find it in the same folder as the referring page. The `"UseHeader"` needs to have its value established because, in the data source file, the first line is not data; this says to ignore that first line and not import it.

```
<object id="tdctest" classid="CLSID:333C7BC4-460F-11D0-BC04-0080C7055A83">
  <param name="DataURL" value="tdctest.csv">
  <param name="UseHeader" value="True">
</object>
```

Now that you have established the data source object, you must bind it to an element on the page. In this case, the bound element is a table. The keys here are the `DATASRC` and `DATAFLD` attributes of the bound element. (Note that these attributes are nonstandard and work only on Internet Explorer.) The `DATASRC` attribute points to the data source object and is the same as the ID of that object, but with the `#` sign in front of it. The `DATAFLD` names the column, or field, in the file from which the data is drawn. These names come from that first line in the comma-delimited file.


```
<table datasrc="#tdctest" border="1" width="100%">
  <tr>
    <td width="33%"><span datafld="NAME"></span></td>
    <td width="33%"><span datafld="ADDRESS"></span></td>
    <td width="34%"><span datafld="PHONE"></span></td>
```

```
  </tr>
</table>
```

Although the table has only a single row, all the records in the data source file are still displayed, as shown in Figure 40.6. It is called a repeating table.

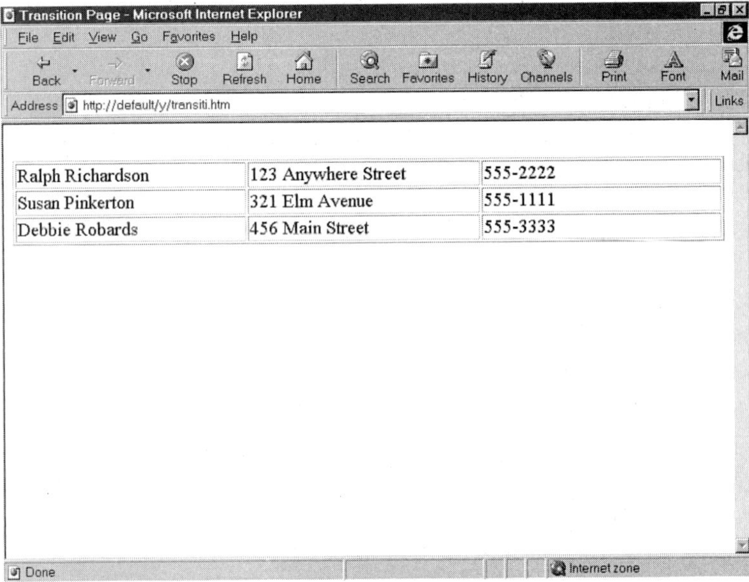

FIGURE 40.6.
Repeating table.

The Tabular Data Control has many other possible uses (you can even replace the comma with some other delimiter if you want), and you can develop scripts for sorting or filtering the screen output from the data source file.

The full range of possibilities for using dynamic HTML is far beyond the scope of this book. For a fully detailed exploration of this exciting new technology, see the book *Dynamic HTML Unleashed* in this same series.

Summary

In this chapter, you learned about the new dynamic HTML features of FrontPage 98, including animation of text and other page elements, page transitions, collapsible outlines, dynamic form labels, and access keys. You then read a general overview of dynamic HTML, the document object model, and the application of such dynamic HTML modes as dynamic styles, dynamic content, absolute positioning of page elements, three-dimensional placements, and data binding, looking at specific examples of all these different modalities.

CHAPTER 41

Using Push Channels

by David and Rhonda Crowder

IN THIS CHAPTER

- Creating Push Channels *678*
- Managing Multiple Channels *688*
- Designing Push Channel Content *691*
- Learning by Looking *692*
- Learning from Tutorials and References *693*
- Facing Dual Standards *694*

Push channels bring a whole new level of power to the World Wide Web, and FrontPage helps you take advantage of it. Essentially, this new technique allows Web designers to open their own international superstation, just as though they owned a vast cable television network. Or perhaps the metaphor of a global magazine publishing empire would be more appropriate. Whatever your perspective, you can now have a far-flung group of subscribers who are kept aware of changes to your Web site through this new technology.

In the past, you had to depend on someone repeatedly visiting your Web site in order to keep them up to date. Because this took all the power out of the hands of Webmasters, it was common for a great deal of effort to go to waste. Sites lovingly and skillfully constructed with hours, days, weeks, or even months of toil might yield little or nothing in the way of repeat visitations. With push channel technology, however, any visitor can become something new—a subscriber.

Unlike random visitors, subscribers are automatically kept current. When a Webmaster makes a change, updates a site, or adds new information, anyone who has expressed an interest will know about it right away—or at least very shortly afterward. Despite the terminology, information is not actually pushed from your server to subscribers' clients as with the PointCast approach; what actually happens is that their clients check for and pull new information from your site on a preset schedule. Depending on that schedule, the information may be present on their desktops in minutes, or it may take days. Normally, each subscribed channel is checked at least once per day.

Depending on your subscribers' settings, they may receive an e-mail message (either containing or attaching your updated HTML page, whichever their e-mail software supports), or they may actually download the changes to their hard disk for offline browsing.

Will push channels replace the traditional pull approach entirely? That seems unlikely. Web surfers are too used to exploring and enjoying the vast amount of information and entertainment available to give it up easily for canned content. The end result will probably be the best of both worlds: the freedom to go wherever in the vast World Wide Web you want, and the convenience of having interesting material delivered to your desktop with no effort on your part.

Creating Push Channels

The easiest way to allow visitors to subscribe to your site is to do nothing at all. Internet Explorer 4.0 will let visitors to your site subscribe to it without any effort on your part. So why should you go to the trouble of developing an official channel? Two reasons: 1), the presence of a Subscribe button prompts the visitors to take an action they might not otherwise consider while passing through your site; and 2), it gives you a degree of control over the subscription process, enabling you to set default values for the notification process and update schedules.

The Channel Definition Format

Channel Definition Format (CDF) files are the vehicle whereby you control the variables of channel subscriptions. CDF files contain information that push-capable browsers or other clients can use to manage the channel update process. The most basic CDF file simply points to the Web pages you want the subscribers to receive updates on. More complex ones contain information on other items. The following listing includes additional data for Internet Explorer to use, such as what images to use for the channel icons, as well as other items like abstracts for the channel and individual pages:

```
<?XML Version="1.0" Encoding="iso-8859-1" ?>
<Channel HREF="index.htm" BASE="http://default/fputestweb/" SELF="channel.cdf">
    <A HREF="http://default/fputestweb/index.htm">
    </A>
    <Title>FPU Test Web</Title>
    <Abstract>This is an example of a personal Website.</Abstract>
    <Logo HREF="images/city.gif" Style="Image" />
    <Logo HREF="images/sunset.gif" Style="Icon" />
    <Schedule>
        <IntervalTime HOUR="3" />
    </Schedule>
    <Item HREF="index.htm">
        <A HREF="http://default/fputestweb/index.htm">
        </A>
        <Title>Home Page</Title>
        <Abstract>The home page for the personal site.</Abstract>
        <Usage Value="Channel">
        </Usage>
    </Item>
    <Item HREF="interest.htm">
        <A HREF="http://default/fputestweb/interest.htm">
        </A>
        <Title>Interests</Title>
        <Abstract>Personal interests page.</Abstract>
        <Usage Value="Channel">
        </Usage>
    </Item>
    <Item HREF="favorite.htm">
        <A HREF="http://default/fputestweb/favorite.htm">
        </A>
        <Title>Favorites</Title>
        <Abstract>Favorite websites.</Abstract>
        <Usage Value="Channel">
        </Usage>
    </Item>
    <Item HREF="photo.htm">
        <A HREF="http://default/fputestweb/photo.htm">
        </A>
        <Title>Photo Album</Title>
        <Abstract>Family photo album.</Abstract>
        <Usage Value="Channel">
        </Usage>
    </Item>
```

```
    <Item HREF="myfav3.htm">
        <A HREF="http://default/fputestweb/myfav3.htm">
        </A>
        <Title>My Favorite Site 3</Title>
        <Abstract>Placeholder for link to external site.</Abstract>
        <Usage Value="Channel">
        </Usage>
    </Item>
</Channel>
```

NOTE

Microsoft has made much of the "CDF standard." In fact, CDF is not an official standard, and has not been accepted or enacted by any official standards body whatsoever. It is, simply and plainly, a Microsoft-developed file format. This fact is easy to overlook in the vast amount of hype Microsoft has laid down over this topic. CDF has indeed been "proposed" as a standard to the World Wide Web Consortium (W3C), the official standards development committee for the Web, but this is not the same thing as being accepted by it. Many standards are proposed to W3C; few are adopted. Even if it were a standard, adoption of a standard by W3C is meaningless because W3C has no power to require the use of its official standards, and both Microsoft and Netscape routinely add things (new HTML tags, for instance) without W3C approval.

Although you can, of course, write your own CDF files and incorporate them into your site by manually adding hyperlinks to them, FrontPage 98 makes the process nearly effortless with the Channel Definition Wizard.

Using the Channel Definition Wizard

The Channel Definition Wizard walks you through a welcome screen (see Figure 41.1) and seven simple steps to create your own push channel. This example uses a basic web created with the Personal Web Wizard (see Chapter 29, "Instant Web Sites with FrontPage 98"); you can, of course, apply the same techniques to a web of your own.

NOTE

One item you might want to cover before you begin, although you can always add it later: You may want to develop icon and logo images for your channel. The logo image will be displayed to differentiate your channel from all the others in Internet Explorer's channel listings; otherwise, the standard, boring channel logo will be used automatically. The icon image is used to identify the pages in your channel. These images are not necessary for your channel to function, but they can add a professional look.

If you do want to use them, your logo needs to be 80×32 pixels, and the icon should be 16×16; these sizes are required by Microsoft. Both have to be GIF files. Place them in your images folder for the web you want to use them on. You will have to import them to the web, or their filenames will not be displayed when you attempt to select them in the Channel Definition Wizard.

It should be noted that, at the current early stage of channel development, the images will not always display in Internet Explorer.

To add these images after you have created a channel, simply use the modification option in the following procedure.

To use the Channel Definition Wizard, follow the procedure outlined in the following sections describing Steps 1 through 7.

Step 1: Channel Description

Select Tools|Define Channel from the menu in FrontPage Explorer. This will bring up the Welcome screen. The Welcome screen offers only two choices. The first (default) choice is to create a new CDF file. The second is to modify one you have already created. If there is no channel in existence on your web, select the first option. If, on the other hand, you have already created a channel and want to make changes in it, select the second option. Click the Next button.

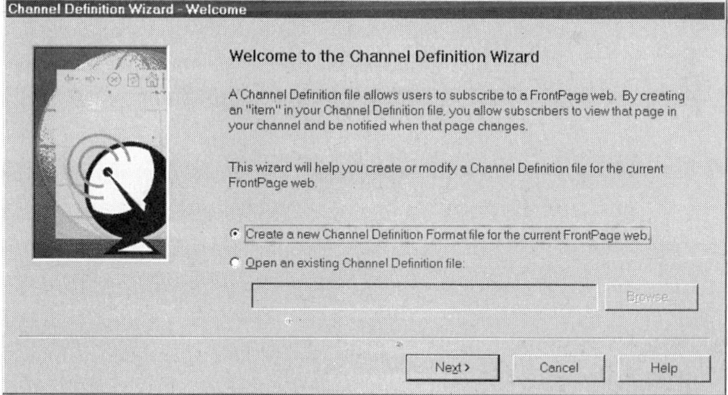

FIGURE 41.1.
The Channel Definition Wizard—Welcome screen.

CAUTION

It is possible to put more than one channel up per site by repeatedly selecting the Create a new Channel option. Although it might seem that this would overwrite an existing CDF file for the web, it will actually create as many new ones as you ask it to (the first file will be named `channel.cdf`, the second, `channel0.cdf`, and so on). If this is not your intent, then

continues

continued

make sure you use the Open an Existing Channel option to modify your existing channel. If you do want to add more than one channel to your web, see the section "Managing Multiple Channels" for further information.

You are now looking at the Channel Description dialog box (see Figure 41.2). The Title edit box is already filled in for you, using the title of the current FrontPage web. If you want your channel to have a different title from the web itself, just type it in over the default one. Likewise, the Introduction Page edit box is filled in by default with the URL of your home page. Generally, you'll probably want to leave this alone, but you can click the Browse button next to the edit box and select a different channel introduction page from a listing of the other pages in the current web instead.

Add an abstract (a brief description) of your channel if you want. This is also where you select the logo and icon images discussed in the Note at the beginning of this section. When you have finished, click the Next button.

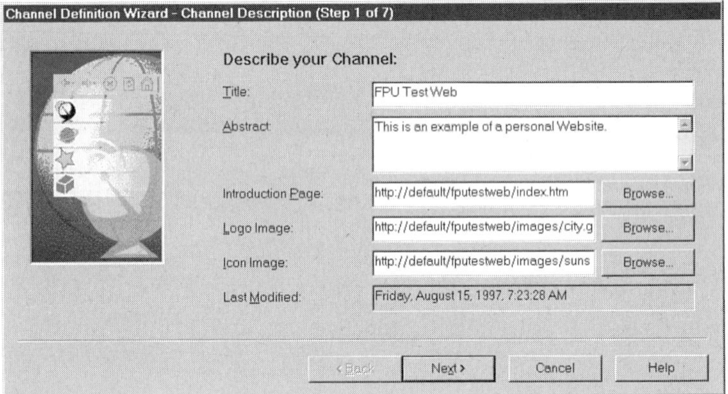

FIGURE 41.2.
The Channel Description dialog box.

Step 2: Choose Source Folder

The Choose Source Folder dialog box displays (see Figure 41.3). By default, this is the folder containing the current FrontPage web. You can have pages in subfolders that you would like to include in your channel. If you want to include subfolders of this in addition to the main folder, then click the Include Subfolders check box. If you want to use a subfolder instead of the main folder, then use the Browse button to select it. When you are finished, click the Next button.

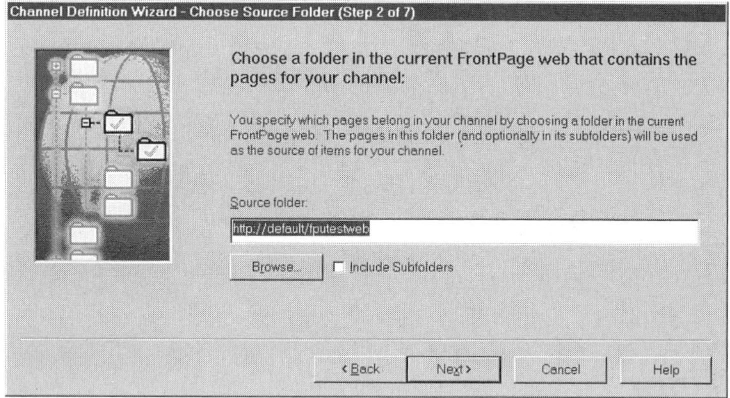

FIGURE 41.3.
The Choose Source Folder dialog box.

Step 3: Edit Page List

You will now be presented with the Edit Page List dialog box (see Figure 41.4). By default, all pages in the folders selected in Step 2 are included in the channel. If you want to exclude any of them, select them and click the Exclude button. If you change your mind about excluding a page, select it and click the Restore button.

This works a little bit differently if you are modifying an existing CDF file. In that case, the pages listed here are the ones you excluded previously, or new pages added since the CDF file was originally developed, or old ones that have been renamed. Just treat them the same way as with an original channel development, excluding the ones you do not want and leaving in the ones you do want.

When you are finished, click the Next button.

NOTE

This time, there's a potential catch. If there are pages that have been moved, renamed, or deleted from the web, you will get a nearly identical dialog box labeled Missing Page List (see Figure 41.5) instead of moving on to the next regular step. Your only real choice is to delete these, then click the Next button. The best course of action is to make sure your FrontPage web is fully up to date before starting the Channel Definition Wizard.

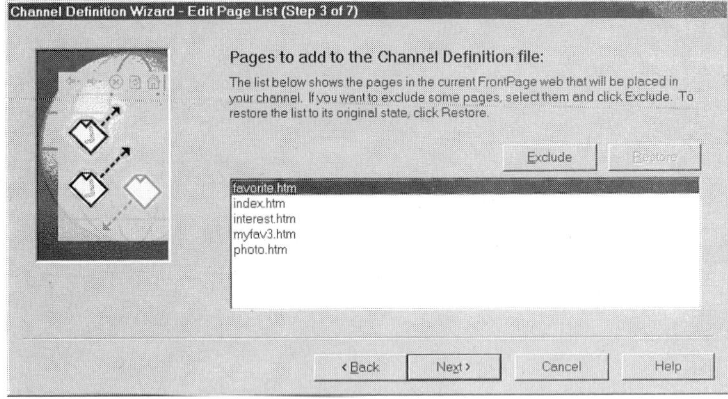

FIGURE 41.4.
The Edit Page List dialog box.

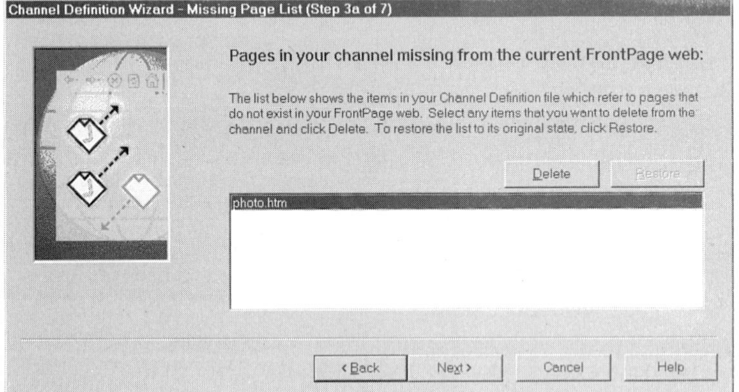

FIGURE 41.5.
The Missing Page List dialog box.

Step 4: Channel Item Properties

The Channel Item Properties dialog box (see Figure 41.6) has many choices for you. As with Step 3, you can choose to exclude or restore pages from your channel (except that the Exclude button has been renamed Delete). Here, the pages are called Channel Items.

As with the earlier addition of an abstract for the entire channel, you can add individual abstracts for each page in the channel. To do so, simply select the page in the Channel Items listing, then type the abstract into the edit box located in the center. Repeat this for each page you want to create an abstract for.

For Page Cache, you will generally want to leave the setting at User Default, which accepts each individual subscriber's Web browser cache settings. The Don't Use Cache setting prevents the subscriber from browsing your channel offline, and Use Cache forces a download to the subscriber's hard drive.

The Usage section defines how each channel item will work in a subscriber's Web browser. By default, Channel is selected, so if you make no changes here, each page in the channel items listing will be available as a separate part of your channel. The Email Notification check box will cause a message to be sent to your subscribers when changes are made to that page. If you select Screen Saver, then those of your subscribers who have selected Channel Screen Saver for their display will receive your selected page as their screen saver. You can also choose to have your channel item sent as a Desktop Component by clicking the check box of that name; if you choose this option, you must also specify the height and width in pixels for the component. Your last option under Usage is to make the channel item Hidden—that is, to include it as part of the overall download for offline browsing, but not to set it as a channel, screen saver, and so on.

Finally, the Reset button will undo your changes to the currently selected page. Selecting another page disables the reset button; if you change your mind after selecting another page, you will have to manually change the settings back.

When you have completed your decisions, click the Next button.

NOTE

You can select multiple options under Usage, such as having the channel item show up as a desktop component and sending an e-mail notification.

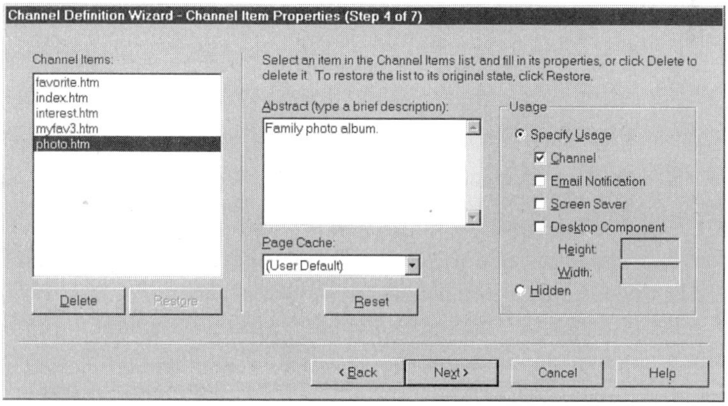

FIGURE 41.6.
The Channel Item Properties dialog box.

Step 5: Channel Scheduling

You should now be looking at the Channel Scheduling dialog box (see Figure 41.7). In most cases, you will only need to set the Check every setting. Type a number into the first box after these words, then select minutes, hours, or days from the drop-down list box to the right (for instance, type 1 and then select Days to have your subscribers check in once a day).

However, if you have an unusual situation, you might need to alter some of the other settings as well. The From start date setting is, by default, the current date. You may, however, have a case where you know there will be no changes until a certain date (as in the case of a launch date for a software product), so you would then set the start date to an appropriate one. The same is true of the Until end date setting. The default is forever and this is what most Webmasters would want. If you had created a temporary channel, though, such as an election results site, you would want to set the final date for election day.

Also, if you find your server is overloaded by all those subscribers checking in at midnight, you can set things so that updates are randomly staggered. To do this, click the Delay checks check box. This works just like the Check every settings, except that there are two numbers. Type in the numbers for the amount of time delay you want (lower number first), and then select minutes, hours, or days from the drop-down list box on the right. For example, you might select a delay of from 1 to 3 days for a channel that is updated weekly.

When you have adjusted things to your satisfaction, click the Next button.

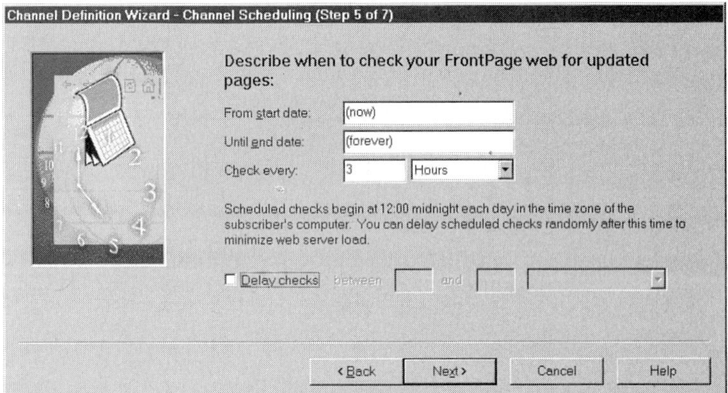

FIGURE 41.7.
The Channel Scheduling dialog box.

Step 6: Log Target

The Log Target dialog box (see Figure 41.8) is used to specify the URL of a form handler, if you have created one, which will log information about your subscribers' browsing habits (see Chapter 24, "Handling Form Output and Saving the Results," for information on form handlers). Use the Browse button to locate your form handler; if you have not created one, just ignore this dialog box. Either way, click the Next button to continue.

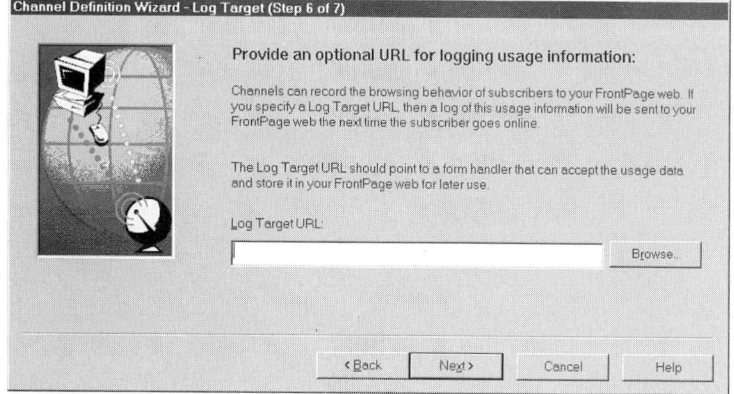

FIGURE 41.8.
The Log Target dialog box.

Step 7: Finish

The Finish dialog box (see Figure 41.9) is, of course, the final step. By default, FrontPage 98 will provide you with a filename of `channel.cdf`, located in the current web's folder (if this is not your first channel in this web, it will be named `channel0.cdf` or `channel1.cdf`, and so on.). If you want to change the name, you can do so, or you can use the Browse button to locate, select, and overwrite another CDF file.

There are two check box items under the heading of Additional Options. The first is to place a Subscribe button on the navigation bar on your home page (see Figure 41.10). The second, Prepare for publishing to, is only used if you are finished testing the channel locally (or are not going to do so) and want to set the CDF file to only respond to subscription requests at the specified URL. Because this setting does not have Web browsing capability, you have to type the URL in.

When you are finished, click the Save button to complete the Channel Definition Wizard process.

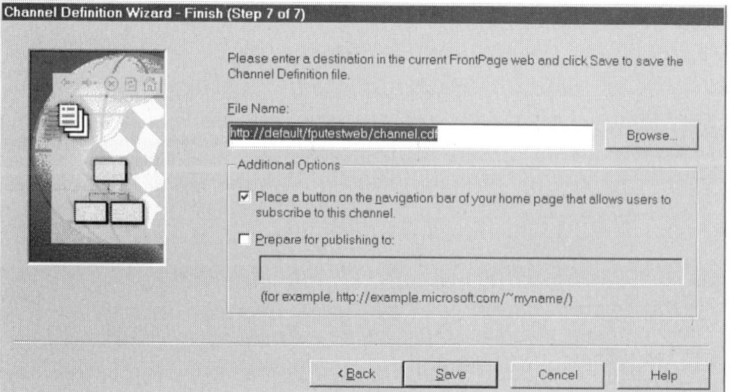

FIGURE 41.9.
The Finish dialog box.

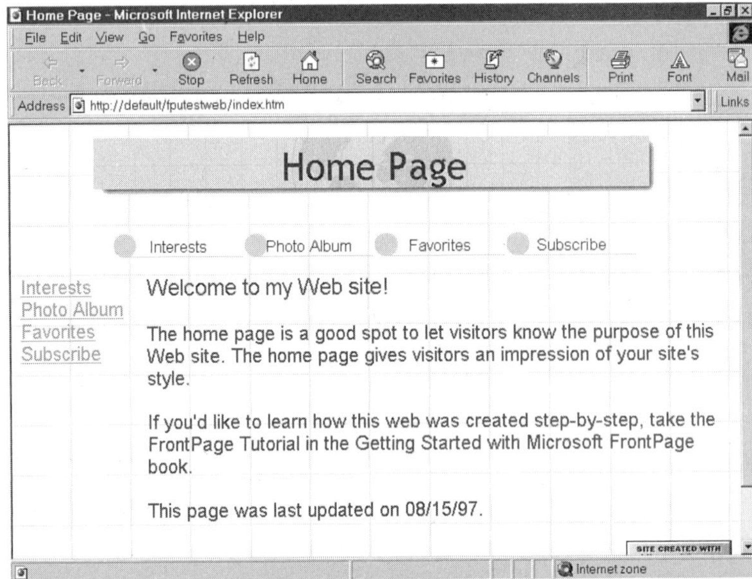

FIGURE 41.10.
Navigation bar with Subscribe button.

TIP

The option to put a Subscribe button on your home page's navigation bar works only if your web has shared borders. If you do not have shared borders or do not use a navigation bar, you can still add a channel subscribe option to your page. Simply make a hyperlink the usual way, but select the CDF file as the destination. You can even design your own Subscribe button and make an image hyperlink using it.

Managing Multiple Channels

Although most sites will do fine with one channel per web, in some cases multiple channels could be offered. For example, a news station's Web site might offer separate subscription channels for sports scores, weather information, local or national news, and so on. They might even establish a channel for updates on a single hot story. If you want to have multiple channels available from a single web, the process is still just as easy as developing a single channel, but requires more careful planning to avoid potential snags.

Once you have decided what channels you want, you will probably want to develop separate logos for each one of them. Also, it would be preferable to create subfolders under the main web folder to hold each of the pages and images for each channel, or, at the very least, draw up lists of which ones belong with which channel so you can check them off as you add them. Pick descriptive names for the subfolders, and use the same names for the CDF files.

Of course, you must also decide if all the channels will share the same characteristics. Should weather be updated more frequently than sports? Would financial information be more appreciated as a desktop component? Each channel deserves complete consideration in its own right as a totally separate function. It is quite possible that the only characteristic the different channels will share is the web page with the Subscribe buttons on it.

Once you have done all that, simply follow the steps in the section entitled "Using The Channel Definition Wizard" once for each channel.

The results (multiple, identical Subscribe buttons on your navigation bar, see Figure 41.11) will probably confuse visitors to your site unless you change them to be more descriptive.

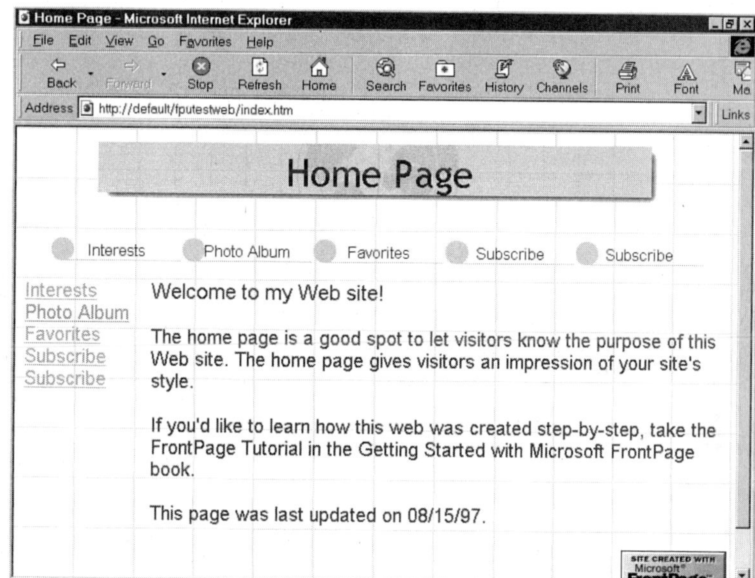

FIGURE 41.11.
Navigation bar with two Subscribe buttons.

Fortunately, this is easy to do in FrontPage Explorer:

1. Enter Navigation View. You will see something similar to Figure 41.12.
2. Click the Subscribe button you want to rename. From here, you can hit the F2 function key, or select Edit|Rename from the menu, or click one more time on the Subscribe button. Any of these approaches will put you in renaming mode, but be careful if you use the "two clicks" approach. If you make them too close together, you are double-clicking, and that will launch the Channel Definition Wizard, preset for modifying the channel the button references. Once you are in renaming mode, the name of the button will be highlighted, and you can simply type the new, more descriptive name in its place (see Figure 41.13).
3. Click anywhere outside the highlighted area to complete the task.

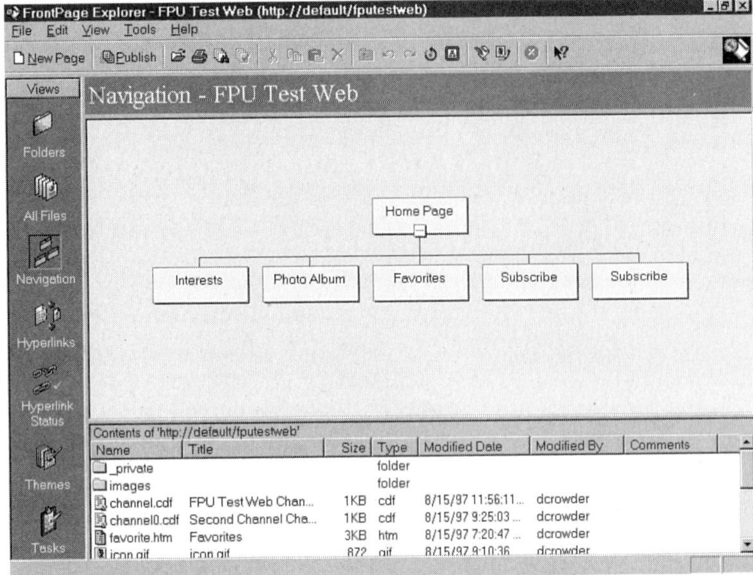

FIGURE 41.12.
Navigation View of Subscribe buttons.

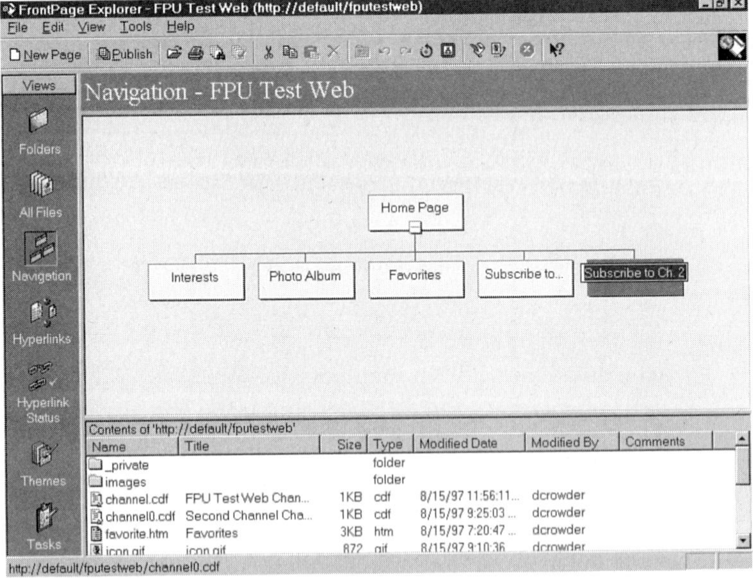

FIGURE 41.13.
Renaming Subscribe buttons in Navigation View.

The finished product, when viewed in Internet Explorer, should look something like Figure 41.14. Note that, although the left margin has expanded to allow for the increased length of the button names, the top navigation bar is pressed to the limit to fit them. Bear this in mind when renaming your own subscribe buttons.

FIGURE 41.14.
Navigation bar with renamed Subscribe buttons.

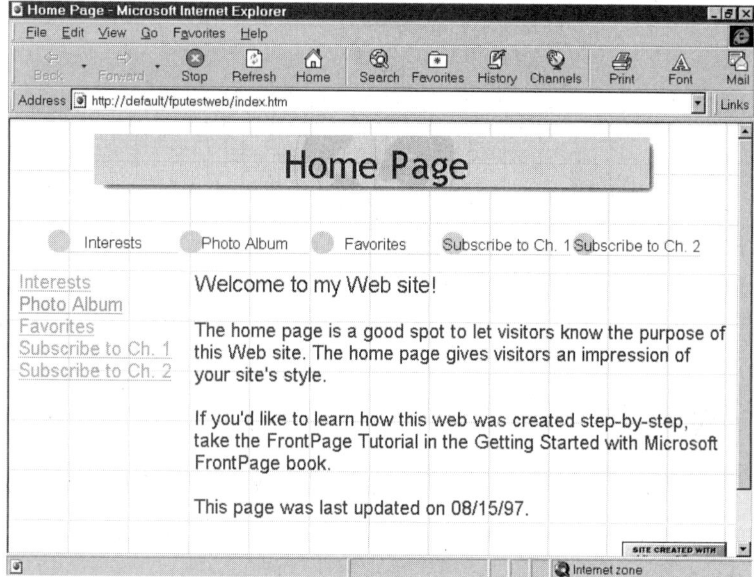

Designing Push Channel Content

What can be made into a channel? That's the same question as "What can a Web site be?" What makes a good Web site, though, may not make a good channel. It all depends on the content. Static content, even if it produces a good Web site, produces boring channels. Constantly changing content—as long as it is meaningful to your subscribers—is the key. Take a look at some examples.

A printed book that has been converted to HTML format could make a very good site, so long as it is a very good book. The hypertext format adds immeasurably to the functionality of most books (at least nonfiction ones). However, this would be a terrible idea for a channel. Why? Because it just lies there, unchanging, monolithic. This is definitely a case for plain old pull technology.

What about the case of a work in progress, though? If the book were being made available on a chapter-by-chapter basis over a period of time, then you would have an ideal situation for a channel. This would be true for fiction or nonfiction alike, and would work particularly well for a serial.

Periodicals fit the channel model perfectly. A magazine, newspaper, or newsletter format, with a variety of interesting material being constantly updated, practically defines what push channel technology is all about.

A catalog site may or may not make a good channel, depending on its content. Apply the "does it just lie there" rule to it. If it isn't static, then apply the "who cares" rule to the changes. If the changes themselves really matter to your subscribers—and it is critical here to recognize that the fact of change alone is not enough, that the material of the change is more important—then you have the makings of a channel. For example, the fact that you altered the order in which you displayed your products would bore your subscribers to tears, but the acquisition of a warehouse full of highly sought-after items at a bargain cost would be a delight. For a catalog, you might want to remember that you are not required to make the entire site into a channel, but you can also create a push channel for a single page. It might be best in this case to make a channel out of an update page where you list the latest incoming bargains.

The best channel possibilities are situations where subscribers have a real need for up-to-date information. A channel could supply stock prices to investors, for instance, or election results to news outlets.

How often you should update your channel depends partially on the nature of your material. A stock ticker needs to be updated continually, a newspaper daily, a magazine or newsletter weekly or monthly. The other main consideration is the work load. Unless you have a large organization behind your efforts, such as a string of reporters feeding you stories on a continual basis, along with at least a few people assisting you in maintaining the channels, then keep your effort small. It is very unlikely that a mom-and-pop operation run out of a spare room will be able to effectively compete with CNN.

If you are starting a Web site from scratch, it is fairly easy to apply these principles in advance. What about an existing site, though? Adapting a conventional pull-based site to the new push-based technology can be a daunting prospect. Unless the site is coincidentally one of the handful of information providers that were just born to be channels, it will likely require a tremendous amount of tearing down and rebuilding to effectively change to meet the new challenge. In many cases, it might be best to go right back to the drawing board and redesign with the new technology in mind.

Finally, when planning your content, never forget that subscribers can become former subscribers in a flash if you do not keep them happy. Never bore them, anger them, or abuse their trust if you want to keep a large readership. You may get away with it once or twice, but you must remember that you are taking up their limited time and resources. If they start perceiving your channel as a waste of time, they can and will pull the plug on it.

Learning by Looking

As with any new technology, you can learn about push channel technology best by looking at what other developers are doing with it. Although the number of channels currently in existence is small, it will grow rapidly as push channels become more accepted and developers and users alike become more comfortable with them. Although this is not an exhaustive listing, Table 41.1 lists some sites that either offer channels to which you can subscribe or list links to channels.

Table 41.1. Channel sources.

Site Name	Site URL
Celebguide.com	`http://celebguide.com`
Developer.com	`http://www.developer.com`
Dreamcatcher	`http://www.mdmax.com`
Entertainment Drive	`http://www.edrive.com`
InvestorsEdge	`http://channels.irnet.com`
Microsoft Channel Guide	`http://channels.microsoft.com/guide/chguide.asp`

Learning from Tutorials and References

Although FrontPage 98 makes channel development incredibly easy, there is a great deal of material available for those who want to delve more deeply into the topic. Although there will be many more references relating to push channels as the technology becomes more common and stable, several good sites are already dealing with this emerging technology. Table 41.2 offers a list of useful starting points—Web sites and online articles—related to channel technology in general and the Channel Definition Format in particular.

Table 41.2. Channel references.

Site Name	Site URL
Browser Wars on Again	`http://www.cnnfn.com/digitaljam/9707/15/yusuf_intv/`
Channel Definition Format (CDF)	`http://www.microsoft.com/standards/cdf-f.htm`
Internet Explorer 4.0 Technologies	`http://www.microsoft.com/workshop/prog/ie4/channels/cdf1-f.htm`
Microsoft Gets Pushy in Content Fight	`http://www.news.com/News/Item/0,4,10957,00.html`
Push Technology	`http://www-us-east.intel.com/drg/hybrid_author/cookbooks/push/`
Submission Request to W3C	`http://www.w3.org/Submission/1997/2/Overview.html`
Webcasting in Microsoft Internet Explorer 4.0 White Paper	`http://www.microsoft.com/ie/press/whitepaper/pushwp.htm`

Facing Dual Standards

In their never-ending battle for Web dominance, Microsoft and Netscape have, as usual, taken different approaches to push channel technology. Although there are those who argue that neither company has actually begun to use it properly, pointing out that both techniques would be more properly called "managed pull" rather than "push"—and technically, they are right—no other vendors of channel systems have the market presence of these two giants. Therefore, the systems put forth by Netscape and Microsoft are the ones most Webmasters will have to deal with.

Microsoft's offering in the push channel client arena is called Active Channels and is part of Internet Explorer 4.0. Netscape's is called Netcaster, and is part of the new Netscape Communicator. Both are still in the very early stages of development. FrontPage 98, being a Microsoft product, is of course designed to work with the Active Channels system, but Netcaster users will still be able to subscribe to your channels.

At this point, the differences between the two approaches do not matter much to you as a FrontPage developer because the Web browsers and other channel clients being used are subject to the usual rapid upgrades the Web as a whole has become used to. Basically, because both systems are capable of reading a basic CDF file, you can go right ahead and develop your channels, confident that they can be used.

Summary

Push channels offer a new ability to keep site visitors up-to-date on changes through channel subscriptions. Subscriptions cause the client to access the server on a regular basis, checking for new material. Depending on options set, notification may be made by e-mail, or the new pages, images, and so on may be immediately downloaded for offline browsing. The Channel Definition Format (CDF) file is a proposed standard Microsoft developed for handling subscription processing. The Channel Definition Wizard built into FrontPage 98 eliminates the need for developers to write CDF files because it handles this task automatically. Push channels are currently accessible only by clients such as Internet Explorer 4.0 and Netscape's Communicator. Multiple subscription channels can be set up on a single FrontPage web. This chapter also covers design considerations in channel development and provides tables of links to currently available channels as well as to articles and references on CDF and push technology.

PART VIII

IN THIS PART

- Web to Database Connectivity with FrontPage 98 *697*
- Advanced Database Setup and Custom Scripts *713*
- Working with SQL and Database Management Systems *739*
- Moving Up to Visual InterDev *763*

Working with Databases

CHAPTER 42

Web to Database Connectivity with FrontPage 98

By Craig Eddy

IN THIS CHAPTER

- Web Database Access: Past and Present *698*
- Creating ODBC Data Sources *699*
- Database Access with Internet Database Connector Pages *702*
- Database Access Using Active Server Pages *709*

The growth of the Internet in general and the Web in particular is due in no small part to the vast amount of information that is available in cyberspace. Ask any Web surfer what the best and the worst part of surfing the Web is, and you'll probably hear the same answer: A ton of information is available on the Web.

From its infancy, the Web was designed as a client/server database engine. The original intention was the sharing of scientific information across many platforms by standardizing the presentation of data with HTML and the transportation of data with HTTP. Client machines would (and still do) request specific HTML documents from an HTTP server. Thus, Web browsers become de facto database clients, and Web servers become database servers.

Originally, the Web was relatively static. A document was created in the HTML format, placed somewhere that a Web server had access to it, and it was left alone for all of eternity. Many (perhaps most) sites on the Internet are still of this static variety. The content doesn't change very often, and therefore, the site becomes stale rather quickly.

These days, however, most companies that are serious about the Internet will tell you that their presence on the Web is two-fold: first to provide information and the company's "message" to the buying public, and second to collect information about the buying public. Both of these purposes are accomplished by connecting the Web server to a corporate database. In this chapter, you learn ways to use FrontPage 98 to assist you in connecting your Web pages to your databases.

Web Database Access: Past and Present

As the Web has evolved, so have the means used to access and compile data using the Web. In the past, most Web servers operated on a UNIX platform machine. Although UNIX has its advantages over Windows-based operating systems such as Windows 95 and Windows NT, it also has some severe limitations.

The early database access applications for Web servers were written using what's known as a Common Gateway Interface, or CGI for short. Web servers can launch applications written as CGI applications and both send data to and receive output from these applications. The output is returned to the Web browser that requested that the CGI application be initiated. Part V of this book, "Forms and Advanced Form Handling," covers the HTML aspects of CGI and its counterparts.

CGI applications are typically very specific to their input, their data source, and their output. Therefore, a new CGI application must be written and compiled each time a new feature or function needs to be added to the Web site. Similarly, if the back-end database changes, the application more than likely must be recompiled as well.

Eventually, Web servers for Windows-based platforms became available, and along with them came the capability to access data from the hundreds of database systems and applications available for Windows machines.

Along with the access to existing database systems came access to the underlying architecture of Windows. Web application writers now can access all the functionality of the Windows API and services, thus enabling them to create more robust Web applications.

One of the biggest advances for Web-based database access was the development of the Internet Database Connector (IDC) and Active Server Pages (ASP). The IDC is a generic database connector that, through a template and an SQL script file, allows you to connect a Web page to any ODBC-compliant database accessible to the Web server machine.

ODBC stands for Open Database Connectivity. This is a standard to which most databases used in the Windows environment adhere. An ODBC-compliant database management system (DBMS) is guaranteed to respond to a standard syntax for both data definition language (DDL), which is the programming language used to define a particular database's structure, and data manipulation language (DML), which is the language used to update and retrieve the data in that database. Using ODBC, application developers can write their applications using a single set of DDL and DML constructs; and be assured that their applications will work on any DBMS platform adhering to the ODBC standard.

Active Server Pages allow expanded access by extending server-side scripting and an open, extensible object model to the Web server. Using ASP pages, you can access any in-process OLE object that is registered on the Web server machine. One of the standard objects installed on an Active Server machine is the ActiveX Data Object. This object allows you to use ODBC to access databases through a relatively flat object model. It has all the necessary properties and methods for retrieving practically any data from these databases, as you'll see in this and the following chapter. You can find more information about ASP development on the Microsoft SiteBuilder Web site at `http://www.microsoft.com/sitebuilder`.

In this chapter, you learn about retrieving data from an ODBC-compliant database using both the Internet Database Connector and Active Server Pages. Although you won't learn about entering and updating databases using these mechanisms, the techniques are not very much different from retrieving the data.

Creating ODBC Data Sources

The first step in using either the Internet Database Connector or Active Server Pages is to create an ODBC data source that the Web server can use to open the relevant database. The data source tells the ODBC driver manager how to connect to the physical data. This information includes which database management system (DBMS) the database uses, where the data physically resides, and which transport mechanism (if applicable) should be used to access the data.

NOTE

You must create the data source on the machine that is running the Web server software because it is the Web server application that will actually access the database specified by the data source. You don't need to set up this data source locally (if you're developing your site on a different machine) because FrontPage 98 does not require a connection to the database.

To create an ODBC data source, you must first gather several key pieces of information. First and foremost, you must know on which DBMS the database resides. This information determines which ODBC driver you must use to connect. The second piece of information is the name of the server (if you're using a client/server DBMS such as SQL Server or Oracle) on which the database resides. Third, you need to know the name of the database. In the case of an Access or other file-system database, you need either the filename or directory name. Finally, if the database has any security implemented, you need to have the proper logon credentials handy. Typically, you need a logon name and password combination.

After you gather the necessary information, you can create the data source. The steps vary depending on the needs of the DBMS and the ODBC driver that connects to it, as well as the version of the ODBC driver manager you have installed, but they probably follow the general path presented here.

1. Start the Control Panel application by clicking the Windows Start button and choosing Settings and then Control Panel.
2. Double-click the 32-bit ODBC icon. The ODBC Data Source Administrator application appears, as shown in Figure 42.1. Note that the ODBC Administrator dialog has changed many times with the different revisions of ODBC. Your machine's dialog might look different than that of Figure 42.1, but the key pieces of information will be present somewhere within the dialog.

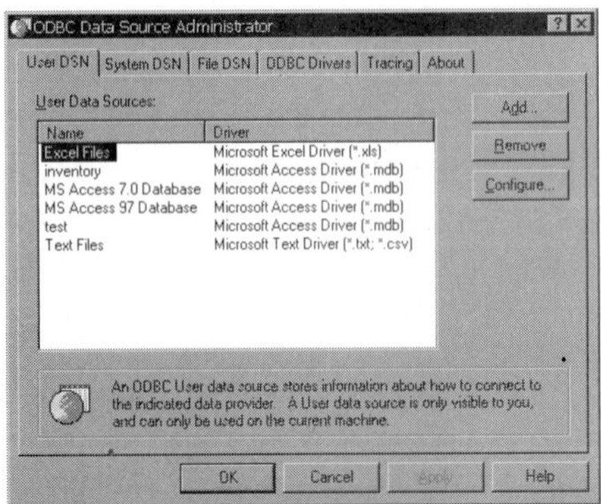

FIGURE 42.1.
The ODBC Data Source Administrator.

3. Select the System DSN tab. You need to create a system DSN as opposed to a user DSN because the Web server runs as a system service, not as a logged-in user. A system DSN is valid for every user of the particular system as well as any service running on the system.
4. Click the Add button. The Create New Data Source dialog box, shown in Figure 42.2, appears.

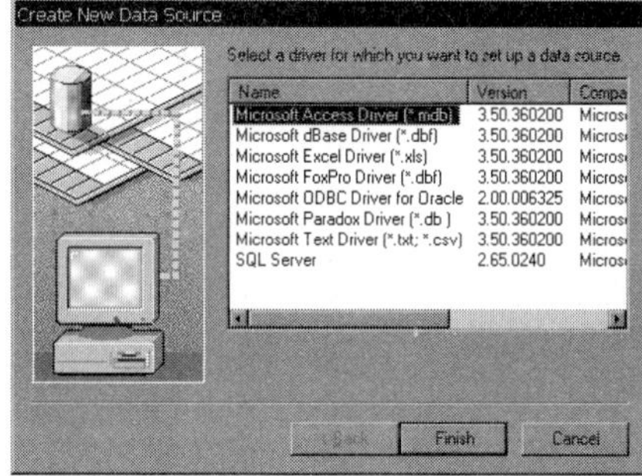

FIGURE 42.2.
The Create New Data Source dialog box.

5. In the list box, select the ODBC driver that matches the database to which you're connecting.
6. After selecting the driver, click the Finish button. The ODBC data source setup dialog box for the driver chosen in Step 5 appears. Although this dialog box is different for each driver, they all have two things in common: a data source name and a database location. Some drivers may require additional information to complete the definition of the data source. Figure 42.3 shows an example data source configuration for an SQL Server database being accessed using TCP/IP. If you need help defining the data source, click the Help button. The driver-specific help file is then displayed.

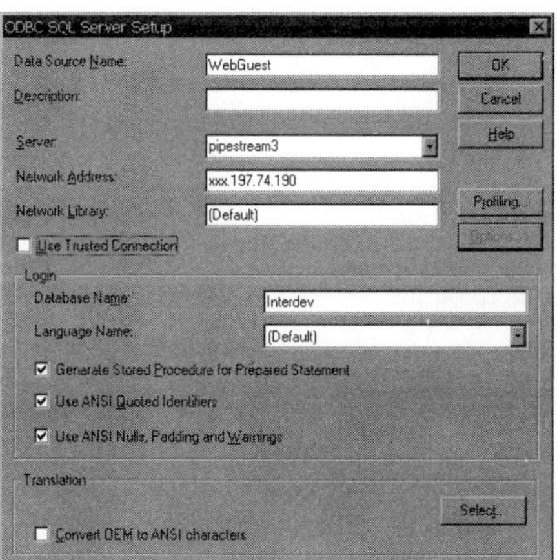

FIGURE 42.3.
The ODBC SQL Server Setup dialog box.

7. After you enter the necessary information, click the OK button to save the data source information and return to the ODBC Data Source Administrator.

Now that you've created the data source, you can use it with the Internet Database Connector or with Active Server Pages containing ActiveX Data Objects.

Database Access with Internet Database Connector Pages

The Internet Database Connector (IDC) is a specialized application that you can install on either the Microsoft Personal Web Server (for Windows 95), Peer Web Services (for Windows NT Workstation), or the Internet Information Server (for Windows NT Server). Using the IDC, you can produce Web pages that display live data. You can also design a form that can be used in conjunction with the IDC to add to or update data in a database. For this chapter, you concentrate on displaying information already contained in the database.

NOTE

The FrontPage Personal Web Server does not support IDC or Active Server pages. You need to upgrade to Microsoft's Personal Web Server to do so. The Personal Web Server is part of the Internet Explorer Suite and can be downloaded from `http://www.microsoft.com/ie`. You can find instructions for upgrading from FrontPage Personal Web Server to Microsoft Personal Web Server at `http://www.microsoft.com/frontpage/upgrade/engupgrade.htm`.

To use the IDC, you need two files, a template file and a script file. The template file is a special file that, in addition to standard HTML and scripting, contains tokens for each of the database fields to be included in the output as well as other tokens that instruct the IDC on how to display the data. The script file contains the information necessary to connect to and retrieve data from the database. The template files have the extension `HTX`, whereas the script files have the extension `IDC`.

When you create a link to an IDC page, the link should specify the URL for the IDC file. A Web server that has the Internet Database Connector properly installed knows to provide the requester with the database-aware Web page.

Creating the Template File

The first step in using the Internet Database Connector is to create a template, or HTX, file. This file provides the IDC with information about which fields should be displayed, as well as where and how to display them. The template file combines HTML and scripting with special IDC tokens. These tokens can be embedded anywhere within the HTML.

You set tokens apart from the rest of the HTML by surrounding them with `<%` and `%>`, similar to the Active Server Page tokens for distinguishing Active Server Script from plain HTML.

Two of the standard IDC tokens specify the start and end of a detail section. The detail section contains a single record from the database query's result set. These tokens are `<%begindetail%>` and `<%enddetail%>`.

To output a database field, simply enclose the field name in `<%` and `%>` brackets. For example, placing the token `<%Company%>` instructs the IDC to replace the token with the value of the Company field from the result set. This replacement is a literal replacement. The IDC inserts the field's data directly into the text stream of the HTTP response message. Any fields that are specified in the HTX file must be included in the IDC file, which you learn about in the following section.

To create an HTX file using FrontPage 98, follow these steps:

1. Open the destination web using the FrontPage Explorer.
2. Select the folder into which you want to create the template file. The folder must have Execute permissions enabled. You can view and set this permission by right-clicking the folder name and choosing Properties from the pop-up menu. The Allow scripts or programs to be run check box must be checked.
3. Click the New Page button. Give the template a meaningful name and the extension `HTX`.
4. After FrontPage Explorer finishes renaming the file, double-click its name to open it in the FrontPage Editor.
5. Use any of the necessary features of FrontPage 98 to design your template file.
6. Choose Edit|Database to insert the detail section markers and the database field tokens. Or you can use the HTML tab of the editor to enter these tokens manually.
7. After you finish creating the template file, be sure to save it.

A simple template file is provided in Listing 42.1. This file was created with the Access 97 Northwind sample database's Customers table in mind. It prints some of the fields from this table into an HTML table.

Listing 42.1. A simple HTX file for the Northwind Customers table.

```
<html><head>
<meta http-equiv="Content-Type" content="text/html; charset=ISO-8859-1">
<title>New Page</title>
<meta name="Microsoft Theme" content="blueprnt 111, default">
</head>
<body>
<h1 align="center">Northwind Customers</h1>
<div align="center"><center>
<table border="1" width="761" height="76">
<tr>
```

continues

Listing 42.1. continued

```
<td align="left" width="152" height="30"><big>CustomerID</big></td>
<td align="left" width="219" height="30"><big>Company Name</big></td>
<td align="left" width="194" height="30"><big>Contact</big></td>
<td align="left" width="172" height="30"><big>City</big></td>
</tr>
<%begindetail%>
<tr>
<td width="152" height="34"><%CustomerID%></td>
<td width="219" height="34"><%CompanyName%></td>
<td width="194" height="34"><%ContactName%></td>
<td width="172" height="34"><%City%></td>
</tr>
<%enddetail%>
</table>
</center></div>
</body></html>
```

You can also create more sophisticated template files by using the If-Then Conditional Section command when you choose Edit|Database. This command allows you to easily specify a region of the HTX file that will be displayed if the Boolean expression you construct evaluates to `True`. For example, suppose you want all the customer records in a specific city to have their data appear in boldface or in a different color. Using the If-Then Conditional Section, you can accomplish this task by simply comparing the value in the City field with the name of the city you want to highlight.

When you use the If-Then Conditional Section menu item, FrontPage 98 presents you with the dialog box shown in Figure 42.4. After you complete this dialog box, FrontPage 98 inserts special markers in the Normal view, as shown in Figure 42.5. You can place any content you want between these markers.

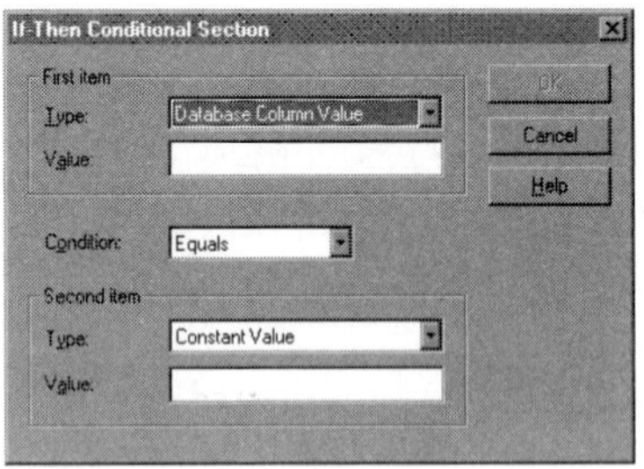

FIGURE 42.4.
The If-Then Conditional Section dialog box.

The Boolean expression to be evaluated for the section can be constructed using a database column value, an IDC parameter value, a constant value, or any of the available IDC or HTTP variables. You specify two such items and then specify how you want to compare these items. You can specify a comparison operator chosen from equals, less than, greater than, or contains.

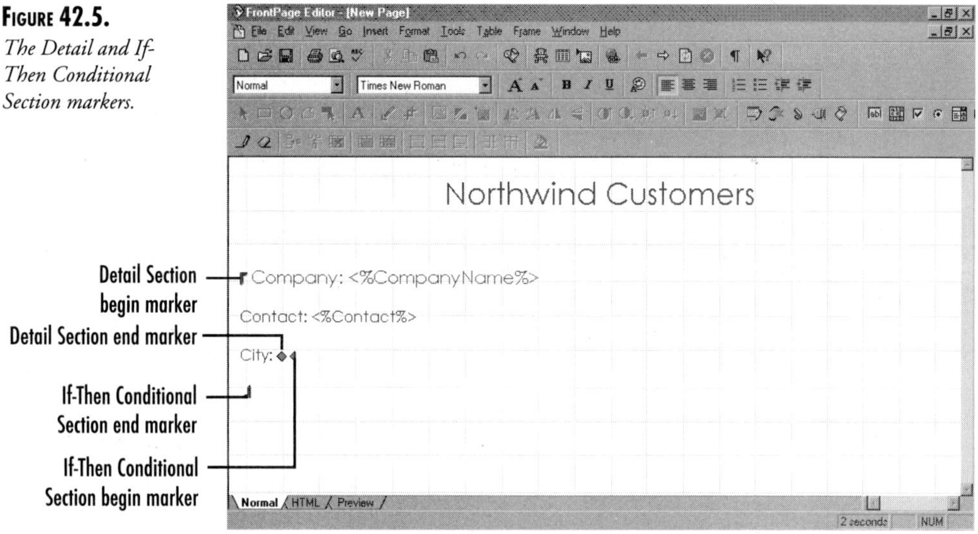

FIGURE 42.5.
The Detail and If-Then Conditional Section markers.

You can also create an Else Conditional Section. To do so, place the cursor within an If-Then Conditional Section and use the Edit|Database|Else Conditional Section. Between the markers placed by FrontPage 98, enter the content to be inserted if the Boolean expression specified in the If-Then Conditional Section evaluates to `False`.

Creating IDC Files with the Internet Database Connector Wizard

After you create the template file, you're more than halfway home. Creating the IDC file is a piece of cake compared to creating the template file. If you have included a fair number of fields in the template file, you might want to print the file's HTML using the FrontPage Editor so that you don't leave out any fields when creating the IDC file.

NOTE

You cannot proceed past the initial Database Connection Wizard dialog box without specifying a template (HTX) file that is present on the current web. If you have not yet created a template file, do so now by following the instructions in the preceding section.

FrontPage 98 provides an Internet Database Connector Wizard that assists you in setting up your IDC files. However, as you'll see after you finish creating the IDC file, there's really not much to the wizard. After you create a few IDC files and learn how to construct them, creating one manually is probably easier.

To create a new IDC file using the Internet Database Connector Wizard, return to the FrontPage Explorer and follow these steps:

1. Navigate through the FrontPage Explorer to a folder that has Execute permissions enabled. The IDC file must be placed in an executable directory. You can view and set this permission by right-clicking the folder name and choosing Properties from the shortcut menu. The Allow scripts or programs to be run check box must be checked.
2. Click the New Page button, choose File|New|Page, or press Ctrl+N.
3. Rename the file from the default name to a meaningful name, and give it the extension `IDC`.
4. After renaming the file, double-click its name to open it with the Internet Database Connector Wizard.

NOTE

If the Internet Database Connector Wizard does not launch when you double-click, be sure that the file has the extension `IDC`. If the file does have `IDC` as its extension, then the default editor for IDC files has been modified. To remedy this situation, choose Tools | Options and then select the Configure Editors tab. Find IDC in the Type column and click the Modify button. Enter a name and the path to a file named `fpidcwiz.exe`. By default, this file is installed in the `\pages\fpidcwiz.wiz` subdirectory of the directory to which FrontPage 98 was installed (`Program Files\FrontPage` by default).

The initial dialog box of the Internet Database Connector Wizard appears, as shown in Figure 42.6.

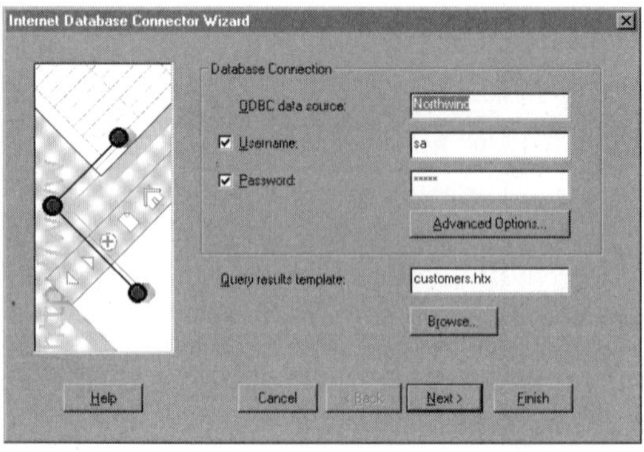

FIGURE 42.6.
The initial dialog box of the Internet Database Connector Wizard.

5. On this dialog box, specify the ODBC data source name, any login credentials that are required to open the database, and the template file to use. You can also use the

Advanced Options button to set up optional information about the query, about the database connection, or to set limits on the amount of data that will be returned to the user.

6. After you enter the appropriate information, you can use the Browse button to display a file dialog box showing the HTX files present in the current web.
7. Click the Next button to move on to specifying the query or queries that will provide the data result set you want. This dialog box is shown in Figure 42.7. If the query will be based on any parameters supplied by the requesting page or by parameter defaults, you can insert them into the SQL query using the Insert Parameter button. Alternatively, you can enter the parameter name, enclosed in `<% %>`, directly into the query box. Enter the appropriate query and click Next.

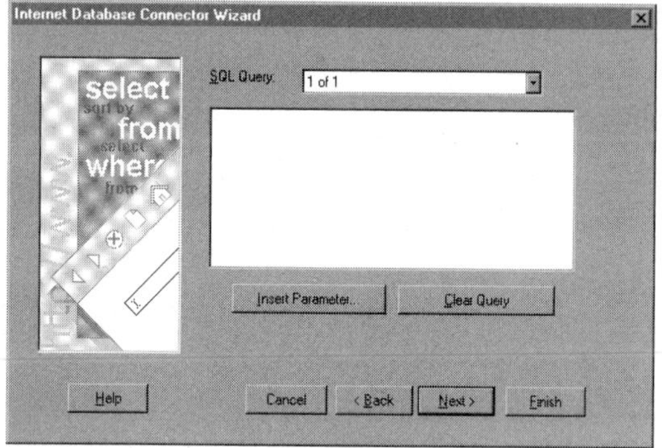

FIGURE 42.7.
Creating SQL queries using the Internet Database Connector Wizard.

NOTE

You can specify multiple queries in the IDC file. Each query is output into sequential detail sections. Your template file should have one detail section for each query you plan to output using the IDC file. The SQL Query drop-down list box informs you which detail section the contents of the text box apply to.

WARNING

The Microsoft Personal Web Server supports only one query in the IDC file. For more information on this topic, see Microsoft's Knowledge Base Article Q160809 (`http://www.microsoft.com/kb/articles/q160/8/09.htm`).

8. On the next wizard dialog box, you specify any default parameter values. If the SQL query relies on parameters, and there's a chance that they will not be provided when the IDC file is requested from a Web browser, you should take this opportunity to enter some default values for them. To add a default parameter value, click the Add button. A dialog box appears with text boxes for entering the parameter name and the default value to be used. After you enter all the necessary default parameters, click Finish to update the IDC file and return to the FrontPage Explorer.

A sample IDC file to accompany the HTX file from the previous section (refer to Listing 42.1) is provided in Listing 42.2. As you can see, this file doesn't contain much information. Also, the contents don't change much from query to query within the same database. If you're working in the same database, you can create another IDC file by copying an existing one and simply modifying the SQL statement and any default parameters.

Listing 42.2. An IDC file for the Northwind Customers table.

```
Datasource: Northwind
Template: customers.htx
Username: sa
Password: secret
SQLStatement: Select * from Customers
```

Viewing the Results

To view the results of an IDC page, you must request the page from a Web server having the IDC application files installed. You cannot open the file in the browser using the file system and see the results of the query because the database interactivity is actually performed by a process that runs on a Web server machine, not by the Web browser application itself.

After you complete your IDC pages, therefore, you must make sure that they're accessible by a Web server application. If you open your FrontPage web by connecting to a Web server anyway, then simply saving your files causes the Web server's content directories to update. If, however, you edit your files locally and then post them to your Web server using the Publish FrontPage Web dialog box or the Web Publishing Wizard, you must publish your files before you can view them.

After the files are available in one of the Web server's content directories, you can fire up your favorite Web browser and enter the URL for your IDC file in its address box. Any browser will do because IDC files are as browser independent as the HTML in the template file. The page loads and shows you the results of your database query or any error message if an error occurs.

A sample IDC results page is shown in Figure 42.8.

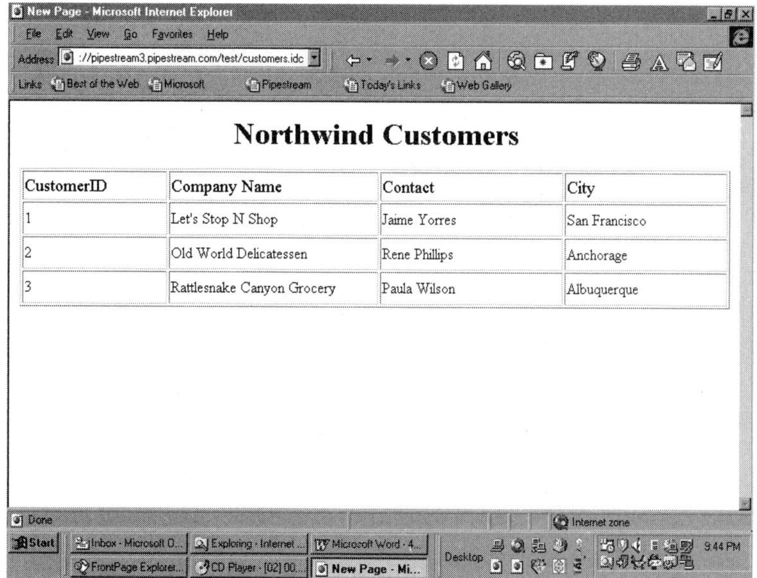

FIGURE 42.8.
A sample IDC results page.

Database Access Using Active Server Pages

In addition to the Database Connection Wizard used for creating IDC pages, FrontPage 98 also provides support for connecting to database with Active Server Pages. Active Server Pages (ASP) are HTML pages with server-side script embedded in them. Active Server Pages are supported by Microsoft's Internet Information Server platform.

The Web server, prior to returning any data to the user's browser, executes the Active Server Page's script. None of the script code is actually returned to the browser. The user sees only the HTML that was either a part of the original ASP or was generated by the script code. This capability allows you, the Web site developer, to hide critical details such as database login names and passwords from the user. The resulting Web pages don't look any different from what you can create with an IDC/HTX page, but the underlying architecture of ASP provides you with greater functionality than the Internet Database Connector.

Using FrontPage 98, you can create a new ASP file on the Web using the FrontPage Explorer. The FrontPage Editor provides a Database Region Wizard, which you can use to combine FrontPage WebBots with Active Server script. In the following section, you learn how to use the Database Region Wizard to connect a Web page to a database using an Active Server Page.

NOTE

In addition to supporting Active Server Pages, the Web server must also have the FrontPage 98 server extensions installed to use the WebBots.

Creating a New Active Server Page

Creating an Active Server Page is as simple as creating any other page in a FrontPage web. Open the destination web using the FrontPage Explorer, and click the New Page button or choose File|New|Page. Then simply rename the page and give it an ASP extension. You can then edit the page using the FrontPage Editor by simply double-clicking its name from the FrontPage Explorer.

Alternatively, if you're already in the FrontPage Editor, choose File|New and select Normal Page on the new page dialog box that opens. Save the page with the extension ASP so that the Web server knows to use its Active Server Script parser when a browser requests the page.

Running the Database Region Wizard

Now that you have a new Active Server Page available, open it in the FrontPage Editor. To use the Database Region Wizard, you must be on the editor's Normal tab. The menu item for the Database Region Wizard is disabled on any other tab. You can enter any other content you want on the page before or after the area into which you will place the database region.

To use the Database Region Wizard, follow these steps:

1. Position the pointer at the place on the page where you want to insert the database region.
2. Choose Insert|Database|Database Region Wizard.

   The first dialog box of the wizard, shown in Figure 42.9, appears.
3. In this dialog box, as with the Database Connection Wizard, you enter the ODBC data source name and any necessary login credentials. Click Next after you enter the necessary information.

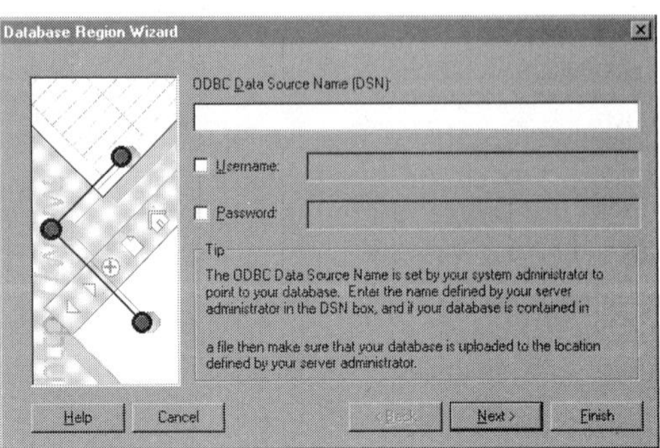

FIGURE 42.9.
The initial dialog box of the Database Region Wizard.

4. In the second dialog box of the Database Region Wizard, shown in Figure 42.10, enter the SQL query to be executed by the Active Server Page. You can enter the SQL manually, or you can paste it from the Windows Clipboard. You can also enter any parameters to be used either by clicking the Insert Form Field Parameter button or entering the parameter name enclosed in %%. After you enter the query, click the Next button.

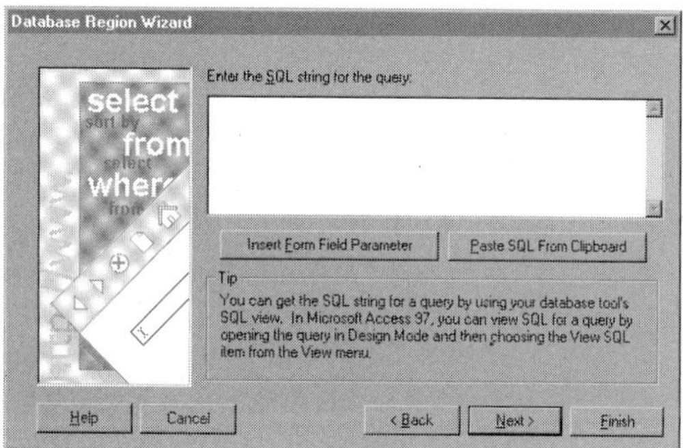

FIGURE 42.10.
The Database Region Wizard's SQL query dialog box.

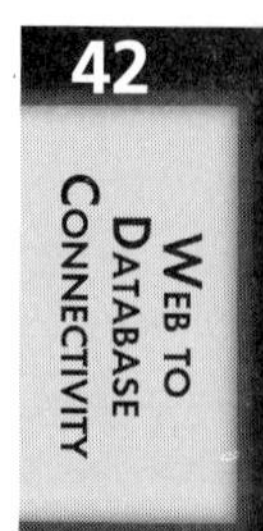

5. On the Database Region Wizard's final dialog box, enter the names of the fields to be output to the region. These fields must also have been included in the SQL query you entered on the preceding dialog box. Enter each field name by clicking the Add Field button. You can remove a field by clicking the Remove Field button. Click Finish after you enter all the field names.

   The Wizard outputs HTML for a table, several WebBot components and some Active Server script code. You can view the HTML and script on the HTML tab of the editor. You can view the graphical representation of the output fields using the Normal tab.

After the database region is in place, you can invoke the Database Region Wizard to modify the region by right-clicking over any of the database field indicators shown on the Normal tab and choosing Database Region Properties from the shortcut menu.

You can also insert fields elsewhere on the page by choosing Insert|Database|Column Value. To replace an inserted field with another field, either click the field's indicator and choose Insert|Database|Column Value, or right-click the indicator and choose FrontPage Component Properties from the shortcut menu. Using any of these actions, you can invoke the Database Column Value dialog box, which is shown in Figure 42.11.

After you enter the content for the page in this dialog box, be sure to save it! Then load up a Web browser (again, Active Server Pages are browser independent unless you add some browser-dependent content) and point it to the page you just created.

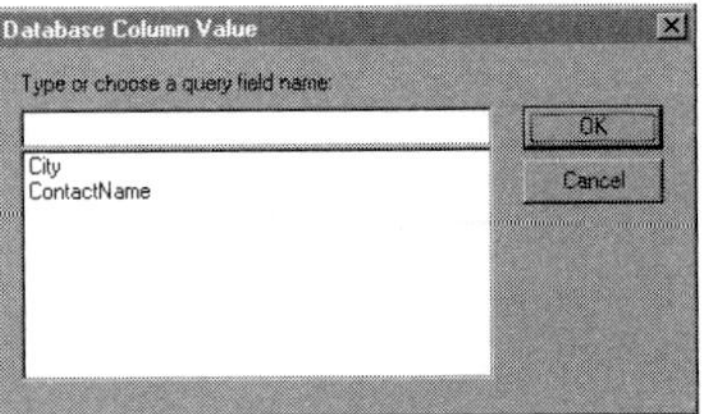

FIGURE 42.11.
The Database Column Value dialog box.

A sample page is shown in Figure 42.12. It was created using the Database Region Wizard with the Adventure Works database that is installed with the Active Server Page installation. I set the border for the region's table by right-clicking over the database region table, using the Table Properties menu item, and setting the Border value to 1.

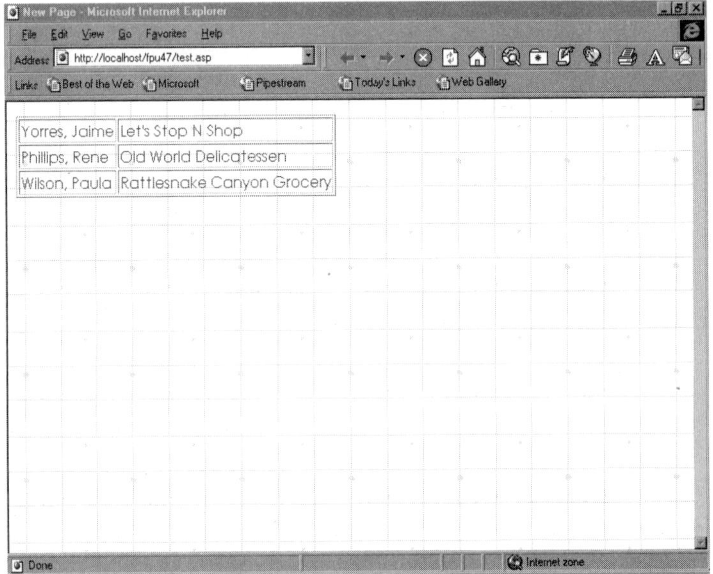

FIGURE 42.12.
A sample page created with the Database Region Wizard.

Summary

In this chapter, you learned about the database capabilities provided by FrontPage 98. In the next chapter, you'll learn about some of the advanced features provided by the Database Connection Wizard as well as some more advanced database topics, including creating forms to use in conjunction with your IDC and Active Server Pages.

If you plan to do a large amount of database integration into your Web site, you should read Chapter 45, "Moving Up to Visual InterDev," for an introduction to Microsoft's Visual InterDev. This package is a complete Web application development environment including full-featured design-time controls and the Visual Database Tools.

Advanced Database Setup and Custom Scripts

by Craig Eddy

IN THIS CHAPTER

- The Internet Database Connector Wizard's Advanced Options *714*
- Using a Database Search Form *718*
- Introducing the ActiveX Data Objects *725*
- Using the ActiveX Data Objects *734*

Chapter 42, "Web to Database Connectivity with FrontPage 98," introduced you to FrontPage's database connectivity features. This chapter digs deeper into database connectivity. The chapter explores some of the advanced features of the Internet Database Connector Wizard, discusses database search forms, and teaches you how to use Active Server Pages with the ActiveX Data Objects.

The Internet Database Connector Wizard's Advanced Options

As you saw in Chapter 42, the Internet Database Connector Wizard assists you in setting up an IDC file to use with the Internet Database Connector. The Internet Database Connector is one means of connecting the Microsoft Personal Web Server, Peer Web Services, or Internet Information Server to an ODBC database.

If you're setting up a simple, generic IDC file, the Internet Database Connector Wizard can actually take longer to run than if you manually created the IDC file with Notepad. However, if you want to fine-tune the Internet Database Connector, specify timeouts, or set limits on the amount of data returned by the IDC, the Wizard's Advanced Options dialog is invaluable.

This section describes the four tabs of the Advanced Options dialog. You'll learn about setting query options, specifying how the ODBC connection operates, specifying limits on the amount of data returned, and setting driver-specific options.

The Query Tab

The Query tab contains options for setting how the SQL query is executed by the ODBC driver and how the template file is returned to the Web browser. Figure 43.1 shows the Query tab.

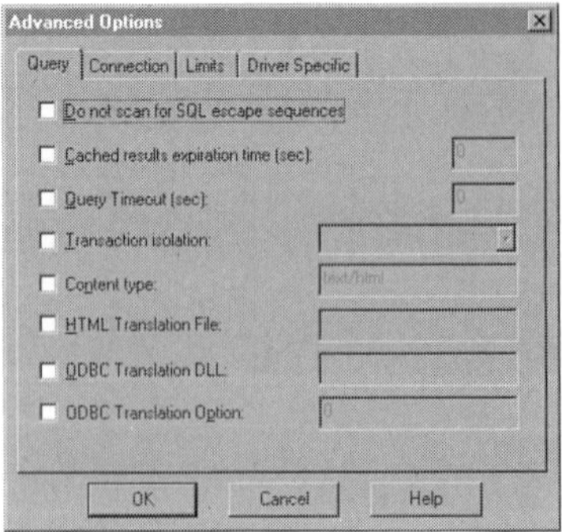

FIGURE 43.1.
The Query tab of the Advanced Options dialog box.

The first option regards scanning for escape sequences. In an ODBC SQL statement, you can place escape sequences that denote portions of the SQL statement requiring special handling. Escape sequences are used most often to specify *scalar functions*. Scalar functions provide a database-independent query to the ODBC driver. By checking this option, you're instructing the driver not to scan for the escape sequences. This will improve performance slightly. You should only check this option if your query will not contain any escape sequences.

The second option, Cached results expiration time, specifies how long (in seconds) the Internet Database Connector should store the results of a query in its cache. If an identical query is subsequently run within this expiration time, the IDC will not requery the database. Instead, the cached results will be returned to the user. By default, the IDC does not cache its results. You must enable this option and specify a timeout period in order to have the results cached.

The Query Timeout option is perhaps the most important option in this dialog. If the database query takes longer to execute than the time specified by the query's timeout, the execution of the query will be canceled. By default, the IDC will use the query timeout specified in the ODBC data source. If you select this option and enter a value in the text box, the IDC will use this value as the timeout. There are cases when you may want to provide a longer timeout or a shorter timeout. This option allows you to specify the timeout value for each IDC page you create.

The Transaction isolation option allows you to control which records and which versions of those records are retrieved in a database environment that utilizes transaction-based processing. Transactions are used to encapsulate data updates that involve several discrete operations. You can roll back the entire set of operations or commit the entire set should an error occur. By setting the Transaction Isolation to Read Uncommitted, the query will see changes that haven't yet been committed to the database. The other settings all have to do with how records are reread from the database if those records were involved in a transaction that took place outside of the IDC's query. In general, the IDC will only be reading records in a single pass, and these settings don't have much value.

The Content type setting allows you to specify how data is sent to the IDC when the requesting page uses a POST request. The type of request is specified in the ACTION element of an HTML form, as you'll see later in this chapter. If the IDC page was reached by clicking a link or entering the URL in an address box, the HTTP request is a GET request and this setting will have no effect. Typically, the default (html/text) is correct.

The HTML Translation File option specifies the path to a file that translates characters in the HTML output to international characters. This is useful if you're publishing your database in a language other than English. Using the translation file, Web browsers can correctly display the characters.

The ODBC Translation DLL setting specifies a DLL that will be used to translate data from one format to another. The ODBC Translation Option allows you to supply any necessary option to that DLL. The translation DLL converts all of the data that passes between the data source (the database) and the ODBC driver. In the vast majority of cases, you will not need to use these settings. When these settings are used, ODBC calls the `SQLDriverToDataSource` and `SQLDataSourceToDriver` functions that reside in the DLL.

The Connection Tab

On the Connection tab, shown in Figure 43.2, you can specify several options, which affect how the ODBC connection is opened and maintained.

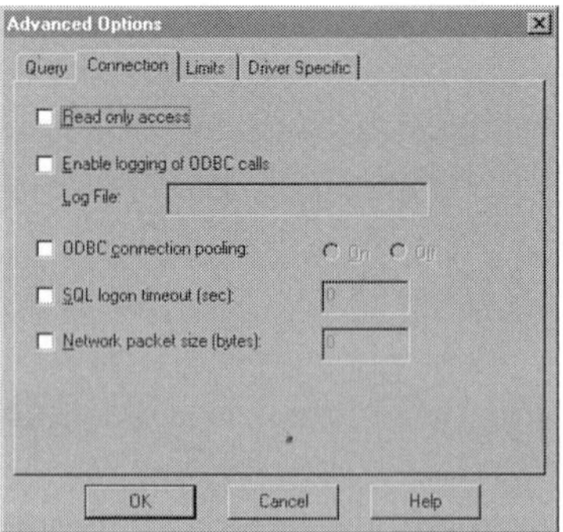

FIGURE 43.2.
The Connection tab of the Advanced Options dialog box.

Enabling the Read-only access setting will prevent the IDC request from being able to update or delete any data in the database. It can also increase the performance of the connection, both for the IDC request and other users connecting to the database. The results of attempting to update data when this option is set depend on the driver.

To log all of the connections ODBC calls to a file, check the Enable logging of ODBC calls setting and enter a filename in the Log File text box. If the file specified already exists, ODBC will append the new calls to the file. If you think there might be a lot of activity on your site, you should carefully consider whether or not to enable logging. The ODBC log files can become quite large in a short period of time if there's a lot of database activity.

The ODBC Connection Pooling option instructs the IDC to keep the ODBC connection open after the request has been completed. Subsequent connections can use this open connection without having to go through the connection opening and logon processes. As you can probably guess, this will increase the performance of your IDC pages.

The SQL logon timeout specifies the amount of time the IDC will wait when it is attempting to connect to the data source. If this setting is not selected, the data source's default will be used. If the setting is specified as 0, the IDC will wait indefinitely for the connection to complete. If the setting is set to a value greater than the maximum timeout for the data source, the data source's maximum timeout value will be used instead.

The Network Packet Size setting specifies the number of bytes to use in each data packet sent between the Web server and the database. Not all data sources support this option. If the value specified falls outside the range set in the data source, the data source's settings will be used instead.

The Limits Tab

On the Limits tab (shown in Figure 43.3), you can help to reduce network traffic and decrease the amount of time a user has to wait while an IDC request is fulfilled. By setting limits on the amount of data and the number of records returned, you can ensure that the user is not overwhelmed with unnecessary data. Typically, if these values are exceeded, the user needs to refine his searches anyway.

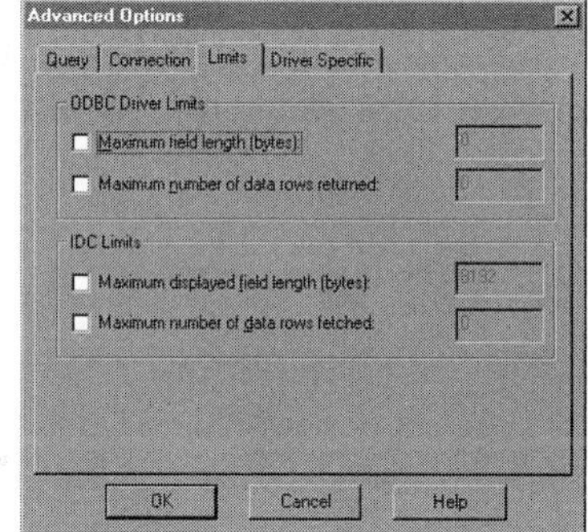

FIGURE 43.3.
The Limits tab of the Advanced Options dialog box.

The ODBC Driver Limits settings allow you to limit the amount of data returned by the ODBC driver. You can limit the number of bytes returned in a character or binary field using the Maximum field length setting. This should only be used to reduce local network traffic (between the Web server and the database server) and is not supported by all data sources. The Maximum number of data rows returned setting limits the number of rows that the data source will return to the IDC system. Again, this should only be used if supported by the driver and only to reduce local network traffic.

The IDC Limits section allows you to limit the amount of data returned to the Web browser. This will reduce traffic between the Web browser machine and the Web server machine. You should typically use these settings instead of the ODBC Limits.

To limit the amount of data returned for each field in the result set, enter a value in the Maximum displayed field length. To limit the number of data rows returned to the browser, enter a value in the Maximum number of data rows fetched setting.

The Driver Specific Tab

On the Driver Specific tab, you'll enter any driver-specific options. You'll need to refer to the documentation for the ODBC driver being used to determine what, if any, options need to be entered here.

To add an option, click the Add button. On the dialog that appears, enter an option number and a value to use for that option. Click OK.

To change an existing option, select the option and click the Modify button. To delete an option, select it and click the Remove button.

Using a Database Search Form

In the previous chapter, you learned how to use FrontPage 98 to create a simple Web page that returns a set of data to the user. In this chapter, I'll show you how to create a database search form that you can use with either the Internet Database Connector or with an Active Server Page containing the Database Region Wizard's WebBots.

The examples in this chapter use the Adventure Works sample database that's included with the Active Server Page installation application. If you haven't installed Active Server Pages for your Web server, or if you are running a server that does not support Active Server Pages, it's a simple task to convert the examples to another database.

Creating A Database Search Form

The first step in this process is to create the search form. This is an HTML page containing an HTML form. The form will be used to pass the information entered into its input elements to the IDC or Active Server Page that performs the database query.

You can place any of the form elements discussed in Chapter 22, "Working with Forms," as input elements on the form. You should give the elements a name that makes it easy to identify the field or query parameter to which the element corresponds. For example, if you have a text box for entering a last name, `lastname` would be a good name for this form element.

If a data field has a fixed list of possible values, you should use either a list box or option buttons when creating a search or update page that includes this field. This ensures that the user will not enter an invalid value into the search or update page.

For this example, you'll create a page used to enter search criteria for the Adventure Works Products table. This table's structure is shown in Table 43.1.

Table 43.1. The Adventure Works Products table.

Field	*Data Type*	*Size*
`ProductID`	AutoNumber	Long Integer
`ProductCode`	Text	10
`ProductType`	Text	20
`ProductIntroductionDate`	Date/Time	
`ProductName`	Text	50
`ProductDescription`	Text	255
`ProductSize`	Text	5
`ProductImageURL`	Text	255

Field	Data Type	Size
`UnitPrice`	Number	Double (currency)
`OnSale`	Yes/No	

You'll create a form that allows the user to select a product type to look up in the database. You'll use a drop-down list box (known in FrontPage 98 as a drop-down menu) that contains all of the available product types. Initially, you'll set the form's properties to work with an IDC page (which you'll create in the next section), but later you'll edit this form so that it will work with an Active Server Page created using the Database Region Wizard.

To create a search form for this table, follow these instructions:

1. Open FrontPage Explorer and click the New Page button. Give the new page an appropriate name, such as `search.htm`.
2. Double-click the name to open the page with the FrontPage Editor.
3. Enter whatever content you want at the header of the page. When you're ready to begin the actual search criteria entry portion of the form, use the Insert|Form Field|Drop-Down Menu menu item to insert a drop-down menu.
4. Double-click the drop-down list box to open the Drop-Down Menu Properties dialog. Change the Name property to `ProductType` to match the name of the field we'll be using in the SQL query.
5. Enter the following items into the Choice list by clicking the Add button for each one. For the values with spaces in them, click the Specify Value check box on the Add Choice dialog and remove the spaces from the value. Do not set any of the items as Selected.

Choice	Value
Backpack	`Backpack`
Boot	`Boot`
Carabiner	`Carabiner`
Crampon	`Crampon`
Harness	`Harness`
Pants	`Pants`
Parka	`Parka`
Rock Shoes	`RockShoes`
Shirt	`Shirt`
Sleeping Bag	`SleepingBag`
Supplies	`Supplies`
Tent	`Tent`

6. Enter a caption to the left of the Drop-Down Menu and some white space between the Drop-Down Menu and the Submit and Clear buttons. Your form should now appear similar to Figure 43.4.

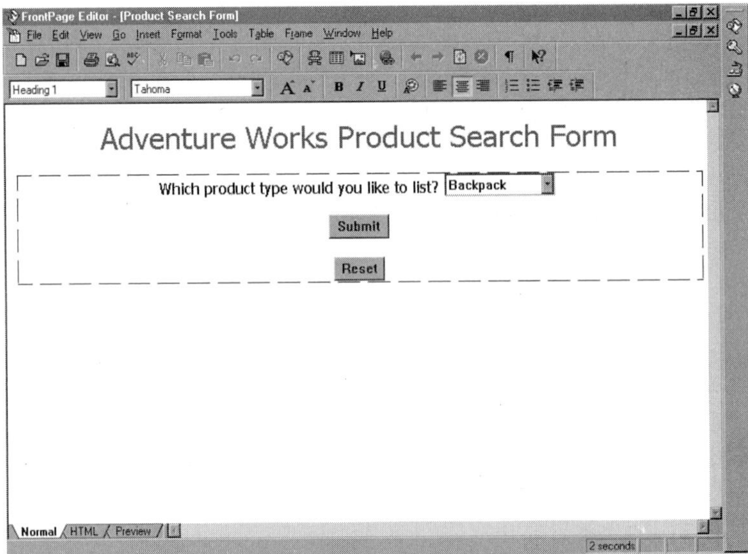

FIGURE 43.4.
The sample search form.

7. Now you'll change the properties of the form to point to an IDC page. Right-click anywhere within the dotted lines that make up the border of the form. Select Form Properties from the shortcut menu, and the Form Properties dialog box shown in Figure 43.5 appears.

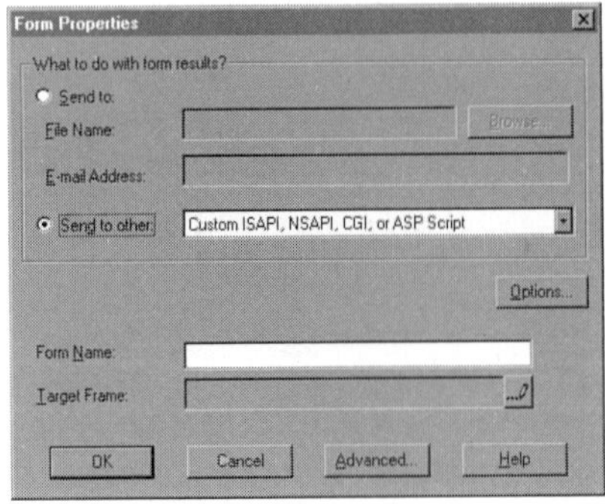

FIGURE 43.5.
The Form Properties dialog box.

8. Click the Send to other option button. Leave the default item in the drop-down list as is (Custom ISAPI, NSAPI, CGI, or ASP Script) and click the Options button.

9. On the Options for Custom Form Handler dialog, type `products.idc` in the Action text box. Set the Method list box to `POST`. Leave the Encoding Type text box empty. Click OK.
10. Click OK on the Form Properties dialog to close the dialog. Save the page.
11. Switch to the Preview tab to view the page. For this page, the preview is very similar to the design view.

Now that you have a simple search page, it's time to create the pages that will do the actual database searching for you. Both of the following sections assume that you have an ODBC data source named `AdvWorks` and that this data source points to the Adventure Works database (named `advworks.mdb`) or at least to a database with a Products table structured as shown in Table 43.1.

Searching with the Internet Database Connector

As you learned in the previous chapter, the Internet Database Connector relies on two files to do its work: a template file and a query definition file. The template file defines how the output page will look and which fields it contains. The query definition file specifies the ODBC data source to use, the SQL query to execute, and the parameters to use in the query.

First you'll create the template file. Follow these steps:

1. If you still have the FrontPage Editor open, click the New toolbar button. If you've closed the editor, click the New Page button in the FrontPage Explorer. Rename the file to `PRODUCTS.HTX`.
2. On the first line of the page, type `Product Type:` and a space character. Use the Edit|Database|IDC Parameter Value menu item. On the IDC Parameter Value dialog, type `ProductType`. This will cause the data entered in the search form's Product Type drop-down menu to be output at this spot in the page. Press the Enter key to create a new paragraph.
3. Select Edit|Database|Detail Section to insert an IDC detail section. Position the cursor between the start and end marks of the detail section.
4. Create a three row by two column table within the detail section. Edit the table properties (right-click with the pointer over the table and select Table Properties from the shortcut menu) to give it a border and pad and space the cells. I used values of five for the Cell Padding and three for the Cell Spacing. Set the first column to be right-justified.
5. In the first column, enter `Product Name:` on the first row, `Product Code:` on the second row, and `Description:` on the third row.
6. Move the cursor to the second column of the first row. Select Edit|Database|Database Column Value. Enter `ProductName` in the Database Column Value dialog. Move to the second row and repeat this process, entering `ProductCode`. For the third row, enter `ProductDescription`.

7. Your template file should now appear similar to Figure 43.6. Save it, giving it the name `PRODUCTS.HTX` (if you started Step 1 with the editor already open).

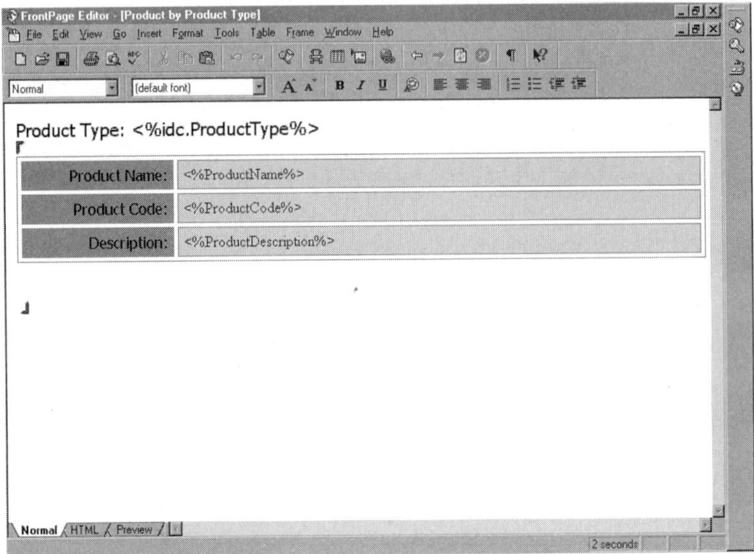

FIGURE 43.6.
The `PRODUCTS.HTX` *template file.*

The next step is to create the IDC file. Follow these steps:

1. Return to the FrontPage Explorer and create a new page named `PRODUCTS.IDC`.
2. Double-click the filename to run the Internet Database Connector Wizard. See the previous chapter for the complete details on this wizard.
3. In the ODBC data source box, enter `AdvWorks` (or the name of your data source if you're not using the Adventure Works sample).
4. In the Query results template box, enter `PRODUCT.HTX`. Click Next.
5. In the SQL Query text box, enter `select * from products where ProductType = '%ProductType%'`. The `%ProductType%` is the parameter that the IDC will receive from the search form. So, if the user selects `Supplies` in the drop-down menu on the search form, the query that gets executed will be `select * from products where ProductType = 'Supplies'`. Click Next.
6. What will happen if no data is entered into the form? Although this is very unlikely with the search form you've designed, it is possible to request the IDC page from a Web browser using just the URL to the page. Therefore the IDC should have some default values to work with. This dialog is where they are entered. Click the Add button and enter `ProductType` for the parameter name and `backpack` for the value. Click OK. Click Finish to save the IDC page.

That's all there is to it. Now test the IDC page. Load the search form you created earlier into the FrontPage Editor. Switch to the Preview tab. Select a product type in the drop-down menu and click the Submit button. The IDC page will execute the query and return the results to the Preview tab. You should see something similar to Figure 43.7.

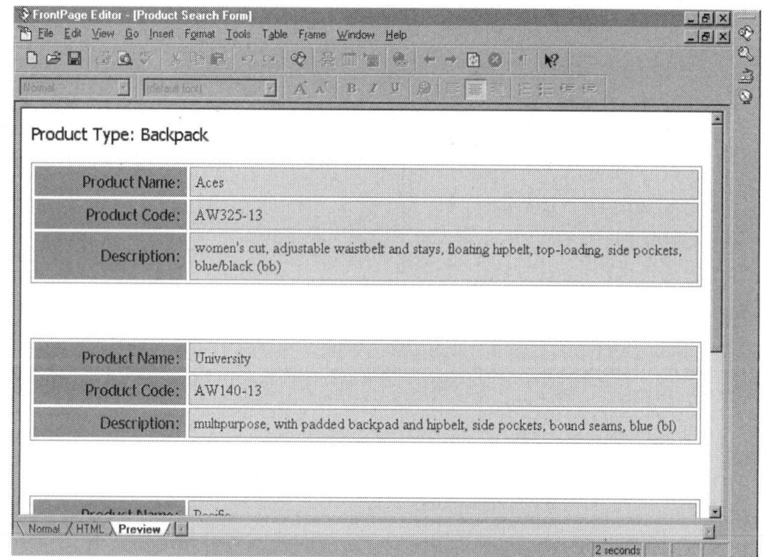

FIGURE 43.7.
The output of the IDC search.

Searching with Active Server Pages

This section shows how easy it is to take the search form and use it with an Active Server Page. You'll use the Database Region Wizard as well as a small amount of server-side VBScript to create a results page very similar to the IDC results page (`PRODUCTS.HTX`).

Create a new page in the FrontPage Editor. If you start from the Explorer, name the page `PRODUCTS.ASP`.

On the first line of the file enter `Product Type:` and a space. Use the Insert|Advanced|Script menu. The Script dialog appears. Check the Run Script on Server check box. Enter `= request("producttype")` in the Script text box. Click the OK button.

Press the Enter key a couple of times to leave some space between this line and the Database Region you're about to create. To create the region, follow these steps:

1. Use the Insert|Database|Database Region Wizard menu item.
2. Enter `AdvWorks` or the name of your data source into the first dialog. Click Next.

3. In the SQL text box, enter `select * from products where ProductType = '` and click the Insert Form Field Parameter button. Type `ProductType` in the Insert Form Field Parameter dialog and click OK. Enter a single quote at the end of the line. The query should now read as `select * from products where ProductType = '%%ProductType%%'`. Click Next.
4. On the dialog that appears, click the Add button for each of these fields: `ProductDescription`, `ProductCode`, `ProductName`, in that order.
5. Click Finish to return to the FrontPage Editor. Right-click over the fields that were added to the page and choose FrontPage Component Properties to verify that the fields appear, from left to right, as `ProductName`, `ProductCode`, and `ProductDescription`.
6. Right-click again and select Table Properties. Give the table some fancy effects, such as a border. Click OK.
7. Move to the HTML tab. Scroll to the top of the page and locate the lines that read

```
<table width="443" border="1">
  <!--webbot bot="DatabaseRegionStart" startspan
```

8. Place the pointer at the end of the `<TABLE>` element. Enter the following HTML:

```
<tr>
    <th width="74">Name</th>
    <th width="98">Code</th>
    <th width="259">Description</th>
</tr>
```

9. Save the page. Give it the name `PRODUCTS.ASP`. It should appear similar to Figure 43.8.

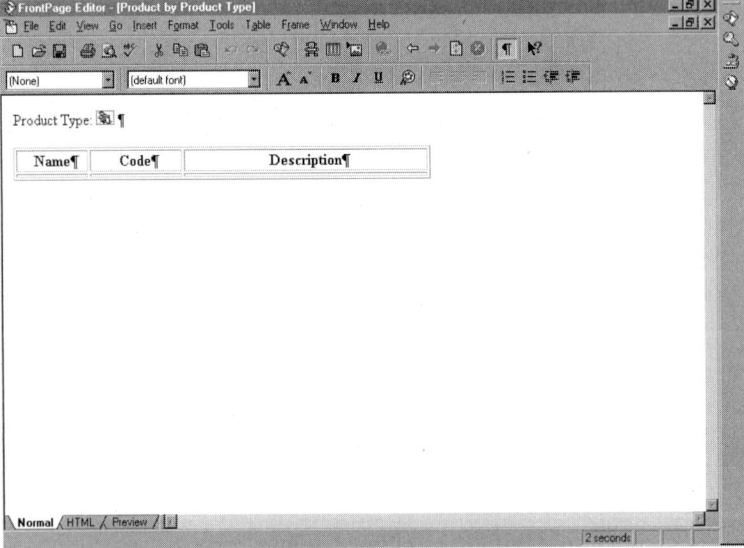

FIGURE 43.8.
The product search results Active Server Page.

Now it's time to edit the search form. You'll need to point the form to the PRODUCTS.ASP page you just created. Open the search form in the FrontPage Editor. Right-click over the form area and select Form Properties. Click the Options button and replace the text in the Action box with the name of the Active Server Page you just created (PRODUCTS.ASP). Click OK to close the options dialog. Click OK to close the Form Properties dialog. Save the form and move to the Preview tab.

Select a product type in the drop-down menu and click the Submit button. If all is well with your server, you'll see the results as shown in Figure 43.9.

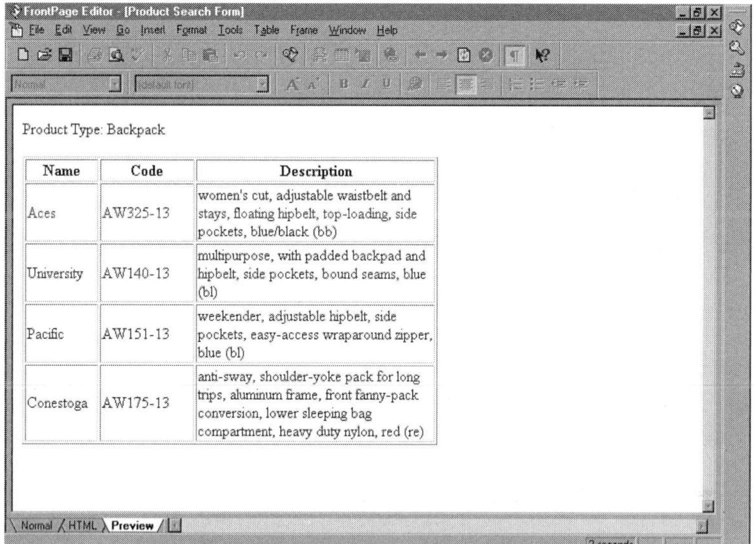

FIGURE 43.9.
The product search results in action.

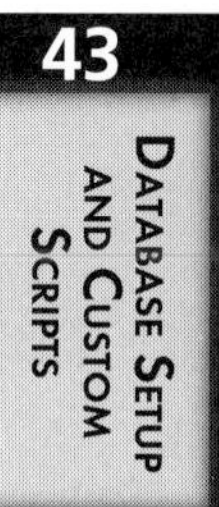

Introducing the ActiveX Data Objects

In the flurry of development tools and Web server tools that Microsoft introduced in 1996 and 1997 came the introduction of a new database technology called OLE DB. OLE DB is a set of OLE interfaces that provide a consistent means of access to many different types of data sources. OLE DB is similar to (and rides on top of) the Open Database Connectivity (ODBC) platform in that it is intended to provide a common means of accessing a variety of diverse data service providers.

The ActiveX Data Objects are provided with the Active Server Page installation and are optimized for use with OLE DB. The ActiveX Data Objects provide several key advantages to the Active Server developer:

- Objects can be created independently of one another. The flat object model does not require you to create and maintain an entire hierarchy of objects.
- Support for batch updates.

- Support for stored procedures, including those that return multiple result sets.
- Support for many different cursor types, including some server-side cursors.
- Free-threaded objects, which are more efficient for use in Web server applications.

NOTE

All of the script code samples provided in the remainder of this chapter should be entered into your pages either using the Editor's HTML tab and enclosing the scripting portions in `<% ... %>` or using the Script Wizard with Run at Server checked.

The ADO Object Model

As mentioned earlier, the ActiveX Data Objects utilize a flat object model. You do not have to create objects that are the children of other objects. Instead, you can create independent objects and then associate them using properties such as `ActiveConnection`, which relates a `Recordset` object with a `Connection` object. Another advantage to the ADO model is that it provides you with the full capabilities exposed by the underlying data provider, but also provides quick methods of performing command operations.

Figure 43.10 shows a diagram of the ADO object model. If you're familiar with the Data Access Objects or the Remote Data Objects included with Microsoft Visual Basic, you'll immediately appreciate the simplicity of the ADO model.

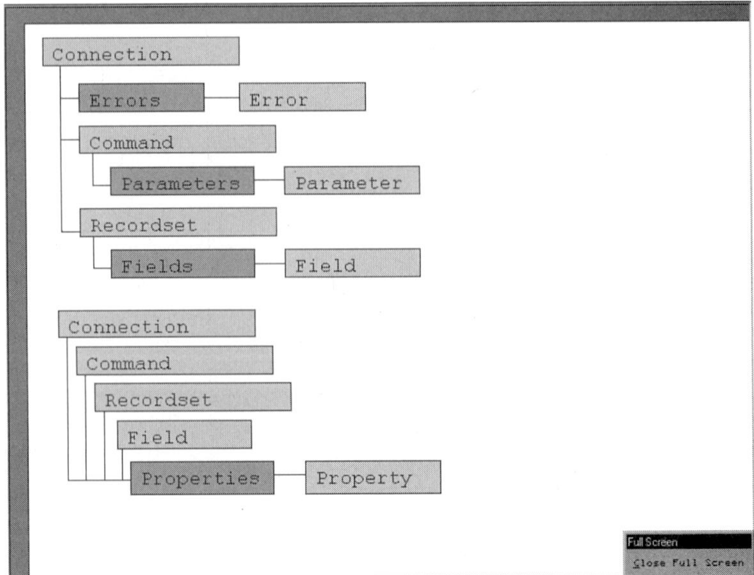

FIGURE 43.10.
The ADO object model.

Although the object hierarchy is flat, Figure 43.10 seems to imply that the `Command` and `Recordset` objects are children of the `Connection` object. This is not the case, however. What Figure 43.10 illustrates is that the `Command` and `Recordset` objects cannot do their work without a corresponding open `Connection` object. If a `Command` or `Recordset` is created independent of an active connection, however, the ADO engine will create a `Connection` object but won't assign that object to an object variable.

NOTE

If you will be creating multiple `Recordset` and/or `Command` objects that will access the same `Connection` object, you should explicitly create a `Connection` object. You will then use this `Connection` object as the source for creating the `Recordset` and/or `Command` objects.

Another aspect of the simplicity of the ADO model is that it contains only a few objects. This set of objects, though, can be used to completely model any imaginable data source. The fact that there are fewer objects in the collection makes it easier to code your Active Server pages—you can get the same work done while having to learn and remember the usage and syntax of fewer objects.

ADO Collections

The remainder of this section will introduce you to the various objects within the ADO model. Although this can't be considered an exhaustive study of the ADO objects and collections, it will provide you with a base upon which to utilize the ADO within your Active Server pages.

All of the ADO collections contain the `Item` and `Count` properties found in most OLE object collections. The `Item` property references a specific member of the collection. The `Count` property evaluates to the number of member objects currently defined on the collection. To reference a specific member of a collection, you can use any of the following:

- `object.collection.Item(0)`
- `object.collection.Item("name")`
- `object.collection.(0)`
- `object.collection.("name")`

Additionally, a few of the collections provide other means of accessing their member objects. The sections that follow explain these in detail. Each of the collections has its own set of methods, depending upon the nature of the collection. These are explained individually in the following sections as well.

The `Connection` Object

The `Connection` object provides an open connection to an OLE DB data source. An explicit `Connection` object is not required for the ADO to function. However, if an explicit `Connection` object is not created, an implicit one will be created by the ADO whenever a recordset is opened or a `Command` object is executed. Figure 43.11 shows the hierarchy of the `Connection` object.

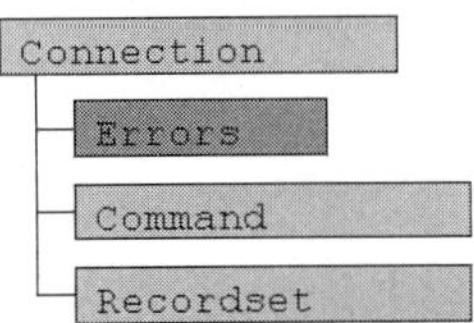

FIGURE 43.11.
The ADO `Connection` *object.*

Each open `Connection` object represents a connection to the underlying data source. You can establish and break the physical connection using, respectively, the `Open` and `Close` methods. These methods are discussed in the upcoming section "Using the ActiveX Data Objects."

The type of physical connection used to access the data depends, of course, upon what the data source is and where it is located relative to the machine on which the ADO `Connection` object is instantiated. The connection may be attaching to a local Microsoft Access database or to a remote server database residing on a SQL Server machine on the other side of the continent.

The Execute Method

In addition to the `Open` and `Close` methods, the `Connection` object also has an `Execute` method. This method allows you to run a query against the underlying data source. The query can either return results into a `Recordset` object or it can perform some action upon the underlying data. The syntax for the `Execute` method takes either of the following forms:

```
Set recordset = connection.Execute(CommandText, [RecordsAffected], [Options])
```

or

```
connection.Execute CommandText, [RecordsAffected], [Options]
```

The `CommandText` parameter is a string representing the query, table name, or stored procedure to be executed. The format of this string is specific to the underlying OLE DB data source. The `RecordsAffected` optional parameter provides a means for the data source to return the number of records that were affected by the operation. The data type for this variable is `Long`. Finally, the `Options` parameter provides a means of instructing the data source how it should interpret the contents of the `CommandText` parameter. The available choices are

- `adCmdText` (1): The `CommandText` parameter contains a textual command.
- `adCmdTable` (2): The `CommandText` parameter contains a table name.
- `adCmdStoredProc` (4): `CommandText` contains a call to a stored procedure.
- `adCmdUnknown` (8): (Default) The type of the command is not known.

Connection Object Properties

The `Connection` object has several useful properties. However, you'll probably find that in practice you'll use them infrequently. This is due to the fact that the most useful property,

ConnectionString, is set when you use the object's Open method. This section outlines some of the more useful properties.

The ConnectionString property contains the information necessary to actually open a connection to the underlying data source. This information includes user name and password for access control, the data source name if ODBC is being used, a provider-specific filename used to identify the exact source of the data, and the name of the OLE DB provider. Not all of this information is required for every OLE DB provider, however.

The ConnectionTimeout property indicates how long the ADO engine should wait while attempting to establish a connection. Should this time period expire without a successful connection, an error will be generated. This time is specified in seconds, and the default value is 15.

The CommandTimeout property is similar to the ConnectionTimeout property. It specifies the length of time to wait for a command to complete before generating an error. This property also specifies seconds and the default value is 30.

The Mode property is a read/write property that specifies what kinds of modifications can be made to the underlying data in a connection. This property must be set only when the connection is closed.

Transaction Management

The Connection object also provides methods that allow you to use transaction-based processing on the data source. These methods are BeginTrans, CommitTrans, and RollbackTrans.

Transactions are used to group commands together. If any one of the commands fails, the entire group of commands can be rolled back and their effects undone. Likewise, if all commands succeed, the entire group can be committed to the data source at one time. If no transaction processing is used, the OLE DB provider will commit the operations to the data source as soon as they are performed.

The BeginTrans method starts a new transaction. From the point that BeginTrans is executed, all operations against the data source are wrapped together in the transaction. The CommitTrans method instructs the OLE DB provider to actually commit the transactions to the data source and to end the current transaction. On the opposite side, RollbackTrans informs the provider that the transaction should be canceled. All operations that took place since the BeginTrans method was invoked will be wiped out.

The Recordset Object

The Recordset object is used to view and manipulate the data in an underlying data source. The recordset's data can be derived from a base table or from an executed query. Using a recordset, you can perform a variety of operations on the data, including updating, deleting, and inserting records, providing the data source and the query executed permit such functions. This section won't provide an exhaustive reference to the Recordset object, but it will get you started in using it effectively.

As you can see in Figure 43.12, the `Recordset` object requires a `Connection` object in order to function. You can, of course, create a `Recordset` independent of a Connection, but in doing so the ADO engine will create an implicit `Connection` object. This `Connection` object just won't be assigned to an object variable.

FIGURE 43.12.
The `Recordset` *object.*

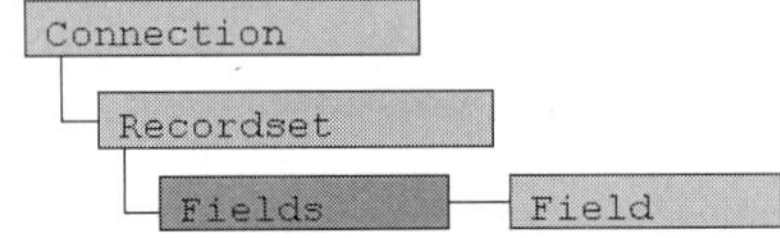

The Fields Collection

Each `Recordset` object has a Fields collection that contains a `Field` object for each column in the underlying data. Using the Field object's `Value` property, you can set or return the data in the current record for the specified column. Use any of the following to retrieve the `Value` for a specific Field:

- `recordset.Fields.Item(0)`
- `recordset.Fields.Item("name")`
- `recordset.Fields(0)`
- `recordset.Fields("name")`
- `recordset(0)`
- `recordset("name")`
- `recordset![name]`

In addition to the `Value` property, the Field object also sports a number of other useful properties. These include the `Type`, `Precision`, and `NumericScale` properties, which provide you with some basic attributes about each Field. There are also properties for `DefinedSize` and `ActualSize`, which return the declared size of a field and the size of the data stored in the field for the current record, respectively.

Navigating the `Recordset` Data

The ADO model provides several methods to navigate the data in a `Recordset` object. These consist mainly of `MoveFirst`, `MoveNext`, `MovePrevious`, and `MoveLast`. There are also two properties, `AbsolutePosition` and `AbsolutePage`, which can be used to move to different records in the recordset.

The `MoveFirst` method moves to the first record in the recordset. `MoveNext` moves the record pointer to the record following the current record. `MovePrevious` moves the record pointer to the record preceding the current record. `MoveLast` moves the record pointer to the last record in the recordset. There is also a `Move` method, which allows you to move a specified number of records, either relative to the current record or relative to a record bookmark specified by the method's optional second parameter.

The AbsolutePosition property sets the current record pointer to a specified record number within the recordset. Normally you would not discuss absolute positioning with a database management system such as SQL Server because the concept of a numeric record pointer is nonexistent. This is especially true of dynamic recordsets whose membership can be changed based upon the actions of other users of the database. However, the AbsolutePosition property allows you to specify that for the current sort order on the current recordset, move to record number *x*. This is a 1-based property, meaning that to move to the first record in the recordset, you would use

```
Recordset.AbsolutePosition = 1
```

The upper limit to the AbsolutePosition property is the value of the recordset's RecordCount property.

Using the ADO's paging feature, you can divide a recordset into pages each containing the same number of records. The number of records contained in a page is controlled by the PageSize property. Using the AbsolutePage property, you can specify which page, from 1 to PageCount, to set as the current page. The first record on that page then becomes the current record.

While navigating a recordset, you can check the BOF and EOF Boolean properties to determine if you've reached the beginning or end, respectively, of the recordset. When the record pointer is positioned at the first record and you execute the MovePrevious method, the current record will become invalid and the BOF property will be set to True. Likewise, if the record pointer is positioned at the last record in the recordset and you execute MoveNext, the record pointer becomes invalid and the EOF property is set to True.

Miscellaneous Recordset Methods and Properties

The Recordset object has far too many properties to explain all of them in the context of this chapter. However, this section introduces you to some of the more important of these properties.

First, the CursorType property determines what type of cursor is created for the Recordset object. The property is read/write when the recordset is closed and read-only after the recordset is opened. You can specify a value for this property using the property itself or by setting the CursorType parameter when you invoke the recordset's Open method. The possible values for CursorType are

- adOpenForwardOnly (0)—a forward-only cursor. It's similar to a static cursor, but allows you to move through the recordset in the forward direction only. This type of cursor is ideal when you need to make a single pass through the records in the recordset. This is the default value for the CursorType property.
- adOpenKeyset (2)—a keyset cursor. It's similar to a dynamic cursor except that records added by other users are not visible to the recordset. Data changes to records in the recordset are visible, however, and records deleted by other users become inaccessible to the recordset.

- `adOpenDynamic` (3)—a dynamic cursor. Any modifications, additions, or deletions made by other users are visible in the recordset. Also, every form of record navigation is available. Bookmarks are available only if the OLE DB provider supports them.
- `adOpenStatic` (4)—a static cursor. It produces a static copy of the recordset. No additions, deletions, or modifications are visible to the recordset.

To determine which operations an opened recordset object will allow, you can invoke the `Supports` method. This method's syntax is

```
SET boolean = recordset.Supports(CursorOptions)
```

where *`CursorOptions`* is any of the constants specified by `CursorOptionEnum`. The method returns `True` if the specified cursor option is valid for the recordset.

The possible *`CursorOptions`* values are

- `adAddNew` (16778240)—The `AddNew` method is available.
- `adApproxPosition` (16384)—The `AbsoluteRecord` and `AbsolutePage` properties are available.
- `adBookmark` (8192)—The `Bookmark` property can be used to access specific records.
- `adDelete` (16779264)—The `Delete` method is available.
- `adHoldRecords` (256)—You can retrieve more records without committing all pending changes and releasing all currently held records.
- `adMovePrevious` (512)—You can use the `MovePrevious` or `Move` methods to move backwards in a recordset.
- `adResync` (131072)—You can update the recordset's data with the data currently available in the database.
- `adUpdate` (16809984)—You can invoke the `Update` method to commit record changes to the database.
- `adUpdateBatch` (65536)—You can use batch updating to commit changes to the database in groups.

The `ActiveConnection` property allows you to create a recordset independent of a `Connection` object. You can create one `Recordset` object that will be used with multiple `Connection` objects, for example. To assign the `Recordset` to a `Connection`, set the `ActiveConnection` property to a reference to the `Connection` object. The syntax is

```
Set recordset.ActiveConnection = connection
```

This property is read/write when the recordset is closed. It is read-only after the recordset has been opened or the `Source` property has been set to a valid `Command` object.

The `Source` property is where the source for the data is set. You can set this property to a `Command` object, a SQL statement, a table name, or a stored procedure name. Like most recordset properties, `Source` is read/write when the recordset is closed and read-only when the recordset is opened. If you set the value to a valid `Command` object, the recordset inherits the `ActiveConnection` property from the `Command` object. Viewing the `Source` property in this case does not return the name of the `Command` object, but rather the `Command` object's `CommandText` property.

The Command Object

The final ActiveX Database Object discussed in this chapter is the `Command` object. A `Command` object is created to hold a command you want to execute against a data source. They are typically used with parameterized queries or stored procedures thanks to the availability of the Parameters collection discussed in the section "The Parameters Collection."

You can create a command object that returns results to a `Recordset` object, performs a batch process on the data, or makes changes to the database structure. Like a `Recordset`, `Command` objects can be created independent of a `Connection` object. Like the `Connection` object, the `CommandText` property can be a SQL statement, a table name, or a stored procedure.

Properties and Methods of the Command Object

The `Command` object has only a few properties and methods, which this section introduces.

The `CommandText` property holds the text of the command to be executed. The `CommandType` property indicates what this text is. As mentioned with the `Connection` object, the `CommandType` property can take one of four values:

- `adCmdText` (1): The `CommandText` parameter contains a textual command.
- `adCmdTable` (2): The `CommandText` parameter contains a table name.
- `adCmdStoredProc` (4): `CommandText` contains a call to a stored procedure.
- `adCmdUnknown` (8): (Default) The type of the command is not known.

The `ActiveConnection` property is identical to the `Recordset` object's `ActiveConnection` property. Setting it to a valid `Connection` object will associate the `Command` object with that `Connection` object.

The `CommandTimeout` property behaves identically to the `Connection` object's `CommandTimeout` property—it specifies the amount of time the ADO engine will give a command to complete its execution.

Finally, the `Prepared` property specifies whether or not the provider should prepare (compile) the command before executing it. If this is set to `False`, the provider should execute the command directly, without compiling it. If this property is set to `True`, having a compiled version of the command will allow subsequent executions of that command to operate faster (though the *first* execution may be a little slower due to the time it takes to compile the command).

There are only two methods for the `Command` object: `CreateParameter` and `Execute`. The `Execute` method executes the SQL query or stored procedure specified by the `CommandText` property. If the query returns results, a `Recordset` object can be created to hold them. The syntax for the `Execute` method is either

```
Set recordset = command.Execute(RecordsAffected, Parameters, Options)
```

or

```
command.Execute RecordsAffected, Parameters, Options
```

where `RecordsAffected` is an optional variable to hold a count of the number of records affected by the `Command` object, *`Parameters`* is an optional Variant array of parameter values, and *`Options`* is an optional parameter used to specify the `CommandType` property for the `Command` object.

The `CreateParameter` method is used to create a new `Parameter` object, as discussed in the next section.

The Parameters Collection

The Parameters collection is used to specify any parameters that may be required during the execution of a `Command` object. The Parameters collection is made up of Parameter objects. The necessary Parameter objects are defined by the query or stored procedure being executed.

The Parameters collection has the standard properties and methods: `Count` and `Item` properties and `Append`, `Delete`, and `Refresh` methods. The `Append` method is used to add a Parameter created with the `Command` object's `CreateParameter` method to the Parameters collection. The syntax for the `CreateParameter` method is

```
Set parameter = command.CreateParameter(Name, Type, Direction, Size, Value)
```

The Parameter object has properties that correspond to the parameters for the `CreateParameter` method. They describe the Parameter and its usage in the current `Command` object. These properties include `Name`, `Type`, `Value`, `Direction`, and `Size`. To define a parameter for a `Command` object, use the following code

```
Set myCommand = Server.CreateObject("ADODB.Command")
Set myParameter = myCommand.CreateParameter("Param1", adVarChar, adParamInput, 50,
➥"Parameter Value")
MyCommand.Parameters.Append myParameter
```

Using the ActiveX Data Objects

Now that you've been introduced to the ActiveX Data Objects, it's time to put them to use. This section provides some brief examples of opening an ADO `Connection` object and creating an ADO recordset.

Opening an ADO Connection

A simple example illustrating how to open an ADO `Connection` object is provided in Listing 43.1. Figure 43.13 shows the results of this page. This example uses the AdvWorks data source, which you used earlier in this chapter.

Listing 43.1. An ADO Connection example.

```
<%@ LANGUAGE="VBSCRIPT" %>

<HTML><HEAD><TITLE>Connection Properties</TITLE></HEAD>
<BODY>
<%
set conn = Server.CreateObject("ADODB.Connection")
conn.open "DSN=AdvWorks;", "", ""
%>
<font face="Comic Sans MS">
<CENTER>
<H2>Connection Properties</H2>
<table border=1>
<tr><td align=right>Provider:</td><td><%=conn.Provider %></td></tr>
<tr><td align=right>Connection Timeout:</td><td> <%=conn.ConnectionTimeout %>
➥</td></tr>
<tr><td align=right>Command Timeout:</td><td> <%=conn.CommandTimeout %></td></tr>
<tr><td align=right>Isolation Level:</td><td> <%=conn.IsolationLevel %></td></tr>
<tr><td align=right>Mode:</td><td> <%=conn.Mode %></td></tr>
</table></CENTER></font>
<% conn.close %>
</BODY></HTML>
```


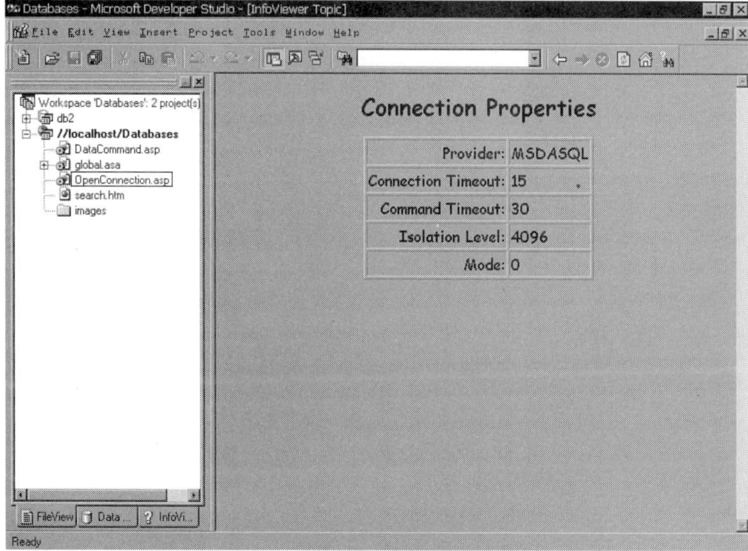

FIGURE 43.13.
The ADO Connection sample Web page.

The easiest way to create the page shown in Figure 43.13 is on the Normal tab. Create a 5-row by 2-column table, give it a `BORDER` of 1, and leave some white space above it. Move the pointer above the table and, using the Script Wizard, enter the script code that opens the connection. In the right-hand column of the table, use the Script Wizard to enter the script code that appears between the `<%` and `%>` markers. This includes entering the equal sign. Finally, below the table enter the script code that closes the connection. Remember, when using the Script Wizard, you do not have to enter the `<%` and `%>` markers.

The script code begins by creating an object to hold the `Connection` object, `conn`. The `Open` method is then invoked, providing an ODBC data source name, a user name, and a password. Following this is the HTML to create a table where you'll output some of the properties of the newly opened `Connection` object. The properties being displayed are `Provider`, `ConnectionTimeout`, `CommandTimeout`, `IsolationLevel`, and `Mode`. The connection is then closed.

Creating an ADO Recordset

Now take a look at returning some results with a recordset. Doing so is not much more difficult than the previous example. Listing 43.2 presents the code. Figure 43.14 shows an example of the resulting Web page. This example parallels the Database Region Wizard example from earlier in this chapter.

Listing 43.2. The Recordset example code.

```
<%@ LANGUAGE="VBSCRIPT" %>

<HTML><HEAD><TITLE>Registered Guests</TITLE></HEAD><BODY>
<%
set conn = Server.CreateObject("ADODB.Connection")
set rs = Server.CreateObject("ADODB.Recordset")
set cmd = Server.CreateObject("ADODB.Command")
conn.open "DSN=AdvWorks;", "", ""
cmd.CommandText = "SELECT ProductName, ProductCode, ProductDescription FROM
➥Products"
cmd.CommandType = 1
Set cmd.ActiveConnection = conn
rs.Open cmd, , 1, 1
%>
<font face="Comic Sans MS">
<CENTER>
<H2>Registered Guests</H2>
<table border=1>
<tr><th>Product Name</th><th>Code</th><th>Description</th></tr>
<%while not rs.eof %>
<tr><td><%=rs("ProductName")%></td>
    <td><%=rs("ProductCode")%></td>
    <td><%=rs("ProductDescription")%></td>
</tr>
<%
    rs.MoveNext
wend
%>
```

```
</table>
<%
rs.close
conn.close
%>
</BODY></HTML>
```

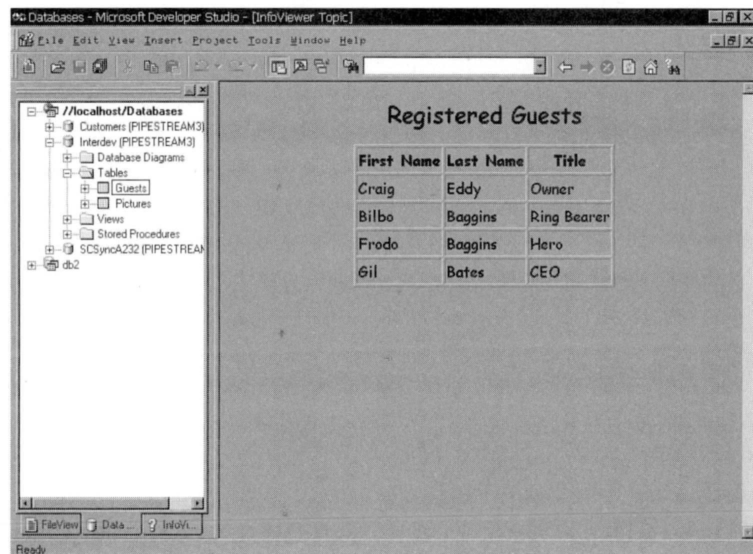

FIGURE 43.14.
The output page from the Recordset example.

This example starts out similarly to Listing 43.1. The first task is to create several objects to use in the page. A `Connection`, a `Command`, and a `Recordset` object are created. The `Connection` object is then opened as in the previous example.

Next, some of the `Command` object's properties are set to define the query that you're going to execute. The SQL statement being used to return results is placed in the `CommandText` property, and the `CommandType` property is set to indicate that `CommandText` contains a SQL string. Finally, the `Command` object's `ActiveConnection` property is set to the connection opened earlier.

Next, the recordset is opened using the `Open` method. Here the `Command` object is specified as the Source parameter, an Active Connection parameter is not necessary (recall that the recordset will inherit the command's `ActiveConnection` value), the Cursor Type is set to 1 (a keyset cursor), and the Lock Type is also set to 1 (a read-only recordset is produced).

Now that the recordset is opened, the code can start to navigate the recordset's returned rows. The page is going to display the results in a table, so first the HTML defining the table's header row is output. Then the code uses a `While` loop to step through each record in the recordset. Each field returned by the query is placed into a different column of the table. After all columns have been output to the HTML, the recordset's `MoveNext` method is invoked to move the current record to the next record in the recordset. When the loop reaches the end of the recordset, signified by the `EOF` property becoming `True`, the table definition is ended. Finally, the code closes down the recordset and connection objects.

One possible extension you may want to make to the code in Listing 43.2 is to add a check on the possibility that the query returns no results. Instead of outputting a table with only a header row, you should output a message to the effect that there are no results for the current query.

Summary

This chapter begins by explaining the advanced options available for the Internet Database Connector. These options provide fine-tooth control over the operation of the IDC. Next, the chapter shows how to create some more advanced database pages using both the Internet Database Connector and Database Region Wizard in conjunction with Active Server Scripting. The next section provides a more detailed explanation of the ActiveX Data Objects, the essential ingredient to database connectivity using Active Server Pages. The last section gives a few examples of how to use the ActiveX Data Objects to produce the same results as the Database Region Wizard.

In Chapter 44, "Working with SQL and Database Management Systems," you'll learn how to deal with the back-end database systems. In Chapter 45, "Moving Up to Visual InterDev," you'll learn about the next step in Active Server development environments, Visual InterDev.

CHAPTER 44

Working with SQL and Database Management Systems

by Armando Flores

IN THIS CHAPTER

- The Reader's Club Case Study *740*
- Creating the Reader's Club Web Site *741*
- Using Microsoft Access 97 to Create the Database *742*
- Generating Web Files with Microsoft Access 97 *749*
- Adding Database Functionality to the Reader's Club Site *752*
- Migrating to SQL Server *760*

In this chapter, you will use the database connectivity concepts covered earlier by creating a simple Web site that uses a database from the bottom up. You will start with a Microsoft Access 97 database and walk through the steps needed to migrate it to Microsoft SQL Server.

You will learn how to design a database, how to generate Internet Database Connector (IDC) files, and how to add them to a Web site. You will then add new functionality to your site by using IDC statements and the Database Region Wizard described in Chapter 43, "Advanced Database Setup and Custom Scripts." Finally, you will review the steps involved when migrating your application to Microsoft SQL Server.

You should have Microsoft Access 97 installed in your system. You also should have a Web server that supports the Internet Database Connector such as Microsoft Personal Web Server or Microsoft Internet Information Server (IIS) version 2 or higher. Personal Web Server is covered in detail in Chapters 49, "Using the Personal Web Server" and 50, "Personal Web Server Administration."

The Reader's Club Case Study

Suppose that your local public school has requested your services to create a Web site to be used by grade school students to enter simple book reports. You get to apply your FrontPage 98 and database skills, and the kids get to use the Web as part of their homework assignments.

This Web site should allow teachers to add books and enroll students to the Reader's Club. The students should be able to view the catalog alphabetically by title or by using any of the following categories: Adventure, Mystery, Humor, Sci-Fi, or Fantasy.

Assume that the school has enough copies of every book in the library to allow students to review as many books as they want and to allow as many students as necessary to review any given book. The books will be rated using one of three possible values: "So-so," "Ok," and "Good." Students can review any book only once.

Finally, the Web site should show how many times each book has been read and which books are the "most liked" books based on the sum of "Ok" and "Good" ratings.

This case study is by no means a complete system, but it should sufficiently illustrate how to use the database features of FrontPage 98. You can extend the functionality of this application as needed and enhance it with themes, navigation bars, and other features.

For now, you will take these steps to create the Reader's Club Web site:

1. Create an empty Web shell for the Reader's Club Web site.
2. Create the database and its corresponding ODBC datasource.
3. Generate a couple of database support files by using Microsoft Access 97.
4. Use FrontPage 98 to create additional database connectivity files as needed.

Creating the Reader's Club Web Site

Before you go any further, verify that the Web server you intend to use supports database connectivity. In the first part of this chapter, you will use the Internet Database Connector (IDC); later you will add a database query using the Database Region Wizard, which is based on Active Server Pages scripting.

Make sure that you review Chapter 42, "Web to Database Connectivity with FrontPage 98," to determine the right configuration for you.

Follow these steps to create the Reader's Club Web site:

1. Start the FrontPage Explorer. Next, select the Create a New FrontPage Web option in the Getting Started dialog box, and then click the OK button.

TIP

The display of the Getting started dialog box is controlled by the Show Getting Started dialog option of the General tab of the Tools | Options menu item.

2. In the New FrontPage Web dialog box, choose the Empty Web item under the From Wizard or Template: heading in step 1 of the dialog box. Then enter **`Reader's Club`** in the Choose a Title for Your FrontPage Web field in step 2. Finally, click the OK button.

To create a new folder for your database and IDC files, follow these steps:

1. Select the Navigation icon in the Views bar, (the vertical bar at the left of the FrontPage Explorer window).
2. Then choose File|New|Folder. In the resulting dialog box, type **`idcfiles`** as the name of the newly created folder.

   An alternative to using the menu option is to move the mouse cursor to the bottom section of the window under the `images` folder. Then right-click to open a context-sensitive menu. From this menu, choose the New Folder option. The resulting screen should look something like Figure 44.1.

A new feature of FrontPage 98 and extensions is the ability to designate whether the contents of a folder can be browsed, whether they can contain a script or programs to be run, or both. For this case, you should designate the newly created `idcfiles` folder only to allow scripts or programs to be run. To do so, right-click the `idcfiles` folder and choose the Properties option from the context-sensitive menu. Then, in the Properties dialog box, select the Allow scripts or programs to be run check box, remove the check from the Allow files to be browsed check box, and then click the OK button.

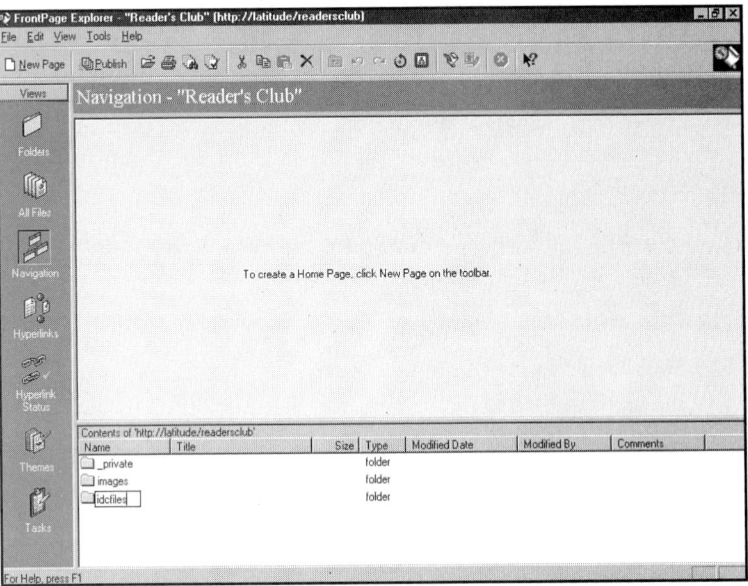

FIGURE 44.1.
Adding the `idcfiles` *folder to the Reader's Club Web site.*

TIP

For security purposes, keeping different types of files in separate folders is always a good idea so that you can determine what types of operations are allowed for a given folder. If you mix HTML and scripting/database files in the same directory, you run the risk of exposing passwords, database names, and other potentially sensitive information hard-coded in your scripts or database files.

Keep in mind that this rule applies not only to HTML and script files, but also to other file types. For example, if your site contains a file-based database such as Microsoft Access, and if the corresponding `*.mdb` file is stored in a directory that can be browsed, a curious user may be able to obtain a copy of the database without your authorization. The best way to address this problem is to put the database file in a directory that is not part of the web directory structure. A second alternative is to place the database in a directory that cannot be browsed, as in this case.

Using Microsoft Access 97 to Create the Database

Now that you have a basic structure for the Web site, you can turn your attention to the database. First, you will translate the requirements stated in the Reader's Club into a database design. Then you will create the database, define its ODBC datasource, and generate a few Internet Database Connectivity files using Microsoft Access 97.

Designing the Database

If you are familiar with the database design process, you might want to skip to the next section, "Creating the Data Tables." Otherwise, read on to look quickly at the process involved in designing a database.

The first step in the design is to identify the entities about which you want to record information. *Entities* are the items that should be represented in the database. After reviewing the system requirements for your Web site, you determine that you need to represent information about students, books, and reports.

Next, you need to determine the properties, or *attributes,* that should be recorded about each of the preceding entities. For now, the student entity will have only one attribute: the student's first name. The book entity will have three attributes: the book name, author's name, and book category.

As you try to define the characteristics of the report entity, you identify the review attribute ("So-so," "Ok," and "Good"). But how do you represent the requirements to have books reviewed by many students and students reviewing many books? In database design terms, this means that the report is not an entity but a *relationship,* in particular a *many-to-many relationship* between the book and student entities. Think about this point for a while: Can a report be created without the corresponding student and book information?

Let me add one final note about attributes. As you may recall, the category attribute of the book entity tells you if the book is an Adventure, Mystery, Humor, Sci-Fi, or Fantasy title. In this design, you will use a category code and a lookup table to represent this information.

Creating the Data Tables

Based on the analysis in the preceding section, the Reader's Club database will contain the four data tables shown in Table 44.1.

Table 44.1. Data tables in the Reader's Club database.

Table Name	*Contents*
`Students`	Student information (first name only in this case)
`Categories`	Lookup table for book categories
`Books`	Title, category, and author name for all books in the library
`Reports`	Book reviews entered by students

The detailed specifications for each table in the database are shown in Table 44.2. Field names followed by the *(pk)* suffix should be the primary keys of the table.

Table 44.2. Specifications for the Reader's Club database.

Table Name	*Field Name*	*Data Type*	*Field Size*
`Students`	`StudentId`*(pk)*	AutoNumber	Long Integer
	`StudentName`	Text	25
`Categories`	`CategoryId`*(pk)*	AutoNumber	Long Integer
	`CategoryDesc`	Text	20
`Books`	`BookId`*(pk)*	AutoNumber	Long Integer
	`Title`	Text	50
	`Author`	Text	50
	`Category`	Number	Long Integer
`Reports`	`ReportId`	Number	Long Integer
	`StudentId`*(pk)*	Number	Long Integer
	`BookId`*(pk)*	Number	Long Integer
	`Review`	Text	10

COMPANION Web site The next step is to create the database. You can either follow the instructions here to create the `Students` table and use the specifications in Table 44.2 for the rest of the tables, or you can download the book's source code from the Companion Web site and move the `readersclub.mdb` file to the `idcfiles` subdirectory of your web.

To create the `ReadersClub` database, follow these steps:

1. Start Microsoft Access 97 and choose File | New Database. Then, in the General tab of the New dialog box, select the Blank database icon and click the OK button.
2. Type **`ReadersClub`** in the Field Name field of the File New Database dialog box. Next, open the Save in drop-down list box, and locate the subdirectory that contains the `idcfiles` folder created in the preceding section. If you're using Microsoft Personal Web Server, you should look for the `C:\WebShare\wwwroot\readersclub\idcfiles` subdirectory. Finally, click the Create button to open the ReadersClub : Database dialog box.

Now that you have created the database, you need to add the tables, as follows:

1. In the ReadersClub : Database dialog box, select the Tables tab. Then click the New button to open the New Table dialog box. In this dialog box, select Design View in list on the right side of the form, and click the OK button.
2. To create the `Students` table, type in the Field Name, Data Type, and Field Size information as shown in Table 44.2. Notice that the Field Size attribute is located under the General tab at the bottom-left section of the form, as shown in Figure 44.2.

FIGURE 44.2.
Creating the `Students` *table.*

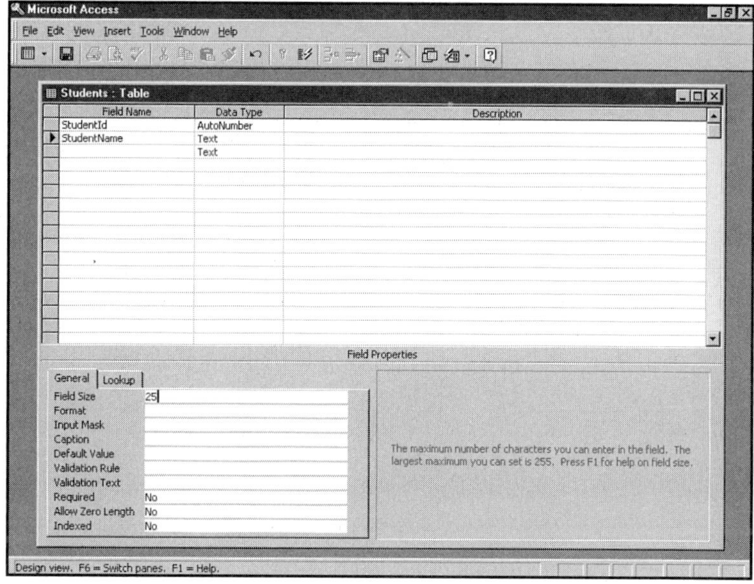

3. Don't forget to set the `StudentId` field as the primary key for the table. To do so, move the mouse cursor to the `StudentId` field, right-click to open the context-sensitive menu, and choose Primary Key. Notice that the leftmost column now contains a small icon depicting a key.
4. After entering the required information for the `StudentID` and `StudentName` fields, click the close button and save the `Students` table.

Repeat the preceding steps to create the `Categories`, `Books`, and `Reports` tables.

TIP

The primary key of the `Reports` table consists of two fields: `StudentId` and `BookId`. Using two fields is one way to enforce the restriction of not allowing any student to report on the same book twice.

To include multiple fields in the primary key, you must select (click) them while holding the Shift key. Then, without releasing the Shift key, right-click and choose Primary Key from the context-sensitive menu.

You can now enter some test data as indicated in Tables 44.3, 44.4, 44.5, and 44.6. Keep in mind that the `BookId`, `CategoryId`, and `StudentId` are generated by the database.

Table 44.3. Contents of the `Categories` table.

`CategoryId`	`CategoryDesc`
1	Adventure
2	Mystery
3	Humor
4	Sci-Fi
5	Fantasy

Table 44.4. Contents of the `Books` table.

`BookId`	`Title`	`Author`	`Category`
1	*Maniac Magee*	Jerry Spinelli	1
2	*The Adventures of Tom Sawyer*	Mark Twain	1
3	*Around the World in 80 Days*	Jules Verne	1
4	*The Westing Game*	Ellen Raskin	2
5	*Amazing Mysteries of the World*	Catherine O'Neill	2
6	*Wacky Spies*	Donald J. Sobol	2
7	*When I Was Your Age*	Ken Adam	3
8	*Fudge-a-Mania*	Judy Blume	3
9	*Amelia Bedelia and the Surprise Shower*	Peggy Parish	3
10	*Norby, the Mixed-Up Robot*	Isaac Asimov	4
11	*Stinker from Space*	Pamela F. Service	4
12	*Mr. Popper's Penguins*	Richard Atwater	4
13	*Winnie the Pooh*	A. A. Milne	5
14	*Charlotte's Web*	E. B. White	5
15	*The Mouse and His Child*	Russell Hoban	5

Table 44.5. Contents of the `Students` table.

StudentId	StudentName
1	Bill
2	Beverly
3	Mariana
4	Stephani
5	Ivan
6	Jonathan
7	Caroline
8	Alex
9	Anthony
10	Amanda
11	Ray
12	Luisa
13	Pete

Table 44.6. Contents of the `Reports` table.

ReportId	StudentId	BookId	Review
1	3	10	Ok
2	5	2	So-so
3	4	5	Ok
4	4	13	Ok
5	3	2	So-so
6	2	13	So-so
7	10	3	Ok
8	6	5	Ok
9	6	10	Good
10	5	3	Ok
11	12	2	Ok
12	1	10	Ok

continues

Table 44.6. continued

ReportId	StudentId	BookId	Review
13	7	12	So-so
14	8	13	Good
15	11	10	Good
16	9	10	Good
17	10	13	So-so
19	7	3	Good
20	9	13	So-so
21	12	14	Good
22	3	13	Good
23	1	15	So-so

Defining the `RdrClubDSN` ODBC Datasource

You can think of an ODBC datasource as a mechanism to establish an indirect connection between a program, the Web server in this case, and the database. The database component of the server issues requests using the ODBC datasource as a handle for the database. The ODBC datasource and the other components of the ODBC architecture communicate with the database to access the data.

Follow these steps to create the `RdrClubDSN` ODBC datasource:

1. Click the Windows Start button, and select the Control Panel item of the Settings menu option. Click the 32bit ODBC icon to launch the ODBC Data Source Administrator dialog box, as shown in Figure 44.3.

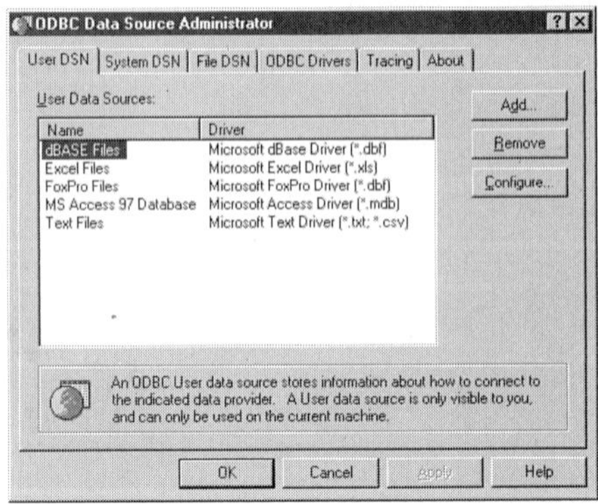

FIGURE 44.3.
The ODBC Data Source Administrator dialog box.

2. Select the User DSN tab. Then click the Add button to display the Create New Data Source Dialog, which contains a list of ODBC drivers currently available in your system. Select the Microsoft Access Driver (`*.mdb`) entry, and click the Finish button.
3. After the ODBC Microsoft Access 97 Setup dialog box appears, type **`RdrClubDSN`** in the Data Source Name field. Then click the Select button in the middle section of the dialog box.
4. In the resulting dialog box, navigate through the directories in your system, and select the `ReadersClub.mdb` file. If you're using Microsoft Personal Web Server, your screen should show a dialog box similar to the one on Figure 44.4.

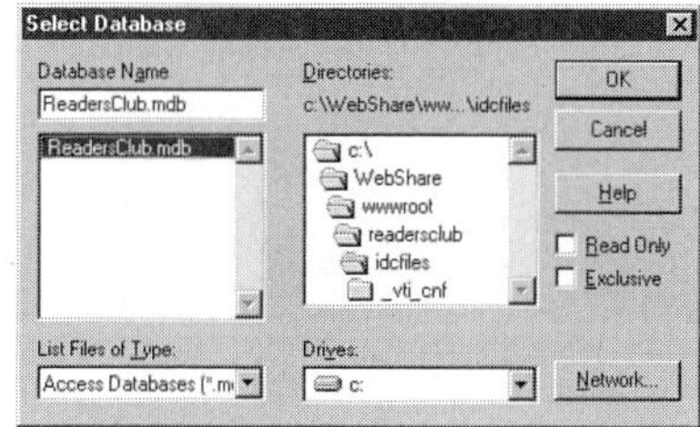

FIGURE 44.4.
Selecting the `ReadersClub.mdb` *file.*

5. Click the OK buttons in the Select Database, ODBC Microsoft Access 97 Setup, and the ODBC Data Source Administrator dialog boxes to close them.

Generating Web Files with Microsoft Access 97

Now that you have the data tables for Reader's Club Web site, you can create a couple of Internet Data Connector (IDC) files to test accessing the database in a web setting. You can use Microsoft Access 97 to create web content based on Microsoft Access tables, queries, forms, and reports. In brief, you can

- Generate static HTML, Internet Data Connector files, or Active Server Pages
- Select an existing HTML document or documents to be used as a formatting template for your Web pages
- Publish your Web pages to a folder or use the Web Publishing Wizard

Generating Internet Database Connector (IDC) Files

In this section, you focus on IDC files as a starting point. I chose IDC files because they provide a good intermediate solution. They allow you to build SQL statements to read from and write to an ODBC-compatible database, and they do not require extensive programming knowledge. The SQL statements can be created with Microsoft Access and Microsoft Query (a query builder included in other Microsoft products such as Microsoft Excel 97).

As you may recall from Chapter 42, IDC requires two file types: Internet Data Connectors (`*.idc`) and HTML templates (`*.htx`). The `.idc` files contain database information: `Datasource`, `Template`, `SQLStatement`, `Username`, `Password`, and other ODBC-related parameters. The `.htx` files, on the other hand, contain HTML tags and Internet Data Connector-specific statements used by the Web server to insert information stored in the database.

You can generate IDC files for the Reader's Club database by following these steps:

1. Start Microsoft Access 97, and open the `readersclub.mdb` database.
2. Choose File | Save as HTML to launch the Publish to the Web Wizard, as shown in Figure 44.5. Click the Next> button to continue.

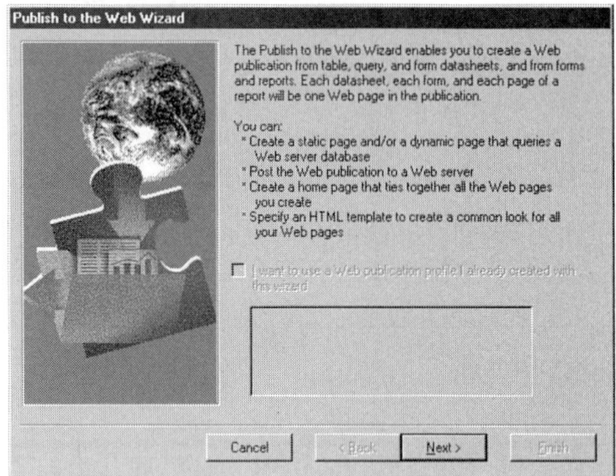

FIGURE 44.5.
The Microsoft Access Publish to the Web Wizard.

3. In the next dialog box, select the Tables tab, and click the Select All button on the right side of the form. Then click the Next> button.
4. For now, skip the selection of a template file in the next dialog box by clicking the Next> button. You can customize your pages later by using the FrontPage 98 features.
5. In the next wizard dialog box, select the Dynamic HTX/IDC (Microsoft Internet Information Server) format type, and click the Next> button. Keep in mind that Microsoft Personal Web Server also supports HTX/IDC files.
6. In the next dialog box, enter `RdrClubDSN` in the Data Source Name field, and click the Next > button to continue.
7. In the next wizard dialog box, use the Browse button to locate and select the `idcfiles` directory you created earlier.
8. Check the Yes, I want to create a home page check box, type **`switchboard`** as its name, and click the Next> button to continue.
9. For now, skip the creation of a Web publication profile in the next wizard dialog box, and click the Finish button.

Testing the IDC Files

Now that you have generated the `.idc` and `.htx` files for the four tables and a switchboard page, you can test them as follows:

1. Start the FrontPage Explorer and open the Reader's Club Web site. Then select the Folders view and open the `idcfiles` folder.
2. Click the `SWITCHBOARD.html` file to open the FrontPage Editor and select the Preview tab at the bottom of the page (see Figure 44.6).

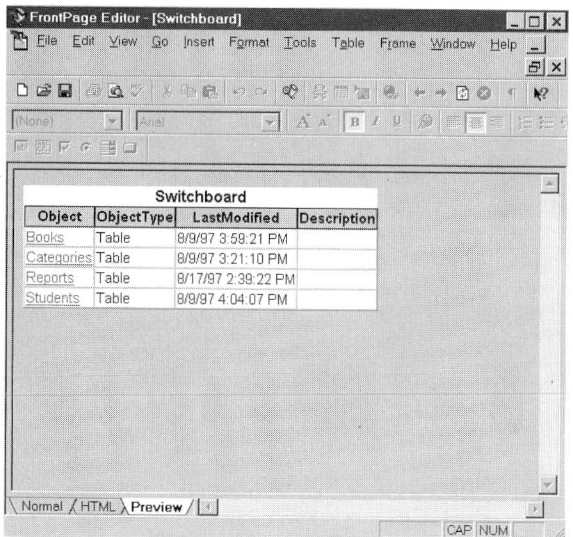

FIGURE 44.6.
The `SWITCHBOARD.html` *file in Preview mode.*

3. Click the `Books` hyperlink to display the contents of the `Books` database table, as shown in Figure 44.7.

> **TIP**
>
> The following are the top two problems that you can run into as you test your site:
>
> If you receive the following message, check to see whether you entered the right ODBC datasource name when you generated the IDC files with the Microsoft Access Web Publishing Wizard:
>
> ```
> Error Performing Query
> ·[State=IM002][Error=0][Microsoft][ODBC Driver Manager] Data source name not
> found and no default driver specified
> ```
>
> continues

continued

If you receive the following message, check the properties of the `idcfiles` folder with the FrontPage Explorer:

```
HTTP/1.0 403 Access Forbidden (Execute Access Denied - This Virtual
Directory does not allow objects to be executed.)
```

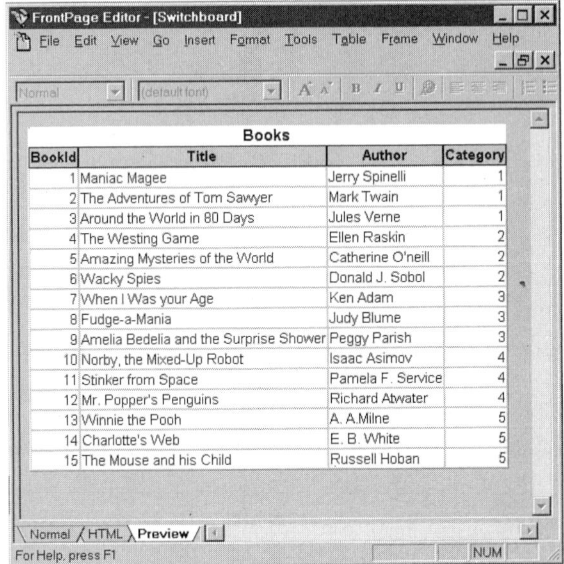

Books			
BookId	Title	Author	Category
1	Maniac Magee	Jerry Spinelli	1
2	The Adventures of Tom Sawyer	Mark Twain	1
3	Around the World in 80 Days	Jules Verne	1
4	The Westing Game	Ellen Raskin	2
5	Amazing Mysteries of the World	Catherine O'neill	2
6	Wacky Spies	Donald J. Sobol	2
7	When I Was your Age	Ken Adam	3
8	Fudge-a-Mania	Judy Blume	3
9	Amelia Bedelia and the Surprise Shower	Peggy Parish	3
10	Norby, the Mixed-Up Robot	Isaac Asimov	4
11	Stinker from Space	Pamela F. Service	4
12	Mr. Popper's Penguins	Richard Atwater	4
13	Winnie the Pooh	A. A.Milne	5
14	Charlotte's Web	E. B. White	5
15	The Mouse and his Child	Russell Hoban	5

FIGURE 44.7.
The Books *table in Preview mode.*

Adding Database Functionality to the Reader's Club Site

In this section, you create additional Internet Database Connectivity files to retrieve and enter information using SQL statements.

Figure 44.8 shows the proposed structure for the Reader's Club Web site along with the filenames that deliver each function. Keep in mind that a corresponding HTML template (or `.htx`) file exists for every `.idc` file.

In the next section, you will learn how to create selected pages of this site. In particular, I have selected pages to illustrate some specific techniques, as you can see in Table 44.7.

FIGURE 44.8.
The Reader's Club Web site structure.

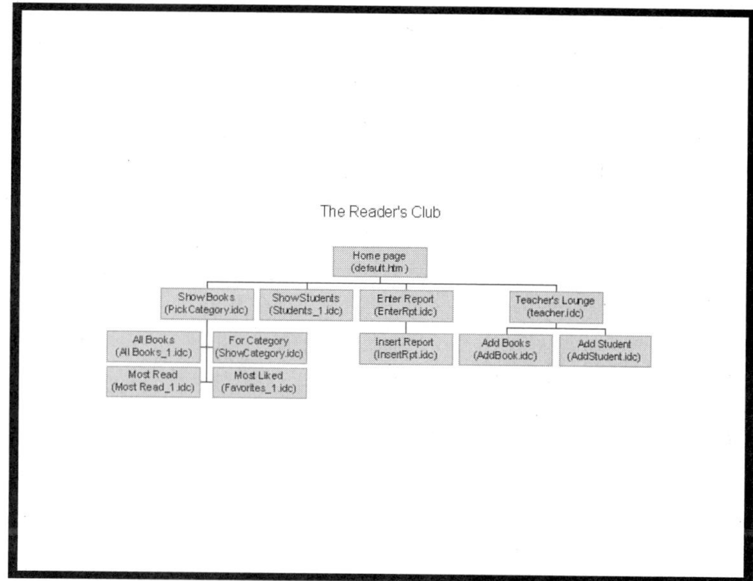

Table 44.7. Database techniques used on selected pages of the Reader's Club Web site.

IDC/HTX Filename	*Technique*
`Most Read_1`	Uses Microsoft Access 97 in a query that combines data from more than one table
`EnterRprt`	Shows how to populate a drop-down menu with items in the database
`InsertRprt`	Issues an SQL `Insert` statement to add data to the database

You can find the entire web in the `Chapter44\Ch44b` subdirectory of the Companion Web site. The `Ch44b` subdirectory contains the `default.htm` file and the rest of the files are located in the `idcfiles` subdirectory.

Using Microsoft Query to Generate SQL Statements

In this section, you use Microsoft Access 97 to create a query and generate the `Most Read_1.idc` and `Most Read_1.htx` files. The query issues an SQL `SELECT` statement to join the `Books` and `Reports` tables and obtain a count of the number of reports entered for each book. The query should list the books in descending "read count" sequence. Follow these steps to create these files:

1. Start Microsoft Access and open the `readersclub.mdb` database.

2. Select the Queries tab of the ReadersClub : Database dialog box, and click the New button.
3. Select Design View on the right side of the New Query dialog box, and click the OK button. The resulting screen should look like Figure 44.9.

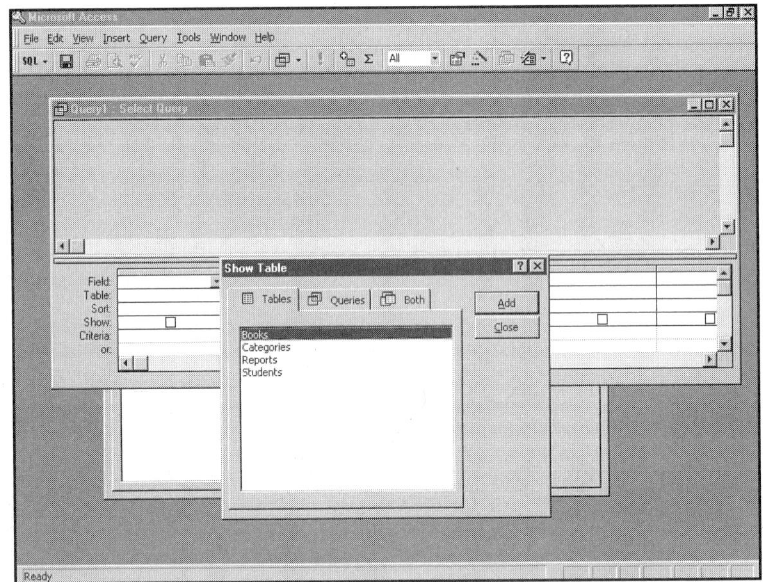

FIGURE 44.9.
The Microsoft Access 97 Query Designer.

4. Select the `Books` table in the Show Table dialog box, and click the Add button. Repeat the same procedure for the `Reports` table, and then close the Show Table dialog box.
5. Move the mouse cursor to the diagram section of the query, and double-click the `Title` field of the `Books` table *twice*.

NOTE

At this point, the `Title` field appears *twice* in the query. Soon, you will modify the query to use one copy of the field to determine the count of books and the other to display the title. Also notice that you do not select any fields from the `Reports` table. Because you included the `Reports` table in the query and the two tables are linked by the `BookId` field, Microsoft Access selects only those records common to both tables.

6. Right-click anywhere on the first copy of the `Title` column to open the context-sensitive menu, and choose the Totals option. Notice that this action adds the `Total:` line to the grid section of the query.

7. Click the `Group By` cell of the first `Title` column, and choose Count from its pull-down list. Do not change the `Group By` setting of the second `Title` column.
8. Click the `Sort:` cell of the first `Title` column, and choose Descending from its pull-down list. The resulting screen should look like Figure 44.10.

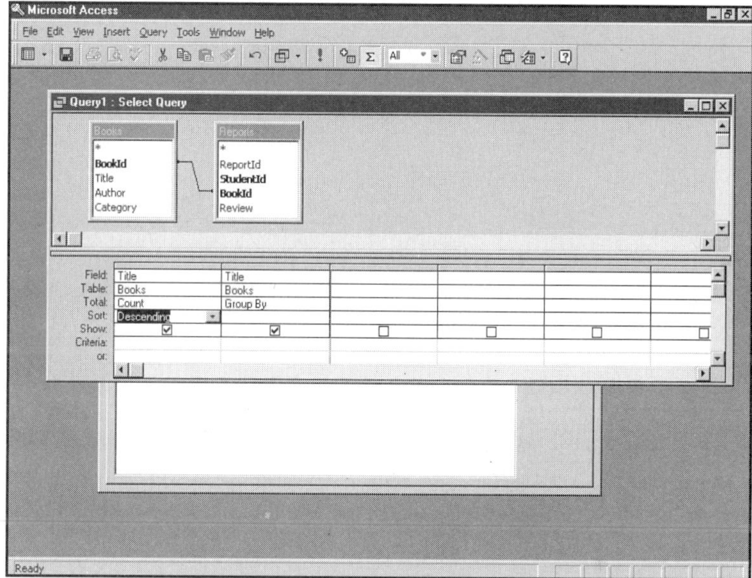

FIGURE 44.10.
Creating the Most Read query with Microsoft Access 97.

9. Run the query by choosing Query | Run or by clicking the exclamation point icon in the Query Design menu bar.
10. Save your new query with the name `Most Read`, and generate the corresponding IDC files by choosing File | Save as HTML.

    You might want to edit the `Most Read_1.htx` file and change the `CountOfTitle` column heading to a more descriptive name such as `Times read` (see Figure 44.11). Notice that Microsoft Access appends the `_1` (underscore followed by the number one) suffix to the filename.

TIP

Look at the `Favorites_1.idc` file, which contains a slightly more complex query of books with "Ok" or "Good" reviews.

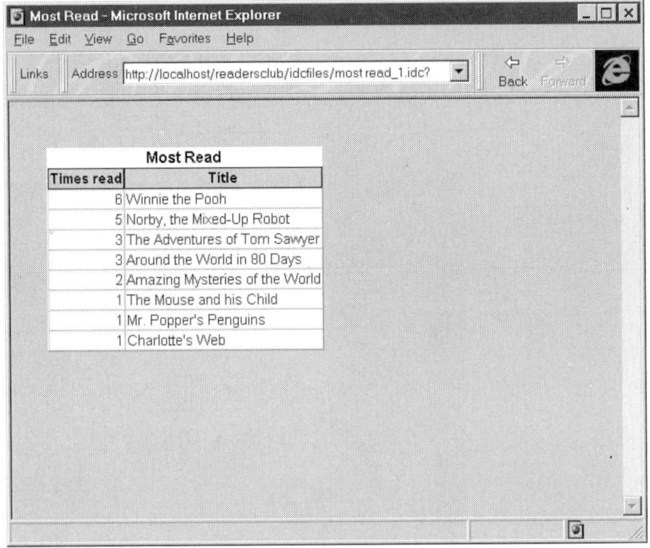

Most Read - Microsoft Internet Explorer
File Edit View Go Favorites Help
Links Address http://localhost/readersclub/idcfiles/most read_1.idc?
Back Forward
Most Read
Times read Title
6 Winnie the Pooh
5 Norby, the Mixed-Up Robot
3 The Adventures of Tom Sawyer
3 Around the World in 80 Days
2 Amazing Mysteries of the World
1 The Mouse and his Child
1 Mr. Popper's Penguins
1 Charlotte's Web

FIGURE 44.11.
The Most Read page of the Reader's Club Web site.

Creating Internet Database Connectivity Files with FrontPage 98

In this section, you create two sets of Internet Database Connectivity files: `EnterRpt` and `InsertRpt`. The `EnterRpt` files illustrate how to populate an HTML drop-down menu. The `InsertRpt` files show how to insert data into the database.

The `EnterRpt.idc` is invoked with the Enter a book report hyperlink of the Reader's Club home page (see Figure 44.12). When processed by the server, the `EnterRpt` files include the list of `Titles` and `BookIds` in the form.

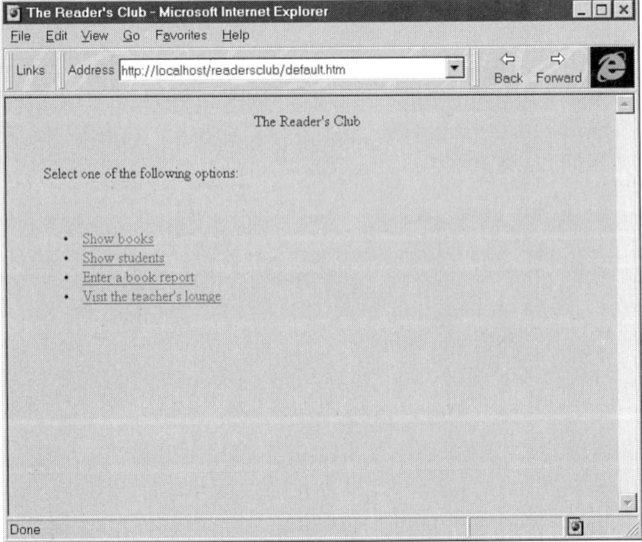

FIGURE 44.12.
A simple home page for the Reader's Club site.

The list of `Titles` and `BookIds` is combined with `EnterRpt.htx` to generate the Enter a book report page shown in Figure 44.13.

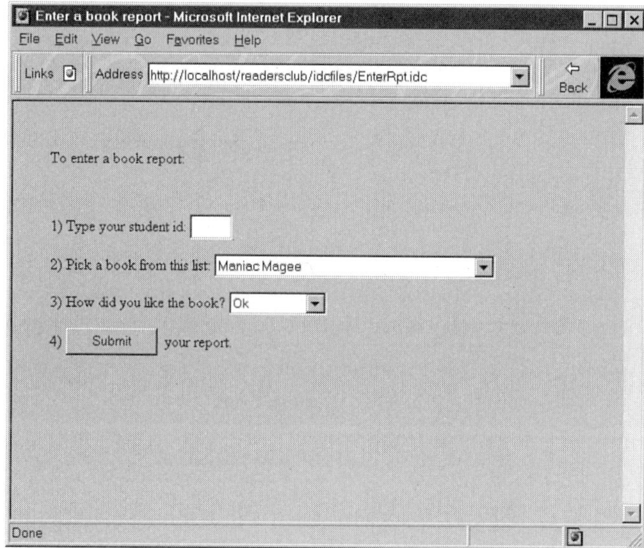

FIGURE 44.13.
The Enter a book report page.

To create the `EnterRpt.idc` file, follow these steps:

1. Start the FrontPage Explorer and open the `idcfiles` folder. Then create a new page.
2. Rename the newly created page `EnterRpt.idc` and open it. This action launches the Internet Database Connector Wizard. Next, type `RdrClubDSN` as the name of the ODBC data source, and type **`EnterRpt.htx`** in the Query results template field, as shown in Figure 44.14. Then click the Next> button to continue.

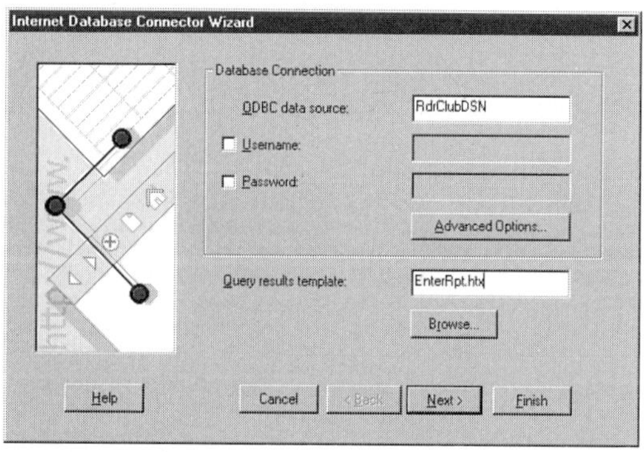

FIGURE 44.14.
The Internet Database Connector Wizard.

3. In the next dialog box, type **`SELECT * FROM`** `Books` as the query, and click the Next> button.

4. Because the `EnterRpt.idc` query does not require any parameters, just click the Finish button in the next dialog box.

Now you can create the HTML template file `EnterRpt.htx` as follows:

1. Click the New Page toolbar button of the FrontPage Explorer or start the FrontPage Editor. Then create a form with one one-line text box, two drop-down menus, and one button. Enter the text shown in Figure 44.13. Refer to the chapters in Part V, "Forms and Advanced Form Handling," if needed.
2. Use `StudentId` as the name of the text, set the width of this field to three characters, and make it a required field.
3. Skip the first drop-down menu for now.
4. Name the second drop-down menu `Review`, and add three entries: `So-so`, `Ok`, and `Good`. Use these entries as both the Choice and the Value. Make `Ok` the default.
5. Set the button type to Submit, and make the form process this request with the following parameters: `Action=InsertRpt.idc?` and `Method=Post`. Refer to the chapters in Part V if needed.

Now go back to the first drop-down menu, and set it up so that it shows the list of books but sends the BookId number back to the server. Here are the steps:

1. Click the first drop-down menu field of the form, open its property page (by pressing Alt+Enter), set its name to `BookId`, and click the OK button to go back to the FrontPage Editor window.
2. Click the HTML tab at the bottom of the FrontPage Editor window to show the HTML text for the drop-down menu field. Replace the highlighted text with the text shown in Listing 44.1, and click back to the Normal tab of the FrontPage Editor window.

Listing 44.1. Populating a drop-down menu with information from a database.

```
<select name="BookId" size="1">
<%begindetail%><option value="<%BookId%>"> <%title%><%enddetail%> </option>
</select>
```

NOTE

Here is a brief description of the code in Listing 44.1:

The `<select>` and `</select>` tags enclose the list of choices for the drop-down menu.

The `<%begindetail%>` and `<%enddetail%>` delimiters surround the text that will be repeated for every row returned by the database query defined in the IDC file.

The `<%BookId%>` and `<%title%>` fields are placeholders for columns of the same name in the result set of the query.

3. Save the file as EnterRpt.htx in the idcfiles directory.

You can now test the EnterRpt.idc file by using your browser and the URL indicated in Figure 44.13. You can click the drop-down menu, but do not click the Submit button yet. The Submit button executes the InsertRpt.idc file that you will create next.

You can create the InsertRpt.idc file as follows:

1. Create a new page in the idcfiles folder, and rename it InserRpt.idc.
2. Launch the Internet Database Connector Wizard by opening the newly created InsertRpt.idc file.
3. Enter RdrClubDSN in the ODBC Data Source field, and enter InsertRpt.htx in the Query results template field. Then click the Next> button to continue.
4. Enter the text shown in Listing 44.2 into the query field of the Internet Database Connector Wizard. Then click the Finish button to save the InsertRpt.idc file.

Listing 44.2. Populating a drop-down menu with information from a database.

```
Insert Into Reports(StudentId,BookId,Review)
Select %StudentId%,%BookId%,'%Review%'
```

5. Create the InsertRpt.htx with one or two lines of text to tell the users that the report was entered.

You can now test the EnterRpt.idc file using your browser and the URL indicated in Figure 44.13.

The Database Region Wizard

The Database Region Wizard, shown in Figure 44.15, is a new feature of FrontPage 98. To a great extent, it is similar to IDC in the sense that it allows you to retrieve information from any ODBC-compliant database. One of the key advantages of the Database Region Wizard over IDC files is that it requires only one file as opposed to the IDC/HTX file combination.

On the other hand, the Database Region Wizard requires a server that supports Active Server Pages. This means that if you want to develop Web pages that use the Database Region Wizard, you have to use IIS or the soon-to-be-released Microsoft Personal Web Server version 4 as a Web server. For additional availability information, check the Microsoft Web site; in particular check, http://www.microsoft.com/iis.

To create a Web page using the Database Region Wizard, follow these steps:

1. Open the FrontPage Explorer and create a new page.
2. Choose Insert|Database and click the Database Region Wizard. Next, enter the ODBC Data Source Name, SQL query string, and query field names when prompted by the wizard.
3. Save or rename the file using the .asp file extension.

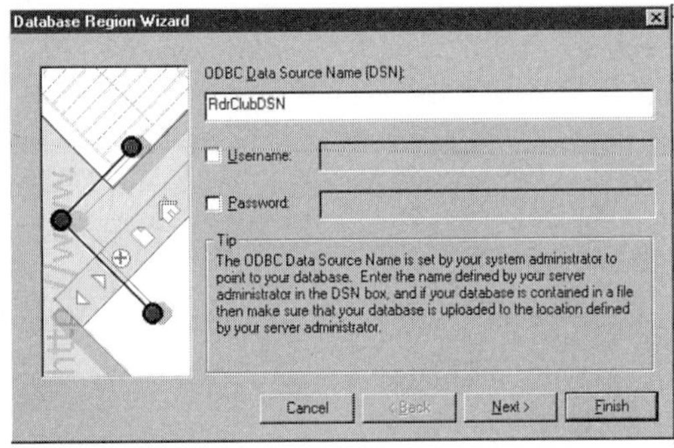

FIGURE 44.15.
The Database Region Wizard.

Migrating to SQL Server

COMPANION Web site

Here are a few points to keep in mind if you ever migrate the Reader's Club to Microsoft SQL Server. The `CrtRdrCl.sql` file in the `Chapter44/Ch44c` subdirectory of the Companion Web site can be executed under Microsoft SQL Server version 6.5 to create the Reader's Club database. The script allocates 2MB in the master database device and grants All authority on the four tables of Reader's Club tables to the Guest login.

If you need to create an SQL Server–based ODBC datasource, you can use the same name as before—`RdrClubDSN`—but make sure that you remove the Microsoft Access version of the datasource to avoid conflicts. Because SQL Server runs under Windows NT, you might want to create a System DSN, as opposed to the User DSN shown in Figure 44.3.

As you move from Access to SQL Server, the whole concept of security takes a totally different perspective. Make sure to review the concept of trusted connections and other server-based security concepts.

Finally, you might need to review the syntax of the SQL query statements generated by the Microsoft Access Web Publishing Wizard and those entered in the IDC and Database Region Wizards. The following are the only two problems I encountered when I migrated the Reader's Club Web site to IIS version 3.0 and SQL Server:

- I had to remove the square brackets generated by Microsoft Access to delimit table and field names.
- SQL Server treated numeric fields enclosed in apostrophes as character strings and rejected them when a numeric value was expected.

TIP

An additional source of valuable information and tools regarding the migration to MS SQL Server from other databases is the Microsoft SQL Server Developer's Resource Kit, available in the Downloads section of the MS SQL Server site at `http://www.microsft.com/sql`.

Summary

In this chapter you learned how to develop a simple Web site using FrontPage 98 and database tools. The chapter begins with a brief introduction to database design concepts and then covers creating the basic framework for the site using Microsoft Access 97 as a database design tool. The chapter then covers enhancing the data access capabilities of the site, using the Internet Database Connectivity and Database Region Wizard features of FrontPage 98. Finally, I review a number of key items to keep in mind when migrating a Web site's database to MS SQL Server.

CHAPTER 45

Moving Up to Visual InterDev

by Keith Leavitt

IN THIS CHAPTER

- What Is Visual InterDev? *764*
- Should I Use Visual InterDev or FrontPage 98 to Develop and Maintain My Web Site? *766*
- How Does Database Connectivity Differ Between FrontPage 98 and Visual InterDev? *767*
- Using ActiveX Controls to Access Databases in Visual InterDev *773*
- Building a Database-Driven Active Server Page with Design Time ActiveX Controls *774*
- Building Database-Driven Active Server Pages with the Visual InterDev Data Form Wizard *779*

The popularity of the Web is at least in part due to its solution to the cross-platform issue. Cool features are no longer developed for exclusively the Mac, PC, or UNIX systems, but are available for use on any machine. However, most of the Web's content is still static, made up of text and graphics that are developed, posted, and often forgotten about. Now, if cross-platform documents popularize a medium like the Web, what would cross-platform applications do for it? Don't you need to be a Java developer to find out? Well, it helps, but you don't need to be. Can you do that over HTTP/HTML? Well, yes. And what's more, if you are at all handy with FrontPage as a content development tool, you are pretty well poised to evolve to the next step in Web development: dynamic content and Web applications. Dynamic content, like static content, is also developed, posted, and forgotten, but only forgotten by the developer. The key advantage of dynamic content is that the content can continue to change over time, customizing itself to the activities of a single user, or drawing information from a regularly updated database. Some of these capabilities are supported in FrontPage 98 , but if you want the full range of development tools available for this endeavor, you should probably take a look at Visual InterDev. With some FrontPage experience under your belt, Visual InterDev could be a big part of the next phase of your evolution as a Web developer.

What Is Visual InterDev?

Because you have delved this far into the book, I'll assume you are quite familiar with the functionality and applications of the FrontPage 98 suite of tools. But you also might have heard of Visual InterDev, the Web development member of Microsoft's Visual Studio tool suite. Throughout this chapter, I will focus primarily on the database connectivity functions available via the Visual InterDev IDE. Database connectivity, however, is only one piece in the larger puzzle that is Visual InterDev.

Visual InterDev is the client component of a suite of tools associated with what Microsoft code-named Denali, or ActiveX Server Scripting. The key component is called Active Server Pages. Active Server Pages work with several servers including Microsoft Personal Web Server, Peer Web Services for NT, and, of course, Internet Information Server. At the risk of oversimplifying, the function of Active Server Pages is to make a Web server to respond dynamically to user requests, and thus act a little less like a static file server. Previously, this result was accomplished with CGI scripts written in Perl (also known as "the Swiss Army Knife of the Web"), REXX, and other scripting languages interpreted on the server. With Visual InterDev, the developer uses ActiveX controls, Active Data Objects, Active Server components, and Visual Data tools to realize more dynamic functionality. I will discuss each of these tools later in this chapter. The upshot of this is still copious amounts of server-side (and, if you like, some client-side) scripting, but it is accomplished with a host of wizards and other Computer Aided Software Engineering (CASE) tools that vastly increase productivity over script editors and language references.

Still, you will find a couple of fundamental performance and functional differences between Active Server and CGI scripting. First, Active Server Pages are implemented as a dynamic link library (`isapi.dll`) on Internet Information Server (IIS) and thus run in the same process as the Web server itself. In contrast, CGI scripts establish their own processes separate from the HTTP daemon. The good news here is that, as a result, Active Server Pages run faster than comparable CGI scripts. The bad news is that a crash in an Active Server Page script may take down the server as well. There is more good news. IIS 4.0 (previously code named K2) fixes this problem by allowing the server administrator to specify whether Web applications run in process or out of process. Thus, you can now pick and choose between the applications you trust, and those you do not.

The second fundamental difference in Active Server Pages is the capability to establish the current state and history of an individual user's sessions in conjunction with those much-maligned cookies. Apparently, folks don't necessarily like the idea of a Web server/browser system surreptitiously writing a lot of data to their hard disks without their express permission (though browsers do this all the time, with or without cookies, but hey, the customer's always right, okay? You can store your own files, thank you very much!). Active Server Applications can retain continuous user history in a server-side file (`global.asa`, which I'll say more about that later too) that tracks session variables as an object, thus overcoming the limitation of HTTP as a stateless protocol. (*Statelessness* just means that standard HTTP has no means of storing information about past events or where a particular user has been surfing.)

NOTE

Active Server Pages can keep track of user sessions and application events on the server side.

The coexistence of Visual InterDev and FrontPage 98 as Web development tools raises many questions for the developer. The key difference between the two tool sets lies in the dichotomy between simplicity and power. In building applications, the developer usually faces at least two mutually exclusive requirements: increasingly extensive functionality versus ease of use. Moving toward one usually means moving away from the other. Projects usually start out conceptually simple, but then a phenomenon known as *requirements creep* sets in. Beta testers start to suggest improvements, and these suggestions are added to the to-do list. Left unchecked, requirements creep can become *requirements avalanche* and drive complexity into the system design. When this situation occurs, the software evolves into something related to, but fundamentally different from, the product it was originally intended to be. Usually, this evolution is away from simplicity and intuitiveness and toward extensive functionality and complexity.

You may have noticed that virtually every function in FrontPage 98 can be implemented with no source-level scripting. Although this is often true in the Visual InterDev development environment, to realize the full power of Active Server Pages, the Visual InterDev developer should bring his or her coding skills. In short, the FrontPage 98 tool set resides mostly on the "easy to use yet somewhat limiting" range of the spectrum, whereas Visual InterDev occupies the "more powerful yet complex" range.

Should I Use Visual InterDev or FrontPage 98 to Develop and Maintain My Web Site?

Deciding the appropriate tools to bring to bear on any software development project depends largely on capabilities and preferences of the developers and the requirements of the system being developed. The importance of requirements definition cannot be understated. Entire systems engineering volumes have been devoted to this subject, and for good reason. Allow me to grossly oversimplify their points with this rhetorical question: Without an objective, how do you ever declare victory? The success or failure of most software development efforts hinge largely on how well the requirements are defined.

To more specifically address the question at hand, you must ask: What is the intended functionality of the site in question, and how comfortable are you and or your development team with writing VBScript and/or JScript? Just like development tools, Web sites can be placed along a spectrum of functionality, from the simple to the not-so-simple. On the simple side are static HTML pages, client-side image maps, and perhaps some animated graphics. Moving away from the simple end, you encounter some server-side functionality such as hit counters and forms. A bit further up the complexity scale, you might find dynamic content via client-side scripting and database connectivity, first read-only, then read-write. Finally, at the upper end, you have full blown server-side applications requiring robust design-time development tools, state management, the works.

Now, in theory, you could use both tool sets across this entire range of functionality. But, applying FrontPage 98 at the upper end, you would spend most of your time handwriting script in the FrontPage HTML markup bot. At the other end, well, let me just say that would be somewhat like driving to work in an F-15; you could do it, but doing so might constitute a questionable application of resources. At this end of this scale, and significantly above it, FrontPage 98 provides far more than adequate functionality. Visual InterDev is designed for application at the high end, where the required functionality necessitates extensive server-side scripting.

FrontPage Components (WebBots) are designed to automate the development of standard Web functions such as server-side includes and search engines. The WebBots and server extensions comprise the functionality that differentiates FrontPage 98 from the myriad of Web authoring tools on the market. Although these bots eliminate a lot of scripting, they are minimally customizable. The Visual InterDev rough equivalent of a FrontPage 98 bot is the design-time ActiveX control. The function of this control is to automate the generation of code, both client and server side. The key difference here is that after the code is generated, it is accessible via the Visual InterDev script editor, and thus fully modifiable, or "re-entrant."

Figure 45.1 depicts the script generated by a the Data Range Header design-time control in an Active Server Page. In the code editing pane, this scripted font is rendered in green to highlight its function. I will cover the use of the Data Range Header and Data Range Footer controls in detail later in this chapter. The script in yellow, delimited with `<%` and `%>` is run at the server. The rest is standard HTML. Web application files are shown at the left in the File View tab, one of three available in a Visual InterDev Web project. The disabled (gray) file icons currently reside only on the server, and the activated (colored) files have been temporarily loaded onto the development client for alteration in the design-time environment. The Data View depicts all database objects connected to the current project. The Info View is a hyperlinked online documentation and help system. This development interface has been standardized across all tools in Microsoft's Visual Studio tool suite.

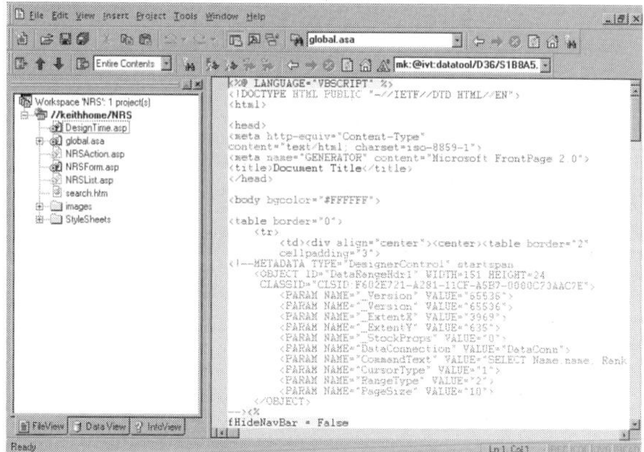

FIGURE 45.1.
Script generated by the Data Range Header control in an Active Server Page as viewed in the Visual InterDev Source Editor.

COMPANION **Web site** Throughout this chapter, I will cite several database connectivity examples using a thoroughly unremarkable MS Access database: `NRS.mdb` or the "Name Rank and Serial Number" database. It consists of three tables—Name, Rank, and Service—that may conceptually have one-to-many or many-to-many relationships. The sample database was kept simple to highlight the functionality if the Visual InterDev tool set. For completeness, I have included the `.mdb` file on this book's Companion Web Site.

How Does Database Connectivity Differ Between FrontPage 98 and Visual InterDev?

The deceptively simple answer to this question is: not significantly. The connection is still via Open Database Connectivity (ODBC) and Data Source Name (DSN) files. However, the development tools available in the Visual InterDev environment are extensive, and thus have a significant learning curve. In the following sections, I have outlined some of the key differences between the two environments.

Data Source Name Files

Both FrontPage and Visual InterDev webs rely on ODBC drivers to access the back-end database. Both use Data Source Name (DSN) files to store information on how to connect to specific databases.

The first difference is in the type of DSN used by each system. The FrontPage Internet Database Connector system requires the use of a machine DSN, where database connection information is stored in the Windows Registration database of the server. Visual InterDev database projects can use either file or machine DSN. The file DSN type is recommended in the Visual InterDev development environment due to its portability between machines. DSN files can be created and modified with the Data Connection Wizard in the Visual InterDev client, or from the 32-Bit ODBC icon in the Win95/NT control panel. By default, file DSNs are buried on the path `<drive>\Program Files\Common Files\ODBC\Data Sources\<filename>.dsn`. The following ODBC stanza from the Name Rank and Serial Number database I use in later examples may serve to remove the shroud of mystery from these obscure files. They simply specify the driver type, database path, and a few other associated parameters.

```
[ODBC]
DRIVER=Microsoft Access Driver (*.mdb)
UID=admin
UserCommitSync=Yes
Threads=3
SafeTransactions=0
PageTimeout=5
MaxScanRows=8
MaxBufferSize=512
ImplicitCommitSync=Yes
FIL=MS Access
DriverId=25
DefaultDir=C:\WEBSHARE\WWWROOT\share
DBQ=C:\WEBSHARE\WWWROOT\share\nrs.mdb
```

FrontPage Internet Database Connector and HTML Template Pages

With FrontPage Internet Database Connector and HTML template pages, database connectivity starts to diverge between the Visual InterDev and FrontPage environments. The `.idc/.htx` file structure of FrontPage 97 is basically a CGI scripting system. The Internet Database Connector (`.idc`) file contains VB script describing the relevant `.dsn` and `.htx` files and the SQL statement specifying operations to be performed in querying the back-end database. Like a UNIX Perl script, the `.idc` file must reside in an executable directory. The `.htx` HTML template file is simply an HTML shell that sits waiting to be filled with the results from the SQL query to the database. (FrontPage 98 introduces Active Server Pages in place of `.HTX` files, but with minimal development tools for their scripting.)

The following is an example of a basic pair of `.idc` and `.htx` files (respectively) that returns each military rank above that of Major and its associated ID from the Rank table of the Name Rank and Serial Number database.

Here is the `.idc` file script:

```
Datasource: NRS 'The system DSN pointing to the Name Rank and Serial Number
database.
Template: ../nrs.htx 'back out of the executable directory
➥and into the parent directory containing the template file
SQLStatement: SELECT ID, Rank FROM Rank WHERE ID > 3 'The SQL statement
```

Here is the `.htx` file script:

```
<html>
<head>
<title> Name Rank and Serial Number Query Results </title>
</head>
<body>
<%begindetail%><%Rank%><%ID%><%enddetail%>
</body>
</html>
```

As is clear from the preceding scripts, the `.htx` file is standard HTML, except the `<%begindetail%>` and `<%enddetail%>` tags, and the fields returned within them. You should note that SQL syntax varies between environments, and the Internet Database Connector environment is no exception. For example, you cannot use the `Like` operator alone in the `.idc` dialect of SQL, even to query a database that supports this syntax. To simulate the `Like` operator, you need to use `%` as a wildcard character. What's more, concatenation of the wildcard operator to a query is not accomplished with `+` or `&` as you might think, but with another `%`. To further confuse matters, the `%` character is also the delimiter for `.idc` query parameters. So to return all records with a field starting with a user-defined parameter, a syntactically correct `.idc where` clause might read `WHERE <fieldname> Like '%[parameter]%%%'`.

TIP

When you're building SQL queries, beware that syntax differs between environments such as IDC and ADO.

With this release, FrontPage 98 is starting the transition to Active Server Pages as the database query-handling mechanism. Active Server Pages are essentially server-side scripts designed to generate HTML dynamically based on user-initiated events. In FrontPage 98, Active Server Pages are used as form handlers to submit the SQL query to the back-end database, and they are returned to the browser as standard HTML. FrontPage 98 offers a Database Region Wizard to author these scripts, and Visual InterDev offers literally a suite of tools to generate Java or Visual Basic scripted programs based on Active Server Pages. Active Server Pages interact with the ODBC back end via a layer called Active Data Objects, or ADO. I discuss the ADO data model in more detail in the next section.

Visual InterDev global.asa Files

A second file in Visual InterDev Web projects also contains information about database connections: the `global.asa` (Active Server Application) file. This script file is loaded into server memory the first time a user views a page in a Web application. A *Web application* is essentially a web that makes extensive use of server-side scripting via active server pages. Four events are tracked throughout any individual user's "session": Session start and end, and application start and end.

By storing these events on the server, an Active Server application can track individual user activities within and even between sessions, varying responses to actions as appropriate. This approach is effective in overcoming one of the main disadvantages of HTTP: the fact that it is inherently a stateless protocol. A database connection is established for a Visual InterDev project by writing the connection information into the `global.asa` file. Of course, Visual InterDev offers a wizard to make this process as painless as possible. The `global.asa` file for the Name Rank and Serial number database project is shown here. The four events are listed at the top, and everything between the `<script>` tags establishes the project data connection.

```
'Sub Session_OnStart
'**Put your code here **
'End Sub
```

'EventName	*Description*
'Session_OnStart	Runs the first time a user runs any page in your application
'Session_OnEnd	Runs when a user's session times out or quits your application
'Application_OnStart	Runs once when the first page of your application is run for the first time by any user
'Application_OnEnd	Runs once when the Web server shuts down

```
</SCRIPT>
<SCRIPT LANGUAGE=VBScript RUNAT=Server>
Sub Session_OnStart
    '==Visual InterDev Generated - DataConnection startspan==
    '--Project Data Connection
        Session("DataConn_ConnectionString") =
        ➥"DBQ=C:\WEBSHARE\WWWROOT\share\nrs.mdb;DefaultDir=C:\WEBSHARE\WWWROOT\share;
        ➥Driver={Microsoft Access Driver (*.mdb)};DriverId=25;FIL=MS
        ➥Access;ImplicitCommitSync=Yes;MaxBufferSize=512;MaxScanRows=8;PageTimeout=5;
        ➥SafeTransactions=0;Threads=3;UID=admin;UserCommitSync=Yes;"
        Session("DataConn_ConnectionTimeout") = 15
        Session("DataConn_CommandTimeout") = 30
        Session("DataConn_RuntimeUserName") = "admin"
        Session("DataConn_RuntimePassword") = ""
    '==Visual InterDev Generated - DataConnection endspan==
End Sub
</SCRIPT>
```

The Newest Data Object Layer: Active Data Objects

The IDC/HTX data access model of previous FrontPage releases is being integrated into the new Microsoft data access programming model: Active Data Objects, or ADO. Internet Explorer and Active Server Pages currently conform to the ADO programming model, and both can be programmed in Visual Basic script. In Internet Explorer, ADO objects are referenced between `<object>...</object>` tags. In Active Server Pages, ADO objects are explicitly declared with the more familiar `CreateObject()` command.

Within the context of Active Server Pages, ADO runs on the Web server and is the basis for all Visual InterDev database connectivity. This component serves as an object layer between Active Server Pages and the application's back-end database. ADO 1.0 is a subset of RDO (Remote Data Objects), but Microsoft plans to expand ADO into a superset of RDO. ADO is also an expansion of DAO (Data Access Objects) but uses another new data access component: OLE DB. In addition to ODBC databases, OLE DB is designed to broker access to several types of data sources including e-mail systems. If you find sorting out the trade-offs between ADO, RDO, and DAO to be as confusing as I did, you might want to get the white paper "Choosing the Right Visual Basic Data Access Strategy" available for free at `http://www.microsoft.com/vbasic/techinfo/choose.doc`.

ADO has a relatively simple object model, exposing six objects and four collections. Many development tools in the Visual InterDev Integrated Development Environment shield the user from the details of ADO. However, any source-level database access development will require some understanding of the ADO object model and syntax. If you're considering the development of data sources compliant with OLE DB, you should check out the latest scoop on OLE DB requirements at `http://www.microsoft.com/oledb`. Microsoft also has the requisite ADO information posted at `http://www.microsoft.com/ado`.

TIP

Choosing a data access model can be a hard-earned talent in itself. Save yourself some headaches and check out `http://www.microsoft.com/vbasic/techinfo/choose.doc`.

The Database Development Environment of Visual InterDev: Visual Data Tools

Although differences between the database connection methods of the Visual InterDev and FrontPage development environments are quite modest, the data management tools employed by both are vastly disparate. The FrontPage 97 Internet Database Connector Wizard steps you through creation of an `.idc` file. FrontPage 97 also offers an `.htx` template file and several database functions such as a detail section and conditional code generation WebBot. The FrontPage 98 Database Region Wizard has similar functionality, but the results are combined with an

Active Server Page rather than `.HTX` files. Design-time ActiveX controls are available to build the `.asp` files, but with all versions of FrontPage, the actual development and management of your back-end database must still be done in the native RDBMS environment of the back-end database.

In addition to database connectivity tools, the Visual InterDev client offers a broad array of database development tools reminiscent of the MS Access RDBMS development environment. Although connections and interfaces to any ODBC-compliant database are supported, the major functions in Visual Data Tools are aimed at SQL Server 6.5 and above. Visual Data tools consist of a huge number of utilities organized into four major components:

- Data View
- Query Designer
- Database Designer
- Source Code Editor

Data View

The left side of Figure 45.2 shows the Data View tab, which provides a folder-based graphical interface to all database components in a web application. Database components available in the Data View include database connections, database diagrams, tables, triggers, views, and stored procedures.

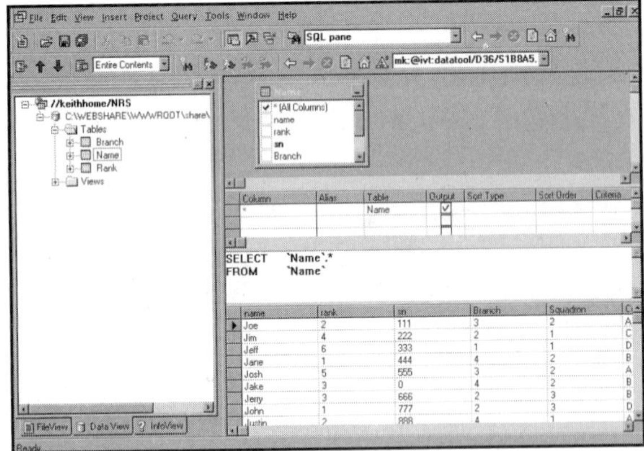

FIGURE 45.2.
The Panes available in the Visual InterDev Data View.

The Query Designer

The Visual InterDev Query Designer was clearly inspired by previous versions of the Access Query By Example, or QBE, capability. The right side of Figure 45.2 shows the four panes available in the Visual InterDev Data View from the View|Show Panes sub menu. The top section on the right is the diagram pane into which you can drag and drop tables, views, or other queries from the Data View on the left. You can also create joins by connecting fields between tables in the diagram pane.

The next section down is the grid pane where any fields selected from tables in the diagram pane are displayed.

The SQL pane displays the live SQL resulting from any changes in the two panes above. You can even perform ad hoc pass-through SQL queries to the connected ODBC database by typing directly into this pane. The diagram, grid, and results panes automatically update to reflect changes made in the SQL pane, as long as they are syntactically correct. The SQL generated in this pane by changes in the diagram pane will vary from ANSI SQL 92 to ODBC SQL, depending on the connected database.

The results pane is displayed at the bottom of the right side.

Database Designer

The Database designer group of tools is, itself, designed to work with SQL 6.5 databases. The centerpiece of this tool set is the database diagram: a graphical representation of all SQL server objects in your database including tables, the relationships between them, and the columns, indices, and constraints within the tables. From within this environment, you can edit the database objects and test your changes. These changes are not applied to the back-end database until you manually save them, when they are stored as transact SQL code. Within the diagrams (as well as virtually every other view in the Visual InterDev development environment), context-sensitive menus are available for any object with a click of the right mouse button. Clearly, the developers of Visual InterDev took extraordinary steps to ensure that help files are ubiquitous in the environment.

Source Code Editor

The Visual Data Tools Source Code Editor is the environment provided to generate and edit and compile stored procedures as well as triggers. Triggers are a type of stored procedure that can be invoked from SQL update, insert, or delete actions.

Using ActiveX Controls to Access Databases in Visual InterDev

If you are new to ActiveX controls, you may not be as new as you think. If you have used OLE Custom Controls (OCXs) or have been around long enough to remember Visual Basic Custom Controls (VBXs), ActiveX controls are simply their Web-ified descendants. Like their ancestors, these self-contained components offer extensible standardized functionality in the form of dynamic link libraries.

ActiveX controls come in two flavors: design-time and runtime. The runtime variants operate on either the server or client at runtime. Those designed to run on the client are usually lightweight versions, due to bandwidth considerations. In my opinion, the use of these controls should be largely restricted to server-side functions, because standardizing server responses is usually easier than ensuring all clients hitting your machine will be doing so with these controls already installed or be willing to allow your server to install the controls on their machines and toy around with the Registry. Maybe I'm too much of a purist, but I believe an HTTP server ought to have a very good reason to stream anything other than the latest standardized HTML and perhaps a client-side Java script here and there. It is up to the individual Webmaster to decide whether the cool animated graphics are worth the bandwidth, but the Web surfer behind the browser will decide whether to risk loading that ActiveX control into his or her Registry.

Editorial aside, the design-time versions of these controls are essentially little CASE tools designed to amplify the coding productivity of the developer. The relatively straightforward Active Server Page you will develop later in this chapter contains over 230 lines of script to produce a Web page with a table populated with data from the NRS database. The more fully functional set of database-connected `.asp` pages you will develop following that contains over 1,800 lines of code. That should make the necessity of coding productivity tools sufficiently evident.

TIP

Unless you know users will be hitting your site with VBScript-enabled browsers, you should probably opt to do any client-side scripting in Java.

The four design-time controls that Visual InterDev installs in the Registry of the development machine are the Data Command, Include, Data Range Header, and Data Range Footer. With the Data Range Header and Footer controls and a minor amount of manual scripting, you can produce Web pages based on the results of SQL queries against the back-end database. The Visual InterDev documentation covers the use of these controls, but I am a firm believer in hands-on experience, so let me walk you through a relatively simple example.

Building a Database-Driven Active Server Page with Design Time ActiveX Controls

Say you want to build an Active Server Page that is populated with content from the Name Rank and Serial Number database. This will leverage the effort already being made to keep the database up to date, without redeveloping the HTML after every change. The following steps represent the direct approach to accomplish this relatively straightforward task.

Setting Up the Active Server Project

You start within the Visual InterDev development environment, in an existing Web project with a connection to the NRS database. Incidentally, arriving at this point is not exactly a trivial matter. You must first set up your server, install Active Server Pages (the `isapi.dll`) on it, and install the Visual InterDev development environment on the client. You then establish a workspace, Web project, and a data connection to the back-end database. For more details on this process, refer to Chapter 5 in the recently released *Microsoft Visual InterDev Unleashed*.

Next, you need to create a view (query) containing the tables and fields you want in your Web page. If all the fields come from one table, no new view is required. You can create a query in the native RDBMS of your back-end database or with the Visual InterDev Visual Data Tools. To create the view in Visual Data Tools, open the Visual InterDev Data View, as shown in Figure 45.2. Drag and drop the tables needed by your query into the diagram pane. Establish joins by dragging and dropping foreign keys between the tables.

For this example, you will display a listing of name, rank, service, and URL, so check these fields in the diagram pane, and they will appear in the grid pane. As you change the query, the SQL statement will be dynamically modified in the SQL pane. In the SQL pane, type `CREATE VIEW <view name> AS` and run the Create View procedure from the Run command on the Tools menu. Your new view will appear as an icon under the `views` folder in the Visual InterDev Data View. You can view all aspects of your new view in the Data View, as shown in Figure 45.3.

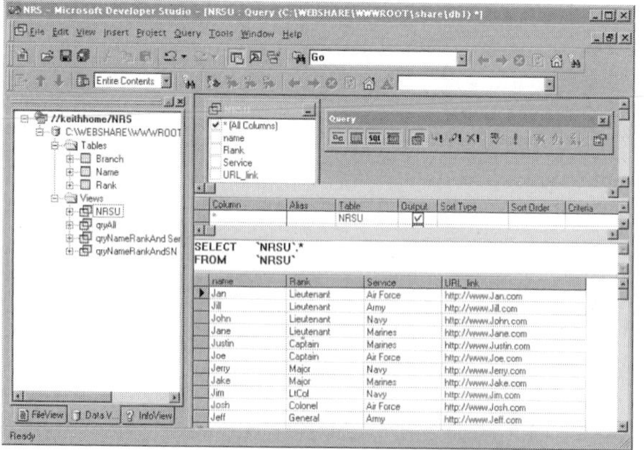

FIGURE 45.3.
The Visual InterDev Data View showing the data you will use to populate the data-driven Active Server Page.

Building the Active Server Page

The next step is to create a shell table to receive the records returned from the database. From here, simply dragging and dropping fields onto an Active Server Page would be nice, but that may be asking a bit too much for the first release of Visual InterDev. Maybe next time. For now, switch to the File View, as shown in Figure 45.1, and choose File|New. Now, rather than select a new HTML file, select a new ASP file instead. The difference is subtle but profound. The basic concept behind Active Server Pages is not to create HTML, but to create programs that create HTML dynamically, dependent on user actions.

On the right pane, you will see a standard set of HTML tags with the comment <!-- Insert HTML here --> between the body tags. Type a title between the title tags and close it. Because you will be building a page to extract data from the name, rank, and service fields of the Name Rank and Serial Number database, enter the title Name Rank and Service. Right-click the new file, and choose Open with. You have several options here, including the FrontPage Editor. Here you get to use your well-earned FrontPage development skills. The FrontPage Editor opens the blank page on the Normal tab, with HTML and Preview tabs in the background.

To extract four fields from the database, insert a table with two rows and four columns. Format the table as you like, and type the names you want at the top of each column into the four fields of the top row. Your table should look something like the one shown in Figure 45.4.

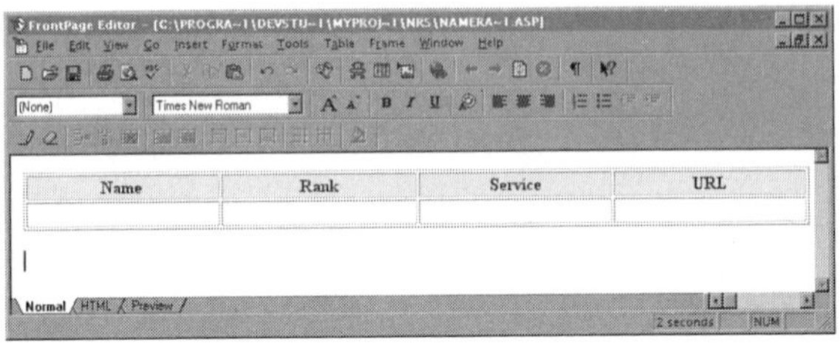

FIGURE 45.4.
Prepare a shell table in the FrontPage Editor to receive the records returned from the code generated by the Data Range Header Control.

Save the ASP file and close the FrontPage Editor. The Source Code View of the .asp page is then updated with the table tags.

Note that although Visual InterDev installs with a version of the FrontPage Editor, you should be careful which files you open in it. Because the FrontPage Editor was created before the advent of Active Server Pages, even the current incarnation is unaware of the <%...%> delimiters for server-side scripts. Unfortunately, these tags have some HTML contexts such as <Table Width=X%>. As a result, the Editor may rearrange these tags in ways that make for neater HTML but have nasty effects on your scripted code.

WARNING

The Visual InterDev client installs its own version of the FrontPage Editor for use in developing Active Server Applications. This editor will perform automatic code reformatting that can change the syntax in your scripts. This makes the HTML prettier, but can blow up your code! This is a case of function following form. Don't edit complex .asp files in the FrontPage Editor, or you might get a big surprise.

Populating the Table with the Data Range Controls

To continue, insert the cursor immediately following the second <tr> tag, right-click, and choose Insert ActiveX control. From the Design Time tab, select the Data Range Header control. The

Properties dialog box for the control then appears; here you specify several control parameters including the data connection and command type. Selecting the SQL command type produces a wizard that leads you through the creation of an SQL statement much like you did by manually creating the new view in the preceding chapter. Because you have already performed this task, select the View command type. After you accomplish this task, the command text dialog box will be populated with a list of views from the database. Select the view you created earlier, and specify the range type as Table because you are populating an HTML table. If you want the records returned to be split between multiple pages, specify record paging and the number of records to be displayed per page. Figure 45.5 shows the Control tab of the Properties dialog box. After you finish specifying properties, close the page showing the Data Range Header object, and you will see over 150 new lines of code in your Active Server page.

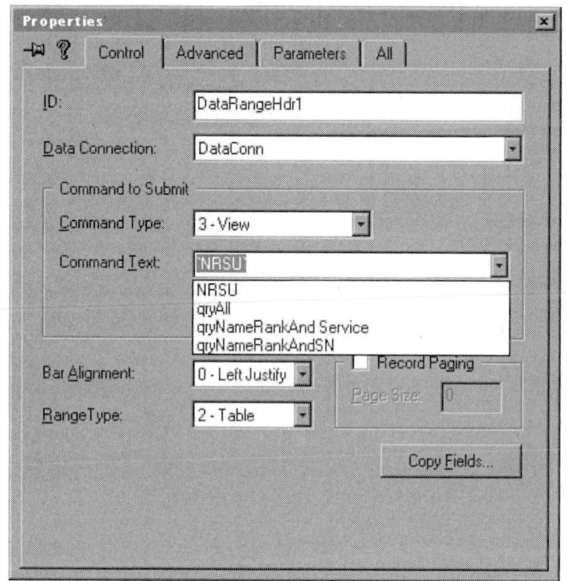

FIGURE 45.5.
The Control tab of the Properties dialog box, from which you can select any table, query, or view for use in the Data Range Header.

In this one place, a bit of manual scripting is required to populate the blank lower four fields with records from the NRS database. Look for the end of the Data Range Header script, where you will find the tag `<!--METADATA TYPE="DesignerControl" endspan-->`. The four table definition tags following the end of the script generated by the data range header should look something like this:

```
<td width="25%"> </td>
<td width="25%"> </td>
<td width="25%"> </td>
<td width="25%"> </td>
```

These blank placeholders for the database fields should be replaced with lines that extract data from the requisite four fields as follows:

```
<td align="center"><strong><%= DataRangeHdr1("name") %></strong></td>
<td align="center"><strong><%= DataRangeHdr1("Rank") %></strong></td>
<td align="center"><strong><%= DataRangeHdr1("Service") %></strong></td>
<td><ahref="<%= DataRangeHdr1("URL_link") %>"><%= DataRangeHdr1("URL_link") %></
a></td>
```

All active server scripts are flanked with `<%...%>` tags and simply extract the field name quoted between the tags. The only twist here is the fourth line. Because this field is a URL, having these links activated and highlighted in blue on the returned page would be nice. You accomplish this task by including the standard HTML `<ahref>...</a>` tags around the field name.

One more step is required to complete the `.asp` page. Insert the cursor after the last `</tr>` tag, right-click, and insert a Data Range Footer control, just as you did the Data Range Header. You don't need to customize any properties here. This control just tells the server to stop when it reaches the end of the recordset. This design-time control inserts another 50 or so lines of code after the four customized field tags. Right-clicking in the source editor produces a pop-up menu, from which you can preview your creation in a browser. You should see something like the view in Figure 45.6.

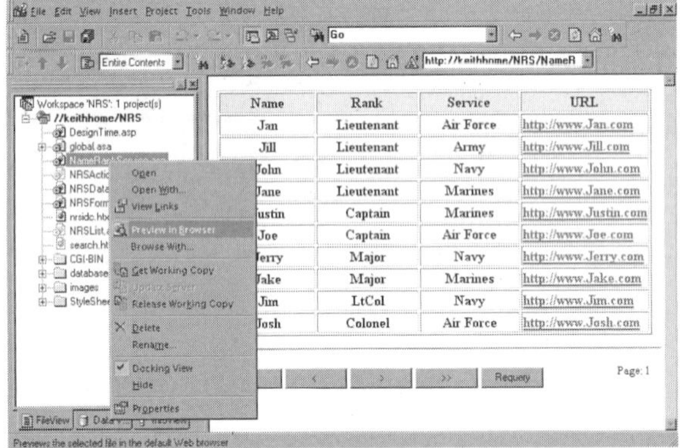

FIGURE 45.6.
Preview the new Active Server Page in a browser view integrated into the Visual InterDev IDE.

TIP

Right-click just about anything in the Visual InterDev Integrated Development Environment, and you'll get a context-sensitive menu.

Building Database-Driven Active Server Pages with the Visual InterDev Data Form Wizard

If using the design-time controls seems like a substantial effort to produce data-driven Active Server Pages, Visual InterDev offers a wizard that generates a set of `.asp` pages possessing all the standard functionality of a two-way HTML database interface. The Data Form Wizard starts by stepping you through the creation of a Domain Name Source and then offers numerous options for both the style and functionality of the pages in question. Figure 45.7 shows a few of the options available in step 4 of the wizard.

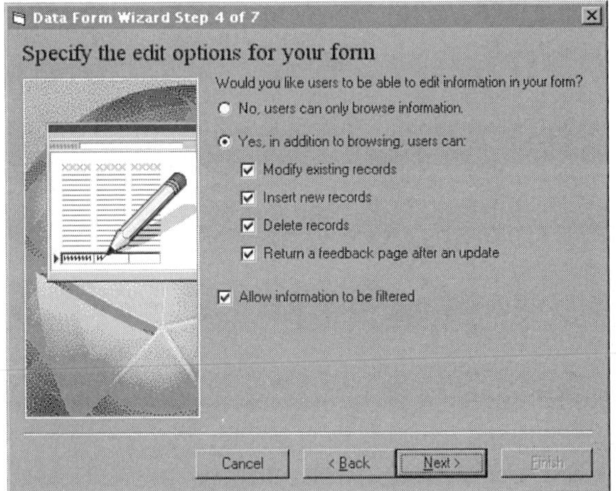

FIGURE 45.7.
Step 4 of the Data Form Wizard. How much scripting would these options take to implement?

Upon completion, the Visual InterDev project contains three new Active Server Pages. The form page embodies about 650 lines of script and presents the single record view of the database, with update options as specified by the developer in the wizard. The list page presents several records at a time, and requires about 460 lines of Visual Basic and HTML script. The third `.asp` page—`action.asp`—contains the server script that handles filter, update, insert, and delete commands from the Form View of a Data Form. It can also echo back confirmation of database operations and report errors. This page contains a whopping 742 lines of code. As a bonus, if your URL field has a title that starts with `URL_`, the Data Form Wizard automatically activates the links from this field in all resultant `.asp` pages.

Figure 45.8 shows the single Record View created by the Data Form Wizard. By clicking the Go to the right of the URL field, you can jump to the address indicated in the field.

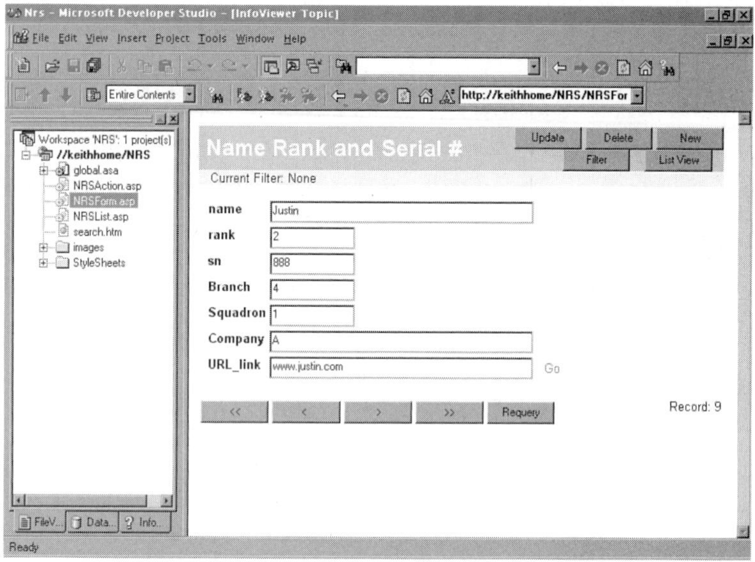

FIGURE 45.8.
The Active Server Form Page generated by the Data Form Wizard.

Summary

The three elements of any successful development project are well-defined requirements, appropriate resources (tools), and the ingenuity to bring the first two elements together. It's debatable which, if any, of these elements drives progress the most (I vote for number 3). Whether FrontPage 98, Visual InterDev, or some combination of the two is the appropriate tool set to apply on your project depends entirely on the other two elements. Odds are, as your Web needs grow, your development capabilities will grow to meet them: a kind of Web-ified version of necessity being the mother of invention. FrontPage 98 is a great place to start if you are new to Web development and/or your needs are relatively simple. As you grow as a developer and start to see new possibilities for porting added functionality and active content to the ubiquitous Web, you'll start to see the relevance of Visual InterDev and the power it brings to the table.

IN THIS PART

- Organizing Your Pages *783*
- Managing Your Web *803*
- Configuring Firewalls and Proxies *815*

Web Site Management with FrontPage Explorer

CHAPTER 46

Organizing Your Pages

by David and Rhonda Crowder

IN THIS CHAPTER

- Shared Borders 785
- Planning Your Page Organization 786
- Creating the Web 790
- Navigation Bars in FrontPage Editor 794
- Modifying the Navigation Structure 799
- Odds and Ends 801

FrontPage 98 introduces a new way to organize your pages. With Navigation View in FrontPage Explorer, Microsoft has achieved a useful and workable combination of automated features and designer control. Just drag the pages into position, establishing peer and parent-child relationships among them, and FrontPage Explorer will do the rest, automatically adding navigation bars to your web. With these new features, your visitors can move with ease among your pages.

Navigation bars are like a selective table of contents, displaying links to only those pages that have certain defined relationships to the page being currently viewed. They are not replacements for the normal hyperlinks used throughout your pages, but they are an adjunct to them, an alternative method for traversing the web.

FrontPage Explorer's Navigation View, as shown in Figure 46.1, allows the web designer to not only graphically portray the layout of the site, but also to plan it like a flowchart.

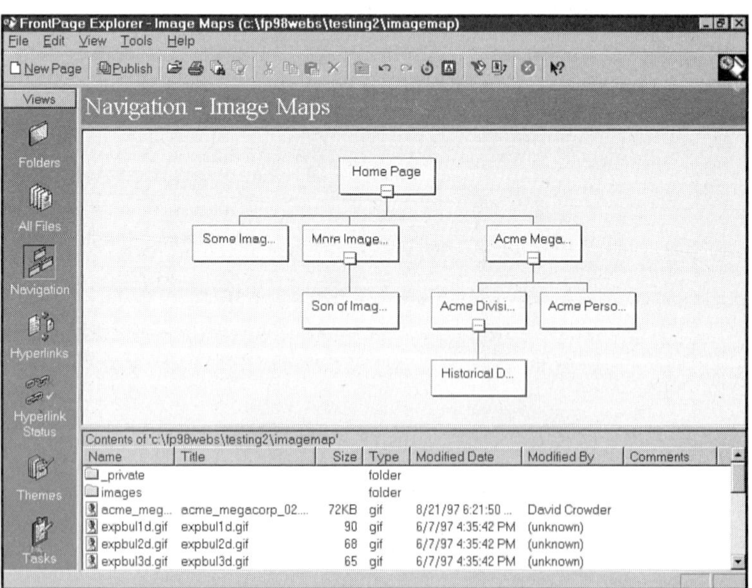

FIGURE 46.1.
Navigation View.

TIP

Before you make any significant changes to your navigation structure, back up your webs on your local drive. Choose File | Publish FrontPage Web, select a local folder, and give the backup copy an easily recognized descriptive name. For example, if the web is named `myweb`, then you might call the backup `myweb_old`. (FrontPage Explorer automatically names it `copy_of_myweb`, and you could do worse for a name.) Once you are certain that you are happy with the new navigation system, you can just delete the backup copy, or if the new navigation system has become fouled up beyond all recognition, you can just delete it and recopy the backup.

Shared Borders

For FrontPage's navigation scheme to work, you must enable shared borders for your web. To do so, just choose Tools|Shared Borders in FrontPage Explorer. The Shared Borders dialog box then appears, as shown in Figure 46.2. In the dialog box shown in this figure, the top and left borders are selected. (The bottom and right borders are designed for comments and do not affect page navigation.)

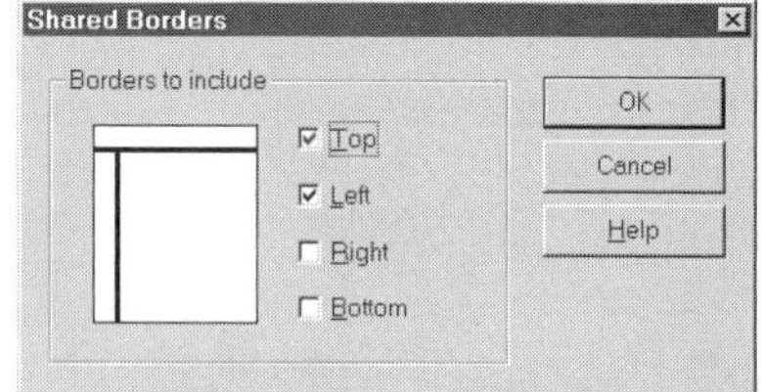

FIGURE 46.2.
Shared Borders dialog box.

The default content of the top border is a navigation bar using buttons that show all pages on the same level, or *peer pages*, in addition to the home page and the parent page. The default content of the left border is a navigation bar using text that shows all pages on the next lower level, or *child pages*.

NOTE

If a FrontPage theme (built-in style sheet) is applied, the appearance of the buttons and text are determined by that theme (see Chapter 14, "Designing Web Sites with Themes.").

If the visual representation reminds you a lot of frames, that is because "shared borders" *are* frames. Microsoft describes them as "page regions reserved for content that you want to appear consistently throughout your pages," but they are frames, plain and simple, with a separate HTML page for each tucked away in a hidden directory. Your pages are actually contained in the central frame, rather than containing "shared borders." For this reason, Microsoft advises you not to use shared borders on frames pages; the potential for conflict and unpredictable results is too high.

When you create a new FrontPage web using a wizard, FrontPage 98 automatically enables shared borders and adds navigation bars to your Web pages. It also follows a preprogrammed design for your navigation setup, so you have little to do unless you're unhappy with the design. Because the navigation arrangements that are already programmed into the wizards' results are optimal, you get little opportunity for learning other than by simply looking at them, and altering them will not improve the affected webs. Thus, in this chapter, you will build a web from scratch, including the navigation system.

TIP

You can change shared borders on a page-by-page basis in FrontPage Editor by choosing Tools | Shared Borders.

Planning Your Page Organization

Although Navigation View is an extremely powerful tool, it cannot take over the task of actually developing a functional and usable interrelationship among your Web site's pages. Without such a scheme, no site, no matter how beautifully wrought the pages, no matter how sophisticated the elements, can possibly fulfill any worthwhile purpose.

Understanding Page Relationships

Unless your site is composed of only a single page, a structural relationship exists among the pages. The two such basic relationships are *parent-child* and *peer-to-peer* (which are simply called *peer relationships* in this chapter).

The parent-child relationship establishes a hierarchy of pages, as you can see in Figure 46.3. In most Web sites, the ultimate parent page is the home page; all other pages are children of it. In FrontPage's navigation system, however, the structure of parent-child relationships is limited to a single level of pages. As far as a FrontPage navigation bar is concerned, the only child level that exists is the one immediately below the page containing the navigation bar. (In FrontPage 98, there is no such thing as an extended family tree, no grandchildren, no grandparents.) Each subsequent level then contains its own child pages, and the pages above it (which are children of the pages above them) become the new parent to the new level. Thus, in the hierarchy illustrated in Figure 46.3, each level other than the top and bottom levels is both a child and a parent; the top level is only a parent, and the bottom level is only a child.

The peer relationship exists among all pages on the same level of the hierarchy. Every child of the same parent is a peer. Peers can have their own child pages, but having them does not alter their relationship with other pages on their own level or with their own parent pages. To a FrontPage navigation bar, all pages on a peer level are available via the Back and Next command buttons, which allow a visitor to your site to move from the first page in your peer level to the last one and back again. Thus, the pages under the home page in Figure 46.4 are all peers of one another and all children of the home page.

In addition to the two basic page relationships in FrontPage's navigational scheme is a sort of variation on the peer relationship that is applicable only to the top level. Any page placed on this level, alongside the home page, does *not* have a direct relationship with any other page whatsoever in the main hierarchy based on the home page. It is neither child nor peer, though it can be a parent. FrontPage 98 calls it a *top page.*

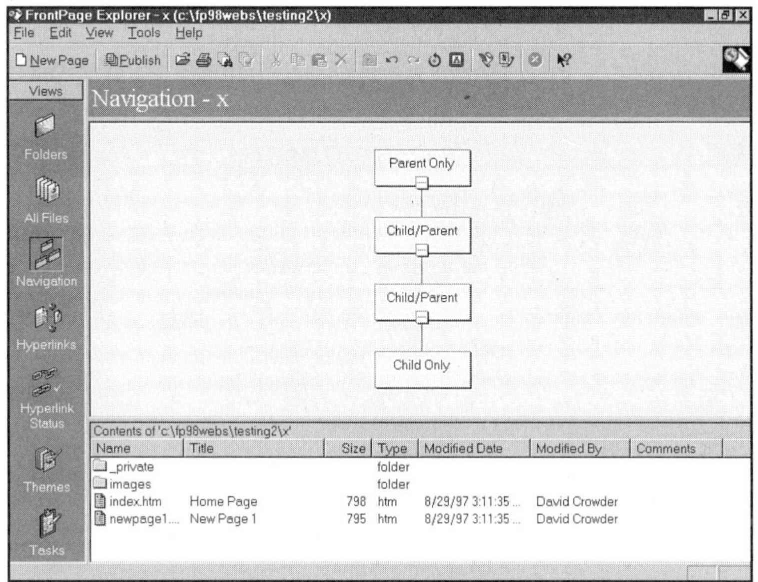

FIGURE 46.3.
Parent-child relationship in Navigation View.

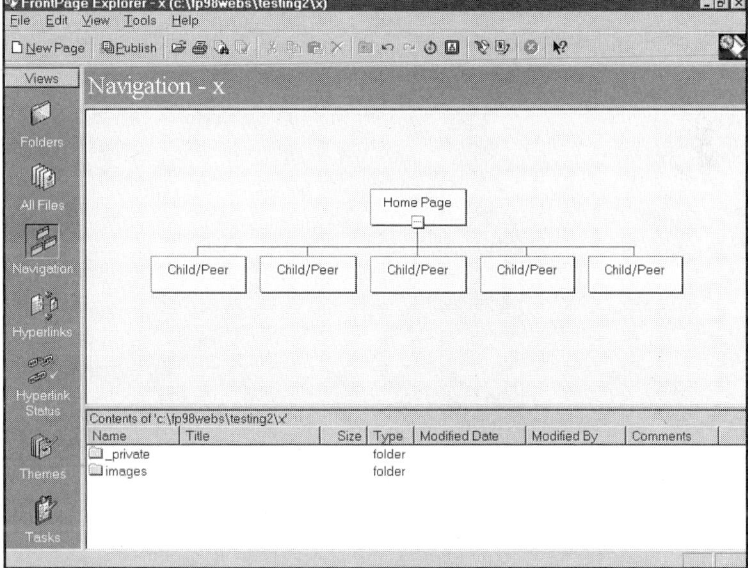

FIGURE 46.4.
Peer relationship in Navigation View.

Top pages are not included in the default navigation bars created by FrontPage Explorer. Thus, if you want top pages to be available, you must add your own navigation bar.

Although top pages are not connected in the Navigation View diagram, and thus not technically in a peer relationship in the sense used by FrontPage 98, they are, like peers, all on the same level. They can be reached, one from the other, by using the Back and Next buttons, and the Top level navigation bar serves much the same function as the Same level navigation bar does for peers.

Applying Page Relationship Theory

A FrontPage web can be satisfactorily developed without using page relationship theory. Prior to FrontPage 98, in fact, all of them were, unless a Webmaster went to a great deal of trouble to put in all the utility of navigation bars by hand on a page-by-page basis.

In the earlier versions of FrontPage, the easiest approach to producing an organized Web site was the haphazard method of using the table of contents to list every page in the entire web. This setup left the Web site visitor with a great deal of work to do to extract meaningful use from the site.

Bearing in mind the two kinds of page relationships, you can easily, using the new FrontPage 98 navigation systems, set up a structured approach to your site, one that can range from a guided tour (see Figure 46.5) to a programmed learning experience (see Figure 46.6).

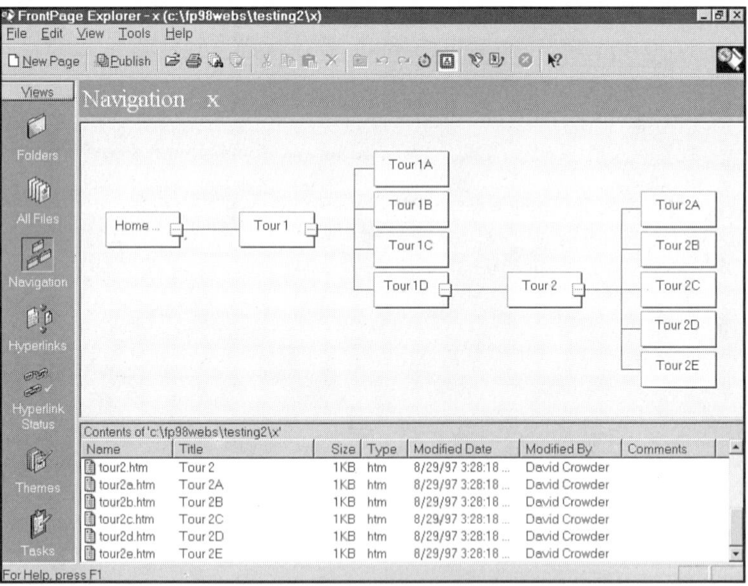

FIGURE 46.5.
Guided tour navigation design.

The first step in designing the navigational structure of your FrontPage web is to develop a basic comprehension of the material and subject matter you are working with. If you're developing a company web to support your work or a personal web to promulgate information on a subject dear to your heart, then you probably already took this step before you ever sat down at the keyboard.

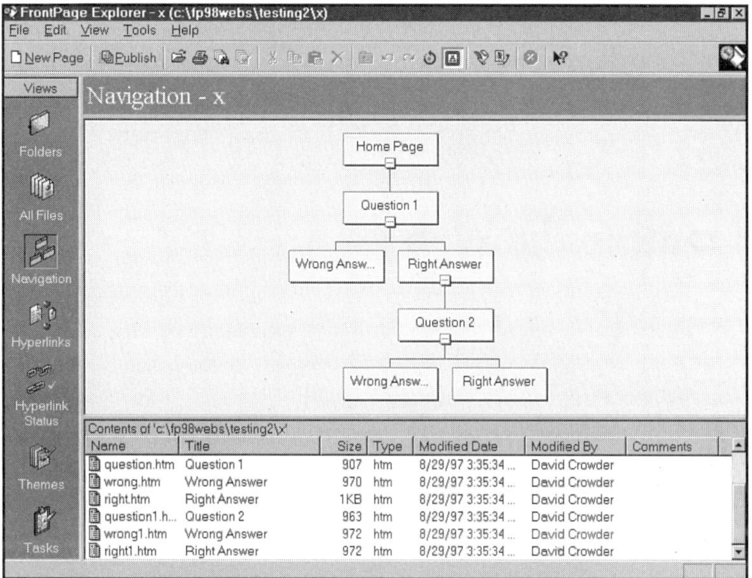

FIGURE 46.6.
Programmed learning navigation design.

If you are a professional web designer, however, you will often have to deal with subjects and material outside your experience. In that case, you have to learn fast. Interviews with people in the field, tours of factories or offices, and library research form the basis for the understanding you must have.

The second step is to shake down all this material to look for the natural relationships that are found in all things. Does the subject have an existing flow? Does one thing inherently follow another? Do established processes help guide you in making your choices?

Say, for example, you are designing a Web site for an art museum. The displays are probably broken down to represent various schools or styles of painting, such as impressionist art. For that matter, some sections probably hold other types of art, such as sculpture or new media. You are likely to find a separate area highlighting the work of the current popular artist of the day. All these facts point you toward a large part of your site design.

You will have other elements to consider as well to offer a truly rounded site. Does the client want you to simply put up an online version of the museum itself? In that case, you could use the home page as the entry door or lobby, and let each of the doors or corridors branching off from it lead into different sections. Obviously, the home page in this case is parent to a group of peers, unless one of the schools of painting is directly derivative of another, in which case it might be a child of that school's page.

How would you handle the setup if the client wanted you to also include a section on the history of the organization? This arrangement obviously requires a different approach than simulating a building, and thus another layer between the home page and the actual exhibits.

What if the client wants you to add a tribute section for major financial supporters or biographies of the staff? Each of these sections will ultimately have its own impact on the structure of the finished site, and in the end, you must decide how each element fits in.

The third step is comparatively simple; just use Navigation View to put all the elements in their proper places.

Creating the Web

To create a new FrontPage web for the demo, choose File|New|FrontPage Web in FrontPage Explorer. The New FrontPage Web dialog box then appears, as shown in Figure 46.7. Select the Empty Web Wizard in the list under the From Wizard or Template radio button, type the title `NavDemo` (or whatever variation suits you), choose a file location or web address, and click the OK button to create the web.

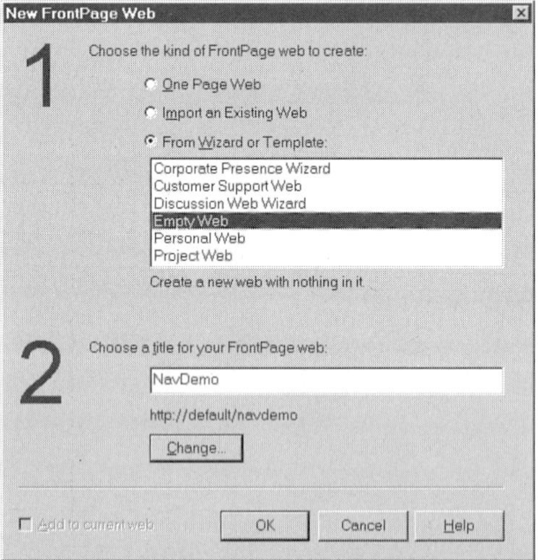

FIGURE 46.7.
New FrontPage Web dialog box.

> **NOTE**
>
> This example uses the "Arcs" theme. You can choose any theme you want, or none at all. However, the buttons are easier to understand if you do use a theme.

If you have not already done so, select the Navigation View from the Views bar. The results should look like Figure 46.8. Because you have not yet established any pages (this being an empty web), the Navigation View is empty, and FrontPage 98 prompts you to select New Page from the toolbar to establish a home page. After you have done so, you should see a Navigation View like the one shown in Figure 46.9.

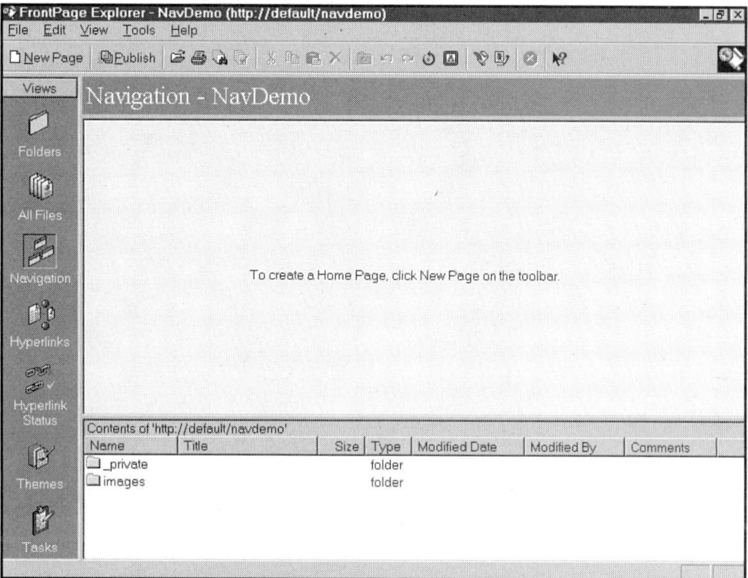

FIGURE 46.8.
Empty Web Navigation View.

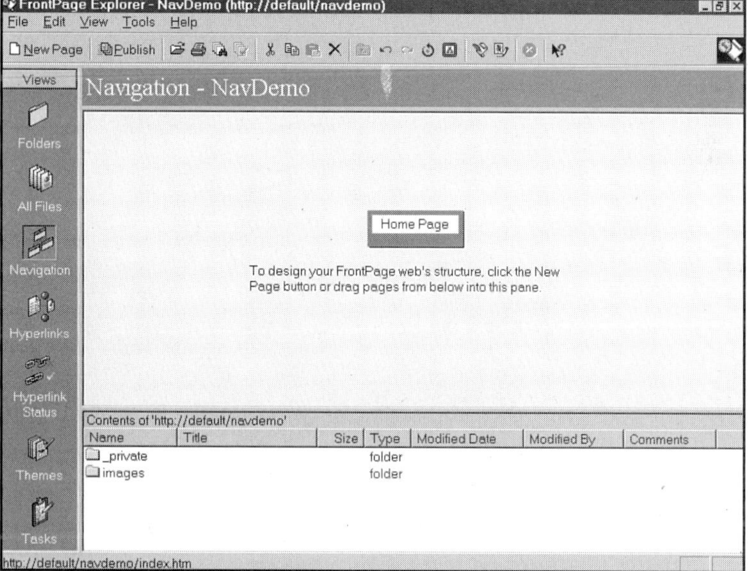

FIGURE 46.9.
Navigation View with home page.

Of course, to have relationships between pages, you need more than just a home page. Make sure that the home page is selected, and then click the New Page button again to create the first child page. At this point, FrontPage 98 asks you whether you want it to establish shared borders and navigation bars (see Figure 46.10). Click the Yes button to proceed. Your screen should now look like Figure 46.11.

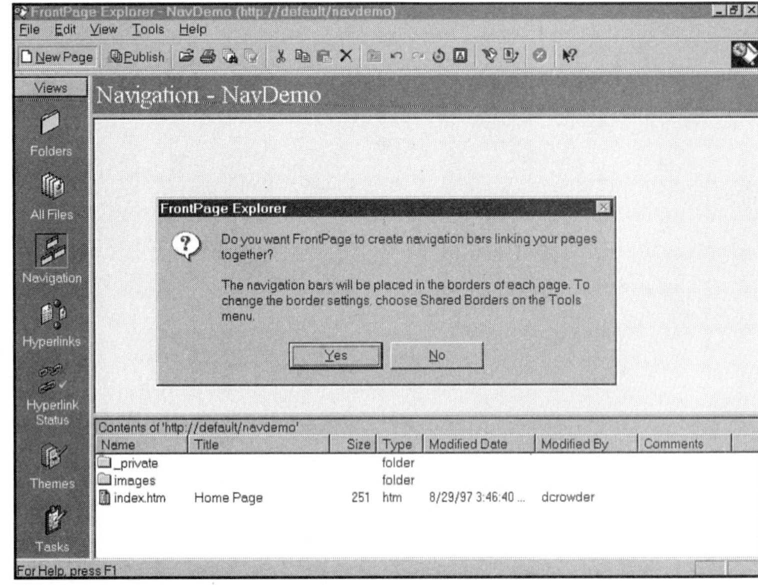

FIGURE 46.10.
Navigation bar message.

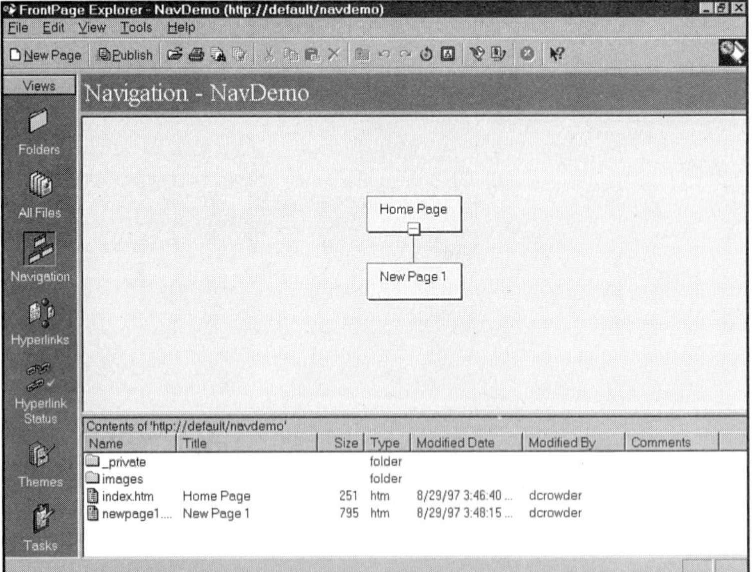

FIGURE 46.11.
Home page with one child page.

NOTE

To add Top pages instead of using the normal hierarchy, click the New Page button when no pages are selected in Navigation View. The Top pages then appear on the same level as the home page, but with no connecting lines.

If you continue to click the New Page button at this point, FrontPage 98 adds a series of child pages on the first level, along with the first one you created. All these pages are peers to one another. For this example web, add three additional new pages for a total of four child pages, as shown in Figure 46.12.

FIGURE 46.12.
Home page with four child pages.

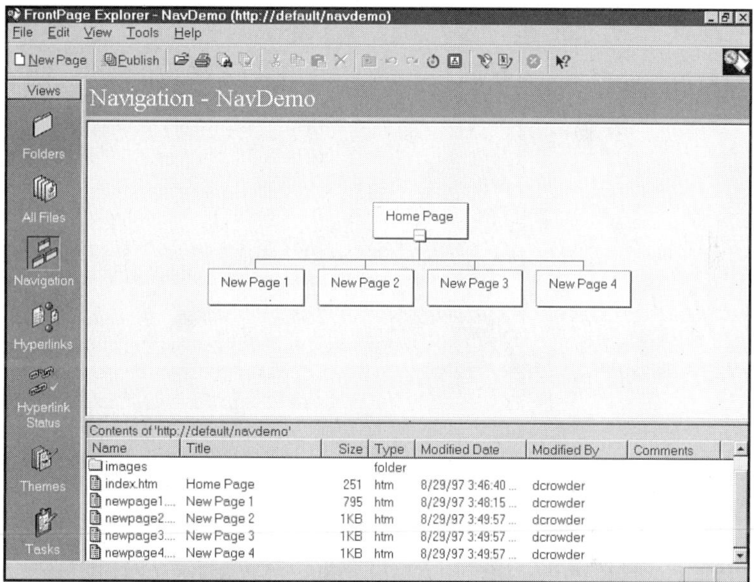

Next, you will add yet another layer of child pages to the hierarchy. The process is the same as before, but this time, select one of the existing child pages instead of the home page before you click the New Page button. Figure 46.13 shows the first one with two child pages added to it, but you can pick any one you like and add as many child pages as you want.

Before you go further, you should change the titles of the pages to reflect their positions. FrontPage 98 automatically tracks these changes. Because the page titles are reflected in the banners and navigation labels on the web pages, this information will make it much easier to see the meaning of the navigation bars and the effects of modifications in their relative positions.

To change the title of a page in Navigation View, select the page, and then either press the F2 key or just click the page again. (If you use the two-clicks method, make sure to pause between clicks; otherwise, you will be doing a double-click, which will launch the page in FrontPage Editor.) Either way, the title on the page representation is highlighted, and you can then type in a new title. Leave the home page alone. For the first child level, name the pages `Child 1`, `Child 2`, `Child 3`, and `Child 4`. For the bottom level, name the pages `Bottom 1` and `Bottom 2`. Of course, if you have created a variant on the example, you should adjust the names accordingly.

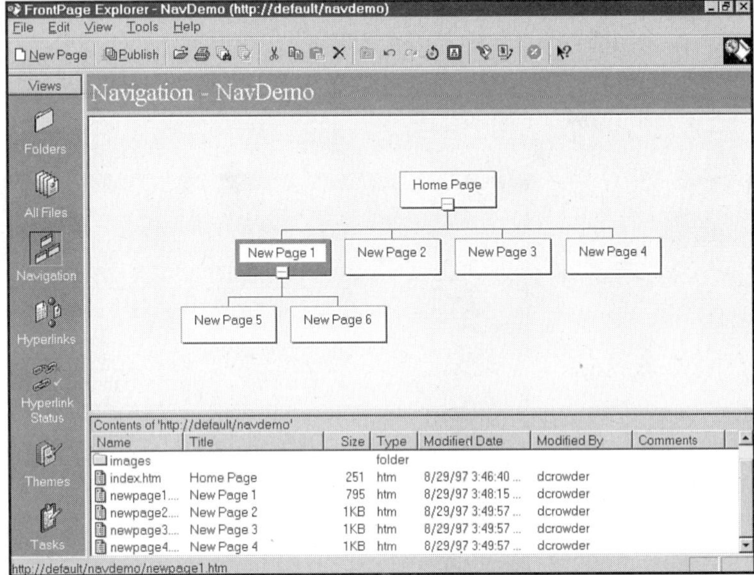

FIGURE 46.13.
Multiple levels.

Navigation Bars in FrontPage Editor

At this point, double-click the home page to launch FrontPage Editor. The page should look like Figure 46.14. The left border shows links to each of the child pages. The top border shows the banner with the page title and three buttons, each simply labeled "Button." These buttons, though they show in FrontPage Editor so that you know they exist, do not appear in Internet Explorer (see Figure 46.15).

These buttons do not show any links because, as you may recall from the section on shared borders, the default content of the top border is a navigation bar using buttons that show peer pages, the home page, and the parent page. Because you are currently viewing the home page, it has no peer pages or parent pages, and having a link to itself makes no sense at all. FrontPage 98, realizing this point, leaves the page blank. On other pages, where such relationships exist, the buttons show as you would expect (see Figure 46.16).

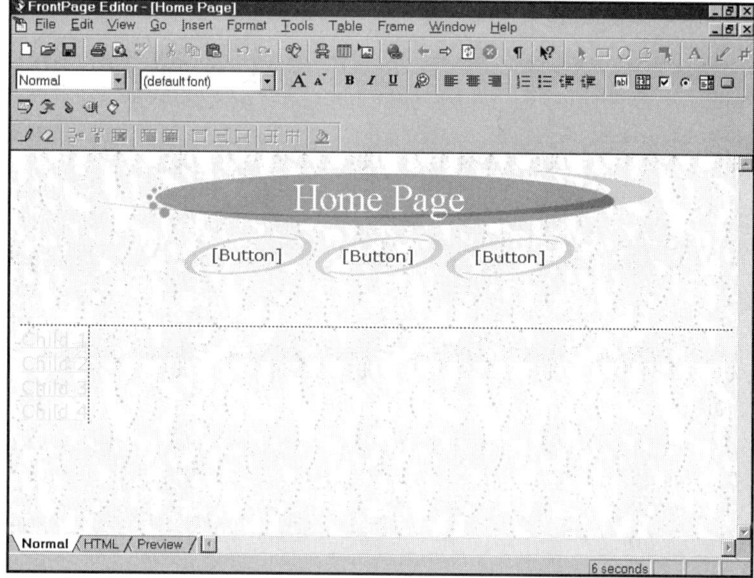

FIGURE 46.14.
Home page in FrontPage Editor.

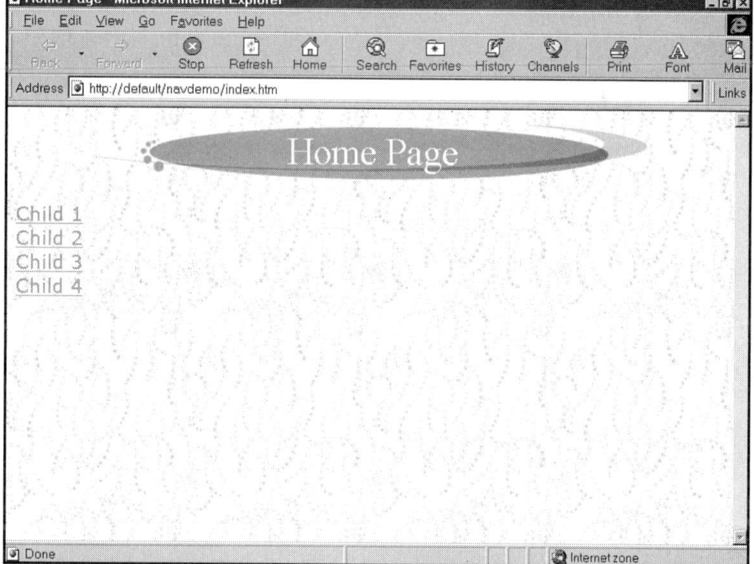

FIGURE 46.15.
Home page in Internet Explorer.

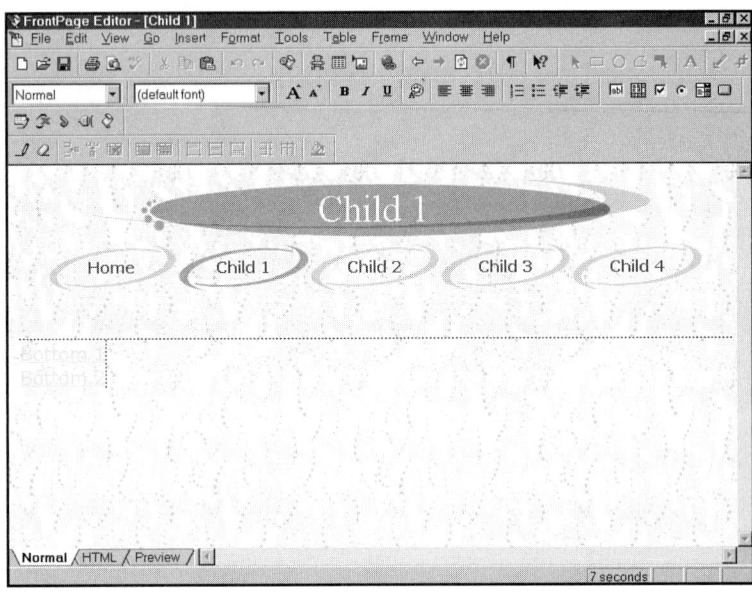

FIGURE 46.16.
Child page in FrontPage Editor.

Similarly, the left border links (which default to text-style buttons for child links) show only the label "Button" in FrontPage Editor and disappear in Internet Explorer for any page that has no child links (see Figures 46.17 and 46.18).

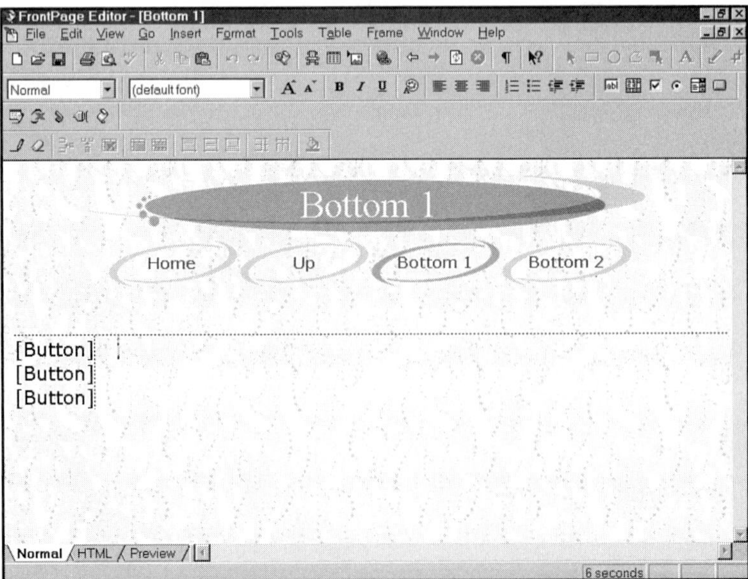

FIGURE 46.17.
Bottom page in FrontPage Editor.

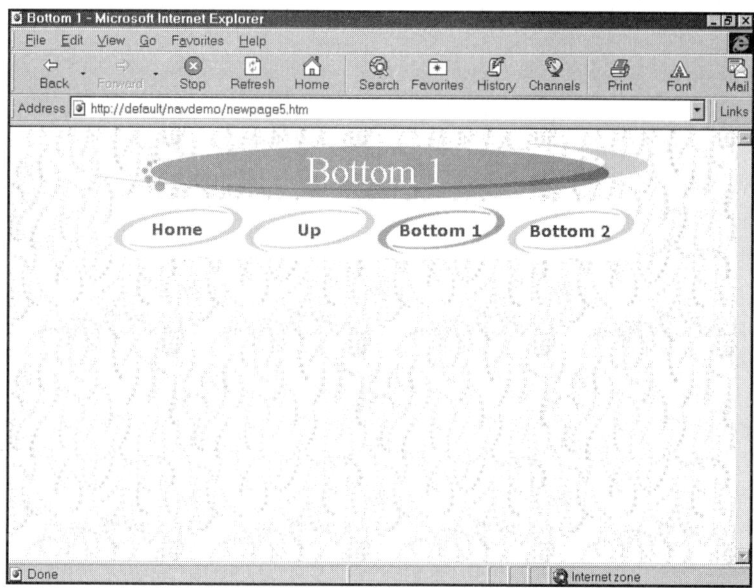

FIGURE 46.18.
Bottom page in Internet Explorer.

You do not, however, have to accept the default settings for the navigation bars in the borders. You have two options: either alter the settings for the existing navigation bars or add your own new navigation bars.

To modify an existing navigation bar, select it and then double-click it. The Navigation Bar Properties dialog box then appears, as shown in Figure 46.19. From this dialog box, you can choose which level of hyperlinks the navigation bar will display. You can also change its orientation (horizontal or vertical), as well as whether it uses graphical buttons or text buttons.

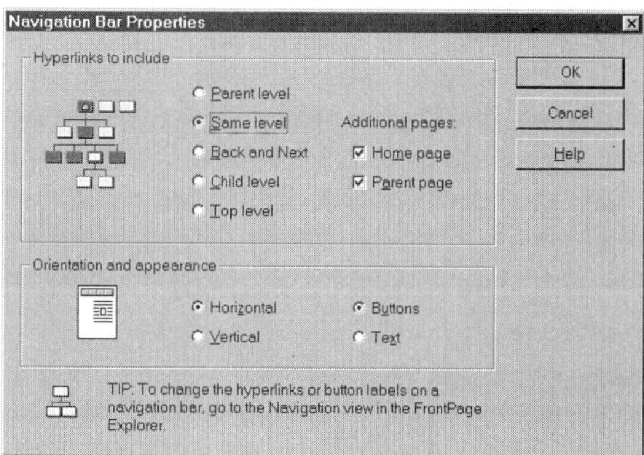

FIGURE 46.19.
Navigation Bar Properties dialog box.

The levels have already been discussed, but the Back and Next radio button is not actually a level. It gives an additional functionality for peer level (Same level) pages, which allows the user to move from one page to another along the level by clicking the buttons.

You cannot choose multiple levels in a single navigation bar; for example, if you choose the Parent level, you are barred from choosing the Child level. If you want to have multiple levels available, you must add more navigation bars, each keyed to a different level in the hierarchy. The one exception to this rule is in the Additional pages check boxes, which allow you to add links to the home page or the parent page in addition to any levels chosen.

TIP

If you select the Parent level radio button, then you don't need to also select the Parent page check box because the parent page is already included in the level choice.

To add a navigation bar, follow this procedure:

1. From the Navigation View in FrontPage Explorer, double-click a page to bring up FrontPage Editor with the page open for editing. Any page will do for this example, as long as shared borders are not deactivated in FrontPage Editor.
2. Click in the border where you want to add the navigation bar, and then move the cursor to the point where you want to insert the new navigation bar. In this example, add a new bar at the bottom of the top border.
3. Choose Insert|Navigation Bar to bring up the Navigation Bar Properties dialog box (see Figure 46.19).
4. Click the radio button for the level you want to choose. For the purposes of this example, choose the Back and Next buttons. You can change the Orientation and appearance settings to be different from the current navigation bar if you like, but having the new ones match the existing ones is better for design coherency. Click the OK button. Make sure you save the page so the new changes will take effect.

   Your top border should now look like the one in Figure 46.20. You should be aware that the page in this figure is in the middle of a row of peer pages and thus shows both the Back and Next buttons. If it were at the beginning of the row, it would show only the Next button, and if it were at the end of the row, it would show only the Back button.

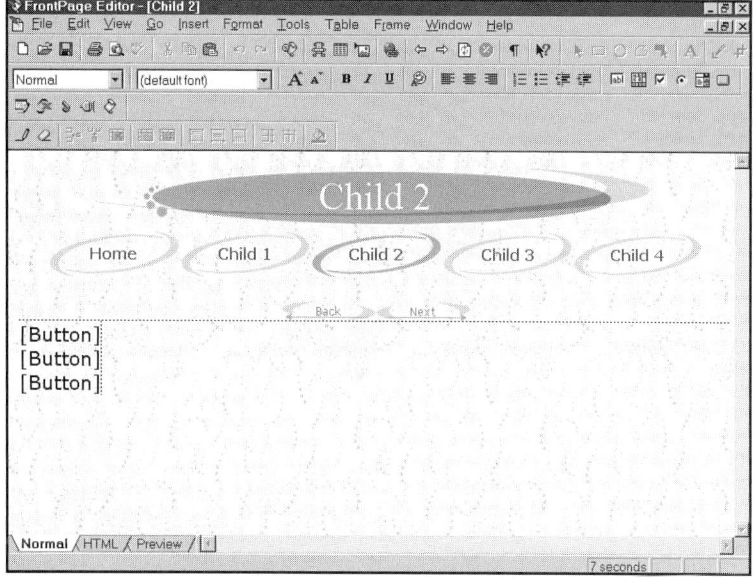

FIGURE 46.20.
An added navigation bar.

CAUTION

You must add navigation bars in the shared border region if you want them to be shown on all the pages in your web. Although you can add a navigation bar anywhere on your page, bear in mind the true nature of shared borders: they are frames. Anything added in the outer frame areas will still be there when the page in the central frame changes, but anything added to the page in the central frame can be shown only when that page is visible.

Modifying the Navigation Structure

Obviously, sometimes you will want to change the structure of a web, perhaps moving pages from one level to another, or adding and deleting pages. FrontPage 98 can accommodate these modifications just as easily as it did when you changed the titles of pages earlier. Its navigation system is designed to keep track of changes automatically and update the navigation bars accordingly.

To illustrate the fact, return to the NavDemo exercise. As you will no doubt recall, you had four child pages under the home page and two child pages at the bottom of the hierarchy (see Figure 46.21). What if you need to change this setup so that one of the four original child pages is moved to the bottom of the hierarchy? Simple. Just click the page and, while holding down the left mouse button, drag it to its new position. As you move the page, the connecting line changes to reflect the possible connections inherent in its current position. Take a moment and drag it all over the screen to observe this feature. When the line shows the new relationship you want, just release the mouse button, and the page will lock into its new place (see Figure 46.22).

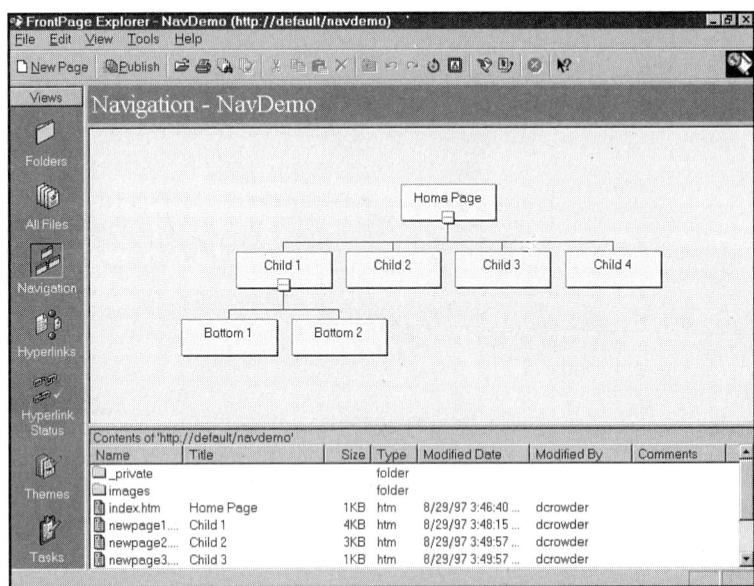

FIGURE 46.21.
Original navigation structure.

If you now go into FrontPage Editor, you will see that the change has registered in many ways. The page titled `Bottom 2` on the third level, which used to show only a Back button, befitting its position at the end of the peer row, now shows both Back and Next buttons, reflecting the new relationships on its level, the addition of another peer to its right, making it no longer the end of the line. Similar changes have taken place on the second level, resulting from the removal of one page and the addition of one to that level's child level.

If you should choose to delete or add pages, FrontPage 98 also automatically keeps track of these modifications, which you will find to be shown in all the navigation bars affected by the changes.

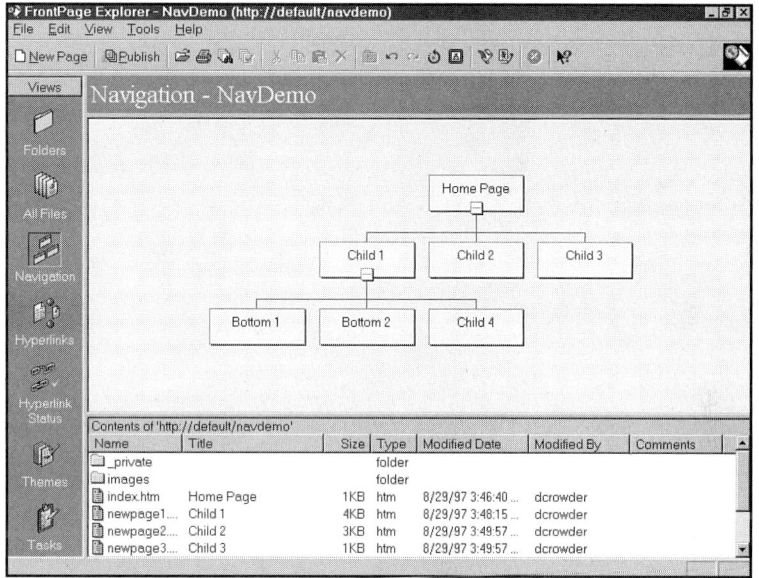

Figure 46.22.
New navigation structure.

Odds and Ends

What do you do if your navigation flow diagram grows too large and runs off the screen as in Figure 46.23? Just click the Size to Fit button in the toolbar, and the diagram is all squeezed into the available space. The drawback to this change, as shown in Figure 46.24, is that, if a large structure is squeezed into a small area, the titles on the pages no longer show.

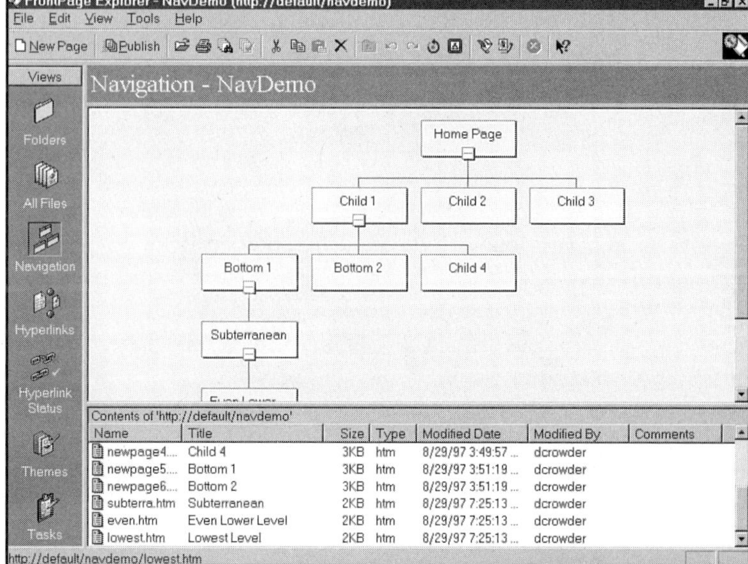

Figure 46.23.
Too large navigation structure.

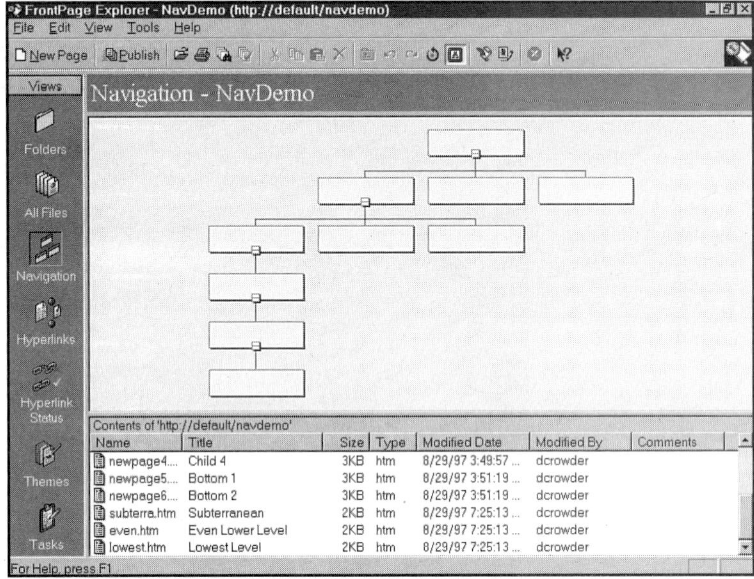

FIGURE 46.24.
Sized navigation structure.

The solution to this problem lies in yet another of FrontPage 98's capabilities. If you click the Printer button in the toolbar while in Navigation View, the entire navigation structure of the web is sent to your printer, including the titles of the pages not shown onscreen.

One more facet of the Navigation View remains: You can change the orientation of the view from portrait to landscape, as it were, by clicking the Rotate button in the toolbar. Depending on the particular design of your site, this change can have a stunning effect.

Summary

The Navigation View is an important part of FrontPage 98; being able to use it well will make constructing complex Web sites much easier. The pages that compose the site are represented visually in Navigation View, and Web developers can simply drag the page icons into position in a flowchart-like arrangement. Pages can be placed in the chart so that they have either peer or parent-child relationships with one another. Different Web site designs require varying approaches to navigational structure. Shared borders, which are frames designed for this purpose, must be enabled so that navigation bars can be displayed in your finished Web pages. These navigation bars, located within the shared borders, provide visitors to your site with the ability to easily navigate among the pages, following the pattern you established in the design phase. You can modify existing navigation bars or add your own custom-designed ones.

CHAPTER 47

Managing Your Webs

by David and Rhonda Crowder

IN THIS CHAPTER

- Automatic Web Updates *804*
- Manual Web Updates *805*
- Using Variables and Includes *810*

Designing, creating, and publishing your Web site is only half the job because, no matter how well designed or executed it is, no Web site is ever truly finished. The nature of the World Wide Web is totally different from that of all other forms of communication, and its component parts are in a constant state of flux. Sooner or later, you will need to change something about your site. Perhaps the change will be necessitated by updated information from your client or company. The need may come from outside influences, such as a broken external link. Whatever the cause, you will find that a Webmaster's work is never done.

Automatic Web Updates

Updating your web is generally a simple operation although a few unpleasant surprises may be in store as well as some simple ways to make your job easier.

In most cases, the best approach is to simply follow the same procedures you did to create and publish the web in the first place. If you need to create a new page, just do it like you always have. If you need to change some text, simply make the alterations, either directly on the remote server or locally on your hard drive, and then republish the web.

Fortunately, FrontPage 98 itself handles most of the changes necessary to update the rest of the web to reflect the modifications you make. If you change the title or location of a page, then all the hyperlinks in your FrontPage web are automatically reset to take account of the differences. If you add or delete a page, navigation bars automatically update.

The table of contents, however, does not necessarily reflect the new arrangement. For it to do so automatically, you have to open the Table of Contents Properties dialog box (see Figure 47.1) and click the Recompute table of contents when any other page is edited check box so that it is checked. If you do not want to make this choice (because having to wait for the table of contents to recompute every time you finish working on any page can be annoying), then you can still force it to do a recomputation when you are ready to by simply saving the home page (or, if you have not put it in the usual place, whatever other page you have put the table of contents on).

FIGURE 47.1.
Table of Contents Properties dialog box.

Table of Contents Properties
Page URL for Starting Point of Table:
index.htm
Browse...
Heading Size: 2
☑ Show each page only once
☑ Show pages with no incoming hyperlinks
☐ Recompute table of contents when any other page is edited
OK Cancel Help

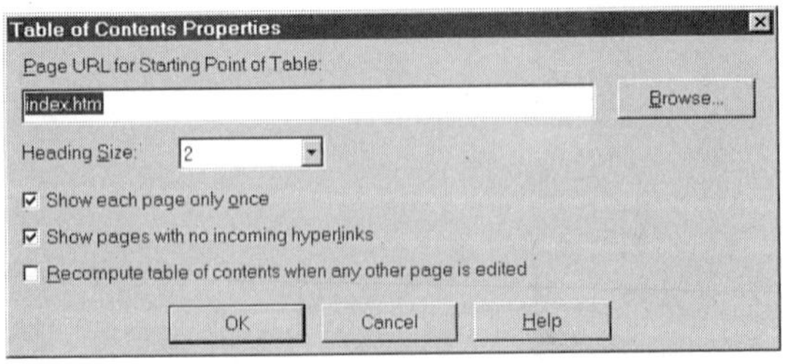

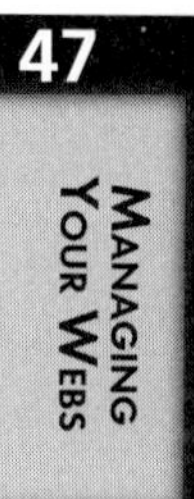

Manual Web Updates

When you're ready to delete a page, though, FrontPage 98 cannot fully handle the situation automatically. True, the table of contents (if you have set it to recompute) and navigation bars will drop the page from their listings without any effort on your part, but any hyperlinks that you have made to that page from other, undeleted pages will still remain.

The same is true of hyperlinks to images and other linkable elements. Additionally, external links, over which you probably have no control, create the same problem when they go down.

Unfortunately, FrontPage 98 does not have a command along the lines of "remove all instances of this hyperlink." Even if it did, the situation would still call for direct hands-on action by the Webmaster because such an action, in many cases, leaves textual references to the removed link.

You can deal with this problem by resorting to a manual solution. In FrontPage Explorer, select the Hyperlink Status View. All local broken links are automatically displayed without further testing (see Figure 47.2). If the same hyperlink reference is found more than once in the web (or even on a single page), each reference is noted separately. If the broken links are not all visible, click the word `Status` at the top of the listing to sort the files so that all the broken ones are on top.

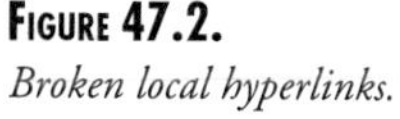

FIGURE 47.2.
Broken local hyperlinks.

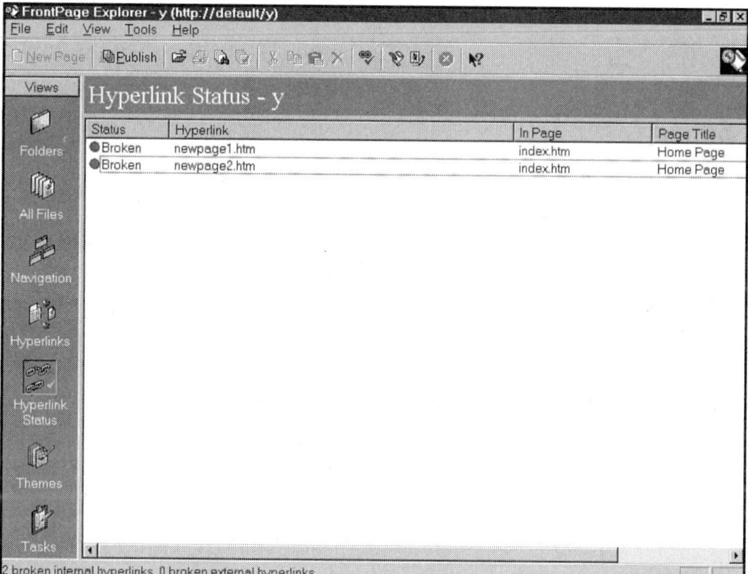

Next, double-click the broken hyperlink to bring up the Edit Hyperlink dialog box (see Figure 47.3).

FIGURE 47.3.
Edit Hyperlink dialog box.

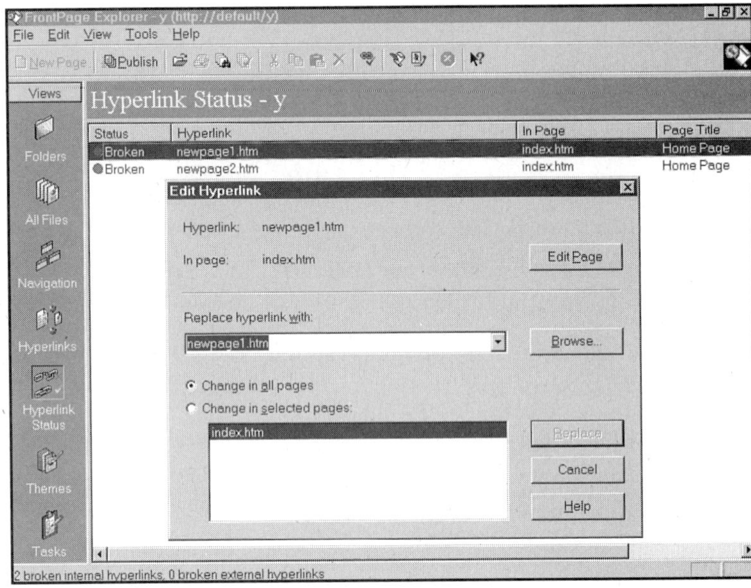

Click the Edit Page button to switch to FrontPage Editor. The page containing the broken link is loaded automatically, and the hyperlink itself is highlighted for easy location (see Figure 47.4).

FIGURE 47.4.
Highlighted broken hyperlink.

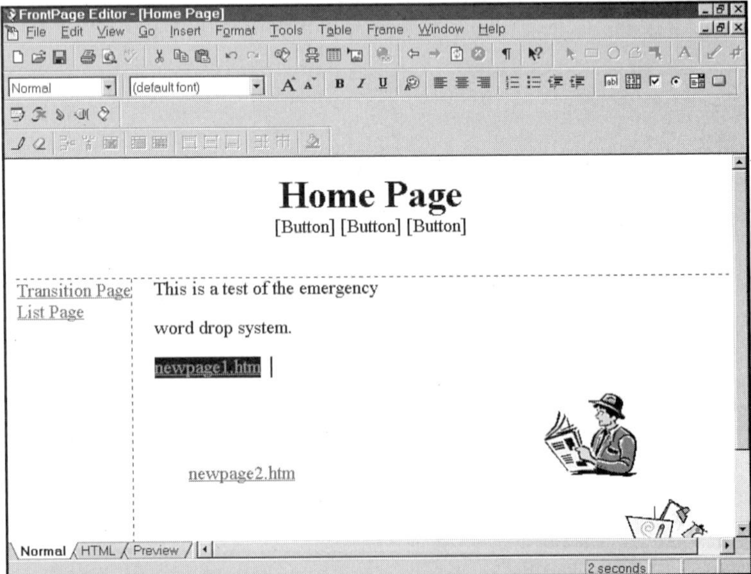

Delete the hyperlink and edit the text as needed to reflect the change, then return to FrontPage Explorer and choose Tools|Recalculate Hyperlinks so that your changes will be reflected in the Hyperlink Status View. You then see a warning that the process will take a few minutes. Click the Yes button to proceed.

NOTE

If, on the other hand, you have a broken link that you do not want to remove completely but want to redirect (such as a new image for the employee of the month), follow the same procedure except that, when the hyperlink is highlighted as shown in Figure 47.4, you need to change the URL to point to the new image. Depending on the particulars of the text involved with the hyperlink, you also might need to repeat the full procedure shown here to edit the hyperlink.

You deal with broken external hyperlinks in the same manner, but first you must test them. To determine whether external hyperlinks are broken, begin by selecting the Hyperlink Status View.

If you want to limit the hyperlinks that are checked, you can select the ones you want prior to continuing with the verification. As with other filename selections, you can use Shift+click to choose a sequence of filenames, or you can use Ctrl+click to choose separate ones. If you want to check all hyperlinks in the web, just don't make any selections.

TIP

Mailto links, although visible in the Hyperlinks View, are not included in the Hyperlink Status View and are not checked by it. You have to test them by sending a message through them and waiting for it to arrive at its destination.

Next, choose Tools|Verify Hyperlinks to bring up the Verify Hyperlinks dialog box (see Figure 47.5).

If you have not selected a set of hyperlinks to be verified, then the Verify all hyperlinks option is automatically selected, and the other options are dimmed, or grayed out. If you have selected a set of hyperlinks, then the Verify selected hyperlink(s) option is automatically selected (see Figure 47.6)—unless only a single hyperlink is selected, in which case you must manually select the Verify selected hyperlinks option. This time, only the center option is grayed out, and you still can choose to verify all hyperlinks instead of just your selected set.

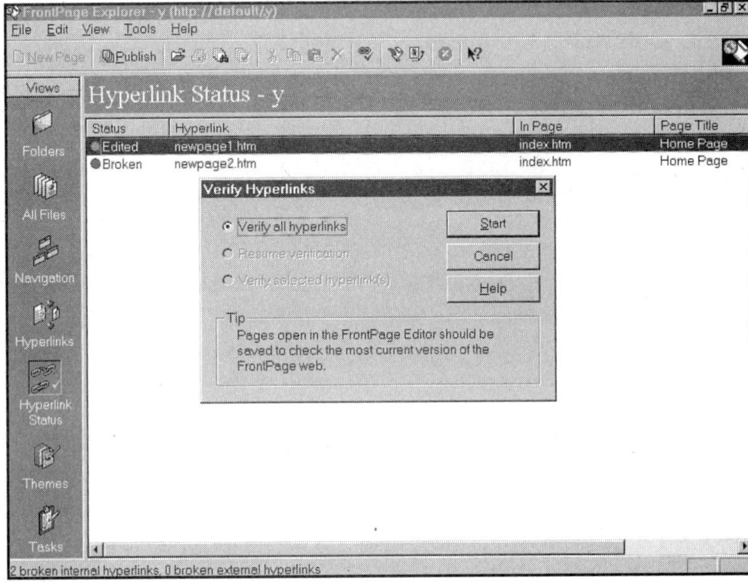

FIGURE 47.5.
Verify Hyperlinks dialog box.

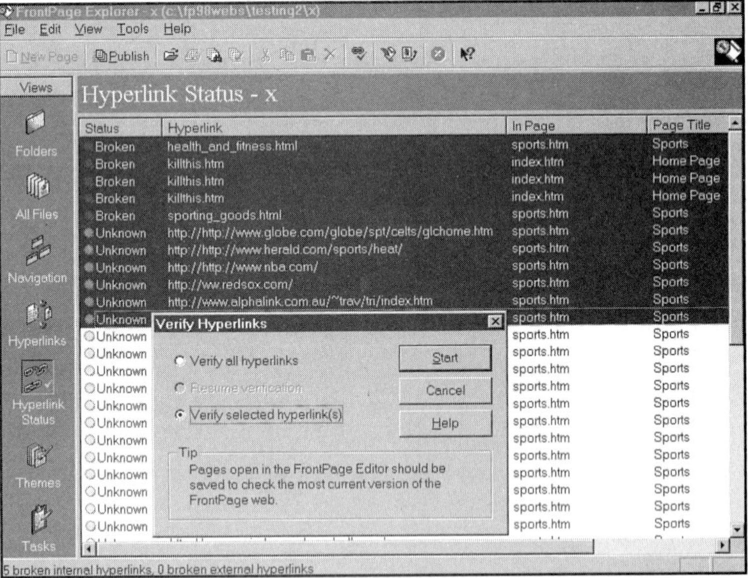

FIGURE 47.6.
Verify selected hyperlink(s).

Either way, you start the process by clicking the Start button, or you can click the Cancel button to abort. When the verification process is complete, your screen should look something like Figure 47.7.

FIGURE 47.7.
Completed verifications.

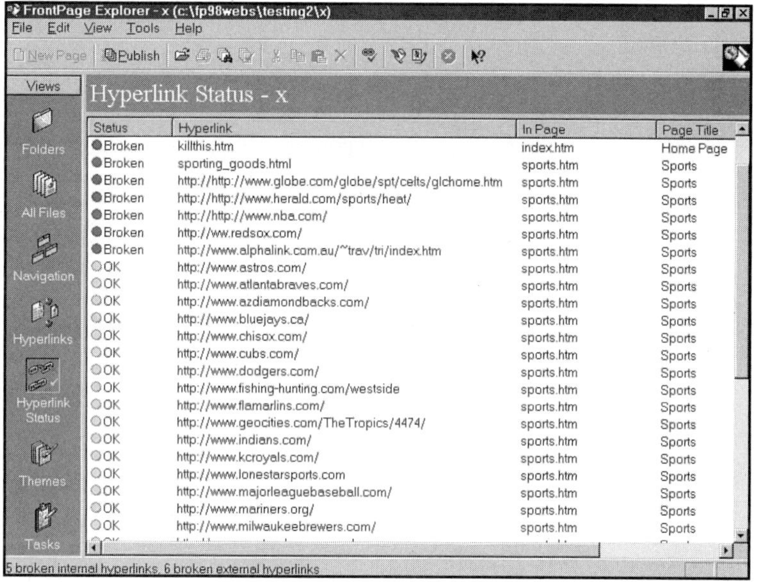

Depending on the size of the web and the number of hyperlinks to be checked, the verification process may take quite some time (especially if several external hyperlinks are involved). If necessary, you can click the Stop button on the toolbar to abort the operation. FrontPage 98 remembers where it left off, so if you want to continue later, you can do so.

To pick up where you left off, follow the same procedure as before, except that the center option in the Verify Hyperlinks dialog box, which was previously grayed out, is now available (see Figure 47.8). Just accept the Resume verification option and proceed with the operation.

CAUTION

Verifying external hyperlinks automatically, although a necessary part of the operation, can be misleading. The fact that FrontPage 98 finds a valid Web page at the linked URL doesn't necessarily mean anything; it could be something other than what used to be there when you first made the link. You should personally follow such links from time to time to verify not only their location, but also their content.

TIP

You can use Internet Explorer as a front end for updating your FrontPage webs while browsing the World Wide Web. All you have to do is surf to a site where you have authoring rights and then click the Edit button on the toolbar. FrontPage Editor then appears with the page ready for editing.

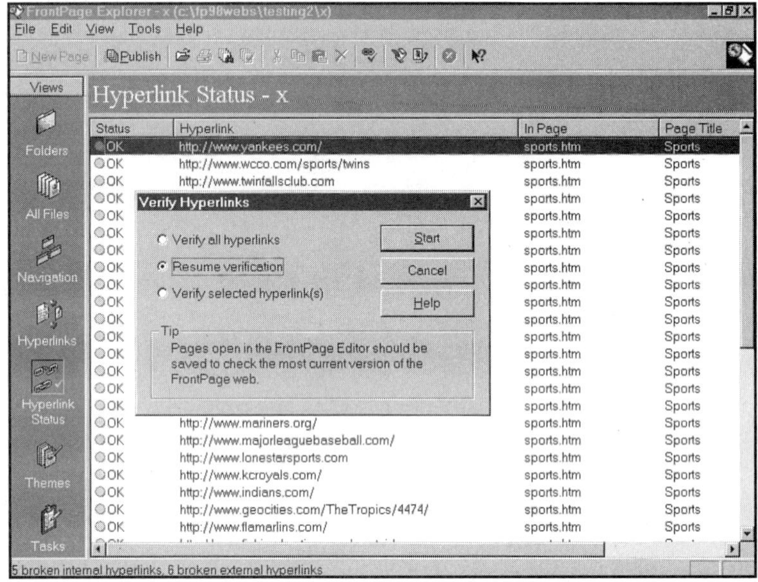

FIGURE 47.8.
Resume verification option.

Using Variables and Includes

Web variables offer a powerful method of controlling updates. In addition to their use for easy updating of FrontPage webs, they can also be used alone to create reusable boilerplate webs or along with templates to increase their functionality. If you use them in conjunction with page and file includes, the possibilities are limited only by your imagination.

Web variables work by substitution, in much the same way as the variables do in a form letter. You decide on a name for the variable and then establish the value for it in FrontPage Explorer. Be sure to pick meaningful variable names; `CompanyAddress` is far preferable to something like `variable427`.

To actually put a variable to use in your web, place the cursor in FrontPage Editor at the place on the page where you want to display the variable's value; then add the variable at that point. FrontPage 98 takes care of the rest. Later, when you change the value of the variable in FrontPage Explorer, every instance of that variable—all throughout the entire web, on every page where it is found—changes to reflect the new value.

To create a variable, follow this procedure:

1. Open the web in FrontPage Explorer.
2. Choose Tools|Web Settings to bring up the FrontPage Web Settings dialog box (see Figure 47.9).

FIGURE 47.9.
FrontPage Web Settings dialog box.

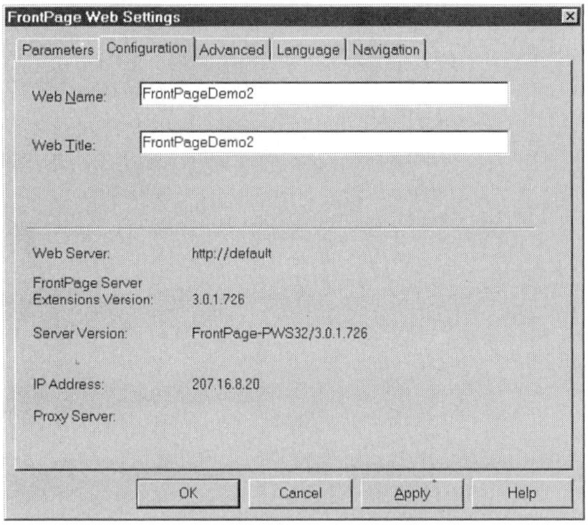

3. Click the Parameters tab. The dialog box should now look like the one shown in Figure 47.10.

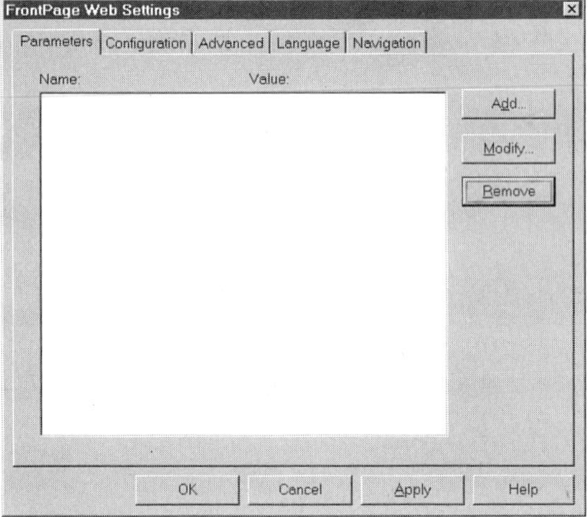

FIGURE 47.10.
Parameters tab.

4. Click the Add button to bring up the Add Name and Value dialog box (see Figure 47.11). Type the name of the variable and the value you want displayed; then click the OK button.

   The name and value you entered are now included in the list of parameters (see Figure 47.12).

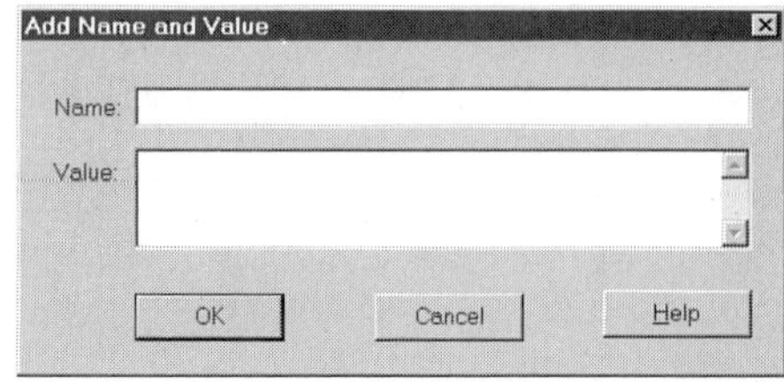

FIGURE 47.11.
Add Name and Value dialog box.

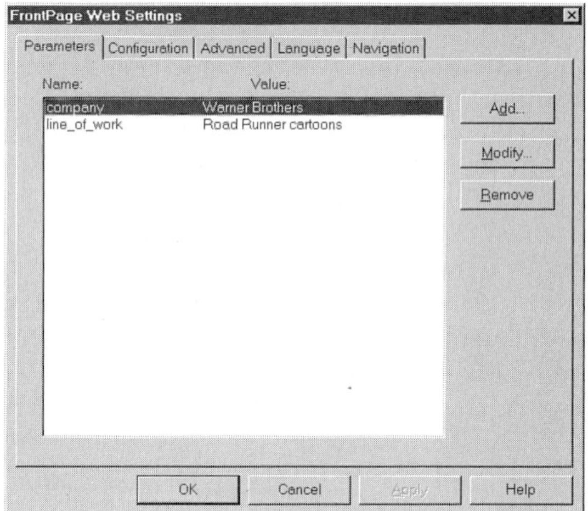

FIGURE 47.12.
Name and Value added to the Parameters tab.

5. Repeat steps 1 through 4 for all the variables you want to add; then click the OK button to complete the task and return to FrontPage Explorer.

When you later need to change the value that the variable displays, follow the preceding procedure, but in Step 4, choose the Modify button instead of the Add button. The resulting dialog box is identical for either method, except for the title at the top and the fact that the Modify Name and Value dialog box entries are not blank; they are already filled in with the selected variable's name and value. Simply alter the value, and then click the OK button.

To delete the variable, repeat steps 1 through 3 of the preceding procedure, and then click the Remove button. Be certain you do want to delete it, though, because no warning box asks you whether you are sure. After you click Remove, the variable is instantly removed from the listing. If you do accidentally delete a variable you do not want to remove, immediately click the Cancel button and start over.

To actually place the variable in the Web page, open the page in FrontPage Editor, then place the cursor where you want to insert the variable. Choose Insert | FrontPage Component to bring up the Insert FrontPage Component dialog box (see Figure 47.13).

FIGURE 47.13.
Insert FrontPage Component dialog box.

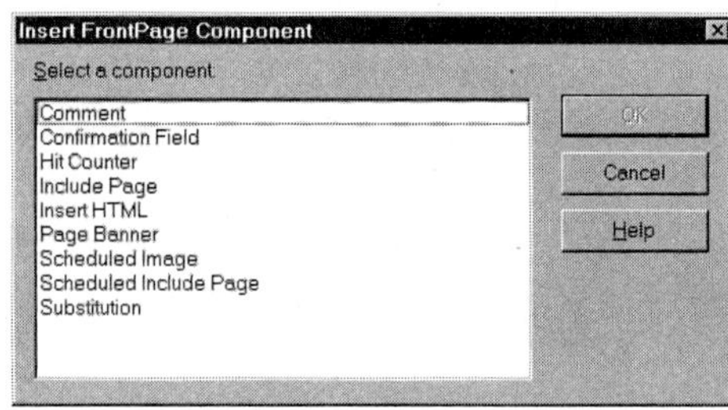

Next, select Substitution in the list box and click the OK button. (Alternatively, you can just double-click `Substitution`.) The Substitution Component Properties dialog box then appears, as shown in Figure 47.14.

FIGURE 47.14.
Substitution Component Properties dialog box.

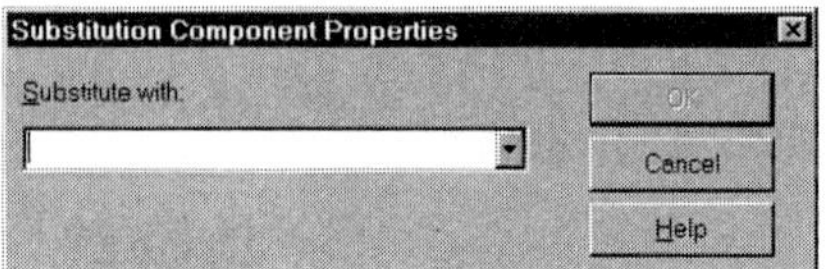

From the Substitute with drop-down list, select the name of the variable you want to insert, and then click the OK button. The value of the variable then appears at the insertion point.

As you have no doubt noticed, variable insertion allows you to manage only small pieces of information. If you need to handle larger amounts of data but like the functionality of variables, you can use the Include Page component in much the same way as a substitution component.

The Include Page component places the value of not just one small variable but an entire HTML page from the same web at the insertion point. The procedure is much the same. Follow the steps as for the substitution component; then choose Include Page instead to bring up the Include Page Component Properties dialog box (see Figure 47.15).

FIGURE 47.15.
Include Page Component Properties dialog box.

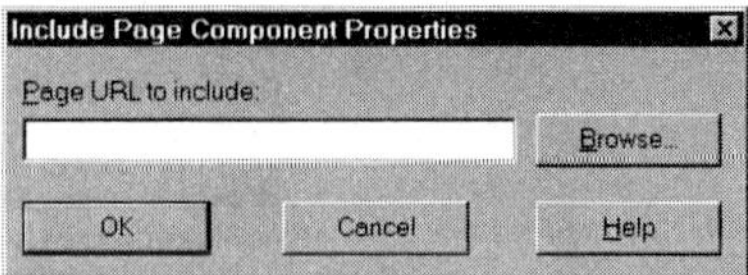

You can either type the name of the page you want into the Page URL to include edit box, or you can click the Browse button. The latter approach brings up the Current Web dialog box (see Figure 47.16), from which you can select the page you want. Clicking the OK button at this point returns you to the earlier dialog box with the URL of the page you want entered automatically in the edit box. Click the OK button to complete the procedure.

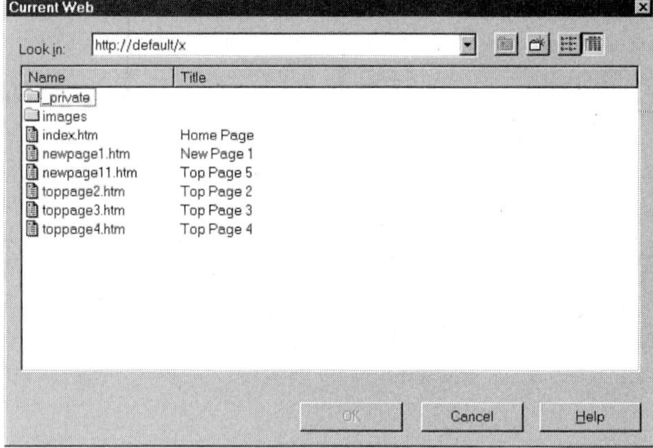

FIGURE 47.16
Current Web dialog box.

You can easily see that these capabilities give you powerful potential for easing the tasks of web management and maintenance. With a little bit more work, you could even use these techniques to improve on the generic templates included with FrontPage 98 by creating a web with one of them, then adding variables and includes in the appropriate places, and finally, creating a new template from the improved web. Alternatively, you could just save the web as a model and work from a copy of it when you want to make a new web from it.

Summary

The work of maintaining a Web site is an ongoing process. Although FrontPage 98 handles many updates automatically, there are exceptions where it does not or where it is best to do the job manually. The table of contents, for example, can be updated either automatically or manually, and there are advantages and disadvantages to either approach. The Webmaster must also handle broken hyperlinks, both local and external. Variables and includes are powerful adjuncts to web management.

CHAPTER 48

Configuring Firewalls and Proxies

by William Robert Stanek

IN THIS CHAPTER

- Firewalls 816
- Proxies 819
- Using Proxies and Firewalls with FrontPage 820
- Encryption 822
- Accessing Your Server 822

Whether you plan to use FrontPage 98 on a corporate intranet or on the Internet, security should be one of your major concerns, especially when it comes to preventing unauthorized people from accessing your system. FrontPage 98 has many built-in security features designed to help you maintain the security of your server and your content. In previous chapters, we explored access controls, secure webs, and other security mechanisms. This chapter looks at how you can use FrontPage 98 with firewalls and proxies, which from your front line in the defense of your corporate data.

Firewalls

When you are working with sensitive information, any slipup could cost you time, money, or both. With businesses where the security of data is crucial, a line is often needed to separate the data from the rest of the world. You need to insure that your important information can never be compromised or leak out into the outside world. In computer security circles, this insurance is called a *firewall.* Firewalls act as a protective measure, isolating regions of a network from the outside world (or perhaps other regions of the same network).

That's where firewalls come in, but a firewall alone does not secure your network. It is only part of a broader area of Web site and networking security in general. The complexities of firewalls, their components, and how to create them are far beyond the scope of this book. However, this section covers some fairly general ground and discusses how FrontPage 98 works with firewalls.

A firewall separates an internal network from the Internet. It screens and filters all connections coming from the Internet to the internal network, and vice versa, through a single, concentrated security checkpoint. You cannot reach the Internet from the internal network, nor vice versa, unless you pass through this checkpoint. Some systems even require you to log on to the firewall. A firewall protects you against the electronic version of vandalism and helps you manage a variety of aspects of your gate to the Web by keeping the jerks out and enabling you to concentrate on your job.

TIP

Using FTP, you can get information on firewalls from mailing-list archives at the following URL:

`ftp://ftp.greatcircle.com/pub/firewalls`

A firewall toolkit and papers are available at the following URL:

`ftp://ftp.tis.com/pub/firewalls`

Protection

A firewall greatly improves network security and reduces risks to servers on your network by filtering inherently insecure services. As a result, your network environment is exposed to fewer risks because only selected protocols are able to pass through the firewall.

For example, a firewall could prohibit certain vulnerable services such as Network File Service (NFS) and Network Information Service (NIS) from entering or leaving a protected network. This prohibition provides the benefit of preventing the services from being exploited by outside attackers while permitting people to use these services with a greatly reduced risk of exploitation. You can use services such as NIS or NFS, which are particularly useful on a local area network, to reduce the server management burden without exposing the network to outside threats.

The problem with firewalls, however, is that they limit access to and from the Internet. In some configurations, you might decide to use a proxy server (which the "Proxy Service" section of this chapter explores in more detail) to filter the inbound and outbound access your policy has determined to be safe. Although not necessary, proxies can be very useful.

Access Control

A firewall can provide access control to site systems. For instance, some servers can be reachable from outside networks, whereas others can be effectively sealed off from unwanted access. Depending on the level of risk you are willing to take in your Web site, you should watch out for outside access to the internal network servers, except for special cases such as mail servers.

When setting up access control systems, keep the following rule in mind: Never provide access to servers or services unless it is required. A good rule of thumb in access control is to keep the available servers and services to a minimum. This limits the number of possible break-in points on your system.

Security

A firewall can be less expensive for an organization than security measures on individual machines in that all (or most) modified software and additional security software can be located on the firewall system instead of being distributed to each server or machine. In particular, one-time password systems and other add-on authentication software can be located at the firewall rather than on each system that needs to be accessed from the Internet.

Other solutions to your Web site security could involve modifications at each server system. Although many techniques are worthy of consideration for their advantages and are probably more appropriate than firewalls in certain situations, firewalls tend to be simpler to implement because only the firewall needs to run specialized software. However, if you have a package-filtering firewall or require your users to log on to the firewall, you need either a router that filters the packages or a dedicated machine.

CAUTION

Don't neglect internal security just because you have a firewall. If a hacker cracks in, your network is exposed unless you have some internal security policies in place.

Privacy

Privacy should be of great concern for every Web site because what is usually considered innocuous information might contain clues that are useful to a hacker. By using a firewall, Web sites can block access from services such as Finger and Domain Name Service (DNS). Finger displays information about users such as their last log on time, whether they've read mail, and other items. Finger can also reveal information to hackers about how often a system is used, whether the system has active users connected, and whether the system could be attacked without attracting the attention of administrators and other monitoring systems.

Some sites have independent internal and external DNS setups. These DNS setups are used to translate a fully qualified domain name (FQDN), such as `www.mcp.com`, into an accurate numeric address (an *IP address*, named after the Internet Protocol) that is used for connection. The internal DNS setups have everything—all the names and IP addresses of your Web site. The external setup, which is the one accessible from the Internet, does not have all the names and IP addresses available, only those important to other Internet servers. Some Web administrators feel that by blocking this information, they are hiding material that otherwise is useful to hackers.

Logging and Statistics

By making all access to and from the Internet pass through a firewall, you can log accesses and provide valuable statistics about network usage.

TIP

A firewall with appropriate alarms that sound when suspicious activity occurs can also provide details on whether the firewall and network are being probed or attacked.

You should have a log of your Web site usage statistics and evidence of probing for a number of reasons. The first reason is to know whether the firewall is withstanding probes and attacks so you can determine whether the controls on the firewall are adequate. Another reason is to track your Web server usage statistics as input for network requirements studies and risk-analysis activities.

Proxies

Most people are familiar with the concept of a proxy, typically in the context of a proxy vote, or something along that line. A proxy stands in the place of another person and carries out an action, all in the name of the requesting party. This concept directly translates into computer security. Proxies are another form of security for networks. Specifically, a proxy server acts as an intermediary between the outside network and the internal client machine. The client requests information via a particular service, so the proxy server takes the request, fulfills it, and returns the data to the requesting client. Proxies are typically used to allow clients inside the firewall to access the Internet at large, without letting the Internet directly access machines behind the firewall. You can think of a proxy as a second line of defense for your network security.

Proxy services can also be used to isolate particular services within the internal network. Proxy servers can enforce what protocols are allowed to interact with the outside network. A proxy can provide only specific services (by acting as the intermediary) to the internal network, while refusing other requests. Each individual service that the proxy server allows can be called a proxy in its own right. If an application gateway only contains proxies for FTP and Telnet, only FTP and Telnet are allowed into the protected subnet. All other services are completely blocked. This degree of security is important. A proxy makes sure that only trustworthy services are allowed through the firewall and prevents untrustworthy services from being implemented on the firewall without your knowledge.

NOTE

If you have used TIA (The Internet Adapter), slirp, or TERM, you probably are familiar with the concept of redirecting a connection. Using these programs, you can redirect a port. Proxy servers work in a similar way by opening a socket on the server and allowing the connection to pass through.

Proxy Service

A *proxy server* is a special server that is typically run on a firewall. A proxy server that provides a web (HTTP) proxy basically does the following:

1. Receives a request from a client inside the firewall
2. Sends this request to the remote Web server outside of the firewall
3. Reads the response
4. Sends the response back to the client

Usually, all the clients in a subnet use the same proxy, which enables the proxy to efficiently cache documents that are requested by several clients.

NOTE

The fact that some proxy services are not transparent to the user means that either the user or the client must be "proxified." Either the user is instructed on how to manage the client in order to access certain services (such as Telnet and FTP), or the client, such as a browser, should be proxy aware.

How Proxies Work with Web Servers

Proxying permits high-level logging of client transactions, which includes logging the client IP address, date and time, URL, byte count, and success code. Another characteristic of proxying is its capability of filtering client transactions at the application protocol level. It can control access to services for individual methods, servers, domains, and so on.

Technically speaking, when a client requests a normal HTTP document, the HTTP server gets only the path and key word portion of the requested URL. It knows its host name and that its protocol specifier is `http:`. When a proxy server receives a request from a client, HTTP is always used for transactions with the proxy server, even when accessing a resource served by a remote server using another protocol, such as Gopher or FTP.

A proxy server always has the information necessary to make a request to remote hosts. The host is specified in the request URL given by the client. Instead of specifying only the path name and possibly searching keywords to the proxy server, the full URL is specified. In this way, a proxy server behaves like a client retrieving a document by calling the same protocol that the client calls to perform the retrieval. However, the proxy creates an HTTP document containing the requested resource to return to the client. A Gopher or FTP directory listing, for example, is returned to the client as an HTML document.

Therefore, a proxy server has a hybrid function. It must act as both client and server—a server when accepting HTTP requests from clients connecting to it and a client (to the remote server) when retrieving the documents for its own client.

NOTE

A complete proxy server must speak all the Web protocols, especially HTTP, FTP, Gopher, WAIS, and NNTP.

Using Proxies and Firewalls with FrontPage

With all the complexities involved in setting up a firewall and proxy server, talking to one might be complicated. It's not. All you really need is to set up a proxy server somewhere on your network. That job is left up to the Webmaster who's also the network administrator. There are entirely too many aspects of proxy servers and firewalls for FrontPage 98 to cover. The only aspect that FrontPage 98 lets you do is define an HTTP proxy.

Defining Proxies

To define an HTTP proxy with FrontPage 98, a Webmaster must load in a particular web. Presuming that he is an authorized Webmaster for that web, he can choose Options from the Tools menu and then select the Proxies tab. You can define an HTTP proxy server by typing in the host name in the HTTP Proxy text box (see Figure 48.1). In addition to the host name, you should specify a colon (:) followed by the port number (typically 80) that the proxy is using. FrontPage 98 automatically takes care of the communication between it and the proxy server.

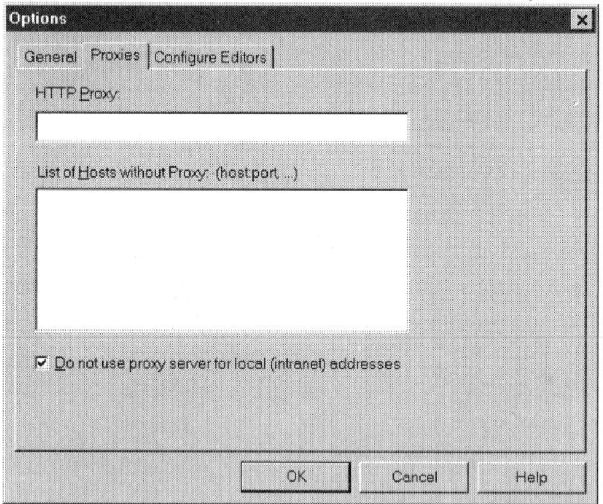

FIGURE 48.1.
To use a proxy server, define its host name and port number.

You can also define other hosts on the same network that are inside the firewall. Simply enter the host names and optional port numbers of the servers in the List of Hosts without Proxy text box. These hosts are then able to use FrontPage 98 as a pseudo proxy. These hosts can talk to the FrontPage host, which in turn talks to the proxy server itself. Use a comma to separate multiple entries in the list.

Another feature is the ability to tell FrontPage 98 not to use the proxy for local addresses. In this way, computers within the company intranet can access the web's content without going through the proxy. To use this feature, select the Do not use proxy server for local (intranet) addresses check box.

When FrontPage 98 Uses Proxies

After you've defined a proxy server, that server name is only used when you try to access the Internet. For example, when you try to use the Open Location command to point to a Web page outside the firewall, the proxy server is used. Similarly, when you try to open a link to an external Web page with the FrontPage Editor, the proxy server is used. Finally, FrontPage 98 accesses the proxy server if you use the Follow Link command in the FrontPage Editor to follow an external Web page.

Encryption

Some people need to send secure data with a Web server. To secure data, the Web server can encrypt the data to be sent. This form of data protection is typically used when you want to conduct transactions across the Net. Most methods of data encryption for Internet transmission are fairly secure. This feature is often the domain of advanced Web servers, so it is not available with all Web servers, which is the case with the FrontPage Personal Web Server. It has no provision for data encryption.

If FrontPage 98 accesses an encryption-capable Web server, the encrypted data merely passes through FrontPage 98, without ever looking at it. What this means is that you can safely send encrypted data through the FrontPage Personal Web Server. You can't send encrypted data with the FrontPage Personal Web Server.

Accessing Your Server

After all the Web pages are created for your web, you'll want to be able to access it. You can access the Web server from both inside and outside the firewall, and each kind of access raises different issues to consider. Fortunately, with proxy servers in place, accessing your Web server is not a problem.

Accessing Your External Server from Inside the Firewall

If you're sitting behind a firewall, accessing an external Web server isn't a problem. Follow these steps:

1. Start the FrontPage Explorer and select File|Open FrontPage Web to display the Getting Started dialog box. Click the More Webs button to open a dialog box similar to the one in Figure 48.2.
2. Type the complete host name of the external Web server that you're trying to access into the Open From Web Server text box.
3. Click the List Webs button to display a list of existing FrontPage webs.
4. Select the web that you want to work on and then click OK.

Accessing Your Server from Outside the Firewall

Suppose you're trying to access a Web server from outside a firewall. If the Web server you're trying to access is Internet accessible, you will have no problems. You can access the internal Web server from outside the organization's domain. However, if the internal Web server you're trying to access is behind a firewall, you'll have a problem. The only way to access an internal Web server from outside the firewall is with a proxy server. If your organization doesn't have a proxy server in place, you won't be able to work on the internal server at all from outside the firewall.

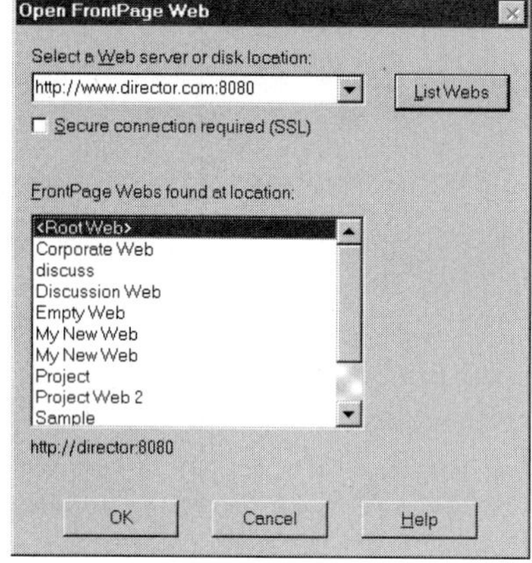

FIGURE 48.2.
You can access an external Web server from behind a firewall without a problem through the Open FrontPage Web dialog box.

Summary

Web server security is a very important part of being a Webmaster. It includes security for the Web server itself as well as its content. For maintaining content security, FrontPage 98 gives you a good set of tools for preventing unauthorized people from accessing your system. Two methods of doing this include using firewalls and proxy servers. FrontPage 98 gives you a very basic mechanism for communicating with proxy servers. Actually setting up firewalls and proxy servers are matters best left to the organization's network administrator. The complex issues involved in setting up firewalls and proxy servers are beyond the scope of FrontPage 98.

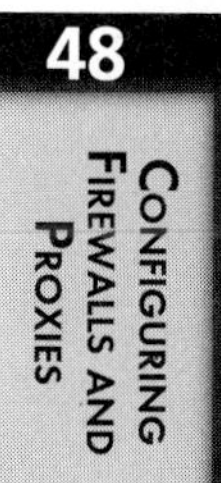

PART

IN THIS PART

- Using the Personal Web Server *827*
- Personal Web Server Administration *845*
- Working with Server Extensions and Multihoming *863*
- Administering FrontPage Server Extensions *875*
- Using IIS with FrontPage 98 *889*
- Using Other Web Servers with FrontPage 98 *895*

Web Servers and FrontPage 98

CHAPTER

Using the Personal Web Server

by William Robert Stanek

IN THIS CHAPTER

- Why You Might Need a Web Server 828
- Installing the Personal Web Server 830
- Running HTTP and FTP Services 834
- Configuring and Running the HTTP Service 836
- Internet Security Issues 837
- Intranet Security Issues 838
- Working with Access Controls 839
- The Authentication Process 842

FrontPage 98, an impressive WYSIWYG HTML editor, is a fine product by itself. However, Microsoft has also thrown in a Windows NT/95-based Web server, called the Personal Web Server, with the FrontPage package. You might be wondering what to do with this server. This chapter explains why you might need a Web server and how to use the one included with FrontPage 98.

Why You Might Need a Web Server

Is it really important to have a Web server along with an HTML editor? Absolutely. The Personal Web Server brings with it many different uses for everybody, from an individual creating his own Web page to an organization looking to create a presence on the Net. The inclusion of a full-fledged Web server makes FrontPage 98 the front-runner as an end-all Web package.

Why an Individual Might Need a Web Server

Although an individual might not really need a Web server, there are times when having one is useful. One such instance is when you're designing and maintaining large Web pages. This situation typically occurs in large organizations where each internal group has its own Web space. In this situation, groups typically have to design their Web pages without direct access to the Web server, so the Webmaster of each group has to maintain the content of the group's Web page. What this all adds up to is a lot of bookkeeping on the part of each group's Webmaster.

Another use an individual might have for a Web server is in creating CGI scripts. Most advanced HTML elements, such as forms and image maps, depend on CGI scripts to work. Directory location, server type, and other technical information are often needed in CGI script creation. Traditionally, creating these scripts required the web author to get this information from the Webmaster. If there were some miscommunication between the web author and the Webmaster, the CGI script would probably fail. Consequently, such scripts were created through trial and error. Also, tracking down buggy parts of CGI scripts could be problematic because the web author might need to look at system files.

By including a Web server with FrontPage 98, both these problems are easily resolved. Complicated Web sites are easier for the Webmaster (presumably you) to manage because she can easily check links when changes are made. If she adds, moves, or removes Web pages, she can easily try the latest links on the Personal Web Server. Also, you can now test and debug CGI scripts without putting them on the actual Web server. Rather than guessing how a particular script might behave, you can test it. All these capabilities make the Personal Web Server an invaluable tool for web authors. Web pages and CGI scripts can now be correct the first time they're pushed out to the actual Web server.

Why an Individual Might Not Need a Web Server

Although there are some good reasons you would find a Web server useful, there are also reasons it's not useful. For one thing, if you're designing very simple Web pages, you really don't need a Web server. You don't need a Web server to see how the <H1> tag looks or how your tables come out. You can correctly view and test these and other simple aspects of Web pages with a Web browser.

Another reason you might not want a Web server is you're low on disk space. The typical Web server uses 6 to 10 megabytes of disk space for the server software alone. The content of the Web server takes up additional disk space. Although having a Web server might be useful, you have to ask yourself if it's a luxury you can afford. Is it worth 10 megabytes of disk space just to verify your CGI scripts?

Why Organizations Might Need a Web Server

Organizations might need a Web server because they're looking to establish a Web presence. A Web presence can be a benefit for a company or organization of any size. For companies that already have an Internet domain, a Web presence can provide great customer support. Along with providing sales material, a web can distribute information for customers. Such information might include frequently asked technical support questions, bug reports, or software updates.

Why Organizations Might Not Need a Web Server

Although a Web server might be beneficial for many businesses, it's certainly not right for all businesses. If you're running a corner drug store, does it really make sense to have a Web server? Probably not. Although it might be interesting to run a server from the store, you would probably do better letting someone else host your Web presence. Having someone host your Web presence dramatically reduces the cost of doing business on the Web.

Why Use the Personal Web Server?

You've decided that you could use a Web server. Why should you use the Personal Web Server that comes with FrontPage 98? (Just because it's included doesn't mean that you should use it.) One reason to use the Personal Web Server is that it's extremely flexible. FrontPage 98 can communicate with other Web servers if server extensions have been installed. This flexibility makes it possible for an organization to use the Personal Web Server as its main Web server. From there, the organization can access other Web servers for different needs. For example, if you're running a Web site that allows people to purchase things over the Net, you can run the catalog of items on a Personal Web Server and access a commerce Web server when needed.

Another strong motivating reason to use the Personal Web Server is for integrated editing with FrontPage 98. FrontPage 98 closely ties with the Personal Web Server and lets you see instantly any changes you've made just as a user would. You can accurately test and develop your sites without concern for working on a live Web site that might break because of your changes. After you have completed your changes, you can then publish your site to your live Web server. In the worst case scenario during your development, your Personal Web Server might contain a site full of errors, but your live Web server will still have the operational site.

Additionally, many large sites for corporations are forced to use a separate web space as a staging area to test their Web site before deploying it to the production server. When you use the Personal Web Server on your own machine, you eliminate the need for this separate staging area as all testing during development can be done in a quick fashion at your own desk. You aren't relying on a network connection to any other Web server—the Personal Web Server is always ready, waiting on your own machine.

Installing the Personal Web Server

The Personal Web Server is easy to install. You can use most of the default options, and at the end of the process, you have a fully functional Web server.

Specifying a Directory

The Personal Web Server is automatically installed as part of the Typical installation of FrontPage 98. You can also use the Custom option to install only certain pieces of the product, such as just the client applications, the Personal Web Server, or server extensions. By default, FrontPage 98 is installed to the `C:\Program File\Microsoft FrontPage` folder and the Personal Web Server is installed to `C:\FrontPage Webs`. You can easily change this location as needed using the Browse button. The installation is very simple, and if the defaults are sufficient for your purposes, there is no reason to change them.

Checking Your Connection

The Personal Web Server operates like most other HTTP servers. Generally, the server communicates over port 80 and requires TCP/IP as a transport for the HTTP information. The server application is a WIN32 application, so a requirement for operation is a 32-bit TCP/IP stack. The Personal Web Server does not operate with 16-bit TCP/IP stacks. If you do not know whether you have the necessary 32-bit TCP/IP stack, FrontPage 98 ships with a TCP/IP Test application that you can run to test whether the Personal Web Server will run on your system. This application, although very simple in scope, provides the most important information you need to set up your Web server, as you can see in Figure 49.1.

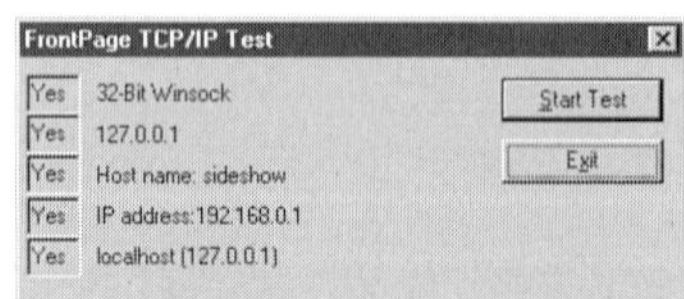

FIGURE 49.1.
The FrontPage TCP/IP Test application details the TCP/IP information for your computer.

To run the TCP/IP Test tool, execute the `tcptest.exe` program located in the bin directory under the FrontPage installation directory (typically `c:\Program Files\Front Page`). Alternately, you can select About the FrontPage Explorer from the FrontPage Explorer's Help menu and click the button labeled Network Test.

NOTE

The Personal Web Server installed on your system might run on port 80 or on port 8080. Port 8080 is an alternate port used only when you have another server installed on your system that is using port 80.

The information that this application captures is the same information that is used by the installation program when you install FrontPage 98. This information is stored in the configuration files for your server and can be changed manually if needed by editing those files, as you'll see later in the chapter. If your TCP/IP stack is configured correctly, FrontPage 98 should discover the information similar to what you see in the TCP/IP Test dialog box. The information that is returned by the TCP/IP Test application is what you use for a URL to your site. The Personal Web Server uses this same information as its identity.

TIP

If you publish your Web pages for others to see, always refer to the host name listed by the TCP/IP Test application, and always include the trailing slash (/) character. Without the slash, the URL path to your server is not complete; it is missing the path portion of the URL. When a server receives a URL without path information, it has to issue a server fix to correct the URL with an assumed path equal to the root of the server. This fix is a potential cause for performance problems because the server has to execute this fix on every URL received in this manner. Following this advice, you reference the URL path to your home page as `http://www.mcp.com/` rather than `http://www.mcp.com`.

You can use either the host name or the IP address for your server, because the host name is actually just a convenient, readable way for people to reference the server. When you enter a host name in a URL, the request is sent to a Domain Name Server (DNS) to translate the host name to an IP address. Then, the request is routed to the appropriate network address. Without the DNS, you would have to remember numbers such as `199.177.202.10` or `198.105.232.30` instead of names such as `www.mcp.com` or `www.microsoft.com`, which are the host names of those same IP addresses.

NOTE

The host name `localhost` and TCP/IP address `127.0.0.1` are reserved names. This host name and IP address refer to the local machine. You should be able to open Web pages on your local machine using a URL of `http://localhost/` or `http://127.0.0.1/` instead of your fully qualified domain name.

After you have your networking information (such as the appropriate TCP/IP stack, and so on), it is quite simple to install the Personal Web Server and begin to build the content using FrontPage. Although you won't be asked during installation to input the test information, FrontPage 98 uses the test information to configure the Personal Web Server. If you chose the Custom installation from the opening dialog when installing FrontPage 98, you have the option to install only the portions of the program that you need to install. You could, for example, install the client software on your main PC and the Personal Web Server and server extensions on another PC that is dedicated to Web traffic.

Defining the Administrator

During installation of the Personal Web Server, you are asked to provide an administrative name and password. You are asked to enter this information before the FrontPage Explorer can open a web for editing. FrontPage 98 enforces this built-in authentication so that only authorized administrators or authors can change the content of your web. If you later add individual authors, they are shown a similar dialog box before access is allowed.

Starting the Personal Web Server

Generally, the Personal Web Server is configured to run automatically at startup for Windows 95. However, you might need to start the Personal Web Server before using it the first time or under Windows NT, using the shortcut for the Personal Web Server from the `Start/Programs/Microsoft FrontPage` folder. If you do not have an icon for the Web server, you can locate the `vhttpd32.exe` executable in the `Front Page\bin` directory of your installation. After you have verified that the server is running as you want it to, you probably want to have the server start automatically.

You can set the server to do this by double-clicking the server icon on the taskbar. This icon depicts a PC with a globe behind it. Double-clicking the server icon opens the Personal Web Server Properties dialog box shown in Figure 49.2 (Windows 95 only).

Click the Startup tab. As you can see in Figure 49.3, you can manipulate the state of the server and its startup options. To have the server run automatically at startup, select the check box labeled Run the Web Server automatically at startup. To ensure you can easily manipulate server properties, you should also select the check box labeled Show the Web server icon on the taskbar. Now, as long as you are logged in to the computer, your server will be running and people can access your content.

The Personal Web Server fully supports basic authentication and Windows NT challenge/response authentication. The authentication mechanisms are used to allow access for authoring as well as to add access restrictions to sections of your web.

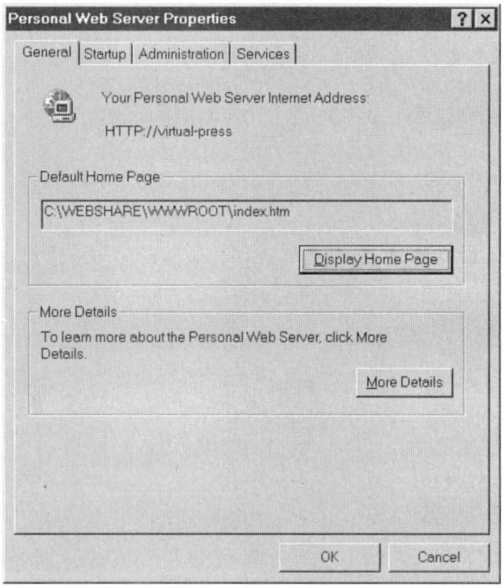

FIGURE 49.2.
Setting server properties is done with the Personal Web Server Properties dialog box.

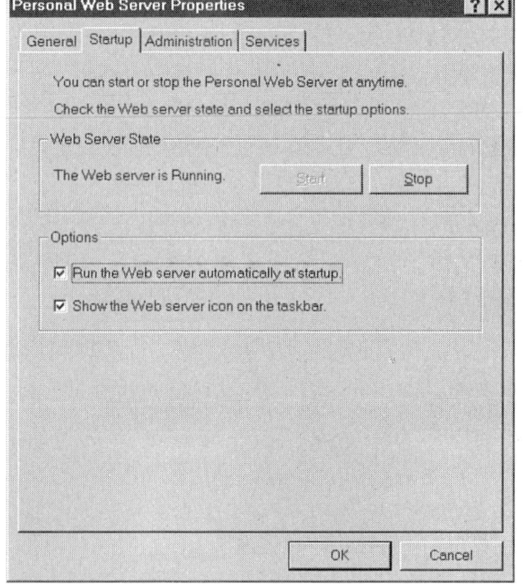

FIGURE 49.3.
You can configure the server to start automatically using the Startup tab.

If you are running Windows NT 4.0 or you have Windows 95 set to provide separate profiles for each user, your Web server only runs when the user who installed the server is logged in. If this is not the behavior you want, edit the Registry in Windows 95 to add the Personal Web Server executable, `vhttpd32.exe`, to the Run key in the Registry. In Windows NT, you can use the `servany.exe` file from the Resource Kit to run the server as an NT service. When run as a service, the Personal Web Server runs no matter who is currently logged in to the PC. You could also log in as the administrator account when you create the Startup folder shortcut so that the shortcut is seen by all users.

CAUTION

If you choose to edit the Registry in Windows 95, the key you need to edit is the following:

`HKEY_LOCAL_MACHINE\SOFTWARE\Microsoft\Windows\CurrentVersion\Run`

You need to add a string value to this key using the information in the other values as examples. Using the Registry Editor incorrectly can cause serious system-wide problems that might require you to reinstall Windows 95 to correct. Microsoft cannot guarantee that any problems resulting from the use of Registry Editor can be solved. Use this tool at your own risk.

After you make the appropriate changes, the Personal Web Server automatically starts so anyone can connect to your server the next time you reboot your PC.

Running HTTP and FTP Services

The Personal Web Server supports both HTTP and FTP services. When you install the Personal Web Server, the only service running is HTTP. Using configuration settings of the Personal Web Server Properties dialog box, it is possible to configure the server to run both HTTP and FTP, to run only FTP, to run only HTTP, or to run neither service. You can also use this dialog box to configure how these servers are started. Generally, the HTTP and FTP services are either started automatically or manually.

Configuring and Running the FTP Service

With the Personal Web Server acting as your FTP server, you gain the ability to locally support FTP file transfers to and from your computer's FTP directories. Just as you can restrict access to the Personal Web Server, you can also restrict access to your FTP server. Access can be restricted by user name and computer IP addresses. To run the FTP service, you need to open the Personal Web Server Properties dialog box and click the Services tab.

As you can see from Figure 49.4, the Services tab is used to start, stop, and set properties for the HTTP and FTP services. In the Services area, click the entry for the FTP service. You can use the buttons labeled Start, Stop, and Properties. Clicking the Start button changes the status of a Stopped service to Running. Similarly, clicking the Stop button changes the status of a Running service to Stopped. Because you want to start the FTP service, click the Start button.

With the FTP service selected, click the Properties button. You can set startup and directory options for the server using the FTP Properties dialog box shown in Figure 49.5. If you want the FTP service to start automatically when the Personal Web Server starts, select the check box labeled Automatic.

FIGURE 49.4.
Configuring HTTP and FTP services is handled with the Services tab.

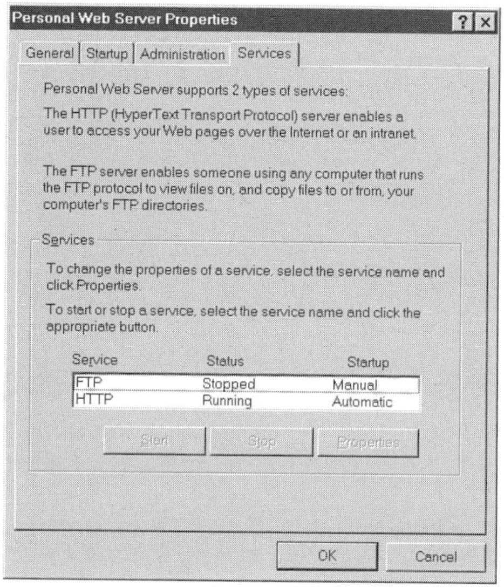

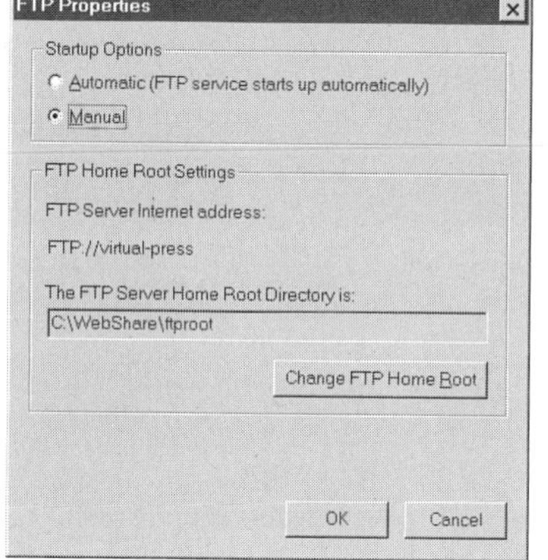

FIGURE 49.5.
Setting FTP service options is easy with the FTP Properties dialog box.

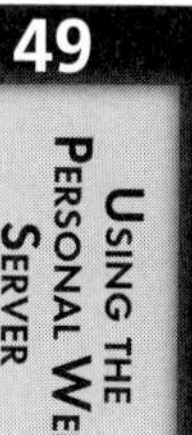

The FTP Home Root Settings area of the FTP Properties dialog box provides information about the Internet address of the FTP server and the server's home root directory. The Internet address is the address you or other users use to access the server. The home root directory is the directory accessed when you log into the server. Sites with a large number of users and content will probably want to immediately create additional folders in this directory to store files by category or type.

By default, the FTP server home root is `C:\WebShare\ftproot`. To change the home root directory, click the Change FTP Home Root button. When you change the home root, users no longer have access to the old home root directory.

Configuring and Running the HTTP Service

HTTP is the key to accessing the Web and HTML pages. Without the HTTP service, no one can access your Web pages, which is why the HTTP service is set to run automatically when the Personal Web Server starts. As with FTP, you can restrict access to HTTP by user name and computer IP addresses.

To change the state of the HTTP service or change the home root directory, you need to open the Personal Web Server Properties dialog box and click the Services tab. In the Services area, select the entry for the HTTP service. After you make the selection, you can use the buttons labeled Start, Stop, and Properties. Click the Start button to change the status of a Stopped HTTP service to Running. Click the Stop button to change the status of a Running HTTP service to Stopped. Click the Properties button to set startup and directory options for the HTTP service.

As you can see from Figure 49.6, the HTTP Properties dialog box for the HTTP service is similar to the properties dialog box for the FTP service. Using the radio buttons labeled Automatic and Manual, you can redefine how the HTTP services starts. Using the Change Home Root button, you can define a new location for Web pages. Additionally, this dialog box contains the Change Home Page button.

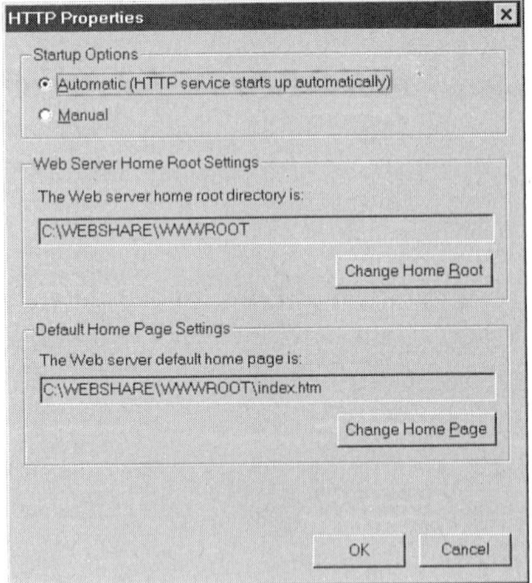

FIGURE 49.6.
Configuring the HTTP service is handled with the HTTP Properties dialog box.

By default, your home page is set to `index.htm`. This means that anyone accessing your Web site using the URL path to your server, such as `http://www.yourserver.com/`, is served a document with the filename `index.htm`. You can change this to one of several widely used defaults, such as `default.htm`, `default.html`, or `index.html`. You can change the home page to any specific page of your liking.

Internet Security Issues

Webmasters typically deal with HTML or scripting questions. They're also expected to maintain the integrity of the Web server itself. Traditionally, Web servers ran off UNIX machines, which made security a very important issue. Sometimes the Web servers had to interface with proxies and talk through firewalls. In some cases, the Webmasters were in charge of the proxies and firewalls themselves.

The security issues that face a Webmaster running the Personal Web Server are much different. Along with the traditional security issues of talking with proxies and firewalls, there are new concerns. The focus in this chapter is primarily on security as it relates to Web page creation. Although there are still some concerns about restricting access to the Web server, this process is not as technical as it once was. This chapter explains the security issues that relate to the use of the Personal Web Server.

Web servers that are directly accessible through the Internet have mainly server access issues. That is, you have to be careful of people accessing the Web server whether they connect from the Internet or a corporate intranet. Webmasters also have to keep a watchful eye on the activities of the Web server itself. They have to watch out for tasks that the Web server performs that might jeopardize its security.

Remote Access

For traditional Web servers that run off UNIX machines, remote users accessing the Web server is always a security issue. The Webmaster must make sure that user accounts on the Web server have secure passwords. He must also be sure that the latest security patches for various UNIX functions have also been applied. UNIX Webmasters have to worry about people being able to hack into their servers.

For people running a Web server on a Windows 95 machine, however, these issues aren't as prevalent. This is because Windows 95 machines don't offer many of UNIX's features; in particular, Windows 95 doesn't offer the capability to remotely log into a computer over the Internet. Consequently, running Web servers from Windows 95 machines is less of a security risk. Because there is no way into a Windows 95 computer, there are fewer risks of the system being hacked into.

For those who want to have some of the power of UNIX but the friendliness of Windows 95, Windows NT is a good option. Windows NT makes much better use of the system's resources and offers better system protection than Windows 95. However, it keeps many of the aspects of UNIX that are missing from Windows 95. These aspects include true user and group permissions and better networking. Although running a Windows NT Web server might be more work than running a Windows 95 server, it's well worth the effort.

Content Control

Being a Webmaster also means being in charge of the content of the entire site. For both large and small companies, this responsibility involves ensuring that whatever is publicly available follows company standards. For example, the Webmaster must make sure that Web pages on an Internet Web server don't hold confidential information. Company Web pages also can't contain copyrighted images, such as those from comic strips, movies, or magazines. Finally, the Webmaster of a corporate Web page must ensure that the content isn't offensive. Pictures of nude people, offensive language, and similar content must be removed.

Another aspect of content control is that not all pages are accessible to everyone. A large business has many different groups, and each group has a particular focus. A particular group might want to limit its Web page access to certain people. This practice is common in large service-oriented companies where groups focus on particular customers. Each group can have a private Web page that only certain, specially designated people can visit. This kind of page enables customers and their corresponding group to be able to view private information.

CGI Scripts

Another security concern with Internet-accessible Web servers is CGI scripts, because the Web server typically runs CGI scripts as itself. This means that whatever permissions the Web server has when it is running, the CGI scripts have as well. Because most UNIX Web servers run as either root (the superuser) or a regular user with extra functions, the CGI scripts can have extraordinary permissions. Consequently, the Webmaster must ensure that all CGI scripts are not potentially malicious. A possible approach to get around malicious CGI scripts is to not allow anyone to create them. This is an acceptable method for many small and medium-sized companies.

Intranet Security Issues

An intranet Web server is one that is accessible from within a particular domain. For large companies, internal Web servers are intranet Web servers. Intranet Web servers allow large companies to distribute private company information easily. Because the information is often sensitive, intranet Web servers aren't accessible to outsiders. Just because the Web server isn't available to the world at large doesn't mean that security can be relaxed, however.

Content Control

For many companies, content control means that the Webmaster must keep track of who has access to what. For example, the Webmaster wouldn't want an author from one group modifying the Web page for another group. Typically, tracking access isn't a problem with UNIX Web servers because UNIX has well-defined user control. If the author of a page didn't want anybody to change her home page, she sets her permissions accordingly.

Unfortunately, Windows 95 doesn't have such controls. Although there are definite user accounts and different user configurations, little file control exists. Anybody can sit down on any Windows 95 machine and delete and modify any and all files. This makes running a Web server for a large intranet site unworkable under Windows 95. The acceptable alternative comes in the form of Windows NT. It does have many of the user control security measures that Windows 95 lacks. Also, because it's built on top of the Windows interface, you don't need to learn UNIX commands.

CGI Scripts

Intranet Web servers, like Internet ones, should also be careful of CGI scripts. It might seem a little strange to be afraid of coworkers, but that's what security is all about. If an employee created a potentially malicious CGI script, the script could cause problems if he leaves the company. If he's laid off or fired, he could easily use his script's malevolent aspects and cripple the Web server. Although this action could simply result in some downtime for the intranet Web server, it could also have more dire consequences.

Working with Access Controls

FrontPage 98 comes with a number of facilities to help you, the Webmaster, control access to webs. This control comes in the form of restricting who creates Web pages, as well as who reads them. Although most of this control takes place in the FrontPage Explorer, where permissions are set on a per-web basis, you also use the Internet Services Administrator to control access.

Controlling Access with User and Computer Accounts

Access control is divided into several broad categories. The first category, called *administrator*, is used to create accounts that have unlimited access to a particular web or to your entire site. Administrators can create accounts for their web, modify web properties, and change web permissions. The second category, called *author*, is used for anyone who can create Web pages but isn't permitted to create webs or perform other administrative duties. The third category, called *browse*, is used for anyone who is permitted to browse controlled areas of the web. To set up accounts in these categories, you use the FrontPage Explorer.

With administrator accounts, FrontPage 98 makes it very easy for the site's Webmaster to delegate authority. For particularly large sites, there's probably a lot of different groups looking to publish a lot of different information. Because it's unrealistic for one Webmaster to watch over all the content, FrontPage 98 allows for lower-level Webmasters so each group can set up its own Webmaster to watch over the content of its particular web. The main Webmaster still has complete jurisdiction over everything.

All accounts can be based on user names or computer IP addresses. When you create an account for a user, you must assign the user a unique password. Whenever users access a secure area of the site, they have to authenticate themselves. When you create an account based on IP address, you restrict privileges based on the location of the computer in the internal or external network.

To better control remote administration and authoring, FrontPage 98 adds an additional layer of security for remote user accounts. You use the FrontPage Extensions Resource Kit to enable authors and administrators to create or manipulate content on your Web site. Complete details for working with the resource kit are provided in Chapter 51, "Working with Server Extensions and Mutilhoming," and Chapter 52, "Administering FrontPage Server Extensions."

NOTE

As you work with access permissions, keep in mind that you can only set access permissions for webs created using a server. This means that you cannot set access permissions for any webs you create on your local file system. Generally, webs you create on the local file system are only accessible from the local system.

Setting Global and Unique Access Controls

Any accounts you create in the root web have privileges in all other webs unless you specify otherwise. The reason for this is that web permissions are based on settings in the root web. Typically, you want someone who can author pages in the root web to be able to author pages in any of the other webs. The same goes for administrators who control webs and users who can browse secure areas of your site.

When you create accounts in the root web, you are creating an account with global privileges, meaning that unless you specify otherwise, the account has identical permissions in all other webs. In an environment where security is a concern, you should not create accounts in the root web unless you are absolutely sure you want to grant complete access to your entire Web site. Instead, assign unique permissions to each web you create using the Permissions dialog box shown in Figure 49.7.

WARNING

The difference between a Webmaster who has control over everything and one who has control only over a particular web is in where you create the account. If you create the administrator account in the root web, you in effect create a do-it-all Webmaster who has access to all webs, unless you specify otherwise. If you create the administrator account in a web other than the root web, the web administrator account holder only has control over that particular web.

FIGURE 49.7.
You can choose to have your web use the same security as the root web, or use its own permissions.

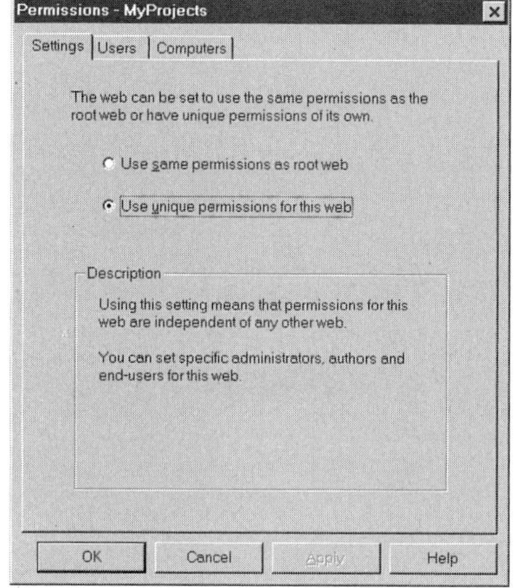

To set unique permissions, do the following:

1. Open the web in the FrontPage Explorer.
2. Select Permissions from the FrontPage Explorer's Tools menu and then click the Settings tab.
3. Click the radio button labeled Use Unique Permissions for This Web and then click the Apply button.

NOTE

The Settings tab is only available when the current web is not the root web. Further, only when you enable unique permissions are you able to edit the contents of a web's Users and Computers tabs.

FrontPage 98 also allows you to create secure webs. In a secure web, all users are required to authenticate themselves before they are granted access to the web. Before you can create a secure web, you must first follow the steps for assigning unique permissions to the web. Next, select Permissions from the Tools menu to display the Permissions dialog box and then click the Users tab.

At the bottom of the Users tab are two radio buttons (see Figure 49.8). To create a secure web, select the radio button labeled Only registered users have browse access. Afterward, click the Apply button. Now all users have to authenticate themselves before they can access the web.

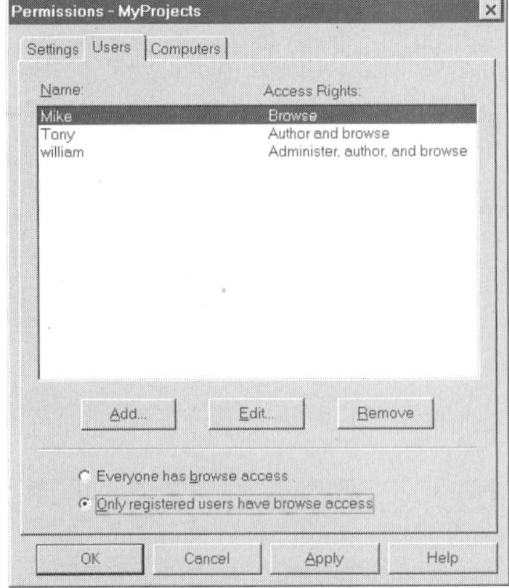

FIGURE 49.8.
Creating a secure web.

NOTE

The password protection extends to the entire subweb, not an individual page. You can't password protect just one page with FrontPage 98. If you want to password protect an individual page, you should create a subweb for it. Then, you can password protect just that subweb.

The Authentication Process

Whenever someone attempts to access the Web as an author, administrator, or user, a process takes place. This process, known as the authentication process, is used for both web modifications and web viewing. This isn't to say that there is one process for intranet accesses and another for Internet accesses. The processes are in place for certain procedures; they are not dependent on where the person accessing the web is.

Internal Authentication

The internal authentication process begins when someone attempts to access the web in order to modify it. Whether this is a modification of the Web page itself or just of its permissions, the internal authentication process occurs. FrontPage 98 controls the internal authentication process. This process begins when someone attempts to access a Web with the FrontPage Explorer. The user sees a dialog box from his Web browser, where he enters his name and password. When he enters the correct information, he is given access to the web.

External Authentication

The external authentication process occurs when someone attempts to access a web for browsing. This process occurs regardless of where the machine requesting the web is located, so both machines on the Internet and intranet are subject to this authentication method. Typically, no authentication is needed on these webs because most Web pages you create are visible by everybody. However, if you password protect a web, the user has to enter a valid user name and password before she can access that web.

Summary

This chapter explains the advantages and disadvantages of having a Web server. Although it gives individuals the ability to write cleaner, and better, advanced Web pages, that might not be enough of a reason to install a server. Although companies could benefit from having an integrated HTML editor and Web server, they might not need one.

If you think a Web server would be useful to you, you should seriously consider using the Personal Web Server. This Web server, which comes with FrontPage 98, is straightforward and versatile. It can communicate and exchange data with other Web servers that have FrontPage extensions installed on them.

Finally, consideration for security in your Web site is an important step. Without insuring the integrity and safety of your site, you risk losing your considerable investment of time and effort. FrontPage 98 makes securing your Web site easy, especially when used in conjunction with the Microsoft Personal Web Server.

CHAPTER 50

Personal Web Server Administration

by William Robert Stanek

IN THIS CHAPTER

- Being a Webmaster 846
- Configuring the Server 847
- The Basics of Web Server Administration 856
- Administering the Personal Web Server from the Command Line 857
- Managing and Verifying Links 859

The inclusion of the Personal Web Server with FrontPage 98 raises a number of administrative issues. These aren't new issues, just issues that many people haven't had to deal with before. Because FrontPage 98 has both a Web server and an HTML editor, it becomes very easy to set up a Web page. Consequently, many people who've never had a chance to be a Webmaster can now be one.

Being a Webmaster

The word Webmaster means different things to different people. The role of a Webmaster is rather nebulous and unclear. Before you can understand what FrontPage 98 lets you do as a Webmaster, you need to understand the various aspects of being a Webmaster.

Webmaster as Web Author

Probably the most traditional definition of a Webmaster is the person who's in charge of Web page design. She knows HTML codes inside and out and can whip out scripts in no time. Most people think of her as the person who develops the organization's main Web page. Oftentimes, she's put in charge of the machine that's running the Web server software. This kind of Webmaster might also be able to use paint programs to create fancy images for Web pages.

She might also know some technical aspects of the Web server. This knowledge enables her to answer commonly asked questions, such as how image map definition files should be formatted. She might also be in charge of the Web server hardware and software itself, but it's unlikely that she is asked to deal with any computers beyond the Web server.

Webmaster as Network Administrator

A lesser-known definition of the Webmaster is a network administrator. Because the Web server must be able to communicate with other computers on the network, certain networking issues relate to managing the Web server. For Web servers that sit on the Internet, the Webmaster has a number of things to worry about. The most obvious is the security of the Web server software and computer itself. The Webmaster must ensure that scripts aren't malicious or can't be manipulated by others to become dangerous.

Another concern for this sort of Webmaster is making sure the computer can communicate with other computers. Because the Web server sits on the Internet, it must be able to correctly resolve host names and perform similar responsibilities. In large companies, this isn't usually a concern because this sort of task should already be done by the network administrator. However, many small companies use one computer to perform multiple tasks. It's common for a small company to have one system serve as the e-mail server, domain name server, FTP server, and Web server. Consequently, if the system is moved, or its functions broken up, the network connection must be maintained.

Web servers that sit on intranets require different concerns. Because they're outside the realm of outside systems, Webmasters don't have to worry about security as much. In large companies, intranet Web server security takes the form of restricting information to only designated people. For example, the research and development group might want to keep the latest specifications under wraps. This secrecy prevents the sales and marketing group from prematurely releasing untested, or unimplemented, features or functionality.

Combining Both Jobs

For small and medium-sized companies, a Webmaster is both a Web author and a network administrator. Because the company's network isn't particularly large, it's still probably managed by one person. Consequently, the company probably doesn't have a budget for two people. Instead, such companies opt to have the systems and network administrator learn HTML. This person is then put in charge of creating Web pages and maintaining the Web server hardware and software.

Larger companies usually divide Webmaster tasks between two or more people. The network administrator often has a number of ongoing issues that he deals with regularly, such as Internet connectivity, intranet connectivity, and network security. He's got a full load of things to do as it is and doesn't have time for Web page design. Consequently, the company would much rather get an HTML expert and make him a Webmaster.

FrontPage Support for Webmasters

FrontPage's Personal Web Server is primarily aimed at Webmasters who are web authors. All the configuration options and variables that the Personal Web Server allows are related to the server itself. There are some settings that relate to the network, but few things of great technical detail. The FrontPage Personal Web Server itself is not involved in networking issues of a large scope, such as routing. This keeps administration of the server fairly simple.

FrontPage's Web server also lets you control user access. You can define other webs underneath the top-level web for your site. The root web is what all other webs are connected to. As Webmaster, you can decide which users get access to which webs. You assign user names and passwords. You can even create lower-level Webmasters by assigning Webmaster-like privileges to people in charge of their group's Web page. These privileges extend only to the webs you specifically designate. This capability lets you empower other users with Webmaster authority in select areas, without complicating matters for yourself.

Configuring the Server

In most installations, there is no need to change the configuration of your server. If you have installed the server properly and you are able to browse its contents using Internet Explorer, the server is running. Sometimes you might need to change the server from its default operation. You might need to run the server on a different port, for example. You might need to add a new MIME type to serve a new data type or add access restrictions to a portion of your web.

You can do each of these tasks in FrontPage 98 by directly editing the server configuration files. If you accept the installation defaults, the server's configuration and access information is located in the `C:\FrontPage Webs\Server\conf` folder. The four main configuration files are called `httpd.cnf`, `srm.cnf`, `mime.typ`, and `access.cnf`. If you are familiar with the UNIX NCSA servers, you should recognize three of those names as similar to the configuration files for those servers, aside from the extension (the UNIX server uses a four letter `.conf` extension). The contents of the configuration files are very similar to the NCSA server's as well, and Microsoft even points you to `http://hoohoo.ncsa.uiuc.edu/` for more details on the configuration. The `mime.typ` file details the MIME types that the server recognizes.

NOTE

In the configuration folder, you might also find several password-related files. These files include `authgrp.pwd`, `authusr.pwd`, and `empty.pwd`. Because editing these files directly scrambles your password tables for users and groups, you should never edit any of these files.

The following sections look at each of the configuration files in turn to see which settings might commonly need changing.

Settings in the `httpd.cnf` File

The `httpd.cnf` file is the main configuration file for your Personal Web Server. This file contains the location of the server root, which is the location of the `vhttpd32.exe` server executable file. The `httpd.cnf` file is also where you find the port number on which the server listens for HTTP requests. Listing 50.1 shows a portion of this file.

Listing 50.1. Partial listing of the `httpd.cnf` file.

```
# ServerRoot: The directory the server's config, error, and log files
# are kept in. This should be specified on the startup command line.
#
# Format: ServerRoot <path>
#
ServerRoot c:/frontpage\ webs/server/
# Port: The port the standalone listens to. 80 is the network standard.
#
Port 80
```

You will probably never need to change any of these settings. If you manually moved the server files from the C: drive to another drive, for example, you could change the `ServerRoot` directive to the new location to allow the server to run and find its other files. The other configuration files use the `ServerRoot` directive to name as the default starting location for their files. Therefore when you change this one directive, you do not need to change the other files. Another common reason to change this file is if you wanted to run the server on a different port from the default port 80. You might already have another Web server installed on port 80, and you just want to install the Personal Web Server for testing purposes. For example, to make the server listen to port 8080 instead of port 80, you could change the Port directive line to read something like the following:

```
Port 8080
```

NOTE

You might have encountered a location on the Web with an URL such as `http://www.someplace.com:8080/`. This URL shows that the server is running on port 8080, which is a common alternative to port 80. Also note that without the `:8080` portion of the URL, a client browser will fail to connect to the server.

After you make any changes to this or the other configuration files, you must stop and restart the Personal Web Server for the changes to take effect. It is always a good idea to make a copy of these files before you make any changes! FrontPage 98 already ships an original unedited version of these files named with an `.org` extension, as in `httpd.org`, but you still should make sure that you have a backup copy of these files for safety's sake.

Settings in the `srm.cnf` File

The Server Resource file (`srm.cnf`) contains settings that control the document layout for your server, and the file and folder names that a client is allowed to see. This file allows you to name your `DocumentRoot` directive, which specifies the location for the content of your web. As you see in Listing 50.2, this file also determines the default directory index file, which is the file that the server attempts to load when an URL ends without a filename, as in `http://www.where.com/`.

Listing 50.2. Partial listing of the `srm.cnf` file.

```
# DocumentRoot: The directory out of which you will serve your
# documents. By default, all requests are taken from this directory, but
# aliases may be used to point to other locations.
#
DocumentRoot c:/frontpage\ webs/content
# DirectoryIndex: Name of the file to use as a pre-written HTML
# directory index. This document, if present, will be opened when the
# server receives a request containing a URL for the directory, instead
# of generating a directory index.
#
 DirectoryIndex index.htm
# AccessFileName: The name of the file to look for in each directory
# for access control information. This file should have a name which is
# blocked from appearing in server-generated indexes!
#
AccessFileName #haccess.ctl
```

In this example, the document root for this server is `c:\frontpage webs\content`. However, as you can see from this listing, the `DocumentRoot` is entered somewhat differently from a conventional DOS path. Notice that instead of normal backslash (\) path delimiters you would expect in Windows NT or Windows 95, the `srm.cnf` file uses the UNIX forward slash (/) character. The forward slash character reveals the UNIX roots of the Personal Web Server and is the way paths are delimited throughout all the configuration files. As with the `httpd.cnf` file, you usually don't have a reason to change the settings in the `srm.cnf` file. For example, however, if you already were using the popular EMWAC HTTPS Web server for NT, whose default directory index filename is `default.htm`, you could change the `DirectoryIndex` line so that you could easily use your existing files without renaming them.

NOTE

The European Microsoft Windows Academic Consortium (EMWAC) created the first popular HTTP server for Windows NT; this server is still easy to use and configure. Dr. Chris Adie was the author of this server and is also responsible for many of the other tools that are available from the EMWAC server at `http://emwac.ed.ac.uk/`.

This same server was eventually shipped by Microsoft as part of the Windows NT Resource Kit and this server was also the base for the commercial Purveyor Web server from Process Software.

Listing 50.3 shows another section of the `srm.cnf` file that might interest you.

Listing 50.3. Another section of the `srm.cnf` file.

```
# AUTOMATIC DIRECTORY INDEXING
# ============================
# The server generates a directory index if there is no file in the
# directory whose name matches DirectoryIndex.
# FancyIndexing: Whether you want fancy directory indexing or standard
#
FancyIndexing off
# IconsAreLinks: Whether the icons in a fancy index are links as
# well as the file names.
IconsAreLinks off
# AddIcon tells the server which icon to show for different files or filename
# extensions. In preparation for the upcoming Chicago version, you should
# include explicit 3 character truncations for 4-character endings. Don't
# rely on the DOS underpinnings to silently truncate for you.
AddIcon /icons/text.gif     .html   .htm    .txt    .ini
AddIcon /icons/image.gif    .gif    .jpg    .jpe    .jpeg   .xbm    .tiff
➥.tif    .pic    .pict      .bmp
AddIcon /icons/sound.gif    .au     .wav    .snd
AddIcon /icons/movie.gif    .mpg    .mpe    .mpeg
AddIcon /icons/binary.gif   .bin    .exe    .bat    .dll
AddIcon /icons/back.gif     ..
AddIcon /icons/menu.gif     ^^DIRECTORY^^
AddIcon /icons/dblank.gif       ^^BLANKICON^^
```

```
# DefaultIcon is which icon to show for files which do not have an icon
# explicitly set.
DefaultIcon /icons/unknown.gif
```

If you are familiar with directory indexing, you might be able to figure out what the settings in this section are used for. Most Web servers have the capability to show you a file directory when a default document is not found. This capability has become a common alternative to an FTP server. If `FancyIndexing` is turned off, and you access a folder that doesn't have a default document, the server generates a display like that shown in Figure 50.1. If you turn on `FancyIndexing`, you will see a display similar to that in Figure 50.2. Another change you can make is to enable `IconsAreLinks`, so that the icons that are shown in these server-generated listings are links to the files as well as the filenames.

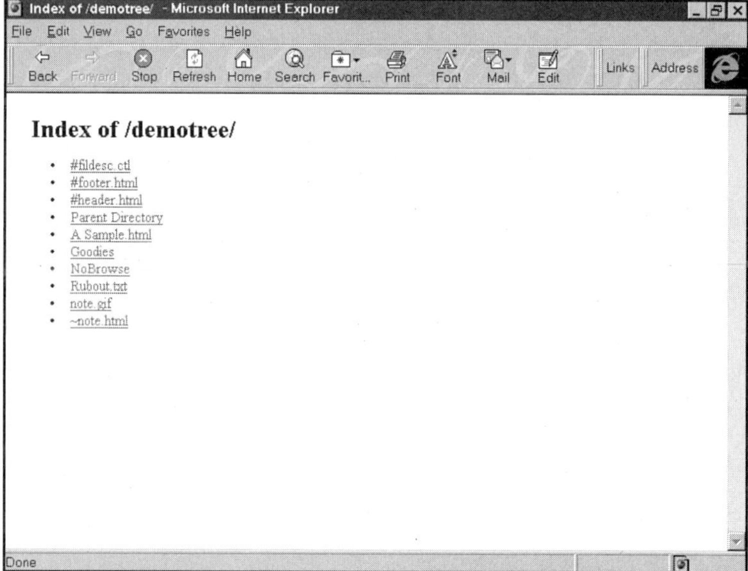

FIGURE 50.1.
A simple directory listing is displayed for folders without default documents when the `FancyIndexing` *directive is set to off.*

You could also create custom icons to use in place of the default icons to represent the types of files you have in these directories. These icons are specified using an `AddIcon` directive as in the following line:

```
AddIcon /icons/text.gif     .html   .htm    .txt    .ini
```

Note that you specify an icon to represent a specific file extension and that you can have a single icon represent multiple file types. If you are going to use this feature a lot and plan on creating multiple icons for different file types, use the default icons as samples so that your icons are the same size. Having icons of the same size provides a uniform display.

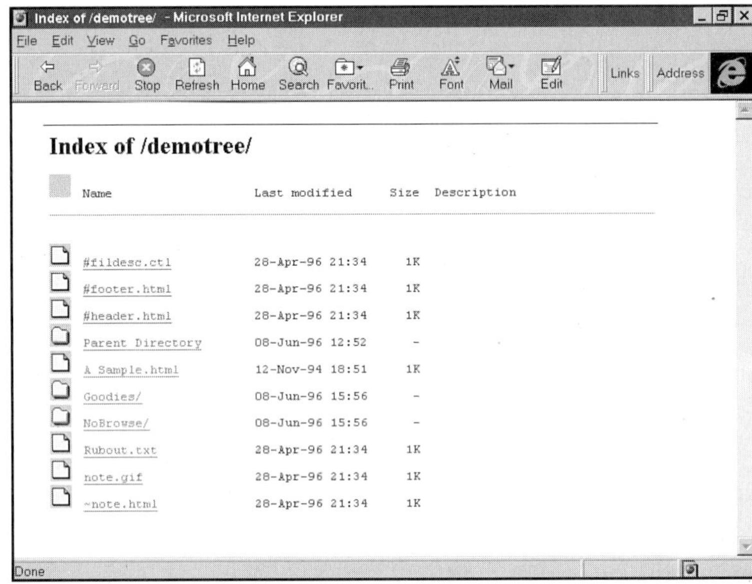

FIGURE 50.2.
A fancy directory listing is displayed for folders without the default document when the `FancyIndexing` *directive is turned on.*

The `mime.typ` File

A Web server is essentially a file pump. It sends a file to the client when requested. This file can be any type of file; the server doesn't care. Without the existence of MIME types, a Web server and client would have a hard time deciding the content of files. MIME types define the content of files so that the Web server and client can communicate consistently. Listing 50.4 is a partial listing of the `mime.typ` file that ships with FrontPage 98. If you need to add a content type to your web, you add a line to this file.

Listing 50.4. Partial listing of the `mime.typ` file.

```
application/activemessage
application/zip               zip
application/x-bcpio           bcpio
application/x-cpio            cpio
application/x-gtar            gtar
application/x-shar            shar
application/x-sv4cpio         sv4cpio
application/x-sv4crc          sv4crc
application/tar               tar
application/x-ustar           ustar
application/x-lzh             lzh
application/x-gzip            gz
audio/basic                   au snd
audio/x-aiff                  aif aiff aifc
audio/wav                     wav
image/gif                     gif
image/ief                     ief
```

```
image/jpeg                      jpeg jpg jpe
image/tiff                      tiff tif
image/x-cmu-raster              ras
image/x-portable-anymap         pnm
image/x-portable-bitmap         pbm
image/x-portable-graymap        pgm
image/x-portable-pixmap         ppm
image/x-rgb                     rgb
image/x-xbitmap                 xbm
image/x-xpixmap                 xpm
image/x-xwindowdump             xwd
message/external-body
message/news
message/partial
message/rfc822
multipart/alternative
multipart/appledouble
multipart/digest
multipart/mixed
multipart/parallel
text/html                       html htm
text/plain                      txt
text/richtext                   rtx
text/tab-separated-values       tsv
text/x-setext                   etx
video/mpeg                      mpeg mpg mpe
video/quicktime                 qt mov
video/msvideo                   avi
video/x-sgi-movie               movie

# Microsoft types
application/msword              doc dot
application/x-msaccess          mdb
application/vnd.ms-excel        xls xlw
application/vnd.ms-powerpoint   ppt pps pot
application/vnd.ms-project      mpp
application/x-mspublisher       pub
application/x-msschedule        scd
application/vnd.ms-works        wdb wks wps wcm
```

This example shows several common file types with which you are probably familiar. MIME types are listed as `type/subtype`, and the most common types are `text`, `application`, and `audio`. When the server gets a request for a specific URL, it parses the URL and if the request resolves to one of the MIME types file, the server sends a content header to the client, defining the data that will follow. The content is then sent to the client, who knows what kind of data to expect.

Remember that undefined MIME types should not be arbitrarily assigned. The MIME RFC1521 specifically requires that undefined types be preceded with an x- to signify the type. If you have an application called myapp that creates `.myf` files that are currently undefined, you need to use a MIME type similar to `application/x-myfile myf` to specify that the content type is not currently accepted as a standard MIME type.

NOTE

For more information on MIME types, check out the hypertext version of RFC1521 at the following URL:

`http://www.oac.uci.edu/indiv/ehood/MIME/MIME.html`

The access.cnf file

The `access.cnf` file controls who can access all the files on the server. You can use the contents of this file to restrict access to individual directories on your server. You can restrict access based on host name or IP addresses so that only clients from certain locations can access your content.

Usually, the settings in this file should only be changed if you want to institute server-wide access restrictions. If you want to restrict access to individual directories, you can use `#htaccess.ctl` files, which you might have noticed earlier in Listing 50.2. The content of these files is similar in format to the content of the `access.cnf` file and allows a very fine granularity to the authentication that the Personal Web Server supports. Look at the `access.cnf` file in Listing 50.5 to understand the format of this file.

NOTE

An alternate to editing this access control file directly is to use the Permissions dialog box accessed from the FrontPage Explorer. Using this dialog box, you can set up access controls for users and computers.

Listing 50.5. Partial listing of the access.cnf file.

```
# The following access configuration establishes unrestricted access
# to the server's document tree. There is no default access config, so
# _something_ must be present and correct for the server to operate.
# This should be changed to whatever you set ServerRoot to.
<Directory e:/frontpage\ webs/server>
Options Indexes
</Directory>
## This should be changed to whatever you set DocumentRoot to.
#<Directory e:/frontpage\ webs/content/>
## This may also be "None", "All", or "Indexes"
#Options Indexes
## This controls which options the #HACCESS.CTL files in directories can
## override. Can also be "None", or any combination of "Options", "FileInfo",
## "AuthConfig", and "Limit"
#AllowOverride All
## Controls who can get stuff from this server.
#<Limit GET>
#order allow,deny
```

```
#allow from all
#</Limit>
#</Directory>
# You may place any other directories you wish to have access
# information for after this one.
```

To understand the format of this file, you need to understand the original NCSA HTTPD server that it is based on. The structure is based on concepts originally developed for a UNIX environment. The file is a simple sequential list of access directives. Because the file is sequentially read when the server starts, the order of the directives in this file is important. If you want to deny unrestricted access to only single folder on your server, it is best to add that directive at the end of the `access.cnf` file rather than at the beginning. If you changed the above `<Directory...>` section in Listing 50.5 to read the following, you would lock out all accesses to your server!

```
<Directory e:/frontpage\ webs/server>
<Limit GET>
deny from all
</Limit>
</Directory>
```

If you are going to require access authentication on your server, you need to think it through before you implement it. There are generally three ways of thinking when it comes to access restrictions for a site. One is the wide open "allow all" approach. Any and all accesses are allowed. The second is just the opposite. Limit access to everyone except certain people. Instead of totally closing the site, you can open the site to certain host names using a format such as the following:

```
 <Directory e:/frontpage\ webs/server>
<Limit GET>
order deny, allow
deny from all
allow from *.mydom.com
</Limit>
</Directory>
```

Remember that the file is read sequentially. Here, you've told the server to deny everybody first, and then to allow those from any host name that has the string `.ingr.com` in the host name. This results in everyone except those from the `ingr.com` domain being denied access to this server. If you reverse the directives in the order: deny, allow line to read order allow, deny instead, the file is processed in such a manner that the deny from all is the last directive, and again, no access is allowed. The following code example demonstrates this principle, where all visitors are allowed except those with the domain shown in the deny line.

```
<Directory e:/frontpage\ webs/server>
<Limit GET>
order deny, allow
allow from all
deny from *.mydom.com
</Limit>
</Directory>
```

The third way that access restrictions are commonly used is a hybrid approach. You start with a wide-open server and add access restrictions on a single directory basis using `#htaccess.ctl` files placed in that directory. If you are not careful, this scheme can become very difficult to keep track of. You might intend to restrict access to a specific subfolder, but place the `#htaccess.ctl` file in the wrong location and therefore lock out a section of the server that you weren't intending. The default `#htaccess.ctl` file is shown in Listing 50.6.

Listing 50.6. Listing of the default `#htaccess.ctl` file.

```
# -FrontPage-
IndexIgnore #haccess.ctl */.??* *~ *# */HEADER* */README* */_vti*
<Limit GET>
order deny,allow
deny from all
allow from all
</Limit>
<Limit POST PUT>
order deny,allow
deny from all
</Limit>
AuthName default_realm
AuthUserFile e:/frontpage\ webs/content/_vti_pvt/service.pwd
AuthGroupFile e:/frontpage\ webs/content/_vti_pvt/service.grp
```

The `#htaccess.ctl` file is a very powerful tool. As you can see from this listing, you can put any directives in this file to modify the standard settings of the server. Because configuration files are read sequentially, settings in this file are loaded when an attempt is made to get a file from the folder in which this file reside.

You can place a copy of this file in any folder to restrict access on a folder and subfolder level. I mentioned that you could also use this file to add or change MIME types on the fly in a given folder. If you want to serve self-extracting archive files from a certain folder, you might need to change the MIME type from the usual `application/octet-stream` to something such as `application/x-sfx-archive` so that the Internet Explorer offers the File|Save As dialog for files of this unknown type. To change a MIME type on the fly like this, you need to place in the folder where you want to change the defaults an `#htaccess.ctl` file with the following single line:

```
AddType application/x-sfx-archive exe
```

Then, anytime a client clicks a link with an `.exe` extension in this folder, the server sends the file with a content type of `application/x-sfx-archive`.

The Basics of Web Server Administration

As a Webmaster, you have a number of issues to contend with. In addition to creating new webs under your root web, you have to work with users. You have to create user accounts and enable whatever privileges you want to grant them. You're also responsible for helping other people when they're having problems with their Web pages. Many UNIX Web servers have built-in facilities, through UNIX itself, to help you handle these tasks. Because FrontPage 98 can run on Windows 95, you must program these capabilities into the Personal Web Server.

You can do most of the day-to-day Webmaster activities from the FrontPage Explorer. Most of the time, you want to change individual webs, not the entire server. The only time you should access the Internet Services Administrator program is when you're affecting the entire Web site by doing such things as changing authentication procedures or logging file access.

You can define administrators that manage individual webs or define another Web site Webmaster, such as yourself. Administrators have other abilities in addition to being able to create Web pages for their particular web. For example, an administrator can manage and verify links every page in the web calls (see the section "Managing and Verifying Links," in this chapter). Administrators can also determine whether they want to make their particular webs password protected.

Along with such routine responsibilities, each administrator can create accounts. These can be accounts for other administrators or web authors. A web author is someone who has access to FrontPage 98 and whose sole responsibility is to create Web pages. Created accounts enable people with access to FrontPage 98 to focus on their tasks. The Webmaster can deal with issues that relate to the entire web, such as creating new webs. The administrators for each web can watch over the content and integrity of their web. Finally, authors focus on creating content for the webs they have access to.

Administering the Personal Web Server from the Command Line

Sometimes you might want to run the Personal Web Server from the command line. You might need to do this when you're logged in from a remote machine onto a Windows NT computer. Perhaps you want to set up a batch file that maintains a Web server. Whatever the case might be, you need to manage the Personal Web Server from the command line. You have to start the FrontPage Personal Web Server Administrator program (`\Microsoft FrontPage\bin\fpsrvadm.exe`) with a set of command-line options. Table 50.1 gives you a complete list of the available switches, their parameters, and their functions.

Table 50.1. Personal Web Server command-line options.

Switch	*Parameter*	*Function*
`-o`, `-operation`	*`operation_type`* (`install`, `upgrade`, `uninstall`, `check`, `recalc`, `enable`, `disable`, `security`, `putfile`, or `recalcfile`)	The specified option is performed.

continues

Table 50.1. continued

Switch	*Parameter*	*Function*
`-p, -port`	*`port_number`*	The `port_number` indicates what port number is to be used for the specified operation.
`-w, -web`	*`webname`*	This option specifies the name of the web. To specify the `<Root Web>`, use `""`.
`-r, -root`	*`front_page_root_dir`*	This option specifies the directory where the FrontPage extensions are installed.
`-t, -type`	*`server_type`* (`ncsa, ncsa-manual-restart, apache, apache-manual-restart, cern, cern-manual-restart, netscape, netscape-manual-restart, or omi`)	This option specifies the server type.
`-s, -servconf`	*`server_config_file`*	This option is the filename of the server configuration file. By default, the server configuration file is located under the directory where the server is installed.
`-m, -multihost`	*`hostname`*	This option is the host name for the multihosting server configuration.
`-u, -username`	*`username`*	This option is the administrator's user name. This option is required in install and security operations.
`-pw, -password`	*`password`*	This option is the administrator's password. This option is required in install and security operations.
`-i, -ipaddress`	*`internet_address`*	This option defines the allowable Internet addresses for a Web administrator. This option follows the standard four-part IP numbering scheme.

Switch	Parameter	Function
`-d, -destination`	*`destination_URL`*	This option specifies the destination URL for a document specified by the `-w` machine.
`-f, -filename`	*`filename`*	This option is the full path name for a file on the Web server.

Some examples might help you understand how to use these command-line options. If you want to create the new web Corporate for an existing `<Root Web>` that's running on port 80, you type the following:

```
fpsrvadm -o install -p 80 -w Corporate
```

To create an administrator for this new web, type the following line:

```
fpsrvadm -o security -p 80 -u Corpadm -pw Corpadm -w Corporate
```

Managing and Verifying Links

Eventually, after each of your webs has been updated and changed numerous times, you'll have broken links. Fixing these links can be a rather daunting task for anybody, especially on large sites. Before FrontPage, there was no easy way to make sure that links in an entire Web site were valid. The best way that a Webmaster could check the links was to follow them by hand. A less tedious method of checking the validity of your links was to wait until someone complained and then fix the broken link. Fortunately, FrontPage 98 makes link management much easier.

Verifying Links

FrontPage 98 can automatically check and verify each link in an entire web. To use this feature, you must load a particular web with Webmaster permissions. Next, select Tools|Verify Hyperlinks to display the Hyperlink Status view and the Verify Links dialog box (see Figure 50.3). The Hyperlink Status view has a complete list of all links that point outside the current web. Even links to webs in another part of the same Web site are considered an outside link. This view also displays any broken links within your own Web site. You can use the scroll bar at the bottom of the dialog box to see more information about a particular link. If you want to view all hyperlinks in your Web site, not just the external and broken links, choose View|Show All Hyperlinks. This updates your display with every hyperlink present in your Web site.

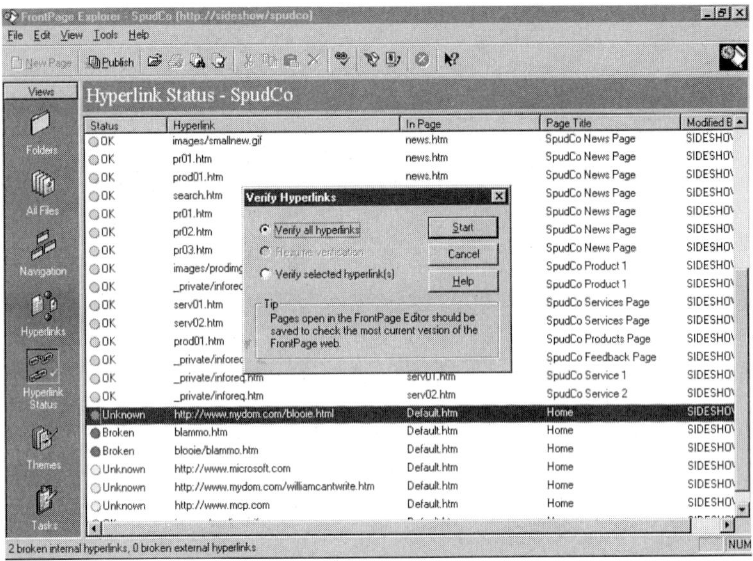

FIGURE 50.3.
FrontPage 98 gives you a list of all the links that it's going to verify.

To begin checking your site's hyperlinks, choose the Verify all hyperlinks radio button (the default choice). If you have multiple hyperlinks from the Hyperlinks or Hyperlink Status view selected, you can choose to Verify selected hyperlinks only. Click the Start button to begin the process. As FrontPage 98 verifies each link, your status line updates with its progress. FrontPage 98 tries to connect to each remote Web site and verify the existence of your URLs. As the verification proceeds, each hyperlink's status is reflected in the Hyperlink Status view. Valid and functional hyperlinks are displayed with a green "OK" status, unknown links (typically not yet checked) in a yellow "Unknown" status, and broken and non-functional links with a red "Broken" status.

You can explore more detail about each link, or directly modify a link, by double clicking it in the Hyperlink Status list. When you double click a hyperlink, the Edit Hyperlink dialog box (see Figure 50.4) appears. This dialog displays the hyperlink's current URL and on what page in your Web site that the URL occurs. You can directly edit the page in question by clicking the Edit Page button, which launches the FrontPage Editor. You can also replace the existing hyperlink with a new one by entering it into the Replace hyperlink with text box, or clicking the Browse button. If you do choose to replace the existing URL, you can replace it in all of the pages in which the URL appears, or in specific pages. To replace the URL in all pages, select the Change in all pages radio button. To replace it in only select pages, click the Change in selected pages radio button and choose your pages from the list. Regardless of what pages you choose to affect, click the Replace button to commit the change. The original URL is then replaced with the new one.

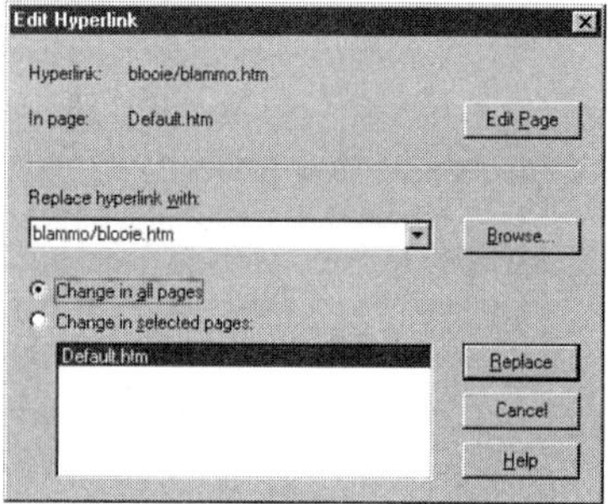

FIGURE 50.4.
You can use the Edit Hyperlink dialog box to replace an existing URL with a new one.

Recalculating Links

Because FrontPage 98 allows multiple authors to work on multiple links, you might need to check out the links from time to time. FrontPage's recalculate link feature updates all the views for the currently selected web. What this feature enables you to do is see the changes that another author has recently put in.

The recalculate link feature also re-creates all WebBots being used in the current web. If that weren't enough, the recalculate link feature also updates the text index that the Search WebBot uses. Because the recalculate link feature does so many things, it can take quite a long time to finish, especially for large webs. When you're in the FrontPage Explorer and select Tools|Recalculate Hyperlinks, you're asked to confirm the procedure (see Figure 50.5).

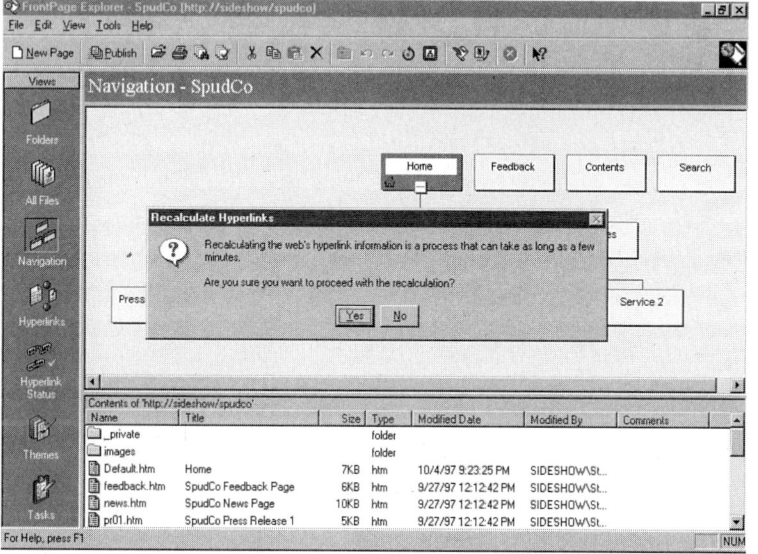

FIGURE 50.5.
Because recalculating all the links in a web can take a while, FrontPage 98 wants to make sure you want to proceed.

Summary

Just because you have a Web server doesn't mean you'll necessarily know what to do with it. Most of the fine-tuning aspects of the Personal Web Server are buried under configuration files. If you've worked on other Web servers, these files are probably very similar.

There's a lot more to being a Webmaster than simply configuring a Web server. As much fun as that might be, you, the Webmaster, have to make sure that the server continues to run well. To this end, FrontPage 98 gives you a number of useful tools to help you keep your Web server working. You can verify hypertext links, take a look at any given web at any time, and run the server from the command line. The command-line options let you run the server remotely or through a series of batch files.

CHAPTER 51

Working with Server Extensions and Multihoming

by William Robert Stanek

IN THIS CHAPTER

- Using the Server Extensions *864*
- Installing and Upgrading the Server Extensions *867*
- Multihoming *869*

FrontPage components and active elements are terrific extras that can help you create a world-class Web site. The most important aspect of any Web site is the server. Because the success of your Web site, and sometimes your business, hinges on the server, you don't want to sail through uncharted waters with unfamiliar server software just so that you can use the advanced features of FrontPage 98. Enter the FrontPage server extensions, which allow you to use FrontPage components, active elements, and all the other goodies in FrontPage 98 with other servers. In this chapter, you look at what you need to know to use the server extensions as well as techniques you can use to take server operations to a new level with multihoming.

Using the Server Extensions

Your Web server is responsible for serving Web pages under varying traffic loads, providing the means to maintain the security of your data, and supplying additional functions as well. The FrontPage Personal Web Server, which is designed to be used with small and medium-sized Web sites, provides a fair amount of functionality. The server runs on Window 95/NT systems, supports the advanced aspects of FrontPage 98, and includes basic security functions.

If your server needs fit these specifications, you can use the Personal Web Server and don't have to worry about compatibility with other servers or the server extensions. If your needs don't fit these specifications, you should look at alternatives to the Personal Web Server. You may need additional functionality or increased security, or you may have a large, busy Web site. You may already have a Web server and don't want to install another server. You may also have different operating system needs. Whatever the case, you can use the server extensions to add the functionality of FrontPage 98 to your preferred Web server.

What Are the Server Extensions?

The server extensions are basically scripts that run on your server. These extensions allow you to browse, author and develop, and administer FrontPage webs. Before you can use the server extensions, you must install them.

Any time you access an advanced function of FrontPage 98 in a Web page, such as a FrontPage component, form handler, or active element, you're using a FrontPage feature that requires the server extensions. When you use the Personal Web Server, these extended features are built in, so you don't need to make any changes. When you use a different server, you can access these extended features only via the server extensions; without the server extensions, the components and active elements simply don't work.

Any time you want to author or administer FrontPage webs, you rely on the extended features of FrontPage 98 as well. You need the extensions to access a FrontPage web on your preferred server using the FrontPage Explorer or FrontPage Editor. You need the extensions to perform general administration and also control access to FrontPage webs.

To ensure that the server extensions can be used with various FrontPage tools and versions, the developers designed the extensions to be backward compatible with previous versions of FrontPage 98. So, you can use the FrontPage 98 Explorer to access a FrontPage 97 web and the FrontPage 98 Editor to edit a Web page created in FrontPage 97. In addition to backward compatibility, the FrontPage server extensions also provide a degree of forward compatibility. You can also use the FrontPage 97 Explorer to access a FrontPage 98 web and the FrontPage 97 Editor to edit a Web page created in FrontPage 98. Keep in mind that the new FrontPage 98 extras aren't supported in older versions of the FrontPage server extensions.

What Servers Can Use the Extensions?

The server extensions are distributed on the FrontPage CD-ROM. You can use the server extensions with Windows 95, Windows NT, and UNIX servers. Because of variances in operating systems and how servers work, specific versions of the extensions are available for different operating systems and servers. Table 51.1 shows a sample of servers that have extensions.

Table 51.1. Servers for use with FrontPage 98 extensions.

Server Software	*UNIX*	*Windows NT*	*Windows 95*
Apache	X		
CERN	X		
Microsoft IIS		X	X
Microsoft Peer		X	X
Microsoft PWS			X
NCSA	X		
Netscape Communications	X	X	
Netscape Commerce	X	X	
Netscape Enterprise	X	X	
Netscape Fast Track	X	X	X
FrontPage PWS			X
O'Reilly Website		X	X

Beyond the standard operating systems and server support, Microsoft has developed architecture-specific versions of the extensions. You can find versions optimized for RISC, PPC, DEC Alpha, Intel x86, and others. To see whether your particular architecture is supported, check the FrontPage CD-ROM. If you can't find what you're looking for, check the FrontPage Web site at `http://www.microsoft.com/frontpage/`.

TIP

Before you install the extensions on the FrontPage CD-ROM, I recommend that you check the FrontPage Web site for updates and patches. Often, you can find a more current version online.

Getting Help with the Server Extensions

In previous versions of FrontPage, the server extensions were one of the least understood aspects of the toolkit. The main problem was that the documentation for the extensions was lacking and difficult to follow. This time around, the developers have thrown in a comprehensive resource kit for the server extensions that is entirely Web-based.

The FrontPage Server Extensions Resource Kit is installed with the server extensions. You can find the main page for the documentation in the `FrontPage` folder. After you fire up your browser and access this page, which is shown in Figure 51.1, you can browse the online documentation, which covers installation of server extensions, security issues, administration, troubleshooting, and more. If you haven't installed the extensions, you can access the resource kit online at the FrontPage Web site.

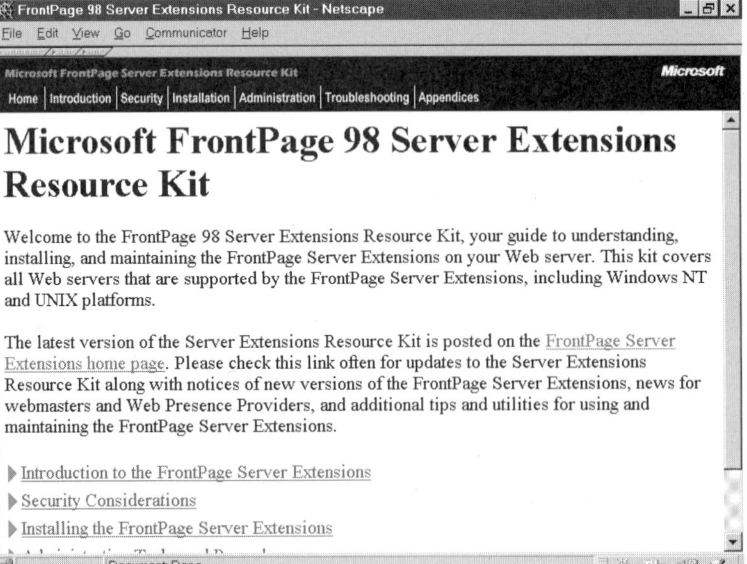

FIGURE 51.1.
Working with the FrontPage Server Extensions Resource Kit.

NOTE

You should turn to the documentation in the Server Extensions Resource Kit if you have any additional questions after reading the chapters in Part X of this book. In this chapter, you find an introduction to the server extensions and tips for installing and upgrading the extensions. Chapter 52, "Administering FrontPage Server Extensions," covers local and remote administration of the server extensions. Chapter 53, "Using IIS with FrontPage 98," covers the specifics of using the extensions with Microsoft Internet Information Server. Finally, Chapter 54, "Using Other Web Servers with FrontPage 98," covers the issues you need to know to use other servers with FrontPage 98.

Installing and Upgrading the Server Extensions

Any time you want to use FrontPage features on a server other than the Personal Web Server, you need to install the server extensions. Installation is generally a two-step process. First, an installer program copies the extensions to a temporary directory on the server. Afterward, the extensions are installed on the Root web of the server and all subwebs as necessary. If the server uses multihoming, the extensions are also copied to each of the virtual hosts.

From then on, the server extensions are available to your FrontPage webs. As you create new webs, the server extensions are either copied to the web automatically or as part of a separate administrative task initiated by the server's administrator.

Because the installation process for Windows and UNIX systems is different, I describe separately how to install the extensions on these operating systems. When a new version of the extensions is published, you can upgrade the extensions simply by repeating the installation process.

Installing the Server Extensions on Windows 95 and Windows NT

To install the extensions on Windows NT, you must have system administration privileges. You install the server extensions by running a self-extracting executable tailored to your server. You can download the executable from the FrontPage Web site or from the FrontPage CD-ROM. To download the executable from the Web, follow the links to the server extensions page from the FrontPage Web site, and then select the appropriate file. To use the executable on the FrontPage CD-ROM, access the `ServExt` folder and select the appropriate file.

On Microsoft IIS, you are asked to enter the name of an existing FrontPage administrator before any files are copied to FrontPage webs. On other Windows servers, you can create a new administrator account during the installation.

In the final step of the installation, dynamically linked libraries (DLLs) and scripts are installed in several directories on your server. The necessary dynamically linked libraries are installed in two directories: `C:\Program Files\Microsoft FrontPage\version3.0\bin` and `C:\Windows\system`. Scripts for administration, authoring, and browsing are installed in `C:\Program Files\Microsoft FrontPage\version3.0\isapi` and `C:\Program Files\Microsoft FrontPage\version3.0\_vti_bin`. After the files are installed here, they are copied to each FrontPage web and subweb. If you're using multihoming, a dialog box appears asking you to select the virtual hosts that should use the extensions.

Scripts and DLLs aren't the only things installed on your server. You will also find the Server Extensions Resource Kit, remote administration forms, and the FrontPage Server Administrator. Although you can access the remote administration forms as part of the Server Extensions Resource Kit, as a security precaution, you cannot use the forms as installed without making some changes.

The FrontPage Server Administrator is a tool for installing and maintaining extensions on FrontPage webs. You can find the administrator in the `C:\Program Files\Microsoft FrontPage\version3.0\bin` directory. You get two versions of the administrator: a windows-based version (`fpsrvwin.exe`) and a command-line version (`fpsrvadm.exe`). You will learn all about local and remote administration using the administration tools and the forms in Chapter 52, "Administering FrontPage Server Extensions."

Installing the Server Extensions on UNIX

On your UNIX server, you can install the extensions only if you are logged in as root. So you can easily get everything you need to use FrontPage 98 with UNIX servers, the server extensions are stored in a compressed TAR file. Along with the server extensions, you will find an installation script, called `fp_install.sh`, and an upgrade script for the Apache Web server, called `change_server.sh`. You can download these files from the FrontPage Web site or from the FrontPage CD-ROM. To download the files from the Web, follow the links to the server extensions page from the FrontPage Web site, and then select the appropriate file. To use the files on the FrontPage CD-ROM, access the `ServExt` folder, and then select the appropriate files.

When you run the installation script, you are asked a series of questions to configure the extensions for your server. By default, the server extensions are stored in the `/usr/local/frontpage` folder. If you change this default, you need a link from `/usr/local/frontpage` to the actual location of the server extensions. Further, the installation directory must be in a local partition that is not mounted with the `NOSUID` flag. After the extensions are installed here, stub files are copied to each FrontPage web and subweb.

The extensions aren't the only things installed on your server. You will also find the Server Extensions Resource Kit, remote administration forms, and the FrontPage Server Administrator. Although you can access the remote administration forms as part of the Server Extensions Resource Kit, as a security precaution, you cannot use the forms as installed without making some changes.

The FrontPage Server Administrator is a tool for installing and maintaining extensions on FrontPage webs. You can find the administrator in the `/usr/local/frontpage/version3.0/bin` directory. The administrator (`fpsrvadm.exe`) is a command-line tool. You will learn all about local and remote administration using the administration tools and the forms in Chapter 52.

Multihoming

A useful, although somewhat limited, feature of the Personal Web Server is its support of multihoming. Multihoming allows you to host and develop for multiple domains on the same machine. Traditionally, multihoming isn't available on all Web server software. Consequently, adding it to some UNIX Web servers requires you to recompile the server itself. Making a computer multihoming-capable also requires some work.

Most people don't need to use the multihoming capability, because they rarely need to host or develop for more than one domain. Even though multihoming is a useful feature, it's still not necessary for everyone. This feature is mainly useful for companies and Internet service providers (ISPs). Even though you might never need to use multihoming, it's a useful tool to have if you need it.

What Is Multihoming?

Multihoming is the capability for one computer on one domain name to pretend to be another domain name. One computer can then appear to be many different computers. Suppose that you're the Webmaster for the company `mycom.com`. The company spawns a subsidiary that makes a different product and has the domain name `mycom2.com`.

Now, traditionally, to provide a Web presence for both companies, you need two computers: one computer to be the Web server for `mycom.com` and another computer to be the Web server for `mycom2.com`. Multihoming enables you to use one computer as the Web server for `mycom.com` and `mycom2.com`. At the same time, both Web sites look different from each other.

Probably the best example of multihoming in progress is with Web Presence Providers (WPPs). A WPP typically offers the service of domain hosting, which means that the WPP makes its multihome-capable Web server act as your server. You don't need to dedicate any computing power to handle Web access. The WPP's computers take care of everything for you.

Multihoming Methods

You can choose from two different methods of multihoming. Each has its advantages and disadvantages. Fortunately, FrontPage 98 supports both methods.

The first method is to run multiple Web servers on one machine. The computer running the many Web servers is already configured to use different domain names. Each Web server is configured to listen for a different domain name so that when a particular domain name is accessed, only that Web server is working. This method of multihoming has the advantage that each Web server can run independently of another. If you need to change the content of one web, you don't have to take down everything else. You also can run one type of server for one customer and another type for another customer. If one customer needs secure data transmissions, you can start a commerce server for him or her only. The obvious downside to this setup is that you can use valuable system resources running multiple instances of the same program. Consequently, you need a fairly powerful and well-loaded computer for this task. Buying the extra necessary hardware could cost you a significant amount of money.

Another method of multihoming is to have one Web server run multiple server processes. Here, the server listens to different domain names and retrieves the appropriate content. The more people who access the multihomed domains, the greater the impact on the Web server. The clear advantage with this method of multihoming is that you're running only one process. Although the process might be running a lot and taking up lots of resources, it's not taking up as much as having many servers running at once. Another advantage of this method is that when you upgrade the software, you upgrade only one program. The problem with this approach to multihoming is that if you do upgrade the software, every domain is affected. Another problem is that you'll have a harder time running specific Web servers for specific customers.

Listening for Other Hosts

Currently, multihoming is most widely supported on UNIX machines. This use isn't because the UNIX Web server software is superior; it is because UNIX features built-in support for listening to multiple domain names. If a UNIX system receives data intended for two different domains, it routes the data correctly. To get a UNIX machine to listen to multiple domains, you have to initialize the network devices to listen to the domains. For example, using a Solaris machine as the root, you have to type something similar to the following:

```
ifconfig le0:1 www.mycom.com up
ifconfig le0:2 www.mycom2.com up
```

This code enables your computer to respond to incoming traffic directed for `www.mycom.com` and `www.mycom2.com`. Once your computer is looking for multiple domains, you have to get the Web server to do the same. This task is often a simple matter of modifying a configuration file; for NCSA-based servers, this configuration file is the `httpd.conf` file. Most Web servers pretend to be a particular host by using the specifications of `ServerName` and `BindAddress` in the `httpd.conf` file. To make a Web server be the server for `www.mycom.com`, you have to add the following code to this file:

```
ServerName www.mycom.com
BindAddress www.mycom.com
```

Connecting FrontPage 98 to a Multihomed System

After you have your Web server configured for multihoming, you can hook it into FrontPage 98. You can do so easily by installing the FrontPage server extensions. Just download the appropriate extension for your Web server, and install it on that machine. After you've done that, a file called `we####.cnf` is placed in the `/usr/local/frontpage` directory. The `####` refers to the port number to which the Web server for that domain is listening. You must rename the `we####.cnf` file to *`hostname`*`:`*`port`*`.cnf`. The *`hostname`* refers to the name of that domain's Web server, and *`port`* is the number on which the server is installed.

Configuring FrontPage 98

After you have the Web server and the FrontPage extensions up and running, you have to deal with some other issues. First and foremost is the fact that the FrontPage server extensions are basically CGI scripts that run under the server itself. Consequently, the Web server's CGI scripts must be run as the same user as the HTTP server itself. Probably the best way to implement this is to have the HTTP server and CGI scripts run as the FrontPage user account. This approach gives your UNIX system the most security and gives FrontPage 98 the most flexibility.

You can also configure the FrontPage server extensions themselves by modifying the configuration files. Because each multihomed server has its own configuration file in `/usr/local/frontpage`, you can configure each system independently. Table 51.2 gives you a complete list of the parameters, what they do, and the acceptable values.

Table 51.2. FrontPage server extensions parameters.

Parameter	*Function*	*Values*
`AccessControl`	Disables FrontPage's normal access controls	`0` = disable controls; `1` = enable controls
`AllowExecutableScripts`	Sets files in executable directories to executable	`0` = files in executable directories will not be executable; `1` = files in executable directories will be executable
`CacheMaxDocMeta`	Sets the maximum number of documents in the cache	Use integer value, such as `256`
`CacheMaxImage`	Sets the maximum size of the image file cache	Use integer value, for file size in megabytes
`CacheMaxInclude`	Sets file size of the include cache	Use integer value for file size in megabytes, such as `8`

continues

Table 51.2. continued

Parameter	*Function*	*Values*
`Logging`	Logs authoring operations	`0` = Do not log author operations; `1` = Log author operations
`MailCharSet`	Overrides the character set parameter of the content-type header in mail messages	Set to specific content type
`MailEncoding`	Sets the encoding for e-mail	Use specific encoding type
`MailSender`	Sets the user name in the From field when sending e-mail	Use full e-mail address for the From field
`NoAbsoluteFile Results`	Prevents Discussion, Registration, and Save Results handlers from writing to a file outside the current folder	`0` = Can write to files outside the current content area; `1` = Can write to files only within the current content area
`NoExecutableCgiUploads`	Prevents authors from uploading and executing active content and scripts	`0` = Files have the execute permission set; `1` = Files don't have the execute permission set
`NoIndexServer`	Prevents use of index server	`0` = Use index server; `1` = Do not use index server
`NoServerFile Results`	Prevents Discussion, Registration, and Save Results WebBots from logging results	`0` = Can write results to logs; `1` = Cannot write results to logs
`PreserveTagCase`	Keeps the existing case (upper or lower) of HTML tags	`0` = Does not preserve the case; `1` = Preserves the case

Parameter	Function	Values
`ReformatHtml`	Allows FrontPage 98 to reformat Web pages that contain WebBots	`0` = Disables reformatting; `1` = Enables reformatting
`SendMailCommand`	Sets the name of the program e-mail should be piped through	Use full file path of e-mail program
`SMPTHost`	Identifies host running SMTP	Set to name or IP address of SMTP host
`TextMemory`	Indicates how many megabytes text indexing allocates for internal indexing.	Any numeric value
`UpperCaseTags`	Converts all HTML tags to uppercase characters.	`0` = Does not convert characters; `1` = Converts all characters

Summary

Server extensions provide a way for you to take advantage of everything FrontPage 98 has to offer even if you don't use the Personal Web Server. Although you can install the server extensions using the files provided on the FrontPage CD-ROM, you might want to see whether an upgrade or patch exists at the FrontPage Web site before you install anything. Server extensions are installed on each FrontPage web and subweb. Multihoming allows a single machine to handle multiple domains. If you use multihoming, the extensions are also installed on each virtual domain.

52

Administering FrontPage Server Extensions

by William Robert Stanek

IN THIS CHAPTER

- Exploring the Server Extension Administration Tools 876
- Local Server Extension Administration 876
- Remote Server Extension Administration 884

The FrontPage Server Extensions Resource Kit is a superb resource that helps you learn the ins and outs of using the server extensions. Within the resource kit, you will find several different tools for local and remote administration of the server extensions. Making sense of when and how to use the administration tools isn't easy, so this chapter provides pointers on how you can make the most of these tools.

Exploring the Server Extension Administration Tools

The Server Extensions Resource Kit provides four tools that are used to perform administrative tasks. Most of the administration tools are command-line tools that you can run from the shell or DOS prompt. One of the administration tools is a Windows-based tool with push button graphical interfaces. You'll use the tools to do the following:

- Install/uninstall server extensions
- Upgrade server extensions
- Check and fix server extensions
- Set permissions for authoring, administration, and browsing
- Recalculate links

Because a few of the administration tools perform the same basic tasks, the factors that really drive your decision as to which tool to use are your server's operating system and whether you want to perform local or remote administration of the server extensions. On Windows 95/NT systems, you have graphical, command-line, and Web-based tools for administering the extensions. On UNIX systems, you have fewer choices because some of the tools simply aren't available.

Another factor that may drive your decision regarding administration tool of choice is the level of security you want to maintain at your Web site. When you restrict your server to local administration only, you ensure tighter security, which is why you must actually enable remote administration before you can use any of the remote administration tools.

Local Server Extension Administration

When you want to run the administrative tools directly on the Web server, you can use one of four utilities to perform your administrative tasks: `fpsvradm`, `iisadmin`, `fpwinsrv`, or `fpremadm`. `fpsvradm` is a command-line utility that is available on Windows and UNIX systems. `iisadmin` is a command-line utility for administering server extensions on Microsoft IIS. The `fpsrvwin` utility has a graphical interface and is available on Windows systems. Finally, the `fpremadm` tool is a command-line program used for remote administration of a FrontPage server. Although `fpsvradm`, `fpwinsvr`, and `fpremadm` are discussed in this chapter, the `iisadmin` utility is discussed in Chapter 53, "Using IIS with FrontPage 98."

This section takes a look at how you can use the `fpsvradm`, `fpremadm`, and `fpwinsvr` utilities. Because these tools perform similar tasks and some material is duplicated in these sections, I recommend reading only the section that covers the tool you want to use.

Local Administration with `fpsvradm`

The `fpsvradm` utility is a command-line tool for local administration of the server extensions. You can run the utility in interactive or noninteractive mode. Using the interactive mode, you rely on a menu system to help you perform administration tasks. Otherwise, you need to supply all the necessary parameters for the utility on the command line. As stated earlier, you'll use the `fpsvradm` utility to perform many administrative tasks. Whether you perform these tasks from the command line or through the menu system, you'll need to enter the same information, just in a different format.

You run the server administration utility by entering the name of its executable file at the prompt. From the command line, the `fpsvradm` utility accepts many options. Each option has a long and a short identifier. When you use the command line, you must specify the operation you are going to perform with either the `-operation` flag or the `-o` flag. Table 52.1 summarizes the valid operations.

Table 52.1. Operations for the server admin utility.

Admin Operation	*Description*
`check`	Checks and fixes the server extensions on a server
`chown`	Sets the ownership of FrontPage files so they work correctly with the server extensions
`disable`	Disables author and administration privileges on a server
`enable`	Enables author and administration privileges on a server
`install`	Installs the server extensions on a server or web
`putfile`	Imports a file into a web
`recalc`	Recalculates all links in a web
`recalcfile`	Recalculates all links in a specified file
`security`	Allows you to set security controls for computers, users, authors, and administrators
`uninstall`	Removes the server extensions from a server
`upgrade`	Upgrades the server extensions on a server

After you specify an operation, you can set additional parameters. Every operation has a group of parameters that the utility expects as well as optional parameters (see Table 52.2). When you put this together, a sample command-line operation would look like this:

```
fpsrvadm -o operation mandatory_parameters [optional_parameters]
```

Table 52.2. Personal Web Server command-line options.

Options	*Parameter*	*Description*
`-a, -access`	*`access_type`*	Specifies the type of account you are setting access privileges for. Valid access types are administrators, authors, and users. You can also use a value of `remove`.
`-d, -destination`	*`destination_URL`*	Specifies the destination URL for a document specified by the `-w` machine.
`-f, -filename`	*`filename`*	Sets the full path name for a file on the Web server.
`-i, -ipaddress`	*`internet_address`*	Restricts the privileges on a web by Internet addresses.
`-m, -multihost`	*`hostname`*	Sets the host name for the multihosting server configuration.
`-n, -noChownContent`	None	Specifies that the server should not change ownership of web files. The exception is for executable files, such as component scripts, `netscape-commerce`, `netscape-enterprise`, `netscape-fasttrack`, and `website`. Valid server types on UNIX include `ncsa`, `ncsa-manual-restart apache`, `apache-fp`, `apache-manual-restart`, `netscape`, and `netscape-manual-restart`.
`-o, -operation`	*`operation_type`*	Performs an operation. Valid operations include: `check`, `chown`, `disable`, `enable`, `install`, `putfile`, `recalc`, `recalcfile`, `security`, `uninstall`, and `upgrade`.
`-p, -port`	*`port_number`*	The *`port_number`* indicates what port number is to be used for the specified operation, such as 80.

Options	Parameter	Description
`-pw, -password`	*password*	Sets the password. This option is required in install and security operations.
`-s, -servconfig`	*server_config_file*	Specifies the filename of the server configuration file. By default, the server configuration file is located under the directory where the server is installed.
`-t, -type`	*server_type*	Specifies the server type. Valid server types on Windows include: `msiis`, `mspws`, `frontpage`, `netscape-communicator`, `netscape-commerce`, `netscape-enterprise`, `netscape-fasttrack`, and `website`.
`-u, -username`	*username*	Sets the administrator's user name. This option is required in install and security operations.
`-w, -web`	*webname*	This option specifies the name of the web. To specify the `<Root Web>`, use `""`.
`-xg, -xGroup`	*user_group*	Sets the user group on UNIX, such as `www`.
`-xu, -xUser`	*user_account*	Sets an account name on UNIX, such as `www`.

Installing and Uninstalling Server Extensions

Installing and uninstalling server extensions are the most common administrative tasks you will perform. When you are configuring your server for use with FrontPage 98, you'll need to install the server extensions on your server. Afterward, you may need to install the extensions on new webs or subwebs. To do this, you can use the `install` operation. The command-line syntax for installing extensions is

```
fpsrvadm -o install -p port_number -m hostname -u username
        -pw password -t servertype -s server_config_file [-w webname
        -xu user_account -xg user_group -n]
```

You could use the installation syntax as follows:

```
fpsrvadm -o install -p 80 -m www.tj.com -u admin -pw admin
        -t netscape-fasttrack -s /usr/local/conf/httpd.conf
```

As you might expect with so many different flavors of server software, some servers expect a slightly different set of options. If you use O'Reilly Website, you do not have to specify the location of the configuration file. If you use Microsoft IIS, you do not need to specify the location of the configuration file or the administrator password.

Additionally, whenever you install extensions on a UNIX server, you will probably want to change the owner and group of the server extension files. To set owner and group to www on an NCSA server, you could use the following command:

```
fpsrvadm -o install -p 80 -m www.tj.com -u admin -pw admin
        -t ncsa -s /usr/local/conf/httpd.conf -xu www -xg www
```

Sometimes you may also want to remove the server extensions from a server. To do this, use the `uninstall` operation. Keep in mind that whenever you remove the extensions for a root web, the server administration utility also removes the extensions for all other webs associated with the root web. No other files or web pages are removed from the web.

The syntax for uninstalling server extensions looks like this:

```
fpsrvadm -o uninstall -p port_number -m hostname
```

Upgrading Server Extensions

Whenever you find a new version of the server extensions, you can download them to your server and run through the installation process for the extensions. If you choose not to upgrade all webs and subwebs at that time, you can upgrade webs individually using the `upgrade` operation. The syntax for upgrading server extensions follows:

```
fpsrvadm -o upgrade -p port_number -m hostname [-w webname
        -xu user_account -xg user_group -n]
```

If you don't specify a web, the root web and all its webs will be upgraded. You could use the `upgrade` operations as follows:

```
fpsrvadm -o upgrade -p 80 -m www.tj.com
```

Checking and Fixing Server Extensions

The server extensions work together to enable all the wonderful features of FrontPage 98. Occasionally, you may find that one of the extension files gets out of whack and things stop working; these things happen. Whether your hover button won't hover or your banners won't swap, you can sometimes fix the problem simply by checking and fixing the server extensions with the `check` operation. The syntax for checking server extensions follows:

```
fpsrvadm -o check -p port_number -m hostname [-w webname]
```

If you don't specify a web, the root web and all its webs will be checked and fixed as necessary. Here is how you could use the `check` operation:

```
fpsrvadm -o check -p 8080 -m www.tj.com -w myweb
```

Adding and Removing Accounts

You create accounts with a specific privilege level. You can give browse access to a secure web by giving a person user privileges in the web. The next privilege level is author. Authors have browse and edit privileges in a web. To give a person permission to create, edit, and browse webs, you would set the permission level to full administrative, author, and browse permissions.

The syntax for adding an account is

```
fpsrvadm -o security -p port_number -m hostname -w webname
         -a access_type -u username -pw password
```

The privilege level is set with the access option. Values for this option are: administrators, authors, and users. You could make a user an administrator for a web like this:

```
fpsrvadm -o security -p 80 -m www.dj.com -w myweb
         -a administrators -u johnnyW -pw changeme
```

Using the `security` operation, you can also remove user accounts. To do this, you would use the `remove` flag as follows:

```
fpsrvadm -o security -p 80 -m www.dj.com -w myweb
         -a remove -u johnnyW -pw changeme
```

When you want to lower an account's privilege level, you should remove the account, and then create a new account. In addition to setting privilege levels, you can also use the security controls to restrict an account's access to a web based on IP address. You can set the IP address to a specific value or use the asterisk character to match all values in a range. To restrict a new account by IP address, you would use the `-i` option, such as

```
fpsrvadm -o security -p 80 -m www.dj.com -w myweb
         -a administrators -u johnnyW -pw changeme -i 201.*.*.*
```

Controlling Authoring and Administering of Webs

To make the lives of administrators a bit easier, the server administrator allows you to disable and enable privileges for accounts on your server with a single command. You disable the authoring and administering of a web with the `disable` operation. You enable the authoring and administering of a web with the `enable` operation. Keep in mind that any changes you make affect the root web and all its associated webs.

The syntax for the `enable` operation is

```
fpsrvadm -o enable -p port_number -m hostname
```

The syntax for the `disable` operation is

```
fpsrvadm -o disable -p port_number -m hostname
```

Recalculating Links

Recalculating links in a web is an all-or-none affair. Using the `recalc` operation, you can recalculate all the internal links in a specific web. An example of recalculating all links is

```
fpsrvadm -o recalc -p port_number -m hostname -w webname
```

Using the `recalcfile` operation, you can recalculate all the internal links in a specific file. An example of recalculating links in a file is

```
fpsrvadm -o recalcfile -p port_number -m hostname -w webname -d file_name
```

When you recalculate links in a file or web, you tell the server to update any included elements, such as included images or included text. You also tell the server to update the index for the web.

Importing Files

Sometimes you'll want to add a file to a web. The easiest way to do this is to import the file into the web with the `putfile` operation. You use this operation as follows:

```
fpsrvadm -o putfile -p port_number -m hostname -w webname -d file_name
```

Local Administration with `fpwinsvr`

The point-and-click counterpart to `fpsvradm` is the `fpwinsvr` utility. If you are on a Windows 95/NT system, you can use `fpwinsvr` to administer the server extensions. Because you are in a graphical environment, many of the options that you have to set individually from the command line can be set to a specific default quite easily, which in turn makes your job easier.

When you run the Windows-based administrator, you will see a dialog box like the one shown in Figure 52.1. In the Select server or port field, you should see a list of all the servers the administrator knows about according to their port number. To get started, select the port that is used by the server you want to administer, and you'll see the additional information to the right of the Select server or port field. Pay particular attention to this additional information; you may be prompted to enter or confirm this information for certain administrative tasks.

TIP

If this is the first time you are running the administrator, there may not be a server port available to select. In this case, click the Install button and follow the installation instructions in the next section.

Installing and Uninstalling Server Extensions

Installing and uninstalling server extensions are the most common administrative tasks you will perform. When you are configuring your server for use with FrontPage 98, you'll need to install the server extensions on your server. Afterward, you may need to install the extensions on new webs or subwebs using the Install button.

FIGURE 52.1.
Working with the FrontPage Server Administrator in Windows.

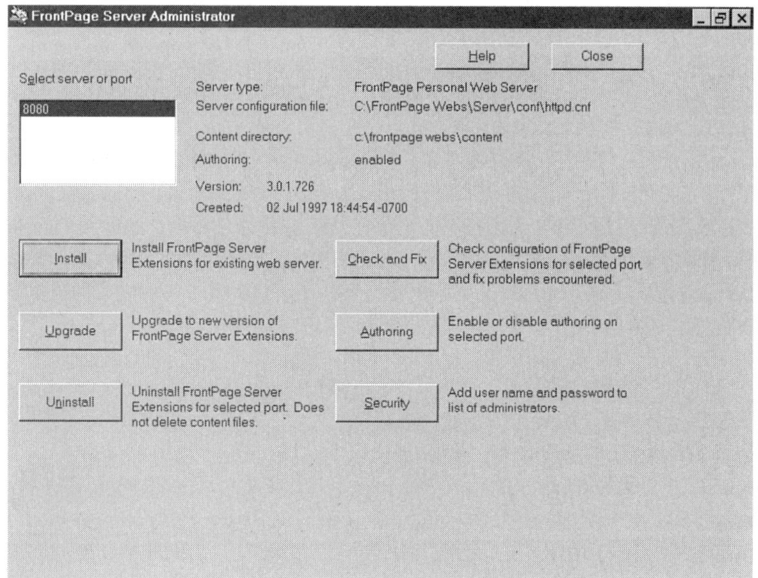

After you click the Install button, you will be asked to select the server type, which should match the value displayed in the Server type field on the administrator's main window. Next, you'll need to enter the file path to the server configuration file. The file path you need to enter should be the same as the one provided in the Server configuration file field on the administrator's main window.

Sometimes you may also want to remove the server extensions from a server. To do this, click the Uninstall button. Keep in mind that whenever you remove the extensions for a root web, the server administration utility also removes the extensions for all other webs associated with the root web. No other files or Web pages are removed from the web.

Upgrading and Checking Server Extensions

Whenever you find a new version of the server extensions, you can download them to your server and run through the installation process for the extensions. If you choose not to upgrade a virtual server at that time, you can upgrade the virtual server using the Upgrade button. You will be asked to confirm that you want to update the server extensions.

The server extensions work together to enable all the wonderful features of FrontPage 98. Once in a while you may find that one of the extension files gets out of whack and things stop working; these things happen. Whether your hover button won't hover or your banners won't swap, you can sometimes fix the problem simply by checking and fixing the server extensions. Simply click the Check button to start this task.

Controlling Authoring of Webs

To make the lives of administrators a bit easier, the server administrator allows you to disable and enable authoring privileges for accounts on your server. Click the Authoring button, and you will see the dialog box shown in Figure 52.2.

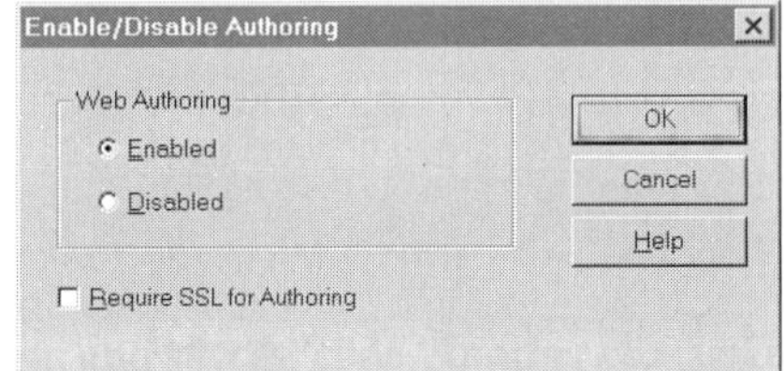

FIGURE 52.2.
You can enable and disable authoring in a snap.

You disable the authoring on a server with the `disable` operation and enable authoring of a server with the `enable` operation. Keep in mind that any changes you make affect the root web and all its associated webs. You can require a secure connection for authoring using the Require SSL for Authoring check box.

Adding Accounts for Administrators

You can create a new administrator account using the Security option. Administrators have create, edit, and browse privileges in the web you specify. If this web is the root web, the administrator will have full permission in all webs associated with the root web. After you specify the web for the account, you'll also need to specify a user name and password.

If you want to restrict remote access to the web using based on IP address, click the Advanced button. You can set the IP address to a specific value or use the asterisk character to match all values in a range, such as `201.*.*.*`.

Remote Server Extension Administration

When you want to make remote updates to a Web server, you will use either the `fpremadm` utility or the Web-based remote administration forms. `fpremadm` is a command-line utility that is available only on Windows 95/NT systems. If you don't want to use a command-line utility, you can access the Web-based remote administration forms with your browser of choice. To access the `fpremadm` or the admin forms, you'll need to know their location and have an administration account.

Take a look at how you can enable remote administration and how you can use each of the remote administration tools. After you learn how to enable remote authoring, don't be afraid to skip ahead to the section that covers the remote administration technique you plan to use.

Enabling Remote Administration

As a security precaution, the remote administration tools are disabled when you first install the server extensions. When you enable remote administration, you open up a can of worms that you may not want to deal with. If your operating environment allows you to use the local administration tools comfortably, I say use them and forget about the remote administration tools. On the other hand, if you find that you or someone on your team needs to remotely administer FrontPage webs, you should consider enabling remote administration.

To ensure that some level of security is maintained in remote administration, you should follow these precautions:

- Store the remote administration forms in a secure web
- Require a secure connection to access the admin web
- Use IP address restrictions

Once you have your security precautions in place, you can move the administration forms to a web on your server. I'll call this your admin web. The default location for administration forms on a Windows server is `C:\Program Files\Microsoft FrontPage\version3.0\admin\cgi`. On a UNIX server, the default location for the forms is `/usr/local/frontpage/version3.0/admin`.

After you set up the admin web, copy the forms directory to the admin web. Within the admin web, you'll find a folder called `scripts`. This folder must have execute permissions.

Remote Extension Administration with `fpremadm`

The `fpremadm` utility is essentially a remote access version of `fpsvradm`, which can be used only on Windows 95/NT systems. Because of this, `fpremadm` supports the same set of operations as `fpsvradm` and the entire discussion on `fpsvradm` applies to `fpremadm`. The only difference is now you have to specify options that verify who you are and what you want to access. The options you use to validate your access are shown in Table 52.3.

Table 52.3. Additional remote administrative options.

Options	*Parameter*	*Description*
`-targetserver`	*`admin_URL`*	Specifies the complete URL to the executable for the remote administrator
`-adminpassword`	*`password`*	Specifies the administrator's password
`-adminusername`	*`username`*	Specifies the administrator's user name

You run the remote administration utility by specifying the filename of its executable at the prompt. When you use the remote options, you simply insert them after the operation you are performing and then use the normal options for the specific task. You could uninstall server extensions remotely as follows:

```
fpremadm -o uninstall -targetserver http://www.tj.com/admin/scripts/fpadmcgi.exe
        -adminusername remadmin -adminpassword adminj12 -p 80 -m www.tj.com
```

Remote Extension Administration with the Web-Based Forms

Remote administration with the Web-based forms is pretty straightforward. The main administration page is called `fpadmin.htm`. After you set up your admin web, enter the URL to the main administration page in your browser, such as `http://www.mydom.com/admin/fpadmin.htm`. If you've set up your web as a secure web, you will need to enter your user name and password before you can perform any administrative tasks.

Installing and Uninstalling Server Extensions

Installing and uninstalling server extensions are the most common administrative tasks you will perform. When you are configuring your server for use with FrontPage 98, you'll need to install the server extensions on your server. Afterward, you may need to install the extensions on a new virtual server or a new subweb.

To create a new virtual server and install the extensions on this server, follow the New Virtual Server link on the main administrator page. After you enter a name and a port number for the new virtual server, you need to enter the user name for your administrator account (see Figure 52.3). When you are finished, click the Create Server button.

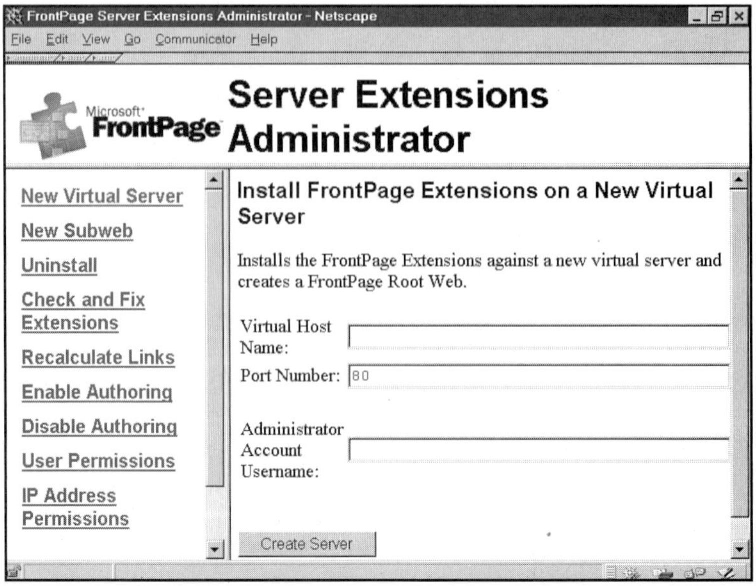

FIGURE 52.3.
Creating a new virtual server.

You create a new subweb in much the same way as you create a new virtual server. First you enter the name of the virtual server and its port, and then you enter a name for the subweb. When you are finished, click the Create Subweb button.

After you click the Install button, you will be asked to select the server type, which should match the value displayed in the Server type field on the administrator's main window. Next, you'll need to enter the file path to the server configuration file. The file path you need to enter should be the same as the one provided in the Server configuration file field on the administrator's main window.

Sometimes you may also want to remove the extensions from a virtual server. To do this, click the Uninstall link. After you enter the host name and port number of the virtual server, click the Uninstall button. Keep in mind that whenever you remove the extensions for a root web, the server administration utility also removes the extensions for all other webs associated with the root web. No other files or Web pages are removed from the web.

Checking Server Extensions

The server extensions work together to enable all the wonderful features of FrontPage 98. Occasionally, you may find that one of the extension files gets out of whack and things stop working; these things happen. Whether your hover button won't hover or your banners won't swap, you can sometimes fix the problem simply by checking and fixing the server extensions. Just click the Check and Fix Extensions link to start this task. In the fields provided, enter the host name and port number of the virtual server, then click the Check button.

Recalculating Links

The remote administrator allows you to easily recalculate links in a specified web. Click Recalculate Links to get started. First you enter the host name of the virtual server and port; then you enter the name of the web. When you are finished, click the Recalculate button.

Whenever you recalculate links in a file or web, you tell the server to update any included elements, such as included images or included text. You also tell the server to update the index for the web.

Controlling Authoring of Webs

To make the lives of administrators a bit easier, the server administrator allows you to disable and enable authoring privileges for all accounts on your server. You can disable authoring by following the Disable Authoring link, entering the host and port information, then clicking the Disable Authoring button. You can enable authoring by following the Enable Authoring link, entering the host and port information, then clicking the Enable Authoring button. Keep in mind that any changes you make affect the root web and all its associated webs.

Adding and Removing Accounts

You create accounts with a specific privilege level. You can give browse access to a secure web, by giving a person user privileges in the web. The next privilege level is author. Authors have browse and editing privileges in a web. To give a person permission to create, edit, and browse webs, you would set the permission level to full administrative, author, and browse permissions.

To create a new account, click the User Permissions link. Start by entering the host name, port, and web to which the user has access. Next, enter a user name and password for the account. Afterward, select the appropriate privilege level, then click the Change Permissions button. Anytime you want to lower an account's privilege level, you should remove the account and then create a new account.

In addition to setting privilege levels, you can use additional security controls to restrict an account's access to a web based on IP address. You can set the IP address to a specific value or use the asterisk character to match all values in a range, such as `201.*.*.*`. Click the IP Address Permissions link. After you enter the appropriate information, click the Change Permissions button.

Summary

Administering the FrontPage server extensions is handled with a family of tools that are designed for different purposes. Your administration tool of choice will depend on your operating system and whether you want to perform local or remote administration of the server extensions. However, you may want to rely on a local administration tool to ensure that you maintain strict security controls on your server.

CHAPTER 53

Using IIS with FrontPage 98

by Craig Eddy

IN THIS CHAPTER

- Introducing Internet Information Server *890*
- Installing the FrontPage Server Extensions for IIS *892*

Microsoft's Internet Information Server (IIS) is considered by many to be the best Web server available today. Certainly, for the Windows platform, there are few Web servers that can compete with IIS. IIS is designed to run on Windows NT Server and is, in fact, tightly integrated with the NT Server operating system.

This chapter explores the reasons you might consider using IIS as your Web server, by covering the system requirements for IIS, and showing just how easy it is to install FrontPage 98's Server Extensions on an IIS machine.

Introducing Internet Information Server

The IIS package is actually a conglomeration of several pieces of software that includes, but is not limited to, Active Server Pages, Microsoft Index Server, Microsoft NetShow, and, of course, the core Internet services. The Internet services, which run as true NT services, include Web, FTP, and Gopher services.

The following section discusses the features and system requirements of IIS. You can learn more details by visiting Microsoft's IIS Web site at `http://www.microsoft.com/iis`.

Version Considerations

As of this writing, the current released version of IIS is 3.0. Microsoft has also made available a Beta version of IIS 4.0 (Beta 3 as of this writing) for download from their Web site. There is a good chance that by the time you read this, IIS 4.0 will have been released.

Some of the cool new features in IIS 4.0 include the following:

- Transactional Active Server Pages, allowing you to use script and components together within a transaction
- Active Server Page script debugging, which means no more `Response.Write` code purely for debugging purposes
- Microsoft Message Queue Server, which provides a reliable method of sending messages over the network between applications
- Broader administration tools and capabilities, including the ability to run multiple Web sites with different administrators on the same IP address

As for the Server Extensions (discussed later in this chapter), the version shipped with FrontPage 98 will work with previous versions of the IIS. You won't need to upgrade to IIS 4.0 (or 3.0 for that matter) to use the features of the FrontPage 98 Server Extensions.

However, if you do upgrade to IIS 4.0, it does require the use of the FrontPage 98 Server Extensions. So, if you've got an older copy of the server extensions and think you can use them on your IIS 4.0 site, think again. Simply install the server extensions that come with FrontPage 98.

Features

As I mentioned, IIS includes several software packages operating under one roof. This conglomeration of software allows the Webmaster to fully utilize the capabilities Microsoft has built into NT Server, as well as easily leverage other NT-platform software packages, including the Microsoft BackOffice suite of applications.

Active Server Pages

Active Server Pages allow you to combine HTML, server-side scripting, and ActiveX server components to easily create Web-based applications. The script code is parsed by the server when the page containing the script is requested. None of the script code is returned to the requester; the browser sees the Active Server Page as a normal HTML document. This allows you to create a browser-independent document. In fact, there is built-in support for browser detection, allowing you to tailor the HTML returned to the browser, based upon its capabilities.

In addition, the ActiveX Database Objects (ADO) are included as part of the Active Server Pages package. These objects allow you to easily connect your Web server to any ODBC-compliant database. The ActiveX Database Objects are discussed in Chapter 43, "Advanced Database Set up and Custom Scripts."

Microsoft Index Server

The Index Server provides a search engine for your Web site. You can create full-text indexes of HTML, text, and Microsoft Office documents that are found on your web. You can also extend this indexing to any other type of file, provided you have the proper Index Server filter for that file type. After the index is built, you can provide querying capabilities to search all of these documents and quickly locate the documents containing information relevant to your query.

Microsoft NetShow

NetShow is the multimedia arm of IIS. It provides streaming of audio and video data to multiple browsers simultaneously. This allows you to do live multicasting from your Web site. You can even coordinate streaming audio with images, allowing you to create an illustrated audio feed.

Internet Server API

The Internet Server API (ISAPI) allows you to write custom server extensions to add new capabilities to your Web server. ISAPI is intended to replace CGI applications and is, in fact, the core on top of which Active Server Pages rides.

System Requirements

The system requirements for IIS are the same as those for NT Server. Of course, you must also have a TCP/IP network in place in order to access the IIS from other machines, but even this is not a requirement: You could certainly run IIS in a stand-alone environment.

The base minimum requirements for IIS are the following:

- Windows NT Server 4.0, service pack 1a or 2
- Intel 486 or better processor, Dec Alpha, or PowerPC (or any compatible system)
- 125MB available hard disk space
- 16MB RAM
- Mouse or pointing device

The following components have additional requirements:

- Active Server Pages requires 20MB of available free disk space.
- Index Server requires 32MB RAM and free disk space equal to 40% of the size of the documents to be indexed.
- NetShow adds a slew of additional requirements, the most significant of which are a Pentium/66MHz processor, 32MB RAM minimum (48MB recommended), and a high throughput Ethernet card. If you're expecting to stream a lot of multimedia content through your NetShow server, spare no expense with the Ethernet card!

Installing the FrontPage Server Extensions for IIS

The FrontPage Server Extensions allow IIS to take advantage of all of the features that FrontPage 98 has to offer. These include functions that support authoring, administering, and browsing your FrontPage webs. For example, when you use the FrontPage Explorer to move a document from one folder to another, the authoring extensions will update the moved document's URL in any documents that contain a link to the moved document.

If the Web server machine already has the FrontPage 97 Server Extensions installed, you only need to install the FrontPage 98 Server Extensions if you wish to take advantage of the new functionality. In addition, the FrontPage 98 Server Extensions are completely backward-compatible with the previous versions of the FrontPage client. Therefore, you can safely update the server without upgrading all of your FrontPage clients to FrontPage 98. For this reason, you should seriously consider updating the Server Extensions.

When you install the Server Extensions on an IIS machine, the following components are installed:

- The Server Extensions DLLs and executables
- The ISAPI components used by FrontPage to implement the Server Extensions
- The FrontPage Server Administrator
- The Server Extensions Resource Kit
- HTML Administration forms

The Server Extensions Resource Kit (SERK) provides a wealth of information about installing and using the Server Extensions. You should review the resource kit documents before installing the Server Extensions. The SERK can be installed with your FrontPage client even if you do not install any of the FrontPage Server components, because the SERK consists of only HTML documents and images.

The Server Extensions can be installed as part of a full installation of FrontPage 98 on the Web server machine or they can be installed by themselves. If you're sure you'll never need to use the FrontPage client tools on your Web server itself, you can install just the Server Extensions. The required files are available on the FrontPage CD-ROM in the `\ServExt` folder. You can also download the Server Extensions from Microsoft's Web site at `http://www.microsoft.com/frontpage`.

When installing the Server Extensions, you should keep the following in mind:

- You must be logged in as an NT administrator.
- The IIS services will be stopped while the extensions are installed and set up. The services will be restarted after the installation has been completed.
- You will be prompted for the account name of a Web administrator. This must be an existing NT account. You will not be prompted for the account's password because it is an existing NT account.
- Immediately after the extensions are installed, all existing content on the Web server will be converted to utilize the new extensions. This might take a few minutes and will increase the processor load significantly.
- You might be required to restart the machine after the extensions have been installed.

If you are installing the complete FrontPage 98 package on an IIS machine, you should select Custom Installation instead of Typical Installation. On the Select Components dialog of the installation, do not select the Personal Web Server. Do select the server extension items, including the SERK. The installation will automatically set up the Server Extensions for any ports on which you have IIS active.

To install the Server Extensions by themselves, follow these steps:

1. Run the Server Extensions setup program for your language and the machine's processor type.
2. On a single-hosted server, the FrontPage Server Extensions are automatically installed on the root folder of the server. On a multi-hosted machine, the Multi-Hosted Server dialog box is displayed. Select the virtual servers on which the FrontPage Server Extensions should be installed and click OK.
3. Enter the FrontPage administrator account name when prompted. At install time, you can only enter a single administrator. To add additional Web administrators, use the Tools|Permissions menu item in the FrontPage Explorer.

4. The Server Extensions are then installed on each Web found on the IIS machine. After this is completed, existing content is converted to the new server extensions.

When the Server Extensions have been installed, you can use the Server Administrator program to install, update, remove, and check the Server Extensions for your web. This program is installed in the `\version3.0\bin` sub-folder of the folder to which you installed FrontPage 98.

Summary

This chapter introduces you to Microsoft's Internet Information Server, which is an Internet server platform that is tightly integrated with the NT Server operating system. It provides a host of features and a high-performance HTTP server.

You've also learned how to install the FrontPage Server Extensions onto an IIS machine. These allow you to take full advantage of all of the features of FrontPage 98, including the server-based FrontPage components.

In Chapter 54, "Using Other Web Servers with FrontPage 98," you'll learn how you can integrate these FrontPage features with other Web server platforms.

CHAPTER 54

Using Other Web Servers with FrontPage 98

by Edward J. Lee

IN THIS CHAPTER

- Reasons for Using Other Web Servers *896*
- Key Considerations for Using FrontPage 98 with Other Web Servers *897*
- Using FrontPage 98 When the Server Extensions Are Unavailable *901*
- Creating New FrontPage Webs on Other Servers *904*
- Updating Non-FrontPage Webs to Work with FrontPage 98 *908*
- Testing Your FrontPage Webs with a Browser *911*

In preceding chapters, you learned how to use FrontPage 98 with Microsoft's FrontPage Personal Web Server (PWS) and Internet Information Server (IIS). You also read about obtaining and installing the FrontPage server extensions in Chapter 51, "Working with Server Extensions and Multihoming." The material covered in this chapter includes information for using FrontPage 98 with other, non-Microsoft Web servers. It highlights some of the key issues to consider when you're using such servers and provides instructions for publishing new FrontPage webs and for updating existing non-FrontPage webs on these servers. In addition, the chapter explores certain compatibility challenges for Web servers that do not support the server extensions and thus might restrict the use of specific FrontPage features.

Although conducting an exhaustive analysis of Web server software is beyond the scope of this chapter, or even this book, the early chapter discussion compares important server features with those of PWS. Knowing these important distinctions can help you better plan your Web site when using FrontPage 98 and can guide you through the overwhelming array of choices available today.

Reasons for Using Other Web Servers

The reasons for using other Web servers can be as varied and as numerous as the number of servers. Many Web developers, though, might have little or no choice in selecting a Web server. You might be a member of a development team in a corporate setting where both the server platform and Web server software are largely predetermined. You could also be a developer for a Web design or consulting company where the Web server is already fixed. If you are an independent consultant or Web hobbyist, the selection might be established by your client, ISP, or the Web-hosting organization of which you are a customer. Finally, you might simply want to use another Web server because of past experiences or because you want richer functionality than that offered by PWS.

Regardless of your reasons, FrontPage 98, as you saw in Chapter 52, "Administering FrontPage Server Extensions," can be used with a number of leading Web servers. For the most part, the FrontPage server extensions make the server platform and Web server software virtually transparent to web authors. Because the extensions are free, no additional software cost is required. As you will see later in this chapter, you can even use FrontPage 98 without the extensions. Because it is an "open" web authoring tool, then, what are the main issues to consider for working with FrontPage webs on servers other than PWS?

NOTE

If you have not already done so, you might want to refer to Chapters 51, "Working with Server Extensions and Multihoming," and Chapter 52, "Administering FrontPage Server Extensions," to develop a better understanding of the FrontPage server extensions. In addition to providing a complete list of all the operating systems and Web servers for which the extensions are available, Chapter 51 offers insights related to the FrontPage Server

Extensions Resource Kit and describes multihoming basics. Chapter 52 covers remote administration and configuration with the server extensions. Together, these two chapters are an excellent guide to installing and maintaining the FrontPage server extensions on your favorite Web server.

Key Considerations for Using FrontPage 98 with Other Web Servers

Ideally, you should select a Web server that is supported by the FrontPage server extensions. FrontPage-supported server platforms allow you to benefit from the full features of the tool, particularly those delivering its interactive capabilities such as threaded discussion groups. Using servers with the extensions installed can also help you avoid additional programming and/or script development, and permit you to leverage FrontPage's built-in content hyperlinking and administration capabilities.

After you narrow your Web server alternatives to those that support FrontPage webs, you might want to evaluate servers or potential Web hosting sites along the following dimensions:

- **Scalability, reliability, and responsiveness.** These evaluation elements are probably the most important because they consider the server's capability to effectively scale up to increasing levels of activity.
- **Richness of Web server functions.** More sophisticated Web server functions can facilitate overall site management efforts.
- **Budget.** Consider operational costs in addition to initial start-up costs.
- **Feasibility of using the same server.** How feasible is using the same Web server for development as using it for hosting or deployment?
- **Level of support.** If your site is hosted by a third party, what is the level of support for and experience with FrontPage webs?
- **Content transfer.** Know and understand in detail the processes for promoting FrontPage webs to the target production environment.

This rather abbreviated list of evaluation criteria is intended to assist the FrontPage developer in quickly sorting through some of the key considerations. Corporate information systems professionals and other commercial Web developers are more likely to use a far more comprehensive list and employ more complex analysis methods. Additionally, the analytical dimensions discussed in this section are in the context of using other servers over PWS.

Assessing the Server's Scalability, Reliability, and Responsiveness

Regardless of whether your site serves as no more than a digital calling card, or offers your company a new way to collaborate with customers, suppliers, and employees, those people accessing your FrontPage web have certain performance expectations. These groups expect high levels of availability, reliability, and responsiveness. Although PWS delivers an excellent starting point for initially organizing your Web site, it does not offer a realistic growth path for actually hosting your production web.

If you are installing your company's first Web server, most likely you will need a solution that, at a minimum, can easily scale to handle multiple concurrent users. In addition, you probably require a more robust environment to ensure greater levels of reliability and responsiveness. Obviously, these factors will lead to solutions that have proven track records under more stressful conditions than those ordinarily experienced or indeed are capable of being handled by PWS. If you are fortunate enough to have a choice in Web server software, then study each alternative with these performance characteristics in mind.

Closely related to the Web server software is the operating system the web itself will run on. For some companies and individuals, the server operating system is among the more critical decision points. Within corporate environments, platform standardization is frequently a key objective, for example. This section leaves this platform debate to the experts. Individuals looking to use FrontPage 98 with their favorite Web server might want to select the operating system with which they are most comfortable.

Establishing Priorities for Server Functions

For more sophisticated Web server functions, PWS is probably not the server of choice. A complete list of server-based features is not presented here although several important server characteristics are described.

Server-side Java, JavaScript, and Active Server Pages are among the more recent "hot" technologies requested by Web developers. Depending on your site's requirements, you might want to consider servers that support these features. Notably, you cannot use PWS if you want to write your own CGI scripts or programs.

A number of Web servers have more comprehensive server administration functions than PWS. Netscape's FastTrack, for example, supports the Lightweight Directory Access Protocol (LDAP), allowing users and groups to be shared across multiple servers.

Other Web servers provide activity and browser logs and can generate reports for performance and usage analysis. These server tools can facilitate site management efforts. PWS does not come equipped with such capabilities.

With PWS, the security model is based on the three access levels of administrator, author, and browser. Simply knowing the right user name and password enables access to authorized functions and webs. Several Web servers feature greater flexibility in governing access to documents and directories. Many Web servers, for example, can provide IP address and host restrictions. This capability adds another dimension to security by restricting access to individual documents and directories based on specific IP addresses or domains.

The preceding are just a few of the server-based functions commonly available with other Web servers. As you analyze your own site's needs, you might want to establish priorities for these or other features. Setting priorities can help you assess the relative strengths and weaknesses of server alternatives as they relate to your specific site requirements and objectives. You can also save time by specifying those criteria that are most relevant to your web. For example, you can quickly come up with a short list of servers if Secure HTTP (S-HTTP) support is mandatory for your project.

NOTE

Secure HTTP is an encryption and user authentication standard proposed by CommerceNet, a consortium of commercial enterprises. The consortium seeks to promote the development of commerce on the Internet. S-HTTP works only with the HTTP protocol.

For more detailed information on CommerceNet and the S-HTTP protocol, refer to the following site:

`http://www.commercenet.net.`

Developing a Budget

Some public domain Web servers such as Apache (UNIX only) are free and offer outstanding performance, functionality, and support. In fact, according to Netcraft in its survey of over one million sites, Apache had a greater than 43 percent share of the Web server market as recently as August 1997. Notably, Microsoft's IIS, bundled with NT 4.0, is also free and enjoyed more than a 16 percent share in the same survey.

Other commercially available Web servers range in price from less than $100 to over $1,000. Some, like WebSite from O'Reilly & Associates, offer free downloads for evaluation. You should note, however, that the initial procurement costs represent only a fraction of the total costs you are likely to incur throughout the operating life of your Web server. Like other software projects, ongoing maintenance, enhancements, and operational costs associated with your web will probably consume the majority of your budget.

Determining the Feasibility of Using the Same Server

Determining the feasibility of using the same server is a specific evaluation dimension that applies to those planning to have their site hosted by a third party. More specifically, it is intended for companies and individuals who have Web site requirements beyond a basic web presence setup. These needs typically drive extensive testing activities before webs are transferred to production. Under these conditions, then, you might want to consider using the same server for development even if the hosting company supports FrontPage webs.

I do not necessarily mean that you need the identical industrial-strength server configuration that your web-hosting partner has. If you or your company can afford a basic development and testing environment, it might be worthwhile, because you can potentially eliminate compatibility (and other unexpected) problems when your site is staged for production deployment. Ideally, you would like to have the same Web server software and operating system.

If even a scaled-down version of a development and testing configuration is not feasible, then discuss which options are available with your hosting source. Expect to pay additional usage fees for a more sophisticated development environment.

Evaluating the Level of Support of FrontPage Web Hosting Companies

Like the immediately preceding section, the discussion here is applicable if you are hosting your Web site with a third party. Even though this section is not directly related to the actual selection of a Web server, it does provide some guidance for FrontPage developers looking to simplify their web authoring efforts.

A number of Web hosting outfits have made substantial investments in supporting FrontPage webs. As a FrontPage user yourself, you might find it advantageous to partner with such companies. Some of these organizations have technical staff dedicated exclusively to handling your FrontPage-related needs and questions, and can even offer insights into development. Other marketing savvy companies are now offering customers alternatives in Web server software and platforms.

If you do have a choice, select a firm that aggressively markets itself as a FrontPage Web hosting company. Then follow up with some of its customers. Of course, you will still need to do some additional homework for ultimately selecting a hosting concern, but you can narrow your search efforts by focusing on FrontPage specialty houses. You can also check out the Microsoft FrontPage site to get a list of organizations that it promotes.

Defining Processes for Transferring Content

Whether you host your FrontPage webs yourself or outsource this function, defining the processes for transferring content to your target Web server is important. Although FrontPage 98 is equipped with excellent content transfer functions, for many developers the tool itself is viewed as only part of an overall process that seeks to minimize errors and disruptions, and to maintain control over site content and functions. Quite literally at the touch of a button, an entire web can be remotely updated. This feature of FrontPage 98 is powerful, but also one that merits careful planning, process definition, and security measures.

In addition to any policy-level constraints with which you should be familiar, you should know and understand the details of the publishing process itself. Generally speaking, the FrontPage publishing process depends on whether the FrontPage server extensions are installed. These scenarios and their corresponding step-by-step instructions are covered later in this chapter.

Summarizing the Key Considerations

Using other Web servers with FrontPage 98 might require some level of research and analysis regarding various servers' performance, functions, and prices. Or, if you have your site hosted by others, you might feel compelled to evaluate FrontPage hosting companies. In either case, as long as the server extensions are properly installed, the server itself should be virtually transparent to the FrontPage author.

With respect to PWS, even though it might not be considered a scalable solution for hosting Web sites, it does offer some distinct benefits. It's useful as a staging area for your content. It offers a way to organize your Web site quickly. Furthermore, it's free. For more details on PWS, refer to Chapter 50, "Personal Web Server Administration."

NOTE

For comprehensive information regarding Web server comparisons, prices, and statistics, visit the following sites:

`http://www.webcompare.com`

`http://www.netcraft.com`

Using FrontPage 98 When the Server Extensions Are Unavailable

If the FrontPage server extensions are unavailable for your favorite Web server, you can still use FrontPage 98 for web authoring, but you should be aware of certain restrictions and potential problem areas. Remember that you can also use PWS to initially structure your web before transferring it to the target server.

This section highlights some of the known issues you might encounter without the FrontPage server extensions installed and how you can get around them. It also identifies alternative ways for publishing content. Notably, this section borrows heavily from some of the documented items made publicly available through Microsoft's Knowledge Base articles.

WebBot Functions That Rely on FrontPage Server Extensions

FrontPage webs that use the browse-time interactive elements delivered via the WebBots should be avoided. According to Microsoft, you should refrain from using the following WebBot components when publishing FrontPage webs to a server that does not support the server extensions or does not have them installed:

- WebBot Confirmation component
- WebBot Discussion component
- WebBot Registration component
- WebBot Save Results component
- WebBot Search component
- WebBot Scheduled Image component
- WebBot Scheduled Include component

Server Compatibility Issues

As noted earlier, you should study the feasibility of using the same Web server software for development and for production hosting, even if the FrontPage server extensions are installed in both environments. When the extensions are not available, you might experience difficulties in the following areas:

- Access control
- Filename extensions
- Default page names

Access Control

As you might recall, access control refers to the security mechanisms used by your Web server. The security model and rules are not replicated from one server type to another. For example, on your local machine's PWS, you might have a user name and password of `Administrator` and `admin`, respectively. When you access the target Web server, you might be prompted for a different set of user name and password combinations, or even totally different information.

Note that you have to enter valid values or additional information on the target server to gain access to the web(s) housed there. Contact your Web server administrator to make sure that you have the appropriate access rights if you encounter problems.

Filename Extensions

When you use FrontPage wizards and templates to design your web, the pages generated by these tools default to the `.htm` extension. Some Web servers, particularly those that are UNIX-based, might recognize only files suffixed with `.html`.

To avoid problems caused by filename incompatibilities between your local or development server and the production server, ensure that the latter recognizes the `.htm` file extension. If this item is not configurable on the production server, you can either rename the files before publishing the web to the target server, or you can use the Save As option when you are in the FrontPage Editor and then modify the filename extension manually.

Neither alternative is perfect, but notably, the FrontPage Explorer and Editor recognize both file extension formats and present no problems in identifying and updating the file.

Default Page Names

FrontPage webs created with PWS assume that the default (home) page is `Index.htm`. Because different servers use different naming conventions for the default page, you should be sure that the production server is configured to recognize this default name.

When you're working on your local machine, you can also configure PWS to designate another file other than `Index.htm` as the default page of your web. This relatively easy configuration modification enables you to map the PWS page name to the name on the target server.

The following instructions have been adapted from the Microsoft Knowledge Base, Article ID: Q150681.

Follow these steps to change the default page name in PWS:

1. Use Windows Explorer to locate the `Srm.cnf` file found in the `FrontPage Webs\Server\conf` folder.
2. Use Notepad as an editor to open and edit the `Srm.cnf` file.
3. Look for the line that appears like `DirectoryIndex index.htm`. Note that the most of the lines are "commented out" with a pound sign (`#`) in the first column. Be sure to remove this character if it is present on the line specifying the default page. Otherwise, any changes you make to the name of the default page will not be recognized when PWS is restarted.
4. Save the `Srm.cnf` file and close Notepad.
5. Stop and restart PWS to allow the changes to take place.

When you open this PWS-based web with your browser, the new default page that you specified in Step 3 is then loaded.

Issues with Transferring Files and Content

Without the FrontPage server extensions installed, you will need FTP services to transfer your content to the target server. If you or your company has decided to host your own site, then ensure that FTP services are available on your production when remote authors are ready to stage their work.

If your site is being hosted by a third party, note that many companies price their hosting plans based on the amount of data transferred during a given time period. Also, if you intend to write customized CGI scripts, you might want to check with your hosting partner. A number of hosting organizations might not allow such scripts. Security and reliability are major concerns for these companies, so you can expect them to require appropriate testing and staging of your content.

Avoiding Server-Based File Conflicts

If you use FTP to transfer your files to your target server, you should be aware of certain Microsoft recommendations. According to Microsoft, you should not transfer the following files and folders:

- **All folders beginning with `_vti_`.** These folders are used exclusively with the FrontPage server extensions.
- **Access control files.** Before you invoke FTP services, you should carefully review the file list you have selected to transfer. For UNIX-based Web servers, do not upload files with names that begin with a period, and for Windows servers, avoid files with names that begin with the pound sign (#).

> **NOTE**
>
> For more details on using FTP to transfer files to your target web, refer to Chapters 51 and 52. There you can also find more information on using the Microsoft Web Publishing Wizard, a tool for transferring FrontPage webs to servers that are not running the server extensions.

Creating New FrontPage Webs on Other Servers

After the FrontPage server extensions have been installed, the process of creating new FrontPage webs on other servers is relatively straightforward. This section focuses on two popular Web servers: WebSite from O'Reilly & Associates and Netscape's FastTrack Server. The former operates on the Windows 95 platform, whereas the latter runs on Windows NT 4.0. Both products were used during the beta evaluation period for FrontPage 98.

Aside from a specific configuration point regarding WebSite, the discussion here assumes that you have already configured either Web server for operation in your own environment. You might want to quickly review some of the multihoming material presented in Chapter 51, because both servers were used in a multihome setting.

Using WebSite 1.1 for Windows 95 to Host Your FrontPage Webs

Earlier in the chapter, you were presented with an overview of various Web server functions. WebSite from O'Reilly and Associates (`www.oreilly.com`) is one of the servers that delivers rich functionality at a relatively low cost.

Version 1.1 was downloaded from the O'Reilly Web site and was used to test the latest FrontPage server extensions. The installation process was fairly simple, but getting the server configured to work properly with the new extensions took just a bit more time than expected. For those readers who might be unfamiliar with this server, the WebSite Server Properties dialog box, shown in Figure 54.1, is the main panel for setting the configuration parameters.

FIGURE 54.1.
Configuring WebSite for FrontPage 98.

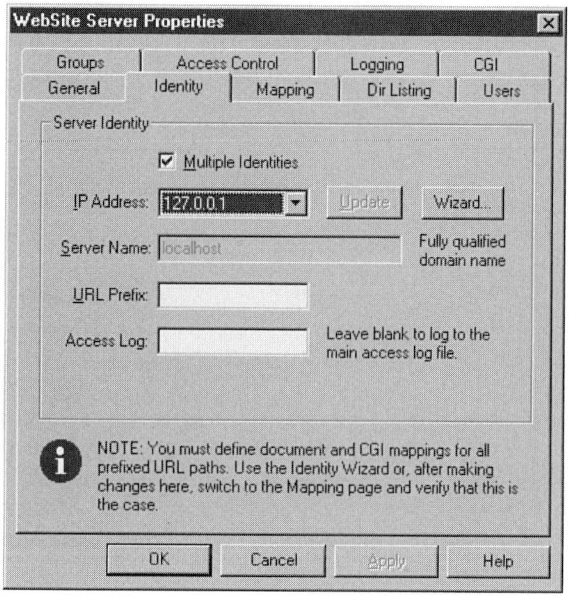

During the server installation process, take particular note of the port number you assign to WebSite Server. This port number is an important qualifier that distinguishes WebSite from PWS, which, as you saw in earlier chapters, typically uses the reserved port number of 80.

CAUTION

Be careful when assigning port numbers to other Web servers. Several reserved values could create conflicts. Your best bet is to select high numbers starting at 8080.

The key fields for getting FrontPage 98 to work with the WebSite Server are the Multiple Identities check box and the IP Address value on the server Identity page. By clicking the check box, you enable an IP address value to be specified. Because the server software was installed on a stand-alone machine for this example, the reserved address of `127.0.0.1` was used. The other fields were left blank, and the WebSite Wizard was not invoked. If WebSite is deployed in a networked environment, then speak with your network administrator or refer to the excellent documentation provided by the vendor.

After installing the FrontPage server extensions (see Chapter 51), you are almost ready to start publishing new FrontPage webs to WebSite. The last task before launching FrontPage 98 is to start the WebSite Server. Following the web creation steps you learned in Part II, you should be able to easily create new FrontPage webs that are actually hosted on WebSite.

From the New FrontPage Web dialog box, choose the kind of FrontPage web to create, type the new title, and click the Change button to specify the new web's location. In the Change Location dialog box, which is shown in Figure 54.2, choose from the pull-down list to indicate the web's location, or type the location in the list box. Note that in the example both the server name and its port number are specified because in this configuration the same physical server is being used to host two Web servers, PWS (port 80) and WebSite Server (port 8080). The servers share the same server name of `localhost`.

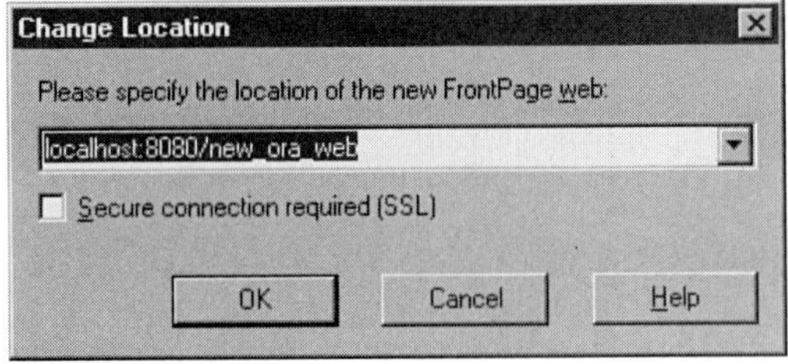

FIGURE 54.2.
Specifying the location of the new FrontPage web.

When you return to the New FrontPage Web dialog box, click the OK button. If you are accessing the web for the first time within this FrontPage Explorer session, you are presented with the familiar Name and Password dialog box. Enter the appropriate information, and the new web creation process is initiated.

FrontPage Explorer should now display the folders and files associated with the kind of FrontPage web you selected a few steps ago in the New FrontPage Web dialog box. In the example, the Personal Web template had been chosen. Figure 54.3 shows the files corresponding to this web type.

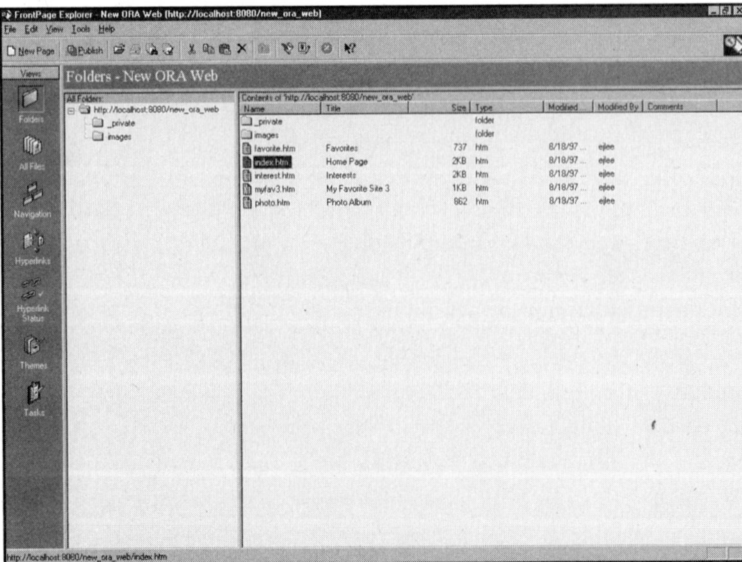

FIGURE 54.3.
Displaying the folders and files from the Personal Web template.

You can now use FrontPage Editor to modify any of these pages. In the example, several of the pages were enhanced by adding a theme, by inserting some hyperlinks, and by including a hit counter to the default page. Figure 54.4, for example, shows the revised `index.htm` page. Everything below the Microsoft FrontPage logo has been added.

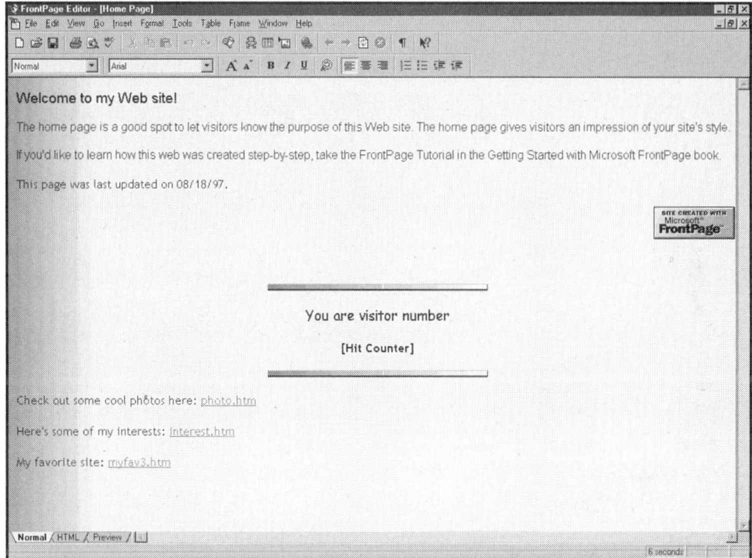

FIGURE 54.4.
Modifying a default page for hosting on WebSite.

After you make your changes and save the individual pages, WebSite Server hosts your new FrontPage web. You have now successfully created a new FrontPage web using a template to set the overall web structure, and have published it to a third-party Web server.

Some Quick Troubleshooting Steps

If you experience any problems, first check that the WebSite Server is running. Then launch the FrontPage Server Administrator. Make sure that the FrontPage server extensions have been properly installed for the WebSite Server and its corresponding port number. If PWS has also been installed, more than one entry should be displayed in the window in the FrontPage Server Administrator dialog box, as shown in Figure 54.5. As a further check, inspect the Authoring parameter. It should be set to `enabled`.

If you feel that you might have missed a step during the installation of the server extensions, you might want to try uninstalling and then immediately re-installing them.

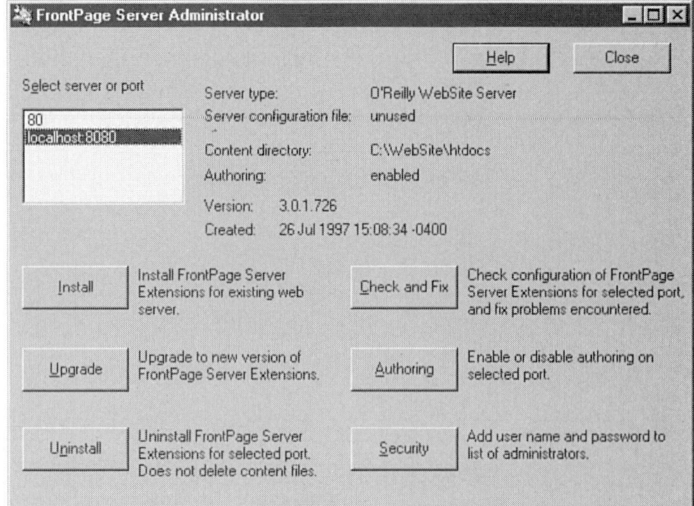

FIGURE 54.5.
Validating the WebSite parameters with the FrontPage Server Administrator.

Updating Non-FrontPage Webs to Work with FrontPage 98

Another scenario you are likely to encounter as a FrontPage developer involves updating existing content. In just a few short years, the sheer volume of information published on the Internet is nearly impossible to contemplate. Fortunately for web authors like yourself, FrontPage 98 allows you to update more of this content than you would probably ever care to imagine.

The point is that FrontPage 98 is flexible enough not only to update this content, but also, as you have seen, to spruce it up at the same time. This section provides instructions for modifying non-FrontPage webs, specifically those residing on Netscape's FastTrack Server.

Updating Content on FastTrack Server 2.01 for Windows NT

FastTrack Server is positioned as Netscape's (`www.netscape.com`) entry-level product in its Web server line. The fact that it sits at the lower end, though, does not necessarily mean that FastTrack is at the bottom of the heap. On the contrary, many reviewers have given the Web server high marks for its ease of installation and management, robust performance, and rich features. For these reasons, including this server in demonstrating FrontPage's "open" authoring capabilities makes sense.

As far as Web servers go, FastTrack must rank among the easiest to install and configure. You can literally get it up and running in minutes. Like O'Reilly's WebSite installation process, though, the same cautionary note applies: Be wary of the port number you assign to the Web server. This advice may be especially important on the NT platform because a version of Microsoft's PWS and IIS might already be installed.

NOTE

If you have come this far without reading Chapters 51 and 52 yet, now would probably be a good time to do so. These chapters provide excellent background material for this entire chapter, particularly because the examples used here are all based on multihoming.

After you start the Web server services on NT, launch FrontPage 98. With the server extensions installed, the FrontPage Explorer offers seamless access to content hosted on the FastTrack Server. Just open the default FastTrack web as you would any FrontPage web, and click the More Webs button in the Getting Started dialog box, which is shown in Figure 54.6.

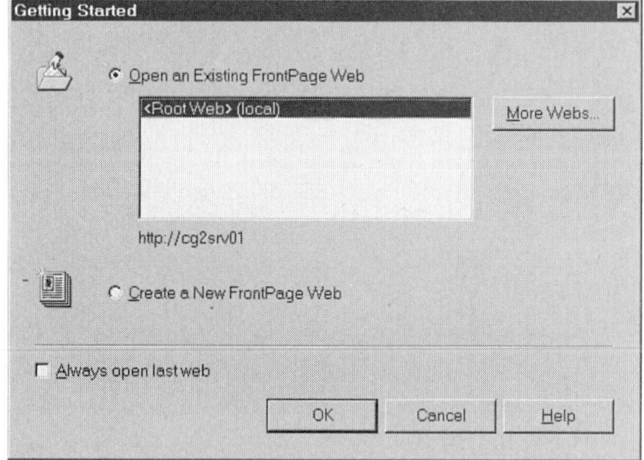

FIGURE 54.6.
Using the Getting Started dialog box to open a web.

Again, because the example is based on a multihomed server, you must specify both the server name and port number. In this example with NT, the server name is `cg2srv01`, and its port number is `8082`.

You can use the pull-down list within the Open FrontPage Web dialog box, shown in Figure 54.7, to select a web, or you can type its location into the list box. If several webs are located on the server, you can also click the List Webs button in this dialog box to view and select the web that you want to update. Click the OK button to retrieve the web. In the example, the FastTrack default home page is loaded into the FrontPage Explorer.

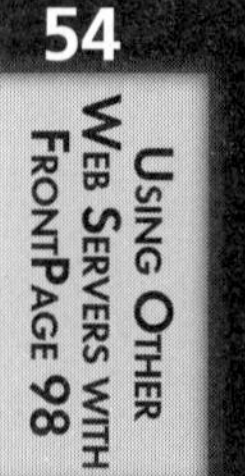

Now that you have successfully retrieved a non-FrontPage web, examine the files listed in the FrontPage Explorer, which is shown in Figure 54.8. Select the page titled FastTrack Home Page, and open the FrontPage Editor. Feel free to make any modifications to the page. After you are done, save the page, close the editor, and exit FrontPage Explorer.

You have just completed the process of updating a non-FrontPage web that is hosted on a non-Microsoft Web server. The next time that you retrieve and update this web, FrontPage Explorer will recognize it as a FrontPage web. Thanks to the server extensions, the process is this easy.

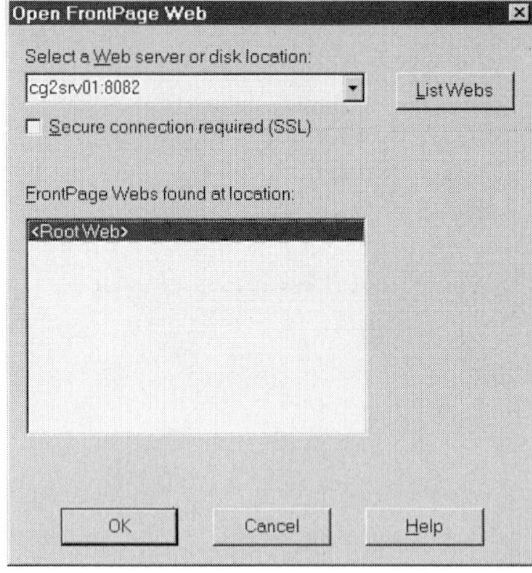

FIGURE 54.7. *Specifying a server name and port number to access a web.*

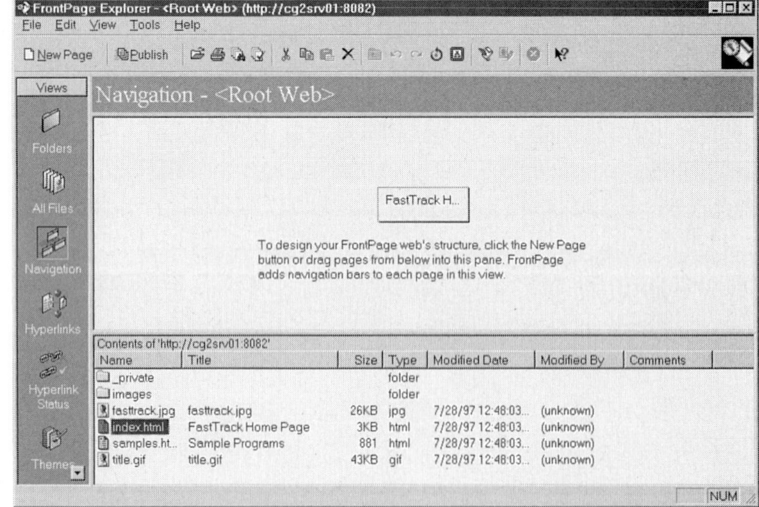

FIGURE 54.8. *Highlighting a Web page to edit.*

Note that FrontPage 98 does not "convert" any pages after they have been edited. Content is organized in directory structures and stored using standard HTML and image formats. For the most part, other authoring tools and HTML editors can coexist with FrontPage 98.

Testing Your FrontPage Webs with a Browser

Now that you have mastered publishing new FrontPage webs and updating non-FrontPage webs on different servers, you can see how the modifications appear and how the webs behave when accessed by your favorite browser. Recall the first example with the WebSite Server. You learned how to create a new FrontPage web using the Personal Web template, made some minor page modifications, and then published the web back to WebSite. For the second exercise, you edited an existing web and published it to FastTrack Server. The new version of FrontPage provides a convenient "preview" feature, but the next level of basic testing involves interacting with the actual webs as most users will, through a browser.

If you're using Windows 95, before launching your browser and testing the WebSite Server content, ensure that the server has been started. Allow your browser to load the home page that you have set as the default. Open the web or its location (but not the local file) by typing `http://` and then the server name and port number. In the example, you might recall that this information was as follows:

```
http://localhost:8080/myweb/
```

Figure 54.9 shows the modifications that were made to the template: A theme was applied; some hyperlinks, text, and lines were added; and a page counter was inserted. If you followed the steps identified earlier, then your modifications should also be visible in your browser.

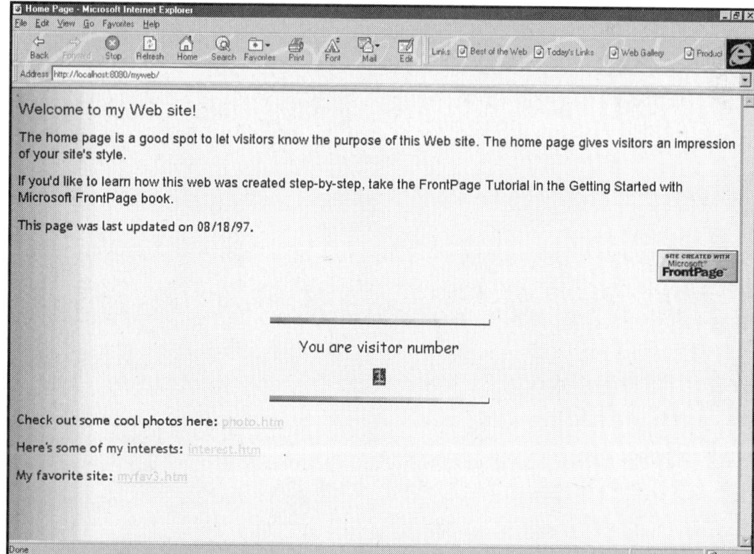

FIGURE 54.9.
Loading a new FrontPage web created with a template and hosted on WebSite Server.

If you're using NT and FastTrack Server, and you also have followed the steps outlined in the second example, then you too should be able to view your modifications. Start the server services on NT, launch your browser, and load the modified web. Figure 54.10 shows the end result of the changes implemented in the second example.

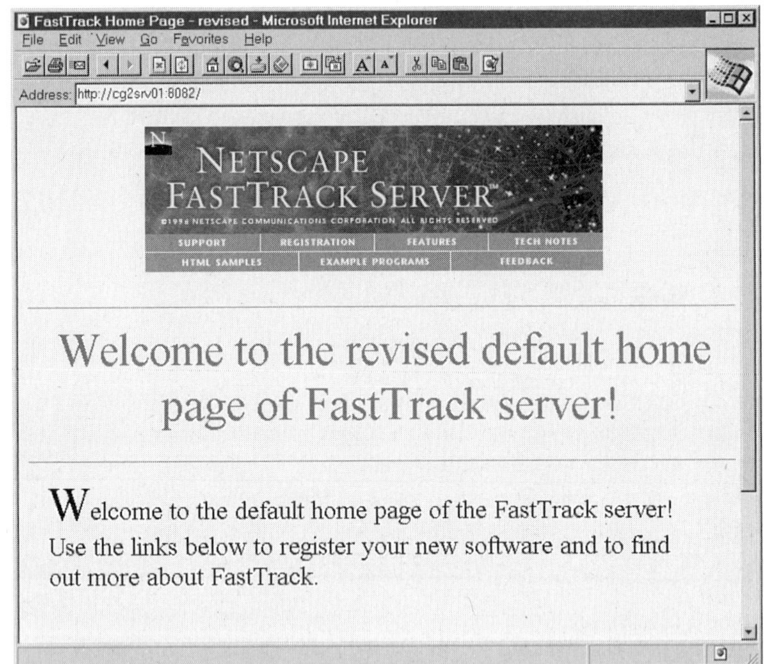

FIGURE 54.10.
A non-FrontPage web hosted on FastTrack Server.

Summary

The FrontPage Personal Web Server (PWS) serves as an excellent starting point for building webs. Most companies, however, have more sophisticated server needs and require more robust solutions. FrontPage 98 itself, though, is a flexible web authoring tool that can be used with a variety of Web server software and platforms. Whatever your Web server preference might be, you can probably find a place for FrontPage 98 in your arsenal of Web technologies.

IN THIS PART

- Introducing the FrontPage Developer's Kit *915*
- Customizing FrontPage Menus *927*
- Creating Your Own Templates *939*
- Creating Your Own Wizards *949*
- Programming the Wizard *961*

PART

Advanced Development for FrontPage 98

CHAPTER 55

Introducing the FrontPage Developer's Kit

by William Robert Stanek

IN THIS CHAPTER

- Using the FrontPage Developer's Kit *916*
- Obtaining and Installing the FrontPage Developer's Kit *917*
- What's in the FrontPage Developer's Kit *917*

FrontPage 98 is the most powerful Web publishing and administration tool available. Not only can you personalize FrontPage 98, you can also create customized tools to meet your specific needs. These tools can include new templates for pages and webs, wizards for creating pages and webs, and programs that automate publishing tasks. To create customized tools for FrontPage publishing, you use the FrontPage Developer's Kit. The FrontPage Developer's Kit has everything you need to help you customize FrontPage publishing.

This chapter introduces the FrontPage Developer's Kit. In addition to learning how to obtain and install the kit, you will get a detailed look at what the kit contains and how to use the kit with FrontPage 98.

Using the FrontPage Developer's Kit

The FrontPage Developer's Kit was created to help developers extend the functionality of FrontPage 98. You use this kit to create templates, wizards, utilities, and CGI scripts for use with FrontPage 98. Although this kit is primarily for developers who have some experience in programming and automation with object linking and embedding (OLE), the kit is meant to be easy to use regardless of your experience.

As you have seen in this book, templates are used as the basis for pages and webs. Using the FrontPage Developer's Kit, you can also create templates for frame-enhanced documents. These templates are called *framesets*. The good news is that you do not need any programming or OLE automation experience to create templates for pages, frames, and webs.

Wizards are also used to create pages and webs. As you have seen in this book, wizards aid the content creation process by presenting options that help you customize pages and webs. Unlike templates, wizards are programs that run on your system and interface with FrontPage 98. To create a wizard, you need to use a programming language, such as Visual Basic or Visual C++. To interface with FrontPage 98, your program uses OLE automation. Thus, if you plan to create wizards, you should be familiar with programming and OLE automation.

NOTE

Visual Basic and Visual C++ are the best programming languages for creating FrontPage wizards, because of their visual development nature. Creating the graphical interface for wizards is easy and quick if you use either of these languages.

Another use for OLE automation is to create utilities that can be used with FrontPage 98. An example of a FrontPage utility is the Web Publishing Wizard, which was originally an add-on developed for FrontPage 97. Using this wizard, you could transfer webs to servers that did not support FrontPage extensions. This wizard is now integrated into the FrontPage Explorer.

The FrontPage Developer's Kit also helps you create CGI scripts that interface with the Personal Web Server. Again, the interface to FrontPage is handled with OLE automation.

Obtaining and Installing the FrontPage Developer's Kit

If the version of FrontPage you purchased does not include the FrontPage Developer's Kit, you can obtain the kit from Microsoft's Web site at no charge. To do so, visit the Microsoft's home page for FrontPage at the following URL:

```
http://www.microsoft.com/frontpage/
```

From this page, you can follow links to the section containing the FrontPage Developer's Kit. Keep in mind that the FrontPage Web site might change occasionally to reflect new versions and information, so make sure that you are obtaining the most current version from the links. If you obtain the FrontPage Developer's Kit from Microsoft's Web site, you will need to install it on your system. All the files in the FDK are compressed into a ZIP file that you have to uncompress using a ZIP utility such as PKZIP.

CAUTION

The FrontPage Developer's Kit's ZIP file contains subdirectories. ZIP utilities that run from the DOS prompt do not automatically unpack your files into multiple directories. So, if your ZIP utility runs from the DOS prompt, be sure to use the `-d` flag to preserve the directory structure, as shown in the following example:

```
pkunzip -d fpdevkit.zip
```

What's in the FrontPage Developer's Kit

The FrontPage Developer's Kit is quite extensive and includes many examples. These examples show you how to create templates, wizards, utilities, WebBots, and CGI scripts that interface with FrontPage 98. Each specific type of example has its own directory under the base installation directory for the FrontPage Developer's Kit.

These directories include:

```
template
wizards
utility
cgi
designer
webbot
```

The sections that follow examine the contents of these directories and discuss how you can use the examples to help you customize FrontPage 98. You might want to review what the FrontPage

Developer's Kit contains, and then read this part of the book in its entirety before studying the examples.

The Template Examples

The `template` directory is in the base installation directory of the FrontPage Developer's Kit. The template directory contains template examples for pages, webs, and frames with each example organized into subdirectories.

The `template/pages` directory has sample page templates. These templates were created with the FrontPage Editor Save as Template option. When you use this option of the Editor, you create an HTML document with the `.htm` extension and a document that stores template information with an `.inf` extension. Files with the `.inf` extension are formatted like Windows INI files and contain parameters for the template, such as the template name and directory.

The `template/webs` directory contains sample web templates that were created with the Web Template Maker Utility. The Web Template Maker Utility is one of the utilities included in the FrontPage Developer's Kit. With this useful tool, you can base a web template on any existing web.

The `template/frames` directory contains sample framesets. All sample framesets have the `.frm` extension. You can use the samples to help you create your own framesets.

The Wizard Examples

The `wizards` directory under the base installation of the FrontPage Developer's Kit contains sample wizards. Most of the sample wizards are programmed in Visual Basic, which is one of the easiest programming languages to learn and use. Because wizards are programs, you can run them just as you would any other program.

TIP

You can use the Windows Explorer to run any wizard. All you need to do is change to the directory containing the executable file and double-click the appropriate icon. Before you run a wizard, you should start the FrontPage Explorer and the Personal Web Server.

To better understand the sample wizards, change to the appropriate subdirectory, list the files, and examine all files (except the binary executable file) using a word processor or standard ASCII text editor. When you list and examine the files in wizard directories, you should see immediately that wizards are more complex than templates, and not only because there are more files involved. Because most of the wizard examples are written in Visual Basic, the wizard directories contain six files that end with the extensions shown in Table 24.1.

Table 24.1. Files in wizard directories.

Extension	*Description*
`.exe`	The binary executable file for the wizard
`.inf`	A Windows INI-formatted file that specifies parameters for the wizard, such as the wizard name and directory
`.log`	A file that logs errors that occur when the wizard runs
`.frm`	A form written in Visual Basic and used to create the wizard
`.frx`	Another Visual Basic file containing program information
`.vbp`	File used to set up program information for wizards written in Visual Basic
`.vbz`	File used to set up flags, dependencies, and so on for wizards written in Visual Basic

Within the `wizards` directory you will find many subdirectories. The `wizards/pages` directory has sample page wizards. The `wizards/webs` directory contains sample web wizards. Sample wizards are not the only programs in the `wizards` directory. The directory also contains directories for Visual Basic modules and Visual C++ object libraries.

The `wizards/vb` directory has utility procedures to help you create wizards. You can use these procedures to add meta information to documents, add files to a list of files you want to update or create, to look up or set parameters for the wizard, and much more.

The `wizards/vc` directory contains object and type libraries for use with Visual C++. You can use these libraries in OLE automation.

The FrontPage Developer's Kit Utilities

There are three very useful utilities in the FrontPage Developer's Kit: the API Test Utility, a helper application called fplaunch, and the Web Template Maker. These utilities are written in Visual Basic and use OLE automation to interface with FrontPage 98. Not only are the utilities useful, but you also can learn a great deal by examining their source code.

The API Test Utility

The API Test Utility is a test suite of all the OLE automation functions you can use with FrontPage 98. You can use the source code in the `utility/apitests` directory as a starting point for any wizard you create. In fact, you can usually cut procedures out of the source code and paste them directly into your wizard's source code.

Each push button in the API Test Utility dialog box enables you to test a specific set of related OLE automation functions. Most functions display a form that prompts you to enter information. For example, if you press the button labeled Web Information, you can test OLE procedures that get a web's title, URL, and meta information.

The fplaunch Utility

The fplaunch utility is an extremely useful helper application that uses OLE automation to create an authoring interface between your Web browser and FrontPage 98. Using fplaunch, you can create HTML documents with links that access the FrontPage Explorer, open a specified web, and then open a page for editing in the FrontPage Editor. To learn how to create your own helper applications, examine the source code in the `utility/fplaunch` directory.

Because you can set an optional user name parameter, fplaunch is a useful utility for Web administrators and anyone else authoring pages in your webs. Before you can use fplaunch, you need to do the following:

1. Configure your Web server and browser so they recognize fplaunch parameter files, which end in the `.fpl` extension.
2. Create an fplaunch parameter file and a document that references the parameter file.

Configuring Your Server and Browser

As with most helper applications, you need to ensure your server and browser correctly identify files used by the helper application. To do this, you must update server and browser configuration files.

Because fplaunch parameter files should end in the `.fpl` extension, you configure your server to send files with this extension as a new MIME type. On most servers, MIME types are stored in a specific configuration file. For the Personal Web Server, the configuration file is called `mime.typ` and is located in the `FrontPage Webs/Server/conf` directory. You need to edit this file and add the following entry to the end of the file:

```
application/x-fplaunch       fpl
```

NOTE

The exact number of spaces between the MIME type and the extension designator does not matter. MIME types are broken down into basic categories, such as application. The application type identifies binary data that can be executed or used with another application. Each data type category has a subtype associated with it. MIME subtypes are defined as primary data types, additionally defined data types, and extended data types. The primary subtype is the primary type of data adopted for use as MIME content types. Additionally defined data types are additional subtypes that have been officially adopted as MIME content types. Extended data types are experimental subtypes that have not been officially adopted as MIME content types. You can easily identify extended subtypes because they begin with the letter x followed by a hyphen, such as x-fplaunch. The x-fplaunch subtype identifies an extended data type in fplaunch format.

After you save the MIME configuration file, restart the Personal Web Server. You are now ready to configure your browser for use with fplaunch. You do this by setting helper application preferences from an options menu within your browser.

Creating and Referencing a Parameter File

Creating a parameter file to use with fplaunch is easy. All you need to do is create an ASCII text file that sets the parameters that enable OLE automation to perform its magic on the FrontPage Explorer. There are three mandatory parameters and one optional parameter:

Parameter	*Description*
`Web server name`	The host name or IP address of the server storing the web you want to access
`Web name`	The name of the web you want to access
`user name`	Optional user name to enter in the login dialog
`page URL`	In the named web, the page URL of the file you want to edit

NOTE

All users must authenticate themselves to FrontPage 98, even if you set the user name parameter. When a user activates a link to fplaunch, she is prompted to enter her user name and password before FrontPage 98 opens the web for editing.

Use each of these parameters in the order presented and enter them on separate lines. The following is a sample parameter file called `startcorp.fpl`:

```
http://www.mcp.com
corpres
william
index.htm
```

When a user clicks a link containing a reference to `startcorp.fpl`, his browser starts fplaunch, fplaunch reads the parameter file, and then the server asks the user to authenticate with the user name filled in as william. The user can enter a new user name and password or enter a valid password for the user william. After authentication, the FrontPage Explorer loads a Web called corpres from the server at `http://www.mcp.com` and opens the file called `index.htm` for editing in the FrontPage Explorer.

NOTE

The parameter file must be placed in the subdirectory for your web. If you installed FrontPage 98 to the default location, the location of your web is `FrontPage Webs\Content\`*`yourweb_name`*. Keep in mind, all entries in the parameter file must be valid. If you are practicing with FrontPage 98, you are probably using a local server with the server name as `http://127.0.0.1`.

After you save the parameter file to the subdirectory for your web, you must create a document that references the parameter file.

TIP

The hypertext reference to the parameter file is best entered as a page link. You can create page links in the Current Web tab of the Create Link dialog box.

The Web Template Maker

The Web Template Maker creates web templates that are based on existing webs. The source code and binary executable file for the template maker is in the `utility/webtmpl` directory. Before you use the Web Template Maker, start the Personal Web Server and the FrontPage Explorer, then open on the server a web that you want to use as the basis for a template.

Next, start the Web Template Maker. The list of existing webs is displayed by title in the Available Webs area of the Template Maker dialog box. Select a web to base a template on by moving the mouse pointer over the name of the web and clicking the mouse pointer. In the New Web Template area of the dialog, enter a title, name, and description for the template. The template name must be unique. You should also enter a unique title for the template.

When you finish defining the template, click the Make Web Template button to create the new template. From then on, when you select New from the File menu in the FrontPage Explorer, your new template will be available for use. To refresh the list of existing webs after you create a new template, click the Refresh Web List button.

Examining the CGI Scripts

CGI scripts are external programs that run on Web servers. Originally, CGI scripts were used to perform advanced publishing tasks, such as processing input from fill-in forms and image maps. Because these tasks are automated in FrontPage 98, you primarily use CGI scripts to do advanced follow-up processing of form input. Also, if your server does not support FrontPage Server Extensions, you might need to use CGI scripts to perform general processing for forms and image maps as well.

The CGI scripts in the FrontPage Developer's Kit are in the `cgi` directory under the base installation of the FrontPage Developer's Kit. Most of the sample CGI scripts are written in C.

Designer HTML and WebBot Extensions

With designer HTML, you gain the capability to select an alternate display for unknown markup in FrontPage 98 and the capability to insert, copy, paste, and drag and drop HTML markup directly into the FrontPage Editor. Using the FrontPage Developer's Kit and FrontPage WebBot extensions, you have access to these so-called designer features.

To get started, examine the designer HTML and custom WebBot examples provided in the FrontPage Developer's kit. In the `designer` directory, you will find examples of pages that use designer HTML. In the `webbot` directory, you will find custom WebBots that are used in the designer HTML examples as well as in the web test examples.

Most of the designer HTML features are built in. For example, if you copy a section of a document in Microsoft Word by using Ctrl+C, you can paste your selection to an open page in the FrontPage Editor by using Ctrl+V. FrontPage 98 automatically converts the text to HTML.

When you want to create an alternate display for unknown markup or new HTML elements not supported by FrontPage 98, you do so using WebBot extensions. WebBot Extensions have a format similar to that of standard HTML and are defined within the context of the WEBBOT pseudo-tag. Like other tags, the WEBBOT pseudo-tag has a begin tag and an end tag.

The begin WEBBOT tag has the following general syntax:

```
<!--WEBBOT bot="HTMLMarkup" StartSpan -->
```

The end WEBBOT tag has the following general syntax:

```
<!--WEBBOT bot="HTMLMarkup" EndSpan -->
```

Between the begin and end tags is where you place elements you want displayed in the alternate format you are defining. Because you are defining an alternate display for HTML, you will always work with the HTML Markup WebBot. This WebBot is responsible for handling unknown markup.

The begin tag has three attributes that let you set the format of the display:

```
U-SRC
ALT
TAG
```

The first attribute, `U-SRC`, lets you define the relative or absolute URL for an image to insert in place of the unknown markup—sort of what FrontPage 98 does with plug-ins, JavaScript, and Java. If the image is on the local file system, the image is imported into the web and displayed. The following is an example of using the `U-SRC` attribute:

```
<!--WEBBOT bot="HTMLMarkup" StartSpan U-SRC="EMBED.GIF" -->
HTML markup that is not supported by FrontPage 98 appears here.
<!--WEBBOT bot="HTMLMarkup" EndSpan -->
```

The HTML or other markup not recognized by FrontPage is then represented by the specified U-SRC image in the FrontPage Editor.

The ALT attribute lets you define an alternative representation for the element FrontPage 98 doesn't support. This alternative representation can incorporate a limited set of HTML tags. These tags include the following:

<A>

<APPLET>

<AREA>

<B>

<BIG>

<BLINK>

<CITE>

<CODE>

<DFN>

<EM>

<EMBED>

<FONT>

<I>

<IMG>

<INPUT>

<KBD>

<MAP>

<MARQUEE>

<OBJECT>

<OPTION>

<SAMP>

<SELECT>

<SMALL>

<STRIKE>

<STRONG>

<SUB>

<SUP>

<TEXTAREA>

<TT>

<U>

<VAR>

Generally, you should not use `U-SRC` and `ALT` at the same time. The following is an example of using the `ALT` attribute:

```
<!--WEBBOT bot="HTMLMarkup" StartSpan ALT="<U><B><STRIKE>Hideous Text</STRIKE></
B></U>" -->

HTML markup that is not supported by FrontPage 98 appears here.

<!--WEBBOT bot="HTMLMarkup" EndSpan -->
```

The final attribute, `TAG`, lets you define the heading or paragraph level for the element you are adding. If you define the element as the equivalent of a level 1 heading, textual portions of the element will be the size of text associated with a level 1 heading. If you define the element as the equivalent of normal text, textual portions of the element will be the size of normal text. Acceptable values for this attribute correspond to the six heading levels and normal paragraph text: H1, H2, H3, H4, H5, H6 and P.

The `TAG` attribute is normally combined with either the `ALT` or `U-SRC` attribute. The following is an example using the `TAG` attribute:

```
<!--WEBBOT bot="HTMLMarkup" StartSpan U-SRC="EMBED.GIF" TAG=H1 -->

HTML markup that is not supported by FrontPage 98 appears here.

<!--WEBBOT bot="HTMLMarkup" EndSpan -->
```

Summary

The FrontPage Developer's Kit was created to help you extend the functionality of FrontPage 98. With the FrontPage Developer's Kit, you can create templates, wizards, utilities, and CGI scripts. Although you do not need to have experience in programming and OLE automation to create templates, you do need this experience to create wizards, utilities, and CGI scripts.

CHAPTER

Customizing FrontPage Menus

by William Robert Stanek

IN THIS CHAPTER

- Menus: Do You Love Them? *928*
- Creating New Menus *930*

With the FrontPage Explorer and the FrontPage Editor, you can access over a dozen menus. These menus altogether have hundreds of options, so you may be wondering why in the world you would ever want to add more options. Well, the answer is simple. Sure, the FrontPage Explorer and Editor have lots of menus, but do the menus do what you want them to? If the answer is no or not always, you can remedy the situation by creating custom menus complete with options of your choosing. But before you dive in, you better know what you're doing, which is the reason this chapter looks at the hows and whys of menu creation first and then walks you through the steps you should follow to add menus to FrontPage 98.

Menus: Do You Love Them?

Menus, you have to love them. Click a menu and up pops a complete set of related options. These options open dialog boxes, start tables, launch other applications, and do lots of other neat tricks. However, when FrontPage 98 doesn't do something you would like it to, you probably want to change the way that FrontPage 98 works—and you can. To do so, you can create custom menus for the FrontPage Explorer and the FrontPage Editor.

What You Need to Know Before You Start

Your custom menu can have its own set of options that do anything—well, just about anything—that you want. So what would you like to add to FrontPage 98? Do you use a tool every time you work with Web pages and you would love to be able to launch that tool from the FrontPage Explorer? Do you hate having to type your company's header and footer repeatedly? Would you love to be able to add these elements at the click of a button?

If you think about this situation, you probably can think of at least one thing you would like to add to the FrontPage Editor or the FrontPage Explorer. To do so, you need to muck around with system-level stuff and the dreaded Windows Registry. The Registry contains a complete database of information on all the applications installed on your computer. Entries in the Registry are rather cryptic but can be sorted out if you are patient. So much stuff is stored in the Registry that entire books have been written on this subject. Instead of droning on and on about the Registry, I'm going to teach you only what you need to know to create custom menus in FrontPage 98.

FrontPage 98 takes a look at its Registry entries whenever you start any of its applications. You can find separate entries for the FrontPage Explorer, the FrontPage Editor, and other FrontPage 98 tools. You will know which entries belong to which application because of a designator key and/or the folder location of the entry. Keep in mind that a single application may have dozens of entries in the Windows Registry. The entries you care about right now deal with menus and menu options.

When you start FrontPage 98, it reads its entries in the Registry and looks for entries that extend its menus. If FrontPage 98 finds such an entry, the menus are updated accordingly. Thus, to add a menu to FrontPage 98, you need to make an entry in the Registry. Next, you need to make an entry for each option the menu will contain.

Because you don't want to muck around in the Registry needlessly, you should plan your menu before you make any changes in the Registry. Start by thinking of a name for the menu and where you will insert the menu or menus into the existing menu system. By default, your custom menus are added before the Help menu, which ensures that the Help menu is always the last option. For example, say you want to create a menu called Extra Stuff for the FrontPage Explorer. When you create this menu, it is added after the Tools menu but before the Help menu. The next menu you create will be added to the menu after the Extra Stuff menu. If you don't want to go with default positioning of the menu, you also can specify an exact position for the menu.

Next, you need to think about the options for the menu. Each option needs a name that clearly identifies the task it performs. You need to arrange the options in a fairly logical fashion. You also need to consider the hot key for the menu and the options on the menu. If you use the Extra Stuff menu, you may logically want to use the first letter of the menu name as the hot key. Well, Alt+E is already taken by the Edit menu, so you might want to use Alt+X to activate your menu.

WARNING

Directly modifying the Registry can be a dangerous proposition. Before working with your Registry, you should always backup your current Registry files in case of a mistake. Your Registry is stored in two files: `system.dat` and `user.dat`. These are located under your `\Windows` (or `\WinNT`) directory structure.

Getting Started with the Registry Editor

Now that you've planned your menu, you are ready to learn more about the Windows Registry and a wonderful tool called the Registry Editor. Using the Registry Editor, you can browse through folders of entries or search for specific entries to learn more about the Registry. You can also use the editor to add new Registry entries and change existing entries.

The Registry Editor (`regedit.exe`) usually lives in the Windows folder. On Windows 95 and Windows NT, you can start the Registry Editor by clicking the Start button, choosing Run, and entering `regedit` into the Run dialog box. When you start the Registry Editor, you see a window like the one shown in Figure 56.1.

The Registry Editor main window has two frames. You can use the left frame to browse the folder structure of the Windows Registry. When you access a folder containing Registry entries, the right frame shows the name and data associated with the entry. Often, you will see the name field set to `(default)` and the data field set to `(value not set)`. Basically, you aren't deep enough in the folder structure to find actual entries and their associated data.

Browsing the Registry is fairly straightforward; the process is similar to the way you browse folders using other Windows tools. When a plus sign appears next to a folder name, you can click the folder to access subfolders. If you wander around the Registry, you can find a complex maze of folders, subfolders, and entries.

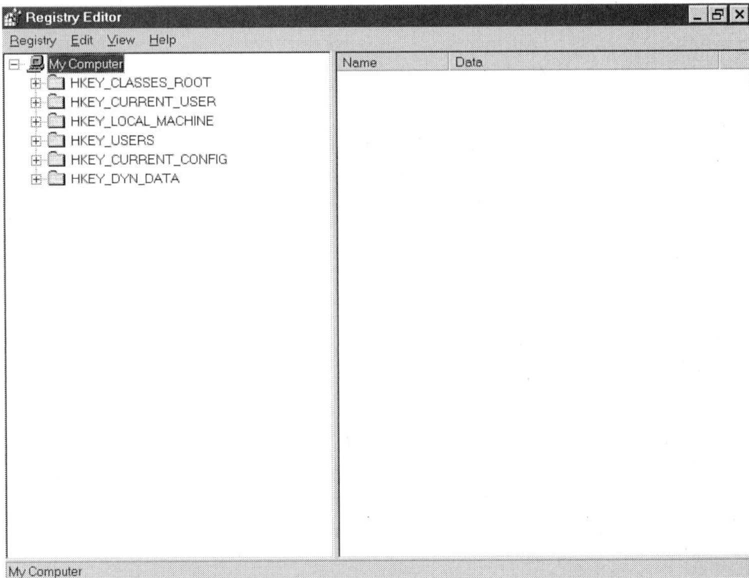

FIGURE 56.1.
Introducing the Registry Editor.

The Registry Editor is definitely not something you should muck around with haphazardly. If you make a mistake in the Registry, you can cause your whole system to freeze up. Before you make any changes to the Registry, I strongly recommend that you print the help instructions for restoring it. You can find these instructions by choosing Help | Help Topics and then clicking the topic titled Restoring the registry. Tape these instructions next to your computer.

Creating New Menus

Now that you've covered the basics, you can begin to create your custom menus. In the sections that follow, you will find instructions for creating a menu and adding options to it. Because you create menus and menu options for the FrontPage Explorer and the FrontPage Editor differently, you'll find separate discussions for each application. If you plan to add a menu to the FrontPage Explorer, jump ahead to the section titled "Building a Custom Menu for the FrontPage Explorer."

Building a Custom Menu for the FrontPage Editor

You will build your custom menu for the FrontPage Editor in two steps. The first step is to create a menu entry. Then you need to create the options for the menu. After you create a custom menu, you need to exit the FrontPage Editor and restart it to see the changes.

Creating the Menu Entry

Custom menus for the FrontPage Editor are stored in a folder called `Init Menus` in the Windows Registry. The path to this folder in the Registry Editor is

```
HKEY_CURRENT_USER\Software\Microsoft\FrontPage\Editor\Init Menus
```

Before you create a custom menu, you need to access the `Init Menus` folder. Start by double-clicking the `HKEY_CURRENT_USER` folder, and continue to follow the folder path to the `Init Menus` folder. This certainly task requires a lot of clicking your way through folders, but eventually, you will end up at the `Init Menus` folder. Double-click this folder to show any current entries. When you first install FrontPage 98, the `Init Menus` folder should be empty, so in the right frame, the name field should be set to `(default)`, and the data field should be set to `(value not set)`.

To create your custom menu, you need to add an entry to the `Init Menus` folder. Choose Edit|New|String Value. This command adds a new value named `New Value #1` to the list of entries in the right frame. Just as when you create a new folder in Windows, the name is highlighted and can be edited. The name is a reference value for your menu. The reference value can be anything you like and is used as a key to obtain the data associated with the entry. Keep it simple, and you'll be much happier. So, for your first menu, go with something like `Menu1`; for your next menu, go with `Menu2`, and so on.

After you name the menu, open the Edit String dialog box by right-clicking and choosing Modify from the pop-up menu. Generally, the first field in the Edit String dialog box, Value name, cannot be edited. The Value name is the name you entered for the reference value and can be changed only if you select the Rename option. In the Value data field, you need to specify the parameters for the custom menu. The general syntax for these parameters is as follows:

```
first_version, last_version, menubar_number, menu_name, menu_position
```

`first_version` is the earliest version of FrontPage that should use your custom menu. Because custom menus were not in version 1 of FrontPage, the only valid values are 2 or greater. If you enter 1, FrontPage treats it as a 2. Any time the current version of FrontPage is earlier than the version you've assigned for this value, FrontPage ignores your custom menu. Version 1 pertains to FrontPage 1 and FrontPage 1.1. Version 2 pertains to FrontPage 2.0 and FrontPage 97. Version 3 pertains to FrontPage 98.

`last_version` is the latest version of FrontPage that should use your custom menu. Any time the current version of FrontPage is more recent than the version you've assigned for this value, FrontPage ignores your custom menu. If you omit this value, FrontPage does not restrict the menu bar based on this value.

`menubar_number` is the number of the menu bar to which you want to add the custom menu. The FrontPage Editor has two menu bars: the empty document menu bar (0) and the active document menu bar (1). Use the empty document menu bar if you want the menu to be available only when no pages are loaded into the Editor. Use the active document menu bar if you want the menu to be available only when a page is loaded into the Editor.

menu_name is the name of the menu. Place the ampersand after the letter or number you want to be the hot key for the menu. FrontPage 98 underlines the hot key letter. If you create a menu called Extra Stuff, for example, you can make the *x* the hot key by using the value `Ex&tra Stuff`; then you can access the menu by pressing Alt+X.

menu_position is the position of the custom menu on the menu bar. You can use a numeric value or the name of an existing menu. If you use a numeric value, the first menu position on the left-hand side has a value of 1; the next, 2; and so on. If you use the name of an existing menu, your custom menu is inserted after the menu. Any time you omit this value, the new menu is placed to the right of the Tools menu.

Understanding the menu syntax is easier if you have an example. Create the Extra Stuff menu. With the Edit String dialog box open, enter the following into the Value data field:

```
3, , 0, Ex&tra Stuff, Tools
```

TIP

To create a menu that is available when no page is loaded into the Editor and when a page appears in the Editor, create two separate entries in the Windows Registry. The entries should be identical except for the values in the *menubar_number* parameter.

Close the Edit String dialog box. You've just created a menu called Extra Stuff that you can access by pressing Alt+X. The menu is used only with FrontPage 98 or later versions of FrontPage. Additionally, the menu is inserted before the Tools menu on the menu bar and is displayed at all times in the FrontPage Editor—even if no document is active.

Adding Options to the Menu

Now that you've created a menu, you need to add options to it. Menu options are stored in a different folder in the Registry, and the file path for this folder is

```
HKEY_CURRENT_USER\Software\Microsoft\FrontPage\Editor\Init Commands
```

In the left frame, the `Init Commands` folder should be visible. Double-click the folder now.

To create an option for your custom menu, you need to add an entry to the `Init Commands` folder. Choose Edit|New|String Value to add a new value to the list of entries in the right frame. Enter a new name for the entry; you can use any name as long as you haven't used it already. As with the menu, keep the name simple and you'll be much happier. So, for your first menu option, go with something like `Menu1Item1`; for your next menu option, go with `Menu1Item2`, and so on.

After you name the menu option, open the Edit String dialog box by right-clicking and choosing Modify from the pop-up menu. In the Value data field, you need to specify the parameters for the menu option using the following syntax:

```
first_version, last_version, menubar_number, menu_name, command_name,
command_line, command_position, insert_flag, status_text, help_reference
```

`first_version` is the earliest version of FrontPage that should use the menu option. Because custom menus were not in version 1 of FrontPage, the only valid values are 2 or greater. If you enter 1, FrontPage treats it as a 2. Any time the current version of FrontPage is earlier than the version you've assigned for this value, FrontPage ignores this menu option. Version 1 pertains to FrontPage 1 and FrontPage 1.1. Version 2 pertains to FrontPage 2.0 and FrontPage 97. Version 3 pertains to FrontPage 98.

`last_version` is the latest version of FrontPage that should use this menu option. Any time the current version of FrontPage is more recent than the version you've assigned for this value, FrontPage ignores this menu option. If you omit this value, FrontPage does not restrict the custom menu based on this value.

`menubar_number` is the number of the menu bar to which you want to add the custom menu. The FrontPage Editor has two menu bars: the empty document menu bar (0) and the active document menu bar (1). Use the empty document menu bar if you want the menu option to be available even though no pages are loaded into the Editor. Use the active document menu bar if you want the menu option to be available only when a page is loaded into the Editor.

`menu_name` is the name or number of the menu on which to add the command. If this parameter is missing or invalid, the option is added to the Tools menu.

`command_name` is the name of the new menu option. Place the ampersand before the letter or number you want to be the hot key for the menu. FrontPage 98 underlines the hot key letter. If you create a menu option called File View, for example, you can make the *F* the hot key by using the value `&File View`.

`command_line` is the fully specified filename and path to the resource file associated with the menu option. If the command is an executable file that should be run when the user chooses this command, set the `insert_flag` parameter to 0.

`command_position` is the position of the command on the menu. You can use a numeric value or the name of an existing menu option. If you use a numeric value, the first menu option has a position of 1; the next, 2; and so on. If you use the name of an existing menu option, your new option menu is inserted after the referenced option. Any time you omit this value, the new menu option is placed at the end of the menu.

`insert_flag` is used to tell the editor how to handle the file pointed to in the `command_line` parameter. Use a value of 0 if the file is to be executed. Use a value of 1 if the file is text that should be inserted into the current document with paragraph breaks before and after it. Use a value of 2 if the file is HTML that should be inserted into the current document without paragraph breaks.

`help_reference` is the filename and topic number for a help topic for the menu option. Separate the filename and the topic number with an exclamation point (`!`).

Understanding the menu option syntax is easier if you have an example. Create a menu option that opens the Registry Editor. With the Edit String dialog box open, enter the following into the Value data field:

```
3, , 0, Extra Stuff, &Registry Editor, C:\WINDOWS\REGEDIT.EXE, 1, 0,
Starts the Registry Editor
```

Close the Edit String dialog box. You've just created a menu option for the Extra Stuff menu that will start the Registry Editor. The menu is used only with FrontPage 98 or later versions of FrontPage. Additionally, the option is displayed at all times in the FrontPage Editor—even if no document is active. When the option is highlighted, the status bar displays the message `Starts the Registry Editor`. The new menu and its option are shown in Figure 56.2.

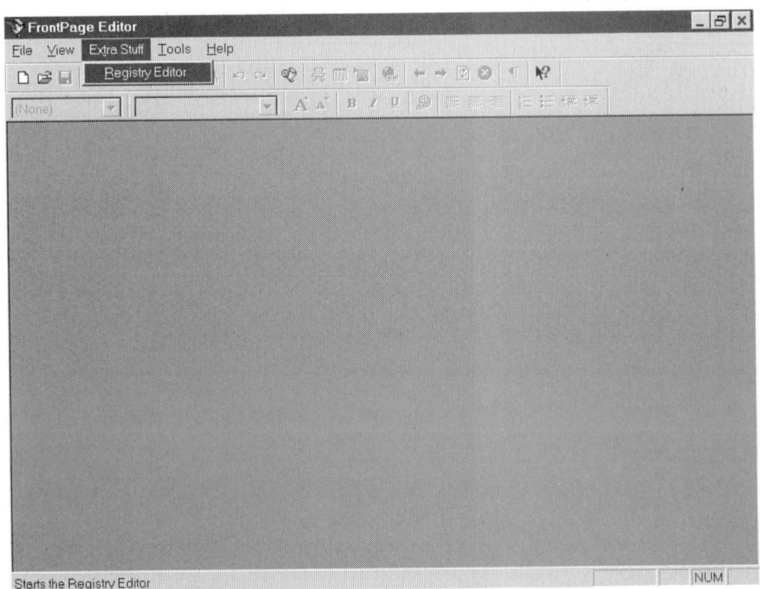

FIGURE 56.2.
The FrontPage Editor with the new menu.

You can create a separator between menu options by entering a dash in the *`command_name`* parameter. After this parameter, the only parameter you need to specify is the position for the option. You can add a separator to a menu as follows:

```
3, , 0, Extra Stuff, -, , 3,
```

Building a Custom Menu for the FrontPage Explorer

You will build your custom menu for the FrontPage Explorer in two steps. The first step is to create a menu entry. Then you need to create the options for the menu. After you create a custom menu, you need to exit the FrontPage Explorer and restart it to see the changes.

Creating the Menu Entry

Custom menus for the FrontPage Explorer are stored in a folder called `Init Menus` in the Windows Registry. The path to this folder in the Registry Editor is

```
HKEY_CURRENT_USER\Software\Microsoft\FrontPage\Explorer\Init Menus
```

Before you create a custom menu, you need to access the `Init Menus` folder. Start by double-clicking the `HKEY_CURRENT_USER` folder, and continue to follow the folder path to the `Init Menus` folder. This task certainly requires a lot of clicking your way through folders, but eventually you will end up at the `Init Menus` folder. Double-click this folder to show any current entries in this folder. When you first install FrontPage, the `Init Menus` folder should be empty, so in the right frame, the name field should be set to `(default)`, and the data field should be set to `(value not set)`.

To create your custom menu, you need to add an entry to the `Init Menus` folder. Choose Edit|New|String Value. This command adds a new value named `New Value #1` to the list of entries in the right frame. Just as when you create a new folder in Windows, the name is highlighted and can be edited. The name is a reference value for your menu. The reference value can be anything you like and is used as a key to obtain the data associated with the entry. Keep the name simple and you'll be much happier. So, for your first menu, go with something like `Menu1`; for your next menu, go with `Menu2`, and so on.

After you name the menu, open the Edit String dialog box by right-clicking and choosing Modify from the pop-up menu. Generally, the first field in the Edit String dialog box, Value name, cannot be edited. The Value name is the name you entered for the reference value and can be changed only if you select the Rename option. In the Value data field, you need to specify the parameters for the custom menu. The general syntax for these parameters is as follows:

```
first_version, last_version, menubar_number, menu_name, menu_position
```

`first_version` is the earliest version of FrontPage that should use your custom menu. Because custom menus were not in version 1 of FrontPage, the only valid values are 2 or greater. If you enter 1, FrontPage treats it as a 2. Any time the current version of FrontPage is earlier than the version you've assigned for this value, FrontPage ignores your custom menu. Version 1 pertains to FrontPage 1 and FrontPage 1.1. Version 2 pertains to FrontPage 2.0 and FrontPage 97. Version 3 pertains to FrontPage 98.

`last_version` is the latest version of FrontPage that should use your custom menu. Any time the current version of FrontPage is more recent than the version you've assigned for this value, FrontPage ignores your custom menu. If you omit this value, FrontPage does not restrict the menu bar based on this value.

`menubar_number` is the number of the menu bar to which you want to add the custom menu. Currently, the FrontPage Explorer has only one menu bar. To ensure compatibility with future versions, set this parameter to 1.

menu_name is the name of the menu. Place the ampersand after the letter or number you want to be the hot key for the menu. FrontPage 98 underlines the hot key letter. If you create a menu called Extra Stuff, for example, you can make the *x* the hot key by using the value `Ex&tra Stuff`; then you can access the menu by pressing Alt+X.

menu_position is the position of the custom menu on the menu bar. You can use a numeric value or the name of an existing menu. If you use a numeric value, the first menu position on the left-hand side has a value of 1; the next, 2; and so on. If you use the name of an existing menu, your custom menu is inserted after the menu. Any time you omit this value, the new menu is placed to the right of the Tools menu.

Understanding the menu syntax is easier if you have an example. Create the Extra Stuff menu. With the Edit String dialog box open, enter the following into the Value data field:

```
3, , 1, Ex&tra Stuff, Tools
```

Close the Edit String dialog box. You've just created a menu called Extra Stuff that you can access by pressing Alt+X. The menu is used only with FrontPage 98 or later versions of FrontPage. Additionally, the menu is inserted before the Tools menu on the menu bar.

Adding Options to the Menu

Now that you've created a menu, you need to add options to it. Menu options are stored in a different folder in the Registry, and the file path for this folder is

```
HKEY_CURRENT_USER\Software\Microsoft\FrontPage\Explorer\Init Commands
```

In the left frame, the `Init Commands` folder should be visible; double-click the folder now.

To create an option for your custom menu, you need to add an entry to the `Init Commands` folder. Choose Edit|New|String Value to add a new value to the list of entries in the right frame. Enter a new name for the entry; you can use any name as long as you haven't used it already. As with the menu, keep the name simple and you'll be much happier. So, for your first menu option, go with something like `Menu1Item1`; for your next menu option, go with `Menu1Item2`, and so on.

After you name the menu option, open the Edit String dialog box by right-clicking and choosing Modify from the pop-up menu. In the Value data field, you need to specify the parameters for the menu option using the following syntax:

```
first_version, last_version, menubar_number, menu_name, command_name,
command_line, command_position, insert_flag, status_text, help_reference
```

first_version is the earliest version of FrontPage that should use the menu option. Because custom menus were not in version 1 of FrontPage, the only valid values are 2 or greater. If you enter 1, FrontPage treats it as a 2. Any time the current version of FrontPage is earlier than the version you've assigned for this value, FrontPage ignores this menu option. Version 1 pertains to FrontPage 1 and FrontPage 1.1. Version 2 pertains to FrontPage 2.0 and FrontPage 97. Version 3 pertains to FrontPage 98.

`last_version` is the latest version of FrontPage that should use this menu option. Any time the current version of FrontPage is more recent than the version you've assigned for this value, FrontPage ignores this menu option. If you omit this value, FrontPage does not restrict the custom menu based on this value.

`menubar_number` is the number of the menu bar to which you want to add the custom menu. Currently, the FrontPage Explorer has only one menu bar. To ensure compatibility with future versions, set this parameter to 1.

`menu_name` is the name or number of the menu on which to add the command. If this parameter is missing or invalid, the option is added to the Tools menu.

`command_name` is the name of the new menu option. Place the ampersand before the letter or number you want to be the hot key for the menu. FrontPage 98 underlines the hot key letter. If you create a menu option called File View, for example, you can make the *F* the hot key by using the value `&File View`.

`command_line` is the fully specified filename and path to the executable file that should be run when the option is selected.

`command_position` is the position of the command on the menu. You can use a numeric value or the name of an existing menu option. If you use a numeric value, the first menu option has a position of 1; the next, 2; and so on. If you use the name of an existing menu option, your new option menu is inserted after the referenced option. Any time you omit this value, the new menu option is placed at the end of the menu.

`insert_flag` is always set to zero in the FrontPage Explorer.

`help_reference` is the filename and topic number for a help topic for the menu option. Separate the filename and the topic number with an exclamation point (`!`).

Understanding the menu option syntax is easier if you have an example. Create a menu option that opens the Registry Editor. With the Edit String dialog box open, enter the following into the Value data field:

```
3, , 1, Extra Stuff, &Registry Editor, C:\WINDOWS\REGEDIT.EXE, 1, 0,
Starts the Registry Editor
```

Close the Edit String dialog box. You've just created a menu option for the Extra Stuff menu that will start the Registry Editor. The menu is used only with FrontPage 98 or later versions of FrontPage. When the option is highlighted, the status bar displays the message `Starts the Registry Editor`. The new menu and its option are shown in Figure 56.3.

You can create a separator between menu options by entering a dash in the `command_name` parameter. After this parameter, the only parameter you need to specify is the position for the option. You can add a separator to a menu as follows:

```
3, , 1, Extra Stuff, -, , 3,
```

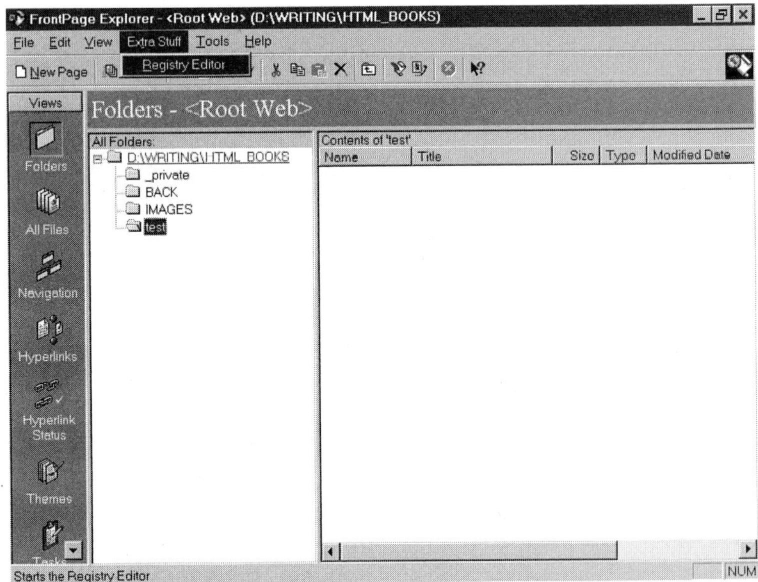

FIGURE 56.3.
The FrontPage Explorer with the new menu.

Summary

Custom menus are great for tailoring FrontPage to meet your needs. Before you create any custom menus, you should plan how those menus will be used and what options they will have. Afterward, use the Registry Editor to make the necessary entries in the Windows Registry.

CHAPTER 57

Creating Your Own Templates

by William Robert Stanek

IN THIS CHAPTER

- Templates: A Basic Overview 940
- Creating Page and Frameset Templates 945
- Creating Web Templates 946

After learning what the FrontPage Developer's Kit contains and how you can use it, you should be ready to create your own templates. There are three types of templates in FrontPage 98: page templates, web templates, and frameset templates. Although it is fairly easy to create page and frameset templates, creating web templates is a fairly advanced subject.

Templates: A Basic Overview

Most template basics you already know. Page templates usually create a single page. Web templates usually create a set of related pages. Frameset templates create a frame-enhanced page. Any page created by a template can contain images, WebBots, references to multimedia objects, and links.

The way you create a new page from a template depends on the type of template you want to use. To create a new page based on a page template, you select New from the File menu in the FrontPage Editor. When creating a new web based on a Web template, you select New|FrontPage Web from the File menu in the FrontPage Explorer. Finally, if you want to create a frame-enhanced page, you use the FrontPage Editor's Frames Wizard, which can be started by selecting New from the File menu and then clicking Frames Wizard in the New Page dialog box.

Although FrontPage 98 includes a wide variety of templates for you work with, you might be looking for something different. Perhaps you have a Web site that uses a common appearance between pages, and a template would be ideal for expanding your site. Thankfully, the creation of most FrontPage templates is fairly simple and lets you expand your template selection.

Template Directories

All templates are stored in special directories on your hard drive. When you installed FrontPage 98, you had to select a base installation directory (typically `Program Files\Microsoft FrontPage`). The template directories are in this base installation. Any new templates you create must also be located in these directories, so that FrontPage 98 can locate and use your new templates.

If you change to the FrontPage base installation directory or examine this directory with Windows Explorer, you will find the directories used to store templates. Page templates are stored in separate subdirectories under the `pages` directory. Web templates are located in separate subdirectories under the `webs` directory. Finally, frameset templates are stored in subdirectories below the `frames` directory.

All template directories are named with a `.tem` extension, such as `normal.tem` and `glossary.tem`. If you examine the template directories, you will find that all templates are defined by HTML pages named with an `.htm` extension and a parameter file named with an `.inf` extension. Some templates have a structure file associated with them. Structure files usually end with the `.map` extension. All `.map` files contain instructions for an image map.

Creating the Parameter File

All templates must have a parameter file. This file is a plain ASCII text file whose name ends with the `.inf` extension and is formatted similarly to a Windows INI file.

NOTE

When you create parameter files in a word processor, be sure to save the file in ASCII text format.

Because of the way FrontPage 98 looks for parameter files, the parameter file must use the base name of the template directory. If your template is stored in a directory named `mytemplate.tem`, for example, the parameter file for this template must be in a file named `mytemplate.inf`.

As with Windows INI files, your parameter files are broken down into several sections. Each section is named with an identifier set off by square brackets. For example, a section containing information about the template is in a section with the identifier `[info]`.

Template parameters are placed after section identifiers, with one parameter on each line, and are entered as name-value pairs. Each name-value pair identifies a parameter by name and the value associated with the parameter separated by an equal sign (=), such as `title=Sample template`. Parameter files can have four sections: info, FileList, MetaInfo, and TaskList. Only the info section is mandatory for all parameter files. Additionally, because the FrontPage Editor does not refer to the optional sections, you should only use them for web templates used by the FrontPage Explorer.

The Parameter File Information Section

The information section of the parameter file has the identifier `[info]`. This section is used to specify general information about the template, including the title, description, and indexing information.

Whenever you open the New Page dialog box in the FrontPage Editor or FrontPage Explorer, FrontPage 98 reads the information section for all web templates in order to provide you with a title and description of the web templates. If, for some reason, FrontPage 98 cannot find the parameter file, FrontPage 98 displays the base name of the directory in which the template is stored.

The information parameters are designated by the following names:

`title`	The title of the template, such as `Normal Web`.
`description`	The description of the template, such as `Creates a new web with a single page that is based on the Normal page template.`

`NoIndexRenaming`	Tells FrontPage 98 not to rename index files published on external servers. If you do not set this value, files called `index.htm` are renamed automatically to the name used for index files on the external server, such as `welcome.htm`. To disable index renaming, set this parameter as `NoIndexRenaming=1`.
`noframesURL`	Used with framesets, this assigns an alternate page for browsers that do not support frames. Although your frameset file must contain this parameter, you cannot assign it a value. The Frames Wizard assigns this value if necessary.
`layout`	Used with framesets, this specifies the layout of the frameset using a special notation created by the FrontPage developers.
`structure`	Tells FrontPage 98 the name of the structure file associated with the template.

NOTE

Generally, index files are used when users point their browsers to a directory instead of a page. Because FrontPage 98 renames index files automatically, you should not reference index files directly. Instead of using the index filename of `index.htm` in your links, use the link `./`, which forces the server to serve the renamed index document to the user.

The following is a sample information section for a parameter file:

```
[info]
title=Internet Resource Web
description=Create a Web designed to showcase Internet resources
structure=project.map
NoIndexRenaming=1
```

The Parameter File FileList Section

By default, when you create a new web in the FrontPage Explorer, you should use all files in the web template directory to create the web. All you have to do is move the files you want to include on the web into the web template directory, and they will be used to create the web. Generally, all filenames are converted to lowercase. Additionally, the URLs to these files match the file's name.

Using the optional FileList section of the parameter file, you can selectively include files from the template directory and specify the URL for the files, which can be different from the filename. The FileList section can also enable you to include files that are in subdirectories of the web template, such as files you've placed in the web's `_private` or `cgi-bin` directory. If you do not make specific entries for files in template subdirectories, the files will not be included in any webs based on your template.

Keep in mind that whenever you use a FileList, you must explicitly specify all the files you want to include. If you omit any files that are in a template directory, FrontPage 98 assumes you don't want to include them.

NOTE

Only valid web subdirectories can be used in the FileList. Valid subdirectories for webs include `_private` for hidden files, `cgi-bin` for CGI scripts, and `images` for images used in the web.

You enter files in the FileList section one per line in the form *`filename=URL`*. When you specify only the filename, the file URL will be the same as the filename. The only exception to this rule is that images with the `.gif`, `.jpg`, and `.jpeg` extensions are generally stored in a subdirectory called `images`, which means the URL path to images on most newly created webs is `images/`*`filename`*.

CAUTION

When you include the directory structure in the filename, you use the backslash as the directory separator. However, when you include the directory structure in the URL, you use the forward slash as the directory separator.

The following is a sample FileList section that uses the concepts discussed in this section:

```
[FileList]
pageone.htm=
pagetwo.htm=
pagethree.htm=
pagefour.htm=
header.htm=_private/header.htm
footer.htm=_private/footer.htm
images\newpage.gif=images/house.gif
images\newtext.gif=images/new.gif
```

The Parameter File Meta-Information Section

The meta-information section of the parameter file has the identifier `[MetaInfo]`. Using this optional section, you can specify meta-information parameters for webs created with your template. The primary use for meta-information parameters is to configure variables, yet these parameters can also be used to set variables used by the Substitution WebBot.

To make handling meta-information easier, the parameter names are not case sensitive. The parameter name `WEB_HOST` is interpreted the same as the parameter name `web_host` or `Web_Host`. All parameter names beginning with the prefix `vti_` are reserved for web administration.

The following is a sample meta-information section for a parameter file:

```
[MetaInfo]
WebMaster=webspud@spudco.com
ContactEMail=infospud@spudco.com
CompanyName=SpudCo Industrial Potato Peeling.
```

The Parameter File TaskList Section

Whenever you create complex web templates, you will probably want to provide the user with pointers concerning the best uses of the web based on the template. One way to do this is to provide a series of tasks that the user can perform after creating the new web. Using the TaskList section of the parameter file, you can assign tasks to the to do list.

Each task you assign can have the following six attributes:

`TaskName`	The name of the task to be performed
`Priority`	The priority of the task entered as an integer value from 1 to 3, where 1 is for high-priority tasks, 2 is for medium-priority tasks, and 3 is for low-priority tasks
`CreatedBy`	The name of the person or template that created the task
`URL`	The page or file the task refers to, such as `homepage.htm`
`Cookie`	An additional identifier for a specific bookmark within the referenced page
`Comment`	A description of the task to be performed

As with other parameters, you enter tasks one per line. Each task must be identified by a unique task number, such as `Task01` or `Task02`. Attributes for a task are separated by the vertical bar character (¦) and must be entered in the following form:

```
TaskNum=TaskName¦Priority¦CreatedBy¦URL¦Cookie¦Comment
```

Even if you do not use an attribute, you must account for it. For example, most tasks will not use the `Cookie` attribute. The following is the form for tasks that do not use the `Cookie` attribute:

```
TaskNum=TaskName¦Priority¦CreatedBy¦URL¦¦Comment
```

The following is a sample TaskList section for a parameter file:

```
[TaskList]
task1=Replace Banner Image¦1¦Internet Resource Web¦_private/logo.htm¦¦replace
➥the temporary image on this page with your banner
task2=Customize Home Page¦1¦Internet Resource Web¦index.htm¦¦customize the
➥headings and text to meet your needs
task3=Add Link¦1¦Internet Resource Web¦index.htm¦#resources¦update the bookmark
```

Creating Page and Frameset Templates

The easiest templates to create are the ones used for pages and framesets. You create new templates in the FrontPage Editor by using an existing page or frameset as the basis for the template. Start by opening the page or frameset you want to use as the basis for your template, and then select Save As from the File menu. In the Save As dialog box, click the As Template button. This action opens the dialog box shown in Figure 57.1.

As you can see in Figure 57.1, the Save As Template dialog box has three text boxes: Title, Name, and Description. You use the Title text box to enter a title for the template. The FrontPage Editor displays this title in the New dialog box. By default, the template is named after the template the current page or frameset is based on. You must change the template name in the Name text box to create a new template. In the Description text box, enter a description of the template. The template description is visible in the New dialog box when a user clicks on the template title.

FIGURE 57.1.
Creating a new frameset template with the Save As Template dialog box.

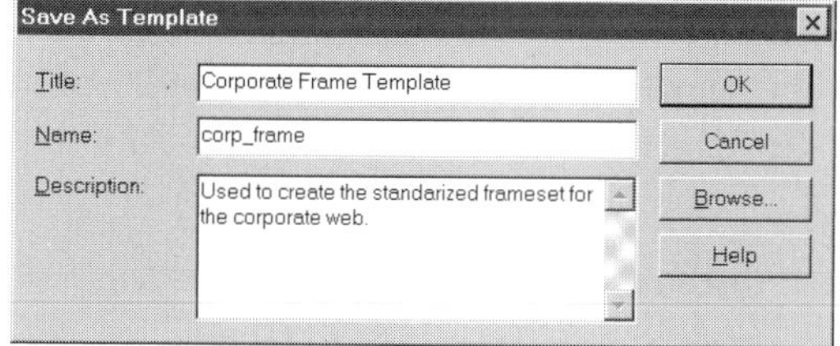

When you use the Save As Template option of the FrontPage Editor, the template and its parameter file are created automatically. All images, HTML pages, and miscellaneous files associated with the template are stored in the same directory. The name of the directory is based on the template name with the `.tem` extension. After creating a page with the template, users can save the page to the current web or to a file. If the page is saved to the current web, the FrontPage Editor will update the page so that the image links point to the `images` subdirectory and will place images in this subdirectory.

Although creating templates with the FrontPage Editor is very easy, sometimes you might want to create your templates by hand. One reason that you might want to do this is to practice with a simple page template before you try to create a more advanced web template.

To create a page template by hand, change to the FrontPage base installation directory, which is usually `Program Files\Microsoft FrontPage`, and then change to the `pages` directory. In the `pages` directory, create a subdirectory for your new template with the `.tem` extension. Keep in mind that template names are based on the name of their related directories, which don't have the `.tem` extension.

Next, move your template page and associated files to the directory you just created. Finally, create a parameter file with the `.inf` extension. Parameter files for pages only have an info section, so a sample parameter file for a page is as follows:

```
[info]
title=Internet Resource Page
description=Create a page that has links to useful Internet resources.
```

Creating Web Templates

Although creating a web template can be a lot of work, it is also very rewarding. After you create a web template exactly as you like it, the template is available to anyone authoring webs on your server. You could also distribute your custom web to others. With the FrontPage Developer's Kit installed on your system, you can create web templates by hand or by using the Web Template Maker.

Using the Web Template Maker

The easiest way to create Web templates is to use the Web Template Maker utility. This utility is discussed in Chapter 55, "Introducing the FrontPage Developer's Kit." When you use the Web Template Maker, you are basing the web template entirely on a web you created in FrontPage 98. The utility does the following tasks:

- Creates a directory for your web template
- Creates subdirectories for images, CGI scripts, private files, and WebBot source files as necessary
- Moves all files in the original web to template directories
- Generates a parameter file based on the original web that includes existing meta-information and to do tasks

Generating a web template automatically is a definite time saver. Keep in mind that before you can generate a web template, you must create a web to base the template on. Additionally, before you use the Web Template Maker, you must perform these steps:

1. Start the Personal Web Server.
2. Start the FrontPage Explorer.
3. Open the web in the FrontPage Explorer.

Sometimes after you create a template with the Web Template Maker, you might want to customize the parameter file. Therefore, even if you plan to use the Web Template Maker, you should read the next section on creating web templates by hand.

Creating a Web Template by Hand

When you create a web template by hand, you have complete control over what is in the web and how parameters for the web are defined. To create a web template, change to the FrontPage base installation directory, which is usually `Program Files\Microsoft FrontPage`, and then change to the `webs` directory.

In the `webs` directory, create a subdirectory for your new template with the `.tem` extension. Template names are based on the name of their related directory. The structure of files and subdirectories within the template directory should follow the structure of FrontPage webs.

The next step is to change to the template directory and create subdirectories for images, CGI scripts, and private files as necessary. The subdirectory for images should be called `images`. The subdirectory for CGI scripts should be called `cgi-bin`. The subdirectory for private or hidden files should begin with the underscore character and is usually called `_private`. After the directory structure for template files is in place, you can move files into the appropriate directories.

To find pages you created in FrontPage 98, change to the base installation directory for web content, which is, by default, `FrontPage Webs\content`. Then change to the web directory containing the file you want to move. Figure 57.2 shows the contents of a web called `custsup` on my file system.

As you can see in the figure, the path to this web is `FrontPage Webs\content\custsup`. Note also that the web has many subdirectories and that you would not move any files from most of the subdirectories. In particular, you should only move files in the `_private`, `cgi-bin`, `images`, and `_vti_shm` subdirectories. Also, you do not want to move any access control files (`#haccess.ctl`) that might be in these directories.

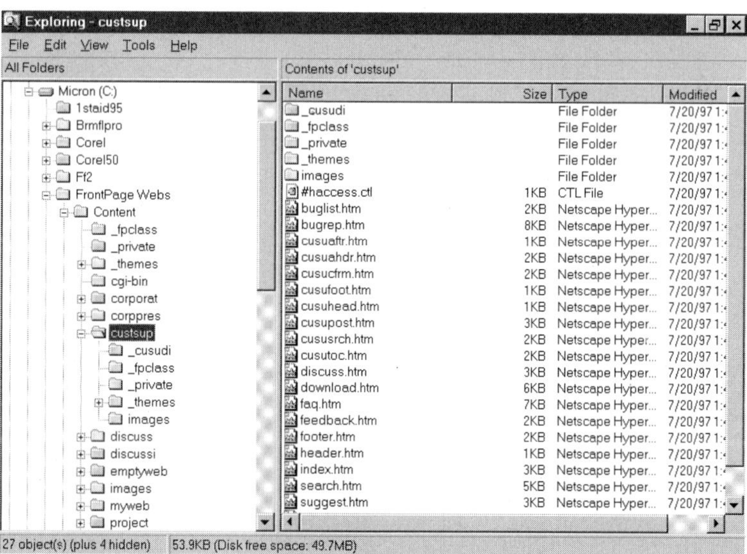

FIGURE 57.2.
Locating web files on your file system.

The main problem you face when moving files created in FrontPage 98 is that pages with WebBots are saved in two forms, source and HTML. The source document for pages with

WebBots is the one you want to move into the appropriate template directory. This document references the WebBots in a usable form. You will use the source document in place of the HTML document, lacks the WebBot information.

TIP

One way to deal with WebBot files is to think of the source files as dynamic files and the HTML files as static files. When you copy files from existing web directories, you copy all static files to the template directories first. Next, you copy the dynamic files from the appropriate `_vti_shm` directory into the template directories, which effectively overwrites the static files.

You will find the WebBot source documents in a private directory called `_vti_shm`. When you move the source document to the web template directory, do not place it in a directory called `_vti_shm`. Instead, place the source file in the same directory you would have placed the HTML document the source file is used with.

After you move all the necessary files to template directories, create the parameter file. The key to creating the parameter file is to ensure all references to files in subdirectories are entered in the parameter file appropriately. To demonstrate this process, suppose you created a template called `sample.tem`. If you move a file called `header.htm` to the `sample.tem\_private` directory, the entry in the parameter file for the header document should read as follows:

```
_private\header.htm=_private/header.htm
```

Parameter files for web templates should have the following sections:

info
FileList

Parameter files for web templates can include the following sections as well:

MetaInfo
TaskList

Summary

Use the examples in this chapter to help you create customized templates. You can create templates for pages and webs. Although page templates are the easiest to create, you can, with practice, create templates for webs. After you create a template, be sure to move it to the appropriate directory.

Creating Your Own Wizards

by William Robert Stanek

IN THIS CHAPTER

- The Basics of Creating Wizards 950
- Creating Your Wizard's Interface 952
- Tracking Wizard Parameters Using Temporary Files 952
- Determining Where Your Wizard Should Look for Key Files 957
- Using OLE Automation in Your Wizards 958

Wizards aid the content development process for pages and webs. Unlike templates, which are based on HTML documents and parameter files, wizards are programs that run on your system and use OLE to interface with FrontPage 98.

Before you create wizards, you should learn the basics of programming and OLE automation. You do not examine these basics in this chapter. Instead, you focus on the specific concepts you use to create wizards.

The Basics of Creating Wizards

Most wizards basics you already know. Using a series of setup pages, wizards help you design pages and Webs. Although page wizards and Web wizards are different, the only real restriction on a wizard is what FrontPage tool it works with.

Generally, you use the FrontPage Editor to access page wizards and the FrontPage Explorer to access Web wizards. To design a new page by using a page wizard, you choose File|New in the FrontPage Editor and then select the wizard you want to use. To design a new web by using a Web wizard, you choose File|New Web in the FrontPage Explorer and then select the wizard you want to use.

All wizards are written in a programming language, such as Visual Basic or Visual C++. Wizards communicate with FrontPage 98 through OLE automation. Just as you put templates in specific directories, you put wizards in specific directories as well.

Wizard Directories

All wizards are stored in special directories under the FrontPage base installation directory. The default path to the FrontPage base installation is `Program Files\Microsoft FrontPage`. If you change to the FrontPage base installation directory or examine this directory with the Windows Explorer, you will find a directory called `pages`. This directory stores the page templates and wizards used by the FrontPage Editor. The FrontPage base installation directory also contains a directory called `webs`. This directory stores the Web templates and wizards used by the FrontPage Explorer.

As with templates, all wizards must have unique names within the `pages` or `webs` directory. All wizard directories are named with a `.wiz` extension, such as `msimport.wiz` and `vtipres.wiz`. If you examine the wizard directories, you will find that all wizards have a binary executable file with an `.exe` extension and a parameter file named with an `.inf` extension. By default, the base name of the executable file and the parameter file must match the base name of the directory in which the wizard is located. Most wizards have other files in their directories as well. For example, the directory for the Corporate Presence Wizard contains all the fancy GIF and JPEG images used with the wizard.

Creating the Parameter File for Wizards

All wizards must have a parameter file. This file is a plain ASCII text file that ends with the `.inf` extension and is formatted similarly to a Windows INI file. Because of the way FrontPage 98 looks for parameter files, the parameter file must use the base name of the wizard directory. If your template is stored in a directory named `mywizard.wiz`, for example, the parameter file for this wizard must be in a file named `mywizard.inf`.

Unlike template parameter files that have several sections, wizard parameter files have only one section, an information section with the identifier `[info]`. This section specifies general information about the wizard including the title, a description, the name of the executable file, and whether the wizard has editing capabilities.

When you open the New Page dialog box in the FrontPage Editor, FrontPage 98 reads the information section for all page wizards to provide a title and description in the dialog box. Similarly, when you open the New Web dialog box in the FrontPage Explorer, FrontPage 98 reads the information section for all Web wizards to provide a title and description in the dialog box. If, for some reason, FrontPage 98 cannot find the parameter file, FrontPage 98 displays the base name of the directory in which the wizard is stored.

Valid parameters for wizards are designated by the following names:

`title`	Specifies the title of the wizard, such as `Corporate Presence Wizard`.
`description`	Describes the wizard; for example, `Design a new Web to help you establish a corporate presence on the Web`.
`editor`	Specifies that the wizard can function as an editor in addition to a content generator. An example of a wizard that is both an editor and a generator is the Frames Wizard. If you do not specify a value of `1` for this parameter, FrontPage 98 assumes that the wizard cannot function as an editor.
`exename`	Specifies the name of the binary executable file for the wizard. You can use this parameter to override the default value that specifies that the name of the executable file must match the base name of the wizard's directory.
`explorerWizard`	Specifies that the wizard is for the FrontPage Explorer. If you do not specify a value of `1` for this parameter, FrontPage 98 assumes that the wizard is used in the FrontPage Editor.

The following is a basic parameter file:

```
[info]

title=My Wizard
description=Design a new page.
```

The following parameter file uses all available parameters:

```
[info]

title=Internet Resource Wizard
description=Design a new resource page.
editor=1
exename.mac=resources.exe
explorerWizard=1
```

Creating Your Wizard's Interface

With wizards, Microsoft developers tried to create programs that let you design advanced content using a self-explanatory interface. As you've seen in this book, the interface is not always self-explanatory, especially when you deal with advanced wizards. However, the interface Microsoft developed goes a long way toward easing the content creation process, and you should consider the general design concepts that went into creating the existing wizards.

The interface used for wizards is fairly standardized; it includes a set of buttons that are displayed throughout the page or web creation process. These buttons are generally labeled Back, Next, Cancel, Help, and Finish. The Back and Next buttons enable users to move to the previous or next phase of the creation process. The Cancel button enables users to quit the wizard without creating the page or web. The Help button opens a Windows Help file. The Finish button enables users to create what they've designed. When a button is not a valid option, the button is usually grayed out to indicate that it cannot be clicked. Other buttons, such as the Finish button, are visible only at certain stages of the creation process.

Beyond buttons, your wizard should allow users to design pages and webs using a series of setup pages. Generally, each setup page lets users select from a set of related design options or enter related information. Each setup page in your wizard should have explanatory text. The most detailed explanatory text is usually found on the wizard's initial setup page.

Another wizard design concept you should study is the use of graphics. Most of the images you find on the existing wizards are positioned on the left side of setup pages and are always above the buttons, which are positioned on the bottom of the setup pages.

Tracking Wizard Parameters Using Temporary Files

An important aspect of any wizard you create is its ability to communicate with FrontPage 98. Part of this communication process means that your wizard should be able to track key parameters and their values.

When you start a wizard in the FrontPage Editor or Explorer, the wizard is passed a single parameter that specifies the path to a temporary parameter file. As with other parameter files, the file is in Windows INI format with section identifiers. Unlike the parameter file discussed in the preceding section, this temporary file exists only when the wizard is running and is updated as necessary to track changes made by the user and other essential system information. The file has three sections related to input, environment, and output settings; they have the identifiers `[input]`, `[environment]`, and `[output]`, respectively.

Input Parameters

The input section is used to track built-in parameters, such as the directory path to the wizard's executable file and the full path to its INF file. When a wizard is started, input parameters are passed to it automatically.

The input parameters for page and Web wizards are identified as follows:

`Dir`	Specifies the full path to the wizard directory.
`Inf`	Specifies the full path to the wizard's parameter file, which has an `.inf` extension.
`Blocking`	Determines whether the temporary file is deleted before the wizard exits. If the parameter is set with a value of `0`, the file is deleted before the wizard exits. If the parameter is set with a value of `1`, the file is not deleted before the wizard exits. Generally, you use a value of `1` when you want to pass output back to the program that started the wizard, in which case the launching program deletes the temporary file after it reads the parameters it needs.
`Editing`	Determines whether the wizard can be used as an editor. This parameter relates directly to the `editor` parameter in the wizard's INF file. If the `Editing` parameter is set with a value of `0`, the wizard cannot be used as an editor. If the parameter is set with a value of `1`, the wizard can be used as an editor. Some input parameters can be used only with the page wizard.
`PageURL`	Specifies the URL the page should be saved with; it is a relative URL in the current web.
`PageTitle`	Specifies the title for the new page.
`PageFile`	Specifies the full path to the file being edited, which is set only if the value of the `Editing` parameter is `1`.

Another useful parameter that you can use only with page wizards is the `destination` parameter. In general, when a page wizard finishes, the page it creates is loaded into the FrontPage Editor. However, if the wizard generates content that cannot be edited by the FrontPage Editor, the wizard should load the page to the current web or to a file on the user's file system instead. You use the `destination` parameter to specify where the file should be loaded or stored.

By default, the `destination` parameter is set to `editor`, which means the page generated by the wizard should be loaded into the FrontPage Editor using OLE automation. You can change the default destination by setting a value of either `web` or `disk`. If the destination parameter is set to `web`, the page is saved to the current web. If the destination parameter is set to `disk`, the page is saved to a file on the user's file system.

Only Web wizards can use the following input parameters:

`WebName`	The name of the current web
`ServerName`	The name of the host server or its IP address
`Proxy`	The proxy server currently being used
`User`	The name of the user who is accessing the FrontPage Explorer

The following is a sample input section for the temporary parameter file:

```
[input]

PageURL=index.htm
PageTitle=My Home Page
Dir=D:\Program Files\Microsoft FrontPage\Pages\FramesWiz.wiz
Inf=D:\Program Files\Microsoft FrontPage\Pages\FramesWiz.wiz\frameswiz.inf
Blocking=0
Editing=0
```

Environment Parameters

The environment section tracks standard environment variables such as the name of the computer or path settings. As with input parameters, environment parameters are set automatically. Additionally, environment parameters are unique to the computer you are using. To check environment variable settings on a Windows 95 or Windows NT system, type the keyword `set` at the MS-DOS prompt.

When I enter the `set` command on my system, for example, I see that the environment variables are set as follows:

```
TMP=C:\WINDOWS\TEMP
TEMP=C:\WINDOWS\TEMP
PROMPT=$p$g
winbootdir=C:\WINDOWS
COMSPEC=C:\WINDOWS\COMMAND.COM
NBACKUP=C:\NBACKUP
CLASSPATH=.;C:\JAVA\LIB\;C:\JAVA\LIB\CLASSES.ZIP;
PATH=C:\MSBOB;C:\WINDOWS;C:\WINDOWS\COMMAND;C:\NBACKUP;C:\JAVA\BIN;
windir=C:\WINDOWS
BLASTER=A220 I5 D1 H5 P330 T6
```

Output Parameters

Unlike the input and environment sections of the temporary file, the output section is empty when the wizard is started and is written to only if the input blocking parameter is set to `1` or the destination parameter is set to `disk`.

The primary output parameter recognized by FrontPage 98 is `ExitStatus`, which sets the status of the wizard. A value of `error` indicates that an error has occurred. A value of `cancel` indicates that the user canceled the creation of the page or web—usually by pressing a button labeled Cancel. A value of `ok` indicates that the wizard completed successfully. If you do not set the `ExitStatus` parameter, FrontPage 98 assumes that an error has occurred. For this reason, you should always set this parameter.

Other output parameters are used only if the destination parameter is set to the value of `disk`. These parameters include the number of files created by the wizard, which is set with the `FileCount` parameter, as well as a `File` and `Url` parameter for each file the wizard creates. The `File` and `Url` parameters are used as keys and end with a suffix that indicates the position of the key, such as `File1`, `Url1`, `File2`, or `Url2`. The `File` parameter indicates the full path to the file, and the `Url` parameter sets the page URL.

A wizard that generates three files might create the following output section:

```
[output]

ExitStatus=ok
FileCount=3
File1=c:\temp\wiz01.tmp
Url1=index.htm
File2=c:\temp\wiz02.tmp
Url2 = banner.htm
File3=c:\temp\wiz03.tmp
Url3=footer.htm
```


Putting Temporary Parameter Files into Perspective

All files generated by your wizard should be written to the `temp` directory under the FrontPage base installation directory. The default path to this directory is `Program Files\Microsoft FrontPage\temp`. So that you can ensure a consistent naming structure, all temporary files your wizard creates should end with the `.tmp` extension.

For the temporary parameter file, you might want to follow the naming scheme used by Microsoft, which consists of the following:

- Naming the file with the prefix `wiz`
- Adding a unique numeric identifier
- Using the `.tmp` extension

A sample filename using this structure is `wiz5190.tmp`.

If you have used wizards, you will find a number of temporary files in the `temp` directory. Examining these files can tell you a lot about how temporary parameter files are used. The following is a sample file from my file system:

```
[Input]

Dir=C:\Program Files\Microsoft FrontPage\pages\framewiz.wiz
Inf=C:\Program Files\Microsoft FrontPage\pages\framewiz.wiz\framewiz.inf
Blocking=0
Editing=0

[Environment]

TMP=C:\WINDOWS\TEMP
TEMP=C:\WINDOWS\TEMP
PROMPT=$p$g
winbootdir=C:\WINDOWS
COMSPEC=C:\WINDOWS\COMMAND.COM
NBACKUP=C:\NBACKUP
CLASSPATH=.;C:\JAVA\LIB\;C:\JAVA\LIB\CLASSES.ZIP;
PATH=C:\MSBOB;C:\WINDOWS;C:\WINDOWS\COMMAND;C:\NBACKUP;C:\JAVA\BIN;
CMDLINE=WIN
windir=C:\WINDOWS
BLASTER=A220 I5 D1 H5 P330 T6

[Output]

ExitStatus=cancel
```

A final note on parameter files is that you should not use a temporary parameter file when you want to retain option settings selected by the user. If you've used the wizards in FrontPage 98, you have probably noticed that the first time you use a wizard you see default settings, but thereafter, you see the last settings you made in the wizard.

To preserve option settings, store the settings in a wizard initialization file. Name this file with the `.ini` extension so that you can identify it as an initialization file, and put it in the `data` directory under the FrontPage base installation directory. The default path to this directory is Program `Files\Microsoft FrontPage\data`.

To get an idea of how you can save option settings, examine the following option settings based on the selections I made using the Corporate Presence Wizard:

```
[Settings]

DoFeedbackPage=True
DoWhatsNewsPage=True
DoProductsPage=True
DoSearchPage=True
DoTOCPage=True
DoHomePage=True
DoHomeContactInfo=True
DoHomeIntro=False
DoHomeMission=True
DoHomeProfile=False
DoNewsArticles=False
```

```
DoNewsPressReleases=False
DoNewsWhatsNew=True
ProductOption=0
NumProducts=3
NumServices=3
DoFeedbackAddress=False
DoFeedbackCompany=True
DoFeedbackEmail=True
DoFeedbackFAX=True
DoFeedbackName=True
DoFeedbackTelephone=True
DoFeedbackTitle=False
FeedbackFileFormat=0
TOCAutoRecalc=False
TOCBullets=True
TOCOrphans=False
DoBottomLinks=False
DoBottomCopyright=False
DoTopLogo=True
DoTopTitle=True
DoTopLinks=True
DoBottomWebmasterAddress=True
DoBottomDateModified=True
DoProductImage=False
DoProductInfoRequest=True
DoProductPricing=True
DoServiceCapabilities=False
DoServiceInfoRequest=True
DoServiceReferences=False
StyleOption=1
UnderConstructionOption=0
CompanyLongName=ACME Industries Inc.
CompanyShortName=ACME
CompanyAddress=123 Web Way, Cambridge MA 02138
CompanyPhone=617-555-1212
CompanyFAX=617-555-1212
CompanyWebMaster=webmaster@yourcompany.com
CompanyEmail=info@yourcompany.com
ShowToDoList=True
LinkColor=0xff0000
VisitedLinkColor=0x800080
TextColor=0x0
BackgroundColor=0xc0c0c0
ActiveLinkColor=0xff
BackgroundImage=0
ColorSettingsOption=0
```


Determining Where Your Wizard Should Look for Key Files

Any wizard you create should be able to run on someone else's computer. Yet, if your wizard references hard file paths, the wizard will work properly only on systems on which FrontPage 98 is installed exactly as you've installed it. The key to ensuring the portability of your wizard is not to use hard file paths.

Instead, you should look up the file paths in the initialization file for FrontPage 98; these paths are always stored in the `Windows` directory. The FrontPage initialization file is called `frontpg.ini`. Using this file, you can determine the location of the FrontPage base installation directory and the base installation directory for FrontPage webs. The `FrontPageRoot` variable tells you the location of the FrontPage base installation directory. The `PWSRoot` variable tells you the location of FrontPage webs. These variables are located in the FrontPage 3.0 section of the INI file.

TIP

You can change the location of the FrontPage webs and pages directories by changing the `WebWizardsDir` and `PageWizardsDir` parameters in the FrontPage 3.0 section of the initialization file.

The following is an example of what the INI file looks like:

```
[FrontPage 3.0]
FrontPageRoot=C:\Program Files\Microsoft FrontPage
DefaultWebTheme=expeditn 001
PWSRoot=C:\FrontPage Webs
UILangAbbrev=enu
BotCacheDir=C:\Program Files\Microsoft FrontPage\BotCache
CheckedHostName=director
HostOverride=

[Internet Explorer Integration]
UseAlternateThemePreview=0
DisablePagePreviewTab=0

[WebPost Publishing]
members.aol.com=;fullwiz

[Ports]
Port 8080=

[Port 8080]
servertype=frontpage
serverconfig=C:\FrontPage Webs\Server\conf\httpd.cnf
authoring=enabled
frontpageroot=C:\Program Files\Microsoft FrontPage\version3.0
```

Using OLE Automation in Your Wizards

The key to communication between your wizard and FrontPage 98 is OLE automation. If you're familiar with Windows programming, you probably already know how OLE automation works. Basically, with OLE automation your wizard can make procedure calls to the FrontPage Explorer, the FrontPage Editor, and the FrontPage To Do List. These procedure calls can cause the program they call to perform specific actions. For example, a procedure call can cause the

FrontPage Editor to start and load a page for editing. Likewise, a procedure call can cause the FrontPage Explorer to launch.

Each of the FrontPage tools you can access with OLE has a specific set of procedures. The set of OLE procedures that a program can use is collectively referred to as its *OLE interface.*

Because the automation interface used in FrontPage 98 is still evolving, your OLE automation code should use macros of function wrappers to localize calls to OLE procedures. In this way, you can easily update your code for compatibility with the next major release of FrontPage.

All applications capable of being accessed with OLE automation must be registered in the Windows Registry. The FrontPage interfaces for version 3.0 have the following identifiers in the Windows Registry:

- `FrontPage.Explorer.3.0`
- `FrontPage.Editor.3.0`
- `FrontPage.ToDoList.3.0`

You use these identifiers to specify which tool you want to connect to. You also can use the FrontPage tools with a generic identifier that resolves to the current release of FrontPage installed on the user's system:

- `FrontPage.Explorer`
- `FrontPage.Editor`
- `FrontPage.ToDoList`

NOTE

You probably will have to update your wizard programs for compatibility with future releases of FrontPage. When you use the specific identifier, you will always have to update your wizard for the new versions of FrontPage. When you use the generic identifier, you might run into compatibility problems if the interface changes in future versions of FrontPage. If you use the generic identifier, however, you might not recognize that the problem is with version compatibility.

Summary

You can use the concepts described in this chapter to help you create customized wizards. Your wizards can use OLE automation to communicate with the FrontPage Explorer, FrontPage Editor, and the FrontPage To Do List.

CHAPTER

Programming the Wizard

by William Robert Stanek

IN THIS CHAPTER

- Establishing a Connection to the OLE Server 962
- Checking the Status of the Explorer When Necessary 963
- Writing HTML Pages to Files 964
- More OLE Automation with FrontPage 98 966

Now that you know wizard basics, what parameters the wizard can use and what files the wizard should create, you are almost ready to program the wizard. Before you begin, consider carefully what programming language you will use. The language you select must support OLE automation. Both Visual Basic and Visual C++ are good choices for programming languages. It's easy to create graphical interfaces with Visual Basic and Visual C++ languages.

After you read about the OLE automation procedures supported by FrontPage 98 and how they are used, you might want to spend a few hours examining the sample wizards included in the FrontPage Developer's Kit. You will be amazed at how much code you can reuse.

Most of the wizards you create will use three common types of routines:

- Routines that establish a connection to the OLE server and perform a procedure
- Routines that check the status of the FrontPage Explorer before performing an OLE procedure
- Routines that write HTML pages to files

Establishing a Connection to the OLE Server

One important step you should perform before calling an OLE procedure is to establish a connection to the automation server's exported object interfaces. Typically, you do this by creating an object with an object type of the application you want to connect to. After the connection is established, you have access to the object's OLE interface and can make procedure calls. When you're finished making procedure calls, release the connection with the OLE automation server.

A key concept when using OLE automation is to minimize the amount of time when an open OLE connection exists. Otherwise, you might run into serious problems when users close the application they are using or change the application's state in a way that will cause your OLE procedures to fail. Most programmers open and close the OLE connection inside a single procedure.

To put these OLE concepts in perspective, Listing 59.1 shows a sample procedure written in Visual C++ that demonstrates these concepts and uses a generalized OLE identifier.

Listing 59.1. An OLE procedure in Visual C++.

```
#include "target.h"

// Initiate the procedure
void IncludeEvent()
{
```

```
// Establish connection to the automation server and handle possible error
IWebber explorer;
COleException error;

if(!explorer.CreateDispatch("FrontPage.Explorer",&error))
{
AfxMessageBox("Error connecting to FrontPage Explorer. Check server status.");
return;
}

// Make procedure call to the FrontPageExplorer
explorer.vtiBringToTop();

// Release the connection with the OLE automation server
explorer.ReleaseDispatch();

}
```

Listing 59.2 shows the same procedure written in Visual Basic.

Listing 59.2. An OLE procedure in Visual Basic.

```
' Initiate the procedure
Function IncludeEvent()
{
Dim explorer as Object

' Establish connection to the automation server and handle possible error
Set explorer = CreateObject("FrontPage.Explorer")

' Make procedure call to the FrontPageExplorer
explorer.vtiBringToTop

' Release the connection with the OLE automation server
Set explorer = Nothing

}
```


Checking the Status of the Explorer When Necessary

The main OLE interface in FrontPage 98 is for the FrontPage Explorer. Whenever your wizards use OLE hooks that access or alter the current web, you will need to write a procedure that ensures a web is open in the FrontPage Explorer. The routine shown in Listing 59.3 checks the URL of the current web in the FrontPage Explorer before adding a task to the To Do List. This routine is written in Visual Basic.

Listing 59.3. Checking the Explorer before calling a To Do List procedure.

```
Private Sub AddTask()

' Initialize variables
    Dim todolist As Object
    Dim webber As Object
    Dim webURL As String
    Dim ret As Boolean
    Dim url As String
    Dim priority As Integer

    MousePointer = 11

' Ensure a Web is open in the FrontPage Explorer
Set webber = CreateObject("FrontPage.Explorer.3.0")
    webURL = webber.vtiGetWebURL

' Close the connection to the Explorer
    Set webber = Nothing

' If the length of the webURL variable is 0, no Web is currently open
' in the FrontPage Explorer. Handle the error by exiting.
    If Len(webURL) = 0 Then
        MsgBox "No Web is currently open in the Explorer."
Exit Sub
    End If

' Set the task priority based in user selection
    If optionHigh Then priority = 1
    If optionMedium Then priority = 2
    If optionLow Then priority = 3

' Add task to the current Web's To Do List
Set todolist = CreateObject("FrontPage.ToDoList.3.0")
    ret = todolist.vtiAddTask(txtTask, priority, txtCreator, txtURL,
    txtCookie, txtComment)

' Display error message if could not add the task
    If Not ret Then
        MsgBox "Failed to add task for To Do List."
    End If

' Close the connection to the To Do List
    Set todolist = Nothing

    frmGetURL.Tag = ""

    MousePointer = 0

End Sub
```

Writing HTML Pages to Files

Your wizards must also generate HTML documents based on the user's selections. Generally, the wizard will write HTML documents to files, with each file containing the HTML markup for one page. Listing 59.4 shows a sample routine written in Visual Basic that writes an HTML page to a file.

Listing 59.4. Writing an HTML page to a file.

```
Public Sub CreatePage(pagepage As String)

' Initialize variable for file
    Dim ff As Integer

' Initialize variable for new line
    Dim nl As String

' Initialize variable for standard string
    Dim str As String

' set new line variable to ASCII new line value
    nl = Chr$(10)

' set file variable to FreeFile
    ff = FreeFile

' set up error handling
    On Error GoTo BadFile

' open file on file system for output
    Open pagefile For Output As #ff

' Build and write the HTML page
    Print #ff, "<HTML>"
    Print #ff, "<HEAD>"
    Print #ff, "<TITLE>" & TitleTag & "</TITLE>"
    Print #ff, "</HEAD>"
    Print #ff, "<BODY BGCOLOR=" & BGColorTag & " TEXT=" & TXColorTag & ">"

    str = "H" & (cmbStyle.ListIndex + 1)   ' H1, H2, or H3
    Print #ff, "<" & str & ">" & ResourceTitle & "</" & str & ">"

    Print #ff, "<P>" & ParaText1 & "</P>"
    Print #ff, "<UL>"
    Print #ff, "<LI>" & P1ListItem1
    Print #ff, "<LI>" & P1ListItem2
    Print #ff, "<LI>" & P1ListItem3
    Print #ff, "<LI>" & P1ListItem4
    Print #ff, "</UL>"

    Print #ff, "<P>" & ParaText2 & "</P>"
    Print #ff, "<OL>"
    Print #ff, "<LI>" & P2ListItem1
    Print #ff, "<LI>" & P2ListItem2
    Print #ff, "<LI>" & P2ListItem3
    Print #ff, "<LI>" & P2ListItem4
    Print #ff, "</OL>"

    If chkCredit Then
        Print #ff, "<HR SIZE=5>"
```


continues

Listing 59.4. continued

```
        Print #ff, "<P><EM>This page was generated by the Internet
        ➥Resource Wizard.</EM></P>"
    End If

    Print #ff, "</BODY>"
    Print #ff, "</HTML>"

' close the page file
    Close #ff

' on error exit the subroutine
BadFile:
    Exit Sub

End Sub
```

More OLE Automation with FrontPage 98

The previous section introduced basic OLE concepts. Wizards use OLE automation to communicate with three FrontPage components: the FrontPage Explorer, the FrontPage Editor, and the FrontPage To Do List. Each component has a specific set of OLE procedures that it recognizes.

Using OLE Automation with the FrontPage Explorer

Most procedures your wizards use will need to interface with the FrontPage Explorer. Using the FrontPage Explorer OLE interface, you can do the following:

- Create a web
- Delete a web
- Add files to a web
- Remove files from a web
- Get the URL of the current web
- Get the title of the current web
- Retrieve a list of files in the current web
- Get meta-information variables for webs and pages
- Set meta-information variables for webs
- Launch the To Do List application

The procedures you use to perform these tasks are restricted by the FrontPage Explorer's OLE interface. For FrontPage version 3.0, the only OLE procedures you can use are the following:

```
vtiBringToTop
vtiCancelRequests
```

```
vtiCreateWeb
vtiEditWebPage
vtiGetDocToFile
vtiGetPageList
vtiGetWebMetaInfo
vtiGetWebPageMetaInfo
vtiGetWebTitle
vtiGetWebURL
vtiIsPageInWeb
vtiOpenWeb
vtiPromptOpenWeb
vtiPutDocument
vtiPutDocuments
vtiPutWebMetaInfo
vtiPutWebPageMetaInfo
vtiRefreshWebFromServer
vtiRemoveWeb
vtiSetWebRecalcDependencies
```

The FrontPage Explorer has the most extensive OLE interface. One of the most common reasons your wizards will access this interface is to open a web. Listing 59.5 shows a sample procedure for opening a web that is written in Visual Basic. As you study the example, pay particular attention to the way OLE procedure calls are made.

Listing 59.5. Opening a web using OLE.

```
Private Sub OpenWeb()

MousePointer = 11

' Initialize variables
Dim webber As Object
Dim ret As Integer

' Open a Web on the specified server
Set webber = CreateObject("FrontPage.Explorer.3.0")
ret = webber.vtiOpenWeb(Server, Web, User)

' Close the connection to the Explorer
Set webber = Nothing

MousePointer = 0

End Sub
```

Another common task your wizards might need to do is to create a web. Listing 59.6 provides a sample procedure for creating a web.

Listing 59.6. Creating a new web.

```
Private Sub CreateWeb()

MousePointer = 11

' Initialize variables
Dim webber As Object
Dim ret As Long

' Create the new Web on the server
Set webber = CreateObject("FrontPage.Explorer.3.0")
ret = webber.vtiCreateWeb(Server, Web)

' Close the connection to the Explorer
Set webber = Nothing

MousePointer = 0

End Sub
```

Listing 59.7 shows a sample procedure for removing a web. Removing a web is trickier than creating a new web or opening an existing web. Before you remove a web, you must ensure that there is an open web in the FrontPage Explorer. You must also ensure that you do not accidentally delete the Root Web. To handle these tasks, check the value returned by the `vtiGetWebURL` procedure before removing the web.

Listing 59.7. Removing webs.

```
Private Sub RemoveWeb()

MousePointer = 11

' Initialize variables
Dim webber As Object
Dim ret As Long
Dim webURL As String

' vtiGetWebURL returns an empty string if there is no current web
' AND if the current Web is the RootWeb
Set webber = CreateObject("FrontPage.Explorer.3.0")
webURL = webber.vtiGetWebURL

' Remove the Web if there is a current Web AND it is not the RootWeb
If Len(webURL) > 0 Then
     ret = webber.vtiRemoveWeb("/" & Web)
     If ret <> 1 Then
     MsgBox "An error occurred while trying to remove the web '" & Web &
      ➥"'. The Web may not exist on the server."
End If
Else
     MsgBox "A Web must be open in the FrontPage Explorer."
```

```
End If

' Close the connection to the Explorer
Set webber = Nothing

MousePointer = 0

End Sub
```

Using OLE Automation with the FrontPage Editor

The FrontPage Editor is used primarily for creating and editing pages. Because pages are not as complex as webs, there is no need for an extended interface between wizards and the FrontPage Editor. You will use the FrontPage Editor OLE interface to perform basic editor tasks including the following:

- Creating a new empty page
- Opening an existing page from the current web or local file system
- Determining whether a page is currently being edited

Although most of the OLE automation hooks to the FrontPage Editor are designed to be used by other FrontPage components, your wizards can use any of the available OLE procedures. These procedures are as follows:

```
vtiBringToTop
vtiNewWebPage
vtiOpenWebPage
vtiQueryWebPage
```

Although the FrontPage Editor OLE interface is not as extended as the FrontPage Explorer interface, you will find many uses for Editor procedures in your wizards. One of the tasks your wizards might need to do is to create a new page. Listing 59.8 shows a sample procedure written in Visual Basic for creating new pages.

Listing 59.8. Creating new pages.

```
Private Sub CreateNewPage()

' Initialize variables
Dim editor As Object
Dim page As Object

'Create new HTML page
Set editor = CreateObject("FrontPage.Editor.3.0")
Set page = editor.vtiNewWebPage("homepage.htm", "", "")

' Close the connection to the Editor
Set editor = Nothing

End Sub
```

Another task you might want to perform is to bring the FrontPage Editor to the front of the display. Listing 59.9 shows a sample procedure to do this task.

Listing 59.9. Bringing the FrontPage Editor to the front.

```
Private Sub BringFront()

' Initialize variable
Dim editor As Object

MousePointer = 11

' Bring editor to front
Set editor = CreateObject("FrontPage.Editor.3.0")
editor.vtiBringToTop

' Close the connection to the Editor
Set editor = Nothing

MousePointer = 0

End Sub
```

A more advanced task you might want your wizard to perform involves checking to see whether a page is currently loaded in the FrontPage Editor. Using the `vtiQueryWebPage` procedure, you query the editor to see whether a page is loaded. Because this procedure can check the URL of the web the page came from, you should ensure that a web is open in the FrontPage Explorer before making the procedure call to the FrontPage Editor.

Listing 59.10 shows a sample procedure for querying the FrontPage Editor.

Listing 59.10. Querying the Editor.

```
Private Sub QueryEditor()

' Initialize variables
Dim editor As Object
Dim webber As Object
Dim webURL As String
Dim ret As Long
Dim url As String

' Ensure a Web is open in the FrontPage Explorer
Set webber = CreateObject("FrontPage.Explorer.3.0")
webURL = webber.vtiGetWebURL

' Close the connection to the Explorer
Set webber = Nothing

' Display error message and exit if no current web
If Len(webURL) = 0 Then
     MsgBox "Cannot continue. No Web is open in the FrontPage Explorer."
Exit Sub
```

```
End If

MousePointer = 11

' Routine for Querying the Editor and displaying a message.
Set editor = CreateObject("FrontPage.Editor.3.0")
ret = editor.vtiQueryWebPage(url, webURL)
If ret = 1 Then
     MsgBox "Document is open in the FrontPage Editor."
Else
     MsgBox "Document is not open in the FrontPage Editor."
End If

' Close the connection to the Editor
Set editor = Nothing

MousePointer = 0

End Sub
```

Using OLE Automation with the FrontPage To Do List

The FrontPage To Do List helps you manage tasks related to creating and editing webs. All tasks have a set of attributes that describe the purpose of the task. When tasks are completed, they are removed from the To Do List.

As with the FrontPage Editor, there is no need for an extended interface between wizards and the FrontPage To Do List. Usually, you use the interface to perform the following tasks:

- Add new tasks to the To Do List
- Remove accomplished tasks from the To Do List
- Hide the To Do List
- Display the To Do List

As with the FrontPage Editor OLE interface, the FrontPage To Do List OLE interface is designed primarily to be used by other FrontPage components. Still, your wizards can use any of the available OLE procedures. These procedures include the following:

```
vtiAddTask

vtiAddTaskAskUser

vtiCompletedTaskByUrl

vtiGetActiveCount

vtiHide

vtiShow

vtiWorkedOnTaskByUrl
```

The most common reason you will use the OLE interface to the To Do List is to add tasks. Listing 59.11 shows a sample procedure written in Visual Basic for adding tasks. As with other code examples in this chapter, you should follow the logic of the code, paying particular attention to the way OLE procedure calls are made.

Listing 59.11. Adding tasks.

```
Private Sub AddTask()

' Initialize variables
Dim todolist As Object
Dim webber As Object
Dim webURL As String
Dim ret As Boolean
Dim url As String

MousePointer = 11

' Ensure a Web is open in the FrontPage Explorer
Set webber = CreateObject("FrontPage.Explorer.3.0")
webURL = webber.vtiGetWebURL

' Close the connection to the Explorer
Set webber = Nothing

' If the length of the webURL variable is 0, no web is currently open
' in the FrontPage Explorer. Handle the error by exiting.
If Len(webURL) = 0 Then
     MsgBox "A Web must be open in the Explorer."
Exit Sub
End If

' Add task to the current Web's To Do List
Set todolist = CreateObject("FrontPage.ToDoList.3.0")
ret = todolist.vtiAddTask(Task, priority, Creator, URL, Cookie, Comment)

' Display error message if could not add the task
If Not ret Then
     MsgBox "Could not add task for To Do List."
End If

' Close the connection to the To Do List
Set todolist = Nothing

frmGetURL.Tag = ""

MousePointer = 0

End Sub
```

Other important procedures you might use with the To Do List interface are those that mark tasks as completed. Note the use of the `URL` and `Cookie` parameters to find a particular task. Listing 59.12 shows how you could use Visual Basic to write a procedure that marks tasks as completed.

Listing 59.12. Procedure for marking tasks as completed.

```
Private Sub TaskCompleted()

' Initialize variables
Dim todolist As Object
Dim webber As Object
Dim webURL As String
Dim ret As Boolean
Dim url As String
Dim priority As Integer

MousePointer = 11

' Mark specific task as completed
Set todolist = CreateObject("FrontPage.ToDoList.3.0")
ret = todolist.vtiCompletedTaskByUrl(URL, Cookie)

' Display error message if could not mark the task
If Not ret Then
    MsgBox "Could not mark task as completed."
End If

' Close the connection to the To Do List
Set todolist = Nothing

MousePointer = 0

End Sub
```

Summary

The FrontPage Explorer, the FrontPage Editor, and the FrontPage To Do List each use a specific set of OLE procedures. You can use these procedures to create wizards that communicate with FrontPage 98. After you create a wizard, be sure to move it to the appropriate directory.

Part XII

IN THIS PART

- Installing FrontPage 98 977
- Troubleshooting FrontPage 98 983

Appendixes

APPENDIX A

Installing FrontPage 98

by William Robert Stanek

IN THIS APPENDIX

- Running the Installation 978
- Choosing Installation Options 979
- Testing the Personal Web Server 982

Before installing FrontPage 98, you should quit all other applications running on your desktop. This ensures that there are no conflicts for files FrontPage 98 must update on your system.

Running the Installation

Installing FrontPage 98 from CD-ROM or floppy disk is easy. The first step is to select Run from the Windows 95 or Windows NT Start menu. Then enter the directory path to the FrontPage 98 setup program on your CD-ROM or floppy drive, such as

```
E:\Setup.exe
```

In this example, `E:` is the location of the CD-ROM drive and `Setup.exe` is the name of the file you want to run. If your CD-ROM is on the D drive, you type the following to run the setup program:

```
D:\Setup.exe
```

NOTE

With the AutoPlay CD-ROM feature enabled, Windows 95 users need only to insert the FrontPage 98 CD-ROM to automatically start the setup program.

When you start the setup program, you'll see one of two startup screens. The setup program for Microsoft FrontPage 98 CD displays an extended dialog box. Using this dialog box, you can install FrontPage 98 and bonus software that includes the Personal Web Server and Microsoft Image Composer.

To install FrontPage 98, click the button labeled FrontPage. You should now see the Welcome page for the FrontPage setup program. If you are not installing FrontPage 98 CD, the Welcome page should display immediately as your startup screen.

Most dialog boxes in FrontPage 98 contain buttons you can use to obtain help, make selections, or exit the program. The Help button accesses the online help. The Cancel button exits the program. To move to the previous or next phase of the setup process, use the Back or Next buttons. When you complete the setup process, you can press the Finish button, and the setup program starts installing FrontPage 98 on your system. You should click the Next button to continue.

You need about 15MB of free space to install FrontPage 98 and the Personal Web Server. By default, the setup program installs FrontPage 98 on the C drive in a folder called `Microsoft FrontPage` under the `Program Files` directory. To change the default, click the Browse button. This opens a dialog box that lets you specify a new folder and path for the base installation. When you are satisfied with the path, click the Next button.

If you are upgrading from an existing installation of FrontPage to FrontPage 98, you do not see the setup page. Instead, you see a page notifying you that a current version of FrontPage exists on your system. You can upgrade the current version by installing FrontPage to the same directory or installing FrontPage to a new directory.

Generally, you simply click the Next button to install the new version as an upgrade. However, if you have the room on your hard drive and you are concerned about changes to your system and existing FrontPage configuration files, you might want to install FrontPage 98 to a different directory. Click the Browse button to choose a new directory.

Choosing Installation Options

FrontPage 98 allows you to select one of two types of installation: typical and custom. The typical installation installs everything most users need, including the client software, the Personal Web Server, and the FrontPage server extensions. The custom installation allows you to select the components you want to install. The client software includes the FrontPage Explorer and the FrontPage Editor. The Personal Web Server is the server you use to provide services for just about everything you do in FrontPage 98. The FrontPage server extensions are used with external Web servers, such as your Internet Service Provider's (ISP) UNIX-based Web server.

NOTE

When you install the Personal Web Server, it is configured to be directly accessible at startup. If you are a Windows 95 user, you should see a new icon on the taskbar that allows you to control and access the server.

TIP

FrontPage 98 makes extensive use of both the client and the server software. The only components you might not need are the server extensions. Unless you are sure you do not need to use an external Web server, you really should install all the components.

Because most users need all the components, you probably want to use the typical installation option. However, the typical installation assumes that you have enough space on your hard drive for the installation. If you want to check the space on your hard drive, you should select the custom installation option and possibly change the destination directory. Furthermore, if you want to use themes and other extras, be sure to take a look at the custom installation.

When you select custom installation and click the Next button, you'll have more options. Not only can you select the FrontPage components you want to install from this page, but you can also see the disk space you need and the amount of free space on your hard drive.

If you choose to install the Personal Web Server and you are installing FrontPage 98 for the first time, the next setup page lets you specify a directory for the server executables and content. Keep in mind that this same directory stores all the files and documents you create or import into FrontPage 98. By default, the server directory is `C:\FrontPage Webs`.

The default directory for server executables is `C:\FrontPage Webs\Server`, and the default directory for content is `C:\FrontPage Webs\Content`.

TIP

Creating content for your Web site is easy with FrontPage 98. It is also easy to get caught up in the content-creation process and quickly eat up several megabytes of disk space. For this reason, I recommend using a drive with 2 to 5MB of free disk space if you plan to create a Web site that is small to moderately sized. This disk space requirement is in addition to the 15MB of free space you need for the base installation.

After you select a server directory or decide to accept the default, click the Next button. You can now choose a name for the folder that holds the program icons.

TIP

The name of the folder is not as important as remembering where the folder is located. This folder holds the icons used to start the FrontPage Editor, the FrontPage Explorer, the Personal Web Server, and other tools provided with the installation.

You need to run the FrontPage Editor, the FrontPage Explorer, and the Personal Web Server just about every time you want to create, manage, or edit FrontPage web files. As a result, most users want to move the entire folder onto the desktop after the installation, which provides easy access to all the programs you need for publishing. If you use your computer exclusively or mostly for Web publishing, you can also move the FrontPage Editor, the FrontPage Explorer, and the Personal Web Server to the `Startup` folder, which ensures that the applications are started every time you turn on your computer.

If you are upgrading to FrontPage 98, the server setup page provides you with the additional options. Click the Upgrade radio button if you want to install the new version of the server software in the same directory as the old version, which effectively overwrites the old version. Click the Install radio button if you want to install the new version of the server software to a new directory.

Generally, you want to upgrade the current Web server software. The primary reason you would not want to use the upgrade option is if you made special configurations for the old server software. Installing the new software in a different location allows you to compare configuration options and ensure you have the same settings.

If you install the server to a new location, the server usually runs on port 8080; the next page you see warns you about this. Because port 8080 is not the default port used by browsers, you have to include the port in your hypertext references, such as `http://www.yourcompany.com:8080/` or `http://localhost:8080/home.htm`.

The next page pertains to the FrontPage server extensions. If you chose to install server extensions, the setup program searches your local file system for installed servers. If you did not install the server extensions, you do not see this page.

Generally, you want to install server extensions on any servers that you plan to use with FrontPage 98. Select servers as appropriate for your system and then click the Next button.

NOTE

Keep in mind the setup program looks only at servers on the local file system. You might need to install server extensions on remote servers.

You are now finished with most of the setup process, and the setup program is now ready to begin installing FrontPage 98. When you click the Next button, you can review the current settings for the installation. If you are not satisfied with any settings, click the Back button. Otherwise, click the Next button, and the setup program begins copying files to your hard drive.

Before the setup completes, you need to set up an account for the server administrator. FrontPage 98 prompts you for this information automatically.

Another name for the server administrator is the Webmaster. The Webmaster is the person who controls access to the server and is also responsible for administering the server. You need to enter a user name and password for the server administrator. You also need to reenter the password in the Password Confirmation field. Remember the user name and password you enter. You need them each time you restart the FrontPage Explorer.

TIP

To protect the security of your web, you should use a secure password. I recommend using a password that is at least six characters long and includes numbers and wild card characters, such as !, @, #, $, and ?.

When setup completes successfully, you have the option of starting the FrontPage Explorer. The Explorer lets you create new webs. Usually, you want to start the FrontPage Explorer immediately. You can click the Finish button to complete the setup process.

After the Explorer starts, FrontPage 98 attempts to determine the IP address and host name of your system. FrontPage 98 uses a tool that checks for a Transmission Control Protocol/Internet Protocol (TCP/IP) connection to a network.

If you are connected to a network and your system has an IP address and host name, FrontPage 98 should return accurate results. If you are not connected to a network but use a TCP/IP dialer to access the Internet (as most Web publishers do), FrontPage 98 might return inaccurate results. For example, on my system, FrontPage 98 returned my login name with my ISP instead of a valid server name.

Testing the Personal Web Server

If you have browsed the Web, you know how Hypertext Markup Language (HTML) documents are served to your browser. The browser is a client application. When you access a file with a client, the client contacts a server and requests a uniform resource locator (URL), such as `http://www.mcp.com/`. The Web server gets the referenced file and passes it to the client. The client displays the file in its viewing window.

FrontPage 98 has two client applications: the FrontPage Explorer and the FrontPage Editor. You can configure both applications to use a server to retrieve files for them. The server included in FrontPage 98 is the Personal Web Server. FrontPage 98 also includes tools for configuring and testing the server: the Server Administrator, the Internet Services Administrator, and the FrontPage TCP/IP Test. You can test the results using the TCP/IP Test tool included with FrontPage 98. To run this tool, execute the `TcpTest.exe` program located in the `bin` directory in the FrontPage installation or select About the FrontPage Explorer from the FrontPage Explorer's Help menu and then click the button labeled Network Test.

To have FrontPage 98 automatically test your TCP/IP connection, click the Start Test button. It takes a few minutes for the Test tool to check your connection. To see a detailed explanation that relates to your system, click the Explain Results button.

FrontPage 98 tests to see whether your system uses a 16-bit or 32-bit Winsock. The Winsock is used in network communications. Next, FrontPage 98 checks to see if the local loopback host `127.0.0.1` is usable on your system. On most networked systems, `127.0.0.1` is the IP address listed in the `/etc/hosts` file for the local host. You use the local host when you want to test your web or publish documents for testing purposes.

The next three tests determine your system's host name, IP address, and local loopback address. The final test ensures that if your local host is different from the standard `127.0.0.1`, you will know about it. You should write down this information if you do not already know it.

Although the Personal Web Server should run automatically at startup, the tested software did not run as advertised. You'll know the server is not running when you see errors.

You might need to start the Personal Web Server by hand from the `FrontPage` folder or directory. The directory path is usually `C:\FrontPage Webs\Server\vhttpd32.exe`.

APPENDIX B

Troubleshooting FrontPage 98

by John Jung and William Robert Stanek

IN THIS APPENDIX

- Solving Problems with the Editor 984
- Solving Problems with the Explorer 986
- Solving Problems with the Personal Web Server 987
- Solving Problems Accessing Your Web: No Network Access 989
- Solving Problems Accessing Your Web on the Network 990
- Solving Problems Publishing Your Web 991
- Problems Moving Your Web 992

No matter how well-documented FrontPage 98 is or how proficient you are in using FrontPage 98, you're bound to run into problems. You can get around some of the problems by digging through the help files. You might even be able to get some help from Microsoft's Internet-based knowledge base, and although you can find the information you're looking for, it could take a while.

As with most other Microsoft products, FrontPage 98 comes with a rather extensive context-sensitive help file. To help you get used to the software, FrontPage 98 even includes its own help file to help you learn about the product. Unfortunately, the help files are broken into different components, some of which are tied to each other. This ensures that when you look up things, you'll come back to something you've already read. Unfortunately, this isn't always what you want. Sometimes you desire a different angle on your problem.

Solving Problems with the Editor

The Microsoft FrontPage Editor is a very versatile WYSIWYG HTML editor. However, using it can occasionally get a little confusing, especially for those who are new to FrontPage 98. The fact that FrontPage 98 makes extensive use of the network frequently causes problems. Fortunately, these problems aren't devastating, and you can easily get around them.

Problems Saving a Web Page

If you started the FrontPage Editor by itself (that is, not from the FrontPage Explorer), you could have a number of problems. One of the more significant ones is that it becomes extremely difficult for you to access any page on a local web. If you know the full URL for the local web page you want to work on, you can access it. Unfortunately, you won't be able to save any changes you make back to the web.

This occurs because FrontPage 98 doesn't know who you are. Consequently, it doesn't know what permissions you have. The best way to get around this problem is to start the FrontPage Explorer. When it's up and running, open the web where you want to save the page. You have to enter your user name and password to the system before you can access any pages. Finally, assuming you have the proper permissions for that web, you'll be able to save your work. If your administrator account is the only account that FrontPage 98 knows, your name will automatically be inserted into the user name field when trying to log into FrontPage 98.

NOTE

The user name and password are case sensitive. This means that if you enter `Administrator` as your user name, the system will not accept `administrator`. This is also true of your password. The confusion arises from the fact the user name in Windows 95/NT is not case-sensitive.

Image Map Display Problem

FrontPage 98 enables you to create client-side image maps right on a Web page. Traditionally, image maps were implemented with a number of files that, when used together, made up the image map. The problem with this approach is that some Web browsers, such as text-based browsers, couldn't handle image maps. Also, people with slow Internet connections who turned off the automatic image loading feature had the same problem. Client-side image maps implement image map capability from within a Web document itself. Consequently, it is suddenly possible for everybody to access an image map. Chapter 21, "Creating and Designing Image Maps," gives you more information about what image maps are used for and how to create them.

If you're creating a client-side image map, it's possible that you won't see the clickable regions. Don't panic. All your hotspots are still in place; you just can't see them. When you put an image on your Web page, the FrontPage Editor suddenly has two display modes: the Web page and the image map. The Web page display mode is shown when you click anywhere on your Web page outside an image. You can navigate through the Web page, and everything you do takes place on it. However, if you move your mouse cursor over an image map hotspot, nothing shows up. The image map display mode shows you the entire Web page as well, but all the links for the image map become visible. If you don't see any image map regions, simply click inside an image and everything should be fine.

Forms and Text

If you're designing complex Web pages, you probably want to add form fields. Unfortunately, because form fields are rather complicated, it's possible that you might not get the results you want. Probably the most common problem you'll encounter when working with forms is trying to put forms and text in the same line. By default, when you create a form field, FrontPage 98 puts it on its own line as its own object. You can't move the form field object into another line with text or graphics. As a result, it might not seem possible to put forms and text on the same line. This is a limitation within FrontPage 98 and not the HTML format itself.

If you're faced with such a situation, don't despair. You *can* put in a form field on the same line as text. When you insert a form field, it isn't inserted into the document at the cursor location. It's inserted into the next blank line after your cursor. If you want to add text before or after the form field, you must create the form field first. After that, you can position your text cursor in the form field region and type in the text you want. This method enables you to put form fields before and after the text in the form field region.

Solving Problems with the Explorer

The best way to minimize the number of problems you might encounter with the FrontPage Editor is to use the FrontPage Explorer. The Explorer takes care of a number of access problems you might encounter with the Editor. However, while you're getting around some problems for the FrontPage Editor, you're getting new problems for the Explorer.

Problems Accessing a Local Web

Suppose you want to add something to a page on your web but can't. A number of problems could be impeding you. First, check to make sure you have an account in the web. If you don't have an account, you'll have to talk to your Web administrator or Webmaster. He can create a Web authoring account for you for the web in question. This account is entirely independent of normal network or share access, and only allows access to the FrontPage web itself.

If you already have such an account, make sure you typed your user name and password correctly. Also, make sure you have an account for the web you're trying to access. Just because you have an account on one web doesn't mean you have access to all webs. This is true even if the two webs are being run from the same Web site. FrontPage 98 enables Web administrators and Webmasters to restrict where Web authors can go. It's possible that you're trying to access a web that's off-limits to you.

You might be unable to access a local web because Web authoring has been disabled. The Webmaster, or Web administrator, has the ability to disable authoring for a particular web. That's not to say that only the page you want to work on is disabled—your entire web might be down. If you're working in a group in a large company, it's possible that your group's web has authoring disabled. This isn't something to panic about because it's possible that the Webmaster is doing some maintenance on your web. He might be upgrading the software or backing up the content.

Problems Accessing Remote Web Pages

One of the most common problems with the FrontPage Explorer is accessing Web pages outside your web. You'll encounter this problem when you try to have FrontPage Explorer verify all the links in your Web page. Unfortunately, if you run into this sort of problem, there's very little you can do about it. In all likelihood, the reason you can't get a remote Web page is because of network issues. Network issues can include many things, from your Internet Service Provider suddenly failing, to the remote server not being up. The best thing to do is to eliminate all of the simple problems first, such as hardware configuration, busy phone lines, and so on. Then move on to more complex problems.

Another possible cause of this problem is that you're running FrontPage 98 from a stand-alone computer. Although FrontPage 98 attempts to connect to the Internet, if there is a connection failure during dial-up, you won't be able to access remote pages. To solve this problem, all you need to do is connect to the Internet.

Web Pages Don't Exist

Because FrontPage 98 is a multiuser environment, you might get a message from one of your colleagues. Suppose that she tells you that she just finished a Web page and that the one you're working on should link to it. If you try to access her new Web page and can't find it, the problem could lie with the FrontPage Explorer.

The FrontPage Explorer loads in the attributes for a particular web when you first access it. This means that if changes are made after you first accessed the web, they won't be seen. Fortunately, you can force the FrontPage Explorer to update the attributes for the current web. This can be done by selecting Tools|Recalculate Hyperlinks from FrontPage Explorer, causing FrontPage 98 to reevaluate all the links and data information for the currently loaded web.

You might also want to use View|Refresh, which updates the current view in the FrontPage Explorer. When you refresh a web, FrontPage 98 checks for pages that have been added or deleted since the web was first accessed.

Solving Problems with the Personal Web Server

The Personal Web Server that comes with FrontPage 98 is a limited version of Microsoft's Internet Information Server (IIS). It features an easy-to-use interface and is fairly easy to run. That's not to say it's a perfect Web server, but the Personal Web Server is at least familiar to veteran Webmasters. Still, when something goes wrong, it might not be easy to fix. The FrontPage Web Server Administrator program doesn't give you an option to work on the files directly. Consequently, you might have to break out a text editor and directly modify the configuration files.

Changing Port Numbers

Although changing port numbers isn't a problem, it is certainly a commonly requested feature. To change the port number of a Web server, you first have to shut down the server that you want to change the port number for. You can do this by double-clicking the Web server icon on the taskbar, selecting the Startup tab, and then clicking the button labeled Stop. Next, start a text editor and modify that Web server's `httpd.cnf` file. However, before changing anything you should make a backup, such as `httpd.bak`, so as to have something to fall back on in case of emergency. Go to the entry that states `Port` and change the value from `80` to some other number, such as `8080`.

By default, Web servers "listen" to port 80 of all machines. However, you might want to change it to suit your particular setup. Situations in which you want a different port number include running a multihoming environment, running a Web server through a firewall, and similar circumstances. Whatever the case may be, changing a port number is easy, but not intuitive. After you save the configuration file, you can restart the server. If you are changing ports, you should probably select one above 6000, so that it doesn't clash with an existing service.

While this isn't a hard and fast rule, it can prevent you from having to diagnose a mystery service outage later. The danger in changing your port number might limit your potential audience, however. A user's browser points to port 80 by default, and it won't know to look for the port to which you've reassigned your HTTP services.

Problems with Internet Information Server

The Internet Information Server (IIS) is a very good intranet package. It offers FTP, Gopher, and Web services in a package that's easy to work with. Your organization could very well be running the Internet Information Server (IIS), and as a result, you might want to have FrontPage 98 hook into it. Fortunately, Microsoft made a FrontPage extension for the Internet Information Server. If you're having problems installing the IIS extension, you simply might not be using the most current version of IIS or the server extensions. Make sure you're using the most current version of IIS and the server extensions.

NOTE

The latest version of the FrontPage server extensions can be found on Microsoft's Web site at `http://www.microsoft.com/frontpage`. Unfortunately though, there is no real method of applying the upgrade remotely. This means you have to run the upgrade locally on whatever server you wish to change.

Problems Accessing Web Pages

As a Webmaster, you might receive complaints about inaccessible Web pages, either on your server or at a remote site. These problems are different; after all, one is a problem with your site, and the other is a possible problem with another site. However, they are similar problems and have some similar solutions.

An internal Web page might be inaccessible because the web in question is password protected. Although you, the Webmaster, can enable or disable password protection on a web, so can Web administrators. It's possible that the Web administrator for the page in question has made his web protected. You can easily get around a page access problem by disabling password protection for a web. This can be done by loading the web in question into the FrontPage Explorer. Next, select Tools|Permissions and choose the Users tab. Simply disable the web password protection and quit the Explorer.

There are four basic classes of security available to FrontPage 98. The first is the administrator class, which has no access restrictions whatsoever. The second is the author class, which can modify files within a particular web, but not necessarily every web. Authors don't have access to administrative functions. Third comes browser, which is essentially an average user who can read files from within a web, but can't influence them in any way. Last comes restricted, which is a user with no access at all and can neither read nor write within that particular web.

There are two ways to create user accounts, depending on how you have security set up for your FrontPage 98 installation. The first is to use the FrontPage Server Administrator to create an account. The problem with this lies in the fact that all accounts created by the Server Administrator are themselves administrator accounts. In order to create more flexible accounts, you need to wean the security away from the Server Administrator and grant control to FrontPage itself.

You do so by loading up the web you wish to modify from the File menu. From there, go to Tools|Permissions. In the Permissions tab, click Use unique permissions for this web. Then click the Apply button. You've now handed control over security for this over to FrontPage. You can create any of the classes of users by clicking the next tab, Users. From there you can create, edit, or remove users as you desire. In order to restrict users you need to go to the last tab, Computers. This allows you to block users wholesale by their IP address and domain names.

If your users also have problems trying to access external Web pages, you must make sure that the host computer of the web in question is actually up. You can verify this by using the standard UNIX utility `ping` and accessing the remote host. If there is no response, the host could be down, or routing to that host could be unavailable. To make sure your site isn't at fault, try to `ping` a computer outside your domain. If it succeeds, it's probably a network problem with the destination host. If it fails, your network connection could be down. You should contact your organization's Internet Service Provider (ISP) and report your problem.

NOTE

For security reasons, many UNIX servers do not allow ping requests to be processed. If a server is hit by several thousand ping requests within a second it can easily crash the server.

A possible cause for Web page access problems both in and out of your site is the proxy server. If your organization uses a proxy server in conjunction with a firewall, the proxy server could be at fault. It could be offline or misconfigured to disallow any communication on port 80, the default port for HTTP. You should talk with your network administrator to verify that the proxy server is running properly. If it is, also have him check to see if proxy servicing is enabled for the ports on which the Personal Web Server is running.

Solving Problems Accessing Your Web: No Network Access

Even though FrontPage 98 was designed to work on a network, it works fine if you're not on one. However, if you're not on a network, you can still have some problems. The most common problem is that webs on the FrontPage server aren't available.

Can't Access a Local Web

If you're trying to access an existing web and you just started a machine, you might have problems. Typically, the Personal Web Server starts up automatically when needed. Sometimes, however, the server doesn't start up immediately and you get an erroneous message that says the server isn't available.

It's not that the server won't start up, but that it starts up too late. Consequently, it's possible that you'll get an error message about a Web server not running on a particular port. Because the Personal Web Server is automatically started when needed, it should be running after you get the error message. If not, simply start the Web server manually. A typical install would place the Personal Web Server executable in `c:\Program Files\Websvr\System\Inetsw95.exe`, if you need to start it manually. After you've confirmed that the Personal Web Server is up and running, try to access the web again. If this happens repeatedly, the underlying problem might be that you don't have enough memory. Make sure that your system has the recommended amount of memory. If it doesn't, seriously consider getting more memory. Personal Web Server requires roughly 1 megabyte of RAM to operate comfortably; if you find your operating system and various programs use too much memory, upgrade.

Can't Open a Web

When you're not on a network, you might sometimes have difficulty starting the FrontPage Editor. This often happens because you have the Personal Web Server and FrontPage Explorer already running. If you try to open a particular Web page, you get an error message about certain modules not being able to run. Although FrontPage 98 recommends that you quit other running applications, that might not be enough.

This problem occurs because, once again, the system you're running has insufficient memory. That's not to say it doesn't have enough physical RAM, but not enough total memory. It's possible that the drive Windows 95 is using for the swap file is filled. You should delete unnecessary files from that particular drive and then try to access the web. FrontPage's minimum system requirement is 12MB of memory. Make sure that you have at least that much in combined physical and virtual memory.

Solving Problems Accessing Your Web on the Network

After you have FrontPage 98 up and running on a network, an intranet, or the Internet, you might still run into problems accessing your web. From time to time, you'll probably get reports about users having problems accessing one of your webs. The Internet is basically a series of interconnected computers, all talking to each other. If one of those computers between you and the person reporting the problem goes down, the network will seemingly go down. Consequently, it's likely that your web will not always be accessible to everyone at all times.

As a result, if you get one or two e-mails complaining about inaccessibility of your web, you can probably ignore them.

On the other hand, if you receive e-mail about your web from a number of different people, there's probably a problem. You should first check your network connection. Using the UNIX utility `ping`, try to reach a random set of computers outside your network. If you can't reach any of them, it could be that you or your ISP are having problems. You also can attempt to track down the specific host that's giving you problems by using the `traceroute` UNIX utility. Whereas `ping` just tells you if it can talk to another computer, `traceroute` tells you how it's getting there. You should inform your network administrator about what you've found as soon you have results.

`traceroute` traces the path that a packet would take in getting from your computer to whatever server you're connected to. It tells you all of the computers that the packet passes through on its route, and how it takes to complete that route. Each journey between machines is known as a hop, with the fewer hops existing between you and your server, the better. The Windows 95 command `tracert` will produce the same results as the UNIX `traceroute`.

Another possible problem arises if you're in a multihoming environment. After you've checked your network connection, you should check each of the computers you're multihoming. Make sure that the Web servers are running on each of those systems. Also, you should check to make sure that the FrontPage extensions are properly installed on each of those systems.

If your system can talk to the Internet and you're still having problems, you might want to look at your proxy server (if you have one). Proxy servers are used, often in conjunction with firewalls, to help watch over network traffic. This is often simply monitoring the traffic between the organization and the Internet. If you are using a proxy server, it's possible that the server has malfunctioned, shut down, or crashed. Whatever the case may be, you should report your problem to the network administrator as soon as possible.

When your Personal Web Server is on the Internet, another problem you might face is an unavailable page. In this case, you should use the FrontPage Explorer, load the web in question, and try to find the page itself. If the page isn't available, you have a dead link. Update the link or notify the person in charge of the web to update the link.

Solving Problems Publishing Your Web

When you try to publish your web, you may run into problems with communications. Before authors can publish their Web pages, they have to be able to communicate with your Web server. If they are complaining that their system isn't established to the Personal Web Server, there could be a few problems. One of the most basic problems occurs when the author isn't logged onto your network. This is especially true if you work for an Internet Service Provider where people dial into your system. Although FrontPage 98 does initiate the dial-up routine, it's possible that the user failed to connect to the Internet and can't upload his Web page because of this connection failure. Make sure the user is logged on to your system to begin with.

Another possible difficulty is that there's a problem between your system and the author's. You can check the network connection through the usual suite of tools. If you're working at an ISP, you probably won't be able to check the connectivity to the author's computer. However, you can have the telephone company check the telephone connection between the remote modem and your company's computer. If there are any problems with the connectivity, they should fix it automatically. If they determine that the connection between your company's building and the remote modem is fine, you should check your building's telephone wiring. (Obviously, checking telephone wiring requires a trained professional from the telephone company.)

One of the most typical methods of publishing your Web pages with FrontPage 98 is to publish the web. That is, the Web author loads his web into the FrontPage Explorer and tries to copy it to the external Web server. This method is a good one because it enables each author to develop his pages independently. This also enables authors to test everything on their systems, minimally impacting the Web server itself. However, because it's probable that you'll have authors from all over the world, the Internet is involved. What this means is that there could be network problems while an author is trying to publish his Web page.

If a few authors can't publish their Web pages, you should check the network connection. Check the network connection between the Web server and the author's computer. You can use the usual `ping` and `traceroute` utilities to help you. It's also possible that the drive with the web content is filled up, and the copy operation is failing. The obvious solution to this problem is to delete or move unneeded files.

Problems Moving Your Web

A possibility exists that you won't always be with the same Internet Service Provider. It's also possible that you won't be working for the same company forever. Consequently, there might come a time when you need to move your web. This obviously only extends to your personal webs because you won't have access to your group's web when you leave. Those duties will be given to someone else to maintain and update.

Missing Files

While you're creating Web pages, you'll almost definitely create links. There are a number of acceptable protocols that a URL can take, such as `gopher://`, `ftp://`, and so on. Another such protocol is `file://`, which refers to a file on the local computer's drive. The file that's going to be accessed isn't the one stored on the server's hard drive, but rather on the client's. Although this might not be used very often on the Internet itself, it's more likely to be used on intranets. It might be practical to have a URL point to a common network drive and access a particular document.

As a result of the way the `file://` protocol behaves, when you move the web, you might suddenly have some broken links. FrontPage 98 usually does a good job of keeping track of which files go where, but the `file://` protocol can easily be overlooked while you're moving your web. Be sure to check your web for any URLs that use the `file://` protocol and manually copy the files over.

Unable to Connect to Web Server

This connection problem typically arises when you move or copy the Web server somewhere else. Some web authors may have hard-coded the address of the Web server. That is, they've put the actual host name in a URL that they used in a link to a file on the same server. Consequently, when you move the web to a new computer and a new host name, those links could very well break. This is especially true if the old Web server has been given to another person. When people try to access once-valid links, they'll try to talk to the old computer. That system might not even be running the Personal Web Server, let alone have the same content.

To fix this problem, first take the old Web server completely off the network. Next, start the Personal Web Server on the new computer and have FrontPage 98 verify all links. If there are any broken links, they are probably due to the hard-coding of the old host name. Correct the problem by eliminating the `http://` protocol and then simply refer to the web from the top level. This makes it easier if, and when, you move the web in the future.

I
Index

Symbols

#htaccess.cnf file listing, 856
*** operator (VBScript), 584**
+ operator (VBScript), 583
- operator (VBScript), 584
/ operator (VBScript), 584
<!--...--> tags, 191
^ operator (VBScript), 584
2D Layout with dynamic HTML, 673

A

<A> (HTML tag), 192
absolute positioning (page elements), 673
absolute values, 149, 172
AbsolutePage property (Recordset objects), 731
AbsolutePosition property (Recordset objects), 731
access
 access.cnf file, 854-856
 administrator accounts, 839
 authentication, 842-843
 author accounts, 839
 browse accounts, 839
 firewalls, 817
 global permissions, 840
 groups, 569-570
 restricted Webs, 560-561
 unique permissions, 841
 Web servers, 822-823, 902
Access 97
 creating
  data tables, 743-747
  databases, 742-749
  files, 749-752
 defining ODBC data sources, 748-749
 designing databases, 743
access keys (form fields), 670
access.cnf file, 854-856
accounts
 computer, 566-569
 user
  adding/removing, 881, 888
  administrator, 839, 884
  author, 839
  browse, 839
  creating, 565-566
  enabling/disabling privileges, 881, 884, 887
  passwords, assigning, 566
  privileges, 566
Active Channels, 694
active elements
 banners
  alignment, 228
  images, 229-230
  linking, 229-230
  size, 227-228
  transitions, 228-229
 hit counters
  alignment, 216
  setup, 216-217
 hover buttons
  audio, 227
  coloring, 225-226
  effects, 226
  images, 227
  linking, 225
  size, 225-226
  text, 225
 marquees
  alignment, 218-219
  animation, 219-220
  colors, 219
  size, 219
 plug-ins
  borders, 224
  embedded, 223
  functionality, 221-223
  hiding, 223
  icons, 224
  priorities, 224
  properties, 224
  seams, 222
  size, 223
  spacing, 224
Active Elements command (Insert menu), 216
Active Hyperlink property, 61
Active Server Pages
 ADO (ActiveX Database Objects), 891
 database
  connectivity, 709-710
  search forms, 723-724
 Database Region Wizard, 710
 NRS.mdb database example, 775
 tracking user sessions, 765
 Visual InterDev
  creating, 774-775
  options, 764
ActiveMovie control, 609, 612
ActiveX
 controls
  ActiveMovie, 609
  adding to webs, 607-608
  Calendar, 609, 613
  changing with VBScript, 613
  Code Source, 609

colors, 610
common controls, 605-606
data sources (URLs), 609
design-time, 766
editing, 610
events, 618-619
functions, 616
known, 609
layout, 608
Macromedia Flash control, 609
methods, 615-617
Microsoft Forms 2.0 controls, 606
Microsoft SiteBuilder Network, 603
Netscape NCompass Script Active, 603
new control settings, 611-612
placing on webs, 605-606, 609
properties, 608
security levels, 603
self-registration, 609
text, 610
unique, 609
Visual InterDev database access, 773
documents, 602
scripting, 602
server framework, 601
technology, 600-601
VBScript interactions, 613
ActiveX Database Objects, see ADO
Add Choice dialog box, 416
Add Computer dialog box, 568
Add File to Import List dialog box, 112
Add Pictures to Clip Gallery dialog box, 262
Add Users dialog box, 566
addition operator (JavaScript), 630
address text, adding to documents, 103
<ADDRESS> (HTML tag), 192
administration
server extensions
fpremadm utility, 885-888
fpwinsvr utility, 882-884
fpsvradm utility, 877-882
local, 876-877
remote, 884-885
Resource Kit tools, 876
Web servers, 856-857
administrator accounts, 839, 884
ADO (ActiveX Database Objects), 725, 891
collections, 727
Command objects, 733
Connection objects, 727
example, 734-737
object model, 726
opening connections, 735
Parameters collection, 734
Recordset objects, 728-730
example, 736
Visual InterDev usage, 771
Advanced Form Properties dialog box, 408
Advanced toolbar
FrontPage Editor, 48
Insert Java Applet button, 648
Adventure Works Products table (database search forms), 718
alignment
banners, 228
hit counters, 216
images, 121-125
Java applets, 648
marquees, 218-219
plug-ins, 224
properties, 148
sprites, 314-315
style sheets, 196-197
tables, 143, 147
captions, 144
cell data, 148
text, 69-70
All Files view (FrontPage Explorer), 17-18
alpha channel (Image Composer), 275
ALT attribute (<WEBBOT> tag), 924-925
Altamira Composer, 274
anchors (links), 72-73
Animated Art (Netscape Web site), 383
Animated GIF Artists Guild Web site, 383
animation (GIF Animator)
Animation tab, 377-378
background, 361-365, 379
comments, 378-380
conceptual overview, 359-360
dithering, 377
drag-and-drop, 376
duration, 378
flying effects, 665

foreground, 365-366
frames
count, 378
creating, 366-368
inserting, 374
loading, 370-372
troubleshooting size, 382
Image Composer, 374
Image tab, 378-380
layering, 365-366
looping, 378
marquees, 219-220
Options tab, 376-377
positioning images, 380-381
previewing, 375-376
size, 377
smoothness, 383
stationary, 381-382
text, dynamic HTML effects, 664-667
toolbar, 373-376
transparency, 380
undrawing, 379
viewpoint, 381
Web sites, 383
Animation tab (GIF Animator), 377-378
Animator applet, 660
annotation bot, 102
API Test Utility, 919
Applet Base URL property (Java applets), 658
applet editor, configuring for FrontPage, 653
Applet Source field (Java Applet Properties dialog box), 648
<APPLET> (HTML tag), 192
example, 661
inserting into webs, 647
applets (Java), 644
alignment, 648
Animator, 660
applet editor, configuring, 653
applications comparison, 647
bytecode verification, 645
classes
color, 656
declaring, 655
font, 656
Graphics, 655
Image, 659
compiling, 653-654
creating, 650, 654-656
displaying, 655
embedding, 647
file access restrictions, 645
graphics, sizing, 660
memory layout control, 645
methods
destroy, 657
drawImage, 660
getImage, 659
Graphics.set, 656
init, 657
paint, 655
start, 657
stop, 657
MyApplet example, 658
non-Java browser issues, 650
parameters, 649, 657
platform independence, 645
properties, 648, 658
safety issues, 644
screening at firewall, 645
showPict, 661
spacing options, 649
testing, 656
AppletViewer, 661
applications (Java)
applets comparison, 647
compiling, 653
Arcs theme (NavDemo web), 790
arithmetic operators
JavaScript, 630-631
VBScript, 583-584
Arrange palette (Image Composer tool), 312
arrays
JavaScript, 628
VBScript, 582
Arts & Crafts (Effects palette category), 322
ASCII text format, converting to HTML, 41-42
assignment operators (JavaScript), 633
attributes
ALT (<WEBBOT>) tag, 924-925
images, 128-129
TAG (<WEBBOT>) tag, 925
webs, changing, 28
audio
hover buttons, 227
streaming (NetShow), 891
authentication, see security
author accounts, 839
authoring, troubleshooting, 986
authors (Webmasters), 846
automatic updating, webs, 804
automation (OLE), 916
Editor
bringing Editor to front, 970

creating pages (listing), 969
querying Editor, 970-971
Explorer
creating Web (listing), 968
opening Web (listing), 966-967
removing Web (listing), 968-969
identifiers, 959
To Do List
adding tasks, 971-972
marking tasks complete, 973
wizards, 958-959
AutoPlay CD-ROM (FrontPage 98 installation), 978
AutoThumbnail command (FrontPage Editor), 45

B

Back button, adding to navigation bar, 798
background
animation, 361-365, 379
colors
copying, 58
setting, 57-58
style sheets, 204-205
tables, 150
Web pages, 59-61
images, 115-116
clip art, 117
keywords, 206-207
repeating, 205
style sheets, 205-207
tables, 151-152
tiling, 117
transparency, 341
transparency, 135-136
washout, 346
Background tab (Page Properties dialog box)
background colors, setting, 57-61
background images, 58-59
text and link colors, 61
Badger's Animated GIF Gallery Web site, 383
Banner Ad Manager, 227
banner and contents template, 179-180
banner template, 161-162
banners
alignment, 228
image maps (navigation bar), 164
images, 229-230
linking, 229-230
size, 227-228
transitions, 228-229
see also marquees
Base Location property, 56-57
BBSs (bulletin board systems), 497-498
BeginTrans method (Connection objects), 729
Bevel button (image toolbar), 348-349
bevels (images), 348-349
Bibliography template, 474
Bill's Animated GIF Collection Web site, 383
black and white images, 346
blinking text, 95
Blocking parameter (wizards), 953
BLOCKQUOTE element, 69-70
<BLOCKQUOTE> (HTML tag), 192
BOF property (Recordset objects), 731
bookmarks
deleting, 79
direct paths, 76
editing, 79
labeling, 79
links, 79-80
relative paths, 75
visiting, 80
borderless frames
creating, 175-177
design, 177-179
templates
banner and contents template, 179-180
contents template, 180
footer template, 180-181
footnotes template, 180-181
header, footer, and contents template, 181-182
header template, 180-181
nested three-level hierarchy template, 183
split templates, 182
top-down three-level hierarchy template, 182
borders
images, 128-129
padding, 211-212
pixels, 147
plug-ins, 224
style sheets, 211-212
tables, 143

bots, 10
bottom-left fly-in text animation, 665
bounding box (sprites), 313
Break Properties window, 91
break statements (JavaScript), 638
brightness (images), 347-348
broken links
- deleting, 805
- redirecting, 807

browse accounts, 839
browsers, 52
- behavior control (JavaScript options), 641
- Browser type field (form output), 436-437
- configuring for fplaunch applications, 920-921
- inline images, 109
- root web, accessing, 15
- style sheets support, 188-189
- testing
  - *for JavaScript compatibility, 625*
  - *Webs, 911-912*

Brush Designer (Image Composer), 303-304
brushes, customizing, 303-304
bulleted lists, 81-84
bulletin board systems, see BBSs, 497
buttons, VBScript uses, 577
bytecode verification (Java applets), 645

C

C/C++ (CGI scripts), 443-444
calculation scripts (VBScript), 578
calculations (JavaScript), 630-633
Calendar control, 609
- command buttons, 616-617
- properties, 613-614

<CAPTION> (HTML tag), 192
captions (tables), 144
Captions Properties dialog box, 144
Cascading Style Sheets, see style sheets
categories (Clip Gallery)
- creating, 258-260
- deleting, 260-261
- editing, 257-261
- naming, 261
- organizing, 257-258

CD-ROM (FrontPage 98 installation), 978
CDF files (Channel Definition Format), 679
Cell Properties dialog box, 148
cells (tables)
- color, 151
- data, 148
- heading, 148
- height drawing tool, 142
- merging, 147
- padding, 143, 147
- properties, advanced settings, 148-150
- selecting, 145, 150
- spacing, 147
- splitting, 145-146
- width drawing tool, 142

cells spacing (tables), 143
CGI (Common Gateway Interface), 428
- directories, 440
- scripts, 439-440
  - *benefits, 445*
  - *C/C++, 443-444*
  - *choosing language for, 440-441*
  - *Developer's Kit, 922-923*
  - *execution, 446*
  - *including in forms, 446*
  - *Perl, 444-445*
  - *providing path to, 447*
  - *security, 838-839*
  - *UNIX shell languages, 441-443*

Change Location dialog box, 26, 490
Channel Definition Wizard, 680-681
channels (push channels), 678-680
- alpha, 275
- as screen savers, 685
- channel item properties, 684
- content design, 691
- creating (Channel Definition Wizard), 680-681
- description, 681
- e-mail updates, 685
- example listing, 679
- item properties, 684
- logging targets, 686
- magazines, 691
- multiple channels, 688-690
- newsletters, 691
- newspapers, 691
- reference sources, 693
- scheduling options, 685

source folders, 682
tutorials, 693
updating, 692
Web site examples, 692
character entities, 102-103
character style tags (HTML), 94-95
check boxes, 412-414
child pages, 785, 791
Choose Theme dialog box, 235
Citation style, 96
classes
Java, inheritance, 657
Java applets
color, 656
declaring, 654-655
font, 656
Graphics, 655
Image, 659
subdirectory (storage), 647
VBScript, system, 594
clickable labels (forms), 670
clients, image maps, 388-390
clip art, 117
Clip Art Gallery, 8, 110
Clip Gallery
categories
creating, 258-260
deleting, 260-261
editing, 257-261
naming, 261
organizing, 257-258
clip packages, importing, 265
Find feature, 254-255
FrontPage 97 clip art, importing, 268-269
image formats, 250-252
images, 252-253
adding, 262
Clip Gallery Live, 265-268
deleting, 262
importing, 262-265
keywords
creating, 256
deleting, 257
editing, 255-257
previews, deleting, 269
Update feature, 269-271
Clip Gallery Live Web site, 265-268
Clip Properties dialog box, 255
Clipart command (Insert menu), 252
Clipboard
images, 115
sprites, 312
Close method (Connection objects), 728
closed Webs
computer accounts (creating), 566-569
passwords, 566
privileges, 565-566
user accounts (creating), 565-566
code, adding comments, 101-102
Code Source property (ActiveX controls), 609
Code style, 96
collapsible outlines, 87-88, 668
collections
ADO, 727
Fields, 730
Color dialog box, 61
Color Enhancement
(Effects palette category), 323
color maps, 133-134
Color Picker dialog box, 288, 352
color swatch (Image Composer), 280-282
colors
ActiveX control properties, 610
background colors, 59-61
copying, 58
setting, 57-58
color amps, 133-134
custom, 61-62
custom palettes, 352-354
Effects palette Color Enhancement tool, 323
hover buttons, 225-226
images, 126
Java applet classes, 656
marquees, 219
sprites, 288
style sheets, 204-207
tables, 150-151
text
sprites, 290
style sheets, 204-205
themes, 246-247
Web pages, 61-63
themes, 238, 243-244
columns (tables)
drawing tool, 142
inserting, 144-146
merging, 147
width, 140, 149
command buttons
Calendar control, 616
dialog boxes (VBScript), 578
command line
fpsvradm options, 878-879
options, 857-859
Personal Web Server administration, 857-859

Command objects, 733
command-line AppletViewer, 662
command-line Java compiler, 654
commands
Edit menu, Hyperlink, 109
File menu
Composition Setup, 361
Import, 112
Save As, 306-307
Save Copy As, 308
Save for the Web, 308
Save Selection As, 307-308
Scan Image, 312
Format menu
Font, 339
Stylesheet, 191
Themes, 235
Frame menu
Delete Frame, 159
Split Frame, 159
Image Composer, 278-279, 282-285
Insert menu
Active Elements, 216
Clipart, 252
Image, 109
Table menu
Insert Caption, 144
Insert Rows or Columns, 144
Insert Table, 141-143
Table Properties, 147
Tools menu
GIF Animator, 360
Options, 333
Permissions, 988
Recalculate Hyperlinks command, 987
Show Image Editor, 275
Web Settings, 389
View menu
Image Toolbar, 336
Options, 119
Refresh, 987
Toolbars, 279
Comment component, 546
comments
adding to documents, 101-102
animation, 378-380
JavaScript, 629
VBScript, 587
CommerceNet Web site, 899
CommitTrans method (Connection objects), 729
Common Gateway Interface, see CGI, 428
common targets, 174-175
comparison operators
JavaScript, 632
VBScript, 585
compiling Java applets, 653-654
components
adding, 546
Comment, 546
Confirmation Field, 546
associating fields with values, 548-549
creating form, 549
URL (setting), 550
Confirmation Field WebBot, 435
extensions
server, 547-548
WebBot, 923-925
FrontPage, 9-10
Hit Counter, 546
Include Page, 479, 546
inserting, 551, 554
start/end dates, 555
updating webs, 813
URLs (entering), 552-554
Insert HTML, 547
installation, 979
Page Banner, 547
Registration, 563-564
Scheduled Image, 547
image URL (entering), 553
inserting, 552-553
start/end dates, 553-554
Scheduled Include Page, 547
Search bot, 461
adding to Webs, 463-465
server extensions, 465
when to use, 465-466
Substitution, 547
configuration variables, 555-557
inserting, 555
web update variables, 813
updating, 547
Web server compatibility, 901-902
WebBots, 766-767
Composition Setup command (File menu), 361
Composition Setup dialog box, 362
compositions, see sprites
compression
lossy, 131
LZW, 130
computer accounts, creating, 566-569

conditional expressions (JavaScript), 636
conditional instructions (VBScript), 587-588
conditional statements (JavaScript), 635-636
configuration variables (Substitution component)
  built-in, 555-556
  defining, 556-557
Configure Editors dialog box, 34-35
Configure External Viewer dialog box, 268
configuring
  FrontPage for multihomed system, 871-873
  Java applet editor, 653
  Personal Web Server
    access.cnf file settings, 854-856
    editing files, 847-848
    httpd.cnf file settings, 848-849
    mime.typ file settings, 852-853
    srm.cnf file settings, 849-851
  Search bot, 463-465
Confirmation Field component, 546
  associating fields with values, 548-549
  creating form, 549
  URL (setting), 550
Confirmation Field WebBot, 435
Confirmation Form template, 476
confirmation pages (guest books), 483
connection errors (opening webs), 27
Connection objects
  BeginTrans method, 729
  Close method, 728
  CommitTrans method, 729
  example, 734-737
  Execute method, 728
  Open method, 728
  properties, 727-729
  RollbackTrans method, 729
  transaction management, 729
Connection tab (Internet Database Connector Wizard), 716
connectivity
  options for databases, 714-715
  troubleshooting, 992-993
content design (push channels), 691
contents pages, 161-164
contents template, 161-162, 180
continue statements (JavaScript), 638
contrast (images), 347
controls
  ActiveMovie, 609, 612
  ActiveX, 601-603
  Calendar, 609
  Data Range Header, 766
  Label, 612
  Macromedia Flash control, 609
  Microsoft Forms 2.0 controls, 606
copying
  images, 114-115
  webs, 29
Corporate Presence Web
  contact information, 542-543
  copyright notices, 540
  Feedback form, 538-539
  headers/footers, 540-541
  home page topics, 534-536
  link options, 540
  logos, 540
  page title options, 540
  presentation styles, 543
  Products pages, 537-538
  selecting pages, 535
  Services pages, 537-538
  Table of Contents page, 539
  task list, 544
  timestamps, 540
  Under Construction icons, 541
  Webmaster address, including, 540
  What's New page, 536
Corporate Presence Wizard, 9, 25, 493, 534
countDays function (VBScript), 593
countSeconds function (VBScript), 593
crashes (Image Composer), troubleshooting, 276
Create Hyperlink dialog box, 76-77, 109
Create New Data Source dialog box, 749
creating
  images, 132
  themes, 241-243
cropping
  images, 343-344
  sprites, 313-314
CSS, see style sheets
curves (spline curves), 294-295

Custom tab (Page Properties dialog box), 64-66
Customer Support Web, 493
- Bug Reporting and Information page, 515
- Discussion area, 519
- Download page, 517
- FAQ page, 514
- Search page, 520
- Suggestions page, 516
- Technical Notes page, 521
- Welcome page, 512-513
- What's New page, 513

Customer Support Web template, 25
customizing
- brushes, 303-304
- colors
  - *creating, 61-62*
  - *palettes, 352-354*
  - *properties (ActiveX controls), 611*
- feedback pages, 485
- frames, 170-173
- FrontPage 98 installation
  - *components, 979*
  - *Explorer, 981*
  - *Password Confirmation field, 981*
  - *Personal Web Server, 980*
  - *server extensions, 981*
  - *upgrading, 980*
- guest books, 481
- menus
  - *FrontPage Editor, 930-934*
  - *FrontPage Explorer, 934-937*
  - *naming, 931*
  - *planning, 929*
  - *Registry Editor, 928-930*
- themes, 241-243
- Web pages
  - *background colors, 57-61*
  - *background images, 58-59*
  - *colors, 61-62*
  - *font colors, 62-63*
  - *META properties, 64-66*
  - *text and links colors, 61*
  - *watermarks, 59*

Cutout tool (Image Composer), 296-300
cutting images, 114-115

D

data
- database search form fields, 718
- Internet Database Connector Wizard Limits tab, 717
- JavaScript, 640
- security (firewalls), 816
- sources
  - *ActiveX control URLs, 609*
  - *ODBC, 699, 702, 748-749*
- tables
  - *binding, 674*
  - *cells, 148*
- types
  - *JavaScript, 627*
  - *numeric, 456-457*
  - *text, 455-456*

Data Form Wizard (Visual InterDev), 779
Data Range controls, 776
Data Range Header control, 766
data tables (Access 97), 743-747
Data View tab (Visual InterDev), 772
Database Designer (Visual InterDev), 773
Database Region, 723
Database Region Wizard, 710-711, 759
databases
- connectivity
  - *Active Server Pages, 709-710*
  - *advanced options, 714-715*
  - *FrontPage options, 698*
  - *historical overview, 698-699*
  - *Visual InterDev differences, 767*
- creating (Access 97), 742-749
- data binding, 675
- designing (Access 97), 743
- folders, 741
- indexers, 460-461
- NRS.mdb (Visual InterDev example), 767
- outputting fields (IDC), 703
- search engines, 460
- search forms
  - *Active Server Page options, 723-725*
  - *Adventure Works Products table, 718*
  - *fields, 718*
  - *IDC files, 722*
  - *template files, 721*
  - *testing, 723*
- Visual InterDev tools, 771

DATAFLD attribute, 675

DATASRC attribute, 675
Day property (Calendar control), 614
DBMS (Database Management System), 699-700
<DD> (HTML tag), 192
declaring Java applet classes, 655
decrement operator (JavaScript), 632
default targets, 173-174
defining
- alternate source documents, 159-160
- proxies, 821
- table colors, 150

definition lists, 81-85
Definition style, 96
Delete Frame command (Frame menu), 159
deleting
- bookmarks, 79
- Clip Gallery
  - *categories, 260-261*
  - *images, 262*
  - *keywords, 257*
  - *previews, 269*
- discussion board messages, 508
- images, 115
  - *hotspots, 397*
  - *text, 340*
- links, 78
  - *broken links, 805*
  - *hyperlinks, 805*
- pages, 805
- table elements, 145
- webs, 28
  - *files, 33*
  - *variables, 812*

design-time controls
- ActiveX, 766
- Visual InterDev, 774

designer HTML, 923-925
designing
- forms, 405-406
- push channel content, 691
- Web pages, 66
- webs, 788

desktop (Image Composer), 276-277
destination parameter (wizards), 953
destination sprites, 318
destroy method (Java applets), 657
Developer's Kit, 916
- CGI scripts, 922-923
- designer HTML, 923-925
- directories, 917
  - *template, 918*
  - *wizards, 918-919*
- installing, 917
- obtaining, 917
- utilities
  - *API Test Utility, 919*
  - *fplaunch utility, 920-922*
  - *Web Template Maker, 918, 922, 946*
- WebBot extensions, 923-925

dialog boxes
- Add Choice, 416
- Add Computer, 568
- Add File to Import List, 112
- Add Pictures to Clip Gallery, 262
- Add Users, 566
- Advanced Form Properties, 408
- Captions Properties, 144
- Cell Properties, 148
- Change Location, 26, 490
- Choose Theme, 235
- Clip Properties, 255
- Color, 61
- Color Picker, 288, 352
- command buttons (VBScript), 578
- Composition Setup, 362
- Configure Editors, 34-35
- Configure External Viewer, 268
- Create Hyperlink, 76-77, 109
- Create New Data Source, 749
- Drop-Down Menu Properties, 415
- Edit Category List, 258-260
- Edit File Type, 119
- Edit Hyperlink, 397, 860
- Edit URL, 114
- Editing Action, 119
- File Format Limitation dialog box, 368
- File Save Option, 306
- Find Clip, 254
- Font, 97, 225, 339
- Font Properties, 98-100
- Form Page Wizard, 420
- Form Properties, 407
  - *Confirmation Page tab, 434-435*
  - *E-mail Results tab, 433*
  - *File Results tab, 431-433*
  - *Saved Fields tab, 436-438*
  - *Send to field, 428*
- Format Stylesheet, 191
- Frame Properties, 170
- FrontPage Component, 102

FrontPage Web Settings, 389
Getting Started, 14, 741
Hit Counter Properties, 216
Hover Button, 225
HTTP properties, 836
Image, 109
Image Properties, 110
Import File to FrontPage Web, 112
Import Web Wizard, 30
Include Page Component Properties, 479
Insert FrontPage Components, 546
Insert Rows or Columns, 144
Insert Table, 142-143
List Properties, 82, 87
Marquee Properties, 218
New Category, 258
New Color Palette, 353
New FrontPage Web, 25-26, 490
New Page, 53
ODBC Data Source Administrator, 748
ODBC Microsoft Access 97 Setup, 749
OnClick event, 578
Open FrontPage Web, 16, 27
Options, 119, 333
Options for Custom Form Handler, 446-448
Output Options, 423
Page Properties, 54, 205
Background tab, 57-61
Custom tab, 64-66
General tab, 55-57
Margins tab, 63-64
Paragraph Properties, 103
Permissions, 23
Personal Web Server Properties, 832
Plug-In Properties, 221, 224
Presentation Options, 422
Publish FrontPage Web, 29
Push Button Properties, 416
Radio Button Properties, 413
Rename Category, 261
Save As, 42
Save As Template, 945
Save Image to Web, 115
Scrolling Text Box Properties, 412
Select Background Image, 117
Show Getting Started, 741
Split Cells, 145
Split Frame, 159
Style, 205
Table Properties, 147
Target Frame, 174
Text Box Properties, 409
Toolbars, 279
Update, 270
VBScript, 577
Verify Links, 859
Web Settings, 22
Dir parameter (wizards), 953
direct paths (links), 74-76
directories
CGI, 440
Developer's Kit, 917
template, 918
wizards, 918-919
JavaApplets images subdirectory, 661
private directories, 28
templates, 940
wizards, 950
discussion form handlers, 431
discussion groups
boards
access restrictions, 501
Discussion Web Wizard, 498
features, 499-500
message display, 503
search results, 502
submission forms, 500-501
Table of Contents, 501
themes, 502
creating, 498-501
file location, 506-507
messages
deleting, 508
modifying, 509
posting, 504-505
open-ended, 496-497
restricted, 497-498
selecting type, 498
threading, 506
Discussion Web Wizard, 25, 493, 498-500
displayError subroutine (VBScript), 594
displaying Java applets, 655
Distort (Effects palette category), 323-324
dithering
animation, 377
images, 351
dividing frames, 158-159
division operators (JavaScript), 631
<DL> (HTML tag), 192
DNS (Domain Name Service), 818
Do Until loops (VBScript), 591

Do While loops (VBScript), 590
document formats (FrontPage Editor), 41
document type definitions (DTDs), 52
documents
ActiveX, 602
bookmarks
deleting, 79
direct paths, 76
editing, 79
labeling, 79
links, 79-80
relative paths, 75
character style tags (HTML), 94-95
comments, adding, 101-102
fonts
sizes, 99-101
types, 98-99
HEAD element, 54-55
hidden documents, displaying, 28
horizontal lines, 92-94
line breaks, 90
non-breaking spaces, 92
properties, setting, 91
lists
bulleted lists, 81-84
definition lists, 81-85
glossary lists, 84-85
nesting, 87-88
numbered lists, 81, 85-86
types, 80-82
types, changing, 87-88
spell-checking, 22
style formats, 95-97
text
address, 103
blinking, 95
formatted, 104-105
special characters, 102-103
subscript, 98
superscript, 98
titles, defining, 55-56
word art, 100
see also Web pages
DOM (Document Object Model), 671
downloading server extensions, 893
Dr.Fun's Page of Animations Web site, 383
drag-and-drop
animation, 376
interface (FrontPage Explorer), 5
Draw Table tool, 141
drawImage method (Java applets), 660
drawing tables, 141-142
drawing tool, 142
Driver Specific tab (IDC Wizard), 717
Drop-Down Menu Properties dialog box, 415
drop-down menus
adding selections, 416
properties, 415
validating, 453
DSN files (Visual InterDev), 768
DSOs (Data Source Objects), 675
<DT> (HTML tag), 192
DTDs (document type definitions), 52
dynamic HTML
content, 672
data binding, 674
Document Object Model, 671
issues and concerns in use, 670-671
outlining, 668
styles, 671-672
text animation, 664-665

E

e-mail
push channel updates, 685
sending form output as, 429, 433
Edit Category List dialog box, 258-260
Edit File Type dialog box, 119
Edit Hyperlink dialog box, 397, 860
Edit menu
command, Hyperlink, 109
FrontPage Editor, 44
FrontPage Explorer, 21
Edit URL dialog box, 114
editing
bookmarks, 79
Clip Gallery
categories, 257-261
keywords, 257
frames, 171
guest books, 480
hotspots, 394-397
navigation bars, 797
properties (ActiveX controls), 610
push channels, 682
style sheets, 193-194
table elements, 145-147
themes, 241-243
webs, 28
wizard pages, 492
Editing Action dialog box, 119
Editing parameter (wizards), 953

Editor (FrontPage)
bookmarks
deleting, 79
direct paths, 76
editing, 79
labeling, 79
links, 79-80
relative paths, 75
visiting, 80
bulleted lists, 82-84
definition lists, 85
files, saving, 42
heading levels, 67
inline frames editor, 6-7
links
creating, 76-77
deleting, 78
following, 78
menus
custom, 930-934
Edit menu, 44
File menu, 43-44
Format menu, 45
Frame menu, 46
Go menu, 45
Help menu, 46
Insert menu, 45
Table menu, 46
Tools menu, 45-46
View menu, 44-45
Window menu, 46
numbered lists, 86
OLE automation
bringing Editor to front, 970
creating pages (listing), 969
querying Editor, 970-971
opening files, 40-42
pages, 39-40
starting, 38
tables, 141-143
toolbars, 47-48
troubleshooting, 984-985
views, 38-39
Web pages, 53-54
editors, files, 34-35
effect colors (hover buttons), 226
Effects palette
applying effects, 321-322
categories
Arts & Crafts, 321-322
Color Enhancement, 323
Distort, 323-324
Gradient, 324-326
Outlines, 327
Paint, 327-328
Patterns, 328-329
Photographic, 329-331
Sketch, 331
Surface, 332
opacity, 321
else statements (JavaScript), 635
ElseIf statements (VBScript), 588
<EMBED> (HTML tag), 192
embedding
Java applets, 647
plug-ins, 223
Empty web, 493
Empty Web template, 25
Empty Web Wizard, 790
entities, 102-103
environment parameters (wizards), 954
EOF property (Recordset objects), 731
equal operator (VBScript), 585
equality operator (JavaScript), 632
Erase tool, merging cells, 147
errors, opening webs, 27
escape sequences (SQL queries), 714
eValue variable (VBScript), 581
events
ActiveX controls, 618-619
Label controls, 618
VBScript, 594-595
Execute method (Connection objects), 728
Exit Function statement (VBScript), 593
Exit Sub statement (VBScript), 594
explicit VBScript variables, 581
Explorer (FrontPage)
checking status (wizards), 963-964
drag-and-drop interface, 5
File view, 5
files
deleting, 33
exporting, 32
moving in web, 33-34
renaming, 33
groups, restricting access, 569-570
installation, 981
links, 77
menus
custom menus, 934-937
Edit, 21
File, 20-21
Help, 24
Tools, 22-23
View, 21-22
OLE automation
creating Web, 968
opening Web, 966-967
removing Web, 968-969

passwords, creating, 566
starting, 14
toolbar, 24-25
troubleshooting, 986-987
user accounts, creating, 565-566
views
All Files, 17-18
Folders, 17-18
Hyperlink Status, 20
Hyperlinks, 18-19
Navigation, 5, 16-17
shortcut menus, 17
Tasks, 20
Themes, 20
webs
attributes, 28
copying, 29
creating, 25-27
deleting, 28
editing, 28
importing, 29-32
opening, 27
publishing, 29
root web, 15-16
exporting files, 32
extensions, see server extensions
external authentication, 843
external hyperlinks, updating, 807
external images, 108

F

FAQ (Frequently Asked Questions)
JPEG, 132
template, 472-473
FastTrack (FrontPage Webs), 908-910
Feedback Form template, 484-485
feedback pages (guest books), 484-485
fields
adding, 408-409
database search forms, 718
hidden, 408
password, 410-411
values relationship, 548-549
Fields collection (Recordset objects), 730
File Format Limitation dialog box, 368
File menu
commands
Composition Setup, 361
Import, 112
Save As, 306-307
Save Copy As, 308
Save for the Web, 308
Save Selection As, 307-308
Scan Image, 312
FrontPage Editor, 43-44
FrontPage Explorer, 20-21
File Save Option dialog box, 306
File view (FrontPage Explorer), 5
File View tab (Visual InterDev), 767
filename extensions, 902-903, 918-919
FileName parameter (ActiveMovie control), 612
files
#htaccess.cnf, 856
access.cnf, 854-856
accessing
direct paths (links), 74-75
Java applets restrictions, 645
relative paths (links), 73-74
creating (Access 97), 749-752
deleting, 33
discussion board, 506-507
editor relationship, 34-35
exporting, 32
formats (FrontPage Editor), 41
httpd.cnf, 848-849
IDC
creating with FrontPage 98, 756-759
increased functionality, 752-753
testing, 751-752
image files
creating, 306
opening, 305
saving, 306-309
size, 350-355
importing, 882
existing webs, 30-32
multiple, 113
to current web, 29-30
mime.typ, 852-853
moving, 33-34
opening (FrontPage Editor), 40-42
paths (wizards), 957-958
renaming, 33
saving (FrontPage Editor), 42-43
srm.cnf, 849-851
themes, 243
Web server issues, 903

Find Clip dialog box, 254
Find feature (Clip Gallery), 254-255
Finger service firewall protection, 818
firewalls
- access control, 816-817
- data protection, 817
- logging options, 818
- screening Java applets, 645
- security benefits, 817
- server access options, 822
- troubleshoooting, 989

Flash control, 609
Flip button (image toolbar), 346
floating images, 135-136
flowing text (tables), 143
flying animation effects, 665-666
folders, 741-742
Folders view (FrontPage Explorer), 17-18
following links, 78
Font command (Format menu), 339
Font dialog box, 97, 225, 339
Font Properties dialog box, 98-100
fonts
- classes (Java applets), 656
- colors (Web pages), 62-63
- sizes, 99-101
- sprites, 289-290
- style sheets, 195-196
  - *faces, 197-199*
  - *size, 200*
- themes, 246-247
- types, 98-99

FontSize parameter (Label control), 612
footer pages (frames), 162-164
footer template, 180-181
footnotes pages (frames), 162-163
footnotes template, 180-181
for loops (JavaScript), 637
For...Next loops (VBScript), 589
foreground animation, 365-366
form handlers, 430-431
Form Page Wizard
- form elements, 421
- input types
  - *overview, 424-426*
  - *selecting, 422*
- launching, 420
- output options, 423-424
- page title, 420
- presentation options, 422-423
- URL, defining, 420

Form Page Wizard dialog box, 420
Form Properties dialog box, 407
- Confirmation Page tab, 434-435
- E-mail Results tab, 433
- File Results tab, 431-433
- Saved Fields tab, 436-438
- Send to field, 428

Form Wizard, 406
Format menu commands (FrontPage Editor), 45
- Font, 339
- Stylesheet, 191
- Themes, 235

Format Stylesheet dialog box, 191
Format toolbar (FrontPage Editor), 47, 67-69
formats
- ASCII, converting to HTML, 41-42
- files (FrontPage Editor), 41
- guest books, 481
- images, 108-109, 129, 350
  - *Clip Gallery, 250-252*
  - *conversion, 131*
  - *file size, 350-355*
  - *GIF, 130-131, 358*
  - *JPEG, 131-132*
  - *Microsoft Image Composer (.mic), 277*
  - *MNG, 358*
  - *PNG, 358*

formatted text, adding to documents, 104-105
formatting text
- line breaks, 90-92
- style formats, 95-97
- subscripts, 98
- superscripts, 98

forms
- advantages, 404-405
- check boxes, 412-414
- clickable labels, 670
- creating, 406-407, 577
- custom scripts
  - *benefits, 445*
  - *C/C++, 443-444*
  - *encoding type, 448*
  - *execution, 446*
  - *including, 446*
  - *languages, 439-441*
  - *paths, 447*
  - *Perl, 444-445*
  - *UNIX shell languages, 441-443*

database search forms
Active Server Page options, 723-725
Adventure Works Products table, 718
fields, 718
IDC files, 722
template files, 721
testing, 723
designing, 405-406
drop-down menus, 415-416
elements, 421
fields
access keys, 670
adding, 408-409
associating with values, 548-549
hidden, 408
password, 410-411
input
overview, 424-426
selecting, 422
multiple, 407
one-line text boxes, 409-410
output
appending data, 436-438
confirmation pages, 434-435
customizing, 431
form handlers, 430-431
options, 423-424
sending as e-mail messages, 429, 433
sending to files, 428-433
presentation options, 422-423
properties, setting, 407
push buttons, 416-417
radio buttons, 412-414
registration (members-only Webs), 561-562
remote administration, 886
scrolling text boxes, 411-412
submission method (specifying), 447
text, troubleshooting, 985
validation, 407
drop-down menus, 453
length restrictions, 457
numeric data types, 456-457
radio buttons, 451-452
selecting script language, 450-451
specifying fields, 451
text boxes, 454-455
text data types, 455-456
value ranges, 457-458

Forms toolbar (FrontPage Editor), 48, 408

fplaunch utility
configuring servers/browsers, 920-921
parameter files (creating), 921-922

fpremadm utility
extensions, 886-887
options, 885
recalculating links, 887
Web-based forms, 886

fpsvradm utility
adding/removing accounts, 881, 888
command line options, 878-879
enabling/disabling privileges, 881, 887
extensions, 879-880
importing files, 882
operations, 877
recalculating links, 881-882

fpwinsvr utility
administrator accounts, creating, 884
enabling/disabling privileges, 884
extensions, 882-883

Frame menu commands (FrontPage Editor), 46
Delete Frame, 159
Split Frame, 159

Frame Properties dialog box, 170

frames, 785
animation
creating, 366-368
loading, 370-372
banners, 161-162
borderless
banner and contents template, 179-180
contents template, 180
creating, 175-177
design, 177-179
footer template, 180-181
footnotes template, 180-181
header template, 180-181
header, footer, and contents template, 181-182
nested three-level hierarchy template, 165-166, 183
split templates, 182
top-down three-level hierarchy template, 182
creating, 157-158

customizing, 170-173
dividing, 158-159
editing, 171
GIF Animator
count, 378
inserting, 374
inline frames editor, 6-7
margins, 173
naming, 171
overview, 156-158
pages
contents pages, 162-164
footer pages, 162-164
footnotes pages, 162-163
frames page, 160-161
header pages, 162-164
No Frames page, 159-160
source page, 156
scrollbars, 156, 171
size, 158-159, 171-173
splitting, 164
targets, 156
assigning, 174
common, 174-175
default, 173-174
templates, 157, 161-166
troubleshooting size, 382
URLs, 160
frameset templates, 916
creating, 945-946
samples, 918
Frequently Asked Questions, see FAQs
FrontPage 97, importing clip art into Clip Gallery, 268-269
FrontPage 98
Components, 766-767
firewalls and proxies, 820
IDC files, 756-759
installation
AutoPlay CD-ROM, 978
components, 979
Explorer, 981
memory requirements, 978-980
options, 979-982
Password Confirmation field, 981
Personal Web Server, 980
running, 978-979
server extensions, 981
startup screen, 978
upgrading, 979-980
Java applet editor, configuring, 653
style sheets support, 187-188
tools, 4
Webs
technology support, 10-11
updating, 908
FrontPage Component dialog box, 102
FrontPage Components, 9-10
FrontPage Editor
bookmarks, 79-80
creating Web pages, 53-54
files
creating, 39-40
editing, 39
opening, 40-42
saving, 42
heading levels, 67
inline frames editor, 6-7
links, 76-78
lists
bulleted lists, 82-84
definition lists, 85
numbered lists, 86
menus
Edit menu, 44
File menu, 43-44
Format menu, 45
Frame menu, 46
Go menu, 45
Help menu, 46
Insert menu, 45
Table menu, 46
Tools menu, 45-46
View menu, 44-45
Window menu, 46
navigation bars, 794, 799
starting, 38
toolbars, 47-48
views, 38-39
FrontPage Explorer
drag-and-drop interface, 5
files
deleting files, 33
exporting, 32
moving in current web, 33-34
renaming, 33
links, 77
menus
Edit, 21
File, 20-21
Help, 24
Tools, 22-23
View, 21-22
Navigation view, 5
starting, 14
toolbar, 24-25
views
All Files, 17-18
File, 5
Folders, 17-18
Hyperlink Status, 20
Hyperlinks, 18-19
Navigation, 16-17
shortcut menus, 17
Tasks, 20
Themes, 20

webs
attributes, 28
copying, 29
creating, 25-27
deleting, 28
editing, 28
importing, 29-32
opening, 27
publishing, 29
root web, 15-16
FrontPage server extensions, see server extensions
FrontPage Web Settings dialog box, 389
FrontPage Web site, 865
FTP (file transfer protocol) service, 834-835
functionality (plug-ins), 222-223
functions
ActiveX controls, 616
JavaScript
getAddress, 628-629
startClock(), 641
Time(), 641
OLE automation testing, 919
VBScript
countDays, 593
countSeconds, 593
getName, 592
IsNumeric, 582
ReDim, 583
UBound, 583

G

gateway scripts, see CGI, scripts
General tab (Page Properties dialog box), 55-57
Get Background and Colors property, 58
getAddress function (JavaScript), 629
getImage method (Java applets), 659
getName function (VBScript), 592
Getting Started dialog box, 14, 741
GIF (Graphics Interchange Format)
GIF24, 130-131
interlacing images, 134
JPEG conversion, 131
LZW compression, 130
overview, 358
transparency, 135-136
GIF Animator
animation
previewing, 375-376
stationary, 381-382
Animation tab, 377-378
background, 361-365, 379
comments, 378-380
dithering, 377
drag-and-drop, 376
duration, 378
Global Palette, 380
foreground, 365-366
frames
count, 378
creating, 366-368
inserting, 374
loading, 370-372
Image tab, 378-380
layering, 365-366
looping, 378
Options tab, 376-377
positioning images, 380-381
size, 377
smoothness, 383
toolbar, 373-376
transparency, 380
undrawing, 379
viewpoint, 381
GIF Animator command (Tools menu), 360
Global Palette, 380
global variables (JavaScript), 627
global.asa files (Visual InterDev), 770
glossary lists, 84-85
Go menu (FrontPage Editor), 45
Gradient (Effects palette category), 324-326
graphical AppletViewer version, 662
graphical Java compiler, 654
graphical menus (images), 126-127
graphics
Java options, 659
Kai's Power Tools, 318
MNG, 358
Photoshop, 318
PNG, 358
sizing, Java applets, 660
themes, 238, 244-246
vector, 255
see also Clip Gallery
Graphics class (Java applets), 655
Graphics Interchange Format, see GIF
Graphics.set methods (Java applets), 656
greater than operator
JavaScript, 633
VBScript, 585
greater than or equal to operator (JavaScript), 633

grids, 210-211
groups, restricting access, 569-570
Guest Book template, 478-479
guest books
confirmation pages, 483
creating, 478-481
customizing, 481
design, 482-483
editing, 480
feedback pages, 484-485
formats, 481
updating, 482
guided tour navigation design, 788

H

<H#> (HTML tag), 192
HEAD element, 54-55
header, footer and contents template, 181-182
header pages (frames), 162-164
header template (borderless frames), 180-181
headers (style sheets), 190-194
defining styles, 190-193
editing, 193-194
grouping, 193
heading cells (tables), 148-149
heading levels, selecting (Format toolbar), 67
headings
creating, 67-68
heading levels, 67
height (tables), 142
Help menu (FrontPage Editor), 46
Help menu (FrontPage Explorer), 24
hidden documents, displaying in webs, 28
hidden fields (forms), 408
hiding plug-ins, 223
highlights (images), 126-128
historical overview of database connectivity, 698-699
Hit Counter component, 546
Hit Counter Properties dialog box, 216
hit counters, 216-217
home position (sprites), 312
horizontal lines, 92-94
horizontal spacing (Java applets), 649
horizontal split template (frames), 164
host names (servers), 831
hotspots
creating, 390, 394
deleting, 397
editing, 394-397
links, changing, 396-397
moving, 394
reshaping, 395-396
size, 394-395
Hover Button dialog box, 225
hover buttons, 225-227
HTML (HyperText Markup Language), 52-53
<!--...--> tag, 191
APPLET tags, 661
BLOCKQUOTE element, 69-70
<DD> tag, 192
designer, 923-925
dynamic HTML, 664
guest book formats, 481
HEAD element, 54-55
pages, writing to files (wizards), 964-966
<P> tag, 68
<STYLE> tag, 191
<TD> tag, 192
<TH> tag, 192
<TR> tag, 192
<WEBBOT> tag, 923
ALT attribute, 924-925
TAG attribute, 925
HTML Reference, see appendix on companion web site
HTML view (FrontPage Editor), 38
HTTP Properties dialog box, 836
HTTP proxies, defining, 821
HTTP service, 836
httpd.cnf file, 848-849
HTX files
differences from Visual InterDev, 768
example listing, 703-704
NRS.mdb database, 769
Hyperlink command (Edit menu), 109
Hyperlink property, 61
Hyperlink Status view (FrontPage Explorer), 20
hyperlinks
broken
deleting, 805
redirecting, 807
external, updating or redirecting, 807
hotspots
changing, 396-397
creating, 390, 394
deleting, 397
editing, 394-397

moving, 394
reshaping, 395-396
size, 394-395
image maps, 398-399
recalculating, 807
troubleshooting, 987, 992-993
Verify Hyperlinks feature, 7
verifying, 807
see also links
Hyperlinks view (FrontPage Explorer), 18-19
hypertext links, 72-73
anchors, 72-73
direct paths, 74-75
relative paths, 73-74
URLs (uniform resource locators), 72
see also links
HyperText Markup Language, see HTML

I

icons
FrontPage Explorer toolbar, 24-25
navigation, 128
plug-in, 224
push channels, 680
Under Construction, 541
IDC files
creating, 741, 749-752
creating with FrontPage 98, 756-759
database search forms, 722
differences from Visual InterDev, 768
increased functionality, 752-753
Internet Database Connector Wizard options, 705-707
NRS.mdb database, 769
testing, 751-752
template, 704
tokens, 702
if statements (JavaScript), 635-636
If Then conditionals, 704
if...else statements (JavaScript), 635
if...Then conditions (VBScript), 587
if...Then...Else conditions (VBScript), 588
Internet Information Server, 890, 988
Active Server Pages, 891
Index Server, 891
ISAPI (Internet Server API), 891
NetShow, 891
server extensions, installing, 892-894
system requirements, 891-892
troubleshooting, 988
versions, 890
Web site, 890
Image command (Insert menu), 109
Image Composer, 132
animation, 374
channels, 275
color swatch, 280-282
commands, 278-279, 282-285
crashes, troubleshooting, 276
desktop, 276-277
files
creating, 306
opening, 305
saving, 306-309
formats (Microsoft Image Composer), 277
launching, 275-276
layers, 274
menus, 282-285
opening, 119
overview, 274
palettes, hiding, 280
plug-ins, 332-333
sprites, 274
aligning, 314-315
Clipboard, 312
colors, 288
combining, 312
creating, 288-291, 294-306
cropping, 313-314
extending, 313-314
flipping, 314-315
fonts, 289-290
grouping, 315
home position, 312
inserting, 311-312
opacity, 290
opening, 305
placing, 312-313
rotating, 314-315
saving, 306-309
scanning, 312
sizing, 313-314
stacking, 315
text alignment, 289
text colors, 290
terminology, 274-275
toolbar, 277-280
toolbox, 280-282
tools, 281-282
Arrange palette, 312
Brush Designer, 303-304
Cutout tool, 296-300
Effects palette, 321-332
Paint palette, 300-303, 334

Select Color Region palette, 298-300
Shapes palette, 291, 294-295
Stencil tool, 298
text palette, 289-290
Texture Transfer palette, 318-320

image composer, 7-8

Image dialog box, 109

image maps
banners (navigation bar), 164
client/server comparison, 388-389
client/server selection, 389-390
design, 399
guidelines, 398
hotspots
changing links, 396-397
creating, 390, 394
deleting, 397
editing, 394-397
moving, 394
reshaping, 395-396
size, 394-395
navigation bar, 164
overview, 386-388
troubleshooting, 985

Image Properties dialog box, 110

Image tab (GIF Animator), 378-380

image toolbar
Bevel button, 348-349
Black and White button, 346
Crop button, 343-344
Flip button, 346
FrontPage Editor, 47
Less Brightness button, 347-348
Less Contrast button, 347
Make Transparent button, 342
More Brightness button, 347-348
More Contrast button, 347
Restore button, 336-338
Reverse button, 346
Rotate Left button, 346
Rotate Right button, 346
Undo button, 336-338
Washout button, 344-346

Image Toolbar command (View menu), 336

images, 108-109
alignment, 121-125
animation, positioning, 380-381
attributes, 128-129
background images, 115-117
background images (Web pages), 58-59
copying, 58
setting, 57-58
banners, 229-230
bevels, 348-349
black and white, 346
borders, 128-129
brightness, 347-348
Clip Art Gallery, 110
Clip Gallery, 252-253
adding, 262
deleting, 262
importing, 262-265
Clip Gallery Live, importing, 265-268
Clipboard, 115
color maps, 133-134
color schemes, 126
contrast, 347
copying/pasting, 114-115
creating, 132
cropping, 343-344
deleting, 115
external, 108
file size, 350-355
flipping, 346
formats, 108-109, 129, 350
Clip Gallery, 250-252
conversion, 131
GIF, 130-131
JPEG, 131-132
GIF, 358
graphical menus, 126-127
guidelines, 117-119
highlights, 126-128
hover buttons, 227
Image Composer, 132
importing, 112-114
inline, 108-109
inserting, 109-112
interlacing, 134
Java options, 659
JPEG (text), 338
links, 109-110, 121
loading (speed), 120-121
MNG, 358
navigation icons, 128
Paint Shop Pro, 132
Photoshop, 132
PNG, 358
properties, 110-112
resampling, 354-355
resolution, 129
restoring, 336-338
reversing, 346
rotating, 346
saving, 115
scanning, 110
scheduling display time, 552-554
searches (Clip Gallery), 254-255
selecting, 114

silhouettes, 348
size, 120-121, 125
spacing, 129
style sheets, 205-207
tables (background), 151-152
text, 338-341
textual alternatives, 119-120
themes, 238, 244-246
thumbnails, 119
tools, 336-342, 345-346, 349
transparency, 135-136, 341-343
background, 341
internal, 342
removing, 342-343
troubleshooting, 136
troubleshooting, 269-271
undoing, 336-338
washout, 344-346
see also graphics
images subdirectory (javaApplets directory), 661
<IMG> (HTML tag), 192
implicit VBScript variables, 581
Import command (File menu), 112
Import File to FrontPage Web dialog box, 112
Import Web Wizard, 30-32
Import Web Wizard dialog box, 30
importing
Clip Gallery, 265, 268-269
existing webs, 30-32
files, 882
multiple, 113
to current web, 29-30
images, 112-114
Clip Gallery, 262-265
Clip Gallery Live, 265-268
subdirectory, 114
troubleshooting, 114
text (FrontPage Editor), 41-42
Impressionist plug-in, 333
Include Page component, 479, 546, 551-555
inserting, 551, 554
start/end dates, 555
updating webs, 813
URLs (entering), 552, 554
Include Page Component Properties dialog box, 479
increment operator (JavaScript), 632
indenting
style sheets, 196-197
text, 69
Index Server, 891
indexers, 460-461
inequality operator
JavaScript, 633
VBScript, 585
Inf parameter (wizards), 953
inheritance (Java classes), 657
Init Menus folder (Registry), 931
init method (Java applets), 657
inline frames editor, 6-7
inline images, 108-109
inline style sheets, 189-190
input parameters
Blocking, 953
destination, 953
Dir, 953
Editing, 953
Inf, 953
PageFile, 953
PageTitle, 953
PageURL, 953
Proxy, 954
ServerName, 954
tracking (wizards), 953-954
User, 954
WebName, 954
Insert Caption command (Table menu), 144
Insert FrontPage Components dialog box, 546
Insert HTML component, 547
Insert Java Applet button (Advanced toolbar), 648
Insert menu (FrontPage Editor), 45
Insert menu commands
Active Elements, 216
Clipart, 252
Image, 109
Insert Rows or Columns command (Table menu), 144
Insert Rows or Columns dialog box, 144
Insert Table command (Table menu), 141-143
Insert Table dialog box, 142-143
inserting
applet tags into webs, 647
sprites, 311-312
installation
Developer's Kit, 917
FrontPage 98
AutoPlay CD-ROM, 978
components, 979

Explorer, 981
memory requirements, 978-980
options, 979-982
Password Confirmation field, 981
Personal Web Server, 980
running, 978-979
server extensions, 981
startup screen, 978
upgrading, 979-980
Personal Web Server
administrator (defining), 832
checking connections, 830-832
specifying directory, 830
starting, 832-834
TCP/IP Test tool, 830
server extensions, 867-869, 879-883
for IIS, 892-894
remotely, 886-887
UNIX, 868-869
Windows 95 and NT, 867-868
Instant Web sites, 488-492
instantiation of Java objects, 654
Integer variables (VBScript), 581
interactive menus (VBScript uses), 577
interfaces
wizards, creating, 952
see also desktops
interlacing images, 134
internal authentication, 842
internal links, see bookmarks
Internet Database Connector, 699
database access options, 702-705
database searches, 721-722
outputting database fields, 703
template files, 702
Internet Database Connector Wizard
advanced database options, 714-717
Connection tab, 716
Driver Specific tab, 717
IDC files, 705-708
Limits tab, 717
queries, 707
Query tab, 714
SQL queries, 707
viewing IDC page results, 708
Internet Explorer ActiveX controls, 603
Internet Information Server, see IIS
Internet security, 837-838
CGI scripts, 838
content control, 838
remote access, 837
Internet Server API, see ISAPI
intranet security, 838-839
CGI scripts, 839
content control, 838-839
IP addresses, 831
Is operator (VBScript), 586
ISAPI (Internet Server API), 891
IsNumeric function (VBScript), 582
ISPs, 992-993
issues and concerns with dynamic HTML, 670
item properties push channels, 684
iValue variable (VBScript), 581

J-K

Java
graphics options, 659
methods, overriding, 657
objects (instantiation), 654
stand-alone applications, 646
Java Applet Properties dialog box, 648
Java applets, 644
aligning on pages, 648
Animator, 660
applet editor, configuring, 653
bytecode verification, 645
classes, 654
color, 656
declaring, 655
font, 656
Graphics, 655
Image, 659
compiling, 653-654
creating, 654-655
creating with JDK, 650
differences from applications, 647
displaying on page, 655
embedding in pages, 647
file access restrictions, 645
graphics, sizing, 660
horizontal spacing, 649
memory layout control, 645

methods
destroy, 657
drawImage, 660
getImage, 659
Graphics.set, 656
init, 657
paint, 655
start, 657
stop, 657
MyApplet example, 658
non-Java browser issues, 650
parameters, 649, 657
platform-independence, 645
properties, 648, 658
safety issues, 644
screening at firewall, 645
showPict, 661
spacing options, 649
testing, 656
vertical spacing, 649
Java AppletViewer, 661
Java classes inheritance, 657
javaApplets directory, 661
JavaScript, 624-626, 647
adding to webs, 638-640
addition operator, 630
arithmetic operators, 630-631
arrays, 628
assignment operators, 633
break statements, 638
calculations, 630-632
comments, 629
comparison operators, 632
conditional expressions, 636
conditional statements, 635-636
continue statements, 638
data types, 627
decrement operator, 632
displaying data and time, 640
division operators, 631
else statements, 635
equality operator, 632
functions, 628-629
getAddress, 629
startClock(), 641
Time(), 641
greater than operator, 633
greater than or equal to operator, 633
if statements, 635-636
if...else statements, 635
increment operator, 632
inequality operator, 633
less than operator, 633
less than or equal to operator, 633
logical operators, 634
loops, 637
modulus operator, 631
multiplication operator, 631
objects, 630
operator precedence, 631
return statement, 629
strings, 627
subtraction operator, 630
testing browsers for compatibility, 625
unary negation operator, 631
unary operators, 632
variables, 626-629
Web browser behavior control, 641
writing to webs, 639
JDK (Java Developer's Kit), 650-652
JavaScript Reference, see appendix on companion web site
JPEG (Joint Photographic Expert Group), 131-132
GIF conversion, 131
lossy compression, 131
quality settings, 132
text, 338
Web site FAQ, 132
Kai's Power Tools, 318
Keyboard style, 96
keywords (Clip Gallery), 255-257

L

Label controls
caption changing (VBScript example), 619-620
FontSize parameter, 612
updating with events, 618
labeling bookmarks, 79
launching Image Composer, 275-276
layering animation, 365-366
layers (Image Composer), 274
layout properties (ActiveX controls), 608
layout templates, 475
Less Brightness button (image toolbar), 347-348
Less Contrast button (image toolbar), 347
less than operator
JavaScript, 633
VBScript, 585
less than or equal to operator (JavaScript), 633
levels (navigation bars), 798

<LI> (HTML tag), 192
Limits tab (Internet Database Connector Wizard), 717
line breaks, 90-92
 non-breaking spaces, 92
 properties, setting, 91
linking
 banners, 229-230
 hover buttons, 225
 troubleshooting, 987, 992-993
links, 72-73
 anchors, 72-73
 bookmarks, 75-76
  creating links to, 79-80
  deleting, 79
  direct paths, 76
  editing, 79
  labeling, 79
  relative paths, 75
  visiting, 80
 broken, redirecting, 807
 color, 61
 creating, 76-77
 deleting, 78
 direct paths, 74-75
 following, 78
 hyperlinks (Verify Hyperlinks feature), 7
 images, 109-110, 121
 recalculating, 861, 881-882, 887
 relative paths, 73-74
 replacing, 860
 targets, 173-175
 URLs (uniform resource locators), 72, 78
 verifying, 807, 859-860
 see also hypertext links
List Properties dialog box, 82, 87
listings
 #htaccess.cnf file, 856
 ActiveX control properties:setting with VBScript, 614
 ADO connection example, 735
 access.cnf file, 854-855
 adding tasks to To Do List, 972
 bringing Editor to front, 970
 checking Explorer status, 964
 creating pages with OLE automation, 969
 creating Web using OLE, 968
 httpd.cnf, 848
 HTX file example, 703-704
 IDC file, IDC Wizard example, 708
 JavaScript array values, 628
 JavaScript assignment operator examples, 634
 JavaScript logical operators, 635
 JavaScript while loop example, 638
 live clock function, JavaScript, 640
 marking To Do List tasks complete, 973
 mime.typ, 852-853
 MyApplet example, 658
 OLE proceudre in Visual Basic, 963
 OLE proceudre in Visual C++, 962-963
 opening Web using OLE, 967
 push channel example, 679
 querying Editor, 970-971
 Recordset example code, 736
 removing Web using OLE, 968-969
 sales tax calculation, VBScript, 578
 showPict applet, 660
 simple Applet tag example, 661
 srm.cnf, 849-851
 VBScript sales tax program, 596-598
 writing HTML pages to files, 965-966
lists, 80-82
 bulleted lists, 81-84
 definition lists, 81-85
 glossary lists, 84-85
 nesting, 87-88
 numbered lists, 81, 85-86
 types, 80-82, 87-88
loading images, 120-121
local files, accessing
 direct paths, 74-75
 relative file paths, 73-74
local variables
 JavaScript, 627
 VBScript, 592
logging options
 firewalls, 818
 ODBC calls, 716
logging targets (push channels), 686
logical operators (JavaScript), 634
logical styles (HTML character style tags), 95
logos (channel icons), 680
looping (animation), 378

loops
JavaScript, 637-638
VBScript, 589
loose typing, JavaScript, 627
lossy compression, 131
LZW compression, 130

M

Macromedia Flash control, 609
magazines (push channels), 691
mailto links, verifying, 807
Make Transparent button (image toolbar), 342
manual web updates, 805
margins
frames, 173
setting in Web pages, 63-64
style sheets, 208-211
Margins tab (Page Properties dialog box), 63-64
Marquee Properties dialog box, 218
marquees, 218-220
alignment, 218-219
animation, 219-220
colors, 219
size, 219
members-only Webs, 561-564
Registration component, configuring, 563-564
registration form, 561-562
memory
FrontPage 98 installation, 978-980
troubleshooting, 990
memory layout control (Java applets), 645
menus
custom, 928-930
FrontPage Editor, 930-934
FrontPage Explorer, 934-937
naming, 931
planning, 929
Registry, 928
Registry Editor, 929-930
drop-down, 415-416
FrontPage Editor
Edit menu, 44
File menu, 43-44
Format menu, 45
Frame menu, 46
Go menu, 45
Help menu, 46
Insert menu, 45
Table menu, 46
Tools menu, 45-46
View menu, 44-45
Window menu, 46
FrontPage Explorer, 20
Edit menu, 21
File menu, 20-21
Help menu, 24
Tools menu, 22-23
View menu, 21-22
graphical menus, 126-127
Image Composer, 282-285
merging
cells (tables), 147
columns (tables), 147
rows (tables), 147
message parameter (Java applets), 657
META property, 64-66
methods
ActiveX controls, 615-617
Command object, 733
Java, overriding, 657
Java applets
destroy, 657
drawImage, 660
getImage, 659
Graphics.set, 656
init, 657
paint, 655
start, 657
stop, 657
Recordset object, 731
VBScript, 595
Microsoft Active Channels, 694
Microsoft Access 97 Query Designer, 754
Microsoft Access Web Publishing Wizard, 751
Microsoft Forms 2.0 controls, 606
Microsoft Image Composer format (.mic), 277
Microsoft Query SQL statements, 753-755
Microsoft SiteBuilder Network (ActiveX controls), 603
Microsoft SQL Server Developer's Resource Kit, 761
migrating SQL Server, 760-761
MIME types (form data), 448
mime.typ file, 852-853
MNG (Multiple Network Graphics), 358

modifying
navigation scheme for webs, 799
push channels, 682
see also editing
modulus operator (JavaScript), 631
Month property (Calendar control), 614
More Brightness button (image toolbar), 347-348
More Contrast button (image toolbar), 347
Move method (Recordset objects), 730
MoveFirst method (Recordset objects), 730
MoveLast method (Recordset objects), 730
MoveNext method (Recordset objects), 730
MovePrevious method (Recordset objects), 730
moving files in current web, 33-34
Msgbox statement dialog box display, 578
multi-dimensional arrays (VBScript), 582
multihoming, 869-873
configuring FrontPage, 871-873
connecting FrontPage to system, 870
defined, 869
listening for hosts, 870
multiple processes on one server, 870
multiple servers on one machine, 869-870
troubleshooting Webs, 991
WPPs, 869
multilevel undo and redo feature (FrontPage Editor), 44
multimedia plug-ins, 221
Multiple Network Graphics, see MNG
multiple push channels, 688-690
multiplication operator (JavaScript), 631
MyApplet (Java applet example), 655, 658

N

naming
bookmarks, 79
Clip Gallery categories, 261
custom menus, 931
frames, 171
pages (default names), 903
parameter files, 955
NavDemo web, 790
Arcs theme, 790
home page, 790, 794, 796
modifying navigation scheme, 800
navigation
design for webs, 788
icons, 128
scheme for webs, 802
navigation bars, 784, 794
adding, 798
Back button, 798
editing, 797
levels, 798
Next button, 798
Parent level button, 798
push channel buttons, 689
Navigation view, 784
adding navigation bars, 798
NavDemo web home page, 790
parent-child page relationship, 787
peer page relationships, 787
Navigation view (FrontPage Explorer), 5, 16
NCompass Script Active (ActiveX controls for Netscape), 603
negation operators (JavaScript), 631
nested if statements (JavaScript), 636
nested lists, creating, 87-88
nested three-level hierarchy template (frames), 165-166, 183
Netcaster push channels, 694
Netscape Navigator
ActiveX controls, 603
Netcaster push channels, 694
NetShow, 891
network administrators (Webmasters as), 846-847
network access, troubleshooting, 989-990
New Category dialog box, 258
New Color Palette dialog box, 353
New FrontPage Web dialog box, 25-26, 490
New Page dialog box, 53

newsletters (push channels), 691
newspapers (push channels), 691
Next button (adding to navigation bar), 798
Next Day button
Calendar control, 617
Next Month button
Calendar control, 617
Next Year button
Calendar control, 617
<NL> (HTML tag), 192
No Frames page, 159-160
non-breaking spaces, 92
non-Java browsers Java applet issues, 650
Normal Page template, 471
Normal view (FrontPage Editor), 38
NRS.mdb database
Active Server Page example, 774-776
Data Range controls, 776
DSN file, 768
global.asa file, 770
HTX file, 769
IDC file, 769
Visual InterDev example, 767
numbered lists, 81, 85-86
numeric data types, validating, 456-457
numeric entities, 102-103

O

objects
Java, 654
JavaScript, 630
ODBC (Open Database Connectivity), 699
data sources, 699-701, 748-749
driver options (Internet Database Connector Wizard), 717
DSN files (Visual InterDev type), 768
ODBC Data Source Administrator, creating data sources, 700
ODBC Data Source Administrator dialog box, 748
ODBC Microsoft Access 97 Setup dialog box, 749
<OL> (HTML tag), 192
OLE (object linking and embedding)
automation, 916
Editor, 969-971
Explorer, 966-969
identifiers, 959
testing functions, 919
To Do List, 971-973
wizards, 958-959
servers, connecting to, 962-963
Visual Basic procedure listing, 963
Visual C++ procedure listing, 962-963
OnClick events dialog box buttons, 578
one-dimensional arrays (VBScript), 582
one-line text boxes, 409-410
properties, 409-410
validating, 454-455
One-Page web, 493
opacity
Effects palette, 321
sprites, 290
Open FrontPage Web dialog box, 16, 27
Open method (Connection objects), 728
open-ended discussion groups, 496-497
opening
ADO connections, 735
files, 305
FrontPage Editor, 40-42
Image Composer, 119
sprites, 305
webs, 27
operators
JavaScript
precedence, 631
VBScript, 584
arithmetic, 583
comparison, 585
precedence, 584
Option Explicit statement (VBScript), 581
Options command
Tools menu, 333
View menu, 119
Options dialog box, 119, 333
Options for Custom Form Handler dialog box, 446
Action field, 447
Encoding Type field, 448
Method field, 447
Options tab (GIF Animator), 376-377
organizing webs, 786
Outlines (Effects palette category), 327
outlines, collapsible, 87-88

output (forms), 428
appending data, 436-438
confirmation pages, 434-435
customizing, 431
form handlers, 430-431
sending as e-mail messages, 429, 433
sending to files, 428-433
Output Options dialog box, 423
output parameters, tracking (wizards), 955
outside firewall server access options, 822
ovals (sprites), 292
overriding Java methods, 657
overview of
ActiveX technology, 600-601
Java, 644
JavaScript, 625
VBScript, 576
Visual InterDev, 764-765

P

<P> tag, 68, 192
packages (JDK), 650
padding borders, 211-212
Page Banner component, 547
page elements (selectors), 191
Page Properties dialog box, 54, 205
Background tab
background colors, setting, 57-61
background images, 58-59
text and link colors, 61
Custom tab, 64-66
General tab
Base Locations, 56-57
document titles, 55-56
page location, 55-56
Margins tab, 63-64
page templates, 9
page transitions, 667
page wizards, 9
PageFile parameter (wizards), 953
pages
background images, 115-117
confirmation pages (guest books), 483
creating, 53-54
OLE automation, 969
templates, 940
with FrontPage Editor, 39-40
customizing
background colors, 57-61
background images, 58-59
custom colors, creating, 61-62
META properties, 64-66
text and link colors, 61
watermarks, 59
default names (Web servers), 903
deleting from webs, 805
designing, 66
feedback pages
font colors, defining, 62-63
FrontPage Editor, 38, 43
Advanced toolbar, 48
creating pages, 39-40
Edit menu, 44
editing pages, 39
File menu, 43-44
Format menu, 45
Format toolbar, 47
Forms toolbar, 48
Frame menu, 46
Go menu, 45
Help menu, 46
Image toolbar, 47
Insert menu, 45
moving toolbars, 47
opening existing pages, 40-42
saving pages, 42
Standard toolbar, 47
starting, 38
Table menu, 46
Table toolbar, 48
text import options, 41-42
toolbar, 47
Tools menu, 45-46
View menu, 44-45
views, 38-39
Window menu, 46
headings
creating, 67-68
displaying heading levels, 67
selecting heading levels, 67
HTML, writing to files (wizards), 964-966
inline style sheets, 190
margins, setting, 63-64
paragraphs, creating, 68-69
properties
Base Locations, 56-57
document titles, 55-56
page location, 55-56
setting, 54-55
remote, troubleshooting, 986
saving, troubleshooting, 984

text, 69-70
titles, changing, 793
troubleshooting access, 988-989
PageSize property (Recordset objects), 731
PageTitle parameter (wizards), 953
PageURL parameter (wizards), 953
Paint (Effects palette category), 327-328
paint method (Java applets), 655
Paint palette, 300-303, 334
Paint Shop Pro, 132
palettes
color palettes, creating, 352-354
Image Composer, hiding, 280
Paragraph Properties dialog box, 103
paragraphs, creating, 68-69
parameter files
templates, 941-944
FileList section, 942-943
information section, 941-942
meta-information section, 943-944
TaskList section, 944
wizards, 952-957
creating, 951-952
environment parameters, 954
input parameters, 953-954
naming, 955
output parameters, 955
parameters
Java applets, 649, 657
new ActiveX controls, 612
VBScript, 592
Parameters collection, 734
Parent level button (navigation bars), 798
parent page, 785
parent-child page relationships, 786
Password Confirmation field, 981
password fields, 410-411
passwords
assigning, 566
protection, troubleshooting, 988
pasting images, 114-115
Patterns (Effects palette category), 328-329
peer page relationships, 786
peer pages, 785
Perl (Practical Extraction and Report Language), 444-445
permissions
global, 840
setting, 23
unique, 841
user (members-only Webs), 561
Permissions command (Tools menu), 988
Permissions dialog box, 23
Personal Web Server, 7
administration, 856-859
advantages, 829-830
authentication, 832
command line options, 878-879
configuring
access.cnf file settings, 854-856
editing files, 847-848
httpd.cnf file settings, 848-849
mime.typ file settings, 852-853
srm.cnf file settings, 849-851
FTP service, 834-835
HTTP service, 836
installation, 830-834, 980
administrator (defining), 832
checking connections, 830-832
specifying directory, 830
TCP/IP Test tool, 830
multihoming
configuring FrontPage, 871-873
connecting FrontPage to system, 870
defined, 869
listening for hosts, 870
multiple processes on one server, 870
multiple servers on one machine, 869-870
WPPs, 869
root web, accessing, 15
security, 837-838
CGI scripts, 838
content control, 838
intranets, 838-839
remote access, 837
starting, 832-834
testing, 982
troubleshooting, 987-989
troubleshooting Webs, 991
see also server extensions

Personal Web Server Properties dialog box, 832
Personal Web template, 26, 493
Photographic (Effects palette category), 329-331
Photoshop, 132, 318
physical styles (HTML character style tags), 95
Ping (troubleshooting Webs), 991
Ping requests (security), 989
pixels (table size), 143
planning web organization, 786
platform-independence of Java applets, 645
Plug-In Properties dialog box, 221, 224
plug-ins, 221-222
- alignment, 224
- borders, 224
- embedded, 223
- functionality, 222-223
- hiding, 223
- icon, 224
- Image Composer, 332-333
- multimedia, 221
- properties, 224
- seamlessness, 222
- size, 223
- spacing, 224

PNG (Portable Network Graphics), 131, 358
polygons
- hotspots, 395-396
- sprites, 295

port numbers, troubleshooting, 987-988
Portable Network Graphics, see PNG
posting to discussion boards, 504-505
Practical Extraction and Report Language, see Perl
<PRE> (HTML tag), 192
precedence of operators
- JavaScript, 631
- VBScript, 584

Presentation Options dialog box, 422
Preview view (FrontPage Editor), 38
previews (Clip Gallery), deleting, 269
Previous Day button (Calendar control), 617
Previous Month button (Calendar control), 617
Previous Year button (Calendar control), 617
printing navigation scheme, 802
privacy via firewalls, 818
private directories, 28
privileges
- computer accounts, 568-569
- enabling/disabling, 881, 884, 887
- users (closed Webs), 565-566

procedures (VBScript), 591-594
PRODUCTS.ASP page (Database Region), 723
programmed learning web design, 788
Project Web, 493, 524-530
- Archive page, 528
- Discussion area, 530
- Home page, 524
- Members page, 525
- Schedule page, 526-527
- Search page, 529
- Status page, 527
- template, 26

properties
- ActiveX controls
  - *changing with VBScript, 613*
  - *Code Source, 609*
  - *color, 610*
  - *editing, 610*
  - *known, 609*
  - *layout, 608*
  - *new control settings, 611-612*
  - *text, 610*
  - *unique, 609*
- alignment, 148
- Calendar control, 613-614
- captions, 144
- cells, 148
  - *advanced settings, 148-150*
  - *multiple cells, 149*
- Command object, 733
- Connection objects, 728-729
- forms, setting, 407
- FTP service, configuring, 834
- horizontal lines, setting, 93
- images, 110-112
- Java applets, 648, 658
- line breaks, setting, 91
- plug-ins, 224
- Recordset object, 731
- style sheets, 194
- tables, resetting, 147
- Web pages
  - *Base Locations, 56-57*
  - *document titles, 55-56*
  - *page location, 55-56*
  - *setting, 54-55*

protecting data transfer via encryption, 822
protecting data via firewalls, 816-817
proxies, 819-821
defining, 821
pseudo proxies, 821
servers, troubleshooting, 989-991
working with Web servers, 820
Proxy parameter (wizards), 954
pseudo proxies, 821
Publish FrontPage Web dialog box, 29
Push Button Properties dialog box, 416
push buttons, 416-417
push channels, 678-680
alpha, 275
as screen savers, 685
channel item properties, 684
content design, 691
creating (Channel Definition Wizard), 680-681
description, 681
e-mail updates, 685
example listing, 679
item properties, 684
logging targets, 686
magazines, 691
multiple channels, 688-690
newsletters, 691
newspapers, 691
reference sources, 693
scheduling options, 685
source folders, 682
tutorials, 693
updating, 692
Web site examples, 692

Q-R

queries
database-independent, 714
Internet Database Connector Wizard, 707
Microsoft Access 97 Query Designer, 754
timeout options, 715
Query Designer (Visual InterDev), 772

Radio Button Properties dialog box, 413
radio buttons, 412-414
properties, 413-414
validating, 451-452
Recalculate Hyperlinks command (Tools menu), 987
recalculating hyperlinks, 807
recalculating links, 861, 881-882, 887
recalls (Shapes palette), 295
RecordCount property (Recordset objects), 731
Recordset objects
AbsolutePage property, 731
AbsolutePosition property, 731
ADO, 728-730
BOF property, 731
EOF property, 731
example code, 736
Fields collection, 730
methods, 731
Move method, 730
MoveFirst method, 730
MoveLast method, 730
MoveNext method, 730
MovePrevious method, 730
PageSize property, 731
properties, 731
RecordCount property, 731
ReDim function (VBScript), 583
redirecting broken links, 807
redo option (FrontPage Editor), 44
reference sources (push channels), 693
Refresh command (View menu), 987
Registration component, configuring, 563-564
registration forms (members-only Webs), 561-562
Registry
browsing, 929
entries, 928
Init Menus folder, 931
modifying, 929
Registry Editor, 929-930
browsing Registry, 929
main window, 929
starting, 929
relationships in subject matter (web design), 789
relative paths (links), 73-75
relative values, 149, 172
Rename Category dialog box, 261
renaming files, 33
requirements avalanche, 765
requirements creep, 765
resampling images, 354-355

resolution (images), 129
restoring images, 336-338
restricted discussion groups, 497-498
restricted Webs, 560
accessing, 560-561
group access, 569-570
see also closed Webs; members-only Webs
return statement (JavaScript), 629
Reverse button (image toolbar), 346
RollbackTrans method (Connection objects), 729
Root web, opening, 562
root web, 15-16
Rotate Left button (image toolbar), 346
Rotate Right button (image toolbar), 346
rotation (banners), 228-229
routines (wizards), 962
rows (tables)
drawing tool, 142
inserting, 144-146
merging, 147
selecting, 145, 150

S

safety (Java applets), 644
sales tax calculations (VBScript), 578
Sample style, 96
Save As command (File menu), 306-307
Save As dialog box, 42
Save As Template dialog box, 945
Save Copy As command (File menu), 308
Save for the Web command (File menu), 308
Save Image to Web dialog box, 115
Save Selection As command (File menu), 307-308
saving
files
frames page, 160-161
FrontPage Editor, 42-43
Image Composer, 306-309
troubleshooting, 984
images, 115
sprites, 306-309
scalability (Web servers), 898
scalar functions (database-independent queries), 714
Scan Image command (File menu), 312
scanning
images, 110
sprites, 312
Scheduled Image component, 547
image URL (entering), 552-553
inserting, 553
start/end dates, 553-554
Scheduled Include Page component, 547
scheduling options (push channels), 685
screen resolution (tables), 143
screen savers (push channels), 685
screening applets (firewalls), 645
Script Wizard, initializing web clock, 641
scripts
ActiveX, *see* ActiveX
CGI, *see* CGI
Data Range Header control example, 766
forms
benefits, 445
C/C++, 443-444
encoding type, 448
execution, 446
including, 446
languages, 439-441
paths, 447
Perl, 444-445
UNIX shell languages, 441-443
validating, 450
JavaScript, *see* JavaScript
VBScript, *see* VBScript
scrollbars (frames), 156, 171
scrolling marquees, see marquees
Scrolling Text Box Properties dialog box, 412
scrolling text boxes
default text, 412
properties, 411-412
validating, 454-455
seams (plug-ins), 222
Search bot, 461-462
adding to Webs
customizing form, 463-465
search page, 463
guidelines, 465-466
server extensions, 465
search engines
Index Server, 891
WAIS, 460

search forms (databases), 718
Search Page template, 463, 475
searches (Clip Gallery), 254-255
security
- access.cnf file, 854-856
- accounts
  - *administrator, 839*
  - *author, 839*
  - *browse, 839*
  - *computer, 567*
- authentication
  - *external, 843*
  - *internal, 842*
  - *Personal Web Server, 832*
- classes, 988
- data transfer encryption, 822
- firewalls, 816-817
- folders, 742
- Internet
  - *CGI scripts, 838*
  - *content control, 838*
  - *remote access, 837*
- intranets
  - *CGI scripts, 839*
  - *content control, 838-839*
- Java applets, 644
- levels (ActiveX controls), 603
- passwords, troubleshooting, 988
- permissions
  - *global, 840*
  - *unique, 841*
- Ping requests, 989

Select Background Image dialog box, 117
Select Case statements (VBScript), 588
Select Color Region palette (Image Composer), 298-300
selecting
- images, 114
- table elements, 145, 150
- themes, 235-239

selectors (page elements), 191
self-registration (ActiveX controls), 609
SERK (Server Extensions Resource Kit), 893
server extensions, 7
- administration
  - *fpremadm utility, 885-888*
  - *fpsvradm utility, 877-882*
  - *fpwinsvr utility, 882-884*
  - *local, 876-877*
  - *remote, 884-885*
- checking, 880, 883, 887
- components, 547-548
- defined, 864-865
- downloading, 893
- installation, 879-883, 981
  - *IIS, 892-894*
  - *remote, 886-887*
  - *UNIX, 868-869*
  - *Windows 95/NT, 867-868*
- multihomed systems, 871-873
- Resource Kit, 866, 876
- server compatibility, 865
- upgrading, 880, 883

Server Resource file, see srm.cnf file
ServerName parameter (wizards), 954
servers
- access options, 822-823
- ActiveX framework, 601
- configuring for fplaunch applications, 920-921
- host names, 831
- IIS, (Internet Information Server)
  - *Active Server Pages, 891*
  - *ADO (ActiveX Database Objects), 891*
  - *Index Server, 891*
  - *ISAPI (Internet Server API), 891*
  - *NetShow, 891*
  - *server extensions, installing, 892-894*
  - *system requirements, 891-892*
  - *troubleshooting, 988*
  - *versions, 890*
  - *Web site, 890*
- image maps, 388-390
- IP addresses, 831
- OLE connections, 962-963
- proxy servers, 819, 989-991
- testing, 982
- Web servers
  - *access options, 822-823*
  - *administration, 856-857*
  - *cost, 899*
  - *creating Webs, 904*
  - *data encryption, 822*
  - *exporting to, 900-901*
  - *extensionless, 901-904*
  - *FastTrack, 908-910*
  - *functions, prioritizing, 898-899*

hosting companies, 899-900
PWS alternatives, 896
proxies, 820
reliability, 898
responsiveness, 898
scalability, 898
transferring content, 900-901
users, 828-829
WebSite, 904-907
see also Personal Web Server
setup (hit counters), 216-217
SGML (Standard Generalized Markup Language), 52
shading (tables), 150
Shapes palette (Image Composer tool), 291
ovals, 292
polygons, 295
recalls, 295
rectangles, 292
spline curves, 294-295
Shared Borders (Webs), 785
shortcut menus (FrontPage Explorer views), 17
Show Getting Started dialog box, 741
Show Image Editor command (Tools menu), 275
showPict applet, 661
silhouettes (images), 348
sites
Animated Art for Netscape, 383
Animated GIF Artists Guild, 383
Badger's Animated GIF Gallery, 383
Bill's Animated GIF Collection, 383
Clip Gallery Live, 265-268
CommerceNet, 899
creating, 488-492, 740-742
Dr.Fun's Page of Animations, 383
FrontPage, 865
IIS, 890
JPEG, 132
push channel examples, 692
Tru Realities, 383
URLs (creating), 490
viewing with FrontPage Explorer, 4-5
Wagon Train Animated GIFs, 383
Web Wizard's World Animation Station, 383
size
animation, 377
banners, 228
frames, 158-159, 171-173
graphics (Java applets), 660
hotspots, 394-395
hover buttons, 225-226
images, 120-121, 125
dithering, 351
files, 350-355
marquees, 219
plug-ins, 223
sprites, 313-314
style sheet fonts, 200
tables, 140, 143
sizing navigation scheme chart, 801
Sketch (Effects palette category), 331
source (frames), 156
source code, adding comments, 101-102
Source Code Editor (Visual InterDev), 773
source documents, alternate, 159-160
source folders (push channels), 682
source sprites, 318
spacing
cells (tables), 147
images, 129
options (Java applets), 649
plug-ins, 224
style sheets, 196-197, 208-212
special characters, 102-103
Specify Background and Colors property, 59
speed, loading images, 120-121
spell-checking, 22
spiraling fly-in text animation, 666
spline curves (sprites), 294-295
Split Cells dialog box, 145
Split Frame command (Frame menu), 159
Split Frame dialog box, 159
split templates, 182
splitting
frames, 164
table elements, 145-146
sprites
aligning, 314-315
bounding box, 313

Clipboard, 312
colors, 288
combining, 312
creating, 288-291, 294-306
cropping, 313-314
Cutout tool, 296-300
destination sprites, 318
extending, 313-314
flipping, 314-315
fonts, 289-290
grouping, 315
home position, 312
inserting, 311-312
opacity, 290
opening, 305
Paint palette, 300
Brush Designer, 303-304
tools, 302-303
placing, 312-313
rotating, 314-315
saving, 306-309
scanning, 312
Select Color Region palette, 298-300
Shapes palette
ovals, 292
polygons, 295
recalls, 295
rectangles, 291-292
spline curves, 294-295
sizing, 313-314
source sprites, 318
stacking, 315
Stencil tool, 298
text
alignment, 289
colors, 290

SQL queries
Database Region Wizard, 711
escape sequences, 714
Internet Database Connector Wizard, 707, 714
Microsoft Query, 753-755

SQL Server, 760-761
srm.cnf file, 849-851
stacking sprites, 315
stand-alone applications (Java), 646
Standard Generalized Markup Language (SGML), 52
Standard toolbar (FrontPage Editor), 47
start method (Java applets), 657
startClock() function (JavaScript), 641
starting
FrontPage Editor, 38
FrontPage Explorer, 14

startup screen (FrontPage 98 installation), 978
statelessness, 765
statistics tracking (firewalls), 818
Stencil tool (Image Composer), 298
stop method (Java applets), 657
streaming audio/video, 891
String variables (VBScript), 581
strings
JavaScript, 627
VBScript, 586

structural relationship of web pages, 786
Style dialog box, 205
style formats, 95-97
style sheets
background colors, 204-205
borders, 211-212
browser support, 188-189
FrontPage 98 support, 187-188
grids, 210-211
headers
defining styles, 190-193
editing, 193-194
grouping, 193
images
background, 205-207
keywords, 206-207
repeating, 205
inline, 189-190
margins, 208-211
overview, 186-187
properties, 194
spacing, 208-212
text, 212
colors, 204-205
fonts, 195-199
size, 200
spacing, 196-197
themes, 239

<STYLE> tags, 191
Stylesheet command (Format menu), 191
subroutines (VBScript), 593
subscript text, 98
Substitution component, 547
configuration variables, 555-557
inserting, 555
web update variables, 813

subtraction operator (JavaScript), 630
superscript text, 98

Surface (Effects palette category), 332
switches (command line), 857-859
system classes (VBScript), 594
system variables (META property), 65

T

Table menu (FrontPage Editor), 46
Table menu commands
Insert Caption, 144
Insert Rows or Columns, 144
Insert Table, 141-143
Table Properties, 147
table of contents, updating, 804
Table of Contents template, 473-474
Table Properties command (Table menu), 147
Table Properties dialog box, 147
Table toolbar, 48, 141
<TABLE> (HTML tag), 192
tables
advanced, 140
alignment, 143, 147
background images, 151-152
borders, 143, 147
captions, 144
cells
color, 151
data cells, 148
heading cells, 148-149
height, 142
merging, 147
padding, 143
selecting, 145, 150
spacing, 143, 147
splitting, 145-146
width, 142
color, 150-151
columns/rows
inserting, 144-146
merging, 147
selecting, 145
width, 149
creating (FrontPage Editor), 141-143
data binding, 674
data tables, 743-747
deleting elements, 145
drawing, 141-142
editing elements, 145-147
height (drawing tool), 142
overview, 140-141
properties, resetting, 147
screen resolution, 143
selecting elements, 145
size, 140, 143
splitting elements, 145-146
text, flowing, 143
values, 149
width (drawing tool), 142-143
TAG attribute (<WEBBOT> tag), 925
tags (HTML), 52-53
<!--...--> tag, 191
APPLET tags, 661
BLOCKQUOTE element, 69-70
<DD> tag, 192
designer, 923-925
dynamic HTML, 664
guest book formats, 481
HEAD element, 54-55
pages, writing to files (wizards), 964-966
<P> tag, 68
<STYLE> tag, 191
<TD> tag, 192
<TH> tag, 192
<TR> tag, 192
<WEBBOT> tag, 923
ALT attribute, 924-925
TAG attribute, 925
Target Frame dialog box, 174
targets
assigning, 174
common, 174-175
default, 173-174
frames, 156
Tasks view (FrontPage Explorer), 20
TCP/IP Test tool, 982
<TD> (HTML tag), 192
TDC (Tabular Data Control), 675
templates
banner, 161-162
Bibliography, 474
borderless frames
banner and contents template, 179-180
contents template, 180
footer template, 180-181
footnotes template, 180-181
header, footer, and contents template, 181-182
header template, 180-181
nested three-level hierarchy template, 183

split templates, 182
top-down three-level hierarchy template, 182
Confirmation Form, 476
contents, 161-162
creating, 945-946
Customer Support Web, 25, 493, 512
directories, 918, 940
Empty Web, 25
FAQs, 472-473
Feedback Form, 484-485
files
database searches, 721
IDC, 702
If...Then conditionals, 704
frames, 157, 161-166
Guest Book, 478-479
layout, 475
nested three-level hierarchy (frames), 165-166
Normal Page, 471
overview, 470-471
page templates, 9, 940
parameter files
FileList section, 942-943
information section, 941-942
meta-information section, 943-944
TaskList section, 944
Personal Web, 26, 493
Project Web, 26, 493, 524
Search Page, 463, 475
Table of Contents, 473-474
top-down three-level hierarchy (frames), 165
Web, 9
FrontPage Webs, 946-948
pages, 39-40, 53-54
sites, 488-490
see also frameset templates

testing
database search forms, 723
IDC files, 751-752
Java applets, 656
JavaScript compatibility, 625
mailto links, 807
Personal Web Server, 982
TCP/IP, 982
Webs, 911-912
Winsock, 982

text
addresses, 103
aligning, 69-70
animation, 664-666
blinking, 95
colors
style sheets, 204-205
themes, 246-247
Web pages, 61
data types, validating, 455-456
flowing around tables, 143
fonts, 98-101
formatted text, 104-105
forms, troubleshooting, 985
horizontal lines, 92-94
hover buttons, 225
images, 338-341
deleting, 340
JPEG, 338
textual alternatives, 119-120
importing (FrontPage Editor), 41-42
indenting, 69
line breaks, 90-92
sprites, 289-290
style formats, 95-97
style sheets, 194-200, 212
fonts, 195-196
spacing, 196-197
subscript, 98
superscript, 98
word art, 100

Text Box Properties dialog box, 409

text boxes
one-line, 409-410
scrolling, 411-412
validating, 454-455

text palette (Image Composer tool), 289-290

text properties (ActiveX controls), 610

Text property, 61

Texture Transfer palette, 318-320

<TH> (HTML tag), 192

Theme Preview window, 235

themes, 8
choosing, 239-240
colors, 238, 243-244
creating, 241-243
customizing, 241-243
editing, 241-243
files, 243
fonts, 246-247
images, 238, 244-246
overview, 234-235
selecting, 235-239
style sheets, 239
text colors, 246-247
viewing, 235-236, 239

Themes command (Format menu), 235
Themes view (FrontPage Explorer), 20
threading discussion boards, 506
thumbnails, 119
tiling
background images, 117
Texture Transfer palette, 320
Time() function (JavaScript), 641
timeout options for queries, 715
titles, 55-56, 793
To Do List (OLE automation), 971-973
tokens (IDC) files, 702
Toolbars dialog box, 279
toolbars
Format toolbar, 67-69
Forms, 408
FrontPage Editor, 47-48
FrontPage Explorer, 24-25
GIF Animator, 373-376
Image Composer, 277-280
image toolbar
Bevel button, 348-349
Black and White button, 346
Crop button, 343-344
Flip button, 346
Less Brightness button, 347-348
Less Contrast button, 347
Make Transparent button, 342
More Brightness button, 347-348
More Contrast button, 347
Restore button, 336-338
Reverse button, 346
Rotate Left button, 346
Rotate Right button, 346
Undo button, 336-338
Washout button, 344-346
Table toolbar, 141
Toolbars command (View menu), 279
tools
GIF Animator Global Palette, 380
image tools, 336-342, 345-346, 349
Java Developer's Kit, 652
TCP/IP Test tool, 982
toolbox (Image Composer), 280-282
tools (Image Composer), 281-282
Arrange palette, 312
Brush Designer, 303-304
Cutout tool, 296-300
Draw Table tool, 141
Effects palette
applying effects, 321-322
Arts & Crafts category, 322
categories, 321
Color Enhancement category, 323
Distort category, 323-324
Gradient category, 324-326
opacity, 321
Outlines category, 327
Paint category, 327-328
Patterns category, 328-329
Photographic category, 329-331
Sketch category, 331
Surface category, 332
Paint palette, 300-303, 334
Select Color Region palette, 298-300
Shapes palette, 291, 294-295
Stencil tool, 298
text palette, 289-290
Texture Transfer palette, 318-320
Tools menu
commands
GIF Animator, 360
Options, 333
Permissions, 988
Recalculate Hyperlinks, 987
Show Image Editor, 275
Web Settings, 389
FrontPage Editor, 45-46
FrontPage Explorer, 22-23
top border
adding navigation bars, 798
NavDemo web home page, 794
top pages
adding to NavDemo web, 792
webs, 786
top-down three-level hierarchy template, 165, 182

<TR> (HTML tag), 192
traceroutes (troubleshooting Webs), 991
tracking user sessions (Active Server Pages), 765
trailing comments (animation), 378-380
transaction management (Connection objects), 729
transferring files (Web server issues), 903
transitions (banners), 228-229
transparency
animation, 380
images
background, 341
internal, 342
removing, 342-343
troubleshooting, 135-136
troubleshooting
animation
frame size, 382
Image Composer, 374
authoring, 986
crashes (Image Composer), 276
Editor, 984-985
Explorer, 986-987
firewalls, 989
forms (text), 985
GIF Animator frames, 374
IIS, 988
image maps, 985
images, 269-271
importing images, 114
ISP transfers, 992-993
linking, 987, 992-993
memory, 990
network access, 989-990
server connections, 993
system connections, 992
pages
access, 988-989
remote pages, 986
saving, 984
passwords, 988
Personal Web Server, 987-989
port numbers, 987-988
proxy servers, 989
publishing, 991-992
transparency, 136
user accounts, 989
Webs
access, 986, 990-991
multihoming, 991
Personal Web Server, 991
Ping, 991
proxy servers, 991
traceroutes, 991
Tru Realities Web site, 383
tutorials (push channels), 693

U

UBound function (VBScript), 583
<UL> (HTML tag), 192
unary operators (JavaScript), 631-632
Under Construction icons, 541
undo option (FrontPage Editor), 44
undoing images, 336-338
undrawing animation, 379
uniform resource locators, see URLs
unique properties (ActiveX controls), 609
UNIX
server extensions installation, 868-869
shell scripting languages, 441-443
Update dialog box, 270
Update feature (Clip Gallery), 269-271
updating
guest books, 482
Label controls, 618
push channels, 692
table of contents, 804
Webs, 804, 908
Include Page component, 813
manual updates, 805
variables, 810-811
upgrading
FrontPage, 980
FrontPage 98 installation, 979
server extensions, 880, 883
URLs (uniform resource locators)
ActiveX control data sources, 609
changing links, 78
defining Form Page Wizard, 420
frames, 160
links, 72
relative file paths, 73-74
Web page properties, 55
Usenet, 496-497
User parameter (wizards), 954

user variables (META property), 66
userAddress variable (JavaScript), 629
users
- accounts
  - *creating, 565-566*
  - *troubleshooting, 989*
- frames, editing, 171
- passwords, assigning, 566
- permissions (members-only Webs), 561
- privileges (closed Webs), 565-566
- tracking sessions (Active Server Pages), 765

V

validating forms, 407
- drop-down menus, 453
- length restrictions, 457
- numeric data types, 456-457
- radio buttons, 451-452
- selecting script language, 451
- specifying fields, 451
- text boxes, 454-455
- text data types, 455-456
- value ranges, 457-458

values, absolute/relative, 172
Variable style, 96
variables
- JavaScript, 626
  - *global, 627*
  - *local, 627*
  - *userAddress, 629*
- META property, 65-66
- VBScript, 581-582, 592
- web updates, 810

VBScript
- ActiveX controls
  - *adding buttons, 617*
  - *property settings, 613-614*
  - *interactions, 613, 616*
- arrays, 582
- buttons (interactive), 577
- calculation scripts, 578
- classes, 594
- comments, 587
- conditional instructions, 587-588
- dialog boxes
  - *command buttons, 578*
  - *display code, 577*
- events, 594-595
- functions
  - *countDays, 593*
  - *countSeconds, 593*
  - *getName, 592*
  - *IsNumeric, 582*
  - *ReDim, 583*
  - *UBound, 583*
- Label control captions, 619-622
- language, 576
- loops
  - *Do Until loops, 591*
  - *Do While loops, 590*
  - *For...Next loops, 589*
- menus (interactive), 577
- methods, 595
- operators, 584-586
- parameters, 592
- procedures, 591-593
- sales tax program, 596-598
- statements
  - *ElseIf, 588*
  - *Exit Function, 593*
  - *Exit Sub, 594*
  - *If...Then, 587*
  - *If...Then...Else, 588*
  - *Option Explicit, 581*
  - *Select Case, 588*
- strings, 586
- subroutines, 593-594
- variables, 581-582, 592
- webs, 577, 580-581

VBScript Reference, see appendix on companion web site
vector graphics, 255
Verify Hyperlinks feature, 7
Verify Links dialog box, 859
verifying links, 807, 859-860
vertical spacing (Java applets), 649
vertical split template (frames), 164
video, streaming, 891
View menu
- commands
  - *Image toolbar, 336*
  - *Options, 119*
  - *Refresh, 987*
  - *Toolbars, 279*
- FrontPage Editor, 44-45
- FrontPage Explorer, 21-22

viewing
- IDC page results, 708
- themes, 235-236, 239
- Web sites (FrontPage Explorer), 4-5

viewpoint animation, 381
views (FrontPage Explorer)
- All Files view, 17-18
- Folders view, 17-18
- Hyperlink Status, 20
- Hyperlinks view, 18-19
- Navigation view, 16-17
- shortcut menus, 17
- Tasks, 20
- Themes, 20

Visited Hyperlink property, 61
visiting bookmarks, 80
Visual InterDev
- Active Server Pages options, 764
- ADO usage, 771
- components, 764-765
- Data Form Wizard, 779
- Data Range controls
- Data View tab, 772
- Database Designer, 773
- databases
  - *ActiveX control access, 773*
  - *connectivity, 767*
  - *tools, 771-772*
- design-time controls, 774
- DSN files, 768
- examples
  - *database-driven Active Server Page, 774-775*
  - *NRS.mdb Active Server Page, 774-775*
  - *NRS.mdb database table, 776*
- File View tab, 767
- global.asa files, 770
- NRS.mdb database, 767
- Query Designer, 772
- sites, creating, 766
- Source Code Editor, 773

W-X-Y-Z

Wagon Train Animated GIFs Web site, 383
WAIS (Wide Area Information Server), 460
washout, 344-346
watermarks, 59
Web browsers, 52
- behavior control, JavaScript options, 641
- Internet Explorer, ActiveX controls, 603
- testing for JavaScript compatibility, 625

Web pages
- background images, 115-117
- creating, 53-54
- customizing
  - *background colors, 57-61*
  - *background images, 58-59*
  - *colors, creating, 61-62*
  - *META properties, 64-66*
  - *watermarks, 59*
- designing, 66
- font colors, defining, 62-63
- FrontPage Editor
  - *Advanced toolbar, 48*
  - *creating pages, 39-40*
  - *Edit menu, 44*
  - *editing pages, 39*
  - *File menu, 43-44*
  - *Format menu, 45*
  - *Format toolbar, 47*
  - *Forms toolbar, 48*
  - *Frame menu, 46*
  - *Go menu, 45*
  - *Help menu, 46*
  - *Image toolbar, 47*
  - *Insert menu, 45*
  - *moving toolbars, 47*
  - *opening existing pages, 40-42*
  - *saving pages, 42*
  - *Standard toolbar, 47*
  - *starting, 38*
  - *Table menu, 46*
  - *Table toolbar, 48*
  - *text import options, 41-42*
  - *toolbar, 47*
  - *Tools menu, 45-46*
  - *View menu, 44-45*
  - *views, 38-39*
  - *Window menu, 46*
- headings, 67-68
- margins, 63-64
- paragraphs, 68-69
- properties
  - *Base Locations, 56-57*
  - *document titles, 55-56*
  - *page location, 55-56*
  - *setting, 54-55*
- saving, troubleshooting, 984
- text
  - *aligning, 69-70*
  - *colors, 62-63*
  - *indenting, 69*
- titles, changing, 793
- troubleshooting access, 988-989
- *see also* documents

Web Presence Providers (WPPs), 869
Web Publishing Wizard, 11
Web servers
- access options, 822-823
- administration, 856-857
- cost, 899
- creating Webs, 904
- data encryption, 822
- exporting to, 900-901
- extensionless
  - *access control, 902*
  - *compatibility issues, 902*
  - *conflicts (avoiding), 904*

default page names, 903
file/content transfer issues, 903
filename extensions, 902-903
WebBots and, 901-902
FastTrack (FrontPage Webs), 908-910
functions, prioritizing, 898-899
hosting companies, 899-900
proxies, 820
PWS alternatives, 896
reliability, 898
responsiveness, 898
scalability, 898
transferring content, 900-901
users, 828-829
WebSite (FrontPage Webs), 904-907
see also Personal Web Server
Web Settings command (Tools menu), 389
Web Settings dialog box, 22
Web sites
Animated Art for Netscape, 383
Animated GIF Artists Guild, 383
Badger's Animated GIF Gallery, 383
Bill's Animated GIF Collection, 383
Clip Gallery Live, 265-268
CommerceNet, 899
creating, 488-492, 740-742
Dr.Fun's Page of Animations, 383
FrontPage, 865
IIS, 890
JPEG, 132
push channel examples, 692
Tru Realities, 383
URLs (creating), 490
viewing with FrontPage Explorer, 4-5
Wagon Train Animated GIFs, 383
Web Wizard's World Animation Station, 383
Web technologies (FrontPage 98 support), 10-11
Web Template Maker utility, 918, 922, 946
Web templates, 9, 946-948
Web wizards, 9, 488
accessing, 490
Proxy parameter, 954
ServerName parameter, 954
User parameter, 954
WebName parameter, 954
Web Wizard's World Animation Station Web site, 383
<WEBBOT> tag, 923
WebBots, 9-10
annotation bot, 102
see also Components
Webmasters, 846-847
WebName parameter (wizards), 954
Webs
closed
computer accounts, creating, 566-569
privileges, 565-566
user accounts, creating, 565-566
closing (OLE automation), 968
Corporate Presence
contact information, 542-543
copyright notices, including, 540
Feedback form, 538-539
headers/footers, 5 40-541
home page topics, 534-536
link options, 540
logos, inserting, 540
page title options, 540
presentation styles, 543
Products pages, 537-538
selecting pages, 535
Services pages, 537-538
Table of Contents page, 539
task list, 544
timestamps, 540
Under Construction icons, 541
Webmaster address (including), 540
What's New page, 536
creating on other Web servers, 904
Customer Support, 493
Bug Reporting and Information page, 515
Discussion area, 519
Download page, 517
FAQ page, 514
Search page, 520
Suggestions page, 516
Technical Notes page, 521

Welcome page, 512-513
What's New page, 513
Empty, 493
hyperlinks, verifying, 807
members-only
Registration component, 563-564
registration form, 561-562
One-Page, 493
opening (OLE automation), 967
Project Web, 493
Archive page, 528
Discussion area, 530
Home page, 524
Members page, 525
Schedule page, 526-527
Search page, 529
Status page, 527
removing (OLE automation), 968-969
restricted
accessing, 560-561
group access, 569-570
see also Webs, closed
Root Webs, opening, 562
Search bot, adding, 463-465
templates (Personal Web), 493
testing, 911-912
troubleshooting
accessing, 986, 990-991
multihoming, 991
Personal Web Server, 991
Ping, 991
proxy servers, 991
traceroutes, 991
updating for FrontPage 98, 908

webs
ActiveX controls, 605-609
adding JavaScript scripts, 638-639
collapsible outlines, 668
copying, 29
creating, 25-27
data and time display (JavaScript options), 640
database connectivity (IDC options), 702-705
deleting, 28, 33, 805
designing, 788
documents, hidden, 28
dynamic styles, 671-672
editing, 28
elements, positioning, 673
forms
access keys for form fields, 670
clickable labels, 670
database searches, 718-720
hyperlinks, recalculating, 807
importing
existing webs, 30-32
to current web, 29-30
Java applets
alignment, 648
displaying on page, 655
embedding, 647
horizontal spacing, 649
inserting tags, 647
parameters, 649
spacing options, 649
vertical spacing, 649
links, 805-807
modifying navigation scheme, 799-800
moving files, 33-34
navigation bars, 784
adding, 798
editing, 797
Parent level button, 798
navigation scheme, printing, 802
opening, 27
pages
child pages, 785
deleting, 805
parent page, 785
parent/child page relationships, 786
peer pages, 785-786
top pages, 786
transitions, 667
permissions, setting, 23
planning organization, 786
publishing, 29
push channels, 680-683
renaming files, 33
root web, 14-16
Shared Borders, 785
text animation, 664-666
troubleshooting connection errors, 27
updating
Include Page component, 813
manual updates, 805
table of contents, 804
variables, 810-811
variables for site updates, 812
VBScript, adding scripts to pages, 580-581
Visual InterDev options, 764

WebSite (FrontPage Webs), 904-907

while loops (JavaScript), 637

Wide Area Information Server, (WAIS), 460
width (tables), drawing tool, 142
Window menu (FrontPage Editor), 46
windows
Break Properties window, 91
Theme Preview, 235
Windows 95/NT server extensions installation, 867-868
Winsock, testing, 982
wizards, 9
Channel Definition Wizard, creating push channels, 680-682
connecting to OLE server, 962-963
Corporate Presence Wizard, 9, 25, 493, 534
creating, 916, 950
Database Region Wizard, 710, 759
directories, 918-919, 950
Discussion Web Wizard, 9, 25, 493, 498-500
editing commands, 492
Empty Web (NavDemo web creation), 790
Explorer status (checking), 963-964
file paths, 957-958
Form Page Wizard
form elements, 421
input types, 422-426
launching, 420
output options, 423-424
page title, 420
presentation options, 422-423
URL, defining, 420
Form Wizards, 406
HTML pages, writing to files, 964-966
Import Web Wizard, 30-32
interfaces, creating, 952
Microsoft Access Web Publishing Wizard, 751
OLE automation, 958-959
closing Webs, 968
Editor, 969-971
Explorer, 966-969
opening Webs, 967
removing Webs, 968-969
To Do List, 971-973
option settings, 956-957
page wizards, 9
parameter files
creating, 951-952
environment parameters, 954
input parameters, 953-954
naming, 955
output parameters, 955-957
programming languages, 962
routines, 962
Script Wizard, initializing web clock, 641
Web pages, creating, 39-40
Web Publishing Wizard, 11
Web wizards, 9, 488
accessing, 490
Proxy parameter, 954
ServerName parameter, 954
User parameter, 954
WebName parameter, 954
word art, 100
WPPs (Web Presence Providers), 869
writing to webs (JavaScript), 639

Year property (Calendar control), 614

z-order dynamic layout, 674
zoom text animations, 666